The SAGE Handbook of
Youth Work Practice

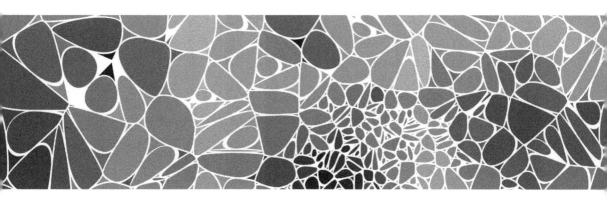

The SAGE Handbook of
Youth Work Practice

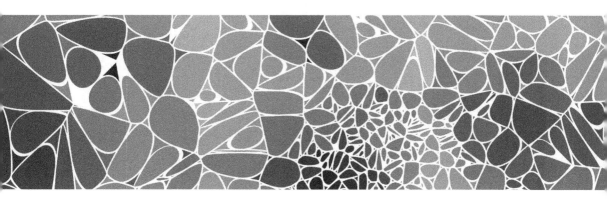

Edited by
Pam Alldred, Fin Cullen, Kathy Edwards and Dana Fusco

Los Angeles | London | New Delhi | Singapore | Washington DC | Melbourne

Los Angeles | London | New Delhi
Singapore | Washington DC | Melbourne

SAGE Publications Ltd
1 Oliver's Yard
55 City Road
London EC1Y 1SP

SAGE Publications Inc.
2455 Teller Road
Thousand Oaks, California 91320

SAGE Publications India Pvt Ltd
B 1/I 1 Mohan Cooperative Industrial Area
Mathura Road
New Delhi 110 044

SAGE Publications Asia-Pacific Pte Ltd
3 Church Street
#10-04 Samsung Hub
Singapore 049483

Editor: Kate Keers
Editorial Assistant: Colette Wilson
Production Editor: Rudrani Mukherjee
Copyeditor: Rosemary Campbell
Proofreader: Derek Markham
Indexer: Richard Walker
Marketing Manager: Camille Richmond
Cover Design: Wendy Scott
Typeset by: Cenveo Publishers Services
Printed in the UK.

Library of Congress Control Number: 2017962340

British Library Cataloguing in Publication data

A catalogue record for this book is available from the British Library

ISBN 978-1-4739-3952-3

Contents

List of Figures

List of Tables

Notes on the Editors
and Contributors

THE EDITORS

Pam Alldred is Reader in Education and Youth Studies in the Social Work Division at Brunel University London, UK. From 2012 to 2016 she was Director of the Centre for Youth Work Studies which had delivered Youth & Community Worker education for thirty years. Pam taught there for its final ten years. Her own formation was through critical psychology and cultural, psychosocial, then childhood studies. She has researched sexualities education, teenage motherhood, home-school relations, lesbian parenting and the notion of *fitness to parent*, focusing in each case on how policy is negotiated by those whose lives it governs. She has led two large international projects on gender-related or sexual violence with European Union co-funding and recently published *Sociology and the New Materialism* (with N.J. Fox, Sage, 2016). She has edited special issues of *Sex Education*, *Sociological Research Online* and many issues of *Feminist Review* and been a member of four book collectives on feminist methods and critiques of psychology. Pam and Fin co-convened the *Sexualities* Special Interest Group of the *British Educational Research Association* and together have researched student carers and supervised many youth and community work research projects. She brought the editorial group together on the strength of her collaborations with Fin and knowing Dana and Kathy through their work.

Fin Cullen is Senior Lecturer in Education and Social Science at St Mary's University, Twickenham, UK. She is a qualified Youth & Community Worker and has worked in practice settings across the UK for over fifteen years. For eight years she was involved in youth work education as part of the Centre for Youth Work Studies, Brunel University, UK. Her research and practice interests focus on drugs education, sex and relationship education, youth policy and sexuality and gender. She has long been involved in the work of the Gender and Education Association and was previously involved in the UK arm of the EU-Daphne co-funded project developing training to help educators challenge gender-related violence (http://sites.brunel.ac.uk/gap). Fin has published in *Gender and Education*, *Pedagogy*, *Culture and Society*, *Girlhood Studies* and *Sex Education*, amongst others. In recent years, she has co-edited a collection with Simon Bradford on research methods for practitioners (2011) and a special issue on the theme of youth policy in austerity Europe (2013).

Kathy Edwards is Senior Lecturer in Youth Work at RMIT University, Melbourne, Australia, where she teaches subjects related to youth sociology, professional ethics, policy studies and social action. Her research background is in women's studies and political sociology and for the past 15 years she has researched in youth studies, her introduction to this being when she was involved in an Australian Research Council funded project that considered young people's attitudes to politics and voting. Kathy has published extensively in the areas of youth participation, civic engagement, civic education, social inclusion and government policies in respect to these. Her research focuses on the nexus between policy and young people's lives. Current research interests include the effects of globalisation on young people and on developing forms of youth work practices that take 'southern perspectives' into account. She has co-edited a collection of research papers on youth participation and published widely in *Youth Studies Australia*, the *Journal of Youth Studies* and *Sociological Research Online*, amongst other journals. She is on the International Editorial Board of the *Journal of Applied Youth Studies*.

Dana Fusco has worked in the fields of education and youth work for over 25 years as a practitioner, college teacher and researcher. She has served as editor and author for several major works in the area of youth work, including *Youth and Inequality in Education: Global Actions in Youth Work* (2016); a special issue of *Child & Youth Services* entitled 'Professionalisation Deconstructed: Implications for the Field of Youth Work' (2013); and *Advancing Youth Work: Current Trends, Critical Questions* (2012). She served as the Howland Endowed Chair in Youth Development Leadership at the University of Minnesota Extension Center for Youth Development during the 2012–2013 academic year, during which time she studied the professional education of youth workers in the United States. Dr Fusco brings to this project an array of skills as a writer, researcher and educator and a breadth and depth of knowledge in the field of youth work both within the continental US as well as globally.

THE CONTRIBUTORS

Björn Andersson has a PhD in Social Work and Associate Professor at the Department of Social Work, University of Gothenburg, Sweden. Björn is a trained social worker and has been working in detached youth work and community work. He has for many years taught university courses in social pedagogy, community work and youth work. Björn has written extensively on outreach approaches in social work and current research projects include issues around young people's participation in society and social sustainability in urban planning.

Helen Bartlett is a youth worker based in Brighton & Hove. Having developed her practice in a community development setting, she is now working in a busy youth centre. Helen has a background in informal education, international youth exchanges and conflict transformation work and has interests in class, poverty, feminism and queer politics.

Janet Batsleer works at Manchester Metropolitan University in the Faculty of Education, as Reader in Education and Principal Lecturer in Youth and Community Work. She has written and published extensively on youth work/girls work/community work from a critical and feminist anti-racist perspective. Current research collaborations include: 'The Loneliness Project' – a UK study, using creative methods to explore young people's experience of loneliness – and Partispace (http://partispace.eu/) – a study of young people's participation practices in eight European cities. In her chapter she draws on work more fully developed in *Youth Working with Girls and Young Women in Community Settings: A Feminist Perspective* (London Ashgate Arena, 2013).

Fiona Beals currently works as a senior staff member on the Bachelor of Youth Development in Aotearoa New Zealand. She has research interests in critical pedagogy, the sociology of youth and performances of edgework. Her recent publications have explored the whakapapa of youth development knowledge and the impact of that knowledge on current practices and policies in colonised spaces such as those in the Pacific. Fiona has a PhD in Education from Victoria University of Wellington. Outside of research, Fiona enjoys doing grassroots youth work in her local community of Wainuiomata in the Wellington region. She also sits as a governing board member to the youth sector's peak body Ara Taiohi.

Brian Belton is a senior tutor at the YMCA George Williams College, London. Coming from an East London/Gypsy family, Brian played a leading role in the youth gang life of that area in the late 1960s/early 1970s. However, with the help of a couple of tough but fair coppers he entered youth work as a volunteer and part-time practitioner in the docklands of the late 1970s. While working in youth-work-related situations around the world, including Israel, the Falkland Islands, Germany, the USA, Thailand, Hong Kong, Zambia, South Africa, China and Canada, Brian's interest in identity and ethnicity flourished and today he is an internationally recognised authority on Gypsy ethnicity and the rights of Roma in Europe, having written widely and delivering papers on that subject, most recently in the USA, Austria, Greece, Sweden and Slovenia, as well as around the UK. He has recently concluded a three-year research programme focusing on the social exclusion of Roma with partners in Spain, Germany and Turkey. Having just completed baseline research into youth work in 35 nations (as lead writer) and a 3 year project developing detached youth work in Malta, Romania and Holland, Brian is embarking on research into and development of Roma led youth work responses with a number of agencies in the European context.

Judith Bessant is Professor at RMIT University, Melbourne, Australia. She has taught, researched and published in policy studies, sociology, politics, youth studies, media and history. She has designed higher education curricula in universities and developed secondary school curricula for the state government. Judith has worked in various governance, policy and advisory positions in universities and with various national and international governments and non-government organisations. Her recent books include *The Precarious Generation: A Political Economy of Young People*, with Rys Farthing and Rob Watts (Routledge, 2017) and *The Great Transformation, History for a Techno-Human Future* (Routledge, 2018).

Simon Bradford is Associate Reader in Social Science in the Department of Clinical Sciences at Brunel University London. His main research interests lie in social policy initiatives that affect young people and communities, the history and organisation of professional work in the public services (particularly education services) and aspects of youth culture. He is the author, with Fin Cullen, of *Research and Research Methods for Youth Practitioners* (Routledge, 2012) and *Sociology, Youth and Youth Work Practice* (Palgrave, 2012). Simon Bradford lives in Kecskemét, Hungary.

Gregory Brender is Co-director of Policy & Advocacy at United Neighborhood Houses – New York City's federation of settlement houses. In this role, Gregory works with settlement house leaders and programme participants, including youth, to advocate for community-based services such as early childhood education and after-school programmes. He has written about ways to strengthen neighbourhood-based services and led campaigns to expand access to community programmes. Prior to UNH, Gregory worked as an aide to New York State Assembly Member Deborah Glick and then Manhattan Borough President Scott Stringer. He lives in Astoria, Queens.

Graham Bright is Senior Lecturer in Childhood and Youth Studies and Youth and Community Work at York St John University, UK. His PhD with Durham University explores youth workers' life and practice narratives. Graham is editor of *Youth Work: Histories, Policy and Contexts* (Palgrave, 2015) and co-editor, with Carole Pugh, of *Youth Work: Global Futures* (Sense, forthcoming). His practice continues to support work in the voluntary and faith sectors.

Steph Brocken is a part-time doctoral student at the University of Chester. She is engaged in research around Youth Theatre, its political context and the way in which it develops young people socially, personally and politically. She combines her studies with work as a freelance drama practitioner, arts manager and consultant. Since 2009 she has run her own arts organisation, Minerva Arts, based in Chester. She also works for Peshkar, a National Portfolio arts organisation based in Oldham and consults for Curious Minds and CapeUK.

Katie Byrne worked as a research assistant on the state-funded project on youth and gang violence intervention that is the subject of this chapter while completing her Masters in Community Development and Planning at Clark University. She graduated from Clark in 2016 and now works with the Department of Youth Services as a local coordinator for the Juvenile Detention Alternatives Initiative.

Stephen Case is Professor of Criminology in the Department of Social Sciences at Loughborough University, having previously been an Associate Professor and Director of Undergraduate Studies at Swansea University. His primary research interests are youth justice, youth crime prevention and social justice, particularly the promotion of positive, children-first ways of working with children embroiled in the youth justice system. He has published in a range of international journals and conducted research for the Youth Justice Board, Home Office and Welsh Government.

Kodzo Chapman is a multi-skilled NGO Management and Technical Support Consultant with hands-on social and child protection expertise, having worked in partnership with the UNHCR, Ghana. Kodzo is a member of the Ghana Journalists Association (GJA) and an effective communicator whose professional life has, however, centred on human rights, social justice and equity, as well as gender and development. He worked as a Programme Manager for Gender-Based Violence with the American Refugee Committee in Bong County, Liberia. In partnership with a Canadian popular educator, Marion Thomson, he developed the Young People's Human Rights Project which became Young People's Experience for Change – YPEC.

Philippa Collin is Senior Research Fellow at the Institute for Culture and Society, Western Sydney University. She researches children and young people's use of digital media, participation and citizenship and their relationship to health and well-being. She has worked extensively with youth and allied services, including as Managing Director, Research and Policy at online youth mental health initiative Reachout.com. From 2011–2016 she was a Research Program Leader with the Young and Well Cooperative Research Centre working with hundreds of young people, professionals, advocates and policy makers looking at the role of digital technologies for the mental health and wellbeing of young people. Philippa is the author of *Young Citizens and Political Participation in a Digital Society: Addressing the Democratic Disconnect* (Palgrave Macmillan, 2015) and co-author of *Young People in Digital Society: Control Shift* (with Amanda Third, Rosalyn Black and Lucas Walsh, Palgrave Macmillan, forthcoming).

Paula Connaughton is Lecturer in Community Development and Youth Work at the University of Bolton. She has many years of experience working in the field of community development, community education and youth work. She is a Secretariat member of the Professional Association of Lecturers in Youth and Community Work and Editorial member of the *Youth & Policy* Journal. She is also actively involved in Defence of Youth Work and is a trustee member of a local voluntary organisation.

Susan Cooper is Senior Lecturer in the Faculty of Education and Social Science at the University of St Mark & St John, England. She has over thirty years' experience in youth work, as a practitioner, a manager and for the past ten years as course leader for Youth & Community Work at the University. She completed her doctoral studies in the field of participatory evaluation in 2011 and has conducted several evaluations of youth work. Her research interests focus on enabling young people, community members and practitioners to engage meaningfully with evaluation processes. She is currently co-ordinating a European research project using transformative evaluation to demonstrate the impact of youth work. Her publications include 'Putting Collective Reflective Dialogue at the Heart of the Evaluation Process' (*Reflective Practice Journal*), 'Transformative Evaluation: Organisational Learning through Participative Practice' (*The Learning Organization Journal*) and *Participatory Evaluation in Youth and Community Work* (Routledge, 2018).

Trudi Cooper is Associate Professor of Youth Work at Edith Cowan University, Australia, where she is Director of the Social Program Innovation Research and Evaluation (SPIRE) group and leads the youth work programme, in addition to teaching postgraduate research. Her research includes youth work education, youth work theory and programme evaluation. In 2016, she became an Australian Learning and Teaching Fellow. Previously, in 2010–2014, she led a national project to harmonise and renew the Australian youth work curriculum. Before her academic career, she was a youth and community worker in Lancashire in the UK and has also been a play-worker. She has taught at the University of Lancaster, and at institutions that became the University of Cumbria and the University of Central Lancashire.

Jen Couch is Senior Lecturer in Youth Work at the Australian Catholic University (ACU). She has established a national reputation for her work in the area of young refugees and resettlement and has recently completed the first longitudinal ethnographic study of homelessness amongst refugee young people. Before beginning at ACU, she worked extensively in the youth and international development sector in Australia and South Asia including India, Nepal, Afghanistan, Pakistan and Thailand. Jen has worked with, and on behalf of, young people in the areas of refugee settlement, displacement, homelessness, rights and participation, torture and trauma, and capacity building. Jen was the Director of the Australian Clearinghouse for Youth Studies. More recently Jen has been teaching youth work to Burmese refugees and migrants on the Thai/Burma border. Jen's current work is focused on youth work in conflict zones, decolonising youth work practice and embedding Southern Theory into youth work pedagogy.

Tania de St Croix has been a youth and community worker for over two decades, and in recent years has combined practice with research and teaching in youth work, education policy and child studies. She is a Lecturer in the Sociology of Youth and Childhood at King's College London. Her book, *Grassroots Youth Work: Policy, Passion and Resistance in Practice* was published in 2016 by Policy Press. She is actively involved in 'In Defence of Youth Work' and volunteers with a small youth workers' co-operative in East London, Voice of Youth.

Kate D'Arcy has been working in education for many years as a youth worker, teacher and researcher. Kate's working practice has always been situated in the margins of education, supporting a variety of vulnerable and often disengaged children, young people and communities in a variety of settings. She is committed to equality and diversity and continues to work to promote an agenda for change for marginalised individuals and groups. She has a particular interest and expertise in exploring race and ethnicity and ensuring the active participation of marginalised children, young people and adults in research. Kate joined the University of Bedfordshire in October 2010 to undertake teaching about equality and diversity. She has led on numerous projects which have an agenda to improve social justice and circumstances for marginalised groups, including children and young people.

Bernard Davies is a qualified and experienced youth worker who has also worked as a local authority youth officer and as a lecturer and tutor on full-time youth work, teaching and social work qualifying courses. He has been a trustee of a number of voluntary organisations and until 2015 was a director of the National Coalition for Independent Action. Currently he is active in In Defence of Youth Work, including facilitating its youth work story-telling workshops. His publications include a three-volume *History of the Youth Service in England* and *Youth Work: A Manifesto for Our Times – Revisited*.

Ronnie Djupsund works as the head of the youth department in Kokkola, Finland. His expertise lies in the field of non-formal education. Djupsund, together with the youth department and Finnish Youth Research Network, has developed the first process-based curriculum of youth work in Finland. He was one of the writers of the book *Why Is There Youth Work?*, published in Finnish in 2015. As the head of the youth department, Djupsund is responsible for several projects, including outreach youth work and preventing exclusion and dropout in education. As a youth director and the president of the board of Youth Centre, Villa Elba he collaborates with numerous organisations related to education, guidance and counselling.

Leo Fieldgrass is CEO of the Youth Affairs Council of Victoria (YACVic). As a youth worker and policy advocate, his work in the UK and Australia has covered diverse themes, including youth participation, civic engagement, flexible education, sexual health, alcohol and other drugs, financial inclusion and music technology.

Peter-Clinton Foaese currently works for the New Zealand Office of the Children's Commissioner as a community and young person's engagement specialist. He is dedicated to supporting marginalised young people and their families to find and use their voice to transform their situations. He also works as a youth worker with 'Whakaoho' and 'Pacific All Stars' – initiatives created and led by youth with family and community. Through his role as an Executive Council member in ASPBAE he has observed and experienced youth development practice throughout Asia and the Pacific.

In the past working for council and social services, Peter witnessed Māori and Pacific youth being alienated, their lived-experiences marginalised and ignored. The Bachelor of Youth Development enabled him to go beyond traditional engagement theories to support young people to read their reality to transform it. He journeys with rangatahi affected by generations of oppression, disconnected from their whenua (land), struggling to survive in a fast-changing world. Peter works with marginalised young people to share stories, generate research and evidence that exposes the injustice they live and to find the real solutions.

Ellen Foley is Associate Professor of International Development and Social Change at Clark University. She is trained as a medical anthropologist and she has been conducting action research on youth violence intervention programmes since 2006. Her other research examines health disparities and access to sexual and reproductive health care in West Africa.

Jennifer Fuqua is a former youth worker and author of 'The Curtain Rises' (*After School Matters*, 2008). She recently completed a doctorate at the University of Delaware in Urban Affairs and Public Policy and teaches in the Organizational and Community Leadership Program at UD. Her research interests are Positive Youth Development systems, non-profit management and the role of arts in youth programmes.

David Giles is Professor of Educational Leadership and Management in the College of Education, Psychology and Social Work at Flinders University, South Australia. After teaching in primary and secondary schools, David began teaching undergraduate and postgraduate courses in educational leadership, teacher education and higher education. He has taught in four universities within New Zealand and Australia and currently teaches educational leadership in China. David's research interests focus on the phenomenological nature of relationships in education, curriculum, pedagogy, leadership and organisational culture. To this end, he employs Appreciative Inquiry, as a strengths-based lens on current praxis, alongside Hermeneutic Phenomenology, as a means of researching the essence of students', teachers' and leaders' everyday lived experiences.

Pauline Grace is Senior Lecturer and MA Programme Leader of Youth and Community Work at Newman University and Chief Editor of the *International Journal of Open Youth Work*. With over 28 years of face-to-face youth work experience in the UK, she is a founding member of the Professional Open Youth Work in Europe group and actively involved in In Defence of Youth Work. Her research interests include challenging the neoliberal in everyday life, feminism, reflective practice and international youth work.

Anu Gretschel works as Senior Researcher in the Finnish Youth Research Network. Her research career started in 1996 in youth centres where young people were offered the possibility to develop their living environment. Her doctoral thesis about the participatory methods used was published in 2002 in the University of Jyväskylä. Interests in youth participation, youth work, action research and evaluation have taken her to a variety of contexts from the local to the national and the European level. Publications with several co-authors include 'Municipalities of Children and Young People', 'Whose Arena is the EU Youth Policy?' and 'Youth Centre as Enabling Near Community'. She recently led a research process called 'Network-based Development of Youth Work Statistics and Key Characteristics'. Currently, she is developing methods to evaluate quality and impact in different kinds of youth work processes.

Angel Guzman is the Director of Outreach at Straight Ahead Ministries. Angel is a skilled trainer in topics such as Juvenile Delinquency and its Contributing Factors; Engaging High-Risk Youth: Transformational Approaches; and Juvenile Justice Institutional Ministry Models. He sits on the Worcester Police-Clergy Partnership and the Worcester Re-entry Initiative.

Ken Harland is a Consultant, Trainer and Researcher in youth work practice specialising in the development of innovative approaches to work with boys and young men. For 20 years Ken lectured in Community Youth Work at Ulster University where he was also co-founder and co-director of the Centre for Young Men's Studies. His research areas include masculinities, violence, educational attainment and youth work in contested societies.

Peter Hart completed his doctoral research, titled 'An Ethnographic Study of Ethical Practices in Relationships Between Young People and Youth Workers' at Durham University and is now a research fellow in character education, researching the subject through English Literature curricula at the University of Leeds. His practice experience includes faith-based and statutory settings.

Kieron Hatton has previously worked as a community worker and social worker, where his focus was on preventative work with young people entering the criminal justice system. Since 1992 he has been employed at the University of Portsmouth. He was Head/Professional Lead for Social Work between 2004 and 2013. He is currently Principal Lecturer in Social Work and Social Care. He has written extensively around social pedagogy, social work, community development and youth work. His current research interests include the reintegration of school-excluded young people through engagement with a Third Sector project, social pedagogy and service user/carer involvement in social and community work.

Bethany Hayden is an undergraduate student in Christian Theology at York St John University, UK, where she was employed on the 'Students as Researchers' programme. Bethany previously spent time working with a Christian youth work charity and continues to volunteer with a local church.

Jo Heslop is Lecturer in Education and International Development at the Institute of Education, University College London. Jo teaches on issues related to gender, health promotion and research methodologies in developing country contexts. Her research interests are gender violence, sexuality and young people in developing country contexts and using mixed methods and participatory research. She has worked on several multi-country projects aiming to better understand and address gender inequalities and violence experienced by young people in and around schools. These have involved partnerships with NGOs and governments internationally and in several countries in sub-Saharan Africa, and Jo is interested in the research-policy-practice interface and better understand how change happens. She recently co-authored *A Rigorous Review of Global Research Evidence on Policy and Practice on School-related Gender-based Violence*, published by UNICEF.

Frances Howard is a doctoral researcher from the University of Nottingham's School of Education. She has worked previously in local authorities, arts education and youth work. For her PhD research she is undertaking an ethnographic study of 'dis-engaged' young people's experience of the Arts Award programme within three youth project settings.

Tony Jeffs was until recently a full-time member of staff within the Department of Applied Social Sciences, University of Durham (England) where for a number of years he was Head of the Community and Youth Work Unit. Although now retired, he continues to teach part-time at Durham University on post-graduate programmes. He also teaches part-time on a post-graduate programme at the University of Bolton (England). The founding editor of the journal *Youth and Policy*, he remains an active member of their Editorial Board. *Youth and Policy* since 2017 has been an open-access and online journal.

Helen M.F. Jones is Director of Graduate Education at the University of Huddersfield, West Yorkshire, UK. She teaches on undergraduate (BA) and postgraduate (MA) youth and community work courses. Her work includes supervising PhD, EdD and MA research students. She has been a trustee of The Youth Association (originally Leeds Association of Girls' Clubs) for many years and has published several articles concerning aspects of the organisation's century-long history and also their ongoing work. Currently she is working on an evaluation of the Association's work with Roma Slovak young people. She lives with two cats who conspire to hinder her progress.

Daniel Jupp Kina currently undertaking a PhD degree at University of Dundee, and is also a qualified Social Psychologist with over 12 years experience in community development in favelas in São Paulo, Brazil. This includes five years working and managing an interdisciplinary child protection team dealing with complex and serious reports of abuse. He has also had three years' experience on a trustee board and as a board of directors' member for three human rights organisations in Brazil and the UK. He has specialist practice and research knowledge of participatory and inclusive practice working in challenging environments. The combination of professional expertise and experience as a qualitative researcher brings an in-depth understanding of subjective vulnerabilities. His recent work is on interdisciplinary applied research, utilising action research to develop studies embedded in praxis.

Richard Kennedy is Senior Lecturer in Education at De Montfort University, specialising in social justice, race, social class and critical consciousness. He is currently studying for a PhD at De Montfort University, examining the educational experiences of black young people in predominantly white areas. Richard was previously a Youth and Community development worker for Lincolnshire and Nottinghamshire County Council, with over twenty years' experience of working with disadvantaged groups in non-formal settings.

Tomi Kiilakoski is Senior Researcher in the Finnish Youth Research Network and an Adjunct Professor at the University of Tampere. His areas of expertise include youth work, youth participation, educational policy, school violence and its prevention, school as a societal institution, cultural philosophy and critical pedagogy. He has written numerous books and articles in Finnish, English, German, Russian and Turkish. He engages actively in promoting participation and developing youth work at the local and state levels in Finland. He devotes his leisure time to family life and his ambition to be an amateur folk musician, playing guitar, mandolin and glockenspiel.

Viljami Kinnunen has twenty years of practical experience in working with youngsters, ten years of which as a youth worker. He also has a pretty annoying tendency to ask why. He has been a project manager in charge of developing an authentic youth work curriculum for Kokkola and other towns in Finland. During his professional career he has worked in multiple projects dealing mainly with well-being, peer dynamics, employability and motivation. He is a co-author of the book *Why is There Youth Work?*, published in Finnish in 2015, and the author of articles on the nature and meaning of youth work.

Girish Lala is a Research Fellow in the Institute for Culture and Society, Western Sydney University. His research interests include identity and online interaction and technological mediation of social cohesion and social change. Girish's current work explores using new communications technologies to create innovative methodologies and interventions to facilitate young people's health and well-being.

Heather L. Lawford is Associate Professor in the Psychology Department at Bishop's University and an Adjunct Professor of Child and Youth Studies at Brock University, specialising in Social Developmental Psychology in youth and adolescence and the Co-Director of Research at the Centre of Excellence for Youth Engagement. She received her doctorate in Psychology from Concordia University. Her major research interests and the focus of her publications, include moral behaviour, development of concern for future generations and narrative identity formation.

Miguel Lopez is a Lieutenant in the Worcester Police Department (USA); the highest ranking Latino police officer in the department. Miguel has spent much of his 23-year career in the gang unit and his work has focused on gang prevention, youth programme development and evaluation and juvenile court diversion. Through these initiatives Miguel is working with community partners and city leaders to shape a city-wide youth violence reduction plan.

Wendy Luttrell is Professor of Urban Education, Sociology and Critical Social Psychology at the Graduate Center, City University of New York. She is the author of two award-winning books on this topic, *Schoolsmart and Motherwise: Working-Class Women's Identity and Schooling* (1997) and *Pregnant Bodies, Fertile Minds: Gender, Race and the Schooling of Pregnant Teens* (2003) and is also the editor of *Qualitative Educational Research: Readings on Reflexive Methodology and Transformative Practice* (2010). Her visual longitudinal project, Children Framing Childhoods and Looking Back, examines the role that gender, race and immigrant status play in how diverse young people growing up in working-class communities portray their social and emotional worlds through photography and video. Throughout her career, Luttrell has directed community-based, university and teacher inquiry projects that are dedicated to advancing social justice in and around schools and that promote innovative research and teaching practices.

Tim McConnell is a trans-masculine person with lived experience of mental health issues, substance misuse and trauma. They have previously worked as a peer support worker and substance abuse counsellor at a youth residential addiction treatment facility in New Brunswick, and as a community outreach worker and workshop facilitator with several agencies in Toronto. They write extensively on trans accessibility, institutional cisgenderism and Insidious Trauma, and have presented their work at Grounding Trauma 2014 and the Canadian Conference on Child and Youth Care. Tim is a project coordinator with Pieces to Pathways, a peer-led initiative creating Canada's first substance use support programme for LGBTTQQ2SIA youth aged 16 to 29 years old in Toronto. Tim recently compiled a zine on trans and gender non-conforming experiences of sexual violence.

Catherine McNamara is Pro-Dean and Director of Learning, Teaching and Student Experience at The Royal Central School of Speech and Drama (University of London). She is a Reader in Applied Theatre, Principal Fellow of the Higher Education Academy and teaches on various undergraduate and postgraduate courses at Central as well as supervising at

Doctorate level. Catherine is one of the co-founders and Directors of Gendered Intelligence, an organisation engaged in encouraging the cultural shift needed to develop a more intelligent approach to gender and sexuality across society as a whole. Catherine's recent projects include 'TransActing', a project that nurtures trans talent by facilitating performer training master-classes for trans and/or non-binary actors and connects those actors with industry professionals.

Susan Matloff-Nieves is a youth and community worker who has created and implemented programmes for over thirty years. Currently Deputy Executive Director of Youth and Aging at Goddard Riverside Community Center in New York City, she has a commitment to developing programmes that are responsive to youth and community voice. She is interested in integrating research, theory and practice and has previously presented and published on the intersection of social justice and youth work, preparing girls to confront gender bias in science, technology, engineering and maths (STEM) and staff development.

Eliz McArdle is Lecturer in Community Youth Work at Ulster University. Eliz has worked in partnership with Susan Morgan for over 15 years focused on maintaining and developing work with young women in Northern Ireland. Eliz worked as Team Leader for the Equality Work with Young Women team in YouthAction Northern Ireland (previously the Gender Equality Unit) and co-created 'Gender-conscious work with young people' advocating the use of gen-der-conscious approaches in youth work settings. Her research interests are in feminist youth work; gender and mental health; how youth work processes can impact on peace-building in Northern Ireland.

Martini Miller is a youth worker and experiential educator from Aotearoa New Zealand. He received his bachelor's degree from the Wellington Institute of Technology in Wellington, New Zealand and has been involved within the New Zealand youth work sector for over seven years. As an indigenous youth worker, Martini identifies strongly with the South Island based Maori tribe of Ngai Tahu and strives to incorporate indigenous perspectives into all aspects of his practice. Martini is currently studying towards a Masters in Childhood Studies and Children's Rights in Berlin, Germany. His academic interests include traditional child-rearing practices, post-colonial hybridity and children's rights perspectives within an Aotearoa New Zealand context.

Susan Morgan is Lecturer in Community Youth Work at Ulster University. Susan has worked in partnership with Eliz McArdle for over 15 years focused on maintaining and developing work with young women in Northern Ireland. Susan is co-creator of 'The Gender Lens Model' outlining perspectives and methodologies in gender-conscious practice. Morgan and McArdle have recorded a local chronicle of feminist youth work, entitled 'Long walk from the door: A history of work with girls and young women in Northern Ireland since 1969.' Her research interests are in feminist youth work; gender and formal education; and widening access to further and higher education for under-represented groups.

Rachel Morris is Lecturer in the Department of Social Policy and Social Work, University of York. As a criminologist, her research interests focus on the relationship between youth justice policy and practice and the criminal careers of young people. She also teaches undergraduate students, focusing on criminal justice, youth justice and prisons. She is the Executive Secretary of the British Society of Criminology.

Adam Muirhead has been a youth worker since 2002, specialising in detached and community development methodologies. Having professionally qualified in 2010, he currently works as a Projects Manager for a community development charity in Brighton, UK, overseeing the organisation's work with young people. Adam also lectures on the Youth Work degree course at the University of Brighton and is the Chair of the Institute for Youth Work, the professional association for youth workers in England.

Roshni K. Nuggehalli is Executive Director at Youth for Unity and Voluntary Action (YUVA), a non-profit organisation in India that works on issues of urbanisation, urban poverty and the right to the city. YUVA facilitates people's organisations towards their empowerment and conducts research and advocacy on issues of housing, livelihood, children and youth. Roshni's interests include youth and child rights, migration, informal labour and gender justice. She has published on themes of urbanisation, children's participation, youth work and governance.

Mike Ogunnusi is interested in transformative pedagogies that explore and promote solutions for peace in our communities by bringing together youth work, critical peace education and public engagement. Michael offers university-, school- and community-based learning, workshops and project management with young people, practitioners and educators across the UK and internationally. His background includes lecturing, social work, community development, research, civil rights work and police monitoring. Michael continues to deliver youth work and peace education and is currently a PhD student at De Montfort University using Photovoice to investigate how young people understand peace through youth-led advocacy and public engagement.

Rajesh Patel is currently Senior Lecturer in Youth and Community Work at Manchester Metropolitan University. He was a practitioner and youth work manager in the North of England for over twenty years, with interests including working with BAME (Black and Minority Ethnic) communities, youth and community arts and international exchange work. In his academic career he has continued to develop work on reflective practice – the subject of his PhD (2015); the use of visual methods; arts-informed research methodologies; creativity and partnership work in education settings; and, most recently, youth work in hospitals, with assistance from the UK health-based youth workers' support group.

Helen Perkins was born in Essex, England and moved to Aotearoa New Zealand in 2005. Helen has worked with young people for twenty years in England and Aotearoa in a variety of projects that have included alternative education, youth justice support, outdoor activities, community-based youth work, detached youth projects, youth courses and establishing a number of pilot projects. Helen currently works for a community organisation coordinating programmes based in South and West Auckland supporting parents and delivering a programme for young mums. Helen lives in West Auckland with her two young daughters after spending a few years living and working in Christchurch in the South Island. Helen is interested in research concerning informal education, changing behaviour and community development work. She is interested in further study of Tikanga Māori (Māori customs and ways) and in postgraduate research concerning informal education, changing behaviour and community development work.

Egbert Pinero has been in youth work for ten years and is currently an outreach worker on Worcester's Byrne Criminal Justice Innovation Program (in the USA). He was an outreach worker and case manager at the Worcester Youth Center prior to his work on the Byrne programme. He has developed a speciality in utilising social media in targeted street outreach strategies.

Steve Pullano is Director of Education, Employment and Outreach at Queens Community House (USA) where he founded a unique programme that conducts street outreach among young people. A junior high school teacher in public schools for many decades, he has worked to create a nexus between traditional education modalities and youth work. He has mentored youth workers and teachers and has learned and developed a myriad of methodologies to engage young people, particularly those who have developed a distrust of adult institutions.

Marisa Ragonese is a PhD candidate in the field of social welfare at the CUNY Graduate Center and Silberman School of Social Work, where she is working on a dissertation exploring the reproduction of gender inequity among teens at the intersection of the aggression commonly known as bullying and sexual harassment. A long-time feminist activist and advocate with and on behalf of girls and LGBT youth, she opened and ran the first and only drop-in centre for LGBTQ youth in her native Queens, NYC. Currently she serves as Director of the Westchester County Youth Councils. She is also a research fellow at QuERI, the Queering Education Research Institute of the LGBT Social Science Center and Policy Institute at Roosevelt House, Hunter College, CUNY. She lives in Yorktown, NY with her partner and their daughter, Holly.

Heather L. Ramey is Professor in the School of Social and Community Service at the Humber Institute of Technology and Advanced Learning, an adjunct professor of Child and Youth Studies at Brock University and the Co-Director of Research at the Centre of Excellence for Youth Engagement. She received her doctorate in lifespan development psychology from Brock University. She began her working life as a child and youth worker and has worked in a variety of roles in direct work with youth, including youth-adult partnerships. Her research has focused on youth engagement and youth community mobilisation and the bidirectional relationships between youth and larger contexts, including organisations and communities.

Victoria Restler is Assistant Professor of Educational Studies and Director of the Master's Program in Youth Development at Rhode Island College. Since 2002 she has worked in schools, juvenile justice facilities, galleries, neighbourhoods and non-profits to address social justice issues through participatory art-making. Victoria received her PhD in Urban Education from the CUNY Graduate Center in 2017. Her multimodal dissertation explores the visual culture of teacher evaluation by zooming in on the images and experiences of educators grappling with new evaluation policies. She was awarded the 2018 AERA Outstanding Dissertation Award in Arts-Based Educational Research.

Laurie Ross is Associate Professor of Community Development and Planning at Clark University (USA). She is also Director of the Youth Work Practice professional certificate programme at Clark. She engages in community-based action research projects on topics such as youth and gang violence, youth and young adult homelessness and youth worker professional education.

Jennifer Safford-Farquharson serves as the Outreach Coordinator/Community Resource Liaison focusing on creating, maintaining and supporting a collective approach to outreach work, which includes training, organising, advocating and managing. This work falls under her broader work as Youth & Gang Violence Initiatives Projects Coordinator for Clark University (USA) where she also works as Adjunct Faculty.

Momodou Sallah is Reader in Globalisation and Global Youth Work at the Social Work, Youth and Community Division, De Montfort University, UK. He is also the Chair of the Board of Directors of Global Hands, which is an INGO operating in The Gambia and the UK. In June 2013, he was named a National Teaching Fellow by the UK Higher Education Academy. In November 2015, he was named the 'Most Innovative Teacher' in the UK in the Times Higher Education Awards. He has more than twenty years' experience working with young people at the local, national and international levels; from being the Youth Director of The Gambia Red Cross Society to a Senior Youth Worker at the Leicester City Council, UK. Dr Sallah has numerous publications in the fields of working with black young people and young Muslims and globalisation/global youth work. His research interests include diversity, participation and globalisation, especially in relation to young people.

Natalie Sargent is a passionate youth worker, with vast experience working alongside youth in a variety of contexts. She graduated from Wellington Institute of Technology with her Bachelor of Youth Development in 2016. Her drive for positive outcomes for youth has led her to engage in further study focusing on youth development, whilst continuing to work in the New Zealand youth sector.

Alastair Scott-McKinley is Lecturer in Community Youth Work at Ulster University. He has practitioner experience in a range of youth work settings, including youth justice, political education, community relations work and centre-based youth work. He has written on curriculum use in youth work and is currently researching epistemic culture amongst youth work professionals.

Howard Sercombe is a youth work academic and practitioner. He has been a pioneer internationally in thinking about professional ethics for youth workers and was involved in drafting codes of ethics for youth work associations across Australia and in Scotland, England, South Africa, Zambia and New Zealand. His book, *Youth Work Ethics* was the first text on the subject by a major publisher (other than edited collections) and has been widely influential. He has also published widely on the sociology of youth, including the construction of youth in the media and the emerging influence of neuroscience. He is currently honorary Professor of Education at the University of Glasgow.

Ismail Shaafee came to Australia to study youth work in 2008. He has a Diploma in Youth Work (Holmesglen TAFE), a B.Soc.Sci (Youth Work) and a B.Arts (International Studies) (Hons) from RMIT University. His honours dissertation, for which he was awarded a distinction, considered the international transfer of youth work knowledge. In 2014 Ismail moved back to his home, in Male, the Maldives, to take up the position of Senior Youth Officer in the Ministry for Youth and Sports. In this capacity, he managed Youth Centres across the Maldives and designed and facilitated programmes for these, while also being involved in reviewing the existing Youth Department framework and developing and drafting the Youth Bill. Aside from his official work, in his free time, Ismail loves to help young people in activities such as finding work or accessing health care.

Nicola Sim is a PhD candidate with Tate and the University of Nottingham. Her work investigates partnerships between visual arts organisations and the youth sector, using a Tate-led programme called Circuit as the context for her ethnographic study. Nicola was formerly Curator, Public Programmes at Whitechapel Gallery and a freelancer in the Youth and Adult Programmes at Tate Britain.

Hans Skott-Myhre is Professor in the Social Work and Human Services Department at Kennesaw State University. He is cross-appointed to the graduate programme in psychology at the University of West Georgia and holds appointments at Brock University and the University of Victoria. He is the author of *Youth and Subculture as Creative Force: Creating New Spaces for Radical Youth Work* and co-editor with Chris Richardson of *Habitus of the Hood*, co-editor with Kiaras Gharabaghi and Mark Krueger of *With Children and Youth*, as well as co-editor with Veronica Pacini-Ketchabaw and Kathleen Skott-Myhre of *Youth Work, Early Education and Psychology: Liminal Encounters*.

Kathleen Skott-Myhre is Associate Professor of Psychology and Associate Dean of Social Sciences at the University of West Georgia. She is the author of *Feminist Spirituality under Capitalism: Witches, Fairies and Nomads* as well as the co-author of *Writing the Family: Women, Auto-ethnography, and Family Work*. She is co-editor with V. Pacini-Ketchabaw and H.A. Skott-Myhre of *Youth work, Early Education and Psychology: Liminal Encounters*. She has published multiple articles, reviews and book chapters.

Joshua Spier is Research Associate in the College of Education, Psychology and Social Work at Flinders University, Australia. He has practised in community development, music and education for over 17 years across a variety of contexts, including youth work, local government and the international development, relief and advocacy sector. He has taught community development, sociology and youth studies as a lecturer within various tertiary programmes. Joshua's doctoral research crafted a hermeneutic phenomenological analysis of Australian educators' everyday experiences of teaching pre-service youth workers in university contexts. His recent book conveys the findings from this study: *Heidegger and the Lived Experience of Being a University Educator* (Palgrave Macmillan, 2018). Joshua's current research agenda seeks to advance equity and ethical practice within higher education, community development, health and human services.

Helmut Steinkellner's perspective on youth work practice is informed by almost two decades of experience in the field of 'Streetwork', where he has undertaken both direct-work and management roles. Helmut is a long-standing member of the international Streetworkers network, 'Dynamo International' and has fulfilled a variety of roles within numerous European Union youth programs. Through his practice roles and his involvement in various international networks Helmut proactively lobbies for the rights of the child and has a particular interest in the rights of refugees and asylum seekers. Helmut is currently completing a Masters in Political Education at Danube University Krems.

Tony Taylor is the coordinator of In Defence of Youth Work, having been previously a youth worker, trainer, community education adviser, chief youth officer and lecturer. Throughout his career he has been a prominent trade union activist. He has written extensively on such subjects as anti-sexist practice with young men and the relation of class politics to youth work. Most recently he has focused on the illusions of the outcomes-led agenda, speaking to this theme in Europe and Australia.

Paul Thomas is Professor of Youth and Policy at the University of Huddersfield, UK and a professionally qualified youth and community worker. Paul's research focuses on how multiculturalist policies such as Community Cohesion and Prevent have been mediated and implemented by local policy-makers and practitioners (particularly youth workers) and experienced by youth and their communities. It has led to the books *Youth, Multiculturalism and Community Cohesion* (Palgrave, 2011) and *Responding to the Threat of Violent Extremism – Failing to Prevent* (Bloomsbury, 2012), as well as journal articles. Paul has recently researched the barriers faced by young adults in different communities when it comes to sharing concerns with authorities regarding someone close to them having an involvement in violent extremism and also how the 'Prevent legal duty' has been understood and implemented by schools and colleges in England.

Roma Thomas is Research Fellow at the Institute of Applied Social Research (IASR) at the University of Bedfordshire. She joined the International Centre: Researching Child Sexual Exploitation, Violence and Trafficking in IASR in 2013. She is Course Coordinator for a Masters in International Social Work and Social Development and her teaching interests include adolescence, gender, research methods and academic skills. Her research interests include family support, social work, young masculinities and emotional methodologies. Her past research work includes a range of projects with children, families and practitioners. Roma is currently completing her doctoral studies, focusing on young masculinities, at the University of Sussex.

Naomi Thompson is Lecturer in Youth and Community work at Goldsmiths, University of London. She has previously worked at Middlesex University, YMCA George Williams College and The Open University and she has a professional background in local authority youth work. Her research specialisms include young people, youth work, crime and religion. She edits for the online journal, *Youth and Policy*. Her research monograph on *Young People and Church since 1900* was published by Routledge in 2017.

Marion Thomson has extensive experience in developing and facilitating education programmes with youth and community workers, community organisations, unions, social housing tenants and staff. This work has focused on such areas as equity and human rights, community and international development, popular education, children's rights, barriers to educational success, gender, oral history, participatory research and evaluation. These innovative programmes were developed for various continental contexts in urban and rural communities in Canada, the UK and Ghana, West Africa. The latter programme is the focus of our chapter drawing on Marion's experience working in partnership with Kodzo Chapman and YPEC using arts-based methods and popular theatre. She has worked extensively with young people and children of all ages and believes in the transformative power of critical and participatory approaches to education and youth work. Marion has a Masters and a PhD in Education with a special interest in critical youth work, equity and social justice, popular education and arts-based education, qualitative research and social history.

Jo Trelfa is the Head of Academic Professional Development at the University of Winchester, UK, supporting lecturers in their teaching and facilitation of undergraduate and postgraduate students on a range of degree programmes, including work with children and young people. Prior to this she was senior lecturer in youth and community work programmes for 20 years, having worked for 12 years as a youth worker, community worker and psychotherapist in the

UK and Middle East, and on projects in South America and the Caribbean, with individuals, groups and communities around issues of abuse, violence, mental health and being well. The anchor of her work has always been the process leading to decisions that she/professionals make, referred to as reflective practice. This became the focus of her teaching and research. She is in the final stages of a part-time PhD and has a number of papers published in this area, more recently in Japan where she has supported an initiative to establish reflective practice as part of university programmes there. She is the full-time mother to a wonderful daughter and enjoys living near the sea.

Wolfgang Vachon has been working with children and youth as an advocate, ally, artist and educator for close to three decades. Community arts practice has informed his work with diverse young people including those who are street involved, homeless, LGBTQ+, survivors of trauma and in detention as well as state care. Wolfgang is a full-time faculty member in the Child and Youth Care programmes at Humber College in Toronto, Canada and is the host of CYC Podcast: Discussions on Child and Youth Care (www.cycpodcast.org)

Ron Waddell is Director of Aftercare at Straight Ahead Ministries. He has been continuously involved in serving disadvantaged youth. His commitment to young people resulted in him leaving his high-paying job as a project manager to focus on his passion for young adults. He also recently founded the Finding Cain Fatherhood Initiative, which has a mission to maximise the potential of fathers, spiritually, socially, economically and psychologically.

Candice T. Wallace is an avid Child Protection Advocate, International Development Consultant and Certified Mediator. Her expertise is centred on the research, development, implementation, monitoring and evaluation of social policies, programmes and projects. She has a Bachelor of Laws and a Masters in Children, Youth and International Development. She has a strong blend of experience in child and youth development, restorative and juvenile justice, judicial reform, conflict resolution, human rights and gender equality. She is the President and Founder of RISE – a Child Protection Foundation and co-founder of XDA, a youth organisation that uses dance as a medium to empower at-risk youth. Candice has contributed to several policies and programmes and the development of procedures, protocols and standards to enhance child well-being in Trinidad and Tobago. She has also worked with organisations and communities in South Africa, Zimbabwe and the UK strengthening child protection systems, building monitoring and evaluation capacities and designing community-based approaches to address gender-based violence.

Rob Watts is Professor of Social Policy at RMIT University. Rob teaches in policy studies, criminology, ethics and good practice, the history of ideas and applied human rights. He was a founding member of the Greens Party in Victoria, a founding editor of the journal *Just Policy* and he established the Australian Center for Human Rights Education at RMIT in 2008. His books include *The Foundations of the National Welfare State* (1987), *Arguing About the Australian Welfare State* (with M. Considine and P. Beilharz) (1992), *International Criminology: A Critical Introduction* (with J. Bessant and R. Hil) (2009), *Sociology Australia* (3rd edition, with J. Bessant) (2007) and *Talking Policy: Australian Social Policy* (with J. Bessant, T. Dalton and P. Smyth) (2007). His *States of Violence and the Civilising Process: On Criminology and State Crime* was published in 2016 and *Public Universities, Managerialism and the Value of Higher Education* in 2017.

Michael Whelan's professional background is in youth work where he has gained an international perspective on the development of services for young people through his experience of working as a qualified youth worker in the Republic of Ireland, Australia and the UK. In 2008 he completed his PhD research project, which focused on researching the issue of 'street violence amongst young men in London'. Public space, social geography, youth violence and detached youth work are all important themes within Michael's work and this is reflected in his professional practice background, his research and publication interests and his teaching focus with higher education.

Tanya Wiggins has twenty years' experience as an educator, during which she has supported youth through middle school instruction, professional development, non-profit leadership and higher education. Tanya currently serves as Clinical Assistant Professor of Foundations and Adolescent Education in the School of Education at Pace University. Her research interests seek to bridge the worlds of research and practice by exploring the ways in which young people create their own forms of social capital in support of educational achievement, as well as examining the role of community-based youth organisations as educational spaces.

Mark Wood has worked with young people for thirty years in Europe, the UK, USA and New Zealand. He has trained youth workers in both the UK and New Zealand. He is a published author, having written a guide to working with young men for the UK charity UKYouth. He has many years' experience in group work and individual work with young people, their families and communities. He is passionate about youth development and its ability to make services more responsive to young people's needs.

Dan Woodman is the TR Ashworth Associate Professor in Sociology in the School of Social and Political Sciences at the University of Melbourne. He is President (2017–18) of The Australian Sociological Association (TASA) and also Vice-President for Oceania of the Research Committee for the Sociology of Youth (RC 34) within the International Sociological Association. His work focuses on the sociology of young adulthood and generations, social change and the impact of insecure work and variable employment patterns on people's relationships. His recent books include *Youth and Generation* (with Johanna Wyn, Sage) and the four-volume collection *Youth and Young Adulthood* (with Andy Furlong, Routledge) and the edited collection *Youth Cultures, Transitions, and Generations: Bridging the Gap in Youth Research* (with Andy Bennett, Palgrave).

Johanna Wyn is Redmond Barry Distinguished Professor, FASSA, FAcSS, at the University of Melbourne, Australia. She leads the Life Patterns longitudinal study of two cohorts of Australians and her research focuses on the impact of social change on young people's lives, with particular reference to the relationships between education and work, and gender and well-being. Recent books include *Youth and Generation* (with Dan Woodman, Sage), *Handbook of Children and Youth Studies* (with Helen Cahill, Springer) and *Youth and Society* (4th edition, with Rob White and Brady Robards, Oxford University Press).

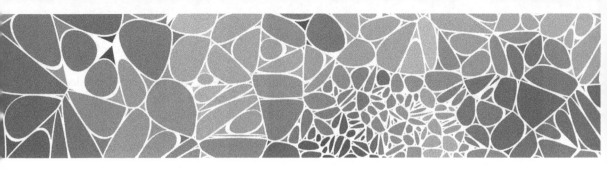

Introduction

Pam Alldred, Fin Cullen,
Kathy Edwards and Dana Fusco

This *Handbook* documents and celebrates professional work with young people as it is practised in diverse forms around the world (although the relations to 'the professional' are varied and contested). It argues for recognition of the value of youth work for communities, and for societies, as well as for individuals. It demonstrates the urgency of this work in times of increasing globalisation, social division and entrenched nationalism, racism and individualism, in the context of the prevalence of neoliberalism and global capitalism – and of macho posturing by international leaders that most of us would not accept in a youth project, classroom, playground, office, or around the dinner table. Much of this social context correlates with an overall detachment and de-investment from youth services and youth work, hence the importance and timeliness of this *Handbook* as a way to elevate a practice tradition currently endangered.

Some challenges will already be apparent in this project. SAGE seeks global reach for

its *Handbooks* and while we editors accept that global coverage is neither possible nor palatable in an Anglophone collection edited by four white women from industrialised nations, most in the Global North, we celebrate the diversity of forms of practice included here and the culturally situated perspectives they represent.

The collection illustrates the wide range of approaches that identify as youth work, or community work or community development work with young people, youth programmes, and work with young people within care, development and (informal) education frameworks. Across these differing approaches, the *Handbook* explores the ways practitioners work with young people and the type of projects, services, campaigns and relationships that are possible. It examines how specific contexts (geographical, economic, regional and political) shape and enable specific forms of practice and organisation, and authors were asked to consider how unique, indigenous or common certain modes of practice are. We have encouraged contributors to locate their practice clearly in their local context and to recognise different perspectives among young people or practitioners in any given location, as well as differences and the intersections of privilege within a locale, such as the differential impacts of poverty, exclusion or discrimination. We have also sought to explore the political histories of what has been called youth work and how its colonial export to fields of existing practice created neo-colonial strands, sometimes in dialogue with indigenous practice, and the tensions between these and local conditions, understandings or practices as well as with more established, dominant, 'old world' understandings.

In the collection that results from four years of dialogue with potential contributors, then chapter drafts and editorial exchanges, we have chapters about practice with Roma youth, and with young people in Aotearoa New Zealand, Austria, Australia, Brazil, Canada, 'Europe' in general, Finland, Ghana, India, Kenya, Mozambique, South Africa, the Maldives, Sweden, Tanzania, the United Kingdom (and specifically England and Northern Ireland), the United States of America, and Zambia.

The *Handbook* therefore offers a wide-ranging and experience-based resource for practitioners, researchers and educators. It provides an insight into some of the major paradigms, histories, issues and debates in Anglophone youth practice, as well as practice that is that sometimes written about in English, and it reflects critically on the current challenges facing those working with young people. Specific discourses and traditions, such as Positive Youth Development from the USA, the Albemarle tradition from the UK, or Social Pedagogy from Europe, come up in many different chapters, but practices, issues and in particular young people inflect each chapter uniquely. The *Handbook* does offer some mapping of a discipline, albeit a pluri-vocal discipline, and identifies some new directions for the future of youth practice or professional work with young people.

Each chapter presents a rich and substantial account of the pressures and perspectives that have shaped, or continue to shape, the discipline or mode of practice. They speak from particular locations and forms of practice with young people in that and/or other locations, and often explicitly consider (rather than assume) the potential relevance to other places. Each discussion of practice is contextualised, along with the practices or theories it discusses, not just nationally, but historically, culturally and geo-politically.

What unites these chapters is not writers engaged with 'the problem of youth', but activists and writers engaged with the problems that young people face in their daily lives. This emphasis pervades the whole collection. While some contributors employ developmental discourses of youth and others critique this, all are critical of the treatment of young people in their societies: their marginalisation, infantilisation, desexualisation or oversexualisation, exploitation or the *conditional* ways in which they are finally granted citizenship.

The *Handbook* has 44 chapters and is divided into four sections. Part I introduces approaches within 'youth work' and considers enduring themes and questions. Part II illustrates some of the range of practices these inform. Part II discusses the politics and ethics of practice in different locations, and Part IV looks to the future in tracing the current tensions and developments in practice. We editors each took responsibility for a section. At the end of this Introduction is a list of the members of the international Advisory Board, to whom we were very grateful to draw on to invite and review contributions.

Part I, *Approaches to Youth Work across Time and Place*, introduces different approaches to youth work, considers enduring themes and problems, and focuses on how these manifest in modern times. It is telling that, despite the diversity of subject matter, almost all chapters discuss the pernicious effects of globalism (especially global capitalism) and/or neoliberalism, and highlight the necessity for youth work to respond to the challenges posed by these. Sub-themes that emerge across the chapters include the state's impetus towards controlling young people and the complexity of youth work's relationship with the state, the exacerbation of old and the creation of new inequalities, and the need to adapt older or create new approaches to youth work. Underlying this is the perennial question of 'what is youth work?' and, in an increasingly precarious and globalised world, whether any consensus on this can be reached. Importantly, places and spaces for hope, creativity, regeneration and resistance also feature.

The challenges posed to youth work by neoliberalism and/or globalisation are central to three chapters: Woodman and Wyn focus on changes to youth labour markets, now characterised by precarity, unemployment and underemployment, and consider the capacity of young people to build lives and make positive transitions in this context. They see the potential for youth work to draw on generational awareness to facilitate young people to control their own lives and be part of collectively shaping the future of their respective communities. Drawing from post-Marxist and postmodern ideas and aligning with the tradition of radical youth work, Skott-Mhyre and Skott-Mhyre focus on the necessity for youth work to confront global capitalism, arguing that we should be working with young people for system change. They urge eschewing the state and instead developing creative, community-focused 'DIY' approaches. A team from In Defence of Youth Work (Taylor, Connaughton, de St Croix, Davies and Grace), document the destructive impacts of neoliberalism on English youth work. Focusing on a shift from youth work that prioritised voluntary association, open-ended work and relational approaches, to that characterised by an austerity agenda of competition for funding and

structured formal programmes designed to create 'resilient' young people, they argue for the creation of international alliances to secure the future of radical youth work praxis founded on social justice and democracy.

The effects of neoliberal policy agendas and globalisation on youth work are seen in a range of other chapters with broader foci too. Regarding the impetus of the state towards control, but concentrating on European youth policy and programmes, Cullen and Bradford consider the enduring issue of youth work and risk. They argue that the precarious economic and social climates engendered by neoliberalism are resulting in policy regimes that foreground 'risk' and which aim towards turning young people into responsible citizens, creating a range of new and old challenges and dilemmas for youth workers. Jones tells the story of the bid to professionalise English youth work and how this fell victim both to austerity in the name of neoliberalism and the desire of both Labour and Conservative governments to harness youth work to regulate and control young people. Jones also interrogates bigger questions, such as whether youth work should be professionalised and the potential impacts of professionalisation on the character of English youth work. Writing from India, Nuggehalli foregrounds the shift of the Indian state towards a neoliberal developmental agenda in the 1990s, resulting in an impetus to consider young people instrumentally. Nuggehalli counterposes state-driven youth work that seeks to professionalise, regulate and control, with youth work in independent NGOs that is guided by the principles of justice and participatory democracy and aimed at ensuring young people's agency and purposeful action.

Working with girls and boys and Black, Asian and minority ethnic (BAME) young people have long been central concerns in youth work education and research, as has practice oriented towards ending the oppression of girls and BAME youth. Sallah, Ogunnusi and Kennedy take up the issue of youth work, race and racism through the lenses of Critical Race Theory, Critical Peace Education and Global Youth Work to argue that globalism is increasingly creating gross inequalities, including those relating to race. Emphasising an intersectional approach, they argue that youth work needs to operate as a pedagogy of disruption and hope. Batsleer considers English youth work, girls and sexism and describes three different, necessary 'moments' in youth work practice, 'equality', 'ideology critique' and the 'affirmation of difference' and considers how each plays a role in dismantling sexism and women's oppression.

In considering old and new forms of youth work, as noted above, some chapters focus centrally on the United Kingdom, the crucible of youth work. Often, these emphasise the need to *defend* youth work. Others consider youth work in the new world, a world shaped by modern globalisation and also by older patterns of colonisation. In these contexts, the issue is more about how best to create approaches to youth work that complement local conditions and customs. Fusco considers youthwork in the United States, aspiring to map its history and to create dialogue about its future. She argues that youth work in the US has been shaped by definitions and problematisations of youth and is deeply located in historical, cultural and economic contexts. Edwards and Shaafee consider difficulties inherent in transferring youth work from the old world and the Global North (especially the UK) to the Global South, particularly to the small island nation of the Maldives. They ask crucial questions about the potential for youth work to be a colonising rather than emancipatory practice and argue for the creation of diverse, culturally specific youth works. Youth work as informal education or 'social pedagogy' is also a mainstay of youth work in the UK and some other contexts. Drawing on European approaches, Hatton argues that framing English youth work as social pedagogy in the current neoliberal climate can contribute by reframing activities with young people around three central notions of criticality, creativity and community.

Two chapters focus on the 'big picture' of how we understand youth work and how youth work understands itself. Jeffs makes the observation that to understand our present and future we must understand our past. He aims to understand how youth work in the UK considers the practices and ideas that shape its history and delineate it as 'youth work'. Cooper grapples with complex questions of why we should and how we might define youth work across geopolitical borders as a distinctive form of practice. She considers unifying and distinguishing characteristics – finding holism, positive regard and concern for flourishing as three of these – as well as areas of difference and disagreement. Cooper's aim is to spark curiosity and debate, with the chapter acting as a discussion piece for the way forward.

In Part II, *Professional Work with Young People: Projects and Practices to Inspire*, chapters consider the methods and approaches for contemporary youth work practice in diverse contexts. Key themes that emerge throughout this section are around professional space, young people's rights and the need to develop responsive praxis to changing times – and such themes are again drawn on in later sections. In the opening chapter Collin, Lala and Fieldgrass consider the challenges raised by youth participation approaches and the need to consider broader questions of citizenship while arguing for a deeper political project of youth engagement. Within many regional and (inter)national contexts, youth work arose from faith-based settings and Bright, Thompson, Hart and Hayden explore the motivations and reflections on practice of UK-based staff from a range of world faiths. They view faith-based settings as responsive and inclusive sites for professional praxis that can challenge dominant neoliberal regimes of 'targeted' practice.

Questions of colonialism in relation to theory and practice are raised by Beals, Foase, Miller, Perkins and Sargent.

Starting with the work of Freire, they consider how personal and professional praxis in Aotearoa/New Zealand might draw on new stories and conceptualisations of practice, and highlight how these can create counter-narratives to dominant Western views of youth development. Couch reflects on effective practice with refugee youth in an Australian context and highlights the need to develop supportive relationships that value young people's experiences, especially when working in often hostile political contexts.

Two chapters consider detached or street-based youth work. Whelan and Steinkellner reflect comparatively on power, space and territory in work in public spaces in Austria and the UK. This issue of territoriality in relation to professional identities is also developed by Andersson writing from a Swedish context. Using the concept of 'fringe work', he traces the history of 'outreach work' to consider the border work of developing relationships with young people when navigating complex political tensions regarding disadvantaged and refugee youth.

Issues of space and purpose are a key theme in Howard, Brocken and Sim's chapter on youth arts work, in which they draw on Soja's 'Thirdspace' to argue for productive dialogue with young people based on a nuanced, deep understanding of youth work pedagogy. Case and Morris explore youth justice practice within the UK and argue that new child/youth-centred practices can promote and support young people's rights and create more progressive and equitable youth justice contexts.

Single sex and feminist-based practice has a long tradition within youth work in many contexts and two chapters highlight why sex-gender matters in contemporary work. Morgan and McArdle reflect on decades of work in a Northern Irish context and broader debates on feminist activism and youth work practice to argue for an 'alchemy' of transformative practice in supporting young women. McNamara's chapter on the work of UK-based Gendered Intelligence with trans, gender diverse and/or non-binary young people documents the emergence of new practices to revalue stigmatised identities, support trans young people in developing a sense of pride and promote greater intelligence about gender for all. Overall, this section traces models and approaches to practice, not to provide new orthodoxies of 'good practice', but to promote dialogue about the complex and shifting political and professional challenges faced by youth workers, young people and their communities across regional and international contexts. It reflects on local and global anxieties, new funding regimes and broader political and theoretical debates regarding professional expertise and the purpose of work with young people.

In Part III, *Values and Ethics in Work with Young People*, the politics and the ethics of practice are considered by practitioners in various locations, and working with varied theoretical and disciplinary resources. The opening chapters consider the centrality of relationship to youth work or to the work of social educators in reflections on practice in Australia, Brazil and the UK, respectively: Spier and Giles offer an ethics of care which they see as central to professional involvement with young people; Jupp Kina highlights the contribution of relationship for young people who have experienced violence from their family or community; and Trelfa scrutinises our resources for professional reflexivity. Each of these chapters explores the challenges of voluntarism, non-coercion and letting young people choose what to share and when, and each offers an alternative theoretical toolbox.

Chapters by a group of collaborators in the USA (Foley, Guzman, Lopez, Ross, Safford-Farquharson, with Byrne, Pinero and Waddell), and then by Thomas consider the politics of gang intervention work and in particular, the politics of working with police and government agencies, scrutinising work in the USA and the UK respectively. In both locations, these forms of practice raise issues about the politics of working with targeted and minority youth, and dilemmas that can arise as a result of funding arrangements or the rhetoric of policy that practice is to enact.

Informal educational approaches are identified as central to working with young people around sexual politics and against sexual violence. Two chapters discuss the dilemmas facing child protection activists in contexts in Sub-Saharan Africa and in the UK. Heslop shares case studies of universal and of targeted youth or community education projects in Ghana, Kenya and Mozambique to examine the pedagogies for social change that might seek to promote sexual consent, reduce stigma or challenge the sexual double standards surrounding girls who are believed to be sexually active compared with boys. D'Arcy, Thomas and Wallace examine approaches to tackling child sexual abuse, sexual exploitation and abuse in interpersonal relationships. Interventions might be framed as educational, or as experience-sharing, and might be conducted in schools, in homes, in independent community spaces or even in a car parked outside a parental home.

What can other social movements teach us about challenging normativities? How can young people work across difference and how can adults work with young people across their difference(s) from them – does the notion of *ally* help? Vachon and McConnell consider what can be learned from the experience of trans and disability activists regarding coalition working. Another type of resource that can be deployed to recognise difference or to reframe stigma is visual research, and Restler and Luttrell illustrate this through work that can talk politics through intimate home space imaging.

Sercombe's chapter considers internationalism as a resource in itself and addresses the challenges of developing an international ethical code for youth workers that can transcend Eurocentrism and colonialism. This he founds within a humanistic and essentialist ideal type of youth work, characterised by an ethic of service to young people as clients, a focus upon their immediate social

environment, and the goal of achieving young people's self-actualisation by encouraging their own agency.

Finally, two chapters in this section consider the ethical issues raised – and cultural resources available – to support young people with particular needs, emerging variously from the use or misuse of drugs and alcohol and the complex issues that arise regarding young people's health or mental health needs (Wood) or at the end of their life for those young people with a terminal illness (Patel). The resources of indigenous (Māori) culture and recent policy on youth, and of medical ethics or of wider *social* models of health – and the notion of well-being – are some of the frameworks that help to identify resources or priorities for supporting young people in these circumstances.

Overall, this section offers examples of practice and case studies of locations where practitioners strive for fully participatory or youth-led approaches to work for social justice with young people or in their lives. There is much reflection on the value and skills of relationship building, especially with socially marginalised youth. Even the most individualised of support work, such as that with young people needing palliative care, shows the value of political analysis to identify priorities and projections that others have for these young people in order to better hear what young people themselves want. This enables us to deconstruct discourses of support to see how they draw more strongly from protectionist palettes for sick young people than empowerment palettes. It is in this sense that some of the disciplinary resources on offer show their merit. Whereas sociology helps practitioners to recognise the structural pressures facing young people, the psychological influence in policing and law (and psychology) focus on the individual, locating the deficit or problem there.

Part IV, *Current Challenges, Future Possibilities*, includes nine distinct chapters. The chapters illustrate the challenges faced by youth and, by extension, youth workers, in a variety of settings and contexts, and point to future possibilities for youth work as a way to help create a more just, inclusive and decent society. Each chapter in its own way identifies professional responses that enable young people to overcome, face, live with, thrive, and to change violence, oppression, racism, ageism, and dearth of expectation and opportunity through a range of youth work practices. As with the rest of the *Handbook* collection, each narrative paints a deeply contextualised story in which youth work responses are interwoven in a complexity of socio-political, historical, economic and cultural factors.

Read in this way, one might examine how macro-levels of contextuality (politics, history, economic conditions, etc.) intersect and play out on a local community and neighbourhood level, particularly as they pertain to making decisions that impact the lives of young people: What is the broader organisational and social/cultural/political/historical context(s) within which young people and youth work reside? How does that context shape and even limit organisational responses and practices with young people in positive or negative directions? And, how does all of that shape the lives of young people (for better or worse)? As the reader will shortly note, societal conflict and post-conflict (e.g., in Northern Ireland), colonialism and post-colonialism (e.g., as in 'Roma' communities and in Ghana), and notably, neoliberal economic policies (e.g., in most of Europe, Australia and the United States) have had enormous impacts on young people, communities and youth work – and disproportionately, youth and communities of colour. Yet, it is all too typical that decisions about practice, policy, research and funding are made in isolation from these broader realities.

Each chapter draws attention to the need to take into account the nuanced and grounded intersection between the micro context (the situation, area and context for a particular group of youth and the practice of youth work that responds to these young people's realities), the mezzo context (the nature of organisations in their particular context; the

articulated values and ethics within the profession; the conditions of the sector including social/economic capital; professional education and professional status; and how each of these is set up to support or possibly impede the social progress of young people), and the macro context (the larger political, cultural, economic, social factors that cast a shadow on how we see/shape/respond to youth and youth work). By addressing all three aspects within a specific context, we envision future decision-making about youth work that has the capacity to be responsive to the actual conditions of young people's lives, to the organisational challenges faced by those doing the work, and to the larger social forces that support or impede the ability of all young people to thrive.

The stakes are higher than many recognise in terms of multiple layers of loss when attention to context is ignored: loss to youth, to communities, to society, to our global village and to democracy. Youth work in many places not only has withered away through enormous funding cuts for youth services, but in its place systems have been introduced that work against democratic practices with young people. The losses over the past twenty or so years to young people, to communities and to the field are itself enough to lament over; but the loss to potential representative democracies is also staggering as young people are not prepared for embracing their place in the world as equal citizens of a shared and fair society. Participation in pre-packaged programmes does not get at the pedagogical practices and principles that most here hold up as the critical core of the youth work tradition, discipline and profession. In each youth work context, the relationship between youth and youth worker(s) is the vehicle for expressions of care and concern, the basis for trust, the foundation for dialogue, and the tool for communication and learning. Further, the relation(s) between and among youth worker(s), young person(s) and the community (whether the immediate geographical surrounding or an interest-based community) has an immediate role in defining the purpose of youth work as a practice that is closer to traditional social work than more current educational iterations and re-shapings of youth work. Each of these types of social relations requires 'partnering' (see Ramey and Lawford) and participation (see Cooper and Gretschel), and challenges the notion of empowerment (see also Belton), which is embedded in individualistic notions of growth and advancement.

Bartlett and Muirhead illustrate how young people's own priorities are placed at the heart of a youth work approach inspired by community development, while linking into wider structures and processes and emphasising social and collective as well as individual outcomes; something that some strands of youth work have lost sight of in recent times. Youth workers in this arrangement are called back to a place of responsiveness to young people (see Matloff-Nieves et al.), facilitative (see Belton) and ethical (see Bessant and Watts) in their actions.

Youth work has no subscription to a particular content: it can reside in everything from basketball, hip hop, ping pong/table tennis, theatre and film, literacy, or service learning. However, in many areas, there is a specific need and a call to engage youth in political and historical analysis, because without so doing there is no way to heal and restore. Of course, analysis without action may not yield the sorts of youth and community actions that many would aim for, and certainly runs short of democracy building and peace, as many in this section point out. Thomson and Chapman illustrate there is no such thing as 'common sense', for our sense is always limited to our experiences, which themselves can be contradictory and complex. It is essential for self-growth, as well as the growth of communities to engage in critical analysis and reflection in order to challenge the epistemological frameworks upon which prior learning has been built. They view the questioning of 'why' and 'what if' as the 'training ground for democracy'.

The implications for a responsive, democratic practice for the professional education of youth workers as well as the evaluation of youth work programmes is then discussed in the final two chapters. Kiilakoski, Kinnunen and Djupsund provide a call to action for youth workers to articulate the form and function of youth work. The chapter offers an interpretation of how youth workers can explicate the tacit knowledge of the profession as supporting the individual and social identities of young people through their participation in curriculum development. Cooper and Gretschel draw on their respective research in England and Finland, where both are exploring models for participatory evaluation. The chapters urge us to consider how the principles of youth work can also be the bedrock for youth work education, research and evaluation, with all methods based on participation and dialogical relationships.

This *Handbook* is among the first books about youth work practice that is truly international. That is hugely significant, and not before time. As Tony Jeffs, a member of our Advisory Board as well as contributing author, says 'Youth work is a long rope comprising many strands. One that remains unfinished'. The vigour and resilience of this emanates from a blending of fieldwork and research which broadens our understanding and deepens our awareness, and from a process, whereby theory changes practice and practice changes theory, in what philosophers and others refer to as praxis. As Howard Sercombe remarks in his chapter, we hope the *Handbook* initiates new dialogues and sustains the conversation. We look forward to seeing the collection of chapters in conversation with each other across the four Parts and then to the conversations within youth studies and youth work/development scholarship and practice. With so many challenges facing the world today, our conviction is that work of the types illustrated here can help societies to listen, to cooperate, to heal, ultimately to be more just and to exclude and discriminate less. We hope that you will find the inspiration for practice for social justice in each of the chapters that we do.

PART I

Approaches to Youth Work
Across Time and Place

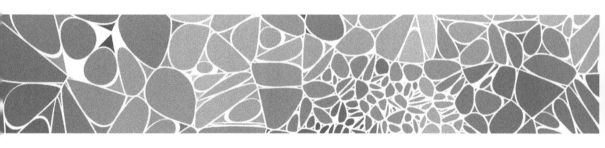

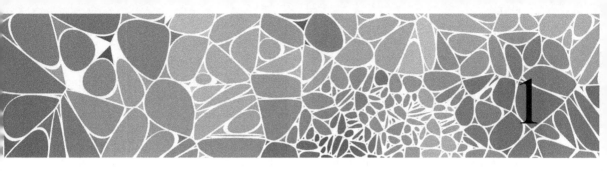

Defining Youth Work: Exploring the Boundaries, Continuity and Diversity of Youth Work Practice

Trudi Cooper

INTRODUCTION: DEFINING YOUTH WORK – THE NEED AND THE DIFFICULTIES

The general public, politicians and novice youth workers do not find it easy to understand how youth work relates to other forms of work with youth in the education, welfare and recreation sectors. A definition of youth work that delineates boundaries between youth work and other types of work with young people would have a number of benefits. It would make it easier for those outside youth work to understand and value what youth workers do, and to support the conditions required for successful youth work, and would increase the likelihood that youth workers' roles, skills and expertise would be publicly supported (McKee, Oldfield, & Poultney, 2010). Without this clarity, it is more difficult to challenge the various forms of dubious practice publicly labelled as youth work to the detriment of genuine practice, and youth workers find it difficult to resist the attempts of other professions to colonise youth work and redefine youth work to reflect the purposes and interests of other profession groups.

Politicians, the public and novice youth workers often seek a simple operational definition of youth work, however, as others have recognised, this is not possible (Butters & Newell, 1978, p. 17). To illustrate why this is so, consider the following comparison. People understand what teachers do because schools and teaching are part of the social fabric of contemporary societies. Teachers are employed by particular types of *institution* (schools); work in a single *context* (the classroom); perform a particular socially recognised *role* (teach pupils/students in a particular age-range); and are referred to uniformly as *teachers*. Schools as institutions have been found in most societies for generations, even before universal education became normalised. In the contemporary world, most adults have personal experience of schooling, and consequently easily recognise these institutions, contexts, roles and job titles. This means that although schooling systems and teaching methods vary considerably between schools, between countries and over time, the shared social knowledge of schooling and teaching endures even though the characterisation may change.

By contrast, for youth work there is no similar *institutional or contextual coherence*, and no universally shared social familiarity with youth work practice. Youth work occurs in varied institutional and contextual settings that appear dissimilar to observers. Many adults have little personal experience of youth work. People who are called youth workers are employed by many different types of organisation (schools, charities, other government and non-government organisations, including local government, community organisations, churches, health departments, international development agencies, shopping centres and even in custodial youth settings). Contexts of employment are varied. Youth workers may be found almost anywhere young people can be found. Locations for youth work include both specialist youth facilities (such as youth centres, residential centres or camps, and youth refuges and youth accommodation services), and non-specialist facilities (like school premises in alternative or mainstream schools, in cafés, on the streets, in shopping centres, in hospital wards, in employment or drug and alcohol services, online and sometimes in young people's homes). Given these circumstances, it is little wonder that casual observers of the everyday activities of youth workers might see little commonality in the structure, activity and purposes of youth work.

From an international perspective, the situation is further complicated because the boundaries of what is considered as youth work vary between and within countries and over time. In some languages, youth workers may have a title that makes no reference to youth (for example, animateur, Sozialpädagogik) (Hamalainen, 2015). In addition, the rationale, purposes, methods and forms of practice, and the age range of the clientele, vary between countries, and have changed over time within the same country.

Unlike teaching, it is not possible to define youth work by how it is funded. Internationally, funding for youth work comes from a wide variety of sources. Although traditionally the education department was the primary funder for modern youth work in the UK, in other countries sources of government funding have been much more diverse. In Australia, for example, multiple federal and state government departments fund youth work. Funds are provided by government departments responsible for youth justice, crime prevention, health, community development, urban renewal, civic inclusion, cultural diversity, Indigenous affairs, sport and recreation, employment, welfare, arts, homelessness, youth, families, child protection and sometimes, education. Internationally, youth work projects are funded by non-government sources, including philanthropic charitable trusts; directly by religious congregations; by business donors; through local fundraising and street collections; through contributions from young people themselves; from proceeds of gambling or crime; or from levies raised through taxation on alcohol and tobacco. In addition, not all youth work is funded. Some forms of youth work depend upon the unpaid labour of volunteers, as still occurs in village and church youth clubs, or by unpaid youth workers working alongside paid youth workers, as in youth mentoring programmes where unpaid volunteers are coordinated, trained and supported by paid youth workers (MacCallum, Beltman, Cooper, & Coffey, 2017).

In summary, shared operational definitions of youth work that cross national borders are not possible. An alternative is to seek conceptual definitions of youth work processes that encapsulate essential features of practice.

MODELS OF YOUTH WORK

Models and definitions of youth work developed independently in various countries, responded to local conditions, and were grounded in differing disciplinary perspectives. A recent Council of Europe conference report emphasised the importance of youth work theory to make sense of the diversity of contexts and practices (Williamson, 2015) and hence, this discussion draws primarily upon conceptual literature concerned with youth work processes and purposes.

Youth work academics in various countries have used schema and models to show how apparently diverse youth work practices are linked, and to differentiate between types of practice informed by different values. These schema developed independently and draw upon different theory and organising principles. Models of youth work practice attempt to systematise and contextualise youth work as a distinctive set of practices linked to other bodies of theory. This section provides an overview of how various schema have been used to make sense of youth work in different countries, and where possible link these models to definitions of youth work found within each country. More detailed discussion of these models can be found in Cooper (2012).

In the UK, Butters and Newell (1978) provided one of the earliest attempts to theorise traditions within British youth work. Butters and Newell drew upon the sociology of education, to position youth work as a countervailing force against the reproduction of social inequalities, which the mainstream education system magnifies. They distinguished five approaches to youth work, which they named 'Character-building', 'Cultural Adjustment', 'Community Development', 'Institutional Reform' and the 'Radical Paradigm' (self-emancipation). Critical pedagogy, radical social work and Marxian social action theory informed their approach. Although their schema has theoretical problems (Cooper, 2012; Leigh & Smart, 1985; Smith, 1988) it was influential in the UK until the 1990s and influenced the language and terminology of several subsequent models.

Ten years later, Smith (1988) used a historical perspective as the main organising principle of another UK model of 'youth work traditions'. Smith's model responded to deficiencies in the Butters and Newell model, and set out to describe, compare and contrast youth work traditions and processes found in Britain. This approach avoids the historicism of Butters and Newell's model. In Smith's model, history provides a means to understand relationships, tensions and boundaries between different traditions or strands within youth work, including religious and political traditions, political activism, leisure, service organisations, welfare and informal education (Cooper, 2012; Smith, 1988), see Figure 1.1. Histories of youth work demonstrate there has been continuity in some methods, especially the emphasis on positive supportive relationships between youth workers and young people. Discontinuities can be found in the purposes of youth work relationships, and the extent to which the relationship was intended to encourage conformity to social norms and engagement in wholesome leisure activities, to support religious conversion or to bring about political, social and personal change.

Since the introduction of neo-liberal post-welfare state policies beginning in the 1990s, both the institutional structure and the previously accepted consensus about youth work values have been disrupted in the UK (Cooper, 2013). This has been met with renewed interest in research into histories of youth work (Gilchrist, Hodgson, Jeffs, Spence, Stanton & Walker, 2011; Gilchrist, Jeffs, Spence & Stanton, 2013; Gilchrist, Jeffs, Spence & Walker, 2009; Spence, 2010) and with the emergence in 2009 of 'In Defence of Youth Work' (IDYW), which is a campaigning movement to defend youth work 'as a distinctive educational practice founded on a voluntary relationship with young people and shaped by their agendas' (https://indefenceofyouthwork.com/about/).

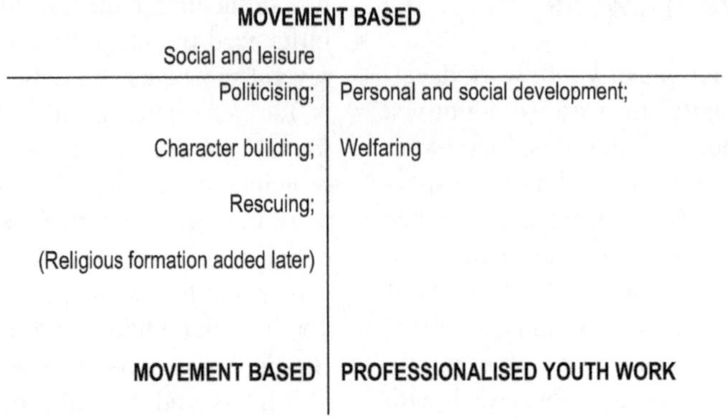

MOVEMENT BASED

Social and leisure

Politicising;	Personal and social development;
Character building;	Welfaring
Rescuing;	
(Religious formation added later)	

MOVEMENT BASED	PROFESSIONALISED YOUTH WORK

Figure 1.1   Youth work traditions (adapted from Jeff & Smith, 1988)

Definitions of youth work are offered in several UK texts and IDYW, and include varying degrees of specificity. Common features include informal educational intent, and the use of techniques such as trust-building, conversation and dialogue as dominant methods (Batsleer, 2013; Jeffs & Smith, 2005; Sapin, 2013). Based upon an analysis of common themes in youth work, Smith (2013) proposed that 20th-century youth work can best be described as a 'form of informal education' that involved:

1 Focusing on young people.
2 Emphasising voluntary participation and relationship.
3 Committing to association.
4 Being friendly and informal, and acting with integrity.
5 Being concerned with the education and, more broadly, the welfare of young people.

The substance of this definition was endorsed by a speaker at the recent Council of Europe conference on youth work (Kovacic, 2015).

In Ireland, youth work is also conceived as a form of education, but the institutional context of youth work differs because youth work is provided by non-government organisations. Youth work is defined within the Youth Work Act (2001) as a planned educational programme

for the purpose of aiding and enhancing the personal and social development of young people through their voluntary involvement, and which is complementary to their formal, academic or vocational education and training and provided primarily by voluntary youth work organisations.[1] (National Youth Council of Ireland, 2017)

In the Irish context (Hurley & Treacy, 1993) adapted a radical sociology model developed for organisational analysis by Burrell and Morgan (1979) to provide the basis of a model of youth work. This model included both detailed elements drawn from contemporary Irish programmes, policy and institutional contexts, and 'big picture' elements that differentiated programmes according to their overall socio-political purposes. This schema differentiated between youth programmes that intended to fit young people into society, and those that intended to bring about social change. The schema also contrasted programmes that focused on internal intra-personal change with those that focused on external inter-personal or extra-personal change. Hurley and Treacy's model captures the multi-faceted nature of youth work interventions. The original document is out of print, but a simplified version can be found in Cooper (2012), see Figure 1.2. The discussion and examples are framed in the Irish context of the era, but conceptually could be applied in other contexts where it is useful to differentiate

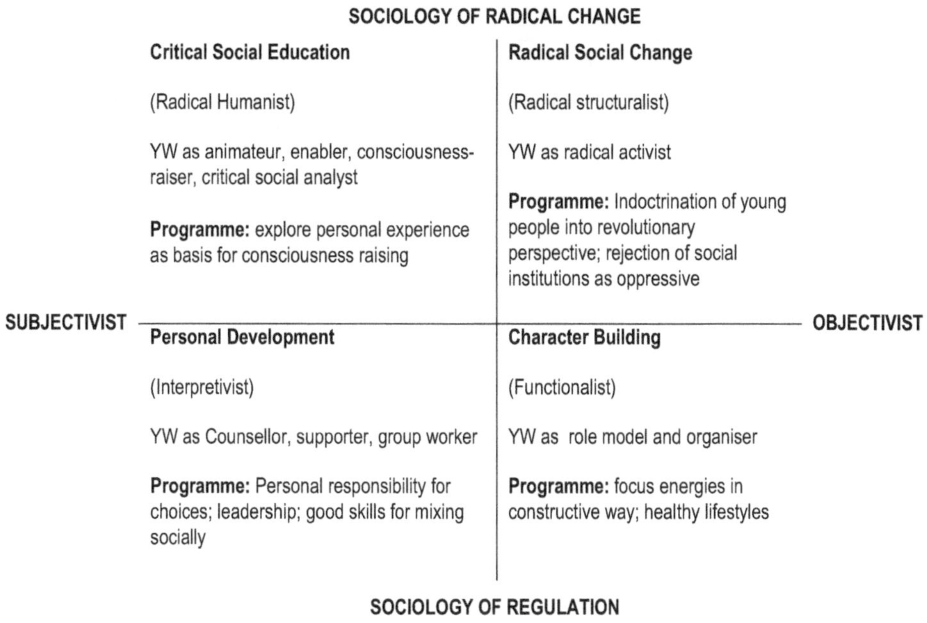

SOCIOLOGY OF RADICAL CHANGE

Critical Social Education	**Radical Social Change**
(Radical Humanist)	(Radical structuralist)
YW as animateur, enabler, consciousness-raiser, critical social analyst	YW as radical activist
Programme: explore personal experience as basis for consciousness raising	**Programme:** Indoctrination of young people into revolutionary perspective; rejection of social institutions as oppressive

SUBJECTIVIST ———————————————————————————— **OBJECTIVIST**

Personal Development	**Character Building**
(Interpretivist)	(Functionalist)
YW as Counsellor, supporter, group worker	YW as role model and organiser
Programme: Personal responsibility for choices; leadership; good skills for mixing socially	**Programme:** focus energies in constructive way; healthy lifestyles

SOCIOLOGY OF REGULATION

Figure 1.2   Sociological model of youth work (adapted from Hurley & Treacy, 1993)

between various youth work purposes (social change vs. social conformity) and approaches to personal and social change (changes to how young people see themselves vs. changes to what young people do).

In Australia, and other countries with a federal structure (like the USA and Canada) a greater variety of institutional arrangements for youth work coexist. It does not make any sense to discuss 'the Australian youth service', because youth work provision is very different in each state. Australian youth work is embedded in the welfare sector and includes youth homelessness support and youth addiction and mental health services, as well as employment services, crime prevention initiatives, school-based youth work, youth centres, youth participation projects, street work and recreation provision. Bessant, Sercombe, and Watts (1998, p. 239) defined youth work as:

the practice of engaging with young people in a professional relationship in which: the young person(s) are the primary constituency, and the mandate given by them has the priority; the young

person(s) are understood as social beings whose lives are shaped in negotiation with their social context; the young person is dealt with holistically.

This definition emphasises a holistic approach to working with young people and the importance of understanding social context. Another definition developed by the Australian Youth Affairs Coalition has an explicit emphasis on young people's rights.

Youth work is a practice that places young people and their interests first; Youth work is a relational practice, where the youth worker operates alongside the young person in their context; Youth work is an empowering practice that advocates for and facilitates a young person's independence, participation in society, connectedness and realisation of their rights. (Australian Youth Affairs Council, 2013)

Neither definition mentions education.

In the Australian context, Cooper and White (1994) published a model of youth work that linked various youth work orientations to practice to particular worldviews, see Table 1.1. Worldviews included how young

Table 1.1   Political models of youth work

	Political traditions	Human nature	Vision/Goals	Values	Language
Treatment	Conservative, Fascism, also some forms of Socialism	Negative, people are naturally selfish and anti-social	Individual fitting in to society for greater social good	Social cohesion,	Deviancy, misfit , inadequacy, 'bad' or 'mad' 'trauma' 'at-risk'
Reform	Liberal, Social democratic	Malleable, young people can overcome adversity	Social mobility Meritocracy	Equal opportunity,	Disadvantage, poor social environment, 'at-risk', need
Advocacy (Non-Radical)	Liberal, Social democratic	Neutral	Social contract, Individual rights	Rights as due under existing law	Rights, social justice, need
Advocacy (Radical)	Social democratic Liberal feminism	Positive, people naturally seek social justice	Gradual social change towards just society. Law reform	Social justice, Positive rights	Rights, social justice, self-efficacy, need
Empowerment (Non-Radical)	Classical liberal Anarcho-capitalism, Neoliberal	Neutral or negative, people are naturally competitive	Small government	Freedom from interference Negative rights	Empowerment, enfranchisement, 'take control'
Empowerment (Radical)	Anarcho-syndicalism, Feminism Socialism (some forms)	Positive, people are naturally cooperative and altruistic	Self-government, grassroots democracy Well-being	Equality of social power	Empowerment, consciousness-raising, Anti-oppressive, Positive identity

Source: Adapted from Cooper and White (1994)

people are viewed, and how the causes of their 'problems' were explained. Within this schema there are six different orientations to practice. These are treatment, reform, advocacy (radical and non-radical) and empowerment (radical and non-radical). For example, in the treatment model, the assumption is made that the young person is the problem and it is the young person who needs to change, whereas in the advocacy models assumptions are made that the young person's problem has arisen because they live within a complex socio-technical bureaucracy and no one in their life is sufficiently skilled to advocate on their behalf to support their rights. In non-radical advocacy, the youth worker advocates on behalf of the young person, whereas in radical advocacy, the youth worker supports the young person to advocate on their own behalf for better protection of their rights. Like the previous model

by Hurley and Treacy, this model discusses how youth work can be used for different purposes (promoting social conformity, vs. social change; enhancing social equity, youth participation, self-determination and social solidarity vs. promoting competitive individualism). Discussion and examples were framed in the Australian context of the era, but conceptually this model could be applied in other contexts. A benefit of this model is that it highlights the contested political nature of 'youth work values' and discourses about rights, social justice, equality, participation and social inclusion. The discussion of political values also clarifies different meanings and priorities accorded to these concepts within particular political traditions.

In the USA, youth work is an umbrella term (Baizerman, 1996) applied to working with young people in a variety of settings, traditionally including after-school services (Fusco, 2008), residential care youth services (Brendtro, 2002) as well as street work (Baizerman, 1996), mentoring (Wells, Gifford, Bai & Corra, 2015) and activist traditions (Kirshner, 2007). In the USA, youth work education is frequently subsumed into social work, because of a shared welfare orientation. In both the USA and New Zealand, youth work has been discussed in the language of Positive Youth Development (PYD). In the USA, interpretations have been linked to positive psychology and the psychology of resilience (Sanders, Munford, Thimasarn-Anwar, Liebenberg & Ungar, 2015). This direction has been welcomed by some as providing a positive paradigm to replace the older deficiency-based conceptions of young people (Damon, 2004; Larson, 2000; Silbereisen & Lerner, 2007). However, Sukarieh and Tannock (2011) contend that the preoccupation of the PYD movement with youth 'at-risk', demonstrates this approach is merely a re-packaging of deficit concepts of deviancy and deficiency. For a critique of labelling young people as 'at-risk', see te Riele (2006) and te Riele and Gour (2015). In New Zealand, the Circle of Courage model is widely referenced and PYD is framed in terms of ensuring the social conditions required for human flourishing; encouraging supportive peer relationships; and providing individual support (Martin, 2002).

The Circle of Courage (Brendtro, 2002) intervention model was developed in the USA and has been influential in parts of the USA, Canada, New Zealand, South Africa and Australia, see Figure 1.3. The Circle of Courage model outlines a framework for youth work that focuses on how youth workers can maintain a positive social ecology and offer personal support to help young people flourish and overcome trauma. According to this model, both personal support and social ecology support a young person's basic needs for belonging, generosity, mastery and independence. The model emphasises the importance of positive relationships between young people and adults, and the importance

of a supportive social ecology around young people, including inter-personal dynamics between young people. It is informed by several traditions including PYD, mainstream social psychology, and Bronfenbrenner's social ecology, combined with an anthropological approach related to Native American traditional practices.

The practices and concepts were pioneered at Starr Commonwealth and applied primarily in controlled residential settings (total environments), many of which are involuntary, such as children's homes, residential care, custodial facilities and alternative education settings, where youth workers had extensive contact with young people and had control over their social environment. The model has an explicit therapeutic orientation. The approach has been adapted to less intensive contexts, where it has gained popularity in some parts of the youth sector in North America, South Africa (Brendtro & du Toit, 2005), Australia and New Zealand (Bruce et al., 2009). A contribution of this model is that it emphasises the importance of social ecology and discusses how youth workers can influence the young person's social ecology directly through their work with young people, and indirectly through their support for the development of beneficent relationships between young people and other adults in the young person's social environment.

European approaches to youth work have become more available to English-language audiences through the work of the Council of Europe (Williamson, 2015), SALTO and Erasmus projects and histories (Council of Europe, 2011; Coussee, Verschelden, Van de Walle, Medlinska & Williamson, 2010; Taru, Coussee, Williamson & Verschelden, 2014; Verschelden, Coussee, Van de Walle & Williamson, 2009). These reports document the variety of approaches adopted in member states (Huang, 2015; Kovacic, 2015; Petkovic & Zentner, 2015; Siurla, 2015), most of which differ considerably in approach from the traditional British model of youth work. European approaches to youth work often

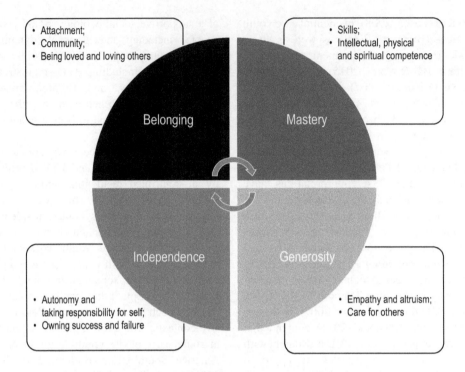

Figure 1.3   Circle of courage (adapted from Brendtro et al., 2002)

focus on employment, health or crime prevention (Coussee et al., 2010). In scope and diversity European youth work is not dissimilar to youth work in other parts of the world, including New Zealand and Australia. In Europe, social pedagogy in particular articulates an approach to working with young people that does not make sharp divisions between education and welfare. Social pedagogy is not a single 'European' tradition and variations are found between countries and in different contexts (Regional Youth Work Unit – North East, 2010). Education for social pedagogy involves four or five years of study at university and includes both theoretical and practical work. Social pedagogy is not a youth-specific methodology but a way of working that can be applied with any age group. It takes a whole-person perspective, sometimes referred to as 'head, hands and heart'. Social pedagogy is applied in contexts beyond the traditional scope of UK youth work, including residential settings and

children's homes (Slovenko & Thompson, 2016). For further theoretical discussion of the connections between UK youth work traditions and social pedagogy see Regional Youth Work Unit – North East (2010) and Slovenko and Thompson (2016).

FRAMING TRANSNATIONAL DEFINITIONS OF YOUTH WORK

Several disciplines contributed to the conceptualisation of youth work practice in the models examined. Each model and the various definitions drew preferentially from a particular mix of disciplinary perspectives. This is not a criticism, it is the essence of what good models should do (Sterman, 1991). In the British model the focus was upon informal education, and theory was drawn primarily from critical pedagogy. The Australian model focused upon rights and social justice, and theory was drawn from political philosophy. In the Circle of Courage from the USA the focus was social ecology, with theory drawn from social psychology. In the Irish model, the focus was on the interplay between structural and personal change in elements of youth work policy and practice, and drew upon theory drawn from the sociology of organisations. Social pedagogy consciously uses a multidisciplinary perspective. The models reflected aspects of practice relevant to particular context, and used language drawn from the parent discipline.

These models and definitions share important similarities but have differences in substance, emphasis and language. A synthesis of these definitions highlights shared characteristics of contemporary youth work, including:

1   A focus on young people's lives and their concerns (also 'starting from where young people are'; 'young people as primary constituency');
2   Attending to the social connection ('association', 'belonging') and the context of young people's lives ('social ecology');
3   Positive regard and processes for working through supportive and friendly relationships;
4   A holistic approach to young people that includes commitment to
    i   informal education (also, 'mastery', 'independence', 'generosity', 'hand, head and heart');
    ii   an ethic of care and concern that young people should flourish ('physical, emotional and spiritual', 'generosity', 'heart');
    iii facilitation of youth participation, rights and social justice ('anti-oppressive', 'advocacy', 'empowerment', 'consciousness-raising');
5   Acting with integrity (from Smith, 2013).

Smith (1999, 2002) suggested that the context of youth work is education and welfare. If welfare is understood as care for wellbeing or human flourishing (Jeffs & Smith, 2005), this statement is inclusive of all forms of youth work encompassed in the compound definition. If welfare is understood narrowly as the provision of welfare services, this statement excludes many forms of youth work such as recreational or activist youth

work. Smith also included the requirement to act with integrity. This expectation is not explicit in other definitions, despite discussion of youth work ethics in the literature. The requirement to act with integrity implies a higher ethical standard than simply abiding by a code of ethical conduct, and this is fitting. Definitions of youth work leave open the definition of 'youth'. Age ranges for youth work vary between countries and between services (usually within the range of 10–25 years old, but sometimes younger, as for example in Ireland, or older, as in Italy), so this omission masks another potential point of difference.

Two other characteristics, voluntary participation and a mandate from the young person, are features of some types of youth work, but in a transnational context these characteristics are not universal. Voluntary participation has been central to UK youth work (IDYW, 2014), but not in some other traditions, for example, social pedagogy (Slovenko & Thompson, 2016). There are two possible responses to this observation. The first is to insist that these are essential characteristics of youth work, and to exclude *prima facie* all forms of practice that do not have these characteristics. The second is to examine how these characteristics relate to youth work practice.

Even in traditions that emphasise the importance of voluntary participation and the primacy of the young person's mandate, contextual factors, legal responsibilities, and collaboration agreements may limit realisation of these principles. A voluntary relationship is best epitomised by detached youth work, where youth workers make contact with young people in their territory. In this environment the relationship between youth workers and young people is genuinely voluntary, and young people can walk away without consequences. This type of voluntary engagement is contrasted with contexts where young people are mandated under threat of sanction to engage with youth workers (Davies & Merton, 2009). In some circumstances, however, judgement about whether the young person's relationship is really voluntary is less clear cut. In Australia, youth workers are employed in emergency youth accommodation services. They uphold values and practices consistent with youth work, see themselves as youth workers, and are seen by others as youth workers. Is a homeless young person who presents themselves to a service doing so voluntarily? Is a young person who is referred to the service by a social worker or the police voluntarily interacting with the youth worker? The young person can technically refuse, but a lack of alternatives limits their choice.

A second area of contention is whether taking a mandate from the young person is a defining feature of youth work. Certainly, it is a guiding principle in many contexts. However, other factors limit the capacity of youth workers to respond only to the mandate of young people. For example, legislation often requires youth workers to report sexual abuse, even when it is against the young person's wishes. In some circumstances youth workers' duty of care for the young person or for other people, means that they cannot accept the young person's mandate of confidentiality, if, for example, a young person plans to hurt themselves or others, or is too intoxicated to care for themselves. More contentiously, information-sharing policies are often a feature of interagency work with young people. Where such policies exist, as is commonplace when youth workers are employed in schools or with youth justice teams, this restricts the freedom of youth workers to be responsive only to the young person's mandate about confidentiality. This issue is highly contentious within youth work. Some argue that youth workers should not become involved in any contexts where their ability to respond to a young person's mandate is restricted in any way, even if this means that youth work becomes an unfunded activity. Others argue that despite the limitations, it is better for youth workers to engage in these arrangements and attempt to ameliorate them, than to remain outside. A position

that honestly acknowledges the complexities of some youth work situations might recognise the value of voluntary relationships and of the primacy of the mandate from a young person, whilst also acknowledging how factors in their context limit these values in practice. This might be captured in the following commitment:

Youth workers aim to:

1 Maximize the possibility for voluntary participation, but are aware of how a lack of alternatives may limit young people's real choice;
2 Respond to a mandate from the young person, but be explicit with young people about any limitations to their mandate imposed by particular youth work contexts.

This position may be unacceptable to some youth workers who believe that voluntary engagement with young people and the primacy of their mandate are absolute and inviolable features of youth work. For youth workers in other contexts, this statement represents an acknowledgement of the realities of their situation.

FRAMING TRANSNATIONAL BOUNDARIES OF YOUTH WORK

The synthesis of these definitions provides a means to differentiate youth work from most other forms of work with young people. For example, teaching and youth work can be differentiated through differences in focus (intellectual development for teaching vs. holistic development for youth work); and through differences in the curriculum (a predetermined curriculum in teaching vs. informal education responsive to young people's interests in youth work). Similarly, youth work can be differentiated from youth justice work through differences in goals (a narrow focus on prevention of re-offending in youth justice vs. a broader focus of starting with the young person's concerns in youth work). In some settings, however, the boundaries between professions are blurred, as for example, when youth workers and youth social workers work together, have the same goals and use the same methodologies.

People sometimes ask whether the Hitler Youth movement was a form of youth work. As a fascist movement, its assumptions and practices were holistic (and totalising) and the Hitler Youth movement shared associational features with youth work. However, the requirement to adhere to an ethic of care means that the Hitler Youth movement and similar fascist youth organisations would not qualify as youth work by the synthesis of definitions I have presented here. This demonstrates that a definition of youth work, even with contested elements, can be useful to exclude harmful forms of practice with young people.

There are three other points of difference about the boundaries of youth work that are not addressed by this compound definition. The first relates specifically to British youth work, the second concerns the relationship between youth work and traditional indigenous practices with young people, and the third concerns the relationship between youth work and therapeutic practices with young people.

In the UK there are customarily boundaries between youth work and social work whereby youth work focuses on informal education, and social work focuses on welfare work with young people. When key axioms of British youth work theory were laid down, British youth work was strikingly dissimilar to youth work in most other countries. Between the late 1960s and the late 1990s, British youth work had a stable institutional form firmly embedded in the post-war welfare state model of service provision, and was an integral, fully funded component of core mainstream education provision (Cooper, 2013). This institutional linkage helped shape British youth work practices and defined the conventional boundaries between youth work and other forms of work with young

people, especially social work. This process resulted in a narrower conceptualisation of where youth workers might operate, which allowed social workers to set the norms of practices for welfare work with young people. In other countries, where youth work is conceptualised to include a greater variety of roles with young people, youth workers are better placed to influence practice in welfare work with young people. This is a sphere of influence that youth workers in the UK might beneficially reclaim.

Countries like New Zealand, the USA, Canada and Australia have indigenous populations and examples of indigenous youth work. In some locations, there remain active living systems of indigenous social knowledge, whereby elders and other community members work holistically with young people (and older people) using traditional methods for cultural transmission and human development. Some of these methods have been adapted by indigenous and non-indigenous youth workers (Brendtro, 2002; Collard & Palmer, 2006), and the perspectives and practices have influenced youth work with both indigenous and non-indigenous young people (Brendtro & du Toit, 2005; Martin, 2002). The composite definition intends to include indigenous youth work but not necessarily traditional indigenous practices in work with young people.

Finally, both the Circle of Courage model and social pedagogy have an explicit therapeutic orientation. In social pedagogy, therapy is accepted as part of the holistic approach where it meets a young person's needs. In the Circle of Courage, it is used to help young people overcome the effects of trauma. Both use a therapeutic environment in conjunction with approaches that fit easily with informal education methods. The question of whether therapy has a place in youth work is contentious. Many youth workers would not consider therapy as part of a youth work role. However, within youth work there have always been some who work close to the boundaries with therapy, including youth workers who provide formal or informal counselling, some forms of developmental group work with young people, some forms of consciousness-raising and some interventions where a young person is exploring an aspect of their identity. This is an issue on which there is no agreement, and opinion is shaped by context, and the norms in different types of youth work practice.

CONCLUSION

This conclusion is offered tentatively, to begin discussions, rather than to close them down. I have suggested that youth work is a pluralistic occupation. Models of youth work have developed in various countries, based upon different bodies of theory, and use different language to express commitments and to describe practices. Despite differences of language and theorisation, I believe there is benefit in synthesising diverse models and this uncovers a core of values and practices. In plain language I have suggested these include:

1 A focus on young people's lives and their concerns;
2 Attending to the social connection and the context of young people's lives;
3 Positive regard and processes for working through supportive and friendly relationships;
4 A holistic approach to young people that includes commitment to:
    i   informal education;
    ii   an ethic of care and concern for the flourishing of young people;
    iii facilitation of youth participation, rights and social justice;
5 Acting with integrity.

When youth work is viewed transnationally, institutional arrangements are diverse and the roles of youth workers are varied. On some issues there are strongly held differences of opinion. For some, voluntary engagement by young people and the primacy of the young person's mandate are fundamental commitments. However, few contexts are completely

free of limitations on the young person's mandate, and free choice about voluntary engagement presumes there are equally attractive alternative options. Many youth workers are aware of the complexities of these issues, and one aspect of working with integrity is to be sensitive to constraints and open about consequences for work with young people. Because of the acknowledged difference of opinion on this issue, these two commitments are more contentious and may not be accepted by all youth workers:

1 Maximise the possibility for voluntary participation, but be aware of how a lack of alternatives may limit young people's real choice;
2 Respond to a mandate from the young person, but be explicit with young people about any limitations to their mandate imposed by particular youth work contexts.

The relationship between youth work and therapeutic work with young people is another area where models indicate that practices vary and opinion differs. Therapeutic approaches are integral to the Circle of Courage approach (used in the USA, Canada, South Africa, New Zealand and parts of Australia) and to social pedagogy (used in parts of Europe and in parts of the UK). Counselling, consciousness raising and developmental group work have at different times also been part of mainstream youth work practice in the UK. For some youth workers therapeutic practice is part of a holistic approach that supports the young person's flourishing. For other youth workers therapeutic practice is perceived to be incompatible with informal education. This is noted as an area of potential disagreement.

Finally, a few words about things that I have omitted from this description that some people might expect to see. In this chapter I have tried to use plain language and avoid technical language that might not be understood in everyday life. This eases communication with non-youth workers and maintains a degree of neutrality between different discourses on youth work. There are many different methods in youth work, as there are many different methods in teaching or in social work. Some methods in youth work are specific to particular models. For this reason I have not singled out anti-oppressive practice in the description of youth work, even though it is an important method. Similarly, I have not listed generosity, which in the Circle of Courage model has a particular meaning, and is an essential method of this approach. My hope in writing this chapter is that as people consider alternative ways of thinking about youth work, this will spark curiosity rather than defensiveness, and encourage dialogue that will enrich practice.

Note

1   In the UK and Irish contexts 'voluntary organisa-tions' refers to what would be termed non-gov-ernment organisations in most other countries

REFERENCES

Australian Youth Affairs Council. (2013). *The AYAC Definition of Youth Work in Australia*. Retrieved from: http://www.ayac.org.au/uploads/131219%20Youth%20Work%20Definition%20FINAL.pdf [11 June 2017].

Baizerman, M. (1996). Youth work on the street: community's moral compact with its young people. *Childhood*, *3*(2), 157–165. doi:10.1177/0907568296003002003.

Batsleer, J. (2013). Youth work, social educa-tion, democratic practice and the challenge of difference: a contribution to debate. *Oxford Review of Education*, *39*(3), 287–306. doi:10.1080/03054985.2013.803960.

Bessant, J., Sercombe, H. & Watts, R. (1998). *Youth Studies: An Australian Perspective*. Melbourne: Addison Wesley Longman.

Brendtro, L. K. (2002). *Reclaiming Youth at Risk: Our Hope for the Future*. Bloomington, Ind.: Solution Tree.

Brendtro, L. K. & du Toit, L. (2005). *RAP: Response Ability Pathways: Restoring the Bonds of Respect*. Cape Town: Pretext.

Bruce, J., Boyce, K., Campbell, J., Harrington, J., Major, D. & Williams, A. (2009). Youth work that is of value: towards a model of best practice. *Youth Studies Australia*, *28*(2), 23–31.

Burrell, G. & Morgan, G. (1979). *Sociological Paradigms and Organisational Analysis*. London: Heinemann Educational Books.

Butters, S. & Newell, S. (1978). *Realities of Training: A Review of the Training of Adults Who Volunteer to Work with Young People in the Youth & Community Services*. Leices-ter: National Youth Bureau.

Collard, L. & Palmer, D. (2006). Kura, yeye, boorda, Nyungar wangkiny gnulla koor-langka: a conversation about working with Indigenous young people in the past, pre-sent and future. *Youth Studies Australia*, *25*(4), 25–32.

Cooper, T. (2012). Models of youth work: a framework for positive sceptical reflection. *Youth & Policy*, *109*, 99–117.

Cooper, T. (2013). Institutional Context and youth work professionalization in post-welfare societies. *Child & Youth Services*, *34*(2), 112–124. doi:10.1080/0145935X.2013.785877.

Cooper, T. & White, R. (1994). Models of Youth Work Practice. *Youth Studies Australia*, *13*(4), 30–35.

Council of Europe. (2011). History of Youth Work in Europe, Volume 3: Relevance for Today's Youth Work Policy. Council of Europe.

Coussee, F., Verschelden, G., Van de Walle, T., Medlinska, M. & Williamson, H. (2010). *History of Youth Work in Europe, Volume 2: Relevance for Today's Youth Work Policy*. Council of Europe.

Damon, W. (2004). What Is Positive Youth Devel-opment? *The Annals of the American Acad-emy of Political and Social Science*, *591*(1), 13–24. doi:10.1177/0002716203260092.

Davies, B. & Merton, B. (2009). Squaring the circle? Findings of a 'modest inquiry' into the state of youth work practice in a changing policy environment. Retrieved from http://www.dmu.ac.uk/documents/health-and-life-sciences-documents/research/squaringthecir-cle.pdf [11 June 2017].

Fusco, D. (2008). School vs. afterschool: a study of equity in supporting children's development.

Journal of Research in Childhood Education, *22*(4), 391–403. doi:10.1080/025685408095 94635.

Gilchrist, R., Hodgson, T., Jeffs, T., Spence, J., Stanton, N. & Walker, J. (2011). *Reflecting On The Past: Essays in the History of Youth and Community Work*. Lyme Regis, Dorset, UK: Russell House Publishing.

Gilchrist, R., Jeffs, T., Spence, J. & Stanton, N. (Eds.). (2013). *Reappraisals: Essays in the History of Youth and Community Work*. Lyme Regis, Dorset, UK: Russell House Publishing.

Gilchrist, R., Jeffs, T., Spence, J. & Walker, J. (Eds.). (2009). *Essays in the History of Youth and Community Work: Discovering the Past*. Lyme Regis, Dorset, UK: Russell House Publishing.

Hamalainen, J. (2015). Defining Social Pedagogy: Historical, Theoretical and Practical Considerations. *British Journal of Social Work*, *45*(3), 1022–1038. doi:10.1093/bjsw/bct174.

Huang, L. (2015). *Reflections on Seven Youth Work Themes: The Scope and Boundaries of Youth Work*. Paper presented at the Second European Youth Work Convention: Similarities in a World of Difference, Brussels.

Hurley, L. & Treacy, D. (1993). *Models of Youth Work: A Sociological Framework*. Dublin: Irish YouthWork Press.

IDYW. (2014). In Defence of Youth Work Statement. Retrieved from https://indefenceofyouthwork.com/idyw-statement-2014/ [11 June 2017].

Jeffs, T. & Smith, M.K. (2005). *Informal Education: Conversation, Democracy and Learning* (3rd edn). Nottingham: Education Now Publishing Co-operative Ltd.

Kirshner, B. (2007). Introduction: youth activism as a context for learning and development. *American Behavioral Scientist, 51*(3), 367–379. doi:10.1177/0002764207306065.

Kovacic, M. (2015). *Reflections on Seven Youth Work Themes: Patterns and Practices of Youth Work*. Paper presented at the Second European Youth Work Convention: Similarities in a World of Difference, Brussels.

Larson, R.W. (2000). Toward a psychology of positive youth development. *American Psychologist, 55*(1), 170–183. doi:10.1037/0003-066X.55.1.170.

Leigh, M. & Smart, A. (1985). *Interpretation and Change. The Emerging Crisis of Purpose in Social Education*. Leicester: National Youth Bureau.

MacCallum, J., Beltman, S., Cooper, T. & Coffey, A. (2017). Taking care of youth mentoring relationships: red flags, repair and respectful resolution. *International Journal of Mentoring and Coaching in Education, 25*(3), 250–271.

Martin, L. (2002). *The Invisible Table: Perspectives on Youth and Youthwork in New Zealand*. Palmerston North: Dunmore Press.

McKee, V., Oldfield, C. & Poultney, J. (2010). *Benefits of Youth Work*. Retrieved from http://www.cywu.org.uk/assets/content_pages/187799973_Benefits_Of_Youth_Work.pdf [11 June 2017].

National Youth Council of Ireland, N. (2017). What is youth work? Retrieved from http://www.youth.ie/nyci/what-youth-work [11 June 2017].

Petkovic, S. & Zentner, M. (2015). *Reflections on Seven Youth Work Themes: Education and Training for Quality*. Paper presented at the Second European Youth Work Convention: Similarities in a World of Difference, Brussels.

Regional Youth Work Unit – North East. (2010). *A Study on the Understanding of Social Pedagogy and its Potential Implications for Youth Work Practice and Training*. Retrieved from http://www.socialpedagogyuk.com/images/pdf/northeastyouthwork_may2010.pdf [11 June 2017].

Sanders, J., Munford, R., Thimasarn-Anwar, T., Liebenberg, L. & Ungar, M. (2015). The role of positive youth development practices in building resilience and enhancing wellbeing for at-risk youth. *Child Abuse & Neglect, 42*, 40–53.

Sapin, K. (2013). *Essential Skills for Youth Work Practice* (2nd edn). London: Sage.

Silbereisen, R.K. & Lerner, R.M. (2007). *Approaches to Positive Youth Development*. London: Sage.

Siurla, L. (2015). *Reflections on Seven Youth Work Themes: The Meaning of Youth Work*. Paper presented at the Second European Youth Work Convention: Similarities in a World of Difference, Brussels.

Slovenko, K. & Thompson, N. (2016). Social pedagogy, informal education and ethical youth work practice. *Ethics and Social*

Welfare, *10*(1), 19–34. doi:10.1080/174965 35.2015.1106005.

Smith, M.K. (1988). *Developing Youth Work: Informal Education, Mutual Aid and Popular Practice*. Milton Keynes: Open University Press.

Smith, M.K. (2013). What is youth work? Exploring the history, theory and practice of youth work. *The Encyclopedia of Informal Education*. Retrieved from www.infed.org/mobi/what-is-youth-work-exploring-the-history-theory-and-practice-of-work-with-young-people/ [31 January 2018].

Spence, J. (2010). Collecting women's lives: the challenge of feminism in UK youth work in the 1970s and 80s. *Women's History Review*, *19*(1), 159–176. doi:10.1080/0961202090 3444734.

Sterman, J.D. (1991). A Skeptic's guide to computer models. In G.O. Barney (Ed.), *Managing the Nation: The Microcomputer Software Catalog* (pp. 201–229). Boulder, CO: Westview Press.

Sukarieh, M. & Tannock, S. (2011). Journal of Youth Studies: The positivity imperative: A critical look at the 'new' youth development movement. *Youth Studies Australia*, *30*(4), 63.

Taru, M., Coussee, F., Williamson, H. & Verschelden, G. (2014). *History of Youth Work in Europe, Volume 4*. Council of Europe.

te Riele, K. (2006). Youth 'at risk': further marginalizing the marginalized? *Journal of Education Policy*, *21*(2), 129–145. doi:10.1080/02680930500499968.

te Riele, K. & Gour, R. (Eds.). (2015). *Interrogating Conceptions of 'Vulnerable Youth' in Theory, Policy and Practice*. Rotterdam: Sense Publishers.

Verschelden, G., Coussee, F., Van de Walle, T. & Williamson, H. (2009). *History of Youth Work in Europe and its Relevance for Youth Policy Today, Volume 1*. Council of Europe.

Wells, R., Gifford, E., Bai, Y. & Corra, A. (2015). A Network Perspective on Dropout Prevention in Two Cities. *Educational Administration Quarterly*, *51*(1), 27–57. doi:10.1177/0013161X13511110.

Williamson, H. (2015). Finding Common Ground. Mapping and Scanning the Horizons for European Youth Work in the 21st Century Towards the 2nd European Youth Work Convention: Summary Paper. Paper presented at the Second European Youth Work Convention: Similarities in a World of Difference, Brussels.

2

How to Support Young People in a Changing World: The Sociology of Generations and Youth Work

Dan Woodman and Johanna Wyn

INTRODUCTION

In this chapter we revisit the idea of generations as a tool for thinking about the unequal lives of young people in changing times and extend this to the question of how a generational awareness can be helpful in the context of youth work. Young people today are likely to be living very different lives to their parents at the same age. Many changes are positive but some are not. In general, young people are more educated, physically healthier and have greater mobility and expanded cultural options compared to their parents. The opportunities for young women, LGBTI young people, and other minorities have improved, although a backlash is emerging in some places. But as in the past, some young people have greater access to the new opportunities afforded to their generation. The young people that have missed out often have parents who were similarly denied opportunities. Yet there have been significant changes in how these inequalities are manifested. In our work we have argued that the sociology of generations can provide the tools to think about the impact of social change on young people, without neglecting the essential step of recognising the significant and increasing inequalities between young people today (Woodman and Wyn, 2015a). Across the areas of education, work and leisure many young people face barriers to creating the relationships and ways of living they desire. Here we contend that, at its best, youth work can facilitate intergenerational relationships built on joint learning, where both young people and those who work with them make an effort to understand the similarities and differences in their life worlds. Generational awareness can be a catalyst for youth work supporting young people to control their own lives and be part of collectively shaping the future of their respective communities.

THE SOCIOLOGY OF GENERATIONS

The use of generations as a tool to help understand the relationship between individual lives and social conditions emerges from the foundational work of Karl Mannheim (1952 [1927]), a Hungarian born sociologist who aimed to link the subjectivities of groups of people to the historical and structural conditions that shape lives and livelihoods. In this sense Mannheim's sociology was a forerunner to C. Wright Mills's (2000 [1959]) concept of the sociological imagination – which advocates for a sociology that explicitly links historical change, social structure and individual lives. One of Mannheim's insights was that the pace of social, structural and cultural change is uneven, and intersects with the life course and the age stratification of human societies. His conceptualisation of generations was not of a 'natural process' in which one biological generation replaces the previous generation through a cycle of births and deaths, but sociological; new generations emerge as previous ways of life become impossible or unacceptable, and new subjectivities and possibly new social movements arise, and shape society in novel ways. Thus one of the important aspects of having a generational sensitivity in youth research and working with young people is an openness to the ways in which young people are shaping new realities and ways of being.

It is important to acknowledge at the outset that the usefulness of the concept of social generation is debated. Critics of our approach to social generation argue that a generational approach homogenises youth, washing out class, gender and race-based inequalities and overstating the case for social change (see for example Roberts, 2007; France and Roberts, 2015). We dispute this, arguing the critique is based on a misrepresentation of the sociology of generations (Wyn and Woodman, 2007; Woodman and Wyn, 2015b).

Within a generation there are groups of people with very different experiences and holding different, even radically opposed, views (Mannheim called these groups 'generational units'). These differences are related to dimensions such as different class position, gender or race. What unites a generation is not that they think the same way or have the same priorities, but that they have no choice but to orient around and struggle over a distinctive set of economic, cultural or political stakes that are 'theirs', different from the previous generation (Mannheim, 1952 [1927]: 306–307). As such, the subjective dimension of a generation does not mean that all young people share the same beliefs or values, or that these will stay constant as they age. A sociological conceptualisation of generations is based on the assumption that experiences in youth and young adulthood create a set of distinctive dispositions and ways of living, which can be built on and changed over time.

In our work we have used and developed the concept of social generations as a heuristic for understanding youth and inequalities between young people in the context of social change. We have argued that it provides a more nuanced approach than the one that sees youth as primarily a period of transition (Woodman and Wyn, 2015a).

THE EXPERIENCE OF YOUTH IS CHANGING

Concern about the educational and employment futures of the young is not new. The link between education and employment has been a core social and youth policy focus for several decades (Quinlan, 2012). Yet, until the late 1980s, youth transitions in Western countries were considered straightforward. In a famous study that was part of the formation of youth transition studies, British scholars Ashton and Field (1976: 115) asserted that although the transition from school to work 'involves inevitable stresses and strains, [it] does not normally create serious problems'. The minor strains they had in mind were 'learning the ropes' and 'getting on with older workers' in the workplace. In Australia through the 1960s, full-time employment was widely available, even to teenage job seekers, and this supported a relatively straightforward transition into work for young men, and for many young women, at least before they started a family, providing a foundation for other successful transitions into 'adult' statuses (Cuervo and Wyn, 2012: 8).

Now it is relatively common to read that youth transitions into employment, and young people's achievement of adulthood lives have reached a point of crisis (Denny and Churchill, 2016). Anxiety over contemporary youth transitions has a solid basis. In the Australian case, youth unemployment rates show peaks and troughs, but have remained high for decades, particularly impacting on those with less education. In the 1980s and 1990s casual employment grew significantly, with younger employees among the most affected. More recently, underemployment has grown explosively, particularly since 2000, and is now affecting almost 20 per cent of 15–24-year-olds in the labour force (ABS, 2015). The underemployment rate is approximately double the unemployment rate. Underemployment now ranks alongside unemployment and insecure conditions as the major challenges facing young people entering the labour market (Campbell and Price, 2016). Job and income insecurity impacts on other aspects of young people's lives, including housing and relationships (Woodman and Wyn, 2015a). This is part of the explanation for the increasing trend for young people to live in the family home into their twenties and exacerbates the housing stresses driven by rapid house price and rent rises.

Although our own research is based in Australia, and our suggestions in this chapter are most applicable to Australia and similar countries, the patterns highlighted are mirrored, and often more stark, in other parts of the world. Globally, youth unemployment rates have been growing over the past five years, driven in part by a slowdown in employment growth for young job seekers, even in nations in the Global South that have had very rapid economic growth (ILO, 2016). In the European nations worst hit by the economic crisis of 2008–2009, particularly Spain and Greece, youth unemployment rates hover around 50 per cent. Rates are similar in other parts of the world, such as South Africa (OECD, 2016). Underemployment rates are not as easily available across nations, but working poverty rates are particularly high among young people, at almost 70 per cent in Southern Africa, 50 per cent in South Asia and almost 40 per cent in Arab States (ILO, 2016), even as many nations in these regions have invested significantly in raising levels of secondary and tertiary education (Brown et al., 2011). So, while the degree of hardship faced varies markedly, there are global trends towards underemployment and precarious employment for young people, despite an equally worldwide trend of growing levels of education. The failing nexus between education and work creates new challenges for youth workers, as even the well-educated can find it difficult to obtain secure enough work to build a life.

GENERATIONAL CONDITIONS, SUBJECTIVITIES AND INEQUALITY

Within the field of youth studies these changes are largely, and mistakenly, understood as delaying the (inevitable) transition to adulthood. While this makes intuitive sense, we have challenged whether the concept of individual 'transitions' to adulthood is the best framework for understanding these changes and their significance (Andres and Wyn, 2010; Blatterer, 2007; Cuervo and Wyn, 2014; Woodman and Wyn, 2015a). The foundations of adulthood (such as secure employment and home ownership) for the landmark 'baby-boomer' generation (against which subsequent generations have been judged) were available across society. The legacy of 'the' transition to adulthood lies in the specific conditions available to the baby boomers, who could leave secondary school at age 15 and find a secure job. At that time, undertaking post-secondary educational qualifications pretty much guaranteed a secure, professional job. The traditional markers of adulthood (leaving home, full-time work, marriage) were relatively within reach by the age of 23. However, today these markers of adulthood are more difficult to achieve for young Australians across all social classes, and for those with fewer resources, increasingly out of reach (see for example Crofts et al., 2016).

As it becomes normative for young people in many countries and locations to spend longer in education, they experience common generational effects. This includes increased or new forms of dependence on their families, or the state, for a longer time than the previous generation, and increased levels of financial stress as they struggle to finance their education and to meet debts incurred during their education years (ILO, 2013). Young people are also increasingly mobile, as they shift from rural to urban areas to access secondary and tertiary education, and an elite go offshore to access educational institutions in other countries. Finally, spending longer in education contributes to a pattern of increased precarious work, as young people seek flexible employment to survive financially through the student years and yet, as noted, often remain stuck in less secure employment after they graduate, despite their credentials (Crofts et al., 2015; Furlong, 2015).

There is some evidence that young people are responding to these conditions by adjusting their expectations, developing new understandings of adulthood not reliant on traditional markers like marriage and family, and placing their hope in their personal resilience to succeed (Blatterer, 2007; Silva, 2012). Some young people are developing new understandings of career and family, and refusing to invest too much of their sense of self in their education, their job, or even in their relationships (Howie and Campbell, 2016).

Given the global nature of new patterns of education and work, in recent years it has become common to talk of a global generation

(Edmunds and Turner, 2005). While it is possible to talk in generalities about shared generational conditions, and emerging new attitudes, it is essential to recognise differences among groups of young people (which, as noted above, Mannheim referred to as 'generational units'). In the face of the changes mapped out above, inequalities in resources and opportunities are significant and in many cases are exacerbated by the global trend towards income inequality (ACOSS, 2015), and the benefits of increased participation in education are not even. Some young people are living (physically) healthier lives than any previous generation (AIHW, 2016), while others are caught in protracted and deadly conflicts (UNICEF, 2012; WHO, 2016).

There continue to be great differences in the resources available to young people in different parts of the world and at local and national levels, and inequalities are often stark. Parents who were not supported in school, or excluded from the labour market, are more likely to have children who are also excluded (Lamb, Jackson, Walstab and Huo, 2015). Supporting young people through these transitions, often with a social justice aim of improving outcomes for the least well resourced, has been one of the major aims driving youth research and youth work (Williamson, 2011). Yet focusing on these continuities alone can mask important changes that help us understand and work with young people. For example, notions of 'extended transitions' (from youth to adulthood) create the false impression that adulthood is simply a phase of life that has shifted further along the life course because of circumstances. It is far more helpful to understand that, for *everyone*, adulthood has changed, its boundaries have become increasingly unclear and the stability and securities that once (in the days of baby-boomer transitions) underpinned adult life, for many have disappeared. Youth workers (and others working with young people, such as teachers), have an important role in grasping the nature of adult life that young people are facing and understanding and supporting the kinds of social, emotional and material resources that are now required to manage lives characterised by insecurity, especially for those who are the most disadvantaged.

FROM INDIVIDUAL TRANSITIONS TO (GENERATIONAL) TRANSITION REGIMES

Some of the most compelling work on youth transitions goes beyond focusing on patterns of transition among individuals, to identifying the institutional 'transition regimes' that structure young lives, often with life course effects (du Bois-Reymond and Stauber, 2005). Young people across the world are increasingly subject to a shared transition regime that is built on the completion of secondary education and achievement of post-secondary qualifications within a neoliberal policy framework. This approach shows how government policies and institutional practices in education, labour markets and welfare create the youthful experience, as well as the horizons of identity available to young people (see for example Hodkinson et al., 2013; Kelly, 2007; Mizen, 2004).

Across most countries, young people's subjectivities are shaped by institutional patterns in education and the youth labour market that valorise 'the market', competition, and the notion of reward for investment, creating a shared set of 'transition regimes' (du Bois-Reymond and Stauber, 2005: 63). These transition regimes concurrently provide a structural set of pressures leading to unequal outcomes, and propose an individualised discourse about the causes of, and responsibility for, these outcomes. These changes have done more than reshape the economy, or even the institutions of the welfare state, they have reshaped the life course, giving both youth and adulthood distinctive new features. Education provides a particularly powerful example of global transition regime.

Across the world, governments have responded to the pressures of global competition and 'neoliberalism' by facilitating the expansion of higher education. Largely this expansion has been paid for by expecting students (or their families) to cover a greater share of the costs of their education. Post-school education has become the norm in North America, Europe and Australasia, and has expanded most rapidly in North and West Asia (the 'Middle East') (Cole and Durham, 2008; Anagnost et al., 2013). Despite this greater investment in education, in the current context of high unemployment and rapidly expanding rates of underemployment, many young adults, even with reasonable levels of education, are unemployed, or if they do find employment, it is more likely to be insecure, or for fewer hours than they want.

In this context, achieving educational credentials becomes less of a guarantee of success, but is even more important than before in the competition for jobs. Finding quality employment and financial security, or even work at all, is much harder than previously for those who do not finish high school; while a higher degree continues to provide most with better quality employment and higher pay, it is far from the pass to middle-class success that it was for baby boomers (Brown et al., 2011).

The concept of personal investment for reward is the foundation of the neoliberal model of education (and the economy). Education is positioned as a tool for both personal and national development and international competitiveness. This model aims to increase individual 'choice' and competition between providers. As Connell (2013) highlights, notions of choice and competition depend on inequality to be meaningful, hence within a neoliberal framework of education, individuals have to face consequences for their 'poor choices'. For choices to matter some options have to be considered better than others (and hence can command a price premium) and some choices better than others.

This section has drawn attention to global and local processes impacting on young people in the current generation. We hold that educational institutions and labour markets today increasingly constitute a global transition regime that is part of the new (if variable) generational conditions. These processes include the expansion of transition regimes in which universal completion of secondary education is a reality in developed countries and a goal in developing countries, and in which tertiary education is increasingly normative.

As we have suggested above, a generational approach has value because it opens up the question of what adulthood now means. The idea of a 'new adulthood' (Blatterer, 2007; Dwyer and Wyn, 2001), that all young people (and adults) must contend with, makes the work of youth workers all the more crucial, because many of the insecure 'transitions' young people are seen to pass through (and sometimes need support with), are not the developmentally based uncertainties of a protracted youth phase, but institutional and systemic insecurities that continue to mark their lives well into adulthood.

Youth work can play a significant role in supporting young people to (a) understand the local and global context of their situation, (b) develop the personal resources they (like their generation) will need to thrive in 'the new adulthood', and (c) gain access to the material resources that may support this. This attention to understanding one's generation and developing the capabilities to be part of that generation is controversial, because it is often conflated with simply conforming to the imperative to develop 'neoliberal' identities (see for example Roberts, 2007). However, our experience is that young people are deeply immersed in generational practices (many of which are supported by online applications) and seek to understand themselves, their worlds and those of the older generation. It is important that youth workers understand the specific generational identity work that young people are compelled to do.

An example is the account of young homeless people by Farrugia and Watson (2011), who show how they try to manage their extreme structural inequality by building relationships (both intimate ones and with friends), actively taking up the sense of responsibility and reflexivity that is common to their generation. We develop these suggestions for youth work practice in the final section of the chapter.

THE SOCIOLOGY OF GENERATIONS AND YOUTH WORK: IMPLICATIONS FOR SUPPORTING BELONGING AND SOCIAL AND ECONOMIC INCLUSION FOR YOUNG PEOPLE

Concern about young people's behaviour, and efforts to intervene, have a long history. Youth work has traditionally been driven by a philanthropic class who wanted to save children from poverty, and more importantly 'immorality' (Bessant, 1997). The recent past of such interventions has been shaped by the use of a risk and resilience framework that has continuities with traditional concepts of youth as 'adolescence', implying that youth is a developmental period dominated by risky transitions, and characterised by storm and stress (Bessant, 2008; Furlong and Woodman, 2015).

Youth work is fraught with tensions, and performed in this context of rapid change, needing to rethink its purpose while operating with budgets that are being continually squeezed and often overly simplistic, but onerous, reporting requirements (Sercombe 2004). Youth workers are frequently positioned as a point of intervention to bring young people's behaviour into line – particularly as they are often employed to support young people who are defined as 'risky' and making this 'risky transition'. Yet this is combined with a youth work ethic that also champions supporting young people's critical engagement with the status quo (Williamson, 2011;

Sercombe, 2010). There is no easy way to resolve the tensions involved in youth work, but attention to generational elements can provide a tool to critique the focus on managing risky transitions that shapes many youth programmes and a tool to frame productive interventions.

The approach to youth and young adulthood that we have described above is one in which failure to conform to the timelines of transition regimes is not due to the risky nature of youth (or 'adolescence') as such. Nor is it suggested that variations in transition patterns should be characterised as 'delayed transitions' (or for that matter transitioning to adulthood too early). For many of the young people youth workers are engaging with, the insecurity and stress that characterises their current life cannot be considered a transitional situation. Insecurity and stress are also a characteristic of young adulthood and this situation is unlikely to pass as young people's lives progress. Rather, the attitudes they form to accommodate or resist the elements that characterise young adult life will have lifelong generational characteristics. The challenge for youth workers and youth researchers alike in understanding the impact of social change on young people, is to recognise how changing social conditions makes it necessary for young people to use new strategies and ways of thinking, even to achieve many of the same things as their parents' generation have.

In popular formulations of generational change, the young and old often appear alien to each other, conflicting groups holding such different understandings of the world that communication is difficult. Such crude generationalism (Davis, 1999) obscures more than it makes visible and the concept of generations is limiting if it fails to recognise the positive interactions and solidarities between age groups as well as the conflicts. While we have argued that new generational dispositions are emerging, we do not see strong evidence of 'generational wars' (as is suggested in the media). Young people are not

developing a set of values and beliefs radically opposed to those held by their parents. Our research shows that young people in Australia have hopes that are fairly modest and were in large part available to their parents. They rank a secure job, to own a home, to have a long-term intimate relationship and to start a family as among the most important aims for their future (Crofts et al., 2015). Yet as we have tracked our participants through their twenties and thirties, these goals have taken a long time to eventuate for many, and for a significant minority appear to be forever out of reach. It is in this context that they are having to reinvent adulthood (Dwyer and Wyn, 2001).

From the outset, the sociology of generations has offered a more nuanced understanding of how younger and older people can work with each other than the crude generationalism that is common in the popular press, and sometimes academia (Eckersley et al., 2007). In Mannheim's (1952 [1927]: 301) foundational work he identifies the interaction between the emerging and previous generation as one of the key sociological problems of generations. Mannheim recognises that generation is only one social division, and those of different generations can share other aspects of their social positions that might lead to shared experiences. Yet he also claims that if rapid social change has taken place, an older teacher (or youth worker) will confront challenges in doing their job. A new generation is defined by the different set of institutional demands, obstacles and cultural elements they experience (and shape) to those that existed for older cohorts, such as the baby boomers, when they were young, who are themselves living a different version of older age to the generation before them. By definition, a new generation will have a different understanding of and disposition towards acting on the challenges they face. Yet, for Mannheim (1952 [1927]: 301), the 'compensating factor' that can overcome this challenge is that 'not only does the teacher educate his pupil, but the pupil educates his teacher too. Generations are in a state of constant interaction'. This principle is documented strikingly in research that brings two generations into dialogue about values and futures (Eckersley et al., 2007). The facilitated dialogue between young people from a Melbourne Secondary School in a disadvantaged area and older people who were community members and academics resulted in a profound reassessment for both generations. Being positioned as 'experts', the young people rose to the occasion and offered considered, thoughtful and provocative assessments of their worlds and their futures. The older people connected with the younger generation on the issue of adapting to change, promoting 'generational intelligence' (Biggs and Carr, 2016). Other research shows how learning partnerships between young people and trainee teachers and medical practitioners enable both groups to learn things of value. Young people, especially those whose voices are not traditionally heard, have important insights to offer, given the opportunity to work with respectful adults within a facilitated environment (Cahill and Coffey, 2013).

Youth workers, like all who work with young people, are required to be 'generationally intelligent' (Biggs and Carr, 2016). In the context of intergenerational workplaces, Biggs and Lowenstein (2011) define generational intelligence as an ability to reflect and act, drawing on an understanding of one's own and other's life-course, family and social history, within a contemporary social context. The value of generational intelligence is amplified by the reality that all age cohorts have been influenced by rapid changes over recent years. For example, few youth workers today have the type of job stability that was commonly available to social service providers thirty years ago. The emergence of different generational conditions does not mean that the values of today's young generations around the world will be radically alien to those of their parents. They may inherit a set of values, such as progressive or conservative,

but will have to operationalise these values in a new context (Dunham, 1998).

One way that the tension between control and empowerment in youth work has been managed is to instigate various levels of youth participation into youth work practice, and this resonates with the need for generational intelligence. This potentially opens a space for young people to understand the context they find themselves in, such as the transition regime discussed above, and for intergenerational learning. However, critique and advocacy through various forms of youth participation can also reflect privilege, with well-resourced and privileged young people having greater opportunities to have their views heard. Youth participation can have the potential to open up new ideas that bring benefits to young people, especially those who are marginalised or disadvantaged. An example is the initiatives supported by UNICEF in the Asia Pacific to counteract gender-based violence and HIV (Cahill and Beadle, 2014). However, as long as the idea of youth is framed by a developmental model that positions young people as not completely formed and adults as 'complete', young people's contributions to decision-making and problem-solving will remain under-valued.

The lines between youth and adulthood are increasingly difficult to define, and the fluidity and complexity traditionally associated with the idea of an extended period of youth are, we suggest, now a characteristic of many adult lives for this generation – not a precursor to it. Economic, employment and housing insecurity is now spread throughout the youth cohort; these conditions are 'transitioned' beyond by fewer people and inequalities are expanding. What this means in practice for youth workers is complex. Some of the same economic pressures that are shaping young lives in new ways are also squeezing funding for youth services. All of this will create significant challenges for the allocation of resources and difficult tensions to manage. The research on young people in the current generation provides strong evidence of new generational conditions, which means that the age range that youth workers engage with will need to be flexible. For example, initiatives to support young people will fall short if they are simply to 'see them through the risky stage of youth', because young people need to develop lifelong skills in a context of widespread insecurity.

Welfare and income support measures that are based on outdated information about the conditions faced by young people (such as measures that fail to support young people in out of home care beyond the age of 18) are counterproductive and often harmful. An understanding of how social change contributes to generational change opens up new understandings of the contemporary situation of young people. In the context of youth work, this approach raises the question of whether older-generation social policies and measures are fit for purpose as conditions change.

CONCLUSION

Youth researchers who study 'transitions to adulthood' have shown that, in general, these transitions are taking longer and are less linear (than was the case for that unique generation, the baby boomers). Yet the changes to young lives are of a greater magnitude than this. Lacking generational intelligence, many commentators have suggested that transitions are simply 'extended' and have given little thought to the nature of the adulthood young people now have access to. A greater proportion of young people face these transitions with few resources, or with additional barriers. For example, an increasing proportion of children in Australia are in out-of-home care, or in sole parent households.

There are radical disparities between young people, within particular countries and across the world. The generational conditions we have traced show that while difficult transitions through school might correlate within families across the generations, the impact of

marginalisation from education is heightened in a world where educational credentials have never been more significant.

Youth work is about more than supporting a particular age category through a defined period of time. Across their diversity, young people's lives in a majority of cases will be very different in significant ways to those of their parents. We have used the concept of generations to think through what this means for youth work. Understanding young people through the lens of youth transitions has been very important in youth studies, and identifying the transition regimes that shape young lives remains central. Yet these regimes are changing, and those in the youth field need the right conceptual resources to ask 'transition to what' and to understand what the patterns they discover mean for the life course, as well as the tangible ways that young people may be supported to creativity understand and manage the context of the social change they are living through. Generational intelligence provides a lens through which young people's insights and contributions can be valued, because increasingly it is not the older generation who will tell young people about the world they will live in, but young people who will have insights into the world for us all.

ACKNOWLDEGEMENTS

The research that this chapter draws upon is and has been supported by numerous grants from the Australian Research Council – Grant numbers: DP160101611, DP1094132, DP0557902, DP0209462 and A79803304.

REFERENCES

Anagnost, A., Arai, A. and Ren, H. (Eds) (2013) *Global Futures in East Asia: Youth, Nation and the New Economy in Uncertain Times*, Stanford: CA: Stanford University Press.

Andres, L. and Wyn, J. (2010) *The Making of a Generation: The Children of the 1970s in Adulthood*, Toronto: University of Toronto Press.

Ashton, D. and Field, D. (1976) *Young Workers*, London: Hutchinson.

Australian Bureau of Statistics (ABS) (2015 update) *6265.0 – Underemployed Workers, Australia*, September 2013, ABS: Canberra.

Australian Council of Social Services (ACOSS) (2015) *Inequality in Australia 2015*, Strawberry Hills: ACOSS.

Australian Institute of Health and Welfare (AIHW) (2016) *Australia's Health 2016*, Australia's Health Series No. 15. Cat. no. AUS 199, Canberra: AIHW.

Bessant, J. (1997) 'Free market economics and new directions for youth workers', *Youth Studies Australia*, 16(2): 34–40.

Bessant, J. (2008) 'Hard wired for risk: neurological science, "the adolescent brain" and developmental theory', *Journal of Youth Studies*, 11(3): 347–360.

Biggs, S. and Carr, A. (2016) 'Age friendliness, childhood, and dementia: toward generationally intelligent environments', in T. Moulaert and S. Garon (Eds) *Age-Friendly Cities and Communities in International Comparison: Political Lessons, Scientific Avenues, and Democratic Issues*, Switzerland: Springer International Publishing, 259–276.

Biggs, S. and Lowenstein, L. (2011) *Generational Intelligence: A Critical Approach to Age Relations*, London: Routledge.

Blatterer, H. (2007) *Coming of Age in Times of Uncertainty*, New York: Berghahn.

Brown, P., Lauder, H. and Ashton, D. (2011) *The Global Auction: The Broken Promises of Education, Jobs and Incomes*, New York: Oxford University Press.

Cahill, H. and Beadle, S. (2014) *NewGen: A Leadership Training Course for Young People from Key Populations at Higher Risk of HIV in the Asia-Pacific Region*, Melbourne: Youth Research Centre.

Cahill, H. and Coffey, J. (2013) *Learning Partnerships*, Melbourne: Youth Research Centre.

Campbell, I. and Price, R. (2016) 'Precarious work and precarious workers: towards an improved conceptualisation', *The Economic and Labour Relations Review*, 27(3): 314–332.

Cole, J. and Durham, D. (Eds) (2008) *Figuring the Future: Globalization and the Temporalities of Children and Youth*, Santa Fe: SAR Press.

Connell, R. (2013) 'The neoliberal cascade and education: an essay on the market agenda and its consequences', *Critical Studies in Education*, 54(2): 99–112.

Crofts, J., Cuervo, H., Wyn, J., Smith, G. and Woodman, D. (2015) *Life Patterns: Ten Years Following Generation Y*, Melbourne: Youth Research Centre.

Crofts, J., Cuervo, H., Wyn, J., Woodman, D., Reade, J., Cahill, H. and Furlong, A. (2016) *Life Patterns: Comparing the Generations*, Melbourne: Youth Research Centre.

Cuervo, H. and Wyn, J. (2012) *Young People Making it Work: Continuity and Change in Rural Places*, Melbourne: Melbourne University Press.

Cuervo, H. and Wyn, J. (2014) 'Reflections on the use of spatial and relational metaphors in youth studies', *Journal of Youth Studies*, 17(7): 901–915.

Davis, M. (1999) *Gangland: Cultural Elites and the New Generationalism* (2nd edition), Sydney: Allen and Unwin.

Denny, L. and Churchill, B. (2016) 'Youth employment in Australia: a comparative analysis of labour force participation by age group', *Journal of Applied Youth Studies*, 1(2): 5–22.

du Bois-Reymond, M. and Stauber, B. (2005) 'Biographical turning points in young people's transitions to work across Europe', in H. Helve and G. Holm (Eds) *Contemporary Youth Research: Local Expressions and Global Connections*, Aldershot: Ashgate, 63–75.

Dunham, C. (1998) 'Generation units and the life course: a sociological perspective on youth and the anti-war movement', *Journal of Political and Military Sociology*, 26(2): 137–155.

Dwyer, P. and Wyn, J. (2001) *Youth, Education and Risk: Facing the Future*, London/New York: RoutledgeFalmer.

Eckersley, R., Cahill, H., Wierenga, A. and Wyn, J. (2007) *Generations in Dialogue about the Future: The Hopes and Fears of Young Australians*, Youth Research Centre and Australia 21, Melbourne.

Edmunds, J. and Turner, B. (2005) 'Global generations: social change in the twentieth century', *The British Journal of Sociology*, 56(4): 559–577.

Farrugia, D. and Watson, J. (2011) '"If anyone helps you then you're a failure": youth homelessness, identity and relationships in late modernity', in S. Beadle, R. Holdsworth and J. Wyn (Eds) *For We are Young and …? Young People in a Time of Uncertainty*, Melbourne: Melbourne University Publishing.

France, A. and Roberts, S. (2015) 'The problem of social generations: a critique of the new emerging orthodoxy in youth studies', *Journal of Youth Studies*, 18(2): 215–230.

Furlong, A. (2015) 'Unemployment, insecurity, and poor work: young adults in the new economy', in J. Wyn and H. Cahill (Eds) *Handbook of Children and Youth Studies*, Singapore: Springer, 531–542.

Furlong, A. and Woodman, D. (2015) 'Youth studies: past, present and future', in A. Furlong and D. Woodman (Eds) *Youth and Young Adulthood*, London: Routledge, 1–20.

Hodkinson, P., Hodkinson, H. and Sparkes, A.C. (2013) *Triumphs and Tears: Young People, Markets, and the Transition from School to Work*, London: Routledge.

Howie, L. and Campbell, P. (2015) 'Guerrilla selfhood: imagining young people's entrepreneurial futures', *Journal of Youth Studies* (online first, doi: 10.1080/13676261.2015.1123236): 1–15.

International Labour Organization (ILO) (2013) *Global Employment Trends 2013: Recovering from a Second Jobs Dip*, Geneva: ILO.

International Labour Organization (ILO) (2016) *World Employment and Social Outlook 2016: Trends for Youth*, Geneva: ILO.

Kelly, P. (2007) 'Governing individualized risk biographies: new class intellectuals and the problem of youth at-risk', *British Journal of Sociology of Education*, 28(1): 39–53.

Lamb, S., Jackson, J., Walstab, A. and Huo, S. (2015) *Educational Opportunity in Australia 2015: Who Succeeds and Who Misses Out*, Melbourne: Centre for International Research on Education Systems, for the Mitchell Institute.

Mannheim, K. (1952 [1927]) 'The problem of generations', in *Essays on the Sociology of Knowledge*, London: Routledge, 276–322.

Mills, C.W. (2000 [1959]) *The Sociological Imagination*, New York: Oxford University Press.

Mizen, P. (2004) *The Changing State of Youth*, New York: Palgrave.

OECD (2016) *Youth Unemployment Rate (Indicator)*. doi: 10.1787/c3634df7-en (accessed on 7 December 2016).

Quinlan, M. (2012) 'The "pre-invention" of precarious employment: the changing world of work in context', *The Economic and Labour Relations Review*, 23(4): 3–24.

Roberts, K. (2007) 'Youth transitions and generations: a response to Wyn and Woodman', *Journal of Youth Studies*, 10(2): 263–269.

Sercombe, H. (2004) 'Youth work: the professionalisation dilemma', *Youth Studies Australia*, 23(4): 20–25.

Sercombe, H. (2010) *Youth Work Ethics*, London: Sage.

Silva, J.M. (2012) 'Constructing adulthood in an age of uncertainty', *American Sociological Review*, 77(4): 505–522.

UNICEF (2012) *Progress for Children: A Report Card on Adolescents*, New York: United Nations Children's Fund.

Williamson, H. (2011) 'A complex but increasingly coherent journey? The emergence of "youth policy" in Europe', in L. Chisholm, S. Kovacheva and M. Merico (Eds) *European Youth Studies: Integrating Research, Policy and Practice*, Innsbruck: EYS Consortium, 136–148.

Woodman, D. and Wyn, J. (2015a) *Youth and Generation: Rethinking Change and Inequality in the Lives of Young People*, London: Sage.

Woodman, D. and Wyn, J. (2015b) 'Class, gender and generation matter: using the concept of social generation to study inequality and social change', *Journal of Youth Studies*, 18(10): 1402–1410.

World Health Organization (2016) *Adolescents: Health Risks and Solutions* (WHO factsheet), Geneva: WHO.

Wyn, J. and Woodman, D. (2007) 'Researching youth in a context of social change: a reply to Roberts', *Journal of Youth Studies*, 10(3): 373–381.

3

Looking Over Our Shoulders: Youth Work and its History

Tony Jeffs

To remain ignorant of what has been transacted in former times is to remain always a child. (Cicero)

INTRODUCTION

Words and concepts have their own histories. Precision regarding the appearance of a 'marque' such as 'youth work' is seldom readily to hand. Definitive answers may elude us but even partial ones are helpful. For example, these can help us demarcate youth work's borders, thereby gaining a grasp of where it, as an entity, begins and ends. Youth work is not a walled well-manicured garden. The fences are ramshackle and intermittent; the borders porous with neighbouring welfare and educational professions who work with young people and often utilise the same techniques. Youth justice, community, social and play workers, and youth ministers are merely five examples encountered in the UK and elsewhere of practitioners operating in a

similar fashion but who refrain from describing their practice as youth work. These neighbours share many antecedents. For example, Mary Carpenter in Britain (Manton, 1976) and Jane Addams in America established ground-breaking juvenile justice programmes and girls' clubs (Meigs, 1970). Prior to 1935, club workers (as youth workers were commonly known) and social workers shared the same professional qualification and consequently the former often identified as 'social workers'. In some European countries an analogous situation exists with those undertaking what elsewhere might be designated adult education, community, social or youth work being described as social pedagogues (Kornbeck and Jensen, 2011, 2013). Youth work's boundaries may be permeable but they exist. In the UK and most settings it is characterised by:

- young people choosing to engage *voluntarily*;
- interventions focused upon the *education* and *welfare* of young people;

- a primary concern with *young people*, making it an *age-specific* activity;
- the work being underpinned by a desire to encourage participants to come together to foster *association* and *relationships*;
- workers who are *educative role models, friendly and responsive*; and
- workers who act with *integrity*. (Jeffs and Smith, 2008: 277)

Nothing in this list is unique to youth work. What is exceptional is the fusion of the characteristics, creating an amalgam that practitioners in many countries opt to identify with. Therefore, describing oneself as a 'youth worker' in the UK and numerous other locales signals a commitment to working with specific methodologies and clientele. However, those methodologies that have been appropriated by youth work as their own predate the emergence of the term; consequently, to comprehend what youth work is, and may become, one must scrutinise their history. This chapter will now consider the events but also more importantly the ideas that have shaped youth work, in the UK and elsewhere, both as a way of working and a concept. It will discuss these because the present always depends on the past, hence it is an essential object for our study. As Chaucer explains: 'From oute of the olde fields, as men sey, comyth all this newe corn from yere to yere' (*Parliament of Foules*).

ORIGINS

Most literature traces youth work's origins to late 18th-century Britain (Davies, 2009; Jeffs, 1979; Jeffs and Smith, 2002). Usually linking this to the emergence post-1780 of Sunday schools, which besides religious instruction offered young people leisure activities, welfare services, basic education and meeting places wherein they might relax with friends and 'caring' adults (Laqueur, 1977). The concept rapidly took flight. Within barely two decades Sunday schools

were operating in the USA (Boylan, 1990) as well as throughout the British Empire and much of Europe (Orchard and Briggs, 2007). Britain was the first nation to endure the traumas of industrialisation and urbanisation, which accompanied the market economies' rise to domination. Polanyi (1944) called this 'the great transformation'. There were benefits, notably greater productivity but also 'diswelfares' – i.e. heightened mortality rates, epidemics, poverty and homelessness – which prompted an unparalleled flowering of philanthropy and social action (Prochaska and Prochaska, 1980). The rationale for both were not pre-set; some sought to generate progressive change – others prevent it; some promoted democracy – others endeavoured to halt its advance; and some wished to emancipate the proletariat and women – others to erect bulwarks to ensure neither occurred. Despite their ideological differences, practitioners tended to create and adopt a similar armoury of techniques to accomplish diverse ends, because their first priority was to make and sustain contact with young people who often rightly distrusted their motives. During this period, Sunday schools (religious and secular alike), Missions, Friendly Societies, Ragged Schools, Mechanics Institutes and Evening Schools collectively fashioned procedures and skill sets that still comprise the basic *modus operandi* of youth work. Outreach and detached work, clubs, school-based provision, uniformed groups, drop-ins, residential work, sporting and cultural programmes, and more besides, were all tried and tested before 1870 (see Montague, 1904). However, youth work as a term and concept was unknown in the UK and elsewhere until the late 1930s, apart from a brief interval during the 1860s.

In 1863 Arthur Sweatman, a London based curate, delivered a widely circulated paper to the Annual Meeting of the Social Science Association concerning the Islington Youths' Institute opened in 1860 which referred to it and similar provision as Youth's Clubs.

Which sought to attract working lads aged 13 to 19 uninterested in attending 'Night Schools' and Mechanics Institutes. Staffed by two paid managers and gentlemen volunteers Islington Youths' Club had a well-stocked reading room and hall for activities. Members paid a subscription and were expected to engage in its management. In return they enjoyed a mix of 'recreation, companionship, reading, instruction' (Sweatman, 1863: 3) plus social events, lectures 'of an entertaining and instructional' bent, and access to welfare assistance such as a penny bank. The programme contained many stalwarts of contemporary youth work – exchange visits involving other clubs, sporting competitions, musical evenings and summer excursions. The model proved attractive but the title was soon abandoned in favour of 'boys' club'. A switch which coincided with the emergence of girls' clubs; the first opened in Bristol in 1861 (Jeffs, 2018a). Those running these became boys' and girls' club workers or leaders; paid staff were called superintendents, managers or secretaries.

The term youth club re-surfaced in the 1930s, after which individuals began describing themselves as 'youth workers' and their calling as 'youth work'. Cunningham therefore with justification argues that 'youth work' like 'teenager' is 'a mid-20th-century invention' (2012: 14). Indeed, it was only during the early 1940s that official documents, books and agencies in Britain and elsewhere first talked of 'youth work' and 'youth workers' – a decade after *Methods in Youth Work*, authored by Walkey, Wills and Motley (1931), the earliest text to employ the term appeared. Based on three talks delivered to the National Assembly of the Baptist Union the book, like so much subsequently written on 'youth work', emphasised the merits of: working with small groups; listening to what young people said; responding to their interests; and meeting, where possible, their expressed needs. It called for workers to possess 'personalities' that made them attractive to be with and warned

that you 'cannot standardise leadership, nor turn it out by mass production' (1931: 14–15). Finally, the authors urged readers to 'take a long view of your work' (ibid.: 17) and avoid judging impact via short-term outcomes. Although its content had, and retains, a familiar ring, it embodied a break with tradition. Hitherto the literature had been gender-specific focusing exclusively on either the boys' or girls' clubs. Indeed it was not until Brew's *In the Service of Youth* was published in 1943 that that dam was finally breached. Why Walkey et al. opted for a mixed model they called 'youth work' in preference to the single-sex club is not difficult to unearth. Post-1920 Baptist congregations and Sunday school attendance, like those of other denominations, was declining year on year (Brown, 2001). One possible means of staunching this decline was to offer those who traditionally left the Sunday school when they entered employment an alternative, hence the formation of mixed Baptist Youth Fellowships. It was for leaders of these and similar clubs that *Methods in Youth Work* was penned. Pearl Jephcott's research undertaken in Birmingham around this time found girls' clubs, mostly linked to churches, chapels or synagogues, faced a comparable predicament (Jeffs, 2018b). The proportion of members aged 14 plus was waning, primarily, Jephcott learnt, because most young women once they entered employment favoured spending their leisure time in mixed, commercially run, settings. By 1937 the National Council of Girls' Clubs' (NCGC) leadership sensed single-sex girls' clubs had a limited future; therefore, they held club work's survival necessitated the promotion of mixed units (Jeffs, 2018a).

Probably the earliest mixed 'youth organisation' was the Young People's Society of Christian Endeavor, founded in Portland, Maine, by a Congregational Minister, Francis Edward Clark, in 1881, who shortly afterwards published a text advocating discrete 'youth' provision (Clark, 1882). Christian Endeavor, which remains active, was created as a 'club' to which Sunday School members might transfer at 14. Here was an idea whose time had come. Within four years a Maine Christian Endeavor convention drew 15,000 members; the 1896 World Convention attracted 75,000, including delegates from the UK, Australia, China, Japan, Mexico and South Africa (Meadows, undated). By 1905 there was a European Union incorporating 16 national bodies and London alone had over 500 branches. US membership declined post-1910, principally because Clark's idea had been adopted by 'mainline denominations' (Senter, 2010). Others also followed in Clark's footsteps. For example the British Conservative Party in 1906 launched the mixed Junior Imperial and Constitutional League – simultaneously Britain's first political and secular youth organisation. The 4-H movement (the 'H' stands for head, heart, hands and health) was probably America's first mixed secular youth organisation. One cannot confidently identify its year of commencement, as units emerged independently post-1890. Each offered meaningful leisure-time activities whilst preparing young people for life in a rural environment. When finally a national organisation was formed in 1914 it inherited an emblem, title, well-established format and branches in nearly every state. Activities were frequently gender-specific but branches overwhelmingly mixed (Wessel and Wessel, 1982).

Two years after the appearance of *Methods in Youth Work*, the first youth centre opened on a new housing estate in Dagenham, managed by a full-time 'youth worker', Mrs C. Langley, possibly the UK's first. Construction costs were met by a charitable trust whilst the NCGC in collaboration with the NABC (National Association of Boys' Clubs – founded 1925) produced the building's design. Divided into three segments: two comprising specialist rooms equipped for gender-specific activities and a third communal area with a library, social space and canteen. Youth clubs proved popular but few prior to the late 1940s occupied purpose-built premises. Some had their own modified buildings, but the overwhelming majority made do with borrowed premises – usually schools, church halls or community centres.

Although the NABC and the NCGC cooperated with respect to the Dagenham Youth Centre, the NABC's membership were implacably opposed to mixed clubs. This hostility was not simply the by-product of boorish misogyny. They firmly believed the case for separation was vindicated by the writings, research and 'scientific' evidence assembled by G. Stanley Hall and his followers. Hall's two-volume text *Adolescence*, published in 1904, played a decisive role in the development of youth work. An unwieldy compendium of research findings, it nevertheless sold so briskly that Hall and others hastily penned shorter accessible versions (Hall, 1906; Slaughter, 1911). Hall's promotional tours of the United States and Europe combined with the book's sales meant that he virtually single-handedly crafted the concept of adolescence as a discrete developmental stage, thereby manufacturing a superficially unanswerable case for specific leisure and social provision for young people. His model called for single-sex clubs and uniformed troops where conscientious, wise adults could help guide members through the turbulent waters of adolescence (Savage, 2007). *Adolescence* supplied the intellectual buttressing for an unprecedented expansion in the number of clubs and uniformed organisations during the two decades following publication – not least for the Boy Scouts and Girl Guides, launched in 1907 and 1910 respectively by Robert Baden-Powell, a forthright advocate of Hall's theories (Jeal, 1989). Baden-Powell, like a majority of boys' club leaders, accepted as a given Hall's belief that only boys were destined to scale the highest intellectual and physical peaks, and that women, inherently weaker in both spheres, must be protected from the rigours of life and equipped for sheltered domestic roles. In accordance with this stance, Hall campaigned for 'the school and all institutions' to 'push sex distinctions to its utmost' (1903: 6). Co-education and mixed clubs were not merely wrong, they were, Hall and his numerous supporters counselled, detrimental to the well-being of individuals and society. This dogma prompted the NABC to rebuff every overture from the NCGC to collaborate in the development of mixed clubs. The latter, whose leadership knew girls' clubs would haemorrhage membership if they failed to adapt, went their own way and post-1939 actively promoted 'youth clubs' and 'youth work' (Jeffs, 2018a). By 1950 less than 5 per cent of their much enlarged membership attended girls' clubs. Eventually the NABC and the boys' uniformed youth organisations yielded to the inevitable and post-1980 began admitting young women in the hope of turning their fading fortunes around. For the Boy Scouts it worked, for the NABC it proved too late. Eventually in 2017 the rump merged with UK Youth the direct descendent of the NCGC. In the USA the respective organisations advantageously amalgamated in 1990 to form the Boys' and Girls' Clubs of America.

Dagenham Youth Club's opening in 1933 helped highlight the reality that girls, who traditionally carried the dual burdens of employment and work in the home, enjoyed far less 'leisure' than boys (Fowler, 1996; Todd, 2005). Moreover, at this time domestic service, frequently involving evening work, remained by far the largest employer of teenage girls (Rooff, 1935). This lack of free time contributed to the majority of girls' clubs opening only one or two evenings per week. In Birmingham (UK) in 1934, out of 60 NCGC-affiliated girls' clubs just one operated for six evenings per week and during the day, and it alone employed a full-time leader (Jeffs, 2018b). Nationally, an acute shortage of women leaders, paid or unpaid, meant that many girls' 'clubs and fellowships are run almost entirely by young people' (Rooff, 1935: 3). Consequently whilst boys' clubs tended to have had their own buildings, often with playing-fields and gymnasia, plus a full-time leader; girls' clubs invariably met in borrowed premises with a voluntary leader. Similarly with regards uniformed youth organisations, whereas Scout and Boys' Brigade troops commonly had their own huts, this was unknown amongst their sister organisations. Unsurprisingly, the NCGC failed to recruit a woman leader for Dagenham and was obliged to ask the YWCA to 'loan' them one of their general secretaries. This difficulty helped convince the NCGC that if youth work and youth centres were to fulfil their potential, a national training programme for youth leaders was needed. This they launched in 1935 (Jeffs, 2018c).

The experimental design adopted for the Dagenham Youth Centre was, for whatever reason, never replicated. However, the existing NABC architectural model was unsuitable for a mixed membership. The possible alternative was that of the YWCA, who had run their own premises since 1855. However these, like those of the YMCA (founded 1844), catered for a largely middle-class clientele able to afford costly membership fees. Based on the layout of a London ladies' or gentlemen's club, complete with restaurants and often residential accommodation, they were neither appropriate nor affordable for a neighbourhood youth centre. It took decades of trial and error in Britain and elsewhere before suitable designs emerged (Pietsch and Muller, 2015). Unfortunately by the time the conundrum was solved in the 1960s the era of the youth centre was drawing to a close (Ord, 2011; Robertson, 2009).

THINKING ANEW

It would be naive to assume that youth work in Britain or elsewhere is solely the by-product of industrialisation and urbanisation. Equally, it was shaped by a philosophical and intellectual revolution of similar magnitude – the Enlightenment. Philosophy like most human activities has heightened periods of vibrancy. Gottlieb (2016) identifies two junctures when the greatest leaps forward occurred: one the Athenian era of Socrates, Plato and Aristotle; the other the *le siècle des Lumières* (the Century of Lights) or Enlightenment, which flourished from approximately 1700 to 1825. Before focusing on the second we should acknowledge youth work's debt to the first. An 'extended' history of youth work and informal education would commence with the contribution of the Athenians. The golden thread that fuses each successive manifestation of informal education with young people is that it seeks via dialogue and conversation to offer participants educational experiences that enable them to flourish – socially, spiritually and intellectually. Primarily this educational core is what unifies such disparate entities as informal education, social pedagogy, youth work, liberal adult education and community work. Etymologically 'education' derives from the Latin 'educere' or 'educare', which translates to 'leading or bringing out'. Although Latin provides our root, the ideas incorporated within the terms emerged not in Rome but Ancient Greece. There many believed we are born with immortal souls, which, following our death, return to a 'world' inhabited by the gods wherein all things become known to it. Afterwards the soul is reborn in a new body and during the trauma of birth this knowledge and wisdom is forgotten but not erased. Thereafter, learning becomes a process of recollecting. Articulated by Plato and Socrates, amongst others, this theory held that acquiring knowledge and wisdom entailed 'bringing out' what is immemorially lodged in our souls. Presumably few reading this chapter share Plato's and Socrates' belief in the transmigration of souls or the theory of 'recollection'. However, before dismissing 'recollection' out of hand it is worth pausing to ask why so many have long found the teaching methods it cultivated attractive. One who did, for example, was Bruner, author of two of the 20th-century's most influential

education texts, *The Process of Education* and *The Relevance of Education*. In the latter Bruner advocates 'discovery teaching', involving 'not so much the process of leading students to discover what is "out there", but rather their discovering what is in their own heads' (1971: 72). So why do individuals who reject the beliefs on which the methodology resides believe it to be germane?

The first reason is because it furnishes an alternative to the dominant view that education amounts to merely pouring 'knowledge' and 'facts' into empty heads; and that young people must be force-fed a curriculum and drilled to pass tests with pre-ordained answers. Plato (1941) long ago warned that this model consistently failed because nothing 'learned under compulsion stays in the mind' (*The Republic*, 536.D; see also Grove, 2014; Jones et al., 2015). 'Recollection' remains alluring because it bids us to view those we teach as possessing knowledge and talents we can help to 'lead out' and nurture. It invites youth workers to set aside a deficit view of young people and commence from an appreciation of their 'hidden' talents and expertise. A second reason is that 'reflection' and 'leading out' suggest we sidestep narrowly didactic approaches and embrace dialogue, conversation and discussion. A technique with a protracted history, and employed by Socrates, it was known as *elenctic* or *elenchus*. It entails posing probing questions to help our partners in dialogue reveal what they know. *Elenchus* necessitates individuals interrogating their beliefs and embarking via dialogue on a search for truth. Skilful youth workers have long cultivated learning by applying this method. Dialogical education may struggle to co-exist with an outcome-driven school and college system, but it is congruent with the world beyond the classroom where youth workers operate. Indeed the spaces they construct, such as clubs, or find within the outside world are perfect sites for the fostering of dialogue and educative conversations. The foundations upon which a concept of education as 'leading out' rests may be improbable, but as a guiding principle for how youth workers function it remains an attractive methodology – not least because it is one that enables participants to acquire some mastery of the arts of reasoning and the making of sound judgements.

Kant, in an essay written in 1784 sought to answer the question *Was ist Aufklarung* [What is Enlightenment?]. His response began:

> Enlightenment is the emergence of man from his self-imposed infancy. Infancy is the inability to use one's reason without the guidance of another. It is self-imposed, when it depends on a deficiency, not of reason, but of the resolve and courage to use it without external guidance. Thus the watchword of enlightenment is Sapere aude! Have the courage to use one's own reason. (1996: 11)

Sapere aude, borrowed from Horace, translates as 'Dare to Know' or 'Dare to be Wise'. It is an axiom that encapsulates much of the spirit of the Enlightenment which held that:

1　Reason is an individual's central capacity which enables them to think and most importantly act correctly;
2　People are by nature rational and good therefore 'evil' can be overcome;
3　Individuals and society have the potential to progress to perfection;
4　Beliefs should be adopted only on the basis of reason, not taken on the authority of others, including religious leaders and texts.

Enlightenment thinkers broke through barriers of prejudice by urging tolerance towards the views and lifestyles of others, and the removal of injustice. Condorcet, a leading Enlightenment thinker, was not atypical in advocating an end to discrimination against homosexuals, the granting of full political and social equality to women, the provision of free education for all and the abolition of slavery (Schapiro, 1963). By adopting these and similar liberal positions he and others radically re-orientated the way many perceive their place in the world, and our attitudes to young people and the role of education. If we examine the list above we can see how the better elements of contemporary youth work are not a mere by-product of technological, social and economic change but also of the Enlightenment's re-conceptualisation of the relationship between human beings and their world. In line with John Locke's belief that 'no man's knowledge can go beyond his experience' (2000: 71) those who sought wisdom and understanding were encouraged to turn, at least in part, towards the physical world for guidance and inspiration. This growing acceptance of a sensory basis for ideas promoted not only a greater respect for the natural world but the earliest stirrings of a belief that subsequently became a cornerstone of youth work, that young people learn best from experience via outdoor activities, craftwork, music, dance, sport, drama and group interaction.

For youth work the Enlightenment proved important for two reasons: first it initiated a profound re-alignment in social attitudes towards the role of education. Enlightenment thinkers were aware their ambitions to set aside prejudice and ignorance and create a new world order founded upon reason and justice required an educated populace – one possessing, as Locke explained, 'a sound mind in a sound body' (1693: 33). Although few might disagree in the abstract with this premise, in reality the balance he advocated has never been prioritised within schooling. The need for a 'sound body' has always been subservient to the task of teaching 'employment skills' and 'examinable subjects'; an over-sight which fostered alternative forms of pedagogic practice embraced by youth work. These sought to help young people acquire a 'sound body' via voluntary engagement in sports and healthy activities. So it came about that club and settlement workers such as Octavia Hill played a central role in creating organisations that secured access to the countryside for the whole population, much as they invented new low-cost sports such as table tennis, basketball and volleyball and codified traditional sports so that participation increased via leagues.

The second reason for the importance of the Enlightenment to youth work was that its supporters prioritised the need to equip people to think for themselves and fulfil their destiny as autonomous citizens. Early advocates of democracy held that if an electorate were not to be presided over by self-perpetuating elites or manipulated by charlatans, thereby making a mockery of this system, high-quality universal education was essential. Herein emerged a difficulty, one never fully resolved; namely if young people were to acquire the arts and knowledge required to be sovereign citizens how can this be accomplished if the educational institutions are controlled by the religious bodies, governments and employers who long denied them liberty and equality and whose self-interest is served by producing a supine easily manipulated populace. Various writers outlined solutions to this dilemma. Thomas Jefferson, principle author of the American Declaration of Independence, believed the answer resided in ensuring education was controlled by locally elected and accountable officials; Condorcet opted for education to be provided by independent Guilds of Teachers (Schapiro, 1963: 211). Rousseau held that the solution lay in allowing children to develop 'naturally', which meant sheltering them from unwarranted and excessive interference. It is in his writings that we encounter the modern origins of 'experiential education', the rudiments of an analysis that morphed into a substantive strand within the theoretical underpinnings of contemporary youth work. Rousseau's rule of thumb when it came to giving young people guidance with respect to their learning was 'let it be very little' and, if it was called for, to 'arrange some practical situation' that they will need to address (1979: 13). Here we encounter the foundations of an educational model that rested upon a belief that young people have a natural proclivity towards activity, inquisitiveness, inventiveness and self-discovery. Rousseau assumed this format was best suited for young men, but those who followed, such as Pestalozzi and Froebel

(1907), not only put flesh on the bones of his thinking but saw that young women would similarly benefit from this approach, which strove for the education of the whole person – mind and body. Pestalozzi's (1885) version was summarised as an approach that engaged the hands (via creative activity), heart (via the experience of feeling and emotion) and head (by the process of thinking).

Boys' and girls' clubs at their best catered for the members' 'hands, hearts and heads', as places where activity, learning and dialogue fed upon each other. 'Clubs' or YMCA and YWCA associations also embodied another Enlightenment value – a faith in democracy. Adult clubs are entities wherein members have an equal say, via voting and discussion, in determining rules and policy. By embracing the club concept, youth workers expressed a commitment to democracy in an era when all women and most men were denied the franchise. In Europe and the United States this commitment to democracy was reflected in the prominent roles many club workers played in the struggle to extend the franchise to those denied it. But also, along the way, clubs became places where members gained their first opportunity to practice citizenship's arts.

MANY STRANDS

Youth work is a long rope comprising many strands; one still unfinished. Thanks chiefly to the creativity of practitioners, it is being elongated as long-standing modes of practice are remodelled and renewed, and broadened as new approaches are woven into the fabric to meld with traditional formats. In essence, its strength emanates from the fusion of accumulated experiences and practitioners' theories seamlessly transferred, via conversation, observation, the written word and tuition, from worker to worker – generation to generation. Just as conversations and dialogues with colleagues help us to acquire insights into unfamiliar ways of working and untried techniques, so via these routes we come by new theories and ideas. Wise practitioners develop their practice by joining what some call 'invisible colleges' – informal networks that facilitate the exchange of information, experience and knowledge via electronic devices, conversation and personal communication (Zuccala, 2005). Irrespective of the medium, these help us accumulate the wisdom of our peers and acquire useful theories and concepts. This is why 'professional' conversations are so productive. Just as wise practitioners value the chance to learn from peers so will they wish to learn from those who went before. Newton, in a letter to his fellow scientist and rival, Robert Hooke, reminded him, and us, that one can see 'a little further' by 'standing on the shoulders of Giants'. It is a maxim that applies equally to youth work.

Holding on to the rope metaphor we can envisage an entity that takes ideas and activities, history and vision, analysis and action and draws these strands together so each acquires strength one from another. This interplay of theory and practice, ideas and action, with each nurturing and modifying the other, is not unique to youth work; indeed, it is the hallmark of all vibrant professions or arenas of study. The process, whereby theory changes practice and practice changes theory, is what philosophers and others refer to as *praxis*. It is not a new concept. Aristotle, 2,300 years ago, maintained there were essentially three fundamental human activities – *theoria* (thinking), *poiesis* (making), and *praxis* (thoughtful doing) – and that 'life is *praxis*, not doing. Mere doing is the function of the slave' (1999, 7.2: 1325). Praxis entails making prudent practical judgments regarding 'how to act' in given situations. Arendt (1958), one of the last century's most influential political philosophers, and incidentally a youth worker with Youth Aliyah in Paris from 1935 to 1940, argues that it is this application of *theoria* via *praxis* that uniquely makes us human. Freire, who acquired a comparable status in relation to adult and informal education, spoke similarly of humans 'as beings of *praxis*' who alone possess an ability to 'transform' and 'humanise' the world (1970: 455). It is the development of such abilities that lies at the heart of constructive and ethical youth work.

UTILISING HISTORY

Nothing stands still, including youth work. Unrelentingly 'praxis' – the interplay of theory and practice, ideas and activity, policy and procedure – has re-shaped it as much as have pressures emanating from the wider social, economic and physical environment. At best this perpetual state of flux is exhilarating, at worse unsettling, but we are better able to obtain a heightened grasp of what is taking place and marshal an inkling of the trajectory of travel by acquiring an awareness of how the building blocks of practice abrade one against another. An essential starting point for doing so is by cross-examining our history. Therefore, besides teaching us a measure of 'humility' and a sense of 'awe' by confronting us with the scale of the accomplishments of those who preceded us, like the totality of history itself, a sense of our own history affords 'a political and psychological treasury from which we can draw reserves' that will equip us to better 'cope with the future' (Lasch, 1979: xviii).

It is important however to avoid adopting a teleological narration that promises us that as time unfolds, usually with a measure of inevitability, we will arrive at a positive outcome. Nor must we ever assume youth work's future will be better than its past. Histories of play work (Frost, 2009) and liberal adult education (Holford, 2016) certainly leave us with evidence that sectors can lose momentum and embark on journeys of sustained, even terminal, decline. Indeed, examples within our past offer stark warnings that things can go awry. The first relates to how Soviet

Russia and Nazi Germany with consummate ease and unquestionable expertise embraced the methodologies of youth work and utilised them to entrench their power and murderous ends. In the former, state-sponsored organisations, notably the Pioneers, annexed existing provision and exploited a 'monopoly position' to create the 'assertive young person' exhorted to actively 'campaign and exercise leadership over "backward" adults', including family members (Kelly, 2007: 77). Unsullied by a bourgeois past, such young people were to build a new order and to help them do so they were given 'staggering' freedom to undertake 'outreach work', including construction projects, child care, organising propaganda programmes and managing their own leisure activities. Pioneer Palaces opened in urban centres often lavishly equipped with facilities for relaxation, activities and self-directed learning (Kelly, 2007: 551–552; Reid, 2015). Despite their ideological differences, the German Nazi Party operated comparable programmes post-1933. Social pedagogy, youth and social work were recalibrated to serve the Third Reich (Sunker and Otto, 1997). Some youth organisations and prospective recruits resisted incorporation within the Hitler Youth, but it was a conflict neither could ultimately win. Becker (1946) recounts how groups of young people such as 'The Pack' fought the Hitler Youth, whom they despised, until their leaders were eventually arrested. By 1939 the Hitler Youth had 'achieved the allegiance of a substantial majority of German youth' (Stachura, 1981: 137), via judicious application of stick and carrot. The stick was compulsory membership, requiring cunning or courage, often both, to avoid. The carrot was access to well-equipped centres, holidays, adventure and sports (Donath, 2015). A second example is the embarrassing history of American youth organisations, notably, but not exclusively, in the South, prior to the 1960s in relation to racial segregation. With few exceptions many tamely helped prolong segregation and discrimination by condoning discrete provision for blacks and whites over large swathes of the country (see for example Canady, 2016; Hinnershitz, 2015; Jordan, 2016; Mjagkij, 1994; Neverdon-Morton, 1989; Robertson, 2007; Thompson, 2012; Wolcott, 2012). Such examples, plus similar ones from elsewhere, remind us that youth work's techniques and practice are neither axiomatically liberal nor progressive; and like other welfare and educational formats they can always be employed to facilitate either the oppression or liberation of individuals and groups.

GUIDES TO ACTION

The INFED website launched in 1995 now contains archival documents, histories of organisations and modes of practice, plus biographies of key individuals, thereby forming an invaluable resource for anyone wishing to study youth work's narrative – as are the six volumes comprising contributions to the *Youth & Policy* History of Youth and Community conferences (Gilchrist, 2001 onwards) and the five volumes of essays on *The History of Youth Work in Europe* (Verschelden et al., 2009 onwards). The latter volumes in particular have filled long-standing gaps by publishing accounts of youth work's development in most European states and regions. Modern youth work, like universal schooling and welfare provision, initially surfaced where industrialisation took off – Britain, Flanders, Germany and the north eastern United States. Consequently, the literature disproportionately focuses on events in those places. Certainly they are the subject of our 'general histories' – Flanders (Coussée, 2008), the UK (Jeffs, 1979; Davies, 1999a, 1999b, 2008) and Germany (Becker, 1946; see also Spatscheck, 2009). The other material falls into three categories:

1 Texts produced by pioneers as practice manuals for new entrants or accounts written to raise

awareness of youth work; outstanding examples include: Maude Stanley's *Clubs for Working Girls* (1890); Charles Russell and Lilian Rigby's *Working Lad's Clubs* (1908); Lily Montagu's *My Club and I* (1941); Winifred Buck's *Boys' Self-governing Clubs* (1903); Charles Bernheimer and Jacob Cohen's *Boys' Clubs* (1914); Helen Ferris's *Girls' Cubs: Their Organization and Management* (1918); and Renee B. Stern's *Clubs, Making and Management* (1925). Within this category we encounter easily the most widely read texts: Baden-Powell's *Scouting for Boys* (1908) and *The Cross and the Switchblade* (1962) by David Wilkinson, founder of Teen Challenge.

2 Biographies recounting the achievements of leading practitioners from Raikes onwards. We surely have sufficient on Jane Addams, 12 when last counted, and possibly also on Hannah More and Don Bosco, who along with his co-worker Maria Domenica Mazzarello remains youth work's only canonised saint and the subject of a full-length film. Outstanding contributions include: Jeal's (1989) on Baden-Powell; Binfield's (1973) on George Williams; and Darley's (1990) on Octavia Hill.

3 A mix of histories relating to specific youth organisations plus a few longitudinal studies of discrete practice formats; examples include: Senter (2010) on youth ministry; Miller (2007) on American girls' organisations; Eagar on boys' clubs (1953); and Ogilvie (2013) on outdoor education. No histories exist of detached, club or school-based practice, but we have abundant national accounts of the work of the YMCA, YWCA, Scouts and Guides. The major omission remains, as Thompson notes in relation to 4-H, the absence of the 'voices from club members themselves' (2012: 16) – an oversight that exposes the need to unearth accounts of young people's encounters with youth work.

CONCLUSION

The overall tenor of recent material embodies a faith in the value of history as a guide to action, reflecting a belief that by interrogating our past we will acquire a steer regarding current trends. Here we encounter what might be termed 'applied history' – scholarship partially sustained by the premise that history will offer a 'recompense' equipping authors and audience alike to better read the undertow of contemporary practice and policy.

Perhaps this explains why the flow of historical material has multiplied at an almost exponential rate post-1990 in line with a widespread contraction in the sum total of provision, notably in the UK and parts of Europe. In Europe this period has witnessed the decline and, in some locales the almost total disappearance of state-run youth services. In Eastern Europe this was precipitated by the ending of communist rule. The resultant vacuum was partially filled by a return to the 'past' which led to the 're-entry' of scout and guide movements, and agencies such as the YMCA and YWCA. In western Europe and elsewhere a shrinkage in state provision has occurred as a consequence of austerity measures designed to lower state expenditure on welfare and the election of politicians ideologically committed to 'rolling back the state'. Irrespective of the causation, the outcome has been similar – a forced re-structuring plus widespread closures of programmes and facilities. However, austerity is not the sole causation, for during this period we have witnessed what may prove to be the culmination of a long epoch of decline in the numbers engaging with youth workers and organisations. In the UK, apart from the period 1939–1945 when unique circumstances prevailed, year-on-year the average age of those involved with youth work agencies has fallen since the 1930s (Jeffs, 2018a). Therefore with each passing year youth work has become less about serving 'youth' and more about 'managing' children. As the proportion of those under 21 in full-time education grew in every industrialised nation, so the need for clubs and projects as sites for adolescent socialisation diminishes. Now, the pace of retrenchment has quickened as this client group acquires access to increasingly sophisticated means of electronic communication. Smartphones, tablets and computers have fundamentally altered young people's lifestyles. These, plus improvements in material well-being have produced a sharp diminution in the time spent outside the home, working part-time and physically 'hanging-out' with friends. Twenge (2017) argues that consequently 18-year-olds are now acting more like 15-year-olds used to and the latter's patterns of behaviour now closely resemble those of 13-year-olds a decade ago. We also appear to be living in an era when people of all ages are becoming less collectivist and more individualistic regarding their choice of leisure and social activities (Elliott and Lemert, 2006; Putman, 2000). A cultural shift that has cultivated a decline in participation in team games, group activities and social interaction, and fostered a turn towards pursuits which individuals undertake in isolation, for example, cycling, playing on a computer and visiting a gym – an adjustment that does not auger well for youth work's future well-being. An optimistic reading tells us that just as youth work pushed aside boys' and girls' clubs, which had earlier displaced Sunday schools, so we are now witnessing another period of transition, during which new practice genres will come to the fore, i.e. *positive youth development* (Damon, 2004), *targeted youth work* (Scanlon et al., 2011), *digital youth work* (Melvin, 2015) and *missional youth work* (Kirk and Thorne, 2011).

Or maybe not; for robotics, AI (Artificial Intelligence) computerisation, and electronic communications and entertainment are setting in motion a second 'great transformation'. Out of the first grew what eventually became youth work. Possibly now we are witnessing that epoch's closure and must therefore be prepared to acknowledge that, like other formats before youth work, has run its course. Whether or not this is so, we can extract from our history the optimistic message that dialogical education, of which youth work has been a component for two centuries, has a history stretching back four millennia – during which time it has outlived many great Empires and ridden the surf of the last great transformation. Perhaps we should be quietly assured that it will emerge intact from the next. In the poem 'Mutability' Shelley warned that 'man's yesterday may ne'er be like his morrow', but that does not mean there will be no place or need for those willing to engage in dialogical education with young and old alike.

REFERENCES

Arendt, H. (1958) *The Human Condition*, Chicago: University of Chicago Press.
Aristotle (1999) *Politics* [translated B. Jowett], Ontario: Batoche.
Becker, H. (1946) *German Youth: Bond or Free*, London: Kegan Paul.
Binfield, C. (1973) *George Williams and the YMCA*, London: Heinemann.
Boylan, A.M. (1990) *Sunday School: The Formation of an American Institution*, New Haven: Yale University Press.
Brew, J. Macalister (1943) *In the Service of Youth*, London: Faber.
Brown, C. (2001) *Death of Christian Britain: Understanding Secularisation 1800–2000*, London: Routledge.
Bruner, J. (1971) *The Relevance of Education*, New York: Norton.
Canady, A. McNeill (2016) *Willis Duke Weatherford: Race, Religion, and Reform in the American South*, Lexington: University of Kentucky Press.
Clark, F.E. (1882) *The Children and the Church and Young Peoples' Society of Christian Endeavor as a Means of Bringing Them Together*, Boston: Congregational Sunday School and Publishing Society.
Coussée, F. (2008) *A Century of Youth Policy*, Gent: Academia Press.
Cunningham, H. (2012) 'Youth in the life course – a history' in F. Coussée et al. (Eds.), *The History of Youth Work in Europe: Relevance for Youth Policy 3*, Strasbourg: Council of Europe.
Damon, W. (2004) 'What is positive youth development?', *Annals of the American Academy of Political and Social Science*, 591(1): 13–24.

Darley, G. (1990) *Octavia Hill: Social Reformer and Founder of the National Trust*, London: Faber.

Davies, B. (1999a) *From Voluntaryism to Welfare State: A History of the Youth Service in England 1939–1979*, Leicester: Youth Work Press.

Davies, B. (1999b) *From Thatcherism to New Labour: A History of the Youth Service in England 1979–1999*, Leicester: Youth Work Press.

Davies, B. (2008) *The New Labour Years: A History of the Youth Service in England 1997–2007*, Leicester: Youth Work Press.

Davies, B. (2009) 'Defined by history: youth work in the UK' in G. Verschelden et al. (Eds.), *The History of Youth Work in Europe: Relevance for Youth Policy Today*, Strasbourg: Council of Europe.

Donath, M. (2015) 'The Home of the Hitler Youth at the Exhibition' in S. Piethsch and A. Muller (Eds.), *Walls That Teach: On the Architecture of Youth Centres*, Heijningen, Netherlands: Jap Sam Books.

Eagar, W. McG. (1953) *Making Men: The History of the Boys' Clubs and Related Movements in Great Britain*, London: London University Press.

Elliott, A. and Lemert, C.C. (2006) *The New Individualism: The Emotional Costs of Globalisation*, London: Routledge.

Fowler, D. (1996) *The Life-style of Young Wage-earners in Interwar Britain*, London: Woburn Education.

Freire, P. (1970) 'Cultural Action and Conscientization', *Harvard Educational Review*, 40(3): 452–477.

Froebel, F. (1907) *The Education of Man* [translated by W.N. Hailmann], New York: Appleton.

Frost, J.L. (2009) *A History of Children's Play and Play Environments*, New York: Routledge.

Gilchrist, R., Jeffs, T. and Spence, J. (2001) *Essays in the History of Community and Youth Work*, Leicester: Youth Work Press.

Gottlieb, A. (2016) *The Dream of Enlightenment: The Rise of Modern Philosophy*, Harmondsworth: Allen Lane.

Grove, J. (2014) 'New students have forgotten bulk of A-level knowledge', *Times Higher Education Supplement*, 25th June.

Hall, G. Stanley (1903) 'Attack on co-education', *New York Times*, 11th July.

Hall, G. Stanley (1904) *Adolescence*, New York: Appleton.

Hall, G. Stanley (1906) *Youth: Its Education, Regimen and Hygiene*, New York: Appleton.

Heafford, M.R. (1967) *Pestalozzi*, London: Methuen.

Hinnershitz, S. (2015) *Race, Religion and Civil Rights: Asian Students on the West Coast 1900–1968*, New Brunswick NJ: Rutgers University Press.

Holford, J. (2016) 'The misuses of sustainability: adult education, citizenship and the dead hand of neoliberalism', *International Review of Education*, 65(5): 541–561.

Jeal, T. (1989) *Baden-Powell*, London: Hutchinson.

Jeffs, A.J. (1979) *Young People and the Youth Service*, London: RKP.

Jeffs, T. (2018a) *A Century of Youth Work. Volume One: From National Organisation of Girls' Clubs to UK Youth; 1911 to 1960*, London: Y&P Publishing.

Jeffs, T. (2018b) 'Pearl Jephcott: club worker', *Women's History Review* (forthcoming).

Jeffs, T. (2018c) 'Ups and downs: a history of youth work training' in P. Connaughton and T. Jeffs (Eds.), *Then and Now: Essays in the History of Youth and Community Work*, London: Y&P Publishing.

Jeffs, T. and Smith, M.K. (2002) 'Individualism and youth work', *Youth & Policy*, 76: 39–65.

Jeffs, T. and Smith, M.K. (2008) 'Valuing youth work', *Youth & Policy*, 100: 207–302.

Jones, H., Black, B., Green, J., Langton, P., Rutherford, S., Scott, J. and Brown, S. (2015) 'Indications of knowledge retention in the transition to higher education', *Journal of Biological Education*, 49(3): 261–273.

Jordan, B.R. (2016) *Modern Manhood and the Boy Scouts of America: Citizenship, Race, and the Environment 1910–1930*, Chapel Hill: University of North Carolina Press.

Kant, I. (1996) *Practical Philosophy* [Cambridge Editions of the Works of Immanuel Kant], Cambridge: Cambridge University Press.

Kelly, C. (2007) *Children's World: Growing up in Russia 1890–1991*, New Haven: Yale University Press.

Kirk, B. and Thorne, J. (2011) *Missional Youth Ministry*, Grand Rapids: Zondervan.

Kornbeck, J. and Jensen, N.R. (2011) *Social Pedagogy for the Entire Lifespan – Volume One*, Bremen: EHV.

Kornbeck, J. and Jensen, N.R. (2013) *Social Pedagogy for the Entire Lifespan – Volume Two*, Bremen: EHV.

Laqueur, T.W. (1976) *Religion and Respectability: Sunday Schools and Working Class Culture 1780–1850*, New Haven: Yale University Press.

Lasch, C. (1979) *The Culture of Narcissism: American Life in an Age of Diminishing Expectations*, New York: Warner.

Locke, J. (1693) *Some Thoughts Concerning Education* [reprinted 1830], Boston: Gray and Bowen.

Locke, J. (2000 [1689]) *An Essay Concerning Human Understanding*, London: Routledge.

Manton, J. (1976) *Mary Carpenter and the Children of the Streets*, London: Heinemann.

Meadows, P.R. (undated) 'How it all began' in *A Brief History of Christian Endeavor*, http://www.worldsceunion.org/files/CE-Americas.pdf

Meigs, C. (1970) *Jane Addams: Pioneer for Social Justice*, Boston: Little, Brown.

Melvin, J. (2015) 'Youth work in digital age' in G. Bright (Ed.), *Youth Work: Histories, Policy and Contexts*, Basingstoke: Palgrave.

Miller, S.A. (2007) *Growing Girls: The Natural Origins of Girls' Organisations in America*, New Brunswick: Rutgers University Press.

Mjagkij, N. (1994) *Light in the Darkness: African Americans and the YMCA, 1852–1946*, Lexington: University Press of Kentucky.

Montague, C.J. (1904) Sixty *Years of Waifdom or, the Ragged School Movement in English History*, London: Charles Murray.

Neverdon-Morton, C. (1989) *Afro-American Women of the South and the Advancement of the Race, 1895–1925*, Knoxville: University of Tennessee Press.

Ogilvie, K.C. (2013) *Roots and Wings: A History of Outdoor Education and Outdoor Learning in the UK*, Lyme Regis: Russell House.

Orchard, S. and Briggs, J. (2007) *The Sunday School Movement*, Milton Keynes: Paternoster.

Ord, J. (2011) 'The Kingston Youth Service: space, place and the Albemarle legacy' in R. Gilchrist et al. (Eds.), *Reading the Past: Essays in the History of Youth and Community Work*, Lyme Regis: Russell House.

Pestalozzi, J.H. (1885) *Leonard and Gertrude*, Memphis: General Books.

Pietsch, S. and Muller, A. (2015) *Walls That Teach: On the Architecture of Youth Centres*, Heijningen: Jap Sam Books.

Plato (1941) *The Republic* (trans. F.M. Cornford), Oxford: Oxford University Press.

Polanyi, K. (1944) *The Great Transformation*, New York: Farrar and Rinehart.

Prochaska, F. and Prochaska, F.K. (1980) *Women and Philanthropy in Nineteenth-Century England*, Oxford: Oxford University Press.

Putman, R. (2000) *Bowling Alone: The Collapse and Revival of American Community*, New York: Simon and Schuster.

Reid, S.E. (2015) 'Khrushchev in Wonderland: the Pioneer place in Moscow's Lenin Hill, 1962' in S. Piethsch and A. Muller (Eds.), *Walls That Teach: On the Architecture of Youth Centres*, Heijningen: Jap Sam Books.

Robertson, N.M. (2007) *Christian Sisterhood, Race Relations and the YWCA 1906–1946*, Champaign: University of Illinois Press.

Robertson, S. (2009) 'Withywood Youth Centre' in R. Gilchrist et al. (Eds.), *Essays in the History of Youth and Community Work: Discovering the Past*, Lyme Regis: Russell House.

Rooff, M. (1935) *Youth and Leisure: A Survey of Girls' Organisations in England and Wales*, Edinburgh: T. and A. Constable.

Rousseau, J-J. (1979) *Emile*, New York: Basic Books.

Savage, J. (2007) *Teenage: The Creation of Youth Culture 1875–1945*, London: Chatto and Windus.

Scanlon, M., Powell, F., Geoghegan, M. and Swirak, K. (2011) 'Targeted Youth Work in Contemporary Ireland', *Youth Studies Ireland*, 6(1): 3–16.

Schapiro, J.W. (1963) *Condorcet and the Rise of Liberalism*, New York: Octagon.

Senter, M.H. (2010) *When God Shows Up: A History of Protestant Youth Ministry in America*, Grand Rapids: Baker Academic.

Slaughter, J.W. (1911) *The Adolescent*, London: George Allen.

Spatscheck, C. (2009) 'The German perspective: youth work, policy, integration and policy' in G. Verschelden et al. (Eds.), *The History of Youth Work in Europe:*

Relevance for youth Policy Today, Strasbourg: Council of Europe.

Stachura, P. (1981) *The German Youth Movement 1900–1981: An Interpretative and Documentary History*, London: Macmillan.

Sunker, H. and Otto, H-U. (1997) *Education and Fascism: Political Identity and Social Education in Nazi Germany*, London: Falmer.

Sweatman, A. (1863) 'Youths' clubs and institutes' in H. Solly, *Working Men's Clubs*, London: Simpkin, Marshall, Hamilton, Kent & Co.

Thompson, E.N. (2012) '"The changing needs of our youth today": the responses of 4-H to social and economic transformation in twentieth-century North Carolina', unpublished PhD, University of North Carolina Greensboro.

Todd, S. (2005) *Young Women, Work and Family: 1918–1950*, Oxford: Oxford University Press.

Twenge, J. (2017) *iGen: Why Today's Superconnected Kids are Growing Up Less Rebellious, More Tolerant, Less Happy – and Completely Unprepared for Adulthood*, New York: Atria.

Verschelden, G., Coussée, F., Van de Walle, T. and Williamson, H. (2009) *The History of Youth Work in Europe: Relevance for Youth Policy Today*, Strasbourg: Council of Europe.

Walkey, F.J., Wills, W.H. and Motley, H. (1931) *Methods in Youth Work*, London: Kingsgate Press.

Wessel, T.R. and Wessel, M. (1982) *4-H: An American Idea 1900–1980. A History of 4-H*, Chevy Chase: 4-H National Council.

Wolcott, V.W. (2012) *Race, Riots and Roller Coasters: The Struggle over Segregated Recreation in America*, Philadelphia: University of Pennsylvania Press.

Zuccala, A. (2005) 'Modelling the Invisible College', *Journal of the American Society of Information Science and Technology*, 57(2): 152–168.

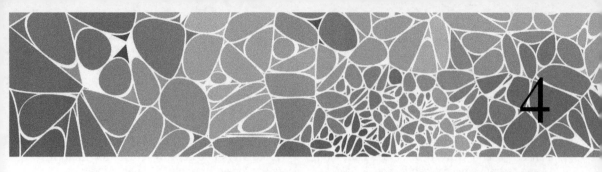

4

Some Conceptions of Youth and Youthwork in the United States

Dana Fusco

INTRODUCTION

In the United States, there is no one philosophy of youthwork practice, no overarching concept or theory, no sole ethos, and no single site for the delivery of youth services. Like the United States itself, youthwork here is a diverse and varied set of practices that are of immigrant as well as, native origin, and are multicultural, multi-linguistic, and multi-genred. These diverse youthwork practices go by many names, come from many traditions, have different beliefs and values, and emerge as part of citizen action at least as often as organized professional activity. This heterogeneous mix can look chaotic, without coherence and integration to the outsider. To us Americans, it fits within a cultural and political heritage that marks our identity as a pluralistic nation that is also deeply conflicted about its diversity. To understand its history is to accept a contested and incomplete history at best, with plenty of untold, forgotten, and/or silenced stories.

Within this incompleteness, and with the full realization that history will continue to write itself, the aims of this chapter are twofold: first, the chapter aspires to map a history that has not yet been mapped – an important addition to the academic discourse and discipline of youthwork in the US and elsewhere. With the complete understanding that there is no such thing as the one and final 'telling' of history, as history is always shaped through the eyes of the re(constructor), the chapter hopes to initiate a dialogue and debate that will help add to the thinness of this existing historical literature in youthwork. The second, and perhaps more poignant, aim is to illuminate US youthwork in the context of how 'youth' is constructed through a myriad of cultural, political and economic influences. While the 'youth' category has been discussed, the two (youth and youthwork) have not been aligned within the US historical context. I ask: what is the relationship between how youth and youth problems are conceived, and then, how is youthwork constructed as a response, both real and symbolic? The chapter cannot adequately address the full breadth of literature on the history of youth (see Sercombe, 2016 for a more recent thorough account) or the complete varieties of professional youthwork identities, particularly in the US, but hopes to continue to add to a growing historical literature (Fusco, 2016). In short, the chapter argues that youthwork is responsive not only to the actual behaviors of young people, but also to the social definitions and problematizations of those behaviors by adults, all of which are deeply interwoven within historical, cultural, political, and economic contexts.

To say the least, our relationship with and to youth is profoundly paradoxical: youth are at once romanticized and disenfranchised, loved and feared, nurtured and ignored. The paradox signals societal expectations for young people and where we believe responsibility for their well-being lies. The primary belief of many Americans, regardless of class, is that it is the role of parents to take care of their young and ensure their offspring are not a burden to society. Educating and caring for 'other' people's children is considered tolerable at best and only in the most severe and unfortunate situations. This belief likely stems from earlier legal conceptions about the care of the poor. The parliamentary approval in England of the 1601 Poor Relief Act, commonly known as the 'Elizabeth Poor Law', distinctly divides poor people into the impotent poor (those unable to work), the able-bodied, and the idle or vagrants. This law was the basis for the treatment of the poor in Colonial America as well as England, and is likely to have carried forward into an underlying influence on American culture. It is also deeply rooted in a racist and classist rhetoric of welfare systems as governmental waste. While Americans will evoke their moral or spiritual beliefs, generosity, and/or good nature to help their less fortunate neighbors, there is a quota to their charity and they will quickly push back against perceived ingratitude, irresponsibility, and/or

greed. Resulting anger when this does occur, whether real or perceived, leads to a classist/racist backlash that comes in many covert and overt forms of (mis)behavior. The attack on public services is one such response and youthwork is no exception. Youthwork, like other social services, has suffered from drastic and perpetual cuts over the past two decades, and small cuts to already small budgets have even bigger impacts.

Understanding societal expectations for the care and well-being of young people then is no small part of understanding socially constructed programmatic responses: how youthwork practices are conceived, supported, implemented, and either continued or defunded. Societal expectations for youth, their welfare, education, and general well-being, are bound within history, culture, institutional systems, and ideologies: a complexity now also fully reflected sociologically through the density and richness of intersectionality (Heathfield & Fusco, 2016). Recognizing the complex relationship between conceptions of youth as a sociological category; youth problems, particularly those that interfere with achieving prototypical adulthood; and conceptions of youthwork in the US is the focus of this chapter. I begin by looking at the onset of youth as a social category and then discuss how different understandings of youth and youth problems have defined and impacted practices for working with young people. Finally, I consider how the goals and imperatives of youthwork have changed over time while remaining on a macro level, always responsive to the broader adult and societal concerns, visions and priorities of the times.

CONCEPTIONS OF YOUTH

Language exerts hidden power, like the moon on the tides. (Brown, 1988)

Referential terms for young people – juveniles, adolescents, teenagers, youths, millennials, Generations X, Y, and Z – each emerged at different points in US history, carrying with them particular ideologies, and hidden power, about young people as individuals and as a group, and always in relation to adult and societal perspectives, values, and priorities. Of course it is easy to lose sight of the fact that such terms could only be invented because there existed an 'object' to which they referred: the teenager. This objectification of youth within an age category has not always been the case. In the 1700s, a boy of seven years of age became a man with no particular youth period to speak of. American-born children worked either in the home or on the farms, and sold their crafts and goods (wool, soap, jam, and the like) in the city markets and streets. Their individual labor served the family and was thought important to the development of good moral and ethical character. They often created families of their own before the end of their 'teen years. It was not until the 1800s that historical accounts of 'youth' as a distinct group appeared.

Early uses of youth-related terms began a tradition of the youth category as inherently problematic. Passionate and articulated claims from well-educated, powerful men and women began to instill fear of youth by associating young people with uncivilized, savage, and racist notions. For instance, to Charles Loring Brace, the founder of the Children's Aid Society, urban street kids (or street Arabs as they were also dubbed) were '… the young ruffians of New York' who would soon form the 'great lower class of our city' (Marten, 2005). As Chinn (2008) points out, the youth problem was essentially an immigration problem. At that time, boys immigrating to Colonial America were likely to be indentured servants or, if from better circumstances, apprentices. They relied on adults outside of their families for their well-being. But, there was also an emigration problem of sorts as American-born youth from rural areas flocked to the cities looking for employment opportunities. Emigration

and immigration led to overcrowded, under-resourced urban areas and created 'the dangerous classes of New York': the underclass that needed to be contained in order to maintain order in society (Brace, 1872). The street children of the late 1800s were the first American 'teenagers' (Chinn, 2008), related to not as children but not quite as adults. They were 'boys' mostly, referenced in relation to their behaviors of criminality and immorality, and what each implied about their underlying character or lack thereof. Such a perspective was deeply wedded to the theological underpinnings that many philanthropists and missionary workers brought to their work. For instance, it was believed that idle time along with 'weak character' was the perfect playground for the devil to do his work.

With the onset of Darwin's theory of evolution in 1877, theology would give way to (or at least share the stage with) science, and in 1879 to the birth of psychology. 'Adolescence' would emerge as a psychological explanation of the differences between teens and children, and understandings of teenagers would prioritize natural stages of development in relation to their physical and psychosocial needs. American psychologist, Granville Stanley Hall, is most notably remembered for his discussion of adolescence as a period of 'storm and stress' (Hall, 1904). At that time psychiatry and psychology were largely responsible for drawing upon medical diagnoses and biological processes to explain adolescent behavior (an alternative to the stained character that was the devil's work). The onset of puberty would shape the next decade of one's life, causing turmoil and strife. Hall (1904) discussed a wide variety of issues pertaining to the adolescent period (14–24 years of age), not all of which were biologically based. For instance, he attributed increased depression to poor peer relations and increased crime to social risk factors such as media and parental divorce (cited in Arnett, 2006). A look at today's journals in adolescence provides insight into the focus of psychological youth study: the effects of violent video games on hostile behavior; building psychosocial assets and well-being among adolescent girls; friendship dyads; civic engagement in adolescence; cross-cultural difference in parent-adolescent relationships. The topics and perspectives are vast, with interdisciplinary roots, though still deeply wedded to early notions of youth as vulnerable to the impacts of their physical and social environments.

As Americans began to accept adolescence as a new period of the lifespan, popular conceptions of the 'teenager' emerged. Denoting the chronological period between thir*teen* and nine*teen* years of age, the use of the term 'teenage' (originally hyphenated, teen-age) may have first been used to identify teen-age Sunday Schools as early as the 1900s. As young people moved toward semi-autonomy, with time and leisure on their hands, 'teens took on a new social meaning (Savage, 2007). These young consumers were employed or employable white, middle-class, suburban young people who had money in their pockets to burn. When not in school or working, they spent their leisure time dating and daydreaming. This was the classic American teenager of the 1920s (Hine, 2000). Interesting to note: they were the consumers of youth culture, but not necessarily the producers of it. In fact, much of white suburban youth culture, particularly the expressive cultural manifestations in music, dress, and dance, owes a debt of gratitude to Black and Latino culture (Chang, 2005; Chinn, 2008).

From Sunday School to pop culture, the term itself did not make its way into public consciousness until about 1941. The first printed use of the term in popular culture emerged when Edith Stern wrote an article for *Popular Science* on the democratic educational method of movie making being used in a Denver high school. During her interview with the head of the state board of health where students were researching the health lab for their movie, Dr Mitchell noted: 'I never knew 'teen-agers could be so serious'. The term, teen-ager, was popularized in

a democratic youth-led context, but lost its potency as a result. Youth as consumers was a more comfortable (and passive) position and role for young people than youth as producers of culture. The daters and daydreamers went un-problematized (as also witnessed by the lack of social programming for youth in the 1930s).

This all changed in post-war times, when youth and youth culture was contextualized in criminality. In 1946, the US Attorney General appointed a panel on juvenile delinquency. Interestingly, the data of the time showed no particular increase in youth-related crime post war. But the moral panic had set in and potential youth dissension and radicalization was of major concern. This panic held true through the 1950s and 1960s when public sentiment was steeped in media sensationalizing of fascism and the second wave Red Scare. Youth perceived to be alienated in any way from mainstream society were an immediate threat to the dominant social order. 'Prevention' programs skyrocketed.

While the term 'youth' was already in use, it was Kenneth Keniston (1971) who theorized it as a stage of life different from adolescence. Keniston's work signified a new understanding of the youth period that helped explain and examine perceived youth alienation outside of internally located pathologies. In the prologue to his book, *Youth and Dissent*, he writes: 'Millions of young people today are neither psychological adolescents nor sociological adults; they fall into a psychological no man's land, a stage of life that lacks any clear definition' (p. 3). Keniston believed that socially an extension of human development had been created that had no clear definition, theory, or terminology. He proposed that 'youth' was a stage of life that emerged from a lack of congruence between one's sense of identity and the incongruous demands and opportunities within post-industrial US society. The resulting tension between self and society was not to be mistaken for a definitive rejection of existing systems, but rather a refusal or ambivalence to be socialized. Youth culture and subculture became an interest among sociologists, and 'youth studies' emerged as its own sub-discipline within sociology. The discipline of youth studies seeks to understand the 'material and subjective conditions associated with the youth period' (Cote, 2014, p. 9). The discipline helps us to identify the micro and macro contexts of youth issues but also to recognize youth as a socially constructed phenomenon. These social scientific perspectives, compared to previous behavioral scientific, scientific, and theological ones, offered for the first time a way of reading 'youth' as situated in broader social, cultural, and economic contexts and conditions that impact what it means to be young, how to do youth/hood, what opportunities and challenges are available to those within the category of 'youth', and how 'youth' are related to by adults as individuals, within communities, and within society at large.

Yet, beyond academic circles this sociological positioning of youth was still held as secondary to the more dominant psychological models. As youth crimes increased through the 1980s, particularly in the larger cities of the US, deviant models of behavior remained popular. In 1999, youth incarceration hit an all-time high; 2.5 million juveniles were arrested, according to Office of Juvenile Justice and Delinquency Prevention statistics (OJJDP, 1999). The over-criminalization of youth during this period is attributed in part to the strengthening of a neoliberal ideology put in place during the Reagan administration. The marketization of prison meant incarcerations produced profit; in fact, the labor of prisoners results in billions of dollars in the pockets of multimillion-dollar corporations such as IBM, Microsoft, Macy's and Target (Pelaez, 2014). Though arrests have since decreased, the continued criminalization of youth, clearly linked to race and gender, continues to have devastating effects in urban communities of color throughout the country, and is an issue that spurs much youth-related activism, along with immigration, poverty,

and public education: areas also gravely impacted by a neoliberal agenda.

In short, 'youth' in all its linguistic variations (adolescents, teenagers, juveniles, etc.) can refer to a state of being, a chronological age, a developmental period, or a culture of its own. Each term comes with its own set of markers, perspectives, and academic discourse. It carries meaning intricately woven in history and social scientific and popular understandings, as well as the economic and political conditions of the times. At the same time, youth problems are always counter-hegemonic threats to dominant cultural agreements. The youth category from inception was an invention of adult engineering meant to deal with these perceived social problems (Chinn, 2008; Hartinger-Saunders, 2008; Hine, 2000; Savage, 2007; see also Sercombe, 2016 for similar historical rooting of 'youth' in the European context). In categorizing youth as a group separate from other groups (children, adults), the youth problem appeared and required a set of responses. Theological, and later scientific, paradigms would provide the interpretations of such behaviors and with it the location of the problem as either individually or socially rooted, or some combination thereof. It is in this context and with these understandings that youthwork practices in the US emerged.

CONCEPTIONS OF YOUTHWORK

There is no professional association of youthwork at a national level in the States; no organizational labor structure or defined career trajectory; no journal of youthwork; and perhaps most importantly, no public understanding or recognition of the work/field. Today, youthwork is mostly funded by private and corporate donations, fee-for-service structures, and some public funding for specific initiatives such as teenage pregnancy or college readiness; hence it is often encapsulated in 'programs,' which are easiest for attracting funds. If you asked a typical American to define youthwork, they are very likely to associate it with youth employment.[1] Thus, framing the conceptions of youthwork within the US is largely unchartered territory in our literature and, as such, is a key contribution of this chapter. Singular youthwork areas and their corresponding history, purpose, and philosophy have been discussed but there has been no 'field' of youthwork per se in the US. To move in that direction, one approach has been to create broader schemes that are inclusive of the various and multiple contexts of youthwork such as youth clubs, afterschool programs, recreation centers, residential care, community education, and street or gang work, from which common principles might be gleaned (Fusco, 2012), and imperatives that are the underbelly of the work such as a moral, educational, or social justice imperatives (Fusco, 2016). A third categorization scheme, and the one considered here, is to organize youthwork by 'approach'. Approaches occur within and across contexts. Butters and Newell (1978) have organized UK conceptions of youthwork historically and in so doing found three general approaches. All three are found also within the US: character building, social education, and radical paradigms. Respectively, the goals of these approaches are: to help young people build good moral character, become capable members and participants of society, or to critically analyze their social and political worlds in order to change them.

Character Building

From the mid-1800s to the early 1900s, a time of rapid expansion which saw the doubling of the population, there was a boom in the development of youth organizations (the YMCA in 1844; Children's Aid Society in 1853; Boys' Brigade in 1883; Hull House in 1889; 4-H clubs in 1902; Scouting in 1907; Boys Town in 1917). From 1900 to 1920,

Presbyterian neighborhood houses, many conversions of existing missions and Sunday Schools, also sprang up throughout the country to offer girls' and boys' clubs (Presbyterian Historical Society, 2008). In New York City, lodging-houses for boys were the first non-formal setting for intentional social interventions that would address urban poverty. Without the daily guidance and support of their families, missionaries (known also as 'child savers') felt that street children needed a range of provisions: basic living necessities, education, religious instruction, and discipline (Sheldon, 1922). These youth were thought to need services but also character development. 'Eventually they are drawn into the neat and comfortable Boys' Lodging-houses, and there find themselves, imperceptibly changed into honest and decent boys' (Brace, 1872, p. 630).

This was the prime of the Progressive Era: a time of reform and activism, modernization and science. These early youth programs had religious and philanthropic roots grounded in missionary work and in the pursuit of character development as well as provision of services. They were organized by well-educated men and women who believed change was possible, and used the latest scientific theories to justify programmatic responses. Prevention of vagrancy and delinquency through literacy instruction and character development were the cornerstones of these 19th-century youth programs.

While character building has long and deep roots, it is still discussed today as an important area of focus for both formal and informal education. Character strengths such as kindness, loyalty, and reverence, for instance, are still critical to the philosophy of the Boy and Girl Scouts of America. Also, positive youth development is conceptualized as including competence, confidence, connection, *character*, and caring (Lerner, Phelps, Forman, & Bowers, 2009). Touted as a virtue with multiple facets, character development remains a prime goal of American society and is embedded still in many youth-serving organizations.

The Radical Paradigm

In the US we might interpret the radical paradigm to mean those approaches that take into
consideration the structural inequalities and
social conditions that impact young people
and communities, sometimes in devastating
ways. Here the role of the youthworker is to
ally with young people, to identify, examine
and ultimately change such conditions so that
their opportunities for well-being are better
secured. New York City was an early leader
in such a position (Sonnenfeld, 1995). In
1946 the US Attorney General established a
Panel on Juvenile Problems. New York State
already had a commission with heads of state
from correction, education, welfare, and later
health. The commission was working to
define issues of delinquency in relation to
social considerations that were beyond existing legal definitions. At the time New York
was the only state to distribute significant
resources to municipalities for youth services. In 1947, the New York City Youth
Bureau was established for the prevention
and control of juvenile delinquency. Its pilot
projects focused on coordinated efforts
across agencies, but also research and evaluation in order to improve working knowledge
of youth issues. By the 1950s, there was
growing attention to juvenile delinquency
and support of community-centered
responses. 'Street club workers' or 'detached
workers' built relationships with members of
street clubs (gangs), and sometimes their
families, in an effort to prevent or reduce
antisocial behaviors (McCloskey, 1959).
Summer employment and year-round recreation programs were also sponsored as a way
to ensure low youth crime. Some municipalities were encouraged to establish local youth
councils (mostly made up of educated professionals and citizens) to help assess local
services and find ways of reaching the most
vulnerable. Such work laid the foundation
for intersectional understandings of youth
problems in relation to economic conditions,
family issues, employment, health, and

education. Pilot projects were strategically
focused on areas of high delinquency, and
cross-agency services were coordinated to
tackle issues in structural ways, and were
found to be quite effective (Sonnenfeld,
1995). There are parallels here in Chicago
with Clifford Shaw and others from the
University of Chicago who created the Area
Project model back in the 1930s. Shaw was a
sociologist 'who believed every neighborhood could reduce juvenile delinquency by
improving community life' (http://www.chi-
cagoareaproject.org/about-us).

The existing Settlement House model
had already provided a basis for understanding youth services in the context of
broader community action. The Settlement
House movement began in Great Britain as
a Christian response to the growing rates of
poverty caused by increased industrializa-
tion. Toynbee Hall, the first 'house', was the
result of a group of students from Oxford
and Cambridge, who were influenced by
Arnold Toynbee to begin a residence program in the East End of London (Reinders,
1982). The residence hall was meant to
remove the distance 'that makes friendship
between classes almost impossible' (Canon
Samuel Barnett, vicar, cited in Reinders,
p. 4). Many American visitors to Toynbee
in the late 1800s brought the residence idea
back to the States: Stanton Coit, who founded
the Neighborhood Guild in 1887, later to
become the University Settlement in 1892;
Jane Addams, who started Hull House with
Ellen Gates Starr; Vida Scudder, who with
colleagues started the College Settlement
in 1889; Everett Wheeler, who with support
from the Episcopal Church formed East Side
House in 1891; and there are many more
examples in the cities of Chicago, Boston,
New York and Philadelphia. As Reinders
(1982) points out, the American Settlements
responded to a huge influx of immigrants and
'viewed the poor not as a permanent underclass but as a group capable of improving
their economic and social status' (Reinders,
1982, p. 48).

Unfortunately, as Hounmenou (2012) notes, 'African Americans who migrated to the urban areas from the poor southern regions did not get as much attention as European newcomers' (p. 650). African American female activists took matters into their own hands and started the Black Settlement Houses. Christianity had always been a source of social activism among Blacks; now the Settlement Houses were another institution that would take on a similar role (Hounmenou, 2012). The Settlements provided a context for Black women to use their shared identity and struggle and exhibit leadership in confronting oppressive structures of inequity and advocating for the necessary resources for their communities.

Civic activism was nourished within the Settlement Houses and Settlement workers recognized the need for young people to express themselves outside of hegemonic structures. Rather than public dance halls, for instance, Settlements created their own dance halls, in part as a statement of resistance to the commercialization of youth culture (Chinn, 2008).

In the era of McCarthyism, many Settlement leaders had to resign under speculations of radicalism and Communism (Trolander, 1987). Wealthy white donors were not interested in supporting immigrant working-class men and women to participate in democracy; their voice was of less interest than their 'behavior', which should simply disappear into the throes of hegemony without the disruption of dominant culture. The decline of philanthropic support necessitated government funding. Trolander attributes this shift to the professionalization of social work, which led to social workers no longer being interested in frontline reform. Either way, the dual commitment to social services and social reform was no longer possible, and single-problem-focused funding took over. The essence of Settlements as centers for not only educational, vocational, and recreational services, but also as community mobilization centers, was 'under siege' (Fabricant & Fisher, 2002).

Youth organizing is another practice of youthwork that falls within 'the radical paradigm'. With an explicit social justice focus, youth organizing is considered the most engaged strategy to work with young people (LISTEN, Inc., 2000). As young people examine social, economic, and political systems that challenge their capacity to engage democratically, they become active agents of change. Although it had a long history, it wasn't until the 1990s that there was an emergence and significant growth of youth-led organizing (Delgado & Staples, 2008). The trend corresponded with the definition of 'youth' as a political interest group (Hosang, 2003) as well as a surge in funding to support youth campaigning. Many of the founders were young people of color from low-income urban neighborhoods and immigrants addressing social injustices affecting their own communities. Finding financial support for such efforts in today's political and economic climate has been next to impossible.

Social Education

Social education is a broadly inclusive set of practices that aims to help young people become healthy adults by providing learning opportunities that facilitate successful accomplishment of life-stage tasks. Both the field of child and youth care (CYC) and current youth development approaches easily fit within this category. CYC practice includes but is not limited to 'skills in assessing client and program needs, designing and implementing programs and planned environments, integrating developmental, preventive and therapeutic requirements into the life space' (http://www.cyc-net.org/profession/pro-definitions.html). It begins with practitioners assessing both the 'normal' and 'special needs' of the infant, child, or adolescent and then working within the developmental space to design and implement programs. Today the field is organized around five domains of competence: applied human development; relationship and communication; developmental practice methods; cultural and human diversity; and professionalism. Residential youthwork and youth development have some basic tenets in common with Settlement youthwork and youth organizing in that all are interested in working with young people where they are at and in the life space. Much of this work occurred in the 'youth clubs' or community centers.

At one time, youth clubs flourished in US neighborhoods. They were often multi-generational, multi-racial hang-outs that allowed young people to engage in a range of leisure and recreational activities from ping pong to chess. Within this seemingly non-purposed informal gathering, mentoring, guidance, support, and positive peer and adult relations occurred. With increased concerns about educational outcomes, these spaces became increasingly focused on homework and academic enrichment. During the 1990s, with the marketization of all forms of education, clubs came to be called after-school programs and many teen programs lost funding or were encapsulated under the guise of afterschool programs. Eventually most of these youth clubs would be relocated to school buildings, changing even further the nature of youthwork practice.

In 2002, the National Research Council and Institute of Medicine published a volume that synthesized youth development research. It suggested that youth development programs should include features such as physical and psychological safety, appropriate structure, supportive relationships, opportunities to belong, positive social norms, support for efficacy and mattering, opportunities for skill building, and integration of family, school, and community efforts (National Research Council and Institute of Medicine, 2002). This set of developmental imperatives emerged from several bodies of research. First, in the early 1990s, research by the Search Institute found that the more 'developmental assets' young people reported, the less likely they were to be engaged in drug and alcohol use, violence, and sexual activity, and the more likely they were to succeed in school, exhibit leadership, and engage in pro-health behaviors (Scales & Leffert, 1999). Second, a science of positive psychology was launched as a challenge to the overreliance on pathological explanations of human behavior of the times (Seligman & Csikszentmihalyi, 2000). The field of positive psychology is about valued subjective experiences such as well-being, hope, and happiness (Seligman & Csikszentmihaly, 2000). Such experiences are the result of nurturing strengths, rather than fixing deficits and pathologies. From this nascent field, grew the positive youth development (PYD) movement in the United States, with its focus on nurturing those aspects of human nature that predict 'thriving' behaviors among young people. The goal of youthwork from this stance is to help young people become healthy, well-adjusted adults through the successful accomplishment of life tasks where strengths and assets are accumulated. This is the dominant model in play today – a model not without its critics.

While the PYD theory also purports that the lack of external assets (e.g., caring neighbors, positive family communication, a supportive 'educative' school climate) is equally related to poor youth outcomes, it offers little contextualization for the sociopolitical and economic factors that play a role in family, school and community well-being. Structural factors are ignored leading to a micro-contextual grounding of development and no implied methodology for community action or activism. This is in stark contrast to community movements such as Hull House where activities were civic as well as educational, political as well as familial. New versions of youth development models are emerging that deal with this critique. For instance, Travis and Leech (2013) provide a strong argument for adding 'community' and 'citizenship' to the existing 5 C model of positive youth development, and Bulanda, Tellis and Tyson (2015) argue for co-creating space with African American youth in order to develop an afterschool curriculum that is culturally relevant.

UNDERSTANDING YOUTHWORK IN RELATION TO 'YOUTH'

These are some of the youthwork practices that are spread across the US landscape. By no means is this a complete listing of the complex and dynamic practice landscape. Rather, it encompasses those approaches outlined within the Butters and Newell (1978) framework, and helps to draw out some of the common differences found there (see Table 4.1 for a comparative chart). Four areas for comparison are noted: the context, imperative, content, and the targeted level of change.

1 *Context*: whether the practice draws from a focus on individual traits like character or development, or takes a more sociologically and contextualized approach to understanding the worlds of young people.
2 *Imperative*: each practice is driven by different and sometimes overlapping imperatives – moral obligation, developmental imperatives, community action, democratic imperatives, and ending global oppression (Fusco, 2016). These imperatives can be more or less linked to youthwork approaches, providing an added dimension of understanding to the purpose of youthwork in targeting levels of individual, group, community, society, and global change.
3 *Content*: practices with young people are wrapped in content – media production, sports, recreation, tutoring, service learning, etc. The content is less important to the integrity of youthwork than how it emerged. Predetermined content, even when fascinatingly interesting, will lose the potential to fully illuminate authentic issues of most concern to young people. It is tied to societal and organizational goals and priorities, which may or may not be what the young people feel connected to in that particular place and at that moment in time. A packaged curriculum has its place and young people and/

or their parents will voluntarily find programs of interest to them to attend, but when we formulate youthwork I am in agreement with Bulanda et al. (2015), we want holistic and dynamically constructed spaces that youth can own, lead, direct, and produce.

4 *Level of change*: The end goal of practices varies. Most often the hope is personal growth (or youth development, in trendy parlance). But sometimes, the goal is group change, community change or even global change.

As understandings of youth change so too does the specific approach as well as the context, imperative, content, and targeted level of change. Yet, we also see that the approach is always connected to these broader concepts and definitions. Youthwork always responds to how 'youth' as a social category is constructed and how youth problems are defined. In some ways, this reality seems unproblematic and likely to continue in the future no differently from other social forms of governments: healthcare professionals respond to a new virus and educators are called upon to respond to low literacy levels. That said, it is difficult to not also wonder: how does youthwork deal with the tension between being in many ways artificially constructed (that is, designed at a policy level to meet the needs of 'youth' not youth) while maintaining authenticity with actual young people at a practice level? What might youthwork look like when constructed by youth and youthworkers in local communities to meet actual real-time needs and desires?

CONCLUSION

'Youth' is a modern invention that appeared on the American scene as a constructed response to very specific adult concerns about the behaviors of young people. The youth category is immersed in a history of youth as problems. The young ruffians were engaged in dangerous criminality; juveniles were delinquent; adolescents were sex

Table 4.1 A comparative chart of conceptions of youth and youthwork

Youth	Youth problem	Approaches	Context	Imperatives	Content	Level of change
'Ruffians' 'Juvenile delinquents'	Criminal or deviant behavior	Character building	Individual traits	Moral	Predetermined	Personal growth
'Adolescents' 'Teens'	Risk(y) behaviors	Social education	Individual development, with ecological models focused on 'environment,' 'community' and 'culture'	Development	Most often predetermined	Personal growth; group growth sometimes a vehicle for personal growth but not an end goal in itself
'Youth'	Alienation from institutional arrangements	Radical paradigm	Sociological, understands youth issue in context of macro issues: historical, political, economic	Community action Democratic imperatives Ending global impression	More often emergent but can be predetermined	Personal as well as community, societal, and even global

crazed; teens were lazy daydreamers; and youth disengaged from society were potentially fascist/radicals and a threat to the dominant social order. Whether penology, criminology, psychology, or sociology, each view casts its methodological gaze upon young people in order to study, explain, and diagnose 'the youth problem' and offer solutions and prescriptions for adult-youth interactions and interventions. Such interventions are reactive less to the actual behaviors of young people and more to the social definitions and problematizations of those behaviors by adults. They are also situated in historical, political, economic, and cultural understandings of youth and adulthood. Through such definitions and understandings, youthwork helps fulfill societal expectations of how we envision successful youth(hood), adult(hood) and the ideal pathways and choices along the way. Whether through character building, social education and youth development, or radical paradigms, each approach was designed to help solve the youth problem. Today, one can easily find all paradigms at play. With different goals, agendas, priorities, and methods, it is hard to imagine this as one field. But what makes a pediatrician, a podiatrist, and an oncologist all doctors, or a dance instructor, a math tutor, and coach, all educators? Can we find the common goal in youthwork? In the States, the answer is not yet at least.

One reason for the lack of coherence and commitment to a field might be the way that youth are constructed, e.g., as a temporary holding pen for later adulthood. The current experience of American adolescence can be described as one of waiting. High school is a moratorium of sorts. While the adolescent invention might hold value to adults and society at large, what is contested is whether it holds any value for young people. Is the teenage experience one of nourishment and enriched opportunities, or, as Hine (2000) warns, is it a 'predicament' to live not in, but through? The question is not a myopic one

as it opens for consideration how we arrived at such a defined period of the lifespan, why, and the types of responses we as adults, including youthworkers, have had in relation to this historically situated but modern-day invention. Interestingly, youth themselves have not changed much over time. Much attention has been given to differences across generations (Strauss & Howe, 1991). These provide interesting and valid illuminations of typical characteristics of whole groups of youth situating individual characteristics in the historical, social, economic, and political conditions of the times. But youth across generations are also remarkably similar, not because of biological or neurological bases, certainly this is not to be discounted, but more because the American adult and his/her relationship to 'youth' as a concept and a practice has shown remarkable consistency from the 1800s to present day. As Zuckerman (2011) illustrates, there is little actual evidence that American teens as a whole are really experiencing storm and stress. That is, while teens do engage in risky behavior and while this currently has been attributed to the ongoing brain development of the prefrontal cortex, such a post-hoc theoretical explanation does little to explain why adults also engage in risky behavior at least as often, if not more often, than adolescents. Yet, American adults (this author included) have consistently bought into all sorts of moral and social panics about teen behaviors and outcomes. We relate to young people as vulnerable to outside influences and without agency and control over their choices. What value does this relationship to young people serve *young people*?

While we have defined and accepted adolescence as an important period of life, society continues to deny teens any real role in society, except as consumers and trendsetters. As Hine (2000) argues, before the invention of youth, young people were not incompetent, needing long periods of life to prepare them for adulthood. Rather, they worked alongside adults as 'beginners'.

We tend to believe that young people are not fully formed and that there is still time to help them correct any mistakes they have made. But this optimism becomes distorted when, seeing the teen years as the last chance to perfect troubled young people before they turn into vicious adults, our drive to perfect the young becomes coercive and arbitrary. (Hine, 2000, p. 20)

Discussing the alternative is beyond the scope of this chapter. At best we might here consider what the role of the youth category is in the US when we are so conflicted about our relationship to young people and have not committed any real resources to 'the problem.' We adults have created the conditions for 'youth' to be contained, very likely making them more vulnerable than if they were integrated into society as younger people alongside older people. Youth remain in waiting and in preparation for the next stage of life, and youthworkers' aim is to help them arrive. What is to occur then when young people find the current institutional arrangements stifling of their voice, their creativity, their courage? Where do young people go to find pathways that are of their own making, that are deliberate in their own intentions? What then of democracy when such avenues are only available to the most rare and privileged? So maybe I can indulge the question a second time: What might youthwork look like when constructed by youth and youthworkers in local communities to meet actual real-time needs and desires? Maybe history will do more than rewrite itself.

Note

1   It is for this reason that I have opted to use 'youthwork' instead of the more popular 'youth work.'

REFERENCES

Arnett, J.J. (2006). G. Stanley Hall's Adolescence: Brilliance and nonsense. *History of Psychology*, 9(13), 186–197.

Austin, J.A. & Willard, M. (Eds.) (1998). *Generations of youth: Youth cultures and history in twentieth-century America*. New York: NYU Press.

Barton, W.H., Watkins, M. & Jarjours, R. (1997). Youths and communities: Toward comprehensive strategies for youth development. *Social Work*, 42(5), 483–493.

Brace, C.L. (1872). *The dangerous classes of New York: And twenty years' work among them*. 1973. Reprint: NASW classic series.

Brickell, C. (2013). On the case of youth: Case files, case studies, and the social construction of adolescence. *Journal of the History of Childhood and Youth*, 16(1), 50–80.

Brown, R. (1988). *Starting from Scratch*. New York: Bantam Books.

Bulanda, J., Tellis, D., & Tyson, K.M. (2015). Cocreating a social work apprenticeship with disadvantaged African American youth: A best-practices after-school curriculum. *Smith College Studies in Social Work*, 85(3), 285–310.

Butters, S. & Newell, S. (1978). *Realities of training: A review of the training of adults who volunteer to work with young people in the Youth and Community Services*. Leicester: National Youth Bureau.

Chang, J. (2005). *Can't stop. Won't stop. A history of the hip-hop generation*. New York: Picador.

Chinn, S. (2008). *Inventing modern adolescence: The children of immigrants in turn-of-the-century America*. New Jersey: Rutgers University Press.

Cote, J. (2014). *Youth studies: Fundamental issues and debates*. Houndmills: Palgrave Macmillan.

Delgado, M. & Staples, L. (2008). *Youth-led community organizing: Theory and action*. Oxford: Oxford University Press.

Fabricant, M. & Fisher, R. (2002). *Settlement houses under siege: The struggle to sustain community organizations in New York City*. New York: Columbia University Press.

Fusco, D. (2012). Framing trends, posing questions. In D. Fusco (Ed.), *Advancing youthwork: Current trends, critical questions* (pp. 216–238). New York, NY: Routledge.

Fusco, D. (2016). History of youth work: Transitions, illuminations and refractions. In M. Heathfield & D. Fusco (Eds.), *Youth and inequality in education: Global actions in youth work* (pp. 36–52). New York, NY: Routledge.

Fusco, D. & Heathfield, M. (2015). Modeling democracy: Is youth 'participation' enough? *Italian Journal of Sociology of Education*, 7(1), 12–31.

Hall, G.S. (1904). *Adolescence: Its psychology and its relation to physiology, anthropology, sociology, sex, crime, religion, and education* (Vols. I & II). New York: D. Appleton & Co.

Hartinger-Saunders, R.M. (2008). The history of defining youth: Current implications for identifying and treating delinquent youth. *The New York Sociologist*, 3, 88–103.

Heathfield, M. & Fusco, D. (2016). (Eds.) *Youth and inequality in education: Global actions in youthwork* (pp. 19–35). New York: Routledge.

Hine, T. (2000). *The rise and fall of the American teenager*. New York: Harper Collins Publishers.

Hosang, D. (2003). *Youth and community organizing today*. Washington, DC: Funders Collaborative on Youth Organizing, Occasional Paper Series on Youth Organizing, no. 2.

Hounmenou, C. (2012). Black settlement houses and oppositional consciousness. *Journal of Black Studies*, 43(6), 646–666.

Keniston, K. (1971). *Youth and dissent: The rise of a new opposition*. New York: Harcourt Brace Jovanovich.

Koerin, B. (2003). The Settlement House tradition: Current trends and future concerns. *Journal of Sociology and Social Welfare*, 30(2), 53–68.

Lerner, J.V., Phelps, E., Forman, Y.E. & Bowers, E.P. (2009). Positive youth development. In R. Lerner and L. Steinberg (Eds.), *Handbook of adolescent psychology* (pp. 1–15). New York: Wiley.

LISTEN, Inc. (2000). An emerging model for working with youth. Occasional paper series on youth organizing, No. 1. Washington, D.C.: Funders Collaborative on Youth Organizing.

Marten, J. (2005). *Childhood and child welfare in the Progressive Era: A brief history with documents*. New York: Bedford/St Martin's.

McCloskey, M.A. (1959). State and municipal youth authorities (or commissions) and their role in juvenile delinquency prevention. *The Journal of Negro Education*, 28(3), 339–350.

Morrison, J.D., Alcorn, S. & Nelums, M. (1997). Empowering community-based programs for youth development: Is social work education interested? *Journal of Social Work Education*, 33(2), 321–333.

National Research Council and Institute of Medicine (2002). *Community youth programs to promote positive youth development*. Washington, DC: National Research Council and Institute of Medicine.

OJJDP (1999). *Statistical briefing book*. Retrieved from http://www.ojjdp.gov/ojstatbb/default.asp

Pelaez, V. (2014). The prison industry in the United States: Big business or a new form of slavery? El Diario-La Prensa, New York and Global Research. Retrieved from http://www.globalresearch.ca/the-prison-industry-in-the-united-states-big-business-or-a-new-form-of-slavery/8289

Presbyterian Historical Society (2008). In response to their communities: Presbyterian neighborhood houses and the Settlement movement, 1890–1965. *The Journal of Presbyterian History*, 86, 27–34.

Reinders, R.C. (1982). Toynbee Hall and the American Settlement movement, *Social Service Review*, 56(1), 39–54.

Sallah, M. (2014). *Global youthwork: Provoking consciousness and taking action*. Dorset: Russell House Publishing.

Savage, J. (2007). *Teenage: The creation of youth culture*. New York: Viking Adult.

Scales, P. & Leffert, N. (1999). *Developmental assets: A synthesis of the scientific research on adolescent development*. Minneapolis, MN: Search Institute.

Seligman, M. & Csikszentmihalyi, M. (2000). Positive psychology: An introduction. *American Psychologist*, 55(1), 5–14.

Sercombe, H. (2016). Youth in a global/historical context: What it means for youthwork. In M. Heathfield & D. Fusco (Eds.), *Youth and inequality in education: Global actions in youthwork* (pp. 19–35). New York: Routledge.

Sheldon, F.M. (1922). The Congregational Education Society. *Christian Education*, 6(3), 163–165.

Sonnenfeld, K. (1995). Changing perspectives on youth services as seen through the historical development of the New York City youth board. Dissertation, Teachers College, Columbia University.

Strauss, W. & Howe, N. (1991). *Generations: The history of America's future, 1584 to 2069*. New York: Harper Perennial.

Travis, R. & Leech, T.G.J. (2013). Empowerment-based positive youth development: A new understanding of healthy development for African American youth. *Journal of Research on Adolescence*, 24(1), 93–116.

Trolander, J.A. (1987). *Professionalism and social change: From the settlement house movement to neighborhood centers, 1886 to present*. New York: Columbia University Press.

Zuckerman, M. (2011). The paradox of American adolescence. *Journal of the History of Childhood and Youth*, 4, 13–25.

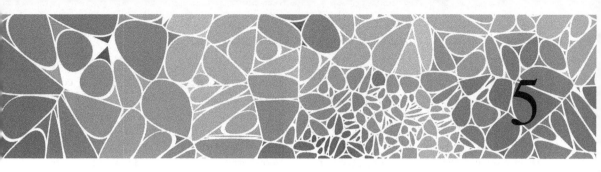

5

Youth Work as a Colonial Export: Explorations from the Global South

Kathy Edwards and Ismail Shaafee

INTRODUCTION

This chapter explores the export of youth work as practices and as knowledges from colonising nations, the 'old world' or the metropole of the global North, to colonised nations, the 'new world' or peripheral nations in the global South. It makes the claim that youth work has been, and remains in some contexts, a practice with colonising potential. It explores this potential, first in a historical context, with regard to the transfer of youth work knowledges and practices from Britain to Australia in the 19th century. Next, it turns to the current era. Here, we ask whether youth work has potentially continued its colonising impetus through conduits such as the international education market and some international development initiatives. As a primary case study, we focus on the transfer of youth work knowledges via Australia's higher education industry from Australia to the Maldives. Colonising practices and the project of decolonisation have been

discussed within literature concerning allied occupations such as social work (see for example Gray et al. 2013), and international and community development (see for example Ife 2002), but apart from a few tentative beginnings (for example Belton 2014a; Martin 2002) these subjects remain relatively unexplored within youth work. We are keen to throw open questions concerning the ethics of transferring youth work knowledge, to consider the challenge of decolonising youth work knowledges and practices and to consider also what the global youth work community could learn from youth works from the global South.

It is useful at the outset to situate ourselves as authors of this chapter and to provide some reflections on its origins. Our arguments are mostly shared, so we frequently use the term 'we' to describe what we say. Our identities and experiences, however, are vastly different, thus we also speak in our own voices when this becomes relevant to our stories. Kathy is an Australian youth work educator, and Ismail is a Maldivian citizen and graduate of the degree programme that Kathy teaches in. In this programme, youth work is considered in the context of social science knowledge. Ismail also produced an undergraduate (Honours) dissertation on the subject of transferring Australian youth work knowledge, principles and practices to the Maldives.[1] In his thesis, for which Kathy was his academic supervisor, Ismail was concerned to consider how this might be achieved in order to build a youth service in the Maldives. It was in the creation of Ismail's thesis that both authors were inspired to consider, and reflect on, from their respective standpoints and experiences of teacher and student, and positions of citizens of developed and developing nations, questions relating to their own work, teaching, learning and lived experiences. To this end, this chapter very much intertwines the personal, intellectual and political. It describes journeys for both authors that called us to question our own understandings of youth work knowledges and practices that we accepted or took for granted, and reconceptualise how we understand the story of youth work, and, to some degree what youth work is.

THEORETICAL FRAMEWORK

As a theoretical basis for telling our story, we borrow from Connell's (2007) text *Southern Theory: The Global Dynamics of Knowledge in Social Science*. Here, Connell challenges the practices of production and circulation of social science knowledge across the global regions. Connell describes these regions as the global North (also the 'metropole') and the global South (also the 'periphery') (Connell 2007, p. 212). 'Metropole' pertains to mainly European and North American countries and 'periphery' describes poorer and/or developing countries which show patterns of dependence on, and paths of development from, European and North American

countries (Connell 2007, p. 212). A core precept of *Southern Theory* is that knowledge from privileged, metropolitan societies includes primarily 'Northern' knowledges and theories, hence a claim to the 'Northernness' of this knowledge. As authors, we consider that Connell is useful in drawing attention to the dynamics of how and where youth work knowledge has been produced, how it has been disseminated, and the relations of power inherent in and reproduced by this knowledge and these processes as part of the colonising story.

In making the claim of 'Northernness', Connell (2007) identifies four main 'moves' in the production of social science knowledge in the metropole. The first of these, *claims of universality*, suggests that there is a strong and repeated claim to universal relevance when producing social science knowledge. The second, *reading from the centre*, suggests that contributions to social science knowledge are often presented as resolutions of problems in previous metropolitan theoretical literature (in other words, metropolitan literature, and problems, are centred). The third, *gestures of exclusion*, suggests that scholars from the colonised periphery are very rarely cited and are notably absent in metropolitan texts; further, these texts do not introduce ideas from scholars from the periphery, with the result that these ideas are excluded from the realm of what is understood as world-scale knowledge. The fourth move, *grand erasure*, suggests that erasure of the experiences of communities from the periphery, which make up the majority population on a global scale, occurs in social science as it uses the empirical knowledge wholly or mainly driven from the metropole, and where theorists' concerns arise from the problems of metropolitan society to the exclusion of the periphery.

Connell suggests, however, that knowledge creation occurs not only in metropolitan societies, but also in the periphery. She uses the notion of Southern theory to describe this knowledge creation. She contends that texts from the periphery have to be taken seriously – 'as texts to learn from, not just about' (Connell 2007, p. viii), and that knowledge from peripheral and colonised societies has as much intellectual power as metropolitan social thought. In other words, she advocates that scholars in the metropole consider intellectual thought from the periphery by including texts from these communities when knowledge is produced on a global scale. Connell also suggests that we need to understand the way this knowledge from the periphery communicates beyond its immediate contexts, and the way it might enter a global communication of knowledge, as an equal partner with knowledge from the metropole.

Connell's core claim relevant for this chapter is that the realm of social science knowledge (in which we can include youth work knowledges) embeds the viewpoints, perspectives and problems of 'the privileged' from the metropole whilst excluding perspectives from less privileged communities from the periphery. Thus, she finds that current and dominant social science knowledge accounts for only a fraction of people of the world and has limited validity on a world scale. In other words, she suggests that social science knowledge from privileged societies falsely represents itself as universal knowledge applicable to all communities in the world. Following from Connell, we now consider the process of the transfer of youth work knowledges from the global North to the global South.

TRANSFERS OF YOUTH WORK KNOWLEDGES AND PRACTICES FROM THE OLD WORLD TO THE NEW COLONIES

In telling the intertwined stories of how we 'know' young people and how we understand what youth work *is* to her students, Kathy begins in Imperial Britain. Her story is explicitly one of globalisation and of colonisation. She identifies the origins of youth work in 19th-century Britain, following rapid industrialisation and urbanisation, with the establishment of ragged and Sunday schools, closely followed by clubs and societies established for young men, and providing opportunities for education and leisure. Also at issue here were changing social, technological, legal and economic circumstances, particularly the Factory Acts that prevented children from working and the rise of schooling that created the categories of 'children' and 'youth' (Savage 2007; Thane 1981). Young women's organisations followed shortly thereafter, and then, as the stories go, some became more formalised as 'uniformed' societies, such as the Scouts and Guides in 1908 and 1910. Early pioneers of these initiatives were influenced by a complex mix of Christian, Enlightenment and Victorian progressive thinking. This is an oft-told story. Less explored, but still recognised, is the cross-fertilisation between British and US ideas and practices of youth work. Youth clubs were formed in the United States too, and Scouting organisations were established in the early years of the twentieth century, following Baden-Powell's model. Youth work also developed there as part of the Settlement movement (see Fusco in this volume), often resulting in 'child-saving' initiatives (Platt 1969) that were also present in philanthropic movements in Britain. At the same time, Granville Stanley Hall's work conducted in the US on adolescence, which conceptualised the life-stage as imbued with angst and potentially dangerous outcomes, provided a framework for highlighting the necessity of youth clubs and organisations, not only in the US and North America, but in Britain, Australia and beyond. Later, British educational psychologist Cyril Burt added to the repertoire with his concerns about potential delinquency. Later still, the rise of youth culture in the 1950s spurred another moral panic about wayward youth and, in England, the Albemarle Report heralded the rise of local youth centres and youth work as it is known, practised and vigorously defended today. Modern youth work in Britain is practised as informal education and its value base relies on criteria such as voluntary association and centring young people's agendas (IDYW 2014).

Thus, the problem that defined English youth work and its incipient knowledge base was clear. For the state, the problem was how to control young people in order to save them from delinquency and create citizens who would provide the foundations for prosperous societies. For nascent youth work, especially where it was funded by the state, there was a struggle between enacting the state's agenda and emerging ideas that youth work was about more than control, but should, in order to be considered *youth work*, be something emancipatory. This struggle is on-going today. As chapters in this volume attest (see Taylor et al., Jones and Jeffs) youth work in austerity era Britain is currently under severe threat with cuts to services and a neoliberal state-driven impetus to once again put youth work to the task of 'controlling' young people deemed at risk. As a result, much focus in activism and literature is being put on the need to defend valued practices and delineate *real* youth work from that which is corrupted by the state.

In telling the story of how youth work reached Australia, Kathy is faced with some difficulties. The first of these is that whereas there are some extremely valuable Australian texts, most knowledge production about youth work takes place in the global North, in the United Kingdom (and to some extent the United States).[2] Thus, whereas there are a plethora of rich, detailed histories and conceptual studies of English youth work, many examples of which line her bookshelves (for example, Batsleer and Davies 2010; Bright 2015; Davies 1999; Gilchrist et al. 2001), there is comparatively little on the Australian experience (and less still that concerns indigenous perspectives), *and* these texts carry with them a core conception of

what youth work *is* forged in the English metropole. Nevertheless, Kathy explains that during the 19th century, as youth work as a distinctive set of knowledges and practices was forming and taking shape in Britain, so it was also being exported as part of earlier patterns of globalisation in the form of the colonial expansion of the British Empire, expansion that also included the resettlement of many British young people, sent abroad to new colonies such as Canada and Australia as orphans or children of the state as part of initiatives to 'save' these young people from lives of poverty and crime (Coldrey 1999; Maunders 1984). Imported initiatives included ragged schools and Scouts as well as child-saving initiatives such as various Societies for the Protection of Children and many charitable organisations such as the homes and institutes set up by the Try Society and Berry Street in Melbourne (Maunders 1984). As youth work was imported in this way, so was its core, defining problem. As Bessant notes, like in Britain, much early colonial youth work in Australia 'involved what some historians ... describe as a class-based project driven by "respectable fears" about "social degeneration" and social order with an interest in pacifying the urban poor' (2012, p. 3). In Australia there was the added complexity that indigenous young people were deemed especially problematic and fell victim to a particular regime of social control that included, but was not restricted to, the practices that gave rise to the stolen generations (Van Krieken 1999).

The story of youth work has differed in Australia, however, as Australia has steadily moved away in terms of identity and policy from her colonial mistress. Australia did not have an Albemarle Report equivalent and no statutory youth service was established. In Australia, youth work has developed a more 'inchoate character' than in Britain (Bessant 2012), and can describe many activities including (but not limited to) informal education, as well as formal, individual or group advocacy (including in policy spaces), casework with a variety of young people in service delivery organisations, statutory and youth justice settings, programme development and community work. Thus, the telling of the story of youth work in Australia as part of her teaching involves Kathy in some contradictions, not the least of which is that much of what is accepted as youth work in Australia falls outside of the increasingly tightening English-led definition of what youth work *is*.

As Kathy tells it, the story of youth work in Australia has been heavily influenced by a post-1960s rights-based model, drawing heavily also on ideas about youth participation. There are similarities and differences with the English model here. In attempting to draw together and define youth work for an Australian context the (now defunded) national peak body, the Australian Youth Affairs Coalition (AYAC), decided on: that which places young people and their interests first; is relational where the youth worker operates in the young person's context; is empowering and which 'advocates for and facilitates a young person's independence, participation in society, connectedness and realisation of their rights' (AYAC 2013, p. 3). In Victoria, the YACVic Code of Ethical Practice is developed from a human rights basis and is built on a series of principles that include empowerment, participation and social justice. It centres the young person as a youth worker's primary consideration (YACVic 2007). Thus, in Australia, youth work is frequently couched in the language of rights, with the young person as a 'rights bearing' citizen with distinct interests at its centre, a clear reflection of the liberal individual of Enlightenment origins. Indeed the model of youth work that Kathy implicitly or explicitly reflects in her teaching is one of youth work as radical advocacy for and empowerment of individual young people, groups of young people, or young people collectively, through service provision, policy advocacy and social action.

Obviously, the above is a potted history only and represents the skeleton of the story as Kathy teaches it to her students. Despite its necessarily incomplete nature, though, it is possible to draw four important conclusions necessary to our joint story here. First, both youth work practices and knowledges have a colonial history, imported from Britain to Australia, although following the end of Empire and the forging of Australia as a nation in its own right, Australia developed its own knowledges and practices. What counts as 'real' youth work, though, still largely relies on English foundations. Second, related to this, youth work knowledges have been part of the production and circulation of knowledge more generally across the global regions, with most (still) emanating from Britain. Third, the core defining 'problem' that engendered English youth work was a problem of the newly emerging industrialising metropole: how to develop emancipatory practices in working with young people that countered state practices of saving and control. This problem has been the driver of youth work knowledge since youth work began to emerge as a distinct set of knowledges and practices and it remains as such today. Finally, transferring knowledges and practices across regions often results in contradictions when local conditions differ. Our story, however, does not end here and it is time to consider Ismail's perspective.

THE MALDIVIAN CONTEXT

In studying for his youth work degree qualification in Australia, as one of a large number of international students who partake of offerings in Australia's global education market, so Ismail learned from this mishmash of mainly British, some North American and some Australian sources. It is important to note here that Ismail studied youth work in Australia as part of an international aid

programme administered by the Australian
Government. There are currently no universities in the Maldives offering a youth work
degree programme and none also in nearer
neighbouring countries. Similarly, there is
scant literature concerning Maldivian youth
and none that considers youth work in the
Maldives. As Ismail noted in his dissertation:
'in examining the background (or perspectives) and locations from which youth work
theories, identities, and practices are
spawned, it can be identified that these generally include mainly a few privileged countries which are both comparatively wealthy
and also secular' (Shaafee 2013, p. 15).
Perhaps more importantly, he noted, 'current
youth work research draws conclusions about
"youth work" without including young
people and their communities from outside
these privileged, 'metropolitan' contexts'
(p. 17). Thus, Ismail's experience was a very
personal one of travelling from a developing
country in the periphery to the metropole, not
to learn local knowledge, but to learn from
knowledges shaped in the metropole. Ismail's
experience was also one of globalisation and
arguably of colonisation. In travelling to
Melbourne, Australia, Ismail became
enmeshed in the global web of knowledge
production and transmission that, as Connell
(2007) notes, generally flows from North
to South.

As Ismail tells the story of his thesis, he
initially considered that upon his return
he would need to bring the knowledge he
gained in Australia back to the Maldives.
He also 'thought that the problem in knowledge transfer was due to the backwardness
of the thinking of the Maldivian society,
and that the Maldives needed to advance
to 21st-century ideals', further stating: 'As
we learn in youth work studies, I felt that I
must employ concepts of "social change",
in order to advocate for a fairer world for
the Maldivian young people' (p. 9). Here, it
is perhaps possible to see this as a story of
ostensibly benevolent colonisation, a relatively wealthy country, although arguably a

Southern nation, providing financial aid and
educational opportunities to a citizen of the
periphery.[3]

It was through reading some sociological and community development literature
(Connell 2007; Ife 2002; Reichel 2008) that
does centre the periphery that Ismail realised that the situation could be understood
differently, and indeed *needed* to be understood differently. In both sociology and youth
work, we often talk about 'critical moments'.
A critical moment in the story of Ismail's thesis was when after considering the realities
of how metropolitan youth work knowledge
might be received by decision-makers in the
Maldives, he asked Kathy how she would
resolve an ethical dilemma. Ismail and Kathy
co-created this story, 'The story of the Jinni
Avalun', which Kathy now uses in scenario
form in her teaching deliberately in order
to unsettle students' Northern/metropolitan
preconceptions of what youth work is and
to encourage students to consider Southern
perspectives. It serves here to introduce the
Maldives and to provide context for the next
part of our story; creating peripheral knowledges and considering the challenges inherent in this.

Ismail challenged Kathy to respond to
this story, which is a true one and reported
in various stories in *Haveeru*, the Maldivian-
language (Dhivehi) newspaper.[4] He then challenged her to think about how her response
may differ if she believed in the Jinn and the
power of the *fanditha*, and then finally to
think about the possibilities of a youth work
that centred rather than marginalised this, as
well as being sensitive to the social location of
young people in Maldivian culture and to this
culture more broadly. This conversation led
to a consideration of the differences between
problems encountered in transferring youth
work knowledge and thinking about what a
Maldivian youth work might look like. At the
core is that this scenario looks very different from 'within' and 'without' and a 'youth
work solution' from the metropole might be
very different from one developed from the

Box 5.1   The Story of the Jinni Avalun

The Maldives is an Islamic nation, comprising of some 1,192 islands, in the Indian Ocean. The most populated of these, and the capital, is Malé. Other islands are less populated and mostly smaller. The island of Makanudhoo in the North of the Maldives on the atoll of Haa Dhaalu has a population of around 1,400 people and has a school, health centre and a mosque. It is typical of many Maldivian Islands.

When he created the world, Allah created humans, the angels and the Jinn (the hidden) – creatures made as best as we can describe from a smokeless flame and fire. Unlike Angels, and like humans, the Jinn are capable of free will, and thus of good and evil. They are invisible to humans, although they live on Earth and can interact with humans. They have powers and abilities that Allah has not given to humans, including their ability to possess human beings, thus, humans must avoid upsetting them.

There are a number of stories about how the young people of Makunudhoo upset the Jinn of their Island. One tells of a young girl taken to a local beach by her mother accidentally stepping on the head of a Jinn baby, and that way becoming possessed. Another recounts a tale of a group of boys playing and, by accident, hitting a ball into a tree inhabited by the Jinn, wounding a Jinn boy. In this case, the human boy suffered a distortion of the hand, the identical injury to the Jinn child. In reference to the same tree, another account tells of the children of the school damaging the tree, and so upsetting the Jinn. A final, confusing, version tells of two local criminals invoking the Jinn to assist with a curse. The written curse was buried in a bottle, near the tree. This story has the possessed children being able to locate the bottle, and the curse being lifted when it was removed.

Whatever the origin, the case came to light when students at the school, mainly girls, began exhibiting symptoms that to some indicated possession by the Jinns, known as 'Jinni avalun': fainting, fits, unusual strength, crying out. That this was recognisable to some as being indicative of possession draws upon a long folkloric tradition, extending through the Maldives and beyond. Others, of a more 'Northern' bent, noted that the possession began with one student, and spread, gradually, suggesting mass hysteria and demanding psychological attention.

Two strategies were thus employed by those who intervened. On the one hand, Island leaders asked for practitioners of *fanditha* to assist. This is a mixture of folk medicine, charms and black magic based on ancient beliefs and superstitions that allows communication with the Jinn to treat the sick and to cure those who are possessed. In this case, the practitioners tried to banish the Jinn to outlying, uninhabited islands to cure the students, and they attempted, with success, to locate the bottle with the curse. Various health workers and a youth worker were also sent to the Island to provide counselling and advice. A number of the local peoples were unhappy with this, preferring the old ways. Yet, these old ways are regarded with some scepticism in modernising Maldivian culture, and even some locals consider it as antithetical to Islam as currently practised in the Maldives.

You are the youth worker in this scenario. While the other health workers were talking to the Island's leaders, you spoke with the young people, who told you that they were afraid of the Jinn, but comfortable that the finding of the bottle with the curse would release their classmates from their Jinni avalun. The young people were suspicious of the other health professionals. They told you they realised that by custom they would need to respect the decisions of the leaders, but they would prefer that the situation be left to the *fanditha* practitioners. How would you approach this?

---

knowledges, experiences and cultural specificity inherent in Maldivian society. More centrally, both Ismail and Kathy came to realise that youth work knowledge from the metropole was not universal and not necessarily transferrable to the global South. Some of the operations of power in the transfer of this originally Imperial knowledge between the global North and South started to become clear, as did the practical and ethical necessity of developing youth work knowledges and practices from the peripheries of the global South.

Indeed, in his thesis, Ismail eventually concluded that it was problematic to transfer youth work knowledge as currently constituted from the metropole to the Maldives. One key pragmatic issue here is the age bracket for youth understood in the metropole differs greatly from that which characterises young people in the Maldives. This issue can be explored through one of the few sources of information available on young people in the Maldives, *Youth in the Maldives*, a report published by the World Bank in 2014 (after the completion of Ismail's dissertation). Although not the focus here, this provides a clear example of the way that knowledges from the metropole frame interpretations of and 'ways of knowing' young people in the Maldives. As the World Bank acknowledges, 'according to the prevailing policy framework, youth in the Maldives span the 18–35-year-old age group' (World Bank 2014, p. 11). 'Worldwide', they continue, 'it is not uncommon for youth to cover such a large spectrum of the population' (World Bank 2014, p. 11). However, they contend 'this is not practical, as it spans 17 years and covers many stages in the lives of young people' (World Bank 2014, p. 11). Thus, their report 'focuses on the 15–24-year-old cohort, consistent with the UN definition' (World Bank 2014, p. 11), despite this not capturing youth as understood and experienced in the Maldives and indeed in many other nations in the periphery. The report continues to examine young people and the condition of youth in the Maldives using common criteria for measuring development, health, education, participation and the like. Issues facing young people in the Maldives, according to the report, include drug use, lack of employment opportunities and participation in gangs and gang culture (amongst others). Most of the references drawn upon in the report consider metropolitan research and knowledge and apply this to the Maldives.

Beyond pragmatic issues, a particular difference influencing the difficulty of knowledge transfer is the Maldives' Islamic foundation. Again, we start with perspectives from the metropole. There is some literature discussing youth work and Islam, or Islamic youth work (Belton 2011; Cressey 2007; Khan 2006; Seddon and Ahmad 2012), all of which Ismail considered, but again this is produced in the metropole and the main focus of these authors is on considering the situation of potentially alienated and socially excluded young British Muslims. Again, this is a problem of a multicultural

metropole, where the debate concerns an old problem in new clothes: the perceived potential of young, in this case, Islamic people, for social disruption. Very few studies from the periphery consider youth work in contexts and cultures that are primarily or wholly Islamic. Al-'Uthaymeen (2011), for example, writing from Saudi Arabia considers the Qur'an and Sunnah as core sources for working with young people around issues such as joblessness, good behaviours and predestination. Similarly, Haruna (2011), writing from Ghana, considers that education (secular and Islamic), and personality development of youth and the role of Muslim leaders are important factors in developing work with Muslim young people. However, these are tentative steps, and, importantly, are culturally specific and do not necessarily speak for the Maldives. We must not fall into the colonising Imperialist trap of homogenising an Islamic periphery.

A further complication is that modern globalisation has brought with it problems from the metropole as well as knowledges. The Westernising of Maldivian society has led to a clash of cultures and values and there are now those who desire to control young people in order to save them from delinquency and create citizens who can provide the foundations for a prosperous Maldivian society, a problem familiar in the history of youth work from the metropole. A case study as described by the blog 'Dhivehi Sitee' (2014) illustrates this conundrum as well as paints a picture of a complex contemporary Maldivian society as many young people experience it. In 2014, some young people in the Maldives attended the OTUM Music Festival on Anbaraa, Vaavu Atoll. Following a police raid, many were arrested on suspicion of being in possession of or affected by alcohol or other illegal substances (forbidden according to Maldivian Law). This attracted the attention of several Maldivian bloggers who alleged the raids were aggressive and did not follow any due procedure. Also at issue was that the western-style of clothing worn by female party-goers raised the ire of the police. There are also national-ist responses. *The Guardian* reports that radi-calisation of young people in the Maldives is seeing many join radical forces in Syria, a problem the World Bank blames, perhaps ironically, on more Western problems; drugs, alcohol, unemployment and the rise of gang culture (Burke 2016).

Put briefly, a core problem in transferring youth work knowledge from the metropole to the Maldives is that the young person of the Maldivian culture, framed as it is by a mixture of Islamic and other local traditions, is not the young rights bearing individual who is the subject of an emancipatory youth work, framed by opposition to a controlling state premised by youth work knowledge from the (British or Australian) metropoles. Nor are Maldivian young people the poten-tially disaffected or socially excluded young person understood by the literature concern-ing Islamic youth work written from the (British) metropole. Young Maldivians expe-rience youth differently and for a different period of their lives. They are enmeshed in a milieu where the roles they play as young people involve paying respect to Islam, par-ents, family, community, government and more local traditions. At the same time, no culture is static and globalisation is bringing changes to the way that young Maldivians live their lives and to the choices and challenges they face. Young people in the Maldives are subject to the lure of youth culture and free-doms from the metropole as this is exported as part of a globalising world and they are pulled too by the forces of nationalist fun-damentalism. These are the complex, diverse and driving problems to which youth work in the Maldives could be responsive. There are some overlaps with the core problems that shaped youth work in the metropole, but also many core differences. However, their distinctiveness demands particular, local solutions rather than the imposition of falsely universal, but really metropolitan, knowledge.

CONSIDERING KNOWLEDGE TRANSFER

Although a brief departure from the narra-tive, it is important to note at this point that Ismail's experience of knowledge transfer via higher education in Australia was just one instance of knowledge transfer from a metro-politan to a peripheral nation. There are many other youth work students from coun-tries in the periphery also undertaking higher education in countries in the metropole. Also, youth work education has been exported to the global South via a range of other educational and development initia-tives. These include knowledge as packaged in books that inform practice (most of which, as noted come from the United Kingdom). The Commonwealth, a remnant of the British Empire and comprising of ex-colonies, has also been instrumental here, driving initia-tives to professionalise youth work and train professional youth workers across this sector and as part of the Commonwealth Youth pro-gramme. The Diploma in Youth Development was introduced in 1973 and has been sup-plemented by much other professional devel-opment and training. Many youth development initiatives are undertaken by numerous NGOs and intergovernmental organisations, many in the name of youth work and reliant on youth work knowledges. The report on youth in the Maldives pub-lished by the World Bank has already been discussed and is an example of this.

All of these knowledge transfer initiatives have colonising potential to construct the periphery through the eyes of the metropole, robbing nations of identity, specificity and the ability to create their own knowledges. Connell reminds us that knowledge transfer must be seen as part of this process of glo-balisation, not something that sits objectively outside of it. An insight from Sallah, who, in considering global youth work, notes the tendency for youth work to operate from the 'missionary position' where civilising is a core goal and with its roots in 'colonial subjugation' (Sallah 2014, p. 73) is also pertinent here. Sallah argues for the necessity to infuse youth work with critical Southern perspectives and he warns against the spectre of 'negative neutrality', instead moving Southern perspectives from the periphery to the centre.

At this point, it is useful to return to Connell's four 'moves' in order to make sense of the story so far, particularly as it concerns knowledge transfer to the Maldives. Although there have been no explicit *claims of universality* made in youth work knowledge, or the transfer of this, there have at the same time been implicit assumptions made about the *potential* for the transferability of this knowledge, and limited interrogation of its specificity or universality, first as it was transferred from Imperial Britain to the colonies of Australia and then from Australia to the Maldives. Arguably, youth work in both English and Australian terms, assumes at its core a universal Platonic idea of a young person, perhaps best understood as a liberal, Enlightenment-project individual who is possessed of a range of 'rights'. Most nations in the metropole, being loosely based on liberal democratic principles, also interpret young people as 'rights bearers' and (to some degree) autonomous beings possessing (limited) citizenship. The current understanding of young people and of the goals of youth work in both Australia and Britain is influenced also by the emergence of words such as 'democracy', 'citizenship', 'participation' and 'community' into the vocabulary of youth work (Bessant, Sercombe and Watts 1998). In terms of claims of universality, a Maldivian perspective on youth work from the metropole finds it foreign to cultural and social practices and religious beliefs. It cannot be shoehorned in as a way of working with young people. That 'Muslim youth work' as it exists in the metropole is named as such suggests that it is peripheral to the main referent, 'youth work', that is at the centre and which provides the model from which variations derive. Yet, as noted above, those

who produce youth work knowledge in the metropole are rarely aware of the specificity of the knowledge they produce and this specificity has certainly not been interrogated. In other words, youth work knowledge from the metropole, by omission, gives a false impression that it is universal and transferable.

With respect to *reading from the centre*, as shown above, much of the story of youth work has been shaped by a desire to resolve an initial, but on-going problem, where young people were understood as potentially disruptive and were subject to methods of social control. In the metropole, youth work stands in opposition to this, constructing ideas and practices that variously, broadly put, position youth work as about voluntary engagement, informal education and young people's agendas (in England) or about rights, advocacy and young people as the primary consideration (in Australia). Whereas there are some similarities, this is simply not the same problem that might drive youth work responses in the Maldives. Further, reading from the centre reveals that conceptions of 'rights' and autonomy derived from the metropole do not transfer easily to the Maldives. Revealed here is the necessity to interrogate youth work knowledge from the metropole for its biases before assuming it can be simply transferred to other contexts.

In terms of *gestures of exclusion*, most youth work literature is produced in the global North. There are nascent efforts to understand young people, youth and youth work from outside this metropole, but they are emergent only and certainly not centred within the literature (see for example Belton 2014b; Heathfield and Fusco 2016). As a result of this practice, invaluable ideas from the peripheral communities, in particular their values, skills, roles and ideologies, are currently excluded in producing youth work knowledge. Connell suggests dialogue with indigenous and diverse thoughts from peripheral societies, and a collective learning process in producing knowledge, as these practices will contribute to the expansion and enrichment of the field of knowledge. In other words, this will contribute to the development of 'universal' knowledge that is more applicable to diverse global regions.

The reluctance to cite texts from the periphery in producing youth work knowledge is problematic because the periphery actively imports youth work knowledge from the metropole, and the metropole actively exports this knowledge, through the mechanisms described above. Connell (2007) suggests the knowledge is incomplete and results in problematic truthfulness when we do not learn from intellectual works from all communities equally, especially when knowledge is considered on a world scale. She highlights that there are more than 10,000 cultures across the world, and contends that we must recognise the diversity and dynamism of these communities when producing 'world-scale' knowledge and transferring this knowledge to global regions. Otherwise, only incomplete knowledge, imbued potentially with problematic truthfulness, is being transferred to the periphery.

Thus, it can be argued that a *grand erasure* has occurred, with the experiences of communities from the periphery being excluded in the production and transfer of youth work knowledges. In this case, the transfer of youth work knowledge from Britain to Australia and from Australia to the Maldives risks the tendency of exporting and applying a youth work model that erases the particularities, specificities and experiences of the population of the Maldives, as well as creating a barrier in the formation of youth work knowledge by neglecting the potential opportunities for reaching understandings of this community.

In his thesis, Ismail summed up by saying that in undertaking youth work studies in Australia as an international student from the Maldives, he shifted from thinking that he would need to push for changes to ideas and practices in the Maldives to realising that knowledge produced and circulated by 'privileged' countries largely neglects to account

for the people of less developed communities. What became clear to Ismail, and to Kathy as she learned from him, is that current youth work knowledge is 'incomplete' and it is wrong to assume that this knowledge is universally applicable across the globe. Transferring youth work knowledge from the metropole with the assumption that it is 'universal' knowledge could reinforce a hegemonic relationship between the metropole and the periphery, operating exactly as a colonial missionary. There is also rich creative potential being neglected here. As Connell emphasises, by silencing the vast majority of the world's peoples, those in the metropole are neglecting the vast potentials of knowledges from the periphery.

WHERE TO FROM HERE? CHALLENGES AND QUESTIONS FOR YOUTH WORK EDUCATORS, PRACTITIONERS, RESEARCHERS AND OTHERS

So, where to from here? We conclude by suggesting some issues to consider and some potential ways forward for producers of youth work knowledge, including academics, researchers and those who derive knowledge from practice.

As a start, we argue that those in the metropole responsible for the creation and transfer of youth work knowledges should be aware, conscious and reflective regarding the genesis and genealogy of that knowledge, as well as its underlying assumptions. At the very least, it is necessary to be aware that knowledge is not neutral and cannot necessarily be universalised. This is especially true where individuals can potentially be wearing the mantle of the colonial, teaching, researching or practising in the periphery or with those from nations of the periphery. This is an ethical as well as a practical precept. We contend that, as well as being impractical in many contexts, it is highly unethical to make assumptions about the transferability of core precepts and concepts inherent in youth work knowledges.

There is some emerging research (from the metropole) on youth work epistemology that considers how youth work knowledge is created (O'Donovan 2010; Seal and Frost 2014). We contend that youth workers and scholars engaged in the interrelated endeavours of knowledge creation and practice consider epistemological issues more centrally in respect to the creation of youth work knowledges, and with the kinds of cultural, political and ethical questions engendered by older styles of colonialism and potentially perpetuated through newer practices made central. In this context, questions need to be asked about what kinds of problems and issues precipitated the formation of youth work knowledges and how these continue to drive and shape practice, as well as about foundational concepts such as 'individual', 'rights', 'community' or 'society', etc. with respect to these knowledges.

As well as engaging in 'meta' epistemological inquiry, we contend there are some debates about youth work knowledge here that should be engaged in by scholars and practitioners of youth work in the metropole. These include discussions about the genesis and transfer of the aforementioned foundational concepts, and what it might mean to talk about social or individual goods across places and cultures, particularly in the periphery and global South. For those in the metropole, this will require a degree of reflection about one's own meta-narrative, roots and often (dearly held) preconceptions about what youth work is, possibly all the more challenging in times and places when youth work is under threat. For all of us this could involve some uncomfortable considerations of where we might consider that practices with young people may not constitute 'youth work'. Some of these debates have been started in other genres such as in childhood studies, development studies, critical race studies and children's geographies, and

we contend that these need to be more central to youth work scholarship also (see for example Holloway and Valentine 2000; Ife 2002; Twum-Danso Imoh and Ame 2012).

Finally, we argue that it is important to be part of the process of engendering authentic youth work knowledges from the periphery or 'global South'. In writing about sociology, Connell (2007) emphasises the importance of considering genealogies and histories of knowledge as well as actively looking for knowledges under construction and for points of disruption in these where perspectives from the periphery are or might be found. These might be in foundational knowledges, in youth research or in research and scholarship (including that derived from practice) that directly concerns youth work from the periphery. This is to benefit those in the periphery so that those knowledges can best inform practice in specific geographical and cultural contexts, but it is also so that those in the metropole may learn from these rich knowledges.

Notes

1   In Australia, honours degrees are either a final year to an ordinary degree or a separate degree undertaken after an undergraduate degree. Undergraduate degrees range in length, but youth work degrees are three years in duration.

2   See for example Bessant, Sercombe and Watts (1998) as well as the three volumes of *Doing Youth Work in Australia* collated from articles published in *Youth Studies Australia* by White (2009, 2010). *Youth Studies Australia* was defunded by the Australian government in 2013 and has been replaced by the *Journal of Applied Youth Studies*, which is published by the not-for-profit Centre for Applied Youth Studies and which focuses on Australasia, the Pacific and South-East Asia.

3   Australia's position in conceptions of the global North and global South is somewhat complex and contested. For his thesis, Ismail accepted it as an intermediary nation, Southern and peripheral in some ways, but also a metropole in others. In this chapter, we tend towards using 'metropole' and 'periphery' because we find these terms more useful for our purpose.

4   As these articles do not appear in translation, interested readers are advised to consult the blog of a sceptical expatriate Maldivian for discussion of the event: <http://www.jawish.org/blog/archives/298-Makunudhoo-Jinns-The-story.html>

REFERENCES

Al-'Uthaymeen, S.M.S. 2011, *Youth's Problems: Issues that Affect Young People Discussed in Light of the Qur'an and the Sunnah*, International Islamic Publishing House, Riyadh, Saudi Arabia, http://www.kalamullah.com/youths-problems.html (viewed 20 April 2013).

Australian Youth Affairs Council (AYAC). 2013, The AYAC Definition of Youth Work in Australia.

Batsleer, J. and Davies, B. 2010, *What is Youth Work?*, Learning Matters Ltd, Exeter, UK.

Belton, B. 2011, *Youth Work and Islam: A Leap of Faith for Young People*, Sense Publishers, Rotterdam.

Belton, B. 2014a, 'Compassion and the Colonial Mentality in Pretoria' in B. Belton (ed.), *Cadjan-Kiduhu: Global Perspectives on Youth Work*, Sense Publishers, Rotterdam.

Belton, B. (ed.) 2014b, *Cadjan-Kiduhu: Global Perspectives on Youth Work*, Sense Publishers, Rotterdam.

Bessant, J. 2012, 'Youth Work and the Education of Professional Practitioners in Australia' in D. Fusco, *Advancing Youth Work*, Routledge, New York.

Bessant, J., Sercombe, H. and Watts, R. 1998, *Youth Studies: An Australian Perspective*, Longman, South Melbourne.

Bright, G. (ed.) 2015, *Youth Work: Histories, Policies and Contexts*, Palgrave, Basingstoke.

Burke, J. 2016, 'Paradise Jihadis: Maldives Sees Surge in Young Muslims Leaving for Syria' *The Guardian*, https://www.theguardian.com/world/2015/feb/26/paradise-jihadis-maldives-islamic-extremism-syria (viewed 10 April 2017).

Coldrey, B. 1999, *Good British Stock: Child and Youth Migration to Australia*, National Archives of Australia, Canberra.

Connell, R. 2007, *Southern Theory: The Global Dynamics of Knowledge in Social Science*, Polity, Cambridge.

Cressey, G. 2007, *The Ultimate Separatist Cage? Youth Work with Muslim Young Women*, National Youth Agency, Leicester.

Davies, B. 1999, *From Voluntaryism to Welfare State: A History of the Youth Service in England*, NYA, London.

Dhivehi Sitee 2014, 'Maldives: The Hypocrites' Paradise', http://www.dhivehisitee.com/people/hypocrites-paradise/ (viewed 10 April).

Gilchrist, R., Jeffs, T. and Spence, J. 2001, *Essays in the History of Community and Youth Work*, NYA, London.

Gray, M., Coates, J., Yellow Bird, M. and Hetherington, T. 2013. *Decolonizing Social Work*, Farnham, Ashgate, UK.

Haruna, SZS 2011, *A Case of Social Re-engineering for the Ghanaian Muslim Youth*, AC Concepts, Accra, Ghana.

Heathfield, S. and Fusco, D. 2016, *Youth and Inequality in Education: Global Actions in Youth Work*, Routledge, New York.

Holloway, S. and Valentine, G. (eds) 2000, *Children's Geographies*, Routledge, London.

Ife, J. 2002, *Community Development: Community-Based Alternatives in an Age of Globalisation*, 2nd edn, Pearson Education, Frenchs Forest, NSW.

In Defence of Youth Work (IDYW), 2014 'Revised Purpose' – see online at http://indefenceofyouthwork.com/idyw-statement-2014/ (viewed 14 February 2016).

Khan, M.G. 2006, *Towards a National Strategy for Muslim Youth Work*, National Youth Agency, Leicester.

Martin, L. 2002, *The Invisible Table: Perspectives on Youth and Youthwork in New Zealand*, Dunmore Press, Palmerston North.

Maunders, D. 1985, *Keeping Them Off the Streets: A History of Voluntary Youth Organisations in Australia 1850–1980*, Phillip Institute of Technology, Melbourne.

O'Donovan, D. 2010, 'Reflective Action in Youth Work: Constructing an Inquiry into the Epistemology of Youth Work as an Action' in P. Burgess and P. Hermann (eds), *Highways, Crossroads and Cul de Sacs: Journeys into Irish Youth and Community Work*, Europäischer Hochschulverlag GmbH & Co. KG, Bremen.

Platt, A. 1969, 'The Rise of the Child-Saving Movement: A Study in Social Policy and Correctional Reform', *The ANNALS of the*

American Academy of Political and Social Science, 381, pp. 21–38.

Reichel, P. 2008, *Comparative Criminal Justice Systems: A Topical Approach*, 5th edn, Pearson/Prentice Hall, Upper Saddle River, NJ.

Sallah, M. 2014, *Global Youth Work: Provoking Consciousness and Taking Action*, Russell House: Lyme Regis.

Shaafee, I. 2013, *Transferring Youth Work Knowledge From Australia to the Maldives: Perspectives and Problems*, Thesis submitted in partial fulfilment for the degree of Bachelor of Arts International Studies (Hons) RMIT University, Melbourne.

Savage, J. 2007, *Teenage: The Creation of Youth Culture*, Viking, London, pp. 62–73.

Seal, M. and Frost, S. 2014, *Philosophy in Youth and Community Work*, Russell House Publishing, Lyme Regis, UK.

Seddon, M.S. and Ahmad, F. (eds) 2012, *Muslim Youth: Challenges, Opportunities and Expectations*, Continuum International Publishing Group, London.

Thane, P. 1981, 'Childhood in History' in M. King (ed.), *Childhood, Welfare and Justice*, Batsford, London, pp. 6–25.

Twum-Danso Imoh, A. and Ame, R.K. (eds) 2012, *Childhoods at the Intersection of the Local and the Global*, Palgrave Macmillan, Basingstoke, UK.

Van Krieken, R. 1999, 'The "Stolen Generations": On the Removal of Australian Indigenous Children from their Families and its Implications for the Sociology of Childhood', *Childhood*, 6(3), pp. 297–311.

White, R. (ed.) 2009, 2010, *Doing Youth Work in Australia* (Vols 1–3), ACYS, Hobart.

World Bank 2014, *Youth in the Maldives: Shaping a New Future for Young Women and Men Through Engagement and Empowerment*, http://documents.worldbank.org/curated/en/460551468263693729/Youth-in-the-Maldives-shaping-a-new-future-young-women-and-men-through-engagement-and-empowerment (viewed 10 April 2017).

Youth Affairs Council of Victoria (YACVic) 2007, Code of Ethical Practice – A First Step for the Victorian Youth Sector, Youth Affairs Council of Victoria, http://www.yacvic.org.au/sector-info/yacvic-s-code-of-ethical-practice (viewed 13 May 2013).

6

Let Principles Drive Practice: Reclaiming Youth Work in India

Roshni K. Nuggehalli

INTRODUCTION

Amidst shifting political and social contracts in India, young people are positioned as a peg onto which several aspirations are simultaneously hooked. They are viewed as a labour force that can propel economic growth, as a troubled homogeneity that must be restrained, and also as a canvas to be imbued with an often divisive political agenda. The meanings and manifestations of youth work in this context have moved along the spectrum of inertia to dynamism. This chapter will open with a critical comparison of the Indian context with global trends (Bradford and Cullen, 2014; Davies, 2013; among others), emphasising the similarities between the South and North, in terms of decreasing funding and increasing State control. Unique features include the complete absence of disciplinisation and relegation of youth work as an add-on to other programming. At the level of the State this translates into bundling it with sports (under the Ministry of Youth Affairs and Sports) and in the non-governmental sector space youth work is viewed as a generalist role. The implications of this context on youth work practice and the ability to co-create empowering pathways for young people in India is considered.

The chapter proceeds to argue for locating youth work within a framework that can ensure young peoples' agency and provide space for their critical reflection and purposeful action. It uses an example from the Youth for Unity and Voluntary Action's (YUVA, an Indian non-governmental organisation)[1] experience of working with marginalised youth guided by principles of justice and participatory democracy to highlight the challenges and possibilities that exist for contemporary youth work in India. The need for conceptual clarity on the why and how of youth work (Walther et al., 2002) is emphasised through a case that points to the influences of a rapidly changing political economy juxtaposed on youth transitions.

The chapter profiles 'Anubhav Shiksha Kendra' (ASK), an experiential learning programme that is still running, twenty years since its inception as a funded intervention. It argues that a focus on building democratic organisations and political consciousness for marginalised youth, alongside collaboratively defined and upheld values, is responsible for the longevity and continuing impact of this programme. Successful examples of ASK youth transforming their realities are shared, while foregrounding the need for intensifying these forms of pluralistic youth work in the prevailing climate of sectarian and divisive politics in India. This process differs from direct service-based youth work, and examples are shared on how youth workers can constructively engage with governments while ensuring independence of voice and autonomy.

The chapter proceeds to identify challenges to non-service-based youth work, including reduction in funding. Professionalisation poses a significant challenge to the inclusive and expansive nature of programmes like ASK and the chapter questions the rationale and relevance of a professionalisation journey for these forms of youth work in India. The chapter concludes by speculating on key contestations that are relevant for contemporary youth work in India and also in other countries. The imperative for bringing conceptual and normative clarity to youth work in India is reiterated alongside the need to ensure flexibility and a recalibration of the measures of youth work's success. Methods by which youth workers can support young people's journeys through democratic processes and reclaim the shrinking space for youth voices are highlighted. The challenges of balancing the principles driving youth work with prevailing financial and politico-legal constraints are raised.

HISTORY OF YOUTH WORK IN INDIA

Since the 1990s India has pursued a purposive and focused neoliberal developmental agenda, accompanied by an increasing retraction of the welfare mandate of the State. A simultaneous demographic transition means that over 64 per cent of the country will be of working age by 2020 (UN-Habitat, 2012). In a country with the largest population of young people in the world, the persistent marginalisation of youth is one fallout of the shifting political and social contracts inherent in India's development model. Young people are positioned as a peg onto which several aspirations are simultaneously hooked. They are viewed as a driving force for economic growth, while at the same time as a group that must be managed in order to limit the perceived consequences of their disruptive tendencies. For political groups, youth are often the easiest entry point for driving and spreading ideologies and agenda.

The purpose and manifestations of youth work in this context cannot be assumed – they need to be interrogated. Several sources have examined the history and definitions of youth work globally and within specific country contexts (for an overview, see Belton, 2014; Edginton et al., 2005; Hurley and Treacey, 1993; Smith, 2013; among others). This chapter focuses on the historical progression of youth work in India. For the purposes of the chapter, youth work is referred to in its broadest sense as encompassing a diversity of approaches and models.

India has a long history of identity-based engagement with young people. As in Britain and other countries (Smith, 2013), faith-based youth work is widespread, particularly in terms of mobilisation to spread religious messages and for participation in formal politics. Prominent in this environment are the youth clubs and 'shaka' (branches) of the Hindu right-wing Rashtriya Swayam Sevak Sang (RSS) and several Islamic and Christian groups. Caste-based youth mobilisation is a unique feature in India and its focus on social transformation cannot be ignored in the history of the youth development landscape. A significant part of student politics is coloured by religious and caste affiliations as well as left-leaning ideologies.

State-driven work with young people was initiated in the 1960s and 1970s partly in response to the rise in student activism. Interestingly, this trajectory is comparable to countries in the North like Britain (Smith, 2013) and America (Edginton et al., 2005). In India, State-sponsored youth work took the form of an integrated Youth Plan delivered through a nodal Ministry. The Ministry that houses youth services has changed over the years and the responsibility currently rests with the Ministry of Youth Affairs and Sports. The first National Youth Policy of 1988 set the tone for training an instrumental lens on young people as an important input into economic growth, to facilitate which, services, socialisation and training was assumed to be necessary. Youth clubs, the National Social Services, Nehru Youth Centres are a few of the platforms for youth mobilisation towards programmes to improve developmental outcomes. Successive versions of the 1988 National Youth Policy (in 2003 and 2014) also focused on the delivery of services towards building a productive workforce, developing a healthy generation, instilling social values, promoting community service, facilitating participation and engagement, and supporting at-risk youth (NYP, 2014). While there is no direct reference to youth work as a profession in the policy document, the implications of the nature of State engagement with young people is clear.

Smith (2013) attributes the rich and varied history of youth work within and across countries to the existence of different forms of youth work rather than a single deterministic version of youth work. This is most definitely true in India, particularly when the youth work promoted by the State and faith-based groups is contrasted to the nature of working with youth promulgated by young people themselves. In the 1960s and early 1970s, there were a series of student strikes across the country, which began to coalesce into a larger movement towards the late 1970s. This dissent was directed at the prevailing conditions of poverty, hunger and lack of employment that jarred with the welfare promises of State. Several non-governmental organisations that were established in the late 1970s and early 1980s were in some ways born out of this climate of dissent. Many began their work with an emphasis (both stated and unstated) on the human rights approach, and a clear understanding of the systemic nature of the problems facing the country.

Youth for Unity and Voluntary Action (YUVA) was one such organisation, and, like many others, it aimed to support reclaiming values of democracy and social justice for those groups oppressed by caste- and class-based inequities. These organisations and movements were born out of and rooted in a strong ideological framework of participatory democracy, with an approach towards the empowerment of marginalised groups. This frame was positioned as an alternative vision to liberal technocracy and runaway neoliberalism.[2] YUVA worked through a climate of increasing globalisation, and approached both the State and the private sector as players who need to be engaged with in order to impact on structural change. Driven by this framework, youth work seeks to ensure young people's agency and provide space for their critical reflection and purposeful action.

Youth work thus has what Bradford and Cullen (2014) call universalistic aims and is framed within a radical theory of impacting larger societal change by working beyond the individual level and as a collective (Jeffs, 2002). Guided by a clear purpose and intent, the practice of youth work is similar to the Cooper and White (1994) framework of positive sceptical reflection, where the youth worker constantly uses questioning and reflection as a tool to appreciate his role in the life of a young person, and ensure that in the midst of the youth worker's own bias and subjectivity, a space is created for meaningful empowerment. Youth workers look at 'social hierarchy as constructed, rather than as inevitable' (Miller, 2012, n.p.), and seek a shift in traditional, and often entrenched, ways of socio-economic structuring. Youth work, in this context, is a political act and the politicisation of young people is seen as a positive process, as opposed to something to be avoided or ignored.

However, as the engagement of State-led work with young people grew, it was accompanied by collaborations with non-governmental organisations as well. These joint efforts focused on skill building for entry into the job market; to remove 'deficits' in at-risk youth; to facilitate their integration into the economy; and to implement schemes of national and local governments for skills development towards job preparedness. Although jobs are a critical need for youth development, these processes view young people solely as fuel for the production and consumption model of the economy. In India this translates to reaching out to large numbers and focusing on tangible outputs achievable in short time frames, as opposed to process-oriented, dialectical engagement methods. Larger non-governmental players were able to adhere to these guidelines and grew their programmes, while many others had to reduce their scope of work or adapt, contrary to their core principles.

India's trajectory affirms that youth work manifests in many ways, where each manifestation is the result of a conscious decision on the 'why'; the purpose of engaging with young people. The example from YUVA's work points to the transformational potential housed in a form of youth work driven by an ideology of participatory democracy, social justice and human rights, recognising young people's right to self-determine and question. This threatens the status quo, and is challenged by State- and donor-led efforts to reduce its outreach and impact, both deliberate and incidental. One of the most serious challenges facing 'radical youth work' in India today is the push towards the professionalisation of youth work. This challenge will be detailed and possible pathways for marrying the advantages of a professional approach to youth work with the disruptive

potential of radical youth work will be suggested. For several youth-focused NGOs in India, ensuring that youth work which challenges the establishment exists and thrives is important to enable pathways for alternative futures.

THRIVING AMIDST CHANGE: *ANUBHAV SHIKSHA KENDRA* (EXPERIENTIAL LEARNING CENTRE)

Anubhav Shiksha Kendra (ASK) is a multi-stakeholder programme with young people that has been ongoing since the early 1990s, with a goal of facilitating the movement of youth towards social transformation. Youth workers across different non-governmental organisations in the Indian states of Maharashtra and Madhya Pradesh (MP) have come together to engage with urban and rural youth from marginalised caste and income groups. Young people are exposed to the changing landscape of an information-driven society, alongside growing consumerism and identity politics. ASK is a civil society process that supports young people in unpacking the meanings of their external world, while enabling live examples of democracy, citizenship, secularism, and gender and social justice. ASK aims to provide a space for young people to express themselves and find meanings beyond the mainstream imagination promoted by the State and market.

ASK has evolved over the years, however the core purpose has been supporting youth development and youth for development. As of 2017 the programme is implemented by seven participating organisations (through eight outreach centres) in 28 districts (26 in Maharashtra state and two in Madhya Pradesh state) (Bokil, 2012). The stated goal of the programme is 'to build capacities of young people to become concerned, responsible citizens for asserting rights and responsibilities as well as to engage them in the development process of social transformation'.

The programme believes that if provided the space and support to develop critical thinking and experiential reflection, young people have the ability to change their lives and communities. The motivation driving youth work in ASK, is similar to what is according to Tony Jeffs (2002), is '… about offering young people opportunities for lived democracy, those tiny, small pockets in which real democracy grows' (p. 6).

The thematic focus in ASK programming is centred on governance, livelihoods and gender. These have stayed relevant throughout the period for which the programme has been implemented. Governance, particularly at the local levels in urban and rural areas of India, has not been able to realise the expected outcomes due to a lack of people's participation. Hence, in order to reverse the decreasing focus on equity-oriented policies and programmes, pressure from people can lead to beneficial outcomes for the most marginalised. Livelihoods are often the first priority of young people, and ASK addresses issues of declining agricultural productivity and low wages in urban areas. The programme moves beyond the limited development of specific skills for jobs, and facilitates a holistic focus on economic resilience. This enables young people to explore alternative, innovative sustainable livelihoods. By talking about gender and sexuality with young people, ASK youth workers break the taboos that exist in Indian society. In an integrated way, youth workers support young people not only in their personal journeys, but also in their social and political selves.

The strategies adopted for youth work practice in ASK can be broadly classified into four interrelated processes. First and most intensive is outreach and mobilisation of youth in chosen communities, all which have high degree of socio-economic marginalisation (including groups of *dalits*, women, religious minorities, urban and rural poor). Young people who come in contact with the programme proceed through three levels of participation – *Mitra* (concerned friend), *Sahayogi* (change agent) and *Sathi* (leader). Parameters exist for each level of participation, however these are not looked at as rigid or deterministic categories. Progression is non-linear, process-driven and left to the autonomous decisions of the youth worker and the young people. A basic aim is that any young person who comes in contact with ASK will at least be seen as a concerned friend.

A second core component is designing processes, events and activities that create space for both critical reflection and creative expression of young people. Youth workers collaborate with participating youth to co-create activities that help in the sensitisation to and internalisation of the core values of ASK. Through exposure tours across the country, young people meet activists to learn about social movements: they understand different civil society processes and also interact with government officials. They build perspectives through actual experience on internal and external realities about self and society. They also access opportunities for life-long learning through formal and non-formal processes and generate insights for development theory and practice through individual and group projects in their own communities.

Youth workers also build capacities and offer strategic support for a Youth Forum that is independently managed and led by young people themselves. Over the years the Youth Forum in the state of Maharashtra has emerged as an alternative and vibrant youth-led group. It is a medium for organising youth, as well as a platform for advocating for social change by engaging in existing political and governance mechanisms. The Forum operates in a federation model, with member groups from different tribal, rural and urban areas. In terms of impacting on the local and larger policy environment, the facilitation of the Youth Forum has emerged a significant outcome of the ASK programme over the years.

In an external evaluation of ASK in 2012, Milind Bokil (2012: 10) reflects on the relevance and impact of processes like ASK for India. He says:

> ... at present there is no other process which aims to engage with youth the way ASK does. The decade of [the] seventies was charged with students' and youth movements. These movements not only helped to overthrow the dictatorial regime in 1977 but also opened the gates for thousands of youths to devote their energies ... [to] national reconstruction. In the later years, students and youth movements got slowly dissipated ... Movements and agitations create great amounts of energy but they are transitory. What could be permanent is the steady process of engagement, skill development and capacity building, with special focus on values. Organisation of students and youths has been happening but influencing the youth with democratic values and principles has not been conspicuous. Hence, a process like ASK becomes relevant.

ASK's relevance is reflected in tangible outcomes. The last externally evaluated details of ASK show that the total outreach of the programme from January 2008 to March 2011 (over 646 villages and 122 colleges of 27 districts) was 109,469. Over the years ASK has created concerned citizens, change agents and community leaders who participate in the Youth Forum as well as existing forms of government from local to national levels (Bokil, 2012). Several young people who have passed through the ASK process have set up their own independent groups, practices and non-governmental organisations that focus on many of the principles upheld by the ASK experience.

ASK challenges the mainstream perspective of young people as being deficient or lacking in certain critical conditions for social and economic success. This is a perspective pushed by the State, and it results in a form of youth work that is seen as a way to deliver services that correct deviant behaviour and focuses merely on mainstreaming. Bokil (2012: 15) recounts an example of challenging this perspective:

> [The impact] does not remain restricted to the young people's personalities alone. It impacts their families, relatives, friends and the community. In Sehore district of Madhya Pradesh, when some of the young men joined ASK and were influenced by its principles, they encouraged their sisters to study further and also join [the] ASK programme in the college. They also established youth groups in their village and started monitoring government programs like the rural employment guarantee scheme of the national government.

This translates into a practice that is more 'dialectical than dialogical' (Belton, 2009). The support provided by ASK youth workers leads to different forms of 'generative politics' (Giddens, 1994) that push the traditional boundaries of social and civic action by young people. As a result, social inequalities are addressed in uniquely youth-driven and -centric ways. Opportunities for young people to exercise their right to participate in decision making and self-determine the course of their own lives is what distinguishes ASK from several other youth work programmes, leading to empowering possibilities, as is evident in the outcomes emergent over the years.

Simultaneously, ASK also presents a contrast to what Belton (2010) calls the 'relative political neutrality' of the youth work field. By presenting a 'clear statement on the political purpose and social function of non-formal education' (p. xi), youth workers in ASK are able to define the contours of their practice within a participatory democracy and critical theory. With its structural analysis frame, ASK emphasises addressing social issues head on; for instance, overcoming caste barriers to mobility in remote rural areas, spreading the message of peace and religious harmony in communally sensitive areas, and building coalitions of *dalit* and other caste youth in opposing GMOs in agriculture. Through these, ASK affirms its belief in secular and egalitarian values and seeks to preserve 'creative and pluralistic youth work from prescribed and predictable outcomes' (Belton, 2009). It reaffirms the community-wide benefit of contextual youth-led politics elegantly argued for by Jeffrey and Dyson (2014). When this happens in the presence of youth workers, it is common for young people to challenge youth workers themselves. ASK has seen youth resisting established knowledge and arriving at outcomes far removed from what were imagined at the start of the process.

An example of how ASK youth workers have addressed the dilemmas and contradictions faced in facilitating an empowering process is the drafting of the Maharashtra State Youth Policy. Youth workers and young people together enabled an intensive and participatory policy-drafting process from across the state of Maharashtra. The draft supported by ASK youth was one that considers the contextual needs of a diversity of identity and interest groups, thus encompassing the breadth of vulnerabilities faced by young people. Despite consistent advocacy, the drafts released by the Government did not consider these recommendations in their entirety. Rather, there were further efforts to dilute the plural intent of the Policy and it was positioned as a means to push a political agenda, in spite of ostensible references to youth empowerment. Several youth groups and organisations were left frustrated as they felt co-opted into supporting a draft Policy that was against their principles.

This led them to critically assess the outcomes of their engagement with the government, and to find ways to measure the real impacts of advocacy engagements. They realised the need to re-strategise constructive engagement with the government while ensuring their independence and autonomy. For instance, the shift in policy making towards an 'evidence-based' approach[3] (Sivakumar, 2012) means that young people need to be equipped to critique accepted forms of knowledge and evidence, while simultaneously innovating and engaging in participatory knowledge-creation processes. Social education is described by The Commonwealth Youth Programme as the 'intellectual and personal means to interact and develop in the social context', which, it is argued, facilitates political education (Belton,

2012). The experience with the Maharashtra Youth Policy shows how youth engagement in governance has developed through an experiential and reflective process. The role of youth workers has been central in facilitating this evolution, so that unfettered participation in political spaces without co-option can remain a reality for young people.

PROFESSIONALISATION OF YOUTH WORK?

In spite of their longitudinal impact and enduring rationale for continuity, specific processes like ASK and the overall ecosystem of autonomous, non-service-based youth work in India are challenged by several factors. Primary amongst these is the shrinking space for dissent and freedom of speech throughout the country (Unmüßig, 2016). Draconian laws, a culture of fear and the police State aim to limit the free expression of civil society and restrict the heterogeneity of perspectives and practices. Funding priorities shift from empowerment-based processes to those that are directly focused on service delivery, like de-addiction, health care and education. Those who speak up against the status quo are subject to institutionalised forms of confrontation and repression. Additionally, I argue that professionalisation is another significant challenge for Indian youth work.

The use of a question mark in the section title may seem a moot point in the case of those for whom professional youth work is not an option, but a living, breathing reality. It may seem like turning back the clock, or ignoring the experiences of many decades of professional youth work, including the creation of frameworks for assessing the benefits of professionalisation (recognition, quality, compensation and building a discipline for assessing benefits) (Johnston-Goodstar and Robolt, 2013). I refer to, in the Indian context, questions raised by Johnston-Goodstar and Robolt (2013) on the empirical outcomes of professionalisation, whether it supports quality practice and what, if any, could be the unintended consequences. I argue that if we do not interrogate the purpose and potential impacts of the professionalisation of youth work, we stand to lose the transformational potential of decades of work with young people across India.

In both sociological and lay terms, a profession can be broadly defined as an exclusive group, where entry is determined by the judgement of other similarly educated experts. Being part of a profession entails recognition of qualifications along with a career pathway. Kritzer (1999: 717) says the key features of a profession are the '... creation and recognition of trained expertise, and structuring of occupations around this expertise'. The Commonwealth Youth Programme (CYP), which has been at the forefront of professionalising youth work across the Commonwealth, lays out its rationale thus:

> Enhancing the impact of collective professional efforts to improve youth services is at the core of the CYP's mandate ... at the foundations of a successful professionalising process lies the collective strength of youth work practitioners participating in defining the parameters of their profession. This could include participatory decisions on required competencies for youth work, establishing parallel qualifications, and assuring the quality of training and practice. Such collective decision-making ensures the establishment of a vibrant and responsive youth service that serve[s] young people optimally. (Belton, 2012, p. 5)

There is undoubtedly a value in youth workers coming together, sharing experiences and emerging as a strong collective. The CYP argues that professionalisation can play a role in improving services for youth. This would imply in areas of care work, health work, education and other similar services, for which quality standards, indicators for success, and common and comparable parameters can undoubtedly result in improved outcomes for young people. Since 1950 the CYP has trained youth workers across member countries with this very premise, that trained youth workers result in better outcomes for youth. Professionalised youth workers differentiate between the youth worker and the 'client', where the essence is that the central aspect of the association is on a service that is to be provided, while the relationship- and rapport-building processes are either incidental or secondary in nature. When professionalisation is applied to provision of youth-relevant services, the question arises whether the same logic can be effectively extended to youth work that focuses on building independence and agency, affording spaces for the positive disruptive potential of youth.

A critical examination is required into whether the forms of youth work that are less amenable to be systematised or less likely to fit into defined frameworks should be professionalised. This mirrors a long-standing debate in the professionalisation of social services work, for instance as articulated by Johnston-Goodstar and Robolt (2013), Fusco and Baizerman (2013) and Weiss-Gal and Welbourne (2008), among others. Johnston-Goodstar and Robolt (2013) show that arguments in favour of professionalisation are not necessarily based on empirical data, and attribution of any benefits to quality improvements in practice are difficult to correlate to professionalisation, for instance in the fields of teaching and social work. More importantly, by documenting the loss of practices that question and address structural change, they highlight the role that dominant norms are likely to play in the professionalisation trajectory of youth work. Further, in the words of Fusco and Baizerman (2013), 'Because professionalisation requires standardised structures to select, monitor and evaluate all aspects of the profession, the process created may run counter to the essence of youth work as an inclusive, democratic and participatory practice' (p. 93).

An unpacking of these experiences is necessary for the Indian context – what are the forms of youth work that can empirically produce better outcomes through professionalisation? Is professionalisation a necessary precursor to the decision to pursue the programme of enabling young people's participation towards their transformation? Can professional youth work in any way impede the autonomy and diversity of non-service based forms of youth work? Specifically, what would professionalising youth work mean for processes like ASK and others by organisations driven by principles of social justice and participatory democracy? And if we choose to professionalise, what are the implications for the possibility to create new meanings and new outcomes, outcomes that are difficult to predict and harder to make tangible? Similar questions have been raised during the professionalisation history of social work, and reflecting on the lessons learnt will be important by those promoting professionalisation of youth work.

I raise a related question on the risks and implications of youth work in India getting institutionalised alongside the professionalisation trajectory. Tucker (2004) and others have shown how professional identities arise and develop within prevailing socio-political contexts. How Indian youth work gets professionalised and contoured into a separate specialisation will depend on the underpinning ideologies and principles. If the State takes the lead in professionalisation, it is likely that the primary motivation will be to ensure the creation of youth workers who can mainstream young people into the production- and consumption-driven economy. The indications for this in India are many since government universities are already designing course work and curricula for a youth work degree under the aegis of the Ministry of Youth Affairs and Sports. If the private sector lends support to this process, then adding economic and business value to their corporate mandate will be at the core of the endeavour. Finally, if professionalisation proceeds as a collaborative exercise, with participation from the state and civil society, the likelihood

of co-option into the State mandate is high. Hence, alongside the debate on professionalisation, it is necessary to include reflection on the institutional framework within which professionalisation will be realised.

CONCLUSION

In the long history of youth work in India, a stream of pluralistic and autonomous engagement has had a strong presence and impact, alongside service-based work with young people. Processes like ASK, carried out across multiple states and stakeholders is an example of this, and there are many more. They have contributed to building citizenship among young people in the country to challenge and uproot discriminatory systems. If located as an expression of a larger political ideology and theoretical exploration, there is a strong probability that youth work will retain principles of plurality and autonomy. However, these processes are increasingly challenged by attempts to homogenise civil society interventions and limit spaces for dissent, both from the State and certain non-state actors. In the context of youth work, reductions in funding alongside the push towards professionalisation can result in similar limitations in pursuing the entire breadth and depth of the youth work agenda.

Where the primary purpose of professionalising youth work is to simplify our parameters of measurement and employ standard measures of success, the work we do with young people risks losing its grounding in an equity and justice frame. The advantages of creativity, innovation and interdisciplinary linkages can also be reduced through this approach. Are we willing to trade in 'a bigger cage of subjugation for a smaller cage of freedom'?[4] We must reflect deliberately and deeply on this question.

Notes

1 For more information see: http://yuvaindia.org/
2 Including John Gaventa (2003) among others.
3 This was the focus of the National Youth Policy of 2012, and a similar approach was advocated for the Youth Policy of different States.
4 Sharlene Swartz, University of Cape Town. Personal Conversation.

REFERENCES

Belton, Brian (2009) *Developing Critical Youth Work Theory: Building Professional Judgement in the Community Context*. Rotterdam: Sense Publishers.

Belton, Brian (2010) *Radical Youth Work: Developing Critical Perspectives and Professional Judgement*. Dorset: Russell House Publishing.

Belton, Brian (2012) *Establishing a Professional Youth Worker Association: A 12-Step Guide and More*. Commonwealth Secretariat, Commonwealth Youth Programme Asia Division, Chandigarh, India.

Belton, Brian (ed.) (2014) *Cadjun – Kiduhu: Global Perspectives on Youth Work*. Rotterdam: Sense Publishers.

Bokil, Milind (2012) *External Evaluation Report on Anubhav Shiksha Programme, for Katholische Zentralstelle fur Entwicklungshilfe (KZE) and Youth for Unity and Voluntary Action (YUVA)*. Navi Mumbai.

Bradford, Simon and Cullen, Fin (2014) 'Positive for youth work? Contested terrains of professional youth work in austerity England', *International Journal of Adolescence and Youth*, 19(1): 93–106.

Cooper, Trudi (2012) 'Models of youth work: A framework for positive sceptical reflection', *Youth & Policy*, 109: 98–117.

Cooper, Trudi and White, Rob (1994) 'Models of youth work practice', *Youth Studies Australia*, 13(4): 30–35.

Davies, Bernard. (2013) 'Youth work in a changing policy landscape: The view from England', *Youth & Policy*, 10: 6–32.

Edginton, Christopher R., Kowalski, Christopher L. and Randall, Steven W. (2005) *Youth Work: Emerging Perspectives in Youth Development*. Urbana: Sagamore Publishing.

Fusco, Dana and Baizerman, Michael (2013) 'Professionalization in youth work? Opening and deepening circles of inquiry', *Child & Youth Services*, 34(2): 89–99.

Gaventa, John (2003) 'Participatory development or participatory democracy? Linking participatory approaches to policy and governance', *PLA Notes*, 50. Available at: http://pubs.iied.org/G02106.html?k=PLA%2050 (accessed 1 June 2016).

Giddens, Anthony (1994) *Beyond Left and Right: The Future of Radical Politics*. Stanford: Stanford University Press.

Hurley, Louise and Treacey, David (1993) *Models of Youth Work: A Sociological Framework*. Dublin: Irish YouthWork Press.

Jeffrey, Craig and Dyson, Jane (2014) '"I serve therefore I am": Youth and generative politics in India', *Comparative Studies in Society and History*, 56(4): 967–994.

Jeffs, Tony (2002) 'Whatever happened to radical youth work?', *Concept: The Journal of Contemporary Education Practice Theory*, 2(2): 1–7.

Johnston-Goodstar, Katie and Robolt, Ross VeLure (2013) 'Unintended consequences of professionalising youth work: Lessons from teaching and social work', *Child and Youth Services*, 34(2): 139–155.

Kritzer, Herbert M. (1999) 'The professions are dead, long live the professions: Legal practice in a postprofessional world', *Law and Society Review*, 33(3): 713–759.

Miller, Ron (2012) Towards participatory democracy, *Education Revolution blog*. Available at: http://www.educationrevolution.org/blog/toward-participatory-democracy/ (accessed 1 June 2016).

National Youth Policy (NYP) (2014) Ministry of Youth Affairs and Sports, Government of India.

Sivakumar, P. (2012) 'Knowledge production and dissemination: An analysis in the context of the National Youth Policy', *Journal of Management and Public Policy*, 4(1): 33–41.

Smith, M.K. (2013) 'What is youth work? Exploring the history, theory and practice of youth work', *The Encyclopedia of Informal Education*. Available at: www.infed.org/mobi/what-is-youth-work-exploring-the-history-theory-and-practice-of-work-with-young-people/ (accessed 17 June 2016).

Tucker, Stanley (2004) 'Youth working: Professional Identities given, received or contested?', Chapter 9 in Roche, J., Tucker, S., Thomson, R. and Flynn, R. (eds), *Youth in Society: Contemporary Theory, Policy and Practice*. London: Sage, pp. 80–89.

UN-Habitat and IRIS Knowledge Foundation (2012) *State of the Urban Youth, India 2012: Employment, Livelihoods, Skills*. India.

Unmüßig, B. (2016) *Civil Society Under Pressure – Shrinking – Closing – No Space*. Heinrich Böll Foundation. Available at: https://www.boell.de/sites/default/files/uploads/2015/12/20160601_civil_society_under_pressure_shrinking_spaces_englisch.pdf (accessed 20 January 2017).

Walther, A., Hejl, G.M. and Jensen, T.B. (2002) 'Youth transition, youth policy and participation: State of the art report', *Working Paper 1*, Research Project YOYO. IRIS, Tubingen.

Weiss-Gal, Idit and Welbourne, Penelope (2008) 'The professionalisation of social work: A cross-national exploration', *International Journal of Social Welfare*, 17(4): 281–290.

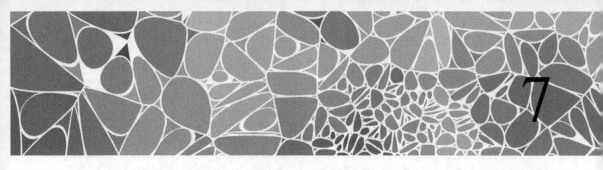

The Impact of Neoliberalism upon the Character and Purpose of English Youth Work and Beyond

Tony Taylor, Paula Connaughton,
Tania de St Croix, Bernard Davies and
Pauline Grace

INTRODUCTION

This chapter argues that the present state of English youth work exemplifies the corrosive influence of neoliberal capitalism upon its character and purpose. It is offered as a contribution to a collective understanding of how youth workers might criticise and resist on a national and international level neoliberalism's arrogant contention that there is no alternative. Our analysis is politically committed, stemming from our involvement in the In Defence of Youth Work (IDYW) campaign, born in 2009, whose history is woven into our narrative. In the founding letter the cornerstones of youth work are defined as:

- the primacy of the voluntary relationship, from which the young person can withdraw without compulsion or sanction;
- a commitment to a critical dialogue, to the creation of informal educational opportunities starting from young people's agendas;
- the need to work with and encourage the growth of young people's own autonomous networks,

recognising the significance of class, gender, race, sexuality, disability and faith in shaping their choices and opportunities;
- the importance of valuing and attending to their here-and-now as well as to their 'transitions';
- the nurturing of a self-conscious democratic practice, tipping balances of power in young people's favour;
- the essential significance of the youth workers themselves, whose outlook, integrity and autonomy is at the heart of fashioning a serious yet humorous, improvisatory yet rehearsed educational practice with young people.

Inimical to the neoliberal desire for certainty, IDYW extols a practice that is 'volatile and voluntary, creative and collective – an association and conversation without guarantees' (IDYW, 2009).

NEOLIBERALISM

Neoliberalism appeared on the world stage during the 1970s, a conscious and collective political project to restore the power of the ruling class in the face of post-1945 working-class organisation and the impact of Keynesian economics. Dressed as Thatcherism in the UK, neoliberalism offered the leading role in the dramatic overturn of the social-democratic settlement to the City of London and finance capital. Its watchwords were liberalise, privatise and financialise. It sought to free the market from regulation and particularly trade union influence; to privatise public services, shrinking the welfare state; and, contrary to Shylock, it advised, 'a borrower and a lender be', drawing companies, banks and individuals into a speculative casino capitalism, the hoi polloi playing their part via credit cards, loans and mortgages. At the height of its success it presided over an astonishing development of information technology, whilst restoring levels of inequality close to those of the early 20th century. Its bubble was punctured in 2007–8 by a global banking crisis, amid a criminal excess of exposed and hidden debt. To survive, neoliberalism broke its own rules, bailing out private banks with public money. Meanwhile it has imposed austerity upon its citizens, cutting benefits and keeping wages stagnant, whilst saddling the younger generation with either zero-hour contracts or substantial student loans. The 'invisible hand' of the market has created the precarious society (Mason, 2015).

Neoliberalism seems a broken economic model. However, its ideology, the values and ideas it has promoted across three decades, remains hegemonic, the common-sense of our age (Hall and O'Shea, 2013). Few remain untouched by a behavioural modification project conducted on the grandest scale, the manufacturing of a possessive and self-centred, satisfied yet never satiated consumer for whom a notion of the common good is almost blasphemous. Individuals are forced to deal with the social problems outsourced by the state – of poverty, health, housing and indeed education. As for the last of these, neoliberal ideology is instrumental and reductive, deeply suspicious of critical thinking. Teachers teach to test, lecturers cram consumers and, as we shall see, youth workers are led by outcomes.

YOUTH WORK

Our starting point is that youth work is a contested ideological and pedagogical arena – a clash played out differently across the globe with specific circumstances determining the significance of differing paradigms of practice. Thus this paper will explore the tensions between informal and non-formal interpretations of youth work, especially as the latter assumes increasing importance in England. In this context the IDYW definition of youth work represents a compelling strand in a pluralist tapestry of predominantly informal education within the UK as a whole, summed up as follows:

> For those involved in doing it, whether voluntary or paid, whatever their ideological differences, there has long been a consensus. It ought to be founded on a voluntary engagement with young people in their leisure time. (IDYW, 2011: 2)

The basis of this agreement lies in 'the indigenous tradition' of the early 19th-century working class seeking to educate itself through, for example, Sunday Schools, both secular and religious. As the state took more responsibility for mass education this self-help activity was overtaken by late 19th- and 20th-century forms of 'provided' youth leadership, shaped by a largely conformist, Christian, character-building approach, focused on young people's welfare and their acceptance of prevailing societal norms. Yet, from the beginning, compulsory attendance was seen as an anathema; getting to know the young boy and girl as individuals was vital; members' self-government was encouraged; and the peer group, even the street gang, was accepted as 'in some sense the school for the poor' (Davies, 2009: 71–72).

At first glance this hierarchical 're-moralising' and 'child-saving' tradition may seem to have little in common with the IDYW politicised 'horizontal' conception of youth work. Yet a closer examination reveals a genuine continuity between the defining features of that early practice and IDYW's cornerstones. Both assert free-willed engagement, respect for young people's terms and the nurturing of authentic involvement – commitments underpinning a legacy of religious and humanist youth work at odds with neoliberalism's soulless functionalism. It is a tradition which continues to embrace Josephine Brew's questions about its purpose, 'how can the desire for truth be awakened, the love of beauty stimulated, the passion for righteousness quickened?' (1943: 6), and her prescient concern that 'a youth leader must try not to be too concerned about results' (1957: 183).

FROM SOCIAL DEMOCRACY TO NEOLIBERALISM

To understand the remarkable volte-face in both provision and ideology over the last three decades we need a sharp sense of what went before. The voluntary youth organisations created by the 19th-century pioneers continued to be the dominant providers through to 1939 – until wartime conditions persuaded state policy-makers that, in partnership with them, they needed to create a 'Service of Youth'. With weak legislative recognition in the 1944 Education Act, this was far from fully integrated into the UK's social democratic welfare state settlement. Facing extinction it was given fresh life by the 1960 Albemarle Report, which brought increased funding, a major building programme, a doubling of the full-time workforce and nationally recognised training, qualifications, salaries and conditions for workers.

Among the key features of post-Albemarle youth work were:

- a commitment to a distinctive, process-led social education whose rhythm was determined ultimately by the young person;

- a belief in the virtue of association, caught in Albemarle's edict that nurturing 'young people to come together into groups of their own choosing is the fundamental task of the Service' (Ministry of Education, 1960: 52);
- an acceptance of the autonomy and integrity of the professional worker – 'the first adult not to be an authority figure';
- whilst classically concerned with a young person's character, a move away from inculcating social conformity to facilitating both self and social awareness;
- a ringing endorsement of the centrality of young people's voluntary participation 'because it introduces adult freedom and choice' (Ministry of Education, 1960: 10).

Following the publication of the Milson-Fairbairn Report (1969), many local Youth Services rebadged themselves as Youth and Community Services, often without embracing the radical forms of 'critical involvement of young people in their community' it advocated. More influential in politicising youth work were activists from contemporary social movements whose interventions led to

- a recognition that young people were heterogeneous, social individuals, their age being qualified by the interaction of their class, gender, race, sexuality, disability and faith;
- autonomous work with young people centred on their experience of oppression and exploitation.

However, all was not harmony and light, particularly as the journey from social democracy to neoliberalism was no overnight affair. Across the 1980s, as neoliberalism strengthened its grip nationally, social democracy hung on locally through 'municipal socialist' councils, where a radicalised youth work sought refuge. In parallel, many within both the statutory and voluntary organisations, sceptical about the 'anti-oppressive and anti-discriminatory' agenda, discovered that even their mix of character-building and person-centred practice was viewed with suspicion. As this retreat unfolded, youth work's often naive analysis of the state was exposed, with calls for increased government intervention to resolve its marginality backfiring.

If youth workers believed that a Labour government's election in 1997 would change their fortunes, they were misled. Under Blair the social-democratic party embraced neoliberalism, introducing 'performance measures' requiring local Youth Services to 'reach' 25% of their 13–19-year-old age group, with 60% expected to achieve an 'accredited outcome' (DfES, 2002: 16). Youth work's integration into multi-disciplinary teams dominated by child-protection concerns weakened its educational commitment, as did policies developed ever more systematically to prioritise 'early intervention' and the 'targeting' of young people 'at risk'. Increasingly youth workers saddled with caseloads of referred young people described their practice as 'social work lite'. As the shallow roots of the 1980s' anti-oppressive practice were unearthed, a so-called 'Prevent' strategy demonised all Muslim young people, pressurising youth workers, amongst others, to report signs of an ill-defined un-British 'extremism' (Mohammed and Siddiqui, 2013). More broadly, surveillance of young people's activity became an accepted norm (de St Croix, 2016).

Implicitly or explicitly, informal youth work was judged to be antagonistic to this instrumental project, voluntary engagement with young people defined as inherently out of control. As central government cut its financial support for local authorities by some 40%, between 2012 and 2016 over 600 youth centres were closed, 139,000 youth service places lost and some 3,660 youth worker jobs abolished (Unison, 2016). A survey of three thousand community and voluntary sector workers found that 5% had more than four jobs at a time, 9% were on zero hour contracts and 24% did not receive the living wage (Unison, 2014). The part-time youth workforce, considered under social democracy 'the lifeblood of the Youth Service', was reduced to permanent precarity, standard short-term contracts often assuming workers would register as self-employed. Faced with this turbulence many local authorities sought to pass the buck by outsourcing their responsibilities to local community groups, pretending an emergent wave of volunteers would replace 'disappeared' paid and trained staff.

The Conservative government's intention to recast informal youth work in its own image is symbolised by the launch of a National Citizen Service (NCS). Aimed at 15–17-year-olds, this comprises an unremarkable month-long programme of team-building and volunteering kicked off by a residential outdoor activities week. In 2014–15, on a budget of £140 million the take-up was just 58,000, compared with the up to a million young people sampling or regularly using local Youth Service provision (NCVYS, 2013). Crucially, NCS replaced this open access, year-long informal youth work with a time-limited non-formal practice infected by neoliberal assumptions. Marketed as a 'once in a lifetime opportunity' with an advertising budget in 2015 of £8 million, delivery contracts were awarded only to private and voluntary organisations. Spurious 'monetised' claims about its outcomes suggested its social return was worth almost three times its cost (de St Croix, 2016). In the real world its participants, lauded as NCS graduates, found that with the collapse of the Youth Service infrastructure a dead end was often reached. Yet, ignoring both youth work's long-standing pressure to strengthen those services' legislative basis and its own declared anti-statism, the Conservative government introduced in 2016 legislation requiring local authorities, schools and other state bodies to promote a programme, failing palpably to meet its targets. In the teeth of the evidence £1.2 billion was set aside to fund NCS through to 2020 – more than enough to restore the previous five years' cuts to open access youth work provision.

In common with much of the so-called Third Sector, national voluntary youth organisations such as the National Youth Agency (NYA), the National Council for Voluntary Youth Services (NCVYS) and UK Youth, increasingly compromised their independence by acting, largely uncritically, as agents delivering government policies like NCS and by allying themselves with global corporations tainted by seriously flawed ethical records, such as Serco, G4S and Barclays Bank (Davies, 2014). As part of this process of recuperation, and fearful for their futures, they were prominent in redefining youth work as any form of practice with young people for which funding could be achieved. Ironically, the long-standing NCVYS, formerly the voluntary youth sector's independent voice, ceased to exist, merging with AMBITION, the former National Association of Boys' Clubs, only for this fledgling organisation to be assimilated into UK Youth, which consolidated its role as the corporate conduit for neoliberal assumptions into practice.

In stark contrast to the social-democratic youth work summarised earlier, key features of the neoliberal state's malevolent equivalent include:

- the imposition of prescribed outcomes on targeted groups via structured, time-limited initiatives and the conscious uncoupling of youth work from the Department of Education (Jeffs, 2015);
- a deep distrust of young people's own peer groups;
- a stress on the worker as entrepreneur, 'inspiring young people with dreams of "making it"' (de St Croix, 2016: 31).
- whilst classically concerned with the character of the young person, an explicit return to inculcating social conformity;
- a loss of faith in the voluntary relationship on the premise that as young people make poor choices their options are better predetermined;
- a depoliticisation of practice, a return to a generalised notion of young people;
- a desire to limit participation to agreed formal channels, reduce social action to volunteering and suppress direct political activity.

FROM PROCESS TO OUTCOMES

Whilst neoliberalism's influence on youth work globally is by no means uniform, revealing itself most visibly via the privatisation and

outsourcing of provision, in England it might be summed up in one managerialist word, uttered thrice, which has rendered doubt heretical, 'outcomes, outcomes, outcomes'. Outcomes-based management (OBM) is a neoliberal concoction that is only a couple of decades old, its *raison d'être* being supposedly to measure the efficient use of funding in meeting identified targets. OBM has been utilised to marketise both the public and voluntary sectors and to discipline the workforce, distorting the endeavours of practitioners across education, welfare, health and even the police (Lowe, 2013). It seems ill-suited to the fragile, yet fertile world of process-led, young-people-centred youth work.

Undaunted, within English youth work, the Catalyst consortium, led by the now defunct NCVYS, supported by the NYA and the Young Foundation (YF) harboured no doubts. It announced a commitment to strengthen the youth sector market to work in partnership with government and to establish a social finance retailer, charged with promoting a specific social investment approach based on evidence of impact (Young Foundation, 2012).

This opportunistic embrace of neoliberal tenets is expressed in the ideologically-laden advice espoused in the 2013 NYA publication, *The Future for Outcomes*. Before a young person even meets a youth worker, a project is advised to define its audience, agree the evidence needed and select accordingly from its portfolio of outcomes, all with an eye on the competition. Prioritising the collection of the right data is seen as crucial to surviving and perhaps prospering in a world of commissioning and payment-by-results. In this way the market is forced into the very soul of youth work. Young people are commodified, becoming no more than objects, bearers of 'data for exchange'.

The basis of the influential YF's Framework of Outcomes for Work with Young People (McNeil et al., 2012) is a matrix of social and emotional capabilities: communication, managing feelings, resilience and determination, creativity, relationships and leadership, planning and problem solving, and confidence and agency. None break new ground, although the absence of any reference to sexuality is staggering, any reference to collective political activity less so. The YF argues that these outcomes can be measured and compared via a range of recommended tests, such as the Life Effectiveness Questionnaire, the goal being to convince workers and managers of the objective, robust and rigorous nature of the outcome-led enterprise.

The claim however does not stand up to scrutiny.

- The meaning of any outcome for a young person can only be understood in relation to the totality of their lives, the complexity of influences upon their existence.
- An outcome cannot be the property of a youth worker or agency. By its very social nature an outcome is the product of multiple causality.
- Contrary to the YF's assertion, capabilities do not become straightforwardly an integral part of a young person's character. Confidence, for example, ebbs and flows, waxes and wanes and is often situation-specific.
- The process of worker and young person getting to know each other cannot be presumptuously packaged. It is organic in its authenticity, fully aware of its limitations.
- To prescribe outcomes is to stifle the improvised and creative character of practice, which can produce unforeseen outcomes, initially never imagined by any of the participants.
- The world of desired outcomes and demanded data cannot bear failure.
- Increasingly, collecting of the data means monitoring a worker's performance, seductive in its simplicity for management.
- The need to meet targets and outcomes leads managers and workers into 'gaming', falsifying the figures – a systemic dilemma.

Underpinning the pursuit of outcomes and the data gathering is the fashionable construct, a theory of change (Anderson, 2005), whereby a project establishes its long-term goal, before 'mapping backwards' to identify the outcomes necessary to realising that aim. The YF makes plain its goal – to produce the 'emotionally resilient' young individual who,

through the planned interventions of youth workers, will shrug their shoulders at adversity. Utterly in tune with neoliberal policy, this manufactured individual will need public services less and will be willing to work for whatever wages, zero-hour contracts or indeed benefits are on offer. Nowhere does the alleged theory acknowledge that to talk of change demands a serious engagement with the social and political circumstances underpinning young people's lives (Taylor and Taylor, 2013).

YOUTH DEVELOPMENT: FRIEND OR FOE?

The vehicle for this fundamental shift in philosophy is youth development. Noting its growing influence a decade ago, Jeffs and Smith (2008) illustrated its congruence with the increasing emphasis on 'managing transitions' and the need to address through positive activities and pre-determined programmes recalcitrant youth. They suggested that the development approach favours formation rather than education, being 'less open-ended and more oriented to delivering a message' (Jeffs and Smith, 2008: 288); or, in the light of our critique of outcomes, the delivery of an approved type of young person.

Little has been written from the point of view of those practising youth development in England, although, for example, in the USA and the Commonwealth, it is a major and respected presence with its own conflicting interpretations of problematic versus positive adolescent development (Walker and Dunham, 1994). Given English youth work's suspicion of adolescent psychology, the model was introduced, often without being named as such, by management and consultants, arguing that it brought much-needed order to a practice perceived to be unruly and rudderless. Stuart and Maynard (2015) echo this prejudice in the first serious definition to appear, proposing that, rooted in non-formal learning and education, youth development is a structured and planned intervention into young people's lives with identified and intended measurable outcomes. It can for them be shown to be robust and rigorous in both theory and practice. Whilst rooted in informal learning and education, youth work is then no more than unintentional learning, having little need for an educator or for preparation. Given a failure to evidence achievement, youth work is less than fit for purpose.

Davies, Taylor and Thompson (2016) refute this assertion. They argue that Stuart and Maynard fail to recognise the central role played in youth work as informal education by the purposeful, improvisatory and reflective practitioner, who relates to individuals and groups at a pace appropriate to both changing needs and shifting circumstances. The areas of intervention pursued by youth development in England – employability, challenging anti-social behaviour, developing well-being, engagement in social action – do not result from dialogue with young people but are imposed categories linked to neoliberal funding streams and stuffed full of contradictions. Thus, does challenging anti-social behaviour include opposing the profoundly anti-social policies of a neoliberal government waging a 'war on youth'? Their proffered olive branch from the informal to the non-formal is that both youth work and youth development need to be self-critical, supportive friends rather than hostile rivals.

EMPOWERMENT AND PARTICIPATION

Empowerment was introduced into the English vocabulary of youth and community work by activists involved in the social movements of the 1970s. Explicitly it rejected the idea that the more powerful could empower the less powerful; that the youth worker could empower young people. Whilst the youth worker could seek to facilitate, the acid test was whether young people, typically in

those days, young women or black young people, started to organise autonomously and collectively. Today's overwhelming neoliberal emphasis on 'empowering' individuals from above masks the structural inequalities which restrict most young people's choices. Empowerment reduced to the gaining of self-confidence feeds into a neoliberal diet of possessive individualism.

Empowerment's contemporary bed-fellow is participation. The desire to involve young people dates from youth work's origins. In the era of social democracy Albemarle proclaimed that young people should be the 'fourth partner' in running the Youth Service, a plea mostly honoured in the breach. Under neoliberalism youth participation is close to being a tyrannical orthodoxy (Farthing, 2012) – expected to provide young people with the social skills necessary to compete in a labour market where the odds are stacked against them and to restore their faith in a representative democracy revealed increasingly as corrupt and unaccountable. Young people are asked to contribute to improving the 'doing more with less' efficiency of public services, to 'youth-proofing' government policy. Specialist teams such as Young Advisors are now employed as trained young consultants, commissioned to help organisations and local services improve their products and delivery, to make them more young people friendly (Sheffield Young Advisors, undated). In this form participation is commodified, narrowed to the input of young entrepreneurs selling themselves as the voice of young people.

Participation is dressed up also in the garb of volunteering and social action, exemplified by the charity, Step up to Serve, founded in 2013. From the perspectives of social democracy and neoliberalism, volunteering and social action emerge as very different phenomena. In the past individuals and groups volunteered out of a sense of duty and concern about the common good. Social action born of the 1970s was a collective, agitational and politicised practice undertaken by and for communities seeking to change their circumstances (Harrison, 2014). Under neoliberalism, Step up to Serve argues that social action improves academic outcomes and prepares young people to be successful in the workplace. As Buchroth and Husband maintain, 'young people volunteering has become one of the predominant features of the neoliberal mindset, which regards volunteering as an output with measurable returns' (2015: 107).

TRAINING VERSUS EDUCATION

Inevitably such an ideological transformation has posed increasing dilemmas for the training agencies tasked to produce youth work's professional cadre. Bradford (2015) indicates a move from welfare professionalism under social democracy to performative professionalism under neoliberalism. The former was characterised by a tension between a romantic-humanistic discourse which prioritised personal development and the need for a body of knowledge, conscious of society's underlying power relations. Its informed welfare professional sought to be relatively autonomous and questioning, siding with the young people's agenda. The latter, sceptical both of 'self-actualisation' and critical theory, has sought its legitimacy by embracing competency-based training, which 'privileges *doing* over *knowing* and *practice* over *knowledge*' (Bradford, 2015: 33, italics in original). Its obedient, performative professional accepts monitoring, inspection and control, siding with the State's agenda.

Training often lags behind practice, but increasingly the conflict in the workplace is reflected in academia. On the one hand many lecturers still wish their students to be welfare professionals. The training agencies have largely held to a curriculum inspired by the 1970s and 1980s politicisation of the social-democratic ideology. Humanistic psychology, critical theory and critical pedagogy remain influential, complemented by

the concept of intersectionality (Crenshaw, 1989). This radical tradition continues with contemporary UK-based academics exploring and extending the understanding of youth work as informal education within a socially fraught and divisive context (Batsleer, 2008).

On the other hand, employers, university bureaucrats, an increasing number of lecturers and well-meaning organisations within youth work itself either welcome or see no alternative to the rise of the performative professional. The National Youth Agency's validation of professional courses is premised on the institution's acceptance of the National Occupational Standards (NOS) – a framework reliant on the notion of accepted competencies and prescribed outcomes, which is intended to establish 'comprehensive standards and qualifications frameworks' for assessing youth work in the UK. Inexorably the employer has moved to the centre of the validation process, representing yet another incursion of the market into the culture of Higher Education.

Jeffs and Spence (2008) argue that the impact of modularisation, the increasing fragmentation of knowledge and the fixation with competencies combine to usurp a theoretically informed, argumentative youth worker education. Teaching to predetermined outcomes instrumentalises the relationship between lecturer and student. The latter become 'customers' and the process of learning is redefined as 'knowledge transfer'. As the youth work landscape fractures and the workforce fragments, placements, where informal education is the guiding philosophy, are ever more difficult to find. The rehearsed resolution of this dilemma is that, wherever placed, the student carries with her youth work's values and skills.

Oft neglected amidst the graduate profession's anxieties about its standards and the currency of its qualifications are part-time youth workers. Under social democracy the training of home-grown part-time workers via free, locally delivered and person-centred qualifying courses was responsive to and respectful of their plurality of experience. By the beginning of the 21st century neoliberalism's fixation with performance was in the ascendancy as accredited National Vocational Qualifications (NVQ) in Youth Work were offered by a range of voluntary sector, further education and private providers. Nowadays workers have to take personal responsibility for their training in order to hone their transferable skills as competitors in an insecure jobs market. In common with Higher Education, trainers find themselves torn between the formalistic demands of employers and their commitment to the informal. Perversely, part-time youth work is peopled by workers who are not necessarily trained at all or who are overqualified, possessing graduate and postgraduate degrees but unable to find full-time employment.

FACING CONTRADICTION

Earlier we recognised that our passionate defence of informal youth work was being challenged by both the shifting circumstances and our engagement with differing interpretations of youth work as non-formal education. The demise of the local education authority Youth Service and the rise of targeted work has meant that youth work is described increasingly as occurring in a diversity of settings – social care, schools, even prisons.

Readers from as far apart as North America and Australia can be forgiven for wondering what our fuss is all about. For example, the International Child and Youth Care Education Network states that:

> Professional practitioners promote the optimal development of children, youth and their families in a variety of settings, such as early care and education, community-based child and youth development programs, parent education and family support, school-based programs, community mental health, group homes, residential centers, rehabilitation programs, pediatric health care and juvenile justice programs. (CYC, 2016)

Closer to home our growing involvement in Europe has forced us to acknowledge the diversity of approaches, outlined by Williamson (2015), from self-governed youth organisations under the banner of the European Youth Forum, sometimes explicitly political as in Flanders, to street work in Austria and what are deemed Open Spaces in Lithuania. Stimulated and challenged we have sought to contribute to the European debate through conferences and publications (Davies, 2009). Most directly IDYW has been involved in the emergence of an association of youth workers, the Professional Open Youth Work in Europe (POYWE). However, youth work policies and practices across Europe are not homogeneous but reflect the continent's rich cultural, ethnic, religious, and political heritage and its specific responses to the neoliberal desire 'to formalise the informal' (Coussée, 2012). POYWE negotiates across a range of differing national realities and in a climate of flux, rendering its search for a collective statement of purpose an arduous undertaking.

Within this dialogue IDYW has had to listen and learn, guarding against being seen as the apostle of a 'pure' Anglocentric youth work. Grappling with these differences constructively has led to the launch of both POYWE's practitioner-led online magazine of information and the European Research Network's International Journal of Open Youth Work, notable for its emphasis on collaborative writing. At home we have sought to awaken English youth work to the unifying possibilities present in the European Declaration of Youth Work, which reminds us that 'youth work engages with young people on their terms and on their turf, in response to their expressed and identified needs, in their own space or in spaces created for youth work practice' (2015). Our effort to be outgoing is now suffused with complications, following the Brexit decision to leave the European Union. On the ground, as youth workers, we must engage afresh with both alienated young people from working-class communities 'left behind', who voted to leave, and young people, frustrated with the prospect of diminishing opportunities abroad, who wished to remain. Both groups will be disadvantaged if the ERASMUS+ programme, combining the EU's schemes for education, training, youth and sport, disappears. Uncertainty prevails.

ACCOMMODATION AND RESISTANCE

Throughout this chapter we have been unashamed in owning our critique of neoliberalism and its distortion of youth work policy and practice. It is necessary to reflect, however, on how far this critique is shared by fellow practitioners. Are people accommodating to or resisting the neoliberal imperative?

The uncomfortable truth we hear time and again in IDYW gatherings and Story-telling workshops is that workers, their managers and their national bodies have accommodated, willingly or unwillingly, to greater or lesser extents. Perhaps this is partly because the structured and targeted forms of practice preferred by policy become an attractive option as youth work becomes more precarious, particularly given the challenging nature of open-ended encounters with young people. Other forms of accommodation are more clearly oppressive; with striking frequency, workers tell of senior managers who consciously suppress dissent, transforming the staff meeting from a forum of shared reflection to an exercise in obedience.

Nevertheless, young people and youth workers have demonstrated in support of democratically accountable local authority youth services, embedded local voluntary organisations and valued youth spaces. In 2011 the Choose Youth campaign, an alliance of over thirty civil society organisations, organised a series of rallies, culminating in a major lobby of Parliament. In this national setting and in a diversity of Save our Services groups – from Oxfordshire to Newcastle via Camden – young people have been the creative, driving force, with many youth workers forbidden from involvement. One youth service volunteer interviewed within a research project, one of us led, commented:

At the moment there are a lot of things people are saying you shouldn't do, like protesting for example, 'You shouldn't do this because you're a council employee'. And therefore they have been told if they are caught protesting in work time … then it can be classed as a disciplinary. … So they've been told not to. They've also been told not to tell the young people.

The same research suggested that committed grassroots youth workers, while rarely being involved in overt protest, frequently engaged in 'everyday' forms of resistance – small examples of practising differently, at odds with employers or in ways subversive of dominant practices. For example, an LGBT youth group refused to compromise the young people's privacy and anonymity by implementing local authority requirements to record young people's personal details and outcomes on a database (de St Croix, 2016).

Unexamined in our earlier comments on participation was the government support for formal initiatives such as youth councils and parliaments which mimic the institutions of representative democracy. There are moments when these seem to be utterly compromised, recuperating young people's enthusiasm in the service of a democratic charade. Yet Shukra, Ball and Brown (2012) stress the contradictions of a state, both local and national, which hungers for, yet fears, young people's involvement. Citing the success of a ground-breaking Young Mayor's Project, they suggest a crucial distinction between programmes which see young people as consumers, garnering their consent for the status quo, and initiatives which view young people as creators, as critically conscious agents. The latter constitute embryo forms of defiance.

The era we are analysing has also witnessed a revival of faith-based youth work, not surprising given neoliberalism's moral amnesia. Within its diversity flows a significant radical Christian current articulating a commitment to the oppressed and to the common good (Pimlott, 2015). For Bright and Bailey (2015: 157) this involves developing 'a social ethic, which transcends the rigid and performative prescriptions of contemporary social and policy frameworks and which re-elevates the humanity of relationships and relatedness'. Tellingly they are critical of the danger under neoliberalism of ethical concerns being divorced from politics, ending up as rigid rule-books rather than flexible frameworks for practice. At the 2015 IDYW conference on the relationship between faith and secular youth work, Muslim, Christian and atheist contributors all spoke of the need to resist neoliberalism's undermining of relational practice.

The turmoil of cuts and closures has led to the emergence of local autonomous youth projects initiated often by redundant youth workers drawing upon a variety of funding streams and grasping the nettle of social enterprise whilst seeking to maintain their independence. Amidst controversy and suspicion, different ways of organising youth provision surface as councils slash budgets. Mutuals and charitable foundations have appeared, with the Third Sector assuming a more prominent role, whilst some local councils – Nottinghamshire and Ealing in London – have maintained their state-funded youth services. In short, a new social economy of youth work is coming to pass, which, though little researched and riven with contradictions, potentially contains opportunities for re-imagining our work with young people.

We would be playing coy if we did not suggest with some humility that resistance to the pervasiveness of neoliberalism demands the creation of something like IDYW. A fragile venture, counting on the labour of the few, it has nonetheless been a collective reference point for many. Our seminars and conferences provide rare opportunities for workers to reflect upon practice, whilst our blog and Facebook page, followed by thousands, offers a continuity of information and argument. Indeed our presence on social media has woken us to the collective possibility, alongside the 'networked' young person, of nurturing the 'networked' youth worker in the struggle against neoliberalism (Mason, 2015).

On more traditional ground we have failed so far to develop the chain of local and regional IDYW groups that would strengthen immeasurably our efforts. More optimistically our Story-telling project provides a locus of resistance to the 'tick-box', often fake objective claims of the Outcomes fetishists. Building on the centrality of conversation in the youth work process, workshops committed to creating a subjective, qualitative and comparable appreciation of the distinctiveness of informal youth work have been held in the UK, Ireland, Finland, Kazakhstan and Argentina. In parallel a web resource has been created, drawing together the lessons from this collective undertaking, supported by partial translations of its contents into Russian, Kazakh, Finnish, Spanish and Japanese (IDYW, 2014).

CONCLUSION

Using England and IDYW as intertwined case studies, we have tried to communicate our heartfelt concern about the continuing detrimental influence of neoliberalism on youth work and wider practice with young people. We are cautious about claiming that practitioners elsewhere in the world should learn lessons from our experience. Nonetheless we hope our thoughts will resonate with people's experience, and will be taken up and criticised in a burgeoning international debate.

A neoliberal way of seeing the world has so insinuated itself into our psyches that it is experienced as being the natural order of affairs. It is nigh impossible to underestimate neoliberalism's ability to recuperate our alternative discourse. Thus, within youth work the idea of equality is no longer about the struggle for a social outcome in the interests of all, but about equality of opportunity for individuals to compete in the marketplace. To take another example, the Centre for Youth Impact in England talks of youth work achieving 'collective impact', which when stripped of its conceit, means no more or less than working together to achieve agreed goals, albeit with neoliberal 'mission-driven' consultants on hand to measure performance (Kania and Kramer, 2011). In the absence of critique, 'collective impact' is likely to become the fashionable vehicle for 'thought-less action' (Ledwith, 2007) and continued appeals to be 'pragmatically principled'.

Within youth work we cannot give any more ground to an economics and ideology which doesn't give a shit (Mason, 2016), to the denial of access to alternative understand-ings of the world. We need to renew an open and pluralist form of youth work, both infor-mal and non-formal, within which a radical and reflective practice prospers. To do so will be to paddle against the current, requiring the renaissance of that collective spirit despised by neoliberalism. In a limited way as IDYW we have sought to do this in the English and UK context by building links across education and welfare through such bodies as Choose Youth, the Training Agencies Group, the Social Work Action Network and Positive Youth Justice, organisations of workers in youth work, higher education, social work and juvenile justice. It demands also that we remain in criti-cal dialogue with key players in the English youth sector like the aforementioned Cabinet-Office-funded Centre for Youth Impact, lest we be consigned utterly to the margins.

Of course, too, it means that the perspec-tive outlined in this chapter has to be open to criticism. Within our own ranks dissenting voices chastise us for not buying into youth work as a special set of values and skills and for exaggerating the import of the volun-tary principle. As for the former we dispute the claim that youth work possesses a dis-crete set of corporate values and skills. The insistence on this, the implication that youth workers get social justice or practise empa-thy in ways unbeknown to other profession-als, is counterproductive and an expression of an historic inferiority complex. As to the latter, our defence of the voluntary principle has led authors, normally sympathetic to our views, to suggest that the notion is a pervasive

'hidden unknown', a taken-for-granted, even a destructive force, limiting youth work's potential scope and impact. Taking us to task, they suggest we are grieving for the loss of the established meaning of our practice. Using the example of youth work in schools, claiming to follow Giroux (2005), they argue for a bor-der pedagogy which helps youth workers to reconceptualise their practice and forge 'new ways of knowing' (Coburn and Gormally, 2015: 212) – or perhaps helps rationalise their required presence in other agencies?

This is no abstract disagreement. It sym-bolises the tensions dominating English youth work and beyond. In taking up these criticisms we will attempt to end our analy-sis on a hopeful note. We read Giroux's call for a 'borderless' pedagogy as being in tune with our interpretation of the relationship between youth work and the wider worlds of education and welfare across the globe. Our starting point is not youth work per se. It is a radical educational praxis, often described as critical pedagogy, which does not belong to any particular profession or institution. At heart it is about the struggle for authentic democracy, about the continued question-ing of received assumptions. It is obliged to oppose neoliberal capitalism. Educators committed to this radical praxis do so in a diversity of settings, under differing con-straints and across the board.

Youth work is one such setting whose character, not some pretentious argument about the exceptional understandings of its workforce, is its distinctive feature. As neo-liberalism assaults critical thinking wher-ever it rears its cussed head, it has no time for an argumentative youth work. It has used English youth work as a laboratory to test out how to silence and incorporate the radi-cal and liberal traditions of autonomous work with young people. Our duty is to refuse to be silenced and incorporated. Our desire is to resuscitate our collective imagination and autonomy. We hope this chapter is a contribu-tion to that struggle, both within and without of youth work.

REFERENCES

Anderson, A. (2005) *The Community Builder's Approach to Theory of Change: A Practical Guide to Theory and Development*. New York: The Aspen Institute Roundtable on Community Change.

Batsleer, J. (2008) *Informal Learning*. London: Sage.

Bradford, S. (2015) 'State beneficence or government control?', in G. Bright (ed.) *Youth Work: Histories, Policy and Contexts*. London: Palgrave Macmillan.

Brew, J.M. (1943) *In the Service of Youth*. London: Faber and Faber.

Brew, J.M. (1957) *Youth and Youth Groups*. London: Faber & Faber.

Bright, G. and Bailey, D. (2015) 'Youth work and the church', in G. Bright (ed.) *Youth Work: Histories, Policy and Contexts*. London: Palgrave Macmillan.

Buchroth, I. and Husband, M. (2015) 'Youth work in the voluntary sector', in G. Bright (ed.) *Youth Work: Histories, Policy and Contexts*. London: Palgrave Macmillan.

Coburn, A. and Gormally, S. (2015) 'Youth work in schools', in G. Bright (ed.) *Youth Work: Histories, Policy and Contexts*. London: Palgrave Macmillan.

Coussée, F. (2012) 'Historical and intercultural consciousness in youth work and youth policy – a double odyssey', in F. Coussée, H. Williamson and G. Verschelden (eds) *The History of Youth Work in Europe, Volume 3*. Strasbourg: Council of Europe.

Crenshaw, K. (1989) 'Demarginalizing the intersection of race and sex: A black feminist critique of antidiscrimination doctrine, feminist theory and antiracist politics', *The University of Chicago Legal Forum*, 140: 139–167.

CYC (Child and Youth Care Education Network) (2016) 'The profession: Definitions', http://www.cyc-net.org/profession/pro-definitions.html

Davies, B. (2009) 'Defined by history: Youth work in the UK', in G. Verschelden et al. (eds) *The History of Youth Work in Europe: Relevance for Youth Policy Today*. Strasbourg: Council of Europe.

Davies, B. (2014) 'Independence at risk: The state, the market and the voluntary youth sector', *Youth & Policy*, 112: 111–122.

Davies, B., Taylor, T. and Thompson, N. (2015) 'Informal education, youth work and youth development', *Youth & Policy*, 115: 85–86.

de St Croix, T. (2016) *Grassroots Youth Work: Policy, Passion and Resistance in Practice*. Bristol: Policy Press.

Declaration of the 2nd European Youth Work Convention (2015) http://pjp-eu.coe.int/documents/1017981/8529155/The+2nd+European+Youth+Work+Declaration_FINAL.pdf/cc602b1d-6efc-46d9-80ec-5ca57c35eb85

DfES (Department for Education and Skills) (2002) *Transforming Youth Work: Resourcing Excellent Youth Services*. London: DfES/Connexions.

Farthing, R. (2012) 'Why youth participation? Some justifications and critiques of youth participation using New Labour's youth policies as a case study', *Youth & Policy*, 109: 71–97.

Giroux, H. (2005) *Border Crossings*. Abingdon, Oxon: Routledge.

Hall, S. and O' Shea, A. (2013) 'Common-sense neoliberalism' in S. Hall et al. (eds) *After NeoLiberalism?* London: Soundings.

Harrison, M. (2014) Social Action – *Co-creating Social Change: A Companion for Practitioners*, http://socialaction.info/docs/social_action_co_creating_social_change.pdf.

IDYW (In Defence of Youth Work) (2009) 'The open letter', In Defence of Youth Work website, http://indefenceofyouthwork.com/the-in-defence-of-youth-work-letter-2/

IDYW (In Defence of Youth Work) (2011) *This is Youth Work: Stories from Practice*, London: Unison, http://indefenceofyouthwork.com/the-stories-project/

IDYW (In Defence of Youth Work) (2014) 'Story-telling in youth work', https://story-tellinginyouthwork.com

Jeffs, T. (2015) 'Innovation and youth work', *Youth & Policy*, 114: 75–95.

Jeffs, T. and Smith, M. (2008) 'Valuing youth work', *Youth & Policy*, 100: 277–302.

Jeffs, T. and Spence, J. (2008) 'Farewell to all that? The uncertain future of youth and community work education', *Youth & Policy*, 97/98: 135–166.

Kania, J. and Kramer, M. (2011) 'Collective impact', *Stanford Social Innovation Review*, Winter, 9(1), https://ssir.org/articles/entry/collective_impact

Jeffs, T. and Smith, M. (2008) 'Valuing Youth Work', *Youth & Policy*, 100: 277–302.

Ledwith, M. (2007) 'Reclaiming the radical agenda', *Concept*, 17(2): 8–12.

Lowe, T. (2013) 'The paradox of outcomes: The more we measure, the less we understand', *Public Money & Management*, 33(3): 213–216.

Mason, P. (2015) *PostCapitalism: A Guide to our Future*. London: Allen Lane.

Mason, P. (2016) 'Steel crisis: They do not give a shit', https://medium.com/mosquito-ridge/steel-crisis-they-do-not-give-a-shit-86516750a1e0#.4ohfydwja

McNeil, B., Reeder, N. and Rich, J. (2012) *A Framework of Outcomes for Young People*. London: Young Foundation.

Milson-Fairbairn Report (1969) *Youth and Community Work in the 70s*. London: HMSO.

Ministry of Education (1960) *The Youth Service in England and Wales*. London: HMSO.

Mohammed, J. and Siddiqui, A. (2013) *The Prevent Strategy: A Cradle to Grave Police State*. London: CAGE, http://www.cageuk.org/wp-content/uploads/A4_PREVENT_CAGE_REPORT_WEB.pdf

NCVYS (2013) *Youth Report 2013*. NCVYS, http://www.ncvys.org.uk/sites/default/files/Youth%20Report%202013v2.pdf

NYA (2013) *The Future for Outcomes: A Practical Guide to Measuring Outcomes for Young People*. Leicester: NYA.

Pimlott, N. (2015) *Embracing the Passion: Christian Youth Work and Politics*. London: SCM Press.

Sheffield Young Advisors (undated), http://sheffield.youngadvisors.org.uk/

Shukra, K., Ball, M. and Brown, K. (2012) 'Participation and activism: young people shaping their worlds'. *Youth & Policy*, 108: 36–54.

Step up to Serve (undated) 'Making a case: Creating a double benefit through youth social action', http://www.iwill.org.uk/about-us/making-the-case/

Stuart, K. and Maynard, L. (2015) 'Non-formal youth development and its impact on young people's lives: Case study – Brathay Trust, UK', *Italian Journal of Sociology of Education*, 7(1): 231–262.

Taylor, T. and Taylor, M. (2013) *Threatening Youth Work: The Illusion of Outcomes*, https://indefenceofyouthwork.files.wordpress.com/2009/05/threatening-yw-and-illusion-final.pdf

Unison (2014) *Community and Voluntary Services in the Age of Austerity: Unison Voices from the Frontline*. London: Unison.

Unison (2016) *The Damage – a Future at Risk: Cuts in Youth Services*. London: Unison.

Walker, J. and Dunham, T. (1994) *Understanding Youth Development Work: Center for 4-H Youth Development*, College of Education and Human Ecology. University of Minnesota Extension.

Williamson, H. (2015) 'Finding common ground' http://eryica.org/sites/default/files/FINDING%20COMMON%20GROUND_Final%20lay%20out.pdf

Young Foundation (2012) http://youngfoundation.org/projects/catalyst/

8

Youth Work in England: A Profession with a Future?

Helen M.F. Jones

In 2010 youth work in England[1] joined the range of occupations requiring a university honours degree. In youth work's case this was additional to a professional qualification validated by the National Youth Agency (NYA) and recognised by the Joint Negotiating Committee (JNC).[2] The requirement for an honours degree added to youth work's status as a profession and set it alongside other graduate jobs such as school teaching and social work. At the same time, other initiatives towards professionalisation were made. In 2013 the Institute of Youth Work (IYW) was established purporting to offer 'a voice in the changing times our sector has and will continue to experience', continued professional development opportunities and a variety of resources. These include the Code of Ethics that 'demonstrates a set of principles and standards of practice and behaviour [which] will indicate to prospective employers the high standards to which members operate' (IYW, 2014). This chapter considers the implications of these moves towards professionalising youth work in England. Is youth work a profession? What qualifications should be required? Where should the funds come from? Should youth workers be paid by the state or should youth work be located in the voluntary sector?[3] Is there an inherent contradiction in a 'profession' that emphasises its informality alongside its educational foundations? Is it possible to predict the future? England's situation today may present some salutary lessons for other nations: a series of missed opportunities and abandoned policies have left most young people with few opportunities to engage with youth workers. Despite the profession's hard won status, its long-term future is in some doubt.

IS YOUTH WORK A PROFESSION?

Youth work has just been described as a profession, but is it actually a *profession* rather than an *occupation*? There are nuanced debates around precisely what constitutes a 'profession'. Many years ago Greenwood explored the attributes of a profession in the context of social work. He identified five: a 'systematic body of theory', 'professional authority', control over training and hence over who enters the profession, a code of ethics and a 'professional culture' (Greenwood, 1957: 45). This last feature might include a professional association and also a belief 'that the service is a social good and that community welfare would be immeasurably impaired by its absence' (Greenwood, 1957: 52).

It could be argued that youth work in England has some – but not all – of the five characteristics. First, there is now a 'body of theory' to inspire and explain practice, as research and literature that explore youth work theory and practice have developed exponentially since the early 1980s. However, secondly, 'professional authority' does not characterise youth workers' engagement. Indeed relationships with young people are successful specifically because the power invested in teachers, social workers, police officers and other professionals is not present. Where youth work crosses into other professional areas, forming hybrid professions, the issue is highlighted. For example, youth workers within schools or youth offending teams may be given authority and obliged to implement rules that have not been negotiated with young people, which can compromise the quality of relationships. Bradford and Byrne (2010) investigated the impact of youth workers situated alongside teachers in schools in Northern Ireland, showing the tensions between teachers' formal and youth workers' informal educational approaches and emphasising differences in resultant relationships. This is epitomised by approaches to names: teachers are addressed formally whilst youth workers are known by first names.

Thirdly, Greenwood listed training and entry to the profession. In England, youth workers study for their professional qualifications at university. These degree-level courses may be pre-service or in-service. This is a topic of complexity that will be revisited

later. Fourthly, during the 1990s, youth work acquired its code of ethics and, more recently, the Institute for Youth Work (IYW). The IYW does not play the regulatory role usually associated with a professional association (IYW, 2014) and its Code of Ethics is – at best – a set of useful guidelines. Its professional development opportunities are not compulsory. As there is no obligation to join the IYA and its register is voluntary, youth work in England does not have 'controlled entry'. Many youth workers have studied at university for professional qualifications, but, once qualified, there is no system of obligatory membership of a register that can be rescinded: youth workers cannot be 'struck off'. Other youth workers have either completed lower-level certificates or not undertaken formal study: their knowledge has been generated by practical experience alone.

The National Youth Agency and the Joint Negotiating Committee play additional roles. The NYA is a charity and is the 'national body for youth work'. Its work includes 'professionalising youth work' which it does through 'training youth workers, setting occupational standards, offering accreditation for professional development and constantly researching, innovating and improving the methodologies and practice of youth work in all its forms' (NYA, 2016b). The Joint Negotiating Committee is responsible for the negotiation of pay and conditions and is discussed later in this chapter.

Youth workers certainly share a belief in the importance of their work. They see the significance of achieving parity of esteem with other professionals working with young people. Several years ago Alan France and Paul Wiles focused on youth workers' embrace of the term 'social education' and observed that it 'was useful in the professional development of youth work because its use of "education" and "curriculum" gave its members entry into the world of professional education and hence higher status' (France and Wiles, 1997: 73). However, in relation to Greenwood's fifth attribute, the nature of the 'professional culture' differs from that of most traditional professions and is best described as radical and socialist (for a developed, albeit partisan, discussion see Nicholls, 2012). This is not new: workers in the late 19th and early 20th centuries championed improved welfare for young workers and supported women's right to vote. Hence youth workers would tend to be uncomfortable with the idea of the professional privilege, power or prestige that characterise traditional professions.

Ronald Barnett has raised questions about professionalism in the public sector. In particular, language has shifted. Nowadays 'efficiency', 'performance indicators', 'standards' and 'smart' management have replaced 'trust', 'integrity', 'commitment' and 'loyalty'. Young people have become 'clients' rather than 'members'. This reflects 'a lurch from an ethic of service to an ethic of performance' (Barnett, 2008: 197). These changes do not sit well with youth workers' internalised values and vision; the old focus on association and working with groups has been replaced by a focus on individuals.

QUALIFICATIONS FOR YOUTH WORK

As indicated, 'professions' require qualifications and those required for youth work have developed gradually. Training courses originally grew out of meetings and discussions. Over a hundred years ago Flora Freeman recommended regular meetings not only to discuss dealing with difficult members but also to inculcate appropriate values amongst the workers (Freeman, 1908). Such meetings gradually evolved into training sessions. Leaders began to develop appropriate theoretical bases for the work. Early pioneers established the importance of empowering young people: for example Maude Stanley believed girls could have formed a committee to 'manage the club entirely alone' if they had had time (Stanley, 1890: 47) and a few years later Baden-Powell delegated power to

senior boys who became 'Patrol Leaders' (Baden-Powell, 1908: 344). This began to establish youth work's ideological foundation as informal education and development rather than welfare: in England social work and youth work evolved as parallel strands of work with different value bases.

During the 1920s and 30s attitudes to the idea of training differed along gendered lines. The National Association of Boys' Clubs (NABC) 'believed that the girls' organisations overemphasised the value of training. The NABC tended towards the view that (male) leadership was a *natural* capacity rather than something achieved through training' (Bradford, 2007: 298). This arguably initiated the anti-intellectualism which has tended to characterise some strands of youth work ever since. Skilled and experienced youth workers can make their expertise appear straightforward, giving rise to the notion in observers that there is nothing to be learnt, whilst those who are unconsciously competent may struggle to put the thinking underpinning their work into words.

By the Second World War youth work had developed considerably and the urgent need to train workers of both genders was highlighted. Unpublished archive documents dating from 1941 concerning the content of training show the development of dual strands of theory (social policy, psychology) and 'club work' (YAGC, 1941). The West Riding Association of Girls' Clubs outlined training opportunities, which brought universities into the picture:

> The full *professional* [my italics] club leaders' training ... takes about two to two and a half years and involves taking the Social Science Certificate or Diploma in a University Social Science Department, and doing at least six months' practical work ... (WRAGC, 1942: 8)

This initiative saw the birth of formalised training for youth work as a profession. In 1942 there were also three-month and six-month Emergency Courses in Youth Leadership in London. A short time afterwards the Ministry of Education approved two courses (one in England and one in Wales), which ran between 1945 and 1960. This expanded to six between 1961 and 1970 (NYA, 2016a). During the 1970s, 80s and 90s the number grew greatly.

By the final decades of the 20th century, school teaching and social work had become university-graduate-status professions in England, requiring practitioners to have honours degrees, which represent three years' university-level study. Holding only their diplomas, which took two years to complete, some youth workers felt that their lesser status was highlighted particularly in agencies where they worked closely with teachers and social workers. Others felt that youth work would be endangered by the conventionality of academia, that imagination and dynamism would be stifled and homogeneity imposed; they believed in using their own instincts and ingenuity rather than studying and risking being domesticated. Arguably these sceptics follow in the footsteps of youth work's pioneers: they too were activists who saw a need and got to work setting up provision. Nonetheless youth work became an honours-degree-level profession in 2010, requiring the equivalent of three years' full-time study rather than the previous two. Some established workers who returned to study to complete their degrees saw the move as very positive. They found that their new knowledge and confidence as graduates could be seen in the quality of their own practice and proved advantageous in dealing with other professionals: nobody regretted their changed status. Interestingly, comparable reservations and experiences affected nursing during the same period (Staines, 2008).

In broad terms, the curriculum has remained consistent since the 1920s, comprising practical work placements in youth settings together with social policy, sociology, psychology and research methods. Courses require students to link theory with practice and vice versa, although, as Mike Seal comments, youth work's professionalism continues to be undermined by its tendency to take an 'anti-intellectual and anti-theoretical stance' (Seal, 2014: 3). Some youth workers do not appreciate the significance and relevance of theory, but a developed understanding of the abstract concepts, ideas and explanations underpinning practice is central for any profession. As Tony Jeffs and Jean Spence point out, practitioners need to be able 'to make their own theory, to engage in critical investigative conversations and construct alternatives to the status quo' (Jeffs and Spence, 2008: 159). University courses have scope to foster rather than stifle creativity.

The total number of courses burgeoned during the late 20th and early 21st centuries but has decreased since 2010. Several reasons could be suggested for this. The bureaucratic demands mentioned above also include the necessity of arranging relevant work placements totalling over 800 hours over the duration of a three-year programme. This is costly in terms of staff time. In addition, youth work students typically reflect local populations in terms of ethnicity, culture and class. Many are 'mature' (aged over 20 on entry). Although some universities value these 'non-traditional' students, there are concomitant issues around retention and progression. In England full-time students are expected to complete their studies in three years. Failure to do so for any reason (for example, caring responsibilities, financial difficulties, domestic problems) reflects poorly on the university and teaching staff. Many students are 'first in family', lacking the cultural capital to deal with unfamiliar educational terminologies and systems. Furthermore, the reduction in the number of jobs for youth workers has led to potential students questioning the wisdom of studying the subject.

Universities delivering professionally accredited courses have to balance various sets of requirements. Documentation has to meet the university's own requirements for validation. Separate documentation also has to meet the requirements set out by the National Youth Agency, which validates courses on behalf of the Joint Negotiating Committee. In 2017 a university's submission for NYA initial validation or revalidation (required every five years) might comprise a 25,000 word document accompanied by an extensive collection of supporting documentation, presenting a considerable administrative challenge. Benchmarks set by the Higher Education Quality Assurance Agency, standards identified in the Professional and National Occupational Standards for Youth Work and the course outcomes identified by the university each have to be met and mapping has to show how course elements meet each. In addition, each year every course has to undertake an annual evaluation using its university's format and also a separate annual monitoring for the NYA. Hence, professional validation generates substantial bureaucratic requirements, which universities are increasingly reluctant to support. The processes can be seen as a guarantee of quality but there are sometimes tensions between the competing institutional and organisational demands.

FUNDING YOUTH WORK AND PAYING WORKERS

A century ago most youth workers were unpaid and the state was scarcely involved in youth work: it was essentially unregulated and relied on volunteers. Over the subsequent period state funding and state involvement burgeoned. For example, in 1941 the Board of Education '[confirmed] its interest in "professional" youth work by holding a conference on training': the wartime environment had shown that 'young people required leaders with something more than "personality" and "natural flair"' (Bradford, 2006: 145). In the second decade of the 21st century, however, the imposition of politically motivated austerity has impacted on funding whilst the state's vision of youth work's purpose has shifted along party political lines, leading to the creation of programmes which reflect politicians'

ideals. Nonetheless the role of finance in the development of the profession of youth work can be traced back to the earliest days.

In the late 19th and early 20th centuries, pioneering workers motivated by a range of welfare-focused, faith-based and philanthropic concerns, engaged with young people. Most clubs were linked to churches, chapels or synagogues, which provided the premises. Some were open to all but others stipulated that members should attend worship. Usually club members paid a small fee each week, covering refreshments. In 1908 Freeman observed that aspirational girls in London were suspicious if they thought that subscriptions were too low: they suspected 'kidding' or 'getting at them for religion' (Freeman, 1908: 12). Public performances, concerts and competitions helped to bring in money, together with donations, subscriptions and appeals. In general the workers were middle class and they were not usually paid. Some men undertook youth work as part of their church ministry whilst others (men and women alike) were independently wealthy or supported by their families. Davies describes work with lads in the 1890s, 'The clubs ... were founded and initially run by middle-class philanthropists, whose motives combined a sense of civic duty with a Christian compassion for the youth of the slums' (Davies, 2008: 339). Maude Stanley however suggested paying 'a superintendent' to work in girls' clubs. She observed that 'large pay [would] not be required' for 'a working woman' taking the position, as she would have paid work elsewhere by day. Astonishingly to 21st-century eyes, she added, 'should the superintendent be a *lady*, [my italics] her salary need not be much more' (Stanley, 1890: 31–32). Although club workers were volunteers, richer clubs (those able to collect higher subscriptions from members) might pay specialist tutors to coach groups singing or doing drill or dance. Whether this was fair when clubs competed against each other was the topic of lively discussion: richer clubs' members might have been trained by skilled tutors.

By the outbreak of the First World War in 1914 there were clubs throughout the UK but provision was uneven and piecemeal as it relied on individuals taking initiatives. Throughout the war (1914–18) clubs attempted to keep running although often members were unable to attend due to working overtime; male club workers had joined the forces, women workers had taken on war work and premises had been commandeered for war purposes. Concerts and competitions were scaled down. Meanwhile there was 'a serious juvenile crime wave' (Davies, 1999: 15) perpetrated by younger teenagers. This served as an impetus for the state to begin to take an interest in providing activities and after the war local authorities were given the go-ahead to establish committees. Such committees were in a position to map provision and encourage groups to start, whereas volunteers could not be corralled to undertake tasks designated by the state.

During the 1920s, 30s and 40s money was channelled from the Ministry for Education to national organisations such the National Association of Boys' Clubs and National Council of Girls' Clubs (NCGC). They in turn channelled funds through their regional offices to local clubs. Most of the work continued to be undertaken by volunteers but government became more interested in ensuring provision was made.

The Second World War (1939–45) encouraged the government to establish work with young people on a still firmer footing. The wartime situation led to large-scale mobility of the population: children were evacuated from cities to the countryside, young adults were frequently employed away from home and people were forced out of their homes by bombing. The UK's streets were unlit at night to deter bombing and this environment had the potential to facilitate crime and anti-social behaviour. Learning from the problems attributed to young people during the First World War, action was taken to provide activities during leisure hours. There was an increase in the number of secular civic youth clubs; more paid full-time youth leaders and part-time workers were recruited hastily. According to one education authority internal document, 'the emphasis was on the quantity of Youth Work rather than quality' and 'grants were being made to clubs without any detailed investigation into the work they were doing' (West Riding Education Authority, 1948). Civic clubs were established in school buildings: the urgency of wartime conditions necessitated quantity rather than quality so workers were not always skilled, able or trained. Associations of mainly church-based youth organisations appointed regional organisers. They visited and supported clubs with a view to raising the quality of practice, setting them apart from the civic programmes.

During the latter stages of the war, preparations were made to build a better nation for peacetime. The final months of the war and the years following saw the establishment of the UK's Welfare State. The population needed a vision of what the future would bring and wanted a more satisfactory outcome than they had experienced after the First World War. Politicians wanted to combat the 'five giants' of 'want, disease, ignorance, squalor and idleness' (Timmins, 2001), in other words: 'poverty, poor health, poor education, poor housing and unemployment'. The Welfare State replaced charitable and voluntary endeavours in many fields: people now had free access to services such as health, education and pensions as a right. Working adults paid National Insurance and provision no longer relied on philanthropic rich people and charity. However, the range of services covered by the Welfare State's statutory responsibilities did not include those for young people outside school. The Youth Service did not become a statutory service because Section 53 of the Education Act (1944) only required each local education authority to 'secure … sufficient educational leisure-time activities which are for the improvement of their well-being, and sufficient facilities for such activities' and also 'sufficient recreational leisure-time facilities'

(Education Board, 1944). This phrasing has been a point of contention ever since and set in place the scope for authorities to justify their provision of little or nothing: the Youth Service was denied a legally binding professional footing. Nonetheless during the later 1940s and 1950s many youth workers were positive.

By this time, paid youth workers staffed civic youth clubs although unpaid volunteers were frequently involved too. The youth workers' trades union, the Community and Youth Workers' Union (CYWU), highlighted the fact that rates of pay and terms and conditions varied across the country and were not consistent with comparable professions (Nicholls, 2012: 112). Many of the paid workers were schoolteachers supplementing their salaries with hourly paid evening work rather than people qualified in youth work. Qualified youth workers questioned the fact that qualified school teachers were *ipso facto* regarded as professionally qualified in terms of youth work. This situation continued for many decades.

In most parts of England three strands of provision emerged. First were long-established uniformed organisations like Scouts and Guides. Secondly, local authorities created youth services including civic youth clubs. Thirdly, older voluntary or third sector organisations began to receive funding from local authorities rather than via national bodies. The West Riding of Yorkshire, in the north of England, did not see a similar peaceful co-existence. Politicians whose belief in the Welfare State was absolute led the County Council. They believed that the state could, should and would provide for young people and 'believed the days of voluntary clubs had ended because a really progressive LEA should have taken all their work over' (Graham, 1947). They were suspicious of the motivation of other organisations including the old girls' clubs and boys' clubs, which were often linked to churches or chapels (Jones, 2014b: 68–69). On the other hand, the local voluntary organisations were proud of their long history of work with local youth

and suspicious of state provision for young people. They cited the Hitler Youth as a terrifying example of the dangers posed by state involvement. It took several years for the generation of leaders on both sides to move on and for equilibrium to result.

The later 1950s marked a turning point. The birth of youth culture alarmed adults who came to regard young people as troubled and troublesome. In 1958 there were riots in London and other English cities when gangs of right-wing white young men attacked people who had recently arrived from the Caribbean. The Government established two committees, which reported in 1960. The Crowther Report focused on teenagers and their formal education whilst the Albemarle Report looked at the teenagers' leisure hours and paid particular attention to 15–21-year-olds (at the time, most young people left school aged 15). The Albemarle Report was of particular significance in the development of professional youth work and concerned workers, premises and approaches. New purpose-built youth centres were constructed around the country: association was at the core of the vision. The centres tended to have a hall for large-scale social events, a coffee bar and kitchen area, a room or two for small group activities and an office. Most centres were staffed by a 'warden' and one or more assistants. These were all jobs for youth workers who also managed the facilities. The era saw a considerable investment in provision for young people outside formal education.

Recommendations in the Albemarle Report and campaigning by the union led to the creation of the Joint Negotiating Committee (JNC) in 1961. The JNC brought together organisations representing workers, trades unions and employers in the public and voluntary sectors to negotiate and establish conditions and rates of pay. The resulting conditions included the total number of hours per week and the fact that no more than ten sessions (a morning, afternoon or evening) should be worked per week. A key aspect was the stipulation that a worker should only work eight evenings per fortnight. The JNC set up separate pay scales for men and women (Nicholls, 2012: 114), arguably disgraceful at a time when equal pay for women was being introduced across the public sector (the civil service had already finished phasing in a single pay scale). Gender pay equality was introduced only gradually. The JNC also took on the role of approving qualifications although it was not an awarding body: it relied on colleges and universities to devise and award the qualifications. Its role in the negotiation of pay and conditions together with its central position in the recognition of qualifying courses contributed to the professionalisation of youth work. Indeed, in terms of the growth of youth work as a profession, the creation of the JNC was a significant development.

During the decades following the Albemarle Report a *modus vivendi* emerged and survived for many years until the early years following the millennium. First, local councils headed large and often over-bureaucratic local authorities, which included Youth Services. These varied considerably in terms of efficiency and vision. Within the public sector there could be a sense of a basic binary division in which state provision was good whilst other providers were viewed with some suspicion. Working for a local authority provided the security of JNC terms and conditions but some stuff found that the bureaucracy stifled innovation and initiative. For example, a youth worker and young people with a news story might need to contact line management who would involve a local authority's publicity department rather than making direct contact with a local newspaper. Many professionally qualified youth workers acted as centre wardens and the management of decaying premises could be time-consuming and draining. Expertise in working with young people did not necessarily correlate with expertise in managing buildings.

Secondly, voluntary (third sector) organisations sometimes employ paid workers. These include churches and other religious bodies. In addition, national charities such as the National Society for the Prevention of Cruelty to Children (NSPCC), Barnardo's and the Terrence Higgins Trust bring paid and unpaid workers together in projects. Smaller local projects seek grant aid from a range of state and other sources and employ paid and unpaid workers. Some voluntary sector organisations choose to use JNC terms and conditions. Organisations' funding came – and comes – from a range of sources that are frequently short term. Such sources may be seen as having both positive and negative aspects. The temporary nature of many funding streams removes the element of continuity, which has been shown to be an important dimension for young people (Jones, 2014a: 222) and may tempt organisations to adapt their work to fit the funding. Thirdly, traditional uniformed youth organisations are supported by small staff teams in national offices and rely on large numbers of unpaid volunteers at local level – a situation which is ongoing.

Since the millennium, local authorities have moved away from JNC terms and conditions and implemented 'single status agreements'. These aim to employ all employees, from head teachers to street cleaners and from park keepers to housing officers on a single pay scale, thus attempting to ensure that they receive equal pay for work of equal value. This has impacted on youth workers' conditions, for example by removing restrictions on the number of evenings that full-time employees can be required to work each week. Jobs may be open to people with a range of qualifications rather than restricted to qualified youth workers. In parallel, austerity has been forced on the public sector and swingeing cuts have impacted on long-established local authority provision. Funds have been focused on provision required by law: youth work's non-statutory basis has proved problematic. The voluntary sector variously has been co-opted, drafted and enlisted to undertake work hitherto forming parts of the provision formerly undertaken by the Welfare State. Some youth centres have been mothballed and others have been signed over to community groups whose capacity to manage them can be limited. There are no definitive figures recording the reduction in the number of youth workers remaining in the public sector, but all local authorities' workforces have been reduced drastically and there are predictions of further cuts in future years. Unison (a major UK trades union) has recorded the loss of over 3,500 youth work jobs between 2014 and 2016 and suggests further cuts will follow (Unison, 2016). Unqualified and casual workers are cheaper to employ than professionals but they may not have a developed knowledge and understanding of techniques or theories. Austerity is seeing the de-professionalisation and casualisation of youth work in some sectors, although the field has not 'come full circle' as regulation and the knowledge underpinning the profession remain in existence.

THE FAILURE OF A 'NEW PROFESSION'

In 2000, the New Labour Government led by Tony Blair announced that a new profession was required to work with young people as part of a new service intended to contribute to combatting social exclusion. The new profession of 'Personal Adviser' (PA) would staff the new 'Connexions Service'. The PA's role was intended to ensure that each young person only had to deal with a single professional who would represent them and re-tell their situation to other agencies including housing, health and education. The PA was required to broker arrangements on the young person's behalf. To staff the new service, youth workers (often with existing professional qualifications in youth work), careers guidance workers (often with existing professional qualifications in guidance) and workers from related fields were brought in (Smith, 2000). None was deemed qualified until they had secured the new qualification: the PA Diploma. The civil servants responsible for

designing Connexions had a range of experience but none had a background in professional youth work or careers guidance. Youth workers who met with the civil servants behind the scheme observed that they seemed not only unaware of the curricular content of the existing qualifications in youth work and careers guidance, which many of the workforce held already, but also lacking in understanding of the nature of the professions.

Connexions focused on individual young people rather than groups and introduced a new level of bureaucracy and record keeping. Rather than building relationships, youth workers who became PAs found themselves interrogating 'new' young people about various aspects of their lives, including education, housing and health in order to complete all the boxes on their Assessment, Planning, Intervention & Review (APIR) sheets. This process was intended to flag up areas of concern that would result in referrals to appropriate professionals. Young people were reframed as 'clients' rather than members or participants – something which reflected the move away from 'service' mentioned earlier. Connexions workers were required to prioritise those who were deemed to be 'at risk'. This resulted in the comparative neglect of, for example, careers guidance for well-qualified young people struggling to decide on their future options. Connexions felt extremely well-funded and new office furniture and fittings and free gifts proliferated: the purple and gold branding became widely recognised amongst young people. Critics voiced concerns about the levels of surveillance associated with the links being made between attendance at appointments, travel passes and records being shared by different departments (see, for example, Garrett, 2002).

The New Labour Government assured youth workers that Connexions was the equivalent of a statutory service but when they lost the 2010 election its demise was rapid. The new government (2010–15) was a coalition formed by the Conservative Party and Liberal Democrats. New Labour's social policies were largely abandoned. The end of Connexions served as an illustration of the extent to which youth work could be harnessed to ideological ends. Hundreds of thousands of young people were left with reduced youth work provision as well as woefully inadequate careers guidance in schools and colleges. Thousands of youth workers and careers guidance workers were left with valueless qualifications, which no longer carried any currency in the professional arena. Connexions was the ultimately failed policy of the New Labour Government (1997–2010): its association with party political policies designed to tackle social exclusion guaranteed its downfall.

THE NATIONAL CITIZENSHIP SERVICE

Whilst the Connexions Service was in its death throes, the Coalition Government was launching its own policies: the 'Big Society' and the National Citizenship Scheme (NCS). When Prime Minister David Cameron announced the Big Society initiative, he explained that public expenditure had to be reduced, and stated memorably 'we're all in this together' (Cameron, 2009). The 'Big Society' was marketed as a way to return power to communities and to support people who wanted to run things for themselves, but from the beginning it was widely regarded as a smokescreen for the implementation of cuts. There was talk of a large workforce of local volunteers being recruited and trained but the policy lacked clarity and gently sank without trace. Within three years it no longer formed part of the agenda and nothing took its place: the Big Society arguably had little or no impact except in generating increased public cynicism concerning politicians.

The National Citizenship Scheme was better funded. The Government insisted that money was being invested in youth work and cited the NCS. Formerly, local Youth Services had provided year-round provision, but

NCS is an intensive three-week experience. Broadly speaking, it is a programme of outdoor pursuits, team building and social action intended for 16-year-olds. Some staff have youth work qualifications, but the programme also recruits many people whose suitability is less obvious. Developed academic critiques of NCS are few but Tania de St Croix has investigated the programme. She has drawn attention to many matters including the ideologically loaded statements contained in the participant evaluation sheets (de St Croix, 2011, 2015). David Ainsworth's research suggests that around a quarter of places have not been filled and a significant percentage of participants fail to complete the full three weeks (Ainsworth, 2015). Some young graduates of the scheme recount positive experiences and are articulate advocates, although brief comments on the decidedly middle-class online discussion forum Mumsnet suggest wider scepticism as the following example shows:

> I think it's a shocking use of money that could have been allocated to the Youth Service for really useful work amongst youngsters who haven't had those opportunities. (Backforgood, 2013)

Despite this, the scheme is being extended, and one of David Cameron's final actions as Prime Minister was to make NCS statutory: in 2016 it was established on a permanent footing. Moreover Cameron went on to become (unpaid) Chair of Patrons of NCS (Weaver, 2016). This happened alongside NCS's failure to recruit the numbers envisaged, which led to the creation of some more flexible models: optimists predict spaces which youth workers can make their own. Anecdotal evidence suggests that greater levels of success are achieved when professional youth workers are responsible for local programmes.

WHAT WILL HAPPEN NEXT?

The approach to organising youth work in England has become linked closely to political ideologies, and young people (who cannot vote for change) have become the victims. The Connexions Service was killed off when New Labour lost the election in 2010. The ill-thought-through Big Society faded away before the Coalition Government ended with the election in 2015. It remains to be seen whether NCS collapses following a future election. Its strong association with Cameron may prove unattractive to any future government formed by a different political party. Furthermore, the government department responsible for youth work was changed. For many generations it was located in the Department for Education, reflecting youth work's foundation. In 2013 the responsibility for youth strategy and policy (including youth work) was shifted abruptly to the Cabinet Office, whose priorities include '[building] a stronger civil society' and '[driving] efficiencies' (Gov.UK, 2016). Equally suddenly, responsibility moved again – to the Department for Culture, Media and Sport (Offord, 2016). The detaching of youth work from education emphasises the governmental idea of the function of work with young people and goes against the vision held by many workers.

In the second decade of the 21st century severe cuts are being implemented across the public sector. Neo-liberal governments (the Coalition Government, 2010–2015, and the Conservative Government, 2015 onwards) persuaded the population that austerity was a necessity and that public spending needed to be reduced hugely. Although the UK's debt may be attributed to the global banking crisis, it is popularly believed that overspending in the public sector is to blame. Councils' budgets have been reduced hugely and their response has been to close non-statutory provision such as youth clubs, family centres, libraries, museums and swimming pools. Many local authorities have ceased to fund any youth work. They focus only on individual young people who have been identified as being 'at risk' (for example, of becoming involved in crime) and have been 'targeted'.

Although youth work's professional status has been established in some ways, the destruction of the Youth Service has removed the majority of opportunities for employment in posts with the title 'youth worker' and with appropriate remuneration and recognition. Nonetheless, professionally qualified youth workers are employed in a range of capacities. In many situations they are not doing youth work but their specialised skills and knowledge are valued and they stay true to the code of ethics. Their skills in engaging with young people are found useful by schools, colleges, housing associations, drugs and alcohol agencies and even a range of specialist areas in hospitals. They are working with young people and they are using their youth work skills. They are often working with targeted individuals and groups. They might be working with young people and also with their families. All too rarely are they working with groups of young people who are involved of their own volition. Nonetheless, they may succeed in adapting the context to suit their professional skills and values. Through demonstrating what they can achieve, some succeed in making spaces where youth work can develop in future.

Of course, most young people are not concerned about the professional status of workers or the structures employing them: they are interested in the quality of their encounters. Youth workers, who value their professional autonomy, find state systems require the containment rather than the liberation of young people. Listening to young people's voices rather than policy makers' views can only be undertaken in alternative locations. Over a century ago, youth work developed through voluntary initiatives. Perhaps the most innovative work can only be created outside state structures.

SHOULD YOUTH WORK BE A PROFESSION?

This chapter started by asking questions about whether youth work in England is a profession and considering the criteria that characterise a profession. It was suggested that youth work boasts some – but not all – of the attributes associated with professions. However, also at issue is the question of whether it should be one in the first place. This has been debated since the days of the Second World War when it was first thought that professional input was required to help to 'manage' young people's lives (Bradford, 2006: 133). Today youth workers value their professional autonomy and independence, although for some, the notion of protecting an esoteric body of knowledge is anathematic. Many years ago Ivan Illich and his fellow writers raised fundamental questions about the nature and impact of professions, showing how needs are defined and solutions (requiring professional implementation) are identified or even created. They identified a key paradox in that many professions led to the generation and identification of further need (Illich, 1977). Before the creation of the National Health Service in 1948, many British people believed its cost would decrease as people grew healthier (Timmins, 2001: 206). Of course, the opposite was true. John McKnight asked, 'Why are we putting so much resource into medicine while our health is not improving? Why are we putting so much resource into education and our children seem to be learning less?' (McKnight, 1977: 75). In the case of youth work, arguably this is not the case: youth work presents a contradictory exemplum. When more funding was available for youth work, young people were – for example – less unhappy. Now spending on youth work in England is diminishing and, at the same time, the nation's young people are increasingly unhappy: they are now amongst the least happy in the world (ISCWeB, 2016; The Children's Society, 2016). Although research has not examined whether a correlation between these facts exists, it presents a topic for exploration.

In 2009 the campaign In Defence of Youth Work (IDYW) formed in response to the perceived hostile political environment and cuts. It continues to be a lively and partisan body that is somewhat ambivalent towards professional status due to its impact on the 'army of volunteers' and 'range of autonomous practice' (IDYW, 2014). Many other voices continue the debate. Graham Bright (2015) revisited the matter and suggested that youth work is still 'striving' for acceptance as a full member of the panoply of people professions. In his book on professional ethics, Howard Sercombe expressed personal ambivalence concerning 'whether youth work ought to consider itself a profession and whether it ought to organise itself as one' (Sercombe, 2010: 7), although he concluded that it fits the criteria to be seen as a profession.

Illich wrote of professionals' protection of their 'secret knowledge' and outlined the results of professionals assuming responsibility for aspects of people's lives: 'In any area where human need can be imagined these new professions, dominant, authoritative, monopolistic, legalised – and, at the same time, debilitating and effectively disabling the individual – have become the exclusive experts of the public good' (Illich, 1977: 19). He includes 'educators' in the list of disabling professionals, yet the example of youth work introduces a second contradiction. Youth workers take pride in their expertise in working effectively with young people, including the most challenging, yet they also strive for transparency (as opposed to 'secrecy'), informality and inclusivity and emphasise the role of empowerment in their practice. They foster relationships based on equality rather than power. Hart's 'Ladder of Participation' (Hart, 1992: 8) provides a popular framework for measuring the extent to which children and young people's involvement is 'real' or cosmetic. Youth workers aspire to reach the higher rungs where young people exercise real power over activities. This provides a clear demonstration of the sharing of knowledge: unique amongst the professions, youth workers' 'secret knowledge' is that 'there is no secret'.

CONCLUSION

In England the profession of youth work has evolved and reached maturity ironically coterminously with the withdrawal of much state funding. The skills, values and knowledge that underpin youth work degree courses remain relevant to contemporary society but the future is impossible to predict. Employers value youth workers' skills in communicating with young people without necessarily embracing the entire value base and professional youth workers are facing situations where there is clear scope for their skilled interventions. However, there is no clear vision of what types of provision would best meet the needs of young people who are less likely to find open access youth clubs and youth centres appealing.

Arguably in England there has never been a perfect balance between four key elements: the young people, the workers, the funding of the work and the work itself. A utopian youth-friendly nation would ensure first, professionally qualified trained youth workers who are able to base their practice on traditional values of voluntary engagement by young people, an educational foundation and work with groups (association). Secondly, there would be a secure funding base for youth work, which insulates provision from shifting party political ideologies. Thirdly, opportunities would be designed to suit all young people living in a particular locality, including both adult-led and youth-led provision, and finally the workforce would reflect the nation's youth in terms of gender, ethnicity, sexuality, (dis)ability, faith and culture. Sadly, in England's current neo-liberal political environment it appears unlikely that the perfect balance will be reached.

Youth work in England provides a case study of what can happen when policy becomes a party political plaything: for several decades each government's reaction to electoral success has been the cancellation of the previous government's policies for young people. Reports published under previous administrations are archived and no longer easily accessed; successful initiatives are jettisoned seemingly on ideological grounds. Funding appears to be redirected to politicians' pet programmes that are rarely grounded in empirical research into young people's needs and aspirations. In England the formal establishment of youth work as a profession has been a significant achievement and ideally the next steps should be to involve youth workers and young people in designing future initiatives. Time alone will tell whether youth work has a future that sees qualified, paid professionals working with young people who are participating of their own volition. Imagination and vision need to be employed to ensure that a profession originally born out of conditions generated by the 19th-century Industrial Revolution responds to the challenges of the 21st.

Notes

1   England, Scotland, Wales and Northern Ireland comprise the United Kingdom. In areas such as education and youth work, systems differ. This chapter focuses on England.
2   Until 2010 the professional qualification was achieved after students had completed two years of full-time study. At this point, an academic Diploma in Higher Education was awarded together with the professional qualification. After 2010 both the academic and professional qualification required three years' study. Nowadays the qualification is validated by the individual university as an academic honours degree and validated by the NYA on behalf of the JNC as a professional qualification.
3   In England the 'voluntary sector' is the collective term applied to charities/third sector and non-governmental not-for-profit organisations.

REFERENCES

Ainsworth D (2015) National Citizen Service to serve 300,000 a year and cost £1.1bn by 2020. Available at: https://www.civilsociety.co.uk/news/national-citizen-service-to-serve-300000-a-year-and-cost-1bn-by-2020-

Backforgood (2013) It all starts at yes. NCS. Available at https://www.mumsnet.com/Talk/secondary/1773666-It-all-starts-at-yes-NCS

Baden-Powell R (1908) *Scouting for Boys: A handbook for instruction in good citizenship*. London: Horace Cox.

Barnett R (2008) Critical professionalism in an age of supercomplexity. In Cunningham, B. (ed) *Exploring Professionalism*. London: Institute of Education.

Bradford S (2006) Practising the double doctrine of freedom: managing young people in the context of war. In Gilchrist R, Jeffs T and Spence J (eds) *Drawing on the Past*. Leicester: The National Youth Agency, 132–149.

Bradford S (2007) The 'good youth leader': Constructions of professionalism in English youth work, 1939–45. *Ethics and Social Welfare* 1(3): 293–309.

Bradford S, Byrne S (2010) Beyond the boundaries: resistances to school-based youth work in Northern Ireland. *Pastoral Care in Education* 28(1): 19–31.

Bright G (2015) In search of soul: where now for youth and community work? In Bright G (ed) *Youth Work: Histories, Policy and Contexts*. London: Palgrave, 236–252.

Cameron D (2009) Full text of David Cameron's Speech to the Conservative Conference. Available at: www.theguardian.com/politics/2009/oct/08/david-cameron-speech-in-full

Davies A (2008) *The Gangs of Manchester*. Reading: Milo Books.

Davies B (1999) *From Voluntaryism to Welfare State*. Leicester: Youth Work Press.

de St Croix T (2011) Struggles and silences: policy, youth work and the National Citizen Service. *Youth and Policy* 106: 43–59.

de St Croix T (2015) Volunteers and entrepreneurs? Youth work and the Big Society. In Bright G (ed) *Youth Work Histories, Policy and Contexts*. London: Palgrave, 58–79.

Education Board (1944) *Education Act*. London. Available at: www.legislation.gov.uk/ukpga/Geo6/7-8V31/contents/enacted

ESRO (2016) *Children's Media Lives – Year 2 Findings*. Available at: www.ofcom.org.uk/__data/assets/pdf_file/0021/80715/children_media_lives_year2.pdf?lang=cym

France A, Wiles P (1997) Dangerous futures: social exclusion and youth work in late modernity. *Social Policy and Administration* 31(5): 59–78.

Freeman F (1908) *Our Working Girls and How to Help Them*. London: A.R. Mowbray & Co. Ltd.

Garrett PM (2002) Encounters in the new welfare domains of the Third Way: social work, the Connexions agency and personal advisers. *Critical Social Policy* 22(4): 596–618.

Gov.UK (2016) Cabinet Office: about us. Available at: www.gov.uk/government/organisations/cabinet-office/about

Graham RB (1947) *Mrs R.B. Graham's Interview with County Councillor Hyman 30th October 1947*. Unpublished manuscript.

Greenwood E (1957) Attributes of a profession. *Social Work* 2(3): 45–55.

Hart R (1992) *Children's Participation from Tokenism to Citizenship*. Florence: UNICEF.

IDYW (2014) *For a Critical Emancipatory and Democratic Education*. Available at: https://indefenceofyouthwork.files.wordpress.com/2014/05/new-revised-purpose-2014.pdf

Illich I (1977) *Disabling Professions*. London: Marion Boyars Publishers.

ISCWeB (2016) *Children's Views on their Lives and well-being in 17 Countries: Key messages from each country*. Available at: www.isciweb.org/_Uploads/dbsAttachedFiles/Key-Messagesfromeachcountry_final.pdf

IYW (2014) Welcome to the Institute for Youth Work. Available at: www.iyw.org.uk

Jeffs T, Spence J (2008) Farewell to all that? The uncertain future of youth and community work education. *Youth and Policy* 97–8: 135–162.

Jones HMF (2014a) 'Counting young people is not youth work': the tensions between values, targets and positive activities in neighbourhood-based work. *Journal of Youth Studies* 17(2): 220–235.

Jones HMF (2014b) 'The voluntary organisation forms ... a unique feature of the British way of life': one voluntary organisation's response to the birth of the Youth Service. *Youth & Policy* 113: 60–75.

McKnight J (1977) Professionalized service and disabling help. In Illich I (ed) *Disabling Professions*. London: Marion Boyars Publishers, 69–91.

Nicholls D (2012) *For Youth Workers and Youth Work*. Bristol: Policy Press.

NYA (2016a) Historical list of all schemes, courses and programmes recognised from 1945 onwards. Available at: www.nya.org.uk/wp-content/uploads/2016/05/MASTER-historical-validation-Database-Mar-2016V2.pdf

NYA (2016b) Our purpose. Available at: www.nya.org.uk/about-us/ourpurpose

Offord A (2016) 'Loughton: youth policy transfer to DCMS "a mistake"'. *Children and Young People Now*, 25 July.

Seal M (2014) Introduction: it's more than just common sense … the relevance of philosophy to everyday youth and community work. In Frost S and Seal M (eds) *Philosophy in Youth and Community Work*. Lyme Regis: Russell House Publishing, 1–7.

Sercombe H (2010) *Youth Work Ethics*. London: Sage.

Smith M (2000) Personal Advisers within the Connexions Service. Available at: www.infed.org/personaladvisers/pers-adv.htm

Staines R (2008) Nursing to become degree-only profession. *Nursing Times*. Available at: www.nursingtimes.net/nursing-to-become-degree-only-profession/1832902.fullarticle

Stanley M (1890) *Clubs for Working Girls*. London: Macmillan and Co.

The Children's Society (2016) *The Good Childhood Report*. Available at: www.childrenssociety.org.uk/what-we-do/research/the-good-childhood-report

Timmins N (2001) *The Five Giants*. London: Harper Collins.

Unison (2016) *The Damage*. Available at: www.unison.org.uk/content/uploads/2016/08/23996.pdf

Weaver M (2016) David Cameron to work with National Citizen Service in first post-politics role. *The Guardian*. Available at: www.theguardian.com/politics/2016/oct/12/david-cameron-to-chair-national-citizen-service-in-first-post-politics-role

West Riding Education Authority (1948) *Policy Sub-Committee – The Service of Youth General Report Memorandum September 21st 1948*. University of Leeds Special Archive Collections. MS 731. Box 31. Doc G13. Unpublished manuscript.

WRAGC (1942) *Annual Report*. Wakefield: West Riding Association of Girls' Clubs.

YAGC (1941) Minutes of Meeting of the Yorkshire Association of Girls' Clubs Training Sub-Committee. Unpublished.

9

Precarious Practices with Risky Subjects? Policy and Practice Explorations in the UK and Europe

Fin Cullen and Simon Bradford

INTRODUCTION

This chapter explores peril, blame and fear to consider how youth work funding regimes and logics of practice are predicated on managing young people and risk. Youth has been understood as an inherently risky social category since the late 19th century and varying ideas of risk have been offered to justify youth work's development in the UK in the 20th century (Cohen, 1972; Pearson, 1983; Bradford, 2014). Here, we explore theoretical and policy discourses of risk before considering implications for practice. This chapter poses questions for critical reflection in youth policy and practice, and considers the theoretical, policy and practice dilemmas raised by such discourses framing interventions with young people.

The chapter builds on sociological literature exploring youth as a social problem in determining how discourses of risky youth and individual choice have increasingly framed the youth work policy and practice

arena. We focus mainly on the impact on UK and European Union (EU) youth policy formations and funding regimes. We consider the future of a risk-based or risk-averse youth work and critique policy and practice notions of resilience and risk to consider how various youth work practices might be mobilised as sites that quell intergenerational anxiety. We also reflect on how new spaces of precarious engagement may be developed where practice boundaries may be increasingly uncertain because of contradictory or ambiguous policy and institutional imperatives. Precarious space and practice implies contingency and instability, demanding careful and creative exercise of practitioner discretion in competing discourses of public professionalism (Evetts, 2009).

It is difficult to predict the impact of Brexit on youth and youth work in Europe and the UK. The UK has been part of the European Economic Community (latterly the EU) since 1973, and there has been a gradual shift towards proximity in relation to EU youth and social policy for education, community and youth projects, through grants via the European Social fund, for example, although these policy and funding streams are themselves increasingly precarious.

THEORISING YOUTH AND YOUTH WORK

Youth work is poorly defined, ambiguous and contested with a broad range and diversity of approach within and across national contexts. Such work can overlap formal schooling and welfare and be delivered by a variety of practitioners: volunteers, clergy, pedagogues, social workers and professionally qualified youth workers. Across Europe there are multiple and overlapping definitions of youth work. However, as a recent EU report notes:

> ... at the heart of youth work there are three core features that define it as youth work distinct from other policy fields:
>
> • a focus on young people,
> • personal development, and
> • voluntary participation. (European Commission, 2014, p. 4)

This emphasises participatory informal learning based on relationship building with others. Yet as noted in a European Commission report, there has been a shift in the practices framed as youth work across Europe (European Commission, 2014). This includes a decline in 'traditional' youth work, less upfront funding and an increased focus on targeted and intervention-based practices with young people considered to be problematic in some way (European Commission, 2014).

A tension that arises here is the liminal status of youth and, moreover, that of youth work itself (Bradford, 2011a, 2011b; Bradford and Cullen, 2014). Youth's liminality is evident in the imprecision of this age category within wider scholarly, policy and practice literatures. The markers for entering adulthood are vague, with indicators such as the

age of criminal responsibility differing across national contexts, for example from age 10 in England and Wales to 16 in Portugal. Similarly, the age of consent varies widely, from 12 (the Netherlands) to 18 in Malta. Such legal markers highlight how notions of responsibility and agency, though chronologically marked, are socially and culturally constructed. These variations render problematic inflexible and vertically structured rights-based policy and practice interventions (for example the UN Rights of the Child).

Since the 19th-century 'discovery' of adolescence by G. Stanley Hall (1904) in the United States, an ambiguity has existed regarding this so-called life stage (again, culturally determined and structured) and its relation to earlier and later stages. Arguably, Western social science (psychology especially) has been obsessed with understanding human life as naturally constructed in 'stages' to the extent that this has now become common sense. The discovery of youth located adolescence as a life-stage rooted in physiological and psychological change and instability. Work by Arnett (2000) calls for an inclusion of a *new* stage, that of *emerging adulthood* to be positioned post adolescence and prior to early adulthood, and completing Erikson's (1968) staged model in contemporary developed societies. This new stage is supposedly necessary in highlighting incipient complexity and ambiguity for young adults in traversing the contemporary cultural landscape, with its prolonged dependency on parents and delayed labour and housing transitions alongside later marriage and parenthood. Such culturally elongated transitions are typically a product of broader shifts within the socio-economic realm of the industrialised West.

This cultural fluidity of transitional stages between childhood and adulthood suggests how youth is culturally constructed in liminal time and space, positioning those within it as troubled and troubling (Griffin, 1993, 1997). The wider sociological literature has described the positioning of young people as 'folk devils' (Cohen, 1972) posing a perceived (often media-driven) risk to the wider social fabric. Such concerns (so-called moral panics), whether they be about mods and rockers, rave culture, football hooliganism or radicalisation, attest to the particular and acute positioning of youth as a source of crisis and peril. After a time such concerns abate and shift to a new focus of societal and media anxiety. However, individual and groups of young people are thus no longer constructed as 'children' in need of protection and care but become positioned as potentially threatening and socially deviant.

These generational crises have, historically, created the demand for a range of professionals with overlapping occupational responsibilities to ameliorate the risky bodies, minds and conduct of young people (Bradford, 2014). As Jeffs and Smith (1999) note, young people are often positioned in policy discourses in three identities: 'thugs, users, and victims'.

> As *thugs* they steal cars, vandalise estates, attack older (and sometimes, younger) people and disrupt classrooms. As *users* they take drugs, drink and smoke to excess, get pregnant in order to jump the housing queue and, hedonistically, care only for themselves. As *victims* they can't find work, receive poor schooling and are brought up in dysfunctional families. Yet so many of the troublesome behaviours associated in this way with young people are not uniquely theirs. (Jeffs and Smith, 1999, p. 1)

Jeffs and Smith's three discursive positions frame young people as deficient, requiring professional support (or containment) to remedy their failings, protecting young people from themselves and others, as well as protecting the wider community. Balanced between these precarious positions of troubled/troublesome means that young people are imbued with perceptions of greater (or, at least, more *urgent*) risk than other generational groups. Of course generational risk is also classed, gendered and racialised, with certain permutations of these being regarded as more risky and in need of intervention. As Clarke (2008) notes, the concerns of troubled youth extend bourgeois discourses that

problematise working-class men's conduct in public space. The fear of dangerous young men created an increase of experts in youth (youth workers have seen themselves as the exemplars) to deal with the perceived 'youth problem' through welfare, semi-therapeutic or educational approaches. There has been a simultaneous call for methods emphasising law and order, framing a historical tension between welfare and justice from which youth work has not been immune. Recent approaches to youth crime have assumed an *actuarial* orientation (Muncie, 2009, p. 322). This privileges the identification of 'risky' groups (young men, Black young people, drug users and so on) and, on the basis of various aggregate data analyses, seeks to calculate the probability of such groups' *actual* engagement in criminal behaviour and activity. This invariably entails more young people and more youth conduct becoming understood as actually or potentially problematic and in need of intervention of some kind.

Partially reflecting the tension between welfare and justice across Europe, professional educators, including youth workers, have been tasked with educating to re-moralise youth within national and EU transnational youth policy. By *re-moralise*, we argue that these agents' responsibilities have been concerned with encouraging young people to understand themselves and their relations with others in new ways that animate an underlying notion of responsible citizenship. Diverse professional positions and responsibilities can be understood as shaping a broad spectrum of work, spanning semi-therapeutic interventions to much more punitive attempts in shaping and reorienting the moral worlds and future characters of young people as potential and actual risk-takers. For example, other professional groups tasked with managing aspects of this youth problem include youth justice and detached youth workers:

> ... the youth problem and problem youth are always/already framed by the intersecting fields of experience (and the institutionalized sites of their interventions). We can never come to these issues

'fresh' because they have been colonized by psycho-logical, pedagogical and criminological knowledges (assembled and mobilized in different professions, practices and settings). (Clarke, 2008, p. 2)

So what might this mean for youth work? Youth practitioners, produced through and because of youth problems, have been his-torically tasked and funded to 'rescue' and re-moralise those who are regarded as at risk or have transgressed normative transitions to adulthood. In his history of English youth work Davies (1999) wrote of the ongoing ten-sions between empowerment and social con-trol (another evocation of the welfare/justice couplet) that underpin the origins of youth work. Of course, so-called 'empowerment' should not always be seen as purely benign and can be understood as implying the exer-cise of power, often concealed within pro-fessional interventions (Cruickshank, 1999). However, actuarial discourses have signalled the predominant thrust of funded practice as the amelioration of risk for nation, state and economy in rescuing young people from themselves (Bradford and Cullen, 2014). Such a move, and perhaps a return to a risk-based practice, has also begun to shape gender-specific work with girls (Batsleer, 2006; Cullen, 2013). Post-feminist youth work practice with young women focuses less on empowerment and more on protection and rectifying the individual girl's perceived problems (Batsleer, 2006). Individual girls' imperilled minds and bodies (especially their wombs) become a key site for policy and practice intervention, and policy discursively plays out and reconstitutes neoliberal notions of 'risk', as well as 'stigma' (Hanbury and Ronan, 2014).

WHAT IS RISK?

Risk is, perhaps, one of the most overworked concepts in recent sociology. Earlier work in the sociology of youth has highlighted how discourses of youth at risk are threaded throughout late modernity (Kelly, 2001, 2006;

Te Riele, 2006; Clarke, 2008; Kemshall, 2010). Mary Douglas (1994) notes that cultural assumptions inevitably shape ideas of risk, alongside broader ethical, political and moral judgments that blame particular groups. Indeed, Douglas points to the cultural and political load that the notion of risk carries in the contemporary world. Commenting that risk discourse has emerged in societies that have shifted from predominantly *local* to *global* social relations, Douglas identifies how the coding of risk and its attendant relations of accountability (creating the potential for *blame*) has filled the hiatus left by globalised social relations. She points out that this estab-lishes the need for protective mechanisms (to deal with multiple social perils) and that the notion of risk '... could have been custom-made. Its universalizing terminology, its abstractness, its power of condensation, its scientificity, its connection with objective anal-ysis, make it perfect' (Douglas, 1994, p. 15).

Douglas's argument makes clear the cen-tral role of risk discourse in contemporary actuarial practices, especially in the invoca-tion of probability. One influential contribu-tor to this has been Farringdon whose data analyses have sought to develop evidence-based policy in relation to youth crime. Notions of risk and probability animate this work. Farringdon attempts to identify vari-ables (*risk* factors) that are believed to predict the emergence of crime amongst particular groups, and so-called *protective* factors that purportedly counteract risk (Farringdon, 1996). Scholars from other perspectives have brought theories of reflexive modernisation (Beck, 1992; Giddens, 1991) together with work on governmentality (Foucault, 2008; Rose, 1999), analysing how risk in late modernity positions individual subjects *and* produces them as self-regulating actors. For Kelly, the emergence of neoliberal govern-mentality has provided 'a new articulation of risk' (2006, p. 20) framed within a climate of increased uncertainty and individualisation.

Interrogating such discursive framings pro-vides scope to consider how young people are positioned within these self-reflexive projects, but also how youth itself is produced via the products of institutionalised risk. Perhaps the question here is 'what are young people at risk of not becoming?' (Kelly, 2006, p. 25). The crux of the issue is how risk and youth-at-risk entail concerns about the future and wider, jeopardised futures as young people become 'the embodiment of crisis' (Clarke, 2008). Some youthful identities are perceived as particular crisis identities in the renewed anxiety about problem youth, particularly those young people considered to be of marginal, criminal or migrant origin (Clarke, 2008). Youth as a category is thoroughly problematised, but, within this group, certain subcategories are seen to be at particular risk (of criminalisation or radicalisation, for example) and thus a perceived threat to the wider social order.

The youth transitions literature has attempted to explore the sociological positioning of youth as a life stage in later modernity in relation to housing, labour and employment transitions (MacDonald et al., 2001). Key tensions arise here between agency and the choice biographies of young people in late modernity as they move into adulthood, and how these are positioned in relation to established structural formations. A host of terms has sprung up to explain the contingency and complexity of young people's lives as they move into education and employment to describe these transitions in the industrialised West including *fractured, multiple* and *looped* transitions (MacDonald, 1998; MacDonald et al., 2001). Late capitalism is characterised by broader global restructuring of markets by neoliberal forces predicated on a free flow of capital and labour. These forces have shaped new labour market formations, a rise of credentialism and increasingly precarious transitions into employment for young people. The global crash of 2008 further destabilised an already weakened youth labour market leading to rising youth unemployment and consequent limited opportunities within various consumer markets, especially housing.

EU YOUTH IN TIMES OF PERIL

All crises are socially constructed. National and international responses to these produce new ways of understanding and responding to social problems: in effect, new 'regimes of truth' (Rabinow, 1991, p. 54). Ideological and financial responses to 'austerity' provide insights into national concerns and focus around ideas of renewal and youth. As Walby (2015) argues, crises and responses to them are invariably gendered. These crises are also clearly generational. Recent documents regarding the wider EU youth strategy focus on the challenges facing EU youth and the potential role of youth work (Dunne, Ulicna, Murphy and Golubeva, 2014; European Commission, 2014, 2016). Currently, the EU population of young people aged between 15 and 29 stands at almost 90 million (European Commission, 2016) with the EU youth unemployment rate as of July 2016 running at 18.8 per cent (Eurostat, 2016).

Late modernity's economic storm and stress positions youth in a curious and precarious position (reflecting a similar *internal* storm and stress), tying generational inequality into the wider social fabric, with some scholars predicting increased inter and intra-generational conflict (Roberts, 2012). Recent EU Youth reports highlight a number of potential perils emerging mainly from the 2008 economic crisis and the attendant impact of this on the welfare, health and social inclusion of young people in EU states (European Commission, 2014, 2016). One clear source of peril is the declining number of EU young people. If the wealth of the nation is built on the individual nations' and the continent's youth, then a declining population signals an ominous warning for stability and productivity across the EU. However, there remains movement between EU states as young people attempt to seek employment or migrate for study (Cairns, 2014). Moreover, the new migrant population *into* Europe comprises predominantly young people aged 20–29, and, through internal and inward migration into Germany, Sweden and the UK is swell-ing the youth populations of some EU states.

Some EU countries, such as Ireland, have experienced mass youth emigration (McAleer, 2013; Cairns, 2014). This repre-sents a continuation of an older history of youth emigration that shaped Ireland over the 20th century. However, unlike earlier waves of migration, Irish young people have migrated beyond the UK to other EU states, Australia, Canada and the US. This had a sig-nificant impact in the revival of a depressed economy post-crisis and brought pessimism to the broader youth policy context shaped by such an acute transnational 'brain drain'. Similar processes are occurring in other parts of the EU. In Hungary, for example, Sik has shown young people's ambivalence about modernisation, especially in relation to poli-tics and the labour market and the attraction of right-wing political parties in these cir-cumstances (Sik, 2015, p. 117). The dynam-ics and structure of migration are complex (Bodnár and Szabó, 2014), but there is con-siderable evidence of young people's desire to leave Hungary for 'the West'. A high pro-portion of those leaving are graduates and thus a considerable and valuable source of a nation's human capital (Blaskó, Ligeti and Sik, 2015). The Hungarian Government has attempted, largely unsuccessfully, to provide incentives to attract young Hungarians back from Western countries.

In a reflection on potential responses of young people in Europe to austerity, Williamson (2014) suggests that there is a range of potential risks and reactions to the diminished life chances 'of all but a relatively small minority of the younger generation' (Williamson, 2014, p. 15). For some, this might be a political move rightwards – as groups turn against minorities in the form of the 'white political right' (p. 11) – and Williamson notes the rise of far-right groups in response to continuing economic uncer-tainty. For others, this might lead to a grow-ing radicalisation and violent extremism as material conditions and experiences of racism

exacerbate existing issues of poverty and mar-ginalisation for some minority young people. Others still, Williamson suggests, might move to challenge austerity through their involve-ment in anti-globalisation movements such as Occupy[1] or Indignados[2] or in urban revolt, as seen in the 2011 English riots.[3]

Another response is that of 'retreat' where Williamson notes in the recent Greek context, the rising number of suicides and poor mental health of young people facing bleak economic times. While we might question whether sui-cide is best understood as a form of 'retreat', other potential responses include young peo-ple realigning their aspirations with harden-ing conditions and accepting their diminished opportunities (Williamson, 2014). Although Williamson does not discuss youth migra-tion, we suggest that the mass transnational mobility of young people chasing economic and life chances outside their home nations also suggests a pragmatic response to broader economic conditions and high rates of youth unemployment. Williamson paints poten-tially a rather depressing picture. The move towards racist and extremist movements, especially in post-communist Europe (Csillag and Szelényi, 2015), or the declining mental health of Europe's youth positions young people, in the wake of austerity, in peril.

YOUTH WORK AS PRECARIOUS PRACTICE

At this time of economic crisis there has been a renewal of interest in the potential of youth work by the EU (Williamson, 2011; Dunne et al., 2014; European Commission, 2014, 2016; Council of Europe, 2015). Youth work is seen as a potential space to ameliorate some of these difficulties and perils, yet the fuzzi-ness around its purpose, direction, content, methods, funding and impact suggest that it remains a marginal and precarious practice.

Much has been written about tensions and challenges within the UK Youth sector

(Wylie, 2010; Davies, 2011, 2013; Bradford and Cullen, 2014). Other national contexts such as Spain, reflect austere times and have experienced cuts in youth services, decreasing youth worker salaries, the deskilling of the youth work profession and savage cuts to the Spanish Youth Council and other local youth bodies (Soler, Planas and Feixa, 2014). A creeping privatisation has also entered the Spanish youth work sector with competition and a marketisation of public services favouring larger corporate providers that can weather future financial storms (Soler et al., 2014). Within the Irish context, extensive cuts in youth funding have changed the direction of remaining state-funded practice, as reported in a recent EU case study:

> With the reduction in funding streams and amounts, youth work is now being asked to deliver on that and youth work has become increasingly under pressure to be intervention and prevention based. This can lead to the view that young people are to be 'contained' and that young people are being 'serviced' by youth work rather than [it] being a space for learning and development. (Dunne et al., 2014, p. 57)

These concerns have been echoed elsewhere. Drawing on the 2011 European Youth Work Conference, Williamson (2011) raises a series of critical questions about the 'core business' of contemporary European youth work that framed the recent debates regarding purpose and direction of policy and practice:

> Is it about preventing risk or promoting talent? Is it about reducing early school leaving or delivering non-formal education? Is it about guiding young people towards active citizenship, or towards education, training and employment? Is it for all young people, or just for young people 'at risk'? (Williamson, 2011, pp. 201–202)

Williamson's questions reflect well on the historical problem of youth work. Namely, that in an era where the division of labour is characterised by increasing specialisation and narrowness of knowledge, the position of the 'generalist' is perhaps inevitably precarious. Again historically, and consequentially,

youth work has found it difficult to colonise a specific area of work (competing with other, powerful professional groups in this) and has never been entirely successful in persuading political powers that it has a specific capacity or capability. Such tensions emerge in much of the EU and local national literature exploring the nature and purpose of youth work. Moreover, the emphasis on risk frames policy, practice and funding regimes but may take on different emphasis in the various (trans)national settings. For example, the notion of enterprise and entrepreneurialism runs deep within the current UK Conservative Government policy for youth work, Positive for Youth (HM Govt, 2011), reflecting its own political preferences. The young people identified in that policy document might not be seen as active and critical citizens but often as little more than consumers and wealth creators: Beck and Giddens's enterprising, individualised subjects fabricating their own choice biographies. UK initiatives such as the National Citizenship Service aimed at 15–17-year-olds are predominantly led by a series of third sector organisations with a clear aim and aspiration of producing resilient, career minded and enterprising citizens for the new economic realities of precarious employment. Interestingly, these organisations eschew a *professionalised* approach to youth work, assuming that these aspects of young people's lives (citizenship education in its broadest sense) can be adequately maintained by voluntary organisations and volunteers, although perhaps co-ordinated by small numbers of professionally qualified workers. This departure from at least a token acknowledgement of the need for professional youth work intervention is a significant development in England and Wales.

Government responses to global economic crisis and high levels of youth unemployment in particular have been varied. For some the individualising and responsibilising thrust of neoliberal government policy has pushed discourses of individual entrepreneurship and enterprise as the seed for individual young people to seek ways out of this generational bind. This 'can do' attitude predicates success and has become increasingly engrained within funding for youth projects, and education settings. Indeed, iterations of youth practice that emphasise this apparent innovativeness and flair in the guise of so-called Positive Youth Development (National Youth Agency, 2007) have been enthusiastically received in some quarters.[4]

For those young people who are seen to be low achieving, the language of character building and resilience has re-entered policy and practice discourse. Of course, such an emphasis is not new (it was central to the public school and university education of the upper classes) and was evident within the early 20th-century roots of youth work – in the Scout movement, for example. This response to a new crisis of youth and young people is interesting in so far as it has begun to frame what counts as effective youth work practice in the contemporary world. Rather than a focus on young people as potentially critical, politically educated agents in seeking change, this policy focus reformulates the global crisis as one of individually deficient subjects who through 'grit' and resilience can shape their singular futures as human capital. The UK all-party Character and Resilience Manifesto (Patterson, Tyler and Lexmond, 2014) offered no further funds to support this work, in the wake of savage cuts to youth services, but rather highlighted the space for uniformed youth groups (Scouts, Guides), existing projects such as the National Citizenship Service[5] and the patronage of state schools by elite private schools as an approach that might strengthen and develop the work of building character in disengaged youth. This work is framed by the assertion that '… there is a growing body of research linking social mobility to social and emotional skills … empathy and the ability to make and maintain relationships to application, mental toughness, delayed gratification and self-control' (Patterson et al., 2014, p. 4). This highly individualised approach certainly

appears to challenge orthodox sociological analyses of the structures and patterns of social mobility.

Such redirection in policy, focusing on individual character and skill, again mirrors Brooks's (2013) observation that UK education policy has returned to a combination of laissez-faire notions of enterprise and the family as key sites for combatting the creeping generational inequality between children and their parents in the post-crisis West. This is similarly reflected in broader EU youth strategy with its focus on enterprise (a predominantly individualising discourse) as a way of tackling youth unemployment and social exclusion.

> Entrepreneurship can constitute an important element with regards to the autonomy, personal development and wellbeing of young people. Entrepreneurship can be seen as one of the solutions to combat youth unemployment. (Council of the European Union, 2014)

Enterprise discourse places the focus on individuals becoming recuperated via their own graft and initiative. Young people emerge discursively as agentic and entrepreneurial subjects who can achieve despite enormous (structural) economic and generational inequalities. Such a framing posits risks on individual subjects and their ability to navigate such complex and tortuous transitions.

European Union policy has contributed to mapping the capacity and scope for European youth work within and beyond individual states. Some of this incorporates positive commitments to youth work based on equality, rights and social justice and is expressed in language with which many youth workers would be familiar and would welcome (e.g. Council of the European Union, 2010). However, the neoliberal language of enterprise and risk also frames policy. There is a danger that in some jurisdictions youth work might depart from its educational roots and become a peripatetic service to support transitions into the labour market and provide remedial support to those failed by formal schooling. Within the UK, a mixture of directed funding into preferred services and a channelling of funding away from universal provision means that youth work has become a marginalised practice within state-funded youth services. However, the work of uniformed groups, social work and youth justice work with individual 'problem' young people and their families, commercialised for-profit youth sport and arts activities and youth provision targeted at problem populations continue. However, young people may become divided between the 'can do' category who are perceived to have sufficient grit, determination and enterprise, and a broader residual category of young people who have failed in relation to their labour market and economic positioning. They are, perhaps, regarded as having insufficient character to make a successful transition into the adult world. What then for youth work? How might a rather different iteration of youth work be imagined in the face of such complexity and challenges?

BEYOND RISK? TOWARDS NEW PRACTICES?

So far, this chapter has outlined the range of critical challenges facing contemporary youth work practice. The question arises, however, *how* might youth work respond so that its purpose and rationale is not risk-led, but rather engages with broader questions of democratic renewal, equality and a valuing of young people. While there has been a tension within youth work that emerges as a response to crisis and fear of troublesome youth, another tradition has co-existed within the helping professions from 1960s onwards, that of the romantic humanist orientation, 'celebrating personal growth and emancipation' (Bradford and Cullen, 2014, p. 6).

However, such 'emancipatory' work is vulnerable to economistic ideological shifts. For example, as youth work scholars reflecting on the history of feminist girls' work in

the UK have noted, recent years have seen a broader discursive backlash against feminism and a rechanneling of funds and attention away from explicitly feminist work towards concerns around masculinity and 'at risk' male youth (Batsleer, 2006; Cullen, 2013; see Chapters 10 and 22, this *Handbook*).

Reflecting on the possibilities in the face of crushing ideological and financial cuts to UK services, Hughes, Cooper, Gormally and Rippingale (2014) suggest a need to generate 'a new language and new ways of thinking about how to measure the worth of community and youth work, and what it really means to "care"'. Such an approach, they argue, entails re-envisioning success and creating counter discourses to dominant deficit models presented by the market. For existing youth work caught in the bind of ideological and financial austerity, which brings new, for-profit youth providers and a neoliberal individualised orientation to practice, this can create considerable challenge. The faith-based youth sector is the most rapidly growing section of UK youth work in the face of government attempts to shrink state-funded and -run services (Smith, Stanton and Wylie, 2015). There remain potential tensions between faith groups' agendas and young people's needs, and indeed faith-based settings may find it challenging to offer, for example, LGBTQ youth work and sexual health services. However, such contexts do offer valuable space beyond target driven, risk-based services in which to think critically about creating such a counter-discourse.

Other potential and paradoxical spaces for resistance and establishing and maintaining the 'romantic' drive within earlier youth work for social justice are uniformed groups such as the Girl Guides. The paradox emerges, as again in recent youth policy discourse such groups have been deployed by recent administrations to shrink the state. In an earlier article, Cullen (2013) suggested that uniformed groups such as the Girl Guides could reinvigorate areas of feminist youth practice. Indeed, Girl Guiding UK's *Girls Matter* campaign attests to this more explicitly feminist focus and strive for gender equality in British girl guiding. However, such campaigns often remain framed within wider concepts of risk and resilience. As Hanbury and Ronan argue:

> There remains a need for a space for the core youth work principles and practice of encouraging discussion, debate and challenging 'norms'. We continue to reflect upon the (im)possibility of being a critical feminist youth worker in neo-liberal times and we ask; what is the role of professional youth and community work in creating a critical and feminist site for exploration? (2014, p. 84)

Of course, notions of 'core youth work principles' are contested across time and space in this amorphous and imprecise practice. Similarly, the notion of 'professional' youth workers is also contentious, as across Europe a range of different professionals and volunteers with different roles and job titles deliver 'youth work'. However, following earlier approaches to critical and Freirian pedagogy (Freire, 1972; Giroux, 2011) this focus on unpacking 'norms' to provide alternative structures in order for young people to explore concepts and interrogate existing social power dynamics continues to provide fruitful sources of critical engagement in some arenas, particularly with minority and marginalised groups, see, for example, Busche's reflections on the use of queer theory and deconstructivism in feminist girls' work in Germany (Busche, 2013; see also Chapters 10 and 22, this *Handbook*). Batsleer (2012) also uses the lens of queer theory to explore opportunities and challenges in non-heteronormative youth work for social justice in a UK context.

Other scholars have noted the decline of sociality and association in the industrialised West (Smith, 2001; Jeffs and Smith, 2002), a central aspect of much group-based youth work practice. For example, Putnam's reflection on modern US society suggests the decline of popular sociality and the rise of an atomised existence with weak social ties. His exploration of modern suburban US life acquired some resonance within the European context (Putnam, 2001). Putnam's

work predates much of the more recent rise of new technology, and thus fails to fully reflect on the powerful effect of social media and the 'network society' (Castells, 1996). New technology allows for a reconfiguration and formation of new (virtual) social ties with new individual and group identities, and communities formed and information shared across global spaces around shared interests (Crowe and Bradford, 2006). Other networked sites spring up around local communities and shared campaigns and actions, as demonstrated in the use of social media in many youth social movements in recent years (Cohlmeyer, 2014).

The potential of digital youth work has been noted by a number of scholars and is discussed in more detail later in this volume. More optimistic commentators highlight how the Internet can provide helpful and cost-effective pedagogic strategies to engage with large groups of geographically distant young people on their own virtual territory (Melvin, 2015). However, it is also noted that there is a 'digital divide' on a local, national and international level in terms of access to net resources, how young people might use new technologies, and the capacity for digital youth work to reach a broader section of young people (Boonaert and Vettenburg, 2011). In relation to offline sociality, the increased atomisation of youth and a move from established collective leisure pursuits, from parks and streets to the bedroom gamer (Lincoln, 2015), might create tensions for traditional youth clubs and other forms of youth association. Indeed, there are questions regarding the role of contemporary youth work in fostering associational life (and what constitutes this in a digitised context) as these possibilities provide new forums beyond the twin concerns of risk and resilience, as well as, perhaps ironically, contributing to the increased 'material individualisation' of young people. As Smith (2001) notes:

> We ... also have to attend to creating (or rediscovering) ways of working with groups that take account of a new environment. One element of this is coming to terms again with the notion of

the club. Here three areas present themselves immediately for exploration: the 'club-like' qualities of spontaneous groups; the potential of 'organizing around enthusiasms' especially the enhancing of mutual aid in leisure; and working to open up associational spaces for young people in existing organizations and groups. (Smith, 2001)

SOME CONCLUSIONS

This chapter has attempted to tease out some of the critical challenges facing youth work within the UK and wider European context. Policy and practice agendas have increasingly and predominantly positioned young people as deficient and have tasked youth workers to 'fix' the errant bodies and minds of unruly and risky 'youth'. Such discursive framings of practice shape transnational and local iterations of the various national and transnational configurations and formations of youth work.

Ideological shifts and global anxieties for the future continue to frame the funding and policy arena, and young people come to embody these very concerns. The 'risk' in risk-based youth policy and practice projects these anxieties onto the bodies, minds and brains of individual, atomised young people. However, this individualised risk-management also fails to engage with broader global concerns beyond the local, the threats posed by ecological concerns, social and intergenerational injustice, and enduring structural high levels of youth unemployment as an essential by-product of global capitalism. A final more positive point is that the European Commission appears to have a growing commitment to valuing youth work in its variety of forms, both across and within EU states. As the Declaration of the 2nd European Youth Work Convention concludes:

Youth work is not a luxury but an existential necessity if a precarious Europe is to effectively address its concerns about social inclusion, cohesion and equal opportunities, and commitment to values of democracy and human rights. Youth work is a central component of a social Europe. (Council of Europe, 2015, p. 10)

Such a heartening vision of an inclusive and *essential* youth work signals the intergenerational commitment to young people and begins to discursively move beyond risk and anxiety towards a vision of hope for Europe's youth. Perhaps it reflects Karl Mannheim's view that youth is a 'revitalizing agent ... a kind of reserve which only comes to the fore...[in] quickly changing or completely new circumstances' (Mannheim, 1943, p. 34). The challenge is to uphold Mannheim's optimism and retain an inclusive and hopeful practice, within and beyond Europe at a time of economic and social uncertainty.

Notes

1 The Occupy Movement is an international anti-globalisation movement protesting against multinational corporate power and social and economic inequality and calling for the redistribution of economic and political power.
2 Indignados is a Spanish anti-austerity movement rejecting global capitalism and national political structures.
3 Following the police shooting of Mark Duggan in London in August 2011, public protests and later widespread urban unrest broke out across London and major English cities. Various explanations have included anger at police brutality, gang violence and social exclusion.
4 A letter welcoming the UK Positive for Youth policy was published in the *Guardian* newspaper in December 2011. Signatories included key figures in UK youth sector and heads of companies such as Telefonika and Starbucks see: http://www.theguardian.com/society/2011/dec/20/be-positive-about-young-people?CMP=twt_gu
5 The National Citizenship Service is a short-term social action project for 15–17-year-olds in England and Northern Ireland. It has faced much criticism as it has received considerable government funding while open access year-round youth provision has faced savage cuts (de St Croix, 2015, 2017).

REFERENCES

Arnett, J.J. (2000) 'Emerging adulthood: A theory of development from the late teens through the twenties', *American Psychologist*, 55(5): 469–480.

Batsleer, J. (2006) 'Every Girl Matters! Young Women Matter! A feminist comment', *Youth & Policy*, 90(Winter): 59–63.

Batsleer, J. (2012) 'Dangerous spaces, dangerous memories, dangerous emotions: Informal education and heteronormativity – a Manchester UK Youth Work vignette', *Discourse: Studies in the Cultural Politics of Education*, 33(3): 345–360.

Beck, U. (1992) *Risk Society: Towards a New Modernity*. London: Sage.

Blaskó, Z., Ligeti, A.S. and Sik, E. (2015) *Magyarok külföldön – Mennyien? Kik? Hol? (Hungarians abroad – how many? Who? Where?)*. Budapest: TÁRKI.

Bodnár, K. and Szabó, L.T. (2014) *The Effect of Emigration on the Hungarian Labour Market*, MNB Occasional Papers 114, Budapest: Magyar Nemzeti Bank.

Boonaert, T. and Vettenburg, N. (2011) 'Young people's internet use: Divided or diversified?', *Childhood*, 18(1): 54–66.

Bradford, S. (2011a) 'Anomalous identities, Youth work amidst "trashy daydreams" and "monstrous nightmares"'. In R. Gilchrist, T. Hodgson, T. Jeffs, J. Spence, N. Stanton and J. Walker (eds) *Reflecting on the Past Essays in the History of Youth and Community Work*. Lyme Regis: Russell House Publishing, 102–118.

Bradford, S. (2011b) 'Current policy and practice imaginations in English Youth work', presentation at The First International Conference on Youth Development (IC Youth, 2011), 1/11/11, Putrajaya, Malaysia.

Bradford, S. (2014) 'Managing the spaces of freedom: Mid-twentieth-century youth work'. In S. Mills and P. Kraftl (eds) *Informal Education, Childhood and Youth*. Basingstoke: Palgrave Macmillan, 184–196.

Bradford, S. and Cullen, F. (2014) 'Positive for youth work? Contested terrains of professional youth work in austerity England', *International Journal of Adolescence and Youth*, 19(sup1): 93–106, DOI: 10.1080/02673843.2013.863733

Brooks, R. (2013) 'The social construction of young people within education policy: Evidence from the UK's Coalition government', *Journal of Youth Studies*, 16(3): 318–333.

Busche, M. (2013) 'A girl is no girl is a girl_: Girls-work after queer theory', *Pedagogy, Culture & Society*, 21(1): 43–56.

Cairns, D. (2014) 'Here today, gone tomorrow? Student mobility decision-making in an economic crisis context', *Journal of International Mobility*, 14: 185–198.

Castells, M. (1996) *The Rise of the Network Society. The Information Age: Economy, Society and Culture Vol. I*. Cambridge, MA; Oxford, UK: Blackwell.

Clarke, J. (2008) 'What's the problem? Precarious youth: marginalization, criminalization and radicalization', *Social Work & Society, International Online Journal*, 6(2) at http://www.socwork.net/sws/article/view/62/364 (accessed 29/2/16).

Cohen, S. (1972) *Folk Devils and Moral Panics: The Creation of the Mods and Rockers*. London: McGibbon and Kee.

Cohlmeyer, D. (2014) 'Developing a technology philosophy for digital youth work', *Concept, the Journal of Contemporary Community Education Practice Theory*, 5(1): 1–7.

Council of Europe (2015) *Declaration of the 2nd European Youth Work Convention: Making a World of Difference* at http://pjp-eu.coe.int/en/web/youth-partnership/convention (accessed 19/02/17).

Council of the European Union (2010) *Resolution of the Council and of the representatives of the governments of the member states, meeting within the Council, on youth work* at http://pjp-eu.coe.int/documents/1017981/8641305/Resolution+of+the+EU+Council+of+18-19+November+2010+on+youth+work/065f18e1-7392-4d88-b4f1-f0fcf2d33cc0 (accessed 19/02/17).

Council of the European Union (2014) *Conclusions on promoting youth entrepreneurship to foster social inclusion of young people* at http://www.consilium.europa.eu/uedocs/cms_data/docs/pressdata/en/educ/142702.pdf (accessed 29/2/16).

Crowe, N. and Bradford, S. (2006) '"Hanging out in Runescape": Identity, work and leisure in the virtual playground', *Children's Geographies*, 4(3): 331–346.

Cruickshank, B. (1999) *The Will to Empower*. Ithaca: Cornell University Press.

Csillag, T. and Szelényi, I. (2015) 'Drifting from liberal democracy: Traditionalist/neo-conservative ideology of managed illiberal democratic capitalism in post-communist Europe', *Intersections, East European Journal of Society and Politics*, 1(1): 18–48.

Cullen, F. (2013) 'From DIY to teen pregnancy: New pathologies, melancholia and feminist practice in contemporary English youth work', *Pedagogy, Culture and Society*, 21(1): 23–42.

Davies, B. (1999) *From Voluntaryism to Welfare State (History of the Youth Service in England), Vol. 1*. Leicester: NYA.

Davies, B. (2011) 'What's positive for youth? A critical look at the Government's emerging "youth policy"', *Youth & Policy*, 107: 99–104.

Davies, B. (2013) 'Youth work in a changing policy landscape: The view from England', *Youth & Policy*, 110: 6–32.

de St Croix, T. (2015) 'Volunteers and entrepreneurs? Youth work and the Big Society', In G. Bright (ed.) *Youth Work: Histories, Policy and Contexts*. London: Palgrave Macmillan.

de St Croix, T. (2017) 'Time to say goodbye to the National Citizen Service?', *Youth & Policy* at http://www.youthandpolicy.org/articles/time-to-say-goodbye-ncs/ (accessed 2/7/17).

Douglas, M. (1994) *Risk and Blame: Essays in Cultural Theory*. London: Routledge.

Dunne, A., Ulicna, D., Murphy, I. and Golubeva, M. (2014) *Working with Young People: The Value of Youth Work in the European Union Case Studies*. Brussels: European Commission.

Erikson, E.H. (1968) *Identity: Youth and Crisis*. New York: Norton.

European Commission (2014) *Working with Young People: the Value of Youth Work in the European Union* at http://ec.europa.eu/assets/eac/youth/library/study/youth-work-report_en.pdf

European Commission (2016) *Youth Report 2015*, European Union at http://ec.europa.eu/assets/eac/youth/library/reports/youth-report-2015_en.pdf (accessed 19/02/17).

Eurostat (2016) Unemployment figures (July) at http://ec.europa.eu/eurostat/statistics-explained/index.php/Unemployment_statistics (accessed 27/9/16).

Evetts, J. (2009) 'New professionalism and new public management: Changes, continuities and consequences', *Comparative Sociology*, 8(2): 247–266.

Farrington, D. (1996) *Understanding and Preventing Youth Crime*. York: Joseph Rowntree Foundation.

Foucault, M. (2008) *Birth of Biopolitics. Lectures at the College de France 1978–79*. New York: Palgrave Macmillan.

Freire, P. (1972) *Pedagogy of the Oppressed*. Harmondsworth: Penguin.

Giddens, A. (1991) *The Consequences of Modernity*, Cambridge: Polity Press.

Giroux, H. (2011) *Critical Pedagogy*. New York: Continuum.

Griffin, C. (1993) *Representations of Youth*. London: Polity Press.

Griffin, C. (1997) Troubled teens: Managing disorders of transition and consumption. *Feminist Review*, 55(Spring): 4–21.

Jeffs, T. and Smith, M.K. (1999) 'The problem of "youth" for youth work', *Youth & Policy* 62: 45–66. Available in the informal education archives, http://www.infed.org/archives/youth.htm. (accessed 20/6/16).

Jeffs, T. and Smith, M.K. (2002) 'Individualization and youth work'. *Youth & Policy* 76: 39–65. Available in the informal education archives: http://www.infed.org/archives/e-texts/individualization_and_youth_work.htm (accessed 20/2/17).

Hall, G.S. (1904) *Adolescence: Its Psychology and Its Relations to Physiology, Anthropology, Sociology, Sex, Crime, Religion, and Education*, 2 vols. New York: Appleton.

Hanbury, A. and Ronan, A. (2014) 'Risk and resilience: Exploring the necessity and (im)possibility of being a critical and feminist youth worker in neo-liberal times', *Youth & Policy*, 113: 80–85 at http://www.youthandpolicy.org/wp-content/uploads/2014/11/hanbury-risk-and-resilience.pdf (accessed 22/3/15).

HM Govt (2011) *Positive for Youth: A New Approach to Cross-government Policy for Young People aged 13–19* at https://www.education.gov.uk/publications/eOrdering-Download/DFE-00133-2011.pdf (accessed 24/4/16).

Hughes, G., Cooper, C., Gormally, S. and Rippingale, J. (2014) 'The state of youth work in austerity England – reclaiming the ability to "care"', *Youth & Policy*, 113: 1–14 at http://www.youthandpolicy.org/wp-content/uploads/2014/11/hughes-youth-work-in-austerity.pdf

Kelly, P. (2001) 'Youth at risk: Processes of individualization and responsibilisation in the risk society', *Discourse; Studies in the Cultural Politics of Education*, 22(1): 23–33.

Kelly, P. (2006) 'The entrepreneurial self and "youth-at-risk": Exploring the horizons of identity in the twenty-first century', *Journal of Youth Studies*, 9(1): 17–32.

Kemshall, H. (2010) 'Risk rationalities in contemporary social work policy and practice', *British Journal of Social Work*, 40(1): 1247–1262.

Lincoln, S. (2015) '"My bedroom is me!" Young people, private space, consumption and the family home'. In E. Casey and Y. Taylor (eds) *Intimacies, Critical Consumption and Diverse Economies*. Basingstoke: Palgrave Macmillan, 87–106.

MacDonald, R. (1998) 'Youth, transitions and social exclusion: Some issues for youth research in the UK', *Journal of Youth Studies*, 1(2): 163–176.

MacDonald, R., Mason, P., Shildrick, T., Webster, C., Johnston, L. and Ridley, L. (2001) 'Snakes & ladders: In defence of studies of youth transition', *Sociological Research Online*, 5(4), at http://www.socresonline.org.uk/5/4/macdonald.html (accessed 15/3/16).

Mannheim, K. (1943) *Diagnosis of our Time: Wartime Essays of a Sociologist*. London: Kegan Paul, Trench, Trubner and Co. Ltd.

McAleer, M. (2013) *Time to Go? A Qualitative Research Study Exploring the Experience & Impact of Emigration on Ireland's Youth*. National Youth Council of Ireland at http://www.youth.ie/sites/youth.ie/files/NYCI_Youth_Emigration_Report.pdf (accessed 13/3/16).

Melvin, J. (2015) 'Youth work in digital spaces'. In G. Bright (ed.) *Youth Work: Histories, Policy and Contexts*. London: Palgrave Macmillan, 216–235.

Muncie, J. (2009) *Youth and Crime* (3rd edition). London: Sage.

Nagy, A. and Szekely, L. (2011) 'Online youth work and eYouth – a guide to the world of the digital natives', *Children and Youth Services Review*, 33(11): 2186–2197.

National Youth Agency (2007) *Evidence of the Impact of the 'Youth Development Model' on Outcomes for Young People – a Literature Review*, Leicester: National Youth Agency.

Patterson, C., Tyler, C. and Lexmond, J. (2014) *Character and Resilience Manifesto*, The all-party parliamentary group on Social Mobility, London: House of Commons.

Pearson, G. (1983) *Hooligan: A History of Respectable Fears*. London: The Macmillan Press.

Putnam, R.D. (2001) *Bowling alone: The collapse and revival of American community*. New York: Simon and Schuster.

Rabinow, P. (ed.) (1991) *The Foucault Reader: An Introduction to Foucault's Thought*. Harmondsworth: Penguin Books.

Roberts, K. (2012) 'The end of the long baby-boomer generation', *Journal of Youth Studies*, 15(4): 479–498.

Rose, N. (1999) *Powers of Freedom: Reframing Political Thought*. Cambridge: Cambridge University Press.

Sik, D. (2015) 'Incubating radicalism in Hungary – the case of Sopron and Ózd', *Intersections, East European Journal of Society and Politics*, 1(1): 100–121.

Smith, M.K. (2001) 'Young people, informal education and association', *the informal education homepage*, at www.infed.org/youthwork/ypandassoc.htm (accessed 23/4/16).

Smith, M.K., Stanton, N. and Wylie, T. (2015) *Youth Work and Faith: Debates, Delights and Dilemmas*. Dorset: Russell House Publishing Ltd.

Soler, P., Planas, A. and Feixa, C. (2014) 'Young people and youth policies in Spain in times of austerity: Between juggling and the trapeze', *International Journal of Adolescence and Youth*, 19: 62–78.

Te Riele, K. (2006) 'Youth "at risk": Further marginalising the marginalised', *Journal of Education Policy*, 21(2): 129–145.

Walby, S. (2015) *Crisis*. Cambridge: Polity Press.

Williamson, H. (2011) 'The Emperor still has no clothes: Some realities about youth work interventions in the lives of "vulnerable" young people in the 21st century', *Psihološka Istraživanga [Psychological Research]*, XIV(2): 193–207 at http://www.komunikacija.org.rs/komunikacija/casopisi/Psiholoska%20istrazivanja/XIV_2/05/download_gb (accessed 30/3/16).

Williamson, H. (2014) 'Radicalisation to retreat: responses of the young to austerity Europe', *International Journal of Adolescence and Youth*, DOI: 10.1080/02673843.2013.812041 at y

Wylie, T. (2010) 'Youth work in a cold climate', *Youth & Policy*, 105: 1–8.

10

Undoing Sexism and Youth Work Practice. Seeking Equality. Unsettling Ideology. Affirming Difference. A UK Perspective

Janet Batsleer

INTRODUCTION

This chapter draws on and summarises arguments I have developed in my book *Youth Working with Girls and Women in Community Settings: A Feminist Perspective* (Batsleer, 2013) and research undertaken since then on a variety of projects. It is also strongly influenced by my reading of the work of Sara Ahmed (2017). I am seeking to chip away at the wall of sexism and to show how youth work practice can both be complicit in building that wall of sexism and can chip away at it. I introduce three moments in the practice of undoing sexism. The first concerns equality; the second concerns ideology critique; and the third is concerned with the affirmation of difference. Each of these three moments is necessary in the practice of chipping away at sexism. I argue that it is essential to situate the practice of engagement with young women and young men in the neoliberal policy context and wider contexts of governance (Gewirtz, 2002; Ball, 2016), as well as in the

context of wider cultural messages, in order to chip away at sexism. It is the institutionalised patterns and framings of practice that need to be unsettled and it is a mistake to locate the challenge to sexism primarily in a challenge to internalised sexism among the young. The terms 'sex' and 'gender' are used somewhat interchangeably in what follows as there is not space here to interrogate the rich discussion which accompanies their use (Oakley, 2015). As I understand youth work as an embodied practice of socio-cultural accompaniment, the term 'sex-gender regime' (Hill-Collins, 1990) seems to usefully show that there are relations of ruling at stake here, which have to do in complex ways with culture and embodiment, and is used at various points in what follows.

Before the term 'sexism' was invented it was called 'the problem that has no name'. But the pressure of the problem was felt widely and so it came to be named. The process of naming sometimes appears to bring what is named into being. If it has no name, it can appear to be not there. The same process of naming needs to occur in the contemporary moment, sometimes designated as 'postfeminist': a time when women and girls can claim equality under the law and ask to be treated as individuals in their own right. So naming the pressure that can be called and is usefully called sexism happens once more (Ahmed, 2015). This pressure is deeply caught up in other pressures which control the lives of women and men. That reality is taken for granted in this chapter. And it remains useful to tease out the forms of sexism, naming it in order to undo and abolish it. I therefore offer a perspective which recognises the persistence of institutionalised sexism and its changing forms, making a contribution to the archive of both the nature and manifestation of sexism and of the challenges to it mounted within youth work.

Most of the research drawn on in this chapter was undertaken in the United Kingdom but the chapter also draws on knowledge developed as part of my involvement in a European research project called *Partispace* (http://partispace.eu/). Especially in the section on unsettling ideology I seek to show the complicity of marketised and individualised practices in sustaining a wall of sexism in work with young people.

What is now termed Youth Work emerged in the context of community-based and philanthropic social initiatives as a response to conditions of the poor under industrial capitalism. Now, in the period of transformation being wrought by the computer and post-computer based, networked global capitalism, youth work, like the young people with whom youth workers seek to work, is newly positioned (Jeffs, 2015). The networks and flows of power which are re-shaping social life globally, particularly those associated with new technologies and forms of communication, are being harnessed by young people in new ways (Bessant, 2014). Everything is different, it can easily be said. And yet, oddly, so much remains the same (Bates, 2014, 2016). This paradox of the persistence of old entrenched forms of inequality and

power difference alongside radically new ways of being-in-the-world is a paradox with which youth work practice must necessarily engage. It has been said that we now live in a period of 'gender (and sexism) without women', 'racism' without 'race', social class without class solidarities, into which children and young people are being inducted through their experience, especially of the 'virtual world' (Braidotti, 2006). In other words, these social hierarchies persist and take forms of control over widespread populations, without at the same time bringing into being peoples who seek to undermine them. It may be the case that in youth work therefore there is encountered a curious passivity, a lack of activism, as the grids of control over practice deepen. The problem has to be named again; the archive of responses to the problem re-covered.

SEEKING EQUALITY

The Audit

One simple way of understanding institutionalised sexism is as a claim to a natural hierarchy: in Audre Lorde's terms: 'The belief in the inherent superiority of one sex and with it the right to dominance' (1984: 114); a definition Lorde presented alongside her definitions of other hierarchical practices of dominance including racism. Youth workers involved with countering sexism have first of all to ask how terms connected with 'sex' or 'gender' are being used, and whether they are being used to reinforce ideas of a natural hierarchy in which males are seen to be stronger or cleverer or genetically better adapted to certain tasks than females or vice versa (Ivinson, 2014). When this is the case, the term 'essentialist' is used, and women's movements have sought in a variety of ways to challenge such essentialism. Boys are not essentially and inevitably stronger or more powerful; girls are not essentially and inevitably weaker or more caring.

'Sex Equality Strategies' refer to ways of noticing and responding in situations when girls and boys are not being treated equally, usually so that girls are being given a lesser set of opportunities than boys. In youth clubs and youth groups equality audits are the basis for strategies to develop. The audit concerns the question of equal access to resources and asks questions about money, activities, and allocation and use of space (Hanbury, Lee and Batsleer, 2010).

In a typical large modern sports centre cum youth club (Youth Centre), such an audit might include the following: who is using the various sports facilities and activities on offer and at what times; who is positioned where in the club in terms of the use of the social areas and canteen; who is using the arts and crafts areas and dance studios; how much space and time is allocated to each of these activities. It also involves a simple count of numbers of boys and girls using the facilities. It can consider the overall budget of the provision and what is spent on the activities currently associated with boys and girls.

The equality audit can be extended in a variety of ways, to include the use of questionnaires with young people exploring their experience of family life, school, work and leisure time and the expectations of boys and girls in those contexts. It can also be extended to consider the staffing of the facility; to what extent do men or women occupy senior positions in the staffing hierarchy and who fills the main support roles such as cleaning and catering. Furthermore, in the funding bodies which support the Centre, who directs and controls their funding decisions. The audit can ask questions about pay inequalities also, if such information about pay grades and hours allocations of staff at different levels is available.

It would be an unusual Youth Centre where there was a strong form of sex segregation and inequality, but it would be an equally unusual Centre in which there were no forms of marginalisation and no limiting of opportunities in relation to which part-time and migrant workers came off worse. It would

be an unusual Centre in which it was girls rather than boys who dominated the pool and snooker table and the outdoor football spaces. It would be unusual to see boys filling the arts and crafts spaces. Such designations and valuing of spaces and activities through gender form the bricks in the wall of sexism and the turn to autonomous work is one response to this. This is based on the premise that in gathering, naming and enquiring into shared experience, the problems associated with inequality are named and then can be undone (Batsleer, 2013).

Autonomous Group Work

In 'Mixed Clubs' (open to all) there is a perceived need to manage sex and sexuality, specifically heterosexuality, among the working class, through greater social education and supervised encounters (Tinkler, 1995; Butterfield and Spence, 2009). This has often been accompanied by a persistent fear that single sex spaces are spaces of homoerotic experimentation and even encourage an unhealthy form of love between adults and young people, especially between men and boys. Shared space for boys and girls comes at the cost of intensifying the pressure to conform to fairly conservative heterosexual norms which silence same sex desire and make 'masculinity' active and agentic and 'femininity' attractive, nurturing and attentive. Although much has changed since the inception of mixed youth clubs almost one hundred years ago, my own research observations in open access mixed youth clubs suggest a persistent assumption that these are spaces in which heterosexual relationships are taken as normal and in which early practice in dating happens. In these patterns there is a persistent assumption that girls are less active than boys and that when girls are actively sexual and non-monogamous there is a problem (Holland and Thomson, 2010).

A great deal of youth work as social education in practice has become compensatory.

That is to say it seeks to make up for certain 'lacks', especially in morality, that are felt to be present among the young and disadvantaged. Girls need to be encouraged not to get pregnant and boys need to be encouraged to curb their aggression. This is all too readily seen as a matter of instilling morality and good character. Youth work becomes concerned with meeting and fulfilling norms and expectations already laid down by previous generations. This conservative tendency in social education means that 'mixing' alone does not strengthen the access to experience and opportunities or equalise the position of girls and boys. Girls' role at the sides and edges of the mixed club – classically watching the boys at play rather than playing themselves – became embedded in mixed club provision. Further strategies to promote equality therefore need to emerge, just as they did in the context of an emerging new feminist wave in the 1970s.

Since 'mixed' club work seems paradoxically to build inequality into its structures, the movement for autonomy is a necessary response. With the 'second wave' of the women's movement came a concern that the move to 'mixed' clubs had not strengthened the position of girls. Legal changes to prevent discrimination in education and the provision of services, and to ensure pay equality, consequent on a renewed period of activism, created a context in which feminist activism could go still further and open up the space of the 'private sphere' for scrutiny. Patterns of discrimination and harassment evident in social spaces such as clubs became a focus for attention. In making sexual violence and inequality in personal and domestic life visible and contested, feminist organising also made visible the ways in which informal practices of violence, harassment and control were present in schools, workplaces and social and recreational spaces, including mixed youth clubs (Wood, 1984).

This form of activism which took as its focus the systematic presence of violence and control has been associated and linked through ideas and people with other movements against injustice with strong and emerging commitment to and consciousness of the power of autonomous organising – the Black Consciousness Movement and Disability Activism being among the most important examples. The power dynamics involved in arguments for both integration and autonomy or 'separatism' as it came to be called are complex. The slogan from the Disability Rights movement: 'Segregation we Hate. Autonomy we Choose' sums up the spirit of such movements well. It was from the maelstrom of these movements across Europe and across the world that the autonomous Girls Work movement in youth work emerged with its claim: 'Girls are People too!' (Spence, 2010; Batsleer, 2013).

Sex Equality strategies in club work have therefore gone beyond the mere presence of both boys and girls to engage in the positive action needed to ensure girls could access all the opportunities the clubs offered and try activities usually confined to boys. The purpose of this work is not to allocate particular closed spaces to girls and boys and confirm sexist allocations of resources through stereotypical gendered activities. Rather it provides an opportunity to be and speak together and address all the ways in which 'it is not fair'. In this, it is powerfully connected to the second aspect of undoing sexism explored here: unsettling ideology.

UNSETTLING IDEOLOGY AND YOUTH WORK PRACTICE

'Unsettling Ideology' refers to the ways that femininity and masculinity is taken for granted and given norms are repeated through the structuring of youth work. Norms are always present in groups but sometimes they are only recognised when they are not conformed to. Our understanding of sexism has become very much associated with the ways in which norms are lived, come up against,

chipped away at. What does it mean to allocate pink to girls and blue to boys? What
happens when we do it differently? What
happens when the girls in a youth club say
they want their room to be painted anything
but pink? What happens is that sexism is
chipped away at.

But the force and pressure of norms are
sustained in powerful processes which are
usually invisible to us, they are so taken for
granted. These processes are the 'sex–gender
regime', the structures which are 'in place'.
It is here that I find the term 'ideology' useful. I use it to refer to the naturalisation of a
sex/gender hierarchy. Another way of stating
this is to say that sexism is operating silently;
it does not draw attention to itself; it does
not announce itself; it exerts its pressures in
ways that seem so natural and normal as to
pass unnoticed, and undoing sexism means
that nevertheless we do notice them, both
as an inarticulate pressure and intuition and
in occasionally hesitant verbalisations. For
example, we notice that 'girls don't want
to ...' or 'boys don't want to ...'. Or that we
are talking about the boys again. Or, when
it comes to pregnancy, not talking about the
boys again.

The difficulty of supporting girls and boys to
access non-conventional opportunities relates
to the power of ideological framings of femininity and masculinity within institutionalised
sexism. Even if girls and boys are offered
equal access to opportunities, those trying to
access them will rapidly encounter the invisible wall. The sex-gender regime becomes
naturalised ideologically. So there are certain
things boys and girls just don't do: only when
they transgress the norms do they discover the
'gender trouble' they are in (Butler, 1989).
Much of this occurs well beyond the power
of youth work through the poisonous pedagogies of corporate culture. The investigation of
popular culture and the strengthening of the
capacities of young people to engage with
both pleasure and critique in popular culture
has long been a significant focus for youth
workers who are undoing sexism.

Policy Framings and Invisible Walls of Sexism

'Unsettling ideology' as a strategy for practice addresses the experience of governance
in projects, the way the work is formulated
and framed. It makes this open to question in
order to create openings and opportunities
otherwise likely to be denied to both young
women and young men.

Sexism as ideology and practice sometimes operates when sex–gender regimes are
visible, taken for granted and reinforced as
a basis for social action and for the deroga-
tion of women in public life. A youth worker
active in challenging sexism via a Twitter
campaign was told on Twitter by her local
MP 'Silly little girls should keep their pretty
little heads out of politics'. Much of the time,
however, the sex–gender regime is invisible
and needs to be made visible, if inequalities
and oppressive power dynamics are to be
addressed. Making a sex–gender regime and
its forms of control and violence (towards
both boys and girls) visible opens up a range
of questions concerning the modalities of
inequality, injustice and oppression.

Although, as already stated, neoliberal
policy and governance can seem to operate
in a world of gender (and sexism) without
women, racism without race and social class
without class solidarities, I argue that these
ideological framings need to be unsettled. As
well as carrying a general power to shape and
frame practice away from earlier more collective and associational goals, neoliberal forms
of governance can be recognised as deepening and changing patterns of sexism which
youth work practitioners need to address.

Open Access Work and Targeting as Ideological: Making Sexism Visible

The distinction between 'open access' and
'targeted' work in youth work has become
one of the defining distinctions in the field of

UK Youth Work, and yet the influence of these different models in constructing or chipping away at sexism is rarely discussed.

By 'open access' is meant something like the old club or 'youth house' provision; it may also refer to street work projects (historically termed 'detached work') or other outreach programmes. As discussed above, one of the issues for such 'open access' provision is that apparently open social spaces tend to become the preserve of particular groups and become dominated by them and so positive action to challenge this needs to be consistently built in to the programmes of work.

This is particularly evident for example in the new generation of large open access Youth Centres in England which were developed in the UK towards the end of the 'New Labour' period of Government in 2007 as part of the 'MyPlace' programme (Wright, 2015). 'My Place' centres offer a strange re-enactment and embodiment of early and mid-20th-century ideologies concerning young people in a 21st-century building programme. The new aspects reflect the struggles over the meanings of shared social space discussed earlier in relation to 'mixing' and autonomous work: a girls' room seems necessary now in a way it never was previously, though it remains still smaller than other spaces and is typically dedicated to beauty and pampering. The focus on beauty for girls embodies prevailing and conservative gendered messages. The emphasis on sport and fitness (where boys predominate) is stronger than ever. Positive steps have been taken to embrace 'inclusion' for children and young people with disabilities, whether physical, cognitive or developmental, with dedicated times and staffing in all the centres. The curriculum which the buildings propose is one in which sport predominates, but it also includes drama and performance, cooking and eating, socialising with snooker and pool tables as well as coffee bars, beauty, music technology, art, dance.

'Targeted' work was developed in apparent contrast with open access work as a means of responding to young people whose lives were seen to be particularly vulnerable. All members of 'targeted groups' came to be defined through their 'lacks' or 'deficits', or through an analysis of the 'blocks and barriers' they faced in finding a voice. In the US models of 'positive youth development' have particularly arisen in this context, and here there still remains a powerful tendency to see gender as an essentialised form of difference, as measures of positive identity development are explored (Catalano et al., 2016). 'Targeting' of specific interventions towards disadvantaged youth can be seen as a way of addressing the systemic inequalities and exclusions thrown up by globalised neoliberal systems without requiring or even seeking any real transformation of those systems.

In the policy language of 'targeted work' it is unusual to find explicit discourses of gender, and yet the 'targets' and themes for the work are often implicitly gendered. Work with young people 'Not in Education Employment and Training' can become a channel for strongly gendered expectations about workplaces, from manual trades to health and social care and hair and beauty courses. Work concerned with young people's mental health works with an embedded 'difference' in diagnoses along gender lines as well as with a set of assumptions about the forms of bullying, abuse and violence which frequently accompany mental and emotional difficulties in the teenage years. These tend to make girls seem 'mad'/victimised and boys seem 'bad'/persecutory. Since funding for work follows these discourses it is not surprising that practice in youth work as social education is so often drawn to an uncritical rehearsal of conventional gendered messages in a persistent sex-gender regime. With an increased emphasis on measurement and comparison of outcomes, the conservative goals of such practice become further entrenched.

Most obviously, work which aims to reduce rates of teenage pregnancy is gendered, with work with girls and boys taking different forms, and condom distribution being its most measurable form. Work which targets 'young parents' and focuses on parenting strategies as a form of early intervention can create a focus on young mothers and a subsidiary engagement with young fathers, which takes different forms. When there is an apparently gender-neutral focus to the policy it is harder to engage with the ways in which sexism and a set of practices which lower the status of women are being reinforced. However, it has been widely argued in the years following the adoption of the Teenage Pregnancy Strategy that being subject to hostile scrutiny and the gaze of others, whether of professionals or simply of older women, is one of the most demeaning aspects of the experience of being a young mother (Arai, 2009; Duncan, 2010).

Similarly, even when the framing of young women's contributions as active citizens emphasises their assets and their pro-social behaviour, it can be experienced as placing a burden of responsibility on young women which is not expected of their male peers. Even when 'girl power' is affirmed, it is frequently as a means of enabling girls to limit the violence and control they experience in order to sustain them in their role as supporting the family. Internationally, therefore, the advocacy of girl power as a means of addressing all kinds of poverty and inequality is increasingly being subjected to important critical scrutiny (Shain, 2013).

So all of these practices form part of the archive of sexism, usually without ever mentioning the terms 'sex' or 'gender'. When projects challenge prevailing assumptions which underpin funding they are part of a movement against sexism in youth work. This happens when youth workers explore sexual pleasure in workshops funded as part of 'teenage pregnancy prevention', explore anger with women as well as depression with men to understand oppression and not simply to provide 'anger management strategies', and when they offer support to work experience in IT and building trades to girls and hairdressing and health and social care to boys.

Individualism and Sexism: Against Role Models and for Dissidence

The reorganisation, fluidity and deconstruction of social life and inherited forms of social solidarity has been accompanied by an intensification of individualisation and 'responsibilisation' of young people and especially of young women (Scharff, 2012). Whereas consideration of sexism most often leads to a focus on the injustice inherent in structural patterns and norms, a persistent focus on role modelling and mentoring has emerged which can suggest that individual change is the most significant aspect of youth work. The idea of the 'role model' has emerged powerfully as a basis for practice in two apparently contrasting contexts; that of normative masculinity and that of non-conformist sexuality, specifically in relation to 'coming out' as not straight. However, it is emerging too in discussions of girls as needing to develop confidence to cease being 'self-censoring' and 'under-aspirational'. Such motivational practices are present now in almost every youth work project to some degree, including in the form of peer mentoring. Used to support 'coming out' processes and the aspirations for social mobility of individuals held back within the current system by 'glass ceilings' of various familiar kinds, for young people aligned with groups whose lives have been stigmatised or rendered invisible and apparently unliveable it is clearly the case that mentoring or the simple presence of adult 'possibility models' is immensely valuable.

But the idea of the role-model has become part of the widespread common-sense of professional youth and community work practice. The idea of role-modelling has been mobilised in relation to mentoring and coaching projects (Colley, 2003) where docility in relationship is sought as the vehicle for achieving employability and other social goals such as a reduction in anti-social behaviour. What is offered can seem to be a re-moralisation rather than a challenge to systemic patterns of power and control. 'Bullying' as anti-social behaviour rather than harassment as an outworking of racism or sexism or class power becomes the focus of youth work intervention. Characteristically it is mentoring programmes in which someone has 'converted' their lives which are offered as the best forms of practice. For young men, the anti-role models of criminal gangs, with the appeal of instant gratification, are set against a masculine discipline of work and sport and deferred gratification or militarism and glory. In the UK, the work of The Prince's Trust, Outward Bound, Brathay and One-to-One programmes regularly figure strongly in reporting of the youth work constructed as the positive alternative to gang involvement. Following the UK riots of 2011, news reports focused predictably on this theme. Here too a strengthened emphasis on the measurability of outcomes of interventions will tend to reinforce conventionally gendered practice.

However, the learning relationships in such contexts need not be constructed as 'modelling' or even 'mentoring'. When the significance of one-to-one work of various kinds is constantly affirmed it can be difficult for project workers to affirm the importance of association and groups as relationship. Yet over and over again it is relationship rather than 'gender specific modelling' which is affirmed by young people as important to them (Robb et al., 2015). Relationships with trusted adults both within and beyond the immediate family context; mutual support and self-help within peer groups: these are identified and valued by young people despite the silencing of their value within much public discourse and also within professional common-sense. When young people find a dissident peer group it is not so much about modelling as about the opening up of possibilities to live differently and otherwise than by the norms expected by sexism. Yet the ideological framing of 'modelling' continues to suggest powerfully normative routes that are to be followed, and resisting the power of these norms is resistance to the pressure of sexism.

Since 2009, the Feminist Webs network has been using resources generated by second-wave feminists in the Girls Work movement to resource current practice. The first project 'Done Hair and Nails? Now What? challenged the association of femininity with beauty, pampering and body image. It would be difficult for a mentor to avoid the issue of dress codes but this is what Feminist Webs insists on confronting in a dissident practice. The book created as part of 'Feminist Webs' *The Exciting Life of Being a Woman: A Handbook for Women and Girls* (available from www.feministwebs.com) gives a clear sense of the range of dissident challenges to normative ways of working with girls that the network has enabled and supported (Batsleer, 2010). This emphasis on dissidence suggests a strong connection with the third strategy for undoing sexism: opening up to difference.

Affirming Difference

'Affirming Difference' refers to the refusal of binary oppositions, in which the masculine is the positive term and the feminine is simply its opposite. Anti-sexist work soon opens up exploration of a whole palate of difference which affirms the possibilities of life for many young people who dissent from this binary. Here the term 'binary' does not refer primarily to those living as non-binary persons, but rather to all expressions of masculinity or femininity which do not construct these terms as opposites or shaped by a hierarchy of dominance and subordination.

Within neoliberal systems, the power of naming, categorising and measuring has become a means of allocating diminishing resource and at the same time a means of classification and social abjection (Tyler, 2013). 'Diversity' may be valued at the expense of 'equality', yet this is a form of commodification of difference which entrenches injustice. Among young people in 'targeted groups' the sense that they are being involved in projects 'in order to tick your boxes' is palpable, and increasingly expressed with frustration and anger. Classifications of this kind are experienced as a form of violence. By affirming difference, I am referring to practices which are other than expected, other than the norm. Tick boxes of diversity can be seen as a way of reinforcing a norm.

Youth working which focuses on the politics of recognition and affirmation of complex identities can sometimes be at the expense of a focus on justice and fairness in which identity claims are necessarily discounted. Both of these approaches in turn can divert attention from consideration of the need for redistribution and social transformation as a basis of social justice (Fraser, 2013). Whilst for some writers, the space of 'gender-conscious practice' remains one of exploring the complexities of the socio-cultural formation of identities (Morgan and Harland, 2009), there is a good case to be made for a rejection of identity claims as the basis for gender-conscious practice and a return to issues of justice and of the even more fundamental issue of supporting liveable lives. Opening up to difference may enable a swerve away from classification, with its fixation on identities, whilst affirming a range of experience of identity itself, in both its more solid and more fluid forms.

Queer and Anti-Sexist Spaces

The establishment of Girls Work groups seems a rebellious act, concerned with challenging the relations of ruling which mean girls come second and are only concerned with care and cosmetics. When girls are seen as the second sex it is also often the case that an ethics of care is seen as secondary rather than fundamental. Girls Work practice wants to turn this round and put an ethic of care first.

Girls Work spaces across Europe have often been spaces with a significant presence of lesbian youth workers and where alternative and more dissident female identifications were supported. However, when anti-sexist politics disappears from practice, and girls groups focus mainly on arts and crafts, cooking and pampering and other activities which were and remain strongly aligned with normative femininities, lesbian identification also becomes marginalised once more (Busche, 2013).

The flourishing of an anti-sexist men's movement and the development of Boys Work as a partner to Girls Work has been a small but highly significant and supportive response to these concerns. Boys against sexism work can offer a focus on some of the same themes for boys as Girls Work does for girls. The challenge is one of timing – not running girls' sessions only at times when the football leagues are running – and there is also a challenge concerning the register of response – not responding to boys' complaints of being left out of girls work sessions only by picking up a football and taking it to the local park. The challenge is to develop sessions which are open and in which all can explore the pressures and violences which sexism inflicts and which they endure.

The challenges to hegemonic masculinity and especially to sexual violence against both girls and boys can make it difficult to discuss sex and relationships and emotion and mental health with boys in a supportive way. Currently, much activism in relation to questions of gender, power and normativity is developing first through online spaces and in a connected way through older forms of organising, especially through student spaces. It is typically led by young women, but masculine support for feminist organising is no longer taboo, either from the point of view of feminist organising or from the point of view of manhood. Nevertheless, young men are less present in these spaces than young women and shared space on an equal basis is still difficult to find (Bates, 2014, 2016).

Spaces to Encounter Difference: Against Religious Discrimination

In current student politics in the UK the covering of women and their seclusion in their own 'separate space' (including chosen 'self-seclusion') is seen as an act of aggression not so much against women as against liberal values of freedom, openness and mixing. The affirmation of the right of Muslim women to sit covered in public and separately from men is seen as an affirmation of religious tolerance too far. The 'mixing' of public space comes to be seen as a marker of liberal values. In this context, the organisation of 'girls groups' in youth clubs in inner city areas with significant Muslim populations takes on new and charged meanings. There is activism here too which both mirrors and unsettles student activisms.

It is apparent that many young women live in communities where the expectation of shared social space between men and women is limited and in which both men and women expect to live separate lives as adults in their own spaces, with women's lives being lived in the family space primarily. This does not necessarily mean lives lived directly under the thumb of male partners. Many Muslim women from Somali communities for example head single-parent households. Youth workers who seek to connect with young people 'where they are' have been drawn to organising *Girltalk* groups as a means of offering legitimacy to their work with some communities. Whereas there is a legal requirement to send children to school there is no such requirement for engagement in non-school spaces and so other means of engagement are found by youth workers. This usually means engagement from the beginning on the terms of the community, and this involves offering single-sex spaces. It is clearly the case that when such opportunities are created the voices of school girls and university students blend closely to challenge harassment.

Girltalk is a group within The Hideaway Youth Project, Manchester, UK. It attracts girls from a number of the communities to be found within inner Manchester. In 2015 girls from Hideaway were involved in a number of projects which took their perspectives into the wider community. They were involved in 'Consent Workshops' and joined a panel on the theme of 'Consent' at a local WHY? Festival. The WHY? Festival linked initiatives led by young people to celebrate and explore the United Nations Declaration on the Rights of the Child. With Odd Arts, Hideaway Girls made a film (*Why can't it stop?*) about their experience of street sexual harassment: being called out to sexually in the streets and about the way they were being treated (especially after the Paris attacks) as a result of wearing the headscarf. All of these forms of violence are closely connected for girls attending the Hideaway Youth Project. They respond to attacks on their religious identity by affirming the meaning and value of the headscarf more strongly. In turn the affirmation of dignity and modesty through covering becomes part of the protest against sexual harassment. Identity, but also exploration of that identity, and a politics of justice are deeply intertwined. There is a crying out for communication too across some of the barriers created by the current political climate, based on a call for love rather than hate towards those who see their headscarves as the mark of difference which disguises a potential terrorist.

In discussing this example I seek to show how the concern with sex/gender and challenge to sexism opens up the possibility of new and affirmative practice. Challenging sexism cannot be done by one group of women on behalf of another group who are already active in confronting oppression, but only in solidarity. It is therefore in dialogue that the possibility emerges of women and men from a range of backgrounds acting in solidarity with one another and as allies in movements which challenge sexism. It can be argued that it is an engagement with a politics of difference rather than a politics of identity which has enabled this, even though the affirmation of identity is strong within the space, itself a fragile dwelling in which people of all ages have gathered over four decades to confront institutionalised racism and support each other.

CONCLUSION

In this chapter I have highlighted three key strategies which counter sexism: sex equality work through audits and through autonomous groups, clubs and associations; ideology critique to unsettle sex/gender hierarchies and assumptions in prevailing policy agendas, including those which focus on targeting and on individual progress; and affirmation of difference and the possibilities of living differently. All of these strategies can support the continued interconnection of youth work and women's movements in an inescapably globalised future, for the sake of the girls to come.

In creating an archive of sexism in the fields of youth work, informal learning and community learning, therefore, activists also create the possibility of imagining new ways of being and even new possibilities of joyful living.

Some contemporary materialist feminisms, like earlier emancipatory feminisms, see a joyful movement of life and connection as the ground of feminisms: 'moving into and beyond feminism just for the joy of it' as bell hooks once put it (hooks, 1994). But in the development of multi-faceted practices of care for all living beings there is a need to acknowledge the impact of loss and of the precariousness of lives lived in the underbelly of the capitalist system. Loss of home for migrant communities and loss of work over generations are part of the story in many of the places where youth work and informal learning happens. This is the context in which new kinds of youth work practice will happen which seek equality, seek to unsettle sex/gender ideology and which seek to support and generate new ways of being girl (Gonick and Gannon, 2014), being boy, being non-binary. It is a practice which is by definition open to new connectivities between Girl and Machine; Girl and Animal; Girl and Sex; Girl/Girl; Girl/Boy; Girl and Power; Girl and Divine; Being Infant/Young/Queer. Being sensible of the ways in which these connectivities are enabled and are to be enabled globally is one urgent task for current utopian practice in youth work which proposes that undoing sexism and other oppressive and life threatening practices as well as affirming difference is possible. The Brownies and Guides did and still do that in the traditional Thinking Day; emancipatory open youth work looked for opportunities to build those connections through international journeys and exchanges; now is the moment in which online space opens into such solidarities. Dancing in the streets as a flash mob from the youth club against violence against women, as happened in the 'Fifteen Days against Violence against Women Actions' in 2014, is a possible taste of the future.

REFERENCES

Ahmed, S. (2015) 'Sexism: A Problem with a Name'. *New Formations* 86, pp. 5–13.

Ahmed, S. (2017) *Living a Feminist Life*. Duke University Press: Durham North Carolina.

Arai, L. (2009) Teenage *Pregnancy: The Making and Unmaking of a Problem*. Policy Press: Bristol.

Ball, S. (2016) 'Neoliberal Education? Confronting the Slouching Beast'. *Policy Futures in Education* 14(8), pp. 1046–1059.

Bates, L. (2014) *Everyday Sexism*. Simon and Schuster UK: London.

Bates, L. (2016) *Girl Up*. Simon and Schuster UK: London.

Batsleer, J. (2010) 'Feminist Webs: A Case Study of the Personal, Professional and Political in Youth Work' in M. Robb and R. Thomson (eds) *Critical Practice with Children and Young People*. Bristol: Policy Press, pp. 217–33.

Batsleer, J. (2013) *Youth Working with Girls and Women in Community Settings: A Feminist Perspective*. London: Ashgate Arena.

Bessant, J. (2014) *Democracy Bytes: New Media and New Politics and Generational Change*. London: Palgrave.

Braidotti, R. (2006) *Transpositions: On Nomadic Ethics*. Cambridge: Polity.

Busche, M. (2013) 'A Girl is No Girl is a Girl_: Girls-work after Queer Theory'. *Pedagogy Culture and Society* 21(1), pp. 43–56.

Butler, J. (1989) *Gender Trouble: Feminism and the Subversion of Identity*. New York: Routledge.

Butterfield, M. and Spence, J. (2009) 'The Transition from Girls Clubs to Girls Clubs and Mixed Clubs' in R. Gilchrist, T. Jeffs, J. Spence and J. Walker (eds) *Essays in the History of Youth and Community Work: Discovering the Past*. Lyme Regis, UK: Russell House Publishing, pp. 60–92.

Catalano, R.F. et al. (2016) 'Positive Youth Development in the United States: Research Findings on Evaluations of Positive Youth Development Programmes'. *Annals of the American Academy of Political and Social Science* 591(1), pp. 98–124.

Colley, H. (2003) *Mentoring for Social Inclusion: A Critical Approach to Nurturing Mentor Relationships*. London: Routledge.

Cullen, F. (2013) 'From DIY to Teen Pregnancy: New Pathologies, Melancholia and Feminist Practice in Contemporary English Youth Work. *Pedagogy, Culture and Society* 21(1), pp. 23–42.

Duncan, C., Alexander, C. and Edwards, R. (2010) *Teenage Motherhood: What's the Problem?* London: Tufnell Press.

Fraser, N. (2013) *Fortunes of Feminism: From State-managed Capitalism to Neo-Liberal Crisis*. New York: Verso.

Gewirtz, S. (2002) *The Managerial School: Post Welfarism and Social Justice in Education*. London: Routledge.

Gonick, M. and Gannon, S. (2014) *Becoming Girl*. Canada: Women's Press.

Hanbury, A., Lee, A. and Batsleer, J. (2010) 'Youth Work with Girls: A Feminist Perspective' in Batsleer, J. and Davies, B. (eds) *What is Youth Work?* Exeter: Learning Matters, pp. 116–128.

Hill-Collins, P. (1990) *Black Feminist Thought: Knowledge, Consciousness and the Politics of Empowerment*. London and New York: Routledge.

Holland, J. and Thomson, R. (2010) 'Revisiting Youthful Sexuality: Continuities and Change over Two Decades'. *Sexual and Relationship Therapy* 25(3), pp. 342–350.

hooks, b. (1994) 'Moving Into and Beyond Feminism: Just for the Joy of It' in *Outlaw Culture Resisting Representations*. New York: Routledge, pp. 283–328.

Ivinson, G. (2014) 'How Gender Became Sex: Mapping the Gendered Effects of Sex-Group Categorisations onto Pedagogy, Policy and Practice'. *Education Research* 56(2), pp. 155–170.

Jeffs, T. (2015) 'Innovation in Youth Work'. *Youth & Policy 114 Special Issue The Next Five Years*, pp. 75–95.

Lorde, A. (1984) *Sister Outsider: Essays and Speeches*. New York: Falling Wall Press.

McIntosh, M. (1993) 'Queer Theory and the War of the Sexes' in J. Bristow and A. Wilson (eds) *Activating Theory: Lesbian, Gay, Bisexual Politics*. London: Lawrence and Wishart, pp. 30–52.

McRobbie, A. and Nava, M. (eds) (1984) *Gender and Generation*. London: Macmillan.

Morgan, S. and Harland, K. (2009) *The Lens Model: A Practical Tool for Developing and Understanding Gender Conscious Practice. Youth & Policy* 101, pp. 67–79.

Oakley, A. (2015 [1972]) *Sex, Gender and Society*. London: Ashgate.

Robb, M., Featherstone, B., Ruxton, S. and Ward, M. (2015) *Beyond Males Role Models? Gender Identities and Work with Young Men*. Milton Keynes: Open University and Action for Children.

Scharff, C. (2012) *Repudiating Feminism: Young Women in a Neoliberal World*. London: Routledge.

Shain, F. (2013) '"The Girl Effect": Exploring of Gendered Impacts and Opportunities'. *Sociological Research Online* 18(2) article 9, pp. 1–11.

Smith, D.E. (1990) *Texts Facts and Femininity: The Relations of Ruling*. London and New York: Routledge.

Spence, J. (2006) 'Working with Girls and Young Women: A Broken History' in R. Gilchrist, T. Jeffs and J. Spence (eds) *Drawing on the Past: Essays in the History of Community and Youth Work*. Leicester: NYA, pp. 242–261.

Spence, J. (2010) 'Collecting Women's Lives: The Challenge of Feminism in UK Youth Work in the 1970s and 80s'. *Women's History Review* 19(1), pp. 159–176.

Spence, J. (2014) 'Feminism and Informal Education in Youth Work with Girls and Young Women 1975–85' in S. Mills and P. Kraftl (eds) *Informal Education, Childhood and*

Youth Geographies, Histories, Practices. Basingstoke: Palgrave Macmillan, pp. 197–215.

Tinkler, P. (1995) 'Sexuality and Citizenship: The State and Girls' Leisure Provision in England, 1939–45' in R. Gilchrist, T. Jeffs and J. Spence (eds) *Essays in the History of Youth and Community Work.* Leicester: Youth Work Press, pp. 283–262.

Tyler, I. (2013) *Revolting Subjects: Social Abjection and Resistance in Neoliberal Britain.* London: Zed Books.

Vicinus, M. (1985) *Independent Women: Work and Community for Single Women 1850–1920.* Chicago: University of Chicago Press.

Wood, J. (1984) 'Groping Towards Sexism ...' in A. McRobbie and M. Nava (eds) *Gender and Generation.* London: Macmillan, pp. 54–60.

Wright, D. (2015) 'Falling Back: Youth Policy in England'. *Jeugbeleid* 9(2), pp. 105–112.

11

Intersectionality and Resistance in Youth Work: Young People, Peace and Global 'Development' in a Racialized World

Momodou Sallah, Mike Ogunnusi and Richard Kennedy

INTRODUCTION

This chapter is framed by the concepts of Critical Race Theory, Critical Peace Education, and Global Youth Work. It departs from a premise that Youth Work can be an effective tool to provoke consciousness (Sallah, 2014) and redress power imbalances as an instrument of resistance (Scott, 1990) in a grotesquely unequal and increasingly globalized world. In this context, we argue that globalized hegemony exists in personal, local, national and global acts of, and reactions to, violence, and that this necessitates a shift from a singular binary of oppression to an intersectorial approach recognizing multiple interconnections such as age, race, structural violence, 'development' and global situatedness. In making this argument, we focus on the way that hierarchies of oppression, enacted within society, are linked to micro aggressions and the framing of majoritarian stories within the consciousness of the oppressor and the oppressed that

negate human potential as direct and structural violence (Galtung, 1969). Crucially, we argue that resistance to oppression should also shift from a mere critical understanding of this intersectionality, to generating pedagogies of disruption, and in turn pedagogies of hope.

Starting from the experience of Youth Work in England, this chapter will deconstruct the lure of 'whiteness' as a cultural marker (Fanon, 1986; Giroux, 1997), and explore the causal and emergent properties (Archer, 1995; Carter, 2000) of racial hierarchy to understand the generative mechanisms that influence the structure and agency of the individual. It is cardinal to understand at this juncture that ethnicity/whiteness is only one of many variables that intersect to generate discrimination and oppression at the personal, local, national and global levels. Due to imposed word limits, we will explore only ethnicity/whiteness in detail, out of all the other variables, to illustrate our core points. This will permit us the opportunity to position Critical Peace Education and Global Youth Work as experiencial, informal and critical spaces to disrupt the configuration of ways of knowing, in order to generate new ways of being. Key questions that frame the chapter include, 'how do we initiate a critical dialogue between the hidden transcript of subordinate groups into the public transcript (Scott, 1990) of Youth Work?' and 'how do we make them one, anti-oppressive and mutually libratory script?'

CRITICAL RACE THEORY

Youth Work and youth workers remain uniquely placed and historically positioned to challenge the status quo (Smith, 1988). In the context of race and racism, Youth Work can provide a voice for Black young people to share their experiences, talk back to power, and allow the real-time experiences of Black people to be expressed. This further provides the Black young people with whom we work an opportunity to discuss and explore counternarratives as a fundamental part of Youth Work (Giroux, 1983; Smith, 1988), challenging young people through Youth Work practice to enter the discourse and investigate the overarching themes of racial disadvantage and advantage (Giroux, 1983; Hiraldo, 2010; Taylor et al., 2009). The crucial part of this process is to contextualize these counternarratives and abstract them from the majoritarain stories which have been built and sustained, over recent centuries, on 'meritocracy', 'equality' and white privilege.

We begin with an exploration of race and racism through the lens of Critical Race Theory (CRT). CRT is used within this chapter to position the centrality of race within society. This centrality is presented as the ideology of whiteness (Garner, 2010; Gillborn, 2010; Vawda, 2013). CRT has its origins in Critical Legal Studies (CLS) in the US in the late 1970s and developed out of the dissatisfaction with the traditional Marxist structuralist class-based analysis of society, which was perceived as too narrow for not fully acknowledging the interactions between ideology, power and 'race' (Gillborn and Rollock, 2011) as part of the process of control designed to perpetuate white privilege (Chapman, 2013; Dovemark, 2013).

Any developments in race relations over the last 400 years need to be understood from this standpoint. Patton (2016) argues the 'wall' of racism has been built as a defence of privilege and of whiteness. Exposing these hidden transcripts imposed by the dominant culture allows for the explanation of how multiple dimensions of oppression work together to form what Hill-Collins calls a 'matrix of domination' (Hill-Collins, 1989). Whiteness, as described by Edwards (2008), has interlocking parts that develop and reaffirm the white hegemony within society. The structural dimension stratifies the racial hierarchy with whites placed at the top; this advantage affords whites unearned privileges. These can be the ability to visualize and see oneself represented in the media, education or legal system, and this practice becomes institutionalized through the development of social policy and an educational curriculum which emphasizes white history and experience (Bonnett, 1992; Edwards, 2008).

A white value base has become white normativity (Gaertner and Dovidio, 2005; Leonardo, 2012), in which whiteness is redefined as unseen and a given within society (Garner, 2007). It is the process of normalization of cultural practices and ideologies. These become homogeneous and accepted as the status quo (Edwards, 2008; Gillborn and Rollock, 2011), minority culture becomes labelled as 'othered', defined as 'exotic' and 'ethnic' whilst white culture is normative and thus unseen (Blee, 2002; Garner, 2007). This process of white normativity has become so hegemonic that it is positioned as common sense (Dovemark, 2013; Picower, 2009); the practices have become normalized, and the system reaffirms white interests (Edwards, 2008; Mirza, 1997). This is further expanded by Garner (2007) who suggests that whiteness is not only linked to a phenotype or skin colour but also to a value base. This has become a Westernized view of the world, which has within its foundations colonialism, imperialism and ultimately the capitalist mode of production (Hill, 2008). The 'othered' can integrate or more aptly, assimilate, as long as the dominant values are adhered to. This limited stage of integration exaggerates the difference between groups to reproduce the hierarchy (Garner, 2007; San Juan, 2001). Nationalism and whiteness are synonymous with the oppression of the other (Harvey, 2007; Sherwood, 2001; Tyler, 2012); they both form a grouping that restricts the entry but solidifies the group members. This is then a default position and cultural marker (Garner, 2007; Giroux, 1997) that develops into 'us and them'. It remains important to explore how this recreates membership in the image of the dominant group, and how this is reflected within the wider community and the nation. Garner supports this recreation and goes further to suggest that it has become a normative ideology as whiteness:

> In theory, the members of a given nation share a common identity of some kind. The idea of nation stretches across time to include the dead and yet unborn in a continuous narrative of belonging. Thus, the use of we and our to describe history, heritage, armies, victories, etc. is a normal part of this idea. (Garner, 2010: 50)

This dominant ideology is enacted throughout society as a celebration of things Western, British and thus white. What is conveniently forgotten or whitewashed from this narrative of dominance is the exploitation that took place during the development and construction of the historical narrative (Giroux, 1997; Tyler, 2012). These symbols act and develop into a mythical idea of a cohesive white superiority, grounded in historical subjugation and exploitation.

The positionality of race and now whiteness has its foundations in what has always been part of reproduction theories and the fact that the distinction between races is deeply seated in our social construction (Akom, 2008; Garner, 2010; Gillborn, 2008; Mizra, 2005). This social construction has been transformed into the lure of whiteness as the standard to measure all things against (Fanon, 1986; Gillborn, 2008). This dominant structure creates a narrative of oppression which perpetuates whiteness as an ideology and develops into a position of being constantly under attack from the 'other'. Gilroy (1987) states that there has been an exaggerated need to protect the national identity, the white majority and their value base, which has protected their privilege. The discussion about who is included and excluded in the debate about national identity developed into a re-emergence of deep-seated racist views, and has culminated in the structural demarcation of the 'enemy within' as part of the hegemony of whiteness (Gilroy, 1987; Vawda, 2013). The effects of this are twofold; whiteness is seen as constantly being under attack (Garner, 2010; Giroux, 1997) and in need of defending under the auspices of national identity, negating the need for a full debate of structural oppression. Second, the debate becomes one of acceptability and openly treats the others as suspect communities and questions their rights to engage as part of the political state (Garratt, 2011). This process has developed into collective paranoia that enemies are everywhere, as Gilroy et al. suggest, 'It connects with common sense ideas about why racial problems arise by identifying "racial violence" as a result of an illegitimate alien presence' (Gilroy et al., 1986: 29).

White transparency is the culmination of the structural and value-based understanding of whiteness within society, the inability of whites to view themselves and the consequences of the societal arrangements made in their favour (Aleman and Aleman, 2016; Flagg, 1998). The privilege afforded to some and not to others is a 'public and psychological wage' that insulates individuals from the lowest status within society (Du Bois, 1935).

As Black people continue to strive for equal treatment, it has become more and more evident that contemporary theoretical approaches to racism highlight the illusion of equality (Dixson and Rousseau, 2005). The work of Crenshaw (Crenshaw et al., 1995), Brooks (2009), Lentin and Titley (2011) reinforce the idea of a lack of racial development within society. Society has moved away from the crude Darwinian scientific basis of difference to the development of a post-racial colour-blind approach to race (Garner, 2010; Mirza, 2005). Both these concepts – Darwinism and colour blindness – have their ontological positions based on white superiority; both negate challenge to fundamental notions of white privilege and how the system is organized to relocate and justify that privilege. The literature surrounding colour blindness presents the argument that this perpetuates the othering of groups who are non-white (Gillborn, 2004; Lentin and Titley, 2011); but also provides a tool to argue that race is no longer an issue, and forms the process of social inoculation (Dyson et al., 2014), which then promotes meritocracy. This links the two dominant ideologies, capitalism and whiteness. Although the appearance is homogeneous and taken for granted, the links between capital and exploitation have a marked history of Western thought; racism finds its roots in capitalism and imperialism (Du Bois, 1962). They confuse and hide the oppressive systems from the workers that ferment the process of fragmentation, pitting working against worker (San Juan, 2001).

The system of racism in which Black young people have to interact or negotiate is not elemental or out-there; it is invasive and fundamental to human activity (Du Bois, 1903; Fanon, 1986). Racism is manifested using the hidden transcript of macroaggressions, this becomes the sphere in which it operates; it is in the realm of the hidden and subconscious. Microaggressions are outlined as being 'an insidious form of cultural bias, which include the experience of a variety of

direct and indirect (conscious and unconscious) insults, slights, and discriminatory messages' (Owen et al., 2014: 283). Owen et al. go on to explain that these microaggressions are expressed in three distinct categories. They are microvalidations that deny racism exists at all; microassaults as overt racism that happens in a safe space; and microinsults that take cultural norms as being pathological (Owen et al., 2014). This is further supported by Sue et al. (2007: 271) who assert that:

> Racial microaggressions are brief and commonplace daily verbal, behavioural, or environmental indignities, whether intentional or unintentional, that communicate hostile, derogatory, or negative racial slights and insults toward people of colour. Perpetrators of microaggressions are often unaware that they engage in such communications when they interact with racial/ethnic minorities.

Black young people experience microaggressions daily, it becomes an acceptable defence of the racial privilege within society. Statements such as 'there is only one race, the human race' or 'when I look at you, I don't see colour', not only deny the experiences of Black people, but also deny the racial advantage given to some groups and denied to others. Esposito's (2011) study explores the counter-narratives in which Black students share their experiences; they talk about the feeling of anger, being looked at in an odd way and their presence being discounted. It is clear that we are not in a post-racial society, as Esposito (2011: 156) explains 'from subtle microaggressions to the more blatant instances of discrimination – race has to be negotiated because of a clear system of power and privilege'. Black young people are negotiating these dynamics as they interact with institutions shaped and constructed to perpetuate whiteness and white privilege.

It is essential that youth workers and informal educators recognize this code or veil of whiteness (Du Bois, 1962), decolonise it, and explore how it is constructed and maintained. It becomes much more than simply working in an anti-oppressive and reflective manner. It is about a positioning and an understanding of self or place within the world. This develops into a situatedness, or positionality, outside the internalized hegemony of racial hierarchy and oppression. The use of counter-narratives within Youth Work, which challenge the post-racial dogma of progress, needs to be firmly explored (Ladson-Billings and Tate, 1995). The construction of society to benefit one group has become an unseen, undocumented and accepted element of the hierarchical social system (Calmore, 1997; Miller, 2015).

CRITICAL PEDAGOGIES OF RESISTANCE

In this next section, we want to introduce two methodological approaches that encourage the construction of counter-narratives as well as present disruptive pedagogical approaches to the sometimes toxic and grotesque prevailing normalities. In this light, we will present Critical Peace Education (CPE); and Global Youth Work, to counter the issues identified in the first half of this chapter.

Critical Peace Education

This section introduces Critical Peace Education (CPE), influenced by Galtungian peace theory (1969, 1971, 1990, 1996, 2000) to critically engage with race/racism as a form of direct, structural and cultural violence. Here, we explore the possibilities for Youth Work in adopting principles and practices of CPE in order to consider the intersectionality of race/racism and its associated powers as a form of violence.

As previously stated, there is a continued need for race/racism to be explicitly recognized as part of the process, content and pedagogy of Youth Work in Britain. Although, there is current anxiety in England regarding

the continued existence of Youth Work as a distinct practice (Davies and Merton, 2009; Fyfe and Moir, 2013), it can be summarized as a non-formal dialogical approach that is framed by ethical and professional principles (Connaughton, 2014: 90) derived from voluntary and participative relationships that value young people, and strive to keep their needs and interests central to the learning process (Batsleer and Davies, 2010; Jeffs and Smith, 2010; Sapin, 2009; Wood and Hine, 2009).

Youth Work has traditionally accepted that society is both stratified and conflicted (Batsleer and Davies, 2010; Young, 1999) and guides practice 'towards the promotion of social justice for young people' (NYA, 2004: 6). This requires youth workers to challenge 'discriminatory actions and attitudes on the part of young people, colleagues and others' (NYA, 2004: 8) and act 'in a way that does not exploit or negatively discriminate against certain young people on irrelevant grounds such as "race", religion, gender, ability or sexual orientation' (NYA, 2004: 7). Historically, English youth work has primarily understood racism in terms of multi-culturalism (1970–1980), anti-racism (1980s–1990s) and integration/assimilation (2000–the present), which provides a limited response to some of the issues identified earlier in the chapter, 'within the everyday struggles' (Sallah and Howson, 2007: 17) of white normativity (Leonardo, 2012) and social constructs of white power and privilege.

The tradition of Peace Education (PE) is well documented (Harris, 2008) and includes peace research, conflict resolution, democratic participation, social justice and human rights; international relations, peace and security; non-violence and disarmament; sustainable economic and social development; global education, environmental studies and critical pedagogy. Definitions of PE remain contested, but it is generally understood as a vehicle for young people and adults to develop knowledge, skills, attitudes, and behaviours to promote peace (Hicks, 1988), by drawing out people's desire for peace, promoting non-violent alternatives for managing conflict, and analysing structural arrangements that legitimize and perpetuate the risk of personal, social and environmental violence, injustice and inequality.

Writers such as Bajaj (2008, 2015), Bajaj and Brantmeier (2011), Brantmeier (2011), Diaz-Soto (2005) and Hantzopoulos (2011) have contributed to a renewed critical pedagogic approach to PE. Rooted in the Frankfurt School of Social Research, Critical Peace Education (CPE) posits an epistemological assumption that peace can be encouraged and taught, whilst emphasizing a need for learners to 'critically analyse power dynamics and intersectionalities among race, class, gender, ability/disability, sexual orientation, language, religion, geography, and other forms of stratification' (Bajaj and Brantmeier, 2011: 221). CPE accepts that our social sense of peace, social peacefulness and social justice calls for a deeper consideration of the tension between social structure and agency due to 'issues of power, domination, and symbolic violence or cultural imposition' (Bajaj, 2008: 142). Disrupting the unequal and oppressive reproduction of society calls on learners and educators alike to actively uncover and challenge 'structural impediments' to advancing peace (Bajaj and Brantmeier, 2011: 221) as a genealogy of resistance, i.e. the dialectic between theory and practice achieved by raising critical consciousness for educators and participants to become transformative agents; and a presupposition that change comes from within the affected community (Bajaj, 2008, 2015).

CPE understands race/racism as a socially constructed incompatibility (Galtung, 2000) alongside other forms of oppression and injustice, derived through difference and elaborated through intersectionality, to reinforce and create personal, structural and cultural forms of violence. It offers a praxis that interrogates the role of peace education in relation to white privilege and global disparity (Pluim and Jorgenson, 2012),

encouraging a critical discourse 'beyond a Eurocentric colonizing/*saviour* lens' (Diaz-Soto, 2005: 96; our italics). Educators are tasked to expose and confront their motives and values in ways that enable them to create participatory and co-constructed learning throughout the entire pedagogic process based on a commitment to social justice.

Galtung (1969) provides a paradigm for social justice that seeks to challenge and eradicate direct and indirect forms of violence, i.e. social relations and structures that undermine fundamental human needs and promote inequalities of power and resources. Galtung offers three typologies of violence: direct *events* of mental and/or somatic violence (e.g. assault, terrorism, war); *processes* of structural violence built into the structure of society (e.g. poverty, discrimination); and the historical *invariance* of 'any aspect of a culture that can be used to legitimise violence in its direct or structural form' (e.g. the symbolic violence of ideology, art, language) (Galtung, 1990: 291). These ideas can be located in the wider discussion of race/racism.

Direct microaggressions are regularly presented through the micro dynamics of body language, speech, disregard and ridicule. These behaviours carry the constant threat of violence, along with more recognized instances of physical attacks (foreigner hatred and xenophobia), or the damage of lives and property. The ethics and purpose of Youth Work dictates the active re/development of intra/inter-group relationships that ask us to unmask and critically reflect on how we experience ourselves, and our encounters with others/otherness. Youth Work can enable the centrality of young people's narratives to be shared, heard and valued – exploring the intersectionality of race, class, gender, religion, sexual orientation, etc. and complicating existing stereotypes to 'understand learnt behaviours and socially constructed difference, intergroup relations and conflict, and intrapersonal values and conflicts' (Iram, 2003: 22). It is an evolving pedagogic approach that seeks to enhance self awareness and critical thinking, compassion and empathy, cooperation and conflict resolution, underpinned by a commitment to personal, social, and environmental justice (Hicks, 1988; Navarro-Castro and Nario-Galace, 2010), in ways that are non-violent, whilst promoting shared resistance to racism and intersecting forms of oppression (Yosso, 2005).

Race/racism is built into social systems as macroaggressions purposefully created with 'actions that are meant to exclude, either by action or omission' (Osanloo et al., 2016: 6), Structural racism can be less apparent as it includes both 'human inaction' and 'intended acts' (McCandless et al., 2007: 87) to socially position and legitimise race/racism through identification, power, meritocracy, opportunities, accountability, etc. Taken from the conceptual process of praxis (Freire, 1974), this work approaches and analyses social problems that young people and their communities face. Critically exposing the invisible effects of structural violence through reciprocal dialogue and engagement can allow young people to pose critical questions of their social reality, which may produce self, and social, transformation as action (Freire, 1974) as they move from individual to collective positionality and agency. The aim is to trigger meaning and action for change that seeks to redress power imbalances. In the context of race/racism, this requires educators and young people to move away from 'a deficit view of Communities of Color as places full of cultural poverty or disadvantages', but rather focus on and learn from 'these communities' cultural assets and wealth' (Yosso, 2005: 82). Freire (1974: 12) describes this as learners becoming aware of their sociocultural reality and recognizing their capacity for action as 'agents of their own recuperation'. This is Youth Work that prioritizes collaborative social action with young people as a 'necessary outcome' (Baja, 2015: 154).

Finally, cultural violence reproduces the means by which norms of race/racism translate into daily and routine values to justify in/direct violence. This is where cultures of white normativity (Leonardo, 2012) accommodate legacies of racial purity, racial superiority and postcolonial ideologies of race/racism as forces and activities that restrict agency and elaborate oppression. Cultural violence holds the power to eclipse asymmetrical power relations and create the type of false consciousness that unquestioningly perpetuates injustice, inequality and brutality. Galtung (1990: 295) uses the following example to illustrate the insidious nature of cultural violence:

> Africans are captured, forced across the Atlantic to work as slaves: millions are killed in the process – in Africa, on board, in the Americas. This massive direct violence over centuries seeps down and sediments as massive structural violence, with whites as the master top dogs and blacks as the slave underdogs, producing and reproducing massive cultural violence with racist ideas everywhere. After some time, direct violence is forgotten, slavery is forgotten, and only two labels show up, pale enough for college textbooks: 'discrimination' for massive structural violence and 'prejudice' for massive cultural violence. Sanitation of language: itself cultural violence.

The historicity and permanency of culture creates 'a perceived sense of social cohesion' (Bajaj, 2008: 143) as a dominant ideology so deeply entrenched in the plethora of our day-to-day stories and politics that it sits 'unnamed' as normal (Ani, 1994). This is challenged by the praxis of CPE, which asserts that there are no neutral spaces. A fideistic approach to peace (Gur-Ze'ev, 2010; Page, 2004), peace education and Youth Work, can obscure the cultural dominance that 'silences, ignores and distorts epistemologies of People of Color' (Yosso, 2005: 72). It is important that Youth Work remains open to other forms of critical inquiry such as Global Youth Work, CRT, feminist perspectives (Brock-Utne, 1989), critical multiculturalism (Leicester, 1992; May, 1999), environmental racism (Kaza, 1999; O'Sullivan, 1999), and human rights education (Reardon, 1977).

If Youth Work in Britain chooses to maintain transformative pedagogy, then Galtung's structuralism (1969) can help it to understand the causal relationship of race/racism as direct and structural violence rooted in existing culture. Numerous writers provide case studies of CPE with young people to illustrate how it works in practice (Bajaj, 2015; Bajaj and Hantzopoulos, 2016). In communication with CPE, Youth Work can adopt a pedagogic approach to race/racism that invests in each young person's potential and power (Ardizzone, 2003; Del Felice and Wisler, 2007) to foster 'an inclusive alternate paradigm' (Diaz-Soto, 2005: 96) for peaceful social transformation.

This section has briefly introduced CPE in the hopes that these ideas can strengthen a general discourse of peace within Youth Work that talks directly to issues of race/racism; and the broader discourse of power, inequality and injustice.

GLOBAL YOUTH WORK AND GLOBAL EDUCATION THEORY – A DISRUPTIVE PEDAGOGY

Global Youth Work (Sallah, 2009, 2014) has been variously labelled by a number of writers who have attributed multiple terminologies to the practice (Bourn, 2015; Cotton, 2009; Dare to Stretch, 2009; North-South-Centre, 2010). As a process, there is broad agreement that it is concerned with how the concept and process of globalization impacts on young people's realities; is based on the principles of informal education; promotes consciousness and action; challenges oppression and promotes social justice; and is located in young people's realities (Bourn, and McCollum, 1995; DEA, 2004; Sallah, 2014; Sallah and Cooper, 2008).

This process described above, when configured into a whole, can emerge as the distinct practice of Global Youth Work. Terms such as International Youth Work, Development Education (Sallah, 2009) and Global Leaning (Bourn, 2015) have been used to label this

practice; however, the term Global Youth Work (GYW) was coined in 1995 (Bourn and McCollum, 1995), and its prominence has grown in recent times as a distinct way of working with young people, incorporating both the principles of Development Education and Youth Work. As previously noted, there appears to be efforts to decapitate Youth Work in the mainstream through government policy in England; GYW, whilst still widely practiced, must be understood in this context. The DEA (now 'Think Global') positions GYW as:

> Informal education with young people that encourages a critical understanding of the links between the personal, local and the global and seeks their active participation in actions that bring about change towards greater equality and justice. (DEA, 2004: 21)

Similarly, The North-South Centre (2010: 10) identifies GYW as an educational approach that 'opens people's eyes and minds to the realities of the globalised world and awakens them to bring about a world of greater justice, equity and Human Rights for all'.

GYW is a methodological approach that explores the personal, local, national and global interconnections between young people and the five faces of globalization (economic, political, cultural, environmental and technological) interactively to generate a critical understanding (Freire, 1993), which hopefully leads to the second prerogative of promoting action as a result of that consciousness which attempts to change the world (Sallah, 2014).

GYW is used interchangeably with Global Education given our focus on the process. The North-South Centre (2010: 16) argues that Global Education enables the development of the skills, knowledge and attitudes needed for everyone to fulfil their potential and live in a just and sustainable world. This concept proposes the reimagining of the content, form and context of education, with a focus on developing the necessary skills, knowledge, values and attitudes. In presenting his theoretical framework, Woolley (2011) highlights the three interlinked dimensions of global issues, global experiences and global perspectives that must be configured as a whole for the distinct practice of GYW to emerge. The DEA (now Think Global, 2010) posit that GYW supports young people to connect with local/global issues, and then encourages them to challenge their own construction of reality, the normalization of inequality and injustice, starting from their own realities and experiences; and then to bring about change. Following from this, one of the authors (Sallah and Cooper, 2008; Sallah, 2014) has argued that GYW must first attempt to engage with young people's constructed realities and then support young people to make the links between the personal, local, national and global, and the five faces of globalization (economic, political, cultural, technological and environmental) to provoke critical consciousness and then support them to take action; whatever the concerned young people deem appropriate in creating a more just world for themselves and the rest of humanity.

From this discourse, whilst some conceptual frameworks focus on the development of skills and attitudes (for example the North-South Centre) and others focus on connecting with the young people as key (for example Sallah, 2014), all of the four conceptual frameworks focus on process, based not on a fixed curriculum, but on the constructed realities of the young people engaged and the need to develop critical literacy and support action that young people choose, to interact with and change the world. Therein lies the disruptive potential of GYW as a pedagogic tool as it focuses on decentring the established and reconstructing new realities. It calls for a decolonization of the conceptual frameworks we use as a basis to engage young people, given the intersecting variable of race, class, gender, religion, sexual orientation, etc., and a skewed globalized hegemony.

In deconstructing race and racism, and all other associated discriminatory variables, the increasing interconnectedness of the world calls for a more fluid and critical understanding of our relationships to the 'death of distance'. Both in terms of 'whiteness' and direct/indirect/cultural violence, as earlier discussed; these can no longer be played out in just personal, local or national spaces. It is essential that the personal, local, national and global links are established in any local-global issue that is explored. In order to understand the link between Empire and current white privilege, or the link between current refugee presence in the streets of Europe and the conflicts in Afghanistan, Iraq, Syria and Somalia, a globalized pedagogical approach is needed that links to the personal, local, national and global, in line with engendering transformative and disruptive pedagogies. It is in this light that we advance GYW as an approach that provokes consciousness in the people most affected by violence in all its manifestations, in order to support them to be at the centre of the transformation they seek.

CONCLUSION

To conclude, this chapter highlights how the dominant ideology of whiteness, has become inextricably linked with forms of violence built into the structure of society that impede human potential and deny human needs and rights on the basis of race and assertions of racial superiority (Bajaj, 2015). The protection of whiteness is outlined as being hegemonic and unseen; created and recreated as white normativity (Gillborn, 2006; Picower, 2009). We explore how Critical Peace Education and Global Youth Work can help to understand issues of race/racism and its associated powers. Critical Peace Education encourages and equips practitioners and young people to challenge the paradigm of both direct and indirect violence (Galtung, 1969) and introduce pedagogies of resistance that call on youth workers and young people to affect change for peace (personal, social and enviromental) through relationships and social conditions in their communities (Bajaj, 2015; Snauwaert, 2011). Similarly, Global Youth Work is a pedagogic tool to generate critical consciousness within young people, to understand oppressions at the personal, local, national and global levels as well as equip them in practically building a fairer world, based on the principles of social justice. Both of these approaches are particularly important when we recognise that the art of youth work often occurs in contexts that are characterised by conflict and enveloped by wider social contradictions and incompatibilities (personal, local, national and global) that perpetuate young people's disproportionate experience of violence and social injustice. We hope to reinforce the need to revisit, and stay aware of, young people's experiences and perspectives of violence (direct, indirect and structural) and peace in their communities as part of the multiple interconnections of oppression (Ogunnusi, 2006), as well as offering a combined approach to encourage social action more widely in youth work for the purpose of bringing about learning and development linked with critical awareness, peace and social justice in an increasingly globalized world; one that also generates active acts of resistance.

The chapter highlights a common commitment present in critical pedagogy to change our beliefs and behaviours through counter-narratives that seek to expose the reproduction of power dynamics and inter-sectionalities, and disrupt 'structural impediments' to advancing peace (Bajaj, 2013: 145). The hope is that young people, youth workers and educators, can address issues of whiteness and violence in ways that are meaningful and transformative by positioning CPE and GYW as pedagogies of resistance. It is from these critical positions that youth workers can start to develop an understanding of race/racism as a significant organizing feature of society which ultimately dehumanizes both Black and white (Du Bois, 1903).

REFERENCES

Akom, A.A. (2008) Ameritocracy and infra-racial racism: racializing social and cultural reproduction theory in the twenty-first century. *Race Ethnicity and Education*, 11(3), pp. 205–230. Available at: http://www.tandfonline.com/doi/abs/10.1080/13613320802291116 [accessed November 27, 2014].

Aleman, S.M. and Aleman, E. (2016) Critical race media projects: counterstories and praxis (re)claim Chicana/o experiences. *Urban Education*, 51(3), pp. 287–314. Available at: http://uex.sagepub.com/cgi/doi/10.1177/0042085915626212

Ani, M. (1994) *Yurugu: An African-Centred Critique of European Cultural Thought and Behavior*. New Jersey: Africa World Press.

Archer, M. (1995) *Realist Social Theory: The Morphogenetic Approach*. Cambridge: Cambridge University Press.

Ardizzone, L. (2003) Generating peace: a study of nonformal youth organizations. *Peace & Change*, 28(3), pp. 420–445.

Bajaj, M. (ed.) (2008) *Encyclopedia of PE*. Charlotte: Information Age.

Bajaj, M. (2015) 'Pedagogies of resistance' and critical peace education praxis. *Journal of Peace Education*, 12(2), pp. 154–166.

Bajaj, M. and Brantmeier, E. (2011) The politics, praxis, and possibilities of critical peace education. *Journal of Peace Education*, 8(3), pp. 221–224.

Bajaj, M. and Hantzopoulos, M. (2016) *Peace Education: International Perspectives*. London: Bloomsbury Academic.

Batsleer, J. and Davies, B. (eds) (2010) *What is Youth Work? Empowering Youth and Community Work Practice*. Exeter: Learning Matters.

Blee, K.M. (2002) *Inside Organized Racism: Women in the Hate Movement*. London: University of California Press Ltd.

Bonnett, A. (1992) Anti-racism in 'white' areas: the example of Tyneside. *Antipode*, 24(1), pp. 1–5.

Bonnett, A. (2000) *Anti-Racism*. London: Routledge.

Bourn, D. (2015) *The Theory and Practice of Development Education: A Pedagogy for Global Social Justice*. Abingdon, Oxon: Routledge.

Bourn, D. and McCollum, A. (eds) (1995) *A World of Difference: Making Global Connections in Youth Work*. London: DEA.

Brantmeier, E. (2011) Toward mainstreaming critical peace education in U.S. teacher education. In C.S. Malott and B. Porfilio (eds), *Critical Pedagogy in the 21st Century: A New Generation of Scholars*. Greenwich, CT: Information Age Publishing, pp. 349–375.

Brock-Utne, B. (1989) *Feminist Perspectives on Peace and Peace Education*. New York: Teachers College Press.

Brooks, R.L. (2009) *Racial Justice in the Age of Obama*. Princeton, NJ: Princeton University Press.

Calmore, J.O. (1997) Exploring Michael Omi's messy world of race: an essay for naked people longing to swim free. *Law and Inequality*, 15(1), pp. 25–82.

Carter, B. (2000) *Realism and Racism*. Abingdon: Routledge.

Chapman, T. K. (2013) You can't erase race! Using CRT to explain the presence of race and racism in majority white suburban schools. *Discourse: Studies in the Cultural Politics of Education*, 34(4), pp. 611–627.

Connaughton, P. (2014) Review: A Concept Journal Youth Work Reader. *Youth & Policy*, 113, pp. 88–91.

Cotton, N. (2009) *Global Youth Work in the UK: Research Report*. London: DEA.

Crenshaw, K., Gotanda, N., Peller, G. and Thomas, K. (eds) (1995) *Critical Race Theory: The Key Writings that Formed the Movement*. New York: The New Press.

Dare to Stretch (2009) *Promoting Development Education in Youth Work Training, A Research Report on Development Education in Community Youth Work Courses at the University of Ulster*. Jordanstown. Belfast: Centre for Global Education.

Davies, B. and Merton, B. (2009) *Squaring the Circle? Findings of a 'Modest Inquiry' into the State of Youthwork Practice in a Changing Policy Environment*. Leicester: DMU.

DEA (Development Education Association) (2004) *Global Youth Work: Training and Practice*. London: DEA.

Del Felice, C. and Wisler, A. (2007) The unexplored power and potential of youth as peace-builders. *Journal of Peace Conflict & Development*, 11.

Diaz-Soto, L. (2005) How can we teach peace when we are so outraged? A call for critical peace education. *Taboo: The Journal of Culture and Education*, 9(2), pp. 91–96.

Dixson, A. D. and Rousseau, C. K. (2005) And we are still not saved: critical race theory in education ten years later. *Race Ethnicity and Education*, 8(1), pp. 7–27.

Dovemark, M. (2013) How private 'everyday racism' and public 'racism denial' contribute to unequal and discriminatory educational experiences. *Ethnography and Education*, 8(1), pp. 16–30. Available at: http://bada.hb.se/handle/2320/10537

Du Bois, W.E.B. (1996 [1903]) *The Souls of Black Folk*. New York: Penguin.

Du Bois, W.E.B. (1998 [1935][1962]) *Black Reconstruction in the United States, 1860–1880*. New York: Free Press.

Dyson, S.M., Atkin, K., Culley, L. and Dyson, S.E. (2014) Critical realism, agency and sickle cell: case studies of young people with sickle cell disorder at school. *Ethnic and Racial Studies*, 37(13), pp. 2379–2398. Available at: http://www.tandfonline.com/doi/abs/10.1080/01419870.2013.809130 [accessed November 27, 2014].

Edwards, K. (2008) *The Elusive Dream*. Oxford: Oxford University Press.

Esposito, J. (2011) Negotiating the gaze and learning the hidden curriculum: a critical race analysis of the embodiment of female students of color at a predominantly white institution. *Journal for Critical Education Studies*, 9(2), pp. 143–164. Available at: http://www.jceps.com/archives/679

Fanon, F. (1986) *Black Skin, White Masks*. London: Pluto Press.

Farmer, P. (2003) *Pathologies of Power: Health, Human Rights, and the New War on the Poor*. Berkeley: University of California.

Flagg, B.J. (1998) *Was Blind, but Now I See: White Race Consciousness and the Law*. New York & London: New York University Press.

Freire, P. (1970) *Pedagogy of the Oppressed*. New York: Continuum.

Freire, P. (1974) *Education: The Practice of Freedom*. London: Writers and Readers Publishing Co-op.

Freire, P. (1993) *Pedagogy of the Oppressed*. London: Penguin.

Fyfe, I. and Moir, S. (2013) Standing at the crossroads – what future for youth work? *A Concept Journal Youth Work Reader.*

Gaertner, S.L. and Dovidio, J.F. (2005) Understanding and addressing contemporary racism: from aversive racism to the Common Ingroup Identity Model. *Journal of Social Issues,* 61(3), pp. 615–639. Available at: http://doi.wiley.com/10.1111/j.1540-4560.2005.00424.x

Galtung, J. (1969) Violence, peace and peace research. *Journal of Peace Research,* 6(3), pp. 167–191.

Galtung, J. (1971) A structural theory of imperialism. *Journal of Peace Research,* 8(2), pp. 81–117.

Galtung, J. (1990) Cultural violence. *Journal of Peace Research,* 27(3), pp. 291–305.

Galtung, J. (1996) *Peace by Peaceful Means: Peace and Conflict, Development and Civilization.* London: Sage.

Galtung, J. (2000) *Conflict Transformation by Peaceful Means (The Transcend Method).* Geneva: UN.

Garner, S. (2007) *Whiteness.* Abingdon, Oxon: Routledge.

Garner, S. (2010) *Racisms.* London: Sage.

Garratt, D. (2011) Equality, difference and the absent presence of 'race' in citizenship education in the UK. *London Review of Education,* 9(1), pp. 27–39.

Gillborn, D. (2004) Anti-racism: from policy to praxis. In G. Ladson-Billings and D. Gillborn (eds.), *The RoutledgeFalmer Reader in Multicultural Education.* London: Routledge, pp. 35–48.

Gillborn, D. (2005) Education policy as an act of white supremacy: whiteness, critical race theory and education reform. *Journal of Educational Policy,* 20(4), pp. 485–505.

Gillborn, D. (2006) Critical Race Theory and Education: Racism and anti-racism in educational theory and praxis. *Discourse: Studies in the Cultural Politics of Education,* 27(1), pp. 11–32.

Gillborn, D. (2008) *Racism and Education: Coincidence or Conspiracy?* London: Routledge.

Gillborn, D. (2010) Reform, racism and the centrality of whiteness: assessment, ability and the 'new eugenics'. *Irish Educational Studies,* 29(3), pp. 231–252. Available at: http://www.tandfonline.com/doi/abs/10.1080/

03323315.2010.498280 [accessed February 11, 2014].

Gillborn, D. (2012) The White working class, racism and respectability: victims, degenerates and interest-convergence. In K. Bhopal and J. Preston (eds), *Intersectionality and 'Race' in Education.* London: Routledge, pp. 29–56.

Gillborn, D. and Ladson-Billings, G. (2010) 'Critical Race Theory'. In P. Peterson, E. Baker and B. McGraw (eds), *International Encyclopedia of Education, Volume 6.* Oxford: Elsevier, pp. 341–347.

Gillborn, D. and Rollock, N. (2010) Education. In A. Bloch and J. Solomos (eds), *Race and Ethnicity in the 21st Century.* Basingstoke: Palgrave Macmillan, pp. 138–165.

Gilroy, P. (1986) Police and Thieves. In Centre for Contemporary Cultural Studies, University of Birmingham (eds), *The Empire Strikes Back: Race and Racism in 70s Britain.* London: Hutchinson, pp. 143–182.

Gilroy, P. (1987) *There Ain't No Black in the Union Jack.* London: Hutchinson.

Giroux, H.A. (1983) Theories of reproduction and resistance in the new sociology of education: a critical analysis. *Harvard Educational Review,* 53(4), pp. 257–293.

Giroux, H.A. (1997) White squall: resistance and the pedagogy of whiteness. *Cultural Studies,* 11(3), pp. 376–389. Available at: http://www.tandfonline.com/doi/abs/10.1080/095023897335664

Gur-Ze'ev, I. (2010) Beyond peace education: toward co-poiesis and enduring improvisation. *Policy Futures in Education,* 8(3–4), pp. 315–339.

Hantzopoulos, M. (2011) Institutionalizing critical peace education in public schools: a case for comprehensive implementation. *Journal of Peace Education,* 8(3), pp. 225–242.

Harris, I. (2008) History of PE. In M. Bajaj (ed.), *Encyclopedia of PE.* Charlotte: Information Age, pp. 15–23.

Harvey, J. (2007) *Whiteness and Morality.* New York: Palgrave Macmillan US.

Hicks, D. (ed.) (1988) *Education for Peace: Issues, Principles, and Practices in the Classroom.* London: Routledge.

Hill, J.H. (2008) *The Everyday Language of White Racism.* Oxford, UK: Wiley-Blackwell. Available at: http://doi.wiley.com/10.1002/9781444304732

Hill-Collins, P. (1989) A Response to Inequality: Black Women, Racism, The Social Construction of Black Feminist Thought. *Signs: Journal of Women in Culture and Society*, 14(4), pp. 745–773.

Hiraldo, P. (2010) The role of critical race theory in higher education. *The Vermont Connection*, 31, Article 7.

Iram, Y. (ed.) (2003) *Education of Minorities and Peace Education in Pluralistic Societies*. Westport: Greenwood Publishing Group.

Jeffs, T. and Smith, M.K. (eds) (2010) *Youth Work Practice*. Basingstoke: Palgrave.

Kaza, S. (1999) Liberation and compassion in environmental studies. In G. Smith and D. Williams (eds), *Ecological Education in Action*. Albany: State University of New York Press, pp. 143–160.

Ladson-Billings, G. and Tate, W. (1995) Toward a critical race theory of education. *Teachers College Record*, 97(1), pp. 47–68.

Leicester, M. (1992) Antiracism versus the new multiculturalism: moving beyond the interminable debate. In J. Lynch, C. Modgil and S. Modgil (eds), *Cultural Diversity and the Schools. Volume 1: Education for Cultural Diversity, Convergence and Divergence*. London: Falmer Press, pp. 215–229.

Lentin, A. and Titley, G. (2011) *The Crises of Multiculturalism: Racism in a Neoliberal Age*. London: Zed Books.

Leonardo, Z. (2012) The race for class: reflections on a critical raceclass theory of education. *Educational Studies*, 48(5), pp. 427–449.

May, S. (ed.) (1999) *Critical Multiculturalism: Rethinking Multicultural and Antiracist Education*. London: Falmer Press.

McCandless, E. (2007) Synopses of Major Concepts in McCandless, E., Bangura, A., King, M. and Sall, E. (eds.) *Peace Research for Africa: Critical Essays on Methodology*. Addis Ababa: University for Peace, pp. 83–109.

Miller, E.T. (2015) Discourses of whiteness and blackness: an ethnographic study of three young children learning to be white. *Ethnography and Education*, 10(2), pp. 137–153. Available at: http://www.tandfonline.com/doi/abs/10.1080/17457823.2014.960437

Mirza, H.S. (ed.) (1997) *Black British Feminism*. London: Routledge.

Mirza, H.S. (2005) 'The more things change, the more they stay the same': assessing Black underachievement 35 years on. In B. Richardson (ed.), *Tell It Like It Is: How our Schools Fail Black Children*. Stoke on Trent: Trentham Books, pp. 111–119.

Navarro-Castro, L. and Nario-Galace, J. (2010) *Peace Education A pathway to a culture of peace* (2nd ed). Quenzon City: Miriam College.

National Youth Agency (2004) *Ethical Conduct in Youth Work*. Leicester: NYA; New York: Routledge.

North-South Centre (2010) *Global Education Guidelines, Concepts and Methodologies on Global Education for Educators and Policy Makers*. Lisbon: North-South Centre.

Ogunnusi, M. (2006) Keep it together, keep it safe: violence, peace and young people. *The Development Education Journal*, 13(1), pp. 12–14.

Osanloo, A., Boske, C. and Newcomb, W. (2016) Deconstructing macroaggressions, microaggressions, and structural racism in education: Developing a conceptual model for the intersection of social justice practice and intercultural education. *International Journal of Organizational Theory and Development*, 4(1). Available at: http://www.nationalforum.com/Electronic%20Journal%20Volumes/Osanloo,%20Azadeh%20Deconstructin%20Racism%20in%20Education%20IJOTD%20V4%20N1%202016.pdf

O'Sullivan, E. (1999) *Transformative Learning: Educational Vision for the 21st Century*. London: Zed Books.

Owen, J. et al. (2014) Addressing racial and ethnic microaggressions in therapy. *Professional Psychology: Research and Practice*, 45(4), pp. 283–290. Available at: http://dx.doi.org/10.1037/a0037420

Page, J. (2004) Peace Education: exploring some philosophical foundations. *International Review of Education*, 50(1), pp. 3–15.

Patton, L.D. (2016) Disrupting postsecondary prose: toward a Critical Race Theory of higher education. *Urban Education*, 51(3), pp. 315–342. Available at: http://uex.sagepub.com/cgi/doi/10.1177/0042085915602542

Picower, B. (2009) The unexamined Whiteness of teaching: how White teachers maintain and enact dominant racial ideologies. *Race Ethnicity and Education*, 12(2), pp. 197–215. Available at: http://www.tandfonline.com/doi/abs/10.1080/13613320902995475

Pluim, G. and Jorgenson, S. (2012) A reflection on the broader, systemic impacts of youth volunteer abroad programmes: a Canadian perspective. *Intercultural Education*, 23(1), pp. 25–38.

Reardon, B. (1977) Human Rights and Education Reform. *Bulletin on Peace Proposals*, 8(3), pp. 247–250.

Rollock, N. and Gillborn, D. (2011) Critical Race Theory (CRT), British Educational Research Association online resource. Available at: https://www.bera.ac.uk/researchers-resources/publications/critical-race-theory-crt [accessed June 06, 2017].

Sallah, M. (2009) Conceptual and pedagogical approaches to the global dimension of youth work in British higher education institutions. *The International Journal of Development Education and Global Learning*, 1(3), pp. 39–55.

Sallah, M. (2014) *Global Youth Work: Provoking Consciousness and Taking Action*. Lyme Regis: Russell House Publishing.

Sallah, M. and Cooper, S. (eds) (2008) *Global Youth Work: Taking it Personally*. Leicester: National Youth Agency.

Sallah, M. and Howson, C. (eds) (2007) *Working with Young Black People*. Lyme Regis: Russell House Publishing.

San Juan, E. (2001) 'Problems in the Marxist Project of Theorising Race', in E. Cashmore and R. Jennings (eds) Racism: Essential Readings. London: Sage, pp. 225–246.

Sapin, K. (2009) *Essential Skills for Youth Work Practice*. London: Sage.

Scott, J. (1990) *Domination and the Arts of Resistance*. New Haven, CT: Yale University Press.

Shaw, I., Lynch, J. and Hackett, R. (eds) (2011) *Expanding Peace Journalism: Comparative and Critical Approaches*. Sydney: Sydney University Press.

Sherwood, M. (2001) Race, empire and education: teaching racism. *Race & Class*, 42(3), pp. 1–28. Available at: http://rac.sagepub.com/cgi/doi/10.1177/0306396801423001

Smith, M. (1988) *Developing Youth Work: Informal Education, Mutual Aid, and Popular Practice*. Milton Keynes: Open University Press.

Snauwaert, D. (2011) Social justice and the philosophical foundations of critical PE: exploring Nussbaum, Sen, and Freire. *Journal of PE*, 8(3), pp. 315–331.

Sue, D.W. et al. (2007) Racial microaggressions in everyday life: implications for clinical practice. *American Psychologist*, 62(4), pp. 271–286. Available at: http://doi.apa.org/getdoi.cfm?doi=10.1037/0003-066X.62.4.271

Taylor, E., Gillborn, D. and Ladson-Billings, G. (eds) (2009) *Foundations of Critical Race Theory in Education*. New York: Routledge.

Think Global (2010) *Connect – Challenge – Change: A Practical Guide to Global Youth Work*. London: DEA.

Tyler, K. (2012) *Whiteness, Class and the Legacies of Empire*. Houndmills: Palgrave Macmillan. Available at: http://www.palgraveconnect.com/doifinder/10.1057/9780230390294 [accessed March 3, 2014].

Vawda, S. (2013) A matter of differences: researching race, ethnicity and class. *Education as Change*, 17(2), pp. 243–259. Available at: http://www.scopus.com/inward/record.url?eid=2-s2.0-84879642454&partnerID=tZOtx3y1.

Wood, J. and Hine, J. (eds) (2009) *Work with Young People: Theory and Policy for Practice*. London: Sage.

Woolley, G. (2011) *The Global Dimension in Youth Work: A Conceptual Model*. Derby: Global Education Derby.

Yosso, T. (2005) Whose culture has capital? A critical race theory discussion of community cultural wealth. *Race Ethnicity and Education*, 8(1), pp. 69–91.

Young, K. (1999) *The Art of Youth Work*. Lyme Regis: Russell House.

12

Youth Work and Social Pedagogy: Reflections from the UK and Europe

Kieron Hatton

INTRODUCTION

This chapter seeks to engage with debates around the meaning of contemporary youth work and look at ways in which the radical agenda of many practitioners and theorists can be maintained and enhanced in the unsympathetic environment of contemporary neo-liberalism (Slovenko and Thompson, 2016). It will do so by examining European notions of social pedagogy (drawing particularly on Danish and German traditions) and examining the ways in which social pedagogy draws on some of the same traditions as English youth work (radical youth work, the writings of Paulo Freire, (1973) and Skott-Myhre (2006)). It does so by framing the discussion around notions of criticality, creativity and community and looking at how they intersect with social inclusion, social justice and diversity. Such an approach, the chapter argues, maintains the traditional place of young people at the centre of youth work discourses and allows us to recognise the sense of agency that young people exhibit in their interactions with the external environment.

Criticality suggests an approach to working with young people which moves beyond the parameters laid down by the state and which engages with young people in partnership (through concepts such as the Common Third (Denmark) and *Haltung* (Germany)), which gives them voice and which, in particular, emphasises young peoples' agency

Creativity focuses on the need for what Vygotsky (2004) terms the '*creative imagination*', the understanding that not only should things be better than they are but that a concept should be developed of how they could be made better. *Creativity* is about moving from targeted interventions to ones closer to those of traditional English youth work, and based on young peoples' capacity to express themselves through music, drama (including the use of techniques such as Forum Theatre), writing, poetry, sculpture, public expression or the social media.

Community reflects the site of our interventions. It suggests that individualised approaches not only isolate the young people from their external environment but also preclude the effective involvement of young people in wider processes of social change and thus mitigate against their empowerment and their ability to effect significant change.

DEFINING SOCIAL PEDAGOGY

The Social Pedagogy Development Network say that, in essence:

[social pedagogy] is concerned with well-being, learning and growth. This is underpinned by humanistic values and principles which view people as active and resourceful agents, highlight the importance of including them into the wider community, and aims to tackle or prevent social problems and inequality...

This perspective of social pedagogy means that it is dynamic, creative, and process-orientated rather than mechanical, procedural, and automated. It demands from social pedagogues to be a whole person (Social Pedagogy Development Network, downloaded from www.thempra.org.uk/ on 16/04/18).

Hämäläinen (2003) argues that social pedagogy has a distinct contribution to make to the conceptualisation of welfare practice. He argues that social pedagogy starts from the premise that, 'you can decisively influence social circumstances through education' (p. 71). Further, he suggests social pedagogy's focus is on:

The integration of the individual in society ... it aims to alleviate social exclusion. It deals with the processes of human growth that tie people to the systems, institutions and communities that are important to their well-being and life management. The basic idea of social pedagogy is to promote people's social functioning, inclusion, participation, social identity and social competence as members of society. (p. 76)

By taking account of what Marynowicz-Hetka (2007) calls the '*transversalism*' of social pedagogy it may be possible to integrate a social pedagogic perspective into youth and community development (Slovenko and Thompson, 2016). Transversalism she describes as constructing a broad social movement which integrates issues of race, class, gender and community within our work, again elements core to English youth work. Rosendal Jensen (2009) argues that social pedagogy consists of social policy and social practice and represents, as does youth work, an example of the tensions between care and control. Lorenz (2008) argues that:

Pedagogy-inspired intervention must not take its bearings from institutional objectives but network with and build upon the countless moments of 'expertise' with which people demonstrate their coping abilities in everyday informal and non-formal learning programmes. (p. 639)

This also means developing an approach premised on social justice (Jordan and Drakeford, 2012) which recognises processes of marginalisation and exclusion and which seeks to replace them with more solidaristic, communal and emancipatory ways of ensuring people's involvement (Stepney and Popple, 2008). Such an approach will be based on ideas of inclusion and a recognition of the agency of users of welfare services (Hatton, 2013), and that their 'voice' should be heard in all discussions about modes of intervention. Central to such an approach is a focus on people as having diverse experiences and cultures and a refusal to homogenise that experience, but to also recognise the ways in which these experiences intersect (Goodley, 2011).

Hatton (2013) suggests that this means a wider definition of social pedagogy, a structural social pedagogy needs to be adopted. Such an approach would seek to integrate 'humanistic interpersonal, inclusive and relationship based focus ... with a more radical vision which recognizes the importance of using partnerships with service users to empower people to take control of the services on which they depend' (p. 100).

Such a focus complements the informal education tradition which has been so influential in the development of UK youth work (Slovenko and Thompson, 2016). Thus, social pedagogy has been attracting increasing interest in the UK since around 2000. For example, the Thomas Coram Research Unit was commissioned by the Departments of Health and Children, School and Families (now the Department of Education) to look at the efficacy of social pedagogy as a form of intervention in children's residential services (Cameron et al., 2010). This follows a gradual, but increasing, understanding of the importance of listening to different approaches to the provision of social work and in particular learning from our European neighbours (Lorenz, 1994; Hatton, 2000(b), 2001a, 2008; Lyons, Manion and Carlson, 2006).

Reporting on the initial stages of the Thomas Coram Research Unit (TCRU) report, Petrie (2001) argued that 'the pedagogue, exercising an emancipatory pedagogy and respecting children as social agents, could ensure that children and young people were themselves brought more fully into the discussion' (p. 25).

Community and Social Pedagogy

Eriksson (2011) has pointed to the differences and similarities between community development and social pedagogy, some of which can also be traced in discourses around work with young people. She points to the way in which social pedagogy can be formulated as an individual intervention while community development is, by definition, a collective response to the problems people face. However, she argues that there are clear similarities. Both provide a holistic understanding of education, development and learning. She suggests that in both traditions, there is 'a tension between a radical and a conservative side' and that they both raise the question of whether the individual, society or both should be the focus of change (2011: 414–417).

Lone (2010) raises similar issues when discussing the use of treatment collectives in residential care for people who misuse substances. She argues that because of the lack of hierarchy in these agencies there has been a 'strong and radical political bias' (p. 62) which has allowed them to provide an alternative social pedagogy to the medicalised services available elsewhere in Norway. She quotes Edle Ravndal, who in a review of the working of collectively organised services suggests that, 'The collective model seems still to defend its place as an important component in a larger treatment system for the most challenged youths' (Lone, 2010: 70).

Social pedagogy and community development appear to share the potential to transform people's experience and create new ways of delivering and experiencing welfare services. They can connect with traditions whose focus has been on promoting change not merely ameliorating the impact of inequality and disadvantage (Hatton, 2015). It is worth remembering the words of the authors of *In and Against the State*, who noted:

> Our struggle is therefore in part the assertion of our own ways of doing things, ways which are rooted in people's lived experience rather than betraying it, ways that strengthen rather than whittle away people's confidence, and foster collectivity rather than individualism. (London Edinburgh Weekend Return Group, 1979: 53)

This emphasis asserts the right of people to be involved in transforming and recreating their own situations. This may happen through the process Freire has called 'conscientisation', the notion that when the person becomes aware of their oppression they develop the capacity to take action to change their situation (Freire, 1973; Mayo, 1999).

In Europe as well as the United Kingdom, we now face neo-liberal governments intent on dismantling the state and paradoxically forcing us to look to altruism rather than state funding for services. In responding to this, the language of social pedagogy can combine with those of youth work and community development to promote a shared language where localism, empowerment and social action are emphasised.

Creativity

Central to the concept of social pedagogy is the idea of creativity. Creativity is envisaged as an active process in which the social peda-gogue/social worker, etc. works with the person using their service in a way which seeks to maximise their potential, increase their ability to make decisions and improve their life chances. In the Danish context it is based on theoretical concepts around the 'Common Third'. This is described by Aabro as a descriptive project or ambition within the pedagogical tradition of relations in social work in which there is a 'deliberate focus on the object as something outside the subject. The object being a "common thing" which "both parts in the relation" can con-nect with' (see Hatton, 2006, 2015). Aabro describes the work of Husen who sees the key element of social pedagogy as being:

> To be sharing something, to have something in common, implies in principle to be equal, to be two (or more) individuals on equal terms, with equal rights and dignity (subject–subject relation). In a community you don't use or exploit the other (subject–object relation). (Husen, 1996: 231, trans-lated by Aabro, 2004, cited in Hatton, 2015: 114)

In Germany one of the key pedagogical prin-ciples is 'Haltung', which includes a com-mitment of attitude, mindset and ethos. This was seen as expressing 'an emotional con-nectedness to other people and a profound respect for their human dignity' (Eichsteller and Holthoff, 2011). Haltung was seen as encompassing, among other elements, notions of acceptance, equality, humanistic democratic values, the child as expert, love,

empathy, child (person) centredness and respect.

Eichsteller and Holthoff (2011) demon-strate how Haltung connects to the concept of Lebensweltorientierung, which they trans-late as life-world orientation and which is drawn from the social constructionist tradi-tion. They argue that the idea of life-world, 'demonstrates social pedagogy's commit-ment to social justice by aiming to improve living conditions and social circumstances' (p. 37). In turn, 'social pedagogic Haltung does not refer to an attitude to individuals but provides the context for social pedagogy's aims and purposes at the level of community and society' (p. 38). As suggested above, this provides a way of understanding the broader, structural, purpose of social pedagogy. Social pedagogy seeks to integrate the individual perspective (the focus on the whole world of the person we are working with in the context of their own needs/aspirations) with a focus on social justice (equality, respect, dignity, democracy) and the centring of the person with whom we engage as experts in their own life. Young (1999) has suggested that youth work also in its own way is an art, as it is based on the 'ability to make and sustain … relationships with young people' (p. 6). Slovenko and Thompson (2016) suggest that these elements of both traditions can also be found in informal education and youth work.

At the core of the relationship between the providers and users of services are notions of equality and respect and the eradication of unequal power relations. Cacinovic Vogrincic (2005) talks about how the social pedagogue or social worker needs to develop new lan-guage and concepts but makes, 'the co-cre-ation of solutions together with the client possible' (p. 336). He suggests that such an approach is based on a focus on participation, a focus on strengths rather than weaknesses and finally what he calls co-presence, which he says is about, 'confrontations, understand-ing, agreements … [as] sources of new expe-rience and possible changes' (p. 338). He suggests that the key to these elements is the transfer of professional knowledge into professional action.

Boddy and Statham (2009) noted that in France the profession closest to pedagogy, *education specialise*, was more 'practical than that of the social worker. It was about *doing*, and doing *with* someone ("C'est le faire avec") and about working with relationships ("travailler avec des relations")' (Petrie and Statham, 2009: 8). Ott, a French social pedagogue said 'I use the framework of social pedagogy as a source of inspiration. We are influenced by Paulo Freire, Korczak and Freinet' (2012). Elsewhere he has also suggested that the role of the social pedagogue involves a combination of transmitting ideas, transforming society and education (p. 26) (Ott, 2011: 66–67).

Notions of equality and respect and the eradication of unequal power relations are central to ideas about social pedagogy being developed in the UK, as demonstrated in the work being produced by the Social Pedagogy Development Network (Eichsteller and Holthoff, 2011 – see also www.social-pedagogyuk.com). Coussée, Bradt, Roose and Bouverne-De Bie (2010) argue that an emerging social pedagogical paradigm in the UK has to be conscious not to separate interventions from 'the structures and institutions of society ... pedagogical analysis [they suggest], cannot be separated from social analysis' (p. 799).

This approach is consistent with a wide range of activities which have been taking place across the social sectors in Europe. In the editorial for the spring 2009 edition of *Homeless* in Europe, the magazine of the European Federation of National Organisations Working with the Homeless (FEANTSA), projects featured 'share the common achievement of having improved people's self-esteem, self-awareness and motivation, while challenging mainstream perceptions of homelessness' (FEANTSA, 2009: 3).

This creative and inclusive approach to social pedagogy can have beneficial effects in terms of improving self-belief and self-confidence. This chapter is concerned to look at how social pedagogy can help sustain improved outcomes within the youth service. Over the last few years the UK and Europe (France, Belgium) has seen an explosion of violence and disengagement in a significant number of communities. Early indications suggest that this can at least partly be explained by young peoples' sense of dislocation and alienation from mainstream society (Tyler, 2013a). A key feature of social pedagogy is the recreation of relationships, an attempt to increase social integration and a commitment to ensuring that the people pedagogues work with engage and/or re-engage with the communities in which they live. As such it can begin to provide solutions, or at least part solutions to this sense of displacement and dislocation.

SOCIAL PEDAGOGY AND YOUTH WORK

As noted above, there are similarities in genesis and practice principles between English youth work and the European tradition of social pedagogy described here. English youth work emphasises voluntary relationships, critical dialogues, democratic practices and the like (see the IDYW 2014 Statement for a full description), and both stem from wider traditions of social education. In the climate of neo-liberal challenge to youth work, which is seeing a shift towards more targeted, state-driven interventions with young people, a range of authors (Eichsteller and Rapey, 2006; Slovenko and Thompson, 2016) have argued that social pedagogy can help strengthen the case for more traditional ways of working with young people. This is put most clearly by Slovenko and Thompson (2016) who argue that social pedagogy, 'fits well with the theory and practice of informal education and, alongside it, may help to strengthen the case for holistic and ethical youth work practice' (p. 21).

Langager (2009) describes the work of the Danish-based Academy for Untamed Creativity (AFUK), 'a creative socio-educational environment … [which] represents a contemporary social-pedagogical approach to the vulnerable adolescents' (Langager, 2009: 91). As Langager says:

> The basic idea is to empower the participants trying to strengthen their self-esteem, their acting, their … competence and individual development of constructive new life strategies by working with creative projects – theatre, music, poetry, design, cooking (as an art) etcetera. (2009: 92)

One participant said, 'What I most of all have learned in this school, is to turn a problem [in]to something you can work with' (p. 94).

Such outcomes have encouraged the providers of youth work in the UK to examine the usefulness of social pedagogy in their youth services. A report of the Regional Youth Work Unit North East and the University of Sunderland examined a six-month review of the implications of social pedagogy for youth work. The unit interviewed professionals, young people and collated information from local authorities carrying out social pedagogy pilot programmes.

Respondents to the survey were asked why they did or did not think social pedagogy would benefit children or young people in England. They noted that:

> Social pedagogy underpins good quality youth work and social work practice, so it is already happening here – we just haven't called it social pedagogy. The key benefit for children and young people is to be regarded as competent individuals who are treated with respect and supported/enabled to learn and develop as they grow into adults. (RYWUNE/UoS, 2010: 33)

The respondents note how social pedagogy helps people who are dislocated and disconnected gain direction and support, improves communication, helps people make informed decisions and become competent individuals, is person centred and contributes to the integration of service delivery.

The report is notable also for its focus on the views of young people themselves. They point out that young people suggested to them that social pedagogy courses could be beneficial to services in the UK. They suggested that social pedagogy was beneficial in building positive informal relationships, that it enabled professionals to see people in a holistic manner and that it could contribute positively to the basic training of all professionals involved with young people (pp. 47–48).

The report also looked at the opinion of youth work professionals on social pedagogy. One said, 'for me the principles of social pedagogy are quite similar to the principles of youth work … I think it could really help actually in making our workforce more creative and responsive to young people and their own needs and aspirations' (p. 52). Another commented that:

> in terms of young people being influential on what happens to them, not just having things done to them, it will be a really positive thing … [in a social pedagogy framework] young people are far more influential in services. And that can only improve services for them because they are the only ones that know what services they need, want and will use. (p. 54)

They quote one area manager of integrated services as saying:

> good youth workers have always put the young person at the centre of their work … they have the young people helping in terms of planning. They give them choices. They try not to bring their own prejudices into their work … good youth work is based on social pedagogy. (p. 56)

The report notes that 46 per cent of professionals who completed their questionnaire believed that social pedagogy would benefit the children and young people's workforce (p. 58).

The report's authors warn, however, that the drawbacks to introducing social pedagogy into the UK may include that it is seen as too idealistic; it is not sufficiently well understood or effective in a UK context; and the possible resistance of the workforce if proper account is not taken of the cultural differences between the UK and European countries more familiar with the pedagogic tradition. They call for an increased awareness of social pedagogy across the children and young people's workforce, the development of further pilot projects, the review of existing pedagogic training in the UK to ensure consistency across the sector and adequate funding for the development of pedagogy as a profession.

RISK, SOCIAL PEDAGOGY AND YOUTH WORK

One of the key issues in identifying ways in which social pedagogy can be integrated within youth work is by looking at issues of risk. In Care Matters, a UK government policy paper on the possible future of services for young people who have been through the care system, one of the more noticeable responses came from young people asked their views about the way services meet or fail to meet their needs. They consistently comment on wishing to be heard more and, in particular, articulated strong views around issues of risk. The Commission for Social Care Inspection report from 2006, which looked at the views of young people leaving the care system suggested that, 'to reach their potential an individual must be allowed – and supported – to take risks, have new experiences and make mistakes' (Hatton, 2015: 16).

Eichsteller and Rapey (2006) point out how notions of risk are formulated differently in the UK and in Europe (particularly Germany which is their primary comparator). They suggest that:

> The level of risk assessment is also a large difference between UK and German practice. In the UK there is a strong tendency both in culture and policy to view the child as vulnerable and to protect it from all kinds of risks. The child as competent model really falls down within this kind of culture and is unusual for visitors from Europe or Scandinavia (Danish pedagogic tutors are still bemused by British parents who put their kids on leashes [reins]!)

For some young people in the UK, in order to receive a service they first have to have a problem, have that problem identified and then have it labelled. There is an argument that UK risk-based (deficit model) policy has extended the 'at risk' label to a much wider range of young people, and being labelled 'at risk' legitimises government intervention, which again moves more young people into the 'vulnerable' and controlled category, therefore affecting the type of services offered to them (Eichsteller and Rapey, 2006, Slovenko and Thompson, 2016). Jeffs and Smith (2002) have suggested that this was related to wider processes of uncertainty which has produced a world, 'that is ever less secure and predictable in terms of its outcomes' (p. 52), and which in turn fosters an individualism predicated on a precarious life style, 'devoid of the certainties once imparted by mutuality, community and emotional commitment and attachment to place and locality' (p. 53). (These are not processes impacting only on youth work, a similar neo-liberal agenda impacts across welfare services throughout Europe (Jordan and Drakeford, 2012)).

Coussée, Roets and De Bie (2009) have made similar points about youth work in Flanders, suggesting that as currently constituted youth work can become:

> [a] de-contextualised praxis, disconnected from the process of the empowerment of the young people it works with, and from desirable outcomes like transformational changes in societal institutions ... Youth work becomes unsupportive and even disempowering, in particular for vulnerable youth. (p. 433)

It is however possible to identify similarities between social pedagogy, informal education and youth work. Table 12.1 highlights these points and shows how the three traditions can be seen to complement each other.

Table 12.1 provides a brief framework for considering these similarities. The similarities are clearer at the micro and mezzo levels, and can be seen in the majority of discourses around the three forms of intervention,

Table 12.1 Similarities between social pedagogy, informal education and youth work

Social pedagogy	Informal education	Youth work
Micro level	**Micro level**	**Micro level**
Holistic view of young person	Holistic view of young person	Holistic view of young person
Belief in young people's agency	Commitment to young people's capacity	Focus on agency/capacity of young people
Mezzo level	**Mezzo level**	**Mezzo level**
Common Third	Co-production of activities	Co-presence, working together
Creativity, outdoor activities	Creativity, art, outdoor activities	Creativity, focus on young-people-led activities
Partnership	Focus on non-traditional, experiential learning	
Head, Hands and Heart		
Macro level	**Macro level**	**Macro level**
Equality – belief that young people have agency	Education as the practice of freedom (Freire), social education	Focus on social change – more noticeable in radical interventions, which emphasise need for social struggle, more limited foci in mainstream work
Transversalism		
Structural change pedagogy of the oppressed (Freire)		

although clearly they are expressed differently, for example creativity is a shared focus but the cognitive, emotional and physical aspects are more clearly articulated in the Danish concept of the 'Common Third'. The social change or macro focus is more visible in the more radical interpretations of social pedagogy and youth work (see below).

LINKING YOUTH WORK AND SOCIAL PEDAGOGY

How then can we align youth work with an approach which can integrate social pedagogy in a positive and beneficial way for young people? A Quartet report from 2009 positively highlighted the ways in which services in Denmark adopted what they regarded as a radically different approach (in Danish terms) to caring for children and young people, which was 'based on nurturing relationships, individuality and creativity' (Gulati and King, 2009: 17).

Key to the Danish approach is the formulation 'Head, Hands and Heart'. The head enables the pedagogue to develop an understanding of the reasons for their intervention, the heart indicates the regard for and empathy

with the person or group with whom the pedagogue is intervening and the hands indicate the range of practical and creative activity which the pedagogue uses in any intervention (Boddy and Statham, 2009).

Social pedagogy can be seen as a form of social education and much of the discussion of social pedagogy is formulated through the work of IEIJ, FESET (association Européenne des Centres de Formation au Travail Socio-Educatif and the various fora for social educators which make up FESET). The Nordic Forum for Social Educators argues that:

> Social education is the theory about how psychological, social and material conditions and various value orientations encourage or prevent the general development and growth, life quality and welfare of the individual of the group. (Nordic Forum for Social Educators, 2003: 8)

The NFFS suggests that central to social education processes are issues of integration. The general aim is to ensure the integration of excluded and marginalised people. Their focus is on working in ways which ensure the people they engage with benefit from, rather than become dependent on, the services they use. This is achieved through them connecting 'critical analysis with constructive actions' (p. 10). At the core of social education work (and informal education and youth work) is the notion of becoming reflective practitioners.

SOME CONCLUDING IDEAS

This chapter will conclude with a brief look at potential ways of achieving links between social pedagogy in its European manifestation and English youth work. The first is the idea of positive youth development which has emerged over the last two decades. Flannagen, Syvertsen and Wray-Lake (2007) suggest that positive youth development is, in a similar way to a strengths perspective, an attempt to focus on young people's assets and not their deficits. They suggest that this approach can be extended by recognising young people as agents of change and that political activism should be seen as an important element in such positive youth development. They argue that we would need to legitimise marginalised identities, a similar point to that made by Bill Jordan in his work on poverty and social exclusion (Jordan, 1996). They argue that we should support young people in contesting race and class inequalities in a wide range of welfare services including public spaces (this would mean developing a much more resistant discourse to the paradigms which problematise young people, such as the ways in which behaviour is characterised as anti-social or problematic).

Coussée, Roets and De Bie (2009), writing about youth work in the Flemish part of Belgium, argue that some youth development paradigms can, instead of empowering young people, 'reinforce more negative, targeted forms of intervention and reaffirm a view on the development on vulnerable youth as lacking, deviant and pathological' (p. 425). As they noted, 'youth work that was originally set up with the aim to engage with hard to reach, vulnerable youth in the end deepened social stratification, reinforced social dividing lines and isolated people from each "other"' (p. 430).

Tyler (2013b) suggests that an important area of analysis when discussions of young people's experience take place is the process through which 'public consent is procured for the policies and practices that are effecting these deepening inequalities within the state' (s 2.1). A similar point is made by Waquant (2001) when he talks about the 'penalisation of precariousness' a process which he says is:

> designed to manage the effects of neo-liberal policies at the lower end of the social structure of advanced societies ... precipitated by the overturning of the inherent balance of power between classes and groups fighting over control of employment and the state. (Waquant, 2001: 401)

Skott-Myhre (2006) suggests that such processes can lead to the development of power relationships in which the young person who resists adult domination or authority and engages in a 'display of opposition or resistance in a sustained performance of resistance to adult authority [risks] ... incarceration for "treatment"' (p. 223). This, he suggests, presents a challenge to youth work because, 'people are punished not just because they are poor but because they are ... [seen to be] living like savages and not behaving in a civilized manner' (p. 224). This construction of young people as 'other' or separate from society results in forms of youth work intervention which are prescriptive and punitive rather than creative and inclusive.

De St Croix (2016) argues that the function of grassroots youth work should therefore be to create counter-discourses which embody new ways of thinking about young people, recognition of the need for 'refusal and rebellion' and the need to re-imagine youth work in a way in which instead of individualising young peoples' experience recognises how they interact with the community and wider environment. These ideas align closely with the social pedagogic discourse described in this chapter.

Flanagan, Syvertsen and Wray-Lake (2007) argue that young people are currently, and will continue to be, involved in environmental and global justice activism. They argue that young people can be encouraged to critically analyse the societies around them. They suggest that, 'with the proper knowledge and skills, youth can move beyond individual acts of service and link their sense of social responsibility to constructive political action' (p. 251).

Danish pedagogy and youth work across the UK and Europe has been influenced by the work of Paulo Friere (Hatton, 2001a; Eriksson and Markstrom, 2003; Belton, 2009; de St Croix, 2016). Friere (1973) argues that a key way in which people without power are marginalised is through a process in which their behaviour becomes pathologised and their human nature is constructed in a distorted way through what Friere describes as processes of indoctrination, manipulation and 'dominated consciousness'. Freire argues that as a result they lack the consciousness or understanding to decode their situations. He argues for a process of de-individualisation, by which he means encouraging people to see the commonality of their situation. He suggests that this focus on the common interest can only be achieved through a process which he describes as *conscientanzo*. This is a process through which people not only become aware but act on that awareness. Noting the influence of Freire, Eriksson and Markstrom (2003) suggest that the key contribution of Freire to social pedagogy is his emphasis on social mobilisation and emancipation. In this context they see social pedagogy as a means of initiating a process through which people mobilise their own resources. De St Croix (2016) similarly describes the influence of Friere on grassroots youth work (pp. 140–141).

An example is provided by a youth worker at the Blaeksprutten (Octopussy) youth project in Copenhagen (Hatton, 2001b) (the project is part of the SSP (School, Social services, Police) model widely used in Denmark – see Langager (2009)). This is a project which focused on the experience of a poor, marginalised community with a high proportion of black and minority young people living within its boundaries. The project aimed to break down the barriers between the police, social welfare agencies and local young people. The project leader said that they seek to provide the young people with an increased sense of self-worth.

One of the project workers describes how:

> When we give these kids more confidence and a strong identity they go out on the streets and in social society and can be like normal people, they do not have to be afraid and do not have to pretend to be tough guys, because they know from the inside that they are good enough. After giving these kids self-confidence they can do more things for other kids and adults in social society. We are showing the social society that the kids around here are OK. (Hatton, 2013: 72)

A similar approach is suggested by Perkins, Borden and Villarruel (2003) when they talk about community youth development. They suggest that community youth development:

> shifts the emphasis from a dual focus of youth being problem free and fully prepared, to a triadic focus for youth being problem free, fully prepared and engaged partners. More importantly, this focus recognises that there is an interdependent relationship between positive and healthy youth outcomes and positive and healthy communities. (p. 43)

They suggest that at the core of community youth development is a focus on the young persons' capacity to both understand and act upon the environment, a recognition that this involves the active support of people across the community, and that central to this is the engagement of youth in 'constructive and challenging activities that build their competence and foster supported relationships with peers and with adults' (p. 48).

The author is not suggesting that these approaches have been absent from developments in youth work. What is being suggested is that over the last ten years we have seen developments that have challenged the traditional values and practice principles of English youth work – including the development of neo-liberal policies which atomise and individualise welfare while problematising the recipients of welfare (Ferguson, 2008). In the context of young people this means a focus on young people as problematic rather than as people with capacity. We have seen the growth of organisations such as youth parliaments, and through Care Matters and Youth Matters (in the UK) recognition of the importance of listening to and engaging with young people. This has occurred increasingly against a backdrop in which young people have been, and continue to be seen as, a threat, rather than a resource within our societies (Skott-Myhre, 2006; Tyler, 2013b).

As we have seen, social pedagogy can complement youth work to allow us to reframe these debates, if only by reminding us that youth work, similar to other welfare professions, has a radical history (de St Croix, 2016; Ferguson and Woodward, 2009; Hatton, 2015). This will allow us to focus on the creativity of young people, their capacity to act (in a positive rather than negative way) and the importance of including, engaging with and promoting young people as active citizens. Recent foci within UK and European youth policies on targeted interventions with the most vulnerable young people can result in us reinforcing negative images of young people rather than seeing the positive outcomes which social pedagogy and youth work can attain (Coussée et al., 2009).

Aluffi-Pentini and Lorenz (1996) pointed to the importance of social professionals, including youth workers and social pedagogues, challenging structural as well as individual oppression when addressing racism. They described how 'racism was a challenge to educators in all parts of the country, that all pedagogical interventions had to be embedded in a clear political analysis, [and] that cultural differences reflected power differentials' (p. vi).

Participation and Empowerment

This means, among other things, engaging with young people and ensuring their participation in all levels of decision-making (Checkoway, 2011). The United Nations Children's Fund (UNICEF) (2001: 9–11) suggested that participation had a number of important values for young people. These included a focus on human rights and self-development as a way of building effectiveness and sustainability while recognising young people's contribution to society. The UNICEF paper refers in particular to the way young people 'will be better equipped to deal with abusive, threatening or unfair situations because they will be in a better position to seek advice, exit a harmful situation when necessary or cope creatively when there is no exit' (p. 10). They quote the Dominican Youth Group who argue that:

> participation implies decision making and is viewed as a strategy for human development as it is closely linked to the promotion of leadership (with transforming capacities) at the social level, that empowers adolescents, adolescent groups, communities, provinces, and the country to get involved in the processes towards individual and collective development. (p. 12)

This view of work with young people as potentially empowering at a structural as well as an individual level reinforces our understanding of social pedagogy and youth work as activities which needs to engage with social change as well as individual development. This suggests that, as long maintained by youth workers from a range of traditions, the agenda in our work with young people needs to be participatory, inclusive and oriented towards social action rather than focusing on young people as a problem which needs to be solved or fixed. A bridge between these two approaches can be seen in the links between community development and social pedagogy discussed above (Hatton, 2011).

Social pedagogy can remind us of informal education's focus on relationship work. We can learn from pedagogic traditions in that they 'may allow us to see the similarities as well as the differences between us, to recognise that truth does not reside in one set of culturally specific values but that ways of understanding, methods of working and commitments to social justice are often shared' (Hatton, 2001a: 276).

Fook (2002) describes this as a process of 'transferability', or 'the ability of ... theory to transfer meanings between different contexts' (p. 82). Coussée et al. (2009) argue for a form of youth work influenced by the German tradition of critical '*Socialpedagogik*', which they argue can help to overcome the individual/social divide in much current discussion. As de St Croix (2016) argues, this means bringing young people into contact with alternative discourses and ways of living. Social pedagogy, with its commitment to creativity and co-creation and its focus on structural as well as individual approaches to changing people's lives can be an important part of this process (Hatton, 2011, 2013). However, in the final analysis it is the capacity of youth work and social pedagogy to learn from each other's *strengths* in shared opposition to neoliberal policies that have threatened the ethos and principles of English youth work that provides the best way forward.

REFERENCES

Aabro, C (2004) *The Common Third*, correspondence with author.

Aluffi-Pentini, A and Lorenz, W (1996) *Antiracist Work with Young People: European Experiences and Approaches*, Lyme Regis, Russell House Publishing.

Belton, B (2009) *Developing Critical Youth Work Theory: Building Professional Judgement in the Community Context*, Rotterdam, Sense Publishers.

Boddy, J and Statham, J (2009) *European Perspectives on Social Work: Models of Education and Professional Roles: Nuffield Foundation Briefing Paper*, London, The Nuffield Foundation. Retrieved from http://discovery.ucl.ac.uk/10000717/.

Čačinovič Vogrinčič, G (2005) Teaching Concepts of Help in Social Work: The Working Relationship, *European Journal of Social Work*, 8(3), 335–351.

Cameron, C, Jasper, A, Kleipoedszus, S, Petrie, P and Wigfall, V (2010) *Implementing the DCSF Pilot Programme: The Work of the First Year*, London, Thomas Coram Research Unit, Institute of Education.

Checkoway, B (2011) What is Youth Participation? *Children and Youth Service Review*, 33(2), 340–345.

Coussée, F, Bradt, L, Roose, R and Bouverne-De Bie, M (2010) The Emerging Social Pedagogical Paradigm in UK Child and Youth Care: Deus Ex Machina or Walking the Beaten Path, *British Journal of Social Work*, 40, 789–805.

Coussée, F, Roets, G and De Bie, M (2009) Empowering the Powerful: Challenging Hidden Processes of Marginalization in Youth Work Policy and Practice in Belgium, *Critical Social Policy*, 29(3), 421–442.

de St Croix, T (2016) *Grassroots Youth Work: Policy, Passion and Resistance in Practice*, Bristol, Policy Press.

Eichsteller, G and Rapey, D (2006) Social Pedagogy and Youth Work, paper presented to conference organised by the Thomas Coram Research Unit, IOE, University of London, December.

Eichsteller, G and Raper, D (2007) *Treasure Hunt – Searching for Pedagogic Ideas within Youth Work in Portsmouth*. Portsmouth, Portsmouth City Council.

Eichsteller, G and Holthoff, S (2011) The Social Pedagogy Development Network – A Grassroots Movement for Professionals Working with Children and Young People in Social Pedagogical Ways, downloaded from www.socialpedagogyuk.com on 5/03/12.

Eriksson, L (2011) Community Development and Social Pedagogy: Traditions for Understanding Mobilization for Collective Self-Development, *Community Development Journal*, 46(4), 403–420.

Eriksson, L and Markstrom, AM (2003) Interpreting the Concept of Social Pedagogy. In Gustavsson, A Hermansson, HE and Hämäläinen J (eds) *Perspectives and Theory in Social Pedagogy*, Gotenberg, Bokforlaget Daidalos, pp. 9–23.

FEANTSA (2009) *Homelessness in Europe Magazine*, Spring.

Ferguson, I (2008) *Reclaiming Social Work: Challenging Neo-liberalism and Promoting Social Justice*, London, Sage.

Ferguson, I and Woodward, R (2009) *Radical Social Work in Practice: Making a Difference*, Bristol, Policy Press.

Flanagan, C, Syvertsen, A and Wray-Lake, L (2007) Youth Political Activism: Sources of Public Hope in the Context of Globalisation. In Silbereinsen, RK and Lerner, RM (eds) *Approaches to Positive Youth Development*, London, Sage, pp. 243–262.

Fook, J (2002) Theorizing from Practice: An Inclusive Approach for Social Work, *Qualitative Social Work*, 1(1), 79–95.

Foucault, M (1980) *Power/Knowledge: Selected Interviews and Other Writings*, Brighton, Harvester Wheatsheaf.

Freire, P (1973) *Education: The Practice of Freedom*, London, Writers and Readers Collective.

Goodley, D (2011) *Disability Studies: An Interdisciplinary Introduction*, London, Sage.

Gulati, A and King, A (2009) Supporting Vulnerable Young People in Transition, final report to Quartet community foundation for the west of England, in Perspective UK Ltd.

Hämäläinen, J (2003) The Concept of Social Pedagogy in the Field of Social Work, *Journal of Social Work*, 3(1), 70–80.

Hatton, K (2001a) Translating Values: Making Sense of Different Value Bases – Reflections from Denmark and the UK, *International Journal of Social Research Methodology*, 4(4), 265–278.

Hatton, K (2001b) Dialectics of Exclusion and Empowerment: An Examination of the Role of Social Professionals in Britain, Ireland and Denmark. Unpublished PhD thesis, University of Portsmouth.

Hatton, K (2006) Europe and the Undergraduate Curriculum. In Lyons, K and Lawrence, S (eds), *Social Work in Europe: Educating for Change*, Birmingham, Venture Press/BASW, pp. 105–125.

Hatton, K (2011) Changing Professional Identities: Towards a Structural Social Pedagogy. In Seibel, FW, Friesenhahn, GJ, Lorenz, W and Chytil, O (eds) *European Developments and the Social Professions*, Brno, Czech Republic, ECCE, pp. 1237–1250.

Hatton, K (2013) *Social Pedagogy in the UK: Theory and Practice*, Lyme Regis, Russell House Publishing.

Hatton, K (2015) *New Directions in Social Work Practice* (2nd edn), London, Learning Matters/Sage.

Highman, P (2001) Changing Practice and an Emerging Social Pedagogy Paradigm in England: The Role of the Personal Advisor, *Social Work in Europe*, 8(1), 21–26.

Husen, M (1996) Det faelles tredje - om faellesskab og vaerdier I det paedagogiske arbejde , in B. Pecseli (red.): *Kulture & paedagogik*. Kobenhavn Bibliotek, Munsgaard/Rosinante

IDYW In Defence of Youth Work, Facebook. com

Jeffs, T and Smith, M (2002) Individualism and Youth Work, *Youth & Policy*, 76, pp 39–65.

Jordan, B (1996) *A Theory of Poverty and Social Exclusion*, Cambridge, Polity.

Jordan, B and Drakeford, M (2012) *Social Work and Social Policy under Austerity*, Basingstoke, Palgrave Macmillan.

Langager, S (2009) Social Pedagogy and 'At-Risk' Youth: Societal Change and New Challenges in Social Work with Youth. In Kornbeck, J and Rosendal Jensen, N (eds) *The Diversity of Social Pedagogy in Europe: Studies in Comparative Social Pedagogy and International Social Work, Vol VII*, Bremen, Europäischer Hochschulverlag, pp. 83–105.

London Edinburgh Weekend Return Group (1979) *In and Against the State*, London, Pluto Press.

Lone, A (2010) Collectives: A Norwegian Success Story in Residential Care for Drug Addicts Based on a Social Pedagogic Approach, *European Journal of Social Education*, 18/19, 60–72.

Lorenz, W (1994) *Social Work in a Changing Europe*, London, Routledge

Lorenz, W (2008) Paradigms and Politics: Understanding Methods Paradigms in an Historical Context: The Case of Social Pedagogy, *British Journal of Social Work*, 38(4), 625–644.

Lyons, K, Manion, K and Carlson, S (2006) *International Perspectives on Social Work: Global Conditions, Local Practices*, Basingstoke, Palgrave Macmillan.

Marynowicz-Hetka, E (2007) Towards the Transversalism of Social Pedagogy, *Social Work and Society, International Online Journal* 5(3).

Mayo, P (1999) *Gramsci, Freire and Adult Education*, London, Zed Books.

Mayo, P (1999) *Gramsci, Freire and Adult Education: Possibilities of Transformative Action*, Basingstoke, Macmillan.

Morro, RA and Torres, CA (2002) *Reading Freire and Habermas: Critical Pedagogy and Transformative Social Change*, New York, Teachers College, Columbia University.

Nordic Forum for Social Educators (2003) Social Education and Social Educational Practice in the Nordic Countries, Kopenhagen Nordisk Forum for Socialpadeagoger.

Ott, L (2011) Pedagogie sociale: Une pedagogie pour tous les educateurs, Lyon, Chronique Sociale.

Ott, L (2012) Relations Parents/Infants. Paper presented at Innovations Sociales et Terrtoires Conference, Montrouge, Paris, 7–9 February.

Oxtoby, K (2009) How does Social Pedagogy Work on the Continent, and What are the Barriers to its Use in the UK. Available from: http://www.communitycare.co.uk/articles/2009/03/18/111007/social-pedagogy-in-practice.html

Perkins, DF, Borden, LM and Villarruel, FA (2003) Community Youth Development: A Partnership for Action, *The School Community Journal*, 11(2), 39–56.

Petrie, P (2001) The Potential of Pedagogy/Education for Work in the Children's Sector in the UK, *Social Work in Europe*, 8(3), 23–26.

Regional Youth Work Unit North East/University of Sunderland (RYWUNE/UoS) (2010) *A Study on the Understanding of Social Pedagogy and its Potential Implications for Youth Work Practice and Training*, University of Sunderland.

Rosendal Jensen, N (2009) Will Social Pedagogy Become an Academic Discipline in Denmark? In Kornbeck, J and Rosendal Jensen, N (eds) *The Diversity of Social Pedagogy in Europe:*

Studies in Comparative Social Pedagogy and International Social Work, Vol VII, Bremen, Europäischer Hochschulverlag.

Skott-Myhre, H (2006) Radical Youth Work: Becoming Visible, *Child Youth Care Forum*, 35(3), 219–229.

Slovenko, K and Thompson, N (2016) Social Pedagogy, Informal Education and Ethical Youth Work Practice, *Ethics and Social Welfare*, 10(1), 19–34.

Stepney, P and Popple, K (2008) *Social Work and the Community: A Critical Context for Practice*, Basingstoke, Palgrave.

Taylor, K (2006) *The Art of Youth Work* (2nd edn), Lyme Regis, Russell House Publishing.

Tyler, I (2013a) The Riots of the Underclass? Stigmatisation, Mediation and the Governance of Poverty and Disadvantage in Neoliberal Britain, *Sociological Research Online*, 18(4) 6, http://www.socresonline.org.uk/18/4/6.html

Tyler, I (2013b) *Revolting Subjects: Social Abjection and Resistance in Neo-liberal Britain*, London, Zed Books.

UNICEF (2001) *The Participation Rights of Adolescents: A Strategic Approach*, Working Paper series, New York, Programme Division, United Nations Children's Fund.

Vaisanen, R (2010) Social Pedagogical Approaches in Youth Social Work, *Journal Europeen D'Education Sociale*, 18/19, 23–34.

Vygotsky, L (2004) Imagination and Creativity in Childhood, *Journal of Russian and East European Psychology*, 42(1), 7–97.

Waquant, L (2001) The Penalisation of Poverty and the Rise of Neo-liberalism, *European Journal of Criminal Policy and Research*, 9(4), 401–412.

Weedon, C (1998) *Feminist Practice and Post-Structuralist Theory* (2nd edn), London, Wiley-Blackwell.

Young, K (1999) *The Art of Youth Work*, Lyme Regis, Russell House Publishing.

13

21st-Century Youth Work: Life Under Global Capitalism

Hans Skott-Myhre and Kathleen Skott-Mhyre

INTRODUCTION

The question of how we care for young people as we enter the early 21st century is increasingly complex and contested. Without a doubt, life for young people has become increasingly complicated, if not more difficult. The advent of capitalism as a fully global force has significantly altered the social, cultural and economic landscape of everyone's life, as we move from the world of the 20th-century industrial capitalist order into the realm of virtual capitalist rule (Boggs, 2012; Hardt and Negri, 2001; Negri, 1996).

These changes, we would argue, have a profound impact on the world of young people and those who work with them in the context of what has been called youth work. In what follows, we will endeavor to outline the main features of the system of rule designated as global capitalism. On the basis of that analysis, we will trace some of its effects on young people and make proposals as to how we, who identify as youth/child and youth workers, might shift our practices accordingly.

Writing from a North American context, the terms 'youth work' and 'child and youth care' intersect with each other in rich and complex ways. To be sure, there are differences in North American practices and theories between these frameworks for working with young people. For example, there is significant variation between the characteristics of the child and youth care approach articulated in the work of Garfat and Fulcher (2011) and the much more heterogeneous youth work approaches to practice in the US as noted by Dana Fusco in this volume. However, while our own work can easily be traced on to the characteristics of child and youth care developed largely in international and Canadian contexts, we also find affinity with what Fusco (in this volume) refers to as radical youth work in the US context.

For our purposes here, however, we see conventional understandings of both youth work and child and youth care as rooted in 20th-century understandings of economics, politics and development. It will be our intention to suggest alternative modes of practice and thought more pertinent to 21st-century concerns. To do that, we will utilize a transdisciplinary approach to youth work that draws from post-Marxist and post-modern modes of analysis. While at times these modes of analysis operate outside our traditional understandings of our work, for us they offer the tools we require to think about who we are as youth workers in the 21st century and how we might function in ways that are responsive to 21st-century conditions.

Underlying both the specific historical conditions in question and any proposals for changes to our thinking and practices is an underlying assumption, on our part, that at its root youth work is about youth and adults working together for common purpose. Here, we align ourselves broadly with older traditions in youth work of activism and community transformation (Belton, 2010, 2013; Cooper, 2012; Gilchrist et al., 2009; Jeffs, 2013), but argue for new 21st-century forms of radical activism. We call this DIY Youth Work.

This can happen anywhere that youth and adults come into contact with each other, from institutional settings to casual encounters in the community. For us, it is a question of youth and adults negotiating a set of relationships that works to enhance the creative capacities of us all. To maximize this creative capacity, we will argue, we need to first understand the way global capitalism works as the dominant mode of governance in the 21st century.

In this regard, post-Marxist scholars Michael Hardt and Antonio Negri (2001) refer to global capitalism as Empire and argue that any understanding of the dynamics of power and politics in our current time must account for both the shift in the mode of production and new distributions and concentrations of power. They assert that power, under global capitalism, becomes a decentralized

form of networked deployments of rule, in which the control and regulation of populations, peoples and individuals takes on variable modes and distributions depending on geographies, cultures, social conditions and level of economic immersion in the money form as abstract exchange. Empire, as a decentralized regime of corporate rule with no fixed seat of power, reconfigures features of the global political landscape such as nation states, local and regional political organizations as well as transnational NGOs, stock markets and an increasingly insular and mobile ruling class.

As this emerging system of domination begins the process of articulating its specific mechanisms of control and discipline, the impacts on young people have been profound. Shifts such as the downsizing, relocation or elimination of large sectors of industrial production has had deep ramifications for young people's ability to find stable long-term employment and to sustain themselves economically. Even in parts of the world where there was an initial increase in industrial employment due to the outsourcing of jobs from North America and Europe, such as China, Mexico, Brazil and India, workers have experienced high variability in the sustainability of such employment and extreme fluctuations in economic conditions. Indeed, it often appears as though various local and national economies are moving from crisis to crisis with brief periods of stability in between (Krugman, 2012).

Shifts in the economic and political interests of various multinational corporations and their advocates in powerful nation states have led to what Hardt and Negri (2005) call war between various elements within Empire over who will control appropriate resources that can be leveraged into capital or the money form. They argue that this new form of war, unlike its predecessors, is not about taking or holding territory, controlling any particular population or creating a centralized or permanent mechanism of centralized government. Instead, war under global empire is a permanent feature of rule, through which political instability and social unrest can be deployed as mechanisms of control. Constant fear and anxiety become the emotional indicators of contemporary life, in which no one can count on being exempt from random acts of violence perpetrated at all levels of the social from the local individual acts of mass shootings, terrorist bombings, internecine conflict over various underground economies, to the carpet bombings and drone strikes by powerful nation states against civilian populations. Those young people being born into this world will have no memory of peace in their lifetime under the current conditions of constant violent conflict.

Another effect of economic dislocation, instability and constant war is the movement of massive flows of people across the globe. These flows include young people in significant numbers, placing them at considerable risk of loss of life through assault, sexual and otherwise, starvation and dehydration, as well as drowning, to name but a few examples. These migrant young people are often stateless refugees from wars of one type or another, or economic migrants seeking to better their living conditions. While some of them manage to travel with members of their family, a significant percentage of these migrants are unaccompanied minors. Young people as migrants are subject to the political and economic vagaries of what Georgio Agamben (1998) has termed, in the context of the Nazi holocaust, bare life. Bare life Agamben defines as bodies without the protections of the state in terms of the legal recourse to the rights of citizenship.

Those young people, in movement across borders without the legal status of citizenship, become life that can be killed or incarcerated without due process or legal ramifications. Such young people stand the possibility of being incarcerated in camps of various types, from the refugee camps surrounding the proliferating war zones across the globe, to internment camps for 'illegal' migrants in Europe and the United States.

Outside state or internationally sanctioned modes of incarceration for those young people driven into flight across state borders are the ever-multiplying modes of enslavement as child soldiers, gang inductees, involuntary sex workers and household servants.

Even for young people within the confines of a nation state who have full rights of citizenship, there is no guarantee that one will not be incarcerated or denied due process on the basis of age. Recent legislation within nation states as diverse as the United States, Russia, Guatemala, Algeria and South Korea have targeted transgendered, gay and lesbian young people, refusing accommodation and in some cases resulting in death sentences and incarceration (Woods, 2010). Young women's access to reproductive technologies is being increasingly restricted globally, including both birth control and access to abortion (Locke, 2016). In some instances it is still acceptable to kill a young woman for 'disgracing' her family by defying the will of the father (Smith, 2016). Cases of honor killings for behavior as diverse as listening to rap music, refusing to accept an arranged marriage or entering into a romantic relationship not sanctioned by the young woman's family or dressing in immodest western clothing have been reported in the United States, Europe, the Middle East, Africa and South Asia (Avlon, 2008).

Class and gender is being used both overtly and covertly to restrict access to education (Kabeer, 2016). Overtly, young women in some parts of the world such as Pakistan are being denied the right to go to school, with defiance being punished by death and disfiguration. Covertly, across the globe, education is significantly restricted by economic and class status, with far inferior educational opportunities afforded to poor and disenfranchised young people. For example, in North America, the wealthiest countries in the world systematically underfund schools for African-American, Latino and Indigenous students (Tomlinson, 1998).

As capitalism expands its influence across geographies and peoples there are the obvious effects we have cited so far, but there are also subtler but perhaps even more pernicious effects and tactics. In his prescient work on the disciplinary apparatuses of capitalism, Gille Deleuze (1992) noted what he called the emergence of a society of control. The society of control only becomes possible at the end of the industrial period with the advent of global virtual technology. Up until the end of the 20th century, capitalism focused on the micro-disciplines of the body necessary to develop factory workers and managers. Michel Foucault (1977) traces these developments extensively in his works such as *Discipline and Punish: The Birth of the Prison*.

With the advent of virtual technology, however, something very significant changes. Deleuze (1992) tells us that we move from a system that disciplines our bodies, to an abstract system of control premised almost entirely on the manipulation of various codes. Jean Baudrillard (1994) refers to this as the historical moment at which society becomes a copy of itself and our sense of social reality becomes premised on what he calls simulacrum. What this means is that we begin to model ourselves and our social systems of affiliation such as friends, family, religion and culture on abstract representations of these sets of relations rather than on phenomenological experiences and living material actualities of relations. Niklas Luhmann (2000) argues that this form of society has no direct relation to living beings such as people, but operates on its own logic to extend its various sets of representations.

Luhmann uses the example of the media to make his point. The global system of media which includes, the internet, video games, movies, television, and so on, is premised on the ability to encode representations of actual lived experience and feed them back to the subjects that produced the events portrayed. Of course, as anyone who had ever been interviewed or seen an event in which they participated on a media outlet knows, the representation of the event cannot help but be considerably at odds with the event itself. This is true, if only because no representation of an actual encounter between living beings can ever capture the full complexity of the relations involved.

Luhmann argues that contemporary society operates as an abstract system of code very much like that of a computer. Each social function is defined in binary terms, like the zeros and ones that create information in a computer. Events portrayed in the media have to fit into this kind of binary code. Everything in the world is encoded in terms of this *is* media or this *is not* media. Only those events and phenomena that advance this *is* media as a system of proliferating code will be represented and replicated for consumption. This process of selection produces a global network of information that is highly selective and profoundly influential in terms of what people come to believe is the reality of who we are and what we are becoming. In short, media produces a representation of society and social subjects that is disseminated as real. This version of what constitutes society and social subjects is available for consumption 24 hours a day, seven days a week. It is ubiquitous and provides the main avenue that subjects of 21st-century capitalism have about who they are and what they should do.

Because the media relies on binary codes of difference in order to perpetuate and proliferate itself, there is an emphasis on perpetual change and difference. These are very time limited representations of stable social configurations. It is precisely in the representation of stable social configurations such as the family, democratic governance, economic security, religious faith and various forms of identity that we can see the most pernicious effects of global capitalist media.

Because the media is pure abstract representation based on radical and continual representations of difference, its representations of the relation between change and stable social configurations is highly distorted. The representation of functioning social systems such as families, governments and economic systems are almost always nostalgic recyclings of previous social forms that are posited against current evolving forms in ways that tend to promote cynicism and resentment.

Representations of past social forms are produced as ideal models that are unattainable but highly desirable. The nuclear family, male-headed households, well disciplined and behaved young people, docile women and invisible/uncomplaining minorities and bounded homogenous nation states are juxtaposed with the ostensibly deteriorating social and moral morays of contemporary society.

For young people, this system produces them as abstract symbols of contradiction rooted in portrayals of innocence and deviance, victims and predators. There is a nostalgic impulse for a developmentally ideal child that never existed, as well as a fear of an emerging predatory, amoral, biologically and developmentally flawed future child, that also does not exist, except in the imaginary of the media. However, as these images are fed back to young people, it is inevitable that they will come to understand themselves, to some degree, in relation to these unattainable and highly problematic social imperatives.

This is what Baudrillard (1994) delineates as the force of simulacra. Under a social form premised in abstract systems of signification, we are presented with a mediated representation of social forms. For young people, a significant example of the effects of mediatization is how they view and interact with their family.

Korinne Wiema (Skott-Myhre et al., 2012) explicates this in her work in what she calls her lived with and lived by families. The latter is the version of the family given to her by what she references as the Psy-complex or that social amalgamation of media, psychology and psychiatry disseminated on talk shows such as *Dr Phil* or *Oprah*, as well as in popular media accounts of bio-abnormalities such as undeveloped frontal lobes in young people.

Her lived by family, in contrast, is composed of the actual people and relationships in her family. She writes about the antagonism between the abstract version of her family and the actual sets of living relationships. She discusses how she found it difficult to distinguish her real family from the idealized family being portrayed to her by the media. Her real family always seemed to fail to meet expectation in relation to the mediatized family.

What Baudrillard (1994) argues is that the mediatized family is an abstract copy of actual family relations. However, the copy is structured and shaped to meet the ideological dictates of both the dominant class and the need of the media to create the family as media spectacle worthy of mass media attention. As we encounter the ever present media representations of the family, we come increasingly to shape our expectations of our own families to the template we are absorbing. Over generations the family becomes a copy of the mediatized copy premised almost entirely on abstract symbols of family life rather than actual human relations. We begin to shape our behaviors according to the idealized copy rather than to relations that work for us as living people. This is not a disciplinary regime that is training us to work in a particular segment of the economy any longer. Instead it is a mode of control that is training us to live in a world of pure abstraction – a world perfectly suited to the domination of our lives by an abstract form such as money.

Deleuze (1992) echoes these concerns in his work by suggesting that our lives are increasingly dominated by codes that shape our behavior. For example, in the global North, social insurance or social security numbers are now deeply tied to our credit ratings, rather than our national identity. Our credit rating is now used to determine fundamental necessities such as housing, admission to certain universities and job acquisition, among others. Indeed, the number of times we are asked to provide credit-related information in order to do or acquire things is proliferating exponentially. Of course, this shift in the way we manage the necessities of daily life is a constantly shifting panorama of mediatized demand for new codes, passwords and security verifications. Deleuze indicates that it is just this uncertainty of what will be demanded of us next that is at the heart of the new systems of control. He suggests that the proliferating world of credit will create us not as subjects entrapped within societal apparatuses of physical discipline, but subjects controlled by the abstract regime of debt.

While these trends are particularly pronounced in the global North, these logics are also being disseminated in the global South as well. An excellent example is the recent valorization of the notion of micro-loans for impoverished women who have never experienced institutional monetary debt. While these loans offer opportunity they simultaneously introduce the logic of capitalism into new markets with corresponding new modes of sociality and subjectivity (Rogaly, 1996). Similarly, well-intentioned grants and scholarships administered through NGOs in the global South introduce certain neo-colonial logics of monetary logic and dependence that extend the monetary form with its attendant modes of discipline and control (Hardt and Negri, 2001).

The constantly shifting economic, social and cultural mapping of our lives leaves the future of young people radically indeterminate. Young people entering the world today cannot count on any particular level or mode of education to be adequate in providing them with any measure of social or economic security. Deleuze (1992) refers to this as a society of 'limitless postponements' (p. 5). The logic of indefinite postponement produces an endless array of activities for young people, none of which can be guaranteed to result in anything in particular. The realm of education is producing a dizzying array of educational possibilities, including rapidly differentiating degrees, proliferating institutions (charter schools, colleges, universities – for profit and non-profit, online, brick and mortar etc.) and

endless training opportunities both on and off the job. However, there is no guarantee that once you have obtained any level of degree, certification or licensure that it will provide anything certain socially or financially. This leads to young people being subjected to endless cycles of training and education. However, as Deleuze (1992) points out in horror, 'Many young people strangely boast of being motivated; they re-request apprenticeships and permanent training' (p. 7).

We would argue that we can understand this strange effect as the simulacra or copy of a copy of the independent individual. Indeed, the foregrounding of the individual rather than the community or government is an idea put forward by what has been termed neoliberalism. Neoliberalism is predicated in the idea that good government is premised on the affirmation of individual rights and freedoms over the rule of the common good (Harvey, 2005).

Of course the individual in question is a very specific and rather abstract concept developed to reduce the scope of government regulation of multinational capitalism. In this respect, the neoliberal deployment of a copy of the 19th- and 20th-century independent self-motivated individual who creates the world on his own terms, by pulling themselves up by their own bootstraps, is a very peculiar copy indeed. Such an individual, as Nowile M. Rooks (2012) and Stephanie Coontz (1992) point out, never existed except in the imaginary of the United States and other colonial powers, as a justification for the imperialist subjugation of both people and natural resources. The neoliberal individual who aspires to perpetual training in order to be all they can be is pure social mythology. However, as Foucault points out, just because something doesn't exist doesn't mean it doesn't have force. Indeed, the force it has on young people is doubled in that it drives certain activities and mindsets around who deserves to succeed and what is necessary to succeed, as well as focusing the fault for social and financial inadequacy firmly on the subject. In both cases, global capitalism becomes opaque in its effects while young people become increasingly available for social critique, as we can see in characterizations of the millennials as lazy, self-involved, unmotivated, narcissistic and so on (Schumpeter, 2015).

WHAT IS TO BE DONE?

The good-bad news for those of us involved in working with or caring for young people is that it is quite probable that the system I have just described is unsustainable and may well collapse (Hardt and Negri, 2001). Foucault (1977) points out that, to the degree a system of rule's mode of discipline and control becomes visible, it is quite likely that it is in decline. A system of rule at its most powerful operates invisibly through a thorough integration into the activities, thoughts and beliefs of its subjects.

That said, whether or not global capitalism is on the verge of collapse, it is clearly in transition and as such it has not yet been able to fully and seamlessly integrate its model of rule. Such a situation is good news and bad news for young people coming into the 21st century. On the one hand, the very instability of the system opens the possibility for alternative ways to organize society so that it serves living beings rather than abstract code. The bad news is that periods of transition during which the dominant system of rule is in crisis tend to be periods of immense instability and chaos in which life can become extremely challenging.

For those of us who define our life work in terms of our engagements with young people, I would argue there is no more pressing question than that of how to assist young people in re-shaping the world so that it serves their needs rather than the needs of an abstract signifier such as the money form. In her provocative and inspiring book *The Next American Revolution: Sustainable Activism for the Twenty-First Century*, the 94-year-old

activist Grace Lee Boggs (2012) asks the following question:

> Living at the margins of the postindustrial capitalist order we … are faced with a stark choice of how to devote ourselves to struggle. Should we strain to squeeze the last drops of life out of a failing, deteriorating, and unjust system? Or should we instead devote our creative and collective energies toward envisioning and building a radically different form of living? (p. 134)

Do we as youth workers take adequate account of the actual lived conditions for young people globally? Do those of us ostensibly concerned with caring for young people, hold the capacity to engage substantial accountability to the rapidly deteriorating social and economic conditions facing those young people on a daily basis? How are we making sense of the fact that young people are taking to the streets all over the world in places like Egypt, Great Britain, Brazil, Turkey, Mexico and the US, powerfully demonstrating their dissatisfaction with both the current conditions under which they live and perhaps even more poignantly, their fear that their future will hold economic, ecological and cultural calamity and disaster? What are we doing to care for them under these conditions? Do we have an ethical accountability to their future beyond the immediacy of assisting them to cope and adapt to the failing and deteriorating system in which they live?

If we are to undertake youth work as a relationally founded system of social care, I would argue that these should be the central questions facing our field. Of course youth work itself, as an element of civil society, is under assault through neoliberal efforts to re-shape it in ways that would make it unrecognizable. There are efforts underway to eliminate large sectors of the field through funding cuts and legislative mandates. In areas of the world in which it has a long history such as the United Kingdom, these efforts are accelerating at an alarming rate (see Taylor, Connaughton, de St Croix, Davies and Grace, Chapter 7, this *Handbook*).

In other areas of the global North where youth work has a more recent history, such as North America, where the field appears to be proliferating, it is doing so deeply influenced by the ideological imperatives of the Psy-complex. Youth work or Child and Youth Care, as an element of this pernicious combination of media and psychologically driven simulacra, premises its view of young people using neuropsychology, developmental psychology, psychiatric diagnosis and the perverse narrative of strength-based and competency-driven work founded in the neoliberal motivated individual we have noted above.

Michael Hardt (1995), in 'The withering of civil society' presciently delineates the gradual evisceration of key elements of civil society through the encroaching logic of the abstract money form. He suggests that institutions originally produced by people for their social uses become appropriated by capitalism and emptied of any semblance of service to the community of people who produced them. Government, churches, the family, courts, social services, and so on, become empty vessels that retain their exterior veneer, so that they look like governments etc., but no longer retain any functional center, other than becoming a vehicle for various financial transactions. Youth work and its international variants such as Child and Youth Care may well be in the process of being assimilated into capitalism in this way. The services may still have workers, young people and institutions through which they encounter one another, but the formations of relationship are increasingly turned towards serving the needs of global monetary empire.

So, what would be necessary for the field and for ourselves as individual youth work practitioners and academics, if we were to challenge such trends? How would our engagement with young people shift? One proposal might be to re-center our work by taking the world of 21st-century capitalism seriously and realistically. We would argue that this would require an utterly frank and unvarnished assessment of our relations with young people and each other. We, as youth workers, would need to resist any form of discourse that produces young people as abstraction. We would argue that the strength and force of our work has been founded in the living encounter between living beings. Grace Lee Boggs (2012), in her writing on sustainable activism in the 21st century argues that we need to abandon any talk of the future in our work. Instead, of talking with young people about how to get ahead later in life, we need to focus on engaging young people with us in concrete projects that create real change in our neighborhoods and communities in the present. This would give meaning to life now and offer actual and material reasons to believe in what we can do together. On the basis of this, rather than an abstract promise of inclusion into the world of money, dreams of the future can be envisioned together.

In this sense, youth work would engage the world of young people in its full complexity and contradiction. Those of us who bring with us the logic of the past century may well need to re-think our methods and modes of analysis in order to fully engage the emerging world that young people now encounter. Without a doubt the revolts, both cultural and political, of the 20th century have failed and any nostalgia for the halcyon days of the counter-culture, subculture, new left, hippies, yippies, Maoists and radical pedagogies rooted in outmoded analysis of class struggle is misplaced and insulting to the struggles and political projects being mounted by the young people of today. Similarly, any resentment over the fact that the revolution failed and capitalism is now ascendant is politically suicidal, in that it clouds our vision and embitters our sense of revolutionary possibility.

In his writings from prison to his former comrades in the Italian insurrections of the late 20th century, Antonio Negri (2011) makes precisely this argument about their failed revolution. He reminds them (and us) that society is created by us and no one else. The contemporary reign of capitalism and its devastating effects on young people and ourselves is sustained and built on our backs. It is living people who are producing and sustaining the world of brutal capitalist rule. Without our belief and participation, the money form would have no power and capitalism would collapse. If we don't care for the world of global capitalism and its effects on our lives then we have the power to create a different kind of society premised on a different form of logic. However, any new form of the social cannot be premised in a return to social forms that have passed. There is no going back. There is only our ability to build the world anew by radically rearranging the elements of our current world into new forms.

DIY YOUTH WORK

The notion of reconstituting the social as a set of living relations, rather than an abstract system of proliferating code opens the traditions of youth work as a radical set of possibilities for advancing the desires and capacities of young people. Youth work as a centering of relationships between young people and adults founded in voluntary association and participation, is at fundamental odds with the emerging system of neoliberal control. As such, youth work, as a set of practices built out of collective creative production through work and play, stands as an alternative system of value to the over-determination of social relations under the money form.

However, as we have noted above, this means that youth work as a set of social practices at odds with the dominant system will be under assault. Indeed, all socially collective forms of social organization developed in response to industrial capitalism will be subject to global capitalism's new modes of social control. We can see this in the corruption of political systems, the gradual

evisceration of public education and in the destruction of the labor union movement. For youth work, the object lesson for sustaining and reconfiguring our field of practice as a holding continuing collective value for all of us may well lie in the death throes of unionization.

Deleuze (1992) argued that a key question for labor as it moved out of the 20th century was the 'ineptitude of the unions' (p. 7). He asked, 'will they be able to adapt themselves or will they give way to new forms of resistance against the society of control?' (p. 7). It seems clear, nearly twenty-five years later, that unions have been unable to adapt. In retrospect, we can see that they continued to use the logic of 20th-century industrial capitalism as a foundation for their organization and tactics well beyond their utility. As a result, they have consistently and continually lost ground and membership.

Youth work needs to be profoundly cautious that it does not follow a similar trajectory. We cannot cling to the practices and organizing principles that sustained us in the last century. Ongoing government funding and hopes for economic stability for workers or young people is now both an unrealistic aspiration and an opening to appropriation and accommodation to capitalist incursion. The old tactics of protesting government cuts and speaking truth to power in order to maintain a system of care that is collapsing cannot function in an era of absolute corruption of democratic simulacrum.

Instead, we need to produce an alternative set of practices rooted in the living day-to-day struggles of young people in community. In this, we might well learn something from the failed revolts of the 1960s. Negri (1996) points out that there is a residue left over from failed revolutions that can be used as a compost out of which new revolts can grow. This residue is made up of those unexpended elements of social practice introduced during the period of insurrection and then ignored or cast aside by the new emerging system of rule.

Certainly, one of these is a profound belief in the power of the living collective creativity to be found in generations of people, young and old working together for common purpose. There is considerable social force to be found in returning to our ability as young people and adults to physically modify our immediate environment. Grace Lee Boggs in an interview with Bill Moyers (Boggs, 2008) suggests that one of the most radical political actions that we can take is to work with young people to build community gardens. She proposes that this simple action of preparing the ground, planting seeds, caring for them, harvesting the results and sharing the food with your community has the capacity to fundamentally alter a young person's sense of materiality, time and connection to the broader community.

Boggs's assertion is founded on her work in inner city Detroit after the massive economic collapse of that city. Working as an activist in that community for nearly 70 years, she saw the predations of capitalism and the various modes of resistance through the industrial period. She was politically and socially active in the civil rights movement and the rise and fall of the labor movement through to the demise and abandonment of the people left behind by global capital when the economy failed, the factories left and the city burned.

Oddly, she asserts that the collapse and abandonment by capitalist interests was the best thing that could have ever happened to the people of Detroit. She argues that because they lost all faith in the mythology of neoliberalism and were forced back on their own creativity as a community to survive, they found new social forms and creative capacities. And survive they did. Clearing blocks of burned out buildings to plant community gardens, generating their own power, homesteading abandoned buildings, and so on.

This sort of do it yourself spirit is the living equivalent of the neoliberal simulacrum of the individual. Instead of encouraging the worst sort of narcissistic investment in young people that isolates them and invests them with fear and insecurity, projects like Boggs's work in inner city Detroit engages young people in community as active participants helping to solve the problems of day-to-day living. This kind of youth work is resonant of the work of the Diggers in the latter half of the 20th century. The Diggers were a revolutionary collective of young people and adults who worked and lived in San Francisco during the height of the hippie era (Deransart, 1998). Like Boggs, they refused to submit to the prevailing logic of capitalist rule. Their project was to live as though money was no longer relevant. Their political actions included participatory theater in which they experimented with alternate forms of social organization. They opened free medical clinics, free clothing and food stores and they simply gave away whatever money they accrued. They also opened their homes to homeless and runaway young people. Indeed, a great many of the programs for runaway and homeless youth in the United States were founded on the 'crash pads' developed by the diggers. What is significant for us in our investigation of youth work in the 21st century in the work of the Diggers is the repudiation of the dominant system of value, the refusal of its inevitability, the engagement and care of young people and the insistence that together we can create something else.

The Diggers and Grace Lee Boggs are not isolated instances of DIY political movements. Indeed, there are movements emerging across the planet, both out of necessity and through the force of voluntary social innovation. The appropriation of land, buildings and media by young people and social movements as we enter the 21st century is increasing at an exponential rate (Mason and Mason, 2008). As youth work faces increasing appropriation and evisceration by neoliberal capitalism, it may be time to re-think our relation to the dominant system of rule and begin to re-create our work by seizing back the sets of living relations on which it is founded. Those foundations are in the ability to engage in living relations with young people through acting together in work and play.

Felix Guattari (2005), in his proposals for a new kind of work with people he called schizoanalysis, argues that we need an eco-logic understanding that goes beyond clean distinctions of nature, humans and society. He suggests that we need movements that can work in ways that acknowledge the mutual interdependence of our consciousness, our physical environment and our social relations. Writing at the end of the last century, he forecast a deteriorating ecology for all three interdependent realms. The ecology of the biosphere is demonstrably on a trajectory that threatens large sectors of the globe with flooding, radically dangerous weather patterns, drought, rising sea levels and temperature fluctuations that have already begun to make life for people across the planet quite challenging. Guattari suggested that the relationship between our behavior and the deteriorating global ecology was linked to a crisis in our social ecology. He noted that just as the physical ecology threatens species, including us, there is a similar crisis that creates certain social practices and relations. He marked fraternity, compassion, collectivity and cooperation as on the endangered species list for the social environment. Similarly, he suggested that our consciousness is also suffering from an ecological crisis.

The realm of dominant capitalism as a realm of pure abstraction forces a rupture in the relation between our phenomenological apprehension of the world and our ability to think creatively in relation to our experiences. To the degree our experiences are mediated through abstract code, we gradually lose connection to our actual lived experience and our consciousness becomes increasingly insular and self-reflexive. Guattari argues that, in order to address three ecologies as integrally related, we need to be able to cross between them and see the relationship they hold to one another. We cannot separate thought

from community nor community from interspecies relations.

CONCLUSION

As we enter the 21st century, youth work stands as one of the areas of social engagement that holds the capacity for the kind of work that can pragmatically challenge capitalist logic. To the degree we hold the values of youth work as those relations that are voluntary and relational, then we can begin to valorize our experiences of the world together. In actual terms, this means opening our relations to experimentation with the elements of the world as we encounter them together as members of a community situated in a living inter-species ecology that has direct impact on our day-to-day lives. In this set of relations nothing is excluded. We can mix elements of video games, understandings of intersectionality and entanglements of interspecies relations with the economic imperatives of a particular neighborhood with a specific history and an emerging set of morphing cultural mixes and practices. The trick is not to get stuck in any one register but to keep experimenting with the different elements in material and conceptual ways.

While that may sound quite abstract, in reality it is very simple. Youth work would be a practice of paying attention to the complex emerging world young people encounter every day. Working as a team with young people, families, communities and other workers, we would become artists rather than technicians of care. It could be as simple as planting a community garden or as complex as deconstructing the elements of a video game and working with young people to reconfigure it to a new and unimagined cultural, social or political purpose. The impetus for our work would reside in our willingness to take all elements of our lives and the lives of the young people we encounter in the spirit of very serious play. In this we would refuse the logic of the dominant system in favor of producing an ever-proliferating realm of alternative systems of value. We have the tools. They reside within us and between us. The question is will we put them to work?

REFERENCES

Agamben, G. (1998). *Homo sacer: Sovereign power and bare life*. Palo Alto: Stanford University Press.

Avlon, J. (2008). An American 'honor killing'. *New York Post*. http://nypost.com/2008/07/23/an-american-honor-killing/

Baudrillard, J. (1994). *Simulacra and simulation*. Ann Arbor, MI: University of Michigan Press.

Belton, B. (2010). *Radical youth work*. Lyme Regis: Russell House Publishing.

Belton, B. (2013). Radical youth work: Developing critical perspectives and professional judgement. *Youth & Policy*, 11, 96.

Boggs, G.L. (2008). We are the leaders we have been looking for. https://search.yahoo.com/yhs/search?p=race+lee+boggs+we+are+the+leaders&ei=UTF-8&hspart=mozilla&hsimp=yhs-001

Boggs, G.L. (2012). *The next American revolution: Sustainable activism for the twenty-first century*. Oakland: University of California Press.

Coontz, S. (1992). *The way we never were: American families and the nostalgia trap*. New York: Basic Books.

Cooper, C. (2012). Imagining 'radical' youth work possibilities – challenging the 'symbolic violence' within the mainstream tradition in contemporary state-led youth work practice in England. *Journal of Youth Studies*, 15(1), 53–71.

Deleuze, G. (1992). Postscript on the societies of control. *October*, 59, 3–7.

Deransart, C. (1998). Diggers of San Francisco. https://www.youtube.com/watch?v=i6sPo2Yi3jE

Foucault, M. (1977). *Discipline and punish: The birth of the prison*. New York: Vintage.

Garfat, T. and Fulcher, L. (2011). Characteristics of a Child and Youth Care approach. *Relational Child & Youth Care Practice*, 24(1/2), 7–19.

Gilchrist, R., Jeffs, T., Spence, J., Stanton, N., Cowell, A., Walker, J. and Wylie, T. (2009). *Essays in the history of youth and community work*. Lyme Regis: Russell House Publishing.

Guattari, F. (2005). *The three ecologies*. London: Bloomsbury Publishing.

Hardt, M. (1995). The withering of civil society. *Social Text*, 45(14), 27–44.

Hardt, M. and Negri, A. (2001). *Empire*. Cambridge, MA: Harvard University Press.

Hardt, M. and Negri, A. (2005). *Multitude: War and democracy in the age of empire*. New York: Penguin.

Harvey, D. (2005). *A brief history of neoliberalism*. New York: Oxford University Press.

Jeffs, T. (2013). Whatever happened to radical youth work?. *Concept, 7*.

Kabeer, N. (2016). Gender equality, economic growth, and women's agency: The 'endless variety' and 'monotonous similarity' of patriarchal constraints. *Feminist Economics*, *22*(1), 295–321.

Krugman, P. (2012). *End this depression now!* New York: WW Norton & Company.

Locke, C. (2016). Discursive challenges: Reproductive rights and women's well-being in developing. In G. Boswell and F. Poland (eds) *Women's minds, women's bodies: Interdisciplinary approaches to women's health*. Houndmills, UK: Palgrave Macmillan, 208–220.

Luhmann, N. (2000). *The reality of the mass media*. Palo Alto: Stanford University Press.

Mason, M.J. and Mason, M. (2008). *The pirate's dilemma: How hackers, punk capitalists, graffiti millionaires and other youth movements are remixing our culture and changing our world*. London: Penguin UK.

Negri, A. (1996). Twenty theses on Marx: Interpretation of the class situation today. In S. Makdisi, C. Casarino and R.E. Karl (eds), *Marxism Beyond Marxism*. New York: Routledge, 149–180.

Negri, A. (2011). *Art and multitude*. Cambridge: Polity.

Rogaly, B. (1996). Micro-finance evangelism, 'destitute women', and the hard selling of a new anti-poverty formula. *Development in Practice*, 6(2), 100–112.

Rooks, Nowile M. (2012). The myth of bootstrapping. *Time Magazine*. http://ideas.time.com/2012/09/07/the-myth-of-bootstrapping/

Schumpeter, P. (2015). Myths about millennials. http://www.economist.com/news/business/

21660110-businesses-should-beware-dubious-generalisations-about-younger-workers-myths-about

Skott-Myhre, K., Weima, K. and Gibbs, H. (2012). *Writing the Family*. Amsterdam: Sense Publishers.

Smith, J. (2016). Honor-based violence: Policing and prevention. *Police Practice and Research*, 17(1), 95–96.

Tomlinson, S. (1998). New inequalities? Educational markets and ethnic minorities [1]. *Race Ethnicity and Education*, 1(2), 207–223.

Woods, J.B. (2010). Reconceptualizing anti-LGBT hate crimes as burdening expression and association: A case for expanding federal hate crime legislation to include gender identity and sexual orientation. *Journal of Hate Studies*, 6(1), 81.

PART II

Professional Work with Young People: Projects and Practices to Inspire

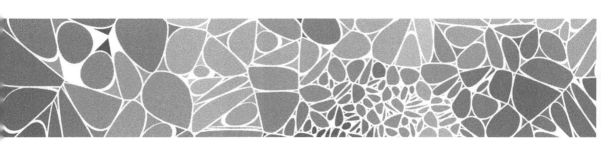

14

Participation, Empowerment and Democracy: Engaging with Young People's Views

Philippa Collin, Girish Lala and Leo Fieldgrass

A key test of participatory initiatives and processes from the perspective of inclusive citizenship is whether they do challenge traditional power relations or simply reinforce them. (Lister, 2007: 439)

INTRODUCTION

One objective of youth work is to facilitate self-formation and awareness in young people through identification and fostering capabilities and agency. When focused on empowerment and enhanced civic engagement, youth work has an explicitly political dimension: to increase civic and political knowledge and skills, but also to foster the conditions by which young people can take action and make claims to citizenship. In its most radical forms, youth work targets broader social and democratic institutions, actors and process as part of a social justice project to increase recognition and responsiveness to young people and their views (Fusco and Heathfield, 2015). As such, youth work as participatory practice views young people as social change agents and aims to

challenge forms of power, social processes and institutions from which they are frequently excluded. However, the theoretical and practical frameworks underpinning policy, organisational and professional practices are diverse and do not always aim for critical or emancipatory outcomes (Fusco and Heathfield, 2015). Even with the best intentions, 'youth participation' can produce unforeseen and problematic consequences (Harris, 2012; Farthing, 2012; Dadich, 2015). Indeed, failure to engage with the politics of youth participation runs the risk of reproducing forms of oppression and exclusion.

This chapter explores new and emergent discourses and practices of youth participation, from within and beyond the field of youth work, and considers some of their unintended consequences. While youth participation means different things and is practised in diverse ways around the world, this chapter considers predominantly the ways participation has been conceptualised and practised in western, Anglophone democracies – specifically Australia where the debates have been rich and diverse. For more than four decades, Australian youth movements, advocacy and non-government organisations, youth workers and researchers have developed and promoted different approaches to participation (Collin, 2015) and Australian governments have actively proscribed policy to shape young citizen practices (Bessant, 2004; White and Wyn, 2004). The Australian focus, therefore, is a means by which to explore more general questions about the prospects for youth participation to enhance both the agency and recognition of young people as well as transform political processes and institutions.

We begin by outlining how participation is a contested concept. We then summarise and critique discourses of youth participation associated with 'empowering' young people as citizens. This section considers how the discourse of 'active citizens' and 'change makers' appeals to ideas of agency and challenges some traditional or mainstream views of young people, but can also re-inscribe them as disengaged or a threat to society and democracy. We then examine how these challenges might be addressed by moving the emphasis from whether – and how – *young people participate* in what is required for institutions and authorities to meaningfully *engage with young people*. The significance of this approach is explored through two Australian case studies, the Koorie Youth Council Yarning Justice Youth Workshop and the Youth Engaged Policy project. We conclude with a discussion of the theoretical, ethical and practical considerations that these examples offer and how the case study findings can be of use to youth work practice concerned with achieving genuine engagement with young people, their perspectives and visions of a good and just society.

YOUTH PARTICIPATION: A CONTESTED CONCEPT

While youth participation has gained salience in the past three decades it has a wide variety of meanings and is advocated for and practised in many ways (Percy-Smith and Thomas, 2010; Collin, 2015). As Ruth Lister (2007) points out, the questions of what participation is (or should be), how it can be fostered and what relationship it has to the state, other social institutions and actors depends on which theory of citizenship is drawn upon. While citizenship is a highly contested concept, broadly speaking, different theories of citizenship define the nature and purpose of participatory acts according to the relative emphasis that they place on 'rights' (liberal theories), 'responsibilities' (civic republican and communitarian) and 'contestation' (radical and post-modern) (see Collin, 2015: 18–22). Additionally, participation can refer to individual or collective actions, in institutional political processes and civil society organisations and in acts that legitimise or contest forms of power and authority. In western countries efforts to promote youth participation have often focused on enabling young citizen voices in government consultations and other formal decision-making processes (Bell et al., 2008). However, Percy-Smith and Thomas (2010) assert that participation is also about various ways of 'being and relating, deciding and acting' in the world and 'as a manifestation of individual agency within a social context' (2010: p. 357). Vromen (2003) has argued that the definition and aims of participation should be rooted in the concept of young people's agency within social structures: as individual or collective acts that are intrinsically concerned with shaping society (Vromen, 2003: 82–83). In this way, we can distinguish between participation as the exercise of 'voice' and participation as 'agency'. Participation as voice or 'having a say' tends to emphasise involvement in formal decision making – both in government and other institutions and organisations. In contrast, articulating agency as a key concept acknowledges the involvement of young people in everyday life settings and how they shape broader social and political processes. How these different ways of conceptualising participation manifest in new discourses of citizenship will be discussed below – highlighting that the distinction between 'voice' and 'agency' is not always a clear one and sometimes the focus on individual agency has the effect of responsibilising young people in problematic ways. Indeed, an emphasis on only one or the other can drive ongoing elitism and exclusion (Bang, 2005; Collin, 2015). The best forms of participation may be at the interface between everyday sociopolitical interactions and formal or institutionalised democratic processes – particularly as online and networked communications technologies are embedded in the practices of everyday life (Vromen, 2003; Harris et al., 2007; Sotkasiira et al., 2010; Third and Collin, 2016). Fusco and Heathfield (2015) have identified that these tensions also feature in youth work: where participation is variously mobilised for youth or community development, cultivating normatively 'good citizens', or as radical practice aimed at challenging hegemonic and oppressive structures that disadvantage or harm young people. In this section of the chapter we explore how and to what effect the latter two approaches play out in the broader literature on youth political participation.

Participation as 'Active' Citizenship

Youth participation in most western countries has been largely operationalised via the policies and programmes of community organisations, advocacy groups and governments with a focus on hearing young people's voices and enabling young people to be actively involved in decision-making processes (Percy-Smith and Thomas, 2010; Harris, 2012). Common strategies have included youth advisory boards, surveys, consultation roadshows, workshops and youth positions on boards and committees. More recently they have manifest as

leadership programmes and initiatives to 'empower' young people in social action and enterprise (Walsh, 2011; Collin, 2015). Increasingly delivered through government or corporate partnerships with NGOs and community groups, these programmes train, mentor and sometimes seed-fund young people to take on leadership roles or develop and lead their own initiatives. Both approaches advocate an 'active' role for young people in democracy, but they represent two distinct goals. The first primarily aims to promote youth voice within existing governance processes. Here, an emphasis on voice can be to socialise young people for 'good citizenship' or to challenge the structures and processes of institutions which often exclude them (Vromen, 2012). The second approach emphasises youth agency via partnerships between young people and adults or the delegation of decision-making to young people (Wierenga et al., 2003), or by positioning young people as changemakers. However, recent programmes and policy initiatives (e.g. the National Citizens Service in the UK) rarely address the systems and structures of power that shape access to such opportunities. In some instances both approaches exercise 'covert power' over young people (Lukes, 1974) as they continue to define the broader terms in which 'youth' can be understood and the forms of participation (even new ones) that are socially desirable.

This can also be thought of as a form of governmentality (Foucault, 1991) whereby policies and programmes contribute to the structuring of ideas about who young people should be, what activities they should be involved in, and, therefore, what they should expect of themselves and their peers. When policies and programmes determine how young people should participate – for example, as youth 'advisers', leaders or entrepreneurs – these modes of participation are given a status and priority over other less conventional or more controversial forms. Young people often become advocates themselves of such models. Some argue this is a form of self-regulation or governance (Bessant, 2004; Walsh, 2016) whereby discourses, policies and programmes operate as methods and practices which facilitate the 'conduct of conduct' of youth (Marston and McDonald, 2006: 4). A governmentality frame demonstrates the challenges young people face in determining for themselves how they want to express their views or make demands to be heard in alternative ways. For example, the strong focus on young people's participation in both adult-led and youth-led initiatives responsibilises young people, often without addressing inherent structural economic forces over which they have no control. This further disadvantages some young people whose low socio-economic status leaves them most exposed to such forces but who are compelled to take personal responsibility for managing the structural conditions of their involvement – including economic and social repercussions. This instrumental model of participation can be detrimental as it socialises young people to the status quo rather than promoting the idea of alternatives. Instrumental participation therefore fails to address broader issues of power and social justice, which disproportionately affect young people when they are marginalised or vulnerable.

Participation as Actualising, Networked and Everyday Citizenship

Youth participation has also been shaped by broader processes of social change, particularly globalisation, individualisation, the internet and digital communication technologies. These challenge the absolute influence that traditional institutions (such as the family, schools and governments) and social forces (class, gender, ethnicity) have over the way people understand and respond to the conditions of contemporary life (Giddens, 1991; Beck, 1992). Issues, individual identities and

networks now have far greater influence on how people think about themselves as citizens and social agents. For example, the affordances of digital media facilitated by the internet have significantly expanded the public spaces in which young people can access information, voice their opinions, discuss and debate ideas and contribute to public agendas and decisions (Bennett, 2003). Moreover, in modern, digital society, young people are increasingly required to employ independent identity management strategies to navigate the risks and uncertainties of social life. Rather than developing 'dutiful' citizenship norms that valorise traditional institutions, actors and processes, they adopt more reflexive, 'self-actualising' citizenship norms and find greater satisfaction in defining their own political paths (Bang, 2005; Bennett, 2007). As a result everyday digitally-mediated, civic and political practices are thought to be more important for youth participation than formal or institutionalised activities (Harris et al., 2007; Harris and Wyn, 2009; Wood, 2014). This includes 'micro' acts of participation online – such as responding to an online poll, contributing to a group on Facebook, blogging or tweeting about an issue or posting images from a rally. In addition, formal and informal youth participation mechanisms in non-traditional settings, such as services, advocacy and research networks, increasingly include digital media to communicate with young people and facilitate their involvement (Collin, 2015).

These new, actualising, every-day and networked forms of participation are generally considered 'good' – to be aspired to and encouraged. However, they also signal potential problems. It is often assumed that digital media equalises participation opportunities, yet gender, class and level of education still play a role in structuring who participates and how they participate online (Xenos et al., 2014). While some organisations and institutions enhance participation via the internet, generally speaking, the barriers to participation that exist offline persist online (Banaji and Buckingham, 2013). In countries such as Australia, governments at all levels have failed to adopt online strategies to involve citizens of any age in meaningful deliberation or decision making (Collin, 2015). Moreover, the discourse of the 'self-actualising' networked citizen may amplify the adoption of a 'self-reflexive experience of inequality' (Threadgold, 2011) – whereby young people assume even greater personal responsibility for addressing structural barriers to participation. Henrik Bang has warned that while 'everyday' political practices – such as ethical consumerism or issues-based social media advocacy – can be empowering for young people, they can also justify the distance policy-makers adopt from the views and acts of ordinary citizens (Bang, 2005). This is a process he calls 'de-coupling': where the politics of the everyday is removed from the politics of formal institutions and actors. For youth services and practitioners, concerns regarding the maintenance of professional boundaries and the navigation of risks associated with communicating with young people via social media may also contribute to a perceived generation gap. Another concern is that alongside discourses of 'active', self-actualising and networked citizenship run equally powerful discourses that construct young people as apathetic or anti-social.

Non-participation, Disengagement and 'Failed' Citizenship

Discourses of non-participation and disengagement are powerful and persistent in Australia and other western democracies. These have been challenged by youth-centred research that has adopted a more expansive conception of politics and participation (Marsh et al., 2007; Vromen, 2007; Collin, 2015). Such studies have shown that disengagement can be a conscious response to experiences of exclusion, loss of trust or desperation with the 'system' (Farthing, 2010; Edwards, 2009). Yet, the underlying

structures that produce such disaffection are rarely examined. The long-standing discourse of 'active citizenship' in Australian policy is one feature of these underlying structures. For example, Kathy Edwards has found that the 1988 Australian Senate Select Committee inquiry into 'Education for Active Citizenship in Schools and Youth Organisations' established the targets (young people), terminology (active citizenship) and methods (education) of youth participation, establishing a powerful policy discourse that has persisted into the 2000s (Edwards, 2010). This includes how 'youth' and participation are defined and what counts as evidence that young people do, or do not 'participate'. Edwards suggests that, by only focusing on youth attitudes and practices, much youth participation literature has ignored the powerful role of the state, adult authorities and institutions. Highlighting how youth participation research and practice is largely concerned with condemning or defending young people according to these parameters, she demonstrates that fundamental assumptions of the debate – who can participate, in what circumstances and to what effect – go unchallenged. The implications of this include the continued valorising of a particular view of democracy (Edwards, 2010) persistent categories of 'non-participation' and 'dis-engagement' (Farthing, 2010), and the production of 'failed citizenship' (Harris, 2012).

Anita Harris argues this is not a new phenomenon, and that young people have been the focus of aspirations and anxieties for the future of the nation state since the turn of the 19th century (Harris, 2012). She suggests that a powerful feature of contemporary, post-welfare-state systems is the rise of self-governance as the underlying logic of late modernity, arguing that the qualities of self-invention, consumption and engagement in mainstream political and civic activities are central to the discourse of 'active citizenship'. As such, those young people who are unable to overcome hardship or exclusion, or comply with normative expectations of a neo-liberal society are constructed as 'failed citizens' (Harris, 2012: 149). Acts that directly challenge the power of adults, institutions and the nation state are rendered invisible or cast as anti-social or anti-democratic (for example, civil disruption or wearing religious dress). This extends to unemployed or minority young people (such as those from indigenous or migrant backgrounds) whose daily and cultural practices may confront the status quo – and who are the main targets of 'youth engagement' policies.

From Participation to Engagement?

Much like discourses of participation, *engagement* typically position young people as the object of concern, without questioning the underlying discourses that structure their position in relation to power and authority. For example, Nenga and Taft (2013) define youth engagement as: 'activities in which children and youth enact a public-spirited commitment in pursuit of the common good'. However, after examining different examples of such activities, they acknowledge: 'it becomes clear that youth engagement is a multifaceted concept with contested social and political goals' (Nenga and Taft, 2013). In policy and practice, two dominant goals of engagement can be discerned.

The first goal is young people's 'engagement in' personal economic, social and civic activities. These are designed to develop good citizens who are 'engaged in employment, education, and positive relationships; involved in community decisions; and in creating cultural activities' (Victorian Government, 2012). While these policies may mobilise an empowerment agenda, they take an uncritical view of good citizenship defined as participation in particular kinds of economic, civic and social structures (White and Wyn, 2004; Collin, 2015). The second policy discourse espouses a model of 'engagement

for' social good, whereby 'youth engagement is the meaningful and sustained involvement of a young person in an activity focusing outside the self' (Canadian Centre of Excellence for Youth Engagement, n.d.). Both these notions of engagement direct young people towards activities that promote self or community/societal development. Broadly speaking, they reflect either liberal or republican notions of citizenship, and position young people – not adult institutions or the state – as the subject of concern. Moreover, youth participation is seen as either 'within' and therefore complicit with existing institutions, or as 'outside' and therefore contesting them. And yet, it is these binaries which close out the possibilities of thinking differently about engagement.

The challenge, as we see it, is to develop a concept of engagement that is informed by, but moves beyond a concern for young people's participation per se to one that focuses on disrupting discourses. Such an approach to participation explicitly questions power relations and interrogates the structures and discourses that define 'youth' and 'participation' in particular ways, rather than determining what participation should be. A concern for engagement with young people is aimed at establishing the very conditions by which young people's involvement provokes ruptures in the structures, spaces, processes and practices in which adult authorities and professionals typically interact. As Sercombe argues, while disrupting discourses is a central feature of youth work practice (2010), the challenge remains how to encourage a focus on *engagement with* young people that can unsettle and contest dominant ideas which delimit young people's participation and citizenship. In other words, engagement is something that occurs *with* young people and adults in the context of already existing relations – but with the intent of recasting established aims, roles and processes. The discussion above highlights three normative goals of a redefined concept of engagement: to maximise young people's agency *within* social and political structures; to transform adult and institutional perceptions of young people in dialogue *with* young people; and, to generate new policy processes and organisational forms via the production of alternative discourses of both 'youth' and 'participation'.

DISRUPTING DISCOURSES THROUGH ENGAGEMENT: TWO AUSTRALIAN CASE STUDIES

The remainder of this chapter looks at the question of what a shift from *youth participation* to *engagement with young people* entails. We discuss two case studies from Australia that illuminate how such disruption can occur, and consider the limitations and implications of these examples for youth work practice more generally.

Recognising Culture, Agency and Voice: Koorie Youth Council Yarning Justice Youth Workshop[1]

The Koorie[2] Youth Council (KYC) is the representative body for Aboriginal and Torres Strait Islander young people in Victoria. It is led by a volunteer Executive of 15 young people and staffed by a small team of paid employees. KYC advances the rights of Aboriginal and Torres Strait Islander young people, positioning them as legitimate citizens with a voice to the state government and the wider community, raising their views, concerns, ideas and aspirations. KYC values the diversity and strength of young people as decision-makers. Membership is open to Aboriginal and Torres Strait Islander young people aged 12 to 25 who live in Victoria. In 2016 there were around 300 members. KYC is an independent, not-for-profit organisation, which operates as an auspiced partner agency of Youth Affairs Council Victoria (YACVic), the state's youth peak body (the leading youth policy advocate and lobbyist for young

people and youth work). KYC's core funding comes from Aboriginal Victoria, a Victorian Government department. It is currently the only youth representative body of its kind in Australia.

A key priority for KYC is to strengthen dialogue between government, other agencies and Aboriginal and Torres Strait Islander young people so that their interests and aspirations are better served by policy. In 2015, KYC partnered with the Victorian Government Department of Justice and Regulation (DJR) to hold a Yarning Justice Youth Workshop in conjunction with Aboriginal Justice Forum (AJF) #43. AJFs are held at least three times a year; they bring together senior representatives of the Aboriginal community and Victorian Government departments of Justice, Education, Health and Human Services to oversee how the Victorian Government and community work together to improve justice outcomes. An important part of each AJF is the community forum, where those in attendance sit and talk together. At AJF43, for the first time, the community forum heard presentations from young people who had participated in the Yarning Justice Youth Workshop, and discussed their questions and ideas.

At the Yarning Justice Workshop 25 Aboriginal and Torres Strait Islander young people from around the state discussed important issues impacting them and their peers, in relation to the justice system. Participants were aged between 15 and 25 and identified in diverse ways. The workshop was facilitated by five young people (four of whom were KYC members). Some participants were supported by parents and/or support workers from different organisations. The workshop focused on four areas: Community Engagement and Cultural Learning; Mental Health Education and Breaking the Stigma; Creating a Safe Environment for Young People; and Creating a Sense of Belonging and Resilience. Participants were split into two groups that each focused on two different themes. Facilitators led groups through a co-design process of active discussion, focusing on why they felt these issues existed, delving more deeply to identify the underlying factors that contribute to key drivers of contact with the justice system, reframing issues and challenges as solutions, and drafting implementation plans for each.

The insights and recommendations of the Yarning Justice forum themselves contributed to new discourses of youth and participation. Presented to Aboriginal Elders and Aboriginal and non-Aboriginal policy-makers, they formed a powerful counter-narrative to the 'evidence that tells truths' about Aboriginal and Torres Strait Islander young people in the context of self-actualising and neo-liberal discourses of successful citizenship. For example, Group 1 identified that cultural learning and community participation was impacted by a lack of genuine connections for young people with community, with their being disconnected from culture and having a lack of resources or facilities that enabled them to stay out of trouble. The group also identified that wider society's lack of Aboriginal cultural knowledge and understanding impacted upon young people's ability to feel belonging and foster resilience. Participants said issues existed because young people often felt as if they did not fit in, were too scared or ashamed to ask for help or support, or were unsure of who to turn to. Participants identified causal factors as racism, stereotyping, lack of available information and limited opportunities, such as cultural awareness training. To address these challenges, participants recommended Aboriginal and Torres Strait Islander youth groups provide culturally safe 'youth spaces' and opportunities for information-sharing, connecting with different agencies, participating in outings and learning about and celebrating Aboriginal culture. They also recommended community development opportunities to address issues arising from gaps in cross-cultural and intergenerational understanding. For example, participants recommended support for

non-Aboriginal people to learn about and understand their culture and feelings, and community events that would create opportunities to foster positive relationships between young people and key people in the wider community (e.g. police or community leaders). The young people in this group also believed that cultural awareness in government departments and other sectors should be embedded into core training, with staff and departments held to higher account. They felt that having traditional custodians run the training in local areas would be a positive way to break down barriers and stigma towards young people and highlight the importance of connection to country.

These insights reveal some things about the forms of participation these young people valued and recommended in order to strengthen dialogue and understanding between different parts of the community and the state structure. For example, in relation to establishing safe and supportive environments for Aboriginal and Torres Strait Islander young people, Group 2 recommended the wider establishment and use of 'Yarning circles' to address stigma, empower young people, provide positive role models and mentors, create safe environments for participation, promote a sense of belonging and strengthen identity. Participants argued that a group of young people should be engaged with the Department of Justice and Regulation to run yarning circles with local mobs, supported by regional Aboriginal Justice Advisory Committees and community Elders. The idea was discussed that these yarning circles could be conducted on country[3] and separated by gender in order to provide cultural safety.

The presentation of these workshop findings to the AJF43 community forum established a precedent for intergenerational and cross-cultural dialogue on youth justice. As a result, the KYC has developed ongoing engagement with the Victorian Minister and Department of Justice, which has integrated Yarning Justice Workshop findings into its policies and procedures. The Yarning

Justice Workshop – and KYC more broadly – help position Aboriginal and Torres Strait Islander young people as legitimate citizens with valued and valuable perspectives on contemporary issues and potential responses. The Yarning Justice Workshop and other KYC activities are not aimed at 'developing' participants, socialising them for western democracy or inserting them into existing institutional structures. While KYC draws on established organisations and approaches (youth work and advocacy organisations) and connects with existing policy actors (Ministers and their departments) and processes (AJF), it is primarily driven by the views of Aboriginal and Torres Strait Islander young people, their culture and experiences.

Importantly the Yarning Justice Workshop established these young people's voices as equally important to those of the senior representatives in attendance at AJF43 – itself a rupture with standard government policy processes. Through the workshop and forum, Aboriginal and Torres Strait Islander young people applied self-determination, giving voice to their concerns, thoughts, ideas and solutions on justice issues that affect them directly. The workshop was an important step towards government and community recognising Aboriginal and Torres Strait Islander young people as participants in the process to create solutions to the policy issues affecting them.

The Youth Engaged Policy Project

In 2014 and 2015 the Australian federal government significantly scaled back support for youth participation by discontinuing key mechanisms, including ministerial-level representation of youth affairs, the national youth peak body and National Youth Week events profiling the positive and valuable contribution young people make in society. In response, a group of youth peak organisations in Australia joined with researchers[4] to investigate how 'youth engagement' is understood and to explore current barriers and enablers to a *youth engaged policy* approach in federal government (full report: Collin et al., 2016). The Youth Engaged Policy (YEP) project was explicitly concerned with bringing together diverse young people and policy practitioners from across Australia to examine youth engagement in policy-making, and identify and design strategies for improvement.

Over three months at the beginning of 2016, young people and policy-makers engaged in a series of group-based activities. Four, two-hour forums in State and Territory capital cities brought together 60 adult policy-makers to discuss professional and institutional views of youth engagement and policy-making. In three, half and full-day intergenerational workshops, in Perth and Sydney, young and adult participants (54 young people and 25 adult policy-makers) explored experiences, barriers and enablers, critical issues and indicators for youth engagement. Workshops were held in broadly accessible locations and unsalaried participants were reimbursed for their time and travel costs. YEP emphasised the involvement of policy-makers and young people as equal contributors. Policy-maker forums encouraged adult participants to reflect on how current attitudes and policy processes position and exclude young people. Intergenerational workshops provided an environment in which adults and young people used these insights and their own experiences to explore and co-design new means through which adult authorities and institutions could be pervious to young people's views and actions. In the final workshop, young people (school students, service users and representatives of advocacy groups), policy-makers, youth work practitioners, researchers and government agency representatives worked in small teams using participatory design methods to generate six specific 'concepts' or 'big ideas' that might be applied to effectively facilitate young people's engagement in policy-making.

For example, one team recommended a Youth Involvement Agency (YIA), funded and overseen by a Federal Minister for Youth in consultation with a youth-led committee. The YIA would commit to engaging with Elders, community role models and intergenerational organisations and agencies, and act as a central point of contact accessible to all young people, connecting them to relevant stakeholders. The agency's key roles would be training, mentoring and consulting with young people to produce policy recommendations and review government proposals on issues affecting young people. A second team proposed Policy (Un)Consultation Groups where young people would be paid to work directly with politicians in agenda and policy development. Resourced by Government and organised via a network of peak organisations, (Un)Consultation Groups would include outreach workers to train and assist young people to communicate their experiences, and generate and utilise digital data to explore, advise and scrutinise issues and policies. One key aim of these groups would be to guard against tokenistic consultations, and ensure young people were permanently represented and involved in policy development from start to end.

Bottom-up processes for setting agendas and generating responses to policy problems were seen as pivotal, as was the provision of training and support for those in authority positions to encourage engagement with diverse, isolated, under-resourced and underrepresented groups. Indeed, in developing strategies for improving engagement in policy-making, participants identified addressing unequal power relations as the most significant concern. Moreover, in contrast with the 'self-made' leader or entrepreneurial archetype increasingly celebrated in official narratives of youth engagement (e.g., Australian of the Year), most of the proposed strategies were aimed at enhancing group – or collective – voice as well as intergenerational collaboration. The project's findings informed a process design and set

of resources to support governments, organisations and youth-led initiatives in engagement (Collin et al., 2016), all of which have been distributed back to project partners and participants.

YEP was designed to engage young and adult stakeholders in discussion and critique of the current state of engagement with young people in policy-making, and develop alternative approaches, centred around the actual needs, experiences and ideas of diverse young people, utilising approaches that resonate with them and which they deploy in their everyday lives. The project recognised significant procedural challenges, but highlighted the desirability and necessity for fundamental structural change in policy-making (recognised by both young and adult stakeholders). Young people saw that intergenerational partnerships were valued by and possible between young and adult stakeholders, and they wanted to engage in cooperatively developing a process and tools through which such partnerships might occur and flourish.

CONCLUSION: WORKING THE LIMITS OF ENGAGEMENT

If one of the key goals of youth work practice is to enable and encourage young people's capacity and agency it must take seriously the challenge of contesting forms of power and authority by critically reflecting on the underlying assumptions and discourses of 'youth' and 'participation'. A practical focus on *engagement with* young people underpinned by an explicit concern to engage critically with the ways 'youth' and 'participation' are constructed – by institutions, policy processes and adult authorities – can produce ruptures in the usual spaces and arrangements of youth–adult relations and generate ways to imagine youth–adult relations differently. Such engagement should consider young people's agency within social and political structures, aim to transform adult and institutional perceptions of young people in dialogue *with* young people, and produce alternative policy processes and organisational forms through new discourses of youth and participation.

The Australian Koorie Youth Council Yarning Justice Youth Workshops and the Youth Engaged Policy project demonstrate the potential for such an approach. Both initiatives unsettled established discourses through generating a range of dialogues between and with young people and adult authorities. Their associated processes and structures might be thought of as 'interrupted spaces' (Bolzan and Gale, 2011) in that they sought to create a break with the 'established way of doing things'. As such, they show the potential and key challenges for youth work practice in other contexts to intervene in dominant discourses of 'youth' and 'participation' by positioning young voices as 'differently equal' (Moosa-Mitha, 2005) to those of adult stakeholders. The KYC Yarning Justice Workshop revealed that engagement based on culture, identity, kinship and well-being exemplify what is required from adult authorities and institutions – whose reimagining is more challenging than the 'socialisation' or 'transformative potential' of young people and their politics. YEP demonstrated that research and design collaborations between adults and young people can generate discourses of youth and participation that do not easily fit the narratives of the 'active', 'everyday' or 'failed' young citizen. This is because the perspectives and proposals developed by the participants were neither simply congruent nor oppositional to existing discourses – seeking, in many cases, new forms of agency that could both contest and cooperate with public decision-makers. The case studies presented here demonstrate how youth work can play a key role in 'disrupting discourse' (Sercombe, 2010) by facilitating new forms of engagement by authorities and institutions of the state with young people and their perspectives. Rather than merely inserting young people and their voices into existing processes or institutions of power, they demonstrate how youth work practice has the potential to contest existing forms of knowledge and power and recast social and political relations *through engagement*.

However, many challenges to this form of engagement remain, with which youth work practitioners must grapple. Who designs, facilitates and participates in such project will always raise questions of representation and power. Material and political commitments to enable engagement processes are crucial and cannot always come from young people or the community itself. How participants use their experiences and project findings in representations to government and other authorities often depends on the ongoing resources available and the priorities of the individuals and groups involved. While the KYC Yarning Justice Workshop demonstrates how incremental discursive change is possible, with specific constituents in mind (in this case, the Department of Justice), the YEP example shows how the possibilities for effecting general shifts in discourse and practice may be more challenging. Yet, while the disruptions produced by an ethic of engagement may be momentary, they are significant in that they contribute to a longer-term process of change nonetheless.

For sure there are considerable challenges associated with entrenched institutional practices and the accepted orthodoxies of adult-defined and controlled modalities that govern youth participation and engagement. Meaningful change in the ideas about and implementation of effective engagement will require significant and sustained shifts in organisational practices and cultures. Without recognition of, and enthusiasm and advocacy for innovative practices by entrenched gatekeepers, recommendations will be difficult to enact. Moreover, shifts in organisational cultures will require concomitant resolve from individual and institutional gatekeepers to support the resourcing of engagement initiatives (e.g., funding, infrastructure, support services). Notwithstanding these challenges, one strategy for turning the spotlight on dominant discourses and their institutions and structures is for youth work practice to undertake a political project of engagement which asks what is required from institutions and authorities, rather than focusing only on young people themselves.

ACKNOWLEDGEMENTS

The authors would like to thank Greg Kennedy, Jessica Bengtsson, Ariadne Vromen, Ramon Marrades, Giulia Maci, Lara Palombo and all the young people and policy-makers who are a part of or work with the Koorie Youth Council and the Youth Engaged Policy project. Their work inspires our thinking.

Notes

1 Adapted with permission from Bengtsson, J. and Kennedy, G. (2015), Yarning Justice: Workshop and forum report, Melbourne: Koorie Youth Council & Youth Affairs Council of Victoria, https://www.yacvic.org.au/assets/Documents/KYC-YJWR-November-2015.pdf
2 KYC uses the term Koorie in its title as inclusive of all Aboriginal and Torres Strait Islander young people living in Victoria.
3 'On country' speaks to place and community. When on country, Aboriginal people can connect with culture, land, spirit and ancestors, environment and community in a safe and meaningful way.
4 The project was supported by the Young and Well Cooperative Research Centre and the Institute for Culture and Society at Western Sydney University, in partnership with the Australian Youth Affairs Coalition, Youth Affairs Council of Victoria, Youth Affairs Council of Western Australia, Youth Action NSW, the University of Sydney and URBEGO.

REFERENCES

Banaji, S. and Buckingham, D. (2013) *The Civic Web: Young People, the Internet and Civic Participation*. Cambridge, MA: Massachusetts Institute of Technology.

Bang, H. (2005) 'Among everyday makers and expert citizens', in J. Newman (ed.), *Remaking Governance*. Bristol: The Policy Press, pp. 159–178.

Beck, U. (1992) *Risk Society: Towards A New Modernity*. London: Sage.

Bell, J., Vromen, A. and Collin, P. (2008) Rewriting the rules for youth participation – inclusion and diversity in government and community decision-making. Canberra, ACT: National Youth Affairs Research Scheme.

Bennett, W. (2003) 'Communicating global activism: Strengths and vulnerabilities of networked politics', *Information, Communication and Society*, 6(2): 143–168.

Bennett, W.L. (2007) 'Civic learning in changing democracies: Challenges for citizenship and civic education', in P. Dahlgren (ed.), *Young Citizens and New Media: Learning for Democratic Participation*. New York, NY: Routledge.

Bessant, J. (2004) 'Mixed messages: Youth participation and democratic practice', *Australian Journal of Political Science*, 39(2): 387–404.

Bolzan, N. and Gale, F. (2011) 'Using an interrupted space to explore social resilience with marginalized young people', *Qualitative Social Work*, 11(5): 502–516.

Canadian Centre of Excellence for Youth Engagement (n.d.). Accessed online: http://archives.studentscommission.ca/index.php

Collin, P. (2008) 'The internet, youth participation policies, and the development of young people's political identities in Australia', *Journal of Youth Studies*, 11(5): 527–542.

Collin, P. (2015) *Young People and Political Participation: Addressing the Democratic Disconnect*. Basingstoke: Palgrave Macmillan.

Collin, P., Lala, G., Palombo, L., Marrades, R., Maci, G. and Vromen, A. (2016) *Creating Benefit for All: Young People, Engagement and Public Policy*. Melbourne: Young and Well Cooperative Research Centre.

Dadich, A. (2015) 'Beyond the romance of participatory youth research', in P. Kelly and A. Kamp (eds), *A Critical Youth Studies for the 21st Century*. Leiden: Brill, pp. 410–425.

Edwards, K. (2009) 'Disenfranchised, not "deficient": How the (neoliberal) state disenfranchises young people', *Australian Journal of Social Issues*, 44(1): 23–37.

Edwards, K. (2010) 'Beyond the blame game: Examining "the discourse" of youth participation in Australia', in D. Bissell, A. Grieg, M. Hynes, D. Marsh, L. Saha, J. Sikora and D. Woodman (eds), *Proceedings of the Future of Sociology*. Canberra: The Australian Sociological Association, pp. 1–12.

Edwards, R., Armstrong, P. and Miller, N. (2001) 'Include me out: Critical readings of social exclusion, social inclusion and lifelong learning', *International Journal of Lifelong Education*, 20(5): 417–428.

Farthing, R. (2010) 'The politics of youthful antipolitics: Representing the "issue" of youth participation in politics', *Journal of Youth Studies*, 13(2): 181–195.

Farthing, R. (2012) 'Why youth participation? Some justifications and critiques of youth participation using new labour's youth policies as a case study', *Youth & Policy*, 109, 71–97,

Foucault, M. (1991) 'Governmentality' in G. Burchell, C. Gordon & P. Miller (eds) *The Foucault Effect: Studies in Governmentality*. Chicago: University of Chicago Press, pp. 87–104.

Fusco, D. (2012) 'Use of self in the context of youth work', *Child and Youth Services*, 33(1): 33–45.

Fusco, D. and Heathfield, M. (2015) 'Modeling democracy: Is youth "participation" enough?' *Italian Journal of Sociology of Education*, 7(1): 12–31.

Giddens, A. (1991) *Modernity and Self-identity*. Cambridge, UK: Polity Press.

Harris, A. (2006) 'Introduction: Critical perspectives on child and youth participation in Australia and New Zealand/Aoteroa', *Children, Youth and Environments*, 16(2): 220–230.

Harris, A. (2012) 'Citizenship stories', in N. Lesko and S. Talburt (eds), *Keywords in youth studies: Tracing affects, movements, knowledges*. New York: Routledge, pp. 143–153.

Harris, A. and Wyn, J. (2009) 'Young people's politics and the micro-territories of the local', *Australian Journal of Political Science*, 44(2): 327–344.

Harris, A., Wyn, J. and Younes, S. (2007) 'Young people and citizenship: An everyday perspective', *Youth Studies Australia*, 26(3): 19–27.

Isin, E.F. (2008) 'Theorizing Acts of Citizenship', in E.F. Isin and G.M. Nielsen (eds), *Acts of Citizenship*. London, UK: Palgrave Macmillan, pp. 15–43.

Lister, R. (2007) 'From object to subject: Including marginalized citizens in policy making', *Policy and Politics*, 35(3): 437–455.

Lukes, S. (1974) *Power: A Radical View*. London, UK: Macmillan.

Marsh, D., O'Toole, T. and Jones, S. (2007) *Young people and politics in the UK: Apathy or alienation?* Hampshire, UK: Palgrave Macmillan.

Marston, G. and McDonald, C. (2006) *Analysing Social Policy: A Governmental Approach*. Cheltenham, UK: Edward Elgar.

Moosa-Mitha, M. (2005) 'A difference-centred alternative to theorization of children's citizenship rights', *Citizenship Studies*, 9(4): 369–388.

Nenga, S.K. and Taft, J.K. (2013) 'Introduction: Conceptualizing youth engagement', in S.K. Nenga and J.K. Taft (eds), *Youth Engagement: The Civic-Political Lives of Children and Youth*. Bingley, UK: Emerald, pp. xviii–xxiii.

Percy-Smith, B. and Thomas, N. (2010) *A Handbook of Children and Young People's Participation: Perspectives from Theory and Practice*. New York, NY: Routledge.

Sercombe, H. (2010) *Youth Work Ethics*. London: Sage.

Sotkasiira, T., Haikkola, L. and Horelli, L. (2010) 'Building towards effective participation: A learning-based network approach to youth participation', in B. Percy-Smith and N. Thomas (eds), *A Handbook of Children and Young People's Participation: Perspectives from Theory and Practice*. New York, NY: Routledge, pp. 174–183.

Third, A. and Collin, P. (2016) 'Rethinking (children's and young people's) citizenship through dialogues on digital practice', in A. McCosker, S. Vivienne and A. Johns (eds), *Negotiating Digital Citizenship: Control, Contest and Culture*. London: Rowman and Littlefield International, pp. 41–60.

Threadgold, S. (2011) 'Should I pitch my tent in the middle ground? On "middling tendency", Beck and inequality in youth sociology', *Journal of Youth Studies*, 14(4): 381–393.

Victorian Government (2012) Engage. Involve. Create. Youth statement, http://www.youthcentral.vic.gov.au/sites/yc.dhsvc/files/Engage_Involve_Create_Victorian_Government_Youth_Statement_2012.pdf

Vromen, A. (2003) '"People try to put us down…": Participatory citizenship of "Generation X"', *Australian Journal of Political Science*, 38(1): 79–99.

Vromen, A. (2007) 'Australian young people's participatory practices and internet use', *Information, Communication & Society*, 10(1): 48–68.

Vromen, A. (2012) 'Youth participation from the top down: The perspectives of government and community sector decision makers in Australia', in J. Van Deth and W. Maloney (eds), *New Participatory Dimensions in Civil Society: Professionalization and Individualized Collective Action*. Abingdon, Oxon: Routledge, pp. 212–230.

Walsh, L. (2011) 'Emergent forms and tools of change-making', in L. Walsh and R. Black (eds), *In Their Own Hands: Can Young People Change Australia?* Camberwell: ACER Press, pp. 107–125.

Walsh, L. (2016) 'Power in contemporary society', in J. Arvanitakis (ed.), *Sociologic: Analysing Everyday Life and Culture*. Melbourne: Oxford University Press Australia and New Zealand, pp. 139–156.

White, R. and Wyn, J. (2004) *Youth and Society: Exploring the Social Dynamics of Youth*. Melbourne: Oxford University Press.

Wierenga, A., Wood, A., Trenbath, G., Kelly, J. and Vidakovic, A. (2003) *Sharing A New Story: Young People in Decision-Making*. Melbourne, VIC: Youth Research Centre, University of Melbourne.

Wood, B.E. (2014) 'Researching the everyday: Young people's experiences and expressions of citizenship', *International Journal of Qualitative Studies in Education*, 27(2): 214–232.

Wyn, J. (2009) 'The changing context of Australian youth and its implications for social inclusion', *Youth Studies Australia*, 28(1): 46–50.

Xenos, M., Vromen, A. and Loader, B.D. (2014) 'The great equalizer? Patterns of social media use and youth political engagement in three advanced democracies', *Information, Communication & Society*, 17(2): 151–167.

15

Faith-based Youth Work: Education, Engagement and Ethics

Graham Bright, Naomi Thompson, Peter Hart
and Bethany Hayden

INTRODUCTION

Youth work represents 'a people-centred, commitment to diversity, anti-oppressive practice and the provision of relational spaces in which individuals and groups can think critically about their lives and worlds, in order that they might act to shape them differently' (Bright, 2015a: xvii). Grounded in critical pedagogical praxis (Freire, 1970), youth work continues to hold the ethos of equity and inclusivity paramount (Batsleer, 2008; Sapin, 2013). Despite these commitments however, there continues to be considerable debate regarding the nature of youth work and its relationship to the various faith-based practices in which much of its history is rooted. This comes at a time of on-going dialogue regarding the telos of the profession – a period characterized, in England[1] and other neo-liberal economies, by continuous restructuring, cuts and uncertainty, to which the faith sector has remained broadly resilient. Interest in the nature of faith-based youth

work and its relationship to wider forms of practice can be seen in the growing number of academic publications and conferences on the subject. Despite a narrative of growing secularization, faith praxis[2] remains a significant, albeit contested contemporary driver. Building on the work of the authors (Bright and Bailey, 2015; Hart, 2016; Stanton,[3] 2012, 2013), this chapter draws on narrative case study interviews with youth workers operating in different faith settings, to explore how they conceptualise and experience some of the joys and challenges of inclusive praxis. It further considers ways in which faith-based youth work attempts to promote social, religious and institutional inclusivity, as well as examining practice motives, and potential conflicts in personal, professional and religious consciences.

The present policy environment in England and beyond has reduced much youth work practice to a 'rump' (Jeffs, 2015: 75). The faith sector has taken its moral duty seriously by developing provision to mitigate recent fiscal effects, yet neo-liberal inducements have led to attempts by states to colonize, marketize and control religion in welfare production (Woodhead, 2012). Such processes are evident in youth work, where civically-minded people of faith, concerned with young people's well-being have engaged in continued voluntarism and localized processes of co-production. Pimlott (2015a, 2015b) in addressing those involved in Christian youth work, argues that people of faith should engage, but do so with active critical political insight, lest they risk accelerating the race to the bottom.

All youth work, in common with all education, is an act of faith (Jeffs, 2011) – full, in equal measure of possibility, uncertainty, hope and adventure. Whether that faith is in something political, social, educational, philosophical, human or 'religious', youth work in its myriad forms, draws in diverse ways on these 'faiths'. Faith gives youth work its dynamism. Jolly (2015) suggests that, whether expressed or not, there are inherent links between these 'faiths' and practitioners' motivations for practice. The motives for faith-based (religious) practice have often been viewed with an external glare of proselytizing suspicion. However, little 'secular' youth work expresses its intended purpose. State agendas are not benign, yet they remain surreptitiously unnamed. This flies in the face of ethical transparency (Sercombe, 2010), and undermines a key tenet of youth work practice: *informed* voluntary participation. In contrast, by virtue of the spaces and places in which it is undertaken, much faith-based practice is, on the surface at least, more teleologically accessible to young people. As an act of inclusive and encompassing faith, all youth work is premised upon, and concerned in the most ethical sense with, espoused processes of conversion – of empowering and enabling young people's potential transformation from one state of learning and being to another. Irrespective of sector, the telos driving these transformative, experiential 'border-crossings' (Coburn, 2010; Giroux,

2005), which open up processes of possibility, requires further interrogation. Drawing empirically on youth workers' practice narratives, the purpose of this chapter is to explore these concerns in relation to faith-based provision.

The origins of faith-based youth work, and indeed youth work more generally, lie in the Sunday School movements of the UK and America and in Jewish youth work, which were developed as lay movements in response to social need (Jeffs and Spence, 2011; Lynn and Wright, 1971; Pimlott, 2015b; Stanton, 2011). The largest sector of the UK youth work field (Brierley, 2003; Green, 2006; Stanton, 2013),[4] and a significant player in community-based provision in other contexts such as Australia and the USA, faith-based practice has had an influential role in youth work's history and development. There is not space in this chapter to explore the full history and internationality of faith-based youth work, however, it remains important to frame recognition of its significance across time and place, rather than as a 'poor relation' to the wider field.

The research informing this chapter focuses on inclusion in faith-based youth work settings. The practice explored is conducted by individuals and small faith organizations rather than large movements with faith-based origins. The present work explores practice in a range of faith traditions, and supports Stanton's (2013) previous findings that inclusive approaches are often more embedded in the youth work provision of religious organizations than in wider faith communities. Our research shows how faith-based youth work challenges and extends the inclusivity of wider institutions (e.g. mosques, Gurdwaras and churches). The role that faith-based youth work plays in extending inclusion is also supported by the wider literature. Singh (2011), for example, found that Sikh youth leaders set up camps and societies for other Sikh young people to explore their faith in more accessible ways. Gould (2015), exploring the practice of the Glasgow Gurdwara, found that its volunteer youth worker had broken new ground in securing young people's representation on the Gurdwara's leadership committee. Ahmed (2015) outlines how the Muslim Youth Helpline was set up as an accessible and inclusive 'space' for Muslim young people to discuss and be offered support around issues that were difficult to discuss in other contexts. Our research found that faith-based youth workers facilitate different forms of inclusive practice – both aimed at young people of particular faith traditions to enhance their sense of inclusion, as well as open access provision for young people more broadly.

We recognize challenges to inclusion in faith-based youth work, as in all youth work, which is never fully neutral or unaffected by the agendas of the state, religious body or other funders (Stanton, 2013). However, whilst retaining a critical academic stance, we resist taking a deficit approach to exploring faith-based youth work in this chapter and to framing it as a sceptical piece within a largely secular text. In doing so, we remain true to the experiences of our research participants, who, overall, view their work positively. Through their accounts, we recognize the role that faith-based youth work plays, how it deals with inclusive practice, some of the challenges it faces, and how it contributes to an inclusive range of provision within a context of wider funding cuts and reduced opportunities for open access provision. However, Clayton and Stanton (2008) and Hart (2016) recognize that there are different approaches and attitudes to professional ethics and boundaries within secular and faith-based provision, largely because of the community-based and vocational nature of the latter. Faith-based youth work has been subject to scrutiny, as all youth work should be, from within the wider profession and beyond. In particular, there have been questions as to its potential role in cementing inequalities, particularly around gender and sexuality (Page, 2015). Similarly, secular youth work has, at times, been found to

work to an agenda of conformity rather than empowerment, with Coburn (2011) finding it can promote 'containment' rather than 'liberation', and Garasia et al. (2016) arguing it can suppress rather than empower young people's voices in political processes. We do not therefore approach either faith-based, or secular youth work as being more superior, or problematic than the other – but recognise the complexities and paradoxes within each.

Overall, we argue that faith-based youth work subscribes to the principles of inclusivity, empowerment and participation, and that it challenges its wider religious institutions, despite some barriers, to become more accessible, inclusive and accepting in empowering young people.

METHODOLOGY

The research underpinning this chapter engaged Interpretative Phenomenological Analysis (IPA) as its methodology (see Bright et al., 2013; Smith et al., 2009). The nine research informants (see Table 15.1) – all who were active youth work practitioners – volunteered to participate in the study as the result of calls made through various professional networks in the UK in spring/summer 2016.[5,6] Interviews, which occurred either face to face or via Skype, were analysed by individual members of the research team using the frameworks outlined by Smith et al. (2009) and Bright et al. (2013). Interview themes from each data item were distilled into three or four major motifs which summarized the essence of each participant's experience. Further in-depth analysis (a process known as subsumption in IPA), across the data set generated three superordinate themes: Education, Engagement and Ethics (see Figure 15.1). Griffin and May (2012: 453) suggest that 'the presentation of analysed [IPA] data should contain substantial verbatim quotations which illustrate the importance of the participant's voice'. The

Table 15.1   Participant information

Name	Participant information
Balraj	Sikh volunteer youth worker
Beth	Christian, church-based youth worker
Daniel	Jewish youth worker
Jim	Christian, church-based youth worker
Kana	Buddhist volunteer youth worker
Mark	Christian youth worker with The Feast – an inter-faith youth work organization
Saori	Buddhist volunteer youth worker
Steven	A Revert Muslim youth worker with The Feast – an inter-faith youth work organization
Warsan	Muslim volunteer youth worker who has initiated a Scouts group for Muslim young people

Note: Some names are elected pseudonyms. Other participants and organizations made explicit requests for real names and locations to be used. Ethical protocols, as consented by York St John University for this research, have been followed throughout.

data and contextual commentary that follow, attempt therefore to illuminate participants' experiences of contemporary faith-based practice, and provide a basis for the critical analysis with which the chapter concludes.

EDUCATION: FAITH IN DIALOGUE

The sub-themes, like the superordinate themes generated in this research are intricately interconnected. The challenge has been to find appropriate threads with which to begin navigating a way through the data, and to select a cross-section of examples from the significant amount generated. Research always necessitates compromise. In this case, it has been to balance out the richness of the data produced through IPA with the space afforded by, and the focus of, the chapter. For this reason, particular sub-themes will be explored in this work. Our hope is however that the data is presented in a way that resonates with the reader, and, which remains true to the contributors' experiences.[7]

Faith in Informal Education

It became encouragingly apparent in analysing the data that a deep commitment to relationally-grounded informal educational

practice with young people lies, in various ways, at the centre of participants' practice. In many instances, this was framed by connecting young people's everyday experiences to issues of faith through dialogue, and, to exploring young people's perceptions and understanding of faith in a safe and respectful manner.

> … we had a boy who came the other day who has joined us and is part of our team now … but he'd suffered with bone cancer at 17, and we'd seen this stuff that Stephen Fry had presented online, and this whole discussion started, and as the boys filtered in and they joined in. And we talked about what we believe about creation, and 'Was there a God?' and 'Could there be a God?' 'And if there was, did he create anything, or was that just luck, but he's still around?' So we really talked, and I would say the conversation was for about an hour and a half, which to get young people to sit down and talk for an hour and half, like, orchestrated, you just, you couldn't do that at all. (Beth)

Other examples included Daniel having an open exchange of ideas around atheism and allowing everyone's opinion to be heard, and Saori who creates space for informal dialogue amidst opportunities for study and prayer. This dialogical commitment extends to ethical and moral issues, and often leads to action in the wider community, and, in some cases, to a committed engagement with global concerns. This, many of the participants highlighted as key to developing critical pedagogical practice, and as resulting in young people generating a greater sense of

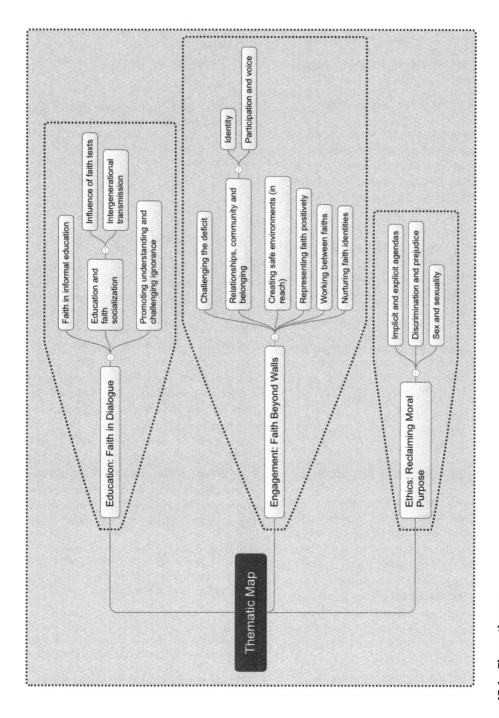

Figure 15.1   Thematic map

possibility, agency and critical civic responsibility.

> … one of the first things we did back in 2012 was a charity event, and we raised funds for a local children's hospital … So we did a fundraising event and we fundraised almost £8000 for that because we managed to get all of the community together. So that was a real kind of taste of, oh wow, we can actually make things happen. (Balraj)

In a further example, Steven described how he engages young people from different faith backgrounds in critical discussions regarding human trafficking and fair trade. His focus is on developing a pedagogy that challenges young people to '… look at things on a local, national and global scale…'. The programme he currently runs encourages young people to consider ethical choices in terms of shopping. He suggests that irrespective of young people's particular faith traditions:

> … this stuff affects you, so the questions that we're posing are: 'As young people of faith, what does your faith teach you about the issue of caring for other people? What does your faith teach you about treating other people well?' So it's really asking people to reflect upon themselves and their own belief system, and look at the world that they're living in through the context of the faith that they belong to.

Education and Faith Socialization

The central importance to participants (albeit to different degrees) of processes of faith socialization as an educational concern, can be seen in the majority of the data. This is evident in the place given by participants to the influence of faith texts, mentoring and the intergenerational transmission of faith values and practices via dialogue and experience. Many of the participants highlighted the centrality of applying faith texts in their youth work curricula in enabling young people's learning and development in navigating personal, social and moral issues.

> … we also do Jewish text learning so we do stories from famous Rabbis, and people talk personally

about how this relates to them, and so last time we had some really amazing discussions about, like, authenticity and lying and being fake and to what extent you should, sort of, fully reveal everything about yourself, or should you keep some stuff more hidden, and more personal. And a lot of people have some amazing reflections, particularly on the tensions of revealing Jewish identity in certain contexts. (Daniel)

> There are a lot of stories, Buddhist stories that are applied and used in sort of quite creative ways … to get a message or an understanding across so … in a way it's all Buddhism, or at least Buddhism in daily life and then being able to explore the types of things they're facing. (Kana)

Intergenerational Transmission

Religious socialization can also be seen at the core of respondents' practice. This entails a mixture of direct youth work practice, religious observance and engagement with faith leaders and/or older members of religious communities. Some of the participants expressed this in simple terms; others reflected more fully on the complexities and challenges they faced in this aspect of their work as related to the inclusivity of wider religious bodies. Whilst some of these practices appeared to be more mono-directionally adult to young person, other respondents highlighted a healthy intergenerational ethos, where discussion of young people's experiences and beliefs catalysed dialogue and learning in the wider faith community.

> … so we have like an imam who comes down and he's their spiritual leader … [he] visits them at least once a term, and then they have like questions they can ask him. (Warsan)

> We also practice a traditional Judaism; we do the prayers in Hebrew … we keep the Sabbath, we abstain from work, and we encourage our members to live out as much as they can, traditional Jewish experiences … a lot of our members are not super super-observant, but when they're with us on the summer camps or events we have a high level of observance that we expect everyone, at least in public, to adhere to. (Daniel)

... it's really a movement that comes through young people or adults sharing their own experiences of practising Buddhism in the way that somebody else might become interested or want to know more. (Kana)

Promoting Understanding and Challenging Ignorance

A key sub-theme to emerge was a commitment to deconstruct and challenge misconceptions regarding faith. This can be seen in particular practice examples in which workers endeavour to debunk stereotypical ideas regarding their own faith traditions, and others in which practitioners work to build bridges and learning opportunities between different faiths in the pursuit of inclusive understanding.

> ... it's like well you go to church, you're not really a normal person, you don't know what it's like to do this and to do that, because you're not allowed or whatever, and I think we've really tried to push down those barriers to say, 'Well actually we might not be who you think we are, and maybe we don't believe in the God that you don't believe in either ... Maybe our God is somebody who you haven't discovered yet, you've just got this preconception.' So we really push the social stuff mainly because it's a way to show that Christians are normal people and they enjoy things, they can have a laugh just like you can ... (Beth)

> ...our passion is about helping young people to learn how to talk to one another about faith, share their beliefs, share their experiences, build bridges, make friends, change lives, you know, create all those experiences they might not ever have had. (Steven)

ENGAGEMENT: FAITH BEYOND WALLS

A spectrum of practice encompassing different purposes and modes of engaging young people within faith-based youth work can be seen in the research. This ranges from open access youth work to more specific faith teaching for those belonging to, or wanting

to explore the beliefs and practices of specific faith traditions. Another realm of engagement was inter-faith work with the purpose of bringing young people of different faiths together.

Challenging the Deficit

Respondents were keenly aware of how their work with young people and communities contributes to civil society. They were aware of gaps in provision for young people, particularly in a climate of austerity, and identified how the work they did was able to challenge this deficit. This work spanned from small social action projects to taking over local authority provision which was no longer funded, as in Beth's case:

> So we have, well we have a centre ... a council property ... that was going redundant because of the lack of youth work that there was in the city. So we took on that and picked up an existing, sort of existing project that they ran as a youth, open access youth project provision there. And we had previously ran one here, which we'd closed down due to residents' complaints, we had a very high volume of young people, roughly about, well between 120 and 140 on a Friday night, and of that about 90% of those were traveller young people. So they caused significant issues in a quite affluent area of York so we had to shut down before, before we were shut down, but the council approached us and asked us to re-open that at this new youth centre which is nearer the traveller sites and also it's a real area of need in York where it is. So, we agreed.

Whilst Beth was the only example of a youth worker taking over the running of local authority provision, others were also keen to frame their work as contributing to civil society. For example, Steven explained how through social action projects such as litter picking, Muslim young people in particular were able to challenge stereotypical perceptions. Similarly, Balraj explained how sociopolitical engagement was a key element of his practice, with his young people engaging in protests and campaigns. Jim, who was more explicit about the ultimate purpose of his work as sharing the Christian faith, runs social provision to serve local young people, which he described as having 'no agenda'.

Relationships, Community and Belonging

Relationships and community were key themes across the youth workers' narratives. Forging relationships with young people, and between young people and the wider faith community, were viewed as key aspects of practice. Whilst this was explicit in all respondents' practice, the idea of mentoring was perhaps most central for the Buddhist youth workers. Here, mentoring was predominantly framed around offering guidance and encouragement to young people with both practical and spiritual issues.

Another dimension of relational practice is to foster friendships between young people.

> Our main focus really is friendship, really to forge the friendship among them because in that, during that kind of teenage time, faith isn't really their focus, in their eyes really ... But friendship is something that they're interested in, that's something that they really connect with ... why we focus on friendship is because when they have a problem or issues, they're not necessarily listen to someone like parents or somebody older, or teacher, or whatever, but they can disclose to their friends, share their problems and encourage each other. (Saori)

The youth workers also often saw their role as a mediator between young people and the faith community. Jim, for example, described how such mediation is a significant part of his role.

> I mean great youth workers are great, like don't get me wrong, but if it's just that, we're missing something. And so ... I have been really proactive in the church, trying to integrate young people with the life of the church, recognising that they need that community ... you think well why do they drop out of church, they obviously don't see it as family or a community that they can connect with, or belong to or be part of, or are valued by. So it's easy to walk away.

Warsan also explained how her role involved mediating between young people and leaders of the Mosque. Other participants also detailed this, albeit to a lesser extent.

Participation and voice were significant in facilitating relationships and community, as respondents, in their intermediary roles, facilitated young people's ability to have a say, and contribute to the faith community. This often necessitated breaking down institutional barriers.

> Well I think one of the roles of the youth work in this context is a sort of mediator and almost as a voice for the young people. So there's a voice for the young people speaking into the systems and infrastructure of the church which can become very rigid, very much like 'this is how we do things' and 'these are the boxes you tick' and all that stuff and obviously young people don't operate like that. So there's a role of kind of balancing the gap I think of, and trying to help young people to recognise that they can have a voice, and they can have a voice within the life of the church and that they, they are a valid, valued part of life at the church and they're not, 'oh those kids' or whatever they might see that they're seen as, or some people might even see them like. So I think that in my role there is very much that voice thing and as the mediator. (Jim)

Similarly, Balraj outlined how he had worked to help Sikh young people have more of a voice at his Gurdwara, and to even sit on the committee.

Representing Faith Positively

This theme overlaps with the educational sub-theme of 'Promoting Understanding and Challenging Ignorance'. It relates also to Engagement, in that, it is about providing a positive representation of the faith tradition or community to the wider public. This was particularly pertinent where youth workers felt a minority faith tradition was misunderstood and subject to negative stereotyping. Mark explained how he had worked with a Muslim community to open up their Mosque to people of other faiths, as well as refusing to do any inter-faith work where responding to 'radicalization' was the starting point. Similarly, Balraj had opened up his Gurdwara with events for the wider public, with the explicit aim of allowing them to learn more about the local Sikh community through charity events, tours and visits from other faith groups.

The positive representation of faith overlaps with 'Working between faiths'. However, the distinction lies in difference in intent – one being to represent minority and, at times, misunderstood faith communities to the wider public; the other being to facilitate relationships between people of different faiths for their own sake.

Working between Faiths

Working between faiths was a key theme across the interviews. This was most pertinent in the practice of The Feast for whom Mark and Steven work. Both independently outlined how creating a sense of community and friendship between young people of different faiths was central to their practice. However, such inter-faith work was also explicit in the other youth workers' narratives. Warsan, for example, outlined how her Muslim Scout group has engaged with the local Christian and Sikh Scout groups:

> Recently we organised a faith show, so like the Mosque, the Gurdwara and the Church which was really good, like they got to speak to like, like I think there was for the Church there was a priest and for the Mosque it was just like one of the boy trustees and I think the same for the Gurdwara.

Daniel was also engaging in inter-faith work:

> We go outside the community and talk to other faith groups and particularly, I think, politically it's very important for Jews and Muslims to be talking as much as possible. So yeah, that's, that's part of the work.

Other youth workers who perhaps weren't engaging in such explicit inter-faith work did

emphasise how young people of other faiths were welcome and had attended their activities.

ETHICS: RECLAIMING MORAL PURPOSE

Inclusion 'Within' and 'Without'

It became apparent from the data that inclusion is multi-faceted, and, to some extent relative. To some respondents, inclusion was expressed as a practice trajectory – of the wider religious community *becoming* more inclusive. This was manifest as either providing a safe place for young people with a faith, or young people challenging the wider community towards greater inclusivity. Whilst this kind of 'with-in' inclusion was prevalent (increasing the level of equality and participation within the community), it also represents a form of inclusion that brings people in from outside.

Inclusion 'with-in' involved creating spaces and structures so young people were not disadvantaged in comparison to their 'secular' peers, and ensuring that impairments did not prevent inclusion in religious experiences. However, respondents were also involved in challenging the wider community to be more inclusive:

> … where young people are they're encouraged, or the meetings or the adults, are encouraged to include them in the meetings in such a way, whether it's from the very young age of doing something that they've prepared or preparing during the meeting with somebody else, or if they're older then participating in the meetings and make sure that they're included in the, sometimes running the meetings with the adults so it's very, the idea is that they're not excluded from that process either. (Kana)

Less prevalent however were organizations' attempts to be overtly inclusive towards people of other faiths (and none). Typically, organizations were engaged in ensuring young people who were part of their faith community were able to be included in wider society or within the religious community. This form of inclusion towards those outside ('with-out') the community was limited to those organizations with a centrifugal mission, or an explicit aim, to work between faith groups. Beth, for example, explains how she and her team came to open a youth centre with universal provision:

> The council approached us and asked us to re-open that at this new youth centre which is nearer the traveller sites and also it's a real area of need in York where it is. So, we agreed. So we run that on a Friday night ... it is open access for anybody from 11 up to age 18, that particular group. We run it as a, quite a fluid group I guess, the activities change depending what's offered, we pick up partnerships with various groups in the city so we run a football project with York City Football Club, they come into the Friday night session, run some training with the young people.

She later comments on how the faith community have a more 'open' attitude towards young people coming in without paying (but later working off the debt) compared to the local authority she works with.

Sex and Sexuality

Workers described their understanding of sexuality through making sense of their faith, doctrine, and young people's lives and norms – and at times living with the tension between them. Daniel, for example, self-identified as a gay man who felt that Judaism in the UK was inclusive of the LGBT community through the legalizing of gay marriage.

Jim was more cautious about sexuality. He appeared to find it challenging to reconcile aspects of his interpretation of the Bible with elements of practice.

> I really believe what the Bible says about homosexuality, that you might want to say I am convinced in the way that I have interpreted it, either, but so that's a struggle with youth work because

in terms of like, youth work values, because I suppose I like, like personally I don't agree with homosexual practice, I don't think it's right. But at the same time, if there's young people who are homosexual, I'd still want to like, love them and kind of, show them that they're welcome and I care about them ... it's easy to be labelled as like anti-gay or homophobic, which I don't [think] I am ... through coming to know God, he has shown that he loves people, and he's given me that love for people ... Well there's a young person who's a lad who's become a Christian and become very involved with the church in the last year or so. And he's absolutely great ... but he wrote little letters to some key people in the church ... basically saying, something like, 'I think I might be gay', or something like that, 'but I fear that the church wouldn't accept me if I am?' ... We're like, Bob, we love you, like, you know, we love you and it's not an issue. And at that point I was thinking, oh this is interesting because this could make or break I think because he's like a really new Christian and all this stuff. And the people just responded with love to him.

Inclusive and pragmatic responses to sexuality and sex can be seen in other practice examples. Beth described working with young people to actively promote safer sex through discussion and condom distribution. And Steven reflected on how he had developed sex education programmes for young Muslims (paid for by the local authority), in order to deliver work that took account of particular cultural sensitivities.

DISCUSSION

Without making claims towards generalizability, the faith-based practice examined in this research bears many of the characteristics of classic informal educational practice with young people. Whilst the idea of exclusion is often rightly problematized via different analytical lenses, the concept of inclusion is uncritically accepted as a given to be strived for. This leads us to pose a number of philosophical questions which need to be considered in regard to practice. 'What do we mean by inclusion?' 'On whose terms is it defined, or negotiated? Young people's? Adults'? Politicians'? As something that is shared? By youth and community work as a profession? Or, in the case of faith-based practice, by the divine?' And, perhaps most fundamentally, 'Does, or can inclusion, by definition, exist without exclusion?' Often, our inclusion in one group necessitates our exclusion from another. It is on the fluid borders of such binaries that belonging and identities are forged, and where the capacity for power to be used for good, or ill is made. These difficult questions have been framed in different ways by our respondents. However, they extend beyond practitioners' heuristic reflections on practice, towards practical and critical educational engagement with young people which recognizes something of the temporal and socially constructed nature of inclusivity, in the pursuit of challenge, justice and change. This can be seen in the present data in a number of ways. Firstly, in participants' pursuit of institutional inclusivity with young people of (or those exploring) faith, where there are mixed experiences of welcome and integration from older members of religious communities (Stanton, 2013). Whilst this form of intergenerational inclusion appears an integral struggle for many of our respondents, it further prompts us to ask questions about the nature of inclusivity and identity. Shepherd (2010), for example, is one of a number of thinkers who has argued the benefits of exclusive inclusivity in faith-based practice – of the importance of providing discrete, safe spaces for young people's faith exploration and identity development. This again can be seen in different examples from the present data; for example, the inauguration of Warsan's Scout group for Muslim young people, or Jim's Bible study group. These youth workers engage young people across a spectrum of practice ranging from targeted faith teaching to open access provision. The Christian youth workers, Beth and Jim, were perhaps the most explicit example of this, with practice developed at both ends of this spectrum. This work reflects, but also

goes beyond, Stanton's (2013) model of faith-based youth work which suggests there are social, spiritual and institutional domains to practice which often lack mutual connectivity. Having exclusive groups may enhance inclusivity for young people of, or those exploring, faith by providing the safe spaces noted above. The practice observed in our research however goes beyond Stanton's model, as this pre-existing work is limited to analysis of Christian youth work provision taking place within church buildings. The youth workers in the present study take their engagement 'beyond walls'. This is particularly the case in the practice of the more 'minority traditions' in their efforts to represent faith positively. This reflects a proactive effort to increase inclusion through engagement with communities and the wider public, often through positive social action.

Secondly, inclusivity can be viewed as being related to the dialogical imperative of informal education (Jeffs and Smith, 2005), where conversation acts as a catalytic vehicle which enables young people to experientially consider, deconstruct and cross physical, linguistic, social, religious, class, gender, sexual and opportunity borders in the pursuit of exchange, understanding and critical insight (Coburn, 2010; Giroux, 2005). Border crossings open up vistas and provide landscapes in which new inter-relationships and identities can be born (Coburn and Wallace, 2011). Borders are meeting points – sites where assumptions and stereotypes begin to be challenged. By crossing borders, we come to meet, understand, and share others' worlds, and, in doing so, understand ourselves and our place in the world more fully. We are enabled to critically recognize the power, intersubjectivities and oppression of differing privileges and positionalities. Border pedagogy challenges our existing, limited worldviews. It is education.

These border crossings are exemplified when respondents move their practices towards inclusively engaging with young people, in order to show their willingness to understand the experiential realities of their lives. Beth and Jim, for example, both describe developing socially-orientated provision designed to engage with, and relationally serve the needs of young people, in the hope that this might encourage young people to cross their own borders, challenge pre-existing worldviews and discover something new. Border crossings are seen in the mentoring undertaken by Kana and Saori, in Balraj's community and political activism, and in Daniel's dialogues between faith and atheism. They are embedded in the various critical discussions fostered by participants on a wide array of issues. Most strikingly perhaps, they are seen in promoting inclusive understanding through inter-faith dialogue. Whilst this is the explicit purpose of The Feast, which, as an organization is engaged in some rather remarkable work, it is something which can clearly be seen in others' practice.

Youth work is about providing relational spaces for border encounters. It is a rich and multi-faceted praxis, which, at its core, is relationally committed to enabling young people's negotiated learning. It is a moral activity which encourages young people to consider how the world is, and how it should be, empowering them towards generating change. Young (2006, 2010) posits this as 'moral philosophising'. Active moral philosophising appears central to various practice narratives in our study. Perhaps the most striking of those cited in this chapter is Steven's account, which describes a pedagogy committed to asking young people of different faiths (and none) to actively engage in considering real-world moral issues and how they might act as a result. It is this form of critical practice in the faith sector which inspires hope and possibility.

Inclusion is not merely philosophical; it is both practical and attitudinal. Many participants highlighted areas where they felt they were able to practically include young people of different faiths and none. Practical inclusion prioritizes the welcome and involvement of young people. Attitudinal inclusion highlights the importance of educating young people about faith values and beliefs, and of educating wider faith communities (and, in some instances, wider communities at large) about young people's experiences, needs and aspirations. Attitudinal inclusion therefore requires changes in thinking about, and attitudes towards, young people from within the faith community, as opposed to simply fostering inclusive institutional practices. The understanding which results creates security and relational reciprocity (Turney, 2007), enables young people's voices to be heard, and furthers work that takes account of their developing needs. Although practical inclusion is a helpful first step, the present data suggests that the usual and desired outcome of practical inclusion is attitudinal. This, in turn, deepens practical inclusion and understanding. This can be seen in Stanton's (2013) research into Christian youth work and in Jim's narrative account of integrating young people with the church – both of which explore how practically bringing young people into church is not the same as there being an attitude of acceptance from the wider congregation. 'Them and us' cultures can exist within 'practically inclusive' settings. These deny attitudinal inclusivity. More broadly, this can occur where the existence of a religious group is tolerated, but no effort is made to engage with, or understand them. Balraj's work to involve his wider community, for example, aims to foster broader attitudinal inclusion.

Faith-based youth work is often accused of proselytization. As proselytization is in its truest sense about asking people to consider changing their minds, it must continue to do so. It promotes learning, understanding and inclusivity. Whilst there are examples of practice in the data that could be described as evangelistic or discipling, these only become indoctrinatory if they successfully deny young people the opportunity to develop – whether cognitively, morally, in identity, or in faith (Hart, 2014). As it is the pedagogic method (rather than content) that is principally indoctrinatory (Thompson, 2017), removing overt acknowledgements of 'faith' from youth work only serves to replace it with other agendas of equally indoctrinatory potential (Copley, 2005). Similarly, it has been argued that all youth work is 'conversionary' in that it seeks to foster change (Brierley, 2003; Clayton and Stanton, 2008), and therefore it is better to be aware of, and accountable to, the agendas of particular work, rather than to deny or hide them. The present data suggests that faith-based workers are acutely aware of personal worldviews allowing them to critically reflect on the role their faith plays in practice. When workers are influenced by more subtly dominant ideologies (e.g. humanism), they are less likely perhaps to reflect critically upon how these impact on their work. Secularism, in particular, is often mistaken as a neutral worldview, when it too makes assumptions about God, the world, and people (Clayton and Stanton, 2008). The promulgation of faith as an aim, however implicitly, provides a powerful motivation to ensure organizations are inclusive – whether that is ensuring the wider faith community is inclusive of young people, or, that youth work provision is accessible and welcoming to those 'outside'.

CONCLUSION

Youth work has its origins in faith-based practice (Bright, 2015b; Pimlott, 2015b; Stanton, 2013). Whilst youth work in the UK was supported by the state from the mid-20th century, state roll-out has been a short chapter in its overall history. Faith-based youth work existed alongside the statutory era, and, as illustrated in our data, is now in many cases filling the gaps left by state-induced local authority funding cuts. At the same time, there are increasing restrictions applied to faith-based youth work and continuing

suspicions as to its intentions. This is seen most particularly within the UK context in the Counter-extremism Strategy (2015) and the associated Prevent Guidance, which suggests all religious organizations engaging young people are soon to be subject to demands for registration, monitoring and inspection (Home Office, 2015).

Youth work, as expressive of the ideals of informal education is alive and well in the faith sector. Given the present climate, it needs to be. The decimation and assimilation of the state and wider voluntary sector has hollowed out youth work's purpose (Jeffs, 2015), and left few spaces in which young people can critically think and act. Given the present environment, perhaps it is the types of practice in the faith-based sector, which this research is representative of, which are now the most inclusive. It appears therefore that the faith sector, from which much youth and community work emerged, is the first and last bastion of civil society.

We have resisted the temptation to present a deficit model of inclusion in faith-based practice. Whilst there are undoubtedly challenges to inclusion and equality across broader religious spheres, faith-based youth work is often at the forefront of promoting greater levels of inclusivity. Young people and their youth workers can drive forward the inclusion of members of faith communities in wider society and religious communities, and challenge orthodoxies regarding justice, gender and sexuality. It would not be fair or accurate therefore, to present faith-based youth work as in need of 'saving' by adopting secular models of inclusion.

The prevalence of neo-liberalism, across much of the Western world (as explored elsewhere in this text), and the concomitant pervasiveness of deficit models, preordained measures of 'success', and monitoring regarding who can access services, place many practitioners in exclusionary positions. Whilst faith-based youth workers have often worked in contexts where they have stood against prevailing cultural conditions, now 'secular' organizations are having to find ways to be inclusive within an exclusionary system. Many of the examples of practice explored in this chapter show a level of openness and inclusivity that wider funding streams often deny. Faith-based practice appears therefore to be promoting young people's inclusion at a time when neo-liberalism is undermining its value by making access to youth work provision increasingly exclusive to targeted subsets of young people.

Notes

1   Cited to denote particular political and professional distinctions between England and other United Kingdom jurisdictions.
2   By 'faith praxis' we mean practice within faith traditions that is based on critical, emancipatory and reflexive thought.
3   Naomi Thompson, one of the chapter authors, was previously Naomi Stanton.
4   It was claimed by the early 2000s that numbers of full-time employed church-based youth workers in England and Wales outnumbered their statutory equivalent (Brierley, 2003; Green, 2006). This was during a time of relative generosity for secular youth work and youth services under the New Labour government. Whilst no current statistics appear to exist on the numbers of faith-based youth workers, it is estimated by the trade union Unison (2016) that at least £387m was cut from local authority youth service budgets between 2010 and 2016, further widening the gap. Jeffs (2015: 11) further argues that Youth Services are likely to be the first public service to completely disappear in the era of neo-liberal austerity, emphasizing, however, that '… whenever discussion of "a youth work crisis" occurs it is important to recall the "crisis" relates almost exclusively to secular units …'.
5   We are particularly grateful to Shelley Marsh from Reshet, The Network for Jewish Youth Provision, for her support for this project.
6   The authors had originally hoped for international contributions; however, despite sustained efforts, this did not materialize.
7   Our participants provided us with a varied amount of rich data for which we are very grateful. We are aware of our struggle to do justice to this in the space afforded in this chapter. We are therefore considering ways in which we might re-visit this data in the hope of producing work which gives further voice to their experience and wisdom.

REFERENCES

Ahmed, S. (2015) The Voices of Young British Muslims: Identity, Belonging and Citizenship. In Smith, M., Stanton, N. and Wylie, T. (eds) *Youth Work and Faith: Debates, Delights and Dilemmas*. Lyme Regis: Russell House Publishing, pp. 37–51.

Batsleer, J. (2008) *Informal Learning in Youth Work*. London: Sage.

Brierley, D. (2003) *Joined Up: An Introduction to Youth Work and Ministry*. Carlisle, Cumbria: Spring Harvest Publishing/Authentic Lifestyle.

Bright, G. (2013) Making Sense of Ologies. In Bright, G. and Harrison, G. (eds) *Understanding Research in Counselling*. London: Sage/Learning Matters, pp. 55–94.

Bright, G. (2015a) Introduction. In Bright, G. (ed.) *Youth Work: Histories, Policy and Contexts*. London: Palgrave Macmillan, pp. xvii–xx.

Bright, G. (2015b) The Early History of Youth Work Practice. In Bright, G. (ed.) *Youth Work: Histories, Policy and Contexts*. London: Palgrave Macmillan, pp. 1–21.

Bright, G. and Bailey, D. (2015) Youth Work and the Church. In Bright, G. (ed.) *Youth Work: Histories, Policy and Contexts*. London: Palgrave Macmillan, pp. 145–160.

Bright, G., Claringbull, N. and Harrison, G. (2013) Making It Happen: Applying Research Methods. In Bright, G. and Harrison, G. (eds) *Understanding Research in Counselling*. London: Sage/Learning Matters, pp. 129–155.

Clayton, M.A. and Stanton, N. (2008) The Changing World's View of Christian Youthwork. *Youth & Policy* 100, 109–128.

Coburn, A. (2010) Youth Work as Border Pedagogy. In Batsleer, J. and Davies, B. (eds) *What is Youth Work?* Exeter: Learning Matters, pp. 33–46.

Coburn, A. (2011) Liberation or Containment: Paradoxes in Youth Work as a Catalyst for Powerful Learning. *Youth & Policy* 106, 60–77.

Coburn, A. and Wallace, D. (2011) *Youth Work in Communities and Schools*. Edinburgh: Dunedin Academic Press.

Copley, T. (2005) *Indoctrination, Education and God: The Struggle for the Mind*. London: SPCK.

Freire, P. (1970) *Pedagogy of the Oppressed*. London: Penguin.

Garasia, H., Begum-Ali, S. and Farthing, R. (2016) 'Youth Club is Made to Get Children off the Streets': Some Young People's Thoughts about Opportunities to be Political in Youth Clubs. *Youth & Policy* 116, 1–18.

Giroux, H.A. (2005) *Border Crossings: Cultural Workers and the Politics of Education* (2nd edn). Abingdon: Routledge.

Gould, G. (2015) *Wasted: How Misunderstanding Young Britain Threatens Our Future*. London: Little Brown.

Green, M. (2006) *A Journey of Discovery: Spirituality and Spiritual Development in Youth Work*. Leicester: The National Youth Agency.

Griffin, A. and May, V. (2012) Narrative Analysis and Interpretative Phenomenological Analysis. In Seale, C. (ed.) *Researching Society and Culture*. London: Sage.

Hart, P. (2014) *Indoctrination and Youth Ministry*. Cambridge: Grove Books.

Hart, P. (2016) Attitudes towards Working 'Out-of-hours' with Young People: Christian and Secular Perspectives. *Youth & Policy* 115, 43–62.

Home Office (2015) *Counter-extremism Strategy*. London: Crown Copyright.

Jeffs, T. (2011) Running Out of Options: Re-Modelling Youth Work. *Youth & Policy* 106, 1–8.

Jeffs, T. (2015) Innovation and Youth Work. *Youth and Policy* 114, 75–95.

Jeffs, T. and Smith, M. (2005) *Informal Education: Conversation, Democracy and Learning*. Nottingham: Educational Heretics Press.

Jeffs, T. and Spence, J. (2011) The Development of Youth Work with Girls and Young Women in the Nineteenth Century. In Gilchrist, R., Hodgson, T., Jeffs, T., Spence, J., Stanton, N. and Walker, J. (eds) *Reflecting on the Past: Essays in the History of Youth and Community Work*. Lyme Regis: Russell House Publishing, pp. 1–33.

Jolly, J. (2015) Christian Youth Work: Motive and Method. In Smith, M.K., Stanton, N. and Wylie, T. (eds) *Youth Work and Faith: Debates, Delights and Dilemmas*. Lyme Regis: Russell House Publishing, pp. 23–36.

Lynn, R.W. and Wright, E. (1971) *The Big Little School: Two Hundred Years of the Sunday School*. New York: Harper and Row.

Marsh, S. (2015) On renewing and soaring: Transformation and Actualisation in Contemporary Jewish Youth Provision. In Smith, M.K., Stanton, N. and Wylie, T. (eds) *Youth Work and Faith: Debates, Delights and Dilemmas*. Lyme Regis: Russell House Publishing, pp. 5–22.

Page, S. (2015) Sex Talk: Discussion and Meaning-making Among Religious Young Adults. In Smith, M., Stanton, N. and Wylie, T. (eds) *Youth Work and Faith: Debates, Delights and Dilemmas*. Lyme Regis: Russell House Publishing, pp. 70–84.

Pimlott, N. (2015a) *Embracing the Passion: Christian Youth Work and Politics*. Birmingham: FYT.

Pimlott, N. (2015b) Faith-based Youth Work and Civil Society. In Smith, M.K., Stanton, N. and Wylie, T. (eds) *Youth Work and Faith: Debates, Delights and Dilemmas*. Lyme Regis: Russell House Publishing, pp. 52–69.

Sapin, K. (2013) *Essential Skills for Youth Work Practice* (2nd edn). London: Sage.

Sercombe, H. (2010) *Youth Work Ethics*. London: Sage.

Shepherd, N.M. (2010) Religious Socialisation and a Reflexive Habitus: Christian Youth Groups as Sites for Identity Work. In Collins-Mayo, S. and Dandelion, P. (eds) *Religion and Youth*. Abingdon: Routledge, pp. 149–158.

Singh, J. (2011) Sikh-ing Beliefs: British Sikh Camps in the UK. In Jacobsen, K.A. and Myrvold, K. (eds) *Sikhs in Europe: Migration, Identities and Representations*. Farnham, Surrey: Ashgate, pp. 253–278.

Smith, J.A., Flowers, P. and Larkin, M. (2009) *Interpretative Phenomenological Analysis*. London: Sage.

Stanton, N. (2011) From Raikes' Revolution to Rigid Institution: Sunday Schools in Twentieth Century England. In Gilchrist, R., Hodgson, T., Jeffs, T., Spence, J., Stanton, N. and Walker, J. (eds) *Reflecting on the Past: Essays in the History of Youth and Community Work*. Lyme Regis: Russell House Publishing, pp. 71–91.

Stanton, N. (2012) Christian Youth Work: Teaching Faith, Filling Churches or Response to Social Need? *Journal of Beliefs and Values: Studies in Religion and Education* 33(3), 385–403.

Stanton, N. (2013) Faith-based Youth Work – Lessons from the Christian Sector. In Curran, S., Harrison, R. and Mackinnon, D. (eds) *Working with Young People* (2nd edn). London: Sage, pp. 193–205.

Thompson, N. (2017) 'Indoctrination'. *Sage Encyclopaedia of Political Behaviour*. Thousand Oaks, CA: Sage, pp. 387–388.

Turney, D. (2007) Practice. In Robb, M. (ed.) *Youth in Context: Frameworks, Settings, and Encounters*. London: Sage, pp. 53–88.

Unison (2016) *The Damage: A Future at Risk – Cuts to Youth Services*, available at https://www.unison.org.uk/content/uploads/2016/08/23996.pdf [accessed 25.01.2017].

Woodhead, L. (2012) Introduction. In Woodhead, L. and Catto, R. (eds) *Religion and Change in Modern Britain*. Abingdon: Routledge, pp. 1–33.

Young, K. (2006) *The Art of Youth Work* (2nd edn). Lyme Regis: Russell House Publishing.

Young, K. (2010) Youth Workers as Moral Philosophers. In Banks, S. (ed.) *Ethical Issues in Youth Work* (2nd edn). Abingdon: Routledge, pp. 92–105.

16

Together We Walk: The Importance of Relationship in Youth Work with Refugee Young People

Jen Couch

INTRODUCTION

In Australia, one in four young people are from a refugee or migrant background (MYAN 2016: 4).[1] Young people from refugee backgrounds are some of the most vulnerable people in our community and they might reasonably be expected to have different complex needs compared with other young people. The purpose of this chapter is to explore and outline some of the key factors in supporting work with refugee young people. This chapter draws on prior research by the author to explore the experiences of refugee young people and youth workers who work with refugees in Australia. Through interview data, the chapter offers insights into the needs of young people, as well as the perceptions of youth workers and the services they use. Central to the chapter's argument is the importance of relationships in developing bonds of trust and building a critically reflective and responsive practice.

Within the resettlement experience youth workers can play an important role in the support of refugees and in their adjustment to a new society. Having an understanding of the specific needs of young refugees and the nature of the difficulties they can experience must influence how youth workers practise in order to assist young people in re-establishing a life which they believe will be meaningful and worthwhile. The quality of the relationship between the youth worker and a refugee young person is the foundation upon which the effectiveness of any intervention rests. A consistent predictable relationship where the worker is caring, genuine and warm provides the basis for allowing the young person's sense of security, value and trust in others to grow.

Regardless of location, the conventional definition of refugees according to the United Nations 1951 Convention Relating to the Status of Refugees, are people who:

... are outside their country of nationality or their usual country of residence; and are unable or unwilling to return or to seek the protection of that country due to a well-founded fear of being persecuted for the reasons of race, religion, nationality, membership of a particular social group or political opinion, and among other things, are not war criminals or people who have committed serious crimes.

The Convention however has been noted as being 'overly restrictive for the purposes of identifying people deserving humanitarian consideration and in need of resettlement' (Coventry et al. 2002: 14). Many young people that come to Australia arrive on visas that do not necessarily classify them as a refugee, but nevertheless have experienced displacement, separation from their family, abuse, exploitation, rape, being forced to witness killing and extreme deprivation. It is common for young people to have spent time in refugee camps where they are denied secure, safe accommodation, safety from abuse, education and health care. For many young refugees, arrival in another country contains many mixed emotions. There is often great anxiety as young people worry for those left behind, try to adapt to a new environment and experience language barriers that can further isolate them.[2]

Therefore, in this chapter 'young people from refugee backgrounds' is used to refer to those who have arrived on humanitarian visas, young people seeking asylum and those who come from refugee backgrounds who arrive on another visa type, including family migration and skilled migration.

In Australia, youth workers have worked specifically with young refugees since the 1980s. Prior to this and the formation of the first ethnic minority youth organisation – the Ethnic Youth Issues Network, young refugees were invisible to mainstream services and ignored by migrant services who only worked with families. Now, youth workers work with young people in both multidisciplinary teams alongside social workers and psychologists and in specific youth services. Organisations span youth centres, migrant resource centres, local government, schools,

community health and arts centres, and are usually NGOs or faith-based services that receive government and philanthropic funding. There is a strong emphasis on assisting young people to 'settle well', however this is more than simply 'fitting in' – the optimal settlement outcome for young people is one of active citizenship:

This is understood to be inclusive: not just about formal citizenship status with associated legal rights and responsibilities, but a proactive approach to engagement and participation in Australian society. It encompasses concepts of participation, power, agency, identity and belonging, and includes activities such as community service and volunteering. It includes structured forms of engagement with political processes, as well as more day-to-day forms of participation in society. Active citizenship assumes the acquisition of social capital and agency, where young people are supported to become active agents of change and in shaping their own futures. Developing a sense of agency is particularly important for refugee and migrant young people as this group of young people have had their capacity for agency diminished by the refugee and migrant experience. This occurs through the development of skills, knowledge and networks. Active citizenship also reflects one of the key developmental tasks of adolescence – negotiating identity, independence and interdependence with family and community. (MYAN 2016: 14)

Whilst many organisations in Australia will provide direct support to young people, others are committed to ensuring young people have every opportunity to have their voice heard, develop skills and lead change in their communities. These services use a range of engagement tactics including advisory groups, forums, arts, sports, leadership training and mentoring to build the capacity of young people to become influential in Australian society.[3]

The process of settling in Australia can be complex and protracted for all refugees and migrants, regardless of age, and is best understood as non-linear, dynamic and not necessarily defined by the number of years since arrival in Australia (MYAN 2016: 12). There are also a number of factors in Australia that affect settlement outcomes, including government policy (e.g. immigration detention, restrictions on family reunion); community and media attitudes towards migrants, refugees and asylum seekers; access to employment, education, housing and community services; and racism and discrimination. Racism can be an ever-present reality for many young people, manifesting as implicit or explicit experiences, and can have a detrimental impact on a young person's sense of identity and belonging, as well as their physical and mental health (MYAN 2016: 12).

Australia has had long-standing migration policies and an underlying deep-seated fear of 'invasion'. Since the mid-1970s, the Australian public has been exposed to negative discourses in the media and from politicians about asylum seekers, and in particular 'boat people'. This negative discourse has firmly constructed asylum seekers and refugees as a 'deviant social group' (Pickering 2001, cited in McKay et al. 2011). The power of this rhetoric has been the construction of popularised labels which shift the public view from the structural reasons for seeking refuge to the individual behaviour of those who arrive in Australia as refugees. This construction has been formed through an overwhelmingly negative and sensationalised focus on the method of arrival, and the constant linking of refugees with labels of 'queue jumpers', 'terrorists', 'boat people' and 'illegals'. Furthermore, media reports often combine politicised labels with extreme images of behaviours: 'unauthorised' boats, overcrowded with predominantly Muslim males; reports of the use of criminal gangs and people smugglers to facilitate the journey to Australia; and extreme protests within detention facilities (McKay et al. 2011). Media reporting reinforces the popularised image of refugees as 'violent', 'different', 'illegal' and seeking to exploit the goodwill of Australians. They present refugees taking 'all' the jobs, emphasising their economic gain and draining of

resources through the provision of welfare services (McKay et al. 2011: 619, 623).

Constructing young refugee people in Australia as a risk and national threat reinforces their difference to normative 'mainstream' Australia. Insinuating that there is deviance from the norm provides the government with further ammunition to implement controlling regulation of this group to avoid further risk (Lupton 1999: 61, 62). The ways in which these young people become cultural, objectified, stereotyped and homogenised in the national conversation, justifies their spatial segregation in communities and contributes to xenophobia and racism.

Young refugees have also often been portrayed as victims, as the passive recipients of the violence of adults (Hart and Tyrer 2006: 9) and as a minority on the periphery, requiring protection from adults, incapable of having opinions and expressing views. Images of trauma and damage dominate the presentations of young refugee people. These images have been reinforced and played upon by agencies in order to draw attention and gain support for projects. On the contrary, however, refugee young people tend to be particularly independent, resilient, opinionated and more than capable of making their own decisions. This should come as no surprise given the determination and personal survival skills required to endure the refugee experience itself. This is not to deny the experience of trauma, but as Hart and Tyrer suggest 'we should learn more about the strategies [young people] employ to deal with their adverse circumstances and maintain material, psychological, emotional and physical wellbeing' (2006: 10) and help them sustain and share these strengths.

Whilst acknowledging that the agency and the contribution young refugees can make is important, given their particular circumstances, their ability to achieve change should not be exaggerated. Young refugees are not all the same, of course, and whilst some will show resilience others will be overwhelmed by life's circumstances.

There is no one-size-fits-all model of good youth work practice with refugee young people.

HUMAN RIGHTS IN YOUTH WORK PRACTICE

From an Australian perspective, human rights are fundamental to contemporary youth work practice. Given the violations that these young people have often experienced, it is paramount that youth workers uphold the rights of refugee young people in every interaction with them.

If we reflect on the rights of the refugee young person as outlined in the various Conventions – the right to asylum, safety, shelter and the right to participate – then the language that is used to discuss the complexities of the resettlement of refugee young people needs to be re-thought. It is more useful in this context to think of a refugee rights model rather than one of refugee needs. Young refugees who have been exposed to a continuum of human rights abuse need more than a welfare-driven notion of needs. The concept of needs has the capacity to further welfarise the refugee and further entrench dependency upon agencies. Additionally, the philosophy of 'needs' fails to acknowledge the right to settle and lead a 'normal' life, which is one of the major concerns for most refugee young people. Young refugees have arrived from countries such as the Sudan, Ethiopia, the Congo, Liberia, Burma and Afghanistan, where contempt for their human rights has been the norm. If we concede that a 'normal' life is a right for all, then in resettlement it is timely that we move away from a needs model and embrace a rights model. Young refugees have the right to access services that are flexible, responsive and committed to working with young people with refugee-like experiences.

Given that the violation of human rights is frequently experienced by refugee young people, the importance of supporting and valuing human rights when working with young refugees cannot be understated. Essential to good settlement is an 'environment that affirms their human dignity and restores a sense of safety and control over their lives' (Mitchell, Kaplan & Crowe 2006: 285). The strengthening of such connections helps to restore the attachments, relationships and sense of belonging that is needed to reduce the fear and anxiety usually caused in the refugee experience. If we recognise this rebuilding of human connection as essential, when working with young refugees the quality of the relationship is vital.

Thus, the next part of the chapter listens to the voices of refugee young people and youth workers to understand the fundamental aspects of building meaningful relationships. These narratives are from interviews conducted with 25 refugee young people (aged between 17 and 25) and ten youth workers as part of a longitudinal ethnographic study into refugee youth homelessness. Interviews were conducted several times between 2010 and 2016. The refugee young people interviewed originated from Sudan, Ethiopia, the Congo, Liberia, Burma and Afghanistan, and had been in Australia between eight months and five years. In addition, ten youth workers were recruited via a snowball sampling technique based on visits to key organisations working with refugee young people. This was facilitated by the researcher having worked extensively with refugee young people and having contacts with a wide variety of services and researchers. The youth workers were employed in a range of services, including advice and advocacy, housing, mental health and counselling, and specific youth service teams. Each youth worker was well regarded by refugee young people and had worked in the refugee sector for a minimum of five years.

BUILDING THE CONNECTION

That trusting relationships are fundamental to good youth work practice is not new,

Martin (2003: 15) suggests that it is 'the place of relationships which defines youth work'. Similarly, the young people and youth workers in my research identified the need to build a relationship with refugee young people as being the most fundamental aspect of the helping relationship regardless of the nature of the presenting problem or the agency context. A consistent and therefore predictable relationship where the worker is caring, genuine and warm provides the basis for allowing the young person's sense of security, value and trust in others to grow. Whether contact is brief or long-term, genuine interest in the well-being of the person conveys respect and helps restore dignity. Encountering an adult who offers assistance and is concerned to understand their feelings can rekindle a belief in the capacity of people to be caring and sincere:

> I can't quite describe what she did. Yes, she helped me with food and school and things like that, but it was more. I just always knew I could rely on her. She remembered things about my life. She always looked glad to see me. Sometimes you would turn up to see someone and they would act like you were taking up their time, but she showed me she really cared and let me come to her when I needed. She knew I had so many problems, but she didn't make me the problem. You know it was heartfelt. That is what made it different.

It is common for a young refugee to have experienced first-hand the failure of the adult world to protect him or her. The witnessing or experience of violence unsurprisingly instils in a young person the sense that the world is unsafe. Youth workers might strive to rekindle a belief in a safe world, but only once that world really is safe for them:

> You know, he approached me as just an everyday young person, because a lot of the time I feel ignored or looked down on. I don't feel I belong in Australia. He didn't say 'you poor thing' or anything. He didn't ask me to tell him anything. He just made me feel normal and safe. Seriously? I think I was hard to work with, sometimes I would turn up … sometimes I would sleep in – I felt tired and it was hard to sleep where I was living. Sometimes I felt shamed. But I would go to play

> basketball and he was so patient, just always there. We would shoot hoops and talk. As I said, it was just normal.

Young refugees' descriptions of their experiences with youth workers in generic organisations showed both similarities and differences with the experiences of young service users generally. Broadly speaking, the young people wanted youth workers to work with them using an approach that was flexible and welcoming. They wanted to feel listened to, heard, responded to and recognised by someone friendly, trustworthy, authentic and respectful. All young people described the importance of a relationship where there was time purely to get to know each other, and where youth workers were guided in practice by the young person's story. The young people appreciated interactions in which they felt a sense of genuine care, and spoke highly of those youth workers who came across as deeply attuned and responsive:

> I received a birthday card from my youth worker the other day. I haven't been there for a while. She asked how I was doing, letting me know I could come back and talk to her. She always stood by me, no matter what I did, or what anyone did to me. She always stood with me. She didn't give up on me. I could call and talk to her all the time, she was just there to listen, even now, I feel like I'm getting down or I can't handle something, can't handle a problem or something I call her. She's like, I don't know, she's always there you know. She is one person I can trust. It made me miss my mum so much; there is no one else like this in my life.

Youth workers consistently identified the youth worker–young person relationship as fundamental in its significance to practice (Rodd and Stewart 2009: 4), outweighing almost everything else. It is here that the youth worker and young person 'engage in an exchange that enriches the available meanings in any situation and the possible courses of action, without pre-determining either' (Rodd and Stewart 2009: 4). Sercombe (2007) suggests that that these exchanges typically occur within an environment that is intentionally limited, which in turn, allows the young person the space to become vulnerable and discuss the embarrassing, dangerous, guilty and/or broken aspects of themselves in order to make the first step towards transformation and healing (p. 13):

> My youth worker always had my back. She never doubted that I could cope. She knew I wasn't a basket case. She knew I was often hungry and tired. I was just so tired dealing with all that shit that I would fall asleep in class. She would bring me lunch … she was interested in me you know. So many people just saw me as a problem. We would talk about my problems, but we would talk about other stuff too. She was such a cool lady. So funny. She would always say 'you know your situation best'.

However, youth workers do not have an automatic right to engage and/or intervene in young people's lives – this is a process of negotiation, building respect and trust 'generally caring about them and being prepared to support them on their terms' (Young 1999: 68). The youth workers interviewed all talked about the importance of 'meeting the young person where they are at', building on the understanding that young people have a range of circumstances, needs and ways of coping. There was emphasis placed on forming a dialogical relationship with young people and one that finds common spaces to build connection. Embedded in this is an acknowledgement that young refugee people are diverse and are the experts on their worlds. Several youth workers spoke about the need to perceive them as people rather than collapsing their identities into the problems of their lives, something that can be easily done when faced with the enormity of a young person's refugee experience:

> I really try to be where young people are at and not impose my thoughts about where they should be at this part of their settlement. Every kid is different, some need lots of help with very basic things, and others need a 'friend' – to rebuild human connection. It's really individual. When I meet a young person, I put my agenda away about what I think is going on. I try to listen.

Thus, to youth workers, the strength and quality of the relationship is the dominant factor in creating change in young people's lives. Given the experiences of refugee young people, the establishment of trust required for a successful relationship dynamic is often difficult and takes resolute persistence, patience and time on behalf of the youth worker. In this persistence, the youth worker demonstrates commitment, integrity, consistency and care towards the young person (Beadle 2009: 25). Young participants noted that the introduction phase of the relationship is very important, commenting that the youth workers who are seen as real and authentic often have a willingness to share aspects of their personal self, so that connections are made on a person-to-person level. In this way, the traditional boundaries so often seen as essential in youth work are more 'widespread and encompassing'.

> I went to other services first; the social worker kept calling me a refugee. When I hear that [refugee] I feel like an outcast, like somebody that had nothing. And most of us … we had something but we lost it, but when they use that word you feel worse and I think that's kind of degrading for me. Like you're putting somebody down. When I met my youth worker she was different, she smiled when I walked in. I was feeling frustrated because I had spent two hours on the train going up and down as I couldn't find the office. She walked over to me and introduced herself and said 'welcome'. She made me a coffee, and we talked about the photos on her desk of her family. She told me about herself and her kids and it all just began to feel OK. She told me what she did, and when she would be there. She told me she had worked with other African kids who have had to settle in Australia. I knew then that she would understand.

Building trust is not without its challenges and several workers noted that the young person's reaction to the worker ranged from one of caution and suspicion to one of clinging and extreme dependency. The Victorian Foundation for Survivors of Torture (1998: 132) notes that this caution is often necessary as a self-protective mechanism because intense fear is evoked by the prospect of a new attachment. Renewed loss and rejection are feared. This manifested itself in young people distancing themselves from the youth worker and failing to attend appointments:

> The young person suddenly stopped turning up which surprised me as I thought we were getting somewhere. I suspected it was because we had begun to talk about things that were distressing to her. I sent her a card saying that I hoped she was well, and that I was here for her and was looking forward to seeing her again ... after a few weeks she returned and we were able to continue our work together.

RESPECTFUL LISTENING

Whilst building a relationship recognises diversity among refugee young people, respectful listening was identified as a process that should be engaged in with all young people. However, for young refugees it had an extra dimension when they talked about the stress involved in having to tell their story over and over. Young people stated that positive intervention rested on more than 'helping them fix some problem' it also needed to help them contextualise and understand the Australian environment. Young people appreciated workers who took an active role in helping them learn the new context they found themselves in – this was about explaining and showing how things are done in Australia, but also 'modelling' what it was to be an 'Australian':

> Most workers have no idea what it is like not to have a place to live or to feel so desperate that you have to humiliate yourself in order to receive help. If I don't want to answer some questions, they think of me as 'uncooperative' or 'not ready for help'. How many of them would feel comfortable walking into a stranger's office and telling them that you were abused or do not have enough food today? They think somehow you know this stuff ... like they tell you in the camps or something. The best thing about my youth worker is that she showed me how stuff works here. How you go to places, how you apply for things, how to talk to

people. We call her our Hazara sister, because she is like Hazara but Australian.

Youth workers noted the importance of valuing and caring for the young person, and what I am calling 'deep listening' allowed them to gain a thorough understanding of how to work with them. This listening allows the young person to have as much control as possible. They should be able to say as little as they like, have a role in saying how much contact they want, and importantly, they need to have control over the depth of the relationship (Victorian Foundation for Survivors of Torture 1998: 146). The youth worker needs to ensure there is time to allow any disclosure to be gradual. Deep listening is fundamental to building a relationship and includes understanding and suspension of judgement or evaluation of what is being said:

> I find that most refugee young people I have worked with like to be approached as just an everyday young person, because a lot of the time I think they feel stigmatised or ignored all together. I think this is dehumanising and contributes to a lack of belonging. Alienation characterises so much of the refugee experience for young people. I find that speaking respectfully, no matter what they look like, and like they are a young adult, it helps them feel empowered. It is so easy to give off an attitude of 'you poor thing'. Not only is it degrading but it's also not true. They are way stronger than most of us. I just take my time; they don't need to tell me their story. I just presume they have been to hell and back.
>
> I was working with a 13-year-old girl from the Congo. She was referred as she was crying continually at school. Her mother had died and she was grieving. When we first met we sat outside in the garden. I asked her how she felt and if there was someone similar to a youth worker where she came from. I explained that her reactions were normal and happened when you went through a loss. I explained to her that I too had lost my mum and so had other young people I know as well and we all felt sad not to see them again. She told me that in the Congo there were no youth workers and she would talk to her mum. I explained that her mum wasn't here anymore, but I could listen and I would be here. For the rest of the session we sat quietly and drew.

These youth workers saw it as essential that they critically challenged the power dynamics in their relationships with refugee young people and interrogated the role of expert 'knower' and the authority of professional knowledge, in order to be comfortable with 'not knowing' what is in the best interests of a young person (Sakamoto 2007: 553):

> Sometimes I have no idea if I am doing the right thing. The person sitting with me has lost everything and I feel a heavy burden to 'fix things' for them. Sometimes, I just fess up and tell them I have no idea where to begin, but we can work alongside each other on the problem and surely two heads are better than one ... I tell them they have so much knowledge about their situation and have learnt so much and we can use those skills to help fix the problem at hand.

Consequently one of the most important things to realise when interacting with a young refugee is that every encounter has the potential to promote the restoration of a meaningful connection with another human being. It is the willingness of youth workers to accept the responsibility for a young person's welfare, as communicated to the young person, that is therapeutic (Victorian Foundation for Survivors of Torture 1996: 68).

DEVELOPING TRUST

Working with young people of refugee background requires an understanding of the historical, political and social influences, both past and present, that affect their lives on a daily basis; pre-arrival experiences characterised by exposure to violence and loss, by systematic persecution, by human rights violations or forced displacement. The effects of war and state-sanctioned violence are planned, systematic ways of destroying, not just individuals and families, but whole communities and races, who represent a threat to the government or group seeking control. In the immediate term such experiences shape psychological and social functioning.

Understanding the profound impact of trauma on young people and their families is critical to good practice with young people from refugee backgrounds, with 'the ultimate effects largely dependent on the opportunities to rebuild lives' (Kaplan 2013: 1). The Victorian Foundation for Survivors of Torture (1996: 39) outline four key ways that persecutory regimes destroy individuals, families and communities – creating a state of terror and chronic alarm; the systematic disruption of basic and core attachments to families, friends and religious and cultural systems; the destruction of central values of human existence; and the creation of shame and guilt. Each of these brings about fundamental changes for young people, in their belief systems – about the self, others and the world. Symptoms and behaviours emerge which are disruptive to everyday functioning and quality of life and they perpetuate the impact of traumatic events.

Young people and youth workers spoke about the key aspects they saw as critical to develop trust, these included providing choices, being counted on, predictability and availability, addressing practical problems and respecting and validating young people's stories.

Seven of the young people talked about being 'cared for' as a form of the help they received and which enabled them to build trust. Caring did not involve trying to solve their problems. Rather, caring involved individualised attention, unconditional acceptance, non-judgemental listening and emotional support. Words and phrases that expressed caring included: 'being there for me', 'staying in touch with me', 'letting me make hard decisions but guiding me', 'reaching out to me'. The caring provided young people with a sense of safety, support, understanding and warmth. Young people appeared to value this relationship very highly and many spoke about the connection in terms of 'friendship' and 'kinship':

> We started off friends. She told me I didn't have to talk to her if I didn't want to. It took several times

for me to come here and really talk, to break my heart out to her. I didn't want to see a social worker. I'm not crazy! But everyone needs a friend and that's what she was to me. We went for walks and she told me to talk about whatever I wanted to. And that is what I would tell youth workers to be for their kids.

Ten of the young people spoke about workers who 'talked straight' to them and challenged them, held them accountable for their actions, confronted them with the consequences of decisions and set boundaries and limits. Young people felt that 'sometimes workers look at you with pity like you are vulnerable and a victim'. Young people said they felt comfortable with workers where they did not need to demonstrate and point out their resilience, but it was taken for granted. Young people appreciated youth workers for encouraging them to take personal responsibility by goal setting, planning and achieving, and giving them clear information:

My youth worker ... she gets stuff rolling, she will keep you going, she will make you get stuff done ... it's so helpful because, like, if I was on my own I would just get lazy. I'm tired of dealing with all this shit.

From these interviews, it is apparent that for many young people youth workers were a primary constant in lives filled with change and confusion. Young people clearly valued a personalised relationship between the young person and the youth worker in which the young person can rely on the worker for multiple levels of support. In this relationship the youth worker is emotionally invested, authentic and committed to the welfare of the young person. The youth worker also accepts fluctuations in the young person's behaviour which may include caution, suspicion, clinginess, dependency, 'testing' the worker and anger:

I began working with a youth outreach worker. She's wonderful. You would love her. A cool lady. There was a point where I was shit scared. I kept feeling like she would leave her job or disappear,

so I just stopped going. I was afraid she wouldn't like me. Then I got this card saying that she hoped I was well, and that she was here for me and was looking forward to seeing me again ... after a few weeks I returned and she never pushed me about what happened ... she acted like I had never gone away. Basically I worked with her and she helped me find a flat. When I first met her I was new to Australia and did not know left from right. I was very angry ... I didn't trust her. I didn't trust anyone ... I was sick a lot ... She helped me in many ways. Everytime I do something she tells me she is proud of me and we celebrate. I feel I have really changed and I have her to thank.

ENCOURAGING PARTICIPATION

White and Wyn (2004: 37) note that the exclusion of refugee young people is exacerbated by the fact that refugee young people are 'considered to be outsiders in their new societies' partly through constructions of racial otherness.

Participation therefore can be a vital and powerful ingredient in helping refugee young people change their often very negative image of themselves and in the process can help to raise their self-esteem (Couch 2007). Involving young people actively as participants can help them value themselves as people who are contributing both to their families and wider society. Collective activities may reinforce this positive identity. It is my experience that when refugee young people value themselves more highly there are two important results. Firstly, young people have more energy to tackle some of the problems and issues that settlement raises:

Being involved in the group and meeting other kids was so cool. You know, there is so much shit at home. At night my father drinks. When he came back home, my parents always fight. I never had time for myself and there was nothing else. Here I made some friends and I can go to the night classes. Being part of something else gives me energy to cope with everything else.

Second, they create bonds with other young people. This often leads to young people looking beyond their own immediate needs and playing a significant role in community development activities:

> So when I first came to Australia it was just a very interesting thing to have someone ask you a question and [be] interested in what you have to say. Where I come from if you are young you are supposed to just respect what an adult will tell you. And even raising your opinion could be considered rude so I always just enjoyed in the fact that I could be near be taking part in different groups and saying what I like. I've now been on three advisory groups as a member. I remember the first one, we talked about something, we discussed it, we researched and all and then we saw the results of what we had talked about. So I remember because we had to spend weeks on trying to put down what are the main issues for young multicultural Victorians. And, it was interesting to see at the end of the strategic plan what had actually been driven from those ideas. That it wasn't a waste of time. That the community may benefit.

If a high level of participation can lead to young people seeing themselves as agents of change in communities and societies, then a traditional welfare approach can instil in young people a self-perception that they are powerless and need to be 'rescued'. If programmes work in such a way as to reinforce young people's image of themselves as passive victims of their circumstances and as passive recipients of services, this may actually make them more vulnerable to abuse and exploitation.

The trauma associated with the refugee experience challenges young people's understanding of the meaning and purpose of life and their identity formation can be damaged. When trauma has shattered a young person's sense of the world an important step can be to involve the young person in activities that build trust and identity. There seems to be good reason to believe not only that participation enhances young people's self-esteem and sense of well-being, but it is also a vital ingredient for resilience.

USING STRENGTH-BASED APPROACHES

Refusing a deficit model of practice and emphasising young people's strength and agency should underpin all youth work however this is not always the case. With refugee young people there is a focus on language and cultural attributes as barriers to integration (Williams & Graham 2014: i8). This tendency to problematise language and culture creates deficit assumptions to the neglect of strengths, skills, resilience and agency (2014: i8). Young refugees are often discussed in the context of having settlement barriers to overcome and as somehow being limited by their pre-migration experience (Skrbis & Chimet 2011: 6).

However, on the contrary, most of the young people interviewed spoke about the skills they had learnt prior to arriving in Australia and several youth workers noted how these skills could be used to provide a platform for social integration. In recognising these strengths and attributes, the basic understanding of the refugee experience shifts, with an acknowledgement that despite the adversities experienced within the pre-settlement context, young refugees are, in many ways, well positioned to thrive upon settlement as they are keen to replicate pre-migration networks and deploy existing skill sets.

If we are to view young people through a strength-based lens, then a reframing needs to occur:

> I am trying to step outside the practice of what I call colonial youth work – I need to try and undo whiteness, decolonise my practice. I realise for these young people I am the gatekeeper to so many things – school, housing, social activities. I want to work as an ally in partnership, not as an adult who tells them what to do. I try to recognise at all time[s] how policies and practice affect the young people I work with and within that I try to give them choices. There is such an assumption that young people should conform and assimilate, and adapt to the wider culture ...

When a youth worker works from a strength-based (as opposed to a deficit) model, power is shifted to the young people themselves and they are able to utilise existing skill sets as a starting point for successful settlement. Young people also become active agents in their settlement pathways (Herbert 2005; Morrow 1999), being able to identify what they need:

> I hate when people say 'empower people' because I feel like people are already empowered you don't need to do that for them y'know? Just show them a way of ... They might already have the solutions coz I feel as though people have the solutions to their problems. But they might not know how to go about it and the different systems and different channels to go through so maybe help them along the way ... But I definitely think that if there is a problem – [the community] would have the solution.

Several youth workers spoke about the importance of creating 'space' for network development – not just between refugee young people themselves, but also between young people and the broader community. These capitalise on young people's existing social skills and ability to meet settlement needs through network synergies:

> I was working with a young man from Liberia and he was telling me how when he was living in the camps, he had to rely on groups of other young people as there were so many things you couldn't do alone (like going out bush or hunting). There simply wasn't success if everyone didn't play a role. This young man had great leadership, social and group work skills and he was keen to be involved in community networks. He ended up training as a mentor to work with other young refugees.

Likewise, it was noted that there was an opportunity to build on the practical skills young people bring with them to help with the transitions of migration and the challenges that come along. In their paper, Skrbis and Chimet (2011: 9) describe a young man who is now doing a plumbing apprenticeship and who developed plumbing skills as a means to acquire water in periods of drought:

> No, it was more because when I was back at the camp it was hard to find water and you thirsty and you always see the men, you know, sitting down putting things together and I thought that was amazing how they put the pipes together. I used to watch them and later try it, you know when they not around. Try to get the water from the pipes. So here, now I know the job already very fast.

CONCLUSION

In this chapter young people and youth workers have provided some signposts for future youth work practice with young people of a refugee background. It seems evident that two key components embody this practice – the formation of genuine human relationships which start at a personal level, and engagement in a relationship where hearing and being heard characterise the interaction. Youth work practice with young refugees must also be embedded in a framework that provides youth workers with an approach to practice that is critical, reflexive and transformative at the personal, professional and structural levels.

This is a practice in which linkages are continuously being made between the personal struggles of a refugee young person and the theories, policy and practice, so that youth workers understand the ethical dilemmas and contradictions that are embedded in everyday youth work practice with young refugees. It therefore requires foresight and commitment to ensure that refugee young people are given the opportunity to realise their full potential. Indeed, history has shown us the incredible contribution that migrants from refugee backgrounds can make to our societies. Crucial to a refugee successfully resettling in a new country is their having the opportunity to regain their sense of power or control over life – regaining a sense of self-worth and purpose.

Having already demonstrated resilience and resourcefulness in the face of enormous difficulties, it would be a substantial loss to society if refugee young people were not

given the opportunities to apply their determination and skills in their new home. Whilst
traditional interventions have focused on
enabling the individual to deal with their
immediate crisis in order to heal, and to be
able to function in and contribute to society,
the youth work relationship actively engages
with the young person and their communities.
Whilst there is no 'one-size-fits-all' model
for the support of refugee young people,
implementation of participatory, strength-
based approaches will ensure that the emphasis remains on the empowerment of young
people and on helping them build lives that
are based on self-reliance and dignity.

Notes

1 This applies to those young people, aged 12–25,
   who settle in Australia through the Refugee and
   Humanitarian Programme or through the broader
   migration programme (e.g. skilled or family
   migration) and hold a permanent resident visa
   (Centre for Multicultural Youth 2014).
2 Whilst resettlement is a challenge for all new
   arrivals, the resettlement needs of young people
   are different to those of adults because of the
   particular life stage of adolescence. Like all young
   people, young refugees between the ages of 12
   and 25 years have hopes and aspirations for their
   future; are defining their personal identity and
   forming relationships outside their family; and are
   laying the foundations for the lives they will live
   as adults. These developmental tasks are compounded by cultural dislocation, loss of established social networks and the practical demands
   of the resettlement process, as well as, for young
   people from refugee backgrounds, the traumatic
   nature of the refugee experience (Centre for Multicultural Youth 2011: 2).
      Young refugees' resettlement experience
   often involves them confronting a number of barriers. Newly arrived and emerging communities
   are often at risk due to limited family and social
   support and because existing support within their
   communities is less developed and has minimal
   infrastructure. Due to the impact of state-sanctioned violence that young people from refugee
   backgrounds may have witnessed or experienced,
   many are suspicious of government authorities or
   those perceived to be in authority roles.
3 Australia also has a national peak body on multicultural youth issues – MYAN which has recently

developed a national youth settlement framework. The MYAN works in partnership with
young people, government and non-government
agencies at the state and national levels to support a consistent approach to addressing the
unique needs of multicultural young people in
policy and practice. The MYAN works across the
youth and settlement sectors because it is at the
intersection of these sectors that good settlement
outcomes for young people are achieved. The
MYAN has representatives from each of Australia's states and territories and facilitates a national
approach to youth settlement through its affiliated state/territory-based organisations/networks
(MYAN 2016: 6). The Australian Government
also provides a range of services to support the
settlement process at the Commonwealth and
state levels, acknowledging the importance of
targeted support for new arrivals. At the Commonwealth level, these services include pre-
arrival training, Humanitarian Settlement Services
to support eligible arrivals in the first six months
of settlement, and Settlement Services and Complex Case Support for support beyond the first six
months, as well as English-language support and
translating and interpreting services. Youth workers are involved at all these stages.

REFERENCES

Beadle, S. (2009) 'Complex solutions for com-
plex needs: towards holistic and collabora-
tive practice', *Youth Studies Australia*, 28(1):
21–28.
Bryman, A. (2001) *Social Research Methods*.
Oxford, Oxford University Press, UK.
Casimiro, S., Hancock, P. & Northcote, J. (2007)
'Isolation and insecurity: resettlement issues
among Muslim refugee women in Perth,
Western Australia', *Australian Journal of
Social Issues*, 42(1): 55–71.
Castles, S., Korac, M., Vasta E. & Vertovec, S.
(2002) *Integration: Mapping the Field*
(Report for the Home Office Immigration
Research and Statistics Service) London.
Centre for Multicultural Youth (2011) *Good
Practice Guide: Youth Work with Young
People for Refugee and Migrant Back-
grounds*. Carlton, Victoria.
Centre for Multicultural Youth (2014) *The
CALD Youth Census Report 2014: The First
Australian Census Data Analysis of Young*

People from Culturally and Linguistically Diverse Backgrounds. Carlton, Victoria.

Checkoway, B. (1998) 'Involving young people in neighbourhood development', *Children and Youth Services Review*, 20(9/10): 765–795.

Couch, J. (2007) 'Mind the gap: considering the participation of refugee young people', *Youth Studies Australia*, 26(4): 37–44.

Couch, J. (2011) 'A new way home: refugee young people and homelessness in Australia', *Journal of Social Inclusion*, 1(2): 39–52.

Coventry, L., Guerra, C., Mackenzie, D. & Pinkney, S. (2002) *Wealth of All Nations: Identification of Strategies to Assist Refugee Young People in transition to Independence – a Report to the National Youth Affairs Research Scheme*. Australian Clearing House for Youth Studies, Hobart.

Hanson-Easey, S. & Augoustinos, M. (2011) 'Complaining about humanitarian refugees: the role of sympathy talk in the design of complaints on talk-back radio', *Discourse & Communication*, 5(3): 247–271.

Hart, J. & Tyrer, B. (2006) *Research with Children Living in Situations of Armed Conflict: Concepts, Ethics and Methods*, RSC Working Paper No. 30, Queen Elizabeth House, Department of International Development, University of Oxford, Oxford.

Herbert, Y. (2005) 'Transculturalism among Canadian youth: focus on strategic competence and social capital', in Hoerder, D., Herbert, Y. & Schmitt, I. (eds) *Negotiating Transcultural Lives: Belonging and Social Capital among Youth in Comparative Perspective*. V & R Unipress, Germany, pp. 103–128.

Kaplan, I. (2013) 'Trauma, development and the refugee experience: the value of an integrated approach to practice and research', in De Gioia, K. & Whiteman, P. (eds) *Children and Childhoods 3: Immigrant and Refugee Families*. Cambridge Scholars Publishing, Newcastle on Tyne, pp. 1–23.

Lupton, D. (1999) *Risk*. Routledge, New York.

McKay, F.H., Thomas, S.L. & Blood, R.W. (2011) '"Any one of these boatpeople could be a terrorist for all we know!" Media representations and public perceptions of "boat people" arrivals in Australia', *Journalism: Theory, Practice and Criticism*, 12(5): 607–626.

Martin, L. (2003) *The Invisible Table*, Thomson Dunmore Press, South Melbourne.

Mitchell, J., Kaplan, I. & Crowe, L. (2006) 'Two cultures: one life', *Community Development Journal*, 42(3): 282–298.

Morrow, V. (1999) 'Conceptualising social capital in relation to the well-being of children and young people: a critical review', *Sociological Review*, 47(4): 744–765.

Multicultural Youth Advocacy Network (MYAN) (2016) *National Youth Settlement Framework*, Centre for Multicultural Youth, Melbourne.

Ogilvie, S. & Lynch, M. (1999) 'A culture of resistance: adolescents in detention', in White, R. (ed.) *Australian Youth Subcultures: On the Margins and in the Mainstream*. Australian Clearinghouse for Youth Studies, Hobart, pp. 148–158.

Olliff, L. (2004) *Pathways and Pitfalls: The Journey of Refugee Young People In and Around the Education System in Greater Dandenong*. Centre for Multicultural Youth Issues/South East Local Learning Network, Carlton.

Parker, S. (2015) '"Unwanted invaders": the representation of refugees and asylum seekers in the UK and Australian print media', *Myth and Nation*, 23: 1–21.

Pickering, S. (2001) 'Common sense and original deviancy: news discourses and asylum seekers in Australia', *Journal of Refugee Studies*, 14(2): 169–186.

Robinson, K. (2014) 'Voices from the front line: social work with refugees and asylum seekers in Australia and the UK', *British Journal of Social Work*, 44(6): 1602–1620.

Rodd, H. & Stewart, H. (2009) 'The glue that holds our work together: the role and nature of relationships in youth work', *Youth Studies Australia*, 28(4): 4–10.

Sakamoto, I. (2007) 'A critical examination of immigrant acculturation: toward an anti-oppressive social work model with immigrant adults in a pluralistic society', *British Journal of Social Work*, 37(3): 515–535.

Sercombe, H. (2007) 'Embedded youth work: ethical questions for youth work professionals', *Youth Studies Australia*, 26(2): 4–10: 11–19.

Skribis, Z. & Chiment, M. (2011) 'Reframing the "refugee experience": the case of African youth in Brisbane', Refereed Conference Proceedings, Local Lives/Global Networks: The Annual Conference of the Australian Sociological Association, Newcastle, Australia.

Victorian Foundation for Survivors of Torture (1996) *A Guide to Working with Young People Who Are Refugees*, Parkville, Victoria.

Victorian Foundation for Survivors of Torture (1998) *Rebuilding Shattered Lives*, Parkville, Victoria.

Valtonen, K. (2004) 'From the margin to the mainstream: conceptualising refugee resettlement processes', *Journal of Refugee Studies*, 17(1): 70–96.

White, R. & Wyn, J. (2004) *Youth and Society*. Oxford University Press, South Melbourne.

Williams, C. & Graham, M. (2014) 'Editorial: "A world on the move": migration, motilities and social work', *British Journal of Social Work*, 44(supplement 1): i1–i17.

Young, K. (1999) *The Art of Youth Work*. Russell House Publishing, London.

17

Screaming Aloud from da Old Plantation Down-under: Youth Work on the Margins in Aotearoa New Zealand

Fiona Beals, Peter-Clinton Foaese, Martini Miller, Helen Perkins and Natalie Sargent

It's just my savage instincts coming back from the brink
Revitalise the knowledge that we lost (you better think)
Culture ebbing's being lost in the ignorance from the ma to the pa to the child
Wonder why your child is running round real wild?
Pass on the knowledge so the tongue leaves its cradle
Or take them back home to the motherland and teach
The ways of our elders, lifestyles and the speech.
(King Kapisi, 2000)

INTRODUCTION

Aotearoa New Zealand (Aotearoa)[1] is geographically isolated in the Southern Pacific Ocean. Sitting in isolation allows for distinctive voices and practices. One such voice is King Kapisi, a hip hop artist of both Aotearoa and Samoan roots. King Kapisi's rap 'Screems from da Old Plantation' (from which the title of this chapter is derived) captures the essence of the margins of Aotearoa, youth work practice and our indigenous/Pasifika[2] youth.

This chapter screams aloud from a history of colonisation. There are stories to be told, there are stories to be heard.

Youth work practice in Aotearoa involves anyone working professionally (even as a volunteer) with young people aged between 12 and 24 (King, 2015a, 2015b; Martin, 2006). This work spans all facets of Aotearoa's social sector: education, welfare, justice, health, community development, cultural development and faith-based settings. Job titles vary to reflect the setting, and while some workers have experience and no qualifications, others have a certificate or diploma in youth work, a non-associated degree or a formal degree in youth development work. Some will work for organisations funded through external sources (such as faith-based organisations), others work for organisations funded through a variety of government funding mechanisms. The diversity of the sector reflects a sector developing and moving toward professionalisation.[3] Within the sector there is one set of words which brings the profession together: 'youth development practice', a form of professional practice drawn from principles of positive youth development and embedded into a formal strategy, *The Youth Development Strategy Aotearoa* (Ministry of Youth Affairs, 2002), or the YDSA.

For many practitioners, the YDSA (Ministry of Youth Affairs, 2002) has the stance of a revered text; those that follow it can cite the key positive youth development principles found in the Strategy by heart and describe the evidence of these principles in their practice. Despite the YDSA now being over ten years old, the youth sector in Aotearoa continues to see it as an essential and foundational document to their practice (King, 2015a, 2015b) simply due to its emphasis on positive youth development. But, here is where a theoretical difference exists. When the YDSA was created, another strategy emerged with a different purpose. The Youth Offending Strategy (Ministry of Justice & Ministry of Social Development, 2002) aimed to intervene early into the lives of youth deemed 'at risk'[4] of criminal outcomes; positive youth development does not feature. The difference between the two Strategies symbolised a tension found within the sector. The strategy embraced by youth workers enabling them to define their practice is the YDSA; other strategies, created at the same time and since then, require youth workers to intervene into the lives of 'at-risk' or 'vulnerable' youth (Beals, 2008); one embraces the positive while the other is concerned with the negative. The tension that youth development workers find themselves in is historically located in the myths that make Aotearoa New Zealand and in the awkward assumption that western theories and approaches can be applied universally.

This chapter explores the tension that exists within the landscape and history of a colonised country and the theories that inform strategies such as the YDSA. Through the use of vignettes, this chapter provides explicit examples of youth workers working within

the dominant global paradigm of youth development practice while pushing at the edges of this paradigm, reading and re-writing it (Freire, 1993). Each vignette is very different, providing a taster into the transformation of practice through theory. Foaese explores how his practice has become one of storytelling, Sargent takes a sociological approach to push the boundaries of society in addressing inequality, Perkins shows how learning indigenous history can change the practice of a girl from Essex (UK), and Miller finishes with a model of practice which brings together theory, experience and the environment. All of these vignettes address three key questions:

1 What happens to your understanding of your own youth development practice when you apply an historical and sociological reading to it?
2 How can the work of Paulo Freire (1993, 1994) inform and improve youth development practice in Aotearoa?
3 What insights for improving practice can the reflections of five youth work practitioners offer?

This chapter argues that youth development practice needs to be informed by history, theory and a sociological re-writing of the world though stories and the breaking of myths, posed as truths. One way this can occur is through the ideas of Freire (1993, 1994). Freire explored how unspoken techniques of oppression have enabled the dominant powerful ruling class (or group) to subjugate others (the oppressed). Freire argued that only the oppressed could free themselves through a critical reading, questioning and re-writing of the causes of their oppression. This chapter will argue that, in the story of Aotearoa's colonialisation, the ideas of Freire have a justifiable use in the context of youth development work. As demonstrated in the vignettes in this chapter, when youth workers move outside of a singular knowledge of positive youth development to engage with complex theories, in the context of their practical work, a space for change opens and the silent stories begin to be spoken and heard.

AOTEAROA: A LAND OF 'TWO' PEOPLES BUT ONE STYLE OF YOUTH DEVELOPMENT

Aotearoa is a country of two predominant groups – the 'us'/'we' and the 'them'/'other' (cf. Smith, 2002). The 'us'/'we' group is the reference group to all things 'normal' within broader dominant discourse. This group tends to be middle-class Pākehā (of European origin, including British). The 'them'/'other' group reflects our Pasifika, Asian and refugee/migrant populations.[5] It also includes our indigenous population, the Māori people. Within these two groups, Aotearoa's population is changing. According to research from Tahu Kukukai (2013), the 'us'/'we' population are having fewer children and will gradually move into a minority grouping. Conversely, Māori and Pasifika communities are growing.[6] Kukukai argues that the population groups that are growing are the marginal groups who feature heavily in statistics of disadvantage. These are the youth that many youth development practitioners are required to work with in order to address their 'at risk' or 'vulnerable' status. So what do they do?

Practitioners describe the style of youth development in Aotearoa as a western approach with indigenous flavours (Baxter, Caddie, & Cameron, 2016). The western approach is found within the positive youth development focus of the YDSA and the theories that support it (e.g. Bronfenbrenner, 1979; Harms, 2010; Hart, 1997; Lerner et al., 2012). These theories are brought into an Aotearoa context with Mason Durie's (1998) Te Whare Tapa Whā (house of four walls) to focus on the holistic (physical/psychological/spiritual/family) development of the individual youth. This is then put into practice through a Native American approach known

as the Circle of Courage (Brendtro & du Toit, 2005). Using the Indian Medicine wheel, the Circle of Courage encourages practitioners to draw upon aspects of belonging, independence, mastery and generosity when working with youth.

Using the YDSA as a driver for evidence-informed practice in Aotearoa, means that youth development workers focus on building developmental strengths within young people. Issues are seen solely through a developmental lens, with the idea that issues can only be addressed through identifying strengths and countering the issue through strengths alone. Despite the practical use of indigenous frameworks and models, this theoretical approach is inherently ethnocentric towards a European/North American (western) concept of what determines healthy youth development (Beals, 2015).

Rather than restricting theoretical understandings of the issues facing youth to developmental theories alone, some youth development workers have begun using a sociological lens to move the problem/issue from the individual youth to the social context surrounding young people in general and in specific demographic groups. Given that Aotearoa's demographic population is changing, and that the largest growing groups are the marginalised 'others', the answer to many of Aoteaora's issues of inequality may come through the work of Freire (1993) and the field of sociology. This is what a critical approach to youth work can achieve; youth workers actively reading their world, the world of Aotearoa, to search for the myths that underpin the ideas that they carry, and engaging in processes of transformation and change.

AOTEAROA: FOUNDED UPON COLONIAL MYTHS

The OECD (2011) notes factors such as globalisation, technological developments and political systems as drivers of inequality within and between countries. Out of all these factors, the political system can either create a fertile space for inequality to flourish or counter the effects of inequality through controlling the influence of globalisation and technological development (OECD, 2011). One factor that is overlooked by the OECD is colonisation. Many of the global relationships between countries were historically put into place through processes of colonisation. Colonisation both stimulated the relationship between countries and established practices of hegemony to protect colonising interests (Consedine & Consedine, 2012). Policies of assimilation put into effect a 'survival of the fittest' model of economic development establishing indigenous peoples as savage and needing to attain a civilised status. This same reasoning informed early theories of youth development (Beals, 2013, 2015; Lesko, 2001).

Aotearoa's historical links to British colonisation enabled our contemporary myths of a 'unique' national identity to flourish; myths that need uncovering to find the truth. Since schooling started in Aotearoa in the 1800s, British history has dominated the history curriculum; the history of New Zealand was, and still is, optional for schools (Consedine & Consedine, 2012). This is where the myths flourish. Many Pākehā find their identity in links back to the myth that England chose to make Aotearoa a colony to make up for the mistakes of Australia by populating it with their finest citizens. In truth, the early settlements did not bring the 'elite' but instead brought working-class peoples hoping for a new start (Simpson, 1997). For many Pākehā and Māori, Te Tiriti o Waitangi (the Treaty of Waitangi) is a unique document which makes the nation different. Te Tiriti established a relationship between the British Crown and the Māori people. While the translations would allow different interpretations, in the Māori version, the Crown promised protection of all rights, including the right to self-determination. Again, a myth exists

in the belief that such a treaty was unique; treaties (even ones written in the style of Te Tiriti) were common throughout the Commonwealth (Indian and Northern Affairs Canada, 2010; Inyang & Bassey, 2014). One of Aotearoa's greatest myths is that the country has healthy race relations (Consedine & Consedine, 2012). Instead, policies have discriminated against Māori, while the urban drift of Māori (and Pasifika peoples) into cities since the 1950s has ignited racial tensions which continue today (Anae et al., 2006; Consedine & Consedine, 2012).

The myths of equity, equality and harmony that dominate New Zealand's psyche also underpin the YDSA. It is naturally assumed within the principles of the strategy that there is a distinctive harmony in Aotearoa – there is no racial/class/gender tension here. There is an assumption that all young people have the same conditions, so are able to naturally make the 'right' choices. Hence, only a mixture of strengths-based practice and indigenous techniques are needed. So how can youth development practitioners become more reflexive and critically conscious in their practice?

Freire (1993) argues that the first step in conscientisation (loosely translated as consciousness-raising) is uncovering the historical moments of oppression buried in myths. This step is essential in critical youth development practice. The principles underpinning developmental psychology have a long tail of history stemming back to the work of Granville Stanley Hall (1908). Hall's theory continues to permeate theories of youth development today (Lesko, 2001), especially the repetition of the conclusion that while youth are equal in age and stage, some youth would struggle through adolescence to the civilised stage of adulthood, while others would remain caught in their savage nature of childhood.

In Aotearoa, policy- and strategy-makers often frame young people from Māori and Pasifika backgrounds as trapped in the social and psychological conditions of their childhood (Beals, 2008). While youth in these communities experience the greatest inequalities, with informed critical practice they do also have the ability to transform their circumstances. Learning the history of youth development theory and how particular social groups were written 'out of the theory' makes it is essential for this re-writing to occur. Take for example, the reflections of Peter-Clinton Foaese. Foaese has had many years of experience in supporting youth in political participation processes. He now works with youth from ethnic gang families and uses Freire's work to enable young people to rewrite their world.

NAVIGATING THE WATERS OF THEORY AND PRACTICE: PETER-CLINTON FOAESE

It is accepted in academic circles that Tangata Pasifika (the Peoples of the Pacific) are descendants of the greatest sea navigators in history. Early European settlers such as Abel Tasman and James Cook were amazed at the variety of sea vessels used by Tangata Pasifika. Louis Antoine de Bougainville who named Samoa the 'Navigator Islands' was in awe of their ability to navigate the whole of the Pacific Ocean. This is the history of our people, stories of innovation, trade and diplomacy stretching across a space larger than the biggest land mass in the world. Through culture and language, generation after generation accomplished the greatest sea voyages and exploration. Through heritage and custom, art and science was passed down to ensure communities would thrive in ocean climates in which 'civilised' nations could not survive. Now, government statistics indicate that Pasifika youth are at risk of negative outcomes and must be 'fixed' so that they can be resilient navigators of their future; a contradiction to their past. Even their history is not spoken in the classroom.

Pasifika youth are bombarded with statistics and the stories of failure for their people. Education is shown to be the only path for Pasifika youth to fix their community. Success is an independent journey of perseverance. The student is to blame if they do not achieve. For years, I bought into this frame of thought. I strived with Pasifika youth to do better in the classroom. If they failed we would try harder. If failure continued, then they were doing something wrong. I adopted this approach because traditional youth development theories emphasised empowering youth and providing them with resources to overcome challenges through strengths-based approaches. When working with young Pākehā, this approach works to achieve the desired outcome. When working with marginalised young people, those young people whose identities and cultures are absent in the stories used by the system, the pathway to success is all but impossible. Simply put, the system is rigged against them.

Culture is a story passed through generations moulding customs, beliefs and social structures. It is a living story shared by a group of people. In formal education spaces, the story that is intertwined with the curriculum is the European story. To achieve in these spaces, students must interact with, and accept, European culture through composers, historians, educators and authors. Cut off from their own experience of the world, Pasifika students quickly become apathetic to learning or worse, defiant. Freire (1993) portrays this well through his work where the student has lost power and is not able to interact positively with their learning because they are alienated by the system. The stories are not theirs; the learning feels more like brainwashing. This is not far from the truth if we recognise the objective of education, socialisation and industrialisation found in Hall's (1908) work. Hall's reasoning continues to be present, Pasifika young people are made to conform to 'civilised' society through their education, and youth workers (with good intentions) strive with at-risk Pasifika youth to align them with the status quo so that they can achieve according to the standards of the dominant cultural story.

For years, I witnessed talented and intelligent young Pasifika fail in the system, gifted in many areas but disengaged from formal education. Freire (1993) revolutionised my understanding by highlighting the real issue Pasifika youth encounter as a minority. It is impossible for young people to be empowered if they do not exist in the story. As a youth worker, I have become more vigilant in supporting young people to live their story and learn from it, encouraging them to write the world as they saw it and read stories that reflected them. I recognise my own job as a change agent, to see how the system alienates youth, and to make change meant supporting young people to use their own experiences to change it. Pasifika youth will continue to fail in a system that is not reflective of their experiences and stories, youth workers must be willing to acknowledge that at-risk youth are really just alienated youth. We have the ability to create environments for those youth to hear and appreciate their own stories. In my own practice, I have begun creating spaces and forums in schools and the community for Pasifika youth to reconnect with our history as navigators. From this, the youth have recognised the value of their stories which has grown their appreciation of other people's stories. The stories are already there. They are alive, and have been alive for centuries, it is our job as youth workers to create spaces for them to be heard and taught.

Alongside the potential stigmatising effects of developmental theory, there is a need to explore the history of oppression and the political practices that occur within a society that enables inequalities to be maintained. In Aotearoa, all youth development training covers the history of colonisation and the place of Te Tiriti (Baxter et al., 2016). The critical exploration of oppression in Aotearoa is not a requirement. When it does occur, it tends to be through a sociological understanding of inequality and deviance. For example, through using maps of local areas and exploring where youth 'issues' cluster in suburbs and towns, youth workers are able to see the boundaries of inequality and how the strain on individuals/families can create limiting situations within geographical boundaries. At these boundaries youth workers can work with marginalised youth to re-write their stories.

Robert Merton's (1994) concept of strain makes it possible to develop an understanding of societal goals and the unequal distribution of resources, and, hence, the limited access to goals for marginalised groups. It is the role of the youth worker to push at the boundaries of success through engaging in practices of innovation and, at times, rebellion to enable the writing of new goals reflecting the aspirations of the youth's culture. Such 'rebellion' is not an outright breaking of social rules, but a questioning of the hidden curriculum that sits within most youth development practice – to socialise and enable a young person to grow into a healthy contributing tax-payer (Jeffs & Banks, 2010). Such rebellion requires the type of reflexivity

that Phil Mizen (2010) calls for in practice where obstacles to resources are reflected on as opportunities to redefine, re-work and bring about social justice.

'Rebellion' may not, therefore, be an outward action of resistance, but rather an inner reflexive attitude of the youth worker, when they know and remain deeply conscious of the agenda of the system in which they are embedded, while actively seeking to empower young people and their communities to see a better world, a different way of thinking. An example of this comes from the practice of Natalie Sargent. Working at the edge of theories such as Merton's (1994) to enable young people to innovate and even challenge the status quo, Sargent's work focuses on empowering youth in community; working with young people and their elders to facilitate change and bring mana (esteem) back into the community (even within the constraints of wider society). This often involves subversive practices of youth work which prioritise community needs first while talking the language that funders need to hear.

A SMALL TOWN GIRL HITS THE AUSSIE OUTBACK: NATALIE SARGENT

I was raised in the 1980s in a small rural community in Aotearoa and was oblivious to the 'us and them' divide within Aotearoa and the world. In my world, I had the same opportunities as my Māori whanau and friends. There was no distinction between ethnicity, we were all one. This belief was soon to evaporate as I left my little community in Aotearoa and headed overseas.

While working overseas with youth, I soon became aware of the 'us and them' concept. Uncomfortable with the injustices I witnessed, I made a conscious effort to rectify what was happening, because in my mind 'we are all one'. I did this by using the sway I held to empower the youth to stand up for their rights within the system that surrounded us. This often meant thinking 'outside the box' and playing the 'system' at its own game.

My passion for working with youth led me to the outback of Australia and working in remote Aboriginal communities as a youth worker. Along with the pressures and labels that society placed on these youth, they were also subject to many injustices because of their ethnicity. I was once told that aboriginal youth had difficulties in reading, my reply was 'In what context?' Because when we are out bush, the youth are able to look at their surroundings and tell me what tracks belonged to what animals and how old the tracks were and so forth. They were able to read their surroundings extremely well; I couldn't do this reading of the land. These types of experiences gave me the drive to right the wrong. I began to focus on building young people's confidence so they could stand up for themselves and not let the pressures and labels placed upon them dictate their futures.

I realised that times were changing and a 'piece of paper' (qualification) was becoming increasingly important. Not being one for conforming to society's ideologies, I struggled with the decision to return to education. The time had come for me to conform, for a qualification would give me a stronger stance in empowering youth and giving them the opportunity to re-write their worlds. It was during my studies that I was introduced to Merton's (1994) strain theory as a reason for innovative practice, a reason to challenge social goals, because only some people had access to these goals; others did not. I was instantly drawn to this theory, being innovative and looking 'outside the box' are key principles for my youth work practice.

When I returned to Aotearoa, I was given the opportunity to work with youth in an alternative education setting. When I saw the high representation of Māori youth in alternative education and I saw the other undesirable statistics for our Māori youth, my belief that 'we are all one in Aotearoa' evaporated. The realisation that in my own country, Aotearoa, there is an 'us' and 'them' and all is not equal has strengthened my resolve to empower youth.

Witnessing the injustices experienced by marginalised youth has formed the blueprint of my youth work practice. As a youth worker, my role is to empower youth, enabling them to build courage and confidence. In my practice, innovation is central. At times, this can be seen as putting the goals of the community ahead of the so-called goals of the system; the goals focused on in funding. Funding goals are often around controlling youth and stopping them entering into negative behaviours, making them docile to the fact that the system marginalises them. A focus on funding

goals denies any young person a chance for genuine success. Small actions of innovation and rebellion give youth opportunities to push at the boundaries of society. Young people need to be given a space to challenge the rules and change the goals in order to create their own future. This has become my driving passion in youth work. I believe that, ultimately, by doing this, we as youth workers can contribute to closing the gap between the minority and majority, working towards equality for all.

Te Tiriti is described as a unique feature of youth development practice in Aotearoa, enabling a partnership between Pākehā and indigenous forms of theory and practice (Baxter et al., 2016). It is this acknowledgement of Te Tiriti, rather than the existence of the YDSA, which permits the myths of equity, equality and harmony to be explored and addressed. This is exemplified in the Code of Ethics for youth workers (Ara Taiohi, 2011), which grounds all youth work in Aotearoa in Te Tiriti and traditional indigenous youth development practices. Understanding the position of Te Tiriti helps build the foundational relationship to enable change and address contemporary inequalities. When engaged with at a critical level, Te Tiriti brings together action, theory and reflection. It enables a form of praxis to occur in one's own practice.

Te Tiriti is so central to the sector that youth workers coming to Aotearoa from other cultural contexts may struggle with understanding why it is seen as so important. Helen Perkins worked in the United Kingdom as a youth worker before moving to Aotearoa. Here, she found herself having to learn another story and set of practices. She now works with young mothers in Aotearoa. Her appreciation for Treaty-centred youth development is central to her work with youth.

JUST A GIRL FROM ESSEX LIVING DOWN-UNDER: HELEN PERKINS

Prior to moving to Aotearoa I can honestly say that I knew nothing about Te Tiriti o Waitangi. It was *never part of my work with youth in England. Before deciding to move to Aotearoa, I had been working in England as a youth worker for years, completing training on the job and working both in volunteer positions and paid employment in many different youth work projects. After emigrating to Aotearoa, my experiences have increased my awareness of people and what life offers. It has opened my world to a greater understanding of cultures, in particular Māori and Pasifika, and built my knowledge and awareness both personally and professionally.*

I have been privileged to have many learning experiences here in Aotearoa with Te Tiriti o Waitangi through quality relationships with people and educational opportunities to learn about Te Ao Māori (Māori worldview; the world of the Māori). I feel that as my life settled here in Aotearoa, my knowledge and understanding of Te Tiriti o Waitangi enabled me to build stronger connections and relationships, not only with the young people I work with but also the wider community. This journey has been one of huge learning, especially about the impact of colonisation on Māori, which continues today. Through this learning, I can now walk alongside young people in their own journey of cultural identity and finding their place in the world.

My role as a youth worker allows me to continue learning, building self-awareness, understanding and a respect for the diversity of this country. This knowledge is important when you have to work in collaboration with others. I am able to now work with young people's whole whnau (close and extended family), involving them in planning and decision-making, and thereby encouraging Māori youth to take control of their own development and well-being.

The cultural and socio-economic influences obviously differ compared to those of the young people in the UK, so adjusting to ways of practising youth work in Aotearoa requires different activities and approaches to those I would have used in England. However, there are lessons that I would take back, particularly around cultural self-awareness and building strong connections. It is important that all youth workers and young people build self-awareness and understanding about their own cultures in order for them to be open to learn about other cultures. Knowing the beliefs and values of young people to help protect their identity and where they have come from is central to this; just as I had to learn Te Ao Māori, it is important to learn the worlds of others. We are able to do this through creating opportunities which enable young people to help others build understanding and respect for ethnic and cultural

diversity. This is often within a variety of cultural settings and involves learning about each other's collective histories and personal stories.

Finally, youth workers need to build strong connections and engage in collaborative work with other services to enable young people to be connected to appropriate cultural services and youth workers. Connecting and collaborating provides opportunities to involve young people and their families in the planning and decision-making for their future. Allowing others to be involved who have cultural connections can better support a young person, both in their development and understanding of their place within the world.

The aim of fusing Freirian critical pedagogy and broader sociological thinking (such as is found in various collected writings (e.g. Calhoun, Gerteis, Moody, Pfaff, & Virk, 2012; Giddens & Sutton, 2010)) into the practice of youth work in Aotearoa allows for new models of practice to be developed, reflecting moments of conscientisation of oneself in practice and of the praxis needed for change. By limiting the YDSA to a sacred text which defines and confines all practice, there is a risk of seeing youth development myopically.

While Freire (1993) is famous for his seminal work on oppression, he reflected on his work later in *The Pedagogy of Hope* (Freire, 1994). Freire noted that the drive behind his first work and his practice was hope. All practice, whether youth development or community development needs to be grounded in hope, and finding hope in the spaces of struggle and marginalisation is crucial for change.

In this final vignette, Martini Miller outlines the development of his unique model of youth development based on place-based education, *whakapapa* (an acknowledgement of your historical connections to people, deities, sea and stars (Warbrick, Dickson, Prince, & Heke, 2016)) and experiential learning. Echoing Freire's reflection on his own work, Miller's model of practice came out of the hope and desperation of a moment of struggle. Miller demonstrates the invaluable role of reflexive reflection, a deep ability to reflect on oneself in the moment and push at the boundaries to create a new story. While his model is distinctly unique to his life story, it demonstrates the need to re-remember the stories behind traditional western theories of development. It also demonstrates how western models of thinking, such as Kolb's cycle of reflection, can be used in an indigenous space of making meaning. It is not about replacing western theory, but knowing where these theories sit within our wider practice stories.

LEARNING TO EMBODY THEORY IN PRACTICE: MARTINI MILLER

I came to be involved in Aotearoa's youth sector shortly after going through a 'cataclysmic' lifestyle shift where I shed my 'challenged youth' typecast, consequently breaking a generational cycle of drug abuse and poor health outcomes. After this experience, I volunteered with a children's holiday programme and discovered the joys of working with people. I began to put into practice the adage that 'the best way to help yourself is to help others'.

As a proponent of learning from my mistakes and viewing them as opportunities for growth, I was drawn to experiential learning theory (Kolb, 1984). Discovering how to implement this knowledge into my own model of practice allowed me to take this knowledge and be able to apply it to a youth development context in a way that was relevant to me and my identity. Growing up, I was fascinated with myths and legends and spent a considerable amount of time reading the tales of other cultures. I had been exposed to Māori myths and legends as a child but it was not until much later that I understood how much the Māori worldview aligned with my own perspective.

My Māori ancestors utilised natural phenomena as mnemonic devices to store complex information. I have continued this tradition with my model, drawing upon the bi-cultural heritage bestowed upon me by my Māori father and European mother to understand my own practice. Through my existence in both worlds, I created a model where western and indigenous paradigms combined to form what Bhabha (1994) referred to as a 'cultural hybridity'.

Entitled Te Wāhi Akotanga 'The place of learning' (Miller, 2014), my model of practice is the result of my own introspective analysis of my practice interpreted through the juxtaposition of Kolb's (1984) experiential learning cycle with the natural setting of my childhood home, Te Wai Pounamu/ the South Island of Aotearoa (Figure 17.1). Joanna Kidman (2012) wrote of the significance of local places as 'cultural incubators' and explored their role in identity formation in an Aotearoa context. As such, the setting I have chosen accurately reflects my cultural identity as a Māori raised in the same mountains as my European and Māori ancestors.

The Southern Alps featured heavily in my formative years and played a role in my lifestyle shift. During a severe period of self-destructive drug abuse, I hit a wall and chose these mountains as the setting for a personal transformation. While there were many challenging moments, I did not miraculously emerge from my time in the mountains with an enlightened view of what I wanted to do with my life. Frustrated and determined to find something of value within my experience, I began a period of intense introspection, musing deeply on the events leading up to and following this event. Kolb (1984) refers to the stage immediately after concrete experience as reflective observation, an unconscious process that, through emphasis, is able to be observed and actively encouraged. I sought to encapsulate this learning within my model.

However, perhaps the most important aspect of my model is not mentioned; the perspective from which it is perceived, from the ocean, looking backwards, towards the mountains. Pre-colonisation Māori viewed the passage of time in a manner far removed from the western understanding, best captured in the traditional whakataukī proverb 'Kia whakatomuri te haere whakamua' – 'I walk backwards into the future with my eyes fixed on the past'. The image of a person walking backwards, blindly into the future, invokes a humility, acknowledging that mistakes and failure can occur, while showing that it is possible to learn from these experiences to better prepare yourself better for the future.

CONCLUSION: WHAT LESSONS CAN AOTEAROA GIVE?

In Aotearoa, the myths of equity, equality and harmony that we hold regarding our status as a country and our youth development practice can limit, and, at worst, distort the story we tell the world about our practice. All countries have the same binaries as Aotearoa, the 'us'/'we' and 'them'/'other'. These groupings have existed throughout

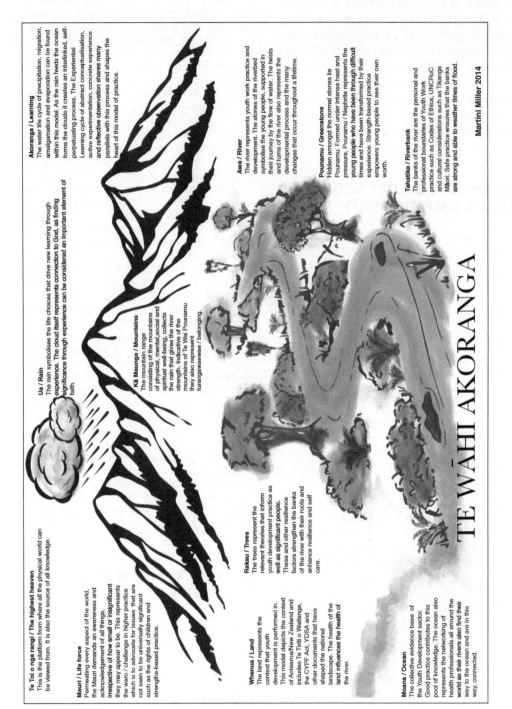

Te Toi o nga rangi / The highest heaven
This is the platform from where all the physical world can be viewed from. It is also the source of all knowledge.

Mauri / Life force
Permeating every aspect of the world, the Mauri demands an awareness and acknowledgement of all things, irrespective of how small or insignificant they may appear to be. This represents the wero / challenge in higher practice which is to advocate for issues that are not seen to be universally significant such as the rights of children and strengths-based practice.

Whenua / Land
The land represents the context that youth development is performed in. This model depicts the context of Aotearoa/New Zealand and includes Te Tiriti o Waitanga, the CYPF Act, YDSA and other documents that have shaped the national landscape. The health of the land influences the health of the river.

Moana / Ocean
The collective evidence base of the Youth Development sector. Good practice contributes to this pool of knowledge. The ocean also represents the networking of health professionals all around the world as their rivers also find their way to the ocean and are in this way, connected.

Ua / Rain
The rain symbolises the life choices that drive new learning through experience. The cloud itself represents connection to God, as finding significance through experience can be considered an important element of faith.

Kā Maunga / Mountains
The mountain range consisting of the mountains of physical, mental, social and spiritual well-being, collects the rain that gives the river strength. Indicative of the mountains of Te Wai Pounamu they also represent turangawaewae / belonging.

Rakau / Trees
The trees represent the relevant theories that inform youth development practice as well as significant people. These and other resilience factors strengthen the banks of the river with their roots and enhance resilience and self care.

Akoranga / Learning
The water life cycle of precipitation, migration, amalgamation and evaporation can be found within this model. As the rain feeds the ocean forms the clouds it creates an interlinked, self-perpetuating process. The Experiential Learning cycle of abstract conceptualisation, active experimentation, concrete experience and reflective observation shares many parallels with this process and shapes the heart of this model of practice.

Awa / River
The river represents youth work practice and development. The stones of the riverbed symbolise the young people, supported in their journey by the flow of water. The twists and turns of the river also represents the developmental process and the many changes that occur throughout a lifetime.

Pounamu / Greenstone
Hidden amongst the normal stones lie Pounamu. Formed under intense heat and pressure, Pounamu / Nephrite represents the young people who have been through difficult times and have been transformed by their experience. Strength-based practice empowers young people to see their own worth.

Tahatika / Riverbank
The banks of the river are the personal and professional boundaries of Youth Work practice such as Codes of Ethics, UNCRoC and cultural considerations such as Tikanga Māori. Safe practice ensures that the banks are strong and able to weather times of flood.

Martini Miller 2014

TE WĀHI AKORANGA

Figure 17.1   Te Wāhi Akoranga

history and are sources of inequality, oppression and war. So what lessons can we draw from Aotearoa and, in particular, these vignettes of practice?

First, there is a need to speak the myths out. Inequality has deep social causes (Engerman & Sokoloff, 2005; Kelsey, 1995). These causes need to be known and the lies that keep these causes hidden have to be spoken. This is evident throughout the vignettes. Sargent's vignette starts directly with the myth that 'we are all one'. This is not the case in Aotearoa. It is not the case anywhere. There are always the haves and the have-nots. There are also the other myths, the hegemonic myths our children of disadvantage receive when they fail in the system of life. It is their fault that they failed in education, their fault that they are poor, their destiny in life is in welfare or in prison (or low-income work). How do we address the myths as part of youth work practice? Some of this will be in actions, like the small actions of innovation that enable cultural goals to be met ahead of dominant societal goals. Myth-busting is what is hardest. It may break or innovate (change) the rules of the game, but it achieves results, such as those evident in Foaese's navigators, where a space is created for young people to tell their stories.

Second, there is an obligation to acknowledge that everyone, and everything, has a story, whether it is the young people who turn up to a community centre, the youth worker, or even the theories that are informing practice. Nothing and no one is outside of a story. It is these stories that need to be told and shared. From the 'Am I in the Story' of Foaese's navigators to 'This is My Story' of Miller's model of practice, in a world that is becoming more and more multi-cultural, it is the stories that will connect us. This is evident in Perkins finding a space in Aotearoa; a space that many mainstream Pākehā struggle to find. Indeed, many Pākehā in Aotearoa are quick to say 'I have no culture'. In a Māori context to have no culture is to have no story. All connections and relationships

emerge through stories. Youth development practice needs to enable the stories to be told. Youth development practice needs to acknowledge the presence of the cultural in order to embrace growing cultural and ethnic diversity globally, and the presence of cultural inequality within – and between – countries.

Third, the hidden challenge in the vignettes relates to the ways practitioners are supported in the youth work sector. It is different everywhere. But everywhere, we need to be asking what Belton (2009) challenges us to do: how do we make youth work, *critical*? The education of youth workers often aligns with requirements from government and key interest groups in society. It is often a socialising project in itself where our practice is aimed at helping the youth 'become' what is socially needed and accepted. The challenge is to not limit sociological theories of struggle, strain and transformation to formal education and degree courses. It is doing what Freire (1993) would desire, getting the learning onto the street and into the hands of those who need it in simple actions such as educators providing short workshops and partnering with major youth development organisations. In this way, as a global sector, youth work practitioners can enable a genuine and authentic dialogue about the messy complex issues which transcend national boundaries but impact our youth locally, such as climate change, conflict and trade. In Aotearoa, this has begun to occur as degree programmes work with a variety of organisations (such as health centres, alternative education providers and community organisations) to provide in-house training and/or development. By taking this knowledge to the street and the spaces of struggle, opportunities are created to enable hope and bring about social change within the organisations and between the organisations and the communities they serve.

Finally, a lesson emerges in the importance of youth workers actively seeking out and understanding the histories of oppression and inequality in the contexts in which they are working. This involves learning the history of space/place and also where particular ideas and knowledge come from and how such hierarchical practices of knowledge production create the boxes for 'us' and 'them'. It is a dialogue that seeks to problem-pose rather than problem-solve, asking the questions like 'why' in order to understand why the present is so complex and why both experiences of inequality and hope are concepts that connect us all. Listening to stories, challenging myths, and finding new practices of education can only occur when we, as practitioners, take a step back and explore our shared histories in authentic dialogue.

There is the word in Māori culture which captures these lessons: *whakapapa*. This word requires us to look back at our social and spatial connections. It is *whakapapa* that gives us our story. It is whakapapa that ignites the hope that is in each of us. It is dialogue about that whakapapa that gives us a window into our brokenness, the conditions that lead to inequality and the moment when our ancestors hoped for something better. It is through dialogue about the whakapapa of youth work that we can learn from our mistakes and endeavour to change the future. Now more than ever we need to stop in this struggle and move towards hope for something better. To know our particular histories of inequality, and the stories that connect us, can bring about this hope. To apply the sociological imagination can help us to push the boundaries and rules so that our practice is more than normative; it is transformative.

> Inā kei te mohio koe ko wai koe, I anga mai koe i hea, kei te mohio koe. Kei te anga atu ki hea.
> If you know who you are and where you are from, then you will know where you are going. (Māori proverb)

Notes

1 Aotearoa is the recognised indigenous name of New Zealand given to the northern island by Hine-te-Aparangi, the wife of the Polynesian navigator Kupe on discovery in early Māori history. New Zealand is the name given to the country by the first European explorer to sight it, Abel Tasman. Except in places emphasising colonial history, in recognition of indigenous histories, this chapter uses the name 'Aotearoa'.

2 Pasifika is a term used to encompass various people groups from the many small island nations throughout the Pacific Ocean.

3 Professionalisation occurred in 2017 with the formation of the professional registration body Korowai Tupu.

4 In recent Government strategies (The Children's Action Plan, 2015) the words 'at risk' have been replaced with the word 'vulnerable' to define the country's most marginalised and disadvantaged children.

5 As of the 2013 Census (Statistics New Zealand, 2013a), people of European descent constituted 74% of the population, Māori, 15%, Asian 12% and Pasifika 7%. This will not add up to 100% as people can indicate more than one ethnic group.

6 Statistics New Zealand (2013b) confirm this; by 2038 the European population will increase by only 2.4%, the Asian population will increase by 72%, the Māori by 69%, and the Pasifika population by 63%.

REFERENCES

Anae, M., Iuli, L., & Tamu, L. (Eds.). (2006). *Polynesian Panthers: Pacific protest and affirmative action in Aotearoa New Zealand 1971–1981*. Wellington: Huia Publishing.

Ara Taiohi. (2011). *Code of ethics for youth work in Aotearoa New Zealand*. Wellington: Ara Taiohi.

Baxter, R., Caddie, M., & Cameron, G.B. (2016). Aotearoa New Zealand's indigenous youth development concepts explored in practice today. In M. Heathfield & D. Fusco (Eds.), *Youth and inequality in education* (pp. 155–172). New York: Routledge.

Beals, F. (2008). Conflicting demands: Reviewing the impact of youth policies on New Zealand schools. *New Zealand Annual Review of Education*, 17, 91–105.

Beals, F. (2013, October). Strengthening the hub of our practice: Replacing policy-centred practice with treaty-centre practice (Keynote Address). Paper presented at the *Voices of the Pacific*, Wellington.

Beals, F. (2015). Tackling the unmarked in youth development: Why settle for the west when a new dawn brings new possibilities. *Journal of Applied Youth Studies*, 1(1), 122–141.

Belton, B. (2009). *Developing critical youth work theory*. The Netherlands: Sense Publishers.

Bhabha, H. K. (1994). *The location of culture*. New York: Routledge.

Brendtro, L., & du Toit, L. (2005). *RAP: Response Ability Pathways*. Cape Town: Pretext Publishers.

Bronfenbrenner, U. (1979). *The ecology of human development*. Cambridge, Mass: Harvard University Press.

Calhoun, C., Gerteis, J., Moody, J., Pfaff, J., & Virk, I. (Eds.). (2012). *Contemporary sociological theory* (3rd edn). Chichester, UK: Wiley-Blackwell.

Consedine, R., & Consedine, J. (2012). *Healing our history: The challenge of the treaty of Waitangi*. Auckland: Penguin. Retrieved from https://store.kobobooks.com/en-ca/ebook/healing-our-history

Durie, M.H. (1998). *Whaiora: Māori health development* (2nd edn). Auckland: Oxford University Press.

Engerman, S.L., & Sokoloff, K.L. (2005). *Colonialism, inequality, and long-run paths of development*. NBER Working Paper No. 11057. Retrieved from http://www.nber.org/papers/w11057.pdf

Freire, P. (1993). *Pedagogy of the oppressed*. New York: Continuum.

Freire, P. (1994). *Pedagogy of hope*. New York: Continuum.

Giddens, A., & Sutton, P.W. (Eds.). (2010). *Sociology: Introductory readings* (3rd edn). Cambridge: Polity Press.

Hall, G.S. (1908). *Adolescence*. London: Appleton and Co.

Harms, L. (2010). *Understanding human development* (2nd edn). Melbourne: Oxford University Press.

Hart, R.A. (1997). *Children's participation*. London: Earthscan.

Indian and Northern Affairs Canada. (2010). *A history of treaty-making in Canada*. Canada: Indian and Northern Affairs Canada. Retrieved from https://www.aadnc-aandc.gc.ca/DAM/DAM-INTER-HQ/STAGING/texte-text/ap_htmc_treatliv_1314921040169_eng.pdf

Inyang, A.A., & Bassey, M.E. (2014). Imperial treaties and the origins of British colonial rule in Southern Nigeria, 1860–1890. *Mediterranean Journal of Social Sciences*, 5(20), 1946–1953.

Jeffs, T., & Banks, S. (2010). Youth workers as controllers. In S. Banks (Ed.), *Ethical issues in youth work* (2nd edn). Abingdon: Routledge.

Kelsey, J. (1995). *The New Zealand experiment: A world model for structural adjustment*. Auckland: Auckland University Press with Bridget Williams Books.

Kidman, J. (2012). The land remains. *Alternative: An International Journal of Indigenous Peoples*, 8(2), 189–202.

King Kapisi. (2000). Screams from da old plantation (Musical Recording). On *Savage thoughts*. New Zealand: FMR.

King, T. (2015a). *Braided pathways: A report on the 2014 Ara Taiohi national youth sector survey*. Wellington: Ara Taiohi.

King, T. (2015b). *Stepping stone: A step on the pathway to professionalisation*. Wellington: Ara Taiohi.

Kolb, D.A. (1984). *Experiential learning*. Englewood Cliffs, NJ: Prentice-Hall.

Kukukai, T. (2013). University of Waikato's NIDEA population research. Paper presented at *Building Pathways*, Ara Taiohi Wananga, Wellington.

Lerner, J.V., Bowers, E., Minor, K., Boyd, M.J., Mueller, M.K., Schmid, K.L., & Lerner, R.M. (2012). Positive youth development. In I.B. Weiner, R.M. Lerner, E.M. Ann, & J. Mistry (Eds.), *The Wiley Handbook of Psychology* (Vol. 6, pp. 365–392). United States of America: Wiley.

Lesko, N. (2001). *Act your age! A cultural construction of adolescence*. New York: Routledge Falmer.

Martin, L. (2006). *Real work: A report from the national research project on the state of youth work in Aotearoa*. Christchurch: The National Youth Workers Network.

Merton, R.K. (1994). Social structure and anomie. In P. Rock (Ed.), *History of criminology* (pp. 389–399). Aldershot, UK: Dartmouth.

Miller, M. (2014). Te Waahi Akoranga: A youth development model of practice developed for the New Zealand Aotearoa context. Unpublished course assessment, Wellington Institute of Technology, Wellington.

Ministry of Justice. (2013). *Youth crime action plan: 2013–2023*. Wellington: Ministry of Justice.

Ministry of Justice, & Ministry of Social Development. (2002). *Youth Offending Strategy*. Wellington: Ministry of Justice, Ministry of Social Development.

Ministry of Youth Affairs. (2002). *Youth Development Strategy Aotearoa*. Wellington: Ministry of Youth Affairs.

Mizen, P. (2010). Working in welfare. In S. Banks (Ed.), *Ethical issues in youth work* (2nd edn, pp. 24–37). Abingdon Oxon: Routledge.

OECD. (2011). *Divided we stand: Why inequality keeps rising*. Paris: Organisation for Economic Co-operation and Development.

Santrock, J.W. (2002). *Life-span development* (8th edn). Boston: McGraw-Hill.

Simpson, T. (1997). *The immigrants: The great migration from Britain to New Zealand 1830–1890*. Auckland: Godwit.

Smith, L.T. (2002). *Decolonizing methodologies: Research and indigenous peoples*. Dunedin: University of Otago Press.

Statistics New Zealand. (2013a, December 03). *Cultural diversity*. Retrieved April 28, 2016, from http://www.stats.govt.nz/Census/2013-census/profile-and-summary-reports/quickstats-about-national-highlights/cultural-diversity.aspx

Statistics New Zealand. (2013b, May 21). *National ethnic population projections: 2013(base)–2038*. Retrieved April 28, 2016, from http://www.stats.govt.nz/Census/2013-census/profile-and-summary-reports/quickstats-about-national-highlights/cultural-diversity.aspx

The Children's Action Plan. (2015). *The Children's Action Plan*. Retrieved June 3, 2015, from http://childrensactionplan.govt.nz/

Warbrick, I., Dickson, A., Prince, R., & Heke, I. (2016). The biopolitics of Māori biomass: Towards a new epistemology for Māori health in Aotearoa/New Zealand. *Critical Public Health*, 26(4), 394–404.

18

Promoting Children First Youth Work in the Youth Justice System and Beyond

Stephen Case and Rachel Morris

INTRODUCTION

This chapter outlines a progressive, participatory and positive model of youth justice called 'Children First Youth Work' We challenge the negative, punitive and correctionalist nature of much contemporary youth justice practice in England by reasserting the status of the youth as a *child* in psychological, emotional, physical and social terms and thus the need to respond to children who offend with this status as primary – hence the apparent paradox of *children* first *youth* work. In particular, the Children First Youth Work (CFYW) model offers an alternative to the adult-centric, system-centric and compliance-focused elements of much youth justice and youth work that can limit children's capacity to contribute to and participate in voluntary and meaningful supportive interventions. CFYW is a holistic practice model developed in Wales through a twenty-year process of engagement and research with children, families, youth justice staff and other key stakeholders such as youth workers, police, teachers and social care practitioners (Haines and Case 2015). The CFYW model coheres youth justice around a series of positive principles that place the child at the centre of practice – prioritising the child's participation, views, rights and achievement of positive behaviours and outcomes. As such, we are arguing for a progressive youth justice practice, which hopefully can be paralleled by a progressive social work and youth work approach – in line with the assertion of the International Child and Youth Care Education Network that 'professional practitioners promote the optimal development of children, youth and their families in a variety of settings, such as early care and education, community-based child and youth development programs … and juvenile justice programs' (CYC 2016).

YOUTH WORK AS A DISTINCTIVE PRACTICE VS. THE NEO-LIBERAL TURN

It is informative to conceive of youth work as a distinctive practice with a rich history in the UK as the basis for considering its relationship with youth justice. This distinctiveness has been characterised by progressive, social democratic practice grounded in voluntarism (i.e. free-willed engagement), creativity and autonomy on the part of the young person, who is placed at the heart of the practice relationship (*In Defence of Youth Work* 2009). In turn, this young-person-centred agenda is facilitated by a creative and autonomous youth worker and young person–youth worker relationship (see Taylor, Connaughton, de St Croix, Davies and Grace, this *Handbook*). Advocates of youth work's distinctive nature are not claiming that youth work is superior or has any claim to be the guardian of a holistic, progressive practice. The claim here is that the setting for youth work, its voluntary basis, gives it its distinctive character (*In Defence of Youth Work* 2009). However, the purported distinctiveness of this young-person-centred, process-led youth work (which the In Defence of Youth Work organisation was established to defend) has been instrumentalised and compromised across the last thirty years by neo-liberalism – placing less emphasis on social contexts, state protection and rehabilitation and more on prescriptions of individual responsibility, an active citizenship and governments governing at a distance. Therefore, much like the youth justice in England and Wales that forms the basis of this chapter, youth work in the UK has made rhetorical claims to be participative and grounded in voluntarism (which the enforcement- and compliance-led youth justice field cannot mirror), when the practice realities may differ (cf. Davies 2005). Neo-liberalism has engendered a more adult-centric and compliance-focused professional youth work characterised by increasingly prescriptive managerialism, inflexibility, and enforcement-led and individualised target-driven approaches visited upon 'at risk' populations. The key features of such an approach lead to:

- the imposition of prescribed outcomes on targeted groups via structured, time-limited initiatives and the conscious uncoupling of youth work from the Department of Education (Jeffs 2015);
- a loss of faith in the voluntary relationship informed by a view that young people make poor choices, so better that their options are predetermined (see Taylor et al., this volume);
- the collapse of local authority youth services, which has seen the workforce dispersed and some youth workers becoming part of Youth Offending Teams (YOTs).[1]

These negative-facing characteristics resonate with much contemporary youth justice in England and Wales, particularly since the Crime and Disorder Act 1998, which has eschewed traditional welfare concerns in favour of prescriptive and tightly-managed control and prevention agendas. In the youth work context, these characteristics run contrary to traditional youth work principles of relationship-based practice that promotes well-being by enabling children to set practice agendas and to function as agents of change (Bradford and Cullen 2014; Bradford 2004). The neo-liberal turn has been reflected in the youth justice practice field, such that, contrary to claims that professional practice promotes the optimal development of children, contemporary practice in both youth work and youth justice in the 21st century has been significantly reconfigured by neo-liberalism.

PUNITIVE YOUTH JUSTICE AND THE NEGLECT OF CHILDREN'S VOICES

The issues of neo-liberal, prescribed adult-centrism and the marginalisation of children's contributions to practice have been seen in the Youth Justice System of England and Wales. Across youth justice systems in the Western world, the punishment of children[2] once they break the law remains difficult to reconcile with notions of the child being in need of support and protection provided by caring adults. The visitation of harmful punishment on children who offend is indicative of dominant understandings of these children as depraved rather than deprived, as risky rather than in need and as requiring control rather than care. In the Youth Justice System (YJS) of England and Wales, historical concerns with children's welfare needs and competing requirements to prioritise a proportionate response to their offence (the 'welfare versus justice' debate – Smith 2005) have been superseded since the 1998 Crime and Disorder Act by an approach which focuses on the punitive correction of perceived 'deficits' and reducing and preventing the 'risk' that children allegedly present to themselves and others (Case and Haines 2014a). This punitive neo-correctionalist, responsibilising, risk-management focus has also become a dominant youth justice paradigm elsewhere across the globe, notably in North America, Australia and developing European countries, in contrast to alternative models of delivering youth justice based on children's participation (e.g. Scotland), welfare-justice hybrids (e.g. Netherlands, Germany) and restorative justice (e.g. New Zealand). There is also a clear contrast here between the ways in which youth justice and youth work are situated in practice in the UK. Contrary to the work practices of informal education, social education and critical pedagogy, which could be seen to be promotional and positive in orientation (see Jeffs and Smith 2002), youth justice in the UK (England and Wales especially) aims to control, to correct and to prevent negative behaviours/outcomes (re/offending, exposure to risk factors for offending, antisocial behaviour, substance use). The promotion of positive behaviours/outcomes (e.g. participation, educational

attainment, employment, citizenship, access to rights) is arguably a subsidiary vehicle for pursuing preventative goals, as opposed to an aim in its own right.

Youth justice practice in the YJS is driven by the 'Asset' risk assessment instrument (YJB 2000). This is a tool that measures a young person's exposure to 'dynamic' social and psychological risk factors (i.e. based in the family, education, neighbourhood, lifestyle, psychological/emotional issues), as well as considering static factors such as criminal history. This risk-based approach to assessment and intervention has enshrined the YJS in a negative, punitive and controlling youth justice context (see Case and Haines 2014a; Morris 2014). This was further amplified by the 'Scaled Approach' risk assessment and intervention framework, introduced in 2009, which requires YOT practitioners to make judgements using Asset on a child's risk of future reoffending and to 'scale' the frequency and intensity of responsive interventions accordingly (YJB 2010). It is argued that the Scaled Approach exemplifies how 'fools rush in' (Morris 2014; Sutherland 2009), in this case the YJB, to create flawed policies based on faulty evidence that 'punishes poverty' (Bateman 2011; Haines and Case 2012). Moreover, Asset is an adult-led (risk) assessment of a child's life and offending behaviour. The tool is designed to be completed following an assessment interview in which the child completes a 'what do you think?' self-assessment section, thus potentially supporting the child to understand their own riskiness and to make prosocial decisions. However, in reality, this self-assessment section is often not completed and the assessment becomes a one-way, adult-driven process. For example, the child does not necessarily see the completed document; therefore they are excluded from the very assessment that is going to dictate the interventions that they will receive. Case (2006: 174) has called this notion, 'prescription without a consultation'. Children's voices have been mostly absent in the wider design and delivery of youth justice services (Case and Haines 2014a). As such perspectives have been neglected so there has been a failure to act upon their wishes across the YJS, leading to adult-dominated, enforcement- and compliance-led youth justice processes and interventions. Recent shifts in youth justice policy and practice in England and Wales since the Coalition Government came to power in 2010 – progressive in our view – have been largely confined to increased diversion from court proceedings; whilst practice with those subject to formal sanctions continues to be disengaging and disempowering. Children who offend continue to be labelled 'offenders' and to be 'othered' from 'normal', non-offending children, thus losing their identities as children, and linked to this is their special treatment by dint of age and (im)maturity. The risk-based approach results in a very narrow and one-dimensional offender first, offence first focus which fails to look at broader issues in children's multi-faceted, complex lives.

FROM NEGATIVE YOUTH JUSTICE TO CHILDREN FIRST YOUTH WORK

Contrary to the negative, deficit-led practices of the YJS, we offer Children First Youth Work (CFYW), a *positive*, principled and progressive model of working with children, underpinned by the promotion of children's participation, positive behaviour and positive outcomes. CFYW is a holistic set of principles for working with children in all areas of their lives, not just in offence- and offender-focused ways based solely on their offending behaviour. Within this chapter, however, we use youth justice as the primary point of discussion as this reflects the context within which the approach was developed. The CFYW model was developed through a longstanding reflective research partnership between researchers at Swansea University and policy makers and practitioners primarily located within Swansea YOT. This relationship began in the mid-1990s, with researchers being granted access from that point onwards to YOT structures, processes, staff and data – operational and strategic meetings (e.g. steering groups, senior management team), frontline practitioners, policy and practice documentation, statistical databases and, most importantly, to the children and families who come into contact with the YJS (Haines and Case 2015). A series of long-term, reflective research and evaluation projects have resulted (cf. Case and Haines 2009, 2014a), with children, families, practitioners, policy makers and researchers working collaboratively in children-first, positive ways to identify issues, strengthen relationships, improve practice and enhance outcomes for local children within and outside of the YJS. Whilst the CFYW model was developed and established in the Welsh city of Swansea, its principles and practices have been evidenced across England and Wales, most notably by Surrey Youth Support Service, an integrated youth work provision discussed later in this chapter.

CFYW conceives of offending as 'only one element of a much wider and more complex identity' (Drakeford 2009: 8) for children, and this 'complex identity', therefore, should be addressed by a series of holistic, joined-up and inclusive *social* policies. The central principles of CFYW directly challenge the main ideas and practices that have characterised contemporary negative youth justice in England and Wales – practices which we see as having no place in the YJS specifically and in the treatment of children generally. Similarly to the principles underlying youth work, the CFYW model has five core principles:

1 Child-friendly and child-appropriate;
2 Promoting the positive;
3 Systems management;
4 Children's participation and engagement;
5 Evidence-based partnerships.

Each of the principles will now be discussed in turn.

Child-friendly and Child-appropriate

CFYW is a child-friendly and child-appropriate model that aims to engage with children who offend in 'child sensitive' ways; in opposition to treating children like adults (adulterisation) and taking an offence-first focus when responding to youth offending. Miniaturising an adult Criminal Justice System in the form of a YJS is an insufficient and inappropriate approach. Traditional ways of treating children who offend can be characterised as punitive, controlling and responsibilising. Children are primarily treated in terms of their offence and/or their offence-related characteristics rather than in the first instance as the child that they are. CFYW does not seek to treat children who offend as if they are (mini-)adults (i.e. in an adulterised manner – see Fionda 1998; Muncie 2008) as this process ignores children's inherent vulnerability and need for protection. Whilst notions of justice in the adult Criminal Justice System are complex and contested (see Sanders et al. 2010), whatever one's view on the justices or injustices perpetrated by this system, it treats those with whom it deals as adults – as people who are independent, capable and responsible for making their own decisions in life and for bearing the consequences of their decision-making. To respond to children who offend simply as an offender reduces them, a social being, to an object or a thing, what O'Malley (2010) refers to as a 'dividual'. In doing this, the child is responsibilised (Garland 1996; Muncie 2006) for their behaviour. It is a process such as this which allows for the state to divest from its duties towards these citizens, and subsequently it negates the responsibilities organisations and adults have towards children.

CFYW rejects the use of the term 'offender', which is why we have taken care to use the term 'children who offend' throughout this chapter. We reject this label because of the constricted, blaming effect and damaging consequences for children that it entails. A child who commits an offence is not an 'offender'; they are first and foremost a child who regardless of their behaviour still warrants the state's care and protection due to the inherent nature of their age and maturity status. By making this recognition, the focus of subsequent responses to such behaviour are 'whole-child'-focused as opposed to being compartmentalised on just one element, i.e. offending.

Key principle: CFYW is child-friendly in all work with children, within and outside of the YJS.

Promoting the Positive

A *positive*, participatory and strengths-based approach that prioritises promotion (rather than prevention) is possible and desirable with all children who come to the attention of the YJS. Prevention policy and practice in the YJS in England and Wales is negative-facing due to it being shaped and driven by the Scaled Approach risk-based assessment and intervention framework. The Scaled Approach concentrates interventions on identifying and responding to measured 'risk factors' for a host of *negative* behaviours (e.g. offending, reoffending, substance use, antisocial behaviour) and *negative* outcomes (e.g. contact with the formal system, conviction, reconviction, custody).

Risk-based assessments and interventions which seek to 'correct' and reduce the 'problem' of offending by targeting perceived deficiencies in the individual (see Goldson 2005; Kelly 2012) – advances an *offender-first* and *offence-focused* approach to the execution of youth justice prevention policy and practice. The resulting individualisation of the claimed causes of offending by children incites the respon-sibilisation of children for their behav-iour and for desisting from it. Combining a punitive neo-correctionalism with respon-sibilisation is a recipe for the negative treat-ment of children in the YJS. Unfortunately, the preoccupation with risk within preven-tion practice has expanded beyond the YJS to encompass the prevention of broader negative personal and social behaviours and outcomes (many of which are perceived as criminogenic) such as social exclusion, academic underachievement and disaffec-tion, psychological and physical ill-health, teenage pregnancy, unemployment and poverty.[3]

A negative prevention model avoids posi-tive and progressive objectives such as pro-tection, facilitating access to rights, support and the promotion of children's strengths, capacities and positive behaviours and outcomes through their participation and engagement (see Haines and Case 2015). In contrast to such negative youth justice and youth work, the CFYW approach asserts that practice with children in and around the YJS should be reframed into work with a child that targets the promotion of measurable, demonstrable and achievable positive behav-iours and outcomes. Simply put, the absence of a negative behaviour/outcome does not constitute or imply the presence of a posi-tive behaviour or outcome and should not be represented as such. It is much more realis-tic and meaningful, in policy, management and practice terms (for both practitioners and children), to establish targets founded on the promotion of positive behaviours (e.g. school achievement, prosocial behaviour, engagement, participation) and positive out-comes (e.g. social inclusion, employment, qualifications, access to rights and entitle-ments – see also Case et al. 2005; Haines and Case 2011).

Key principle: CFYW focuses on pro-moting positive behaviours and outcomes for children who offend and who are considered 'at risk' of offending.

Systems Management

CFYW is enabled by a *systems management* approach (after Tutt and Giller 1987; see also Haines and Drakeford 1998), which views the YJS as an interrelated, mutually-reinforcing series of decision-making points (e.g. deci-sions to arrest, bail, remand, sentence, divert, imprison, punish) that can be targeted to meet specific goals. The processing of chil-dren by the YJS and the outcomes they are subjected to is the product of long sequences of individual decision-making. The power to make these decisions lies in the hands of adults. Although children may be consulted, either in a tokenistic manner (e.g. during assessment interviews) or in meaningful ways (e.g. during diversion panels), adults dominate, shape, drive and make use of jus-tice decision-making processes. It is adults who hold the power to manage systems. Taken together, all the decisions made about all individual children constitute the behav-iour of the (youth justice) system. Systems management thinking teaches us to see the critical outcomes for individual children as the product of this series of decisions. Such thinking explains that each of these decisions is not unchallengeable; that it is possible to influence or change every decision that is made about how the YJS treats individual children. It teaches us that by targeting these decisions, the treatment of individual chil-dren by the YJS and thus the behaviour of the system as a whole can be changed.

Systems management thinking is an influential tool for understanding the way in which the YJS functions and how it pro-duces different outcomes (some good, some bad) for children. It is crucial to employ systems management practice in the ser-vice of CFYW – to animate the objectives and principles of the approach, notably *diversion*. Youth justice practice grounded in CFYW principles operates against the interventionist and net-widening tendencies of the formal YJS (Goldson and Muncie 2006). This should not be interpreted as

CFYW being non-interventionist *per se*; rather it advocates a non-formal intervention model of prevention. Diversion from the formal YJS should mean exactly that; those children who demonstrate problems and problematic behaviour (e.g. low-level offending, antisocial behaviour) are *worked with* by practitioners offering supportive services that promote positive behaviour and are framed around children's rights. This is rather than being *dealt with* by counter-productive, formal youth justice processes, which, as established earlier within this chapter, can stigmatise, label and disengage children from positive, developmental experiences as they grow and develop. By prioritising diversion from the formal YJS, CFYW rejects notions of punishment and its essential retributive quality. Moreover, as youth justice interventions

more often than not have unintended consequences (Kelly 2012; Morris 2014) what may be done to children with good intentions or with their best interests in mind, may be perceived by those children as punitive and may contribute to further offending rather than lessening it.

Within CFYW, diversion animates systems management. The CFYW approach to diversion is that it is holistic and inclusionary, applied to all children, not simply those deemed to have committed low-level offences and those at an early stage in the system (e.g. first-time entrants). It seeks to normalise offending, treating it as an everyday behaviour that exists as only one element of children's complex and multifaceted lives – thus warranting a whole-child approach. It pursues the engagement of key stakeholders in the process to maximise the

---

Box 18.1 CFYW systems management in action: Swansea Bureau diversion programme

The Bureau model is a formal diversionary partnership between South Wales Police and Swansea (now Western Bay) YOT, with three key aims:

1 to divert children out of the formal processes of the YJS;
2 to tackle the underlying causes of offending by promoting positive and prosocial behaviour; and
3 to treat young offenders as children first.

Any local child committing an offence is eligible for the pre-court, diversionary Bureau, which follows a five-stage process:

1 arrest and bail (police-led);
2 assessment of the child and family (YOT-led);
3 assessment of victim's needs (YOT-led);
4 Bureau Panel (police and YOT discuss appropriate response); and
5 Bureau Clinic (police, YOT, child and parents agree appropriate response).

Independent evaluation (Haines et al. 2013) has identified that since the Bureau's inception in 2009, the annual number of first-time entrants into the YJS in Swansea has decreased year-on-year, whilst the annual number and percentage of children who offend receiving a non-criminal disposal (now 'community resolution') has increased year-on-year. Concurrently, the annual number and percentage of children reoffending following Bureau contact and the annual number and percentage of children prosecuted for an offence have decreased year-on-year. These trends have persisted into 2015 (Byrne and Case 2016; Haines and Case 2015).

Child-friendly Bureau decision-making processes (aligned with systems management principles) and positive outcomes for children have been underpinned by the principles of children's inclusion, participation and engagement; principles identified as influential by key stakeholders (e.g. police, YOT workers, parents) in qualitative evaluation (Hoffman and Macdonald 2011). The YJB for Wales has now committed to rolling out the Bureau model across all local authority areas in Wales.

child-appropriate nature of interventions and their potential to promote positive behaviour. In this way, CFYW diversion seeks to divert children *from* system contact, formal youth justice processes (court, custody), offending behaviour and obtaining a criminal record, whilst diverting children *to* youth justice and non-youth justice interventions and supports. Thus, CFYW maintains that any intervention must be child-appropriate and at the minimum necessary level, contrary to contemporary interventionist diversion that does not prioritise diversion from system contact (see Kelly and Armitage 2015). In this way, CFYW does not argue for non-intervention, but rather intervention in appropriate forms and amounts. The potential for just such a principled, informal, non-criminalising, engaging and holistic diversionary model that addresses both the causes of offending and individual needs without recourse to formalised, systemic intervention(ism) is offered by the localised *Bureau* model (see NAYJ 2012; ICYCAB 2010; see also Haines et al. 2013).

Key principle: child-friendly systems management, notably diversion, is a vehicle to promote positive behaviours/outcomes for children and to avoid the potentially criminogenic consequences of contact with the YJS.

Children's Participation and Engagement

There is a duality present between the enforcement and enabling functions of the YJS (Hart and Thompson 2009: 4); this is where the tension between youth work and the CFYW approach lies. The enforcement-led elements of disposals and risk-based interventions, including their content, timing, duration and location, can actively discourage children's participation in and engagement with the YJS. The elements of control and regulation experienced by children during intervention is counter-intuitive

to developing constructive, engaging relationships with adults; relationships that should be based on mutual respect, empathy, trust and legitimacy. Such potential structural and procedural barriers have a particular profound effect on children who have previous negative experiences of youth justice processes. Retributive and punitive enforcement practices can lead children to distrust and lack faith in the behaviour and intentions of the government, the YJS, YOTs and adult staff (cf. Nacro Cymru 2009; Hart and Thompson 2009). It is also possible that existing socio-structural and psychosocial issues that children who offend disproportionately experience may result in a lack of confidence and ability to engage in the youth justice services they receive.

The concept of 'engagement' with youth justice services has been largely understood from the perspective of adult practitioners, rather than prioritising the need to boost children's motivation and commitment to become involved in youth justice activities. Research in related fields (for example, youth work, education, substance use) on the other hand, has identified the value children place on relationships based on trust, respect, fairness and voluntarism/choice (see Ipsos MORI 2010). It is these features that enable children to make the crucial distinction between actual engagement with intervention and token participation in intervention (Ipsos MORI 2010). Although youth justice research has asserted the need for 'understanding in addressing the 'fluid dynamics' of children's 'lived experiences' (Farrow et al. 2007: 87), such research has tended to de-emphasise the role and influence of children's perspectives and experiences in favour of focusing on practitioners and the skills they need (for example, communication and empathy) in order to form engaging relationships with children (Mason and Prior 2008). For example, despite YJB assessment guidance that 'assessors will need to employ individually-oriented interviewing skills which allow them to explore with the young person their own story' (YJB 2008: 15; see also YJB 2004), the self-assessment portion of Asset (entitled 'What do you think?') has been notoriously incomplete or ignored (see Baker 2005), rendering children in the YJS relatively voiceless and powerless in key decision-making processes (Case 2006). Moreover, following a qualitative analysis of the situated knowledge of children subject to YOT contact, Phoenix and Kelly (2013: 419) reconceptualised the notion of responsibilisation as relating to a general lack of engagement by and faith in practitioners, such that children came to know there was no one else to help them change their lives. This meant that children were compelled to address their issues autonomously and independently (see also Birdwell and Bani 2014). Children (unlike adult practitioners) do not privilege programmes and content, but instead value and desire 'a good supportive relationship with an adult who is not judgmental and is able to offer guidance and advocacy ... [T]o gain a greater understanding of these processes we need to listen to the voices and perspectives of young people themselves' (France and Homel 2006: 305–306).

Despite the limited body of engagement research, and guidance having privileged adult perspectives and the skills development of practitioners at the expense of children's perspectives, it is important to acknowledge that a key vehicle for facilitating children's participation and engagement in the YJS is adult practitioner discretion. Drake et al. (2014: 23) advocate: 'maximizing the discretion of youth justice workers to hear and respond to young people's voices, and to "rethink" aspects of practice that impair what can be heard and acted upon'. Enabling children's engagement with decision-making processes and with the design, implementation and evaluation of youth justice services can facilitate strategic planning, enhance the meaningful

and appropriate decision-making of practitioners and services, can improve the quality of the child–adult relationships that influence intervention effectiveness (see also HMI Probation 2009; Nacro 2011). Adult practitioner perspectives offer important reference points for interpreting children's accounts, due to their status as co-determinants of the two-way engagement between children and provider (Case and Haines 2014a; Drake et al. 2014). To this end, it is essential that these knowledgeable, experienced and dedicated practitioners are given the appropriate level of *discretion* to exercise their professional judgement. CFYW further requires that adult practitioners view themselves as working for the children with whom they engage. It is crucial, therefore, that children who come into contact with the YJS are facilitated (by adult practitioners) to express their views on issues that affect them (cf. Article 12 of the UNCRC) and enabled to participate equitably in decision-making regarding their futures, and that access to their universal entitlements as set out in progressive policy statements and international conventions is promoted. These features coalesce to produce a model of delivering youth justice that can be viewed as 'legitimate' to children (i.e. they see their treatment as moral, fair, deserved, equitable), thus increasing the likelihood of them investing in, and committing to, the approach. In this way, children's engagement with youth justice practice and practitioners goes deeper than the fundamentals of voluntarism, trust, respect and fairness (although these remain essential building blocks of the engagement relationship) and moves towards more positive notions of partnership, reciprocity, investment, the legitimate participation in decision-making processes and the achievement of (and recognition for) positive outcomes.

Key principle: CFYW is underpinned by children's participation and engagement, driven by positive relationships between the child and practitioner.

Evidence-based Partnerships

Child-friendly, legitimate services and interventions should be guided by evidence-based partnerships between children (and their families), youth justice practitioners, policy makers and researchers (i.e. key stakeholders in the youth justice process); partnership that enhances the child's potential to contribute to the services they receive through meaningful participation and engagement. Evidence-based partnership also enables academic researchers to engage with key stakeholders in reflective research relationships. The evidential and reflective partnership bases of CFYW seeks to avoid the 'programme fetishism' of criminal justice responses (Morgan 2002: 8) – a systemic tendency to privilege *programme integrity, pseudo-psychological* interventions, '*off the shelf*' accredited packages and *offender- and/or offence-focused* responses. In other words, the evidence that counts is produced, interpreted and disseminated by adults. Whilst Morgan (2002) had focused on adult criminal justice, programme fetishism can be found within youth justice practice, where it has come to dominate and characterise 'effective practice' with children under the guidance of the YJB. Notably, the Scaled Approach to assessment and intervention and the Asset risk assessment tool have been designed (by intent or by default) to deliver programme fetishism. This inevitably produces definitions and explanations of youth offending that are embedded in an adult-centric, pseudo-psychological and risk-focused cloud.[4] These assessments shape subsequent interventions, which are taken from an off-the-shelf menu of (largely pseudo-psychological) accredited 'what works' programmes (e.g. cognitive-behavioural, anger management, victim empathy, moral reasoning, social skills – Wikström and Treiber 2008), in line with the YJB's Key Elements of Effective Practice (KEEPs) (cf. Case and Haines 2009).

Our objections to programme fetishism are rooted in its offender-first focus – the manner in which it responds to children in terms of their offending behaviour and not as whole children with complex lives. We also object on grounds of its frequent reliance on narrowly conceptualised (and individualised) notions of risk and its use of offence- and offender-focused interventions that have been established on limited research and insufficient evidence of their effectiveness (Haines and Case 2015). One way to manage this ongoing dilemma is to move away from the misguided dependence on the limited and seemingly 'evidence-based' programmes that are, in reality, rarely reinforced by a comprehensive, reliable and robust range and depth of actual evidence, particularly evidence generated in meaningful partnership with children. Programmes and interventions recommended by the CFYW model are 'evidence-based' in the sense that they are grounded in research and evaluation conducted in *reflective partnerships* with key stakeholders – practitioners, policy makers, children, families and researchers. Such interventions do not discount psychosocial influences on offending behaviour, but privilege whole child and child-appropriate responses founded on a holistic assessment of the personal, social and structural circumstances and histories of children and their families, generated through research conducted in partnership with children and families. A clear tension emerges, however, where this partnership approach is adopted and children's views may contradict those of practitioners and those promoted by practice guidelines – a tension reflected in the youth work arena. The principles of the CFYW model provides children and youth justice/youth work practitioners with the practice space to explore and reconcile any differences by working in partnership, rather than adopting a default position of inflexible, adult-led, prescriptive practice underpinned by children's compliance. Subsequent intervention does not fetishise risk and the prevention of negative behaviours/outcomes, but instead prioritises the promotion of positive behaviours/outcomes, enabling children's access to their universal rights and working in partnership with children to reflect on and enhance programmes. The collection and use of evidence is critical to this agenda. Nonetheless, the nature of this evidence has to be open-minded, reflexive and bottom-up, developed in locally-sensitive partnerships, rather than restricted, prescriptive and top-down.

The evidence-based partnership principle of CFYW is facilitated by *Reflective Friend Research*. This model of social science research emphasises the *relational* aspects of meaningful, valid and context-specific knowledge development that facilitates (academic) researcher engagement with practitioner expertise, and vice versa, for example, within YOT-University knowledge transfer partnerships. *Reflective Friend*

Research develops through five central relational processes between the researcher and the 'researched' (see Case and Haines 2014b):

- **Situated learning** – researchers actively engage themselves in the everyday contexts of the research partners (e.g. the decision-making structures and processes of YOTs), working with research partners to co-construct their learning, knowledge and understanding of the practical realities of the YJS;
- **Research partnerships** – situating research within the everyday contexts of participants can encourage the co-construction of knowledge and understanding through legitimate and participative research partnerships;
- **Enhanced access** – situated research partnerships can facilitate researcher access to vital aspects of the research process, which, in the

---

Box 18.2   Establishing an evidence-base: YOT–University partnership in Swansea

A long-term programme of localised, evidence-based programme development through Reflective Friend Research began in 1996 at a meeting to discuss local youth crime prevention policies and practices in Swansea. The meeting was attended by practitioners and managers from the local YOT and Community Safety Department, along with researchers from Swansea University's Centre for Criminal Justice and Criminology – all of whom had previously expressed a commitment to developing preventative practice guided by context-specific, child-friendly evidence. A central driver of the meeting from which Reflective Friend Research evolved had been political attempts to undermine prevention-orientated practice with children who offend, on the grounds that it was not 'evidence-based' or demonstrably 'cost-effective' – key elements of the emerging governmental focus on 'effective practice'.

During an interview in 2012, the local authority Community Safety Department Manager (at the time of the original meeting) defined the objective of the approach as developing:

[A] partnership with the University that would give us [Community Safety Department and YOT] that resource to take a more objective look – first of all at the evidence from what we were doing and then secondly the evaluation of what we were doing.

The meeting led to a partnership agreement to pursue sources of funding for the development and independent evaluation and ongoing reflective development of a series of local prevention, diversion and social inclusion programmes (cf. Haines and Case 2015). The preferred mechanism for this partnership was situated and reflective *relationship building* – practitioners and researchers working collaboratively (with each other and with children and families) to identify and target local issues related to offending by children by situating researchers physically and contextually within the YOT working environments (e.g. through the allocation of office space), cultures and practices, both formally (e.g. attending policy and practice development and monitoring meetings, participating in team days, sitting in on assessment interviews, court hearings and family visits with children) and informally (e.g. relationship building in the YOT staff rooms and offices). Situating researchers within YOTs environments, structures and processes provided them with enhanced access to privileged expert contexts and has facilitated the situated learning of both researchers and YOT staff through iterative mechanisms of reflection and critical friendship, such as researchers disseminating and discussing the findings and conclusions of their projects, evaluations and observations with policy makers and practitioners, along with children and families (Case and Haines 2014b).

context of CFYW, can include: research partici-pants/partners (e.g. children, YOT staff), key data sets locally and nationally (e.g. crime statistics, education databases), internal documentation (e.g. minutes, policies) and knowledge-generation processes (meetings, steering groups);

- **Reflective engagement** – regular reflective and reciprocal feedback and dialogue between all research partners, particularly related to evidence-based decision-making processes;
- **Critical friendship** – research partners use situated learning, partnership working, enhanced access and reflective engagement to evaluate and critique the policy, practice and perspectives of their other partners (see also Tuckermann and Rüegg-Stürm 2010). The relational aspect of critical friendship is vital if research partners are to avoid potentially invalidating influences such as bias, lack of independence, friendship, proximity, loyalty, protectiveness and empathy (see Baskerville and Goldblatt 2009).

It is important to balance the promotion of the Reflective Friend Research model with a reflective discussion of the nature of the model. Rather than functioning as a neutral observer, within the Reflective Friend Research model, the researcher is part of the context being described. The situated and participative nature of the researcher role means that this partnership model is vulnera-ble to accusations of *researcher bias* and *lack of researcher independence*. It is possible that situated immersion in practice contexts could exacerbate researcher subjectivity, excessive empathy and a lack of criticality (e.g. 'going native'). Moreover, there is potential for a mutual respect and trust between partners translating into preferential treatment, mis-guided loyalty and over-protectiveness (cf. Fuller 2004). Yet based on experience, critical friendship is the touchstone for Reflective Friend Research. It is possible for the researcher, whilst not 'independent' in the strictest sense, to develop relationships grounded in reciprocity, trust and confidence, which in turn can enhance the quality of the situated learning, practice developments and research impact at the local level (see, for example, Haines and Case 2011).

Key principle: CFYW is underpinned by genuine partnership working that is evidence-based at the strategic and practice levels.

CONCLUSION

This chapter has offered five principles which we propose should underpin responses to children who offend. These principles draw upon principles which have historically char-acterised process-led youth work. A CFYW approach is positive, principled and progres-sive. CFYW challenges and overrides the *system first, offence first* and *offender first* foci of the negative forms of youth justice that characterise youth justice systems inter-nationally, most notably in England and Wales, North America and Australasia. The model advocates for a *systems management* approach wherein all key decisions regarding children are guided by child-friendly *evi-dence* generated in partnership between key stakeholders. In particular, decision-making is informed by empirical evidence obtained through a four-way partnership between chil-dren, youth justice practitioners, policy makers and researchers. Accordingly, *evidence-based partnership* is a central ani-mating feature of CFYW – underpinned by attention to the *relational* aspects of youth justice practice (see Case and Haines 2014a). Child-friendly and child-appropriate evi-dence emerges from empowering and respon-sibilising adult practitioners to facilitate constructive, inclusionary, participative, engaging and legitimate relationships between children and adult decision-makers (e.g. YOT workers, police officers, teachers, parents, researchers). Accessing practitioner perspectives is a crucial means of informing the decision-making processes inherent to effective, evidence-based systems manage-ment, as is accessing children's perspectives through engagement and participation mech-anisms. Crucially, the emphasis of youth justice and youth work in CFYW is placed upon the *promotion of positive behaviours and outcomes* for children, rather than privileging the reduction and prevention of negative behaviours (e.g. offending) and outcomes (e.g. exposure to risk factors).

Children First Youth Work goes beyond youth justice into all areas of the child's life as a holistic, whole-child, normalising and positive approach to children when they offend. We assert that a systematic expansion of the principles established in relation to youth justice into wider spheres of work with children is possible. There is now, more than ever, a strong case for a move from negative youth justice to positive Children First Youth Work.

Notes

1 Placed under statute by the Crime and Disorder Act 1998, Youth Offending Teams (YOTs) are multi-agency teams comprising of personnel from health, education, police, probation and social services with responsibility for the provision of youth justice services in England and Wales.
2 We use the term 'children' across this piece, in accordance with the UN Convention on the Rights of the Child designation of a 'child' as anyone aged below 18 years of age (UNICEF 1989). In the current chapter, the reference population is typically 10–17-year-olds, the age range for criminal responsibility in the Youth Justice System of England and Wales.
3 See for instance UK Government strategy documents such as *Bridging the Gap* (Social Exclusion Unit 1999); *Report of Policy Action Team 12: Young People* (Social Exclusion Unit 2000); *Every Child Matters* (Department for Education and Skills 2004); *Youth Matters* (DfES 2005); see also Turnbull and Spence (2011).
4 This is, in fact, hardly surprising given the theoretical foundations of assessment and intervention in Asset are based on Risk Factor Research, which is dominated by a developmental psycho-social paradigm (see Case and Haines 2009).

REFERENCES

Baker, K. (2005) 'Assessment in youth justice: Professional discretion and the use of Asset', *Youth Justice*, 5(2): 106–122.

Baskerville, D. and Goldblatt, H. (2009) 'Learning to be a critical friend: From professional indifference through challenge to unguarded conversations', *Cambridge Journal of Education*, 39(2): 205–221.

Bateman, T. (2011) 'Punishing poverty: The Scaled Approach and youth justice practice', *The Howard Journal of Criminal Justice*, 50(2): 171–183.

Birdwell, J. and Bani, M. (2014) *'Today's Teenagers Are More Engaged With Social Issues Than Ever …': Introducing Generation Citizen.* London: Demos.

Bradford, S. (2004) 'Management of growing up'. In: J. Roche, S. Tucker, R. Thomson and R. Flynn (eds) *Youth in Society* (pp. 245–254). London: Sage.

Bradford, S. and Cullen, F. (2014) 'Positive for youth work? Contested terrains of professional youth work in austerity England', *International Journal of Adolescence and Youth*, 19(1): 93–106.

Byrne, B. and Brooks, K. (2015) *Post-YOT Youth Justice*, Howard League for Penal Reform, available at: https://howardleague.org/wp-content/uploads/2016/04/HLWP_19_2015.pdf (accessed April 2016).

Byrne, B. and Case, S. (2016) 'Towards a positive youth justice', *Safer Communities*, 15(2): 69–81.

Case, S.P. (2006) 'Young people "at risk" of what? Challenging risk-focused early intervention as crime prevention', *Youth Justice*, 6(3): 171–179.

Case, S.P. and Haines, K.R. (2009) *Understanding Youth Offending: Risk Factor Research, Policy and Practice.* Cullompton: Willan.

Case, S.P. and Haines, K.R. (2014a) 'Children first, offenders second: The centrality of engagement in positive youth justice', *The Howard Journal of Criminal Justice*, 54(2): 157–175.

Case, S.P. and Haines, K.R. (2014b) 'Reflective Friend Research: The relational aspects of social scientific research'. In: K. Lumsden (ed.) *Reflexivity in Criminological Research* (pp. 58–74). London: Palgrave.

Case, S.P. and Haines, K.R. (2015a) 'Children First, Offenders Second positive promotion: Reframing the prevention debate', *Youth Justice*, 15(3): 226–239.

Case, S.P., Clutton, S. and Haines, K.R. (2005) 'Extending entitlement: A Welsh policy for children', *Wales Journal of Law and Policy*, 4(2): 187–202.

CYC (2016) *Ethics of Child and Youth Care Professionals*, https://cyccb.org/ethics/ (accessed July 2016).

Davies, B. (2005) Threatening youth revisited: Youth policies under New Labour. *The Encyclopaedia of Informal Education*, http://www.infed.org/archives/bernard_davies/revisiting_threatening_youth.htm (accessed July 2016).

Department for Education and Skills (2004) *Every Child Matters*. London: DfES.

Department for Education and Skills (2005) *Youth Matters*. London: DfES.

Drake, D.H., Fergusson, R. and Briggs, D.B. (2014) 'Hearing new voices: Re-viewing youth justice policy through practitioners? Relationships with young people', *Youth Justice*, 14(1): 22–39.

Drakeford, M. (2009) 'Children first, offenders second: youth justice in a devolved Wales', *Criminal Justice Matters*, 78(1): 8–9.

Farrow, K., Kelly, G. and Wilkinson, B. (2007) *Offenders in Focus*. Bristol: Policy Press.

Fionda, J. (1998) 'The age of innocence? – the concept of childhood in the punishment of young offenders', *Child and Family Law Quarterly*, 10: 77–88.

France, A. and Homel, R. (2007) *Pathways and Crime Prevention*. Cullompton: Willan.

Fuller, D. (2004) 'Going native'. In: M.S. Lewis-Beck, A. Bryman, and T. Futing Liao (eds) *The Sage Encyclopaedia of Social Science Research Methods*. (p. 435) London: Sage.

Garland, D. (1996) 'The limits of the sovereign state: Strategies of crime control in contemporary society', *British Journal of Criminology*, 36(4): 445–471.

Goldson, B. (2005) 'Taking liberties: Policy and the punitive turn'. In: H. Hendrick (ed.) *Child Welfare and Social Policy*. (pp. 235–269) Bristol: Policy Press.

Goldson, B. and Muncie, J. (2006) 'Rethinking youth justice: Comparative analysis, international human rights and research evidence', *Youth Justice*, 6(2): 91–106.

Haines, K.R. and Case, S.P. (2011) 'Risks, rights or both? Evaluating the common aetiology of negative and positive outcomes for young people to inform youth justice practice', *Social Work Review*, 2: 109–122.

Haines, K.R. and Case, S.P. (2012) 'Is the Scaled Approach a failed approach?', *Youth Justice*, 12(3): 212–228.

Haines, K.R. and Case, S.P. (2015) *Positive Youth Justice*. Bristol: The Policy Press.

Haines, K. and Drakeford, M. (1998) *Young People and Youth Justice*. London: Macmillan.

Haines, K.R., Case, S.P., Charles, A.D. and Davies, K. (2013) 'The Swansea Bureau: A model of diversion from the youth justice system', *International Journal of Law, Crime and Justice*, 41(2): 167–187.

Hart, D. and Thompson, C. (2009) *Young People's Participation in the Youth Justice System*. London: NCB.

HMI Probation. (2009) *Joint Inspection Findings of Youth Offending Teams in Wales 2003–2008*. London: HMI Probation.

Hoffman, S. and Macdonald, S. (2011) 'Tackling youth anti-social behaviour in devolving Wales: A study of the tiered approach in Swansea', *Youth Justice*, 11(2): 150–167.

ICYCAB. (2010) *Time for a Fresh Start*. London: ICYCAB, www.youthcrimecommission.org.uk.

In Defence of Youth Work (2009) Open Letter, available at: http://www.indefenceofyouthwork.org.uk (accessed May 2016).

Ipsos MORI. (2010) *A Review of Techniques for Effective Engagement and Participation*. London: YJB.

Jeffs, T. (2015) Innovation and youth work. *Youth & Policy*, 114: 75–95.

Jeffs, T. and Smith, M.K. (2002) Individualisation and youth work. *Youth & Policy*, 76: 39–65.

Kelly, L. (2012) 'Representing and preventing youth crime and disorder: Intended and unintended consequences of targeted youth programmes in England', *Youth Justice*, 12(2): 101–117.

Kelly, L. and Armitage, V. (2015) 'Diverse diversions: Youth justice reform, localised practices and a "new interventionist diversion"?', *Youth Justice*, 15(2): 117–133.

Mackie, A., Cattell, J., Reeder, N. and Webb, S. (2014) *Youth Restorative Intervention Evaluation: Final Report*, available at: https://www.surreycc.gov.uk/__data/assets/pdf_file/0020/34436/YRI-Report-FINAL.pdf (accessed April 2016).

Mason, P. and Prior, D. (2008) *Engaging Young People Who Offend*. London: YJB.

Ministry of Justice/Youth Justice Board. (2014) *Youth Justice Annual Statistics 2012–13*. London: Ministry of Justice.

Morgan, R. (2002) *Annual Lecture of the National Centre for Public Policy*. Swansea: Swansea University.

Morris, R. (2014) *Did Fools Rush In? Exploring Youth Offending Team Practitioners' Views of the Scaled Approach to Youth Justice*, PhD Thesis [unpublished], University of Lancaster.

Muncie, J. (2006) 'Governing young people: Coherence and contradiction in contemporary youth justice', *Critical Social Policy*, 26(4): 770–793.

Muncie, J. (2008) 'The "punitive" turn in juvenile justice: Cultures of control and rights compliance in Western Europe and the USA', *Youth Justice*, 8(2): 107–121.

Nacro. (2011) *Reducing the Number of Children and Young People in Custody*. London: Nacro.

Nacro Cymru. (2009) *Youth Justice and Participation in Wales*. Cardiff: Nacro Cymru.

NAYJ. (2012) *For a Child Friendly Youth Justice System*. NAYJ, available at: http://thenayj.org.uk/wp-content/uploads/2015/06/2012-A-child-focused-Youth-Justice-System.pdf

O'Malley, P. (2010) *Crime and Risk*. London: Sage.

Phoenix, J. and Kelly, L. (2013) '"You have to do it for yourself": Responsibilization and youth justice', *British Journal of Criminology*, 53(3): 419–437.

Pitts, J. (2003) *The New Politics of Youth Crime: Discipline or Solidarity?* Lyme Regis: Russell House.

Sanders, A., Young, R. and Barton, M. (2010) *Criminal Justice*. Oxford: OUP.

Smith, R. (2005) 'Welfare versus justice – again!', *Youth Justice*, 5(1): 3–16.

Social Exclusion Unit. (1999) *Bridging the Gap*. London: SEU.

Social Exclusion Unit. (2000) *Report of Policy Action Team 12: Young People*. London: SEU.

Stephenson, M., Giller, H. and Brown, S. (2010) *Effective Practice in Youth Justice*, 2nd edition. London: Routledge.

Surrey County Council. (2011) 'Strategic youth justice plan 2011–12', SCC, Kingston upon Thames, available at: http://mycouncil. surreycc.gov.uk/Data/Council/20110719/ Agenda/item%2012%20-%20Annex%20 2%20-%20Youth%20Justice%20plan%20 2011%2012.pdf (accessed March 2016).

Sutherland, A. (2009) 'The "Scaled Approach" in youth justice. Fools rush in …', *Youth Justice*, 9(1): 44–60.

Tuckermann, H. and Rüegg-Stürm, J. (2010) 'Researching practice and practicing research reflexively: Conceptualizing the relationship between research partners and researchers in longitudinal studies', *Qualitative Social Research*, 11(3).

Turnbull, G. and Spence, J. (2011) 'What's at risk? The proliferation of risk across child and youth policy in England', *Journal of Youth Studies*, 14(8): 939–959.

Tutt, N. and Giller, H. (1987) 'Manifesto for management – the elimination of custody', *Justice of the Peace*, 151: 200–202.

UNICEF (1989) *United Nations Convention on the Rights of the Child 1989*. Geneva: United Nations.

Webb, S. (2001) 'Some considerations on the validity of evidence-based practice in social work', *British Journal of Social Work*, 31(1): 57–79.

Wikström, P-O. and Treiber, K. (2008) *Offending Behaviour Programmes: Cognitive Behavioural and Multisystemic Therapies*. Youth Justice Board Source Document.

Youth Justice Board. (2000) *ASSET*. London: YJB.

Youth Justice Board. (2003) *Offending Behaviour Programmes*. London: YJB.

Youth Justice Board. (2004) *Prolific and Other Priority Offenders Strategy*. London: YJB.

Youth Justice Board. (2008) *Assessment, Planning Interventions and Supervision*, Source Document. London: YJB.

Youth Justice Board. (2010) *Youth Justice: The Scaled Approach. A Framework for Assessment and Intervention*. London: Youth Justice Board.

Youth Justice Board. (2011) *Assessment and Planning Interventions: Review and Redesign Project, Statement of Intent – Proposed Framework*. London: YJB.

Youth Justice Board. (2013) *Assessment and Planning Interventions Framework – AssetPlus*, Model Document, London: YJB.

19

Critical Street Work: The Politics of Working (In) Outside Institutions

Michael Whelan and Helmut Steinkellner

INTRODUCTION

The question of how power is distributed within and across groups in society is a central concern in any modern democracy, as it is fundamentally related to the ability of any individual or group of citizens to have a say in or influence the decisions that affect them (Harrison, 2002). If it is accepted that a position of relative powerlessness within any society does not need to be static or permanent, then it should also be accepted that the positioning of certain individuals or groups within dominant power relations might be shifted or realigned through the actions of the individuals themselves, or those who would seek to advocate with or on behalf of them. In as much as youth work practitioners seek to advocate with and on behalf of young people and, in doing so, to challenge dominant power arrangements in the interests of young people, questions of power and politics are central to the practice of youth work.

Aristotle suggested that as human beings we are 'political animals', by which he meant that as individuals with the cerebral capacity to think and to make moral decisions in relation to our own actions and the actions of others, human beings are by nature political. However, even in acknowledging the fundamentally political nature of human existence, it must also be acknowledged that there are variations in people's conscientization to the political nature of their existence, or in their capacity to make effective use of their power to pursue a particular cause (Freire, 1970). It is reasonable to argue, therefore, that despite the fundamentally political nature of youth work practice, there are variations in the extent of the conscientization of workers, and in the extent to which lines of accountability constrain the space for individual workers or groups of workers to engage in political action with or on behalf of young people.

This chapter seeks to explore a form of youth work practice which, although known by different names in different countries, will be referred to here as Critical Street Work (a term which is explored in more detail below). Critical Street Work has traditionally placed questions of power, control and authority as central to its approach to practice. It is argued that by locating themselves on the street, Critical Street Workers create opportunities to challenge or undermine power arrangements which prevent some young people's voices or concerns from being heard. In this sense, Critical Street Workers are actively engaged in political action with and on behalf of the young people they work with, and, importantly, their location on the street is seen as central to their ability to engage in a more 'genuine' dialogue with young people. 'Genuine', in this context, is used to refer to a dialogue which is more directly informed by the needs and interests of the young people themselves, as opposed to some other pre-determined agenda (The International Network of Social Street Workers (INSSW), 2008). A consistent assertion within the UK Critical Street Work literature, for example, has been that by working with young people on the street, Critical Street Workers are meeting with young people 'in their space' and 'on their terms', and that this affords them the ability to engage in a 'genuine' dialogue with young people (Whelan, 2015). Yet, limited attention has been given to a critical scrutiny of the politics of working with young people in public spaces, and that task is at the heart of what this chapter sets out to do.

Discussions within this chapter will focus on the countries of Austria and England, as these are the practice settings for the authors. The intention is not to assume that the observations made here apply to all other international settings where forms of Critical Street Work are practised, but to use these discussions as a way of opening up a critical reflection, which, to-date, has received limited focus. There are two central questions that form the basis of the discussions within the chapter. Firstly, what is the nature of young people's power within urban public spaces, and how does this relate to the kind of relationships that Critical Street Workers seek to establish with young people? And, secondly, what value does the concept of detachment[1] offer in articulating the capacity of Critical Street Workers to challenge dominant power relations within their places and spaces of work? These questions will be addressed in turn here and will structure discussions within the chapter. The key purpose in addressing these questions will be to explore the political opportunities and challenges presented by Critical Street Workers' places and spaces of work.

The authors' approach to developing the ideas explored here was to spend a week together in 'dialogue' in the Austrian city of Graz (the practice setting for Steinkellner). During this week time was spent discussing each other's practice, visiting projects, observing practice, observing public space interactions and, importantly, talking and thinking. The discussions that follow, and the insights they bring to the questions set out above, draw heavily on this week of dialogue between the authors. In this sense, the chapter might be described as a practice dialogue between the chapter's authors that seeks to interrogate and better understand the underpinning principles of Critical Street Work. Given that the term Critical Street Work is being used to refer to a common approach to working with young people evident in both the UK and Austria (and, it is thought, elsewhere), it is important to set out the key features of this common approach before addressing the chapter questions in more detail.

CRITICAL STREET WORK

Critical Street Work is a form of youth work which practice accounts suggest exists in a range of countries around the world (INSSW, 2008), although the practice is not always labelled in the same way and there are variations in practice approaches to be observed. For example, in the UK (the practice setting for one author, Whelan), this youth work approach is referred to as 'Detached Youth Work', while in Austria this youth work approach is referred to as 'Street Work'. Although there are differences in the practice approaches adopted within these two countries, the authors identify a number of common practice features.

- **Street-based working:** The most obvious starting point in identifying common practice features is that its most common setting is the street, or outdoor (usually urban) public spaces. For Detached Workers in the UK and Street Workers in Austria, the street is not just an alternative place to meet with young people, rather it is a space for political action; the location where workers seek to reveal, and often challenge, dominant power relations in the interests of the young people they work with.
- **Critical Youth Work practice:** Accepted knowledge about young people's place in society – who or what they should be, where they belong, or where they do not belong – is shaped, and reshaped, by those in positions of power. Hall suggests that 'knowledge does not operate in a void. It is put to work, through certain technologies and strategies of application, in specific situations, historical contexts and institutional regimes' (1997, p. 49). An important challenge, therefore, for Critical Street Work practitioners is to reveal the agendas and practices through which particular knowledge in relation to young people becomes accepted as 'common-sense' knowledge, and the impact this has on young people's everyday lived experiences.
- **It seeks to explore alternative, innovative or experimental approaches:** The task of engaging and providing support to young people who occupy 'marginal social positions' requires youth workers to think differently about the methods and approaches they are using. The landscape of young people's experiences is constantly changing and, in order to retain a position of relevance within this landscape, Critical Street Workers must also display an ability to continually adapt and innovate in their practice (INSSW, 2008; Whelan, 2015).

- **It challenges barriers to participation, to establish a more 'genuine' dialogue with young people:** A central principle of Critical Street Work practice is a recognition that all young people have an inherent value, worth and place in society. Critical Street Workers, therefore, play an important role in advocating with and on behalf of young people, and are ready to directly challenge those who seek to devalue or undermine young people. Able-Peterson and Wayman (2006) suggest that 'building relationships with young people is part of the process of Street Work itself' (p. 20). In this sense, the pursuit of being 'equal with young people' (in German *'Begegnung auf Augenhöhe'*) is central to genuinely hearing their concerns. The notion of equality, as it is used here, is not used in the literal sense but as an expression of the need for empathy and understanding within professional relationships with young people. There is a strong connection here with Freire's suggestion that 'those who authentically commit themselves to the people must re-examine themselves constantly' (1970, p. 60).

A common thread in each of the points above is the significance of the street as a location for working with young people. The questions that follow, therefore, attempt to critically explore the value brought by locating youth workers in the street and, more specifically, the political leverage, if any, this location brings to Critical Street Work practice. The idea of leveraging power, however, suggests that a person's ability to bring about change in any context relies not just on the power they possess, but the way in which that power is put to use. Power, as it is referred to here, therefore, is not something that some have and others do not, rather it is, as Foucault suggested, 'polymorphous' (1990, p. 11) in nature. That is, power is complex, multifaceted and assumes many different forms. This perspective on power is important in the context of this chapter because it acknowledges that young people's power in public space, and their agency to enact change, is layered and complex, and cannot simply be reduced to a zero-sum equation.

WHAT IS THE NATURE OF YOUNG PEOPLE'S POSITIONS OF POWER WITHIN URBAN PUBLIC SPACES, AND HOW DOES THIS RELATE TO THE KIND OF POWER RELATIONSHIP THAT CRITICAL STREET WORKERS SEEK TO ESTABLISH WITH YOUNG PEOPLE?

The public spaces young people occupy are 'shaped less by the textured edges of bricks and mortar and more by a far less tangible mix of power, control and authority' (Whelan, 2015, p. 192). A central focus for the first question within this chapter, therefore, is to consider the mix of power, control and authority which punctuate young people's positions of power within urban public spaces.

If you have ever sat enjoying an ice cream on a warm summer's day only to have a dollop fall onto your clothes you are likely to have been angered by this unfortunate happening, but in that moment it is possible that you did not stop to consider why it is that the ice cream 'belongs' on the cone and not your clothes, or why it no longer seemed appealing to eat the ice cream off your clothes. You may have even considered that were you to transfer the ice cream back to the cone it might in some way contaminate the remaining ice cream. In travelling from the cone to your clothes the ice cream had not suddenly morphed into some other inedible substance, rather in its new location it had become 'matter out of place' (Douglas, 1966). Douglas suggests that in order to be able to identify something as being out of place a system must exist to determine where 'things' should be; 'where there is dirt there is system' (1966, p. 35). Sometimes the 'system' which helps us determine who and what does and does not belong, is formal and clearly defined, but where this is not the case we draw on less clearly defined lines of separation to distinguish what belongs from what does not.

Central to gaining a better understanding of young people's positions of power in public

space is the task of identifying not only the formal rules which govern the use of public spaces but also the less formal lines of separation which come to define young people's use of those spaces, and their participation in society more generally. There is a growing social geography literature which directly explores the changing nature of urban public spaces and how these changes are impacting young people's public space experiences. This literature will be briefly explored here to draw out the key insights it offers in relation to the 'system' which shapes young people's use of public space.

Whilst the exclusion of certain, less desirable, groups from public spaces is not a new phenomenon, what is different today, perhaps, is the extent to which behavioural expectations have been refined, with behaviour which might be considered unpalatable being increasingly either managed within or managed out of public space (Childress, 2004; Karsten, 2005; Bannister and Kearns, 2013). Childress (2004), for example, draws attention to a number of controlling factors, such as the drive to make spaces more profitable, which are gradually encroaching into what might otherwise be liminal public spaces. She argues that this erodes young people's capacity to appropriate and modify public space as part of what she views as an important 'counter-positioning of experiential and modern cultural norms' (p. 199).

Changes in relation to the corporatization of public spaces are perhaps most sharply seen through the development of malls or shopping centres, which began to appear in many developed countries in the 1950s and have, since then, continued to spring up at an ever-increasing rate and, it appears, in ever increasing sizes. A tour of most developed capitalist (and many non-capitalist) countries today would reveal few self-respecting towns or cities that could not boast at least one large shopping centre or retail-park. Matthews et al. (2000) describe the shopping mall as a 'hybrid' place where young people can hang out in a relatively safe and secure space, but, in doing so, they must also subject themselves to the 'panopticon of the adult gaze' (p. 291), where many adults 'perceive the public and visible presence of young people … as uncomfortable and inappropriate' (p. 292).

Fyfe and Bannister (1998) explore the extent to which CCTV has been used as a tool to make town centres 'safe again', and highlight the way in which CCTV has been used to exclude certain individuals or groups who might detract from the shopping experience for those with more spending power. Millie (2008) also highlights the increasing importance of aesthetics for town centres in attracting business back from out-of-town shopping centres. However, she makes an important connection between aesthetics and efforts to tackle anti-social behaviour (ASB). Perceptions of what counts as ASB are, Millie (2008) suggests, 'strongly influenced by sensory, or aesthetic cues' (p. 383). However, Millie suggests that what counts as adults who, linking back to Douglas's arguments, invariably see young people's presence in public space as matter out of place, largely determine aesthetically pleasing from a public space perspective.

Moore (2008) provides a valuable insight into the process by which certain 'troublesome', unwanted or aesthetically displeasing groups come to be removed from particular public spaces. He highlights the way in which community policing policies pressure police to adopt exclusionary tactics in removing unwanted groups from certain public spaces. Moore suggests that these policies are facilitating or even promoting 'the eliminative ideal'[2] by giving certain sections of the community the power to dictate policing practices.

It is possible to see aspects of the eliminative ideal at work in Goldsmith's (2008) research documenting young people's experiences of CCTV cameras, Anti-social Behaviour Contacts (ASBCs) and 'stop and search' measures on a council estate in southern England. Goldsmith (2008) suggests that

as a consequence of these behaviour management practices, the young people targeted are increasingly spatially marginalized within their own communities, a point echoed in the work of Bannister and Kearns (2013).

The central point emphasized across this literature is the social, cultural and political significance of public spaces for young people; public spaces are central to young people's identity construction and their transitions to adulthood. Yet evidence of adult power and control of public spaces, and the resulting marginalization of young people, has also been consistent throughout. Additionally, the literature which focuses more specifically on 'youth participation' would suggest very mixed progress on questioning adult hegemony and challenging the underlying power dynamics which are undermining young people's place in public space (Rogers and Coaffee, 2005; Gallager, 2008; Percy-Smith, 2010).

It is useful to ground this broader discussion of young people's power in public space by returning to the previously discussed observations and reflections undertaken by the authors in the Austrian city of Graz.

The starting point for the authors' observations and discussions was the public spaces of Graz, and, specifically, young people's use of these spaces. As a visitor to this city, Whelan spent some time independently exploring the city. In addition, time was spent by both authors travelling around different parts of the centre of the city either on foot or by bike. An initial curiosity for Whelan was the extent to which the public spaces of Graz differed from similar urban spaces in the UK. Youth work practice is positioned within wider dominant discourses in relation to young people, which in turn inform youth workers' positions of power within their places and spaces of work. A particular interest within early observations, therefore, was the extent to which the discourse of 'youth presence in public space as problematic', observed by Whelan (2013) in London, was similarly in evidence in Graz.

Initial discussions and observations suggested to Whelan that there were some important disjunctions between the experiences of young people in UK urban spaces and the urban public spaces of Graz. For example, the extent of CCTV coverage in the UK is well documented and its impact on young people's use of public space has been discussed above. CCTV cameras were, therefore, much less in evidence in the public spaces of Graz than in UK cities. Other initial observations made by Whelan prompted the question of whether Graz's public spaces were more democratic, in the sense of offering a broader range of its citizens the scope to make active choices about their use of the city's public spaces, as compared with the UK. For example, Figure 19.1 shows a climbing wall which has been constructed on a river walkway running under one of the city's main roads. The very existence of this publicly accessible climbing wall suggests an openness to members of the public taking creative control of their spaces.

Similarly, the high levels of graffiti, much in English and political in nature, in certain sections of the city of Graz were, to Whelan (a visitor to the city), notable (see Figure 19.2 for some examples). In drawing attention to the prevalence of graffiti around Graz, the intention is not to suggest that this form of expression was welcomed by all, but it does suggest that, first, a relatively large number of people have been moved to express themselves in this way and, second, based on the fact that the graffiti had not been removed from many locations, there appeared to be at least a tacit acceptance of this form of public expression. Banksy, a world-renowned British graffiti artist, makes the point that the right to cover over our walls and public spaces with images and text has been claimed by those in positions of power who often use it to generate profit, by renting out portions of our public space *canvas* to those willing to pay for it (Banksy, 2005). Often this rented space is used by profit-driven enterprises to construct their own commercial aesthetic. The advertisements which pervade modern urban public spaces serve as a daily reminder to the general public of the inadequacy of their lives; our lives could be so much better if only we used the right phone, wore the right clothes or filled our homes with the right products.

The question, therefore, of whether the city of Graz and its people have managed to construct more democratic public spaces, was an important point of reflection within the authors' initial conversations. Walking around Graz it was clear that while the city is far from free of CCTV monitoring of its

Figure 19.1   Public climbing wall in Graz

Figure 19.2 a & b   Public space graffiti in Graz

public spaces, this is much less in evidence than in UK cities. However, Steinkellner suggests that over the period he and his staff team have been working with young people on the streets of Graz (16 years in total) they have observed an increase in the use of CCTV cameras. In particular he notes their use in two of the main transport hubs in the city, which first started recording inside tramways and buses in May 2013. His description of the introduction of CCTV cameras to Graz's central station, combined with the introduction of private security staff, resembles the creation of increasingly sanitized public space experiences, as described above. On our walks around the city Steinkellner identified other factors which are shaping young people's use of public space in Graz, such as increases in the budget allocated to police support officers, who operate in a support role to 'regular' police, and who Steinkellner suggests have at points been used as an additional layer of monitoring and intelligence gathering, and as another point of leverage in removing the displeasing aesthetic of unwanted groups, such as certain groups of young people (those without buying power), from the touristic and shopping areas of the city.

More detailed scrutiny of the city centre revealed other measures which had been taken to manage access to and the use of Graz's public spaces by certain individuals and groups. For example, a popular fast food restaurant in one of the city's major transport hubs was fronted by large potted plants. Without any background to this measure one might speculate that this was an attempt to enhance the aesthetics of the restaurant frontage. Steinkellner's staff team have been meeting young people in and around this location for some time and on visiting this location he agrees that the introduction of the plants was driven by aesthetics, but specifically, the human impact on the location's aesthetic. He suggests that the front of the restaurant had been a popular hangout location for young people, but that this was unpopular with the restaurant management. The restaurant is located on a busy corner with a lot of passing traffic so the large plant pots prevent people from gathering directly at the front of the restaurant. This also pushed potential loiterers into the flow of passing people, making it very difficult to gather at the front of the shop. Steinkellner points to other similar measures, such as the removal of seating areas which had been located along both sides of the main shopping streets in the city centre.

Steinkellner suggests that the cumulative effect of the measures discussed above has been to push certain groups of young people away from the main centres in the city. Instead, some of these groups occupy spaces on the periphery of the main public spaces, which can be less safe and can bring these groups of young people into more direct conflict with local residents and businesses. For example, Steinkellner identifies a small park on the periphery of one of the squares. This park is not big enough to accommodate many people, but because groups have been discouraged from gathering in the main square, larger numbers of young people are brought into closer proximity with each other, which can result in tensions and conflicts within and across groups, what Steinkellner refers to as the 'pressure cooker' effect. Some groups have started to occupy small commercial courtyards and even private car parks as alternative spaces to hang out, creating further tensions with local residents and business owners.

There is a very important point to draw from the discussion above for the wider discussions within this chapter; young people are typically not the dominant power brokers in urban public spaces, and they do not, therefore, typically have a significant say in what spaces they use or how they use those spaces. The social geography literature draws sharply into focus the unstable nature of young people's positions of power in public space, and brings into question the assumption that the choice to engage with a youth worker in public space rests solely, or even primarily, with the young person. It might reasonably be argued that young people have more choice when they *choose* to attend a youth club or *choose* how long to stay there, as opposed to on the street where a young person has no choice when they are approached by a street-based youth worker. The street-based worker may be sensitive to how, why and when they approach a young person but this in and of itself does not amount to enhancing young people's agency to exercise control.

This point is important because it has long been argued by advocates of Critical Street Work that by working with young people in public spaces, as opposed to in a youth centre, that the power relationship between worker and young person is altered in the young person's favour (Able-Peterson and Wayman, 2006; Tiffany, 2007; INSSW, 2008; Whelan, 2015). If locating oneself in a public space does not, in and of itself, shift power relations in the interest of the young people, it is important to consider the basis for the assumed ability of Critical Street Workers to operate outside of, or to challenge, conventional adult-centric power arrangements. In observing and reflecting on Critical Street

Work practice in Graz the authors considered whether Whelan's (2015) emphasis on the potential to gain a level of 'institutional and organizational detachment' by working on the street might provide a helpful explanation of Critical Street Workers capacity to challenge or subvert dominant power relations (including their own lines of accountability) in the interest of young people. The reference to dominant power relations here is not intended to suggest that young people have no power in public spaces, rather that the adult-centric public space discourses explored above serve to consistently undermine young people's positions of power, and their capacity to exercise agency. This is given further consideration within the second key question of this chapter.

WHAT VALUE DOES THE CONCEPT OF DETACHMENT OFFER IN ARTICULATING THE CAPACITY OF CRITICAL STREET WORKERS TO CHALLENGE DOMINANT POWER RELATIONS WITHIN THEIR PLACES AND SPACES OF WORK?

It is worth briefly reminding ourselves at this point of the notion of detachment which is introduced above. Whelan (2015) suggests that Critical Street Work is defined by 'its institutional and organizational detachment' (p. 186). It is through achieving a degree of distance from institutional and organizational agendas that Critical Street Workers carve out a practice space within which they can more effectively 'explore alternative, innovative or experimental approaches to understanding and challenging the barriers to participation experienced by young people in marginal social positions' (Whelan, 2015, p. 186). In this sense, it is argued that the street can offer a more fluid, often uncertain, and potentially creative space for working with young people. Certain more conventional

internal practice spaces, on the other hand, can often become driven by organizational imperatives, which can engender more structured, routine and potentially less critical, ways of working with young people.

An underlying premise for the pioneers of Critical Street Work in the UK was that the way in which a service is delivered can be the very obstacle preventing those who most need that service from engaging with it (Goetschius and Tash, 1967). The concept of detachment, therefore, was seen as central, both in the development of services which were informed by those who most needed them, but also in improving take-up amongst those young people who felt alienated from mainstream services. In conversation about his work Steinkellner was able to identify aspects of his project's activities which were very much aligned with this notion of detachment. This point was of particular interest because although Steinkellner and some of his staff team had had some limited exposure to the UK concept of Detached Youth Work, this was not a core part of their practice conversations, nor was it a central tenet of wider Austrian Street Work practice understandings.

An important question, therefore, which Whelan and Steinkellner sought to explore within their practice reflections, was whether the concept of detachment, as it is described above, can help to more accurately articulate the capacity of Steinkellner and his team to challenge dominant power relations within their places and spaces of work, in the interests of young people. It is important to note that this is not simply an abstract academic pursuit. What will be demonstrated here is that gaining a clearer understanding of power relations within Critical Street Work has fundamental implications for everyday practical considerations in the planning and delivery of work with young people. What follows, therefore, is a more detailed discussion of certain aspects of Steinkellner's work with a view to establishing the relevance of the concept of detachment to that work and a practical consideration of the implications for everyday practice interventions.

Steinkellner works with a large voluntary sector organization that delivers a range of support services to a broad range of young people. We will refer to the organization as 'Charity A'. Charity A's work is categorized (by the organization itself) as falling under one or more of the following three headings: people in need; support and care; and education and inter-cultural work. It is a large and complex organization, employing a broad range of staff to deliver its various services. A detailed analysis of such a complex organization is beyond the scope of the discussion here, but there are some important points worth noting, which are of particular relevance to a more detailed consideration of Steinkellner's Street Work.

The services delivered by the various arms of Charity A are all informed by the organization's centrally driven values, principles, and its related ways of working. For example, Charity A is a Catholic charity, and a visit to its headquarters in Graz was revealing in the extent to which Catholicism, or Christian symbolism at least, was in evidence. For example, most if not all of the rooms visited on various floors of the organization's headquarters had a crucifix hanging or painted on one of the walls. At a more organizational level, many of the projects delivered by Charity A are delivered either in partnership with other Catholic organizations, or with the support of various priests or nuns. So, whether a particular project is a commissioned service delivered on behalf of national or local government, or is funded directly from Charity A's own reserves, the underlying values and principles of Catholicism are likely to filter through from the centre. The point here is not to open up a debate about secularism in the voluntary sector, rather to emphasize the extent to which a set of beliefs, and related values and principles, may filter out from the centre through a form of moral centralization.[3]

The moral centralization in evidence in Charity A is, however, just one dimension of a broader analysis which might be undertaken of the tendency within large organizations (charitable or not) towards making decisions about the planning, organizing and structuring of service delivery from the centre outwards. Every organization, large or small, has its own organizational identity which will, or should, inform the types of services delivered and the way in which those services are delivered. Organizations will, however, vary in the extent to which their organizational identity influences every aspect of their employees' activities. That is, some organizations will allow their employees a level of flexibility in working practices, whilst for others everything from what the employee wears to what they say when they interact with clients is determined by 'the centre'. This centralization tendency should not be surprising in larger organizations given that one of the advantages of being a large organization is the ability to save costs by pooling certain common activities. So, for example, larger organizations can take advantage of economies of scale by centralizing services such as personnel, finance and marketing. Whilst there are undeniable cost benefits that arise out of centralizing common services such as these, it is also important to acknowledge the aggregated effect of such economies on the service user experience. This point is given particular consideration here in relation to Steinkellner work in the delivery of services to marginalized young people.

For Steinkellner, the corporate identity of his parent organization, including its links to Catholicism, represents a potential difficulty or block in working with disengaged young people on the streets of Graz. One example of a challenge presented by the corporate identity of the parent organization is the fact that the young people Steinkellner's team seeks to work with come from a broad range of cultural and ethnic backgrounds, and represent an equally varied range of religious beliefs (or lack thereof). An over-association with Christianity or Catholicism, therefore, may make it more difficult for Steinkellner and his team to engage with the diverse range of young people they seek to work with. One strand in Steinkellner's approach to managing this challenge has been to develop a sub-brand for the street-work project. This sub-branding manifests itself in a number of different ways. For example, the project has its own logo and its own branded leaflets, information booklets and publicity. Distance from the Christian branding which is in evidence in Charity A's headquarters is also apparent in the street-work team's offices, where the crucifix is much less prominently displayed.

Branding involves the use of visual graphics to 'represent' a project or organization to the outside world (Banet-Weiser, 2012). Branding helps to convey what an organization does, but also how and even why it does it. Steinkellner makes the point, however, that a re-branding exercise is a very shallow exercise if it is not also aligned with the actual everyday practices that the branding is intended to convey. In this sense, while the branding of the street-work team reflects detachment from the parent organization, the team's everyday practices must also be consistent with this branding message. The team's detachment, therefore, is also reflected in a broad range of the team's everyday practices, such as: the rules they apply (or more accurately the absence of certain rules); the uniform (or lack of) worn by its staff; the team's attitude to risk; the team's approach to working around more sensitive topics such as sexual health; and the team's willingness to work with certain young people considered by some other projects as too challenging or difficult to work with. Perhaps the most significant feature of the team's detachment, however, is evident in the distance the youth workers gain from the constraints of internal youth club space when they go out on the street to engage and work with young people. It is worth, therefore,

exploring this dimension of their work in a little more detail.

As a starting point, and to state the obvious, the team's street-based encounters happen on the street, and, as has been discussed above, while such street-based encounters do not guarantee detachment from institutional or organizational agendas, they offer a space where the cues to practitioner power are less pronounced. The physical layout of the indoor youth club space out of which the street-based workers operate features a number of quite fixed indicators as to who the power and knowledge holders are in that location. For example, the main club space includes a kitchen/bar area which, though not labelled as a formal 'reception', seems to act as such. That is, it is a staff-controlled space and, although it is not located directly inside the entry door, it faces the main entrance and, as such, it serves as a direct point of reference and orientation for newcomers (or existing users) entering the space. Youth club reception spaces more generally tend to be occupied or managed by practitioners and act as a frontline filter, mediating access to and use of the club space (acting often as both a physical and symbolic barrier to the space that lies beyond). Similarly, the back office in the youth club, out of which Steinkellner and his team operate, is a controlled space, where a locked door demarcates the boundary between what is generally perceived as a more democratic club space and an office space where the movement of people, and the flow of information, is much more tightly managed.

This is not to deny the existence of equivalences of 'reception' and 'back office' spaces for the team's work space on the street. The ID badge, the uniform jacket, or the logo embroidered t-shirt or rucksack may all perform a similar symbolic role to that of the reception desk. The ID badge, for example, provides an official status to its wearer, and it is with the official status conferred by the badge that the street-based worker can assume the authority to engage with his or her target group. In much the same way that a reception space directs those entering a youth club to the gatekeepers of that space, so too the wearing of an ID badge (however subtly it is worn) can serve as an indicator of the authority with which a street-based worker makes an unsolicited approach to a young person. An important difference, however, between the internal club space and the street is the fluid and often unpredictable nature of the street-based setting. This is not to deny the lack of certainty which often characterizes internal club space, but rather to acknowledge the broader range of features of the street-based work environment which are beyond the control of the worker.

The indoor youth work setting might be likened to two people having a conversation where one person has greater scope to dictate how the conversation is opened, to set the direction for how the conversation progresses and to determine how the conversation is brought to a close. The fluid and often unpredictable nature of youth work in street-based settings, means that the ability to dictate the flow of a conversation, or an interaction more generally, is significantly disrupted. In this sense, therefore, it is the detachment of Steinkellner's street-based workers from the more managed indoor club spaces, and the cues to dominant positions of knowledge and power within, which open up the potential for alternative, and possibly even more democratic, interactions with young people. Importantly, it is the street-based worker's willingness not just to experience but to embrace and even actively pursue engagements with young people in these more institutionally and organizationally detached street-based locations that enables them to pursue a form of youth work practice which we have referred to here as Critical Street Work. It is in adopting a Critical Street Work approach, with its emphasis on detachment, that street-based workers can unpick or unsettle established and even taken-for-granted assumptions in relation to positions of power and knowledge, and, in doing so,

open up opportunities to 'explore alternative, innovative or experimental approaches to understanding and challenging the barriers to participation experienced by young people in marginal social positions' (Whelan, 2015, p. 186).

SUMMARY AND CONCLUSIONS

This chapter has set out to explore a form of youth work practice, Critical Street Work, which places questions of power at the heart of its approach to practice. Critical Street Work seeks to develop approaches to working, and working environments, within which its practitioners can proactively advocate with and on behalf of young people who occupy marginal social positions. Two key questions were addressed within the chapter, which sought, firstly to establish the nature of young people's positions of power in public spaces, and the relative positions of power between young person and Critical Street Worker, and, secondly, to consider the relevance of the concept of detachment to the politics of working (in) outside institutions. Three key conclusions can be drawn from the discussions around these areas of debate.

The first key conclusion is that young people's positions of power in public space are less certain or stable than they are often presented as being. Critical Street Workers have often assumed that when they engage with young people in public spaces they are doing this 'in their space' and 'on their terms'. The social geography literature reviewed here, and the authors' observations made in Graz, clearly demonstrate that not only is this a misguided assumption, but that the changing nature of urban public spaces is such that young people's use of public spaces is becoming ever more intensively managed and monitored.

A second key conclusion is that there was nothing in the observations of public spaces or Critical Street Work practice contained within this chapter that suggested that any significant relative loss of power on behalf of Critical Street Workers can be assumed when they locate themselves on the street. That is, if there is any political advantage of locating one's practice in a street-based location, that advantage does not come from assuming a significant shift in the relative positions of power between youth worker and young person. The political advantage of locating oneself on the street, therefore, must lie in the potential offered by street-based locations to leverage practitioner power differently, and this leads on to the final key conclusion.

Thirdly, the concept of institutional and organizational detachment provides a more accurate articulation of the political advantages of Critical Street Work, rather than an assumed shift in the relative positions of power between youth worker and young person by locating oneself on the street. That is, if Critical Street Workers are to challenge dominant power arrangements in the interests of the young people they are working with they must be able to place questions of power and politics at the heart of their practice. This, in turn, requires an acute awareness of the ways in which they manage their institutional and organizational detachment through the strategic and everyday practice decisions they make.

In drawing these conclusions it is also important to draw attention to a limitation of the insights provided within this chapter, the absence of young people's perspectives. What has been set out here is a practitioner dialogue and, as illuminating as it has been to engage with this dialogue, it would be amiss for a youth work approach which seeks a more genuine dialogue with young people not to note the limitation of a dialogue about its approach which has not involved young people. In this sense this chapter represents an opening point for a conversation which must be broadened through further dialogues with the young people with whom Critical Street Workers would seek to work.

In a chapter that has set out to connect a theoretical discussion of a particular Youth Work approach with practical considerations in relation to everyday practices within that approach, it is fitting to finish with a practical consideration in relation to the funding and management of Critical Street Work. A consistent approach to delivering Critical Street Work projects relies on funding organizations to either have some understanding of the underlying principles of the approach, and the flexibility required to pursue its aims, or be willing to fund and manage from a position of blind faith. In a public service delivery context that is increasingly informed by neo-liberal approaches to management, the latter of these options is increasingly rare, and its desirability, in any case, is highly questionable. All the more reason, therefore, that Critical Street Work projects should be able to very clearly articulate not just the value of being on the street but also, more specifically, the importance of adopting particular practices within these street settings.

Without a clearer articulation of the specific aims and related practices which underpin Critical Street Work, its practitioners risk being positioned by those who would fund and manage resources as nothing more than a mobile 'fire-fighting' resource, positioned within dominant practice discourses which all too consistently construct young people's presence in public space as problematic, something to be neutralized and, where possible, removed. With this in mind, the final act of this chapter is to propose that the underlying purpose of Critical Street Work should be to disrupt or challenge dominant power relations in order to engender self-advocacy and provide support and commitment for young people to recognize their circumstances and, ultimately, act in their own interests.

Notes

1 'Detachment in the context of Detached Youth Worker then, is said to relate to workers' avoidance

of the types of pre-determined agendas, which generally accompany other forms of Youth Work' (Whelan, 2015, p. 185).

2 The eliminative ideal refers to efforts to 'solve present and emerging problems by getting rid of troublesome and disagreeable people with methods which are lawful and widely supported' (Rutherford, 1997, p. 116).

3 Centralization refers to the process of administering shared organizational activities (typically finance or human resources related) from a centralized unit, with the benefit of improved efficiency and standardization (Fahy et al., 2005). Moral centralization refers to an extension of this process to include the centralizing of decisions relating to the moral identity of the organization and, arguably, its workers, which are then disseminated out from the centre.

REFERENCES

Able-Peterson, T. and Hooks Wayman, R. (2006) *StreetWorks: Best Practices and Standards in Outreach Methodology to Homeless Youth*. Minneapolis: StreetWorks Collaborative.

Banet-Weiser, S. (2012) *Authentic TM: The Politics of Ambivalence in a Brand Culture*. New York: New York University Press.

Banksy (2005) *Wall and Piece*. London: Century.

Bannister, J. and Kearns, A. (2013) Overcoming intolerance to young people's conduct: Implications from the unintended consequences of policy in the UK, *Criminology and Criminal Justice*, 13(4), pp. 380–397.

Bannister, J., Kintrea, K. and Pickering, J. (2013) Young people and violent territorial conflict: Exclusion, culture and the search for identity, *Journal of Youth Studies*, 16 (4), pp. 474–490.

Childress, H. (2004) Teenagers, territory and the appropriation of space, *Childhood*, 11(2), pp. 195–205.

Douglas, M. (1966) *Purity and Danger*. London: Routledge.

Fahy, M., Weiner, A. and Roche, J. (2005) *Beyond Governance: Creating Corporate Value Through Performance, Conformance and Responsibility*. Chichester: Wiley.

Foucault, M. (1990) *The History of Sexuality: An Introduction*. (trans. Robert Hurley). New York: Vintage.

Freire, P. (1970) *Pedagogy of the Oppressed*. New York: Continuum.

Fyfe, N.R. and Bannister, J. (1998) The eyes upon the street: Closed-circuit television surveillance and the city. In Fyfe, N.R. (ed.) *Images of the Street: Representation, Experience and Control in Public Space*. London: Routledge, pp. 254–267

Gallager, M. (2008) Foucault, power and participation, *International Journal of Children's Rights*, 16(3), pp. 395–406.

Gillich, Stefan (2006) *Professionelles Handeln auf der Straße*. Verlag TRIGA.

Goetschius, G.W. and Tash, M.J. (1967) *Working with Unattached Youth: Problem, Approach, Method*. London: Routledge and Kegan Paul.

Goldsmith, C. (2008) Cameras, cops and contracts: What anti-social behaviour management feels like to young people. In Squires, P. (ed.) *ASBO Nation: The Criminalisation of Nuisance*. Bristol: Policy, pp. 231–245

Hall, S. (1997) *Representation: Cultural Representations and Signifying Practices*. London: Sage.

Harrison, R. (2002) *Democracy*. London: Routledge.

Hinz, P., Simon, T. and Wollschläger, T. (2000) *Streetwork in der Wohnungslosenhilfe*. Schneider Verlag.

Jackson, P. (1998) Domesticating the street: The contested spaces of the high street and the mall. In Fyfe, N.R. (ed.) *Images of the Street: Planning, Identity, and Control in Public Spaces*. London: Routledge, pp. 176–191.

Karsten, L. (2005) It All Used to be Better? Different Generations on Continuity and Change in Urban Children's Daily use of Space, *Children's Geographies*, 3(3), pp. 275–290.

Matthews, H., Taylor, M., Percy-Smith, B. and Limb, M. (2000) The unacceptable flaneur: The shopping mall as a teenage hangout, *Childhood*, 7(3): 279–294.

Millie, A. (2008) Anti-Social behaviour, behavioural expectations and an urban aesthetic, *British Journal of Criminology*, 48(3), pp. 379–394.

Moore, S. (2008) 'Street life, neighbourhood policing and "the community"' in P. Squires (ed.) *ASBO Nation: The Criminalisation of Nuisance*. Bristol: Policy Press, pp. 187–209.

Percy-Smith, B. (2010) Councils, consultations and community: rethinking the spaces for children and young people's participation, *Children's Geographies*, 8(2), pp. 107–122.

Rogers, P. and Coaffee, J. (2005) Moral panics and urban renaissance, *City: analysis of urban trends, culture, theory, policy, action*, 9(3), pp. 321–340.

Rutherford, A. (1997) Criminal policy and the eliminative ideal, *Social Policy & Administration*, 31(5), pp. 116–135.

The International Network of Social Street Workers (INSSW) (2008) *International Guide on the Methodology of Street Work throughout the World*. Brussels: Dynamo International.

Tiffany, G. (2007) *Reconnecting Detached Youth Work: Guidelines and Standards for Excellence*. Leicester: The Federation for Detached Youth Work.

Whelan, M. (2010) Detached youth work. In Batsleer, J. and Davies, B. (eds) *What is Youth Work*? Exeter: Learning Matters, pp. 47–60

Whelan, M. (2013) Street violence amongst young men in London: Everyday experiences of masculinity and fear in public space. PhD, Brunel University.

Whelan, M. (2015) Re-locating detached youth work. In Bright, G. (ed.) *Youth Work: Histories, Policy and Contexts*. London: Palgrave, pp. 182–198

20

Youth Work, Arts Practice and Transdisciplinary Space

Frances Howard, Steph Brocken and
Nicola Sim

INTRODUCTION

For some youth workers, the prospect of a visit to a gallery can provoke a range of emotionally charged reactions. During an observation at an awayday for children and youth services held at a gallery in an English coastal town, youth workers named a number of factors that inhibit their engagement with the art institution. Fear of their groups being reprimanded in the quiet, 'posh' context of the gallery space featured strongly in discussions. Several practitioners also reported feeling alienated by the intellectualising tendencies of gallery interpretation, as well as a concern that their lack of knowledge might be exposed. Many of the youth workers had little prior contact with the visual arts, so galleries were also not perceived as spaces where they could confidently act at their most competent as practitioners.

This example, taken from a doctoral study exploring partnership work between galleries and youth organisations, offers a small insight into youth workers' historically difficult relationship with the visual arts. The social and psychological barriers identified by the practitioners point, for instance, to the classed dimensions of the relationship between the youth and cultural workers. Differences in cultural capital are regularly illuminated in these types of encounters between the visual arts sector (typically understood to be the domain of middle-class values) and the youth sector (increasingly populated by adults and young people who identify as working class) (Batsleer, 2014). The following chapter refers to 'the arts' in the broader sense, to include performance, music and film-making, as well as gallery-based practices. As three doctoral researchers investigating programmes that stage encounters between youth work and informal arts education, we are in a position to reflect upon the forces that characterise these professional fields as both natural allies and uneasy bedfellows. Our enquiry is driven by a belief that these intersections open up a complex space for reflection on disciplinary identity, and produce new sites to support the generation of innovative practice. Aside from acknowledging the personal benefits that interactions with the arts afford, we share a common understanding that the arts and arts-based pedagogies provide valuable collective experiences and creative pathways towards political and social engagement.

Throughout this chapter we explore the compatibility of arts and youth work practices in a UK context, focusing on tensions, pedagogical similarities and differences, and ask how these seemingly distinct regimes of knowledge coexist and influence each other. We do this by looking at three doctoral research sites where the arts and youth work come together: Tate's Circuit programme (Nicola Sim), the young people's Arts Award (Frances Howard) and theatre practice within MyPlace youth centres (Steph Brocken).

Cumulatively, our studies span a five-year time period, from 2011 to 2016, so the fieldwork we draw upon took place against the backdrop of austerity politics. It is commonly understood that austerity measures and policy shifts in the UK and much of Europe have seen youth work become politically deprioritised and severely underfunded. This has led to widespread debate over the value of youth work, and has contributed to the development of youth work's new utilitarian role (Batsleer & Davies, 2010; Coburn, 2011). Arts programmes have experienced similar challenges, often being required to demonstrate social or economic impacts (Belfiore, 2002; Kinder & Harland, 2004; Holden, 2006). So both sectors face external pressures that have forced re-evaluations of the significance and intrinsic benefits of their practices.

Previous research (Ruiz, 2004) has argued for the potential of the youth service for widening young people's access to the arts, and case studies have argued for the value of the arts as methods for engagement within youth work (IDYW, 2014). The arts are frequently used as tools for informal learning

in youth work as a pedagogy of the here-and-now (Batsleer, 2009) and as a means to re-engage reluctant learners (Sefton-Green, 2003). Research has also shown that arts spaces can offer important opportunities for youth work and vice versa (Kiilakoski & Kivijarvi, 2015; Nolas, 2014; Sefton-Green, 2003). However, arguably, there is relatively limited discussion of the arts in youth work literature beyond therapeutic or instrumental framings. There are exceptions, and certainly there is evidence of an increasing academic investment in reframing the role of arts in youth work, although much of this work is concentrated around the performing arts. Current narratives that surround the practice of youth work highlight instrumental shifts, with an emphasis on addressing 'problems' (Coburn, 2011), with priority given to 'child saving' and 'youth control' (Davies, 2010), and with the re-emergence of pedagogical expectations, where youth work becomes more 'organised' and about 'participation' (Van de Walle et al., 2011). One of the questions this chapter asks therefore is whether increasingly instrumental approaches have limited organisational and practitioner capacities for cross-sector collaboration. We argue that the political and economic context both incentivises cross-sector working, and simultaneously restricts it, which adds to the already pressured conditions of a youth–arts alliance.

This chapter also seeks to make a case for increased dialogue and intersection across arts and youth practitioner communities, as spaces for creative, open-ended youth work are consistently squeezed, and arts institutions are working to develop the quality and longevity of these partnerships. We look at the implications of taking arts practices into youth work settings and at projects that create new environments for this work to take place. We identify the professional parameters that distinguish youth work and arts education and discuss the moves undertaken by practitioners and programmes to transgress these boundaries and experiment with hybridised models of practice. Finally, we suggest that arts education practitioners have the potential to be critical advocates for youth work as a form of pedagogy (Batsleer, 2009) that promotes social education and democratic practice.

STUDY SITES AND METHODOLOGIES

The chapter draws upon three doctoral studies, which investigate practical examples, bringing together the arts and youth sectors in work with young people. These three high-profile national initiatives highlight some of the dimensions that characterise the relationships between youth work and arts practice.

Nicola Sim's wider research explores partnerships between galleries and youth organisations, using a four-year programme called Circuit as the primary context for fieldwork. Circuit is led by Tate galleries and is funded by the Paul Hamlyn Foundation (a UK-based charity). It involves organisations in eight towns and cities around England and Wales. The chief goal of the programme is to connect 15–25-year-olds to the arts in galleries and museums, through working together with the youth and cultural sector. Taking a multi-sited, ethnographic approach, Sim followed the development of these cross-sector relationships between 2014 and 2015. Circuit is one example of a number of large-scale initiatives running concurrently in the UK, which have sought to foster sustainable partnerships between arts and youth organisations. While there is a long history of work in this field, gallery education and youth work are arguably less familiar to one another than the performing arts and youth work, where there are more embedded traditions of practice.

Frances Howard explored the young people's Arts Award, a national qualification for 5–25-year-olds, and a growing area of vocational arts education, which is frequently

delivered in the youth sector. Also taking an ethnographic approach, Howard studied three youth projects utilising the Arts Award, aggregating observational and interview data around the value, experience and practice of the award. Fieldwork took place in both open access and targeted youth projects in community and youth centres in a city centre location. The approach to the research was through participant observation focusing on the lived experience of young people undertaking the award, often accompanying them across multiple sites where they undertook their arts engagement. Young people took up different arts activities, from music production to film-making and from street-dance to spray painting. Her stance was based on a youth work approach to research and contained many arts-based and collaborative methods. The youth workers interviewed as part of this study, were responsible for running the award and directing the artistic activities. Many of them came from an arts background or were practitioners themselves, especially in regards to music activities such as rapping and DJ-ing.

Steph Brocken examined the intersection between youth theatre and youth work as part of her wider thesis exploring the conceptualisation of Youth Theatre as a distinct form within applied arts practices. As part of this she drew upon her experience of delivering drama work in a youth sector setting, namely a large-scale 'Youth Zone', funded initially through the government's MyPlace scheme (billed as the largest ever UK government investment in youth facilities, putting £270 million into youth venues around Britain). This particular Youth Zone employed Brocken in 2012, along with a team of practitioners in other art forms, to deliver regular arts activity to its membership of young people between the ages of 8 and 19. In this early period, the arts were highlighted as a particular area of focus for the organisation. This experience influenced Brocken in her doctoral studies and led to several academic papers on the intersection between the two worlds. These intersections included: the role the arts have to play in the youth work setting; how far youth theatre can be characterised as youth work and how far the youth theatre practitioner can be characterised as a youth worker. Some of these concerns will be drawn upon in this chapter.

Taken together, our research explores the interlocking of arts-based work into youth work practice and highlights youth workers' mixed perceptions of the arts and arts spaces. Findings show that in some contexts, youth workers are required to undertake a dual role, employing a united pedagogical approach that is sympathetic to the values and practices of both arts work and youth work. Each example shows the different challenges that youth workers can experience in their job role. We argue that there is sometimes tension between arts- and youth-work-based approaches, and perceived divisions, for instance between drama work as delivered in the process-driven so-called 'youth work tradition', and youth theatre as performed in an allegedly product-focused arts context. Our findings also reflect some of the dilemmas that arise when running semi-structured or structured arts projects within open-access, drop-in youth provision and describe how practitioners navigate artistic and social outcomes, as well as their own occupational identities in these situations. The following section focuses on significant individual qualities of each programme, before concluding with the challenges and opportunities created by all three programmes.

THE YOUNG PEOPLE'S ARTS AWARD AS A TOOL FOR YOUTH WORK

The core purpose of youth work is the personal and social development of young people through informal education (Batsleer, 2009). *An Evaluation of the Impact of Youth Work in England* (Merton, 2004: 6) states that the principal roles of youth workers are as social educators, guides and mentors who offer 'learning, support and challenge to the young people and encourage them to make informed decisions'. Youth work as informal education can help to support emotional and personal development – a young person's rights and needs, identified by Kemmis (2012) as 'double purpose education' (p. 894) … in terms of 'living well and helping to create a world worth living in' (p. 895). The point of engagement between the educator and young people is not the body of knowledge: it is the development of the young people themselves and of their life world (Jeffs & Smith, 1999). Significant characteristics of informal education include the importance of dialogue and relationships, learning through the everyday, learning by doing (experiential learning) and social and relational learning, i.e. from working with, observing and learning from others. Arts programmes such as the Arts Award share this informal education pedagogy and position the arts as a vehicle for the personal and social development of young people.

Conversation, negotiation and the co-creation of knowledge are also shared elements between the arts and youth work. With the Arts Award, the youth worker asks the young person what they want to do, they discuss it, they negotiate and then the youth worker facilitates to make it happen. It has been argued that educational youth work is where young people and youth workers collaborate, through critical and reflective dialogue, in the construction of knowledge, but that this is sometimes restricted by time and resources (Gormally & Coburn, 2014). In the projects that were observed, collaboration ranged from making a music track to creating an album cover and from planning and delivering an arts festival to performing at an open mic night. The programmes facilitated learning through dialogue between youth worker and young person or artist and young person, as close relationships were developed. In this way knowledge was co-created through the young person's experience, as opposed to learning a fixed body of knowledge.

Previous research has argued for the value of youth workers' skills in terms of improvisation for youth work (IDYW, 2014), using the arts as a tool to approach sensitive subjects with young people (Davies, 2011) and as part of their own personal 'tool box' to create activities for their settings (Kiilakoski & Kivijarvi, 2015). Workers interviewed as part of this study viewed the Arts Award as a tool for offering new experiences and a useful framework through which to structure youth sessions. The arts are often seen as vehicles for engaging young people in positive activities and for taking them on personal and emotional journeys, but they also achieve an end product that a young person can take pride in (Davies, 2011). With the Arts Award, the young people reported that they valued working towards something: a creation, an event, as a final product. Also being an accredited award added weight to the activities through recognition of the young people's achievements. However, they also held the process of working with the arts and the time to develop their own arts practice in high regard, in particular when programmes offered the opportunity to work with professional artists, alongside youth workers.

Individual youth workers shared a consensus when reporting back on benefits for the young people from the Arts Award programme, which included participating in new opportunities, new networks, and looking at the 'wider picture'. Workers mentioned taking young people to places they wouldn't normally go, opening up new experiences, putting different groups of youth together, achieving goals, opening up pathways and removing barriers to training and employment that the young person would not have previously accessed. The young people's Arts Award in particular afforded young people the opportunity to develop new arts skills and build up a portfolio. This was a tangible outcome that young people could

see develop throughout the programme and often take pride in, as they documented artistic processes, final creations and public performances, serving as a keepsake after the project had finished.

> It [the Arts Awards] changed our delivery in a positive way, so they're gaining new experiences and we can be flexible with it. So if we get to the session and the kids wanna do dance, then they can do dance around their Arts Award. We don't have to go back and start trawling through, looking for something that's near dance in the NOCN folder and then build up schemes of work and lesson plans ... It allows you to build a framework for your session as well, so we've built projects around the Arts Award. Or elements around the Arts Award. So before we did Arts Award, we would have never taken children out to an art gallery. That's been really nice for us as we've done that and seen some really great results. Mix that in with a project, so if it's a journalism project, we've given them portable recorders and asked them to interview people at the gallery, and each other about their experiences and stuff. So it meets multiple needs there. (Youth Worker)

As well as learning arts skills through the Arts Award, many youth workers reported that it was a useful tool for the personal, social and educational development of their young people. They viewed the arts as a useful vehicle in order to send messages and build bridges. One of the key values of youth work is identity building through interactions with the everyday, where youth clubs provide a culture of participation and a common language which generates a sense of belonging with other young people in the area (Nolas, 2014). With the Arts Award, despite the young people's diverse backgrounds and arts interests, they felt an affinity as a group through undertaking the award in a youth setting. Young people were using their cultural or arts practice to negotiate their identities and to become part of certain communities, which were viewed in a positive light by the workers, as opposed to deficit groupings. As a 'measurable' accredited outcome for young people, their engagement in these programmes was seen as positive and frequently justified their funding through local authority run youth projects. This instrumentalised approach to arts engagement afforded many young people opportunities to take part and develop creatively, but also restricted their experience to what was being offered as part of the programme and the quality of this experience. However, the prioritisation by policy makers and local authorities of social aims, accredited outcomes and 'value for money' arts education programmes such as the Arts Award, has been translated at a local level by youth workers to the privileging of development.

STEPPING ON TOES: ARTS WORK WITHIN THE YOUTH WORK SETTING

Despite the many areas of crossover between arts work and youth work, there are certain clear tensions that emerge when attempting to bring together these two distinct areas. Brocken attempted to make use of both sites of observation (i.e. the MyPlace centre and her Youth Theatre setting) in highlighting areas of both tension and commonality.

In the case of young people, attitudes to the presence of education and learning are particularly significant. An important difference between the youth arts and youth work setting is the imperative within youth arts for the young person to be learning something; developing their skills in a specific arts area or learning about another wider theme through the medium of the arts experience. During week three of Brocken's observations of the group in the youth setting she made the following field notes about a group of boys who had been pushed into her session to give them something to do as they were not engaged in any activities and were perceived to be causing trouble in the building:

> They stayed and participated well in the game although at first their arrival was disruptive to the group. They gradually settled in with body language relaxing and higher levels of eye contact and approval seeking. The group were set a pre-designed script task to block and then finish themselves. The boys group engaged initially then fell away when asked to add imaginatively to the script and rehearse. The rehearsal process is often something that puts new participants off and something that we have had to work on a lot with the regulars. (Fieldnotes)

This demonstrates a clear 'turn off' moment that occurs when young people who are engaging within the youth work environment have their expectations of the environment challenged. Notions of 'learning' within the youth arts and the youth work setting, therefore, must be dealt with in contrasting ways. Batsleer and Davies (2010: 63) have pinpointed this tension between the notion of 'the arts' as a product-focused construct and the freedom inherent in youth work, stating that:

> a narrow definition of creativity places overt emphasis on the use of the arts. When creativity is thus confined then young people may be excluded as the focus is likely to move, for example, on to producing a great performance or a honed and polished manufactured product. This can disenfranchise young people and those who work with them.

However, despite this, benefits can clearly be seen through the development of 'soft skills', such as through confidence and self-esteem building. In defining the different types of development that emerged during observation of the MyPlace group, Brocken labelled them the three Cs: confidence, comfort and connection. All three of these areas can be observed through both settings, however their weighting varies noticeably. In the youth theatre setting, there is a clear and accepted imperative for young people to improve their confidence. Throughout the interviews that were undertaken with this group, this was a topic that they returned to, demonstrating their own awareness of this aspect of their engagement. In the interviews with youth theatre participants, comments such as those below were shared, demonstrating this level of awareness of the idea of confidence and its importance:

> 'I've learnt to be more confident', 'I feel my confidence has grown', 'you'll get people getting to know each other and making friends better and that'll mean they'll be less self-conscious'.

However, confidence is a 'buzz-word' used all too often in youth-related fields with little sense of definition. Some light can be shed on the term by bringing it into the same field as its common bedfellow, self-esteem.

Discourses on self-esteem have varied across the disciplines of sociology and psychology, with the key tension laying in the debate regarding to what degree self-esteem is an internal concept that is regulated only by the individual and to what degree it can, in fact, be influenced by those on the outside such as facilitators and youth workers. Crocker and Wolfe (2001) suggest notions of 'contingencies' of self-esteem, defined as the circumstances on which 'a person has staked his or her self-esteem, so that person's view of his or her value or worth depends on perceived successes or failures or adherence to self-standards in that domain' (p. 594). This suggestion has the potential to impact youth settings greatly as it serves to disrupt our conventional notion that the work we do as practitioners can raise or lower a young person's self-esteem. When the contingencies model is employed it is suggested that in fact the young person must have already chosen to value the person, the setting or the experience before it can have an impact upon self-esteem. This suggestion raises the point that youth work and arts work need to be seen as holistic processes that include those key tenets of relationship building and conversation and that, perhaps, arts work cannot be seen as achieving social goals without involving these commonly held youth work tools.

However, as well as underlining the centrality of the young person and their development, it is also vital to acknowledge the role of the worker in these settings and the tensions that are at play as a result of their status. Brocken reflects that as a defined arts worker within a youth work setting, she has often asked herself the question 'what is my role?' Is the role of the arts worker purely to deliver the arts project and therefore abdicate responsibility from 'youth work-y' things like behaviour management out on the club floor? Or is this role in fact that of an unqualified youth worker who delivers drama? This raises questions of what our expectations are, not only for those delivering in the youth work setting but for anyone delivering arts work with young people. Jeffs and Smith (2002), have suggested that an increased societal move towards individualism and, thus, an uncoupling from traditional community has made it more and more difficult for youth workers to identify their subject, both in terms of age, location and community connection or lack thereof, and have connected this issue to the erosion of the identity of youth work. They suggest that, far from having existing communities to attach practice to and fit in around, it is now the job of youth workers to construct their own communities in which to practice and attempt to sustain impact. Jeffs and Smith (2002) have also highlighted the policy turns that have stripped away the sense of identity from youth workers, stating:

> Government youth policy in Britain and Northern Ireland – especially in England – has taken a major turn away from the fostering of associational activity. Policy-makers have chosen instead to re-brand youth work as a form of individualised case-management, and youth workers as specialists blessed with skills or personalities uniquely fitting them to control, monitor, distract, 'develop' and oversee 'troublesome' young people. (online article)

It may be suggested that such successive alterations in societal structure and government policy have brought youth work and youth arts closer together, causing the two worlds to work in collaboration (or indeed collision) more often. This notion of needing to build a community rather than work within one is a familiar trope to youth arts, with projects, often funding led, being parachuted into areas or institutions. This drawing together can be seen in a variety of different ways – clearly collaboration is a positive movement forward. But that collaboration cannot be achieved until the identities of the partners are solid. It would appear, in fact, that both sectors are having their identities eroded rather than strengthened.

ALTERNATIVE FRAMEWORKS FOR COLLABORATION BEYOND YOUTH AND ARTS SETTINGS

The Circuit programme, which was the subject of Nicola Sim's research, looked specifically at notions of collaboration and partnership across youth work and the arts. The galleries participating in Circuit were all high-profile visual arts institutions with international reputations. Each of these institutions had a dedicated 'learning' team and youth programme. Collectively, these programmes sought to develop new partnerships with youth organisations and services at local levels, which led to collaborations with local authorities, voluntary organisations, alternative education providers and charities. The experiences and reflections gathered from these alliances revealed some of the underlying challenges, as well as the advantages of associations between gallery education and youth work. Some of the projects piloted also demonstrated the consequences of experimenting with new spaces and contexts for partnership between youth workers, young people, galleries and arts practitioners.

As alluded to at the beginning of this chapter, many youth workers who had contact with Circuit initially expressed some degree of reticence when asked to consider visiting a gallery with groups of young people. Some youth workers also reported negative past experiences of working in partnership with arts organisations. During a cross-sector

discussion event organised by one of the Circuit galleries in a large northern English city, youth sector workers recalled being inundated with offers of short-term project funding from arts institutions, and being expected to supply cohorts of young people to populate these projects. One practitioner even voiced concern that artists sometimes exploit young people's personal stories for their creative potential, without putting support structures in place to continue the relationship with the young person at the end of a project. Several participants felt that the needs of their organisations were not taken into account in funding bids, which were usually submitted before a partnership was established. These comments portrayed a common assertion that relationships between arts and youth and community organisations are formed around unequal distributions of control and agency.

Contrastingly, several youth work practitioners involved in Circuit talked very positively about previous associations with visual arts organisations. One practitioner involved in leaving care spoke about the value of meeting groups of young service users in a distinctive, creative context, where they would be encouraged to develop their thinking skills, and feel able to disclose aspects of their lives while creating work. The practitioner did however refer to the ambivalent attitude of his wider organisation to engagements with galleries. This type of work was referred to as 'the cherry on the icing on the cake' for one local authority, particularly during periods of economic uncertainty.

Simultaneously, some gallery programmers within Circuit described a sense of frustration with the typical format of partnership projects between their institutions and youth organisations. They recognised that such projects have a tendency to be structured around a sequence of workshops, located either in a youth setting or at the gallery, for a set period of time with a fixed group and with relatively predetermined outcomes. They also discussed the tendency for some youth workers to withdraw from active involvement (often to get on with other work) if an arts project is run in a youth setting.

By reflecting on and acknowledging some of these recurring issues at the beginning of the programme, Circuit set out to change the conditions under which partnerships between the participating galleries and youth organisations might form. The generous £5 million pound grant from the Paul Hamlyn Foundation and four-year time span of the programme afforded the organisations time and resources to test different models of collaboration, which would encourage both arts and youth practitioners to engage in 'risky trade-offs' (Huybrechts, 2013, p. 3) and extend the boundaries of their practice.

Two of the Circuit sites included in this PhD study developed work in spaces that belonged neither to youth workers nor gallery practitioners. One programme in a large town occupied a former bus station waiting room near the gallery, which had been turned into a temporary creative community hub. This initiative was conceived as an open-access evening social environment, run by members of the gallery's young peer-led group, with the support of the youth service, artists and gallery staff. The programme came about partly in response to the drop-in use of the town's local youth centre, which some of the young people attributed to the reduction in staff numbers and the increased expectation for users to take part in directed activities. The youth service was also in the process of converting to commissioner status, as a strategy for dealing with budget cuts, so they were keen to work with the gallery to resource a weekly offer for young people who often hung out in the gallery's grounds. The gallery's Learning staff were also eager to find a way of engaging with these young people, who were often stigmatised locally for congregating in large groups and displaying so-called 'disrespectful' behaviour. These groups of young people had been reluctant to take part in the workshops and events programmed in and by the gallery, so the bus station nights were also designed to bridge the relationship between the gallery and local communities of young people.

The nights attracted many individuals who were known to the youth service, and some who were not. Visitors could come and go as they wished, spend time with friends, have a hot drink, play games and music and participate in creative activities and interventions prepared by guest artists. These activities included collaging, VJing (visual performance of images, frequently to music) and badge making. Sometimes an artist would leave out playful materials such as hazard tape and rolls of paper for visitors to manipulate. One or two youth workers would always be present and involved in the nights in the first year. The public, collaborative nature of the programme stimulated a range of debates between the practitioners and young people about the social and artistic priorities of the youth nights. Those involved worked hard to negotiate a tricky balance between maintaining the relaxed character of the sessions, while accommodating a varied arts programme. Regular attendees remarked that the youth workers played an important role in making the setting appear 'safe' and 'welcoming' for participants. The young peer-leaders were also able to draw complementary knowledge and skills from their experiences of working alongside both youth workers and gallery practitioners. We use this episode as one example of a transdisciplinary space, modelled as a cross between an open-access youth centre and public workshop. It trialled the concept of a 'hybrid zone' by creating a space which did not belong to one 'expert discipline', but strove to produce an ethos of 'shared ownership' and shared uncertainty (Huybrechts, 2013, p. 166).

DISCUSSION

These studies illustrate three different scenarios where youth work and arts practice come together, through projects rooted in different artistic traditions. These accounts also demonstrate different possible roles for youth workers, as creative facilitators, bystanders and supporters of arts projects. Arts-based pedagogies are shown to be congruent with informal education pedagogies, but the ways in which relationships are set up and situated are key to the efficacy of this type of work. The positioning of the Arts Award programme in youth settings evidently worked well when projects involved the active leadership and mentorship of the youth workers, many of whom had arts backgrounds. These youth workers ensured that the artistic directions of the projects were guided by the participants' cultural tastes and interests, rather than the agenda of an external practitioner or institution. However, as briefly indicated, the accredited nature of the award characterised the arts engagements in a particular educational framework. In many ways this type of framing is compatible with a more instrumentalised, outcome-driven youth work environment. But in drop-in settings, the structured nature of certain arts practices (such as performance rehearsals) are shown to be sometimes in tension with the voluntary principle of open-access youth work.

In the MyPlace centre, some youth workers voiced concern about young people being potentially coerced into participating in an activity that required a degree of commitment, when their primary motivation was to come down to the youth centre 'for a laugh' with peers. Other youth workers felt it was useful to have dedicated arts sessions as this diversified the offer and separated out the informal education from the youth work in the centre. The third site discussed, featuring a partnership venture between a gallery and youth service in a former bus station, sought to create an alternative space for arts and youth work to coexist. The motivation for the project grew out of a joint recognition of areas of need, and a mutual willingness to learn about and work with one another's models of delivery, engagement and evaluation.

What has been observed by all three research projects is the notion of the arts work happening in the 'space' occupied by youth work and the connotations this has for both practitioners and young people. In the case of the first two projects in particular, arts work is 'brought into' the youth work space, suggesting that the youth work setting takes ownership over that space and arts work 'takes over' or perhaps even colonises that space for a set period of time. It is necessary to recognise the importance of how space is conceptualised in order to help us understand some of the responses that arts work receives in these settings from both young people and youth workers.

Edward Soja (1996) sought to define how it is that space is constructed to hold meaning for individuals through his concept of 'Thirdspace'. Soja's key argument is that space has previously been conceptualised in terms of the binaries of real and imagined. Soja instead suggests a 'trialectic' manner of understanding space featuring the 'lived, perceived and conceived'. For Soja, 'Firstspace' describes the 'material or materialized "physical" spatiality that is directly comprehended in empirically measurable configurations' (p. 74), in other words, that which we perceive at face value. 'Secondspace' in Soja's terms is 'ideational, made up of projections onto the empirical world from conceived or imagined geographies' (p. 79). For Soja, Secondspace refers to the interpretations of space that we have that are apart from the material reality of that space. Soja, posits, therefore, that 'Thirdspace' is a 'deconstruction and heuristic reconstruction of the Firstspace-Secondspace duality', not only a critique of the dualist model of thinking but a sense of the 'limitless' (p. 81). Thirdspace is a way of seeing Firstspace mediated through the gaze and ideas of Secondspace. Thirdspace helps to conceptualise the youth work space as not just a combination of these material and interpreted spaces, but as a completely different way of seeing space as a place of potential, with neither the 'perceived, conceived [or] lived' (p. 68) spatiality privileged over the others.

In our context, the Firstspace/Secondspace version of the youth work space demonstrates the importance of both the material construct of the youth work space – the building which young people visit at certain days and times each week – and the feelings that this space elicits for those young people, summed up when young people and staff express a distaste at their space being 'invaded' by arts activity. Not only is physical space (Firstspace) important in terms of the sense of a home for the group, the facilities and resources that are needed to run sessions, etc., but also the Secondspace conceptions of what that space means (i.e. perhaps a chance to relax and be with friends for the youth work setting and the imperative to work towards a final product in the youth arts setting) tell us as much about how that space is going to affect the behaviour and motivations of the young people working within it. To make use of the notion of Thirdspace helps us to see these encounters as taking place within a trialectic space that is tied into both physical, empirical perceptions and those less concrete, more abstract constructions. The trialectic is a concept Soja draws from Levebre's work. It describes a space which is both 'real and imagined' and 'draws upon the material and mental spaces of the traditional dualism but extends well beyond them in terms of scope, substance and meaning' (p. 11). The Thirdspace, therefore, helps us to be able to see the youth work experience as one in which the first and second space cannot be separated from one another and in which neither of these dualisms fully explain the perception of space for the young person.

A further defence for the use of Soja's theory in the bringing together of arts and youth work is his focus on the breaking down of binary structures. Soja's theory not only helps to conceptualise the way in which we

think of space in this particular work, but his thinking around space can help inform the way in which the synthesis of arts and youth work can be seen and conceptualised as a whole. Soja refers to the process of 'thirding-as-othering' and describes how seeing the Thirdspace can introduce something 'more than a 'dialectical synthesis', rather a 'critical "other than" choice that speaks and critiques through its otherness' (p. 60). This is a concept that can not only help to analyse the process of bringing together these two areas but also provide inspiration for seeing the way forward for this synthesis. 'Thirding', for Soja, is not simply a combining of two areas or ways of thinking, it is 'a disordering, deconstruction and tentative reconstruction' which produces an 'open alternative' (p. 61). This suggests, therefore, that perhaps the way forward for viewing this kind of work is to see it as its own Thirdspace, not a combination of two areas, rather a *new* way of working and thinking. It is important to note also that this notion has applications across various different fields, not just the one that is being addressed here. As a mode of thinking and conceptualising experience, not just within certain spaces with certain connotations but also within any environment where differing concepts are drawn together, the Thirdspace can help in theorising and understanding the way in which we can understand experience beyond the mental and material dualism.

CONCLUSION

As a drama practitioner in a youth work setting, Brocken found the challenges of young people's behaviour, the structure of the venue and the politics implicit in the running of a youth work venue to be at times fascinating and at times frustrating in their seeming opposition to the style of youth *arts* work that she had been used to. By conducting comparative fieldwork in the youth theatre and youth work settings, Brocken was able to identify an overt emphasis in the arts setting on skills development and learning. This finding correlated with those discovered by Howard in the Arts Award programme, where the arts within youth work were given an instrumental purpose, with a focus on outcome, controlling the behaviour of the young people and the hotly contested area of 'accreditation' within youth work. However, we do not seek to suggest that the arts are inherently compromised in work with young people, nor that open-access youth work is fundamentally incompatible with arts-based pedagogies (which are certainly not always product- or performance-focused). In the Circuit programme, Sim encountered a number of projects that worked to develop exploratory spaces for process-based creative experimentation, while at the same time enshrining youth work values, policies and practices in a single setting. These efforts were not without conflict, and they relied on the recruitment of co-operative, open practitioners. These collaborative initiatives arguably tend to have least impact when youth workers are not present and engaged in the action, which is telling of the vital role of the youth worker in creating a space of equality, encouragement and safety for young people.

We have also touched upon examples of programmes where youth workers are expected to undertake transdisciplinary roles, drawing upon the pedagogical impulses of both arts practices and youth work. Youth workers with arts backgrounds and interests saw themselves as 'Thirdspace' practitioners, taking on a hybrid identity, which posed both opportunities and challenges for practice. An issue for further investigation is how these practitioners are trained, and to what extent youth work education courses prepare practitioners for working with the arts.

Our chapter argues that arts work within youth work can be seen through our research studies as improving and enhancing practice because it challenges what counts as

learning, youth work and creativity. The inspirational aspects of arts engagement from our studies included the personal and social development of young people by taking part in arts activities, but also the development of youth workers' practice through the experience of engaging with the young people on the programmes. In addition to this, arts programmes and institutions have the potential resources to act as critical allies in the fight to retain forms of youth work that are understood to be consistently under threat due to the encroachment of 'market values' and 'policy diktats' (de St Croix, 2015, p. 59; Norris & Pugh, 2015, p. 95). Artists and arts education practitioners are often adept at working with inventive, improvisatory practices and with youth-led engagement, so they are well placed to function as advocates for critical, creative and democratic youth work. In recent years the arts sector has demonstrated a greater sense of collective awareness of the entrenched barriers and problematic practices that have impacted upon youth practitioners' trust of institutional arts programmes. While these issues are far from resolved, there is a growing appetite for partnership across both sectors, in part due to the broader context of cuts to youth provision (and the arts) in the UK. Our research indicates that more could be done to promote the complex convergences and powerful divergences between these two professional worlds. By assessing their geographies and spatialities of practice, we can generate deeper insights into how these distinct territories overlap and question one another.

REFERENCES

Batsleer, J. (2009) *Informal Learning in Youth Work*. Sage: London.

Batsleer, J. (2014) Educating for a disappearing profession? The case of youth and community work. *BERA Conference*, 23–25 September 2014, London.

Batsleer, J. & Davies, B. (eds.) (2010) *What is Youth Work?* Exeter: Learning Matters.

Belfiore, E. (2002) Art as a means of alleviating social exclusion: Does it really work? A critique of instrumental cultural policies and social impact studies in the UK. *International Journal of Cultural Policy*, 8(1), pp: 91–106.

Coburn, A. (2011) Building social and cultural capital through learning about equality in youth work. *Journal of Youth Studies*, 14(1), pp: 475–491.

Crocker, J. & Wolfe, C.T. (2001) Contingencies of self-worth. *Psychological Review*, 108(3), pp: 593–623.

Davies, B. (2010) Straws in the wind: the state of youth work in a changing policy environment. *Youth & Policy*, 105, pp: 9–36.

Davies, B. (2011) Youth work stories: in search of qualitative evidence on process and impact. *Youth & Policy*, 106, pp: 23–46.

de St Croix, T. (2015) Volunteers and entrepreneurs? Youth work and the Big Society. In G. Bright (ed.) *Youth Work: Histories, Policy and Contexts*. London: Palgrave, pp: 58–79.

Gormally, S. & Coburn, A. (2014) Finding Nexus: connecting youth work and research practices. *British Educational Research Journal*, 40(5), pp: 869–885.

Holden, J. (2006) Cultural value and the crisis of legitimacy: why culture needs a democratic mandate. DEMOS. Available at: http://www.demos.co.uk/files/Culturalvalueweb.pdf

Huybrechts, L. (2013) *Participation is Risky: Approaches to Joint Creative Processes*. Amsterdam: Valiz.

In Defence of Youth Work (2014) *This is Youth Work: Stories from Practice*. UNISON.

Jeffs, T. & Smith, M. (1999) *Using Informal Education*. Buckingham: Open University Press.

Jeffs, T. & Smith, M.K. (2002) 'Individualization and youth work', *Youth & Policy* 76, pp: 39–65 (accessed at infed.org).

Kemmis, S. (2012) Researching educational praxis: spectator and participant perspectives. *British Educational Research Journal*, 38(6), pp: 885–905.

Kiilakoski, T. & Kivijarvi, A. (2015) Youth clubs as spaces of non-formal learning: professional idealism meets the spatiality experienced by young people in Finland. *Studies in Continuing Education*, 37(1), pp: 47–61.

Kinder, K. & Harland, J. (2004) The arts and social inclusion: what's the evidence? *Support for Learning*, 19(2), pp: 52–56.

Merton, B. (2004) *An Evaluation of the Impact of Youth Work in England*. Produced for the Department for Education and Skills by De Montford University.

Nolas, S-M. (2014) Exploring young people's and youth workers' experiences of spaces for 'youth development': creating cultures of participation. *Journal of Youth Studies*, 17(1), pp: 26–41.

Norris, P. & Pugh, C. (2015) Local authority youth work. In G. Bright (ed.) *Youth Work: Histories, Policy and Contexts*. London: Palgrave, pp: 80–101

Ruiz, J. (2004) *A Literature Review of the Evidence Base for Culture, the Arts and Sport Policy*. Scottish Executive Education Department. Available at: http://www.scotland.gov.uk/Publications/2004/08/19784/41507

Sefton-Green, J. (2003) Informal learning: substance or style? *Teaching Education*, 14(1), pp: 37–51.

Soja, E. (1996) *Thirdspace: Journeys to Los Angeles and Other Real and Imagined Places*. Cambridge, Mass.: Wiley, John and Sons, Inc.

Van de Walle, T., Coussée, F., & Bouverne-Du Bie, M. (2011) Social exclusion and youth work – from the surface to the depths of an educational practice. *Journal of Youth Studies*, 14(2), pp: 219–231.

21

Fringe Work – Street-level Divergence in Swedish Youth Work

Björn Andersson

INTRODUCTION

Working with young people means relating to a social space of transformation, transgression and variation. Change and adaptability have always been integral parts of youth work (Jeffs 2015: 75). At the same time, a structured and sustained approach to young people's lives and troubles forms experiences and creates patterns of interventions that function as a basis for youth work methodology. Approaches do not need to be constantly reinvented; there is a working tradition.

In Sweden, detached youth work constitutes such a tradition. Inspired by outreach approaches and gang work in American cities (Calissendorff et al. 1986: 16), the first detached youth workers were engaged in the larger cities during the late 1950s. This approach spread throughout the country and the number of detached youth workers increased during the subsequent decades. In the early 1980s there were about 400 detached youth workers employed in the public sector

(Calissendorff et al. 1986: 39) and today it is estimated that there are 500 positions as detached youth workers available nationwide (RiF 2010: 3). Though there have been tremendous changes since the early days, both when it comes to the social conditions of young people and the way youth work is organized and provided, detached youth workers have managed to keep their efforts alive within contemporary Swedish practice.

The aim of this chapter is to present the tradition of detached youth work in Sweden, but also to investigate how detached youth workers have managed to navigate their occupational role in order to achieve both continuity and change. As Eraut has pointed out, this is a dimension of professional learning that on the one side concerns the tackling of 'well-defined problems' and on the other side requires a problem-solving approach to deal with the 'occurrence of novel and complex situations' (Eraut 2008: 4). Obviously, to generate a living tradition of practice the methodology must not be simply reproduced;

learning the job cannot be a plain process of taking over and doing the same. The work has to be reformulated to meet new conditions, face different problems and relate to new generations of young people (cf. Willis 1977: 2), and this is the focus of this chapter.

It will be argued here that crucial in this context are some of the distinct characteristics of how detached youth work is organized and carried out. Within an outreach approach youth workers are engaged in a constant process to construct meaning in and via their interventions. They also engage in a practice in which they are challenged to move into new areas in order to initiate new and different interventions. This will be discussed in relation to the concept of 'fringe work'. Furthermore, Swedish detached youth workers, through their national association, form what can be understood as a 'moral occupational community' (Evetts 2006), which, together with a relatively stable position inside the public welfare system, helps to accomplish professional continuity.

To contextualize this exploration, the chapter outlines the emergence of detached youth work in Sweden, and two examples of detached youth work in Gothenburg (in the West of Sweden) constitute the empirical basis for the discussion.

DETACHED AND OUTREACH YOUTH WORK

The distinction between 'outreach' and 'detached' youth work is often unclear, both among youth workers themselves and in literature (cf. Crimmens et al. 2004: 14). In Sweden, youth workers tend to use them interchangeably. In general, detached youth work is understood as the most comprehensive effort. It includes working with an outreach approach, but also organizing and being responsible for follow-up work. Outreach work represents a more limited approach, focused on contact-making and signposting to other services and support systems.

The National Association for Detached Youth Work in Sweden provided the following definition of outreach work in their guidance from 2014 (quoted from Andersson 2013: 184):

> Outreach work is a contact-making and resource-mediating social activity, performed in surroundings and situations that the outreach worker does not control or organise, and targeted at individuals and groups who otherwise are hard to reach and who need easy accessible linkage to support.

The aim of the outreach effort is to contact young people, mainly outdoors and in groups, who otherwise are difficult to engage, and to provide them with, and link them to, relevant social support. This includes different forms of assistance, such as arranging counselling concerning personal difficulties at a youth reception or organizing a meeting with a school social worker to sort out issues about school attendance. Often the most important support is to accompany the young person to the meeting. The spatial aspect of this practice is also important. Outreach work is carried out in places not set up by the youth workers, but instead where young people informally gather, or in institutionalized spaces such as the school or the youth club.

In addition, most outreach youth workers also engage in broader efforts for social change and action within the wider community, such as individual support, group work and community organizing. These efforts are often labelled 'follow-up work' and, ideally, there should be a generative coupling between the outreach contact-making with individuals and groups of young people and the signposting and provision of social support arrangements. That is, when meeting and talking to young people while doing outreach work, the youth workers should pick up interests and needs expressed by the young people and transform these into themes that form the basis of the further interventions (cf. Freire 1979: 98–99).

It is this combination of an outreach approach and follow-up work that constitutes detached youth work in the Swedish context. A literal translation of the expression used in Sweden is 'fieldwork'. The youth workers call themselves 'fieldworkers' and they combine an outreach approach with help and support efforts targeted at individuals, groups and the local community.

THE EMERGENCE OF DETACHED YOUTH WORK IN SWEDEN

Detached youth work was introduced in Sweden in the mid-1950s and must be seen as part of the post-war development of welfare policy and services. The work built on experiences from the youth clubs, which at that time had been running for a couple of decades, but inspiration also came from US, Chicago based, gang-work.

When it comes to implementation, organizational affiliation and the understanding of young people and their situation, detached youth work has always been characterized by a certain duality. One side is that in the beginning the work was partly grounded in an interest in the new youth cultures that emerged during the fifties. This was about young people's ways of inhabiting a new world and the new cultural expressions and the patterns of social interaction that this development brought. In this context detached youth work has been working from the start to support young people's participation in society and to engage in projects that aim to create meeting places for young people where they can find ways to express themselves both as individuals and as a collective.

The other side of this duality is that this early detached youth work was influenced by being established within the municipal welfare sector. At the time this was very much governed by an authoritarian tradition and based in a control-oriented organizational culture with a focus on young people as the

source of social problems. One consequence of this was, for example, that youth workers were expected to cooperate with the police in order to detect and report young people who were on the run from juvenile detention.

This historical and contemporary duality of detached youth continues to be an area of much debate. Organizationally, detached youth work is still part of the municipal welfare services. There are examples of organizations and associations within the voluntary sector that run outreach efforts, but these form a very small part of the overall total.

Since 1982, the Social Services Act (re-worked in 2001) has regulated detached youth work in Sweden. This framework law has an opening paragraph which emphasizes a need for social services to be based on democracy and solidarity and to support equality and security among the people to whom it is directed. No doubt this regulation backs a youth work that takes young people's needs and interests as its starting point. However, the social service also retains legal support for compulsory enactment and functions in an authoritarian way in relation to its clients.

Many detached youth workers experience divergent demands within their own organization. They are expected to work as supporters of young people's potential to express themselves, and to be participative and to execute control in relation to what is understood as the social problems of youth. A consequence of this is that outreach workers often have to negotiate their professional position in relation to the management levels within the organization.

One very important occurrence was the formation of the National Association of Detached Youth Work in 1975. This organization functions as a forum to support the professional development of detached youth work and is maintained by voluntary efforts from youth workers. The organization holds annual conferences and arranges regional activities. It has been at the forefront of the issue of defining how detached youth work should be understood and what efforts youth workers should engage. According to the National Association guidelines the key words to describe detached youth work are 'voluntariness, trust and respectful meetings' (RiF 2014: 3). Further, knowledge about the actual social situation and the needs of young people is emphasized, as well as the importance of building relations with young people on the basis of their voluntary engagement with the workers.

The position inside the public sector lends stability to detached youth work. The youth workers are employed on long-term professional contracts and therefore they seldom need to seek continuous funding in order to fund their future project-based work. Although at the national level the number of detached youth workers is relatively stable, locally, changes do occur: some outreach teams are closed down and others are established. Political boards govern each district of the municipality, and although detached youth work is supported by the Social Services Act, it not a part of its statutory commitments. In times of diminishing resources detached youth work sometimes becomes a target for cuts. This puts a pressure on the youth workers to continuously document and evidence their activities.

STREET-LEVEL DIVERGENCE: FRINGE WORK

Working inside the public sector means belonging to a human service organization, which are generally characterized by a high degree of openness when it comes to the implementation of meetings between the employees of the organization and their clients (Hasenfeld 1983). There are difficulties in steering and controlling the 'street-level bureaucrats', as they operate with a certain level of discretion (Lipsky 1980). The effect is that there is often a divergence between the

formal policy of the organization and what is actually happening in the field (Gofen 2013: 473). How street-level employees make use of their discretion has been generally discussed in terms of 'guerrilla government' (O'Leary 2010: 8) and, in connection to social services, as 'deviant social work' (Carey & Foster 2011: 578). This possibility of divergence is important in relation to the earlier mentioned two-sided situation of Swedish detached youth workers. It points at an organizational space where the youth workers can handle the contradictions of their professional role in a self-directed way.

Carmen de la Cuesta has described one example of how street-level divergence can be carried into effect in her study of health visiting in the north west of England (1993). De la Cuesta observed that the health visitors put a great deal of time and effort into adjusting their services in relation to what they interpreted as the needs of their clients. By doing so, they set aside policies and professional principles that regulated the work and these activities were fulfilled hidden from the examining eyes of their bosses (p. 669). De la Cuesta called this 'fringe work' and what was considered as fringe work varied between different settings. However, in general it could be divided into two major types: 'relief work' and 'novel work' (p. 670). Relief work was about meeting basic needs, such as obtaining material resources for poor families. Novel work included setting up new activities, such as starting group work, and was more directed towards mobilizing human competences.

One effect of fringe work was that it developed the professional role of the health visitors, and especially fringe work of the novel type could later be introduced and incorporated as part of the accepted work procedures (p. 672). It also influenced and strengthened the relationship between the health visitors and their clients. In many ways fringe work helped the visitors to feel that they actually accomplished something; that they could contribute to the well-being of people in need. However, de la Cuesta points out that fringe work has 'a double edge' (p. 680). On the one side it helps to improve the quality of the effort and develops the profession. On the other side, it functions 'as an instrument of social control' (p. 680) since it is not directed at everybody, but is targeted at those understood as being the most deserving. It may also result in strain and overwork on the side of the health visitor. Fringe work often involves personal, sometimes even private, commitments that are time-consuming and quite exhausting to fulfil.

There are significant similarities between the occupational roles of health visitors and detached youth workers. Both use an outreach approach to make contact with their target group and they both organize support efforts in close connection to the everyday life of the people they work with.

I will return to the question of how the concept of fringe work can be understood in the context of detached youth work. However, first details of the research approach will be presented.

RESEARCH APPROACH

The empirical basis for this chapter consists primarily of interviews with two different teams of detached youth workers in Gothenburg. The two teams were selected in part because they represent districts in Gothenburg where there has been for several years a stable tradition of detached youth work, and partly because at the time of the interview they worked in a social context that challenged their usual way of working. The idea was that this tension between tradition and innovation would be productive to empirically describe how contradictions in the professional role are dealt with.

From a methodological point of view, my vantage point is descriptive and analytic as well as 'theory-evaluating' (Vennesson 2008: 227–228). The ambition has been to gain empirical material that can both clarify the

tradition of detached youth work in Sweden and at the same time illustrate how the method can be utilized under extraordinary conditions. Thus, both cases represent something general and, at the same time, provide specific 'opportunities to learn' (Stake, 2005: 450–451). It should be mentioned that as a social work academic, I have been in regular contact with the various teams of detached youth workers in Gothenburg and that we have worked together in a research context previously (see Andersson 2014).

I interviewed respective teams on two different occasions. The first interview was documented through detailed notes, and on the basis of these a first draft of the chapter was written. The draft was then sent to and commented on by the teams. Each team was then interviewed a second time and these interviews were taped and transcribed. Then the text was reworked and the new material integrated. In addition to this, one interview was conducted with the manager of one of the teams and a seminar with 25 outreach workers in the Gothenburg area was arranged. During the seminar the concept of fringe work was explored and the youth workers provided examples of how the concept could be applied to their work.

Data analysis was conducted using two complementary approaches. On the one hand I worked with an open thematic analysis where I looked for common themes and patterns, but also for complexity and contradictions (Rapley 2011: 273–278). On the other hand I carried out a theory-driven analysis (Macfarlane & O'Reilly-de Brún, 2012), which has been centred on concepts like 'fringe work' and 'street-level divergence'. I have systematically sought for narratives about how the youth workers deal with methodological issues concerning their professional role and how they handle contradicting demands coming from inside their organization and from the young people they work with.

In agreement with the youth workers interviewed, participants are represented by their real names where quoted. Considering the public positions they uphold and the small number of detached youth workers in Gothenburg, anonymity would not be possible. They have also been interviewed in local media concerning similar issues as discussed here, so their views and experiences have already been made public.

TWO DETACHED YOUTH WORK TEAMS

The two teams selected for this study work in districts that represent typical urban settings where detached youth work is carried out: the city centre and a local neighbourhood. In general, there is a difference between the core groups of young people that the youth workers approach and work with. The young people in the city centre tend to be a little older and do not live in the area where they meet. In contrast, the young people in the neighbourhood tend to have a local orientation, often identifying with the residential area where they live. The age difference is somewhat mirrored in the target group of each team. The city works with young people in the age range 13–21 years, while the neighbourhood team's main focus is on those aged 12–20 years old.

The city unit consists of six outreach workers and to large extent they work in a huge indoor shopping centre – which fulfils an important role as a meeting place for young people in Gothenburg. The shopping centre is located very close to transport links where bus and tram services intersect, so it is easy to reach from different parts of the city. This is a main reason many young people meet there. However, the shopping mall also functions as a hang-out, especially for young people with little connection to their local residential areas. For various reasons many do not feel at home where they live and have few social relations in their neighbourhood. Instead of meeting friends in the local area,

these young people meet with peers in the city centre. The shopping mall is perceived in broader local understandings – particularly in the media – as a risky place to visit, especially after the shops have closed in the evening, since it is considered that it is a site for criminal activities such as drug-dealing.

The neighbourhood team have four full-time members and work in one of Gothenburg's suburban areas. This area was mainly built during the years 1955–65 and has today (2016) a population of about 25,000 people. Gothenburg as a city is heavily segregated and the label 'suburb' normally signifies an area with social and economic conditions below average. Differences in living conditions and health inequalities were recently investigated in Gothenburg (Göteborgs Stad 2014) and the area where the neighbourhood team works was identified as one of the areas with the most pressing inequalities in relation to factors such as education, work, life expectancy and health. In addition, for a number of years, Gothenburg has experienced a very high level of gun crime linked to criminal networks and gangs. The area where the detached team works is one of the neighbourhoods that has been most affected.

DETACHED YOUTH WORK IN THE CITY DISTRICT

During the spring of 2015, the youth workers noticed groups of young people in the centre who they had not met there before, as described by Jenny:

> It was young people with new needs and different experiences. Many of them were unaccompanied children coming as refugees. There were also a group that we understood actually lived on the streets. Most often they had come from North Africa, for example from Morocco, and we realized that some of them had been living as street-children in different European cities. They were very competent young persons who, however, were carrying huge, personal traumas.

The local policy states that the youth workers should direct their work to young people who are residents of Gothenburg, but they felt that they could not ignore the obvious needs of this new group. They especially tried to help the 'street-children', which to a large extent meant engaging in individual help and support efforts. The stories told by the young people were often quite heart-breaking and full of personal tragedies. Annie tells about what they heard:

> They have been on the run for quite a long time and express a pervading feeling of being unwanted. Their families have abandoned them. In their hometowns they have been forced to live on the street and treated really badly. They go to Europe because, in comparison, here is better. However, no one wants them here either. Some are very tired of the life on the street and turn to alcohol and drugs to cope with bad feelings and everyday troubles. Some earn money through criminal activities and probably also prostitution.

What the youth workers found out when they began to engage in the individual situation of these young people, and noted their background and their needs, did not fit into the general model of 'youth in need of assistance' that guides much of the work by welfare institutions and professionals. Many young people had placements and temporary support, but when they had not met the standards or disappeared, they had been written off and forgotten. When the youth workers tried to return young people into the system, the effort was met with significant reluctance from people working in emergency centres and within residential care. The social services did not want these young people back, so the youth workers had to spend considerable time on persuasion and finding creative solutions to locate support. As Annie recalls, it was not always a lucky story:

> We had contact with a 15-year-old boy that had been living on the street for six months. He drank alcohol and used drugs. He expressed suicidal thoughts. We tried to find him a place to stay, but had no success. We had to leave him on the street right in the middle of the night. Could you imagine that happen to a Swedish boy of the same age?

Another approach the youth workers attempted was to map and document the situation of the group. After some time, media attention began to focus on the existence of 'street-children' in Gothenburg and a political decision was taken to undertake a thorough investigation. Extra resources were allocated and additional staff recruited to the detached team to carry out the study. Via the resulting study, the young refugees' situation was investigated and also better recognized. It was also possible to provide a realistic picture of the situation, which was important since reports in local media had exaggerated the number of young people living on the streets, and, by this, contributed to a local hysteria concerning a growing threat to people in central Gothenburg.

The outreach workers also engaged in challenging stereotyping of the young people as sources of danger and risk. One worker wrote a number of posts on a blog run by the National Association for Outreach Workers. One post was called 'Dear child, don't lose your faith in Sweden', and took the form of a letter to all unaccompanied young refugees and newly arrived young people in Sweden. In the blog the youth worker, Annie, described how sad she was about such negative attitudes towards refugees in Sweden and how much she appreciated the meetings with young refugees in the centre of Gothenburg.

This blog post received a great deal of attention and Annie was interviewed by two of the largest newspapers in Sweden. The team was also invited to take part in a conference about unaccompanied refugee children. Through this interest, the team managed to publicize their experiences and views on the current situation for young refugees.

This new interest in the issue of young people living on the streets of Gothenburg had the effect that the youth workers had much less time to spend with the groups of young people they would otherwise interact with. Some young people commented upon this reduction in contact hours; however, it has been possible for the outreach workers to explain their priorities. When they write on the Internet or when they appear in the newspapers, they always receive racist comments. This has also happened in the street when youth workers have been talking to young refugees, but it is rare.

The outreach workers describe one central aim for their work as 'making the unseen visible'. They have managed to do that in relation to the young newcomers they have met in central Gothenburg. However, it has required a great deal of extra time and effort, as well as decisiveness to take on issues that are not really part of the existing prescribed professional agenda.

DETACHED YOUTH WORK IN THE RESIDENTIAL AREA

We spend a lot of time outside in the district, especially during periods like when the shootings occurred. It is important that we are everywhere; that we know many and have relationships with a lot of young people in different parts of the residential area.

Here, Jalil reflects on the approach used by the detached youth work team to which he belongs. Detached youth workers have been based in the area for a long time. However, developments in recent years have led to a decision by the team to work in a partly new way. Central to this new approach is a high degree of presence in the area and having a network of contacts through which they are well known in different parts of the district. The events of recent years have in many ways been a shocking experience for the people who live in the neighbourhood. Although shootings have been mainly directed towards members of various criminal networks, and often are labelled as 'internal affairs', on several occasions, people who are outside these networks have also been injured or killed.

To a large extent, young men dominate the local public environments and the youth workers believe that difficulties regarding school and employment are central to their lives. It is hard for them to find a job when they leave school, partly because the local labour market is very limited. Jalil explains:

We have been very focused on school and work. Many of these guys have great self-confidence when they are in the local area, but they are very insecure beyond the borders. This means that they do not seek to study or look for job opportunities in other parts of the city.

In order to help with contacts outside the neighbourhood and to provide advice about existing education and employment opportunities, youth workers arranged for a number of young people to have an individual meeting with a centrally located unit of counsellors and career officers. However, none of the young people attended. Instead, the youth workers persuaded the counsellors to meet with young people as a group accompanied by the workers. This meeting worked well and resulted in some of the young people engaging with educational opportunities.

The youth workers describe this kind of arrangement as typical. There are facilities that the young people in the area can make use of, but social and personal barriers often prevent them from doing so. In such situations the youth workers must function as mediators and use their relationships with the young people in order to help them overcome such obstacles. The youth workers' presence enabled young people to feel more secure in order to be able to take advantage of services located outside their neighbourhood. This approach works well and the youth workers receive much appreciation for their assistance from the young people. However, at the same time it requires a high degree of personal investment and dedication on behalf of the youth workers.

Another central issue the outreach team has needed to explore is the safety and security of the local district. The goal is to have a high degree of presence; the workers try to cover almost every day of the week. They have worked to initiate activities outdoors in the settings where young people congregate, and many of the young can participate. Often it is physical and contact sport activities such as rugby, basketball and a special form of wrestling.

In spite of these efforts, there are still situations where young people feel unsafe in the area. Therefore, the outreach workers initiated and developed two different projects with what are called 'safety hosts' in schools and 'neighbourhood hosts' working outdoors, mainly during summertime. Both efforts focused on creating relations with young people, initiating activities and support in attempt to mediate conflict situations and local tensions. Many staff recruited to the projects have low levels of formal education, however they have significant local expertise and are well-known in the area. Thus, this has created opportunities for older adolescents and/or adults to be able to gain temporary local employment.

A recent evaluation reports that many working in the area appreciate the two projects with local hosts. The understanding is that they have significantly helped to increase feelings of safety in the area and to enable young people to meet and do things together (Sennemark 2016). For the hosts themselves it has been a both rewarding and stressful experience. During incidents of local unrest, it has been an exhausting mission, and thus emphasizes the importance of the continuous support and counselling they have received from the outreach workers.

Criminal networks have existed and been active in the district for several years, but recent changes in their formation have affected the social life of the whole area. The newest groups involved in crime have been formed on the basis of ethnic affiliation, which previously has not been so pronounced. Since the residential area has a high degree of internal segregation, partly connected to the ethnic background of its inhabitants, gang conflicts have escalated into a geographical contraposition between the northern and the southern parts of the district.

> There are forces that work destructively in the district and we have chosen to appear on the same arena as they do. It becomes a bit of a tug of war when it comes to having influence over young people. We cannot offer cash, but a just life.

In order to discourage and overcome local conflicts between young people, youth workers recruit participants for group activities from both the northern and southern parts of the residential area. The endeavour is to establish youth work on several levels. When needed, they support single individuals, they work with parental contacts, they start groups, and they seek to develop local structures such as the 'neighbourhood hosts' project. To engage with local adults, the youth workers formed local contacts with both the church and the mosque in the area. These institutions also represent important services in many young people's lives, and through this work many new links have been established. In general, the detached team attempts to forge links with businesses and organizations that are active in the area.

The youth workers aspire to build rapport and relate personally with the young people they encounter. They try to remember things they have talked about so they can refer back to these the next time they speak. It is crucial to constantly keep the attention on the local youth they meet, but these relationships are established slowly over time. Indeed many young people need time to change, as Malik says:

> We work with relationships and support; we are not police officers or therapists. We constantly try to think outside the box, but fringe work can't be just anything. Detached youth work can only extend in certain directions; otherwise it becomes a different method.

It is clear that the work the youth workers have carried out during the last few years has been very challenging to them – both at a professional and a personal level. The team consists of young men with no families, and they reflect that being young without a family has probably been a prerequisite in order to meet the high demands that have been asked of them, and that they have made of themselves, during the last years. For example, the sheer volume of work in late evenings has drained their powers.

One key reason why workers have managed to continue, is that they, as a team, have been in total agreement about how to implement and develop the work. They have a very open climate for discussions in the group and are able to both criticize and support one another. The team believe it is vital to think in one's own way and stand up for this, both within the group and externally in relation to other professional and local actors.

BOTH TEAMS: ORGANIZATIONAL POLICY AND MANAGEMENT

One important tension arises between the policy principles embedded within organizational control and the personal and professional values held by the workers themselves. There are policies and job descriptions that regulate the work for each team – and these are agreed by politicians in the district council and at managerial level. However, both teams experience the regulations as vague – using catchwords like 'preventive' and 'confidence building'. It is therefore very much up to the teams themselves to implement and decide the practical consequences and implementation of the policy, and most important in this context is the outreach approach. As Jalil from the neighbourhood team notes:

We work among the young people in the neighbourhood and talk to them about their situation. We start out from their needs and function as mediators between the local district and the youth. We move around where young people gather and listen a lot.

Kim from the city unit says:

We have always focused on the young people that we meet in the city area. The ones who gather in the places where we work and who have some sort of problematic social situation.

A recurrent theme in the interviews is that the youth workers underline the fundamental role of the relationship to the young people with whom they work. They see themselves as spokespersons and advocates for young people and the neighbourhood team also emphasize their commitment to the local area. In this context, the fact that the youth workers are employed by the social services may cause difficulties. Many young people have previous poor experiences from encounters with other representatives of the public services and feel ambivalent about being contacted by youth workers from the local authorities. This is an effect of the earlier mentioned duality of how detached youth work is positioned in Sweden. For example, Joakim of the neighbourhood team says:

It is a balancing act. We are very open with who we are and whom we work for. We always wear clothes that are marked with our occupational belonging and we underline that we work for the local authorities. It is important to show that the municipality actually is doing things in the area.

The city team have the same experience. The only way to handle their position in relation to young people is to be fully open and honest. In most cases young people understand the complex position of the youth workers. In addition, being employed by the social services is connected to certain advantages. It enables access to many resources, such as office space and funding for activities, and it may sometimes give youth workers authority and recognition in relation to other public services.

During the interviews we discussed the concept of fringe work. This was completely new to the youth workers, but they could immediately apply the idea to their own activities. Obviously, the concept covers an important aspect of how the youth workers understand their occupational role and how they consider detached youth work methodology should be implemented. Though they as teams were dependent upon policy decisions from managers and local politicians, they saw it as central that it was their contacts and interpretations of young people's needs that should govern and direct their efforts. Both teams described how they had started up activities and support work, though it was not clear if this was always congruent with the regulations. One example of this was when the city team started to work with the group mentioned earlier living on the streets of Gothenburg. Jenny recalls:

> There was a discussion, started by the management, concerning if we should work with this group or not. It was questioned whether they would have the right to stay in Sweden and was it then the youth we should be working with? But we argued that this is the young people we actually meet during our outreach sessions. If no one else is working with them, who will then do it? We can't just leave them to their fate. This kind of discussion took place. So we had to vindicate the role of the detached youth worker against the system.

The youth workers expressed a strong support for their method based on an outreach approach, and being a detached youth worker was very much a professional identity. They referred to the national organization and the guidelines as important in developing their work. Their identity as a detached youth worker motivated them to engage in their work and the young people they meet, and also to engage in fringe work. This involvement is based upon an understanding of the complexity of what the professional position as a detached youth worker requires. It is both about making personal decisions concerning how to shape your occupational role and about following the standards of a professional community. In this way the professional identity bridges individuality and collective practice (cf. Wenger 1998: 145–146).

However, personal experiences and feelings also functioned as important motivational factors. The neighbourhood team mentioned their own personal histories as important for how they understand and engage in the local situation. They have all been raised in areas similar to the one they are working in; one of them has actually been living in the same neighbourhood. Three of the outreach workers have an immigrant background and through this they recognize a lot of the difficulties and obstacles that young people in the area face.

Similarly, for the city team, emotional engagement was important. Several of the young people they worked with lived in misery and it was an exhausting experience to feel that they really could not help them.

DISCUSSION

In their professional practice detached youth workers meet young people who face many troubles in their everyday lives, and, in response to this, they develop efforts to help the young people to live a better life. For the street-children, a 'better life' is about really fundamental matters: somewhere to sleep and having something to eat. For the young people in the residential area, it is about accessing support to engage with school or having something meaningful to do together with their peers. To a large extent this is precisely what they are employed to do. However, sometimes the youth workers extend their undertakings beyond the limits of their job descriptions and, in debate with their superiors, they defend their right to do so. This kind of divergence in relation to job regulations is not uncommon among officials at the street level of organizations and Gofen sees three analytic dimensions as important in this context: motivation, transparency and collectivity (2013: 482).

The youth workers' 'divergence' is both transparent and collective in character.

They do not try to conceal what they are doing, though, of course, it is difficult for superiors to follow day-to-day what is actually happening in the street. The managerial level is dependent on reports from the youth workers, who often adapt their accounts to serve their purpose and readership. But, none the less, the youth workers do not try to conceal their actions. Here, behaving as a collective is crucial; both teams strongly emphasize the decisiveness of unified action. In this respect they meet several of the indicators that Wenger has listed as formative for a 'community of practice' (Wenger 1998: 125–126).

There are several motivating factors here. One has to do with the relation to young people and the deeply felt need to provide them with immediate support for their needs. This is something that Carey and Foster recognize as a component of deviant social work (2011: 590). The vulnerability and needs of some young people engaged by the youth workers are overwhelming since no other support structures are often available. Important in this context is the proximity and informality of the relation-building process between young people and youth workers. There is an analogy to the health visitors in this respect (de la Cuesta 1993). Both health visitors and youth workers come very close to the everyday lives and the troublesome conditions of the groups they work with. Not being able to contribute with something useful during these circumstances creates a feeling of total powerlessness (Carey & Foster 2011: 679).

This links to another motivating factor: a strong identification with an occupational role with both professional and ideological components (cf. Gofen 2013: 476). The youth workers frequently ground their professional decisions on the fact that they are detached youth workers and that this position both privileges and requires them to act in certain ways. In this context they refer to the national interest organization and to the published guidelines. There is a sense of belonging to something overarching, which can

be described by Evetts's concept of 'moral occupational community' (2006: 136). The community is based on shared occupational positions, but is also built on moral commitments and engagement in social issues concerning young people. This demonstrates the moral character of work in human service organizations (Hasenfeld 1983).

This has both internal and external effects. Internally it keeps the detached youth workers together; there is a 'we' to refer to. In addition, the community via, for example, guidelines, produces images of 'good' detached youth work that individuals and teams have to live up to. Externally, the designation 'detached youth work' is used in relation to young people as well as to managers and politicians to signal who they are and what can be expected from them as professionals.

Finally, there is a personal side to workers' motivation. The young people in various ways personally and emotionally move the youth workers they meet, and this leads to both a deep professional and personal engagement (cf. Carey & Foster 2011: 586). The youth workers in the residential area find it easy to identify with the young people they meet, because they have themselves experienced similar conditions. For the city team, it is rather the opposite. The contrast between their own lives and what can be considered as a 'normal Swedish teenager', and the situation that the 'street children' face, is so upsetting that it functions as a motive to engage. Key here is the wish to understand the young people's standpoint and the need to foster a personal engagement with the community – these are central characteristics of how detached youth workers understand their professional role and has been labelled a 'romantic ethic' (Henningsen 2010: 7).

In her study of 'guerrilla employees', O'Leary raised the question of how managers should act in relation to street-level deviance (2010: 8). Should they try to stop it, or rather does it help develop the organization? What we have seen from the two cases presented here indicates that the latter position seems most reasonable. The initiatives taken by the detached youth workers have had a positive impact on young people's situations, and the initial criticism from managers and politicians has been transformed into support. It seems that the fringe work that youth workers engage in is a product of an avant-garde position that is helped and maintained by the outreach approach.

CONCLUSION

The Swedish tradition of detached youth work is part of broader state welfare services. This provides youth workers a reasonably stable occupational position and resources. However, the means and policies of the public services sometimes are insufficient to meet the needs of young people on the ground, and so youth workers engage in new ways to adapt to new circumstances, here understood as fringe work. This is motivated by young people's immediate need for help, by occupational commitments and by personal engagement. One important outcome of these efforts is that the methodology of detached youth work is kept in motion and flexibly develops to match new and emerging social conditions.

REFERENCES

Andersson, Björn. 2013. Finding ways to the hard to reach – considerations on the content and concept of outreach work. *European Journal of Social Work*, 16(2), 171–186.

Andersson, Björn. 2014. How do detached youth workers spend their time? Considerations from a time study in Gothenburg, Sweden. *Youth & Policy*, 112, 18–34.

Calissendorff, Jan, Staffan Höjer & Per Svensson. 1986. *Grundbok i socialt fältarbete [A Basic Book in Detached Youth Work]*. Stockholm: Liber.

Carey, Malcolm & Victoria Foster. 2011. Introducing 'deviant' social work: contextualising the limits of radical social work whilst understanding (fragmented) resistance within the social work labour process. *British Journal of Social Work*, 41(3), 576–593.

Crimmens, David, Fiona Factor, Tony Jeffs, John Pitts, Carole Pugh, Jean Spence & Penelope Turner. 2004. *Reaching Socially Excluded Young People: a National Study of Street-based Youth Work*. Leicester: The National Youth Agency.

De la Cuesta, Carmen. 1993. 'Fringe work: peripheral work in health visiting'. *Sociology of Health & Illness*, 15(5), 665–682.

Eraut Michael (2008) *How Professionals Learn through Work*. University of Surrey, SCEPTrE. First draft of working paper 22/04/2008.

Evetts, Julia. 2006. Short note: the sociology of professional groups. New directions. *Current Sociology*, 54(1), 133–143.

Freire, Paulo. 1979. *Pedagogik för förtryckta. [Pedagogy of the Oppressed]*. Stockholm: Gummessons.

Gofen, Anat. 2013. Mind the gap: dimensions and influence of street-level divergence. *Journal of Public Administration Research and Theory*, 24(2), 473–493.

Göteborgs Stad. 2014. Skillnader i livsvillkor och hälsa i Göteborg. Rapport. [*Differences in Life Conditions and Health in Gothenburg. Report*].

Hasenfeld, Yeheskel. 1983. *Human Service Organizations*. Englewood Cliffs, NJ: Prentice-Hall.

Henningsen, Erik. 2010. The romantic ethic in outreach work. *Sociétés et jeunesses en difficulté* [En ligne], Numéro hors série | 2010, mis en ligne le 02 avril 2010, Consulté le 07 mai 2010. URL: http://sejed.revues.org/index6615.html

Jeffs, Tony. 2015. Innovation and youth work. *Youth & Policy*, 114, 75–95.

Lipsky, Michael. 1980. *Street-level Bureaucracy: Dilemmas of the Individual in Public Service*. New York: Russell Sage Foundation.

Macfarlane, Anne & Mary O'Reilly-de Brún. 2012. Using a theory-driven conceptual framework in qualitative health research. *Qualitative Health Research*, 22(5), 607–618.

O'Leary, Rosemary. 2010. Guerrilla employees: should managers nurture, tolerate, or terminate them? *Public Administration Review*, 70(1), 8–19.

Rapley, Tim. 2011. Some pragmatics of qualitative data analysis. In: Silverman, David (ed.). *Qualitative Research*. London: Sage, 273–290.

RiF (Riksförbundet för fältarbete, National Association for Detached Youth Work). 2014. *En guide till uppsökande fältarbete med ungdomar*. [*A Guide to Detached Youth Work with Young People*]. Stencil.

RiF (Riksförbundet för fältarbete, National Association for Detached Youth Work). 2010. *Fältarbete och forskning*. [*Detached Youth Work and Research*]. RiF Report 2010:1. Stencil.

Sennemark, Eva. 2016. Utvärdering av uppsökande och trygghetsskapande arbete i Biskopsgården. [Evaluation of outreach and safety work in Biskopsgården]. Contextio Ethnographic. Stencil.

Stake, Robert, E. 2005. Qualitative case studies. In: Denzin, Norman K. & Yvonna S. Lincoln (eds). *The Sage Handbook of Qualitative Research*. London: Sage, 433–466.

Vennesson, Pascal. 2008. Case study and process tracing: theories and practices. In: Donatella Della Porta & Michael Keating (eds). *Approaches and Methodologies in the Social Sciences. A Pluralist Perspective*. Cambridge: Cambridge University Press, 223–239.

Wenger, Etienne. 1998. *Communities of Practice: Learning, Meaning and Identity*. Cambridge: Cambridge University Press.

Willis, Paul, E. 1977. *Learning to Labour: How Working Class Kids Get Working Class Jobs*. Farnborough: Saxon House.

The Alchemy of Work with Young Women

Susan Morgan and Eliz McArdle

INTRODUCTION

'Equality has already been achieved' is the general belief of many young women in Northern Ireland (McAlister, Gray and Neill, 2007). The sentiment expressed in this statement, coupled with their disconnection to an equality struggle that may initially appear irrelevant, presents a complex and challenging picture for feminist youth work practice. Feminist demands for equality have been partially achieved but there remain enduring gender inequalities both locally and globally. The political, social and economic trends for young women reveal notable gains towards equality in a relatively short period of time, but stubborn historic inequalities persist; including the gender pay gap, political representation and violence against women, to name but a few. Holding these perspectives in mind is the starting point for contemporary feminist youth workers. Work with young women in Northern Ireland has a long history, but its distinctiveness has not featured in broader histories of feminist youth work practice (Morgan and McArdle, 2009). Guidance for young women's workers continues to be sporadic with limited structural support. Historically, the practice has been drawn either from feminist and/or informal education theory, and a few lone voices have carried the torch in developing a considered body of theory and practice in a UK context (see: Spence, 1996, 2004, 2010; Batsleer, 2008, 2013; Hanbury, Lee and Batsleer, 2010). This chapter attempts to build on this work and add to the articulation of the principles, methodology and transformative potential of work with young women. We consider the nuances and influence of a specifically feminist youth work approach within Northern Ireland and beyond – concluding with the *Alchemy of Work with Young Women* as a model of practice with both local and international reach and relevance.

The *Alchemy approach* has been built primarily from the thematic analysis of the work practices and insights of ten young women's workers based across a range of youth work contexts in Northern Ireland. Taking inspiration from the ancient transformative process of alchemy, it emphasises an assets-based approach to developing an empowering practice (Kretzmann and McKnight, 1993), transmuting base metals into gold. The base metals are the young women at the centre of the practice; the feminist youth worker is the alchemist who blends systematic deliberate approaches with their intuitive ability. The gold is the transformation from growing self-awareness, through critical questioning of existing structures, towards actions that improve the lives of young women personally, socially and politically. The Alchemy of Work with Young Women is presented as an equation that can be applied across a range of settings; from the youth centre to a detached setting on the street; a conversation through to a structured project. Whilst the Alchemy of Work with Young Women has emerged from Northern Ireland its emphasis on transformation may hold resonance for an international audience.

NORTHERN IRELAND – A PLACE APART: LIVING WITH THE LEGACY OF CONFLICT

Northern Ireland is a small constituency geographically located north, on the island of Ireland. With a population of 1.85 million, this relatively insignificant land has gained some global profile through a local conflict, colloquially known as 'the troubles'. This most recent conflict (1968–1998) springs from the contested legacy of the Anglo-Irish Treaty of 1921 between Great Britain and Ireland. This treaty established the 'new' Irish Free State and made provisions for a new entity called 'Northern Ireland' – a constituent of six counties which continued to be constitutionally aligned to Great Britain. The population of these six counties is mixed, with one section of the community who wish

for a new all-Ireland state and another who wish to maintain the constitutional status quo, with continued membership of the United Kingdom. Community segregation and separation are seen as a societal norm; sectarianism and violence are commonplace; and identities are defended and contested in symbols, flags, emblems and language. In global terms, this conflict paled into insignificance (with over 3,600 people being killed over a 30-year period), yet the connection to the UK, which in world affairs is seen as 'punching above its weight',[1] has provided this local conflict with a global stage. Following the signing of The Good Friday Agreement in 1998,[2] a peace process was begun.

Women and Young Women in Northern Ireland

Women have a quiet voice in Northern Ireland society. Speaking out and taking a leadership role is not the expected norm nor is it encouraged, irrespective of the pivotal role assumed by the women's movement within the establishment of 'The Peace People'[3] and The Northern Ireland Women's Coalition (NIWC).[4] The evolution of the NIWC and the developing voice of women in the political sphere were not welcomed by members of the other political parties (Morgan and McArdle, 2009). This historic default position, that men are better placed to inform peace-building, is one which has developed into a local 'truth'. Galligan (2014: 1) highlights the laboriously slow pace of change politically, with 'women's representation in the Assembly not breaking the 20% mark since powers were devolved to the new power-sharing institutions in 1998'.

The 'invisibility' of young women in Northern Ireland is juxtaposed with the central role occupied by young men throughout the conflict and the subsequent peace machinations. Young men were highlighted in the media and prioritised in the subsequent targeting of resources (McCready and Loudon, 2015). Young women were not considered or recognised as direct or indirect victims or perpetrators of violence. The legacy of the conflict is viewed as being mostly male and as having little impact on young women. This 'invisibility' in conflict has the net result of 'invisibility' in solution, with resources, engagement strategies and interventions focused more towards young men than young women (Gray and Neill, 2010).

The report, *Still Waiting* (McAlister et al., 2007) extensively records the prominent issues in young women's lives in Northern Ireland. Their findings resonate with similar UK studies (Girlguiding UK, 2013; Jackson and Tinkler, 2007), highlighting a continuing persistence in passive attitudes to the endurance of inequality among young women themselves, particularly those experiencing social and economic disadvantage. *Still Waiting* identified continuing levels of inequality experienced by young women in Northern Ireland – stereotyping in careers, unequal pay, lack of access to opportunities for advancement in the workplace, sex stereotyping in domestic roles and double standards relating to sexual practices. It revealed alarmingly high levels of domestic violence and sexual abuse – (a quarter of the young women respondents). The picture painted of young women's lives was of continuous and growing stress from education, work, family, relationships and the expectation on women to 'do it all'.

Two Steps Forward ... One Step Back?

Over the past three decades there have been significant social, economic and cultural changes in the UK and Ireland supported through policy and legislation. Amongst other improvements there are now significantly more women in work, girls are achieving better results than boys at school at all levels, from primary to higher education, and increasingly women are reaching positions of greater power and status than before (Walter, 1998). However, this is not the full picture, either nationally or internationally. The notion that equality has been achieved contrasts to the lived experiences of young women and could arguably point to feminist gains of the past being 'undone' in the present (McRobbie, 2009).

Increasingly, studies show how much of young women's lives are resistant to 'gender equality' (Budgeon, 2001). The most recent economic crisis and government austerity measures have resulted in many facing economic strife; however, recent indicators have shown that young women are amongst the greatest losers across social and economic spheres (Hinds, 2011). Henderson et al. (2007) found that the pull of tradition remains a strong influential force and is experienced more substantially by young women who continue to be more willing to accommodate their careers for family than young men. Despite the wide media coverage that girls are more successful academically, their achievements are not necessarily reflected in the labour market, with young women over-represented in low-paid and casual employment (Thompson et al., 2002; McAlister et al., 2007). Young women continue to have lower self-esteem in early adolescence and are disappointed with their bodies (Orenstein, 2013). There is an alarming increase in easily accessible pornography and young women are now, perhaps more than ever, subjected to unrealistic and increasingly sexualised body images (Walter, 2010). Whilst sexual behaviour and identity is a site of stress for young women (McRobbie, 2009), with contradictory messages of sex as liberation or sex as exploitation, the increasing focus in policy and public discourses on the premature sexualisation of girls is proving to draw attention away from ongoing inequalities and important questions about socially constructed ideas of beauty

(Duschinsky, 2013). The escalating attention to 'celebrity' emerging in popular media and reinforced through television programmes such as 'The X-Factor' suggest that wealth, power and status can be at your fingertips if you 'put yourself out there'. This supports the individualistic perspective of 'if you want it, you can get it' and if you don't 'get it' somehow this is down to your own failings. The message presented to many girls within the dominant popular discourse is that 'you're in control', 'you have choices', often mitigated by their lived experiences and positions, which can create a confusing and isolating climate for girls and young women. This can result in the individuation of personal failure and blame rather than a focus on broader structural influences and inequalities (Duschinsky, 2013; McAlister et al., 2007). The gender territory young women negotiate through adolescence and their transitions to adulthood are laden with these contradictory and confusing messages. It is worth questioning how much agency young women really have in making choices within a neoliberal society that remains predicated on patriarchal norms and fails to engage with structural inequalities that shape these young women's lives.

The global picture presents another perspective where differences in terms of status, power, security and identity continue to emerge (Greer, 2000; Padovic and Reskin, 2002; Walter, 1998; Whelehan, 2007). International treaties and frameworks for gender equality, within a human rights framework, are well established. The UN Security Council Resolution 1325 on Women, Peace and Security, the 1995 Beijing Platform for Action and the UN Commission on the Status of Women present a rolling commentary on the picture for women, nation by nation. More than 1 billion people (mostly women) world-wide live in poverty (WomenWatch, 2015). Violence against women persists both as a weapon of war and a personal tool to wield power. Access to education for girls is a global problem, with long-term impacts on the economic, social and political lives of young women and women internationally. Closer to home, the defiance of reproductive rights across the island of Ireland is an added challenge facing women.

Global social action campaigns 'the girl effect' and 'girl rising' (Bent, 2015) have gained momentum; often coupled with movements driven by large corporations, such as the 'Dove campaign for real beauty' or 'Always, #like a girl campaign'. International development programmes focusing on the empowerment of girls are growing, with project themes of sport, gender-based violence, employment and education most prominent (Hayhurst, 2013; Shain, 2013). Such global programmes' motivations are fundamentally shaped by a neoliberal perspective (Shain, 2013), whereby: 'greater gender equality is also smart economics' (The World Bank, 2012: xiii). Programmes emphasise the economic empowerment of individual girls and young women and further place the weight of substantial social change on the shoulders of girls, whose power is limited. Caution is needed in managing the expectations of *how* the empowerment of girls can realistically achieve the structural development goals tackling poverty and inequality.

Work with Young Women – Surviving against the Odds

Feminist thinking has been disputed in recent decades from a range of different angles. The dominant public discourse is that equality has been achieved, with follow-up inferences that it has gone 'too far', tipping the balance more favourably towards women than men. In the 'post-modern' era, where notions of a 'universal identity' have been challenged, criticism exists of 'old' feminism as failing to recognise the complexity of women's identities, with a growing recognition of a more nuanced intersectional analysis based on race, sexuality, class and location (McCall, 2005; Pilcher and Whelehan, 2004). There are new and contrasting ideas of 'modern feminism' located within a neoliberal climate (Baumgardner and Richards, 2004) contested as a disarticulation of feminism (McRobbie, 2009). The result has been a constant challenge to feminist ideology and action, hostility to feminism in popular culture (Faludi, 1992) and persistent difficulty in making a convincing argument for the specific need for work with young women.

In Northern Ireland the work has endured against the backdrop of both 'the troubles' and feminism, whereby the emphasis and resources of the youth sector were directed squarely at young men, as a response to managing the local civil disorder (Morgan and McArdle, 2009). The challenge to this was taken up by the Gender Equality Unit of YouthAction Northern Ireland[5] in championing feminist work with young women, from the late 1970s. The organisation, not only developed practice with young women, but also built critical evidence to make the case for young women's work (McAlister et al., 2007; NIAYC, 1978; Trimble, 1990; YouthAction N.I., 2014). This body of work has been pivotal in defining the rationale for and the processes of feminist youth work in the Northern Ireland context. It has, however, not been without its challenges. Whilst many young women's workers have been driven and influenced by feminism, tensions and competing agendas within the youth sector often undermine or minimise the practice (see Morgan and McArdle (2009) and Spence (1996) and for examples); the result being that feminist youth work lacks a strong 'foothold' within the youth sector. Feminist insights which motivated the work initially became suppressed by constant challenge, funding pressures and traditional policy perspectives (Morgan and McArdle, 2009). The hostility experienced towards feminism in practice can result in the 'silencing' of workers and their rationale, principles and understanding of the work. Indeed 'work with young women' that develops without this clarity and engagement with feminist

purpose and methodology, can inadvertently *reinforce* and *promote* gender stereotypes and inequality, as opposed to challenging these oppressions – e.g. beauty programmes that fail to explore socially constructed ideas of beauty.

Whilst some important gains have been made for young women, Spence (1996) argues that little impact on structural or organisational change followed. Government policy, even while professing to be gender neutral by using the term 'young people', remains highly gendered (Hanbury et al., 2010). Policy pertaining to anti-social behaviour, drug/alcohol misuse and gun/knife crime is directed towards young men; with protectionist policies directed towards young women, from self-harm to teen pregnancy. Hanbury et al. (2010) argue that work which flows from these policies can *maintain* the gender stereotypes which feminist youth work practices have advocated against. Across UK government departments there is an increasing emphasis on demonstrable outcomes and a desire to fund the defined essentials; with value for money set against predetermined outcomes (Henry et al., 2010). This trend lends itself towards increased managerialism, measurement and 'fix-it' approaches. Practitioners, who set out to do assets-based work focusing on young women in a 'non-problem-centred' way, prompt clashes (or extinction) with policy makers and funding streams consumed with a deficit model of 'fixing' 'problem youth'.

Building a Cacophony of Voices

Morgan and McArdle (2009: 240) have argued that the determination and passion of those central to the practice has been key to its continuity, suggesting that 'stamina and strength, constancy and sustained action and continuous reflection on ideology, vision and practice ... continue to be necessary for a future strategy of work with girls and young women'. It is the workers who are the central protagonists and drivers. Support and development of this collective formed the rationale for a long-standing partnership (from 2003 onwards) between YouthAction Northern Ireland and Ulster University's Community Youth Work department. This began a series of initiatives to combine practice, policy and theory in the field of young women's work. The aim was to amass the groundswell of voices of young women's workers; to build momentum from the collective, to generate gender-conscious theory from their experience and weave these sharper insights back into practice.

This partnership devised a model of gender-conscious practice, proposing an approach to working with young women and young men that proactively challenges societal stereotypes and gendered expectations. The approach recognised that gender-conscious work can be carried out with individuals, groups, or in a large-scale setting, if the principle exists to challenge the social norms of gender that limit the opportunities in explicit and implicit ways. The model was closely followed by 'The Lens Model' (Morgan and Harland, 2009), which accentuated the need for the practitioner to have a keen understanding of how gender impacts on society, on young people, and on their own perspectives and experiences. In using the 'gender lens' to understand the lives of young men and young women, workers can build up an armoury of interventions, programmes and moments to purposefully engage young people in challenging gendered expectations and gender norms.

'The Gender Initiative' seminars ran from 2013 to 2015, open to writers, researchers and practitioners. The purpose of this seminar series was twofold – to develop a support network that would inspire, motivate and develop work with young women; and to sharpen articulation of practice and develop greater confidence in the distinctive qualities permeating practice. These made space for new solidarities to emerge,

either relating to local peace and conflict, or transcending the local context, a collective voice on universal themes. The alliance between research and practice as both a research methodology and a strategic action acted to sustain the practice. From violence to technology, from romance to rights, workers explored, described and critiqued their experiences of work with young women. Two focus groups of ten young women's workers self-selected from the broader group, reflecting feminist practice across a range of contexts – the majority being experienced practitioners in the field, alongside early career young women's workers. Quotes used through this text are from focus group participants. The purpose of focus group discussions was to deepen insights on the defining features of empowering work with young women via an exploration described by Reinharz (1992) as a 'demystification framework'. As lack of knowledge can accentuate and perpetuate powerlessness, in *obtaining* the knowledge the potential for change is created (Punch, 2005: 138). Hence, by demystifying these practices and approaches, confidence and competence to engage in powerful feminist practice is encouraged and embraced. Themes were drawn and analysed from the material transcribed from the focus groups and secondary material from seminar participants. These illuminated the key principles, purpose and methods. Using a constant comparative approach (Thomas, 2009), the ideas were tested by the focus groups and the Alchemy of Work with Young Women emerged, as an equation, with a series of associated processes, herein described.

THE ALCHEMY OF WORK WITH YOUNG WOMEN

The key to unlocking the Alchemy of Work with Young Women was in asking a *different* question. With a starting point of *'what do you like about young women?'* workers immediately focused on what they saw as the *positive* attributes of the young women they encountered in their practice. The exploration then deepened as they uncovered details such as how they used their wisdom and experience to engage young women in a purposeful way; the methods they use; and the potential impact of the work. The research material generated has led to a new language to describe the work: the *alchemy* in practice.

The Alchemy Equation

The simplest definition of Alchemy is the art of transformation. It is a blend of art and science where key elements combine in a perfect ratio, drawing on what already exists. The purpose is changing base metal to gold. It is powerful and magical and at the same time scientific and purposeful. It can be risky and dangerous but can wield valuable results. Alchemy offers a rich metaphor to give form to the practices described. It is best described as the following equation:

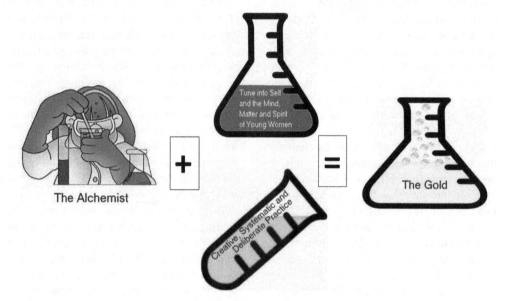

The alchemist refers to the practitioner, who uses their gendered lens to tune into self, and the mind, matter and spirit of the young women; then, through creative, systematic and deliberate practice, engages in purposeful ways with the young women to create gold.

The Alchemist is more than simply a conductor of affairs, using their inspired wisdom in intuitive and spontaneous actions. They are an emotional catalyst, a portal between what already exists and new possibilities. They are disciplined and focused towards building assets and strengths. This assets-based approach views young women as having

latent potential rather than being the problem to be solved. They channel these positive traits, freeing young women to be creative, engaged and motivated towards action. The Alchemist has charismatic capital and young women are attracted to the persona, flare and the empowering style of a worker that encourages them to flourish. This empowering style taps into an inherent self-belief that in turn promotes a 'can do' attitude amongst young women. The starting point for this process is defined by young women themselves. The Alchemist works to bring ideas through to action, in collaboration with young women, inspiring change for individuals, groups, communities and society as a whole. In this transformation, lies the gold.

THE ALCHEMY PROCESSES

Using a Gendered Lens to Appreciate Young Women's Lives

Practitioners reported that young women can have ideas and behaviours about being female or male so deeply ingrained that they become ritualised behaviours, practised and repeated, and act as 'proof of identity' as one sex or another. From shopping to 'gossiping', from make-up to weddings, young women are 'initiated' into these rituals from girlhood. The practitioners **disrupted gender rituals** through noticing, naming them and introducing new ways of being; embracing non-traditional activities and challenges. This disruption can leave young women feeling unsettled momentarily; however, challenge to the established order has liberating properties. New rituals offer space for roles and structures to be re-defined.

The practitioners were intentionally **counter-cultural**. They challenged sexism, cultural norms and patriarchy in planned ways as an expected part of their practice in an attempt to reduce the negative restrictive hold of historical, biographical and cultural experiences. They actively worked against negative gendered messages whilst embracing the positive material the young women brought and presented. Antrobus (2000: 52) concurs that 'the counter-cultural perspective reminds us that asserting women's values and the existence of an alternative, "female" culture is an essential part of the process for transformation'. Inherent in this counter-cultural perspective is an understanding that issues faced by young women are the result of deep-seated historical gender inequalities. The emphasis is on change, not blame – for example, using this approach with young mothers leads to less emphasis

on parenting techniques and more work on building independence; less emphasis on sexual health and more emphasis on health inequalities; less emphasis on 'getting out to work' and more emphasis on lobbying for affordable childcare options. Using their wisdom to identify **real-life situations** led workers towards meaningful engagement centred in the worlds of the young women themselves:

> It's all about using the stuff that is there.
> It's actually something that so many of the group had been affected by, like let's actually hone in on this and let's actually find out more and like feed it into the programme ... (Focus group participant, FGP)[6]

Practitioners in the focus groups spoke of the tales young women brought from local, national or global media that were current and salient. Recognising these 'real-life' current interests provided a powerful source of material to get young women thinking critically about the world around them (Bowler, 2010).

Awakening the Girl Child

Many cultural and social norms have the effect of dampening down the natural exuberance, curiosity or fun that younger girls may freely express. McAlister et al. (2007) identify the 'leisure squeeze' as a feature of young women's busy lives – intrinsically linked to the effects of gender stereotypes on their personal circumstances: the expectation for young women to bear the brunt of household and family chores; the growing caring responsibilities for other siblings or extended family members; and the pressure to do well academically. Girls and young women take on such burdens of responsibility at increasingly young ages. Leisure pursuits are squeezed and the fun and freedom of expression minimised. Young women often become more self-conscious, more anxious and less relaxed. Indeed Batsleer (2013: 26) poses a question to practitioners, asking why girls are so discouraged from 'risk'. She suggests that risk should be re-associated 'with excitement, rebellion, wildness, pleasure and potential'. One practitioner similarly described the need to find ways to enable young women to re-encounter a sense of fun and play:

> Whenever you do see them overcoming their inhibitions and acting the whack, you kind of stand back, when you are doing a gaggy ice-breaker and they are being an eejit, and they don't mind ... you don't get much opportunity to do that ... you become grown up too early. (FGP)

When young women are positively engaged there is an excitement, an enthusiasm, about making an idea happen that can be recognised, harnessed and nurtured:

> I just think that the way whenever they put their heads to something ... how enthusiastic they are and just want to get it done.
>   ... the fact that they are so bright and observant and like notice things around them and then be that enthusiastic to share them thoughts with those around them. (FGP)

This **enthusiasm** is in contrast to a cultural norm of self-consciousness and self-doubt, a pervasive undercurrent which if left can diminish their participation:

> They [the young women] sort of negative self-talk, but then they start to do it [the activity] and they start to change their mind even within a session ... I always recall Amber [pseudonym] within a session on interior design and it was 'I can't do this ... this is going to be crap ... I'm not creative'. (FGP)

The practitioner worked through this self-doubt ...

> ... and she done her table and her table was fantastic and she was 'I can't wait to get this home'. (FGP)

The enthusiasm described by the workers is not necessarily a physical bounding enthusiasm, but nonetheless had a propensity towards action. The practitioners find the fun and give permission for young women to

join in. Through the visceral experience of the physical feeling of enjoyment they engage with each other in light-hearted and laughter-filled interactions. This in turn builds their enthusiasm and desire to be involved.

Encouraging Camaraderie and Collective Wisdom

Practitioners reported the tendency for young women to tell stories of their lives and communities. Through listening to stories they found ways of hearing how **young women made sense of their worlds**. This active listening is the foundation of the relationship and an empowering process whereby young women are liberated to speak about their true lives and experiences:

> I really love that when people are just, kind of just coming to tell stories and stuff but they are just really real about it. I think I really tune into that ... wanting to be more aware of how you feel and own your feelings and things like that. (FGP)

Making sense of these stories is a fully collaborative approach which works by giving value to the sharing, as more than simply idle chat, thus leading to even more dialogue:

> maybe in two weeks down the line, you are talking about an issue and you are able to say 'do you remember you said to me ... such and such and such' and that fits into this and how do the rest of you think that this fits into this' – they start to realise that you are listening to the whole experience and they start to respond then by feeling that it is okay to share more and more because you're interested. (FGP)

The more the practitioner tunes in, the more the young women and worker collaborate to make sense of the wider world.

How young women are, **as a collective**, is a dominant feature of the work and counter to a general stereotype of 'bitchiness' that is often the anticipated persona for young women. One worker made a distinction between what is inherent in young women and what has been learned:

> the friendship and loyalty with young women in some of the groups I think is a really endearing quality that they have. But I know that can go either way ... there are qualities that they kind of learn, like that bitchiness ... you are kind of made to be bitchy. (FGP)

She went on to refer to how group members show sustained and critical support towards each other:

> I've seen young mums being really supportive of each other even with things like you know weaning children or getting them to go to bed ... they are so kind and understanding of where everybody is coming from I suppose. (FGP)

The positive collective not only related to practical advice-giving but moved into positive reinforcement:

> when they have achieved something, they are all chuffed with themselves ... and they are so proud and so supportive of each other 'Jesus, you were brilliant, well done, that was really good'. (FGP)

The **friendship, loyalty and camaraderie** are strong and valued within the psyche of the young women's group, and practitioners tune into and embrace these strong positive attributes.

Organic Conversation

Using conversation is a tried and tested informal education methodology (Jeffs and Smith, 2005). Young women can quickly move into deep conversations, for example, regarding relationships, sex or deeply-felt emotions. Some workers may fear or shy away from real or deep disclosure and tend to keep conversations light and frivolous. However, deep conversations on equality, stereotypes, on sexual and social relationships, on rights and social justice were all part of the repertoire of *these* focus group members. Embedded in these conversations were **a blend of humour**

and gravitas and workers did not fear where conversations might lead. They identified a process whereby young women started to have organic conversations on issues of equality and oppression; they moved through to a deeper exploration, to a point where they made connections from broader concepts to their own lives and vice versa. The practitioners' readiness to embrace these conversations was imperative. Practitioners referred to the tone of the discussions as a two-way respectful conversation, avoiding moralising and judgement. The workers 'joined in' the conversation in the tone already set by the individual or group.

This connects to the role of conversation as an enlightening process, which Blyth describes as 'the spontaneous business of making connections' (2008: 4). The use of stories from social media (Snapchat, Facebook, YouTube) was a powerful tool capturing the imagination of the group whereby they established relevance to their lives, raising consciousness and connecting to wider cultural, social and political agendas. Beginning with conversation based on real-life scenarios brought naturally occurring opportunities for awareness-raising. The practitioners through their inspired wisdom, brought emphasis and gravitas to the meaning behind the story, resulting in both visibility and voice to those things the young women deemed important.

Getting Caught in the Moment

Working with young women is both visceral and cerebral. Culturally, logic is much more valued within society, with discussions, writing and presentations valued as communication and learning tools. The impact of body or sense-filled activities can be underestimated; however, the practitioners reported how young women flourished through these experiences. The new activities, at first, can seem peculiar to young women, as they were not in the habit of taking part in a piece of dance, for example, or playing drums. The body has lost its physical memory of what it feels like to do these things. The worker revives wonder and awe in how the senses can enrich day-to-day living, through ice-breakers involving physical touch or listening to songs in a different way. It is not that these instincts have been lost but they are untapped. There can be therapeutic aspects to this type of sensory work, but coupled with other light-hearted approaches, these are liberating and building rather than fixing and repairing actions. Additionally, for young women who have not found joy and achievement in sport, for example, they often have little experience or **opportunity for immersive activities** – those activities which have a physical component are deeply involving and have the effect of shutting out the world. In these 'flow' activities (Csikszentmihalyi, cited in McArdle and Ward, 2015) losing track of time is a noticeable feature; through them we can be lifted from a self-conscious space into an unconscious or a sub-conscious space. The focus is no longer on 'how do I look?' but rather on 'how am I doing and what is coming next?' This liberating experience for young women provides a chance to develop skills, work towards accomplishments, and take a break from persistent negative self-talk. Practitioners introduced immersive activities to the groups through their own enthusiasm; communicating and demonstrating belief in young women.

Building Fire in the Belly

The practitioners described the strength of spirit that young women bring, combined with strong emotions and an inner conviction towards justice. They connected this to a level of resilience within young women and their ability to endure extreme pressure. It can lie dormant if under-nourished, however it is powerful when embraced:

> See, some of the young women I work with ... they just completely blow me away with what they

have been through. And how they still get up out of bed in the morning ... And I just think if I had been through the care system or been from a broken family or had to care for siblings and then maybe have their own kids now or maybe having trouble from her partner ... You just think Superwoman, like seriously ... into yourself thinking ... how are you still coping, the strength and determination ... (FGP)

The discovery of injustice and inequality can often engage individuals on a cerebral level. But to make the connections between 'self' and the injustice of the world around us is more of a visceral reaction where you feel movement in your belly:

> I love when you get to the point where you've really made your group angry. I think like you say something and until you take it apart a wee bit you don't see the inequalities that are there ... like you don't see that until you think about it. And they don't see that until you are processing it with them as well. (FGP)

This **strength of conviction combined with strong emotions** proved to be a driving force for 'building fire in the belly'. Starting with everyday things and a 'gut feeling' that something is not quite right (a music video, a sexist or homophobic comment), the practitioner compels the young women to explore their emotions. When the gut feeling builds, young women question more closely, building momentum and propelling them towards challenge and action. The process ignites the spark, which builds the fire through making connections that seem so obvious, yet may well have been dismissed as 'just how it is'. One worker described the steady and slow process of walking through issues about gender:

> and all of a sudden, things that they were not interested in, you have got so many stories around the table about that one thing, and I suppose that is good to hone into. (FGP)

Another practitioner identified their own approach of acutely tuning into the movements of the young women and tuning into the ideas and principles which boost their propensity towards action, big or small:

> it is that kind of ownership from the very start that once you throw it out there, and give them the material, that kind of inspires. From that point then on, the rest of the process is theirs in regards to what goes on or what they do with it. (FGP)

The combination of the intense physical feeling, with a new language and logic of how to explain injustice, offers young women the tools for engagement. The practitioner acts as a portal between the young woman's current world and the wider world – encouraging them to break free of the constraints of their current societal context and from those aspects of life that are 'preventing'. Through the use of creativity they can unlock latent ambitions and abilities. The young women learn reflective and noticing skills and consciously note developments in their thinking and action skills. This then helps to build their critical engagement with the wider world.

Repeat and Return

The depth and breadth of the prevailing social norms can be hard to shift. Sometimes young women need to be convinced. To overcome the deeply-seated psychology and unconscious processes of how young women are conditioned to think, feel and act (Walkerdine et al., 2001), practitioners needed a sophisticated understanding of the cycle of self-doubt (e.g. when faced with a new opportunity young women begin enthusiastically; this enthusiasm can wane immeasurably with seeping self-doubt and embarrassment; resulting in indecision and withdrawal). Current gender dis-aggregated statistics show that young women are achieving more highly than young men at GCSEs and A' levels[7] (Burns et al., 2015). This pattern is not surprising when we consider the persistent passivity of young women and their learnt ability to follow rules and

regulations (Orenstein, 2013). School systems and achievements reward the ability to consume information in an unquestioning way. The practitioners discussed how a tacit unquestioning acceptance, alongside embarrassment of being wrong, discouraged young women from challenging the world and the knowledge of others. Acknowledging the pervasiveness of this pattern seemed crucial to practitioners in understanding how young women can disengage before even starting something new. The practitioners talked of the need for **persistence in delivering the same messages** consistently in different ways to counteract the centuries-old entrenched cultural messages. The strategy was therefore to make personal contact close to the beginning of the new adventure in order to nudge the young woman forward. A few repeated nudges might be needed, requiring a gentle persistence and the delivery of the same messages returned to again and again, to strengthen these new alternative messages. Helping young women to be more critical in their way of thinking about the world was inherent in the practice.

The Cogs in a Wheel

Inspiring towards personal and collective action is the purpose of transformative work with young women recognising that individual transformation is a small cog, with collective action a larger cog and structural change as the large wheel to be turned. An example of practice provided by one of the practitioners is an illustration of this. A small group of young women along with their worker started off decorating shoes for International Women's Day, under the theme of 'Move 4 Equality'. They teamed up with young women from four other projects and took the lead position in a rally to Belfast City Hall. One young woman made a speech to the crowd while others were DJ-ing on a bus. Inspired by taking part in the rally, a number of the group took part in a workshop two weeks later on the history of the suffragettes. The principle of 'one thing leads to another' is important within this example. Working to make the connections between the small things that you act upon and the big things you make happen are an important component of empowering practice. For most of the young women the idea of attending a workshop on women's right to vote and the history of the suffragettes was inconceivable at the start of the process, but, incrementally, in learning the language and ideas of equality, it developed more salience for them.

Starting at the right place is the art and moving to the next steps at the right time is the science of work with young women. The analogy for this work is of tributaries running into rivers. The practitioner holds the belief that many small actions can lead to collective action and broader impact as a result. Whilst the worker is a force for inspiration, paradoxically, they must also be realistic. For example, one worker spoke of a young woman, in the week following the International Women's Day Rally, despondently asking '*I wonder when we will see any change?*' The art here is to inspire towards action and retain realism without damaging the optimism and ideals of the young women. The worker's role is to consistently build the resilience and sustainability of the young women. Through reflection (Batsleer, 2013: 54), they can then identify what change is immediately possible and the role of collective action in building towards actual social change.

Building a Public Persona and Voice

The public sphere has historically been an unwelcoming territory for women (Imray and Middleton, 2002). Public exposure feels so threatening that it can lead to young women living and inhabiting the private world rather than having a public persona or face. This can perpetuate the 'invisibility' of young women in everyday life (Batsleer, 2013), in politics and in the many public spheres. Central to the Alchemy of Work with Young Women is **raising visibility**, through working with the personal and the political. In personal terms, building a public persona includes developing ways for young women to communicate and express themselves in the social and public world. Through practising bravery, building fearlessness, deciding upon important messages, developing voices and constant reflection on distance travelled, young women conceive and build a public persona. The practitioner then works collaboratively to find opportunities for **young women to promote this public persona** and engage in meaningful ways in their communities, wider society and the world around them.

CONCLUSION

The Alchemy of Work with Young Women has been created and shaped within a Northern Ireland context. It developed against the backdrop of a society emerging from conflict which resulted in both a low visibility of the work, yet a slow, steady progression and a strong imperative to maintain and sustain practice. The central protagonists of strong empowering practice with young women have essentially been the workers themselves. The need to support and develop these practitioners is central to embedding strong practices, now and for the future. The process, of building momentum from a collective, generating gender-conscious theory from their experiences and weaving these insights back into practice, has strengthened both motivation and focus for the work locally. Strong work with young women has feminist values at its centre as a driving and guiding force. Where feminist values separate from method, work with young women can lose its way. In a context of oppression and continued gender inequality, the Alchemy of

Work with Young Women offers an antidote which is empowering and transformative.

Work with young women in Northern Ireland echoes a range of approaches in both Ireland and the UK, however, the universal themes of empowerment and transformation resonate within a broader global setting. Further insights and wisdom could be generated from using the alchemy equation and processes across a range of social and cultural contexts, or across disciplines. The practices articulated in this chapter are proposed, not as a panacea to world poverty or humanitarian crises, but with a view to the empowerment of girls and young women as a cog in the wheel.

Notes

1 Douglas Hurd, Making the world a safer place: our five priorities, *Daily Telegraph*, 1 January 1992.
2 The Good Friday Agreement, between the UK and Republic of Ireland governments was agreed on Good Friday, 1998 and entered legislation as the Northern Ireland Act, 1998. This heralded the beginning of a peace process for the region, with paramilitary ceasefires and new democratic structures.
3 The Peace People is an organisation based in Northern Ireland that promotes non-violence, peace and justice around the world.
4 The Northern Ireland Women's Coalition (NIWC) was a small political party led by women, which operated from 1996 to 2006.
5 YouthAction Northern Ireland is a 75-year-old regional voluntary youth work organisation, formerly known as the Northern Ireland Association of Youth Clubs (NIAYC).
6 FGP will be used throughout to refer to Focus Group Participant.
7 A' levels are exams for leaving post-primary education.

REFERENCES

Antrobus, P. (2000) Transformational leadership: advancing the agenda for gender justice. *Gender and Development*, 8(3): 50–56.

Batsleer, J. (2008) *Informal Learning in Youth Work*. London: Sage.
Batsleer, J. (2013) *Youth Working with Girls and Women in Community Settings: A Feminist Perspective*. Farnham: Ashgate Publishing Company.
Baumgardner, J. and Richards, A. (2004) Feminism and femininity: or how we learned to stop worrying and love the thong. In Harris, A. and Fine, M. (eds), *All About the Girl*. London: Routledge, pp. 56–69.
Bent, E. (2015) 'Girl rising' and the problematic 'other': celebritizing third-world girlhoods. In Trier, A. (ed.), *Feminist Theory and Pop Culture*. Rotterdam: Sense Publishers, pp. 89–102.
Blyth, C. (2008) *The Art of Conversation*. London: John Murray.
Bowler, R. (2010) Learning from lives. In Buchroth, I. and Parkin, C. (eds), *Using Theory in Youth and Community Work Practice: Learning from Lives*. Exeter: Learning Matters Ltd. pp. 44–61.
Budgeon, S. (2001) Emergent feminist(?) identities: young women and the practice of micro politics. *European Journal of Women's Studies*, 8(1): 7–28.
Burns, S., Leitch, R. and Hughes, J. (2015) *Education Inequalities in Northern Ireland*. Belfast, UK: Equality Commission for Northern Ireland.
Duschinsky, R. (2013) Childhood, responsibility and the liberal loophole. *Sociological Research Online*, 18(2): 7.
Faludi, S. (1992) *Backlash: The Undeclared War against Women*. London: Chatto and Windus.
Galligan, Y. (2014) *Women in Politics – Briefing Paper*. Belfast, UK: Northern Ireland Assembly.
Girlguiding UK (2013) *What Girls Say About... Equality for Girls. Girls' Attitudes Survey 2013*. Retrieved 9th October 2014 from http://girlsattitudes.girlguiding.org.uk/home.aspx
Gray, A. and Neill, G. (2010) Creating a shared society in Northern Ireland: Why we need to focus on gender equality. *Youth and Society*, 43(2): 468–487.
Greer, G. (2000) *The Whole Woman*. London: Anchor.
Hanbury, A., Lee, A. and Batsleer, J. (2010) Youth work with girls: a feminist perspective.

In Batsleer, J. and Davies, B. (eds), *What is Youth Work? Empowering Youth and Community Work Practice*. Exeter: Learning Matters Ltd, pp. 116–128.

Hayhurst, L. (2013) Girls as the 'new' agents of social change? Exploring the 'girl effect' through sport, gender and development programs in Uganda. *Sociological Research Online*, 18(2): 8.

Henry, P., Morgan, S. and Hammond, M. (2010) Building relationships through effective interpersonal engagement: A training model for youth workers. *Youth Studies Ireland*, 5(2): 25–38.

Hinds, B. (2011) *The Northern Ireland Economy: Women on the Edge: A Comprehensive Analysis of the Impacts of the Financial Crisis*. Belfast, UK: Women's Resource and Development Agency.

Henderson, S., Holland, J., McGrellis, S., Sharpe, S. and Thompson, R. (2007) *Inventing Adulthoods: A Biographical Approach to Youth Transitions*. London: Sage.

Imray, L. and Middleton, A. (2002) Public and private: marking the boundaries. In Jackson, S. and Scott, S. (eds) *Gender: A Sociological Reader*. London: Routledge, pp. 155–158.

Jackson, C. and Tinkler, P. (2007) 'Ladettes' and 'modern girls': 'troublesome' young femininities. *The Sociological Review*, 55(2): 251–272.

Jeffs, T. and Smith, M. (2005) *Informal Education: Conversation, Democracy and Learning*, 3rd edition. Nottingham: Educational Heretics Press.

Kretzmann, J. and McKnight, J. (1993) *Building Communities from the Inside Out: A Path towards Finding and Mobilizing a Community's Assets*. Chicago: ACTA.

McAlister, S., Gray, A. and Neill, G. (2007) *Still Waiting – the Stories behind the Statistics of Young Women Growing Up in Northern Ireland*. Belfast, UK: YouthAction Northern Ireland.

McArdle, E. and Ward, S. (2015) *Lifemaps... the Youth Work Journey to Build Mental Health*. Belfast, UK: YouthAction Northern Ireland.

McCall, L. (2005) The complexity of intersectionality. *Signs*, 30(3): 1771–1800.

McCready, S. and Loudon, R. (2015) *Investing in Lives: The History of the Youth Service in Northern Ireland (1844–1973)*. Belfast, UK: Youth Council for Northern Ireland.

McRobbie, A. (2009) *The Aftermath of Feminism: Gender, Culture and Social Change*. London: Sage.

Morgan, S. and Harland, K. (2009) The lens model: A practical tool for developing and understanding gender conscious practice. *Youth & Policy*, 101: 67–79.

Morgan, S. and McArdle, E. (2009) Long walk from the door: a history of work with girls and young women in Northern Ireland since 1969. In Gilchrist, R., Jeffs, T., Spence, J. and Walker, J. (eds), *Essays in the History of Youth and Community Work*. Lyme Regis: Russell House Publishing, pp. 220–242.

NIAYC, Northern Ireland Association of Youth Clubs (1978) *Waiting Our Turn*. Belfast, UK: NIAYC.

Orenstein, P. (2013) *Schoolgirls: Young Women, Self-esteem and the Confidence Gap*. New York: Bantham Doubleday DELL Publishing Group.

Padovic, I. and Reskin, B. (2002) *Women and Men at Work*. Thousand Oaks: Pine Forge Press.

Pilcher, J. and Whelehan, I. (2004) *50 Key Concepts in Gender Studies*. London: Sage.

Punch, K. (2005) *Introduction to Social Research: Quantitative and Qualitative Approaches*. London: Sage.

Reinharz, S. (1992) *Feminist Methods in Social Research*. New York: Oxford University Press.

Shain, F. (2013) 'The girl effect': exploring narratives of gendered impacts and opportunities in neo-liberal development. *Sociological Research Online*, 18(2): 9.

Spence, J. (1996) Feminism in work with girls and women. In Nolan, P.C. (ed.) (2003) *20 Years of Youth and Policy: a Retrospective*. Leicester: NYA, pp. 171–189.

Spence, J. (2004) Working for Jewish girls: Lily Montagu, Girls' clubs and industrial reform 1890–1914. *Women's History Review*, 13(3): 491–509.

Spence, J. (2010) Collecting women's lives: the challenge of feminism in UK youth work in the 1970s and 80s. *Women's History Review*, 19(1): 159–176.

The World Bank (2012) *World Development Report 2012: Gender Equality and Development*. Washington DC: The World Bank.

Thomas, G. (2009) *How To Do Your Research Project*. London: Sage.

Thompson, R., Bell, R., Holland, J. and Henderson, C. (2002) Critical moments: choice, chance and opportunities in young people's narratives of transition. *Sociology*, 36(2): 335–354.

Trimble, J. (1990) *Equality of Opportunity: Provision for Girls and Young Women in the Full-time Sector of the Northern Ireland Youth Service*. Belfast, UK: YouthAction Northern Ireland.

Walkerdine, V., Lucey, H. and Melody, J. (2001) *Growing Up Girl: Psycho-social Explorations of Gender and Class*. Basingstoke: Palgrave.

Walter, N. (1998) *The New Feminism*. London: Little Brown.

Walter, N. (2010) *Living Dolls: The Return of Sexism*. London: Virago Press.

Whelehan, I. (2007) *Overloaded: Popular Culture and the Future of Feminism*. London: The Women's Press Ltd.

WomenWatch (2015) *Thematic Issues and Critical Areas of Concern*. Retrieved 4th April 2016 from www.un.org/womenwatch/directory/critical_areas_of_concern_30.htm

YouthAction Northern Ireland (2006) *An Occasional Youth Work Practice Paper 2. Gender-conscious Work with Young People*. Belfast, UK: YouthAction Northern Ireland.

YouthAction Northern Ireland (2014) *Bullseye – Hitting the Mark in Working with Young Women: A Resource for Working with Young Women*. Belfast, UK: YouthAction N.I.

23

Supporting Trans, Non-Binary and Gender Diverse Young People: UK Methods and Approaches

Catherine McNamara

INTRODUCTION

This chapter takes the work of the UK-based organization Gendered Intelligence (GI) as an example of youth work practice with young people who identify as transgender and/or non-binary. In this chapter, 'trans' is used to mean a broad spectrum of gender identities and gendered expressions and to include people who feel their gender identity does not sit comfortably with the sex they were assigned at birth, including but not limited to transgender and non-binary identified people. Not all non-binary identified people would identify as trans, and, as an umbrella term, trans does not suit all people in the same way. The GI youth groups are described as trans youth groups open to a wide range of people: 'whether you're brand new to identifying as trans, still questioning your identity, or if you consider yourself to be post-transition or as having a trans history. We strive to be fully inclusive of individuals who identify as non-binary/other, as well as male or

female' (Gendered Intelligence website, April 2017). Carrie Davis writes specifically about language relating to trans identities as 'an evolutionary vocabulary that changes inter-generationally, geographically, and within a political context' (2009: 16). For further reading on trans identities see, for example, Bornstein (1995), Stryker and Whittle (2006), GI (2007) and Valentine (2007).

The chapter seeks to consolidate and critically reflect on the experiences gained over a decade from the GI youth group project and share a model of practice that might be used by other practitioner-researchers in this and cognate fields. The discussion in this chapter is based on reflections on historic and present practice and draws on focused conversations with practitioners from GI. The chapter refers specifically to a set of five different monthly youth groups that take place in three cities within England (London, Bristol and Leeds) for people aged 8 to 25. This youth work practice with young people who identify as trans or are questioning or exploring their gender identity has been developing since 2006, and so over ten years has developed to expand, particularly to accommodate younger people, rather than turning families and children away. I offer some contextual detail of GI as a trans-led organization and the GI youth group work specifically. This includes how the youth groups came into being, the geographical spread of the work, the numbers of young people and the staff, and how this work is situated in relation to other similar provision in the UK and internationally. The chapter articulates the broader framework that supports the practice and identifies the specific methods used in this youth work practice. To close, some of the key aspects of the practice are highlighted that could be adapted and adopted to lead to increased trans-inclusive youth work practice more broadly.

Dr Jay Stewart and I were co-founders and Stewart is the Chief Executive Officer (CEO) for the organization. My pedagogic practice and research focuses on gender, particularly trans and/or non-binary gender identities within an arts context. My professional background is in Applied Theatre and Drama Education. GI is based in London and was formally registered as a Community Interest Company (CIC) in 2008. A CIC is a specific type of company structure in the UK which reinvests profits in the company for community and social benefit rather than for shareholders.

THE ORGANIZATIONAL CONTEXT

The aims of GI are to increase the quality of trans young people's lives and to raise awareness of their needs across the UK and beyond. In working towards those aims, we seek to contribute to the creation of community cohesion and strength across the whole of the trans community throughout the UK and to generate discussion and debate around

gender, inequality rooted in gender, misogyny, misandry and sexism. Our position is that gender is a construct and not a natural phenomenon. It is a system which presents challenges in everyday life for the majority of people, regardless of individuals' trans or cisgender status. Here, 'cisgender' is the adjective that relates to a person whose self-identity conforms with the gender that corresponds to their biological sex.

At GI, we try to instigate and participate in discussions at all levels, from the local to the national and international. In order to do this we talk about gender and trans identities in trans youth group sessions, at annual conferences for teachers' unions, with academics and researchers from the UK and in other countries as well as in our own publications (Rooke, 2010; Greer, 2012; McNay and Stewart, 2015). This work has also included acting as consultants for large organizations attempting to develop more trans-inclusive working environments and with Members of the UK Parliament who are involved with improving trans equality in a range of areas of public life (House of Commons, 2016).

In addition to the on-going youth groups, GI carries out specific arts-based projects and creative workshops in collaboration with arts and theatre organizations, with and for young trans people and, on occasion, also with young lesbian, gay, bisexual and queer identified people from across the UK; this includes some opportunities for people over 25. Past projects have included *The Sci:dentity Project*, 2006–2007 (Rooke, 2010); *Brief Encounters* Theatre in Education project run in collaboration with Los Angeles based Fringe Benefits Theatre Company, 2009–2012 (Greer, 2012); the *i:trans: Constructing Selves Through Technology* project run in collaboration with the Science Museum in 2012; the *GI's Anatomy: Drawing Sex, Drawing Gender, Drawing Bodies* project run in collaboration with London Drawing in 2013 (McNay and Stewart, 2015) and the *Transvengers* project, 2014–2015 (Wellcome Collection Blog, 2015).

Building up a body of work as broad-ranging as GI's has happened over time. CEO Jay Stewart notes that it has happened in a relative void. Developing this range of activity, and in particular, the youth work with young trans people, has involved forging new ground. Stewart says:

> It's kind of untrodden ground because obviously we're not just a mainstream youth service, we don't have a massive infrastructure, we're not funded by the local authority ... we are carving out all of that as we go, as a new organization. That for me is the hard work, it's untrodden territory. Well it feels like that anyway, and you find your mentors and you find your people ... but the infrastructural development is happening alongside the service provision. (Focused conversation with Stewart, 2016)

THE WIDER CONTEXT

LGBT youth work run by local authorities or voluntary sector groups existed prior to GI's existence, though there is limited literature in the youth work field that maps LGBT work (Wood, 2009). For example, Lesbian and Gay Youth Manchester (now called The Proud Trust) was established in the late 1970s and provided services for young people in the north of England for over thirty years. LGBT Youth North West started running those services in 2011 and, over time, the inclusion of trans young people gradually increased. It might be fair to say that many LGBT youth groups were inclusive of bisexual, trans and queer-identified young people in name alone, until a cultural shift began to take hold in the early and mid-2000s and local authority youth services began to develop their awareness of the needs of young trans people alongside changes in the law such as the introduction of the Gender Recognition Act 2004. Across the UK, there continues to be other LGBT and trans-specific provision for young people, though LGBT services have faced severe cuts, particularly where they were funded by the

National Health Service or a Local Authority (Colgan, Hunter and McKearney, 2014).

GI is based in London although the work of the organization is carried out nationally, and the youth groups, as previously mentioned, run in two other UK cities. There are differences between London and other UK cities and the more rural areas of the country, but the practices to be discussed within this chapter are nevertheless relevant to a range of cultural contexts within and beyond the UK. In most cities in the UK and in many countries there is one or more youth groups that a young trans person could attend. Often these groups are LGBT youth groups, though historically the extent to which groups were genuinely inclusive of bisexual and trans young people has been variable. The model of practice and the framework that each group operates with varies. For example, a group in Vienna called Young*Trans has a team of staff with psycho-therapeutic backgrounds, whereas a group for young trans people under 27 years of age which operates as part of Transgender Network Switzerland, was founded by young trans people in 2012. 'Youth Break Out!' is a New Orleans based organization founded in 2011 that campaigns against the criminalization of LGBT young people of colour.

In countries where LGBT people face legal and social oppression, far fewer people are openly LGBT and there are fewer services available. In Nigeria, for example, whether under Shari'a law or secular law, same-sex sexual activity is illegal and punishable either by death or by long-term imprisonment. Within such a social and legal framework, identifying as trans is a very different experience. Leading LGBT rights campaigner Bisi Alimi campaigns for change in Nigeria and remarks 'Nigerians have not yet come to the full understanding of the trans identity' (Purvis, 2016).

Since the mid-2000s, despite austerity-related cuts in the UK and in a number of other countries, there has been a growing number of services for trans young people.

There are more groups with a specific remit for working with trans young people, and many LGBT groups have developed more inclusive practice for a full range of young people. The Council of Europe Commissioner for Human Rights notes that the work of support groups for children, teenagers and their parents who have questions around gender identity is crucial (Hammarberg, 2009: Section IV). At the time of publication, such groups exist in the Netherlands, France, Germany and the UK.

In considering the issues that trans young people face and the distinctive challenges that need to be engaged with in youth work that supports them, the Youth Chances Summary of First Findings report (2014) offers valuable data (National Youth Chances Integrated Report, 2016). The report draws conclusions from a survey carried out with the largest sample of lesbian, gay, bisexual, trans and queer-identified young people aged 16–25 in England. There were 6,515 respondents, with 956 identifying as trans in some way. Over half of LGBT respondents (52%) reported self-harming, either now or in the past. This compared to 35% of heterosexual non-trans young people in the sample. 44% of the LGBT respondents reported having thought about suicide. This compared to 26% of heterosexual non-trans respondents (2014: 11). Research carried out in the United States reports that the prevalence of suicide attempts among trans and gender diverse people is 41%, which vastly exceeds the 4.6% of the overall U.S. population who report a lifetime suicide attempt, and is also higher than the 10–20% of lesbian, gay and bisexual adults who report ever attempting suicide (Haas, Herman and Rodgers, 2014: 2). The majority of the young people that we work with face multiple barriers, many of which are similar to those experienced by trans youth in the US and elsewhere. W. Christian Burgess (2009) writes about some of the internal and external stress factors associated with the identity development of transgender youth in the US, saying:

transgender youth are among the most neglected and misunderstood groups in our society today. In addition to undergoing the regular perils of adolescence, these young people face an extraordinary degree of additional internal and external pressures associated with their identity development, centred around a society that is overwhelmingly uncomfortable with gender non-conformity. (2009: 53)

This certainly correlates with what young people typically share with GI in that they experience inequality and discrimination in different areas of their lives. Bullying at school is a common experience for children and young people who do not conform to societal expectations of gender norms and this can lead to low self-esteem and a sense of worthlessness. Indeed, Al-Alami, Turner and Whittle (2007) state that 73% of respondents to the survey of trans young people's experiences had suffered harassment such as threatening behaviour, verbal abuse, physical abuse or sexual harassment (p. 16). The report states that 'young transgender people are particularly vulnerable to discrimination and harassment' (p. 24). Further US-based research also found that transgender youth are particularly vulnerable to harassment and abuse in school and community settings (Rivers and Ryan, 2003; Haldeman, 2000).

Plan UK and Plan Sweden commissioned a scoping exercise that included mapping and analysing the legal, social and other challenges and opportunities facing LGBTIQ adolescents in the world. Their policy report (Middleton-Lee, 2015) puts forward a set of recommendations and considerations for services for young transgender people. They include the suggestion that services should acknowledge and build upon the strengths, competencies and capacities of young transgender people, especially their ability to articulate what services they need. The principles that underpin this research are very much in line with GI practice. Taylor (2004) suggests that relating to children as though they are preparing for adulthood rather than viewing them as people in their own right living full lives in the present, means that young people can be underestimated. This too is echoed in the ethos central to the practice of GI. One core principle of GI's youth work practice is that young people's experiences are acknowledged and valued within the activities at youth group sessions and through the structures in place to facilitate young people's participation and interaction. They are living lives and much as they face barriers and challenges, their collective experience of navigating the social world and finding solutions to problems is a valuable resource.

THE GI YOUTH GROUPS

GI provides a range of youth groups for trans young people (aged 8–25), with the opportunity to gather in real time and space as part of facilitated monthly group sessions. The sessions work to combat social isolation, support young people to gain information that can inform their life choices, enable the development of new skills and encourage the exploration of diverse gender identities.

The GI youth group provision began in 2006 with *The Sci:dentity Project*, a 12-month project funded by the Wellcome Trust. The Wellcome Trust funds projects that improve health through public engagement with science, including projects that involve the Creative Arts. Stewart was the lead facilitator and made a documentary film of the first phase which involved 18 trans young people responding to the question: 'what's the science of sex and gender?' Participants attended a series of creative workshops, interviewed medical professionals, including, for example, an endocrinologist, and met with older members of the trans community to talk about their experiences of transition and of negotiating the world as a trans person.

The participants then began to make work of various forms including installations, live

performance, video and a zine (short for 'magazine', a zine is a form that involves self-publication of original and/or appropriated texts). The work was exhibited for an invited audience and can be seen in the documentary film *Sci:dentity: What's the Science of Sex and Gender?* (Stewart, 2010). In the second phase, specific pieces of artwork were used as stimulus material in workshops, with discussion centring on exploring the science of sex and gender in schools and with youth groups.

Subsequent work with trans young people secured funding from agencies on a project-by-project basis. For instance, with Governmental (Department of Health) funding, young people were invited to participate in workshops to author and design a booklet written by young trans people for young trans people in the UK (Gendered Intelligence and GALYIC, 2007). These project workshops with specific foci enabled us to continue bringing trans young people together, and these sessions were the first iteration of what developed into regular monthly youth groups in 2009, from which time an Equalities and Human Rights Commission grant supported the youth group work until 2011.

The current practice involves a lead facilitator for each of the groups. Depending on the size of the group, there will be a second facilitator and one or more volunteers who support the paid workers by setting up the space and meeting and greeting the young people attending. Having between two and five adults in the space helps us to include a degree of diversity of gender identity and expression, race, ethnicity and other lived experiences among the staff team. One key aspect is that all GI youth group staff identify as trans in some way. Jay Stewart explains why employing trans people in these roles is important to him:

I am not a massive separatist type trans person so it's not about creating a kind of trans-only space that sits outside of mainstream society but it is about giving young people reference points to older people in the community or professional people in the community who identify as trans. I think it's really powerful. It's just a very powerful thing. Some people use the word 'role model' which is a difficult term I think but ... being trans and having a trans experience is a very particular way to navigate the world and when you've done things and made decisions and had discussions in your own life, that is very powerful as a professional person. That's valuable. It's about pathways: not that many people are trans, generally speaking, and have had those conversations that are tricky or awkward. As a young person, you want to know what other people have done, so that they can help you do *your* path, do *your* pathway. (Focused discussion with Stewart, 2016)

As young people begin to engage with GI, we use a membership system which includes an initial assessment to explore each individual's needs and accommodate them accordingly, to ensure participants feel fully included and as safe as possible in our environments. This initial assessment is part of a registration process. A youth group facilitator will have a one-to-one conversation with a young person (and the adult who has accompanied them if they choose this) and will gather information about a range of potential access needs, experiences in different parts of their life (family, school, work, friendships, etc.) and other more practical data (contact numbers; name to be used by us at the group; name(s) that the person may be known by to family members or carers, should we need to contact them; age, etc.).

Many young people accessing GI report that they have never met another trans person before coming to a GI youth group session and that they feel isolated and vulnerable. They tell us this as we first meet them and ask them to register as youth group members. One key indicator of success when we evaluate the impact of the youth group practice is a decrease in the reported sense of isolation and vulnerability after having attended several youth group sessions. I talk about measuring outcomes such as this one in a later section exploring the methods of the practice in more depth.

Some of the young people that participate in GI youth groups have behavioural and psychological difficulties such as anxiety disorders, panic attacks, mild to severe depression, Obsessive Compulsive Disorder, self-harming and/or suicidal thoughts. Some of the young people engage in risky activities such as substance misuse or sexual activity that could put them at risk of emotional or physical harm. At any one time, approximately 60% of the young people attending any of the youth groups will either have a formal diagnosis or self-identify as having one or more of these factors. The membership form does not capture all needs, and ongoing support involves building positive communication such that young people can feel more confident to disclose any difficulties they are experiencing.

THE MODEL OF YOUTH WORK PRACTICE AT GI

As the organization's name suggests there are people who are intelligent about gender in the same way that there are people who have a musical intelligence, for example. One can learn music or can learn about gender but GI posits the notion that some people have an aptitude for being expert and proficient at understanding the complexities of gender. The young trans people that participate in the youth groups and the arts projects at GI tend to demonstrate this type of intelligence relating to gender through the ways they articulate their own identities, and the ways they understand the world around them. Our approach is to work with them to explore solutions to the problems that they face and help them build resilience in order that they can better navigate their social world. In acknowledging the issues that a young person faces by listening and understanding, we seek to explore solutions together. This approach is not unique and draws on Bateman and Milner's description of solution-focused practice which engages with young people as people, not as problems:

> [W]e ask about their hobbies, interests, hopes, aspirations, what they enjoy doing, what are they good at, what the hardest thing they have even done is, and so on. This is not idle chit-chat; we are genuinely curious to learn more about the person we are talking to … we are listening for children's skills, competences, abilities, strengths and resiliences because these are the qualities that will be used in the solution. (2011: 35–7)

The GI youth group practice can be described as a hybrid or as mixed-form of youth work practice. Following Barker and Barker (2009), who talk about social work as a 'specialist element of social care, while social care is a descriptor of the general occupation of those who work within the area of care for people' (p. 149), GI would align the practice of planning and delivering youth groups for trans young people with the area of work termed 'care for people'. The model is more aligned to youth work practice than it is to social work practice in that the emphasis is on the group, or the collective as a set of individuals who come together and connect socially. We concentrate on the potential that young people have rather than using a deficit model. That said, the work can be problem-centred when we seek to explore the challenges faced by members of the group. It can also be more broadly educational when we engage in particular projects. I would suggest there is a degree of boundary-surfing between the professional disciplines of youth work, social work and community work.

One of the GI youth group facilitators, who works with both of the London groups (the under 16 age group and the older age group), commented on this idea of the type or model of youth work practice we provide:

> It's not locally based, so the young people are coming from further afield, so they're making a sort of conscious decision, as opposed to youth work that I guess more traditionally comes from local areas, estate-based work or kind of your neighbourhood provision, which might be open

> five nights a week, four nights a week, once a week and youth workers' longevity in that area is more traditionally like, knowing young people over a long time, their family, you know. So that's the kind of stuff that I might fit more neatly into the youth work category. Whereas ours is monthly so relationship building is slightly harder work, and also young people come from all different areas, all walks of life and so you're dealing with a kind of room of potential strangers as well. (Focused conversation with Greig, 2016)

There are some key differences from the more locally based, generic youth work provision. For example, the group meets monthly, which is relatively infrequent when compared with most mainstream youth provision. Unlike local youth provision that enables young people to meet in a youth or community space close to their homes, trans young people travel long distances from a wide range of geographic locations to attend because of the relative dearth of provision across the UK. Much of the provision takes place in cities and large towns, and those who live outside metropolitan centres need to travel in order to attend.

Another key aspect of GI's approach to young work is an emphasis on creativity and the arts. Creativity often underpins the work that groups engage in. For example, the staff team for the over 16s London group chose to devise a short piece of performance and to perform it for the group as a stimulus for discussion on the topic of intersectionality (the intersections and interactions of identity and cultural status). They drew on their own ethnicity, faith, socio-economic background, immigrant status etc. and performed the short piece as a way to introduce the topic of power and privilege. The staff felt that they could lead by example in sharing their own experiences as a team of three people working together and to facilitate a reflective conversation about being mindful, aware and responsible for one's own privilege. For them, this choice was about understanding the complexity of how oppression and privilege operate and how individual and group positions are produced through such structural formulations.

Trans young people benefit from the opportunity to meet and to explore their identities without anxiety. We use a template structure across all of the groups, regardless of setting or which facilitator is leading. All facilitators use key tools in every session and they are the foundations of our model of practice. One of these tools is the Pronoun Circle. Choice and use of pronouns is important to the trans and non-binary people who attend GI, just as it is to many people irrespective of their gender identity or gender expression. Being 'mispronouned' or referred to as a gender that you do not feel yourself to be can be deeply offensive, upsetting and undermining. An opening circle is a standard element of a practical workshop or group session. Commonly, a group will stand or sit in a circle and play name games, ice-breaker activities, and say something about themselves by way of getting to know each other. The significance of repeating this activity with a group that doesn't meet frequently is that it reintroduces people, and more importantly allows people to adjust and change over time as well as supporting new members to integrate into the group.

Pronoun sensitivity and respect for self-definition, thus treating each individual as the gender they feel themselves to be, is general good practice in most trans youth work in the UK. Thinking back to an early Gendered Intelligence project in 2006, trans youth worker Finn Greig recalls:

> I just remember the first time I was able to say how I identified in a room of people who completely accepted that, the power that that gave me as a young trans person, to be able to say that and people not even blink and move to the next person and totally respect it and the value, how valued I felt in that moment: being able to state it and it being taken completely seriously. (Focused conversation with Greig, 2016)

The Pronoun Circle has been part of our practice ever since 2006, and the custom of acknowledging and inviting self-declaration of pronouns is becoming increasingly more common in LGBT youth spaces in the UK as well as in inclusive feminist spaces, such as conferences and academic seminars.

At the time of writing, GI is the recipient of BBC Children in Need funding to deliver its youth group provision. This funder requires the people and projects it funds to think in terms of identifying three 'priority differences' made to disadvantaged children and young people. This exercise was genuinely productive for us as practitioners. In focusing on three specific things we wanted to change, or make a difference to in young people's lives, we became better able to quantify what activities we would incorporate and how we would be able to measure our success in making those differences. The three key differences that we identified as priorities for the youth groups during the period of the first grant were:

1 Reduce isolation;
2 Increase a sense of pride in one's gender identity;
3 Increase one's ability to manage difficult situations.

I discuss these in the following sections to illustrate the methods we use to effect change and facilitate these differences in trans young people's lived experiences. Hughes et al. (2014) highlight the impact of austerity cuts experienced through the 2000s in the UK, and the way that a culture of 'targets, monitoring regimes and bidding processes ensures that time is taken up with form filling and bids for funds which pit community and youth work projects with the same ambitions against each other, leading to the fragmentation of welfare' (p. 5). One key issue to emerge from the work of Hughes et al. is that of decreased resources, including time, when time is being increasingly taken up by monitoring and evaluating funded project work.

THE METHODS OF THE PRACTICE

We seek to facilitate the development of social networks and friendships through discussion and sharing life experiences within

GI youth group sessions as well as enabling young people to gain access to accurate, up-to-date information that can inform their life choices. By providing a monthly group activity where people can gather, we are facilitating opportunities to form social networks, make friends and find a safe space where young people can be themselves in the company of others who also identify as trans and/or non-binary. We function within a variety of roles including arts facilitation, advocacy, support for young people and their families, information and resource production.

Group activities are carefully facilitated by the team of seven staff. This group of staff works within a model of practice that originated with Jay Stewart and I. The evolution of the model happens with continual reflective evaluation of the practice in situ. The team is alert to the fact that some young people feel extremely anxious at the point of their first attendance at a youth group. 'Welcoming' has been developed from something relatively informal into an actual method. In previous years and with smaller numbers of youth group members, we might have welcomed one or two new people each month. This has developed into a more structured process that is conceived of as a critical phase of engagement for the young people:

> Sometimes welcoming starts before the session on email or phone and that will be 'I'm thinking of coming to the group' or 'I've heard about the group' so whichever worker is most appropriate to respond, will respond and say 'Hey, you know, thanks for getting in touch', and start that building of relationship to say this is what we do. I'll attach a photo of the space, so the physical space, so you know, there's a lot of care taken to help someone figure out where they're going to be, before they even get there ... For the older group, the 16–25 group that will be welcoming the new people into the space, and they get that first half hour to sit in a circle with each other and a worker and go through a bit of like; this is what we do normally, a mini pronoun-around [Pronoun Circle] ... The younger group which is 8–15 year olds, we'll invite the parent into that space for half an hour and hang out with me, [and] the young person, I'll show them around, introduce them to some other young

people who are starting to arrive and they get to look at the membership pack and there's a group of parents who always go to a local pub which is just like a block away, give them my number say; if you don't hear from me, that's a good thing, come back if you need to, you're welcome to come in. (Focused conversation with Greig, 2016)

Establishing trust in the organization and in the individual facilitators at this point is critical for young people and their parents, carers or support workers (where relevant). A trans young person is highly likely to have experienced difficulties and hostility from wider society, and, as part of a process of seeking support, advice and information, people approach groups like this one with apprehension, as well as hope. These experiences can extend to parents. This parent describes the first time she brought her child to a youth group session:

> The day I took our son to his first GI meeting, he was silent and rigid with anxiety. And so was I. What if this wasn't the Promised Land after all? My son still had his girl name and we had no idea what to expect. I mean who were these people? But half an hour later as the other young people trooped in, I could have wept, for there in front of me was a room full of children like my son. Like the ugly duckling who turned out to be a swan, my son had found his people. (Andoh, 2014)

In order to be confident in the methods for facilitating these new connections and friendships and that trust is being actively built and functioning well, we do a number of things. We developed an outcomes-measurement tool called 'Capturing Your Journey'. This tool is a fairly lengthy series of structured questions which we use to support a one-to-one conversation with an individual young person. We use the tool with a smaller number of young people to undertake more in-depth analysis of the impact we are having in relation to our aims. We can explore, for example, the degree to which a person reports their own levels of isolation and the range of social networks they feel part of at six-monthly intervals by talking around the same prompt questions and looking at the differences over time.

In addition, our facilitators reflect and record from their observations made in the sessions to measure the level of participation made by each young person. They notice when participants are interacting more with others or if a participant seems to be struggling to make connections. The emphasis on reducing social isolation is not unique to GI's youth work practice. As Klein states, '[g]roup-work practice with transgender and gender variant teens offers group members a counterforce to the isolation and rejection that many in this population experience' (Klein, 2009: 120).

We operate monthly groups for parents of trans young people in London and have plans to extend this provision. The model here is a volunteer-led group with one or two parents and a GI facilitator 'hosting'. The group offers an opportunity for adults to connect and talk about their experiences of supporting a child or young person who is identifying as trans and/or non-binary or is questioning their gender identity. People meet in a separate space from the youth group sessions and the conversations are self-initiated. Sometimes people just meet up and chat while their children are attending the youth group session in the same building and sometimes the conversation will focus on people's experiences of working with a school or with a Gender Identity Clinic (a UK National Health Service clinic addressing the health needs of trans people that are specific to their trans identities). The peer learning and peer support is relatively informal within these gatherings, and we tend to resist imposing structure, although we encourage the groups to use a consensus approach and some of the core GI ground rules, such as respecting others' views, respecting pronoun use, maintaining the confidentiality of the space, trying to maintain a balance of contributions in discussions and so on.

GI youth group practice incorporates methods of research and inquiry such as peer-to-peer shared experiences, talking with 'expert' invited guests and identifying and critiquing a wide range of resources such as materials aimed at young trans

people and at trans people of any age and materials aimed at trans services providers. GI facilitator, Sabah Choudrey, speaks here about drawing on different sources within a session and the value of supporting young people to access resources that relate to their own identities:

> We had a couple of performances, poetry performance and then we showed a Ted Talk video — it was Taiye Selasi and it was about being from and being brought up in so many different places and having mixed heritage, and then we talked about that and just had a really good discussion ... I feel like there's so little out there for trans BME people and it's really good to bring in other things because then it's like ... actually our community is huge and we're all over the world. (Focused conversation with Choudrey, 2016)

Periodically, we carry out a retrospective evaluation exercise that asks members to consider the impact of the sessions. This allows participants to identify the extent to which engaging with information in this way has empowered them to make choices and decisions about their life. They sometimes report a growing confidence, self-assurance or increased sense of pride in themselves as individuals.

BUILDING TRANS-INCLUSIVE YOUTH WORK PRACTICE

This section turns to consider how trans-inclusive practice might be developed and embedded in LGBT youth work or broader mainstream youth provision. GI has developed practices at a time of significant cultural shifts regarding thinking beyond narrow views of a binary gender, and increasing trans-visibility and recognition of the needs of trans children and young people and their families. It is critical to learn from these practices and identify specific ways of enhancing mainstream youth work practice and LGBT youth work practice, while at the same time continuing to building the trans youth work provision that

GI has developed in order to best serve the greatest number of young people.

All of the facilitators of the trans youth groups at GI are trans-identified themselves, and this is something we identify as a key strength of the practice because young trans people see trans identities represented in the adults they encounter at GI. They know that the professionals who are working to run their youth groups have direct lived experience of what it is to be a trans person, and, although every individual's experience is specific to them, there is more potential for empathy, understanding, practical information and advice. In considering how this can be replicated in other settings, LGBT Youth Scotland offers a different perspective and, in offering information and advice to professionals who are supporting young LGBT people, they say 'you do not need to be an expert in LGBT young people's lives – using a person centred approach will ensure that you will understand their experience and enable you to provide effective support' (LGBT Youth Scotland, n.d.). In our view, a level of specific expertise is important when undertaking this work with young trans people, along with a person-centred approach. This is not to say that the only type of expertise that has validity is that which comes from one's own lived experience, or the only attribute required to be a trans youth group facilitator is that you are trans-identified yourself, but at GI, the expertise gained through years of living as a trans person is an asset that we value highly. Leda Fortier created a self-published website version of a 'Genderism and Transphobia Scale' (Hill and Willoughby, 2005), suggesting its suitability for social work contexts (Fortier, 2013). The scale is an online tool in the form of a simple questionnaire with a scoring system that measures antipathy towards trans people. Rather like analysing unconscious bias, carrying out this exercise could be a useful method of reflection about one's attitudes and beliefs to gender and trans identity as part of working with trans young people.

GI facilitator, Kerri Green identifies as trans-feminine and she facilitates the Leeds GI youth group. In a focused conversation about her facilitation style, she and I talked about the subject of understanding one's client group in youth work practice. Green talked about 'knowingness' and explained that being open to learning and developing one's own understanding of others is key, irrespective of being trans in this role:

> We don't have any trans-feminine young people in the group at the moment and so I've learnt a lot about trans-masculine people, which I didn't know about and I've learnt so much. That was one of the biggest things that I had to learn – other aspects of trans-ness and not just assume that because I'm trans, I know everything about that experience. (Focused conversation with Green, 2016)

Not knowing is as significant an idea as knowing, it seems. Green, in common with other GI youth group facilitators, approaches her role with knowledge and experience of life as a trans person. At the same time, she has only her own lived experience to draw on and she makes an active commitment to be open to multiple perspectives and an ever-evolving range of trans subjectivities and identities. In extending the idea of *knowingness*, a youth group facilitator implements or makes concrete their knowledge through practical actions that enhance the youth group environment. These actions can arise from being in a place of conscious knowing in relation to trans young people's experiences, as well as from thinking about the things that would have improved their own experiences of being in the world when they were younger. Here, Greig explains his thoughts on the 'level of consideration' for practical things which may seem trivial but are, in fact, of critical importance:

> The level of consideration I think that we take as a team to ensure that people feel emotionally safe and safe as far as their identity is concerned, is key, so for me it's really important that we really take time to think about, for example, where the toilets are … that sounds like a practical thing but actually it's an emotional thing when you're trans, so

the fact that we could say to people that there are gender neutral toilets on this floor or downstairs or these are where those toilets are and we've put a 'toilets for anyone' sign over the door or there are other people using the building today but use the toilet of your choice. For me that's about showing that we really understand. (Focused conversation with Greig, 2016)

CONCLUSION

The youth work practice at GI is significant in that it offers opportunities for trans young people to talk about and share their lived experiences, and to bring forth the complex range of experiences of gender among the group of peers. The model of practice is notable and distinctive in providing a space for all participants to contribute, to share and to collaborate in ways that suit them whilst also challenging them to develop new ideas and skills. Where mainstream youth group facilitators are similarly thinking about creating a trans-inclusive space, the extent to which trans young people are being considered and the approach to 'knowingness' that we can take as professionals are key.

REFERENCES

Al-Alami, M., Turner, L. and Whittle, S. (2007) *Engendered Penalties: Transgender and Transsexual People's Experiences of Inequality and Discrimination*. London and Manchester: Press for Change/Manchester Metropolitan University.

Andoh, Adjoa (2014) *Four Thought* (Series 4, 30 July 2014) BBC Radio 4 (http://www.bbc.co.uk/programmes/b04csb0h).

Barker, Richard and Barker, Sue (2009) 'Social Work and Every Child Matters', in Richard Baker (ed.), *Making Sense of Every Child Matters: Multi-professional Practice Guidance*. Bristol: The Policy Press. pp. 147–167.

Bateman, Jackie and Milner, Judith (2011) *Working with Children and Teenagers Using Solution Focused Approaches: Enabling Children to Overcome Challenges and Achieve their Potential*. London: Jessica Kingsley.

Bornstein, Kate (1995) *Gender Outlaw: On Men, Women and the Rest of Us*. New York: Vintage Books.

Burgess, W. Christian (2009) 'Internal and External Stress Factors Associated with the Identity Development of Transgender and Gender Variant Youth', in Gerald P. Mallon (ed.), *Social Work Practice with Transgender and Gender Variant Youth*. 2nd edn. New York: Routledge. pp. 53–64.

Choudrey, Sabah (19 February 2016) Focused conversation with the author.

Colgan, F., Hunter, C. and McKearney, A. (2014) *'Staying Alive': The Impact of 'Austerity Cuts' on the LGBT Voluntary and Community Sector (VCS) in England and Wales*. London Metropolitan University.

Davis, Carrie (2009) 'Introduction to Practice with Transgender and Gender Variant Youth', in Gerald P. Mallon (ed.), *Social Work Practice with Transgender and Gender Variant Youth*. 2nd edn. New York: Routledge, pp. 1–21.

Fortier, Leda (2013) So You Want to Be a Trans* Ally? (http://transallyship.weebly.com/index.html) accessed 15 April 2016.

Gendered Intelligence (n.d.) Trans Youth Work (http://genderedintelligence.co.uk/trans-youth/youth-group) accessed 26 April 2016.

Gendered Intelligence and GALYIC. (2007) *A Guide for Young Trans People in the UK*.

Green, Kerri (31 March 2016) Focused conversation with the author.

Greer, S. (2012) Contemporary British Queer Performance. Basingstoke: Palgrave Macmillan.

Greig, Finn (9 February 2016) Focused conversation with the author.

Haas, Ann P., Herman, Jody L. and Rodgers, Philip L. (2014) *Suicide Attempts among Transgender and Gender Non-conforming Adults: Findings of the National Transgender Discrimination Survey*. American Foundation for Suicide Prevention and the Williams Institute.

Haldeman, D. (2000) 'Gender Atypical Youth: Social and Clinical Issues', *The School Psychology Review*, 29(2): 216–222.

Hammarberg, Thomas (2009) *Human Rights and Gender Identity*. Council of Europe (https://wcd.coe.int/ViewDoc.jsp?p=&id=14

76365&direct=true#P250_65293) accessed 19 April 2016.

Hill, Darryl, B. and Willoughby, Brian, L. B. (2005) 'The Development and Validation of the Genderism and Transphobia Scale', *Sex Roles*, 53(7–8): 531–544. (https://doi.org/10.1007/s11199-005-7140-x)

House of Commons (2016) Women and Equalities Committee, 'Transgender Equality: First report of Session 2015–16', 14 January 2016.

Hughes, Gill, Cooper, Charlie, Gormally, Sinead and Rippingdal, Julie (2014) 'The State of Youth Work in Austerity England – Reclaiming the Ability to "Care"', *Youth & Policy*, 113: 1–14. (http://www.youthandpolicy.org/wp-content/uploads/2014/11/hughes-youth-work-in-austerity.pdf) accessed 14 July 2016.

Klein, Gus (2009) 'Group-work Practice with Transgender and Gender Variant Youth', in Gerald P. Mallon (ed.), *Social Work Practice with Transgender and Gender Variant Youth*. 2nd edn. New York: Routledge, pp. 115–121.

LGBT Youth Scotland (n.d.) Supporting LGBT Young People (https://www.lgbtyouth.org.uk/pro-supporting-young-people) accessed 22 April 2016.

McNay, A. and Stewart, J. (2015) 'GI's Anatomy: Drawing Sex, Drawing Gender, Drawing Bodies', *TSQ: Transgender Studies Quarterly*, 2(2): 330–335.

Middleton-Lee, S. (2015) *Policy Report on the Rationale and Scope for Strengthening Support to Adolescents Who Are Lesbian, Gay, Bisexual, Transgender, Intersex or Questioning*. London and Stockholm: Plan International (https://plan-uk.org/file/plan-uk-lgbt-report-58251117pdf-0/download?token=ZXBGzC5n) accessed 18 May 2017.

National Youth Chances Integrated Report (2016) (https://www.metrocentreonline.org/sites/default/files/2017-04/National%20 Youth%20Chances%20Intergrated%20Report%202016.pdf)

Purvis, Katherine (2016) 'Bisi Alimi on LGBT Rights in Nigeria: "It May Take 60 Years, but We Have to Start Now"', *The Guardian*. (http://www.theguardian.com/global-development-professionals-network/2016/feb/09/bisi-alimi-on-lgbt-rights-in-nigeria-it-may-take-60-years-but-we-have-to-start-now) accessed 19 April 2016.

Rivers, I. and Ryan, C. (2003) 'Lesbian, Gay, Bisexual and Transgender Youth: Victimization and its Correlates in the USA and UK', *Culture Health & Sexuality*, 5(2): 103–119.

Rooke, A. (2010) 'Trans Youth, Science and Art: Creating (Trans) Gendered Space', *Gender, Place & Culture*, 17(5): 655–672.

The Sci:dentity Project: *What's the Science of Sex and Gender?* (2010) [film] London: Jay Stewart.

Stewart, Jay (7 April 2016) Focused conversation with the author.

Stryker, S. and Whittle, S. (2006) *The Transgender Studies Reader*. New York: Routledge.

Taylor, C. (2004) 'Underpinning Knowledge of Child Care Practice: Reconsidering Child Development Theory', *Child and Family Social Work*, 9(3): 225–235.

Valentine, David (2007) *Imagining Transgender: An Ethnography of a Category*. Durham: Duke University Press.

Wellcome Collection Blog. (2015) *Transvengers Review and Interview*. (http://blog.wellcomecollection.org/2015/04/14/transvengers-youth-review-interview/#more-5979) accessed 2 February 2016.

Wood, Jess (2009) 'LGBT Youth from Brighton to Jerusalem', *Journal of LGBT Youth*, 6(2–3): 310–315.

Youth Break Out! (http://www.youthbreakout.org/) accessed 14 April 2016.

PART III

Values and Ethics in Work with Young People

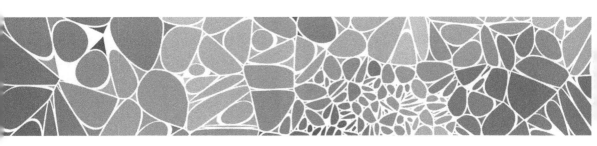

24

An Ethics of Caring in Youth Work Practice

Joshua Spier and David Giles

INTRODUCTION

This chapter shares phenomenological research findings which explore taken-for-granted understandings of ethical youth work practice within human experiences of caring. As researchers, variously located in university youth work education, higher education and educational leadership, we are committed to the application and advancement of a research approach called hermeneutic phenomenology and a form of analysis where the writings of hermeneutic philosophers are drawn into the interpretive processes. We started this journey with phenomenological research in 2003. Since then, we have both completed phenomenological doctorates, and continue to research in our fields, individually and collegially (Giles, Smythe & Spence, 2012; Spier, 2018). Our quest is that others might experience first-hand the transformative and humanising influence that this kind of research can offer. We present the findings of one particular research project to showcase

how phenomenology can deepen thinking on ethical youth work practice (Minister, 2016).

Being a good youth worker always involves discerning, amidst an unfolding moment of practice, an appropriate mode of caring in a young person's life. This was a theme emerging from Joshua's broader research that gathered and analysed lecturers' stories related to the lived experience of being a university educator in Australian university-based youth work education (Spier, 2018). For this study Joshua, with David's guidance, applied hermeneutic (interpretive) phenomenology, a way of researching that seeks ontological meanings (modes of being) that lie within practitioners' stories about their everyday experiences (Giles, Smythe & Spence, 2012; Smythe, 2011; Spier, 2018; van Manen, 2014).

The purpose of phenomenological reflection is to illuminate tacit meanings within people's lived experiences of being in the world (Heidegger, 1962; van Manen, 1990, p. 77; 2014, p. 94). To engage in this kind of inquiry, into the lived meanings of caring in youth work practice, we firstly offer a story from a youth worker who also teaches youth work in higher education. We then explore recent literature applying virtue ethics to youth work practice, noting an apparent absence of phenomenological reflection about lived dimensions of caring. After describing our collaborative research approach and interpretive process, we interweave two ontological insights (*fürsorge* and *phronesis*) to allow the human phenomenon of caring to reveal itself in the everyday context of youth work praxis (Heidegger, 1962). We then circle back to the opening story to see what such insights may bring to light. Finally, we recognise the inescapable tension and limitation of being an ethical youth worker (Hatab, 2000).

ATTUNING TO A PHENOMENOLOGY OF CARING-IN-PRACTICE

As youth workers, do we sometimes sense that we are unable to give the kind of care that a young person is crying out for? To know that even if it could be given, it would never be enough? While Joshua interviewed Peter (not his real name) for his study, he recalled the following story about being a youth worker in an Australian residential care context. Peter recalled responding to what he saw happening for Sarah as a particular situation unfolded.

I am still doing youth work. I work every Sunday night with young people living in out-of-home care: young people that have been removed from their homes and are now living under the 'care' of the department of human services.

A girl Sarah is in care because of domestic violence. Her mother won't tell her who her father is, and the stepfather was very violent, and the mother is verbally very violent towards her. Sarah's got a temper and she swears a lot as a result of that, but she is a wonderful kid. I have great respect for her and we have a really good relationship ...

One night, Sarah had been on the couch. We had been watching a TV show. I think it was

X-Factor. Every Sunday night we all watched the same show and it's a good little community experience. During the ads she was texting someone on her mobile phone. It turns out she was texting her mum. She's got two little brothers, and she had said something like, please tell my brothers I said goodnight and that I love them.

Her mum is really rude to her so I can only guess what she wrote back because she never told me. She got up off the couch, stormed off to her bedroom, and closed the door. And I could tell she was in her bedroom crying ...

When you live in care you have no privacy because she's a self-harmer. She's covered in scars from hurting herself to cope with the stresses in her life. So we go and knock on the door: 'Sarah, are you OK?'

She's not answering. She's locked the door. She [might be] in there hurting herself, and it could go wrong when she's really upset. So we get our keys and we tell her we are unlocking the door. We open the door, and there she is ... not hurting herself. She's curled-up in a ball, on her bed, crying ... And that was it.

That moment of, there she was, vulnerable and hurting and in pain, and completely alone, and she is 15. And I just had this moment of ... She's crying for a home that doesn't exist. She's crying for a belonging or somewhere to be cared for that she doesn't have. And at this very moment, who cares for her? I couldn't even care for her properly right then.

What I wanted to do was give her a hug. We can't go into their rooms unless they are hurting themselves, so we stand at the door and say, oh, are you OK? Of course I was as pastoral as I could be, and I didn't say it superficially, but that is how it felt to me – at that time I was limited by the parameters ... which I had to work in ...

This story can only point to how one youth worker has experienced a moment of doing youth work. And yet this story shows that primary to the profession of youth work is not a set of competencies, but a relationship (Sercombe, 2010, p. 11). Peter's relational encounter with Sarah occurred in a residential care facility for young people who are unable to live with their families. While this is only one of the diverse work situations in which youth workers are currently involved across the world today, it invites thinking about the meaning of caring as a good youth worker.

As youth workers are caught up in the play of particular encounters and situations with young people, they can find themselves dwelling in uncertainty; 'on the edge' between knowing what they 'want' to do and knowing what they 'should' do professionally (Anderson-Nathe, 2008, p. 98). In the increasingly complex occupation of youth work, it is critically important that beginning and experienced youth workers are able to explore in depth what it means to 'care for' young people like Sarah.

Stories like Peter's allow us to ponder 'caring' as integral to the phenomenological world of good youth work practice. We consider this to be an appropriate yet under-utilised way to help people think about ethical practice given that being a youth worker is always being thrown into a context where there is no single way to respond well, but rather a multiplicity of possibilities that bring havoc (Smythe, 2011, p. 36). For such a contingent world of practice, ethical theory in itself is not sufficient to enable a person to know what to do and how to enact helpful caring: each situational encounter with a young person is always unique. We are not suggesting that theoretical ethics should be abandoned, but that phenomenological-ontological inquiry offers a way of thinking about how caring 'is' in the living of it, rather than how it might be theorised away from the world of practice (Hatab, 2000; Sanders & Wisnewski, 2012; Smythe, 2011). For this reason, it is important to situate our discussion within the broader conversation about ethical youth work. Particular attention is given to the place of *caring* in ideas presented about the good, or virtuous, youth worker.

IS 'CARING' A CONTEMPORARY VIRTUE FOR YOUTH WORK PROFESSIONALS?

Within the international literature on ethical youth work practice, there is a growing inclination towards virtue ethics with an Aristotelian orientation (Bessant, 2009; Bessant & Emslie, 2014; Hart, 2016; Ord, 2014; Young, 2010). Modern virtue ethicists point out the limits of act-centred and actor-centred approaches to normative ethics, namely utilitarianism (with its focus on calculating the beneficial outcomes of human action), and Kantian deontology (with its focus on standardising the moral principles that should govern human action). Instead, virtue ethics focuses on distinguishable character traits and dispositions that lie at the heart of human actions, along with existential capacities and virtues that are needed to respond appropriately in contextual relational encounters (Hatab, 2000, p. 117).

Whereas act- and subject-centred approaches tend to prescribe what a person should and *shouldn't do* in a situation (often dwelling on the latter), virtue-centred approaches are primarily interested in 'how' we should dwell ethically in contingent situations (Hatab, 2000). In discussions concerned with being ethical as a youth worker, virtue animates us to think about better and worse modes of practice as an ethical youth worker amidst variable situations instead of merely following a set of invariable rules, principles and codes of conduct (Banks, 2010, p. 16; Hatab, 2000, pp. 3, 117).

Such an approach allows us to ask about the different *practical* virtues, or qualities, that are important to being ethical in a world of youth work (Hatab, 2000). Different ways of answering this question can be found within the contemporary literature. For example Young (2006, 2010), Bessant (2009) and Ord (2014) each apply virtue ethics to think about youth work praxis. In the process, they touch on common and contrasting meanings of virtuous agency as a youth worker. Young, although she does not interrogate the distinct virtues needed to be a good youth worker, suggests the art of being a good youth worker lies in helping young people, through critical dialogue, to reflect on their own development as good people, who question what it means for them to exist in their social world in virtuous ways (2010, p. 97).

In the same vein, Bessant (2009) suggests that good youth workers, by first cultivating their own practice of virtues (such as 'courage, honesty, self-control, critical thinking, generosity, forethought, commitment to justice or fairness, loyalty, and care') animate young people to cultivate theirs (p. 431). The thinking here seems to be that as good youth workers pursue their own excellence and develop virtuous character traits for themselves (including 'care'), they are simultaneously enabling the young people they work with to do the same. Importantly, Bessant also suggests that this task of supporting young people to cultivate virtues requires *phronesis*. Bessant describes this idea, stemming from Aristotle's thought, as 'good judgement' that emerges as a worker's experience grows. As a worker's own *phronesis* comes to the fore, it guides them in knowing how to act in a given situation (2009, p. 434). It appears that, for Bessant, good youth work relies upon a worker's *phronesis*, which guides them to respond to variable situations in ways that exhibit context-sensitive virtues, such as 'courage, fortitude, endurance, generosity, and humility [and care?]' (2009, p. 434).

Resonating with this view, Ord (2014) argues that Aristotle's idea of *phronesis* offers a helpful and more context-sensitive way to understand an elusive relation between the youth worker's work and the profound, albeit immeasurable, outcomes that emerge for young people through the process of such work. Ord draws on an Aristotelian understanding of *phronesis*, as a worker's moral capacity to grasp a way of acting in a given situation that comports towards the best interests of the young person, rather than merely technical 'correctness' (2014, pp. 62–63). With this idea, Ord issues a challenge to dominant discourses that assume a direct causal relationship between measurable service outcomes and a youth worker's competence and technical 'know-how' (*techne*) (2014, pp. 60–62).

Although Bessant, Young and Ord each offer a useful virtue-based approach to youth work ethics, their discussions are theoretical rather than empirical. Furthermore, none of these works offer a full exploration of the practical virtues and existential capacities involved with being a good youth worker. More specifically, none elaborate 'caring' as a possible practical virtue and how it may be integral to what it means to be a good youth worker today in contingent situations. On this point, feminist thinkers such as educational philosopher Nel Noddings (2002) might ask why virtue-based ways of thinking about ethical youth work – often seen as primarily a relational encounter – do not consider how 'caring', or an 'ethic of care', might be a virtue central to being a good youth worker (Banks, 2006, pp. 58–59, 2010, p. 16).

By contrast, Hart (2016) has recently developed an Aristotelian virtue ethics of youth work praxis that is based on his empirical research. This work includes, to some extent, a consideration of the virtue of caring in ethical youth work practice. Informed by his mini-ethnographic study of ethical practices (in relationships between young people and youth workers across four different youth centres in the north east of England), Hart conceptualises and illustrates three virtues that, through his data analysis, emerged as important to being a good youth worker: *phronesis/professional wisdom*, *integrity* and *trustworthiness*. Interestingly, Hart ponders the latter virtue as a precondition for 'caring relationships' to be able to happen in youth work contexts (2016, p. 205) without elaborating on the nature of such relationships in the living of them.

At another point, while discussing the character of a worker as essential for a youth work relationship to be a catalyst for a young person's holistic development, Hart considers 'caring' as a virtue. However, such a virtue seems to be based on a common assumption that caring is primarily an emotive disposition of the worker:

[I]t is true that if 'caring' was considered a virtue in a youth work relationship, that there would be a balance between extremes of 'uncaring' and 'over-bearing' or 'smothering' to maintain. Youth workers need to recognise the role of their emotions in connecting with young people as a basis for offering care, and to prevent the relationships with them becoming distant, while *phronesis* and the idea of a professional relationship ... prevent it from becoming too close. (2016, p. 183)

When we consider caring as a possible virtuous character trait for youth workers from this standpoint, 'caring' in youth work is taken to be the sort or level of emotional attachment a youth worker may (or may not) have for a young person within a professional youth work relationship. From such a perspective, we could go so far as to problematise caring until we see it as more vice than virtue (Curzer, 1993). That is, a youth worker's propensity for 'caring' could be seen as a (non-essential) destructive emotional attachment to a young person they are working with. Seen in this air of suspicion, caring is construed as a dynamic more likely to 'get in the way of', than as an essential dimension of, good youth work (see Curzer, 1993). Critically, such a logic may hold sway if we continue to grasp the nature of human 'caring' in emotional and subjective terms, rather than through an ontological and phenomenological lens.[1]

All of the literature discussed tends to orient us towards the normative theorising of good youth work and the good youth worker. That is, these approaches do not start with the lived experience of the contextual and relational encounters that unfold between youth workers and young people. Furthermore, critical reflection on modes of caring in youth work seems to be marginal in this discussion. Could it be that caring practice has become such a taken-for-granted vitality of what it is that youth workers are already doing every day, that it has become covered over, inviting ontological thinking about elusive ways of being a youth worker? The quest of such a way of thinking does not so much look to

uncover new understandings but rather to awaken understandings of something elusive that people already know, but perhaps have forgotten amidst the familiarity of their hectic practice lives (Smythe, 2011, p. 38). For this reason, we turn now to offer an ontological-phenomenological approach, which may help us to consider afresh good caring-in-action amidst everyday youth work contexts.

AN ONTOLOGICAL APPROACH TO THE EXPERIENCE OF 'BEING' A GOOD YOUTH WORKER

The story offered to open this chapter was gathered as part of Joshua's PhD research, a hermeneutic phenomenological inquiry into the lived experience of being an educator in university-based youth work education (Spier, 2018). The experiential data included practitioners' stories about their experiences of working with young people across diverse situations. Following a hermeneutic phenomenological approach meant seeking to understand everyday experiences in fresh ways, rather than seeking to explain, describe, argue, predict, deconstruct, theorise (Sanders & Wisnewski, 2012, p. 1; Smythe, 2011, p. 38). Philosophically, it was assumed that human phenomena (possible ways of being human), such as being a youth worker, would show themselves in 'lived experience' (*erlebnis*) and be illuminated through eliciting people's stories about how particular situations unfolded for them (Gadamer, 2013, p. 60; Smythe, 2011, p. 39).

The research design and analysis was underpinned by the philosophical writings and insights of Martin Heidegger and Hans-Georg Gadamer. Their works inform our ongoing quest to understand the '*a priori* conditions' of our everyday lives and ways of being human in the world (Heidegger, 1962, p. 31). Particularly foundational was Heidegger's distinction between what he calls 'ontic' and 'ontological' inquiry (1962, p. 31). Heidegger uses the adjective 'ontic' to refer to specific 'beings' (or specific entities), the particular people, things and theories that are intelligible and available for us as we go about our familiar everyday lives and shared practices (Dreyfus, 1991; Heidegger, 1962). Ontic inquiries, therefore, ask about the properties of and information concerning specific 'beings', as well as generating specific theories about them. Ontological inquiries, by contrast, ask about the *ways* beings are – how things are in our (pre-theoretical) experience of them (Dreyfus & Wrathall, 2005, p. 3; Heidegger, 1962, p. 31; van Manen, 2014), they do not ask about specific entities (beings) because *being* itself, in all its elusive and indefinable forms, cannot be conceived as a definable entity (Heidegger, 1962, p. 23). Ontological inquiries do not ask about specific entities (beings) because *being* itself, in all its elusive and indefinable forms, cannot be conceived as a definable entity (Heidegger, 1962, p. 23).[2]

To investigate being a youth worker *ontologically*, as a possible way of being human, means asking how people experience this distinct way of being in a world of practice. An ontological approach starts with the philosophical assumption that the meanings of being a youth worker cannot be considered apart from the experience of 'doing' youth work in a particular background of shared practices (Dreyfus, 1991).[3] Hence, ontological modes of being cannot be reduced to the kind of knowledge we may generate through an ontic inquiry no matter how thoroughly we gather the observable details of specific things, projects or people (Dreyfus & Wrathall, 2005; Harman, 2007). No idea about what ethical youth workers 'should' do, such as those found within a code of conduct, can tell us how it is for a person to be thrown into complex, uncontrollable and unpredictable live situations with young people.

For example, consider the ideal that ethical youth workers should maintain 'professional boundaries' between 'developing supportive and *caring relationships* with young people and the need to preserve the boundaries of the professional relationship' (YACVic, 2008, p. 14). Listening to the voices of workers may reveal how unambiguous ethical principles, which they were expected to recite in university, no longer seem so straightforward when immersed within complex work situations (Shevellar & Barringham, 2016, p. 183). And a person's own practical experience may begin to tell them that a kind of behaviour, which they were encouraged to avoid as students, is the very way that some people tell them is helpful to their care (2016, p. 185). Simply put, creating or reflecting on a specific list of 'dos' and 'don'ts' can never begin to disclose a sense of the everyday experiences of workers, of the constant struggle of being in the uncontrollable messiness of human practice and relationships.

RESEARCH METHOD

The story presented earlier is derived from a collection of transcribed individual interviews. These were conducted with 12 experienced youth workers and researchers across diverse Australian contexts. Participants have also taught student youth workers in a higher education context, and were aged between 30 and 65 years.[4]

The one-off interviews lasted no more than 90 minutes. The aim of these conversational interviews was to elicit a person's concrete stories about particular events and moments that they had lived through, both as youth workers and educators (van Manen, 2014, p. 317). The participants' stories were then transcribed and crafted into nearly one hundred distinct stories of specific lived experiences. After each story had been checked and approved by the participants, we worked hermeneutically with them, a to-and-fro movement between meditative thinking, reading philosophical texts, interpretive writing and dialogue with oneself and with other phenomenological researchers (Smythe, 2011; van Manen, 1990; Wright-St Clair, 2015).

This interpretive process involved allowing philosophical and ontological insights to inform the data analysis process. Specifically, the writings of Heidegger not only guided the methods but also illuminated ontological meanings that had been taken-for-granted, which in turn formed the overarching themes of the findings. It was when ontological insights were brought to bear on the analysis of the stories, not before, that lived dimensions of 'caring' began to emerge as integral to being a youth worker across variable situations. In particular, converging Heidegger's notions of *fürsorge* and *phronesis* helped to reveal taken-for-granted understandings of good caring in the context of youth work practice. We will now discuss each notion in turn.

An Ontological Understanding of Fürsorge

Heidegger uses the term *fürsorge* ('for-concern') to distinguish our concern for other people from our practical concern for useful things (*besorgen*) as we go about our everyday lives and activities (Heidegger, 1962, pp. 83, 157; Sembera, 2007, p. 234). Heidegger's notion of *fürsorge* does not refer to how we think, feel or talk about other people, but to how others always matter to us as we live out our practical lives. We do not have to explicitly hold others in mind, or remain physically by their side for them to be informing our activity (Blattner, 2006; Dreyfus, 1991; Heidegger, 1962). Heidegger further distinguishes 'positive' modes from 'deficient' modes of *fürsorge*, the different and indifferent ways we concern ourselves with other people as we encounter them as we lead our lives. For Heidegger, most of the time we are comporting ourselves towards others in deficient modes, such as when we ignore an email from a stranger (Heidegger, 1962, p. 158).

Importantly for our analysis, Heidegger does identify more 'positive' modes of lived concern for others, suggesting that *fürsorge* has two 'extreme possibilities': '*leaping in for*' and '*leaping ahead of*' the other (1962, p. 158). 'Leaping in' is to act instead of the other, hence taking away the other's responsibility of being (1962, p. 158). Through this extreme mode, the other becomes 'dominated' by or 'dependent' on the person who has leapt in for her or him (1962, p. 158). For example, the carpenter who, when asked for help by his apprentice to do a project, simply does the project himself so he does not have to show his apprentice how to tackle the work himself.

By contrast, an extreme mode of 'leaping ahead' helps the other to 'become transparent [to him or herself in her or his] care and to become '*free for* it' (1962, p. 159). In the example of the carpenter and his apprentice, the carpenter leaps ahead by enabling his apprentice to tackle the project on his own. The carpenter, free to leap ahead of his apprentice, might assist him '*just enough*' to allow him to invest himself in tackling the project, grasping his own abilities to be a carpenter in the world (Simmons & Benson, 2013, p. 206).

Before we move forward in our discussion, it is important to note several key insights emerging from Heidegger's notion of *fürsorge*. (1) *Fürsorge* points to the **practical nature** of our concerned relationships with others. (2) In between the two extremes of *fürsorge* (leaping in and leaping ahead) there are many **mixed forms** (1962, p. 159). (3) The two extreme possibilities of *fürsorge* disclose the **temporal dynamics** in our caring for others: 'leaping in' is more concerned with the present whereas 'leaping ahead' involves a greater sense of the future of others (Tomkins & Simpson, 2015, p. 1017).[5] (4) We think the manner in which Heidegger describes 'leaping-in' modes of concern (and our example above that simplifies the difference between the two extremes) can easily lead to a **misreading** of this sort of concern for others, as somehow 'worse' than 'leaping ahead'. Given a particular situation, immediately leaping in may well be an appropriate form of practical concern, such as when a father grabs his toddler when she suddenly steps into the path of an oncoming car, or a midwife who acts quickly when she sees heavy bleeding after a woman has given birth (Smythe, 2003).

Finally, the phrase *'just enough'* in the example of the carpenter and his apprentice above draws our thinking forward. Does this suggest that caring for others does not simply involve an easy decision-making between *either* leaping in *or* leaping ahead in a given situation? The notion of 'just enough' implies nuanced possibilities between 'too much' and 'not enough', indicating inevitable trickiness in navigating the uniqueness of each situation (Hatab, 2000, p. 107). It is this thought that leads us to integrate Heidegger's notion of for-concern with Aristotle's idea of *phronesis*.

Drawing Fürsorge *and* Phronesis Together

Thought by itself moves nothing. (Aristotle, 2009)

We have already encountered an understanding of *phronesis* earlier in this chapter. So here we expand this idea, joining it with Heidegger's description of *fürsorge*. Aristotle's idea of *phronesis* points to a practical capacity to grasp what response a particular situation is calling for. This kind of wisdom can only be cultivated through our own experience of dealing with similar situations (Gadamer, 2013, p. 327).

We see two points of possible connection between *phronesis* and *fürsorge*, firstly, in relation to Heidegger's indication of 'extreme' possibilities of positive caring (leaping in and leaping ahead). Aristotle articulates virtue as a kind of balancing, or blending, of opposing forces that unveils an otherwise hidden

'mean' of dealing with a given situation, at a particular moment ('mean' for Aristotle refers to a desirable intermediate path of action between two extremes of excess and deficiency) (Aristotle, 2011, p. 19; Hatab, 2000, p. 120). Aristotle's (2009) classic example is thinking about the practical virtue of courage in the context of being a soldier in warfare situations, where *phronesis* is needed for a person to balance between cowardice and recklessness. What is provocative here, in thinking about caring as a virtue for youth workers, is the idea that a good worker's *phronesis* lies in discerning between leaping-in and leaping-ahead extremes of good modes of caring for others, where 'too much' of one (substitution or empowerment) is no longer good caring (Hatab, 2000, p. 120).

This idea prevents us from thinking about extreme possibilities of positive *fürsorge* as a binary that a youth worker must reason between, instead helping us appreciate a temporal interplay between the two (Hatab, 2000, pp. 120–124). Hence, a *phronesis* of good caring in youth work can perhaps be seen as a tension and 'balancing' between two extreme possibilities of 'leaping in' and 'leaping ahead' at a particular moment of decision – that is, as the practical capacity for recognising an appropriate response towards a young person in an unfolding situation (Hatab, 2000, pp. 120–121). Such *phronesis* involves seeing times when a situation is calling for a caring response that is closer to one extreme possibility than the other (2000, p. 121).

But how does a worker discover a balanced way of caring amidst a live situation? Such a question leads us to the second point of connection we see between *fürsorge* and *phronesis*. An Aristotelian (and Heideggerian) sense of *phronesis* does not turn us into a self-governing rational subject/agent (Hatab, 2000, pp. 106–124). An art of finessing balanced responses amidst complex situations does not rest in the 'mindfulness' or 'competence' of the worker. Rather, *phronesis* is much more related to a cultivated attunement towards a temporal movement of practical situations.

In other words, workers always interact in their world of practice with an 'engaged openness' towards the discovery of an appropriate response in relativity to the 'truth' of a situation as it shows itself, rather than to what a worker subjectively makes of it (Hatab, 2000).

The discovery of a good way of caring involves a person's acquired sensibility to 'pick up on' moods, tacit cues and movements of live practical situations with others, rather than involving a self-reliant proficiency for cognitive decision-making. Pure reason – as stable ethical ideas fixed in our minds – not only does not 'move', it does not affectively move *us* either (Hatab, 2000, pp. 85–86). For example, if we witness the beating of a child, we are likely to see this as a situation calling us to leap in, not by way of our cognitive evaluation, but by way of our affective response of disgust and compassion (Hatab, 2000, p. 71). Such a way of attunement may immediately move us to leap in for the sake of the child's care.

And yet, for the most part, everyday youth working is perhaps not punctuated by this kind of urgent situation, animating a response erring towards one extreme of positive *fürsorge*. But rather, youth working is often composed of ordinary situations that require a greater level of *phronesis*, of finesse, in recognising a disclosure of an appropriate balance between leaping in and leaping ahead. Youth workers constantly tread a 'fine line' between 'too much' and 'too little' when taking up a mode of caring in a temporal situation. And with this point, we arrive at an understanding of caring as attunement to a particular moment that calls for a *phronetic* discernment of a balanced mode of caring (between leaping in and leaping ahead).

Ethical situations are always temporal events, meaning youth workers do not respond to them in *chronological* time (quantitative time, from the Greek *chronos*), but as *kairological* time (qualitative time, from the Greek *kairos*). The latter kind of time refers to the right time to act, decisive moments that 'cut time into before and after' (Harman,

2007, p. 174). If this idea of lived time speaks to 'how it is' to experience life as a youth worker (and human being), then *phronetic* wisdom of caring cannot primarily be about 'knowing-how' (competently enacting different modes of caring within ethical situations). Nor can it be reduced to 'knowing-that' (cognitively applying ethical theory to contingent youth work situations). Rather, a practical wisdom of caring as a youth worker emerges as 'knowing *when*'.

As hermeneutic scholar Smythe uncovers: 'it takes skilled judgement [*phronesis*] to know when to leap in and when to leap ahead' (2003, p. 201). Expanding this idea, we argue it takes *phronesis* to enact a mixed form of caring between these two extreme possibilities, at a *kairos* moment of decision in the 'play' of relationships with young people that are lived beyond the rules of engagement (Giles, Smythe & Spence, 2012; Hatab, 2000). Having considered an intrinsically difficult and taken-for-granted *phronesis* of *fürsorge*, we are ready to circle back to our opening story of lived experience. As we revisit Peter (and Sarah's) story, we allow our ontological insights to shed light on how caring is integral to the experience of being a good youth worker.

STANDING AT THE THRESHOLD

Let us ponder again Peter's story (offered at the beginning of this chapter, p. 330) in the light of what we have discussed.

The story starts with the youth worker on the couch with Sarah, enjoying a weekly ritual of 'watching a TV show' *together*. This simple act itself was perhaps a way that Peter was enacting and re-enacting caring for Sarah. In her past Sarah had been uncared for by her family. So this kind of togetherness was perhaps relatively unfamiliar for her.

As this ordinary event unfolded, the youth worker was aware that, during the breaks in watching the TV show, Sarah was watching something else (her mobile phone). There was another storyline, more serious and volatile than that of the TV series, playing out for Sarah on another screen. As Peter was watching the TV show with Sarah, in a deeper sense, he was also always 'watching' out for emotional shifts in Sarah's disposition, allowing his own mode of caring to shift accordingly. And then suddenly, something happens and she is off the couch. Just a moment before, all had been clear. Now, a storm was hitting Sarah. Had Peter sensed it coming?

At this change, Peter attuned to a sharp turn in how this night was playing out. Somehow, Peter guessed that some uncaring words had been exchanged between Sarah and her mother. As it turned out, her mother had been 'there' and 'not there' with them on the couch from the start.

What do untold moments that fall silently within this story tell us? What happened between the moment when Sarah stormed off to her bedroom, and the moment when Peter moved from the couch to follow her? What propelled him towards a different manner of caring? Before following Sarah, did he think through what he should do – to 'let her go' or 'go after her'? Did he consciously retrieve something he had learnt in an ethics class during university? Or, perhaps he responded to a call from the situation itself, not from his thinking about how he 'should' respond. He was attuned to what was disclosed as happening for Sarah, and acted accordingly.

Next, he found himself on the outside of Sarah's locked bedroom. He could tell she was on the other side of the door crying. He already knew of a possibility that Sarah might be in there, 'harming' herself. He called out to Sarah, but she didn't answer. He reached in his pocket for his key to her bedroom, seeing that in this given situation, he must use it. In that moment, he knew this was a time he must cross a normal threshold between respecting her privacy and stepping in to ensure she was safe.

When he turned the key, he was poised, ready to step in even further if necessary. But

seeing she was 'OK' (in physical terms), he stepped back again when he realised that the situation did not call him to enter the room fully. He stood at the threshold of Sarah's bedroom, still watching, still attuning to how she was.

This time, he saw her pain pouring out of her, knowing that as much as he 'wanted' to leap in to hug her, to embody care in another mode, that this way of caring would be inappropriate as a youth worker. Instead, he could only look on, confronted with the limits of caring in youth work practice, experiencing the limitation of being a youth worker.

In this particular moment of lived practice, note how a balancing of possible modes of good caring, as discussed above, was in play. The youth worker's movement of caring can be seen to be balancing both leaping in and leaping ahead, as this temporal event unfolds. Anticipating what might happen 'after the storm' is leaping ahead of the young person, being prepared for what might happen. Whereas 'crossing a line' by unlocking the bedroom door, which in other situations might be considered highly unethical behaviour for a youth worker, is being ready to leap in, to take her agency from her if it means keeping her safe from harm. And in the next moment, seeing she was not harming herself, he resisted stepping in further. He resists a powerful force of human emotion, appealing to him to wrap this young woman up in his arms, a way that lies beyond the threshold and limits of being a youth worker in this situation.

This story reveals how the *wisdom of caring praxis* constantly involves treading a path of action between 'leapings' rather than moving towards an either-or type of response (Tomkins & Simpson, 2015). And yet, *phronesis* occasionally means facing the limitation of one's own ability to enact care for someone as a youth worker. In a sense, wisdom can sometimes take the surprising form of owning up to the limits of one's caring agency and involvement in a young person's life. This leads us to our final reflection.

IS THERE WISDOM IN RECOGNISING THE LIMITATION OF CARING?

In the context of youth work practice, there are times when 'caring is not enough' (Sercombe, 2010, p. 159). Ethical caring praxis cannot undo what may have happened, or change what may be happening, or prevent hardships that may yet happen for a young person in their lives. Whatever caring acts a person may do as a youth worker, however virtuous or emancipatory, they can never safeguard a young person from experiencing domineering relationships with others in the world. While in this chapter we have argued that a practical wisdom of situational caring remains integral to being a good youth worker, we have also pointed to how a person's caring praxis towards young people is always finite in a given circumstance. And yet, this inescapable 'limitation of being' a youth worker is often concealed from us in our work to help people prepare for, and reflect upon, their everyday experiences of being in the world as a youth worker.

CONCLUSION

Our broader aim in this chapter has been to show how hermeneutic-ontological phenomenology can be useful for youth workers, giving them a way to reflect on and enrich their understanding of caring as an essential aspect of being ethical in the world (Hatab, 2000; van Manen, 2014, pp. 104–111). In adopting an ontological approach however, we cannot expect this kind of inquiry to tell us what we should do in the vein of thinking that permeates normative Western ethics (Heidegger, 2011, pp. 173–74, 176; Mulhall, 2010). Ontology is not the kind of thinking with which we evaluate action or from which we draw moral conclusions. Indeed, attempting to extricate specific values, principles and ideals from a lived account of being in the world is perhaps akin to expecting a route on a map to tell us what it is like to walk it.

This means resisting any modern temptation or expectation to 'chisel out' specific theories from the grain of ontological thinking.

Notes

1 There is also limited research that seeks to give voice to young people's views about what 'makes a good youth worker'. Although not explicitly informed by a virtue ethics approach, in 2014 the Australian Youth Affairs Coalition (AYAC) conducted a small-scale online survey of young people, asking respondents to rate 15 statements relating to ethical practice for youth workers in terms of the importance of each quality (virtue) for 'making a good youth worker' (for example, 'A good youth worker is … always on my side', or 'is someone you can trust'). Respondents were asked to rank each quality as 'not important', 'not very important', 'somewhat important', 'important' or 'really important'. The idea of caring, or duty of care, does not feature clearly in the list of qualities provided. However, all preconceived qualities could be considered as possible forms of caring. For example, one of the popular survey responses was the idea of a good youth worker as a person who 'really listens to me' (AYAC, 2014, p. 2). In Sercombe's (2010) brief relating of an 'ethics of care' to youth work practice, he suggests that caring is 'the process of listening to another's world …' (p. 150).

2 An example of an ontic inquiry might be to ask about a specific youth worker. In asking about this person, we might make the following ontic observations: the worker is X gender, aged X, he received his X training from X institution, he currently works part-time with X young people, in X youth centre in X town, his daily role normally involves X and Y, he says that he uses the X code of ethical practice, and that X and Y values underpin his practice.

3 Being a cabinetmaker, for example, means more than merely knowing-how (*techne*) to use certain tools and more than merely knowing-about (*episteme*) the types of things that cabinetmakers build (Heidegger, 1968, p.14). A person cannot be a 'true cabinetmaker' until they are shown how the craft of cabinetmaking essentially responds to the 'shapes slumbering within wood' in relativity to people's everyday lives (1968, p. 14). In a similar way, we could say that a person cannot be a true youth worker without understanding how the craft of youth working powerfully responds to the taken-for-granted mattering of young people's own lives and futures.

4 The Social and Behavioural Research Ethics Committee (SBREC) at Flinders University granted
   approval for this research on 2 May 2013 (Project
   number 6012).
5 We can see a link between Heidegger's notion
   of 'leaping ahead' of others and his idea that,
   as human beings, we are always given over to
   'being ahead of ourselves' as we lead our everyday lives (1962, p. 236). Making sense of the latter may enrich our understanding of the former.

REFERENCES

Anderson-Nathe, Ben (2008). 'It's just a little
  too human: questions of vocation', *Child &
  Youth Services*, 30(1-2): 97–110.
Aristotle (2009) *The Nicomachean Ethics*. Rev.
  edn. Tr. W.D. Ross. Oxford and New York:
  Oxford University Press.
Aristotle (2011) *Eudemian Ethics*. Tr. A. Kenny.
  Oxford: Oxford University Press.
AYAC (Australian Youth Affairs Coalition)
  (2014) *AYAC discussion paper: The values
  and ethics of youth work in Australia*, New
  South Wales, Australia: AYAC.
Banks, Sarah (2006) *Ethics and Values in Social
  Work*. 3rd edn. Basingstoke: Palgrave
  Macmillan.
Banks, Sarah (2010) 'Ethics and the youth
  worker', in S. Banks (ed.), *Ethical Issues in
  Youth Work*. 2nd edn. Abingdon, Oxon and
  New York, NY: Routledge. pp. 3–23.
Bessant, Judith (2009) 'Aristotle meets youth
  work: a case for virtue ethics', *Journal of
  Youth Studies*, 12(4): 423–38.
Bessant, J. & Emslie, M. (2014) 'Why university
  education matters: youth work and the Aus-
  tralian experience', *Child & Youth Services*,
  35(2): 137–51.
Blattner, W.D. (2006) *Heidegger's Being and
  Time: A Reader's Guide*. London and New
  York: Continuum.
Curzer, H.J. (1993) 'Is care a virtue for health
  care professionals?' *Journal of Medical Phi-
  losophy*, 18(1): 51–69.
Dreyfus, H.L. (1991) *Being-in-the-World: A
  Commentary on Heidegger's Being and
  Time, Division I*. Cambridge, MA: MIT Press.
Dreyfus, H.L. & Wrathall, M. (2005) 'Martin
  Heidegger: an introduction to his thought,
  work, and life', in H.L. Dreyfus & M. Wrathall
  (eds.), *A Companion to Heidegger*. Oxford:
  Blackwell. pp. 1–16.
Gadamer, Hans-Georg (2013) *Truth and
  Method*. Trs. J. Weinsheimer & D.G. Mar-
  shall. London: Bloomsbury Academic. (Origi-
  nal work published 1960.)
Giles, D., Smythe, E., & Spence, D. (2012)
  'Exploring relationships in education: a phe-
  nomenological inquiry', *Australian Journal of
  Adult Learning*, 52(2): 214–36.
Harman, G. (2007) *Heidegger Explained: From
  Phenomenon to Thing*. Chicago: Open Court.
Hart, Peter (2016) *An Ethnographic Study of
  Ethical Practices in Relationships Between
  Young People and Youth Workers* (PhD
  thesis). Durham University.
Hatab, L. (2000) *Ethics and Finitude: Heideg-
  gerian Contributions to Moral Philosophy*.
  Lanham: Rowman & Littlefield Publishers.
Heidegger, Martin (1962) *Being and Time*. Trs.
  J. Macquarrie & E. Robinson. Oxford, UK:
  Blackwell. (Original work published 1927).
Heidegger, Martin (1968) *What is Called Think-
  ing?* New York: Harper & Row. (Original
  work published 1954.)
Heidegger, Martin (2011) 'Letter on humanism'
  (tr. F. Capuzzi), in D.F. Krell (ed.), *Basic Writings
  from Being and Time (1927) to The Task of
  Thinking (1964)*. London: Routledge Classics.
  pp. 141–81. (Original work published 1947).
Minister, S. (2016) 'To the people themselves:
  The value of phenomenology for global
  ethics', in J.A. Simmons & J.E. Hackett (eds.),
  *Phenomenology for the Twenty-First Cen-
  tury*. London: Palgrave Macmillan. pp.
  13–32.
Mulhall, S. (2010) 'Heidegger', in J. Skorupski
  (ed.), *The Routledge Companion to Ethics*.
  London: Routledge. pp. 241–50.
Noddings, Nel (2002) *Starting at Home: Caring
  and Social Policy*. Berkeley: University of Cali-
  fornia Press.
Ord, J. (2014) 'Aristotle's phronesis and youth
  work: beyond instrumentality', *Youth &
  Policy*, 112: 56–73.
Sanders, Mark & Wisnewski, Jeremy (2012)
  Ethics and Phenomenology. Lanham, MD:
  Lexington Books.
Sembera, R. (2007) *Rephrasing Heidegger: A
  Companion to Being and Time*. Ottawa: Uni-
  versity of Ottawa Press.

Sercombe, Howard (2010) *Youth Work Ethics*. Thousand Oaks, CA: Sage.

Shevellar, L. & Barringham, N. (2016) 'Working in complexity: ethics and boundaries in community work and mental health', *Australian Social Work*, 69(2): 181–93.

Simmons, J. Aaron and Benson, Bruce (2013) *The New Phenomenology: A Philosophical Introduction*. New York: Bloomsbury.

Smythe, E. (2003) 'Uncovering the meaning of "being safe" in practice', *Contemporary Nurse*, 14(2): 196–204.

Smythe, E. (2011) 'From beginning to end: how to do hermeneutic interpretive phenomenology', in G. Thomson, F. Dykes, & S. Downe (eds.), *Qualitative Research in Midwifery and Childbirth*. London: Routledge. pp. 35–54.

Spier, Joshua (2018) *Heidegger and the Lived Experience of Being a University Educator*. London: Palgrave Pivot.

Tomkins, L. & Simpson, P. (2015) 'Caring leadership: a Heideggerian perspective', *Organization Studies*, 36(8): 1013–31.

van Manen, Max (1990) *Researching Lived Experience: Human Science for an Action Sensitive Pedagogy*. Albany, NY: State University of New York Press.

van Manen, Max (2014) *Phenomenology of Practice: Meaning-Giving Methods in Phenomenological Research and Writing*. Walnut Creek, CA: Left Coast Press.

Wright-St Clair, V.A. (2015) 'Doing (interpretive) phenomenology', in S. Nayar & M. Stanley (eds.), *Qualitative Research Methodologies for Occupational Science and Therapy*. Abingdon and New York: Routledge. pp. 53–69.

Young, K. (2006) *The Art of Youth Work*. 2nd edn. Lyme Regis: Russell House.

Young, K. (2010) 'Youth workers as moral philosophers', in S. Banks (ed.), *Ethical Issues in Youth Work*. 2nd edn. Abingdon: Routledge.

Youth Affairs Council of Victoria (YACVic) (2008) *Code of Ethical Practice: A First Step for the Victorian Youth Sector*. Melbourne: YACVic.

25

Relationship Centrality in Work with Young People with Experience of Violence

Daniel Jupp Kina

INTRODUCTION

This chapter will present the experiences of a support service for young people affected by situations that violate their human rights. The service is delivered by ACER Brasil, a non-governmental organization located in the city of Diadema, São Paulo, Brazil. The experiences presented focus on the relationship-building process between practitioners and the young people accessing the service with particular emphasis on the emotional dimensions of the relationship and how this relates to the development of emancipatory and transformative practice. The chapter is based on data collected during research undertaken as part of two years of postgraduate study in social psychology utilizing critical psychology theory, more specifically the theory developed by Lev Semyonovich Vygotsky. The research was conducted over a period of four months and adopted a qualitative methodological approach through fortnightly in-depth interviews with two practitioners and

monthly interviews with two young people. To be invited to take part in the research two young people and their respective practitioners were selected under two criteria: (1) being engaged with the service for more than two years; (2) gender – one male and one female. Discourse and thematic analysis was used to analyse the data. This chapter presents some selected themes and extracts from the participants' narratives. The chapter will emphasize the participants' voices in the relationship-building process. Their narratives are therefore central to the chapter, and themes will be explored through the lens of discourse analysis. To ensure participant anonymity, all names have been changed.

The chapter is divided into three broad sections. After a brief introduction to the support service that provides the context for later discussion, the relationship-building process is explored focusing on three key developmental stages: initial resistance; establishment of the relationship; and the transformative relationship. Through analysing these stages, the chapter will highlight some of the complexities of the relationship-building process from the perspective of two young people and reflect on the implications of their narratives for ensuring emancipatory and transformative practice.

THEORETICAL BACKGROUND

The service analysed in this chapter utilizes a particular methodology based on engagement as the main tool, applying principles from Latin American Social Education (Gohn, 2009) and 'Spinozist' Critical Social Psychology (Stenner, 2015: 49). The essence of the methodology is the understanding that human beings are a composition of subjective aspects – e.g. emotions, feelings, sensations, illusions – and objective aspects – physical, biological, cognitive – which are interdependent and inseparable, forming one unique unity (Liu & Matthews, 2005). In applying this principle, the relationship between young people and practitioners has a central role in the methodology, making the engagement between young people and practitioners the main tool for transformation.

As illustrated in Figure 25.1, the depth and quality of the relationship are determinants for the process. As a result, engagement between

both parts will evolve and aspects such as identification, trust and legitimacy will be key in the mediation/facilitation of transformation. This is a process that relies on both subjective and objective aspects, making these two dimensions inseparable throughout the process – based on the Vygotskyan 'monistic' approach (Newman & Holzman, 2005: 70). Consequently, the alignment between practitioners' thoughts, emotions and actions is an essential condition for the young people to develop identification, trust and legitimacy in the relationship and to openly reflect and transform behaviour patterns and lifestyles according to their own perceptions. These ideas and their impact on practice will be further discussed through the discussion of two case studies. Before presenting the cases and in order to facilitate an understanding of the process, I will now describe the context and some of the characteristics of the service.

OVERVIEW: THE THIRD SECTOR AND YOUTH WORKING IN BRAZIL

ACER is one of many NGOs that have emerged during the last three decades following the process of re-democratization in the post-military-dictatorship period in Brazil (1964–1985). The years following the end of

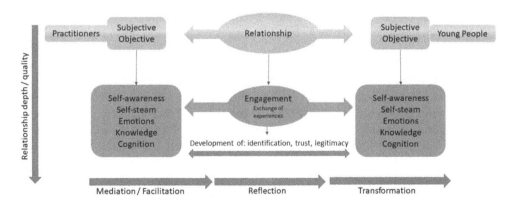

Figure 25.1　Relationship as tool for transformation

the military dictatorship were marked by an intense process of state-building that relied heavily on third sector organizations in addition to state organizations (Garcia Lopez et al., 2011). The creation of the National Constitution in 1988 boosted the third sector, with the establishment of basic rights, and confirmed the importance of the role for both governmental and non-governmental organizations (IBGE & IPEA, 2012). In 1990 the Statute of Child and Young People Rights set specific rights for children and young people as well establishing the rules for the protection services and children's rights organizations.

Alongside the process of re-democratization and development of the third sector, a wide range of socio-pedagogical and community development approaches emerged from a very fertile field of grassroots projects. Paulo Freire's theory and Liberation Theology were two of the most notable theories that have influenced many of the emerging approaches such as Social Education and Street Social Education (Butler, 2008; Rodrigues, 2010). In the same way, youth working in Brazil rapidly developed in the same period and was connected to Social and Street Education from the start, having strong emphasis on 'liberation' and on the development of autonomy. One of the notions that guided the field for many years is the concept of 'protagonism' (Goulart & Dos Santos, 2014: 130). This notion can be considered an ultimate consequence of a strong participatory and inclusive process of education and community development (Jupp Kina, 2012) and shaped youth working methodologies throughout the country, including the methodology presented here. I believe methodologies for youth working – and not only work with young people – should be developed in accordance with the specific needs of each group of beneficiaries, respecting the social, political and cultural characteristics and preferably involving beneficiaries in its development. However, reflections triggered by other experiences can be extremely valuable for opening possibilities, and the exchange of experience between services is essential to the improvement of methodologies. In this way the principles developed by youth work in Brazil, such as protagonism, social education and street education, can make a valuable contribution by triggering debates around effective participatory processes and the importance of relationship-based approaches that fully value the emotional development of young people.

OVERVIEW: ACER

Influenced by this scenario and its rich variety of concepts, ACER has developed its approach based on the needs of local young people. Balancing the power is key in empowering young people and it can be even more complex when dealing with young people who are the victims of violations and live in extreme vulnerable communities. In this way the approach developed by ACER has been effective in providing, through the relationship and engagement some important conditions for the development of protagonism and social transformation.

ACER's aim is to ensure the dignity of young people and their families through promoting the transformation of their social environment. To achieve this the organization delivers a number of services to the local community covering five main areas: sports; education and culture; community development; youth protagonism; and a social support service. Activities delivered vary from football, boxing and karate, to arts courses, percussion and capoeira (a Brazilian martial art), and are run within the organization's premises and in public community spaces. Central to all the services delivered by ACER is a commitment to developing meaningful engagement with the local community, prioritizing long-term interventions and developing deep-rooted connections.

This analysis focuses on the social support service. This service aims to provide support for young people who have had their rights violated in some way. This includes issues such as domestic violence, child labour, drugs misuse, engagement with criminal activities or the neglect of their needs. The service is delivered by a team of support workers comprised of eight practitioners from varied (and sometimes with multiple) professional backgrounds. The support for the young people begins on a one-to-one basis and then expands to include support for the wider family when possible and relevant. An important characteristic of the support provided is the centrality given to developing meaningful relationships and a flexible approach to engagement. The methodology of the service is divided into five phases. Each phase has a different aim and can be adapted according to the specific needs of the young person, as seen in Figure 25.2.

Along the five phases, the practitioner's work focuses on each of the objectives (Figure 25.2) utilizing personalized strategies for each young person. The relationship is the key tool and the intensity and quality of the relationship will provide fundamental conditions for each stage (see relationship intensity in Figure 25.2).

To create conditions for the development of an intense relationship practitioners work with the principle of mediation (Newman & Holzman, 2005) – see Figure 25.1. In this way the relationship is consistently mediated by play activities (such as sports, arts, video games) and beauty activities (such as nail polishing), as well as practical support activities (such as helping with issuing documents), that have a positive meaning for the young person. It is important to move the focus away from the need to talk about themselves and about complicated issues and give the young person the opportunity to choose when, how and to what extent they want to talk about their lives. The activity works as a way to balance power within the relationship, giving young people not only the power to choose but also to lead the activity, explain rules, choose themes and teach something to the practitioner.

Addressing practical issues can be very meaningful for the establishment of the relationship and may act as a point of entry for discussing more complicated issues. Once the young person identifies the practitioner as a source of assistance, the relationship starts

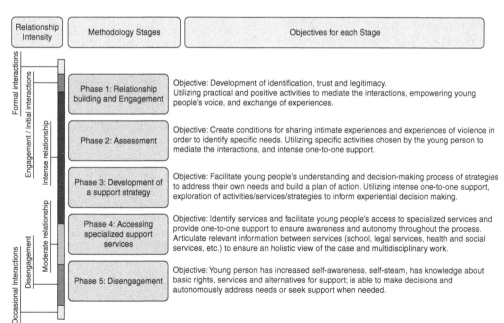

Figure 25.2   Methodology stages, objectives and relationship intensity

to gain a different shape and trust becomes more concrete. It is important to highlight that while the methodology is divided into phases, this is to facilitate the explanation and does not mean that the process runs in distinct steps, or smoothly from phase to phase without disruptions. Breaking away from cycles of violence is extremely challenging and movements back and forward are very common along the process.

THE RELATIONSHIP-BUILDING PROCESS: YOUNG PEOPLE'S NARRATIVES

This section illustrates some of the main aspects of the relationship-building process between young people and practitioners from the perspective of young people. These aspects are organized into three main themes: (1) Initial resistance; (2) Establishment of relationship; (3) Transformative relationship. The two young people who took part in the research were Carla and Lucas. At the time of the research Carla was 14 years old and had been using services provided by ACER for six years. She lived a few blocks away from the organization in one room which she shared with her mother and six siblings. ACER's support service had first come into contact with Carla's family following a referral that had been made as a consequence of violent relations among family members. Initially the focus of the work was towards the relationship between Carla and her older brother Peter, who was responsible for most of the physical and psychological abuse towards other members of the family. When working with families with multiple siblings, the support service always allocated one practitioner to each sibling. While Peter and each of the family members were allocated to other practitioners, Carla was allocated to Mary.

The second young person to take part in the research was Lucas. At the time of the research Lucas was 13 years old and had

been engaged with the service for more than four years. He lived with his mother, three brothers and a niece in a two-roomed house in the neighbourhood surrounding ACER. The concern in the family was the involvement of two of his brothers with organized crime and the consequences that was having for the other family members. According to his key worker, Lucas had difficulties trusting people and was constantly questioning people's intentions, and this had resulted in difficulties in building meaningful relationships. His friendships tended to be constantly disrupted by disagreements and arguments that were often a consequence of power and leadership disputes.

BEGINNING THE RELATIONSHIP: INITIAL RESISTANCE

For Carla and Lucas, the beginning of the relationship-building process was marked by instabilities and some reluctance in engaging with the educators. Through their discourse it was possible to identify some of the feelings that lay behind their resistance and the importance of this phase in building meaningful engagement. In this section I will explore aspects of the relationship-building process with the aim of understanding the initial resistance that young people might have when engaging with educators and the need to respect this as fundamental to the development of meaningful relationships.

Carla when asked about the beginning of engagement with ACER stated:

> [I first came here] because of my sister … I started with capoeira[1], after I did percussion … then, from one point, I started to have an educator[2] to support me. God, I have been in the hands of so many educators (laughing) and I do remember them all. The first one was G and then K who only stayed for a little time working here, later was A and now it is Mary.

The pattern of relationship that Carla built with the practitioners was common among most of the young people who attend ACER. The initial contact with young people is often made by spontaneous initiative with the intermediation of friends or family, and their involvement with the organization tends to be long-term, averaging between two and three years. During this period, it is common that the allocated practitioner changes. This creates a challenging situation for both young person and educator, as highlighted by Carla:

> When I started everybody would say that I was a rebel and rowdy, and then G was the first to come to talk to me, and we started to talk and talk and then she asked me if I wanted her to be my educator and I said yes. In all the final conversations I had with each of my educators I cried, I have this 'marrudinha'[3] face but I am very sensitive and I cry very easily. When G wasn't going to be my educator anymore … because of this and that and then I started to cry and said I didn't want an educator anymore and later I saw K [the next educator] and said 'I don't want that ugly white woman'. But she came to talk to me and we started to talk, talk, talk and then we started to get closer. Then I was getting used to her each day until she came to me and said couldn't be my educator anymore because she would need to move to another city … But then, before she went she introduced me to A and I said 'I don't want, I don't anyone else, I will go away' but A insisted on talking to me and soon we started to get on well and I got used to her a lot, a lot. But one day she came to me and said she was going to leave ACER, I don't remember the reason she told me. I was talking to her downstairs, I remember in details, it was in the computer room in the library, she was talking to me and I was crying, crying, and then Mary came into the room and A told me that Mary would be my educator and I said 'I don't want this skinny four-eyes.' I told her 'I don't want you, I don't want you' and cried.

It is interesting to observe the repetition of the cycle around rejecting the new educator, then 'getting used to' and 'getting on well' with them and all the mixed feelings involved. While describing all these moments Carla was laughing at the situations, especially when she was referring to the moment she was rejecting the new educator. She was emphatic in saying she would remember every detail and she identified that with each of the educators she had learned different things:

> In the beginning I would say: I don't want, I don't want, and then I end up getting used to … I don't know, kind of, in the beginning I feel like, I am strict and 'marruda', I don't know, I don't want to talk about nothing, I feel a bit angry. Like when G came to me to say she couldn't be my educator anymore and then educator K came to talk to me I was like this (crossed arms and side gaze). But then I don't remember what she said afterwards that we started to talk and I was a bit more open. Then, later, we started to talk, talk, talk.

While for Carla the initial feeling was 'a bit of anger', for the educator the initial rejection is understood as part of the process and a consequence of her 'marrudinha' characteristic. This is important as it will determine the dynamic of the relationship along the process. Mary describes it thus:

> She [Carla] took a long time to develop trust [towards me], but after she began to trust then started to look for me for guidance and conversations, but she is not always positive. … she asks for guidance and counselling, she listens and takes it, but then later she does whatever she wants [even if it is the opposite of what was discussed]. … Carla is critical, and doesn't easily listen to other people's opinions.

What Carla calls 'marrudinha' the educator interprets as a sense of critique and self-determination – although not always seen as positive. Carla had been referred to the social support service due to concerns with domestic violence from one of her siblings combined with severe overcrowding within the family home. Carla's tendency to react with anger ('marrudinha') coupled with the hostile home environment resulted in a reluctance to develop relationships as a form of self-protection. In this way, the shifting between rejection and acceptance needs to be understood as an essential part of Carla's way of relating to other people. Understanding the context for her movement between rejection and acceptance of relationships is essential to developing trust. If interpreted differently, the rejection of – and sometimes aggressiveness towards – the educator could prevent the development of trust and consequently the establishment of engagement.

Paul exposes a similar experience at the beginning of the relationship with Lucas:

> to have an engagement with Lucas was very difficult … in the first months … we would have conversations and he would not listen to me, he would pretend he wasn't listening, he would be disguised, would walk away and after five minutes he would start to do things differently than what he had talked about … he is very intelligent and very strategic in his actions; he knows how to mess with the dynamic of a place and how to manipulate people. Our relation was very difficult at the beginning.

According to Paul, Lucas had difficulties trusting people and was constantly questioning people's intentions, which had resulted in difficulties in building meaningful relationships. Educators would frequently utilize the term 'dissimulated' to describe his manipulative way of relating to people:

> He is intelligent, is very good at expressing himself, but has a huge capacity to manipulate people. … he doesn't use his intelligence in a positive way … when something is not the way he wants he tends to be violent. … he doesn't often act as a victim but he is dissimulated and plays the victim when convenient.

The discourse of both Paul and Lucas highlight the initial resistance within their relationship, describing the initial interactions as very difficult and disruptive. While Paul raises Lucas's dissembling attitude and the ability to manipulate as the main barriers to build a relationship, Lucas highlights the importance of trust to overcome this phase, suggesting the reasons and possible solutions for the barriers identified by Paul:

> … it is hard to get used to [a new person]. The person who says they got used to someone overnight is lying, in real life it is different. I think what is most important is the communication, they [educators] try to interact, inviting us to talk, showing that it will be good, showing we can trust … they break the ice, taking [it] very easy and slowly approaching, bit by bit …, if we are [at] one of the activities they come and say hello … Nobody would be open and talk about everything from one day to another, to complain about their mother, or talk about life problems, nobody would do it.

Like Carla, Lucas was constantly looking for something that could define whether the relationship was trustworthy or not. The initial resistance was a way to invite the educator to reach out for them and to test whether the conditions for trust were present. In both Carla and Lucas's discourses, it is clear that at this stage they were the ones dictating how far and how fast the relationship would develop. Although the educator continues to reflect on this process and needs to remain aware of the direction it is taking, the key to this stage is that the educator is able to demonstrate that their understanding of the young person's behaviour goes beyond superficial reactions to the challenges that they present and they instead respect the back and forth movements of rejection and acceptance as part of the relationship development process. This can be interpreted as a form that Carla and Lucas found to 'test' the relationship and find out more about the intentions and willingness of the educator in investing time and effort to build the relationship. Through stressing and challenging this process, other aspects of the educator's subjectivity will emerge, and Carla and Lucas will be able to check the coherence between what they say, and what they actually do and feel. In Vygotsky's words, they will then be able to check the alignment of what is felt, thought and acted by the educator, providing them with a full picture the person, beyond professional identity. It is this acceptance of these challenging behaviours as a spontaneous and important part of the relationship-building process that is key to the development of trust and, therefore, of engagement.

ESTABLISHING THE RELATIONSHIP: IDENTIFICATION, ENGAGEMENT AND TRUST

A vital aspect of the social educator's work is longitudinal and working towards deeply engaged practice. In this sense there is some specificity in the work of the social educator at ACER. As Paul describes:

> To be a social educator here [in ACER] is specific. To be an educator and work with the upper part of a tree is one thing, but it is different if you are an educator working with the roots of the tree and being able to see the problem that the tree has. So here the social educator work is more like this, we work focused on the cause of the problem, we go to the root, we go to visit them at home, we have dialogues, we try to know what is happening, we go to the family and try to reach the soul of the problem.

Emphasizing the importance 'working in the roots', Paul highlights the importance of the longitudinal and in-depth relational work that enables him to understand the reality of the problems faced by the young people and their families. This idea gained more shape when Paul was encouraged to describe the details of the process of engagement:

> The way in which we approach and build the engagement is specific for each case, and this is what makes this work different. Here our work is more individualized, if the problem of that child is related to violence, we work focused on that, if the problem is abuse or if it's socialization then we work on those things. And you are able to identify and assess the issue because you are in the everyday of the child, you visit their home, you are working close to them and trying to strengthen the attachment and this is what makes transformation possible.

This characteristic of the work is essential to overcoming the initial resistance and establishing a strong engagement with young people. It is the presence of the educator in their everyday experiences that provides the young people with opportunities to experiment with new interactions – for example, the movement between rejecting and accepting. These new experiences will generate new reflections, but what is essential to this process is that this can be a gradual process that evolves as the young person begins to feel more comfortable. In understanding and respecting the process of the young person building trust, the educator is able to act as mediator and provide conditions for the young person to, firstly, receive non-violent and constructive responses to their attitude, and, secondly and consequently, to provide a relational space where the young person can experiment with different ways to interact and gradually learn about themselves and about the relationship-building process.

Carla illustrates:

> … but then I started to have conversations with Mary and started to get used to her each day. Later on I discovered that her birthday was the same day as mine and that we liked the same kind of things and that many times we had the same opinion. Now there is one thing she knows about my life that no one else knows and I identify myself with her.

Carla used one term at various moments to qualify the relationship-building process. 'Getting used to' was the expression Carla used as a synonym for getting on well with someone. Another expression Carla used was 'identify myself with' to refer to a stage when she had already got used to the person and started to find common ground between their personalities. This is a significant part of the process: it is at this point that the relationship will either gain depth or will remain superficial. As Carla suggested, more intimate themes will only emerge when there is a moment of identification in the relationship; when the young person begins to see the practitioner as a person with relevant experiences.

Lucas complements this idea, adding another aspect that is essential to the development of the engagement:

> … friendship in first place. What made me believe things were right [in the relationship] is that I knew I could talk about things and I knew who I was talking with, I could feel safe. This was what I needed to be able to relax and be comfortable.

Lucas connects friendship with trust, highlighting the importance of 'knowing' who he is talking with before being open about his life. This exposes how providing conditions and time for young people to 'get used to' the educator is not just about spending time with them, but it is also about allowing them to get to know the educator 'in the round'.

In the process of 'getting used to' and building trust, both Carla and Lucas highlight the importance of getting to know the educator through experience and interaction. More than gathering information about the educator, this is also a process of constructing identities, although understanding the boundaries of the relationship. For Carla, finding common aspects between herself and Mary was a determinant to accepting the relationship. The process of constant identification in the relationship appears in different moments of the narratives, and these are presented as symbolic moments where the relationship gained a different status. As Mary describes:

> ... it was very difficult to have a well-established engagement with Carla. She wasn't open at all and the way we found to build the relationship was ... in trying to make her feel comfortable in the relationship she started to ask questions about my life and started to make comparisons [with other educators]: 'So do you are you in a relationship? Ah OK, because A was in a relationship, and K too'. She would constantly refer to other educators and was always comparing me to them.

The search for common aspects is one of the clear moves that Carla makes in order to accept the relationship. This gives us an insight into the relationship between identification and legitimation. Carla recalls her memories of the other educators with whom she had established a solid relationship, using the comparison as a starting point for finding ways to 'get used to' the new educator. This is interesting, as it provides a strong indication of the effectiveness of the previous relationships. For Carla, these experiences are now providing her with some reference points for building a new relationship. This is a key part in the transformative nature of the educator's work, and will be returned to later.

Through these experiences, Carla is able to make her own analysis of what is relevant to her. Before opening herself to the relationship and revealing details of her life, she needs to first understand the educators' experiences and check if that person fits her expectations and can be trusted. Mary gives more details about this process of identification:

> It was becoming increasingly clear [the search for reference and identification]. One thing that clearly made us have real dialogues was the fact that she started to have the desire to leave home to live somewhere else [and she knew Mary was living by herself, away from family] and for some time this was the subject that we focused on discussing, the good and bad of doing it.

Carla also gave her view of the same moment:

> ... then Mary came and managed to conquer me, she managed to gain my trust and I know we have a lot in common ... I do things that she has already done. ... Among all the things, the one I most like in having an educator is to able to trust. I know if I look for her [the educator] to talk, I will be able trust her. ... I was never comfortable to talk about relationships with my mother, and I talk about everything with Mary, every single thing.

It is possible to observe in the narratives of both Mary and Carla when the relationship began to become viewed as legitimate. The respect and acceptance of the other is dependent on the relevance of their experiences. It is interesting that Carla legitimizes Mary as someone who can provide guidance when she begins to understand exactly where Mary can contribute to her life. More than having someone to give her advice, she is looking for someone who has already 'tested' the advice for themselves and someone who will truly understand her particular reality.

In fact, Carla goes beyond this; in her discourse it is clear that intrinsic to the developing relationship is the acknowledgment of the difference in personalities and life contexts, as Mary describes:

> I think it is nice that Carla has an awareness of the reality ..., she knows how things really are, and many times she threw it in my face. ... Sometimes I would talk about different ways of doing things and she would tell me: 'Mary, this is not possible for me, there are another seven people living at home, so there are things you suggest me to do that because of this simple fact it becomes impossible.

This highlights how Carla developed a sense of identification while still recognizing her particular reality. The process of identification is not about being 'equal' to another person, it is about acknowledging the differences that reveal the boundaries between two people. It is this, the revealing and understanding of difference as well as commonalities, that is essential to developing a transformative relationship. The exercise of mirroring, comparing and reflecting on the realities and personalities, is an important condition to construct alternative ways of understanding, feeling and reacting to the context the young people live in. Through challenging the limits of the relationship, Carla was able to experiment, test, challenge, feel and reflect on new ways of dealing with life situations. By stretching the relationship to the limit she got to know more about her own limits. In Mary's words:

> Sometimes I feel like she [Carla] is challenging me, as if she was asking: 'what credibility do you have to come and tell this?'. [She would] challenge the advice [given by the educator] questioning if they were realistic … she challenged me a lot and still challenges [me].

In challenging the educator Carla is also providing an opportunity to make interventions. The challenging can also be interpreted as a demand for the educator to demonstrate their principles and positionality around certain issues. This process can also be a useful tool for reflection. By getting in contact with different points of view and being able to discuss these in a safe relationship, Carla can reflect about her own principles and expand possibilities and learn from other people's experiences. This is a key element for transformation and can be even more effective if the reflexive interactions are experienced with various people. As Carla highlights:

> … I think it was very good to be with each of the educators, now I know a little bit of each of them and still remember everything, I learned a little bit with each and there are things that I do today that remind me of them. There are things I see that remind me of them, there are things I think that remind me of them. Everything they taught me I teach to other people.

Carla's 'little bit learnt with each of them' presents her experience with the educators as a synthesis of relationships. This is significant to understand how multiple relationships can form a mosaic of experiences and how each one can inform the young person's evolving identity. Although, on initial reading, the way in which Carla expressed these experiences makes it sound like an easy process, it is possible to identify that it is not a straightforward process. The 'little bit' that Carla refers to as having learnt is a result of long-term relationships, and these have gained such a significance that they have helped Carla to rebuild meanings around relationships and about herself. Carla emphasized the influence the relationships with the educators had made in her life, and importantly that this influence was not limited to the moment of the intervention but continued into the present.

In a similar way, Lucas highlights that:

> [to change educators] is good and bad at the same time. Sometimes you are already used to one kind of person, used to having conversations with that person, but on the other hand it is good because you build a friendship with different people, you get to know them better, and you vary [the relationships].

Using the same expression as Carla, Lucas identifies the engagement with the educator as when he is 'used to' the person. He also makes clear the two sides of the variation of educators, highlighting the 'bad' aspect of needing to start a new relationship with a different person and ending the relationship with someone who he was already 'used to'. This reinforces the importance of the variety of relationships as in many cases this provides an opportunity to experience and understand the dynamic of ending relationships in a healthy way and see that it is always possible to re-establish a new and equally valuable one, despite the relationship itself being completely different. These variations in relationships – when dealt with in an appropriate way, with transparency that guarantees the awareness and autonomy of the young people over the process – are essential to encourage the expansion of positive experiences that can later encourage transformation. As highlighted by Lucas, these experiences enable you to get to know and better understand relationship dynamics.

ACHIEVING MEANING: THE TRANSFORMATIVE RELATIONSHIP

The aim of ACER's work is to develop meaningful relationships with young people and the wider community. For the social support service, this means that the aim of their work moves beyond simply supporting young people and into providing them with challenging experiences and ensuring their rights, and towards enabling young people to be autonomous in their own lives, overcoming potential challenges and recognizing the moments when they need to seek help. Part of this process is to expand the young people's experiences to facilitate informed choices. As highlighted by Paul:

> It [transformation] means to show a different reality for the beneficiary. If the problem is violent relationships, then we try to show and provoke experiences with non-violent situations to show relations that are not only based on violence. … we try to show the other side of the relationships often they cannot see because of the environment they are living in. Sometimes they live in an environment in which everybody shouts, hits each other, where there are only negative relationships, sometimes engagement in criminal activities, so we try to show other ways to live and to provide new ways so then they can make choices and make their own way as opposed to following that one path. Sometimes they have not many choices, they live within the possibilities that neighbourhood offers and we try to create opportunities to experience different realities and other ways.

In Paul's words, to transform is to experience new situations and expand the possibilities of choice. What Paul highlights is that the key aspect of the transformational process is the reflection triggered by the experience of new situations. This is essential for developing a process through which the autonomy of the young person is prioritized and so emancipation can be reached at the end of the process. Experiencing new realities is the fundamental aspect to transformation and in many cases it cannot be achieved without the help of someone else. Mary illustrates this idea when narrating an intervention with Carla:

> We [Mary, Carla, Carla's son, and two of Carla's bothers] went [to the public office] to apply for an ID card and we had agreed to go to a park near the office afterwards. … There was a moment when Carla's struggle became very clear. She is now 15 years old but she doesn't have the freedom of a 15 year old … so there was a moment [in the park] when everybody else went to play, there was an event happening in the park and there was some dance performance happening and everybody went for a wander and we set a picnic and stayed there, Carla wanted to go for a wander but she had to stay with her baby. … At some point she saw something in my bag, it was a pencil case that a friend from university have given to me, and Carla remembered the story about the pencil case and started to ask questions about the university and I was telling her that I was still studying and what was it like, and then at some point she told me: 'Oh it is a good thing that I didn't stop my studies [during pregnancy] otherwise it would be very difficult to get back to school.' And then, making the most of that moment I asked: 'And so how do you see your life today?' And she replied: 'Ah, today I don't believe I have left my mother because of him [ex-boyfriend and father of her son], one day my mother slapped me on the face and I took my stuff and went away. From that day he became the most important person in my life but today I don't value him at all. I like my son a lot but if I could choose again I would have had him years later and my life today would be different'…

It is possible to observe in the situation narrated above how a practical activity mediated the interaction between Carla and Mary. The picnic in the park worked as an encouraging context for a reflexive conversation and Carla was comfortable enough to review her choices and share her frustrations. It is also important to highlight the role of Mary's experiences with her friend from university and how this experience was represented by the pencil case and how this worked as a trigger for a conversation about studies, life choices and relationships. In the interaction, Carla had control over the subjects of the conversation and was able to raise her own concerns while also giving space for Mary to explore and encourage her to talk with more depth. As Mary reflects, this situation demonstrates a fundamental principle to transformative practice:

> ... it [the role of the educator] is personal development work, human development, to promote the dignity of people, to help them to know their rights ..., to look around for opportunities that might be available. I think the first thing is for them to look after themselves, to be healthy, and from this move towards stimulating the ambition of realizing dreams ... To show the importance they have for themselves, that they are important to me and to everybody. Getting to this point is something that is only possible if you have a strong attachment with that person. If people come to them and say don't do this, don't use drugs, but you can only make it happen if you are able to show the importance they have [to you].

Mary describes one other important aspect that is essential for empowering people for transformation. Her description suggests the importance of working with people's self-imagery as a starting point for transformation; that changing the way in which they see themselves is the starting point for provoking any change. Like Paul, Mary's discourse about her practice often highlights the importance of a relationship that is based on a deep and meaningful attachment:

> I think the minimum that everybody should have is the awareness of their rights and we are very far from achieving this. This is important to the rest of our work, ... we need to present new options, but before anything we need to understand what is really happening, why are those relations not right or not healthy. ... We need to look at reality, trying to see things through their eyes. It can be someone in the family who is sick and no one is looking

after them, for example, and at first we think this is neglect but we need to understand that ... it can also be that the problem is in the health care system that is not providing the necessary service, but if the person is aware of their rights it is a bit easier for us because we would then deal with the practical arrangements.

It is interesting to observe the connection made between awareness of rights and self-esteem raised by Mary. For her, empowering people is also about increasing their capacities of knowing what is right for themselves and feeling they deserve and own it. This idea is complementary to the definitions offered by Paul and it is one aspect that will determine whether the work will move towards autonomy or to a harmful dependency. To be aware of what they can and should have and at the same time to have the desire for it are the two things that will inform any process of transformation.

CONCLUSION

Throughout this chapter we were able to identify a number of insights from the discourses of Mary, Paul, Carla and Lucas. The narration of their relationship-building processes revealed the emotions, thoughts and actions that facilitated a reflection about the essence of this process. In the beginning of the relationship-building process, Carla and Lucas both showed resistance in getting to know someone new and these initial rejections were a common dynamic in the early stages of the relationships. While for the young people the rejection is part of 'getting used to' the new person, for the educators this is a natural movement through which the young people are testing the limits of the relationship and at the same time checking some of the characteristics of an educator's personality. What came through in the narratives of Carla and Lucas was that the way in which the educators managed these back and forth movements and the dynamic between acceptance and rejection was decisive for the rest of the process of engagement. Through the rejection, the young people took control over the process and challenged the educators to expose their personality and their positionality. What this highlights is that the focus at this stage of the relationship is not on the verbal communication – conversation and orientation – but it is primarily based on non-verbal interaction. This is extremely significant and fundamentally shifts our understanding of practice at this stage of the relationship-building process.

Through the discourses of Carla and Lucas we were able to observe the constant search to identify common and different aspects between their life contexts and personalities and those of the educators. This was vital for the 'identification' between the young people and educators and was an essential part in building trust within the relationship. When Carla and Lucas were able to get in contact with the educator's experiences they felt that they started to get to know the educator as a human being, and it was from this point that they were able to choose whether trust could be established. It is only from this point that the relationship gains legitimacy and therefore the potential to be transformative. Through this legitimacy, trust is established and the relationship then becomes a safe space in which the young person and educator are able to experiment with new forms of interaction. In this space, past experiences are shared and become common, allowing the young people to reflect, construct new meanings and expand their possibilities of choice.

According to Carla and Lucas, the deep relationship has provided them with the opportunity to experiment with different ways of interacting and representing their experiences. In the relationship with the educator they were able to challenge, emphasize, and experiment with ways of interacting within a safe context. In doing this, more than just building a relationship, Carla and Lucas were also building their own identity. Through exploring the educator's life context and personality, the young people were

also able to reflect on their own experiences, allowing them to question, reinforce or confirm their understanding.

Through the reflections of Carla, Mary, Lucas and Paul, we were able to understand more about the challenges of a relationship-based approach. This has demonstrated the importance of the educator bringing themselves, their whole self, to their professional practice; of being prepared to use themselves as a tool for reflection. Naturally, utilizing their own experiences as a tool for reflection is deeply challenging and demands that the educator maintains clarity in their professional position and a coherency between what is said, what the young person may read through non-verbal communication, and what is done. The research indicates that in the end, this alignment between emotions, thoughts and actions constitutes, for the young person, the 'truth' of an educator. If one thing is said and another is done, or if one thing is felt and a different thing is said, trust is undermined; trust cannot be built on incoherence and so the transformative relationship cannot happen. This is what Lucas and Carla were looking for when they were challenging, experimenting, 'getting used to' and 'identifying themselves with' the educators. They have highlighted their need to find 'the truth of' the educator, making us understand that the transformation can only happen when young people build a relationship with someone who is present as a whole human being, present with all the parts that constitutes a person and not just as a professional.

Notes

1 A Brazilian cultural expression that mixes martial art, dance and music.
2 Educador (in Portuguese) and Educator (in English) is the term used by young people to refer to the support workers responsible for the one-to-one and family support.
3 Brazilian slang used to describe someone who is determined, independent, strong and sometimes aggressive in opinions and attitudes.

REFERENCES

Butler, U. M. (2008). Children's Participation in Brazil – A Brief Genealogy and Recent Innovations. *The International Journal of Children's Rights*, *16*(3), 301–312.

Garcia Lopez, F., Leao, L. D. S., & Grangeia, M. L. (2011). State, Third Sector, and the Political Sphere in Brazil: Evolution and Current Scenario. *International Journal of Sociology*, *41*(2), 50–73.

Gohn, M. G. (2009). Educação Não-Formal e o Papel do Educador (a) Social. *Revista Meta: Avaliação*, *1*(1), 28. http://doi.org/10.22347/2175-2753v1i1.1

Goulart, M. V. da S., & Dos Santos, N. I. S. (2014). Protagonismo juvenil e capital humano: uma análise da participação política da juventude no Brasil. *Ciências Sociais Unisinos*, *50*(2), 127–136. http://doi.org/10.4013/csu.2014.50.2.04

IBGE & IPEA. (2012). *De Geografia E Estatística – IBGE Pesquisa Econômica Aplicada – IPEA*. Rio de Janeiro.

Jupp Kina, V. (2012). Participant or protagonist? A Critical Analysis of Children and Young People's Participation in São Paulo, Brazil. *International Social Work*, *55*(3), 320–336.

Liu, C. H., & Matthews, R. (2005). Vygotsky's Philosophy: Constructivism and its Criticisms Examined. *International Education Journal*, *6*(3), 386–399.

Newman, F., & Holzman, L. (2005). Lev S. Vygotsky: Revolutionary Scientist. *Prospects*, 12. http://doi.org/10.1007/BF02195302

Rodrigues, T. (2010). Non-formal Education and Street Youth Empowerment: Pedagogy and Practice of Two Brazilian Non-governmental Organizations. University of Ottowa, https://ruor.uottawa.ca/handle/10393/28578?locale=fr

Stenner, P. (2015). Being Moved beyond the Mainstream. In I. Parker (Ed.), *Handboolk of Critical Psychology* (pp. 43–51). Hove: Routledge.

26

Reflective Practice: Gaze, Glance and Being a Youth Worker

Jo Trelfa

INTRODUCTION

I begin this chapter with a definition of youth work. Whilst definitions of youth work are discussed in more depth and breadth elsewhere in this publication, here I deliberately use an England-centric one to illuminate something of the purpose of and debates around youth work in the whole of the UK, but also, through the brief introductory critical discussion, something of the complexity of youth work. This leads me into discussion of reflective practice, the focus of the chapter.

The definition I draw on is from the National Youth Agency, a registered charity that promotes youth work, occupational standards and accreditation of professional training within England.[1] They describe youth work as 'the science of enabling young people to believe in themselves and to prepare for life'. Emphasis is placed on 'building resilience and character and giving young people the life skills [needed] to live, learn,

work and interact successfully with other people' (NYA, nd, on-line).

The notions of youth work as a 'science' along with 'resilience' to cope with life rather than social activism to change circumstances are problematic. Moreover, 'character' has been taken up within the UK Conservative Party's ideology as shorthand for self-discipline and self-reliance, often linked to assertions of 'British values': all having knotty connotations when applied to youth work. In contrast, rather than a single entity, Smith (1988) advocates understanding the profession as comprising different forms, the dimensions of which have possessed differing priorities throughout its history. Clarity concerning these dimensions elucidates the nature of youth work and what it involves. They are that youth work:

- is young-person focused;
- honours a principle of voluntary participation;
- values community, association and relationship;

- recognises the integrity, approach and values of the youth worker; and,
- focuses on informal education (Smith, 1988).

I qualified as a youth worker in the 1980s and engaged with these dimensions in various contexts for 12 years before moving into higher education as a senior lecturer on programmes for future generations of practitioners. My view of youth work concurs with that of Davies (2005: 4) inasmuch as 'what distinguishes youth work from other related and often overlapping practices is its methods', in other words, the processes by which it practices the dimensions. In the UK these youth work methods are delineated formally through a combination of National Occupational Standards (NOS) and Quality Assurance Agency (QAA) for higher education subject benchmarks because it is a graduate profession.

To illustrate, the NOS (2012: 2), concerning 'the agreed standards of performance and knowledge required in youth work practice across the UK', identify five core areas. The first of these is 'working with young people and others' and the first standard of practice involved is the ability to 'Initiate, build and maintain purposeful relationships with young people'. This is elucidated in the QAA's (2009) subject knowledge and practice skills for youth work as involving power, empowerment and democratic learning; models and methods of youth work and informal education; legal responsibilities; and, communication theory and skills. A practice scenario illuminates this further.

Sami has recently started a three-year university degree programme to qualify him as a youth worker. Before this he had been volunteering in his local Youth Centre, a small organisation based in the predominantly economically privileged town in which he lives. Sami is well known by the employed staff there as well as the young people, having been a user of its services himself since age eight. In contrast, his first compulsory fieldwork experience central to his university programme is based within a large urban residential area characterised by poor quality social housing, high unemployment

and disengagement with statutory services. This, and the other units included in the programme, embody the NOS and subject benchmarks. For example, they introduce him to, and facilitate his engagement in, skilful practice involved in building 'relationship wedges' (Goffman, 1963: 105) with young people, i.e. first contact and formation of relationships. Organisational protocols concerning the nature of that practice, working context arrangements, and legal obligations will also inform his actions.

If I extend this illustration further it highlights the limitations of such formalised delineations of practice, and in doing so it signifies the role of reflective practice.

Sami approaches four young men he has not spoken to before. They are talking together, leaning against the coffee bar with their backs to him. Sami calls out 'Hi, just moved the chairs for the group discussion you were in before, do they look right to you?' This, he feels, is a non-threatening approach to create chat that could lead to conversation, and hopefully open the possibility for future dialogue as he builds his relationship with them. All four turn to face him and stop talking. Two glance at each other and laugh, another aggressively looks him up and down, the fourth takes a drink from the mug he is holding and all turn back and continue their conversation. Sami is uncomfortable in a situation where he is not known. Moreover, his social norms trigger feelings of anxiety and embarrassment when approaching strangers and starting a conversation uninvited, and now he experiences humiliation given their response. This is compounded by the public nature of the encounter, other young people saw what happened. Finally, Sami is not that much older than the young men, he feels clumsy about his own sense of masculinity generally but particularly when confronted by males who have an appearance of surety about them, and is not entirely certain that he understands his role if it is not one of 'helping' which the young men do not appear to need. As a consequence he feels a sense of shrinking inside, of self-image, confidence and purpose. Sami as a person and Sami as a professional are of course one and the same but now confused; Occupational Standards, subject benchmarks and youth work models do not help him in that moment.

Sami's experience is constructed from accounts of student youth workers as they consider what is a most essential moment in the negotiation of their professional relationships, that of initial contact. Unlike other professions where both parties have an expectation (whether accurate or not) of their roles, the informal and voluntary nature of youth work can create confusion for new practitioners and young people alike. Youth workers must negotiate how they relate to young people, be aware of the experiences they bring to that encounter and their emotional responses during practice, as well as cope with the vulnerability of communication. It exemplifies the point that whatever the formal arrangements and requirements in place, the fast-paced, dynamic situations of youth work are such that practitioners must make their *own* decisions in practice. Sami will or will not be consciously aware of benchmark standards and theory in the moment that the young men turn away, but it is his personal reactions that influence whether he continues to try and engage them, or as in this case, withdraw.

The notion of aporia is useful here. From its Greek etymological root: *poros* (path, passage, a way), and *a-poros* (lacking a path, passage, way), aporia describes a 'lack of resource … a perplexity achieved by an encounter with the previously unthought, an uncertainty about where to go next' (Heidegger, 1945/2002: 41) or the dilemma of many possible options. It expresses a notion of practice as messy, a maze of many routes rather than singular paths directed by formal guidance. 'Reflective practice' is the term given to refer to processes involved in bringing to awareness the threads of judgements and decisions behind a particular route being taken. It involves becoming critically alert to the range of internal and external forces that influence one as well as the translation of this into action. I define reflective practice as a rigorous, disciplined approach for noticing, attending to, and inquiring into aspects of practice, where 'practice' means service to others.

REFLECTIVE PRACTICE

The origins of 'reflective practice' is associated with the work of Donald Schön (1983). Challenging a conventional positivist notion that professionals learn about and engage in their work contexts through a linear application of knowledge and theory, Schön took Dewey's (1938: 4) concept of 'enquiry' to understand how professionals 'intertwine thought with action' (Schön, 1995: np). Essentially, his research explains the ways in which practitioners engage with aporic moments of practice. He evocatively refers to it as 'swampy lowlands' in contrast to the 'high ground' where issues and decisions can be managed or resolved via prescribed and applied guidelines (Schön, 1983: 42). Encountering aporic, messy situations, Schön (1983: 50) argues that practitioners engage in two ways: by 'think[ing] about doing something while doing it' (1983: 54), in 'a stretch of time within which it is still possible to make a difference to the outcomes of action (Schön, 1995: np), referred to as 'reflection-in-action'; and by 'reflection-on-action', in which, 'in the relative tranquillity of a post-mortem, [practitioners] think back on a project they have undertaken, a situation they have lived through, and they explore the understandings they have bought to their handling of the case' (Schön, 1983: 61). Through this work Schön presented an 'alternative paradigm' of professional practice, one that 'recognised that every professional encounter is unique and cannot be fully explicated by immanent theory' (Papell & Skolnik, 1992: 20).

Thus, rather than a linear and direct application of standards, benchmarks, agency protocol and theories, Sami's practice can be seen to be inherently complex and messy. His reflection in the moment of the encounter is dominated by embodied embarrassment and humiliation, his need to take himself out of the situation, and a desire instead to occupy himself in something that brings comfort. His university programme would require that later he reflect on the action that he took. Typically, he would do this via writing (diaries, journals, logs, portfolios, blogs) and dialogue (supervision, reflective practice groups, session reviews). Combinations of such activities are also part of continuing professional development and encouraged in work settings. There are a number of potential outcomes and purposes (Moon, 1999) but the underpinning assumption is that engagement in reflective practice will strengthen Sami's practice in (future) action, and ultimately youth work 'will be the stronger if its practitioners learn to plan, execute, accept responsibility for, and critically evaluate their actions' (Barnett, 1990: 76). When writing about the encounter in a journal Sami could consider it from the perspective of the young men, and/or consider specific elements, such as his confusion about his role and purpose, and/or how he might build up capacity as a practitioner, and/or the impact of space and place on his practice. In addition or instead, he might discuss the encounter with a supervisor.

Whilst Sami's encounter will be familiar to those reading this book about youth work, its inclusion is to illuminate the practice of reflective practice, the value of it, and hence why it is characterised as a 'specialised tool' (Moon, 1999: 4) for professional practice in the social professions. Further, it is indicative of how youth work involves limitless nuanced implicit and explicit critical junctures that are suffused with moral and ethical implications (Banks, 2001). Therefore, for youth workers, more than a 'specialised tool', reflective practice must be 'a vital prerequisite' (Banks, 2001: 54).

To this end there is a proliferation of models, theories and approaches in mainstream literature, all of which are dominated by a developmental epistemology wherein individuals must learn how to engage in reflective practice (Bleakley, 1999). Standards, benchmarks and theories do not clarify the direction of a course of action: 'youth workers plot their route … "intuitively", "subconsciously", as part of the second nature of what they do'

(Davies, 2005: 19) in a context where there are 'many conflicting interests, interpretations of reality, moral and ethical standards, visions and hopes for the future [existing] next to each other' (Philippart, 2003: 70).

Given that structural, organisational and institutional arrangements 'constrain, form and organise' (Schatzki, 2001a: 4) and national and global political landscapes shape youth work contexts and activities (Biesta, 2007), as discussed elsewhere in depth in this book, reflective practice offers a 'from within' (Furlong, 2000) response, engaging practitioners in the conscious plotting of their *own* routes.

IDENTITY-OF AND IDENTITY-AS

The assertion is not new that macro-determinants shape professional practice but that individual agency is also involved. Nonetheless, the concepts of '*identify-of*' and '*identity-as*' enable the naming and exploration of processes involved, and thus extend understanding, as well as contributing to a deeper appreciation of reflective practice.

As established, the formalised boundaried categories of 'shared theories, ideas, beliefs or abstractly specified rules or norms' (Barnes, 2001: 17) that delineate youth work are pre-existing 'organised nexuses of activity' (Schatzki, 2001b: 48). It is to these that a youth worker must 'cleave' (Barnes, 2001: 17). *Identity-of* is an epistemological position that explains that 'cleaving', the coming to know and knowing the boundaried categories that define what it is to be a youth worker through the creation of maps in the mind of paths to be taken and likely hazards along the way. *Identity-of* is the process of youth workers 'coming ever more fully into membership of a tradition of practice' (Golby, 1993: 8). They learn, adhere to and adopt the *identity-of* youth worker. Thus, as those institutional orderings become increasingly controlled by macro-social determinants then what it is to be a youth worker is too. In his provocative description of the current landscape of professional practice, Biesta (2007: 2) contends that judgement is no longer 'left to the opinions' of the professionals themselves, but replaced with activity that can be measured, assessed and proved. *Identity-of* describes prescribed and inscribed bodies, shaped and contained by ideologies, discourse, practices and procedures that are subject to control 'from above' (Evetts, 2003: 11).

In contrast, *identity-as* suggests individual agency, an ontological position of an 'imagined or supposed' (Tonso, 2008: 154) sense of what it is to be a youth worker. It is about 'mental states of affairs expressed in behaviour' that 'informs activity by determining *what makes sense* for them to do' (Schatzki, 2001b: 49, emphasis added). Where *identify-of* describes cleaving to an organised, externally controlled, boundaried nexus of actions and behaviours associated with youth work, *identity-as* is about constructing and creating the activities that this involves in ways that might differ entirely or to some extent with those. *Identity-as* also explains how one can hold *identity-as* a youth worker when not formally being employed to do so (Coulter, 2001), as well as explaining how socio-political-historical cultural practices concerning variants of power/powerlessness (such as gender, race, etc.) can support, undermine or eclipse professional role expertise and power (Shohet & Hawkins, 1989). Therefore, *identity-as* not only recognises individual agency but also that 'youth worker' is always-becoming and only one of multiple identities or constructions of selfs (plural used purposefully here) involved when engaging in youth work practice.

Finally, and importantly, through individual and collective regard *-as* their chosen profession, *identity-as* involves the location of youth workers in relation to and positioning around discourse and control from above.

Together *identity-of* and *identity-as* reinforce and promote the significance and role of reflective practice. Whilst *identity-of* suggests an arc commencing from a (variable) start point to an agreed set of practices of youth worker, *identity-as* offers that blurring and agency is possible, indeed enriching, enlivening and essential to professional practice. Youth workers can assume and adopt the *identity-of* youth worker *and* choose what aspects of the profession they wish to embody; they can explore what kind of professional they want to be and can become conscious of the interaction of other aspects of their identity with their professional 'selves' through reflective practice.

In sum, *identity-of* and *identity-as* offers a lens through which to consider professional identity and practice, an analysis that locates and emphasises the significance of reflective practice. Put another way, appreciation of the role and purpose of reflective practice is strengthened by consideration of the ways in which being a youth worker is prescribed and inscribed, shaped and contained by ideologies, discourse, practices, procedures, *and* one's agency in determining one's professional practice and sense of selfs.

THE NATURE OF REFLECTIVE PRACTICE

Having underscored the significance of reflective practice to youth work through an exposition of *identity-of* and *identity-as*, it becomes salient to understand how reflective practice is approached in university education programmes to examine whether it achieves these outcomes. As noted, the typical epistemology underpinning the way that reflective practice is approached in the UK is developmental. In mainstream literature, for example, Brookfield (1995) sees reflection as a learnt skill, and Arredondo and Rucinski (1998) agree but contentiously link the ability to do so with intelligence, inferring that some individuals cannot develop as reflective practitioners. Brookfield (1995: 240) argues that reflection happens through a process that is 'slow and incremental rather than sudden and apocalyptic', whereas for Mezirow (1981) it is the latter, a view shared by Schön (1983). Resting on humanist notions of self as singular, natural, 'true', and 'open to development' (Bleakley, 2000: 406), reflective practice in youth work education centres on the notion of an 'intact coherent self waiting ... to be recorded through language' (Spry, 2011: 503), through skills that are learned incrementally.

Setting aside the obvious disagreement between proponents of a developmental epistemological approach (albeit significant given that education programmes and work settings adopt it as if unproblematic), theory related to reflective practice, and the activities based on these theories, are dominated by reflection-on-action. Substantial attention is given to the shape and content that written and verbal accounts of practice after an event should take, as communicated through models of reflective practice and the *pro formae* based on them. For instance, Rolfe et al. (2001) and Kim (1999) offer models consisting of three stages in which youth workers first consider 'what', with practice articulated through a descriptive narrative; and second 'so what': the reflective stage in which connections are made with espoused theory and knowledge. The aim is that this will result in, or at least facilitate the development of knowledge about practice, processes and applications as well as enhance self-awareness. Similarly, Adams et al. (2002) and Burgoyne and Reynolds (1997: 2) distinguish between the stages or levels of 'effective practitioner' and 'reflective practitioner'. Here, then, youth workers, like Sami, think about a particular practice event, the influences leading to their interventions and responses, and how in hindsight they make sense of it.

It is not until the third stage of 'now what' (Rolfe et al., 2001) or 'critical reflective practice' (Kim, 1999; Burgoyne & Reynolds, 1997) that critical and emancipatory connections are made, thus distinguishing this from

mere reflective practice. These three stages are similar to Mezirow et al.'s (1990) 'non reflectors', 'reflectors' and 'critical reflectors'. Burgoyne and Reynolds (1997: 2) highlight how, for example, a critically reflective practitioner is informed by 'an understanding of a range of rival normative theories to a preferred one'. Issett (2000: 129–130) unpacks the notion further in relation to youth work: youth workers, like Sami, who are engaging in critical reflective practice recognise that professional knowledge can always be improved; are aware of operating within a personal, professional and political value base; and listen and learn from the ways that different cultures and groups experience and perceive the world.

Whilst some construct reflective and critical reflective practice as substantively different, others such as Bolton (2010), Proctor (1993) and Canaan (2005) argue that 'an approach to reflective practice that does *not* adopt a critical perspective would produce poor-quality ... and, in some respects dangerous practice' (Thompson & Thompson, 2008: 26–27, emphasis added). Thus for them, and for me when I use the term 'reflective practice' in this chapter, it is inherently critical.

Those who demonstrate this would be judged as successfully engaging in reflective practice.

A transformative approach to reflective practice is a second, though related, epistemology underpinning the way that reflective practice is approached (Bleakley, 1999). Rather than professions becoming stronger through reflection, here it is suggested that engagement in reflective practice enables practitioners to be 'active, engaged and responsible thinkers capable of developing ... critical consciousness' (Canaan, 2005: 162). This is a powerful aspiration for reflective practice to achieve, and in my previous research students have expressed confusion about how their reflections might attain such heights (Trelfa, 2016). Further, given that this aspiration is incorporated into a developmental approach, any transformative potential is reduced if not eradicated altogether by the 'technical operation' that reflective practice has become due to the 'cognitive and behavioural map' (Bleakley, 1999: 319) provided by 'experts'. For student practitioners, the combination of these elements leads to a preoccupation with impression management in order to stay 'on-map' so that they pass the reflective practice requirement of their education and/or are positively perceived in work settings (Trelfa, 2016; Trelfa & Telfer, 2014). Moreover, regardless of whether reflective practice is *actually* used in assessment of a student's engagement in youth work practice, this is compounded by a neoliberal emphasis in education and employment on implicit and explicit demands to comply with what and how to perform. Indeed, not only are stages prescribed, but what should be expressed through them is too (Hargreaves, 2004). The potential of reflective practice to support *identity-of* and *identity-as* becomes reduced to the former alone, as student youth workers learn and perform the *identity-of* a prescribed so-called reflective practitioner.

ISSUES AT THE HEART OF REFLECTION-ON-ACTION

Having illustrated the importance of reflective practice in youth work via the experience of Sami, subsequent discussion has revealed issues at the heart of reflective practice. These become multiplied when assumptions inherent to reflective practice are considered. Here I briefly touch on four: the unearthing of tacit attitudes, values and beliefs; cognitive processing; memory; and the need to maintain constancy.

Unearthing of Tacit Attitudes, Values and Beliefs

Whilst *identity-of* provides a lens to understand how youth workers learn, adopt and adhere to the given professional practices,

identity-as suggests that this is not a simple matter of application. Youth workers deconstruct the 'meaning and application' (Davies, 2010: 19) that policy, standards, benchmarks and theory hold for their profession, stakeholders, users and themselves. They also consider 'the meaning and application' of skills inherent to the profession, and, for all of this, consider what they individually bring to the work 'personally, politically and professionally' (Davies, 2010: 19). Argyris and Schön (1974: 4) refer to such agency as 'theories of action' to which practitioners give public 'allegiance', which might suggest a conscious process except that they distinguish these from a practitioner's 'theory-in-use', the tacit 'theory that *actually* governs [their] action' [emphasis added]. In fact, one's theory-in-use 'may or may not be compatible' with what is conscious and expressed, and practitioners would be unaware of a conflict between them (Argyris and Schön, 1974: 7). Whilst this could be seen as justification *for* the process of reflective practice, practitioners' accounts are instead 'inaccurate representations of the behaviour they claim to describe' (ibid.). Clearly, this is of vital concern for a process that relies on individuals accounting for their practice after an event.

Cognitive Processing

An explanation for what is happening here can be found in Kahneman's (2011: 13) 'metaphor of two agents', used to describe cognitive processing. 'System 1' is a mode of thinking that 'operates automatically and quickly, with little or no effort and no sense of control' (2011: 20) providing fast impressions and enabling immediate responses; 'system 2' is the deliberate and 'conscious reasoning self' (2011: 21). Whilst practitioners would like to think of themselves as deliberately and consciously reasoning in their actions, an assumption on which on the process of reflection-on-action depends and reinforces, in reality 'only a *fraction* of its capacity is engaged' (2011: 24, emphasis added). System 2 is 'mobilised' when system 1 does not have an answer, is surprised, challenged or 'to increase effort when an error [is] about to be made' (2011: 24–25). This could, of course, explain the emphasis in literature on reflective practice being triggered in single, surprising and challenging moments, at the intersection of routes in the maze of choice. However, Kahneman explains that system 2 is much slower than system 1. System 1 is the mode of thinking we operate with most of the time, and operates via a range of illusions and biases that feed system 2 thinking. Kahneman's analysis of cognitive processing immediately throws up questions about the *practice* of reflective practice. If the aspects underpinning professional action are tacit, then attempts made to identify and express it may not match the actual elements that shaped it if the whole process is based on inherent bias and prejudice not identified by system 2 thinking. Whilst Kahneman's thesis has its critics (Earl, 2012) and further research is indicated (Martin, 2012), it points to questions about the assumptions concerning cognitive functioning inherent in common understandings of reflective practice.

Furthermore, as Cavanagh (2011: 14) points out, we stop paying attention to things as soon as our cognitive processes are overwhelmed by 'attentional load'. In the fast pace of youth work practice, one can suppose that the likelihood of 'attentional load' is great. Thus, it can be presumed that the processes aimed to support reflection *on* that practice are dependent on cognitive processes that are limited, if not 'closed' altogether.

In sum, a more informed appreciation of cognitive processing indicates issues at the heart of reflection-in-action.

Memory

This discussion of reflection is also informed by research into memory. Herlihy et al. (2012: 662) note a literature upon 'explicit memory of an event that occurred in a specific time and place in one's personal past', and this suggests parallels with the material that reflective practitioners draw upon in a work context. Herlihy et al. find that as the gap between event and recall increases, so memories become dominated by associations and familiar emotions rather than the particular and distinct events. Reflection-on-action involves a gap between event and recall. Moreover, the reflective activity of writing can be mundane and tedious such that practitioners put it off until sometime later, and of course supervision can be monthly if not longer (if offered at all). Therefore, given that the activity of reflection-on-action is reliant on memory processes, it will result in representative accounts that are described and engaged with in ways that are familiar and general. As a result, one may question the rhetoric that extols a transformative purpose to reflection-on-practice if not the point of the exercise itself.

Constancy

Finally, whilst reflection-on-action involves thinking after an event in order to learn from experience and make meaning, in their discussion Argyris & Schön (1974: 17) assert that theories-in-use serve to ensure and maintain 'constancy', because practitioners actively 'avoid changing them', reinforcing Herlihy et al.'s (2012) research on memory noted above. The focus then is on the 'maintenance of biographical identity', a sense of self and image that one would like to project. To achieve this, memories are 'modified and refined to maintain and protect' (Herlihy et al., 2012: 63). Individuals are invested in their identities, personal *and* professional, and the maintenance of a consistent account.

Thus, rather than reflection on practice facilitating change, the primary, inherent and tacit function of the cognitive processes involved are to articulate and construct consistency, to recall association and the familiar, and all through a system that is fundamentally structured upon bias. It becomes curious to consider that literature on the practice of reflective practice approaches reflection-on-action unproblematically.

THE NEUROTYPICAL NATURE OF REFLECTIVE PRACTICE IN PROFESSIONAL EDUCATION PROGRAMMES

A final aspect of reflective practice to be discussed in this chapter relates these four critical areas to the way that reflective practice is included in education programmes and practice settings. The assumptions discussed above are translated into reflective practice models and activities and these are applied as if a homogenous body of youth workers engaged with reflective practice in the same way. Thus, current practices of reflective practice centre on an implicit notion of the 'neurotypical' rather than the 'neurodiverse'. The neurotypical is preoccupied 'with social concerns, delusions of superiority, and obsession with conformity', and 'assumes one experience or one correct experience' of the world (Muskie, 2002: np). Thus, a literature and practice around reflective practice that is concerned with defining and maintaining borders between those who effectively engage and those who don't participate, or between those who do so in accepted formats and models and those who do not, can be argued as focusing upon the neurotypical. In contrast, neurodiversity advocates 'the recognition and acceptance of valuable difference' in neurological processing (Runswick-Cole, 2014: 1120–1121). Baron-Cohen (2015: np) discusses neurodiversity as a 'revolutionary concept' that alerts us to 'the huge rich range of brain types'. It is consequently pertinent to a discussion of reflective practice and the way it is embedded in youth work educational programmes and workplace settings.

GAZE AND GLANCE

Having begun this chapter arguing for the importance of reflective practice and of *identity-of* and *identity-as* as a means to understand better the messiness of youth work practice that practitioners like Sami encounter, where does this critique of reflective practice leave us? Is it an empty concept that would best be ignored or removed from professional practice in general and youth work in particular? If so, where does this leave youth workers such as Sami for whom engaging in a rigorous, disciplined approach for noticing, attending to, and inquiring into aspects of practice would clearly be essential if he is to be of service to young people?

One response to this is suggested by my doctoral research (forthcoming), in which student youth workers spoke of their experiences of reflective practice embedded in higher education professional programmes. They described it as staring at an aspect of professional practice to break it into small pieces for analysis, in marked contrast to the fast, fleeting *glances* during professional practice itself, upon which their decisions were taken and interventions made. I developed this difference as that between *Gaze* and *Glance* (capitalised to differentiate them from colloquial uses of the words), a salient distinction when considered in relation to the literature.

Gaze is 'prolonged, contemplative, yet regarding the field of vision with a certain aloofness and disengagement, across a tranquil interval' (Bryson, 1983: 94). It creates 'fissures': the viewer fixes on a single thing at a time and in isolation, as if 'confronting a new scene, one which has broken free of its sequence', and encourages and facilitates a 'particular narrative segment' (1983: 98). Consequently, gaze encapsulates the nature of and processes concerned with reflection-on-action; it is about 'distancing and disengagement' (Craig, 2012: 27).

Gaze may also be connected to feminist theory's critique of objectification and voyeurism, processes that '[demand] a story, [depend] on making something happen, forcing a change in another person, a battle of will and strength, victory/defeat, all occurring in a linear time with a beginning and an end' (Mulvey, 1992: 29). The resonance with earlier discussion about issues at the heart of reflection-on-action are obvious. Youth work becomes examined via reflection-on-action, while what is complex and messy is reduced to a story, accounted for and objectified into constituent parts, through a lens of judgement and a need for improvement.

Gaze also has a benign aspect, and to dismiss it altogether would fall into the very trap of directing reflective practice that I critiqued earlier. Reflecting via 'the relative tranquillity of a post mortem' clearly has its advantages. For Sami the critical distance to consider his reactions to the young people, and space in which to think about his practice and selfs -*as* and -*of* youth worker, might help him. Gaze has a part to play as long as it is understood for what it is and in relation to its limitations, narrowness and partiality.

In contrast to Gaze and its fixity, control and distance, the fast, fleeing, 'flickering, ungovernable mobility' of Glance 'strikes at the very roots of rationalism' (Bryson, 1983: 121). As a process, Glance entails apprehension ('to catch'), perception ('to distinguish'), and comprehension ('to know'); together these 'complete the process of generating meaning' (Craig, 2012: 21). Thus, Glance facilitates a different kind of engagement, one that is relevant to the fast, dynamic 'entangled relationalities' (Barad, 2010: 264) of youth work practice. In her discussion of learning landscapes, Greene (1978: 165) writes of 'an active attention … to life in its multiple phases, not the kind of passive attention in which one sits and stares – not the kind of focalised attention that permits one only to see the track ahead of one'. It is about playfulness, creativity, messiness, and pause in flow.

Here then, I suggest that rather than 'map-drawing' to account for the path taken, a reflective practice is required that more effectively mirrors and enables engagement with aporic and messy youth work practice, one that contrasts with the epistemic focus of reflection-on-action, *identity-of* and Gaze. Glance works in 'epistemic emptiness' (Burbules, 2000: 172); it is a concept and approach that facilitates the capture, articulation and discussion of the messiness and complexity of youth work practice, reflection-in-action, *identity-as* and the liminal third space between it and *identity-of.*

Youth Work and the Significance of Glance

Glance is about noticing the 'uncanny' (O'Neill, 2009) feelings of uncertainty, doubt and aporia: moments in youth work practice when travelling a particular path of professional action that is familiar due to NOS, benchmarks and theory, but finding oneself suddenly thrown off, experiencing discomfort and unease, and not knowing what to do. More than this, however, Glance also captures and conveys the 'canniness of bodily knowing' (O'Neill, 2009: 216). Here, then, in contrast to a Schönian focus on surprising moments alone, Glance is about the body being canny all the time. Proprioception and bodily knowing is typically omitted from mainstream literature on reflective practice and professional practice including youth work, meaning that 'only a small part of professional activity' is included (Vaquez Bronfman, 2005: 13). It is as if body and mind were not 'intertwined' (Kinsella, 2007: 408). Therefore, not only does Glance take reflective practice out of the fixed and routinised limitations of Gaze, it honours bodily knowing. Through this analysis, reflective practice becomes an ontological rather than epistemological practice, one that reclaims reflective practice from its formulation as a reified, cognitively dominated, controlled framing of finite accounts of practice that are used as a form of surveillance, as expounded in mainstream literature and through the dominance of reflection-on-action. *Glance* is a radical concept and practice that returns reflective practice to its transformational roots. Where *gaze* and reflection-on-action are, in essence, an individual practitioner taking something that emerged in a shared process and clinically breaking it up through prescribed forms and discourses, *glance* is about a creative, playful, lightness of engagement in the moment. An analysis of youth work practice through *identity-of* and *identity-as* indicates the need for this new understanding of reflective practice, but also that an appreciation of youth work practice contributes to development of the practice of reflective practice in this way, enabling reflective practice to carry out its radical promise and ultimately be of service to others.

Here, then, I am, and, I argue, youth work educators and supervisors should, incorporate playful and creative approaches to bodily knowing, developing a bodily consciousness and embodied pedagogy together and in their practice, articulating their explorations through a frame of *identity-of* and *identity-as*.

Note

1 Wales, Scotland and Northern/north of Ireland each have different processes and validation bodies.

REFERENCES

Adams R., Dominelli L. & Payne M. (2002) *Critical Practice in Social Work*. Basingstoke: Palgrave.

Argyris C. & Schön D. (1974) *Theory in Practice: Increasing Professional Effectiveness*. San Francisco: Jossey Bass.

Arredondo D.E. & Rucinski T.T. (1998) Using structured interactions in conferences and journals to promote cognitive development among mentors and mentees. *Journal of Curriculum and Supervision*, 13(4): 300–327.

Banks S. (2001) *Ethics and Values in Social Work*. Hampshire: Palgrave Macmillan.

Barad K. (2010) Quantum entanglements and hauntological relations of inheritance: dis/continuities, spacetime enfoldings, and justice-to-come. *Derrida Today*, 3(2): 240–268.

Barnes B. (2001) Practice as collective action. In T.R. Schatzki, K. Knorr Cetina, & E. Von Svigny E. (eds) *The Practice Turn in Contemporary Theory*. London and New York: Routledge. pp. 17–28.

Barnett R. (1990) *The Idea of Higher Education*. Buckingham: Open University Press.

Baron-Cohen S. (2015) One-to-one. BBC Radio 4. Tuesday 17th February.

Biesta G. (2007) Why 'what works' won't work: evidence-based practice and the democratic deficit in educational research. *Educational Theory*, 57(1): 1–22.

Bleakley A. (1999) From reflective practice to holistic reflexivity. *Studies in Higher Education*, 24(3): 315–330.

Bleakley A. (2000) Adrift without a life belt: reflective self-assessment in a post-modern age. *Teaching in Higher Education*, 5(4): 405–418.

Bolton G. (2010) *Reflective Practice: Writing and Professional Development* (3rd edn). London: Sage.

Brint S. (1994) *In an Age of Experts: The Changing Role of Professionals in Politics and Public Life*. Princeton, NJ: Princeton University Press.

Brookfield S. (1995) *Becoming a Critically Reflective Teacher*. San Francisco: Jossey-Bass.

Bryson N. (1983) *Vision and Painting: The Logic of the Gaze*. Connecticut: Yale University Press.

Burbules N.C. (2000) Aporias, webs, and passages: doubt as an opportunity to learn. *Curriculum Inquiry*, 30(2): 171–187.

Burgoyne J. & Reynolds M. (eds) (1997) *Management Learning: Integrating Perspectives in Theory and Practice*. London: Sage.

Canaan J. (2005) Developing a pedagogy of critical hope. *Learning and Teaching in the Social Sciences*, 2(3): 159–174.

Carr-Saunders A.M. & Wilson P.A. (1933) *The Professions*. Oxford: Clarendon.

Cavanagh P. (2011) Visual cognition. *Vision Research*, 51(13): 1538–1551.

Coulter J. (2001) Human practice and the observability of the 'macro-social'. In T.R.

Schatzki, K.N. Cetina, & E. von Savigny (eds) *The Practice Turn in Contemporary Theory*. Abingdon: Routledge, pp. 29–41.

Craig D. (2012) Glance vs. gaze. An investigation into the visual performance of tourism to establish a way of looking through architecture that can cultivate a positive connection with the landscape. Submitted to Victoria University of Wellington, Master of Architecture [on-line]. Available from: http://aro-ha.com/documents/DuncanCraigThesis.pdf (accessed 1/4/2015).

Davies B. (2005) A manifesto for our time. *Youth & Policy*, 88: 5–27.

Davies B. (2010) What do we mean by youth work? In J. Batsleer, & B. Davies (eds) *What Is Youth Work?* Exeter: Learning Matters. pp. 1–6.

Dewey J. (1938) *Logic: The Theory of Inquiry*. New York: Henry Holt & Co.

Earl P.E. (2012) On Kahneman's thinking, fast and slow: what you see is not all there is. *Prometheus*, 30(4): 449–455.

Evetts J. (2003) The sociological analysis of professionalism: occupational change in the modern world. *International Sociology*, 18(2): 395–415.

Foucault M. (1975/1977) *Discipline and Punish*. London: Allen Lane.

Furlong J. (2000) Intuition and the crisis in teacher professionalism. In T. Atkinson & G. Claxton (eds) *The Intuitive Practitioner: On the Value of Not Always Knowing What One is Doing*. Berkshire: Open University Press. pp. 15–31.

Goffman E. (1963) *Behavior in Public Places: Notes on the Social Organisation of Gatherings*. New York: The Free Press.

Golby M. (1993) *Case Study as Educational Research*. London: Fairway Publications.

Greene M. (1978) *Landscapes of Learning*. New York: Teachers College.

Hargreaves J. (2004) So how do you feel about that? Assessing reflective practice. *Nurse Education Today*, 24(3): 196–210.

Heidegger M. (1945/2002) Heidegger on the art of teaching. Excerpt from the transcript of Prof. Dr. Martin Heidegger, submitted before the committee on de-nazification, Albert Ludwig University, Freiburg, IM Breisgau, July 23rd (Trans. V. Allen & A.D. Axiotis). In M.A. Peters (ed.) *Heidegger, Education and Modernity*. Lanham, MD:

Rowman & Littlefield Publishers Inc. pp. 27–46.

Herlihy J., Jobson L. & Turner S. (2012) Just tell us what happened to you: autobiographical memory and seeking asylum. *Applied Cognitive Psychology*, 26(5): 661–676.

Issett M. (2000) Critical professionals and reflective practice: the experience of women practitioners in health, welfare and education. In J. Batsleer & B. Humphries (eds) *Welfare, Exclusion and Political Agency*. London: Routledge. pp. 116–133.

Kahneman D. (2011) *Thinking Fast and Slow*. London: Penguin Books.

Kim H.S. (1999) Critical reflective inquiry for knowledge development in nursing practice. *Journal of Advanced Nursing*, 29(5): 1205–1212.

Kinsella E.A. (2007) Embodied reflection and the epistemology of reflective practice. *Journal of Philosophy of Education*, 41(3): 395–409.

Martin B. (2012) Kahneman in practice. *Prometheus*, 30(4): 457–460.

Mezirow J. (1981) A critical theory of adult learning and education. *Adult Education Quarterly*, 32(1): 3–24.

Mezirow J. & Associates (1990) (eds) *Fostering Critical Reflection in Adulthood: A Guide to Transformative and Emancipatory Learning*. San Francisco: Jossey-Bass.

Moon J. (1999) *Reflection in Learning and Professional Development: Theory and Practice*. London: Kogan Page.

Mulvey L. (1992) Visual pleasure and narrative cinema. In J. Caughie & A. Kuhn (eds) *The Sexual Subject: A Screen Reader in Sexuality*. London: Routledge. pp. 22–34.

Muskie (no initial) (2002) What is NT? Institute for the study of the neurological typical. [On-line] Available from: http://isnt.autistics.org/ (accessed 1/4/15).

National Occupation Standards for Youth Work (2012) [on-line]. Available from: http://www.nya.org.uk/wp-content/uploads/2014/06/National-Occupation-Standards-for-Youth-Work.pdf (accessed 4/4/16).

National Youth Agency (nd) Our purpose [on-line]. Available from: http://www.nya.org.uk/about-us/our-purpose/ (accessed 11/4/16).

O'Neill F.K. (2009) Bodily knowing as uncannily canny: clinical and ethical significance. In J.

Latimer & M.W. Schillmeier (eds) *Un/knowing Bodies*. Chichester: Blackwell. pp. 46–62.

Papell C. & Skolnik L. (1992) The reflective practitioner: a contemporary paradigm's relevance for social work education. *Journal of Social Work Education*, 28(1): 18–26.

Philippart F. (2003) Using Socratic dialogue. In S. Banks & K. Nøhr (eds) *Teaching Practical Ethics for the Social Professions*. European Social Education Training/Formation d'Educateur Sociaux Européens.

Pill R., Wainright P., McNamee M. & Pattison S. (2004) Understanding professions: professionals in the context of values. In S. Pattison & R. Pill (eds) *Values in Professional Practice: Lessons for Health, Social Care and Other Professionals*. Oxford: Radcliffe Publishing Ltd.

Proctor K. (1993) Tutors' professional knowledge of supervision and the implications for supervision practice. In J. Calderhead & P. Gate (eds) *Conceptualising Reflection in Teacher Development*. London: Falmer Press.

Quality Assurance Agency (2009) Subject benchmark statement: youth and community work [on-line]. Available from: http://www.qaa.ac.uk/en/Publications/Documents/Subject-benchmark-statement-Youth-and-community-work.pdf (accessed 4/4/16).

Rolfe G., Freshwater D. & Jasper M. (2001) *Critical Reflection for Nursing and the Helping Professions: A User's Guide*. Hampshire: Palgrave Macmillan.

Runswick-Cole K. (2014) 'Us' and 'them': the limits and possibilities of a 'politics of neurodiversity' in neoliberal times. *Disability and Society*, 29(7): 1117–1129.

Schatzki T.R. (2001a) Introduction: practice theory. In T.R. Schatzki, K. Knorr Cetina, & E. Von Svigny (eds) *The Practice Turn in Contemporary Theory*. London: Routledge. pp. 1–14.

Schatzki T.R. (2001b) Practice mind-ed orders. In T.R. Schatzki, K. Knorr Cetina, & E. Von Svigny (eds) *The Practice Turn in Contemporary Theory*. London: Routledge. pp. 42–55.

Schön D.A. (1983) *The Reflective Practitioner: How Professionals Think in Action*. London: Avebury.

Schön D. (1995) The new scholarship requires a new epistemology. *Change*, 27(6): 27–34 [on-line]. Available from: http://bonnernetwork.pbworks.com/w/file/fetch/59896448/Schoen%2520Scholarship%2520New%2520Epistemology.pdf (accessed 4/4/16).

Shohet P. & Hawkins R. (1989) *Supervision in the Helping Professions*. Bucks: Open University Press.

Smith M.K. (1988) *Developing Youth Work: Informal Education, Mutual Aid and Popular Practice*. Milton Keynes: Open University Press.

Spry T. (2011) *Body, Paper, Stage: Writing and Performing Autoethnography*. Walnut Creek, CA: Left Coast Press.

Thompson S. & Thompson N. (2008) *The Critically Reflective Practitioner*. Basingstoke: Palgrave Macmillan.

Tonso K.L. (2008) Learning to be engineers: how engineer identity embodied expertise, gender and power. In P. Murphy & R. McCormick (eds) *Knowledge and Practice: Representations and Identities*. London: Sage. pp. 152–165.

Trelfa J. (2016) Whatever happened to reflective practice? Current issues and new thoughts on reflective practice. *Journal of Research Institute*, 53: 79–102, Kobe City University of Foreign Studies, Japan [on-line]. Available from: https://kobe-cufs.repo.nii.ac.jp/?action=repository_opensearch&index_id=500

Trelfa J. & Telfer H. (2014) Keeping the cat alive: 'getting' reflection as part of professional practice. In Z. Knowles, D. Gilbourne, B. Cropley & L. Dugdill (eds) *Reflective Practice in the Sports and Exercise Sciences: Contemporary Issues*. London: Routledge. pp. 47–55.

Vaquez Bronfman S. (2005) A Heideggerian perspective on reflective practice and its consequences for learning design. The 11th Cambridge International Conference on Open and Distance Learning. Collected Conference Papers, pp. 13–18. Milton Keynes: The Open University Press.

27

The Challenges for British Youth Workers of Government Strategies to 'Prevent Terrorism'[1]

Paul Thomas

INTRODUCTION

Terrorism, more specifically Islamist terrorism, has been portrayed as one of the greatest challenges facing Western countries since the start of the 21st century. Initially, this Islamist terrorist threat was understood, in the wake of the 9/11 attacks on New York, as something perpetrated by non-Western immigrants. However, it has since been revealed as a domestic threat also, with small but significant numbers of citizens in Western states attempting to carry out Islamist-inspired terrorist acts in their own countries and/or travelling to join foreign conflicts in support of Islamist groups such as ISIS. Alongside this is a growing neo-Nazi terror threat. These threats have been portrayed as the 'new terrorism' (Neumann, 2011), although both the 'newness' and the actual scale of it, as well as the legitimacy of the overwhelming policy response focus on Islamist, rather than broader forms of extremism and terrorism, have been highly contested (Kundnani, 2014; Thomas, 2012).

Within these resulting counter-terrorism policy responses by Western states, the most interesting aspect has been the very significant focus on preventative policies, attempts to prevent domestic terrorist threats at source through programmes of community engagement and education. Britain was the originator of such post-9/11 policies through its 'Prevent' Strategy (previously known as PVE: Preventing Violent Extremism) (DCLG, 2007a; HMG, 2011). Initiated in 2007, Prevent has subsequently been highly influential on the preventative, or 'soft', counter-terrorism strategies adopted by many other Western countries (e.g. Government of Canada, 2011; Ragazzi, 2014). Youth work and youth workers have played a significant role in Britain's Prevent programme, particularly in its initial phase, and the problematic challenges faced by, and experiences of, youth workers have contributed to the highly controversial and contested public image of Prevent (House of Commons, 2010; Kundnani, 2009; OSFJI, 2016).

This chapter aims to explain and critically analyse the challenges Prevent has posed for British youth work. Here, it focuses on Britain, rather than the UK, because Northern Ireland has faced a very different type of domestic terrorism and is consequently not covered by the Prevent strategy (HMG, 2011). In particular, the chapter identifies four key challenges: operational, conceptual, securitisation and pedagogical, that Prevent has had for British youth workers and their organisations. On the basis of youth work's experience of confronting these challenges, it questions the ethical and policy basis for Britain's Prevent programme and offers a cautionary tale for youth workers in other countries who might be directed to support programmes countering violent extremism. To do this, the chapter first factually outlines the nature and content of Britain's Prevent programme. It then uses the four challenges outlined above to critically discuss Prevent's interface with British youth work and youth workers and the ethical dilemmas these four challenges have produced for professional and voluntary youth workers in Britain.

BRITAIN'S PREVENT PROGRAMME

The development of Britain's Prevent programme can be charted through two distinct phases. 'Prevent 1' ran from its inception under the then Labour government in 2007 until the 2011 Prevent Review (HMG, 2011) initiated by the new Conservative-Liberal Democrat Coalition government. 'Prevent 2' has run from 2011 to date. Whilst there have been some aspects of continuity within and between these phases, there have also been significant adjustments during each phase. These adjustments partly reflect unexpected events – Britain did not originally envision a domestic threat and so had to rapidly create Prevent in the wake of the 7/7 London

attacks of July 2005 (Hewitt, 2008); similarly, the Syria/ISIS crisis has provided new challenges. These adjustments also reflect tensions and different perspectives within national government (between different government departments and between different political parties during the 2010–2015 Coalition government: Thomas, 2012; 2014), and particularly between the national state and the local government bodies being asked to implement Prevent.

Prevent 1 was rapidly operationalised through an initial 'pathfinder' year of 2007–2008 and then significantly expanded between the 2008 and 2011 period (Husband and Alam, 2011; Thomas, 2012). This development involved funding to all local authority areas having a certain number of Muslim residents via the Department for Communities and Local Government (DCLG), attempts to develop more polyphonic consultation structures with Muslim communities (particularly with women and young people) both nationally and locally, state promotion of more 'moderate' forms of Islamic practice through initiatives such as the 'Radical Middle Way' roadshow and over 300 dedicated police posts via the security-focused Home Office and its Office for Security and Counter-Terrorism (OSCT). Together, this programme represented almost £150 millions of spending on a programme purely concerned with community engagement, rather than crime detection (Thomas, 2012). Local authorities took a variety of approaches, with some distributing all monies to Muslim community organisations (Kundnani, 2009), while others used it to develop their own programmes, including around the development of Muslim civil society, such as greater training for staff of Mosque schools (Thomas, 2008). A significant priority nationally was developing contact with Muslim young people through youth work (e.g. Lowndes and Thorp, 2010), with virtually all the funded local authorities using their youth work teams (organised in a variety of ways, reflecting both the contingent nature of local state support for youth work in different localities and the variety of national funding streams used to support this local provision) as the key vehicle for establishing and developing this contact. For both Muslim civil society organisations and Youth Work departments within local government, this Prevent funding came just as public spending was being cut, making involvement in Prevent hard to refuse (Ragazzi, 2014). The tactical reasons why the local state foregrounded their youth workers within Prevent are explored below, but indisputably this put youth workers in the front-line of Prevent's implementation.

The rapidly increasing dominance of the police in the direction of local Prevent work prompted hostile media coverage, accusations of 'spying' in youth work settings (Kundnani, 2009) and a critical Parliamentary Select Committee Inquiry (House of Commons, 2010). The incoming Coalition government first paused the programme then launched a revised 'Prevent 2' in June 2011 (HMG, 2011). This removed the DCLG from the programme and focused on a significantly smaller number of local authorities, supposedly identified on an intelligence basis, with much reduced funding. Funding for this work was to be centrally controlled by the OSCT, with this and the continuing police element of Prevent emphasising the increasingly securitised nature of the programme. Prevent 2 supposedly addresses all forms of extremism but, in practice, the focus has remained overwhelmingly on Islamist extremism, and so on Muslim communities. A new priority was the 'Channel' project, a scheme whereby young people viewed as 'vulnerable' to radicalisation would be referred by ground-level professionals, such as youth workers and teachers, for individual counselling. This was supported by training for front-line professionals across the education and health sectors (on a very large scale) on how to spot signs of individual 'radicalisation' (itself a highly-contested concept: Kundnani, 2012).

Nevertheless, the public profile of Prevent seemed to be reducing until the twin events of the 2013 Islamist murder of a soldier named Lee Rigby in London and the Syria crisis led to a re-energising and re-growth of Prevent (HMG, 2013). In particular, the focus was now on a new (and internationally unprecedented) legal duty on all schools, universities and other public bodies such as youth services to 'have due regard to the need to prevent people from being drawn into terrorism' (HMG, 2015: 2), to 'safeguard' people against extremism and to implement Prevent. This was supported by a significantly-expanded programme of the 'WRAP' (Workshop to Raise Awareness of Prevent) radicalisation awareness training for very large numbers of educators and health staff. The possible impacts of this legal duty within education were highlighted by a hard-hitting report (Open Society Foundation Justice Initiative, 2016) that detailed individual examples of unwarranted Channel referrals of Muslim youth based on flimsy or even non-existent evidence (some of these are disputed; see Busher et al., 2017 for empirical data on the duty's implementation in formal education). Whilst the publicised examples stemming from this highly-questionable 'pre-crime' surveillance of youth have come from formal education so far, youth work is likely to be similarly implicated.

OPERATIONAL CHALLENGES

The significant role given to youth work in 2007, as Britain's Prevent programme launched, reflected longer-term operational dilemmas and challenges for state-funded youth work in Britain. In particular, those challenges centred on what state-funded youth work is for and what contribution state funders expect from professional youth workers and their local authority employers. In his sweeping history of the English state-funded Youth Service (the three constituent nations of Britain have always had different youth work arrangements and

these differences have grown more pronounced through formal devolution over the
past twenty years), Davies (1999) highlights
how much of the state-funded youth provision assumed a buoyant youth employment
market. Here, open access, leisure-based
youth clubs were spaces for young people
already in employment (or soon to be) to
socialise with their peers. This model came
under threat in the 1980s as Britain's youth
employment market collapsed through neoliberal, state-sanctioned de-industrialisation.
Mizen (2004) charts how this raised profound questions around the purpose of state-
funded youth work, with the price of
continued state funding being the deployment of youth workers in overt support of
state education and training strategies. Here,
youth workers were to use their established
networks and proven skills of relationship
building with socially marginalised young
people to encourage young people to stay in
the post-16 training or further education now
seen as a necessary pathway to any prospect
of paid employment in the new reality of
severely delayed youth transitions (Furlong
and Cartmel, 2007).

This was seen most clearly under the
Labour government of 1997–2010 and their
'social exclusion' policy agenda. Youth
workers played a central role in key parts
of this policy agenda, including the drive to
reduce teenage pregnancies, efforts to edu-
cationally re-engage so-called 'NEETs' (Not
in Education, Employment or Training), and
roles within formal education doing preventative work with individuals at risk of educational disaffection and school exclusion and
providing the actual alternative education
programme for those young people excluded
by their school. Under the New Labour
regime, this youth work contribution was
increasingly organised under the 'targeted
youth support' label. These roles, especially
the 'Connexions' strategy associated with the
NEET programme, brought very significant
amounts of new money into state-funded
youth work but came at a considerable price

(see DfEE, 2002 and the critique of it in
Smith, 2002). The first consequence was that
youth workers became part of overt monitoring and reporting regimes, for instance
around ambitious local teen pregnancy reduction targets and close scrutiny of the trajectory of each NEET young person. The second
interrelated consequence of such work was
its significant escalation of an individualising focus within youth work (Smith, 2002),
with youth progress out of social exclusion
apparently being dependent on individual
youth agency and coaching/monitoring by
the youth worker rather than on state action
over structural inequalities and lack of opportunities. Here, the first duty of youth workers had apparently become fulfilment of state
targets, rather than the relationship-building
with young people described in youth work
theory (Smith, 2002).

This new role meant that youth work was
the prime candidate to lead local implementation of the Prevent strategy. Youth work
was seen as the vehicle for 'engaging' with
Muslim young people, one of Prevent's key
aims. All local authorities with a certain number of Muslim residents (itself a crude and
stigmatising basis for policy that reveals the
lack of meaningful intelligence about actual
terrorism) received funding, and almost all
used this to fund programmes of work by
their own youth services. Additionally, some
passed money on to local Muslim community organisations, again largely for youth-
focused programmes.

The scale of this new Prevent strategy
should not be underestimated, with a
government-evaluation of the initial
'Pathfinder' year (DCLG, 2008) boasting of
making contact with almost 50,000 young
Muslims nationally. My own evaluation
of one local authority in northern England
(Thomas, 2008) highlighted how their youth
service used their existing citizenship-based
work to develop programmes with wider
groups of Muslim youth. Similarly, Lowndes
and Thorp (2010) charted Prevent's impact
on youth work within the three cities of

their case study region. For one city in particular, Prevent enabled their youth service to develop relationships with Muslim young people previously unknown to them: 'City C recorded a dramatic 87% increase in the uptake of youth services by Muslim young people: from 231 in February 2007 to 432 in February 2008' (Lowndes and Thorp, 2010: 136). This enhanced work included self-esteem work with Muslim young women through residential settings, as well as anger management and boxing coaching with Muslim young men – in short, traditional youth work.

The London borough of Tower Hamlets passed much of their Prevent funding on to local Muslim faith organisations for youth-focused work, so enabling a much higher profile for faith organisations within local government (Iacopini et al., 2011). There was also a strong role for the local authority youth service, despite external evaluators highlighting how: '[t]he Youth Service's perspective seems to challenge the underlying need for Prevent work in the borough in that Islamic extremism may not necessarily be the issue that requires more attention than other broader range of risks/vulnerabilities' (Iacopini et al., 2011: 14). This led to the evaluation (2011: 23) identifying tension between the youth service and the police/local authority leads on Prevent over what could and should realistically be achieved through such activity. In reality, the combination of Muslim community suspicion from the start over Prevent's intention and the difficulty of actually operationalising the flawed model of 'radicalisation' (Kundnani, 2012) to identify which individuals were actually vulnerable, led Tower Hamlets youth workers to have to 'embed' Prevent within normal youth work sessions to get any take-up: 'we used the money for the worker to do a football game after the session as an incentive for people to attend it' (Youth Work project lead quoted in Iacopini et al., 2011: 29).

Similar embedding within 'normal' youth work was found in Kirklees, West Yorkshire

(Thomas, 2008), with another commonality being the reluctance of youth workers to actually use the PVE (later Prevent) name in work with young people – 'pathfinder project' was the opaque title used in Kirklees. Arun Kundnani's (2009) exposée of Prevent, *Spooked*, quotes a youth project manager as saying: 'The work that we do would be discredited, doors would be shut in our face, if people knew that we were Prevent-funded' (cited in Kundnani, 2009: 17).

The lack of transparency within youth work's operationalisation of Prevent was troubling. Here, such capacity and relationship-building through youth work, and the significant funding it involved for both statutory and voluntary sector youth work organisations, could be seen as positive, but the funding for this youth work activity came through an overtly counter-terrorism programme, so posing local authority and voluntary sector youth workers and their organisations with profound ethical dilemmas (Banks, 1999) that went beyond clear connection to wider state policies of 'employability'. In their provocatively-titled essay, 'Resourcing youth work: Dirty hands and tainted money', Jeffs and Smith (1999: 64) pose two fundamental questions to be considered when external funding for youth work is offered: 'Does taking money from certain sources seriously undermine the moral authority of the workers? Does the form funding takes stigmatise the young people?' It is beyond dispute that Prevent was highly controversial from the start, given the fundamental conceptual flaws explored in this chapter. Both the increasing securitisation of the programme's contact with young people and its overt, large-scale focus on young Muslims as inherently 'risky' (Heath-Kelly, 2013), suggest that both of Jeffs and Smith's questions should be answered in the affirmative regarding Prevent. In defence of local authorities, their great reluctance to operationalise Prevent was forcibly overruled by the national state (Thomas, 2012). For Muslim community and youth organisations, there were profound tensions and disagreements over whether to take Prevent money. Some refused point-blank, but others energetically accepted the funding, telling non-Muslim groups, 'Hands off – this is Muslim money' (cited in Lowndes and Thorp, 2010: 134) and seeing it as the one chance to benefit from explicitly Muslim-focused state aid, at a time of wider spending cuts (Ragazzi, 2014). For M.G. Khan, founder of the UK's Muslim Youth Work Foundation, this early acceptance of Prevent funding for community-based youth work was both hypocritical and troubling:

> While there has been consistent condemnation of the use of lottery funding (Britain's National Lottery makes funding from its profits available to charities) by Muslim clergy due to it being seen as 'gambling money', there seems to be comparative silence in relation to PVE funding. (2013: 161)

The development of the Prevent initiative also raised broader, uncomfortable questions and challenges for youth work that are explored below. These include the reality that these significant programmes were for Muslim youth only, so blatantly contradicting wider state approaches to 'community cohesion' (Cantle, 2001; Thomas, 2011), and that they have also led to a clear and significant 'securitisation' (Huysmans, 2009) of youth work's practice with Muslim young people through both the overt involvement of police/security personnel and their demands on youth workers and other professionals to spot and report supposed 'radicalisation' amongst youth. This has involved youth work in Prevent's operationalisation of the highly contested model of 'radicalisation' (Kundnani, 2012) and in an effective characterisation of British Muslims per se as a 'suspect community' (Hickman et al., 2010). On the basis of this critique, many Muslim community organisations refused Prevent funding, but local authority youth workers and their organisations have had no such choice, so effectively becoming part of a new security state.

CONCEPTUAL CHALLENGES

This highly problematic operational role and challenge for youth work stemming from Prevent has also contained what can be termed conceptual challenges. Here, Prevent's initial monocultural focus on Muslims as an essentialised and undifferentiated community directly challenged how youth work, in both theory and practice, has understood and approached young people within Britain's increasingly diverse, multicultural society. Prevent's initial focus on the attitudes and dispositions of British Muslims was overt, with an early government briefing document speaking of the need for: 'demonstrable changes in attitudes amongst Muslims' (DCLG, 2007b: 7). The large-scale engagement with Muslim youth identified above went alongside very significant attempts to create different forms of local and national Muslim leadership, and even state attempts to encourage more 'moderate' forms of worship. The late sociologist Stuart Hall described this package of interventions as 'the most profound internal penetration of an ethnic community' under British multiculturalism (BBC Radio 4, 2011). This focus on Muslims may seem self-evident, given the Islamist threat domestically and internationally, but a very significant number of individuals involved in such terrorism have either been converts or have shown no signs whatsoever of actual Islamic observance or knowledge. Additionally, far-right terrorism is a real and growing threat. Above all, there are profound questions over whether more work with Muslims only is a helpful or realistic way to address the challenge of Islamist violence.

Important here is Prevent's contradiction with Britain's post-2001 multiculturalist policy strategy of 'community cohesion'. This new direction was adopted after riots in northern towns in the summer of 2001 largely involving Muslim young people, and has, in itself, been significantly controversial. The post-riots government reports (Cantle, 2001;

Denham, 2001) identified how previous multiculturalist policy approaches had apparently confirmed and deepened ethnic divides through their focus on the needs of and facilities for distinct and essentialised ethnic 'communities'. This analysis of 'parallel lives' (Cantle, 2001) clearly indicated that strong prejudices about others and moves towards extreme positions are more likely in highly segregated, monocultural communities where norms and assumptions go unchallenged. Such policies had been mirrored by ethnic-specific youth provision in Britain, both a reflection of residential ethnic segregation and a youth work policy belief in the need to work separately with ethnic minority youth (Davies, 1999). The new approach of community cohesion instead foregrounded commonality and the need to build 'shared values'. Such a focus, alongside the explicit moving away from the language of 'multiculturalism' and 'diversity', led some critics to see this new approach as a shift back towards colour-blind assimilationism (Back et al., 2002) that denied both differences and the continued existence of racism.

However, empirical evidence on how youth work was actually understanding and operationalising community cohesion indicates a more positive interpretation. Thomas's (2011) study of youth work in Oldham, Greater Manchester (scene of one of the 2001 riots) highlighted significant youth worker support for the analysis and approach of community cohesion. Here, both the local authority youth service and voluntary sector youth organisations had made community cohesion part of everything they did. Rather than denying difference, they were acknowledging and even celebrating specific youth ethnic and faith identities but were augmenting them with stronger forms of commonality, whilst continuing to challenge racism and intolerance of all types. This was being operationalised through youth programmes based on 'contact theory' (Hewstone et al., 2007), a social psychology-based approach to prejudice reduction. Programmes of experiential youth activities – in many ways traditional, association-based youth work (Smith, 2002) – were used to create safe spaces where contact and dialogue between young people of different ethnic backgrounds (in itself a challenge in a highly segregated town) could take place without any young people feeling threatened or under pressure. Such an approach was understood by the youth workers interviewed as being congruent with core youth work approaches of voluntary association, relationship-building and an experiential curriculum. There was also congruence over the conception of youth identity being deployed. This community cohesion approach saw youth identities as complex and contingent, implicitly working with human-rights-based understandings of individual identity complexity and the need for 'cooler' specific ethnic/faith identities (McGhee, 2010) whilst also acknowledging the lived reality of such group identities (Thomas, 2011). Whilst it is hard to 'prove' that terrorism can be linked to profound ethnic segregation and racial tension, it is clear that wider 'extremism' and intolerance of others stems from such conditions (Eatwell and Goodwin, 2010).

This youth worker support for community cohesion was mirrored by other empirical studies drawing on wider groups of community workers and local officials (Jones, 2013), and it meant that youth workers immediately saw Prevent's monocultural focus on Muslim youth as a counter-productive contradiction. Local authorities in West Yorkshire opposed the creation of Prevent, wanting instead to use community cohesion as a vehicle for anti-extremism work (Husband and Alam, 2011). Some local authorities, such as Rochdale in Greater Manchester initially used Prevent funding to do identity-focused youth work with young people of *all* ethnic backgrounds, before this was explicitly outlawed by central government (Thomas and Sanderson, 2011). Prevent first side-lined the parallel policy approach of community cohesion (Thomas, 2014) before central government washed its hands of cohesion (DCLG, 2012), instead focusing on the now highly centralised Prevent strategy. Here, the remaining modest amounts of funding for local Prevent youth work for young people are rigidly controlled by security officials in London, with no deviation from centrally approved curriculum briefs.

SECURITISATION CHALLENGES

Hand-in-hand with Prevent's monocultural focus on Muslim youth that was imposed on youth workers has come an overt securitisation of youth workers' relationships with young people and their communities. This has subsequently been extended across the education and health sectors through the Prevent Duty (HMG, 2015). This latter development has arguably widened and deepened the securitisation process that Prevent has initiated within the British public sector in general, and within education and youth work in particular. Here, Prevent can be understood as being part of 'processes that securitise everyday relations through the circulation of unease' (Huysmans, 2009: 197). This has been done firstly through the overt involvement of the Police and Security services in the management and even delivery (Knight, 2010) of Prevent's community-based engagement, and latterly through the creation of strictures and an associated climate where all educators are required to 'spot' extremists. For Hussain and Bagguley, 'The securitisation perspective analyses the process by which an issue or group comes to be defined as a security threat so that government and societal resources can be mobilised to counter it' (2012: 76).

The section above highlighted the breadth and scale of Prevent's focus on British Muslims as an undifferentiated and essentialised 'community'. It is argued here that Prevent has involved British youth workers in a state characterisation and treatment of British Muslims as a 'suspect community',

in the way that Britain's Irish community was previously (Hickman et al, 2010). Whilst this analysis has been challenged by what O'Toole et al. (2016) describe as the 'contested practice' within Prevent 1 that saw some Muslim groups playing a leading role in local Prevent delivery, the developments of Prevent 2 around WRAP training and mass (mostly Muslim and many of them under the age of 18) referrals to 'Channel' seem, for many, to confirm this characterisation. Newman (2015) provides a graphic example of where Prevent's gaze is directed within education.

Youth Workers initially found themselves at the forefront of this securitisation process as Prevent was initiated via youth work settings. Counter-terrorism police were centrally involved in the multi-agency local Prevent management structures from the start and rapidly became the dominant player, as a study of Prevent implementation in the West Midlands highlights (Bahadur Lamb, 2012). This was both because of their superior resources and their cultural power of supposedly knowing about extremist threats but being unable or even unwilling to share it with local authority and community partners. For this reason, local empirical studies of Prevent implementation (Lowndes and Thorp, 2010; Iacopini et al, 2011; Husband and Alam, 2011) consistently highlight tensions between the police and local authority youth workers over the focus and effectiveness of projects, as highlighted above. This was clearly shown during the House of Commons Communities and Local Government Select Committee Inquiry into Prevent during 2009–2010 (House of Commons, 2010). Here, police evidence essentially characterised much local Prevent work as a failure because it was 'simply' cohesion work, when they wanted to see harder edged work with individuals supposedly 'at risk' of extremism:

> Much of the PVE funded project work in local areas does not have a specific enough focus on preventing violent extremism and many police authorities question whether, in practice, there is

any real difference between Prevent and community cohesion. (Association of Police Authorities, 2009: 142)

What they meant was that it was youth work with Muslim young people, the only approach local authorities saw as worth attempting, but it was certainly not 'cohesion' as it was with Muslims only! Local authorities, youth organisations and Muslim community groups all criticised Prevent during the Inquiry for very different reasons – that it only focused on Muslims, when they wanted to utilise cohesion approaches. That led me to characterise Prevent at the time as 'failed and friendless' (Thomas, 2010).

One of the key triggers for this Parliamentary Inquiry was a report (Kundnani, 2009) alleging police spying on youth workers and Muslim young people. Arun Kundnani, of the Institute of Race Relations, carried out in-depth interviews with 32 people involved in local Prevent delivery, most of them local authority or voluntary sector youth workers. Within their more general and highly-critical analysis of Prevent were specific allegations about the extent to which the police were expecting youth workers and their organisations to provide intelligence on Muslim young people. Whilst not having a problem with disclosing information when an individual was at concrete risk of involvement in criminality, these youth workers perceived that they were being asked to report on the basis of a much wider and vaguer concept of 'risk'. One youth work manager is quoted as saying:

You have to provide information if an individual is at risk. But you also need to give information about the general picture, right down to which street corners young people from different backgrounds are hanging around on, what mosques they go to and so on. (Kundnani, 2009: 28)

In another case, Prevent funding was approved for a youth centre in a northern town and '"intelligence gathering" was stated as one of the rationales for the centre' (Kundnani, 2009: 29).

Such police expectations of intelligence sharing clearly cut across established youth work professional norms of confidentiality and respecting the wishes of young people. Youth workers also recounted being quizzed by police about their own political and religious views if they demonstrated a reluctance to share information, an echo of what Husband and Alam (2011) describe as the 'chilling effect' of Prevent on Muslim professionals used as sources of insight but not trusted themselves. Here, M.G. Khan succinctly summarises both this state pressure on Muslim-origin front-line professionals, including youth workers, and what he sees as the connivance by some of those professionals in malign state agendas in the:

blurring of the boundaries between personal and professional identities encouraged by employers and used reluctantly or proactively by Muslim, workers ... and with it, the presence of Prevent as an agenda present in the relationship. The trading on identity seemed to be encouraged to take agendas and information into Muslim communities and to mitigate against the impact of the counter-narrative. (Khan, 2013: 166)

A specific allegation of police/security service pressure was identified by Kundnani, whereby five Muslim youth workers in Camden, north London suffered intimidation and even blackmail by MI5 officers determined to turn them into informers. This case in particular brought the *Spooked* report significant media coverage and helped to provoke the Parliamentary Inquiry. At the time, the government categorically denied all charges of spying but Sir David Omand, the government's architect of Prevent, commented to the All-Party Parliamentary Group on Homeland Security in 2010 that:

you can't divide government in two, into those people that go around spying on the population, and there are another lot of people going round to the population and they just don't talk to each other. It just simply doesn't work like that. (APPGHS, 2011: 107)

Omand was even blunter in an interview given to the *Financial Times* weeks before that, when he suggested that it would be naïve of the state to not use any intelligence from community-based Prevent activities in the face of a very serious terrorist threat (Knight, 2010).

This securitising perspective can clearly be seen to have become overt since the 2011 Prevent Review and subsequent policy developments (HMG, 2013, 2015). The Prevent Duty has made providing intelligence to the Police regarding 'at risk' individuals a legal requirement for *all* state professionals. This is backed up by the large-scale WRAP training that some feel has a clear role in amplifying policy concerns about the threat from young Muslims (Blackwood et al., 2012). The initial result was predictable, with more overt Prevent/police involvement in schools (Taylor, 2015) and a large increase in referrals to the Channel scheme by teachers and youth workers, some of them so inappropriate and counter-productive that a comedy writer would struggle to invent them (BBC, 2016; Churchill, 2015; Dodd, 2015; OSFJI, 2016; although some individual cases quoted are disputed).

This significant development of surveillance within youth work and schools, and the large number of resulting referrals of (mostly) Muslim youth (2,127 under 15s and many others aged 16–20 years during 2015/16 alone) apparently confirms that British Muslims are now indeed a 'suspect community' (Hickman et al., 2010). However, this development also poses troubling questions for youth workers and other front-line educators – it is those individual practitioners who are judging individual Muslim young people to be 'risky' and in need of referral, and it is hard to show how the state has directly 'forced' such conduct through an overt use of disciplinary power (for example, see Newman, 2015). Relevant here, arguably, to an analysis of how Prevent has impacted on youth worker/teacher relations with Muslim young people are more complex notions of governmentality (McKee, 2009) that normalise a securitised focus on Muslims as a supposedly 'objective' threat. Here, Prevent can now be understood as neo-liberal governmentality, a policy approach by which front-line practitioners are 'responsibilised' for spotting radicalisation. For McKee (2009: 486), 'Governmentality does not restrict its analysis to the institutions of political power of the state. Rather, it defines the "art of governing" more broadly as the "conduct of conduct"'. In this way, Prevent has 'responsibilised' individual youth workers, teachers and lecturers with monitoring the conduct and disposition of Muslim young people. If a clear pattern of Islamophobic actions can be detected within such policy systems, they *appear* to be the work of individual educators, not the state. This malign impact of Prevent will only worsen until youth workers and other front-line professionals collectively take an ethical stand to question both the referral systems and their underlying logic.

PEDAGOGICAL CHALLENGES

Despite the malign impacts of Prevent on British youth work analysed above, the introduction of this counter-terrorism strategy to youth work spaces *might* be defended in that it has enabled opportunities for anti-extremism education (Davies, 2008). Youth workers, after all, are informal educators first and foremost and Prevent, in its first phase at least, enabled large-scale engagement with Muslim young people. However, in practice there has been little or no evidence of meaningful and overt programmes of anti-extremism education taking place within youth work. Additionally, the way the Prevent strategy characterises and approaches the attitudes and beliefs of young people is, it is argued here, fundamentally at odds with the approach and beliefs of youth work. Here, Prevent can be seen to be repeating the mistakes of previous attempts to operationalise 'anti-racist education' with white young people (Thomas, 2002).

Empirical evidence around the youth-work-based implementation of the Prevent 1 phase showed large-scale engagement with young people (DCLG, 2008) through traditional youth work methods (Thomas, 2008; Lowndes and Thorp, 2010; Iacopini et al., 2011) but little evidence of work that actually focused on the drivers and risks of extremism. That led me to argue that such work fell 'between two stools' (Thomas, 2009), in that it was neither cross-community cohesion work nor actual political education work with young Muslims. In fact, such evidence showed avoidance of the issues underpinning Prevent and youth worker uncertainty over what they were actually being asked to do (Thomas, 2008). This mirrors previous empirical research with youth workers in one region of northern England who mainly worked with marginalised white young people. These workers admitted avoidance and uncertainty over anti-racist educational work because they both lacked confidence and felt entirely uncertain over whether they had been given licence by management to engage in that sort of open and risky dialogue, with the inevitability of strong racist comments by some individuals (CRE, 1999; Thomas, 2002). For Davies (2008), such open dialogue and the absence of worker censure on strong expression is essential to create the conditions where young people are willing to share their prejudices and fears and take part in dialogue that enables them to re-think assumptions.

The absence of such educational dialogue was also identified by Hewitt's (2005) study of the operationalisation of 'anti-racism' within youth work and schools in Greenwich, south-east London. Hewitt found that youth workers and teachers believed anti-racism to be about disciplining and stopping any 'racist' expression or behaviour, rather than exploring it and seeking to change it through debate. The result was that white young people, particularly those from economically marginalised backgrounds, felt a profound 'sense of unfairness', believing that their

'racist' language and behaviour was judged much more harshly than any prejudices and violence from their ethnic minority peers. Such attitudes have been found in more recent, youth-work-based case study research in two areas of northern England (Thomas and Sanderson, 2013). In both cases, white young people felt that their entire community and culture was being negatively judged through the scale and manner of the policy focus.

Prevent can be seen to be replicating these failings, both in its stigmatising focus on young Muslims per se and in its lack of educational content. There has been no national attempt through Prevent to train or support youth workers, teachers and other educators to develop anti-extremism educational processes that can genuinely create resilience against extremist ideologies (Thomas, 2016). In the first phase of Prevent, the UK Youth Parliament, which is the national umbrella body for local youth representation structures, was one of the few Prevent-funded organisations to carry out such open political education dialogue, and with young people of all backgrounds. They subsequently requested funding to train youth workers nationally in facilitating such dialogue but were refused (House of Commons, 2010). Instead, good examples of genuine anti-extremism youth work with young people 'at risk' (Heath-Kelly, 2013) of involvement in extremism have come outside of Prevent funding structures, such as the Welsh 'THINK Project' (Cantle and Thomas, 2014).[1]

The absence of meaningful educational processes in Prevent 1 or tangible evidence as to what the funding had achieved enabled the overt shift towards securitised monitoring of young people within the current Prevent 2 phase. It is here that Prevent's assumptions, based on the flawed model of 'radicalisation' (Kundnani, 2012) can be seen as starkly at odds with youth work's conception of young people and their potential. The 'radicalisation' model offers a simplistic, binary understanding of young Muslims (which replicates anti-racism's binary understanding of young whites as either 'racist' or 'anti-racist') – they are either 'moderate' or 'radicalised', and if they are the latter, they need to be helped/forced to become the former. Its operationalisation through the WRAP training and the Channel process potentially sees any strong, political expression or interest in terrorist actions as prima facie evidence of 'radicalisation'. Relevant here is Cockburn's (2007) research with young activists of the neo-Nazi British National Party in Blackburn, northern England. Not only does Cockburn identify the dispositions of these supposedly far-right activists as fluid and contingent on spatial setting (they also have Asian friends!), but also as performative – their behaviour and even BNP membership can be understood partly as a performative response to Asian street-level rivals or disapproving authority figures. M.G. Khan graphically captures the dangers of such simplistic, external judgments on young peoples' dispositions when he identifies both the reality and, indeed, the importance of young people 'talking shit' (2013: 169) as part of their working out what they actually think and of building their relationships with youth workers and peers. It is the power of this sort of playful and possibly transgressive 'conversation' (Smith, 2002) that enables the possibility of meaningful anti-extremism education, but such open (and possibly performative) youth expression is precisely what Prevent sees as evidence of being 'at risk' of radicalisation and seeks to police through the Channel process. Alongside this, any 'radical' Muslim youth expression is seen as evidence of individual psychological vulnerability (Blackwood et al., 2012), rather than as a response to the collective, structural societal experiences and realities that, for youth work, shape young peoples' lives.

The very weak 'predictive power' of the radicalisation model to identify which individuals will move forward to terrorism highlights the caution needed around youth extremist expressions. Academic literature clearly identifies the lack of consensus of identifiable drivers of terrorism but there is much more consensus on the need for policy to build genuine individual and collective resilience against the appeal of extremism. Here, evidence points to the importance of facilitating both the learning of social respect and tolerance, and the skills of dealing with social, political and identity complexity (Grossman et al., 2016). This highlights the contribution youth work could make within more progressive and inclusive preventative approaches than that currently represented by Prevent.

CONCLUSION

The Prevent Strategy has been highly problematic for British youth workers and their organisations, raising profound ethical dilemmas and a variety of professional challenges, as outlined above. Particularly in its first phase, Prevent posed the increasingly common operational challenge for British youth work – what does the state want for its money? Significant and dedicated Prevent resources were supplied for youth work engagement with young Muslims, but the price was being part of a highly controversial and, for this author, stigmatising and counterproductive initiative. Here, youth work appeared to be the people 'doing' Prevent, with the ethical dilemmas particularly acute for Muslim professionals and Muslim-led youth and community organisations. Closely associated were conceptual challenges around Prevent's stark contradiction to, and undermining of, community cohesion multiculturalist policy approaches that had considerable support from youth workers (Thomas, 2011). Pedagogical challenges have centred on Prevent's simplistic, binary characterisation of young people, so denying the fluid, contingent and performative nature of youth identities and attitudes (Cockburn, 2007), alongside its failure to develop open and progressive forms of anti-extremism educational dialogue that youth work would see as the only realistic from of preventative work with young people. These challenges, core failings of Prevent, all contribute to the most profound failing of Prevent – the challenge of increasing securitisation and its inherent surveillance that Prevent has introduced to youth work's relationship with young Muslims and which have now been deepened by the Prevent legal duty.

Note

1   Funding declaration: the author and Ted Cantle were funded as consultants to the Think Project.

REFERENCES

All-Party Parliamentary Group on Homeland Security (APPGHS) (2011) *Keeping Britain Safe: An Assessment of UK Homeland Security Strategy*. London: The Henry Jackson Society.

Association of Police Authorities (2009) Evidence Memorandum to the House of Commons CLG Select Committee Inquiry to Prevent, in House of Commons (2010) p. Ev 142–145.

Back, L., Keith, M., Khan, A., Shukra, K. and Solomos, J. (2002) 'New Labour's white heart: Politics, multiculturalism and the return of assimilationism'. *Political Quarterly*, 73(4), pp. 445–454.

Bahadur Lamb, J. (2012) 'Preventing violent extremism: A policing case study of the West Midlands'. *Policing*, 7(1), pp. 88–95.

Banks, S. (ed.) (1999) *Ethical Issues in Youth Work*. London: Routledge.

BBC (2016) 'Lancashire "terrorist house" row "not a spelling mistake"', available at: http://www.bbc.co.uk/news/uk-england-lancashire-35354061

BBC Radio 4 (2011) *Thinking Allowed*, broadcast 16 March.

Blackwood, L., Hopkins, N. and Reicher, S. (2012) 'Divided by a common language? Conceptualising identity, discrimination and

alienation' in K. Jonas and T. Morton (eds.) *The Psychology of Intervention and Engagement Following Crisis*. London: Wiley, pp. 222–236.

Busher, J., Choudhury, T., Thomas, P. and Harris, G. (2017) *What the Prevent Duty means for Schools and Colleges in England: An analysis of educationalist's experiences*. Huddersfield: University of Huddersfield.

Cameron, D. (2015) 'Extremism speech', 20 July, Birmingham, available at: https://www.gov.uk/government/speeches/extremism-pm-speech

Cantle, T. (2001) *Community Cohesion – A Report of the Independent Review Team*. London: Home Office.

Cantle, T. and Thomas, P. (2014) *Taking the Think Project Forward: The Need for Preventative Anti-Extremism Educational Work*. Swansea: Ethnic Youth Support Team.

Churchill, D. (2015) 'London child aged THREE in terror alert over radicalisation', *Evening Standard*, 27 July, available at: http://www.standard.co.uk/news/london/london-child-aged-three-in-terror-alert-over-radicalisation-10418455.html

Cockburn, T. (2007) 'Performing racism: Engaging young supporters of the far right in England'. *British Journal of Sociology of Education*, 28(5), pp. 547–560.

Commission for Racial Equality (CRE) (1999) *Open Talk, Open Mind*. London: CRE.

Davies, B. (1999) *A History of the Youth Service in England, Volumes 1 & 2*. Leicester: Youth Work Press.

Davies, L. (2008) *Education against Extremism*. Stoke-on Trent: Trentham.

Denham, J. (2001) *Building Cohesive Communities – A Report of the Inter-Departmental Ministerial Group on Public Order and Community Cohesion*. London: Home Office.

Department for Communities and Local Government (DCLG) (2007a) *Preventing Violent Extremism: Winning Hearts and Minds*. London: DCLG.

DCLG (2007b) *Pathfinder Fund Guidance Note for Local Authorities*. London: DCLG.

DCLG (2008) *Prevent Pathfinder Fund – Mapping of Project Activities 2007/08*. London: DCLG.

DCLG (2012) *Creating the Conditions for Integration*. London: DCLG.

Department for Education and Employment (DfEE) (2002) *Transforming Youth Work: Resourcing Excellent Youth Services*. London: DfEE.

Dodd, V. (2015) 'School questioned Muslim pupil about ISIS after discussion on eco-activism', *The Guardian*, 22 September, available at: http://www.theguardian.com/education/2015/sep/22/school-questioned-muslim-pupil-about-isis-after-discussion-on-eco-activism (accessed 24 September 2015).

Eatwell, R. and Goodwin, M. (eds.) (2010) *The New Extremism in 21st Century Britain*. Abingdon: Routledge.

Furlong, A. and Cartmel, F. (2007) *Young People and Social Change: New Perspectives* (2nd edition). Maidenhead: Open University Press.

Government of Canada (2011) *Building Resilience against Terrorism: Canada's Counter-terrorism Strategy*. Ottawa: Government of Canada.

Grossman, M., Peucker, M., Smith, D. and Dellal, H. (2016) *Stocktake Research Project: A Systematic Literature and Selective Program Review of Social Cohesion, Community Resilience and Violent Extremism 2011–15*. State of Victoria: Melbourne.

Heath-Kelly, C. (2013) 'Counter-terrorism and the counter-factual: Producing the "radicalisation" discourse and the UK Prevent strategy'. *British Journal of Politics and International Relations*, 15(3), pp. 394–415.

Her Majesty's Government (HMG) (2011) *Prevent Strategy*. London: The Stationary Office.

HMG (2013) *Tackling Extremism in the UK: Report from the Prime Minister's Task Force on Tackling Radicalisation and Extremism*. London: HM Government, available at: https://www.gov.uk/government/uploads/system/uploads/attachment_data/file/263181/ETF_FINAL.pdf

HMG (2015) *Prevent Duty Guidance for England and Wales*. London: HM Government.

Hewitt, R. (2005) *White Backlash and the Politics of Multiculturalism*. Cambridge: Cambridge University Press.

Hewitt, S. (2008) *The British War on Terror: Terrorism and Counter-terrorism on the Home Front since 9/11*. London: Continuum.

Hewstone, M., Tausch, N., Hughes, J. and Cairns, E. (2007) 'Prejudice, Intergroup Contact and Identity: Do Neighbourhoods Matter?' In M. Wetherell, M. Lafleche and R. Berkley (eds.) *Identity, Ethnic Diversity and Community Cohesion*. London: Sage, pp. 102–112.

Hickman, M., Silvestri, S., Thomas, L. and Nickels, H. (2010) *'Suspect Communities': The Impact of Counter-terrorism on Irish Communities and Muslim Communities in Britain 1974–2007*, Paper presented at the British Sociological Association Annual Conference, Glasgow, 7 April.

Home Office (2003) *CONTEST: The Government's Counter-Terrorism Strategy*. London: The Home Office.

House of Commons Communities and Local Government Committee (2010) *Preventing Violent Extremism: Sixth Report of Session 2009–10*. London: The Stationery Office.

Husband, C. and Alam, Y. (2011) *Social Cohesion and Counter-terrorism: A Policy Contradiction?* Bristol: Policy Press.

Hussain, Y. and Bagguley, P. (2012) 'Securitised citizens: Islamophobia, racism and the 7/7 London bombings'. *The Sociological Review*, 60(4), pp. 715–734.

Huysmans, J. (2009) 'Conclusion: Insecurity and the Everyday' in P. Noxolo and J. Huysmans (eds.) *Community, Citizenship and the 'War on Terror': Security and Insecurity*. Basingstoke: Palgrave Macmillan, 196–207.

Iacopini, G., Stock, L. and Junge, K. (2011) *Evaluation of Tower Hamlets Prevent Projects*. London: Tavistock Institute.

Jeffs, T. and Smith, M. (1999) 'Resourcing youth work: Dirty hands and tainted money' in S. Banks (ed.) *Ethical Issues in Youth Work*. London: Routledge, pp. 55–74.

Jones, H. (2013) *Negotiating Cohesion, Inequality and Change: Uncomfortable Positions in Local Government*. Bristol: Policy Press.

Khan, M.G. (2013) *Young Muslims, Pedagogy and Islam: Contexts and Concepts*. Bristol: Policy Press.

Knight, S. (2010) 'Preventing violent extremism in Britain', *Financial Times Magazine*, 26 February, available at: http://www.ft.com/cms/s/0/1e684162-1f94-11df-8975-00144feab49a.html

Kundnani, A. (2009) *Spooked: How Not to Prevent Violent Extremism*. London: Institute of Race Relations.

Kundnani, A. (2012) 'Radicalisation: The journey of a concept'. *Race and Class*, 54(2), pp. 3–25.

Kundnani, A. (2014) *The Muslims Are Coming! Islamophobia, Extremism and the Domestic War on Terror*. London: Verso.

Lowndes, V. and Thorp, L. (2010) 'Preventing violent extremism – why local context matters', in Eatwell and Goodwin (eds.) *The New Extremism in 21st Century Britain*. Abingdon: Routledge, 123–141.

McGhee, D. (2010) *Security, Citizenship and Human Rights: Shared Values in Uncertain Times*. Basingstoke: Palgrave Macmillan.

McKee, K. (2009) 'Post-Foucauldian governmentality: What does it offer critical social policy analysis?' *Critical Social Policy*, 29(3), pp. 465–486.

Meer, N. and Modood, T. (2009) 'The multicultural state we're in: Muslims, "multiculture" and the "civic re-balancing" of British multiculturalism'. *Political Studies*, 57(3), pp. 473–497.

Mizen, P. (2004) *The Changing State of Youth*. Basingstoke: Palgrave Macmillan.

Neumann, P. (2011) *Preventing Violent Radicalisation in America*. Washington DC: National Security Preparedness Group.

Newman, M. (2015) 'Preventing far right extremism? Schools in EDL and BNP heartland only monitoring ethnic minority pupils', *The Bureau of Investigative Journalism*, available at: https://www.thebureauinvestigates.com/2015/03/31/prevent-policy-schools-barnsley-edl-bnp-heartland/ (accessed 27 April 2015).

Open Society Foundation Justice Initiative (OSFJI) (2016) *Eroding Trust: The UK's Prevent Counter-extremism Strategy in Health and Education*. New York: OSCJI.

O'Toole, T., Meer, N., DeHanas, D., Jones, S. and Modood, T. (2016) 'Governing through Prevent? Regulation and Contested Practice in State-Muslim Engagement'. *Sociology*, 50(1), pp. 160–177.

Ragazzi, F. (2014) *Towards 'Policed Multiculturalism'? Counter-radicalisation in France, the Netherlands and the United Kingdom*. Paris: SciencesPo.

Smith, M.K. (2002) 'Transforming youth work – resourcing excellent youth services: A critique', *the informal education homepage*, available at: www.infed.org/youthwork/transforming_youth_work_2.htm

Taylor, D. (2015) 'Fury after primary pupils are asked to complete radicalisation-seeking surveys', *The Guardian*, 28 May, available at: http://www.theguardian.com/education/2015/may/28/fury-after-primary-pupils-are-asked-to-complete-radicalisation-seeking-surveys

Thomas, P. (2002) 'Youth work, racist behaviour and young people – education or blame?' *Scottish Journal of Youth Issues*, 4, pp. 49–66.

Thomas, P. (2008) *Kirklees Preventing Violent Extremism Pathfinder: Issues and Learning from the First Year*. Huddersfield: University of Huddersfield.

Thomas, P. (2009) 'Between two stools? The Government's Preventing Violent Extremism agenda'. *The Political Quarterly*, 80(2), pp. 482–492.

Thomas, P. (2010) 'Failed and friendless – the government's Preventing Violent Extremism agenda'. *British Journal of Politics and International Relations*, 12(3), pp. 442–458.

Thomas, P. (2011) *Youth, Multiculturalism and Community Cohesion*. Basingstoke: Palgrave Macmillan.

Thomas, P. (2012) *Responding to the Threat of Violent Extremism – Failing to Prevent*. London: Bloomsbury Academic.

Thomas, P. (2014) 'Divorced but still co-habiting? Britain's Prevent/community cohesion tensions'. *British Politics*, 9(4), pp. 472–493.

Thomas, P. (2016) 'Youth, terrorism and education: Britain's Prevent programme'. *International Journal of Lifelong Education*, Special Issue on 'Youth, Social Crisis and Learning', 35(2), pp. 171–187.

Thomas, P. and Sanderson, P. (2011) 'Unwilling citizens? Muslim young people and national identity'. *Sociology*, 45(6), pp. 1028–1044.

Thomas, P. and Sanderson, P. (2013) Crossing the Line? White Young people and community cohesion'. *Critical Social Policy*, 33(1), pp. 160–180.

28

The Politics of Gang Intervention in New England, USA: Knowledge, Partnership and Youth Transformation

Ellen Foley, Angel Guzman, Miguel Lopez,
Laurie Ross, Jennifer Safford-Farquharson,
Katie Byrne, Egbert Pinero and Ron Waddell

INTRODUCTION

Gang violence intervention has long been the domain of law enforcement. Police and the courts utilize suppression (e.g. gang member identification, surveillance, intelligence gathering, arrest, and sentencing) to get gang members off the streets and disrupt illegal activities. Yet, there is growing recognition that suppression alone is inadequate to prevent gang-related violence over the long term (Peaslee, 2009). A strategy that has shown promise to reduce gang violence is intensive, targeted street outreach. Not all street outreach models, however, are effective in reducing gang violence and criminal activity. 'Detached' street outreach for gang intervention may strengthen the cohesiveness of gangs and in some cases even increase violent criminal behavior (Braga, 2016; Kennedy, 2011; Klein, 1971). Spergel (2007) concludes that, 'neither a single-minded suppression nor a single-minded social-intervention approach has demonstrated

success in reducing gang crime, especially gang violence' (p. 25). Alternatively, street outreach workers (SOWs) that are part of a coordinated, multi-sector approach can be an important component of reducing gang-related violence, shootings, and crime (Decker, Bynum, McDevitt, Farrell, & Varano, 2008; Frattaroli et al., 2009; McGarrell et al., 2012; Skogan, Hartnett, Bump, & Dubois, 2008; Spergel, 1995).

Yet, SOWs navigate a tricky space in these partnerships. They have to be seen as legitimate and effective by two groups that are often in conflict with each other – police officers and gang members (Whitehill, Webster, Frattaroli, & Parker, 2013; Wolf & Gutierrez, 2011). SOWs who are former gang members, have a criminal history, or share other socio-demographic characteristics with gang-involved youth may not be viewed by police as credible partners in violence prevention (Fox, 1991; Kotlowitz, 2008; Wolf & Gutierrez, 2011). SOWs typically have nuanced and extensive knowledge of gangs and gang members, yet police may not value their information or insight (Rios & Navarro, 2010). Police become frustrated when outreach workers learn about violent incidents before they do. Police may also believe that the outreach process lacks transparency and clear goals and outcomes (Decker, Bynum, McDevitt, Farrell, & Varano, 2008). In gang intervention work, these different views and roles create barriers to collaboration (Patterson, 2004; Thatcher, 2001). In the best case scenario, police and SOWs have mutual respect and operate with a clear understanding of their crucial yet distinct roles in violence prevention (Arciaga and Gonzalez, 2012). Yet often, outreach workers are seen by police to be walking a fine line between mediating violence and condoning it (Braga, 2016; Kennedy, 2011; Kotlowitz, 2008).

This chapter explores how SOWs attempt to establish personal, professional, and institutional legitimacy working in partnership with police on a youth violence intervention program located in a mid-sized (180,000 residents), post-industrial city in New England, USA. Co-authored by three street outreach workers, the coordinator of our citywide street outreach team, a Gang Unit police sergeant, and two university-based research partners, we offer our reflections about our experience working together since 2012 on a state-funded program to reduce criminal behavior and violence among very high risk and gang involved young men. Partners focus on approximately one hundred young men aged 17–24 who are most likely to be victims or perpetrators of gun or knife violence and who are often gang-involved.[1] Ninety-eight percent of these men are Latino or African American. The police department provides

limited information to the partners on the young men identified for this program. The program uses intensive street outreach and case management to build relationships and to connect young men to needed services such as mental health, substance abuse, education, and employment with the purpose of reducing their involvement in criminal and violent behavior.

Our aim in this piece is to collectively produce a deeper understanding of how street outreach workers and police conceptualize their roles, the challenges of working with young people, and the obstacles to police and SOW partnerships. The co-authors engaged in a series of dialogues to co-produce a different analysis than that of university partners studying the various actors in youth violence interventions. Taking seriously Patricia Hill Collins's (2015) assertion that intersectional approaches are a knowledge project, we tried to counter the fact that, 'individuals and groups differentially placed within intersecting systems of power have different points of view on their own and others' experiences, typically advancing knowledge projects that reflect their social locations within power relations' (14). Using a collaborative, dialogic approach, we sought to identify shared understandings of our work as well as the ways that our distinct social positions and experiences would impede such shared understandings.[2] Table 28.1 provides brief background information about the program participants featured in this chapter.

Through these dialogues, we learned how outreach workers gain credibility with young people while working in the liminal space between gang-involved youth and law enforcement. We came to realize that this

Table 28.1   Guide to participant's names and roles

Pseudonym	Race/Ethnicity	Role	Length of experience in role
Luis	Latino	Outreach worker	20 years
Eduardo	Latino	Outreach worker	2 years
William	African American	Outreach worker	6 months
Antonio	Latino	Gang unit officer	19 years

space is one with great potential for innovation, creativity, and transformative relationships with marginalized young people. Our conversations also deepened our understanding of the challenges in police–SOW partnerships that also have been identified by other scholars (e.g. Wolf & Gutierrez, 2011).

Examples of the challenges we explore in this chapter include: differing beliefs about youth capacity for change, conflicting views about street outreach and the expertise of outreach workers, and the different advantages and constraints that stem from being situated inside or outside of formal institutions. The dialogues revealed that outreach workers must operate on two fronts simultaneously. They continuously assert their legitimacy to the police who tend to question whether SOWs are professionals with valuable expertise, knowledge, networks and resources.[3] On another front, they engage in the painstaking work of establishing trust and relationships with gang-involved young men, in the hope that these youth might seize upon opportunities to change their life course. As a group, we concluded that SOWs' limited professional legitimacy and institutional recognition leaves them without the structural supports that would bolster their success.

When these tensions can be resolved, or at least made explicit, immense possibilities emerge for street outreach workers and police officers to collaborate for the purpose of youth transformation and gang violence reduction. Nonetheless, our police partner and the outreach workers identified significant obstacles to overcoming these barriers to collaboration. We do not provide definitive answers about how to resolve these tensions. Our chapter offers a rich contextual account of the different perspectives and insight about potential common ground for effective police and SOW collaboration. We imagine that these findings may be relevant in other places that are pursuing comprehensive, collaborative approaches to youth and gang violence intervention.

CONFLICTING VIEWS OF YOUTH

Who are the young people that gang prevention and violence reduction programs aim to reach? What capacity do these young people have to change their lives? The answers that police and outreach workers give to these questions, each rooted in years of personal and professional experience, reveal substantially different understandings of the source of youth violence and gang involvement, the nature of the work at hand, and their responsibilities to young people and the larger community. Outreach workers and police see gang-involved youth through distinct and oftentimes clashing worldviews. These perceptions shape how they approach building relationships with young people, the challenges and frustrations they encounter in their work, and their definitions of success.

The outreach workers in the partnership describe the youth in holistic terms, portraying the challenges they face as embedded in structural factors such as housing vulnerability, poverty, and racism that affect their families and neighborhoods. This perspective is more than an abstract analysis of the structural drivers of crime and delinquency, but is also part of what they *know* (i.e. their expertise as outreach workers and their first-hand knowledge of particular young people). When describing the main challenges of working with gang-involved youth, Luis, an outreach worker with over twenty years of experience, offered a long list of complicating factors, 'They all go through challenges. This identity crisis that they're having … their upbringing, the challenges, you know, socio-economically. The neighborhood that they grew up in, the role models they have.'

The outreach workers' holistic lens derives from the relationships they have with the youth. Their ability to 'go a little deeper with that youth, know them a little more intimately' gives them a particular vantage point. William, an outreach worker with six months on the job, added that youths' challenges are compounded by the complexity and distress of their family situations:

> The amount of time that we're working and pouring into 'em and then consider what they are going back into. What is mom dealing with? What is dad dealing with? So I'm working with these young individuals, but the reality of what they are dealing with is so much broader than just him [sic], there are so many other stresses that are going on. Others don't see that, they just see a behavior, they see the way he is acting, and they're not connecting it to the trauma.

William also spoke about the strengths of the young men that others don't see:

> That's the wealth that I get to see when working with them at that level. When you peel back the layers. Cause he has to put his mask on. When you get to connect with 'em you get to know all of that and the intelligence they have. The compassion and, um, the misguided values. But the drive that they have, the perseverance that these dudes have … to be able to be where they're at, despite what they're going through, is huge, man, it's huge.

This nuanced understanding of young people's lives, and the empathy it produces on the part of the street outreach workers is a result of extended time spent working with them.

While the outreach workers tend to see young men's challenges as part of systemic problems affecting marginalized minority and low-income urban communities, the police tend to view youth primarily as individuals who can be categorized based on their level of dangerousness or risk (e.g. at-risk, high-risk, proven risk). Police may have a keen understanding of the structural conditions that make some young men vulnerable to criminal involvement and gang recruitment (e.g. family cycles of criminality, addiction, and trauma), yet, they focus on the direct link between individual actions and consequences. Unlike the outreach workers who attempt to intervene in the structural aspects of youth realities, the police are charged with monitoring individual behavior and actions in order to keep

dangerous behavior off the streets. Antonio's view was grounded in his primary professional role as a police officer:

> We enforce the laws, it's about accountability. The act or the behavior is our focus – not the person – when a decision to detain or arrest is formulated. It's your behavior. You did X and you were held accountable for X. You break the law, you go to jail.

As a police officer, Antonio explained that he and his fellow officers may understand that the youth grew up with lax parenting and in situations that may not be considered fair. However, as officers become more seasoned, Antonio observes that they increasingly hold the youth accountable for their decisions and actions. He explained that when officers observe occasions in which young men work the system and 'beat a case', or take advantage of leniency or a second chance in order to continue their criminal behavior, they become frustrated with advocates or character witnesses telling judges, 'Oh, he's a good kid, he's turning his life around.' In their minds, the police have ample evidence that the youth in question is capable of serious violence. He explains:

> I think the average cop is thinking, 'I know what this kid did, I know what he's capable of. You might think differently, and you might want to pick up where you know his mom and dad failed, but I know this kid. And you can buy his line like the judges do and release him, but ultimately, when he screws up again, we're gonna get him again.'

In this part of the conversation, Antonio offers insight into how the specific positionality of police officers shapes their perception of youth offenders. His suggestion that youth may 'beat a case' implies that they are guilty and yet managed to 'beat' the criminal justice system. His views echo Collins's argument that what individuals know is a reflection of how they are embedded in power relations. Antonio articulates this viewpoint, which he attributes to his fellow officers, without entirely distancing himself from this interpretation.

One anecdote that was discussed during our two dialogues illuminates the differing vantage points from which officers and outreach workers perceive gang-involved youth. The incident involved several young men in the SOWs caseload. The young men were stopped by the police and frisked as they walked through a local university campus in the early morning on their way to work. They complied with the officers and were subsequently 45 minutes late to work. For one street outreach worker, this incident epitomizes the unfair treatment and harassment that young men experience once they become known to the police:

The kids just let them do what they had to do. The kids said 'we just didn't want no trouble. Didn't want to backtalk, just let 'em frisk us. We knew we weren't doing anything wrong.' As a result though, they were late to their job. These are jobs that are hard for these kids to get and very easy to lose. We're trying to get these kids to stop nickel and dimin' drugs but then we're making them a half an hour late to work just cause we want to frisk them, just cause we know them? Is that fair? I don't think it's fair, but they just kind of gave in.

Immediately after hearing this story, Antonio pointed out the reasons why these young men could have been stopped. He explained that as officers conduct investigations and prepare to serve warrants and make arrests, they often need to make positive identifications, determine current addresses, and photograph suspects, which are all routine aspects of police work. What the outreach worker took as evidence of the daily humiliations that youth may have to tolerate, the police officer surmised was likely the product of officers conducting a legitimate investigation.

Interestingly, the outreach workers were able to empathize with the police's point of view and workplace reality. They have a clear understanding that long histories with particular youth and even particular families will shape officers' approach. Eduardo, an outreach worker with two years on the job, expressed the following:

Police officers are designated to do specific jobs. You have some that deal specifically with gangs and you have general city cops. So the youth that we deal with, the gang-involved kids, the kids that are in violent activities, they are the ones that build relationships with the police officers designated to work with them. So when you have years piling on you from when you were in juvenile detention, to when you age out, and go in and out of the House of Correction, the police officers that know you by name are the ones that are not gonna have a good taste in their mouth when they see you out at 7, 8 o'clock at night with a group of guys. You could just be hangin' out. But what do I know you for? What have I known your father and family for? So, emotions do kick in, and the interactions between gang unit officers and gang kids is going to be very different than the average police officer handling a situation, somebody who doesn't know the history of that kid is going to be very different. There's a police officer that locks up a kid, and then that kid beats his case [the youth is found not guilty in court], he goes in and out, in and out. I'm trying to put myself in the police officer's position, knowing that you're out there going crazy and you're constantly getting away, and now with the way that I'm going to approach you again is not going to be in a general, non-biased and non-judgmental way. I'm gonna go in there with the idea that you're probably doing something you're not supposed to be doing.

Likewise, William, expressed understanding of the police's position, but held on to the importance of staying connected to the whole picture, 'Where I'm looking at the individual as a whole, and saying, OK, this behavior is very real, but what is the source, what is causing that behavior, what is going on, in that individual?' He wonders if being punitive is really helping the individual. He sees in the short term maybe somebody dangerous was taken off the street but he wonders if that individual was really helped and if punishing that young person really changed the community for the better.

Police officers and street outreach workers share a confidence in their first-hand knowledge of the streets and of particular individuals. Yet what they *know* to be true can often produce distinctly different understandings of any individual young person's life chances and potential. And given their distinct institutional positions (or lack thereof) the stakes and consequences of mistaken judgment or risk taking are also quite different.

INSIDER VIEWS OF STREET OUTREACH

We spent a considerable amount of time in our two dialogues talking about what street outreach is and what it takes to be an effective outreach worker. The outreach workers discussed needing to be authentic, persistent, available, positive and patient while earning a young person's trust. Outreach workers need 'street smarts'. They need to know when to be informal (when to 'rock a hoodie') and when to be professional (when to put on a 'button-up'). They need to keep their word to the youth no matter what.

The outreach workers described the purpose of outreach as affecting lasting change in youth's lives, and, in doing so, knowing when rules of professional etiquette need to be bent or broken. They discussed their role as helping youth navigate unfair and unjust systems. They understand that their job is not to be part of investigations of crimes and shootings, but rather to be available in the aftermath and to provide support for rehabilitation and redemption, Luis explains:

> We're there to assist in the re-mending of their life, fixing it, putting it back together and prevention. I don't feel that we are to be the first responders to a criminal act, or a gun shot, but rather after. For family assistance, court assistance, legal assistance, letters of character, meetings to reintegrate them back into society. But when times of crisis happen, I'm not dealing with the call. I really feel it's more of prevention and working with the youth and just keeping them out of trouble and on the straight and narrow.

Eduardo describes the role of the outreach worker as a 'bridge' and as 'the connection to that kid's success'. He explains, 'You have the youth and you have the jail cell and then you have the outreach worker right in the middle. If it was a police in the middle that kid would be going to jail.' Eduardo describes how being in the middle of the youth and jail cell is precarious terrain to navigate:

> When you're an outreach worker and you're responsible for a group of kids and when you're paid to do a certain thing with these kids, in a sense these kids are the sheep and you are the shepherd and letting one go astray because you couldn't do the best that you could – the blood is in your hands. So, that's really how I feel about it especially if you're getting paid for it.

Eduardo acknowledges that as an outreach worker you are in a position that could alter the future for the youth, and that not everybody could do this work. To be in this space,

> you just have to organically know what to do in your head, how to interact. You need to know when to cut the youth off and inform them if they tell you anymore that you will have to go to the authorities with that information and yet still be able to convey to them that you hope they make a smart decision.

The outreach workers act as interpreters and navigators at the edges of what they see as an unjust system, a system in which neither they nor the youth have much power to confront the structural inequalities they face (i.e. poverty, racism, addiction, unstable housing, childhood trauma, familial cycles of violence, etc.). Rather than resisting and challenging the system, street outreach workers often have to counsel young people about the options they do have and the ways that they can give themselves more room to maneuver. Eduardo tells the youth, 'this is what has happened, and because of your previous actions, these are potentially situations you're gonna have to deal with and here's ways to avoid them'. He feels that this is the best advice he can give them because he can't tell law enforcement to change: 'So, it's really to educate the youth on how to avoid those situations'. Eduardo realizes that this is not fair:

Sometimes they have to make unfair life decisions that the average kid who doesn't have that life history wouldn't have to face. Doing basic things, like being in a certain place at a certain time and doing fairly innocent things like playing basketball at a certain court.

He asks, 'How much more freedom are we gonna cut this kid off from, just so he's not harassed by police officers, and he's not targeted because of his previous actions?'

VULNERABILITIES WORKING IN LIMINAL SPACE

Outreach workers operate in a liminal space between gang-involved youth and the criminal justice system. Ambiguity about outreach worker roles seems to come from two directions: (1) law enforcement tends not to understand, recognize, or see the value of outreach; (2) police associate outreach workers with the gang-involved youth they are trying to help. The combination of these factors diminishes the professional legitimacy of street outreach and keeps outreach workers outside of formal institutional arrangements that work with gang-involved youth. This outsider position has some advantages, but on the whole the outreach workers believe greater professional legitimacy and formal institutional partnerships would be valuable to the youth, the police, the outreach workers and ultimately to the community's safety and well-being.

Luis's story illustrates SOWs' structural vulnerability vis-à-vis the police:

I have had police show up at my house. I know they have a job and I respect that job, I really do. I'm not minimizing that at all. But here is the challenge. I got a phone call from a youth when I was on vacation. She was scared. She told me some things that were going on. I told her I'd connect with her once I got back. So long story short there was a crime that had been committed, that person got arrested, and my number was on her phone 'cause she was calling me and texting me. Because I'm an outreach worker, I have a relationship with this person, a detective showed up at my house. I wasn't home, but he asked my wife, 'Do you know what your

husband does? He's jeopardizing the family. He works with gang members.' He gave her a subpoena for me to go to the grand jury. When I got to the grand jury, I got grilled as if I wasn't an outreach worker, as if I wasn't a professional. As if I was just like a common criminal. I got grilled by like ten different people including the district attorney. And not professionally. I was like how are we supposed to counter the at-risk youth who are sayin' this is my experience [with law enforcement], when I'm experiencing the same exact thing?

William reflected on how this lack of relationship and lack of understanding puts street outreach workers in a position of risk:

Thank God it didn't happen, but if there was an incident in which we were trying to interrupt, then I feel like I'd be in cuffs just as quick as the dudes I was trying to help. I'm in a hoodie and maybe that day I forgot to wear my outreach worker shirt. But even if I had that on they might not even care about that. I'm a young African American man, kind of a big dude. Even though I'm here trying to break it up, the police don't understand this and say, 'you're coming with me!'

As William and Luis's stories convey, one of the most basic struggles the outreach workers face is that the police do not know who they are and what they do. Antonio, the police officer, confirmed, 'They don't know you. It could be as simple as "I don't know this dude." You know a lot of these things are based on relationships. And also it could be that they have no idea what street outreach means.' To compensate, outreach workers make an effort to introduce themselves to police officers. The SOWs approach foot patrol officers and give them their business cards. They explain to the police who they are and what they do. They encourage the officers to call them if they encounter youth causing trouble who could be helped by the outreach workers. In spite of these efforts, they say the police never call them or take advantage of the openings they are trying to create. While we do not know the actual reasons that the police do not accept these offers to help, the SOWs perceive a lack of interest and trust from the police. This in turn makes it hard for them to encourage youth to trust the police.

THE POLITICS OF GANG INTERVENTION IN NEW ENGLAND, USA

Another reason SOWs feel vulnerable in this work is that some police officers may fail to distinguish between outreach workers and gang-involved youth. Ironically, the 'street smarts' that outreach workers have, sometimes gained through their own interaction with gangs as they were growing up, is what allows them to do the job of street outreach *and* what renders them problematic partners for police. William's fear that he would end up in cuffs as quickly as one of his clients and Luis's story about being called to the grand jury reveal how street outreach workers may find themselves under scrutiny and subject to the same kinds of criminal investigations as their clients. The blurred boundaries that police may perceive between outreach worker and gang-involved youth can lead to misunderstandings and a conflation of outreach workers with their clients.

Antonio, the police officer, confirms that the SOWs may have cause for their concern. Antonio made reference to a 'fog of illegitimacy' that hovers over the activities of outreach workers, particularly when they work with gang-involved youth. Antonio acknowledged that the 'cloud gets darker and foggier depending on the type of youth you're working with.' He feels that when working with school-based youth in after-school programs, the approach and connections are different. But, when it comes to gang-involved and violent youth, different assumptions kick in:

I guess that kind of floats, and not just in cops' minds, the idea that if you lie down with dogs you wake up with fleas. In other words, does some of the ugliness [associated with gang members] rub off on the outreach worker?

Suspicion toward outreach workers is not just about working with gang-involved youth. Antonio also suggests that it is due to the behavior of some outreach workers:

You know the same things people say about cops, you know when they catch a cop doing something wrong and they paint us all with the same brush, it's the same thing you guys are dealing with. You get one outreach worker who could be doing

anything from fraternizing with a young girl he's supposed to be working with to selling drugs, or using those kids to sell drugs. It's just one more of those, ah-ha, see I told you.

Given their legal and ethical mandate to uphold the law, police officers may be uncomfortable with the idea that outreach workers (who are privy to knowledge of illegal activities) use their best judgement about how to respond with no imperative to enact legal channels. As Eduardo explained, street outreach workers attempt to stand between young people and further systems involvement, acting as a bridge to a different future. Officers must first and foremost attempt to arrest people who commit crimes. These distinct responsibilities lead to different approaches (arrest vs. helping youth navigate away from continued systems involvement) and they may produce significant barriers for productive collaboration.

ON THE OUTSIDE LOOKING IN: STREET OUTREACH AND INSTITUTIONAL LEGITIMACY

There are numerous reasons why police may not perceive street outreach workers as valuable counterparts in their efforts to prevent youth violence and reduce youth involvement in gangs (Braga, 2016). Officers may lack understanding of street outreach as a professional field. They may not have personal or professional connections to SOWs. Yet, one of the most significant obstacles to effective collaboration we learned about in our dialogues was that street outreach workers are perceived as being outside of the circle of legitimate institutional partners within which the police may safely make referrals.

We came to this understanding during an 'ah-ha' moment in our dialogue when Antonio, the police officer, explained why outreach workers have not been incorporated into the network of referral sources for high-risk youth:

The police are in constant motion. They'll get a phone call from a parent that's concerned. The first question is, is the kid court involved? 'Cause that is the quickest, easiest way to get somebody services. 'OK, this is the probation officer you call. She can connect your kid with whatever services.' It's easy enough and safe, because it's institution to institution. The last thing that any officer wants is to go out on a limb and tell a parent, go here, go to this place, see this person [e.g. an outreach worker]. Then they go there and that person's not there. And two or three days later it's a hassle trying to get a hold of them. Then when they get there it's like, 'Who sent you? What do you want?' And it just falls apart. And the cop winds up looking terrible. But when it is in the system where it's institution to institution it's part of the process.

In addition to the police not knowing the outreach workers, not understanding what outreach is, and questioning their professional knowledge and legitimacy, we came to realize that because outreach operates outside of the formal systems, outreach as a scope of work and outreach workers as professionals lack institutional legitimacy. When police officers make referrals to known entities, particularly other institutions that are part of the juvenile justice system, they are protected if the referral fails. On the other hand, if an officer takes a risk and makes a referral to a street outreach worker, any potential mishap reflects poorly on the individual officer who 'went out on a limb' by operating outside of known institutional channels. Antonio reflected on the police's perspective:

I get you're trying to help these kids, but at the end of the day they do something wrong they get arrested. We can't care how much you're working with these kids. We can't care that you know whatever else about him. The police are the only people that have a legal and moral mandate to enforce the laws. We can't push that off or hand that off to somebody and say you do it. At the end of the day we are responsible, we are responsible.

The responsibility for upholding the law necessarily outweighs any other consideration for police officers, which leaves them with little room for imagining alternative outcomes for youth who might benefit over the long term from a relationship with a street outreach worker.

TOWARD A MORE EFFECTIVE PARTNERSHIP?

Is it possible to increase street outreach workers' legitimacy (personal and professional) in the eyes of the police? As we gained insights about the structural challenges of police–street outreach worker partnerships, we explored what it would take to change the dynamic between police and outreach workers in our city. The outreach workers were not overly optimistic about the short term, but could envision a day when they are seen as 'legitimate'. Their vision of legitimacy includes the ability to walk into the courtroom like lawyers and police officers without having to relinquish their cell phones as they enter the court house. Their vision also includes a licensing process for outreach workers. The literature bears out their vision; in places like Boston, MA (Kennedy, 2011) and Houston, TX (Arciaga & Gonzalez, 2012) outreach workers are city employees and benefit from a greater degree of institutional legitimacy.

Striving toward professional and institutional legitimacy is not to bolster outreach workers' egos, but to help them become more effective in their work. Their lack of legitimacy prevents them from receiving reliable, timely information from law enforcement about key individuals and unsafe hotspots in the city; it keeps them out of the referral loop; it jeopardizes the well-being of the youth; and at times it puts the outreach workers in danger. They understand that it may take time for officers to change how they think about gang-involved youth. They are not asking for the police to change their practices or to be more lenient with the youth that have been targeted for street outreach. Rather, they want to be treated like professionals and for law enforcement to distinguish between them and the youth they serve.

Institutionalizing street outreach, which would be one method for increasing its legitimacy, requires developing formalized processes and protocols between outreach and law enforcement. Eduardo stated:

Well if it's not on paper, if you don't have written protocols, if you don't have things like you know standard procedures, no it's not gonna work. The outreach worker who has nobody to report to as far as making those rule-bending decisions, or life-changing decisions or split-second decisions, no it's not gonna work.

Their vision is not just about information sharing. As the street outreach workers point out, most of the information they receive from the police is public information. Instead, legitimacy conveys that the street outreach workers also have expertise that can serve shared objectives. In the absence of this legitimacy, Luis explains that there is a lack of acknowledgment of the work that outreach workers do. Otherwise, police think that '[outreach workers], don't really bring anything to the table'. In addition to respect and acknowledgment of the outreach workers' efforts, they would like police officers to place greater trust in their decision-making abilities, regardless of their close relationships with gang-involved youth.

The outreach workers also recognized that a more formal relationship with the police may be a liability. Operating in the liminal space between gang-involved youth and law enforcement, the outreach workers can disassociate themselves from law enforcement when that is advantageous. William said:

Knowin' that you're working with the police already begins to disintegrate the relationship [with the youth] unless you've built that relationship and that trust to a level where you can have that conversation. But until you've gotten there, and you instinctively know when you're there, to bring up the fact that you're even working with the police disintegrates a level of that trust and ability to connect.

The outreach workers see the advantages that they have in terms of their ability to operate outside of formal protocols and stringent requirements about recording all of their outreach activities and all of their interactions with youth. These flexible aspects of their work would change if they moved toward closer collaboration with the police department:

You wouldn't be able to do anything off the record, I mean, it'd be nice to have your foot in the police department as far as information-sharing and you know to be able to assist these kids, but you're gonna lose the ability to not be accountable for every interaction you have with the kid, I mean everything has to be by the book, everything has to be reported on. But I think the benefits outweigh the cons. Because unless outreach is systematically recognized in the police department, this is not going to change ...

The final segment of our dialogue addressed whether outreach workers' practice would have to change radically to be accommodated and legitimized by the police. Outreach workers are different from state-funded child welfare employees and police officers, and street outreach worker protocols would be distinct. Role-clarification, relationship-building and trust would precede the development of protocols to ensure the core purpose and practices of outreach remained intact (Arciaga and Gonzalez, 2012). The outreach workers and Antonio reflected on their process to develop trust and began to imagine how that could evolve into a city-level conversation.

Luis: For me, it's interesting, right? Because when I first met you, I had this preconceived idea in my head, because you're a police officer. How do you change that? As we work together and we have conversations then we build a relationship there, then we build a certain amount of trust.

Antonio: You have. It's not just a connection with me. You have become part of the system now because of the meetings you go to, who you connect with, and the outcomes of your work. You have basically changed a lot of people's perceptions of outreach. You need more outreach people to do what you're doing. We need more outreach workers to not make rap videos where they talk about shooting people. You know we need more outreach workers sitting in those meetings.

In spite of the trust and mutual respect that has developed between some of the partners, the outreach workers noted the limitations of these isolated relationships. Luis explained the need for more officers doing what Antonio does – to be in regular conversations with the outreach workers:

> To have other officers coming in with you and saying, hey listen this is an outreach worker. This is what they do. It's not just 'hug a thug'. They really have a passion, a calling for this. So I think it's on both ends. Because just like I've changed that perception for me you have changed that perception as well.

In the end, the outreach workers and police partner concluded that it will be a long process, but through training, relationship-building and licensure, there is potential to increase the professional and institutional legitimacy of street outreach workers.

CONCLUSION

As we have sifted through the transcripts of these dialogues, we have seen that the relationships that are forged between police officers, street outreach workers, and gang-involved youth offer some possibilities for transformative professional practice and for altering the life trajectories of young people. These relationships, which take months if not years to build, require trust and rapport to transcend steep gradients of inequality along lines of race, class, education, institutional legitimacy, and criminal histories. We see evidence of the potential of these relationships in our current long-term partnership, which made these frank dialogues possible, and in the positive relationships that street outreach workers forge with youth. Our aim here is not to generalize our findings beyond

our mid-sized city, but to explore the extent to which differentially-situated partners (a gang unit officer, SOWs, and university action-researchers) might come to a shared understanding of the forces that produce youth violence and how to disrupt that violence. Our dialogues suggest that ongoing collaboration helps overcome some of the social distance between law enforcement and SOWs. Nonetheless, even in the context of a very long-term youth violence intervention, structural positions shape perceptions, experiences, and the sorts of knowledge that are produced from each vantage point.

Perhaps our most significant finding is that while these individual relationships between SOWs and police officers may transcend existing power relations, they do little to affect structural change. This finding could very well be relevant to other city's attempts to forge collaborations between law enforcement and SOWs. Even as he was complimentary of Luis, the most veteran member of the outreach worker team, Antonio said, '*you* have now become part of the system' (authors' emphasis), suggesting that it is Luis as an individual who has proven himself trustworthy and a valued partner to the police. While Luis's professionalism may change some police officers' understanding of street outreach, he is perceived by many to be an exceptionally talented street outreach worker and as something of an outlier. His outlier status by its very nature demonstrates that Luis's long and accomplished professional career has done little to increase the legitimacy of street outreach overall.

The liminal space that street outreach workers navigate and their understandings of their work reveal the extent to which this profession is marginalized. Whereas police officers are unwilling to take risks by moving outside of institutional channels, street outreach workers have no institutional safety net. They can be nimble, flexible, and build relationships with gang-involved youth free of constraining protocols, but this is largely a product of their invisibility and lack of professional legitimacy. They have little power to contest the injustices that they may witness as they work with young people. Rather than working toward systems change, SOWs engage at the level of individual youth. They see their responsibilities partially in terms of helping young men adapt to institutionalized inequalities that are unjust but for the moment intractable. Street outreach workers readily admit that they can serve as a bridge to a different future, but this requires teaching youth to tolerate heightened police scrutiny and negative assumptions about their worth as human beings, and to accept an unfair hand without abandoning their efforts to build a better life.

Notes

1 Only men are eligible for this program. While young women are actors in gang-related violence in the community, our conversations centered on this program and for that reason focuses primarily on males.

2 Methodological and authorship note: The authors of this chapter are one and the same as those participating in the dialogues, although names have been changed in the body of the chapter. We collectively agreed on the questions we would explore through two 1.5 hour dialogues that were recorded and transcribed. The research partners transcribed the recordings and wrote the first draft of the chapter. The transcriptions and the first draft were shared with the other participants for their feedback and edits. The final draft represents a consensus piece. The dialogic process proved to be a form of intervention in that the outreach workers, police officer, and research partners gained new insights into each other's positions and momentarily at least opened new possibilities to strengthen the partnership.

3 One of the challenges facing the SOWs in this partnership is that they have no formal professional credentials. Their expertise in street outreach stems from their own life experiences, on-the-job training, and their intuition and instincts. This lack of formal credentialing poses an additional challenge to being seen as a legitimate partner to the police.

REFERENCES

Arciaga, M. and Gonzalez, V. (2012). 'Street outreach and the OJJDP Comprehensive Gang Model'. *National Gang Center Bulletin*, 7, 1–10.

Braga, A. (2016). 'The continued importance of measuring potentially harmful impacts of crime prevention programs: The academy of experimental criminology 2014 Joan McCord lecture'. *Journal of Experimental Criminology*, 12(1), 1–20.

Collins, P. (2015). 'Intersectionality's definitional dilemmas'. *Annual Review of Sociology*, 41, 1–20.

Decker, S., Bynum, T., McDevitt, J., Farrell, A., & Varano, S. (2008). 'Street outreach workers: Best practices and lessons learned'. *Roger Williams University School of Justice Studies Faculty Paper*, Paper 15.

Fox, K. (1991). 'The politics of prevention: Ethnographers combat AIDS among drug users', in Burawoy, M., Burton, A., Ferguson, A. et al., (Eds), *Ethnography Unbound: Power and Resistance in the Modern Metropolis*. University of California Press, Berkeley, pp. 227–249.

Frattaroli, S., Pollack, K., Jonsberg, K., Croteau, G., Rivera, J., & Mendel, J. (2009). *Streetworkers, Youth Violence Prevention, and Peacemaking in Lowell, Massachusetts: Lessons and Voices from the Community*. The Johns Hopkins University Press: Maryland.

Kennedy, D. (2011). 'Whither streetwork?' *Criminology & Public Policy*, 10(4), 1045–1051.

Klein, M. W. (1971). *Street Gangs and Street Workers*. Englewood Cliffs, NJ: Prentice-Hall.

Kotlowitz, A. (2008). 'Blocking the transmission of violence'. *The New York Times*. May 4th.

McGarrell, E. F., Corsaro, N., Melde, C., Hipple, N., Cobbina, J., Bynum, T., & Perez, H. (2012). *An Assessment of the Comprehensive Anti-Gang Initiative: Final Project Report*. https://www.ncjrs.gov/pdffiles1/nij/grants/240757.pdf (last accessed 12/22/16).

Patterson, G. (2004). 'Police–social work crisis teams: Practice and research implications'. *Stress, Trauma, and Crisis*, 7(2), 93–104.

Peaslee, L. (2009). 'Community policing and social service partnerships: Lessons from New England'. *Police Practice and Research*, *10*(2), 115–131.

Rios, V. & Navarro, K. (2010). Insider gang knowledge: The case for non-police gang experts in the courtroom. *Critical Criminology*, *18*(1), 21–39.

Skogan, W. G., Hartnett, S. M., Bump, N., & Dubois, J. (2008). 'Executive summary: Evaluation of CeaseFire-Chicago'. https://www.ipr.northwestern.edu/publications/papers/urban-policy-and-community-development/docs/ceasefire-pdfs/executivesummary.pdf

Spergel, I. (1995). *The Youth Gang Problem: A Community Approach*. New York, NY: Oxford University Press.

Spergel, I. (2007). *Reducing Youth Gang Violence: The Little Village Gang Project in Chicago*. Lanham, MD: Rowman Altamira.

Thatcher, D. (2001). 'Conflicting values in community policing'. *Law & Society Review*, *35*(4), 765–798.

Whitehill, J., Webster, D., Frattaroli, S., & Parker, E. (2013). 'Interrupting violence: How the CeaseFire program prevents imminent gun violence through conflict mediation'. *Journal of Urban Health*, *91*(1), 84–95.

Wolf, A. & Gutierrez, L. (2011). 'Operating and managing street outreach services'. *The California Cities Gang Prevention Network*, Bulletin 22: National League of Cities.

29

Coercion in Sexual Relationships: Challenging Values in School-based Work

Jo Heslop

INTRODUCTION

Over the past two decades work addressing gender and sexual violence with young people has become a global concern. Much international development work has been focused in Sub-Saharan Africa, where research has highlighted girls being routinely exposed to forms of sexual violence, including sexual harassment, touching and peeping by male peers, pressures for sexual relationships from teachers and other men in exchange for better grades, gifts or money, and rape (DevTech Systems, 2007; Leach et al., 2003; Parkes and Heslop, 2011). A UN resolution was passed in 2015 calling on all countries to take action on gender violence in schools (UNESCO, 2015a), whilst funders are investing large amounts of money into interventions that support adolescent girls to challenge gender violence, and projects run by non-governmental organisations are multiplying. This has been accompanied by similar efforts to address HIV and young people's

sexual and reproductive health through education programmes, particularly in sub-Saharan Africa. Whilst sexual violence is an increasing focus of policies and interventions internationally, what it really means is rarely questioned. How do interventions aiming to empower girls and young women understand sexual violence, coercion and consent? How do they disrupt or reinforce existing discourses that shape sexual coercion?

This chapter takes a close look at how young people in four sub-Saharan African countries understand and articulate sexual violence and coercion in heterosexual relationships in their lives, and how projects working with young people to take action on gender violence may disrupt and reinforce discourses circulating within communities. I do this by examining data collected through research linked to international development NGO youth work interventions involving partners in the UK, Ghana, Kenya, Mozambique and Zambia. Different forms of youth work may unwittingly reinforce discourses denying girls sexual agency and making them responsible for sexual safety, whilst under-acknowledging the structures that shape sexual coercion in different contexts in sub-Saharan Africa are all characterised by high levels of gender inequalities, violence and poverty. I am a UK-based, white woman activist researcher working with young people in the field of 'international development work' rather than explicitly within 'youth work' per se. Here I draw out some of the tactical, ethical and political challenges faced by activists in challenging gender violence experienced by young people.

SEXUALITY AND SCHOOLING IN THE LITERATURE

I frame my analysis within discourses that circulate in media, policy and practice on gendered identities and sexuality, and I take a close look at how this relates to violence and coercion. Contradictory expectations are placed on girls to be both sexualised/attractive and 'good', meaning virginal, and evidence shows how girls' bodies and sexuality are regulated in many contexts including in the global North (Duits and Van Zoonen, 2006; Gavey, 2005; Renold and Ringrose, 2013). In international development work sexual activity tends to be seen in opposition to development, and associated with disease, violence and unsustainable fertility rates (Jolly, 2010). This is particularly apparent in work on girls' schooling in the global South. Sexuality tends to be ignored, or education is seen as a way of protecting girls from the dangers of sex, linked to school dropout related to early marriage and pregnancy (Wells, 2015). Whilst research has found that girls living on the streets in Ghana see schools as spaces that can protect them from sexual exploitation and violence (Oduro et al., 2012), other studies have identified how being at school can close down the ability to discuss concerns about sexual

relationships (Chilisa, 2006; Cobbett-Ondiek, 2016). Vavrus (2003) found that young people in Northern Tanzania tended to link hard work with avoiding sexual temptations, whilst 'idleness' upon leaving school (usually due to lack of employment opportunities) was associated with 'bad morals', sexual desire and sexual risk taking. This points to a relationship between schooling and sex that is far from straightforward.

SEXUAL COERCION, DISCOURSE AND AGENCY

In this chapter I situate understandings of sexual violence and coercion as being inextricably linked with those of sexuality. Sexuality is socially constructed, with taken-for-granted aspects of sexuality, including desires, practices and identities shaped by normative discourse and social practices. These discourses are contextual, shared, reproduced through social institutions and sometimes contradictory (Foucault, 2002; Weedon, 1987). What we understand as coercive, consensual or forced sex is shaped by dominant discourses around us, and will influence how we perform, respond to or resist to those experiences (Gavey, 2005). Gavey (2005) argues that the discourses of aggressive desiring males and passive undesiring females within normative heterosexuality act as the cultural scaffolding of rape.

This conceptualisation brings together ideas about structure and agency, and McNay's work, drawing from Bourdieu, is also useful here (McNay, 2000). She looks at how structures of power operate through the habitus: 'the process through which power relations are incorporated into the body in the form of durable physical and psychological predispositions' (McNay, 2008a, p. 12) and come to be internalised. These dispositions are shaped by power relations, with everyday practices that reinforce unequal relationships misrecognised as natural and acceptable. Thus, in this chapter we will see how practices in families, schools and communities, and legal, political and economic processes, reproduce dominant discourses and prohibit forms of agency and choice around gender and sexuality in poverty contexts. However, McNay does not simply see habitus as self-determining, but as creative, and thus as providing space for agency and change. Hence, we are also interested in how girls and young women in these contexts sometimes do recognise, criticise and actively challenge some of these norms and institutions that can produce forms of violence. Choice still may be constrained – agency being realised in different ways as 'cultural and economic forces play themselves out in daily life as constraints and resources for action' (McNay, 2008b, p. 156). In a context of poverty, for example, girls may actively 'choose' because they cannot envisage another option, or because other options may be closed to them. For example, transactional sex may be chosen to ward off hunger or to purchase resources for school (Hallam, 1994), whilst other studies show how girls and young women may make strategic choices in pursuing sexual relationships (Jewkes and Morrell, 2012). This highlights the question of what girls may be 'consenting' to: the sexual interaction or the outcome. Whilst many studies in sub-Saharan Africa highlight asymmetry common in sexual relationships and associated risks such as more difficulty negotiating condom use (Jewkes; Luke, 2005 and Morrell, 2012), they have not tended to examine the concepts of coercion and consent closely, and particularly not in relation to education and youth programmes.

I will explore these questions through looking at two projects addressing gender and sexual norms with young people. I will describe these projects, before discussing coercive processes, the ways in which girls negotiate them, and the potential for different types of youth work to expand the sexual choices they have and make.

TWO RESEARCH PROJECTS INVESTIGATING GENDER AND SEXUAL NORMS FOR YOUNG PEOPLE

The data under discussion comes from two research projects – each linked to a different NGO intervention – 'Stop Violence Against Girls in Schools in Ghana, Kenya and Mozambique', and 'Working with Young People to Improve their Sexual Well-being', set in Zambia. The Stop Violence project worked in schools and communities in Wenje division, Tana River District in the northern part of the Coastal Province of Kenya; Nanumba North and South in the Northern Region, Ghana; and the Manhiça district in Maputo Province in Southern Mozambique. The project areas in Kenya and Ghana were both remote and rural. The communities practised Islam and Christianity and combined different ethnic groups, some of whom had a history of conflict, which was often resource related. One of the groups in the Kenyan site was nomadic pastoralist, and farming was the other main source of livelihood. The project area in Mozambique was on the main road traversing the country, near the capital and therefore with better communications. This brought with it more access to mobile phones and electronic media, higher levels of mobility and migration for work (including to South African mines), more diverse employment opportunities in industry and farming and higher levels of HIV/AIDS. The second project was located in a large village on the main road in Eastern Zambia near the border with Malawi. In many ways it shared some similar contextual features with that of the Mozambique project area, with high levels of mobility, communications and sexual networking. The main sources of livelihoods were cross-border trading, agriculture and brewing beer. However, all sites experienced high levels of poverty, illiteracy and poor access to basic services such as electricity and running water. These harsh material conditions combined with gender inequalities, with women and girls tending to have lower access to education, employment and public life, a high burden of household chores and child-care responsibilities and economic depend-ence on men. Girls and young women in all four sites were at risk of sexual abuse and exploitation, with, for example, a quarter of schoolgirls reporting experiencing some form of sexual violence in the project areas in Ghana, Kenya and Mozambique (Parkes and Heslop, 2011). Very few girls took action to challenge violence, with shame, lack of knowledge about violence and what action to take, a tendency for communities to resolve issues locally and ineffective reporting sys-tems creating barriers to reporting to the authorities (Gordon, 2008; Parkes and Heslop, 2011). It is within these contexts that the projects were initiated.

The Stop Violence Against Girls project was led by ActionAid International and ran from 2008 to 2013. The intervention part-ners worked with schools, communities and government structures to address gender vio-lence and inequalities, with research teams feeding into the project design and investi-gating project impact. The intervention pri-marily targeted girls and boys, aged 8–18[1] in 45 primary schools in the three countries, particularly through school girls' and boys' clubs, and worked with school leadership and teachers to make schools safer and more girl-friendly places. It also worked with ado-lescent girls out of school and community members to deliberate on gender, rights and violence and engaged with community and government structures to improve violence reporting and support systems. Meanwhile, the project in Zambia was implemented by a Zambian NGO 'Young, Happy, Healthy and Safe' and supported by the International HIV/AIDS Alliance between 2003 and 2008. The programme worked with 10–24-year-olds in five communities and pupils in 13 primary schools. The community compo-nent, on which the research was based, used participatory learning and action approaches to train and support young Peer Educators,

and engage traditional initiation advisors, community leaders and health services in reflection on how to enhance young people's sexual well-being.

In addition to a mixed methods baseline and endline study in all 45 primary schools, the research connected to the Stop Violence project also included a qualitative longitu-dinal study, the data from which forms the basis for this chapter. This study took place in 12 schools, following 108 schoolgirls over three years. These girls, their parents, teachers, male and female peers and other key stakeholders were visited in four waves (see Parkes and Heslop (2013) for further detail). Research organisations in each country conducted the research, with sup-port from the UCL Institute of Education. Meanwhile, the research in Zambia was on a smaller scale and used an adapted PEER (Participatory Ethnographic Evaluation and Research)[2] approach. As a researcher attached to the Institute of Development Studies, University of Sussex, I worked in partnership with the international and local intervention partners. I worked with a local counterpart and we recruited and trained three young women and three young men as peer researchers. Instruments were developed together, based on their initial analysis of the challenges young people faced regarding gender and sexuality. In all, 18 young women and 12 young men aged 16–29 – most of whom were unmarried and not in school – were interviewed four times each on different themes by the peer researchers.

Conducting research in post-colonial con-texts, characterised by poverty and inequali-ties is fraught with ethical challenges. As a white British woman/women,[3] whose per-spectives were informed by Western femi-nism and post-colonialism, in leading the research we were sensitive to North/South power dynamics and the potential for diverse perspectives relating to gender and violence. Working in partnership with intervention organisations brought great potential for the research to build locally driven interventions through empowerment of local actors. In both contexts we attempted to develop the research design and methods with local researchers and ensure that research methods would attempt to minimise unequal power relations between children and young people and researchers – bringing in visual and participatory methods such as mapping and transect walks that encourage children and young people to feel comfortable and express themselves (Leach, 2015). Whilst neither were full ethnographic studies, both brought in ethnographic elements, including a mix of observation and direct interviewing approaches, and emphasised building familiarity and trust. Using a phenomenological approach, instead of looking for social facts we were interested in participants' interpretations and meanings attached to experiences. Also central to both these pieces of research was a feminist lens. We tried to draw out research participants' (and researchers') understandings and experiences of gender inequalities and identities and also to privilege the voice of girls and young women given their otherwise marginalised status.

In both pieces of research there was extensive thinking and deliberation with research teams on ensuring high ethical standards, and protocols were drawn up that addressed power dynamics, working with children and young people and ensuring confidentiality and informed consent for research participation in those particular contexts (see Parkes and Heslop (2013) for further detail). A particular concern was addressing sensitive issues on gender violence and the potential for unearthing painful memories or current risk. We worked closely with the local implementing organisations to ensure that specific support was in place for any participants who needed it, and all participants were involved in the on-going interventions. Both pieces of research gained ethical approval from relevant Research Ethics Committees – the UCL Institute of Education for the three-country study and the Institute of Development Studies, University of Sussex for the Zambia study.

In what follows I discuss how young people, particularly girls and young women, talked about gender, sexual relationships and violence to help understand sexual coercion in these contexts.

SEXUAL COERCION AND GENDER DISCOURSES IN THE PROJECT COMMUNITIES

In all four contexts sexual coercion was normative and shaped by discourses of strong, desiring males and passive, undesiring females. This could be seen clearly in the Zambia sexual and reproductive health (SRH) project – where the age of research participants and nature of the project allowed more frank discussion of sex than was possible in the Stop Violence project. Young people explained that men and boys communicated motivations for sex verbally whilst girls and young women were not supposed to express desire in obvious ways for fear of being branded as having loose sexual morals. However, many said that they did sometimes initiate sex in established relationships through subtle, non-verbal cues. Young men and women talked about the impossibility of girls expressing sexual desire or agreement for sex:

A girl will say no even if she wants sex – she can't seem too eager or she will be seen as a prostitute. But they can tell by the way she talks and her actions that she's really interested. (Chikondi,[4] aged 22, Zambia)

He would negotiate, since in tradition no means accepting. He'd do this by using sweet and lovely words, like 'sweetheart', 'darling', 'princess'. She would then accept as she knows he really loves her. (Daniel, male aged 28, Zambia)

Both young men and women said that a 'game' often ensued, whereby men would use persuasion and physical seduction to eventually overpower their female partners.

Young women explained that this was because it was not considered appropriate for girls to be eager for sex, and, secondly, because they enjoyed being chased and flattered by men. This practice of girls and women 'saying no when they mean yes' (also called 'scripted refusal') has been put forward by some studies in the USA (e.g. Muehlenhard and Rodgers, 1998). However, critics have highlighted that although some women in these studies talked about sometimes doing this, they were in the minority, and often such admissions were a result of women having conflicted feelings about whether they wanted to engage in sex – which again highlights the murky area around sexual coercion (Gavey, 2005). Although, in the Zambia study, some men and women explained that men could tell, really, what women or girls wanted, women also talked about often having sex when they didn't want to. Most young women admitted that it wasn't really possible for them to *actually* refuse sex, as they were supposed to ultimately give in to men. On the one hand this could be seen as a way for young women to negotiate the discourses prohibiting sex for them. On the other hand responses showed that it was very common for girls and women to have sex when they didn't want it, or before they were ready, as they had no clear way to genuinely communicate their desires. Many women talked about their experiences of sex without their consent, and how they felt about it:

A man should ask the woman to have sex, not the other way around. Females don't make that decision, they just let it happen to please their partner. However, when it happens women don't feel good. They feel they have been forced when they were not prepared. (Mayeso, aged 23, Zambia)

Whilst there were more taboos that constrained schoolgirls' talk about sex in the Stop Violence project locations, some girls, especially those in the more modernised and peri-urban area in Mozambique, and girls who were out of school, were a little more

forthcoming. These girls spoke about girls having sex for a variety of reasons, but also spoke about the use of force if girls refused to engage in sex, echoing Gavey's assertion that 'violence can be thought of as a technique to enforce one person's will only when other, more subtle forms of persuasion (coercion) are not successful' (Gavey, 2005, p. 10).

In both projects we see how sexual coercion and sexual agency are borne out of dominant discourses of predatory males and fleeing females. This was particularly apparent in the Stop Violence communities, where schoolgirls were positioned as innocent and chaste, and lacking in sexual agency. Sex was seen as something dangerous – leading to disease, pregnancy and failure at school, echoing development discourses discussed earlier:

No, if you have a boyfriend you are a spoilt child and when you are in class you will not concentrate, you will always be thinking about the boy. He may even tell you not to go to school but that you should go for dance. (Fouzia, aged 14, Ghana)

Moses: Children should not engage in sexual issues since they should first go to school.
Goma: Children should abstain from early sex since this will lead to contraction of HIV and AIDS.
Abbo: Education and sex are like oil and water, they don't go together. Abstain.
Said: Sex is bad for children since it makes pupils fail in exams.

(Focus group discussion with boys aged 12–16, Kenya)

Whilst the ideal of sexual abstinence was often placed on pupils in general rather than just girls, in reality boys' sexual interest was often ignored or seen to be natural and was not faced with the same level of policing, and once boys had left school then sexual activity was expected.

These ideas were circulated through families and religious and cultural community institutions and through the learning that girls and boys experienced at school. Whilst some sort of sex education was mandatory in all three countries, delivery varied greatly

(UNESCO, 2015b). For example, in Kenya the Life Skills curriculum is currently undergoing development to meet international standards set by UNESCO. Whilst it touched on issues around gender, sexual relationships and sexual coercion, these were often framed in simplistic or negative ways; for example, presenting sexual coercion as a result of negative peer pressure, and presenting early marriage as a choice that some girls make (UNESCO and UNFPA, 2012). Teachers receive very limited training (UNESCO, 2015b) and there are numerous studies showing how – when sex education is taught – teachers tend to avoid more challenging topics or interpret curricula to reinforce dominant discourses in contexts where discussing sex is taboo (Ahmed et al., 2006; Gordon, 2008; Khau, 2012). In the project areas sex education was sporadic and tended to be limited to issues such as puberty and hygiene, or dealt with sexual relationships in ways that reinforced discourses of chaste schoolgirls:

> In our science lessons, we learned about HIV. We were told that if we follow a lot of men, we will get AIDS. (Aramatu, aged 14, Ghana)
>
> Teachers especially Eliza[5] always talk to us about issues concerning sex or relationships. She last discussed with us in late September this year that sex is only meant for people who are married. She said it can also result into HIV and AIDS diseases. (Asha, aged 15, Kenya)

Girls talked about similar messages coming through religious, community and family institutions:

> No one has talked to me about sex apart from my mother who tells me not to play with boys. (Makorani, aged 12, Kenya)
>
> At the mosque and makaranta [madrasa] they have been preaching that girls should not play with boys because when you are going to school they might impregnate you and when they impregnate you and you go to the house and they won't provide your needs and will not give you money. (Victoria, aged 11, Ghana)

We see how discourses of schoolgirl chastity are reinforced, and how this subsequently

can place on schoolgirls both responsibility for preventing sexual activity and blame when it happens:

> When girls sometimes say that they might bring shame on their family [it] simply means that they can become pregnant when not married. ... Literally I can become a laughing stock, my friends will laugh at me, talk ill of me, the man who has impregnated me might also laugh at me. People will also laugh and mock my parents. Literally this will bring shame to our family. (Betty, aged 15, Kenya)

In the Zambia research area, whilst there was still an overall theme of female chastity and male strength and prowess, other contradictory discourses circulated. Most young people were churchgoers and also talked about the influence of their faith. The messages they received from church emphasised abstinence: 'They feel good about the church as they are taught no sex before marriage. It makes them feel good to strive for that, even though it's not the reality' (Mayeso, aged 23, Zambia). Whilst the religious discourse emphasised abstinence before marriage generally, in reality it was emphasised more for girls than boys. Young people explained that the discourse forbidding sexual activity for unmarried young people, and particularly girls, did not in practice discourage sexual activity but encouraged secretive, furtive, unsafe and coercive sex.

However, initiation processes, which all girls and boys went through upon puberty, were powerful in creating alternative – and sometimes conflicting – discourses about gender and sexuality. Young women explained how they were taught about their roles as women, including personal hygiene and how to undertake their roles as homemakers, but also how to please a man sexually (chimwesho), including using erotic dances (tyoli). Traditionally girls would have married soon after this time, but government and development organisations' efforts to expand access to secondary education are delaying marriage, and girls are thus taught to be sexual and chaste at the same time through their adolescence. Meanwhile boys' learning about masculinity and sexuality was less contradictory – to be hardworking, physically and sexually strong and a provider – and they were taught craftwork and leadership skills. They were given herbs which they associated with sexual arousal and potency – reinforced by being given herbs to put on their bodies whilst jumping on fire during initiation training. Both young men and women considered this to increase the potential for sexual violence, as men believed the herbs made them need sex immediately: 'Traditional herbs can make boys do what they don't intend to, like raping girls' (Limani, male aged 18, Zambia). Young women said that the celebration at the end of their initiation training was a risky time for girls, who were vulnerable to sexual advances and forced and coerced to have sex by men and boys.

We have seen how sexual coercion is produced by the dominant discourses of desiring males and undesiring females and taboos around teenage sex – the intersection of these two creating fertile ground for sexual coercion. We will now consider how girls also sometimes chose to have sexual relationships, but – to muddy the waters even further – how those relationships were constrained by the harsh material conditions characterising the project communities.

TRANSACTIONAL SEX, POVERTY AND MODERNITY SHAPING SEXUAL COERCION

In the Zambian SRH project area the slightly older girls and young women who were not encumbered with the schoolgirl label experienced more space for alternative versions of femininities, whilst these continued to carry a flavour of judgement about them. Young men still talked about young single 'unsullied' adolescent females as the preferred choice for relationships and marriage, whilst

there were many labels placed on young women who were perceived not to follow this standard, either through wearing clothes that were too revealing or having relationships with men. Young people were both admired and judged for their 'Western' or non-traditional dressing. Young women explained the importance of wearing chitenge (a large traditional wraparound cloth) as a sign of respect, but at the same time spoke of the desire for fashionable Western clothes to keep up with friends, and that they were expected to look sexy by their husbands:

> Women are also told that 'if you're always wearing chitenge your man will lose interest'. At the same time girls wearing hipsters, short skirts, revealing tops etcetera do that to entice men or for business. So girls dressing like this are at risk, whatever their motives. (Chikondi, aged 22, Zambia)

Forms of transaction and provision in sexual relationships were normative in all the projects communities. These were often disapproved of, but some girls acknowledged how external forces shaped this: 'I think most girls get into sexual relationship due to influence from other girls, others may be due to poverty levels in their families, they want to have a good life and basic things like "*always*" [sanitary pads]' (Halima, aged 15, Kenya). Girls and young women explained that sexual relations were usually more equal with someone of a similar age, but that these boys and young men were usually unable to provide the material necessities or symbols of modernity that girls and young women were also under pressure to display. So they often engaged in relationships with older men. Girls and young women had some control in these relationships – in terms of what he gave, where they went, what they did, and in the formation and ending of relationships:

> It can be difficult when the girl needs money and the boy doesn't have any. Girls think boys are very strong so can do any job so should have money. If he can't provide in the relationship the girl can dump him or start other relationships with other men. (Daniel, aged 19, Zambia)

However, this agency did not extend to sexual decision-making. For example, many girls said that they could not insist on condom use as they could get more from their partner, materially, by not using condoms, and choosing not to have sex at all was not an option. So girls were caught in a dilemma, and often opted for relationships with economic and age disparities despite the disadvantages:

> In an older man–young girl relationship she has more power, for example by saying she doesn't want to go to the bush but wants to go to a guesthouse. If they are drinking beer together she can say 'let's go' or 'I don't want to – let's stay here'. But when they have sex the man has more power. (Rebecca, aged 19, Zambia)

The hope of marriage was another reason for girls to 'choose' to have sex. Marriage was highly valued in the project communities and there were strong expectations from families for girls to marry whilst they were still young. Girls may be 'choosing' for love, domestic or financial security, or to meet societal expectations (a desirable potential husband would be able to provide financially, including paying a dowry). Occasionally, girls in the Stop Violence communities talked about sexual relationships with teachers. Whilst girls often agreed to sex with their teachers to gain improved grades or material rewards, as salaried educated professionals living in poor rural communities, teachers were seen as having good credentials for marriage and being in a relationship with a teacher could be seen as status- and prospect-enhancing. Often, girls found it difficult to say no or were worried about the consequences, such as being failed in their exams or other punishments that the teacher was able to enact. Our data indicated that girls' expectations of love and marriage were inextricably linked to expectations of financial security and the two could not easily be separated.

We see how local material conditions constrained girls' and young women's ability to refuse sexual relationships, whilst at the same time dominant discourses of female chastity disallowed them. When girls did engage in these relationships, it was thus easy for them to be blamed, although there were some traces of sympathy, as can be seen in girls' acknowledgement of what drives many girls into relationships. We see how sexual coercion can be seen as sexual agency constrained by multiple structural forces: chaste femininities and pursuing masculinities, and taboos around sexuality are reinforced through schools, families and religious and cultural institutions, colliding with desire for symbols of status and modernity in poor communities, all exacerbated by wealth and power inequalities based on gender, age and authority. However, these forces are often neither acknowledged nor questioned – the status quo seen to be natural and 'incorporated into the body' (McNay, 2008a). Despite these constraints being present and powerful in the communities described, this does not mean that all sex is coerced or a violation. Girls and young women in these contexts sometimes do recognise, criticise and actively challenge some of these norms and institutions that can produce forms of violence. It is important for sexual consent to involve an active decision to engage in sex and an understanding of the personal risks and protective measures in sexual encounters, but also a consciousness of the structural constraints to sexual agency. This analysis highlights the necessity for youth work practice to analyse and engage with this complexity around sexual coercion. However, as we see in the next section, there can be many pitfalls and dilemmas in challenging contexts such as these.

DILEMMAS FOR INTERVENTIONS

The Stop Violence project was instrumental in helping girls to challenge violence, through educating girls about laws, rights and reporting and support systems for girls experiencing violence:

I learnt that when somebody meets you in the street saying 'I want to marry you', you should say NO and afterwards stop using that path. Now that I am in the club I learn to read and answer questions, make drawings of a person beating the other. The meaning of the drawing is that the one beating will go to jail. (Maira, aged 10, Mozambique)

You know that was happening before when the girls used to think that when a boy touches your breast then they love you. Now girls know it is wrong and when it happens they report to the teacher or parent. (Zawadi, aged 16, Kenya)

However, this emphasis on how to deal with unwanted sexual aggression, without discussing sexual relationships and sexual agency, reinforced the expectations that girls were not or should not be interested in sex. Girls in Mozambique were sometimes taught about safe sex, and in this more modernised context, with broader networks of information and communication, girls' clubs appeared to be more effective at enabling girls to break silences on taboos around sex and sexual violence, and to report violence with more confidence than in the more remote, rural areas of Kenya and Ghana (Parkes and Heslop, 2013). The risk is that the project, with its emphasis on child protection and challenging violence ends up reinforcing discourses of the chaste schoolgirl, who is responsible for maintaining her own chastity and keeping boys and men at bay.

The Stop Violence intervention was firmly oriented within a rights framework, and this could sometimes emphasise the legal status and consequences of violence rather than examining norms and values around sexual coercion and consent. For example, the age of consent and capacity to consent can be seen as different things. While age acts as a useful guideline, we see how an unthinking application of laws – and laws themselves – around the age of consent can also be problematic and contribute to a discourse denying girls' sexual agency. Although rape (for adult women) is defined in the Kenyan Constitution and Ghana Criminal Offences Act as an absence

of consent, marital rape is not recognised in Mozambique (SADC Gender Barometer – Southern Africa Gender Protocol Alliance, 2015) or Kenya (Kamau, 2013), and laws do not address what consent may mean in relationships characterised by asymmetries in power and status defined by gender, age and/or economic and social standing. The legal age of sexual consent is 18 in Kenya and 16 in Ghana and Mozambique. Any sex (even if consensual) involving a girl below the legal age is considered defilement and the laws have been increasingly applied to punish the boys/men involved – particularly in Ghana and Kenya. The intervention's emphasis on protecting girls from violence also contributed to increased local efforts to punish men or boys who purportedly committed sexual violence. This included when relationships were consensual but resulted in pregnancy, so the sexual relationship became known. In these contexts of poverty, notions of justice were often driven by material concerns, and local customary courts had traditionally mediated informal financial provisions from the baby's father to the young mother's parents for a pregnancy resulting from a sexual relationship whether it was consensual or not. As the complexity of the meaning of sexual consent was not addressed in the intervention, the move to using the formal legal framework to protect girl victims and punish male perpetrators of sexual violence was also applied to consensual sexual activity involving teenage girls. This contributed to a discourse viewing all sex involving schoolgirls as violent, possibly further silencing the possibility of girls' desire or agency in sexual relationships.

This limiting of girls' sexual agency was not the intention of the Stop Violence intervention. In fact in a context where girls experienced a lot of sexual violence and unwanted sexual advances it helped girls to stand up and take action. The intervention was also effective in promoting girls' education and empowerment, female solidarity and high aspirations. The girls' clubs were central in this:

> These days I come to school every day, I don't absent myself from school on market days and my father told my mother not to let me sell things in the market during school hours. I have also learnt a lot from the girls' club and I was part of the advocacy team which went to the market to talk to parents who keep their girls in the market during school hours and so I am happy. (Issah, aged 13, Ghana)

Before the intervention, girls going to school had been disapproved of, as the free mixing of adolescent girls and boys had been seen as dangerous in the Ghana project area. The intervention made great strides in helping to change ideas about girls going to school (by delinking schoolgoing and sexual risk), but this paradoxically made it particularly difficult to address the aspects of sexual relationships needed to help girls understand and negotiate sexual consent.

Meanwhile, the social and economic context of the Zambia location was similar but the framing of the intervention was different. The intervention was primarily set up to facilitate education and discussion about sex and relationships as a way to improve sexual and reproductive health and rights. There were therefore not the same discourses around girls' education constraining frank discussion about sex, and most young people involved in the research were out of school. The emphasis on challenging sexual violence in the Stop Violence project was not there in the Zambia project. However, responses also suggested that girls were at particular risk of sexual violence in the Zambian location. This may well have also been linked to the age of the girls, and the setting, which brought increased mobility and access to resources and modernity, associated with sexual violence risk (Merry, 2009; Walby, 2013). However, it is likely that the discourse of the chaste schoolgirl paradoxically provided some protection from sexual violence and coercion by helping girls to stay away from unwanted sex in the Stop Violence project

locations, whilst in other ways facilitating it, as presented earlier. Other studies have shown that girls can see school as a space to protect them from sexual relationships and violence (Oduro et al., 2012; Switzer, 2010) and this could be at play here.

Whilst the Zambia SRH intervention did pay attention to gender norms, gender was not at the centre of the intervention aims, and sometimes got lost behind the emphasis on safe sex. In fact many interventions oriented within the issues of HIV/AIDS or SRH tend to use behaviour change models that focus on individual values, beliefs, skills and attitudes, such as emphasising identifying personal risk factors and planning a change. These programmes fail to take into consideration how structural factors such as gender and poverty shape discourses around sexual coercion and violence (Edström et al., 2001; Heslop and Banda, 2013). The constraints on girls' and young women's sexual agency are un- or under-acknowledged. Whilst many have been successful in challenging the taboos around discussing teenage sex, gender has been missing, or looked at in a narrow way. Boys and young men are usually involved in such interventions alongside girls and young women, but opportunities around engaging young people in the fight against HIV could do more to address dominant discourses of masculinity, femininity and sexuality and how they shape sexual coercion, consent and violence.

Meanwhile those oriented within girls' education and child protection can also emphasise a version of gender as girls, rather than as structures and identities. Whilst increased efforts were made to work with boys around challenging gender inequalities and violence during the Stop Violence project, the emphasis on girls' responsibility for keeping boys and men at bay and the positioning of girls as victims and boys and men as perpetrators had already implicitly been set. The version of the empowered or agentic girl or woman presented in the Stop Violence and other girls' education projects has not included sexual agency, and has unwittingly contributed to girls' sexual agency being denied.

CONCLUSION

Sexual coercion is very real in the lives of girls and young women in all four contexts, and the discourses of feminine chastity and passivity, and masculine active desire have shaped this. On the one hand it has placed the responsibility for avoiding sex – whether consensual or not – firmly on girls' shoulders, and at the same time has made discussion about the complexity of sexual consent and coercion impossible. This research has shone a light on the multiple constraints on girls' sexual agency. Girls experiencing material deprivation may have little choice about whether to engage in sexual relationships, but that does not make all teenage sex automatically violent. It is vitally important to pay attention to this grey area of sexual coercion and transactional sex.

Some interventions, such as the Stop Violence one examined here, are oriented within girls' education and have emphasised protecting girls from violence. However, we see how these interventions, with their focus on girls, laws and violence, have sometimes reinforced discourses that emphasise female chastity or passivity and closed down spaces for discussion and support. Meanwhile some interventions oriented within sexual health can underplay the structural constraints experienced, linked to gender, age and economic asymmetries which can shape coercion and the context in which 'choices' are made. Interventions with these two orientations could benefit from closer working together and could help to build a vision of girls' empowerment that includes sexual agency and acknowledges the constraints on young people's sexual agency. This would need to include honest discussion around sex – including a positive framing around sexual desire. Discussion around sexual consent and what it may mean would be central to this, and would necessarily include discussion and analysis – with girls – on understanding what the constraints are to sexual agency. Whilst many young people had internalised some discourses that shaped coercion, there were moments of recognition that the status quo was not necessarily fair, natural or inevitable. Interventions can promote discussion that develops critical consciousness of these processes, practices and institutions. The process of learning, questioning and discussing resulted in a transformation for peer researchers during the Zambia research – they started to question inequitable regimes they had taken for granted, and were inspired to plan local action to challenge institutions – such as traditional courts – that reinforced these regimes. Boys and young men need similar opportunities to critically analyse the norms that shape behaviour. We have seen the importance of the roles schools, religious and traditional systems, media and legal frameworks can all play in shaping coercion, and interventions need to be multi-levelled to work with these institutions to create change.

The paradox is that, whilst in some respects the school is a vitally important location to deliver sex education, currently the discourse identified which positions sex in opposition to schooling in some contexts can undermine the approaches which are essential if we are to challenge gender violence and enhance girls' sexual agency. Youth work aiming to address sexual coercion in girls' lives in diverse contexts across the world needs to start with a careful examination of local norms and values and how sexual coercion is shaped by local, national and global structures and institutions. It will be important to not just work with young people in discussing these forces, but to address wider communities and structures themselves if they are contributing to sexual coercion. For example, the Stop Violence project started to work with religious leaders and schools around messages about sex and gender towards the end of the project, and the SRH project worked with initiation advisers who played a powerful role in reproducing gender norms. There is a risk of tension and clashing values, and losing sight of girls' and young women's concerns, but there are emerging examples of successful work in this area, such as the participatory development of a sex education curriculum addressing young peoples' local concerns and school and community buy-in in six countries in sub-Saharan Africa (McLaughlin et al., 2015). These approaches are not straightforward, but further investment in them will be essential to actually stop sexual violence and enhance girls' agency in contexts of poverty.

ACKNOWLEDGEMENTS

I acknowledge the significant contribution of Jenny Parkes, my colleague at the UCL Institute of Education, along with Samwel Oando and colleagues at the Catholic University of East Africa in Kenya, Francisco Januario and colleagues at Eduardo Mondlane University in Mozambique, and Susan Sabaa and GNECC in Ghana, to the research design, execution and analysis for the Stop Violence Against Girls in School project. The research was supported by ActionAid International, ActionAid country offices and implementation partners, and funded by the UK Big Lottery Fund. For the Zambia 'Working with Young People to Improve their Sexual Wellbeing' project, the NGO Young, Happy, Healthy and Safe, especially Rebecca Banda my counterpart, engaged fully in the fieldwork. The International HIV/AIDS Alliance Secretariat and Alliance Zambia provided financial, logistical and technical support for the study, and Gill Gordon provided guidance on study design. Jerker Edström at the Institute of Development Studies provided advice on data analysis.

Notes

1 It is common for girls to be aged up to and over 18 in primary schools due to late entry into the school system and high rates of repetition.
2 Developed by Options Consulting and the Centre for Development Studies, Swansea http://www.options.co.uk/peer/
3 In the Stop Violence project I worked closely with a British colleague Jenny Parkes; in the Zambia sexual health project I received support and guidance from Gill Gordon at the HIV/AIDS Alliance.
4 Pseudonyms are used. All participants quoted are female, unless stated.
5 Name changed to preserve anonymity.

REFERENCES

ActionAid (2004) *Stop Violence against Girls in School: Findings from a Twelve Country Study*. Johannesburg, ActionAid.

Ahmed, N., Flisher, A. J., Mathews, C., Jansen, S., Mukoma, W. & Schaalma, H. (2006) Process evaluation of the teacher training for an AIDS prevention programme. *Health Education Research*, 21(5), 621–632.

Berger, R. & Searles, P. (1985) Victim-offender interaction in rape: Victimological, situational, and feminist perspectives. *Women's Studies Quarterly*, 13(3/4), 9–15.

Burt, M. (1980) Cultural myths and supports for rape. *Journal of Personality and Social Psychology*, 38(2), 217–230.

Caldwell, C. H., Rafferty, J., Reischl, T. M., Loney, D., Hill, E. & Brooks, C. L. (2010) Enhancing parenting skills among nonresident African American fathers as a strategy for preventing youth risky behaviors. *American Journal of Community Psychology*, 45(1–2), 17–35.

Chilisa, B. (2006) Sex education: Subjugated discourses and adolescents' voices. In Skelton, C., Francis, B. & Smulyan, L. (Eds.) *The Sage Handbook of Gender and Education*. London, Sage, pp. 249–261.

Cobbett-Ondiek, M. (2016) Peering into 'spaces for change': Empowerment, subversion and resistance in a gendered violence prevention education programme in Kenya. *Sex Education*, 16(6), 663–677.

DevTech Systems (2007) *The Safe Schools Program: Student and Teacher Baseline Report on School-related Gender-based violence in Machinga District, Malawi.* Washington DC, USAID.

Duits, L. & van Zoonen, L. (2006) Headscarves and porno-chic: Disciplining girls' bodies in the European multicultural society. *European Journal of Women's Studies,* 13(2), 103–117.

Edström, J., Arturo, C., de Soyza, C. & Sellers, T. (2001) 'Ain't misbehavin': Beyond awareness and individual behaviour change. In Cornwall, A. & Welbourn, A. (eds.) *Realizing Rights: Transforming Approaches to Sexual and Reproductive Well-being.* New York, Zed Books, pp. 113–127.

Enriquez, M., Kelly, P. J., Cheng, A. L., Hunter, J. & Mendez, E. (2012) An intervention to address interpersonal violence among low-income Midwestern Hispanic-American teens. *Journal of Immigrant and Minority Health,* 14(2), 292–299.

Foucault, M. (2002) *The Archaeology of Knowledge.* London, Routledge.

Gavey, N. (2005) *Just Sex? The Cultural Scaffolding of Rape.* Abingdon, Routledge.

Gordon, G. (2008) 'One finger cannot kill a louse' – working with schools on gender, sexuality, and HIV in rural Zambia. In Aikman, S., Unterhalter, E. & Boler, T. (Eds.) *Gender Equality, HIV and AIDS: A Challenge for the Education Sector.* Oxford, Oxfam, pp. 129–149.

Gordon, G. & Mwale, V. (2006) Preventing HIV with young people: A case study from Zambia. *Reproductive Health Matters,* 14(28), 68–79.

Grant, M. & Hallman, K. (2006) Pregnancy-related school dropout and prior school performance in South Africa. *Working Paper.* New York.

Hallam, S. (1994) *Crimes Without Punishment: Sexual Harassment and Violence Against Female Students in Schools and Universities in Africa.* London, Africa Rights.

Heslop, J. & Banda, R. (2013) Moving beyond the 'male perpetrator, female victim' discourse in addressing sex and relationships for HIV prevention: Peer research in Eastern Zambia. *Reproductive Health Matters,* 21(41), 225–233.

Jemmott, J., Jemmott, L. & Fong, G. (1998) Abstinence and safer sex HIV risk-reduction interventions for African American adolescents: A randomized controlled trial. *The Journal of the American Medical Association,* 279(19), 1529–1536.

Jewkes, R. & Morrell, R. (2012) Sexuality and the limits of agency among South African teenage women: Theorising femininities and their connections to HIV risk practices. *Social Science & Medicine,* 74(11), 1729–1737.

Jolly, S. (2010) *Poverty and Sexuality: What are the Connections? Overview and Literature Review.* Stockholm, Swedish International Development Cooperation Agency.

Kamau, W. (2013) *Legal Treatment of Consent in Sexual Offences in Kenya.* Toronto, The Equality Effect.

Kelly, L. (1988) *Surviving Sexual Violence.* Oxford, Blackwell.

Khau, M. (2012) Sexuality education in rural Lesotho schools: Challenges and possibilities. *Sex Education,* 12(4), 411–423.

Leach, F. (2015) Researching gender violence in schools in poverty contexts: Conceptual and methodological challenges. In Parkes, J. (Ed.) *Gender Violence in Poverty Contexts: The Educational Challenge.* London, Routledge, pp. 30–48.

Leach, F., Fiscian, V., Kadzamira, E., Lemani, E. & Machakanja, P. (2003) *An Investigative Study of the Abuse of Girls in African Schools. Education Research Report.* London, DFID.

Leach, F., Slade, E. & Dunne, M. (2013) *Promising Practice in School-Related Gender-Based Violence (SRGBV) Prevention and Response Programming Globally.* Dublin, Concern Worldwide.

Lloyd, C. (2007) The role of schools in promoting sexual and reproductive health among adolescents in developing countries. *Poverty, Gender and Youth. Working Paper.* New York, Population Council.

Luke, N. (2005) Confronting the 'sugar daddy' stereotype: Age and economic asymmetries and risky sexual behavior in urban Kenya. *International Family Planning Perspectives,* 31(1), 6–14.

Mackie, G., Moneti, F., Shakya, H. & Denny, E. (2014) *What Are Social Norms? How Are They Measured?* UNICEF and the University of California.

Marteleto, L., Lam, D. & Ranchhod, V. (2008) Sexual behavior, pregnancy, and schooling among young people in urban South Africa. *Studies in Family Planning*, 39(4), 351–368.

McLaughlin, C., Swartz, S., Cobbett, M. & Kiragu, S. (2015) Inviting backchat: How schools and communities in Ghana, Swaziland and Kenya support children to contextualise knowledge and create agency through sexuality education. *International Journal of Educational Development*, 41, 208–216.

McNay, L. (2000) *Gender and Agency: Reconfiguring the Subject in Feminist and Social Theory*. Cambridge, Polity Press.

McNay, L. (2008a) *Against Recognition*. Cambridge, Polity Press.

McNay, L. (2008b) The trouble with recognition: Subjectivity, suffering, and agency. *Sociological Theory*, 26, 271–296.

Merry, S. (2009) *Gender Violence: A Cultural Perspective*. Chichester, Wiley-Blackwell.

Muehlenhard, C. & Rodgers, C. (1998) Token resistance to sex: New perspectives on an old stereotype. *Psychology of Women Quarterly*, 22(3), 443–463.

Oduro, G. Y., Swartz, S. & Arnot, M. (2012) Gender-based violence: Young women's experiences in the slums and streets of three sub-Saharan African cities. *Theory and Research in Education*, 10(3), 275–294.

Parkes, J. & Heslop, J. (2011) *Stop Violence Against Girls in School: A Cross-country Analysis of Baseline Research from Kenya, Ghana and Mozambique*. London, ActionAid International.

Parkes, J. & Heslop, J. (2013) *Stop Violence Against Girls in School: A Cross-country Analysis of Change in Ghana, Kenya and Mozambique*. London, ActionAid International.

Parkes, J., Heslop, J., Oando, S., Sabaa, S., Januario, F. & Figue, A. (2013) Conceptualising gender and violence in research: Insights from studies in schools and communities in Kenya, Ghana and Mozambique. *International Journal of Educational Development*, 33(6), 546–556.

Parkes, J. & Unterhalter, E. (2015) Hope and history: Education engagements with poverty, inequality and gender violence. In Parkes, J. (Ed.) *Gender Violence in Poverty Contexts: The Educational Challenge*. Abingdon, Routledge, pp. 11–29.

Plan International (2016) *Counting the Invisible: Using Data to Transform the Lives of Girls and Women by 2030*. Woking, Plan International.

Renold, E. & Ringrose, J. (2013) Feminisms refiguring 'sexualisation', sexuality and 'the girl'. *Feminist Theory*, 14(3), 247–254.

Southern Africa Gender Protocol Alliance (2015) *SADC Gender Protocol 2015 Barometer*. Johannesburg, Gender Links.

Switzer, H. (2010) Disruptive discourses: Kenyan Maasai schoolgirls make themselves. *Girlhood Studies*, 3, 137–155.

UNESCO (2015a) *196/EX/30 EX/Decisions, Executive Board, Hundred and Ninety-Sixth Session. Paris, UNESCO*.

UNESCO (2015b) *Emerging Evidence, Lessons and Practice in Comprehensive Sexuality Education: A Global Review*. Paris, UNESCO.

UNESCO and UNFPA (2012) *Sexuality Education: A Ten-country Review of School Curricula in East and Southern Africa*. Paris, UNESCO.

van Eerdewijk, A. (2009) Silence, pleasure and agency: Sexuality of unmarried girls in Dakar, Senegal. *Contemporary Islam*, 3(1), 7–24.

Vavrus, F. (2003) The 'Acquired Income Deficiency Syndrome': School fees and sexual risk in Northern Tanzania. *Compare: A Journal of Comparative and International Education*, 33(2), 235–250.

Walby, S. (2013) Violence and society: Introduction to an emerging field of sociology. *Current Sociology*, 61(2), 95–111.

Weedon, C. (1987) *Feminist Practice and Poststructuralist Theory*. Oxford, Blackwell.

Wells, K. (2015) Violent lives and peaceful schools: NGO constructions of modern childhood and the role of the state. In Parkes, J. (Ed.) *Gender Violence in Poverty Contexts: The Educational Challenge*. Abingdon, Routledge, pp. 168–182.

World Bank Group (2016) *Reaching Girls, Transforming Lives. Education Global Practice: Smarter Education Systems for Brighter Futures*. Washington DC, World Bank Group.

30

Youth and Community Approaches to Preventing Child Sexual Exploitation: South African and UK Project Experiences

Kate D'Arcy, Roma Thomas and Candice T. Wallace

INTRODUCTION

This chapter brings together case studies from two pieces of research – an evaluative study in the UK (D'Arcy et al., 2015) and a participatory action research project in South Africa (Wallace, 2015). The chapter aims to provide international perspectives on youth and community approaches to empowering children, young people and their families in preventing and raising awareness of Child Sexual Exploitation (CSE) and Child Sexual Abuse (CSA). It highlights the potential relevance and significance of central tenets of youth and community approaches to prevention work in CSE and CSA by drawing upon the concepts of education, voluntary engagement, participation, strengths-based approaches and rights-based models of working with children and young people.

Both case studies will be used to illustrate community level preventative work. They focus on the innovative methods used to engage children, young people and adults as social actors, collaborators, researchers and change agents, thereby shifting away from didactic approaches of designing programmes and interventions to address the 'problems' of individual young people and families, where there is no consultation or involvement in the process. The two studies: the *Families and Communities against Child Sexual Exploitation (FCASE)* project in the UK, and the *Participatory Approaches to Child Protection (PACP)* study in South Africa, together highlight unique perspectives and approaches in addressing CSA (in South Africa) and CSE (in the UK) through young people's participation, education and empowerment. The frequently hidden nature of abuse and stigma are common factors for both CSE and CSA. The authors believe that this underscores the importance of examining the potential benefits of participatory approaches and of community engagement in sexual abuse and sexual exploitation prevention work. Furthermore, these are areas that remain under-explored in the literature.

Child sexual exploitation is a form of child sexual abuse which occurs where an individual or group takes advantage of an imbalance of power to coerce, manipulate or deceive a child or young person under the age of 18 into sexual activity (a) in exchange for something the victim needs or wants, and/or (b) for the financial advantage or increased status of the perpetrator or facilitator. The victim may have been sexually exploited even if the sexual activity appears consensual. Child sexual exploitation does not always involve physical contact; it can also occur through the use of technology (Department for Education, 2017).

Child sexual abuse is defined according to the World Health Organization (WHO, 1999) as:

> ... the involvement of a child in sexual activity that he or she does not fully comprehend, is unable to give informed consent to, or for which the child is not developmentally prepared and cannot give consent, or that violates the laws or social taboos of society. Child sexual abuse is evidenced by this activity between a child and an adult or another child who by age or development is in a relationship of responsibility, trust or power, the activity being intended to gratify or satisfy the needs of the other person. This may include but is not limited to the inducement or coercion of a child to engage in any unlawful sexual activity; the exploitative use of a child in prostitution or other unlawful sexual practices and the exploitative use of children in pornographic performance and materials. (pp. 15–16)

The chapter is organised as follows. First we describe the context of youth and community work and young people's participation in CSE and CSA awareness and prevention in both countries and give a brief overview of each project. Methods and ethical principles for each of the studies are described and key findings presented. The conclusion confirms that interventions aimed at addressing violence and abuse can and should be situated in parallel to children and young people's (and their families') participation in these efforts. The community's acceptance, support and practice of this can foster a strength-based, empowering approach with regards to addressing child sexual abuse (Wallace, 2015).

YOUTH AND COMMUNITY WORK

The National Youth Association (2016) describes youth work as a process of enabling young people to improve self-belief and life skills preparation. The foundation of traditional youth and community work is underpinned by informal education and a series of values that Jeffs and Smith (1999) described as respect, promotion of well-being, truth, democracy, fairness and equality. They viewed conversations and encounters as important vehicles for empowering young people. Youth work provision in England and Wales has been subject to a large range of financial cuts and restrictions since 2015, which have led to closures and reductions in provision. However, the principles of youth and community work remain intact and its qualities have huge potential for supporting children, young people and their families, and thereby increasing protective factors in the prevention of CSE. The authors observed these principles in operation in their research with children, young people and their families in the FCASE project discussed in this chapter.

Over the past decade a series of high-profile police operations, court cases and on-going investigations into the sexual exploitation of children and young people has drawn attention to the nature and extent of CSE in the UK as a form of abuse (Beckett et al., 2013; Jay, 2014). There is growing research and practice which focuses upon support for victims and prevention of CSE (D'Arcy et al., 2015); and on the prevention of abuse before it occurs (Beckett and Warrington, 2015). While there is evidence of a need to educate and involve children and young people in preventative processes (Bhana, 2008; Cody, 2015), their participation in public-health and other approaches to prevention in both the UK and South Africa has been insufficiently articulated and practised. This principle is further explored in the South African case study presented in this chapter.

'Taking part' is an essential component of youth work practice. The common goal of participation is to create opportunities for young people to be more involved. This involves moving away from situations where young people are recipients of services towards a situation where they are invited to express their views and make a meaningful contribution to activities and decisions. There is now growing consensus that CSA prevention and support approaches must run parallel with children and young people's empowerment and that children have the capacity to deal with matters pertaining to sexuality, power relations and cultural beliefs (Bhana, 2008). CSA affects children, families, communities and entire societies, and its prevention has been listed as a public health priority by WHO (Krug et al., 2002). Although South Africa has advanced legal and policy frameworks, CSA rates are high and efforts have failed to reduce the number of cases, address cultural factors or encourage greater disclosure. Despite the suggested benefits and calls for children and young people's participation in matters affecting their lives, children remain invisible in efforts to address the issue and there remains a general paucity of research focusing on their participation in both CSE and CSA prevention and support for victims (Wallace, 2015).

THE UK STUDY – FAMILIES AND COMMUNITIES AGAINST CHILD SEXUAL EXPLOITATION

In the UK, voluntary sector services have been key players in the prevention and support of CSE (Pearce, 2009; Scott and Skidmore, 2006). Barnardo's is one of the largest non-governmental organisation (NGO) providers of CSE-related services and has for the past two decades been supporting children and young people affected by sexual exploitation.

The *Families and Communities against Child Sexual Exploitation (FCASE)* project emerged out of Barnardo's work with sexually exploited children and young people in the UK. The project was designed both to build on existing expertise and to address the gap in parental/carer support which had been identified. The aim of the project was to embed more effective practice in safeguarding children and young people, including those in foster care, from sexual exploitation, through harnessing the protective factors within a child's family and/ or foster home. The project emphasised the need for work with parents and carers as well as the child or young person in order for early signs of CSE to be identified, and for preventative strategies to be put in place. In doing so it aimed to support processes for the sharing of intelligence and the disruption of abuse.

FCASE was piloted in three sites, as a component of existing Barnardo's services which sit within existing local authority structures and processes for the safeguarding of children and young people. The project built on Barnardo's wider work with sexually exploited young people, with the unique feature of working with parents/carers. The FCASE programme therefore complemented and developed the national UK strategy in supporting CSE prevention by drawing on other areas of work, such as family group work, family conferencing, influencing and awareness-raising strategies.

The three key objectives of the FCASE project were to provide:

1 Awareness training to 1,800 professionals working with children and young people;
2 A six- to eight-week direct work programme with children, young people and their parents/ carers (this includes the introduction of FCASE, initial assessment and incorporation of additional materials);

3 Support and information to representatives from different communities to develop understanding of CSE via 36 community events.

This chapter focuses upon the second aim, the six- to eight-week direct work programme and the voices of young people and their families who participated in the programme to highlight the importance of the educational, participatory process adopted by workers delivering programme. Data collection included interviews with children and young people and their families and their FCASE workers, focus group discussions with FCASE workers and drawing on a range of quantitative data. The research received ethical approval from the University of Bedfordshire and from Barnardo's.

THE PARTICIPATORY APPROACHES TO CHILD PROTECTION (PACP) PROJECT – SOUTH AFRICA

The *Participatory Approaches to Child Protection (PACP)* project was undertaken to explore children's participation and community-based approaches aimed at involving all stakeholders, as essential elements of a holistic and sustainable solution to addressing CSA. It sought to examine whether securing the awareness, commitment and participation of both adult stakeholders and children in protection planning and implementation could serve as a catalyst of change within a South African context. The study utilised several participatory approaches to uncover cultural beliefs and practices; gave children an opportunity to voice concerns and generate solutions, addressing events which affected their lives; and empowered a community to bring about change.

The study was designed as a participatory action research project to address CSA and was undertaken by Candice Wallace as part of a placement for the organisation Project Hope UK, a global health education

and humanitarian assistance organisation which has implemented numerous initiatives within a township in South Africa as part of their Thoughtful Path Programme. The project involved five phases over five weeks that included the participation of children and young people, adult community stakeholders and government stakeholders (see below [p. 420] for a full description of these phases). It ended in a one-day report-back session to foster cross-generational sharing, the establishment and strengthening of community-based protection systems, and the development of a community action plan. The study utilised participatory methods which gave participants the opportunity to choose different methods to express themselves, including art, dance, poetry, short stories, debates, games and song. Methods for the study are described alongside the key findings since the principles of action research make methods an integral part of the change process.

As a researcher, Wallace was cognisant that there was a chance that some contributions/performances referred to real experiences of abuse, which would require heightened awareness throughout the project to ensure that appropriate support was available to participants and that strict ethical guidelines were followed. Participants were reminded at the beginning and end of each session about the need for and importance of confidentiality due to the sensitive subject matter, their age and the familiarity between some group members. Participants had the option of writing down things they did not wish to share with the wider group in notebooks provided, which could be later shared in a more secure and private setting. The ethical process for the project was one of continuous reflection and learning, with clear awareness of the possibility that a child could disclose an incident of CSA, and highlighted the need for local support in the event that this occurred. The study received ethical approval from Brunel University, London (UK).

This study highlights the viability of an approach to strengthening children's protective environments, through recognising and valuing children as agents of change, establishing networks between key stakeholders, and encouraging community ownership and commitment to the sustainability of the initiative.

FINDINGS FROM THE UK STUDY: A PROCESS OF EDUCATION AND EMPOWERMENT

Ingram and Harris (2001) describe good youth work as a learning process whereby youth workers and young people come together voluntarily to form equal caring relationships that can identify young people's needs to enable them to gain autonomy and hence take control of their lives responsibly. Although these youth work principles did not explicitly inform the design of the FCASE model, they do underpin the ethos of the work carried out and we draw on these principles to analyse project findings.

In terms of a *learning process*, the direct work programme included a series of sessions for parents, covering: understanding and living with risk; what is CSE?; abusive relationships and grooming; the Internet and consent. Sessions for young people covered: relationships; risk; abusive relationships; grooming in relationships; consent, law and e-safety, and each one ended with a summary of learning

The project entailed *voluntary engagement*: although families were referred to the programme by a range of agencies, including schools, social workers and police, they chose whether to take part or not. The first step in the programme was to ask if families wanted to be involved. If they agreed, one worker would work with the parent or carer and another with the young person. The time-frame of the programme was six to eight weeks for most families, however for more complex situations the work lasted longer. Workers needed to engage young people and their parents in the programme, and flexibility in time and place (as well as the delivery of the programme) was an important factor. For example, parents and carers appreciated meetings being organised around their work responsibilities and other commitments. Consequently, most of the work with families and young people took place 'out of hours'. Workers focused meetings on the needs of the young person and their parents or carers. For one young man, work was undertaken in a van outside his home because that was the only way he was allowed to engage with FCASE. Workers also focused the learning programme on the needs of young people. There was certainly flexibility in terms of the materials used. For one young woman, aged 14, with a much younger learning age, a whole new set of resources were developed in consultation with the clinical supervisor. The new material involved creative and imaginative forms of play involving collage, drawing and use of the sand tray. For the purposes of the evaluation, the researcher observed a refresher session between this young woman and two FCASE workers and it was clear that the young woman had learnt and retained far more about staying safe than the FCASE workers could gauge during the actual sessions. Another example was where a worker adapted work for a young man on the autistic spectrum, making sure that sessions were more visual and asking him to create a poster summarising what he had learnt as an aide memoire for when the programme had finished.

A central focus of the project was the *meeting of young people's needs*. Some young people found it hard to focus on one thing at a time so the delivery of the programme work was fluid. This tended to be the case for most young people – all aspects of the programme were covered, but some areas might receive more attention than others depending on the young person's needs. Workers' previous experience in working with young people and CSE was clearly advantageous.

The young man on the autistic spectrum praised the approach; he also commented on his relationship with his worker, which was described as helpful because the worker was not a teacher or a member of his family. The fact that the worker was not his social worker or teacher made a difference as they were viewed as independent, even though several FCASE workers were qualified social workers.

> Social workers and teachers they teach you about outside life. The FCASE worker talks about stuff more close to home, outside life and inside life and everything. (Young person)

The approach of the workers demonstrated strong relational skills and high levels of engagement with families, which sometimes were surprising to young people themselves.

> Everyone at school prefers younger teachers and feels younger workers understand young people better. (Young person)
>   However, the young person reflected that somehow they clicked with the FCASE worker and started to enjoy the discussions and going to McDonalds.

Other research has highlighted the importance of such skills in work relating to child sexual exploitation (Shuker, 2012). A number of the families had experienced severe trauma and high levels of harm before the FCASE referral and had, in their words, experienced poor responses from other agencies such as the police, social services and schools. This was contrasted with the support that they felt they received from FCASE:

> FCASE was the only agency that has been consistent and done what they had said they would do. They were honest and kept in contact and returned your calls. (Parent)
>   In CAF meetings – we had been thinking we must be rubbish parents. (Parent)

The nature of the FCASE programme facilitated support for families and this was different to other services:

> I can voice my fears. Social Care and Social Workers are concerned with procedure; they don't deal with me – if I am scared. (Carer)

The combination of voluntary engagement, flexibility and identifying young people's needs resulted in learning. The research found that young people commented positively on the FCASE programme and process, they could recall what they had learnt and made changes to their lifestyles. This reflects the goal of 'good youth work', described by Ingram and Harris as 'achieving the autonomy to take control of their lives in a responsible way' (2001: p. vii). The fact that parents and young people undertook a structured programme was found to be beneficial as family members were learning together about CSE and this made it easier to discuss subjects that are often challenging:

> I used to feel on edge but now I feel much more confident. Now I know what is safe/unsafe, right and wrong so I can say no. But she also knows her mum is there to support her if things go wrong. I would not have realised this person was grooming – that is the word she used – and it shocked me, we did the same session and we were both able to discuss it afterwards. (Parent)
>   I don't complain about my curfew of 7pm, before I thought it was too early but now I realise 8pm is too late and I can still have fun and come in earlier. (Young person)

The UNCRC (1989) Article 12 states that when adults are making decisions that affect children, children have the right to say what they think should happen and have their opinions taken into account. The FCASE programme facilitated a rights-based approach as parents and carers were having conversations with their children and involving them in decisions. Parents and young people noted that this had reduced arguments in the house because it had opened lines of trust and communication. Parents and carers spoke about feeling confident that young people had been given vital information about keeping safe and also felt like they were being treated with respect:

> This house has changed in the way we deal with teenage angst. If we feel angry, we leave it and go back when we've calmed down whereas previously it would get blown out of proportion.

My son had lost even the language at home. He was taking street language into the home. He'd be rude. He has been told he is rude. Hearing this from an outside person has made a difference.

Barnardo's stabilises her and helps her along. [Name of young woman] comes to us now, she informs us of things that are happening. Before she was hiding things but now she has seen we are willing to talk about it.

Similarly, one young person summarised her learning as encompassing the following:

Types of abuse, how to avoid arguments, about internet safety ... and I learnt about myself.

In some cases the study found that both parents and carers and young people were expressing the same views:

We learnt how to deal with our differences. (Carer)
There is less arguing. (Young person)
It has stopped a lot of arguments. We feel more confident. (Carer)
We both learnt to stop and listen. (Young person)
We learnt how to communicate with each other. (Parent)

FCASE concentrated on the strengths of families, rather than what was lacking, leading to improved relationships at home:

We don't fight anymore. I have learnt a lot and it changes my life. I think there should be more services for mums and daughters ... it did help. All her stress was leaving and all mine so we didn't argue. (Parent)

Parents also commented on the improvements in relationships and how the information received had helped them feel equipped with understanding and respect for other family members. Parents explained how relations had improved:

I understand my daughter a little better now and we can all talk about things now things you don't like to talk about. (Parent)

It has improved our home life; we can see each other's opinions and respect them. It has helped the future of my daughter, my son-in-law, me and it extends to family and friends as you talk to them about things. (Parent)

In one case involving a single father using the service, outcomes included learning about internet controls and safety. He noted that this was the most 'prominent thing' and it 'was good to be able to talk to someone else about it, because I'm on my own and it's quite difficult for me to get my head around things, especially for girls'.

This strengths-based process enabled families to reach joint decisions about safeguarding, enabling young people to have a voice in decisions made about them. For example, in reaching agreement over daily routines, one parent was very pleased that her daughter now calls her when she is out and explains where she is and what time she will be back, whereas in the past she would go missing for several hours without contact.

Relationships also improved because FCASE focused on parent/carer strengths. A review (D'Arcy, unpublished; D'Arcy et al., 2015) which explored effective approaches to support the parents of adolescents who have been affected by CSE, suggested that an ideal model of support comprises of helping relationships based on voluntary participation and trust and engagement with young people in the design, delivery and evaluation of support and intervention; both are key principles of good youth work.

Parents/carers spoke of the way that FCASE support had reassured them about their parenting:

It helped with parenting. We feel happier now.

FCASE workers highlighted that the ability to build relationships in a short space of time is key to assessing strengths and enables workers to challenge a parent or carer without them feeling that they are being talked down to or judged.

A rights-based approach was also evident in the final closing meetings at the end of the programme where families sat down with workers and other professionals involved to plan action for the future. These meetings were really valued by young people, parents, carers and workers, as evidenced in the quotes below. Reflecting on this process in a focus group discussion, workers spoke of the opportunity to create a space where conflicts could be resolved and mutually supportive rules could be established. As a worker stated:

> These are good for getting everyone into one room and putting it all up on to flip chart paper, and often parents/carers and young people realise that they have the same objectives. (Worker)

It is striking that this had often been the first opportunity for parents/carers and young people to do this.

> They'd listen to us and take note of what we wanted as a family. (Parent)
> I thought the Safer You meeting was good because it got me back into school, I was frustrated to not be attending school. At the Safer You meeting we talked about harm – I'd probably be in jail now if I hadn't done this programme. (Young person)

To conclude, there is clear evidence that the process of the FCASE model was underpinned by core youth and community principles and values. There was respect, equality and participation for the whole family. The FCASE approach was voluntary and families themselves chose to take part. The programme facilitated a process that was empowering for parents and their child, and as a result of FCASE they were able to take control of their lives together. The holistic mechanisms that brought about change in families also reduced risk behaviours, which supports our argument that community-level preventative work engages children, young people and adults as social actors, collaborators, researchers and change agents in the prevention of abuse and violence.

FINDINGS FROM THE SOUTH AFRICA STUDY: A JOURNEY OF AWARENESS, EMPOWERMENT AND CHANGE

Active and voluntary participation is a key element of the youth work process. It is a way of thinking and working that facilitates joint decision-making by young people and youth workers and promotes personal and social development. This intervention adopted a participatory action research (PAR) approach which involved collaborative research, education and action that is oriented towards social change. Kemmis and Wilkinson (1998) point to some important features of PAR, namely its ability to recognise actors as active agents working towards social action rather than passive subjects; encourage individuals to examine and challenge the role of larger social, political, economic and cultural conditions that shape their identities and actions; inevitably touch on the issues of power, domination and hegemony; as well as its reflexive nature as participants are encouraged to critically examine their own role. These features were embodied in the design of the study through its recognition of the role of children as social agents, encouraging their full participation in the study design, development of prevention strategies, analysis of the power of various actors in CSA, and the reflection of participants on the role they play in addressing CSA. Although the principles of youth work highlighted by Ingram and Harris (2001) did not guide the design of this study, a youth development lens was applied to the process of PAR and the elements of voluntary engagement, meeting young peoples' needs, and a learning process can also be seen in the findings.

The study was conducted in a township in West Rand District, Gauteng Province, South Africa, with an estimated 10,000 or more orphan and vulnerable children. The location was chosen following Project Hope UK's 2010 assessment, which indicated that the population composition reflected a 'microcosm' of a wider orphan and other vulnerable children context across South Africa and much of Sub-Saharan Africa. Access to the community was negotiated through Project Hope UK and formed part of a wider community-based child protection initiative. In line with the principles of PAR, the findings were used by Project Hope UK and the community to propose and initiate local-level changes, such as the establishment of a community-based child rights and protection unit, and of a children's centre established as a safe space in a once-abandoned lot, as well as creating networks between key stakeholders to strengthen the community's response to CSA. The project was implemented in five phases:

Phase 1: A semi-structured focus group was held with an initial group of nine children aged 9–14, selected through volunteer convenience sampling, to gain insight and to pilot research techniques and materials, and to consult with children about the research project and gain their feedback. This assisted in informing the design of the study, allowing children to play a strategic role in the formation and selection of methods used.

Phase 2: A participatory session was held with 27 adult community stakeholders, including representatives from non-governmental organisations, counsellors, community workers, teachers and parents, who received an open invitation to participate. This session allowed the participants to open dialogue between them about the issue of CSA, and establish collaborative relationships and support systems. It also provided insight about the community views, cultural beliefs, perception on actions to tackle CSA, participants' ideas on what is needed and limitations or obstacles to address the issue.

Phase 3: Four sessions were held with 28 children and young people, aged 9–17 years, in participatory activities designed to explore key topics. Children and young people were introduced to a range of participatory techniques and invited to make additional suggestions. Children were able to help shape the agenda, draw upon concrete real-life events, talk about complex and abstract issues, and to interpret social structures and relationships which affect their lives. Thus, participatory methods explored children's capacities, needs and interests from their own points of view rather than viewing them as vulnerable victims. By exploring children's concept of CSA the findings show numerous social

constructs that exist within a child's world that cannot be ignored or overlooked and are a significant source for understanding and dealing with CSA. These included salient factors, beliefs and practices present within children's subculture and gender-based beliefs held by both boys and girls.

Phase 4: Data analysis was dynamic and recursive and occurred throughout the process through open reflection and dialogue with participants during the participatory sessions in Phase 3. Children were asked to explain their submissions, providing the researcher with their interpretation and thus avoiding misinterpretation (Hazel, 1996). Within all of the participatory sessions children were also given an opportunity to write their thoughts before offering spontaneous verbal answers, they were therefore able to take their time and ensure that the finished product was a true representation of their thoughts. A journal was also kept by the participants and the researcher to foster individual reflection and provide a forum for the continuous exploration of developing ideas throughout the study.

Phase 5: At the end of the participatory sessions with the children and young people, a one-day preliminary report-back session was held with the adult stakeholders from Phase 2, where the contributions of the child participants were displayed. The session was part of a four-day Child Sexual Abuse workshop under the PACP project involving the Child Protection Unit of the South African police and social workers, designed to complement the study and simultaneously build adult awareness and capacity on the subject of CSA. The report-back session provided an opportunity for adult stakeholders to review children's submissions, which provided a view of children's subculture to better inform prevention strategies, acknowledge children's capacities in proposing solutions, and highlight the importance of their participation in informing advocacy and action. Due to the date and time of the session, the children were unable to report directly to the community stakeholders. The session was helpful in ensuring the children's ideas were taken on board in community planning and were given the necessary support in prevention initiatives. This allowed the community stakeholders to recognise and value children's perspectives and actively nurture meaningful exchange between adults and children within the community. The children's suggestions and recommendations were all incorporated into the action plan developed by the adults and there was a commitment to establishing a children's ambassador group where the voices of children could always be included in and guide community initiatives so that they would continue to participate in matters which affect their lives.

The stakeholders discussed the contributions and recommendations of the children and young people, and made resolutions to act on some aspects through establishing community-based mechanisms to address CSA, continuing to create spaces for children's participation, and creating safe spaces through strengthening child protective environments. The session contributed to the formation of the Child Rights and Protection Unit, established under The Thoughtful Path programme, as well as a Children's Ambassador Group and an action plan for continued initiatives after the study, including those proposed by the children and young people. A member of the children's ambassador group will represent the group in community planning, and participate in the design, planning and implementation of future initiatives, to ensure the voices of children continue to be heard in matters affecting their lives. These sessions demonstrated the importance of grounding initiatives in local knowledge and experiences, and involving communities in the process.

VOLUNTARY ENGAGEMENT

Participation in all the above sessions was voluntary and invitation letters and consent forms, requiring consent by both parent and child, were sent to children, young people and adults, seeking their willingness to participate. Children and parents were allowed time to reflect on the project and were given opportunities to put questions to the researcher prior to making a decision on whether to participate. The sessions with children were held on Saturdays, which avoided disruption of school attendance. Additionally, participation was flexible, and children and young people chose whether they wanted to attend on any given day and for any number of sessions. On one occasion, four participants who were not issued invitation letters heard about the sessions and attended. Similarly, the adult sessions were held conveniently around the available times of the majority, which allowed for greater participation.

As highlighted by Langhout and Thomas (2010: 61), PAR can be broadly characterised as a theoretical standpoint and collaborative methodology which ensures that those who are involved in research have a voice. This was particularly important as often the voices of children remain unheard in defining issues which address them.

> I like that we were discussing and coming up with our own plans and that shows that it's a team not a crèche. (Young person)

This method proved useful in capturing the voices of both children and community stakeholders when proposing solutions. The researcher drew on her own professional experience as a mediator and child/youth worker, which proved helpful in the sessions. The findings of the study were presented, incorporating children's pictures and excerpts from their written submissions. One such example is the below statement from a campaign message proposed by a young person:

> As South Africans we must stand up [for] these children … The situation is the problem a child's future is blocked. Children don't know what they can do or what they did to deserve this. South Africa's great people. We can help these children. Thank you!!!

The sessions were fluid: participants were introduced to a range of methods and were encouraged to think about additional methods for expressing their feelings and ideas. This recognised the need to tune into children and young people's 'culture of communication' in order to reveal their knowledge (Clark, 2010). Young people were free to choose the type of participatory method that they were most comfortable with and felt would best communicate their views, thereby, as Holloway and Valentine noted (2000), allowing them to construct their views in their own terms. Participants were able to contribute to the design and conduct of the sessions, to break down power imbalances and feel comfortable and unrestricted with regard to sharing information. They decided whether they worked individually or in groups, and the composition of those groups. The researcher acted as a facilitator, introducing key topic areas for exploration, observing and navigating the discourse led by the participants, and stimulating further discussion when necessary.

Children and young people were eager to develop their ideas through whatever method they chose. As such, they created messages, through their various mediums, geared towards educating various stakeholders about CSA. This allowed participants to feel empowered and provided an opportunity for them to express their agency in addressing CSA. Consequently, participants spoke about organising a group to continue working on other CSA initiatives, for example, community marches and posters, as well as finding a way to share the presentations they created with other people, demonstrating child-led advocacy. Below is an example of a message from a child participant geared towards parents.

> Have an open relationship with your child ... teach your child about the privacy of the body ... listen to your children when they try to tell you something and give much attention to your child so that they won't seek it anywhere else. (Young person)

Embedded in their presentations were bold mission statements and calls for the end of child abuse, displaying initiative and recognition of CSA as a social problem by expressing themselves on the issue and the need for its eradication. In reflecting on the project most participants saw it as a *learning process* essential to educating the community and children, as well as to empowering the community to address CSA.

> It was great because I knew nothing about sexual abuse, this campaign has been more educational ... (Young person)
> All these lessons taught me how to avoid CSA and how to prevent it. (Young person)
> As a mother this information helped me a lot to know my kids better and to understand the consequences of abuse and what exactly is sexual abuse. (Community worker)

The design of the PACP project, which included a simultaneous programme for adult stakeholders, had a number of distinct advantages. Through increased knowledge of CSA, parents/carers could create safer environments for their children and take better measures towards preventing the occurrence of CSA in their homes and in the community. Additionally, the participation of both adults and children, as with FCASE, resulted in open discussions on decreasing the secrecy surrounding CSA and stimulating adult–child discussions about sexuality. While most of the adult participants were parents, only a couple were parents of the children participating in the initiative. This was due to the distance and hours of work, which made it hard to attend. In order to expand the reach of the benefits of the project to the parents of the participants, the community worker established relationships with some of the parents and knowledge was shared through informal methods where possible.

The PACP project utilised a rights-based approach by bridging children's right to protection and their right to participation, which are often treated as oppositional thereby limiting the scope and depth of opportunities for them to be heard in matters affecting children's lives (Moses, 2008). The study confirms that children, though often afforded little room to operate as independent actors, are willing to do so with some adult support where necessary. The findings support the need to establish further mechanisms to facilitate the participation of children in decisions affecting them.

The study also showed that children and young people's involvement in the process was an intervention in itself, where participants learned skills through guided participation and active engagement with conditions that facilitated empowerment as well as social change.

> The best thing is to learn about CSA and learn about how you can manage problems facing you in life. (Young person)
> I think the project was very pleasing and very specific about what happens around us. We must always get with things like these and tell the community about these kinds of effects/happenings in our environmental situation. The happy part was when we presented our own thoughts ... (Young person)

As they asserted their knowledge, the children and young people creatively built on strategies to protect themselves (Jewkes et al., 2005). At the end, they shared their desire to become advocates for themselves and others, in particular through expressing their agency and the importance of their participation.

> We have to make adults understand that children can play a role in CSA ... children can talk to their own parents and guardians to show them how children could play a role in CSA. (Young person)
> We must involve ourselves as children to take part in community programmes ... we have the responsibility to show interest and take part. (Young person)

A positive experience of participation can generate confidence and a belief among children and adults that they can make a difference, and may encourage them to become actively involved in their local community and beyond. The PACP project's unique and

holistic approach involving collaboration between government agencies, community stakeholders and children in the development of child protection initiatives can provide meaningful and long-term protection for all children.

> Five years on, based on the evidence revealed through the research, practical and effective solutions to the challenges faced by children threatened by or experiencing abuse in the South African township have been developed to benefit thousands of children each year. (Director, Project Hope UK)

This supports our argument that securing the participation and empowerment of both adults and children as social actors in community-based protection planning and implementation can serve as a catalyst for change.

CONCLUSION

The two studies underscore the value of empowerment, participation and community approaches in addressing CSE and CSA. Together they contribute to a larger argument about the benefits of applying the principles of youth work in working with children and young people on sensitive topics. The effectiveness of these approaches in two very different contexts – a UK child protection framework, a South African community-based systems strengthening approach – demonstrates the potential for these insights to be applicable in a variety of countries and contexts. Evidence from both of the programmes also points to the importance of taking youth work beyond the boundaries of working solely with children and young people and involving parents, carers, community members and other stakeholders in ethical, meaningful engagement.

The importance of ensuring that children and young people remain at the forefront of decision-making and planning along with family members and the community in a programme is demonstrated in the South African study, while the UK study highlights the benefits of children and young people learning together in a parallel programme with their parents or carers. It is useful to see these elements of the two studies as related points for practice which youth workers need to consider as part of a rights-based approach. We do not suggest one 'right' answer for practice but instead hope that the insights from these two studies point up dilemmas that need to be addressed in the design of programmes.

These two studies suggest some advantages of a voluntary, strengths-based approach in supporting children and young people and their parents/carers. These include:

- Clear educational value for young people, parents, carers and even the wider community;
- Improvements in family relations and consequently a reduction in risk;
- Knowledge and confidence about keeping safe;
- Improved self-awareness and self-esteem for parents/carers and young people.

This chapter reveals how practices that encourage joint participation of community stakeholders allows for the creation and strengthening of networks and the establishment of sustainable systems grounded within the community. This reinforces the need for a holistic approach involving children, young people, parents, the community and the government, all working together and playing a significant part in the prevention of CSA and CSE and in child protection to create safer environments.

REFERENCES

Barnardo's (2011) *An Assessment into the Potential Savings from Barnardo's Interventions for Young People who have been Sexually Exploited*, Ilford, Barnardo's.

Barnardo's (2012) *Tackling Child Sexual Exploitation. Believe in Children: Helping Local Authorities to Develop Effective Responses*, Ilford, Barnardo's.

Beckett, H. and Warrington, C. (2015) *Making Justice Work*, University of Bedfordshire.

Beckett, H., Brodie, I., Factor, F., Melrose, M., Pearce, J., Pitts, J., Shuker, J. and Warrington, C. (2013) *'It's Wrong … But you Get Used to It': A Qualitative Study of Gang-associated Sexual Violence Towards, and Exploitation of, Young People in England*, University of Bedfordshire.

Bhana, D. (2008) 'Beyond stigma? Young children's responses to HIV and AIDS' *Culture, Health and Sexuality* 10(7), pp. 725–738.

Clark, A. (2010) 'Young children as protagonists and the role of participatory, visual methods in engaging multiple perspectives' *American Journal of Community Psychology* 46(1–2), pp. 115–123.

Cody, C. (2015) 'Young people affected by sexual violence as change makers in prevention efforts: what are the opportunities and what are the risks'. Available at: https://www.beds.ac.uk/__data/assets/pdf_file/0008/487106/FINAL-Participation-for-Prevention-Colloquium-Report-Low-Res.pdf

D'Arcy, K. (unpublished) *Families and Communities Against Child Sexual Exploitation (FCASE): Exploring Effective Approaches to Support the Parents of Adolescents Who have been Affected by CSE: Mapping and Reviewing the Literature*, University of Bedfordshire.

D'Arcy, K., Dhaliwal, S., Thomas, R., Brodie, I. and Pearce, J. (2015) *Families and Communities Against Child Sexual Exploitation (FCASE): Final Evaluation Report*, University of Bedfordshire.

Department of Education (2017) *Child Sexual Exploitation: Definition and Guide for Practitioners*. Available at: https://www.gov.uk/government/publications/child-sexual-exploitation-definition-and-guide-for-practitioners

Hazel, N. (1996) 'Elicitation techniques with young people' *Social Research* 12, University of Surrey.

HIV/Aids Alliance (2008) *Feel! Think! Act! A Guide to Interactive Drama for Sexual and Reproductive Health for Young People*, Brighton, International HIV/Aids Alliance.

Holloway, S. and Valentine, G. (eds) (2000) *Children's Geographies*, London, Routledge.

Ingram, G. and Harris, J. (2001) *Delivering Good Youth Work: A Working Guide to Surviving and Thriving*, Lyme Regis, Russell House Publishing.

Jago, S. with Pearce, J., Arocha, L., Brodie, I., Melrose, M. and Warrington, C. (2011) *What's Going on to Safeguard Children and Young People from Sexual Exploitation?*, University of Bedfordshire. Available at: http://uobrep.openrepository.com/uobrep/bitstream/10547/315159/1/wgoreport2011-121011.pdf

Jay, A. (2014) *Independent Inquiry into Child Sexual Exploitation in Rotherham 1997–2013*, Rotherham. Available at: http://www.rotherham.gov.uk/downloads/file/1407/independent_inquiry_cse_in_rotherham

Jeffs, T. and Smith, M. (1999) *Youth Work Practice*, Palgrave Macmillan, Basingstoke, UK.

Jewkes, R., Penn-Kekana, L. and Rose-Junius, H. (2005) '"If they rape me, I can't blame them": reflections on gender in the social context of child rape in South Africa and Namibia' *Social Science and Medicine* 61(8), pp. 1809–1820.

Jupp-Kina, V. K. (2010) 'Participant or protagonist? The impact of the personal on the development of children and young people's participation'. Doctoral thesis, Durham University. Available at Durham e-theses online: http://etheses.dur.ac.uk/452/

Kemmis, S. and Wilkinson, M. (1998) 'Participatory action research and the study of practice'. In Atweh, B., Kemmis, S. and Weeks, P. (eds.) *Action Research in Practice: Partnership for Social Justice in Education*, Thousand Oaks, CA, Sage, pp. 21–36.

Krug, E. G., Dahlberg, L. L., Mercy, J. A., Zwi, A. B. and Lozano, R. (2002) *World Report on Violence and Health*, Geneva, World Health Organization.

Langhout, R. D. and Thomas, E. (2010) 'Imagining participatory action research in collaboration with children: an introduction' *American Journal of Community Psychology* 46(1–2), pp. 60–66.

Moses, S. (2008) 'Children and participation in South Africa: an overview' *International Journal of Children's Rights* 16(3), pp. 327–342.

National Youth Association (2016) 'What is youth work?' http://www.nya.org.uk/careers-youth-work/what-is-youth-work/

Office of the Children's Commissioner (2013) '*Sex Without Consent, I Suppose that is Rape': How Young People in England Understand Sexual Consent*. Available at: http://cwasu.org/wp-content/uploads/2016/07/CONSENT-REPORT-EXEC-SUM.pdf

Parents Against CSE (PACE)/Virtual College (2013) *Are Parents in the Picture? Professional and Parental Perspectives of Child Sexual Exploitation*, PACE, London.

Pearce, J. J. (2009) *Young People and Sexual Exploitation: It Isn't Hidden, You Just Aren't Looking*. London, Routledge Falmer.

Scott, S. and Skidmore, P. (2006) *Reducing the Risk: Barnardo's Support for Sexually Exploited Young People. A Two-Year Evaluation*. Ilford, Barnardo's.

Shuker, L. (2012) *Evaluation of Barnardo's Safe Accommodation Project for Sexually Exploited and Trafficked Young People*. University of Bedfordshire.

Smeaton, E. (2013) *Working with Children and Young People Who Experience Running Away and Child Sexual Exploitation: An Evidence-based Guide for Practitioners*. Available at: http://www.barnardos.org.uk/resources/research_and_publications/working-with-children-and-young-people-who-experience-running-away-and-child-sexual-exploitation-an-evidence-based-guide-for-practitioners/publication-view.jsp?pid=PUB-2300

UNCRC (1989) *The United Convention on the Rights of the Child*. Available at: https://downloads.unicef.org.uk/wp-content/uploads/2010/05/UNCRC_united_nations_convention_on_the_rights_of_the_child.pdf?_ga=1.14580532.2052788703.1493206543

Wallace, C. (2015) 'Unveiling child sexual abuse through participatory action research' *Social and Economic Studies* 64(1), pp. 13–36.

World Health Organization (WHO) (1999) *Report of the Consultation on Child Abuse Prevention*, Geneva, 29–31 March. Document WHO/HSC/PVI/99.1.

31

Allies, Not Accomplices: What Youth Work Can Learn from Trans and Disability Movements

Wolfgang Vachon and Tim McConnell

INTRODUCTION

This chapter will discuss trans and disability social justice activist movements, highlighting the ways in which these movements challenge normative agendas and what youth work can garner from them. Through this, we will trouble the normalization agenda embedded in much of youth work, critically interrogating the ways in which the privileging of certain types of knowledge enables the ongoing marginalization of diverse communities. Responding to the marginalization of their own subjective knowledges, members of both trans and disability communities have challenged legal, social, and medical interventions which seek to define and erase us, resulting in two of the most innovative, progressive, and effective social justice undertakings of the past decade and a half.

Tim writes from the location of a young, white, trans person with a history of problematic drug use who is now drawing on that lived experience to develop programmes

for similarly identifying youth. Wolfgang writes from the location of a white middle-age cisgender male with a 25-year history of working with young people. In our lived experiences one, the other, or both of us is, or has a history of being, a 'system-involved youth', disabled, and trans. Through these locations and transitions we will identify learnings from trans and disability movements, encourage (while critiquing) 'ally' as a position for youth workers, and seek ways to adopt an anti-oppressive approach to being in relationship with young people. Although much has been written regarding working with both trans youth and youth with disabilities, our intention is to examine the ways in which the work of trans and disability communities is applicable broadly to youth work.

We have opted to address trans and disability activisms concurrently for a number of reasons. Primarily, these movements resonate with our own lived experiences, and it is our hope to acquaint those in the field of youth work with the complex histories of our communities. It is not our intention to conflate the experiences of trans and disabled people, nor to suggest that experiences of oppression are identical – or even comparable – across communities. Rather, we believe that both the bases of trans and disabled marginalization, as well as the forms of resistance developed in response, are sufficiently similar to identify cross-movement parallels. In both instances, biological essentialism is utilized to identify specific bodies as abnormal, implicitly naturalizing the experiences of those that do not share the distinguishing characteristic(s). Consequently, the latter – on the basis of their normalized identities – are socially privileged to create medico-judicial frameworks that deny the autonomy of the former on the basis of their difference. Similarly, resistance to these discourses in both trans and disability justice communities has prioritized denaturalizing the subject positions of cisgender and non-disabled people (although the term 'otherly disabled' may be more appropriate) while legitimizing the subjective knowledges of trans and disabled people.

We are writing this chapter from our social locations as an attempt to highlight master narratives. A narrative which has historically sought to dominate the discourse, and thus the bodies, of trans, disabled, and young people. As Thorne and McClean (2003) note, 'Master narratives are used by cultural stakeholders as strategies for the 'management of sense-making' (p. 171). This management seeks to legitimize particular voices and minimize others. In challenging master narratives, we have actively sought out perspectives from people who identify as members of specific communities. This means, where possible, we will use texts from people within communities, in addition to, and occasionally instead of, people from outside of those communities. This is a crucial step in listening to and honouring historically marginalized or dismissed voices.

SUBJECTIVE KNOWLEDGES OF TRANS IDENTITY

Knowledge/Power

The term transgender, as it is commonly understood, entered public discourse in the early 1990s. Popularized by Leslie Feinberg, the term was intended to function as a point of political allegiance for 'gender outlaws' – an umbrella term to unite all those marginalized by their divergence from traditional gender norms (Feinberg & World View Forum, 1992). Many texts – both popular and academic – continue to define trans identity in this way. In the context of this chapter, however, we use trans to refer to anyone who does not identify with the sex they were assigned at birth. Trans identity is not contingent upon primary or secondary sex characteristics, sex reassignment surgery (SRS), taking hormones, nor any other form of medical, psychological, or legal intervention. Trans, therefore, is neither an imposed category nor a political expedient, but an identity that one claims.

Although interest in trans experiences has increased in recent years, much of what is presumed to be known does not come from trans-identified people. Instead, the Eurocentric cultural image of trans people is one constructed by cissexist discourses in which the unspoken normativity of cisgender identity casts trans identity as a biological accident. These discourses, invested in the construction of a particular kind of gendered subject, are always 'an exercise in the study of deviance from the standpoint of a normativity that does not have to declare itself' (Stryker, 2011, p. 8). Identities, after all, are not created in socio-political vacuums. Rather, they are 'complex processes, situated in history, through which we enact, create, resist, collude with and change embodied ways of being' (Shotwell, 2012, p. 2).

Trans bodies, therefore, are politicized bodies, 'hotly contested site[s] of cultural inscription, meaning machine[s] for the production of an ideal type' (Stone, 1989, p. 11). These bodies, however, are our bodies: my body belongs to me, yet I am not free to define it. Its meaning has already been declared elsewhere, and is always defined in relation to what it is not. Namely, my body is not a cisgender body, and is therefore not a normal body.

Arguably, although gender variance exists across time, space and cultures, the current Eurocentric conception of trans identity was created in the clinic, when gender non-conformity met modern medicine (Irving, 2008; Stone, 1989). As it is commonly understood – both within and outside of the medical community – trans identity is synonymous with gender dysphoria. According to the diagnostic criteria of the DSM-5, to be trans is to be trapped in the wrong body, to have a body that is defective, and therefore to be sick (American Psychiatric Association, 2013). This so-called 'wrong body model' of trans identity locates a deficiency in the bodies of trans people – or, alternatively, our minds – proposing that trans identity results from a 'misalignment between gender identity and the sexed body' (Bettcher, 2014, p. 383). This conception is espoused by many trans people, and legitimately so. Indeed, it is neither our intention nor our place to question the validity of the self-identification of trans people. If a trans person asserts that they were born in the wrong body, we defer to this description of their experience. We recognize that some trans people see the DSM-5 as 'better' than the DSM-IV, and, further, some want a 'diagnosis' to remain in the DSM. This is often linked to financial rationales (if it is an illness, then medical procedures, such as SRS, may be covered by health care plans) (Davy, 2015). Without minimizing these perspectives, we spotlight the origins of the framework that has proven harmful to many trans people, origins legitimized through psychiatry and the technologies of modern medicine.

Much has been written about the function of power/psychiatry. Writing about the construction of mental health diagnoses, for example, Brown (1994) asserts that:

> The decision to call a cluster of behaviors a mental illness is responsive to many factors that have nothing to do with science but a great deal to do with the feelings, experiences, and epistemologies of those in power and dominance in mental health disciplines. (p. 135)

In the context of trans identity, psychiatry has created an illness that regulates gender and its expressions, and is therefore complicit in a 'long-term biopolitical project of cultivating gender congruence while eliminating incongruity' (Currah & Stryker, 2014, p. 4). For this reason, Arlene Lev (2013) describes the diagnosis of Gender Dysphoria as a 'narrative of an oppressed people and their liberation struggle' (p. 3).

Historically, although sexologists, psychiatrists and physicians have been 'treating' trans people since the late 18th century, gender dysphoria clinics were only institutionalized in the 1960s (Stone, 1989). During these formative stages, the clinic also functioned as a 'charm school', in an attempt to produce 'not simply anatomically legible females [the majority of those engaging with medical technologies were trans women], but women' (Stone, 1989, p. 8). Therefore, those seeking diagnosis and treatment were granted access to medical care on the basis of their ability to successfully adhere to established gender norms. The indication of success, in this instance, was the gender attribution of non-trans people.

A recent example of this being successfully challenged by the trans community is the case of Dr Kenneth Zucker. Zucker was the chair of the workgroup on 'Sexual and Gender Identity Disorders' for the DSM-5 and head of the Child Youth and Family (CYF) Gender Identity Clinic (GIC) at Toronto's Centre for Addiction and Mental Health (CAMH). After years of complaints from the trans community in response to Zucker's 'treatments' of trans children and youth, many of whom went through the clinic as children and youth themselves, CAMH initiated a review of his practices in 2015. Upon receiving the report, CAMH closed the clinic, and terminated Dr Zucker's licence. In the press release they stated 'While the reviewers identified some strengths in the clinic, they found the CYF GIC's approach to providing services to be out of step with current and evolving clinical and operational approaches. The reviewers recommended that CAMH engage with the community to determine future directions' (CAMH, 2015, para. 2).

The marginalization of trans people, therefore, is not simply a function of laws that prohibit certain behaviours. Rather, gendered identities are managed through the diffuse social systems that Foucault refers to as technologies of disciplinary power (Foucault, 1995). This power, according to Foucault is productive rather than repressive. That is, it does not rely simply on legal systems to tell us what we cannot do. Instead, it utilizes knowledge production to create categories that manage and regulate behaviour. This knowledge then creates norms, interfacing with power to transform embodied differences into social hierarchies (Foucault, 2003; Stryker, 2006). In the case of trans identities, the 'subject position of transsexuality' created by the medical establishment 'promotes the creation of norm-abiding gendered subjects' (Spade, 2006, p. 2). Practically, this means that trans identities are always abnormal, always inauthentic, always subject to the scrutiny of the institutions' cisgender gaze.

Access or Authenticity?

All of this, ultimately, limits the ways in which it is possible to express and identify one's gender (Shotwell, 2012). Although all people are subject to gender norms, their impact is usually felt most acutely by trans people. Because our identities are essentially unsanctioned, our bodies become a sort of public property, subject to evaluation by medical professionals who deign to establish our legitimacy.

It is at this point – when trans people enter the clinic – that norms are mobilized through disciplinary technologies to control access to resources. And this interaction begs the question, famously posed by Foucault, 'how much does it cost for the subject to tell the truth about itself?' (as quoted in Butler, 1993, p. 93).

Although trans people may not subscribe to narratives perpetuated by the clinic, we may still want access to its services. Access to trans-specific health care, however, necessitates the recitation of a particular kind of narrative – one that claims our identities are static (masculine or feminine), our bodies defective (penis or vulva), and our genders binary (man or woman) (Spade, 2006; Currah & Spade, 2007). This forces us to be alienated from our own experiences and 'strategically deploy medically-approved narratives' (Spade, 2006, p. 2) in order to access care. A 2012 study surveying the gender identities of an online sample of trans respondents found that the average number of current gender identities endorsed by participants was 2.5 (e.g. female, male, genderqueer, transgender, transsexual, two-spirit, bigender, intergender, etc.), and the average number of past identities unique from current identities was 1.4 (Kuper et al., 2012). Those that endorsed more than one current identity (72.3%) would be unable to access medical transition support – the result of a system that demands stable and singular gender identities (Kuper et al., 2012). Indeed, the very term 'gender identity' is one that places gender as clear and binary. Thus anyone who does not see themself as a man or woman has an identity rather than a gender.

Evidently, the current diagnostic paradigm is not representative of the experiences of trans people. Summarizing the personal narratives of trans people during the formative period of 'gender identity disorder' clinics, Stone concludes that 'each of these accounts is culture speaking with the voice of an individual. The people who have no voice in this

theorizing are the trans[sexuals] themselves'
(Stone, 1989, p. 11).

Resistance

If, as we have claimed, the marginalization
experienced by trans people is based fundamentally in the reification of knowledges
that are both produced by cisgender people
and reproduce cisgender identities, then
opposition must necessarily displace norms
that centre these assumptions. Thereby,
resistance may disrupt the knowledge/power
relationship on which the development of
social hierarchies depends. To do so, trans
people have initiated an academic project
that shifts them/us from the position of
objects of knowledge to subjects of
knowledge.

Beginning in the early 1990s–concomitant
with the emergence of the term transgender
– a new academic field of inquiry began to
develop (Spade, 2006; Stryker, 2006, 2011;
Currah & Stryker, 2014). Influenced by
Sandy Stone's *Posttranssexual Manifesto*,
the subsequently named field of transgender
studies constituted a substantial departure
from the cissexist frameworks that had
previously dominated discussions of trans
identity (Currah & Stryker, 2014). Among
other things, Stone's (1989) text 'called
upon transsexuals to critically refigure
the notion of authenticity by abandoning
the practice of passing as nontranssexual'
(Stone, 1989). In many ways, the espousal
of the term transgender in the years that
followed is emblematic of this spirit.
Namely:

> Transgender represented a resistance to medicali-
> zation, to pathologization, and to the many
> mechanisms whereby the administrative state and
> its associated medico-legal-psychiatric institutions
> sought to contain and delimit the socially disrup-
> tive potentials of sex/gender atypicality, incongru-
> ence, and non-normativity. (Currah & Stryker,
> 2014, p. 5)

Most significantly, transgender studies recognize the legitimacy of subjective knowledges,

arguing that embodied subjects can 'articulate critical knowledge ... that would otherwise be rendered pathological, marginal,
invisible or unintelligible' (Currah & Stryker,
2014, p. 9).

This is certainly not to say that these
developments had not already taken place
elsewhere: trans people have been theorizing
their identities on the basis of their own lived
experience from the imposition of the category itself (Nothing, 2011). Rather, developments within trans communities eventually
infiltrated academia, imported by trans people with the access and privilege necessary to
consolidate the critiques.

Because the academy is a producer
of knowledges – and the reproducer of
hegemony – shifting discourses within an
academic context has allowed for the production of new knowledges (Althusser,
1971). Further, this position allowed the
nascent field of transgender studies to situate itself as one of many discourses initiated by marginalized communities. Finally
taken seriously through the language of the
academy, feminism, critical race theory, and
disability studies all insisted on situating
their constituents as knowledge generators,
rather than simply 'case studies' (Spade,
2006). These fields 'seek to dismantle social
hierarchies rooted in forms of bodily difference' (Currah & Stryker, 2014, p. 9), recognizing bodies not merely as objects of
knowledge, but 'as the contingent ground
of all our knowledge' (Stryker, 2006, p. 9).
Significantly, this is rarely, if ever, a position taken with child or youth studies theory
or practice programmes.

HEARING THE DIS

Disability Justice

Genders that exist outside of normative
binary structures are labelled disordered;
similarly, bodies and minds that do not

adhere to compulsory able-bodied/minded-ness are construed as problems that need to be fixed, eliminated, or pitied. In a description characteristic of the medical model to which much of disability activism runs counter, Wolberg (2014) writes that:

> Disability is a kind of defect or problem inherent to an individual, one that involves deviation from species-typical norms. It is [a] defect directly caused by disease, trauma, or other medical health conditions. The primary objective of medical models is to treat or cure disabilities. (para. 2)

Constructing 'atypical bodies and minds as deviant, pathological and defective' (Kafer, 2013, p. 5), the medical model justifies responses ranging from 'treatment' to eutha-nization (Silberman, 2015). On this basis, disability is understood 'as an exclusively medical problem', and its positioning as such is assumed to be both an 'objective fact and common sense' (Kafer, 2013, p. 5).

Interestingly, prototypical disability activism began by engaging with the medical system to which later activists expressed opposition. Evincing a tension similar to that of trans activism, disability justice continues to struggle internally to navigate the paradox of resisting the imposition of medical discourses while simultaneously accessing necessary health care.

Initially, disability justice was the purview primarily – although not exclusively – of parents of children with disabilities who began to demand better care from the medical system (Solomon, 2012). This sometimes resulted in treatment with the intention of 'curing' the person (National Black Disability Coalition, n.d.), while at others times it resulted in a shift away from the medical and towards a social model. There have been several instances of conflict between these and other competing responses to disability (Solomon, 2012).

Beginning with the work of Oliver in the 1980s, many disability justice advocates began to separate 'disability' from 'impairment', forming the basis of the social model of disability. In this context, 'impairment

refers to any physical or mental limitation, while disability signals the social exclusion based on, and social meanings attributed to, that impairment' (Kafer, 2013, p. 8). Regarding this shift in emphasis, Oliver (1990) states that:

> It is not individual limitations, of whatever kind, which are the cause of the problem but society's failure to provide appropriate services and adequately ensure the needs of disabled people are fully taken into account in its social organization. (p. 3)

In recent years, disability activists have begun to criticize the social model, noting that it fails to recognize both disability and impairment as social, while simultaneously ignoring the 'lived realities of impairment' (Kafer, 2013, p. 8). Alternatively, both Kafer (2013) and Withers (2012a) propose frameworks that extend the arguments of the social model, repoliticizing the experience of disability and interrogating the attribution of deviance to particular bodies.

Kafer, for her part, forwards a political/relational model of disability. That is, she identifies disability as 'implicated in relations of power', the recognition of which allows disability to be incorporated into 'programs of social change and transformation' (Kafer, 2013, p. 8). Departing from the social model's assumption that 'disabled' and 'non-disabled' exist as discrete categories, Kafer advocates instead for what John W. Scott refers to as collective affinities.

> Collective affinities in terms of disability could encompass everyone from people with learning disabilities to those with chronic illness, from people with mobility impairments to those with HIV/AIDS, from people with sensory impairments to those with mental illness. People within each of these categories can all be discussed in terms of disability politics, not because of any essential similarities among them, but because all have been labelled as disabled or sick and have faced discrimination as a result. (Kafer, 2013, p. 11)

As we will argue below, we also think that 'youth' could be included within this list.

Similar to Kafer, Withers (2012b) advocates for the abandonment of the category of impairment entirely. Instead, Whithers contends that 'there is nothing wrong with *any* of us' (para. 5, emphasis in original). All bodies and minds are different, and this does not make one impaired – it makes one divergent. Echoing Kafer's statement that the 'problem of disability' is located in 'logical systems that attribute normalcy and deviance to particular minds and bodies', Withers's radical model recognizes that 'the tragedy of disability is not our minds and bodies but oppression, exclusion and marginalization' (Withers, 2012b, para. 7).

In several notable examples, disabled activists espousing various strains of these competing positions – that is, the social, political/relational and radical models – have begun to challenge the early activism described above. Many people who live with disability have taken positions that differ from both the medical community and parents/caregivers. This trajectory is evident in movements pertaining to deafhood and neurodiversity. Within the deaf community, there is a distinct culture, language and politics, referred to by Ladd as 'deafhood' (Ladd, 2003). Ladd views claiming deafhood, as opposed to 'deaf and hearing impaired', as a means to decolonize the bodies and minds of deaf people. A direct threat to deafhood, cochlear implants – the solution of the medical establishment – would reduce the number of people who are deaf. Some within deaf culture perceive this technology as designed to eliminate deafhood, and therefore view it as a colonialist enterprise. Others (often parents and people outside of deaf culture) view it as a way for deaf people to access broader – read: hearing – society.

Within autism there is a parallel tension, as there are many who seek a cure and/or treatment (Solomon, 2012). This position is changing, as activism and awareness develops. For example, when we started this chapter Autism Speaks identified itself as an organization 'dedicated to funding research into the causes, prevention, treatments and a cure for autism ...' (autismspeaks.org/about-us, para. 1, retrieved, Mar., 2016). The website now reads, 'Today, Autism Speaks is dedicated to advancing research into causes and better treatments for autism spectrum disorders and related conditions to advancing research into causes and better treatments for autism spectrum disorders and related conditions' (autismspeaks.org/about-us, para. 4 – retrieved Feb., 2018). Some people identifying as Aspies or Autistic people (inverting the traditional phrase 'people with autism' and capitalizing the 'A') view themselves as neurodiverse – not disabled. Although not all Autistic people embrace these terms, those that do contend that seeking to treat or cure autism is a eugenic model of responding to disability. The motto of the Autistic Self Advocacy Network is 'nothing about us without us' (Autistic Self Advocacy Network, 2016) – a phrase used by various disability activists (Charlton, 1998) and a concept that has been adopted by many youth workers.

Dominant Design

Universal design is a strategy to provide maximum access for all people, in all facets of life, regardless of ability (Björk, 2014). It recognizes that each individual has specific capacities and seeks to ensure that *every body* has equity, while acknowledging that not everybody is equally abled. It does not negate the ability of the individual, rather it designs for diverse bodies, minds, ages, and competencies. Traditionally, design could be called dominant design; design for dominant bodies, for bodies with power. Dominant design sends a message to those who have difficulty navigating the structures that 'you are not welcome here', a message which perpetuates segregation (Withers, 2012a). Segregation refuses bodies, and then when those bodies are not present it claims those bodies are the problem, dominant design creates disability.

Dominant design is also inscribed upon youth work. Much youth work is based upon a message of acceptable and unacceptable behaviour and seeks to enforce particular social structures. Fusco (2016) writes about a sociology of regulation and a sociology of change underpinning many models of youth work. A sociology of regulation is based upon an agenda of character building, treatment, youth development, and other structures that seek to shape or change the young person. These approaches echo both the charm school model of the early gender dysphoria clinics and the medical model of disability. That is, it identifies the young person as a problem to be treated, resorting to segregation if the problem cannot be cured (read eliminated). For the deaf person, regulation may involve cochlear implants so that they can function as the dominant body does. For the trans person, doctors may refuse hormones or surgery until they adopt a normative gender presentation. For the adolescent, regulation includes imposing positive youth development programmes in order to reduce delinquent behaviours and increase school engagement (Lerner & Lerner, 2013). This framing allows youth workers to avoid examining the structures leading to such behaviours or disengagement.

Conversely, a sociology of change is about empowerment, youth leadership, civic engagement, and youth organizing (Fusco, 2016). In this framing, the problem is with the culture and society that do not value the young person. Such a youth work orientation is analogous to the social model of disability. While less oppressive than regulation, a sociology of change follows a familiar pattern of paternalistic approaches to working with children and youth, one frequently witnessed in early activism within the disability community. In this structure, we – the adults – will empower/advocate for (sometimes with) you the young person, thus re-inscribing power with the adult.

YOUTH AS DISABILITY

The DSM and International Statistical Classification of Diseases and Related Health Problems have a long history of identifying behaviours that are not acceptable, thereby signifying those that are socially approved. The pathologization and disordering of youth behaviour has long been embedded within medicine through these texts, as well as in education (Hattie, 2009), psychology (Robinson, 2007) and popular culture (Lesko, 2001). This is no less true in the history of youth work and allied disciplines (Sercombe, 2016), in which behaviours that fall outside of sanctioned norms are viewed as disorders that need to be modified, treated, or punished. The current positioning of youth as a disorder(ed way of being) is premised upon developmental paradigms (moral, physical, emotional, and cognitive). Seeing age as a disability is predicated upon the construction that young people do not have the developmental capacity to fully understand the implications of their choices; for example, voting, schooling, consuming substances, sex, etc. Because of this incapacity, adults are justified in restricting the decisions that they are allowed to make. Children and adolescents are deemed un-able, which results in them being dis-abled by the social structures in which they live.

This discourse has led to the creation of normative behavioural structures, anything outside of which can be considered abnormal and/or disordered. A popular contemporary example is 'adolescent brain development'. Much has been written recently regarding a lack of development within the prefrontal cortex (among other areas) to explain adolescent decisions and justify imposing restrictions on young people (Brendtro & Mitchell, 2015; Jensen, 2015). It would seem the only cure for adolescence is adulthood. In order for adolescents to become able and ordered, in contrast to disabled and disordered, they require – 'for their own good' – regulations and accommodations, because they are unable to 'self-regulate'. This model makes adolescence itself a disability. Structures have been designed to accommodate this disability; however, if young people do not adhere to this imposed design then remediation is required. As Tuck and Yang write, 'Youth are those who society regards as underdeveloped people not quite ready for self-determination ... around which social institutions are built, disciplinary sciences created, and legal apparatuses mounted' (2014, p. 22). As with gender diversity, neurodiversity, and physical diversity, developmental and behavioural diversity are seen as problems. Youth work is fully implicated in this medico-judicial apparatus and has repeatedly been called upon to regulate adolescent bodies.

YOUTH WORK, ALLYSHIP AND BEYOND

'With Us or Against Us'

As with trans and disability communities, there is a long history of youth movements resisting imposed oppressive structures. Examples of these are numerous, such as the US Newsboys strikes of the 1880s and 90s, the 1976 anti-apartheid Soweto Uprising, or the 2016 Indigenous students' protests in India. A significant difference between these movements and trans or disability movements is the time-bound nature of youthhood. Because all youth age out, much of the knowledge and wisdom also leaves, unless youth activists become adult allies.

Looking at the relationship between youth work and allyship requires an understanding of each. We resist trying to fix either, as both are ever changing, and frequently contested. As Jeffs (2015) writes, 'Innovation is woven into the very fabric of youth work. From its outset, youth work was obliged to remake itself each time the social context and young people's needs changed' (p. 11). Among other ways of understanding youth work, people

have sought to reduce it to a set of competencies (Fusco, 2012); they have presented it as particular values and ideological positions to be held (Jones, 2016) and seen it through particular cultural lenses (Baxter, Caddie & Cameron, 2016). Is youth work defined by an approach, a location, a philosophy, a credential, a set of competencies, or something else? Within these questions sits the debate about whether a social-justice anti-oppression orientation or an (allegedly) apolitical-individual-developmental orientation best serves the needs of young people. Our position is that the individual-developmental orientation is as political a position within youth work as an explicit conscientization agenda. Youth work has never been apolitical.

The experience of the authors is that when one is, or works with, a young person facing discrimination and oppression, a choice is presented. In such moments some choose to adjust themselves to the design that is presenting the obstacles. For example, a trans person can choose to use the 'easier' bathroom (if there is such a thing), try to pass as a cisgender person, or 'hold it in'. This may be a viable option for numerous reasons such as safety, tiredness, or ease. A person with invisible disabilities can pretend they do not have the disability and try their best to get by. A person of colour may alter their name on their resumé/CV, not challenge racist jokes, or live in ways that minimizes their contact with white supremacists. These are all valid choices, and for the youth worker it presents a variety of decisions. What responsibility does the worker have to address discriminatory bathroom polices at their workplace; advocate for universal design structures; or challenge racist colleagues and hiring policies? It is not the role of the worker to determine which toilet a person uses or to demand a person disclose their disability. However, acting in solidarity may mean advocating when a person is misgendered or no adequate accommodations are present. Being an ally in these instances would require the young person and worker to have previously discussed what the young person wants in such situations, and then analysing the interaction(s) afterwards.

Defining Ally

A frequently quoted definition of ally comes from Bishop, 'Allies are people who recognize the unearned privilege they receive from society's patterns of injustice and take responsibility for changing these patterns… Part of becoming an ally is also recognizing one's own experience of oppression' (Bishop, n.d., para. 1). Being an ally, according to Bishop, is an active engagement towards ending injustice. Being an ally requires one to understand one's own social location and the intersectionality of oppressions, while not denying the privilege that one carries in particular contexts. Lynn Gehl (n.d.) created an 'ally bill of responsibilities' looking at Indigenous and settler relationships. Some responsibilities that are directly applicable to youth work include an awareness of privileges, understanding systems of oppression, being a critical thinker, and not taking up space (Gehl, n.d.).

The definition from Bishop and the responsibilities from Gehl are salient for youth work. While oppression of all youth exists, particular youth are impacted more significantly than others (disabled, trans, racialized, Indigenous, gendered, etc.). What are the implications for youth work in recognizing youth as oppressed? Is ally an appropriate role for a youth worker? How can one be in a position of power over, and an ally simultaneously? Recognizing the gendered and racialized nature of the helping professions, and thus the often precarious nature of employment (meaning low pay, insecure, unprotected and inadequate to support a household), what is the responsibility of the individual youth worker in challenging oppression at one's own workplace?

An element of youth work that some regard as essential is voluntary association (Jones, 2016). However, in England (to take but one example) reductions in youth worker funding (Pimlott, 2015) and changes in government agendas have resulted in a shift from a youth work of voluntary association to a youth work of imposed surveillance (Jones, 2016). Under this design, the role of the worker is no longer to respond to the needs of the young person when they reach out; rather, it is to intervene when it is determined there is a problem. The surveillance seeks to identify particular young people (individuals or groups) who are deemed 'at risk'. A more truthful construction would acknowledge that a youth work of surveillance is designed to identify people who are 'of risk' – of risk to the order of the dominant design, be it the pedagogical design of a school, the milieu design of a residence, the binary design of gender, or the medico-judicial design of conduct. Being of risk (to oneself or others) is commonly framed as a behavioural problem, criminal activity, or psychiatric illness. First comes the dominant design, then surveillance of compliance (what Foucault called the panopticon), identification of non-compliance, and then intervention. The intervention is generally imposed upon the young person, because this design positions the individual as the problem. For the worker, the requirement to survey and then impose interventions moves further and further away from a relational, pedagogical, developmentally supportive, voluntary role. Allyship challenges this scheme of youth work.

One form of youth work that moves towards an ally position is detached youth work. Detached youth work is a way of working that waits for the young person to approach the worker, and only after their approach does the worker engage with them (Tiffany, 2012). The worker is present and in an easily accessible space, such as the street, park, or other locale, letting themself be known to the young people, but not imposing upon the young person. Once the child or youth approaches the worker, the worker does all they can to respond to their needs. The only sanction the worker has is the withdrawal of services, the relationship is discretionary for all parties. Direction comes from the young person; the worker uses their privilege and power to respond to the young person's needs. Although, as governments adopt the language of 'detached' and 'street outreach' youth work, there is a corresponding shift towards a more directive and interventionist approach. The original term 'detached youth work' was adopted by workers in opposition to the phrase 'detached youth' (Tiffany, 2012). Workers recognized that young people were not engaged because what they were being offered was not of interest or use to them. However, newer writing would indicate that detached youth work is now being used to again stigmatize young people as disengaged and at risk (see for example the *Outreach and Detached Youth Work Guidelines* from the Belfast Education and Library Board (2012)).

Allyship involves analysis of inequities with an overt social justice stance. With detached youth work, any social justice agenda is covert and only identifiable through resistance to a time- and budget-constricted, surveillance organization-centric approach, rather than being the focus of the relationship. There is no explicit consciousness-raising aspect; indeed conscientization might well be seen by some as antithetical to the nature of a detached youth work approach.

The Problems with Allies

While it is important for youth workers to think about how they may become allies, thought alone is insufficient. Further, the very notion of ally may be inadequate for youth work. Increasingly, the whole construct of ally is being challenged by marginalized and oppressed peoples. Mia McKenzie (2014), who blogs and podcasts at *Black Girl Dangerous*, has written:

> So, henceforth, I will no longer use the term 'ally' to describe anyone. Instead, I'll use the phrase 'currently operating in solidarity with.' Or

something. I mean, yeah, it's clunky as hell. But it gets at something that the label of 'ally' just doesn't. And that's this: actions count; labels don't. (p. 139)

Over the past several years there have been increasing discussions about the roles of allies and even use of the term. While McKenzie's phrase might be seen as another label, we use this quote to highlight the need for action, not the desire to self-identify. Indeed, some argue that those who are currently operating in solidarity with, should not identify themselves as an ally. As Utt writes, 'The moment that we decide "I'm an ally," we're in trouble' (Utt, 2013). Yet, as a way to de-centre youth work, ally has tremendous power. The power lies in questioning and transforming the relationship between professional and young person. If workers see themselves as currently operating in solidarity with young people, then the surveillance shifts from the young person to the dominant design. This begins to move us towards Sallah's (2014) vision of Global Youth Work which:

> ... must first attempt to engage with young people's constructed reality and then support young people to make the links between the personal, local, national and global, and the five dimensions of globalization (economic, political, cultural, technological, and environmental) to provoke critical consciousness; and then support them to take action, whatever the concerned young people deem appropriate in creating a more just world for themselves and the rest of humanity. (p. 74)

This is an iterative worker/youth/ally/youth approach based upon an anti-oppressive socially just orientation.

CONCLUSION

Trans and disability activists have pushed for, and caused dramatic changes in legislation (see for example the work of the Sylvia Rivera Law Project in New York or the Accessibility for Ontarians with Disabilities

Act); education (for example accommodating learning disabilities, integrated classrooms); physical and social structures (ramps, gender-inclusive washrooms, closed captioning, sensory-friendly performance spaces); and language (the constant critiquing and shifting of words that are strength-based and stigmatizing). While certainly there are numerous oppressions that trans and disabled people continue to face on a daily basis, the shifts over the past decade and a half in the West have been massive. This was due to activists from those communities ensuring they were part of the conversation and building relationships with people in power who have the ability to make changes – finding allies. An example of this being the non-trans activists, and eventually senior management, who supported closing the gender identity clinic overseen by Dr Zucker. There are many things that youth workers can learn from disability and trans activist communities, for example:

- *Nothing about us without us*. Despite having been a young person once, adults no longer are. Any time issues related to young people are discussed, young people need to be part of the process.
- It is the responsibility of workers to recognize how the *dominant design* delivers privileges and perpetuates oppression – for both the young person and worker.
- Including young people means developing a *universal design*. The process of including young people must be responsive to the specificities of people's current abilities. Not all people have the same abilities, everyone needs accommodations.
- Because of this, the model of *To-For-With-Without* is a useful structure to use. As people develop capacity there may be times when we have to do to them, for them, or with them, while always resisting fostering dependency upon us.
- In resisting fostering dependence, we accept that *people are experts on their own lives*. When people say they do not need our support, we fade back, but do not disappear or abdicate our role as youth worker. When people ask for support we offer what we can. Youth workers recognize that developing agency will sometimes result in 'mistakes' and unpleasant consequences.

- Allyship is a *transition from the medical, to social, to radical, to global youth work models*. Youthhood is not something that we need to pathologize, we don't need to see being young as a disorder. Youth work can understand age as a distinct identity and social location that enhances the world and adds to human diversity.

Being an ally is a move towards these positions. Yet it is not sufficient. Youth work needs to actively engage to make changes in the master narrative. Dominant design seems ubiquitous; however, it is not inexorable. Universal design is possible and helping to create it is one of the many responsibilities of youth work.

REFERENCES

Althusser, L. (1971). Ideology and Ideological State Apparatuses (Notes Towards an Investigation). In *Lenin and Philosophy and Other Essays*, pp. 170–186. New York, NY: Monthly Review Press.

American Psychiatric Association. (2013). *Diagnostic and Statistical Manual of Mental Disorders* (5th edn). Arlington, VA: American Psychiatric Publishing.

Autistic Self Advocacy Network. (2016). Retrieved from http://autisticadvocacy.org

Autism Speaks. (2016). Retrieved from https://www.autismspeaks.org/about-us

Baxter, R., Caddie, M. & Cameron, G. B. (2016). Aotearoa New Zealand's Indigenous Youth Development Concepts Explored in Practice Today. In M. Heathfield and D. Fusco (Eds.) *Youth and Inequality in Education: Global Actions in Youth Work*. New York, NY: Routledge.

Belfast Education and Library Board (2012). *Outreach and Detached Youth Work Guidelines*. Retrieved from http://www.belb.org.uk/Downloads/y_usap_booklet.pdf

Bettcher, T. M. (2014). Trapped in the wrong theory: Rethinking trans oppression and resistance. *Signs: Journal of Women in Culture and Society*, *39*(21), 383–406.

Bishop, A. (n.d.). Becoming an Ally: Tools for Achieving Equity in People and Institutions.

Retrieved from http://www.becominganally.ca/Becoming_an_Ally/Home.html

Björk, E. (2014). A Nordic Charter for Universal Design. *Scandinavian Journal of Public Health*, 42(1), 1–6.

Brendtro, L. K. & Mitchell, M. L. (2015). *Deep Brain Learning: Evidence-based Essentials in Education, Treatment, and Youth Development*. Sioux Falls, SD: Starr Commonwealth.

Brown, L. (1994). *Subversive Dialogues: Theory in Feminist Therapy*. New York: Basic Books.

Butler, J. (1993). *Bodies that Matter: On the Discursive Limits of 'Sex'*. New York, NY: Routledge.

Butler, J. (2004). *Undoing Gender*. New York, NY: Routledge.

CAMH (2015). CAMH to Make Changes to Child and Youth Gender Identity Services. Retrieved from http://www.camh.ca/en/hospital/about_camh/newsroom/news_releases_media_advisories_and_backgrounders/current_year/Pages/CAMH-to-make-changes-to-Child-and-Youth-Gender-Identity-Services.aspx

Charlton, J. I. (1998). *Nothing About Us Without Us*. Berkeley: University of California Press.

Currah, P. & Spade, D. (2007). The State We're In: Locations of Coercion and Resistance in Trans Policy, Part I. *Sexuality Research and Social Policy*, 4(4), 1–6.

Currah, P. & Stryker, S. (2014). Postposttranssexual: Key Concepts for a Twenty-First-Century Transgender Studies. *Transgender Studies Quarterly*, 1(1–2), 1–18.

Davy, Z. (2015). The DSM-5 and the politics of diagnosing transpeople. *Archives of Sexual Behavior*, 44(5):1165-76. doi: 10.1007/s10508-015-0573-6.

Dunham, J., Harris, J., Jarrett, S., Moore, L., Nishida, A., Price, M. & Schalk, S. (2015). Developing and Reflecting on a Black Disability Studies Pedagogy: Work from the National Black Disability Coalition. *Disability Studies Quarterly*, 35(2).

Feinberg, L. & World View Forum. (1992). *Transgender Liberation: A Movement Whose Time has Come*. New York, NY: World View Forum.

Foucault, M. (1995). *Discipline and Punish: The Birth of the Prison*. New York, NY: Vintage.

Foucault, M. (2003). *Society Must Be Defended: Lectures at the Collège de France, 1975–1976*. New York, NY: Picador.

Fusco, D. (2012). *Advancing Youth Work: Current Trends, Critical Questions*. New York, NY: Routledge.

Fusco, D. (2016). History of Youth Work: Transitions, Illuminations, and Refractions. In M. Heathfield & D. Fusco (Eds.) *Youth and Inequality in Education: Global Actions in Youth Work*. New York, NY: Routledge.

Gehl, L. (n.d.). *Ally Bill of Responsibilities*. Retrieved from http://www.lynngehl.com/uploads/5/0/0/4/5004954/ally_bill_of_responsibilities_poster.pdf

Hattie, J. (2009). *Visible Learning: A Synthesis of Over 800 Meta-analyses Relating to Achievement*. New York, NY: Routledge.

Irving, D. (2008). Normalized Transgressions: Legitimizing the Transgender Body as Productive. *Radical History Review*, 100(1), 38–59.

Jeffs, T. (2015). What sort of future. In N. Stanton (Ed.) *Innovation in Youth Work: Thinking in Practice*. YMCA George Williams College. Retrieved from http://infed.org/mobi/wp-content/uploads/2015/01/Innovation_in_Youth_Work.pdf

Jensen, F. E. (2015). *The Teenage Brain: A Neuroscientist's Survival Guide to Raising Adolescents and Young Adults*. New York, NY: Harper.

Jones, H. (2016). Youth Work in England: An Uncertain Future? In M. Heathfield and D. Fusco (Eds.) *Youth and Inequality in Education: Global Actions in Youth Work*. New York, NY: Routledge.

Kafer, A. (2013). *Feminist, Queer, Crip*. Bloomington, IN: Indiana University Press.

Kuper, L. E., Nussbaum, R. & Mustanski, B. (2012). Exploring the Diversity of Gender and Sexual Orientation Identities in an Online Sample of Transgender Individuals. *Journal of Sex Research*, 49(2/3), 244–254.

Ladd, P. (2003). *Understanding Deaf Culture: In Search of Deafhood*. Clevedon: Multilingual Matters.

Lerner, R. M. & Lerner, J. V. (2013). *The Positive Development of Youth: Comprehensive Findings from the 4-H Study of Positive Youth Development*. Institute of Applied Research in Youth Development at Tufts University and the National 4-H Council.

Lesko, N. (2001). *Act Your Age! A Cultural Construction of Adolescence*. New York, NY: RoutledgeFalmer.

Lev, A. (2013). Gender Dysphoria: Two Steps Forward, One Step Back. *Clinical Social Work Journal*, 41(3), 288–296.

McKenzie, M. (2014). *Black Girl Dangerous: On Race, Queerness, Class and Gender*. Oakland, CA: BGD Press, Inc.

National Black Disability Coalition Models of Disability (n.d.). Retrieved May 11, 2016 from: http://www.blackdisability.org/content/disability-models

Nothing, Ehn. (2011). Queens Against Society. In *Street Transvestite Action Revolutionaries: Survival, Revolt, and Queer Antagonist Struggle* [Zine]. Untorelli Press.

Oliver, M. (1990). *The Individual and Social Models of Disability*. Paper presented at Joint Workshop of the Living Options Group and the Research Unit of the Royal College of Physicians.

Pimlott, N. (2015). Faith-based youth work and civil society. In M. K. Smith, N. Stanton & T. Wylie (Eds.) *Youth Work and Faith*. Dorset, UK: Russell House Publishing.

Robinson, L. (2007). *Cross-cultural Child Development for Social Workers: An Introduction*. New York, NY: Palgrave Macmillan.

Sallah, M. (2014). *Global Youth Work: Provoking Consciousness and Taking Action*. Dorset, UK: Russell House Publishing.

Sercombe, H. (2016). Youth in a Global/Historical Context: What it Means for Youth Work. In M. Heathfield & D. Fusco (Eds.) *Youth and Inequality in Education: Global Actions in Youth Work,* pp. 19–35. New York: Routledge.

Shotwell, A. (2012). Open Normativities: Gender, Disability, and Collective Political Change. *Signs*, 37(4), 989–1016.

Silberman, S. (2015). *Neurotribes: The Legacy of Autism and the Future of Neurodiversity*. New York, NY: Penguin Random House.

Solomon, A. (2012). *Far from the Tree: Parents, Children, and the Search for Identity*. New York, NY: Scribner.

Spade, D. (2006). Mutilating gender. In S. Stryker & S. Whittle (Eds.) *The Transgender Studies Reader*, pp. 315–332. New York, NY: Routledge.

Spade, D. (2007). Methodologies of Trans Resistance. In G. Haggerty & M. McGarry (Eds.) *A Companion to Lesbian, Gay, Bisexual, Transgender, and Queer Studies*, pp. 237–261. Malden, MA: Blackwell.

Stone, S. (1989). The Empire Strikes Back: A Posttranssexual Manifesto. In J. Epstein & K. Stroub (Eds.) *Body Guards: The Cultural Politics of Gender Ambiguity*, pp. 280–304. London: Routledge.

Stryker, S. (2006). (De)Subjugated Knowledges: An Introduction to Transgender Studies. In Whittle, S. & Stryker, S. (Eds.) *The Transgender Studies Reader*, pp. 1–17. New York, NY: Routledge.

Stryker, S. (2011). Transgender Studies 2.0 [PDF]. Retrieved from http://koensforskning.ku.dk/kalender/trans/stryker.pdf

Thorne, A. & McClean, K. C. (2003). Telling Traumatic Events in Adolescence: A Study of Master Narrative Positioning. In R. Fivush & C. A. Haden (Eds.) *Autobiographical Memory and the Construction of a Narrative Self*. Mahwah, NJ: Lawrence Erlbaum.

Tiffany, G. (interviewee). (2012, Nov. 28). *Detached Youth Work: A Conversation with Graeme Tiffany* [Audio Podcast]. Retrieved from http://www.cycpodcast.org/

Tuck, E. and Yang, K. W. (2014). Introduction to youth resistance research and theories of change. In E. Tuck and K. W. Yang (Eds.) Youth Resistance Research and Theories of Change, pp. 17–62. New York, NY: Routledge.

Utt, J. (2013). So you Call Yourself an Ally: 10 Things all 'Allies' Need to Know. Retrieved from http://everydayfeminism.com/2013/11/things-allies-need-to-know/

Withers, A. J. (2012a). Disability politics [web page]. Retrieved from https://stillmyrevolution.org/disability-politics/

Withers, A. J. (2012b). Radical model [web page]. Retrieved from https://stillmyrevolution.org/2012/01/01/radical-model/

Wolberg, G. (2014, April 28). Disability, models of. Retrieved from http://eugenicsarchive.ca/discover/encyclopedia/535eeb407095aa000000021c

Zowie, D. (2015). The DSM-5 and the Politics of Diagnosing Transpeople. *Archives of Sexual Behaviour*, 44(5), 1165–1176.

32

The Trials and Challenges of Using a Youth Development Approach in a Mental Health and Addictions Service for Young People

Mark Wood

INTRODUCTION

I migrated to New Zealand ten years ago and I try to summarise the difference between a Māori world view and a Western world view in acknowledgement that I grew up in the UK, in England. The Western model of (allopathic) medicine sees human beings as individuals with symptoms that need a diagnosis and cure. If someone presents as unwell, medics try to fix the illness without necessarily considering the context within which the illness occurs. In contrast, many indigenous understandings of health see everything as connected (http://www.thenewmedicine.org/timeline/allopathy.html). Māori understanding is that if your physical health is compromised so will be your mental health, spiritual health and family relationships. Māori try to treat the person as a whole person, to situate the person in their family (whānau), extended family, sub-tribe (hapū) and tribe (iwi), and even ancestors are taken into consideration. This wider consideration means that Māori

accept that within this huge extended family there are enough resources to deal with most things.

The New Zealand/Aotearoa context appears unique on the world stage. The Treaty of Waitangi/Tiriti o Waitangi is a framework for how the indigenous people of the land (Māori) are to be respected and treated, and was signed in 1844 by tribal chiefs and representatives of Queen Victoria. It offers basic principles that assert the rights of the first peoples of the land, and establishes a particular and a strong context for participatory work. Its principles are:

- *Partnership:* that the Crown and agencies should work in partnership with Māori for the good of all citizens;
- *Participation:* that all citizens should be able to participate in life fully and to their potential;
- *Protection:* that all citizens are afforded protection by the crown.

The focus of this chapter is on the development of a new youth-friendly alcohol, drugs and mental well-being service within a publicly funded mental health service that is part of the secondary health care setting in Aotearoa/New Zealand. This service was developed for and with young people, and while located within a very particular context, I believe it offers some more general lessons about youth work around drugs and mental health. The chapter begins with a broad overview of youth work in New Zealand. It will then use the Youth Development Model to tell a history of the development of the service.

YOUTH WORK IN THE NEW ZEALAND CONTEXT

New Zealand has a short history in terms of youth development work in the more formal sense, with the establishment of the Ministry of Youth Development in the early 1980s. Many of the longer-standing youth work organisations (such as the YMCA and Boys' and Girls' Institute) were founded at the end of the 1880s and early 1900s and emerged from church organisations with a focus on the physical and spiritual well-being of young people. They were based in strong Victorian values, and to a certain extent these organisations have held true to many of those values and have managed to introduce programmes developing skills and strengths that are still relevant to young people today.

New Zealand has a history of engaging with its young people which has similarities to other countries. In the 1950s it was primarily focused on the idea of how to control and contain young people's immorality and violence. New Zealand at this time saw a rise in concerns about adolescents and their behaviour, leading to a government enquiry and the publication of the Mazengarb Report (Mazengarb, 1952). This era has been reviewed critically by Molloy (1993), who has suggested that there was a series of moral panics at this time concerning

adolescent behaviour, fuelled by the media in a similar way to moral panics seen in the United Kingdom (Cohen, 1973). However, the outcomes were in stark contrast to what happened in the UK, where in 1960 the Albermarle Report (Ministry of Education, 1960) recognised similar issues, but saw the need to build a youth service to aid young people's development, with youth work as a key element. The UK government invested money and encouraged local government to develop statutory youth services under the umbrella of education.

By contrast, in New Zealand the Mazengarb Report blamed lack of parental supervision for juvenile delinquency and advocated a return to Christianity and traditional values. It also provided a basis for new legislation. Mazengarb assisted with the drafting of three Acts recommended by the committee to address perceived immorality and a return to 'wholesome values'. The laws enacted were:

- The Indecent Publications Amendment Act 1954, which widened the definition of 'obscene' and 'indecent';
- The Child Welfare Amendment Act (No. 2) 1954, which enabled the Children's Courts to treat children engaging in sexual behaviour as delinquent; and
- The Police Offences Amendment Act 1954, which made it an offence to sell contraceptives to children under 16 years of age.

This contrast highlights the predominant view in New Zealand about how to deal with the perceived problems that youth were causing. It suggests that the underlying discourse on young people was that they were problematic, and that they therefore needed to be punished and controlled. The social context of young people in New Zealand was that they were living in a society that expected them to follow a very narrow path of development, and that they were a heterogeneous group, which was far from true.

New Zealand finally established a Ministry of Youth Affairs in 1988, acknowledging that young people were affected by social policy decisions. The Ministry's job would be to influence those decisions that impact on young people, and to give young people a voice, and was based within the wider Ministry of Social Development. The Ministry of Youth Affairs was restructured in 2002 as part of a major review of state services, and became the Ministry of Youth Development. The work of the Ministry focuses currently on citizenship, the youth parliament and partnership, working with local authorities to develop youth councils. Its current priorities are:

- Increasing the number of quality opportunities for youth development overall, including those that provide leadership, volunteering and mentoring experiences;
- Increasing the proportion of opportunities targeted to youth from disadvantaged backgrounds;
- Working in partnership with business and philanthropic organisations to jointly invest in shared outcomes.

It is interesting to note, however, that although New Zealand has a Ministry of Youth Development, it does not have a statutory youth service, and the majority of youth development work continues to be delivered in the NGO sector.

This latter change was influenced and supported by the founding document for youth work in New Zealand: the Youth Development Strategy Aotearoa (YDSA) (Ministry of Youth Affairs 2002). This document established the Ministry's focus on building young people's strengths, and is seen as a supportive document for any services working with youth. The YDSA emerged out of a broad literature review which sought to identify the best way to achieve good outcomes for young people. It was hailed as a positive way forward for the youth sector, and is still seen as a founding document for any work with young people in New Zealand. It has been used to develop a code of ethics for working with young people, and it contains some key ideas for youth development across the globe. The YDSA has six key principles:

1 *Youth development is shaped by the big picture:* By the 'big picture' we mean: the values and belief systems; the social, cultural, economic contexts and trends; the Treaty of Waitangi and international obligations such as the United Nations Convention on the Rights of the Child.
2 *Youth development is about young people being connected:* Healthy development depends on young people having positive connections with others in society. This includes their family and whānau, their community, their school, training institution or workplace and their peers.
3 *Youth development is based on a consistent strengths-based approach:* There are risk factors that can affect the healthy development of young people and there are also factors that are protective. 'Strengths-based' policies and programmes will build on young people's capacity to resist risk factors and enhance the protective factors in their lives.
4 *Youth development happens through quality relationships:* It is important that everyone is supported and equipped to have successful, quality relationships with young people.
5 *Youth development is triggered when young people fully participate:* Young people need to be given opportunities to have greater control over what happens to them, through seeking their advice, participation and engagement.
6 *Youth development needs good information:* Effective research, evaluation, and information gathering and sharing is crucial.

These six principles are not hierarchical and are all seen as equally important within the development of quality services for young people. Together, they can help young people to gain a sense of contributing something of value to society, giving them a feeling of connectedness to others and to society, and a belief that they have choices about their future, within a context of feeling positive.

DEVELOPMENT OF THE MENTAL HEALTH AND ADDICTIONS SERVICE

It was within this framework that the new alcohol, drugs and mental well-being service was designed. In mid-2013 I was asked to be involved in writing a proposal for developing a service for young people addressing alcohol and drug issues alongside any mental health concerns they may be having. Having a long background in youth work in Europe and America I thought that using a Youth Development Model as a major approach to this might be interesting and would have positive outcomes for young people. The proposal was accepted in part and so the long journey to service delivery began. The service was developed by myself and a team of young people and health practitioners over a period of 18 months alongside a project manager who was employed for a fixed period to write a project plan.

The YDSA is, as previously noted, a New Zealand/Aotearoa concept that uses some basic youth development in order to deliver better services to young people, so for us its six principles (above) would provide an excellent framework for explaining our progress. The following sections explore how these principles were applied to the new service and allow me to describe some of the challenges arising and solutions found in its development. Some fundamental differences in approach were identified, at the same time as huge developments took place for all involved.

Youth Development is Triggered When Young People Fully Participate

Young people need to be given opportunities to have greater control over what happens to them, through seeking their advice, participation and engagement. In New Zealand the definition of youth development, as set out by the Ministry, is about young people gaining a sense of contributing something of value to society, having a feeling of connectedness to others and to society, a belief that they have choices about their future, and feelings of being positive and comfortable with their own identity. It is also about building strong connections and active involvement in all areas of life including: family and whānau, schools,

training institutions and workplaces, communities (sports, church, cultural groups) and peer groups. Finally, it is about young people being involved and having a say in decisions that affect them, their family, their community and their country, and putting into practice and reviewing those decisions.

Participation has long been one of the fundamental parts of youth development across the world and has the ability to transform any work with young people. It is used as a political tool and leverage against young people, but fundamentally is one of the keys to success. When we set out on this journey of development, we were tasked with developing a youth-friendly, mobile, easily accessible and responsive service for young people. In developing the service, one of the key philosophies we encouraged was that of youth participation and hearing young people's voices in any work we were going to undertake. In health services generally participation is quite a passive thing, you turn up to appointments, and that is participation. In mental health and addiction services there is a growing consumer movement, but this has not led to leadership as yet within the New Zealand context. However, as government continues to review the delivery of services, the voice of the consumer is increasingly given more power and influence, with consumer representatives now sitting at the table in governance positions. However, this is not as often seen in services working with young people.

To fully develop a service which would meet the needs of our community of young people, we believed we would have to get their participation at some level. We thought that one of the ways to do this would be to have a youth leadership group. Their role of this group's members would be to offer suggestions about service development, promotion and models of care. They would be recruited from a broad demographic spread and possibly some of them would have had experience of using the services. Whilst this would encourage participation in the development of the service we were well aware that it would be limited. However, we believed within the team that the service could only benefit from such a move.

The first hurdle was to gain the support for this approach from adults within the health service. The service was to be managed within a mainstream hospital-based child and adolescent mental health and addictions service. The project manager had arranged to have a governance group for the service which was made up of key partners (all adults). Discussions took place about how a youth leadership group would sit outside of this governance group. The discussion was focused on accountability and not on service delivery. It was interesting to note that the adults were clearly focused on how they had to be accountable for the money that was allocated to the project, and not on how they might be accountable for the delivery of a service that was useful to young people. We had discussions about the value in young people shaping their services. In the end it was agreed that we would have a leadership group of young people, and a representative from the youth leadership group would sit on the governance group, to feed in young people's points of view. The discussion focused on what value young people would bring to the discussions about the service, and that we had been tasked with developing a youth-friendly service.

The team were able to hold their position with support from other youth services, such as a youth one-stop shop, youthwork service and police youth service. These services all shared a belief in the power of the participation of young people to help make service delivery more accessible and effective. We brought the discussion back to the YDSA, to the brief for the service and to notions of participation through models such as Hart's (2013) ladder of participation. This discussion was fruitful and those adults who had been opposed to including young people as part of a governance group agreed that young people should be included. Once agreement

had been reached on the need to develop the group, the difficult task of recruiting young people to it began.

This process of moving towards a model of participation in a health service was fundamentally about whether young people had any right to give their opinion on services. It felt very much like the medical institution considered that it did not need to listen to young people, as they are seen as passive in the delivery of health services. They were expected to turn up and be healed. This is in direct contrast to the consumer movement and the Māori models of health, which both believe that the person seeking support knows more about how to help them than anyone else (see The Werry Centre, 2009).

The discussions were difficult, although for people who had always used youth development as their approach it made complete sense and was common practice amongst other youth services. For others this approach seemed to be very scary and fundamentally flawed. It was a huge success to get the idea accepted, even in its very limited form. It is interesting to note that now the service is up and running the need for young people to help lead the service is seen as less important by some of the managers. We are still seeking young people's voices in how the service is developing, this may not be in the same formal way, but the team use feedback from their work to guide developments and all new ideas are shared with groups of young people to get feedback.

We are convinced that we would still be having the discussion about youth participation today, if it had not been for the fact that we were able to convince two senior managers within the service of the value of youth input. They were both from a medical background, which gave them some credibility within the institution and therefore then gave credence to the whole approach. It made the difference in getting the approach accepted, coupled with the evidence from other services in Australia that youth participation was fundamental for success (e.g. 'Headspace' in

Australia). Increasingly there is evidence to support the notion of participation for young people in service development. One of the lessons from this discussion for us was about showing the relevance to the overall goal of the organisation and service. Finding evidence of similar services using this ideology, such as Headspace in Australia, or Jigsaw (the only mental health service that focuses on the 12–25 age group) in Ireland, and showing their success, their consumer feedback loops, their governance and management systems, and ability to engage with their target audience, are what helped win support for the approach.

Once the basic idea was agreed we had to get on with it. Our approach to recruiting young people to help us out was threefold: we approached young people who were currently engaged in the youth alcohol and drug service, we approached young people in all the high schools by talking in school assemblies, and we used personal networks to find young people who might be interested in helping us. These different approaches yielded about twenty young people. The young people all came from different backgrounds, some were users of the services and others knew nothing about it. We immediately recognised that we would need to do some work with the young people to get them working really well together. However, there was also pressure from the adults to get information and results quickly. The project manager needed information quickly to help write a project proposal for the funders, and the young people needed time to build relationships with each other. In order to fulfil both needs it was decided to have formal meetings once a month with the project manager, so that she could get information for the project plan, and the rest of the time the young people would meet together to get a better understanding of the project and service, and each other. This was a very conscious decision on my behalf as it was clear that the young people needed to be able to trust and support each other in order to be able to give their best to the service development. We were

very much reminded of the group development processes highlighted by the work of Tuckman (1965) and the need for the group to be able to go through the forming process in order to get to the performing part.

On reflection, we think the young people were asked some really important questions about service delivery too early in the process; this was to meet adult needs not service needs. If we were to be faced with the same pressures again we would delay the service development discussions until later, therefore allowing the young people enough time to form into a cohesive group. When the project manager came to talk to the group their behaviour was in stark contrast to when they met with others from the service development team. The young people were much more relaxed in the meetings prior to the project manager attending, and when the manager attended, she sat at a desk at one end of the room while they sat at another. Their behaviour was very different. Over time both the young people and the project manager came to sit closer together in meetings. We think that at the start of these meetings the young people's participation was tokenistic and not really understood by the project managers. I think that in hindsight that it would have been helpful for the team to be clear about what our model was prior to the meetings with young people so that our process was understood.

We remember young people saying 'We want to be able to drop in to your service'. The adults started talking about building a drop-in centre and all that might involve. The young people then had to clarify that that was not what they were saying; they wanted to be able to drop in to the service in places where they already went, like schools, etc. Over time, as the young people became more confident in their skills and abilities they started to question the idea of participation with the adults. At times they challenged us on what we were doing, how we were doing it, and whether they really did have any power in the decision-making process. We felt challenged at these times, as the young people asked whether they were being used to make it look like consultation rather than the planners being invested in their real thoughts and suggestions.

This is still a question to ponder on participation and young people. At times they made some really exciting suggestions that the adults felt were too risky, which left the group feeling disempowered. However, we had some amazing successes with a group of nine young people being the recruitment team for the service; the young people also chose the name and designed the logo for the service. They gave clear guidance on how the service would be best received by young people. One of the things that was learnt by the team was to be clear about our model and approach – in order to make it more likely that young people will feel comfortable. Here the young people felt we were still working to stretch the level of participation they have in decisions around the service delivery and development.

Hearing young people's views continues to challenge senior health managers as they think that young people want and expect too much. The question to all of us is when asking young people what they want, are we prepared to hear their answers? I clearly remember a discussion about launching the service and the young people saying, if we do this, is this a good use of public money – and would we be better off spending the money on service delivery?

Participants continue to be enthusiastic about the service, even though their formal input ceased due to individual reasons, such as their moving to new employment or training opportunities. However, this group still has some opportunity to input into the service and some of the group are now working in partnership organisations and in contact with each other. When we have some new idea about service delivery we will make contact with those we know are still around, and see what they think, and then talk to other young people engaged with the service.

Youth Development is about Young People being Connected

Healthy development depends on young people having positive connections with others in society. This includes their family and whānau, their community, their school, training institution or workplace, and their peers. The development of a community-based service for young people could not have been as successful without an understanding of the need for young people to be connected. We understood this as a service development team, and we knew that in order for the young people using the service to be feeling connected socially, electronically and particularly on an emotional level, we would need to ensure a good level of connection with the young people. This was underpinned by our understanding that the therapeutic alliance is one of the strongest indicators of success in therapeutic work with all ages.

Following Norcross (2011), we wanted ourselves to have really strong community connections. This, once again, brought challenges. In the hospital-based services we were growing from, the model of delivery and the accepted way of being was that the hospital is the centre of health care and people come to it to feel better. This new service was to be managed from the hospital site and therefore there was a feeling that it would be hospital based. There was an overriding feeling at times within some parts of health care that the hospital and its staff were not part of a community of health providers and a community of people.

Whilst also trying to develop the governance systems, the team also set about building connections with young people, young people's services and the community at large. One of the ways of doing this was to arrange a series of community meetings in different settings so as to ascertain the feeling about how best to provide services to young people. It was clear from these meetings that in certain areas of our district we would have to spend a lot of time building connections, as these areas felt that they had no connection to the main hospital site and the services provided there.

We also had meetings with young people in schools to get an idea of what they thought about developing a more youth-friendly service. This decision to talk to young people in schools was a recognition that the majority of young people do attend schools and we wanted to get their feelings and thoughts about the focus of the service and how they thought it might best be delivered. This gave us an opportunity to have input from a range of young people from different cultural and economic backgrounds. We were tasked with being youth friendly, and we wanted to know what that meant to 'our'/local young people, and whether the proposed service would be achievable. This process was very useful and helped affirm our decision to move forward as the young people saw a need for the service and gave us great ideas about what and where the service provision might be.

In order to build connections for these young people we knew that we would have to network with as many people as possible in each of our communities so that if the young people accessing support needed wider support we could connect them one to one. The health managers at times struggled with us spending time in the community talking. They did not see it as a necessary thing to do, as they had previously thought that you send a referral and that is enough. Through our practice we were able to challenge this notion and were supported by government ideas about young people being able to access whatever service they needed through whichever service they first enter. The term 'Any door is the right door' has become a fundamental cry for all services working within health, and especially in mental health and addictions in New Zealand (Mental Health Commission, 2012), putting the emphasis on young people connecting to their community, family, schools and friends. This understanding helps services to ensure that young people do

not have to wait to be referred or risk falling through service-delivery cracks.

Even though this is the suggested approach, it is taking time for the health service to understand the value of building connections and that it takes time. The service development team mapped out every service that delivered to young people and looked at who they were funded by and what for and how we might be connected to them. We then spent time talking with the service providers about how we might best be connected to them. During these conversations it was clear that we needed to spend time with some services and just be available on the telephone for others. These connections have been fundamental to the success of our service; our community feel connected to us, on the whole, and are invested in our success.

When talking to young people it became clear that we needed to find a way to be connected to their worlds, especially their virtual worlds. Young people talked about having a virtual life and using Facebook and other social media to connect with it. However, this created another stumbling block. The health service we were working for was extremely hesitant to use social media and had a wholesale ban on its use for services. Young people were constantly asking about our Facebook page, and we had to say we did not have one. It took two years to get permission for the service to have a static Facebook page. It is managed by a communications department, so it is not as up-to-date and real time as young people would like, but it is a step forward as it offers some visibility on social media and gives us an opportunity to share resources and information more quickly than previously.

Once again we used YDSA to support our argument, as well as research on the increasing use and effectiveness of web-based interventions for young people (Tait and Christensen, 2011). Creating a Facebook page focused on one service has been a first and major step into social media for the health service. The challenge for the service is to keep it closely monitored, but we hope that it opens up avenues for other hospital youth services to connect with young people. Fundamentally, the whole area of web-based work is showing us another way forward in connecting young people to services and us to young people.

Youth Development is Based on a Consistent Strengths-based Approach

There are risk factors that can affect the healthy development of young people and there are also factors that are protective. 'Strengths-based' policies build on young people's capacity to reduce risk and enhance the protective factors in their lives. This basic tenet of youth development work has been the most challenging and problematic for us as a service. The main focus of the service is on healing and reducing risks. The way people were generally assessed was in terms of how big a risk they posed to themselves or others and how the service could reduce that risk, if possible to avoid any potential harm.

To this end a lot of time and paperwork is spent on risk assessment. Much of the assessment process focuses on deficits; 'there's something wrong with you, so we need to find out what it is and how we can fix it'. There is a small movement in child and adolescent mental health and addictions work to acknowledge some strengths work, but it is still fundamentally based in the assessment of risk. Into this field we jump, a team of people using a strengths-based model, asking about strengths assessments, looking for ways to engage with young people's strengths and aspirations in order to move them from ill health to well-being.

There are many political and policy reasons why mental health and addiction services have developed risk-averse approaches. Acute harm to a person because of their mental health or addiction raises issues of care and negligence, and this model ensures

that if someone causes themselves serious harm there will be an enquiry to prevent its re-occurrence. By contrast, if services take a more strengths-based approach, they not only ask about what is causing distress, they ask about what is going well, how the young person is doing at school, what they enjoy doing in their free time, who their friends are, how they spend time with those friends, if they get angry and about what. It gives the service provider more information to assess the skills that a young person may have to reduce their distress (Graybeal, 2000; Simmons, 2013). Our belief is that focusing on young people's strengths makes them more likely to achieve wellness. Whilst we do not disagree with risk assessment, we think that it should be given no more emphasis than a strengths assessment. Over the last three years we have tried to shift the emphasis, and have taken small steps forward.

We continue to be challenged to think creatively by a system that looks at a diagnosis as being the end result rather than part of a process. This is in direct contrast to Māori providers, who use a more holistic approach to their assessment and use models such as *Te Whare Tapa Whā* (Durie, 1984), and this gives us hope that we can continue to grow this approach. We ran a series of events for young people at local parks, etc., that focused on being active and engaged. The events were used as a way to promote several services to young people in public places such as swimming pools, skate parks, etc. The events were held during the school summer holidays and were designed to engage with young people and promote services to them, as well as affording opportunities to talk about mental well-being and substance use. This was a unique approach at that time, however, when we talked about it being focused on positive activities for young people, prosocial activities, relationship building and making community connections we were asked what 'actual' work was done. The team spent time sitting and chatting about how young people's days were going. We were questioned about the use of this and how it helps with risk management.

On reflection, this highlighted that our approach and that of our colleagues were very different. Their ideology was based in years of training and practice within the medical paradigm and for us to start talking about alternatives was challenging for them. It remains a challenge for us to work with young people's strengths when under pressure to show outcomes and avoid risks. However, we are at a point where we are able to now start talking about realistic outcome measurement and we look forward to seeing what comes out of this. In trying to approach our work with a strengths focus, we have found we spend a lot less time talking about what is wrong and more about the person as a whole person, this mirroring some of the work Māori talk about in their family-centred work.

The service continues to work to employ a strengths-based approach. When a young person leaves our service for another we talk about the goals they have been working to achieve. The team try to model a strengths-based approach in their everyday work, focusing on the strengths of other organisations etc. We also offer training to other providers that focuses on the sharing of good practice within a strengths-based model.

Youth Development Happens through Quality Relationships

One of the ways we have been trying to develop our service and model is by putting quality relationships at the centre. Previously services such as ours have put measurable outcomes at the centre: how many people use the service? How many assessments were done? etc. We are trying to change this by talking about all the work we do to build relationships with young people, with the community, with families and for and on behalf of young people. Despite evidence that the relationship is the most important part of service delivery (Luborsky, 1994),

many services still focus on assessment. Often services do assessment work in the first two appointments, and then are unable to understand that three months later the picture is different. They are sometimes surprised when service users say that they did not tell them the truth when they first came because they did not trust them.

In the Māori world, who I am and how I am connected to you is the most important question, and one that sometimes never gets answered. In developing our service we are trying to show a model that takes the relationship as the primary goal of service delivery, what follows on from that are strengths and risk assessment, opportunities and transition. However, the most important thing is the relationship. Not only are we working on an individual relationship, but also the relationships the young person has with others, we take a view that family can be anyone that the young person describes as such. We work to strengthen those relationships, and relationships with others such as teachers, etc. This has been a part of mental health and addictions work for a while, but we are saying it is the most important thing. It challenges the notion that you can come and see a doctor once every three months and that is enough. It means you cannot expect a youth worker to deal with a caseload of 40 young people, as they would not have enough time in a 40-hour week to connect with each client.

This means that we have to accept that to build relationships with young people well it is important to be known to do what you say you are going to do. It may take seeing them three times a week, or it may mean turning up three times a week for six weeks and still not seeing the young person, but you came because you said you would. It means sometimes doing some 'off the wall' things: carrying furniture, washing the dog, walking on the beach, standing in the rain talking, texting every day. And it means that you are actively invested in building strong, high-quality relationships with young people. However, it is a skill; it does not come easily to people and it is something you have to work hard at. But, it can have a massive impact if done well (Borowsky et al., 2001).

The other side of the quality relationship agenda is the relationship the service has with other services, the knowing who can help and how to access them. This can be seen as an element of being invested in the community that you are working in. Success cannot be measured on an individual client's record, however it has to be recorded and recognised, as without it, services are withdrawn. If a service believes that its relationships are the foundation of service delivery, then service providers will likely base themselves in an accessible place, will turn up on time and prepared, and aim that the service will become part of the community.

These are our goals and we continue to try to meet them. We have physically moved ourselves out of the hospital site and move around the city in different schools and places where young people go. We drop in to offices to see other providers and we collaborate on projects that benefit the overall well-being of young people in our community. We have been actively involved in education sessions with all high school students on the impact of alcohol on the adolescent brain, alongside other support services to youth. These sessions were held just prior to school ball season. We also are actively involved in public health campaigns around domestic violence and mental health awareness, and place information on these campaigns and our activities on our Facebook page. This to us and our community is what building strong relationships looks like. We are in the fortunate position where the majority of schools and agencies working with young people know one of us directly and will call to talk about particular young people.

Youth Development Needs Good Information

Much of the work that is undertaken by the new service is about providing information that is truthful and complete, and this is key to being understood by young people and the community. We strive to ensure that our information is clear and straightforward. This has been an interesting process for us on several levels – primarily, we need to keep giving information to our young people and community about the service and our aims, how we deliver the service and what the parameters of the work are. During the development of the service sometimes we got this completely wrong, and kept changing our message. This was confusing to would-be service users. When we were working out what the service would look like, we made statements that were aspirational, then as time moved on we had to change our information. These changes in message made it appear that we had changed the parameters of service delivery. The confusion caused meant that we had to work hard to rebuild trust. The lesson learnt was to be really clear about the status of statements to supporters and partners, knowing what you can stand by, and being consistent.

We also learnt that when working with young people in a consultative process, we had to be clear about the message and keep repeating it because each young person was not consistently at meetings. We had been working with a group for about twelve months and suddenly they asked what the service was about – they had got confused as new people had joined and we had not been clear about what the service was; while we had made the mistake of thinking they had been there from the start and knew exactly what we were talking about. We learnt that the more open you can be with young people the better they respond, even if that is sometimes to challenge you and your thinking.

We also learned that our audience for information is not one group. We have had to develop different ways of presenting the same information for different audiences; so, for instance, the information we give to parents is delivered differently to that for young people, which is delivered differently to that for other services. We also learnt that young people are not a heterogeneous group and that we have to give them information based on their needs rather than ours, so we have messaging about helping them, or helping their friends or just helping young people. These lessons are hard learnt at times and bring us into situations with our bigger organisation where we are constantly having to explain why we would not just use one form of information. This has meant that we have to work closely with young people as a communication team to ensure our messages are clear. We are working on making our paperwork more youth friendly, removing jargon from documents we give to young people, and attempting to reduce our paperwork.

We also try to ensure that any web-links we use are from youth-friendly sources. Many Ministry pages contain lots of good information, but their language might alienate many young people so we use these as little as possible. We link to youth-friendly sites so as to meet young people's needs for information and support.

Youth Development is Shaped by the Big Picture

The whole of the service development process was underpinned by an understanding of both the national and international context of working with young people. The service was developed in New Zealand/Aotearoa, however it also sought to apply international understandings of how youth services might best meet young people's needs. This was underpinned by the YDSA locally. The service drew on practices from Headspace, the national youth mental health foundation in Australia, and Jigsaw, the national centre for youth mental health in Ireland.

The service was originally funded to work with 12–20-year-olds. This age range is probably too narrow and will need to be changed to include the 20–24 age range, both because they appear to be a very needy group, and in line with recent understandings of brain development (Arnone, 2014). When we began the service we felt that the age range was too narrow but lost the case to extend it. However, we now see a move towards accepting that the user group needs to be wider.

Internationally, we have been aware of the development of new mental health and addictions plans in the UK in the last couple of years, with proposals for work to raise resilience and making access to support easier for young people, for example in *Future in Mind* (NHS England, 2015). We have been talking with others in Europe, and Australia about being able to collect worthwhile outcome information to show the value of our approach. All this allows us to keep up to date with what is happening in other parts of the world and keep an eye on the 'big picture'. We also monitor developments in the social media space, apps and e-therapy as a way to link young people into a bigger picture. Locally in New Zealand we have the Sparx site (https://www.sparx.org.nz/) which offers therapy online for young people through animated worlds. We await future developments in this space locally, but regularly refer our clients to other apps and sites across the world for information such as NCPIC and the simple screening tool, GoGetter.

We also take time in our work to let young people know of the bigger picture by discussing mental health policy in other countries, or encouraging them to make submissions on possible legal changes to the Misuse of Substances Act here in New Zealand. We aim to ensure that the big picture is localised and that the wider context is seen in order to better understand why changes might be happening at a local level.

CONCLUSION

The development of this service has been challenging and exciting; we have worked with some amazing young people and adults to develop what we think is a responsive service for young people. Young people talked to us about the development of the service, challenging us in our thinking and turning up week after week, despite facing setbacks. They challenged adults in power to think about their perceptions, and made for the best recruitment process I have experienced, with extremely robust conversation about the service and the skills mix needed to deliver it. We continue to evaluate how we are doing against what our original brief was, hearing regular feedback from young people and the community, and are optimistic about the future for young people in our district. Our faith in the ability for long-held practices to be challenged is strengthened by this experience. We are encouraged by what we have experienced, and hope that some of our lessons can be of value to others.

This service development has left us with some key lessons learnt as a team and we hope to hold true to these in the future: having a clear set of key principles that are based in best practice, and communicating those principles to all parties, is a challenge that takes patience and time. Young people's participation in the design and development of services is without doubt the most important part of new service design, and without it I am sure our service would have looked very different. Using young people's voices to help make arguments for change is also imperative, as they will be the clients of the service. Services' relationships with the community is a major influence on success, and without the support of both young people and other professionals within the community we would not have achieved as much as we did. Those relationships take time to build and should be one of the first aims of any service development. We have also learnt to keep an eye on what is happening nationally and internationally, as sometimes this influenced decisions locally, or enabled us to make changes. The final lesson for us has been to make sure as a team that we have kept connected to our purpose and vision, and that throughout the processes that we exercised good self-care.

REFERENCES

Arnone, J.M. (2014). Adolescents may be older than we think: Today 25 is the new 18, or is it? *International Journal of Celiac Disease*, 2(2), 47–48.

Borowsky, I. W., Ireland, M., & Resnick, M. D. (2001). Adolescent suicide attempts: Risks and protectors. *Pediatrics*, 107(3), 485–493.

Cohen, S. (1973). *Folk Devils and Moral Panics: The Creation of the Mods and Rockers*. St Albans: Paladin.

Durie, M. (1984). 'Te taha hinengaro:' An integrated approach to mental health. *Community Mental Health in New Zealand*, 1(1), 4–11.

Graybeal, C. (2001). Strengths-based social work assessment: Transforming the dominant paradigm. *Families in Society: The Journal of Contemporary Social Services*, 82(3), 233–242.

Hart, R. A. (2013). *Children's Participation: The Theory and Practice of Involving Young Citizens in Community Development and Environmental Care*. London: Routledge.

Luborsky, L. (1994). Therapeutic alliances as predictors of psychotherapy outcomes: Factors explaining the predictive success – new directions. In A. Horvath & L. Greenberg (Eds.), *The Working Alliance: Theory, Research and Practice* (pp. 38–50). New York: Wiley.

Mazengarb, O. (1954). *Report of the Special Committee on Moral Delinquency in Children and Adolescents* (The Mazengarb Report), New Zealand Government, pp. 63–68, H–47.

Mental Health Commission. (2012). *Blueprint II: Improving Mental Health and Wellbeing for all New Zealanders: How Things Need to Be*. Wellington: Mental Health Commission, 52.

Ministry of Education. (1960). *The Youth Service in England and Wales* ('The Albemarle Report'). London: HMSO.

Ministry of Youth Affairs. (2002). *Youth Development Strategy Aotearoa: Action for Child and Youth Development*.

Molloy, M. (1993). Science, myth and the adolescent female: The Mazengarb Report, the Parker-Hulme trial, and the Adoption Act of 1955. *Women's Studies Journal*, 9(1), 1–25.

NHS England. (2015). *Future in Mind: Promoting, Protecting and Improving our Children and Young People's Mental Health and Wellbeing*. London: Department of Health.

Norcross, J. (2011). *Psychotherapy Relationships that Work: Evidence-based Responsiveness*. New York: Open University Press.

Simmons, C. (2013). *Tools for Strengths-Based Assessment and Evaluation*. Springer: New York.

Tait, R. J., & Christensen, H. (2010). Internet-based interventions for young people with problematic substance use: A systematic review. *Medical Journal of Australia, 192*(11), S15.

Tuckman, B. W. (1965). Developmental Sequence in Small Groups. *Psychological Bulletin, 63*.

The Werry Centre. (2009). *Not Just Another Participation Model. Guidelines for Enabling Effective Youth Consumer Participation in CAMH and AOD Services in New Zealand* (2nd edition). Auckland: The Werry Centre for Child and Adolescent Mental Health Workforce Development.

Websites

GoGetter: https://www.youthline.co.nz/services/goforward/quizzes/

NCPIC: https://ncpic.org.au/

Sparx: https://www.sparx.org.nz/

33

Gaze Interrupted: Speaking Back to Stigma with Visual Research

Victoria Restler and Wendy Luttrell

INTRODUCTION

Foucault's analysis of surveillance and the disciplinary force of the gaze has inspired a generation of scholars (ourselves included) to examine how ideas about power and subordination get under young people's skin and inside their hearts. The 'inspecting gaze' as he describes it, is expressed through institutionalized arrangements, practices and discourses through which our 'very eyesight [is] pressed into service as a mode of social control' (Wexler, 2000, 5). But there is another side to how young people see, look back, confront, and create new images. This chapter engages the resistive politics of what Mirzoeff (2011) calls, 'counter-visualities',[1] images created by and with youth that interrupt, reverse, or reimagine the gaze. Organized in three sections – each describing a distinct visual research study with youth and youth workers – our chapter offers examples and insights into particular visual methodologies and the 'elbow room' (Rosen,

2012) that art-making provides for moving within, reimagining and resisting stigmatizing labels.

The projects we discuss span twenty years of research, three American cities, diverse educational contexts and distinct participant populations. What draws our work together is a shared commitment to resistive politics, practices and research that interrupts hegemonic gazes. We have an enduring interest in educational settings where dominant gazes are enacted and resisted by various groups of marginalized and stigmatized learners and sometimes teachers. Across the three studies, we take up the critical visual methodology of 'collaborative seeing' as a reflexive and flexible frame for ethically engaging visual work. Collaborative seeing outlines a systematic approach to visual research, analyzing images at their sites of production, content, viewing and circulation, and a commitment to making sense of images with youth, over time and in multiple relational groupings. This approach is designed to preserve the multiple meanings present in young people's images – meanings in flux, fleeting meanings toward transformation. As a practice, collaborative seeing appreciates the limits of what we as researchers can know about young people's images, experiences and life-worlds, and advocates youth (or participant) involvement at each stage, so that young people are able to be producers, interpreters, circulators, exhibitors and social analysts of their own and each other's representations (Luttrell, 2010). In the images and studies we discuss, the tools of collaborative seeing make space to contend with dominant narratives and hegemonic visualities, to resist them but also to dialogue with them, try them on, talk with and talk back. In each project, when given the opportunity to visually represent themselves, participants were able to scrutinize 'inspecting gazes' and to open up complex, layered, counter-hegemonic ways of seeing themselves and others.

1: THE ROOTS OF COLLABORATIVE SEEING

Twenty-five years ago, before visual research with young people had gained popularity, I (Wendy Luttrell) began an ethnographic study in an alternative public school program for pregnant teens in a south-eastern city of the United States, the Piedmont Program for Pregnant Teens (PPPT).[2] I was interested in what led the 'girls'[3] to attend this program, and how they understood and resisted the stigmatizing label of and racialized public debate about teenage pregnancy (Luttrell, 2003).

Stereotypic and flat representations of pregnant teenagers dominated the media. Within the public imaginary, a pregnant teenager was black, urban and poor. Associated with this image was a public narrative (which continues to this day) – she is more than likely herself the daughter of a teenage mother; she

is probably failing in school, has low self-esteem and no aspirations. Public rhetoric pathologized and stigmatized young women's sexuality and pregnancy, casting doubts on her motivations and abilities to mother in the first place. In short, the teenage pregnant self was told and seen as a 'problem'. Within schools, despite Title IX legislation protecting their rights, pregnant girls were objects/targets of institutional surveillance, punishment and shaming.

Knowing that the girls could not step outside the 'stigma wars' and inspecting gaze, that they had to engage these ways of being seen one way or another – whether rejecting, bending, revising, accepting, or defending themselves against dominant images – aroused my interest in critical visual methodologies. I wanted to provide an opportunity for them to not only *respond* to images that others held of them, but to *create* images of their own making and meaning.[4] So, in addition to immersing myself in traditional ethnographic observations in classrooms, eating lunch with the girls, sitting in on parent-teacher conferences, driving the girls on field trips, to their homes and clinic appointments, interviewing teachers and school officials, and reviewing school documents, I designed a series of arts-based activities (theatre and collage) as opportunities/venues for the girls to speak about their experiences, individually and in small groups.[5] These activity sessions were tape-recorded and transcribed so that I could systematically trace the questions the girls asked and free-associations they made about their own and each other's images (without my prompting), and record their insights and debates about the dilemmas of self-representation.

Working with images and art-making offered particular affordances, especially when trying to access experiences and evoke emotions that may be more easily 'seeable' than 'sayable'. As philosopher Suzanne Langer wrote, the arts 'objectify the life of a feeling' (1953: 374). This affective potency comes from the experiential capacity of art, the ability to bring audiences in, arouse emotions, and galvanize alternative ways of seeing.

One of the art activities I designed was a self-portrait collage (accompanied by a written text), all of which were later collected into a collaborative handmade book.[6] This activity served two purposes. On the individual level, the self portrait activity allowed for the girls to place themselves in time and place, and to symbolize or evoke feelings about the pregnant body. After each girl finished her self-portrait, a group conversation was held in which I asked both the 'artist'/image-maker and her 'viewers' what they saw.[7] Engaging with each other's self-portraits made room for collective debate and insight, especially about the gap between how they imagined themselves and how they felt they were being objectified and stigmatized by others, as the following example illustrates.

Tara's Self-Portrait

Tara was the tallest and most full-bodied girl among her classmates. She spoke with a deep, commanding voice. She earned the respect of her classmates through her poetry writing, which she often shared in class sessions. When I met Tara she was living with her maternal aunt because she had recently lost her mother. Her father had died in a car accident when she was a child, and her mother had died of cancer. She spoke openly about her grief during the collage activity. Tara described what had happened when her aunt had learned of her pregnancy as she made her self-portrait:

My aunt cried and cried when she found out I was pregnant. She just couldn't stop crying. My aunt is overly sensitive and emotional; my mother used to say that about her, that she was too soft for the world. Anyway, if my mother was alive I wouldn't be having the baby. You know, how when a family member dies and you get pregnant as a way to deal with it? My mother died in November and I got pregnant in November so I needed to keep the baby (it is April). I always wanted to have a baby,

but not so soon, and since my mother isn't alive I went ahead and decided to have it. You know she (her mother) told me not to cry at her funeral, so I didn't cry. I didn't cry except on my birthday. I can't cry.

Why can't you cry? demanded Shadra. Tara avoided answering and said, My half-sister cries all the time and my half-brother, well he's crazy.

But you might feel better if you could cry, offered Kaela.

Yeah, that's what my counsellor says. But I need to get on with my life. I can't be crying all the time, and besides, there's always somebody worse off than you, you can't spend your life feeling sorry for yourself.

Tara selected a dark blue sheet of construction paper for her background, saying, 'This won't take long. I know just what to make to show how I feel.' From a piece of bright purplish-red paste paper, Tara cut a large round ball, which she pasted in the center of the page. 'Finished', she announced. 'I'll do the writing now and maybe a poem later.' Here is what she wrote:

This picture represents the way I feel. I feel like a big, heavy ball that can't move. I can't pick up things – I can't do what I usually would do, like go out. People look at me as if they've never been feeling like this before. I have nothing to say to them as long as they say nothing to me. The reason for my purple color is because I feel independent. I'm going to have to be independent because nobody is going to do anything for me.

Tara's image embodies, among other things, her feelings about her changing body. Echoing the sentiments of most of the girls, she spoke as if her body was betraying her or was at least a separate entity from herself – big, heavy, motion-less, keeping her from being able to do what she used to do – 'like go out.'

Tara's piece and the conversation it sparked exemplifies the complexities of the 'counter-visualities' that the girls created. Tara's self-representation as a purple ball highlights the way she navigates the inspecting gaze, how she is tugged between the way she is objectified by others, her own self-perception, and the emotions that are mobilized as a result.

As Tara read her piece out loud she spoke with great force about being the object of others' judgments. She raised her voice as she said, 'People look at me as if they've never been feeling like this before.' Tara's them-me formulation ('I have nothing to say to them as long as they say nothing to me') suggests pain, defensiveness, confrontation and perhaps resilience in the face of public ridicule. In light of the conversation about her mother's death that surrounded the making of her portrait, I also see Tara's purple ball reflecting a bounded or toughened sense of self that she has had to develop to cope with unspeakable grief and hardship – her 'you can't be crying all the time' stance toward the world.

But it is the girls' reaction to Tara's picture that drew out the resistive possibilities as they reflect on their bodies as objects of discipline and surveillance. Shadra complimented Tara on her written text, 'It sounds just like you'. But, 'We aren't going to have a big purple circle sitting on a page in the middle of the book. It doesn't look finished', Shadra stated firmly. Ebony disagreed, 'Well, if that is how Tara feels, we can't expect her to change it. Besides, she's talking about feeling like everyone's looking at her, just like in the picture where we're just looking at the ball'. 'That's my picture – if you don't like it, you can change it yourself', Tara said defiantly, shaking her head and shrugging her shoulders.

A heated debate followed and the PPPT girls were split over what should be done. Given the disparaging image of pregnant teenagers in the larger world, what would viewers think about Tara from her picture? How might they judge her? Those who argued that viewers 'might make some wrong assumptions about Tara, like that she is lazy or doesn't care' finally convinced the others. Tara reluctantly agreed to let Shadra add some 'scenery' (Figure 33.1).

Tara's purple ball served as a counter-visuality – a twist on the stigmatized pregnant body that allowed the girls to see and

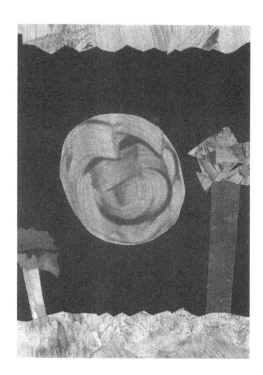

Figure 33.1 Tara's purple ball with 'scenery'

counter-act a dominant narrative about them. Through their image making, the girls were telling about their lives from multiple vantage points: *within* the images; *around* the images as they engaged in making them; and *during* audiencing sessions (when they viewed their own and each other's completed images). A resistive practice of seeing meant preserving all of the meanings and vantage points, including the tensions between how the girls imagined being seen and judged, how they saw themselves, and how they wished to be seen.

2: GIVING KIDS CAMERAS AND INTERSECTING GAZES

In 2003, I (Wendy Luttrell) began a research project with a similar goal of de-centering stigmatizing, blaming and deficit-oriented perspectives about young people growing up in working-class communities of color, including immigrants. This project – Children Framing Childhood (CFC) and its follow-up Looking Back – put cameras in the hands of children attending a local public elementary school in Worcester, MA, serving a racially and ethnically diverse population. Thirty-six children, who represented the diversity of the school were given disposable cameras with 27 exposures and four days to photograph their everyday lives. After the pictures were developed, either I or a research assistant interviewed each child to talk about their images, why they had taken them and which photographs they wanted to show their peers, teachers and a larger public. Then we met in small groups with the children as they discussed each other's photos. Unlike other types of photo-voice/photo elicitation projects, this design not only allowed for multiple opportunities and different contexts for the children to attach meaning to their pictures, but also opened a window into particular ways that the children used their photographs to make identity claims, or vie for status or dignity.[8] This process was followed again when the children were 12, and then again at ages 16 and 18, except that as teenagers, they were given both still and video cameras. The research has generated an extensive audio-visual archive: 2,036 photographs; 65 hours of video- and audio-taped individual and small group interviews; and 18 video diaries produced by a sub-set of participants from ages 16 to 18.

I turned to using photography and video for several reasons, but especially because of my interest in the invisible and undervalued work associated with family, school and community life that sustains and reproduces inequality (DeVault, 2014). The mobility and portability of the camera offered entry into different emotional and geographical spaces of children's life-worlds – into homes, schools, and communities – a chance to see, if only in brief glimpses, through their eyes. Having already learned the power of images to convey what may be seeable, but

not easily sayable, I was anticipating that photography and video would allow special insight into the choreography of everyday life and the children's evolving identities. At the same time, I was acutely aware that, 'The relation between what we see and what we know is never settled', as visual theorist John Berger wrote (1972, p. 7). Thus, I designed a more systematic practice of tracing the complex life of these images – their production, content, viewing and circulation – that is *collaborative seeing* (Fontaine & Luttrell, 2015; Luttrell, 2010, 2016).[9]

Collaborative seeing combines an epistemological stance that complicates the notion of a singular 'child's' voice or 'eyesight'; a set of methodological protocols and ethical practices;[10] and an analytic process which aims to address the structural imbalances of power embedded in adult-child research relationships. Collaborative seeing is committed to preserving the multiplicity of meanings that are co-constructed between researcher and researched, and fueled by the questions: *Whose way of seeing is this? In what context? With what degree of power, authority or control? Toward what purpose? And with what consequences?*

Invited to take pictures of 'what matters most', at ages 10 and 12, the children's images centered largely on home life, with 668 photos of home, 432 of school and 149 of community.[11] In one sense the preponderance of images about family life (people, interiors and exteriors of homes, personal belongings and cherished objects) suggests that the children embraced the prescription that 'cameras go with family life', reflecting what is said to be the earliest use of photography – the establishment of the 'family album' (Sontag, 1977: 8, cited in Luttrell, 2010). But through the collaborative seeing process, a fuller sense of the young people's intentions emerged. They were using their cameras to claim pride in, and the value of, their homes and upbringings against their perception that others might judge them as lacking.

Kendra's Pictures

Two-thirds of Kendra's pictures at age ten are taken of her home, family members and personal belongings, which makes a powerful statement about what she chooses to be identified with, what she wishes to commemorate, and what might be beyond expressing in words. Kendra took two photographs of the exterior of her residence in Terrace Gardens, a public housing complex behind the school. In her individual interview, Kendra explained that she took these photographs because it is where she 'belongs' and 'feels respect'. These connections between belonging and respect are telling, signaling not only the concept but also the politics of belonging. In one sense Kendra's claim to her '*homeplace*' (bell hooks)[12] is an emotional (or even ontological) attachment; it is about feeling 'at home' in a 'safe' space (Ignatieff, 2001, cited in Yuval-Davis, 2011), comfortable, rooted, and among friends. In another sense, her *homeplace* is a badge of pride and dignity.[13] To appreciate this claim means acknowledging that the politics of belonging involve judgment about and in some cases policing of who and who does not belong. Such judgments are accomplished through the construction of stigmatizing boundaries and groupings of people, whether according to origin, 'race', place of birth, language, culture, religion, or shared value systems, to name a few.

Terrace Gardens, where Kendra and a third of the youth participants lived, is one of three public housing projects in Worcester designed after World War II for returning veterans. In 2003, when the project began, Terrace Gardens was in need of repair and had been targeted for capital improvements for several years, but because of cutbacks in state budgets none of the improvements had been completed. A concentration of wage-poor families of color, deteriorating facilities, an educational opportunity gap (the high school drop-out rate of residents is double the city average), and city-wide perceptions of the buildings as crime ridden, presents a potent, stigmatized image of life in Terrace Gardens. Children, like Kendra, who lived there, used their cameras to navigate this axis of social and racial difference (showing that they 'belong' and have dignity). Their photographs and the dialogue that takes place around them work both as tools to negotiate belonging and as counter-visualities, challenging the view of public housing as stigmatized.

During the small group session of six children looking through each other's photographs, Allison picks up the photograph Kendra has taken of stuffed animals, which she has neatly displayed on her bed (Figure 33.2). Allison exclaims that she, too, has Tigger. Kendra was grinning from ear to ear, as this was the photograph she had chosen as one of her five 'favorites' to share with her peers. Kendra said Allison was welcome to bring her Tigger to come play at her house after school. Allison said, 'But my mother won't let me go to Terrace Gardens. She says it isn't safe'. Kendra responded swiftly and matter-of-factly, 'That's not true; it is the safest place that I have lived', and grabbed the photograph from Allison's hand as if protecting her cherished possessions. Allison embraced this response just as quickly, saying, 'Good, then I will tell my mom that I can come to your house'.

Both girls' conversational agility to transcend the negative perception of Terrace Gardens is noteworthy. Allison's view, spoken through her mother's voice, is a commonly held perspective among white, Worcester residents. Allison's family lived in a 'three decker' building across from the school. 'Three decker' light-framed wooden apartment buildings are common throughout New England, built during the late 19th and early 20th centuries to house large numbers of immigrants coming to work in factory mills. Allison, who is white, lived with her family of five on one floor, her grandparents lived on another floor, and her mother's sister's family lived on the third floor. Allison's extended

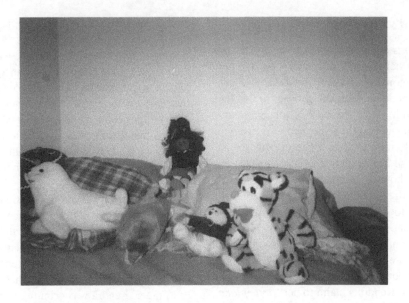

Figure 33.2 Kendra's 'Tigger'

family had resided in the 'three decker' building for all of her life. Kendra's family, who are African American, had moved five times in search of affordable housing. Terrace Gardens was the third public housing unit in which her family of four had lived. This was one among many exchanges between the children where pictures of personal belongings – stuffed animals, games, toys, brand-name clothing – served as a means for them to both uphold and reject social differences between themselves and their peers (Buckingham, 2011; Pugh, 2009). Kendra refutes the construction of her home as unsafe, and Allison is prepared to challenge the stigmatizing boundaries. They also both avoid the sting and scorn of difference, with Tigger serving as the shared token of value and social glue of belonging.

This was not the only way that the children navigated social differences as they examined each other's photographs. One child living in Terrace Gardens expressed envy upon seeing her peer's home, 'I wish I lived here – whose house is this?' and others highlighted expensive objects like computers and televisions to counter the social stigma around public housing. In a culture that equates belonging with

possessions, and being cared for with specific kinds of housing, consumer items and experiences, then dignity is not available to all, and this means that some young people have to work harder than others to achieve it. Using the critical visual methodology of *collaborative seeing* to trace and lift up competing ways of seeing in different contexts also made the politics of belonging more visible. The young people's efforts to re-direct 'inspecting gazes' about their *homeplaces*, even if momentary and fleeting, evidenced their consciousness and complex reactions to being stigmatized.

A final example illustrates the grip of deficit and stigmatizing ways of seeing. Kendra handed her camera to her brother (with whom she and her sister share a bedroom) to take the picture shown in Figure 33.3. It is a photograph she selected as her favorite one to share with a public audience, perhaps because it provides the most intimate glimpse of how she dwells within her *homeplace*. Kendra's account of this photograph during her one-on-one interview featured her most preferred activity – 'reading. I love to read.' She refers to this photograph as another image where she 'feels respect'. She becomes animated

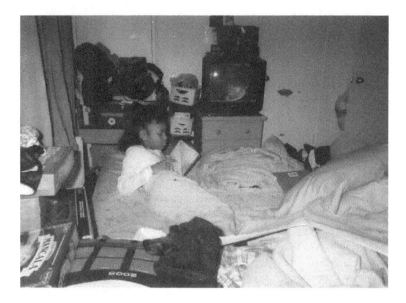

Figure 33.3   Kendra's bedroom

when telling the plot of the book. *Sitting Pretty, True Blue* is a complex story about the demands of a teenage social world organized around shared values and longings – about being athletic, cool, savvy, popular, older than your years (but not an adult), blond ('strawberry blond doesn't count'), and most importantly 'not poor'. It is a story of three teenage girl friends and the possible betrayal of the main character, Sam, who has made a new friend who is wealthy and 'very snobby'. The drama of *Sitting Pretty, True Blue* parallels the drama among the children in their conversations with each other about their photographs, circling around freighted relationships and desires to belong that uphold, reject and circumvent social differences. In the story, as in the way participants spoke of the images they took of their *homeplaces* and belongings, the characters expressed less concern about going without consumer goods or fancy experiences, than about being *shut out* of the social worlds in which young people travel.

Meanwhile, discussions of this image as it circulated among adults were anchored around a different set of readings. I have used the audio-visual archive as a tool for teacher professional development and to train emerging researchers in visual methods. During these audiencing sessions, I invite teachers to look closely at selected images, taking time to notice where they fix their eyes and any questions that come up, before grouping the images into categories of their choosing. Only after this activity are viewers invited to see video clips of the children speaking about their images. Upon hearing what the children have to say, there is a moment of reckoning – surprise, self-satisfaction (for 'getting it right') or embarrassment and guilt for making 'wrong' assumptions. Through this process I have learned just how much the children's frameworks of belonging and care – a central finding of the project – go unseen by a predominantly white, middle-class audience.

Teachers looking at Kendra's bedroom image see 'disorder', 'clutter', 'a lot of stuff', in a 'small, cramped space'.[14] Still others notice the signs of close living – the mattresses on the floor, the bedding, the piling of boxes and storage units, and what looks like a blue curtain dividing the space, suspecting this might be temporary housing or that the family has doubled-up in another household. Whereas a few viewers see 'comfort', most see signs of precarious living. Noting that the child holds a book in her hands, an indicator of 'literacy', many infer its value to the child photographer. Seeing that the television is on, some viewers wonder whether the television is an ever-present backdrop in the room (understood to be less than desirable). Others wonder whether the child can concentrate; or whether she is posing and not really reading but wishing to present herself as such because it is a school project.

The goal of collaborative seeing as a resistive practice for adults working with youth is to invite reflexivity – prompting viewers to notice their identifications with and projections onto the children's images. After hearing Kendra speak about this photograph as a setting where she feels respect, one teacher remarked, 'I just couldn't see past the messiness and the storehouse of stuff. Then again, I wouldn't want someone looking into my son's bedroom before I tidied it up, who knows what they might think.' Coming to terms with the force of hegemonic gazes means engaging adults in new ways of seeing that allow them to reflect on and question assumptions they hold about the young people with whom they work. Collaborative seeing offers an approach that is iterative and dialogic, meant to pry open curiosity rather than judgment. This resistive practice takes practice, for, whoever we are, our eyesight and understanding is always partial.

3: LESSONS FROM TEACHER-ACTIVISTS

My (Victoria Restler) project also engages adults to make, make sense of, and reimagine stigmatizing images of low-wealth youth of color.[15] In 2014, I worked with a group of ten New York City public high school 'teacher-activists',[16] all affiliated with a local social-justice teacher collective. I was interested in

how teachers were managing and making sense of new evaluation policies (which link teacher ratings to student standardized test scores and observations), and the increasingly visual dynamics of school accountability marked by the massive documentation of student and teacher data, the visualization (through graphs, charts and infographics) and publication of this data online and in the media, and video surveillance of schools, among other tactics. The neoliberal educational regime of power has narrowed the lenses through which students (and consequently their teachers) are seen. Contemporary policies and discourses visualize students and teachers through a series of circumscribed and highly racialized performance measures, standardized and overly instrumental definitions of children's achievement. And in the US context, these policies join with 'zero tolerance'[17] disciplinary protocols that criminalize a new range of student activity and conspire to intensify the inspecting gaze upon students of color. This project sought to pry open these narrow lenses through multimodal arts-based research and a collaborative seeing approach. In group workshops, individual interviews and digital spaces we engaged the practice of collaborative seeing to analyze and critique popular media, remix images on an online platform and create new representations of teaching work, students and school life.

Here I want to focus in on two teacher images that decenter the disciplinary gaze and reject dominant, deficit-based lenses on their students. The photo-collages were made by Michelle, a white teacher in her early thirties who favored vintage glasses and sweater vests. She was midway through her fifth year of teaching when she took the pictures, a near-veteran in a field where 50% of US public school teachers leave the profession in their first five years. Michelle teaches at an urban school I call Bronx Humanities, a place whose mission – to educate students who have struggled at traditional schools – she was passionate about. Called by different names – 'second chance schools', 'transfer' or 'alternative schools', Bronx Humanities is one of ten institutions in the borough designed to support students who have dropped out of school, been pushed out, or struggled in other ways. The statistics on Bronx Humanities tell a story of intersecting challenges – 98% of the student body are youth of color, 85% receive free lunches (a marker of poverty in American schools), and only 20% of Humanities' students graduate in four years compared with a 69% city-wide average. Additionally, many of these students face the compounding stigma of having dropped out (Fine, 1991; Silva, 2016) and the condescending label of being 'over-age and under-credited' an official classification that frames students in deficit terms, broadcasting school failures. These are not, however, the stories that Michelle tells about her teaching work, her students or the school community. In the images and narratives that follow, Michelle eschews stereotypical framings, instead painting a picture of her students as social, fun, curious and reflective.

After a workshop where we had discussed teachers' invisible work, our group decided to find or make images about their own invisible and unrecognized labor and share them online (on a password-protected social media platform called VoiceThread). Michelle posted two photographs, initially without the yellow bands of collaged text, and at first, I wasn't quite sure what to make of them. The first image depicts a semi-circle of five girls sitting around a square of hard black plastic tables (Figure 33.4). The space has all the trappings of an urban American public high school – a row of clunky desktop computers, an empty media cart slightly askew at the far wall, border-trimmed bulletin boards posted on the closet doors, and a large white washbasin sink at the back of the room. However, the girls are not engaged in schoolwork. Instead, the table is dotted with backpacks, makeup bags and an assortment of small glass bottles of different colored fingernail polish. Of the five girls, three black and two Latina, only one meets the eye of the camera, smiling and holding up the newly painted turquoise nails of her left hand. The others are all busy painting, fingers curled around bottle-top brushes, looking down at hands resting on the table, thumbs angled just so.

When I saw the image on our shared social media site, my first thought, given our prior discussion of teachers' invisible work, was that the photo was meant to explain the time

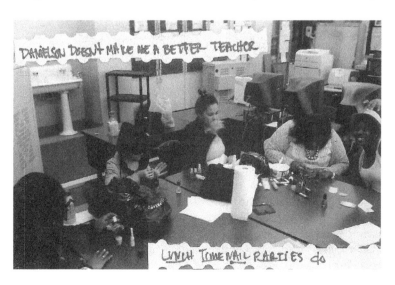

Figure 33.4 Nail parties

(and perhaps cost in the form of polish) that Michelle spends with her students outside of class. I could also see how this photograph might be interpreted as evidence against the young women, proof under the inspecting gaze of neoliberal evaluators that the girls are 'lazy' or 'don't care', as Tara's peers at the PPPT feared she might be judged. Perhaps especially at a 'second chance' school, I imagined outsiders might see these students as squandering 'the chance', as unserious girls who care more about their nails than their grades. When Michelle added in the text, 'Danielson [a shorthand for the new teacher evaluation policy] doesn't make me a better teacher, lunch time nail parties do', I saw the image anew as a kind of badge of teacher pride. Maybe this showed that she was a 'cool teacher', one that students wanted to spend time with during their lunch hour, and also that this part of her practice was not counted within 'Danielson', the extensive teacher observation rubric, a set of standards which frame the evaluator's eye and enforce the disciplinary gaze.

Other teachers saw it somewhat differently. When we viewed the photos during a group audiencing session, Phoebe talked about the educative role of this kind of time and attention.

Nail parties are just one of those examples of an activity that kids actually sort of get something out of. Any social situation where they can interact on a human level that has nothing to do with – everything to do with the educational process, and nothing to do with data.

For Phoebe, nail parties – as representative of activities that foster social interaction – are not a supplement or add-on to teacher work and student learning, but rather form its core. Phoebe distinguishes between 'the educational process' and 'data', a kind of code word for quantitative high-stakes student and teacher evaluation. Her interpretation reframes the representation 'nail parties' as valuable teacher work, claiming the image as a form of resistance to narrow, official conceptions of what counts in teaching practice. For Phoebe,

this group of girls around the table, talking and painting nails is what teaching and learning looks like.

Michelle, for her part, had another take. I spoke about the image with her in a small group interview with Betty and Sarah, two other teachers from her school. Scanning through a stack of her photos and drawings, she held this one up and smiled. 'Yeah. I think this is about the fun things', she said. 'The community building you do. Not during class. You kind of don't even want the administration to come in and see it. You kind of don't want someone to notice you did it.' Betty chimed in, asking sarcastically, 'Right, like, where's the rubric?'[18] And Michelle responded, shaking her head, 'Not even. I just sort of want this special time with my kids.' Here Michelle draws our attention to the picture as evidence of 'special time', narrating the photograph as 'fun' and as a space for 'community building' with her students. In this way, she helps us (as the audience for her image) to see the faces and forms in the photograph as 'kids', as silly and youthful. Dumas and Nelson (2016) write about the state-sanctioned murders of Black American boys, Trayvon Martin and Tamir Rice, and theorize the implausibility and impossibility of Black childhoods, mapping a pattern that persists since American slavery of the social adultification of Black children. Michelle's image and narrative serve as 'counter-visuality' to the dominant representations of these young women of color as already grown, or 'wise beyond their years' – characterizations that facilitate the cultural reading of their culpability as social problems, failing and dangerous (a danger that is necessarily not child-like). By saying that she doesn't 'even want the administration to come in and see it', she rejects the conception of her own teacher-work as something to be calculated or verified from the outside, while she refuses to treat (or see) the girls only as subjects to be disciplined. Michelle's disregard for this stigmatizing storyline and her narrative positioning of her 'kids' as youthful and fun, brings viewers into other ways of seeing her teaching labor and her students – as joyful and as part of a caring classroom community.

Insights, Wherever they Occur

The second image in this series (Figure 33.5) depicts a close-up shot of desktop graffiti – a short phrase scrawled in ball-point pen on a mustardy laminate desk, set against a ground of speckled beige linoleum floor tile. Like the first image, this photograph draws on the unmistakable visual grammar of American public high schools – the desk with its oblong divot for pens, the stretched blue-green reflections of molded florescent light bouncing off the plasticky surfaces, and the desktop doodles just below the center of the frame. The writing on the desk reads, 'We are so hard headed when we in LOVE!' And Michelle's collaged captioning declares, 'Danielson doesn't make me a better teacher, desktop graffiti does'. Like the nail parties

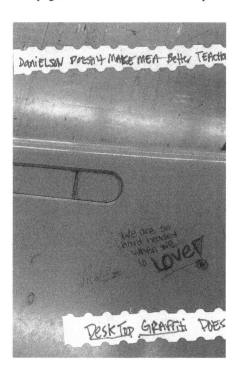

Figure 33.5   Desktop graffiti

photo, this collage calls up ideas of teens behaving badly – using incorrect grammar, shrugging off school work, not paying attention in class – and subverts it, claiming these activities as evidence of learning, thoughtfulness and relational teacher work. These student marks record the defacing of school property, the kind of violation that might exact harsh punishment in the criminalized, 'zero tolerance' climate of school discipline. But in the case of Michelle's 'counter-visuality' they serve to document her own good teaching and the goodness of her Black and Brown students. When we spoke about the image, she said, 'I just love that instead of drawing obscene photos, somebody wrote "We are so hard headed when we are in love"'. Michelle looks past the act of pen on desk to the content of the phrase, comparing it to the kinds of graffiti we might expect teens to write – like curse words or obscene doodles. In contrast to these expectations, to the flattened representations of low-wealth teens in popular culture, this image and Michelle's narrative draw our eyes to the rich inner lives of teenagers. Further, as she claims in the caption, her attention to and support for this kind of reflective practice, serve as evidence of her own good teaching.

Some teachers read different messages into Michelle's collage. As Nisha said of the image with a wry smile, 'Well, I'm a prudish Indian chick, so I'm not a fan of desktop graffiti'. Rebecca too acknowledged the perspective of teachers or administrators who might be upset at a student damaging school materials, but nonetheless, appreciated the desktop drawing as a site of learning and reflection. She commented:

> Forget that it's destroying public property. I think as a teacher you kind of appreciate these insights, wherever they occur, so even if it's in the context of your kid carving out part of a desk that was just bought that year, it's still like, 'Okay'. Also you appreciate it because you understand what it feels like to go through it [falling in love], and the idea that bearing witness, even in sort of a removed way to that moment, is so much more important than this desk.

Rebecca saw the image as evidence of learning, suggesting that as a teacher she appreciates this kind of discovery in any form. She also engaged the image as a way of connecting with the student – coming together around the shared and very human experience of falling in love – what she described as 'the abandon that you feel when you really sort of fall for someone'. This image and the layered teacher interpretations contextualize what might be seen at first glance as the bad behavior of bad kids – 'badness' which is presumed and enforced unevenly along racial lines[19] – and reframes it as testimony to learning, thoughtfulness and good teaching. The counter-visuality of Michelle's collage and interpretation alongside Rebecca's analysis, sidesteps stigmatizing images of historically marginalized youth, while they upend the quantified, instrumentalized portrayals of students (and teachers) as a collection of scores and percentages.

Michelle's images and the narratives that she and fellow teacher-activists exchanged, tell stories about teacher identities, school work and urban youth that are not often promoted within educational discourse. As a white woman teaching at a predominantly Black and Latinx transfer school, Michelle rejects categorizations of her students as failing, at-risk or unreachable. Likewise, she refuses to locate herself in the popular narrative of martyr figure or white savior, further disrupting racialized regimes of power. Her representations subvert these interlocking stereotypes, twisting popular perceptions to present a slice of young people's social worlds, school communities and interior lives that is complex, multi-layered and full of humanity.

CONCLUSION: GAZE INTERRUPTED

We have argued that images and art-making offer particular affordances in qualitative research with and about youth. Making and talking about images can open up space for a different kind of entry into young people's social and emotional worlds, draw researchers' eyes to other frames of view, or make visual and palpable things that are difficult to express in words alone. But it's not enough to roll out the drawing paper or simply 'give kids cameras'. Through the practice of collaborative seeing, we advocate for visual research that lifts up the invisible elements of the inspecting gaze for investigation, revision and refusal.

As critical as youth participation is in making and making sense of images by and about them, we also wish to underscore the value of bringing youth workers, teachers and other adult participants and perspectives into youth spaces of resistive practice. The disciplinary gaze that Foucault describes is dialectical, taking shape in a series of multi-directional interactions between looker, looked-at and selves. It is important to probe this gaze from different vantage points to better understand the back and forth systems of surveillance, catalyze reflexivity and further challenge stigmatizing images of young people. As Wendy shows in the case of Kendra's bedroom photograph, sharing young people's words and images with teachers can prompt them to take note of and challenge the assumptions they hold about their students' *homeplaces* and values. And as Victoria illustrates with Michelle's photo-collages, teachers' angles of vision on their students are not uniform or monolithic. Michelle's images disrupt popular narratives about teacher-student relationships – especially those between white teachers and teens of color in urban environments – and serve as testament to the playful, healing, justice-minded work that teacher-activists and youth workers carry out (Ginwright, 2016). With this chapter we have shown through our own work how the practice of collaborative seeing can take shape across a range of informal and educational settings and powerfully engage both youth and adult populations. We hope this flexible frame for partnering with diverse groups in the making and interpretation of visual research serves the aims of youth workers and researchers working to disrupt stigmatizing policies, practices and public visual and media discourse. The project of decentering deficit-oriented perspectives about historically-marginalized youth of color, immigrant youth, pregnant teens and high school dropouts is a formidable one. We must engage teachers, caregivers, researchers, informal educators and youth workers, alongside youth themselves, to promote reflexivity in the service of disrupting, circumventing and countering the gaze.

Notes

1   Mirzoeff takes up the relations of power and sight through his theories of visuality and counter-visuality. He defines visuality as the means by which authority is sutured to power. Visuality is the way that authority envisions itself and gains and maintains power by constructing and legitimating its own worldview as natural. Counter-visuality therefore, is a kind of rebuff, a refusal to accept visuality's claims to truth, neutrality and authority. We use the term 'counter-visuality' with these meanings in mind to signify a visual companion to the idea of the counter-narrative, images that twist, reject and reframe dominant visualities.

2   All names are pseudonyms.

3   I use the term girls because this is how they referenced themselves and preferred to be called.

4   And for me to re-present what I learned about this process meant that I too had to wrestle with how these hegemonic depictions shaped what I paid attention to and how I interpreted the girls' selves, identities and experiences.

5   See Luttrell (2003) for discussion of these and how I selected the particular forms of visual representation.

6   Robert Shreefter, a book artist, inspired this activity and taught the girls how to make hand-made paste-paper to use in their self-portrait collages and how to bind the colored Xerox-copies of each self-portrait into a collaborative book form. See Luttrell (2003) for more details.

7   See Luttrell (2003) for the set of questions I asked of each girl and of the viewers (e.g. what do you notice about this picture; what's going on in it; and so forth), and how the girls came to mimic this process after a while.

8   Luttrell (2010, 2016) has written elsewhere about the affordances and limitations of 'giving kids cameras' research. See Clark-Ibanez (2004), Burke (2005), Clark (1999) Luttrell and Chalfen (2010), Mitchell (2011), Orellana (1999), Yates (2010), Kaplan (2013) and Thompson (2008) for examples.

9   Collaborative seeing builds on Rose's (2007) concept of intertextual analysis.

10 See Luttrell (2010) for a discussion of ethical procedures, including the importance of on-going rather than one-off consent when working with images.

11 See Luttrell (2010) for the prompts for picture taking that were used at ages 10 and 12.

12 *Homeplace* is a term coined by bell hooks to acknowledge home not as property, but as places where truly all that matters in life take place – the warmth and comfort of shelter; the feeding of our bodies; the nourishing of our souls' (1990: 383).

13 Feeling 'at home' isn't necessarily a positive feeling, as Yuval-Davis notes, and can also lead to a sense of anger, resentment, shame and indignation (Yuval-Davis, 2011: 10).

14 These are direct quotes from viewers across a range of teacher professional development workshops and teacher-education courses.

15 In this piece we use labels such as 'low wealth', 'historically marginalized', and 'poor and working class' to describe young people who have limited financial resources. And yet, in conducting research that seeks to disrupt the stigma these youth face, we realize that these terms are themselves stigmatizing. A primary objective of this piece is to write against labels and offer new, more complex angles of vision onto the images and worlds of these young people. We need new, better words for describing and contextualizing interlocking systems of prejudice, racism and poverty.

16 I use the term 'teacher-activist' following Ginwright (2016) to signal the blurred boundaries between the participants' work as both teachers and activists.

17 The phrase 'zero tolerance' refers to a movement in school discipline beginning in the late 1980s in the United States that mandates specific and harsh punishments for the violation of school rules, including minor infractions like 'insubordination'. The rigidity of these policies, elevated penalties and increasing involvement of law enforcement carried out across a biased system that targets youth of color, has contributed to the formation of a 'school-to-prison pipeline' that pushes students out of school and into the criminal justice system.

18 Betty's use of the term 'rubric' references the Danielson Framework, which consisted in 2014 of a 20+-page checklist of educator skills and practices that were used to observe and evaluate teachers.

19 The disproportionate rates of disciplinary punishment of Black and Latino boys have been well documented (Ferguson, 2000; Gregory, Skiba, & Noguera, 2010; Krueger, 2009; Wallace et al., 2008; Wald & Losen, 2003). In New York City during the 2013–14 school year, out of the 53,504 total school suspensions, only 6.7% were given to white students; while out of the 393 arrests, a mere 5.3% were white set against a figure of 14% total Department of Education enrollment (NYCLU, 2014).

REFERENCES

Berger, J. (1972). *Ways of seeing*. London: British Broadcasting Corporation.

Buckingham, D. (2011). *The material child: Growing up in consumer culture*. Cambridge: Polity Press.

Burke, C. (2005). Play in Focus: Children researching their own spaces and places for play. *Children, Youth and Environments*. 15 (1), 27–53.

Clark-Ibanez, M. (2004). Framing the social world with photo-elicitation interviews. *The American Behavioral Scientist*, 47 (12), 1507–1527.

Clark, C. D. (1999). The autodriven interview: A photographic viewfinder into children's experiences. *Visual Sociology*, 14, 39–50.

DeVault, M. L. (2014). Mapping invisible work: Conceptual tools for social justice projects. *Sociological Forum*, 29 (4), 775–790.

Dumas, M. J. & Nelson, J. D. (2016). (Re)Imagining Black Boyhood: Toward a Critical Framework for Educational Research. *Harvard Educational Review*, 86 (1), 27–47.

Ferguson, A. A. (2000). *Bad boys: Public schools in the making of Black masculinity. Law, meaning, and violence*. Ann Arbor, MI: University of Michigan Press.

Fine, M. (1991). *Framing dropouts: Notes on the politics of an urban public school*. Albany: State University of New York Press.

Fontaine, C. & Luttrell, W. (2015). Re-Centering the role of care in young people's multimodal literacies: a collaborative seeing approach. In M. Hamilton, R. Heydon, K. Hibbert, & R. Stooke (Eds.) *Negotiating Spaces for Literacy Learning: Multimodality and Governmentality*. London: Bloomsbury Books, 43–56.

Foucault, M. (1980). *Power/Knowledge*. C. Gordon (Ed.). New York: Vintage.

Ginwright, S. (2016). *Hope and Healing in Urban Education: How Urban Activists and Teachers are Reclaiming Matters of the Heart*. New York: Routledge.

Gregory, A., Skiba, R. J., & Noguera, P. A. (2010). The achievement gap and the discipline gap: Two sides of the same coin? *Educational Researcher*, 39(1), 59–68.

hooks, bell. (1990). Homeplace: a site of resistance. In *Yearning: Race, Gender, and Cultural politics*. Boston: South End Press, 45–53.

Ignatieff, M. (2001). *The Needs of Strangers*. New York: Picador Metropolitan Books.

Kaplan, E. B. (2013). *'We live in the shadow': Inner-city kids tell their stories through photographs*. Philadelphia, PA: Temple.

Krueger, P. (2009). *Navigating the gaze: Young people's intimate knowledge with surveilled spaces at school*. New York, NY: City University of New York.

Langer, S. K. (1953). *Feeling and form: A theory of art*. New York: Charles Scribner's Sons.

Luttrell, W. (2003). *Pregnant bodies, fertile minds: Gender, race, and the schooling of pregnant teens*. New York: Routledge.

Luttrell, W. (2010). 'A camera is a big responsibility': A lens for analysing children's visual voices. *Visual Studies*, 25(3), 224–237.

Luttrell, W. (2016). Children framing childhoods and looking back. In J. Moss & B. Pini (Eds.) *Visual Research Methods in Educational Research*. Houndmills, Basingstoke, UK & New York: Palgrave MacMillan, 172–188.

Luttrell, W. & Chalfen, R. (2010). Hearing voices: An introduction to dilemmas in visual research. *Visual Studies*, 25 (3), 197–200.

Mirzoeff, N. (2011). *The right to look: A counterhistory of visuality*. Durham: Duke University Press.

Mitchell, C. (2011). *Doing visual research*. London: Sage.

NYCLU (2014). Student Safety Act suspensions factsheet. *New York Civil Liberties Union*. Retrieved from: https://www.nyclu.org/sites/default/files/ssa_suspension_factsheet_2013-2014_edit.pdf

Orellana, M. F. (1999). Space and place in an urban landscape: Learning from children's views of their social world. *Visual Sociology* 14, 73–89.

Pugh, A. (2009). *Longing and belonging: Parents, children and consumer culture*. Berkeley: University of California Press.

Rose, G. (2007). *Visual methodologies: An introduction to the interpretation of visual materials*. London: Sage Publications.

Rosen, C. (2012, May 10). Freedom and art. *The New York Review of Books*. Retrieved from: http://www.nybooks.com/articles/2012/05/10/freedom-and-art/

Silva, R. (2016). *Dropouts drop in: Re-visualizing the 'dropout' stereotype*. Unpublished doctoral dissertation. New York: The Graduate Center City University of New York.

Sontag, S. (1977). *On photography*. New York: Anchor Books Doubleday.

Thompson, P. (ed). (2008). *Doing visual research with children and young people*. London: Routledge.

Yates, L. (2010). The story they want to tell, and the visual story as evidence: Young people, research authority and research purposes in the education and health domains. *Visual Studies, 25(3)*, 280–291.

Wald, J. & Losen, D. J. (2003). Defining and redirecting a school-to-prison pipeline. *New Directions for Youth Development*, 99(Autumn), 9–15.

Wallace, J., Goodkind, S., Wallace, C., & Bachman, J. (2008). Racial, ethnic, and gender differences in school discipline among U.S. high school students: 1991–2005. *Negro Educational Review*, 59(1/2): 47–62.

Wexler, L. (2000). *Tender violence: Domestic visions in an age of U.S. imperialism*. Chapel Hill: The University of North Carolina Press.

Yuval-Davis, N. (2011). *The politics of belonging: Intersectional contestations*. London: Sage.

34

The Ethical Foundations of Youth Work as an International Profession

Howard Sercombe

INTRODUCTION

This *Handbook*, as far as I know, is the first book about youth work practice that is truly international. That is hugely significant, and not before time. A common understanding about youth work as a profession has often developed at a national level, but, usually, that is as far as it has gone, and there are often divergences even at a national level: for example between church-based youth work, uniformed organisations such as the Scouts, and funded, full-time practitioners. Not that there has necessarily been any conflict between youth workers in one country and another: it is more that nobody has really done the work of looking and translating between the different traditions that have emerged across the globe.

There are exceptions: the History of Youth Work in Europe series of conferences and the accompanying published proceedings (Coussée et al., 2009, 2010, 2012, 2014; Siurala et al., 2016) provide a valuable resource for the exploration of this issue as far as Europe is concerned. More generally, the European Union has spent some time and resource considering youth work (Dunne et al., 2014; European Council, 2013; Institut für Sozialarbeit und Sozialpädagogik, 2007), and the energy for this seems to be increasing. Similarly, the Commonwealth Secretariat has been actively promoting youth work across the Commonwealth for around forty years, prompting member states to develop policy and to address such matters as training for youth workers. Beyond these European or Commonwealth communities, the Sociology of Youth Research Committee (RC34) of the International Sociological Association (ISA) is perhaps the only really international vehicle through which youth workers have been able to develop an international community. However, ISA events are expensive and not widely accessible to those outside universities.

An absence of an international perspective affects the profession's accumulation of knowledge, already compromised by the shortage of training in many jurisdictions. The youth work literature has blossomed over the last decade, but still falls far below other professions. Access to understandings and perspectives developed internationally are often limited to those on the conference circuit. That is true of practice methods too. Ingenious programmes developed in Berlin are unknown to practitioners in Perth, and problems solved in Auckland bedevil youth workers in Toronto. Youth work theorists tend to be known only within their national borders, and are often over-used: it can be hard to find keynote speakers for conferences, particularly for long-running conference series. As modernity creates the conditions that make youth work necessary in China, India and elsewhere (Sercombe, 2015), there is an obligation for youth workers from established and resourced jurisdictions to connect and help in the establishment of practice in developing countries.

But is this possible? Youth work is diverse internationally, and there is no consistency about what government department, if any, takes responsibility for it. In some places it is understood as part of education, in others social work or social welfare, in yet others leisure, culture or sport. It can be conducted through charitable organisations, municipal governments, provincial departments or churches. In some places, psychology would stand as its constitutive discipline; in others, it would be sociology, or some other branch of the humanities. Foundation discourses include Positive Youth Development, social pedagogy, human rights, informal education, positive psychology, radical feminism or critical pedagogy. Sometimes it is called youth work explicitly; often it isn't.

It is difficult to represent this diversity faithfully. My own development is rooted in my experience as a detached youth worker in welfare housing estates in Australia, and in the development of university-based training there. Subsequently, I have worked with practitioners on ethics and the constitution of

youth work in New Zealand, Zambia, South Africa, England, Scotland, Singapore, Malta and with representatives from across the Commonwealth. I have also been involved with international communities of practice which have embraced North America and most of mainland Europe, and have been working in Glasgow for the last decade. But we are products of our history, and youth workers from France and Germany, and even more so from China and India, may find that my attempts to move beyond a dominant British discourse of youth work have not been successful. Hopefully, this chapter is the beginning of a conversation, rather than the end of one.

To some extent, diversity is part of the nature of youth work. Youth work is interstitial, happening between the institutional ribs of a society and moving fluidly between them: a practice across borders (Coburn, 2010). At the same time, the territory is contested. The identification of practices as youth work is not uncontroversial. The Child and Youth Care (CYC) tradition in North America and South Africa is closely allied to youth work, and we would immediately recognise the work of many colleagues within CYC settings. Others we might have more doubt about, particularly where young people's participation is mandated in some way. The social pedagogy tradition in Germany and Denmark is the same: there would be many practitioners whose practice and commitments would be indistinguishable from those where 'youth work' is the officially designated title. But social pedagogue is a wider designation, and many social pedagogues are not youth workers. In the Australian Capital Territory, officers in juvenile prisons are called youth workers. Does that mean that they are, or is this a misappropriation, a theft of a professional identity?

Notwithstanding all of this complexity however, it may be argued that 'you know a youth worker when you see one', and 'you know youth work when you see it' (House of Commons Select Committee for

Education, 2011) regardless of whether that is what they are called or what kind of institutions they work for or who funds them. The challenge is to find the *ground* of this commonality, and to see if it is possible to identify the core elements, across the diversity of discourse and structure and identification, that make someone a youth worker.

THE IDEA OF A PROFESSION[1]

Much of the primary work done on the professions has been done by sociologists, rather than philosophers (e.g. Durkheim, 1957; Parsons, 1939; Ritzer, 1975). As sociologists, their primary concern was to look at the professions in terms of their social function, their role in the economy, and the ways that professional status was able to leverage power. Their approach was to study the existing professions, identifying the features they had in common, and the way they worked on the ground. Greenwood's (1957) influential analysis, for example, used a kind of 'ideal type' analysis to paint a picture of the 'typical' or 'iconic' profession, based on the features that most professions had, or at least those that everyone agreed were professions. Occupations were deemed to be professions to the degree that they possessed these common traits, such as a professional association, university training, or recognition in law. Others were classified as para-professions or quasi-professions or emerging professions.

The problem with this analysis is that it confuses the idea of what a profession is at its core, its *essence*, with its external features, or its *attributes*. It's like defining a person by their hair colour. In principle at least, you don't develop a code of ethics or lobby for recognition in law in order to become a profession; rather, you do those things to defend the profession that you already are (Koehn, 1994). An alternative approach is to identify the central core, the engine that drives

the professions, the central logic. According to Koehn (1994), the clue is actually in the name. *A professional is someone who professes*, who makes a profession of some kind. In other words, a vow, a pledge, a commitment to serve some sort of constituency, typically people in some state of vulnerability, with a particular focus on their service. This is essentially a *moral* position, an ethical commitment to serve. All the professions, she argues, are constituted in this way.

This turns the question on its head. *A profession is defined not by a set of practices, but by a relationship*. A dentist isn't someone who fixes teeth. A dentist is someone who works with people to ensure their mouths stay healthy. The implications of this shift are very interesting indeed. First, it means that the term 'professional' does not initially describe a state or a status. It is a relational term, like parent or partner. As a parent must have a child, so there must also be, for a professional, a client. If there is no client, there is no professional (Parsons, 1939).

Second, the relationship is intentionally limited (Bayles, 1981). These limits are in place in order to create conditions of safety within which a client can make themselves vulnerable. Typically, this is through some sort of disclosure: a client is able to tell someone about ugly, guilty, embarrassing, dangerous or broken aspects of themselves. This can be the first step towards healing and transformation. When commentators talk about the importance of trust, they are talking about the process by which a client makes the decision that it is safe to be vulnerable with you. In youth work, the disclosure is often not verbal, and the intervention we make is often not verbal either (Morgan and Banks, 1999). It might just be that we know about some of the circumstances that young people have to live with. We then create a kind of space within which options, alternatives and different ways to be can emerge. Youth work creates spaces within which that can happen well, and walks with young people through the process of it happening.

Third, the usual characteristics of a profession – codes of ethics, professional associations, training and recognition in law – are essentially strategies designed to protect the inner and outer integrity of that circle. In terms of the inner integrity, they are designed to ensure that the intimacy developed within that circle stays within its purpose: the healing, defence and transformation of the client. Sexual expression is excluded from the relationship because it exploits an intimacy which has a different pretext, and which holds a promise that it is protected from the complications and mixed motives of sexual demand. Economic intimacies, such as gifts, inheritances or exchanges are similarly excluded. In terms of the outer integrity, the practice of confidentiality makes sure that the safety of the professional relationship is not betrayed by exposure to the outside world – even to other professionals – without the overt consent of the client. The principle of non-maleficence ('do no further harm') that appears in many professional codes of ethics takes responsibility for ensuring that the relationship does not put the client in further jeopardy.

Fourth, the relationship is not a symmetrical relationship, but a relationship of service. It is in its nature *other-directed* (Brandeis, 1914). The professional is there to serve the client, not the other way round. Professional service certainly has its rewards, and some of them may come from clients, but we aren't hard done by if they don't, and clients aren't responsible for them. Especially, the professional relationship is not a commercial or contractual relationship, though contracts can sometimes be used within them (May, 1975). Clients are not customers, buying a service. Service is primarily a verb, something we do, not a noun, a product we deliver.

In these terms, youth work is a professional practice in which clients, at a point of vulnerability, are engaged in an intentionally limited (and therefore safe) relationship directed towards the transformation of their situation. To borrow Marx's terminology, youth work is

a profession 'in itself' (it meets all the objective criteria) whether or not it is organised as a profession 'for itself' (self-conscious and aware of its identity and its obligations). This is a different approach to defining youth work: or, indeed, any of the professions. Usually, definitions try to capture what practitioners do, and what it is that they do differently from other people. The trouble is that the contexts in which we work are incredibly varied. Defining the profession by identifying its ethical commitment, and what is different in its ethical commitment to other professions, gets us around that. It locates the core of the profession in the relationship with the young person, which is where most of us would want it to be. So then: what should be youth work's ethical commitment? What is the client group, and what are the grounds of their vulnerability? What is the sphere of action? And what transformation are we working towards?

WHO IS THE CLIENT?

Let's start with the question of the client group. We work with young people. But what is a young person? It just isn't good enough to take our client group naturalistically, 'just as young people' (Jeffs and Smith, 1999). The historical and sociological literature describes in great detail how the modern concept of youth has emerged historically and socially (Bessant et al., 1998; Dyhouse, 1981; Epstein, 2007; Kett, 1977; Sercombe, 1996; Springhall, 1984; see also Gillis, 1974). Some societies don't seem to feel the need to define anybody as 'youth' or 'adolescent' (Epstein, 2007; Seig, 1976), and even in societies which have always had a 'youth' category, it has not always meant the same thing as it does now (Dyhouse, 1981; Gillis, 1974; Kett, 1977; Springhall, 1986). The age range embracing young people has changed, the traits attributed to young people have changed, the nature of their position and function within society has changed: and are still changing (Catan, 2004; Nayak, 2016).

Core documents internationally tend to define the client pragmatically, by referring to an age range. So, for example, a New Zealand survey of youth work refers to the World Health Organization's definitions of 'young people as aged 10–24, youth as 15–24 years, and adolescents as 10–19 years' (Martin, 2006: 11). A European policy document notes that the category can begin from 7 years old and end anywhere up to 36 (Institut für Sozialarbeit und Sozialpädagogik, 2007: 23). African countries routinely take the age range to 35, with Malaysian policy going as far as 40 (Roger, 2008).

Age-range definitions are useful administratively, but worthless conceptually. Ten-year-olds have very little in common with 25-year-olds. Most 10-year-olds are biologically children. Most 25-year-olds in the world (notwithstanding the trend to delay parenthood in the West) are parents. And there is no material difference between a 25-year-old and a 26-year-old. The diversity of age ranges proposed to define youth, and the multitude of ages of majority, also indicate that this way of categorising young people is entirely arbitrary. It is an interesting scenario to those of a European mindset when grandparents can still be classified as youth.

Youth is a paradox: young people are at same time adult and not-yet adult. The biology is important: puberty and the capacity to reproduce both signals and drives the emergence of adulthood and establishes adult capacity. There are differences between young people and adults, but they are not fundamentally differences of capacity: there isn't anything an adult can do, from a developmental point of view, that a teenager can't. But while an individual's biological capacity may be adult, their society may not allow them to exercise that capacity. As Conger and Galambos noted, youth 'begins in biology and ends in culture' (Conger and Galambos, 1997: 55). In this analysis, youth is about the gap between the emergence of

biological adulthood and the granting of social adulthood (Seig, 1976).

Recent developments in cognitive neuroscience cast an interesting light on this. According to current understandings, key cognitive circuitry is developing rapidly throughout childhood, with a final surge just before puberty. The teenage years involve a kind of editing process, where some circuits are established and made more efficient, others fall into disuse or are pruned away. So the movement into adulthood involves not so much a change in capacity (your brain will never be quicker than it was when you were 14), as a confirmation of which of those capacities will be foregrounded in the kind of person you become (Sercombe and Paus, 2009).

Adulthood is not a destination: in fact the term itself is deeply problematic. But there is something about 'coming to yourself' or 'coming into your own' or 'being grown up' that the term adulthood describes. Young people are emerging into this sense of identity, of agency, of feeling like their lives are their own responsibility and that they need also to take responsibility for others around them. Some people are already there at 14; others are not when 40.

THE VULNERABILITY

There is an inside story and an outside story to this. There are individual, personal developmental factors at play including genetics and the choices an individual makes. This is also a process that can be facilitated or retarded by the social and physical environment and by experiences. From puberty, young people are *emergent adults*. The process happens discontinuously across a range of capacities, is different from person to person and is, youth workers would argue, deeply dependent on opportunities for responsibility. However, that opportunity is often denied because of the perception of risk, the idea that young people *as a social category* are not ready or will be unreliable.

These factors spiral, creating self-fulfilling prophecies. Environments which give young people opportunities for participation and responsibility find that young people participate and contribute effectively. For example, their elders are routinely astounded by what young people can achieve in wartime (Rosen, 2015). On the other hand, environments which quarantine young people from key social processes because they are unreliable or troublesome find that they are immature, risk prone and irresponsible (Schlegel, 2009; Seig, 1976). Most Western societies correspond to the latter. At a population level, this exclusion creates the youth phenomenon. It also creates a dominant discourse in modern societies that constructs young people in deficit: as troublesome, conflict-ridden, irresponsible, a problem (Griffin, 2013; Maas, 1990; White and Wyn, 1997). This construction is continually reproduced: including, most recently, in neuroscience. Youth work's conception of young people rejects this construction. Youth work is distinguished by the consistent refusal to see youth (or adolescence) as a pathology, a problem or a deficit.

So youth workers do work with a problem: but the problem is not, in the first instance, the young people. The problem is the systems of exclusion that make it difficult for them to participate in social and political processes, or to step up into the roles of citizen and adult which are their birthright. Of course, this system creates problems for young people, and exclusion can easily become disengagement. Youth workers also work with the consequences of exclusion for young people, including the violence, problematic drug use, poverty, isolation, alienation and ill health that predictably follow social disengagement. This experience can cause spiralling cycles of damage which become self-reinforcing and self-replicating, and individual young people and groups of young people can themselves become secondary sources of violence and damage (Searle-Chaterjee, 2000). But at the core, the source of this damage is structural, not personal, and it originated in the decisions of the powerful, not the decisions of young people.

THE PRIMARY CLIENT

Many professions, including teaching, psychology, medicine and social work express a professional commitment to young people. Some may even agree with the understanding of young people above. So what makes youth work distinctive? What distinguishes 'youth workers' from 'workers with youth'? This can be understood with reference to two criteria. (1) in terms of where our primary obligations lie, and (2) the sphere of action.

While we might claim that youth work's clients are young people, they are not its only clients. Because youth work does not have an independent resource base, it is generally dependent on the benefaction of the state or of the wealthy. The state is therefore a stakeholder, and certainly sees itself as a client. Youth workers generally work for organisations, and managers and boards of such organisations are certainly stakeholders as well. Then there are parents, schools, police, shopkeepers, local residents, the community at large – all of whom have a stake in our intervention with young people.

Within this range of very real obligations, I would argue that – ethically – the youth worker should make an active and positive choice about priority such that the interests of the young person are primary, above all others. Fundamentally, the primary client of the youth worker is the young person with whom they engage (Youth Affairs Council of Western Australia, 2003; see also Sercombe, 1997). All other obligations, including those to the funding body, are secondary. Funding bodies should give money to youth work organisations on this understanding.

This places youth work in radical distinction to most other forms of engagement with young people. Social work, for example, does not unambiguously engage the young person as the primary client, even if the young person is in the frame. Their responsibility is to balance the various interests of different stakeholders and try to achieve the best resolution. Teachers have an obligation to the school and to the curriculum which overrides their obligation to an individual young person. Sports development work might be mostly focused on outcomes for the team, and not so concerned with young people who don't make the cut.

The role that these professionals take is essential (and difficult). I am not arguing for any kind of moral superiority for youth workers here. It is just that we take a different position. Young people need to know that someone is unambiguously acting for them, is on their side, and will not act against their interests, whatever the interests of other stakeholders.

THE SPHERE OF ACTION

There are some other professions who would also argue that the young person they are working with is unambiguously their client. Lawyers, doctors and psychologists are (or should be) in this category. If a doctor is treating a young person, or a nurse delivering sexual health education, it should be the interests of the young person (rather than their parents, for example) that have primacy (Alldred and David, 2007).

The difference between these professions and youth workers is in their sphere of action. If youth is a function of social exclusion, then work with young people needs to take this status seriously, and to work with young people around the elements of their social context which impact on them. At the most benign level, young people have to negotiate their accreditation as adults, and to manage the consequences of their exclusion, including, for example, their containment through compulsory school attendance. Youth workers also take seriously young people's place in their peer groups and the positive impact of peer groups on them. So generally, while we work with young people also on an individual level, we work with them in the lifespace, or *en milieu*, as the North Americans would say, or through association, as the British would say. The second condition is therefore that the youth worker engages the young person in their social context.

THE TRANSFORMATION

Though internationally youth work scholars have expressed it variously, I would suggest that the consensus is clear: youth workers seek a transformation in social arrangements so that young people are welcomed into full, active participation in society. This transformation may be described as the transition from dependence to independence or interdependence; achieving positive self-esteem; self-actualisation; achieving one's full potential, social, economic, emotional (etc.) development; building confidence; participation; inclusion; achieving identity; individuation; raising consciousness. At their core, these terms are, I believe, trying to name the same thing. This is a quality in which people are able to see their lives as something belonging to them, in which they can actually decide how they are going to be, rather than be passive recipients, even victims, of a life determined by others or prescribed by circumstance. They take responsibility for those decisions, for the impact they have on others and the world around them, and indeed for the kind of person they become in making them. Sociologists call this quality *agency*.

Liberal philosophies, which still dominate the West, have tended to see agency as a quality of the *individual*: so generating terms like individuation, independence, liberty, self-determination, self-actualisation, individual sovereignty, achieving one's full potential. Youth work has never been satisfied with this. On the one hand, youth workers are intensely aware of the extent to which a person's capacity for agency can be limited (and corrupted) by poverty, oppression, family background, difference, psychological damage and other social circumstances: it is not just a question of choice. On the other hand, this quality of agency is also about a person acting upon their social context: their relationships, their communities. It cannot ever be only individual. A person can be 'successful', but exploitative, uncaring, violent, selfish; or alternatively, caring, supportive, considerate, generous – a constellation of ethical values captured by the South African term *ubuntu*, which has been adopted within the South African Code of Ethics for youth work (South African Youth Workers' Association, 2013). This is why the shape that a young person's agency takes is never ethically neutral, and why our intervention to enable or facilitate young people's agency isn't either (Young, 1999).

The process of agency is also interactive and relational: it is never something that a young person achieves by themselves. Young people cannot become responsible if no one will give them responsibility. Authorities may not do this willingly: not only does it involve surrendering power, but there are layers of myth about how young people are not capable, are too much of a risk. For youth workers, advocacy includes working to open up possibilities for taking responsibility that are currently denied to young people.

Taken together, these four elements – the ethical commitment to young people as the primary client; concern with the vulnerability of young people as emergent adults in an often hostile or dismissive social environment; the sphere of action of young people's social context and environment; and the transformation via young people's agency – establish youth work's professional relationship. This holds whether the youth worker is paid or a volunteer, a student or a manager,

trained or untrained, a bureaucrat or an academic. If a person takes up the challenge of being a youth worker, their primary client is young people, and their sphere of intervention is the social context in which they live. As a policy maker or an academic, for as long as their research or policy work has young people as its primary client, they remain a youth worker. The moment young people cease to be the primary client, they cease being a youth worker, even if they are working with young people every day and their job title says 'youth worker'.

CODES OF ETHICS

In youth work, interest in a code of ethics has been on the agenda since the late 1970s, though globally the impact of codes of ethics upon the profession has varied. In some jurisdictions they have been used powerfully and creatively to clarify and shape practice and to mediate the relationship with the public and with other professions. In many other countries they don't exist, though the broad movement has been in that direction. In the UK, Brunel University's Regional Consultative Training Unit published a 1978 discussion paper on the subject (Banks, 1999). A group of Australian youth workers drafted the Jasper Declaration (a statement on youth work's social and political ethics) at the first National Youth Conference in 1977, and their concerns were developed enough to prompt a major national conference on a code of ethics in 1991 (Quixley and Doostkhah, 2007). Martha Mattingly reports various initiatives in Canada and the United States from about 1985 onwards. New Zealand was later on the scene, with national discussions in 1995, codes of ethics being developed at the regional level from 1997, and a national draft in 2008 (National Youth Workers Network Aoteoroa, 2008). Youth workers in other countries, like Malta, South Africa, Finland and Ireland have been on a similar journey.

A major driver in the formulation of codes of ethics has been the struggle to achieve clarity about what youth work is and what it does. Helena Barwick's review of youth work across Australia, New Zealand and the United Kingdom (2006) identified lack of clarity as a major inhibition on the development of youth work practice and its wider recognition. She recommended two things to remedy this: training and a code of ethics.

It is in this capacity to act as a statement of identity that a code of ethics creates the possibility for the constitution of youth work as an international profession. It may not be possible to achieve agreement about where youth work fits in terms of education or welfare or sport and recreation or health, or which theoretical base is most appropriate for the practice, but once you get beyond the surface differences, an examination of codes of ethics globally reveals strong agreement about the ethical commitments that are central to youth work practice. On this basis, it might be possible to draft a code of ethics that takes us past national or regional particularities and provides a foundation for recognition of each other internationally: and possibly, the basis of international organisation and mutual support.

An analysis of existing codes of ethics indicates that this job might not be as difficult as one might think. Most people who seek to develop a code of ethics begin with an existing piece of work, and modify and adapt it from there. In terms of ratified national youth work codes, there are really only three original progenitors. The National Youth Agency (NYA) code (National Youth Agency, 2002) was drafted by committee, with the expert guidance of social work ethicist Sarah Banks. While it has been replaced to some degree by the Institute for Youth Work code (Institute for Youth Work, 2013), it continues on in Malta's code (Agenzija Zghazagh, n. d.) and perhaps elsewhere. The North American Child and Youth Care code (Mattingly, 1995), under the guidance of academic Martha Mattingly and others, gathered existing documents both within child and youth care circles and in cognate professions such as social work and nursing, and by a combination of committee and individual labour, forged a composite document. Both the North American Child and Youth Care code and the British NYA code rely heavily on the form of social work codes, and on the Kantian ethical theory which has been dominant in that profession.

I was asked to draft the Western Australian code originally as a conversation piece for a conference in 1997. The original draft was refined through a series of workshops and seminars with practitioners and ratified for Western Australia in 2003. The original code has been taken up, elaborated and modified across a range of constituencies and over time, in different forms, in all Australian states except Queensland and South Australia, in the Institute for Youth Work (UK) code, in codes ratified by professional associations in South Africa, Zambia and Scotland, and in much expanded form, in New Zealand. Current conversations in the Commonwealth Secretariat are also taking place around this code.

Youth work practice in each setting is grounded in a particular conceptual framework. Australian and New Zealand codes are based in discourses of advocacy, with implicit connections in the Australian code to concepts of human rights, made explicit in the New Zealand and Victorian variations and in current Commonwealth drafts. Recent New Zealand versions have a more strongly committed connection to Positive Youth Development discourses. The NYA document is based in discourses of education, especially the informal education tradition, and has strong connections to concepts of social justice and equality. The US Child and Youth Care code is grounded in developmental psychology, especially where it connects with social psychology. The influence of the human ecology tradition, especially Ulrich Bronfenbrenner (who was interested in the development of children and young people within their social context [Bronfenbrenner, 1979]) is clear in the conceptual work.

However, despite these differences of language and discourse, none of these codes disagree. Different elements might be emphasised in one or the other, and some might have clauses that are absent in others, but there is clearly a commonality here, a tradition that is recognisably youth work, regardless of the different histories and influences in each country, and some core affirmations that reach across their respective geographies. All of the codes highlight:

- That the young person/young people are at the centre of the work, and that youth workers' first duty is to them.
- The social exclusion of young people, and the need to redress this through giving them the opportunity to make their voices heard, and to participate and be included fully in political and economic processes.
- That youth work practice should avoid discriminating against marginalised groups of young people, and actively redress such discrimination where it occurs.
- That youth workers are obliged to make sure that they are skilled, competent and knowledgeable, that they keep up to date and continue to develop, and that they recognise when they have reached their limits and others need to be brought on board.
- The need to collaborate with other professionals.
- That youth workers need to be scrupulous about confidentiality.
- The need to be careful about the boundary between the professional relationship and other kinds of relationship with the young person, especially sexual relationships. All but the NYA code (National Youth Agency, 2002) ban sexual engagement outright.
- That young people are able and competent to make choices for themselves, and that youth workers should be facilitating and developing their capacity and opportunity to do that.
- That young people exist in a social environment, and that the work extends also to the social environment.
- That the work includes a political element.
- That youth workers need to be aware of their own values, and reflective around those values in their work.
- That youth work environments need to be safe for young people.

This commonality is, I think, powerful. Despite very different histories and structural arrangements, youth workers across the world have come to the same conclusions about how the profession is to be constituted ethically. An international code of ethics, difficulties in wording aside, would be very possible on the basis of these documents. Youth work tends to see itself as a local, geographically specific practice. The documents reveal an international consensus about a youth work identity and what is important in constituting youth work practice, despite local or national variation or specificity.

The trouble is that there is currently no international organisation which is able to convene the conversation, consult internationally among practitioners and their representative organisations, and start to work on getting a draft worked up. It's a catch 22. You need some kind of organisation to find common ground and a common language, but organisations are themselves constituted by discourse, and a common discourse does not yet exist. While that swirls around, youth workers need to do things, and they sink or swim on the basis of whether they are effective or not, whether they are useful.

So, pragmatically, for the purposes of beginning a conversation about this, I have made some suggestions below about what an international code of ethics might look like, based on the code I drafted in 1997; modified for different times and places, it has had the widest acceptance globally. At the purely structural level, it has taken on the discipline of fitting onto a single sheet of paper, on the grounds that one page gets stuck on the wall, two pages go in the drawer. It is designed to be supplemented by commentary and worked examples which may also elaborate further specification relevant to a particular youth work context (for example, residential work, or detached youth work) or to a particular context.

A code like this cannot be imposed, and the draft has no more status than a suggestion. At the same time, it hasn't come from nowhere. Various manifestations of this form of code have been subjected to consultations in Australia, the UK, South Africa, Zambia and New Zealand, and the Commonwealth Secretariat is currently working on a variant. I have not counted exactly, but the number of youth workers who have been involved in consultations on variations of this original form now number several thousand, so it is more than a 'back of an envelope' exercise.

Theoretically, it borrows from several different ethical traditions, and can be read from different points of view. Some existing codes have committed themselves to a central theory, such as human rights (Victoria, Australia) or Kantianism (NYA), but this draft comes from the position that no single ethical theory adequately covers the territory, they are often interdependent, and correct and constrain each other's problems (see Sercombe, 2010, chs 5 and 6). Also, this recognises that the field is pluralist, and that particular fundamentalisms would exclude or alienate some groups of youth workers. While being clear, it does not attempt to be closed. It is meant to begin ethical conversation, not end it. It consciously avoids being couched within specific discourses and traditions, such as Positive Youth Development from the US, the Albemarle tradition from the UK, or Social Pedagogy from Europe, while being philosophically resonant with all of these traditions.

AN INTERNATIONAL CODE OF ETHICS FOR YOUTH WORK

Youth work is a professional practice with a primary commitment to young people, to promoting their place as citizens and full participants in economic, cultural and political life, to the full exercise of their human rights, and to their development as agents in their own lives and in the life of their families and communities. The youth work relationship is protected and shaped by the following principles:

1 **Primary Client:** Youth workers' primary duty is to the young people they work with. Where conflict exists in their obligations between young people, the youth worker should always try to find solutions that minimise harm, and continue to support the young people involved.
2 **Context:** Youth workers work alongside young people in their context, including their culture, family, peer group and community as well as policy and economic environments. Youth work is not limited to facilitating change within the individual young person, but extends to the context in which the young person lives.
3 **Equality:** Youth workers' practice promotes equality for all young people, regardless of age, gender, ethnicity, religion, sexual orientation, disability, location or socio-economic status.
4 **Empowerment:** Youth workers presume that young people are competent in assessing and acting on their interests. The youth worker advocates for and empowers young people by making power relations open and clear; by holding accountable those in a position of power over the young person; by avoiding dependency; and by supporting the young person in the pursuit of their legitimate goals, interests and rights.
5 **Duty of Care:** The youth worker avoids exposing young people to the likelihood of further harm or injury.
6 **Preventing Corruption:** Youth workers and youth work agencies will not advance themselves and their interests at the expense of young people.
7 **Transparency:** The role and expectations established between the youth worker and the young person, and the resulting relationship, will be respectful, open and truthful. The interests of other stakeholders will not be hidden from the young person.
8 **Confidentiality:** Information provided by young people will not be used against them, nor will it be shared with others who may use it against them. Young people should be made aware of the limits to confidentiality. Until this happens, the presumption of confidentiality applies. Wherever possible they should be consulted before disclosure.
9 **Cooperation:** Youth workers will seek to cooperate with others in order to secure the best possible outcomes with and for young people. Youth workers will respect the strengths and diversity of roles other than youth work.
10 **Knowledge:** We will work reflectively, identifying and using the information, resources, skills,

knowledge and practices needed to improve our capacity to meet our obligations to young people.

11 **Self-awareness:** Youth workers are conscious of their own values and interests, and approach cultural and other difference with humility and respect. While the need to challenge may arise, we must first try to understand.

12 **Boundaries:** The youth work relationship is a professional relationship, intentionally limited to protect the young person. Youth workers will maintain the integrity of the limitations of their role in the young person's life. The relationship is not available for sexual engagement.

13 **Self-care:** Ethical youth work practice is consistent with preserving the health of youth workers.

CONCLUSIONS

A code of ethics is a live document, constantly reviewed, able to move with shifts in discourse and understanding but also to resist the winds of mere fashion and the pressure of outside influence. It can be a compass for a profession which is dependent on the powerful for the resources it needs to do its job; a statement of identity for a profession which has earned the right to be what it is; a defence against encroachment from those who would use its reputation to further their own interests; a check for practice in which workers have high degrees of independence and autonomy.

In the current context, a code of ethics could also be a foundation document for an international profession, a form of words not owned by any one nation or jurisdiction but expressing the terms of engagement and the ground of solidarity between them. How that might be progressed internationally is not clear: if youth work's history is anything to go by, an international youth work consciousness will emerge organically and somewhat anarchically until organisation has effectively already happened. In the interim, it is at least a resource for the kind of international conversation about our ethical identity and our core commitment to young people that needs to happen.

For countries where there is not a strong tradition of ethical reflection, the draft might also provide a starting point for the development of their own national code of ethics. The agreement I referred to earlier is made possible in no small part by the willingness of practitioners in very different places to consider whether the reflections offered by people from far away might be useful in their own context, and to borrow, modify, consult, criticise and adopt. That graciousness has time and time again produced a dividend as the conversation is enriched by its diversity and by the contribution of new understandings and reflections from different contexts.

For the future, an international youth work consciousness will be based on our capacity to hear below the differences in language or institutional arrangements a common rhythm, a coherent commitment to young people and to their struggle to find a life that belongs to them – a 'voice, influence and place in society' (National Youth Agency, 2008: 4).

Note

1 The text of this argument is based on the discussion in *Youth Work Ethics* (Sercombe, 2010).

REFERENCES

Agenzija Zghazagh. n. d. *Youth Work Profession Code of Ethics* [Online]. Available at: http://cdn02.abakushost.com/agenzijazghazagh/downloads/Code_of_Ethics.pdf [accessed July 1 2016].

Alldred, P., & David, M.E. 2007. *Get Real About Sex*. London: Palgrave Macmillan.

Banks, S. 1999. Ethics and the youth worker. In: Banks, S. (ed.) *Ethical Issues in Youth Work*. London: Routledge, pp. 3–20.

Barwick, H. 2006. *Youth Work Today: A Review of the Issues and Challenges*. Wellington, New Zealand: Ministry of Youth Development.

Bayles, M. 1981. *Professional Ethics*. Belmont, California: Wadsworth Publishing.

Bessant, J., Sercombe, H., & Watts, R. 1998. *Youth Studies: An Australian Perspective*. Melbourne: Addison Wesley Longman.

Brandeis, L. D. 1914. *Business: A Profession*. Boston: Small and Maynard.

Bronfenbrenner, U. 1979. *The Ecology of Human Development: Experiments by Nature and Design*. Cambridge, MA: Harvard University Press.

Catan, L. 2004. *Becoming Adult: Changing Youth Transitions in the 21st Century*. Brighton, UK: TSA Publishing Limited.

Coburn, A. 2010. Youth work as border pedagogy. In: Davies, B. & Batsleer, J. (eds.) *What is Youth Work*. Exeter: Learning Matters, pp. 33–46.

Conger, J. J. 1973. *Adolescence and Youth: Psychological Development in a Changing World*. Oxford: Harper & Row.

Conger, J. J., & Galambos, N. L. 1997. *Adolescence and Youth* (9th edn). New York: Longman.

Coussée, F., Verschelden, G., Van de Walle, T., Medlinska, M., & Williamson, H. 2009. *The History of Youth Work in Europe and its Relevance for Youth Policy Today*. Strasbourg: Council of Europe Publishing.

Coussée, F., Verschelden, G., Van de Walle, T., Medlinska, M., & Williamson, H. 2010. *The History of Youth Work in Europe and its Relevance for Youth Work Policy Today*, Volume 2. Strasbourg: Council of Europe Publishing.

Coussée, F., Verschelden, G., & Williamson, H. 2012. *The History of Youth Work in Europe: Relevance for Youth Policy Today*, Volume 3. Strasbourg: Council of Europe Publishing.

Coussée, F., Verschelden, G., & Williamson, H. 2014. *The History of Youth Work in Europe: Relevance for Youth Policy Today*, Volume 4. Strasbourg: Council of Europe Publishing.

Dunne, A., Ulicna, D., Murphy, I., & Golubeva, M. 2014. *Working with Young People: The Value of Youth Work in the European Union*. Brussels: European Commission, Directorate-General for Education and Culture.

Durkheim, E. 1957. *Professional Ethics and Public Morals*. London: Routledge and Kegan Paul.

Dyhouse, C. 1981. *Girls Growing Up in Late Victorian and Edwardian England*. London: Routledge and Kegan Paul.

Epstein, R. 2007. *The Case against Adolescence: Rediscovering the Adult in Every Teen*. Sanger, CA, Quill Driver Books.

European Council. 2013. Council conclusions on the contribution of quality youth work to the development, well-being and social inclusion of young people [Online]. Available at: http://eur-lex.europa.eu/legal-content/EN/ALL/?uri=CELEX:52013XG0614%2802%29 [accessed July 1 2016].

Gillis, J. 1974. *Youth and History: Tradition and Change in European Age Relations 1770–Present*. New York: Academic Press.

Greenwood, E. 1957. Attributes of a profession. *Social Work*, 2(3), 44–55.

Griffin, C. 2013. *Representations of Youth: The Study of Youth and Adolescence in Britain and America*. Oxford: John Wiley and Sons.

House of Commons Select Committee for Education 2011. *Third Report: Services for Young People*. London: House of Commons.

Institut für Sozialarbeit und Sozialpädagogik 2007. *The Socioeconomic Scope of Youth Work in Europe*. Strasbourg: Youth Partnership of the European Commission & the Council of Europe.

Institute for Youth Work. 2013. *Code of Ethics* [Online]. Available at: http://www.iyw.org.uk/index.php/about-us/code-of-ethics [accessed July 1 2016].

Jeffs, T., & Smith, M. K. 1999. The problem of 'youth' for youth work. *Youth & Policy*, 62, 45–66.

Kett, J. 1977. *Rites of Passage: Adolescence in America, 1790 to the Present*. New York: Basic Books.

Koehn, D. 1994. *The Ground of Professional Ethics*. London: Routledge.

Maas, F. 1990. Becoming adults: the effects of prolonged dependence on young people. *Youth Studies*, 9(1), 24–29.

Martin, L. 2006. *Real Work: A Report from the National Research Project on the State of Youth Work in Aotearoa*. Christchurch, New Zealand: National Youth Workers' Network of New Zealand.

Mattingly, M. A. 1995. Ethics of Child and Youth Care professionals: a code developed by the Draft Committee for the International Leadership Coalition for Professional Child and Youth Care. *Child and Youth Care Forum*, 24(6), 371–378.

May, W. 1975. Code and covenant or philanthropy and contract. *Hastings Center Report*, 5(6), 49–72.

Morgan, S. and Banks, S. 1999. The youth worker as confidante: issues of welfare and trust. In: Banks, S. (ed.) *Ethical Issues in Youth Work*. London: Routledge, pp. 145–163.

National Youth Agency. 2002. *Ethical Conduct in Youth Work: A Statement of Values and Principles from the National Youth Agency*. Leicester: The National Youth Agency.

National Youth Agency. 2008. *Youth Work National Occupational Standards* [Online]. Available at: http://www.nya.org.uk/wp-content/uploads/2014/06/National-Occupation-Standards-for-Youth-Work.pdf [accessed July 1 2016].

National Youth Workers Network Aoteoroa. 2008. *Code of Ethics for Youth Work in Aotearoa New Zealand*. Wellington: National Youth Workers Network of New Zealand.

Nayak, A. 2016. *Race, Place and Globalization: Youth Cultures in a Changing World*. London: Bloomsbury Publishing.

Parsons, T. 1939. The professions and social structure. *Social Forces*, 17(4), 457–467.

Quixley, S. & Doostkhah, S. 2007. *Conservatising Youth Work? Dangers of Adopting a Code of Ethics*. Brisbane: Youth Affairs Network of Queensland.

Ritzer, G. 1975. Professionalization, bureaucratization and rationalization: the views of Max Weber. *Social Forces*, 53(4), 627–634.

Roger, C. 2008. Youth participation in society. *Asia Europe Journal*, 5(4), 469–477.

Rosen, D. M. 2015. *Child Soldiers in the Western Imagination: From Patriots to Victims*. New Brunswick, NJ: Rutgers University Press.

Schlegel, A. 2009. Cross-cultural issues in the study of adolescent development. In: Steinberg, L., and Lerner, R. (eds.) 2016. *Handbook of Adolescent Psychology: Contextual Influences on Adolescent Development*, Volume 2. New York: Wiley-Blackwell, pp. 570–598.

Searle-Chaterjee, M. (ed.) 2000. *Community: Description, Debate and Dilemma*. Birmingham: Venture Press.

Seig, A. 1976. Why adolescence occurs. In: Thornburg, H. (ed.) *Contemporary Adolescence: Readings*. Monterey: Brooks/Cole, pp. 39–44.

Sercombe, H. 1996. Naming youth: the construction of the youth category. PhD thesis, Murdoch University.

Sercombe, H. 1997. The youth work contract: professionalism and ethics. *Youth Studies Australia*, 16(4), 17–21.

Sercombe, H. 2010. *Youth Work Ethics*. London: Sage.

Sercombe, H. 2014. Risk, adaptation and the functional teenage brain. *Brain and Cognition*, 89, 61–69.

Sercombe, H. 2015. Youth Work in the Context of a Global Sociology of Youth. In: Heathfield, M., & Fusco, D. (eds.) *Unequal age: young people, inequality and youth work*. New York: Taylor and Francis, pp. 19–35.

Sercombe, H., Omaji, P., Drew, N., Love, T., & Cooper, T. 2002. *Youth and the Future: Effective Youth Services for the Year 2015*. Hobart: National Clearinghouse for Youth Studies.

Sercombe, H. & Paus, T. 2009. The 'teen brain' research: implications for practitioners. *Youth & Policy*, 103, 25–37.

Siurala, L., Cousee, F., Suurpaa, L. & Williamson, H. 2016. *The History of Youth Work, Volume 5*. Strasbourg: Council of Europe.

South African Youth Workers' Association. 2013. *The Constitution of Youth Work as a Profession Incorporating the Code of Ethics*. Pretoria: South African Youth Workers' Association and National Youth Development Association.

Springhall, J. 1984. The origins of adolescence. *Youth & Policy*, 2, 20–35.

Springhall, J. 1986. *Coming of Age: Adolescence in Britain, 1860–1960*. Dublin: Gill and Macmillan.

Steinberg, L. & Lerner, R. (eds.) *Handbook of Adolescent Psychology: Contextual Influences on Adolescent Development*, Volume 2. New York: Wiley-Blackwell.

White, R. & Wyn, J. 1997. *Rethinking Youth*. Sydney, Allen & Unwin.

Young, K. 1999. The youth worker as guide, philosopher and friend: the realities of participation and empowerment. In: Banks, S. (ed.) *Ethical Issues in Youth Work*. London: Routledge.

Youth Affairs Council of Western Australia. 2003. *A Code of Ethics for Youth Work* [Online]. Perth: Youth Affairs Council of Western Australia. Available at: https://www.yacwa.org.au/wp-content/uploads/2017/05/Youth-Work-Code-of-Ethics.pdf [accessed April 15 2008].

35

Youth Work at the End of Life?

Rajesh Patel

INTRODUCTION

Approximately 39,000 children under 19 in England are living with a life-limiting condition that may require palliative care (Fraser et al., 2012), while 1.8 million children in Sub-Saharan Africa are living with HIV/AIDS, and between 7 and 20 million children worldwide require palliative support (Chambers et al., 2010). Palliative care is carried out in a variety of health systems, from socialised state systems such as the UK's National Health Service (NHS) to private providers available to those with sufficient incomes or insurance, though this work is frequently carried out by charities and NGOs (Pfund and Kerry-Fowler, 2010). Brennan (2010, 11) highlights how youth palliative care is 'sporadic': even in wealthy countries care can be insufficient (Chambers et al., 2010: 21).

The initial stimulus for writing this chapter came from supervising a youth and community work student employed in a hospice.

Although I had practised youth work and taught undergraduate students for twenty years in the UK, I was not aware of the extent of work with young people or how the values of youth work might be applied in medical settings to help empower and improve their lives. This chapter raises some important questions about the ethics and the dilemmas of working with clinical staff.

Due partly to advances in medical technology, young people with a range of life-limiting conditions in the UK, have extended life spans, leading to extensive health problems and prolonged treatment. This impacts on their social welfare and requires specialist workers who can communicate with and support young adults effectively.

With much public sympathy and elements in popular culture such as the film and book *The Fault in Our Stars* (Green, 2013; Boone, 2014), children with life-limiting conditions are increasingly valorised as brave individuals facing the un-faceable. However, they also experience the same day-to-day emotions as their peers as they continue their development towards, if not into, adulthood. The frustrations of extended hospital care can lead to isolation; even short stays can have a negative impact on behaviour and create anxiety and distress (Livesley and Long, 2013: 129). Harris's (2011: 3) insight that distressed young people harmed by their social environment are often silenced applies also to young people in hospitals, due to the impacts both of their illness and treatment, but also because of the isolation and difficulties faced in communicating with medical practitioners.

It is here that youth workers can offer support, building relationships and offering informal conversation as a means of empowerment. As I heard more from hospital-based workers (White and Walker, 1993; Yates et al., 2009; Hilton and Jephson, 2012), it became clear that ordinary young people coping with extraordinary circumstances might benefit from youth work that provides support, elicits their voice and empowers them, as they endeavour to make the most of the time remaining.

So, while the title of this chapter might appear paradoxical – youth work largely being seen as preparation for a future life course – it outlines the possibilities for practice when it may soon be curtailed. While the medical needs of young people are being addressed through improved technology world-wide, it is the social aspects that will need greater attention for children and young people with life-limiting conditions. At the same time, informal education in health is a growing area (Granholm, 2012) youth workers clearly have a role to play, but the ethical and practice constraints need deeper conceptual grounding. As a British youth and community work lecturer, I shall draw on research from the UK, where youth work practice with this group is developing, though the literature lags behind. To help address the lack of awareness within youth work circles, I will give examples of practice with young people in hospitals. I will then move on to detail some of the conflicts arising from policy

and joint practice with medical staff around patient voice, exploring a case study of a young person who refused treatment. I then consider some of the ethical problems faced by youth workers in medical settings, who are often isolated and have to navigate medical language and clinical institutional values while trying to establish their own ethical principles when faced by dilemmas as they practice. These concerns are likely to emerge for youth workers in international contexts. I examine two issues: supporting young people when consent needs to be informed; and the dilemmas attached to providing group support for young people who have life-limiting conditions.

VOICE, INFORMED CONSENT AND WORKING IN PARTNERSHIP

This part of the chapter will provide some of the background and history of practice, and link that with youth work territory by looking at the themes of voice and empowerment for young people. For youth workers operating in medical settings, conflicts are almost inevitable as they attempt to advocate for young people: this chapter asserts that there is insufficient understanding regarding the consequences of advising and supporting young people on issues related to medical technical knowledge and care. Whilst the youth work social role offers important advantages over medical approaches in communication and using voluntary association to build collaborative knowledge, it also throws up ethical dilemmas for staff.

Youth work in hospitals in the UK is still very new, emerging over the last twenty years, and it brings up many questions. One of the most long-standing projects integrating youth work into hospital settings has been the Nottingham University Hospital Youth Service, which has been running since 1998 (NUHYS, 2016). It has been one of the pioneers, receiving financial support from

Nottingham Hospital Trust (Watson, 2004), and provides open access to any young people in the care of the hospital (Hilton et al., 2004; Hilton and Jephson, 2012) and not purely for those requiring palliative care. Hospital youth work has a longer history in Canada, where youth workers have worked in hospitals since the 1950s (Brooker, 2014: 140). Elsewhere documentation is sparse, and while youth workers may be mentioned in the literature, their roles are more fluid as they overlap with social work functions or health advocacy and the youth work aspect can be unclear, especially for medical staff (Watson, 2004). There is limited academic literature, with articles often written by youth practitioners (Hilton et al., 2004; Smith and Case, 2011; Hilton and Jephson, 2012).

By contrast, the medical literature is relatively well developed, some of which also covers social and emotional support for children and young people, and particularly in nursing there is an interesting body of work (e.g. Miller, 2001; Smith et al., 2007; Pritchard et al., 2011; RCN, 2013; Farrell and Law, 2015), much of it examining ethical questions. Peer support, requiring both one-to-one and group work is viewed largely positively in the medical literature (Grinyer, 2007; Morgan et al., 2010; D'Agostino et al., 2011; Craig 2012). However, encouraging young people to form friendships and promoting association – an integral part of youth work – creates an exposure to loss and potential grief as not all the members of support groups will survive into adulthood; thus, the normalised act of building social relationships (Wood et al., 2015: 30) potentially has negative effects. While this is not inevitably the case, and there is some evidence that association is valued by young people (Smith et al., 2007: 366), this is not a given and there is a need for youth workers to be vigilant to its possible negative effects.

Broader work with young people with both debilitating and life-limiting conditions became supported after the hospice movement in the UK was established by Dame Cicely

Saunders. Helen House, the first UK children's hospice, was set up in 1982 (Grinyer, 2011). This has grown and over forty institutions specifically for children and young people have been established in the UK (TFSL, 2016), with recognition that adult services 'are often poor and vary widely' and are not 'equipped to meet the particular requirements of this group' (Grinyer and Barbarachild, 2011: i). Internationally there are also now many hospices; a key charity – the Children's Hospice International (C.H.I.) – has worked in over forty countries since its inception in 1982. Resources in less developed regions are not well documented.

At the same time, innovations in medical technology and improvements in health care have extended the life spans of young patients. This has, however, led to young people wishing to participate in activities including sex and relationship experimentation (Sargant et al., 2014: 418), experimenting with banned substances or alcohol, and other adolescent pastimes, where previously these young people did not tend to make the transition to young adulthood. How these requests are met in medical settings needs further exploration. In an early piece, White and Walker (1993) outlined some of the needs of young people from Australia who faced long-term hospital care and the difficulties for adolescents in finding their motivation. Certainly there is a focus in social work and care work (Holland, 2009), where adults intervene in order to provide one-to-one support for young people and children and help them to make sense of their care/treatment plans. The role of informal group work is hardly broached, however this is precisely how young people become socialised and understand what is 'normal'. This raises questions about the role of youth workers who are asked to assist young people in accessing semi-legal or even illegal activity or sexual intimacies.

In the UK, youth work in health settings includes national work on advocacy (NHS, 2016), mental health and health education, while, in an innovative example, young people in London who are involved in gangs can receive support from youth workers via hospital or medical contact (Redthread, 2016). The focus of the latter example here arguably consists of education and safeguarding, allowing young people to discuss problems with gang membership whilst accessing health care. While education and safeguarding can be a part of the work in palliative situations, youth work is generally concerned about voice and participation, a tenet of general youth work (Perkins, 2009: 108).

This section has provided a brief overview of supportive work and has identified youth work processes of friendship, association and advocacy as well as dilemmas in assisting young people with their support and in meeting their expressed desires. In many ways, youth work in hospitals suffers from the same identity problems faced elsewhere and in other multi-agency settings when their roles are called into question. Where other professionals might be concerned with more direct outcomes (Banks, 2009: 58), the close cultivation of relationships required by youth workers that leads to more holistic connections with young people to encourage their autonomy can be problematic, with limited understanding of the value of this in engaging and empowering young people.

YOUNG PEOPLE'S INVOLVEMENT IN HEALTH GOVERNANCE AND CONFLICTING VIEWS OF 'VOICE'

A tenet of youth and community work is upholding opportunities for communities to be self-determining, presented often in youth work guidance in terms of rights (Maguire, 2009). For the majority of professionals working with young people, this assertion is subject to the caveat that it is dependent upon guardians' or parents' wishes: 'the views of the child being given due weight in accordance with the age and maturity of the child' (United Nations, 1989: Article 12). Consequently, the rights of young people and children are conditional, and for those who are regarded as being vulnerable (for example those with learning disabilities) this conditionality may be extended beyond the age of majority. This section examines some of the issues associated with 'voice' for young people against the political backdrop of health care.

While carrying out youth work in hospitals seems laudable, the competing forces of medical and social care provide a state of flux of power relations. Patient voice is normatively cited as a means of ensuring that people are involved in their treatment and are able to influence the outcome. This can be problematic for young people, due to a supposed lack of capacity to comprehend medical matters and a legal inability to consent (foregrounding parental authority for young people aged below 18, or beyond for young people with special or additional needs). Livesley and Long assert that this presents difficulties for medical settings and hospital staff 'when their voices were heard, they were often seen as a challenge' (2013: 1292). For youth workers, voice rests in a continuum, and is often applied in relation to democracy and participation (Barber, 2007). When not acted upon, asking for it runs the risk of being seen as manipulation or tokenism and can lead to an abrogation of rights.

'Voice' for young people became a particular issue in the UK in relation to public services including health, when organisations in the post-1997 Labour Government sought to consult young people on matters of policy where it directly affected them. This was part of an ideological enfranchisement of young people (Giddens, 1998) associated with efforts to involve the private sector and not-for-profit organisations in public services, with supposedly democratic safeguards. This move has subsequently expanded internationally as other countries in Europe and Africa also developed partnerships in health care (Mudyarabikwa and Regmi, 2014: 161), with moves towards decentralisation and greater local accountability seeking ways to develop patient 'voice'.

Following the death in 2000 of Victoria Climbié, a child under the care but not custody of social services, the UK government published *Every Child Matters*, a document whose aims included voice and for the child to 'make a contribution', including in terms of health and safeguarding. Particularly pertinent here was the idea that the child should be listened to, given the failures in social care procedures that Victoria had experienced. While this provides an intention that young people should be consulted, I would suggest that for young people in end-of-life care there are a number of possible medical life-threatening and mental health concerns that need to be prioritised. The result therefore is that in wider health and social work circles, voice becomes used to safeguard young people potentially as a site of surveillance for their 'safety', rather than as part of a wider consultation and involvement processes (Munro, 2011). This requires social expertise that is not always present: while youth workers are competent in these areas, it takes time and relationship building, which can be difficult on wards where young people are often being moved. It also requires communication with and support from senior management, touching on wider notions of governance in health care, which there is not sufficient scope for in this chapter, but in partnership situations can make or break work. Lewis and Lenehan suggest that young people requiring end–of–life care and their families 'really struggle to get their voices heard and to be involved in decisions about their own health' (2012: 6). In particular they are critical of the lack of training in working with children and young people for clinical staff. This suggests an imbalance between the differing forms of knowledge that affects the weight that is given to young people's 'voice' and the purposes for which it is used.

THE LIMITS OF 'CHOICE' IN–END–OF–LIFE YOUTH WORK

I shall now illustrate the problems associated with voice as revealed in a highly publicised case of a young woman in the UK, Hannah Jones, who was being treated in the British health care system (Boyle, 2009). This case illustrates professional and institutional problems in relation to voice as she sought to find a way forward with her situation. It introduces 'Gillick competence': a measure used in British health care to examine a child or young person's fitness to make decisions about their care, and examines some of the ethical implications of eliciting voice for young people.

Diagnosed initially with a terminal case of myeloid leukaemia at the age of nine (Boyle, 2009: 140), Hannah Jones was treated successfully, but at the age of 12 was re-admitted and recommended to undergo a heart transplant. Because in her view, she had already suffered 'too much trauma' (Percival and Lewis, 2008), Hannah – with her parents' support refused to consent. The Hospital Trust involved initially considered taking Hannah to court, however they then changed their position, releasing the following statement.

> Hannah appears to understand the serious nature of her condition. She demonstrated awareness that she could die. Treatment options were discussed and Hannah was able to express her clear views that she did not wish to go back into hospital for cardiac treatment. Hannah is clearly attached to her family and wishes to be cared for at home. (Dyer, 2008: 337)

The media interest in this case was widespread and may have been a consideration in the actions of the Trust. The Trust's decision not to challenge Hannah's choice was informed by the application of a test of 'Gillick competence' (sometimes known as Fraser-Gillick), deriving from a case in which Mrs Victoria Gillick sought to enforce her perceived right as a mother to give or refuse consent for her underage daughter to access contraceptive advice and prescriptions. Although Mrs Gillick originally won her case, it was overturned at the Court of Appeal, and the rights of minors enshrined in this judgement subsequently became applied in a variety of medical situations where a young person's consent was required (Maguire, 2009: 30).

For many youth workers this active application of voice for young people is to be applauded. However, there is a need to understand how advocacy for young people becomes constituted in medical settings. Boyle, writing for doctors, demonstrates the variety and complexity of the issues in relation to informed consent pertinent to medical practice: 'There are essentially seven ethical principles with their roots planted firmly in the Oath of Hippocrates, and here there are issues involving six of them; autonomy, beneficence, non-maleficence, justice, preservation of life and truth telling' (2009: 141). So while ideas of 'voice' may appear to youth workers as a simple assertion of a young person's autonomy, there are more complex issues related to the ethical stance taken by youth workers. Youth workers may not fully understand the medical implications of the advice and support that they offer. By refusing a heart transplant, Hannah might have been signing her own death warrant; indeed later on Hannah did recover and opted to receive a transplant with a positive outcome for all concerned (Jones, 2016). Had youth workers been party to advising Hannah then this would suggest some professional responsibility would lie with the staff involved, and whilst rights-based discourses suggest as a direct course of action informing Hannah about the Gillick competence at a level that she might understand, this intervention in itself could possibly lead to her death. Such ethical framing of cases will be further developed later in this chapter.

WORKING IN PARTNERSHIP: A TANGLED WEB

Probably more than in any other situation, youth workers in medical settings will find themselves working in partnership with a wide range of other professionals, from ward care staff to consultants. Sometimes the prevalence of a biomedical model of illness can itself create problems, as Yates et al. (2009: 81) note:

> ... medical staff tend to frame their responses within a biomedical, treatment-focused model of thinking aimed at disease management, but this can be negatively perceived by young people [as it can] limit the possibility of recognising and responding to their often varied and complex needs.

This is not an argument to elevate social knowledge above the biological, but for youth workers the dilemmas become exacerbated as their contribution, as in many settings, is poorly understood. Hilton and Jephson (2012: 14) argue that youth workers' role is to 'work alongside the multidisciplinary team to ensure a greater understanding of the youth worker role and offer a comprehensive response to young people's needs'.

However, a failing in partnership working can derive from an inability of members of multi-disciplinary teams to understand each other's roles and functions clearly (Banks, 2009: 58). When health staff are exposed to youth work practice work their understanding can be almost revelatory, as for instance in the case of a respiratory nurse who, having collaborated with a youth worker to support a 12-year-old patient, said that a purely medical perspective 'would never have allowed her to achieve so much' (Hilton and Jephson, 2012: 18). Moreover, as Yates et al. (2009: 85) highlight, adolescents are regarded as particularly problematic, and the presence of youth workers can enable mediation between young people and health professionals where relationships are difficult. In this way the role of the youth worker in this context is one that is aimed primarily at facilitating communication between young people and medical professionals. This however is dependent on the special relationship that is fostered with young people, in which (to use Young's youth work adage) 'young people are seen as young people' (1999: 117).

Communication is clearly enhanced by the social support that youth workers provide, enabling young people to share knowledge with their peers (Smith and Case, 2011: 29) and allowing 'patients to gain from involvement groups' (Sargeant et al., 2007) where life-limiting conditions are present. Furthermore, as Zebrack's research with cancer patients (Yi and Zebrack, 2010) suggests, having more control and knowledge of health care processes aids patients' long-term survival. Therefore, the social benefits of group work with hospital patients are clearly beneficial.

Conflicts can easily arise with 'each professional often claiming to have the child or young person's interest at heart' (Patel, 2013). Thus partnership working whilst potentially productive is also a site of possible conflict and challenge for youth workers who work in hospitals. Whilst there is a strong tradition of helping young people to assert their rights, this may be viewed differently by medical practitioners.

Health work is clearly a joint enterprise, involving not only the patient and the medical practitioners concerned with treatment, but also family, friends, health educators and the social care staff, including youth workers. It is therefore at heart a partnership with differing influences, motivations and knowledge. As Yates et al. (2009: 84) note:

> The problems regarding young people's interactions with medical staff and institutions relate, in different ways, to a problematic constitution of young people as medical cases in a manner that overrides or leaves unaccounted the wider set of desires, needs, and beliefs that constitute the context of their perceptions and experiences of medical settings, and the manifold challenges associated with chronic conditions and hospitalisation.

It is too easy for youth workers to caricature medical professionals who see young people as 'objects'. Rather than contributing to a 'tribal' schism between youth work and health professionals, it is preferable to try to understand how both scientific and social knowledge and their effects becomes distributed in practice. For young people in hospital the physical symptoms and treatments are often unpleasant and painful (Yates et al., 2009: 79). Although medical procedures may be applied to alleviate the associated physical symptoms, the concomitant social care provided by family, as well as professionals such as nurses, social workers and youth workers, has to help them cope with the feelings of 'depression, anger and hopelessness' (Bhatnagar and Joshi, 2011: 173) that can result.

As noted earlier, research suggests that consulting young people with cancer about their care has major health advantages, including improved post-operative survival rates, in comparison with less holistic models (Yi and Zebrack, 2010; Zebrack et al., 2015). There is no reason to believe that this might not be transferable to other less common life-threatening conditions given the similar levels of intensive care required.

CLARIFYING THE ETHICS OF LANGUAGE

Traced out in the earlier section are a number of the ethical 'dilemmas' that illustrate some of the substance of working with young people in medical settings. It is clear that dominant factors include conflicts with other staff and the day-to-day problems that crop up when working with young people. While these are likely to arise in any youth work context, for young people with life-limiting and debilitating conditions, the moral charge attached is heightened. I have so far used the terms dilemmas, problems and issues freely, but it is helpful to draw on Sarah Banks's (2013) work, which is more precise. She argues for clearer terminology and provides assistance by usefully breaking down the examination of ethics into three areas which she labels 'challenges'. These are:

1 *Ethical dilemmas* – which arise when the youth worker faces a decision-making situation involving a difficult choice between two

equally unwelcome alternatives, often involving a conflict of principles, and it is not clear which choice will be the right one. Any decision leaves a 'remainder' or 'residue'.

2 *Ethical problems* – which arise when the worker faces a difficult situation, where a decision has to be made, but there is no dilemma for the person making the decision – that is, it is clear which course of action to take.

3 *Ethical issues* – which pervade youth work practice in that it takes place in the context of state-sponsored systems of welfare and control, where matters of needs, rights, duties, interests, relationships and the maintenance or transgression of prevailing norms are at stake (Banks, 2013).

This framing can assist in clarifying ethical concerns and breaking them down into various components, and also triggers questions about how to balance care with education – to handle value conflicts with other professionals, dealing with confidentiality and information-sharing as well as the rights and needs of young people.

Returning to the examination of problems cited earlier in the chapter, we can look at the example of a Teenage Cancer Trust (TCT) youth worker who highlighted their concern about whether to set up support groups for young people with cancer or not. In this case providing group support results in an ethical *dilemma*. While peer group work might be supportive, it almost inevitably results in the loss of members (or comrades) as a result of their conditions. However, not providing group work can isolate the young person concerned. As an ethical *problem* youth work values suggest that workers should go ahead with the group. The commitment of youth workers to the social suggests that they are likely to lean towards setting up support with the caveat that a discussion of the potential for loss will be facilitated/conducted with group members. Ethical *issues* might arise when young people disclose dissatisfaction with their health care and request intervention from youth workers to assist in changing situations.

The second challenge highlighted earlier was how informed consent for young people like Hannah Jones, and other international cases (Peekstok, 2012), could best be supported when they want to refuse treatment. In providing advice, the rights of young people to information are seen as a given, however providing details of how to complain or resist treatment may result in the young person's fatality generating a clear *dilemma*. An ethical *problem* is that confidentiality might have to be broken to 'safeguard' the young person; where the actions of a person may result in harm there is a mandate for staff to report. There are ethical *issues* related to 'informed' consent in terms of releasing information at an appropriate level for the young person, which can be subjective. While guidelines may suggest what is acceptable for some young people, this may be beyond their capability to understand or might patronise them.

Having summarised these two situations it is appropriate to ask how ethics can assist youth workers in furnishing solutions. Ethics rarely provides unequivocal answers, but it can assist in delineating the parameters surrounding challenges such as these. Both of the challenges would entail young people firstly giving voice in safe environments; this would be complemented by informal education in which young people explore differing views and alternatives. This educative social process is essential in terms of preparing young people to be able to share ideas with peers or to inform their decisions about consent for medical treatment. While parents' wishes often override those of young people in health care, the relational nature of consent loosens if young people are older and able to participate more in formal decision-making. Thus, informal spaces provided by youth workers allow younger young people in particular to understand and rehearse decision-making and should help them to better make their case with adults.

The use of ethical codes has come to be seen as essential to youth work provision (Banks, 1999), and can offer set guidance that is particularly clear for politicians, policy-makers and managers. Using codes rather than professional traits (Fook et al., 2000) suggests that youth workers practise deontological ethics in which the application of rules provides practitioners with set knowledge to deal with particular situations. In respect of informed consent this suggests that youth workers are able to empower patients by informing them of their rights (Maguire, 2009). There is a strong history of this in youth work and it also encompasses the youth work values of voice, empowerment and participation. Work in this vein has over the years been influenced strongly by sympathetic Marxist, feminist and other critical theoretical traditions (Nicholls, 2012; Batsleer, 2013). Thus, there is a strong weight on providing information to young people as a deontological act to enable decisions to be taken by them, based on their preferences and views, albeit in an informal educative manner. Arguably, this is the preferred choice for many youth workers, partly attributable to a culture that values empowerment through the passing on of knowledge and information. However, the outcomes of providing this information in palliative care are that severe harm or even fatality can result. Deontological models do not examine the results of the action, and this comes under closer scrutiny by consequentialism (see Sercombe, 2010).

Strongly prevalent in health circles and social work is the use of virtue ethics (Gillon, 1985; Hursthouse, 1999; Armstrong, 2007; Banks and Gallagher, 2008; Akhtar, 2013; Ellis, 2014).

Where there are more nuanced issues surrounding patient care, this enables not just the act but the character of the person carrying out the actions to be examined. While some work has been undertaken in youth work (Banks, 1999: 13) there is little evidence that youth workers are being exposed to debates on the virtues associated with youth work in relation to associated professions. It is often stronger in religious contexts (Nash, 2014) and Bessant provides a notable exception in

which she states that '"virtue" itself refers to good habits and dispositions to display character traits like courage, prudence, rationality or temperance' (2009: 429). This suggests that youth workers who practise virtue ethics require a deeper engagement with the character not just of their own conditions but of other professions. Using deontological methods would essentially pit differing rules from diverse professional values against each other, and this will inevitably lead to conflict, therefore a deeper consideration of ethics is necessary.

CONSIDERING BENEFICENCE AND NON-MALEFICENCE

I have briefly outlined the key ethical discourses. There are also a number of well-rehearsed arguments about ethics in medical care, and Boyle (2009) described how there are a variety of different ethical components, two of which are beneficence and non-maleficence. The former means that the doctor or medical practitioner is tasked with carrying out the best treatment in producing a cure. However, also particularly useful in palliative care is the use of non-maleficence. This necessitates the use of inaction, standing by so that the harm may not be increased. There are limits to the power of medicine and thus withholding certain medication may help the patient and some treatments may make the situation worse. While used in terms of medical intervention, the dispensing of advice and knowledge may in some cases exacerbate problems, it is here that the character of the youth worker needs to come into play. The implication is that codes of ethics would entail providing information as of right, with less emphasis on the consequences. In relation to youth mentoring, Rhodes et al. point out that even inadvertently 'mentors may express beliefs or opinions that are at odds with the experiences, values and beliefs of their protégés' (2009: 453). Thus, in acting to support young people it is necessary, especially when they are vulnerable, to examine how we might add to the burdens already experienced by young people.

For youth workers who operate in medical environments the acquisition of medical language is a necessary part of their everyday life, however acquiring language does not necessarily mean that the concepts are thoroughly understood. The examination of the work around 'voice' for example shows that youth work and medical practice don't entirely overlap; for youth workers in health care a closer scrutiny of the terms involved needs to be undertaken. Youth workers may feel that 'giving' voice to medical practitioners introduces an advisory or consultative practice rather than more empowerment/control for the patient. However, using lenses associated with virtue ethics, we can see from the Yates et al. (2009) quote set out above that doctors and nurses might view young people as 'objects' to be treated. The scientific application of knowledge in order to cure disease combined with the pressures associated with working in health care systems limits time and can be expensive. These judgements often have to be made in very short timescales, with much at stake. The management of pain and discomfort requires scientific knowledge, clearly an area that is the domain of medical practitioners, which in relation to virtue ethics helps in some cases to provide a 'good' death (Woods and Hagger, 2013). Of necessity, it may be important for medical practitioners to distract themselves from the human relationship and apply themselves to the science of palliative medicine, and seen in this context viewing humans as objects may be the only way for staff to cope with their duties. Understanding this may help youth workers or others to be less judgemental about medical staff in hospices and hospitals.

Reid and Oliver argue that 'in a target driven context, virtue ethics – or those related to one's personal traits or dispositions, are shrouded by a more consequentialist, or goal-driven stance' (2014: 35). If we begin to unpick this in a hospital context, identified above are the tensions for youth workers who see rights and values as being foregrounded in their day-to-day work. Thus, working with young people where the goals are to 'educate' and 'inform' in relation to health is likely to lead to a desire on the part of the worker to provide information which enables young people to be, for instance, more assertive, particularly where young people are requesting activity which goes beyond the everyday. For work in hospices this may involve requests to go to the pub or attend social events, regarded as normal activity but which can bring institutional disapproval. For young people the negotiation of social boundaries and entry to prohibited spaces are normally seen as part of growing up. Depicted in popular culture, this behaviour often carries humorous overtones associated with 'youthfulness'. For young people in hospitals their institutionalisation can result in concerns being expressed by staff in terms of safeguarding and whether desires such as visiting a night club or roller-skating rink might lead to harm.

Bessant, drawing on Flyvbjerg (2001), suggests that a useful addition to the youth worker's armoury from virtue ethics is *phronesis*, as it 'requires an ability to grasp and recognise the significance or value of the experiences for those involved in that particular situation' (2009: 435). *Phronesis* then, rather than *episteme* or *techne*, products of the Enlightenment which suggest that hard universal scientific truths are more serviceable, offers to recognise the complexities of youth work in hospitals where each case has different circumstances, requiring situated wisdom in providing more flexible solutions to meeting young people's needs and desires.

Reid and Oliver usefully point out that ethics in the helping professions 'can be problematic if issues related to power and position are not considered' (2014: 36). To this, I add the suggestion that a consideration of 'power and position', while helped by critical theoretical traditions cited earlier in relation to partnership working in medical contexts, should encompass differing *intra-professional* ethical stances. A comparison of the values that are extant in partnerships settings, and using the social learning and dialogue that youth workers are adept at, will be of immense benefit in identifying conflicts and allowing staff to work jointly. This would inform a critical examination of the historical, material and social development of related professions and their associated discourses in the literature and may be more productive – particularly where desires become more ardent, for example in requesting sexual relationships, or in cases such as that of Hannah Jones, where deeper questions about mortality and the quality of life emerge that cannot be answered by the application of deontological ethics enacted in codes or through the use of risk-assessments. Clearly, the act of transition to adulthood involves risks being negotiated and taken. It is here that youth workers in hospital might examine what is 'good'. There is a need to enquire further how virtuous qualities might become developed, in concert with medical colleagues, to revisit how medical treatment and practices affect the social. The overt focus on 'rights' through 'empowering' knowledge may enable young people to act, but hard questions need to be asked about the extent to which this allows young people in critical care to make the best use of their precious time.

CONCLUSION

The philosophical nuances have only received a basic coverage here but have produced some highly interesting problems in relation to informed consent and conducting group work.

It is clear that no single group of professionals will be able to meet the multiple needs for physical, mental, social and emotional work required by any young person with a life-threatening condition. This chapter has pointed out gaps in ethical knowledge both

between medical professionals and youth, and for youth workers in their own understanding of professional principles. It has highlighted the tendency of youth workers to draw on rights and values rather than ethics, and the concerns in medical circles about safeguarding that can stifle a young person's 'voice' or agency. This can be partly attributed to youth workers' lack of critical examination of non-maleficence, perhaps seeing this as a term for medical professionals when greater weight needs to be applied to the dispensing or withholding of advice. This chapter has examined how the use of language can lead to conflicts. I have argued that more dialogue about the origins of each other's stances might lead to clearer insights from youth workers to help them move away from reductionist caricatures of medical professionals and towards understanding that there are risks as well as benefits in social intervention; while, in turn, youth workers' stronger communication, advocacy and social support roles could be better understood by medical staff.

REFERENCES

Akhtar, F. (2013) *Master Social Work Values and Ethics (Mastering Social Work Skills)*. London: Jessica Kingsley Publishing.
Armstrong, A. (2007) *Nursing Ethics: A Virtue-Based Approach*. Basingstoke: Palgrave Macmillan.
Banks, S. (1999) *Ethical Issues in Youth Work*. London: Routledge.
Banks, S. (2009) Ethics and values in work with young people. In Hines, J. and Wood, J. (Eds.) *Work with Young People: Theory and Policy for Practice*. London: Sage, pp. 48–59.
Banks, S. (2013) *Ethics, Professionalism and Youth Work*. Available at http://www.lide-share.net/POYWE/key-note-speech-1-sarah-banks [accessed 05/03/2017].
Banks, S. and Gallagher, A. (2008) *Ethics in Professional Life: Virtues for Health and Social Care: Character, Conduct and Caring*. London: Palgrave Macmillan.

Barber, T. (2007) Young people and civic participation: A conceptual review. *Youth & Policy* 96, pp. 19–40.

Batsleer, J. (2013) *Working with Girls and Young Women in Community Settings.* London: Ashgate.

Bessant, J. (2009) Aristotle meets youth work: A case for virtue ethics. *Journal of Youth Studies* 12(4), pp. 423–438.

Bhatnagar, S. and Joshi, S. (2011) Palliative care of young adults: An issue which needs higher and better awareness. *Indian Journal of Palliative Care* 17(3), pp. 173–174.

Boone, J. (Dir.) (2014) *The Fault in Our Stars* [Film] Fox 2000 Pictures.

Boyle, L. (2009) Gillick competence – just where to draw the line available. *Journal of Northern Ireland Ethics Forum* 6(1), pp. 140–152.

Brennan, F. (2010) Paediatric palliative care as a basic human right. In Pfund, R. and Fowler-Kerry, S. (Eds.) *Perspectives on Palliative Care for Children and Young People: A Global Discourse.* Oxford: Radcliffe Publishing.

Brooker, J. (2014) Current issues in youth work training in English-speaking countries. In Belton, B. (Ed.) *'Cadjan – Kiduhu': Global Perspectives on Youth Work.* Sense Publishers: Rotterdam, pp. 133–150.

Cannella, G. S. and Lincoln, Y. S. (2009) Deploying qualitative methods for critical social purposes. In Denzin, N. K. and Giardina, M. D. (eds) *Qualitative Enquiry and Social Justice.* Walnut Creek, CA, USA: Left Coast Press, pp. 53–72.

Chambers, L., Boucher, S., Downing, J., Mwangi-Powell, F. and Kraft, S. (2010) The International Children's Palliative Care Network (ICPCN). In Pfund, R. and Fowler-Kerry, S. (Eds.) *Perspectives on Palliative Care for Children and Young People: A Global Discourse.* Oxford: Radcliffe Publishing, pp. 27–41.

Craig, F. (2012) Adolescents and Young People in Goldman, A., Hain, R. and Liben, S. (Eds.) *Oxford Textbook of Palliative Care for Children.* Oxford: Oxford University Press, pp. 108–118.

D'Agostino, N. M., Penney, A. and Zebrack, B. (2011) Providing developmentally appropriate psychosocial care to adolescent and young adult cancer survivors. *Cancer* 117(10), pp. 2329–2334.

De Castella, T. (2009) Hospital youth work: A place to forget about illnesses. *Children and Young People Now* March, pp. 14–15.

Dyer, C. (2008) Trust decides against legal action to force girl to receive heart transplant. *The British Medical Journal*, 337.

Ellis, P. (2014) *Understanding Ethics for Nursing Students (Transforming Nursing Practice Series).* Exeter: Learning Matters.

Farrell, C. and Law, K. (2015) Role of specialist liaison nurses in caring for young adults. *Cancer Nursing Practice* 14(9), pp. 14–19.

Flyvbjerg, B. (2001) *Making Social Science Matter – Why Social Inquiry Fails and How it Can Succeed Again.* Cambridge: Cambridge University Press.

Fook, J., Ryan, M. and Hawkins, L. (2000) *Professional Expertise: Practice, Theory and Education for Working in Uncertainty.* London: Whiting and Birch.

Fraser, L.K., Parslow, R.C., McKinney, P.A., Miller M., Aldridge, J.M., Hain., R. and Norman P. (2012) *Life-Limiting and Life-Threatening Conditions in Children and Young People in the United Kingdom. Final Report for Together for Short Lives.* Bristol: TfSL.

Giddens, A. (1998) *The Third Way.* Cambridge: Polity Press/Blackwell Publishers.

Gillon, R. (1985) *Philosophical Medical Ethics.* London: Wiley.

Glendinning, C. and Coleman, A. (2004) Joint working: the health service agenda. In Snape, S. and Taylor, P. (Eds.) *Partnerships between Health and Local Government.* London: Frank Cass, pp. 51–72.

Granholm, C. (2012) Young people and mental health when ICT becomes a tool of participation in public health in Finland. In Loncle, P., Cuconato, M., Muniglia, V. and Walther. A. (Eds.) *Youth Participation in Europe: Beyond Discourse, Practices and Realities.* Bristol: Policy Press, pp. 173–188.

Green, J. (2013) *The Fault in Our Stars.* London: Penguin.

Grinyer, A. (2007) *Young People Living with Cancer: Implications for Policy and Practice.* Maidenhead/New York: McGraw Hill/Open University Press.

Grinyer, A. (2011) *Palliative and End of Life Care for Children and Young People: Home, Hospice and Hospital.* London: Wiley-Blackwell.

Grinyer, A. and Barbarachild, Z. (2011) *Teenage and Young Adult Palliative and End of Life Care Service Evaluation*. Commissioned report. London: Teenage Cancer Trust.

Halliday, J. (2014) Ashya King's father 'treated like criminal' on return to UK, *The Guardian*, 1 December.

Harris, B. (2011) *Working with Distressed Young People (Empowering Youth and Community Work Practice)*. Exeter: Learning Matters.

Hilton, D. and Jephson, S. (2012) Evolution of a youth work service in hospital. *Nursing Children and Young People* 24(6), pp. 14–20.

Hilton, D., Watson, A.R., Walmsley, P. and Jephson, S. (2004) Youth work in hospital: The impact of a youth worker on the lives of adolescents with chronic conditions. *Paediatric Nursing* 16(1), pp. 36–39.

Holland, D. (2009) Teenage and young adult oncology: Challenges for the specialty. *Paediatric Nursing* 21(4), pp. 38–41.

Hursthouse, R. (1999) *On Virtue Ethics*. Oxford: Oxford University Press.

Jones, H. (2016) *The Brain Tumour Charity* available at https://www.thebraintumour-charity.org/get-involved/supporter-groups/groups/the-hannah-louise-jones-fund [accessed 05/03/2017].

Lewis, I. and Lenehan, C. (2012) *Report of the Children and Young People's Health Outcomes Forum*. London: Department of Health.

Livesley, J. and Long, T. (2013) Children's experiences as hospital in-patients: Voice, competence and work. Messages for nursing from a critical ethnographic study. *International Journal of Nursing Studies* 50(10), pp. 1292–1303.

Maguire, M. (2009) *Law and Youth Work*. Exeter: Learning Matters.

Miller, S. (2001) Facilitating decision-making in young people. *Paediatric Nursing* 13(5), pp. 31–35.

Morgan, S., Davies, S., Palmer, S. and Plaster, M. (2010) Sex, drugs, and rock 'n' roll: Caring for adolescents and young adults with cancer. *Journal of Clinical Oncology* 28(32), pp. 4825–4830.

Mudyarabikwa, O. and Regmi, K. (2014) Public–private partnerships as decentralization strategy in health sector. In Regmi, K. (Ed.) *Decentralizing Health Services: A Global Perspective*. New York: Springer-Verlag, pp. 161–182.

Munro, E. (2011) *The Munro Review of Child Protection: Final Report: A Child-Centred System*. CM, 8062. London: The Stationery Office.

Nash, P. (2014) Ethical dilemmas and practice. In Nash, S. and Whitehead, J. (Eds.) *Christian Youth Work in Theory and Practice: A Handbook*. London: SCM Press, pp. 227–244.

Nicholls, D. (2012) *For Youth Workers and Youth Work: Speaking Out for a Better Future*. Bristol: Policy Press.

NHS (2016) *Health and High Quality Care for All, Now and For Future Generations* NHS England: London.

NUHYS (2016) *Welcome to the NUH Youth Service*. Available at http://www.nuhyouth-service.org.uk [accessed 05/03/2017].

Patel, R. (2013) Informed consent? Patients, partnerships and professional dilemmas. Keynote speech at *Teenage & Young Adults in Oncology*, The Christie, Manchester, 23 July.

Peekstok, K. (2012) Rights of Ohio mothers: Best practices for the pediatric patient with a life-threatening illness. Unpublished Master of Public Health thesis, Wright State University.

Percival, J. and Lewis, P. (2008) Teenager who won right to die: 'I have had too much trauma', *The Guardian*, 11 November.

Perkins, D.F. (2009) Community development. In Hines, J. and Wood, J. (Eds.) *Work with Young People: Theory and Policy for Practice*. London: Sage, pp. 104–113.

Pfund, R. and Kerry-Fowler, S. (2010) *Perspectives on Palliative Care for Children and Young People: A Global Discourse*. Boca Raton, FL: CRC Press.

Pritchard, S., Cuvelier, G., Harlos, M. and Barr, R. (2011) Palliative care in adolescents and young adults with cancer. *Cancer* 117(10), pp. 2323–2328.

Redthread (2016) A and E work. Available at: http://www.redthread.org.uk/ [accessed 28/04/2016].

Reid, H. and Oliver, J. (2014) Beyond rhetoric: Asserting the importance of professional ethics and values in the training of Youth Support Workers in challenging times. *Youth & Policy* 113, pp. 31–47.

Rhodes, J., Liang, B. and Spencer, R. (2009) First do no harm: Ethical principles for youth mentoring relationships. *Professional Psychology, Research and Practice* 40(5), pp. 452–458.

Royal College of Nursing (2013) *Adolescence: Boundaries and Connections. An RCN Guide for Working with Young People*. London: RCN.

Sargeant, A., Payne, S., Gott, M., Small, N. and Oliviere, D. (2007) User involvement in palliative care: Motivational factors for service users and professionals. *Progress in Palliative Care* 15(3), pp. 126–132.

Sargant, N. N., Smallwood N., and Finlay F. (2014) Sexual History Taking: A Dying Skill? *Journal of Palliative Medicine* 17(7). https://doi.org/10.1089/jpm.2013.0046

Sercombe, H. (2010) *Youth Work Ethics*. London: Sage.

Smith, S. and Case, L. (2011) The benefits of involving young patients in service development. *Cancer Nursing Practice* 10(3), pp. 26–29.

Smith, S., Davies, S. and Wright, D. (2007) The experiences of teenagers and young adults with cancer – results of 2004 conference survey. *European Journal of Oncology Nursing* 11(4), pp. 362–368.

TCT (2016) *Support Outside Our Units*. Available at https://www.teenagecancertrust.org/about-us/what-we-do/support-outside-our-units [accessed 05/03/2017].

Together for Short Lives (2016) *About Us* Together for Short Lives [accessed 12/04/2017]. Available at http://www.togetherforshortlives.org.uk/about-us/

United Nations (1989) *Convention on the Rights of the Child*. Available at: http://www.unicef.org.uk/UNICEFs-Work/UN-Convention/ [accessed 28/04/2016].

Watson, A. (2004) Hospital youth work and adolescent support. *Archives of Disease in Childhood* 89(5), pp. 440–442.

White, J. and Walker, K. (1993) 'It's too clean in here!' Motivating adolescents in hospital. *Youth Studies Australia* 12(2), pp. 14–17.

Wood, J., Westwood, S. and Thompson, G. (2015) *Youth Work: Preparation for Practice*. London: Routledge.

Woods, S. and Hagger, L. (2013) *A Good Death? Law and Ethics in Practice*. London: Routledge.

Yates, S., Payne, M. and Dyson, S. (2009) Children and young people in hospitals: Doing youth work in medical settings. *Journal of Youth Studies* 12(1), pp. 77–92.

Yi, J. and Zebrack, B. (2010) Self-portraits of families with young adult cancer survivors: Using photovoice. *Journal of Psychosocial Oncology* 28(3), pp. 219–243.

Young, K. (1999) *The Art of Youth Work*. Lyme Regis: Russell House Publishing.

Zebrack, B., Kwak, M., Salsman, J., Cousino, M., Meeske, K., Aguilar, C., Embry, L., Block, R., Hayes-Lattin, B. and Cole, S. (2015) The relationship between posttraumatic stress and posttraumatic growth among adolescent and young adult (AYA) cancer patients. *Psycho-Oncology* 24(2), pp. 162–168.

PART IV

Current Challenges, Future Possibilities

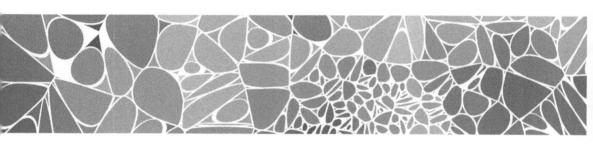

36

Youth Work Practices in Conflict Societies: Lessons, Challenges and Opportunities

Ken Harland and Alastair Scott-McKinley

INTRODUCTION

Throughout the world, children and young people increasingly grow up and exist within a context of conflict and warfare (Batsleer, 2010; Stein & Baizerman, 2007). Recent examples of this include Syria, Iraq, South Africa, Sierra Leone, Mali, Liberia, Burundi, Bosnia, Israel, Palestine, Russia, Croatia, Afghanistan, Egypt, and within our own local context, Northern Ireland. Living in conflict societies has been shown to have residual negative impacts on children and young people, with a complex interaction of risk factors (Muldoon, Trew & Kilpatrick, 2000), particularly for marginalised children and young people (Browne & Dwyer, 2014; McGrellis, 2011; Muldoon, 2004), that includes the enlisting of children into armed groups (Leonard, McKnight & Spyrou, 2011).

While there has been much critique, debate and research into 'the Troubles' in Northern Ireland, to date there has been a paucity of documentation that captures the unique way in which youth work practices, policy and curriculum developed since the onset of conflict in 1969. We have been particularly exercised by a lack of shared learning and knowledge exchange that captures experiences and lessons from youth work practices in other global conflict areas. This is not to say that youth work practices in other regions throughout the world have not experienced and responded to their own specific conflicts and contexts (e.g. Buzinkic et al., 2015; Crownover, 2009). However, as noted by Hamber and Kelly (2005), most research and writing about conflict has attended 'to political negotiation, at the expense of reflection on the role of civil society groups' (p. 15). Magnuson (2009) also previously identified 'a considerable gap between ideas about youth in conflict societies and empirical research' and suggested the need for more description of youth work practice. Magnuson (2007) further argued that for societies in conflict, and emerging from conflict, 'youth work is a moral and existential necessity, since youth are both vulnerable to, and contributors to violence' (p. 4).

Despite entering a new political phase of peace building and hope as a result of paramilitary ceasefires in 1994, Northern Ireland remains a deeply divided and contested society. The pathway towards peace necessitated engaging in post-conflict transformation work that included addressing complex and sensitive issues such as reconciliation, reintegration, decommissioning, police reform, prisoner release, security and a drive towards ending paramilitarism (Harland & McCready, 2015). This complexity has shaped political development, government structures and economic investment sourced primarily through increased levels of European and international funding. These factors also significantly influenced the formation and delivery of youth work practices and policy, including the establishment of professional training for Community Youth Workers at Ulster University in 1972.

In this chapter we draw specifically upon the role, development and experiences of youth work practices during a period of protracted ethno-political conflict in Northern Ireland known locally as 'the Troubles'. However, this paper is not an account of 'the Troubles' in Northern Ireland; nor is it an exploration of concepts of transitional justice, truth-telling, reparations, restorative justice and processes to promote healing. More accurately, it is an exploration of how youth work practice evolved distinctively and separately from other regions, and subsequently influenced the direction and formation of a specific youth work curriculum and wider youth work policy. We discuss how the conflict in Northern Ireland shaped a distinctive statutory basis for youth work practice and the emergence of vibrant voluntary and community youth sectors, and highlight how those practices moved through distinct phases of peace-keeping and peace-making. We argue the need for youth work practices in conflict societies to become 'peace-sustaining' in order to accrue for young people the gains made by peace-building and political processes. We also identify a number

of tensions that emerge in youth work practice in conflict societies for practitioners to be conscious of and prepared to navigate. Finally, we reaffirm the need for more robust politically engaged youth work practices centred on the values of equity, diversity and interdependence, and the need to find creative ways for youth workers to apply these to their relational work, group work and organisational structures (Morrow et al., 2003; Wilson, 2015).

YOUTH WORK AS A BODY OF KNOWLEDGE

The fledgling roots of youth work as a method of non-formal education in the United Kingdom have their origins in mid-19th-century Victorian Britain (McCready & Loudon, 2015). While it is difficult to say exactly when the term 'youth work' became prevalent, the Young Men's Christian Association (YMCA) set up in 1844 has been identified as the first dedicated youth organisation in the UK (Smith, 2002). Fusco (2012) notes that while every profession rests on a body of knowledge, 'understanding how a body of knowledge comes into being is surprisingly complex' (p. 115). Despite the history of youth work, the same can be said of daily youth work practices, which have been difficult to define, and therefore have produced competing and complex views as to the profession's fundamental purposes and nature (Davies, 2010; Fusco & Baizerman, 2013; Harland & Morgan, 2006; Sercombe, 2004; Walker & Walker, 2012).

Baizerman (2007) describes youth work as a 'family of practices' that has a 'craft orientation' grounded in situational and ongoing enquiry structured in the shape of questions. Wilson (2015) speaks of the central importance of youth workers building open, inclusive and accepting relationships with and between young people. Harland and McCready (2014) also discuss how youth work is a critical, relational-driven encounter with young people built on respect, trust and choice that is characterised by a specific value system relating to social justice and participative democracy. This includes involving and supporting young people in public decision-making about institutions, policies and programmes and encouraging them to accept their responsibilities as individuals and group members. VeLure Roholt and Cutler (2012) use the term 'civic youth work' as a process of engagement that aims to introduce new understandings of young people as citizens. Through engagement in intentional and reflective small group action, VeLure Roholt and Baizerman (2013) argue that youth work aims to create learning spaces that engage, stimulate, excite and motivate. Youth work recognises young people's different abilities and extracts knowledge and meaning from their experience and ideas. Youth work practices enable the creation of 'safe spaces' where, through conversations and dialogue, young people can explore their fears, hopes and aspirations (Smith, 2010). It is an approach that enables young people to extract knowledge and meaning from their everyday lived experiences, often de-prioritised within formal education (Friere, 2006), and is concerned about how young people feel, which helps to distinguish it from other approaches to learning (Blacker, 2010; Spence et al., 2006; Young, 2006). Ledwith (2011) suggests youth work is founded on principles of empowerment and participation that aim to bring about desired changes in individuals, communities and society. This does not mean however that youth workers have, or should have, all the answers to the questions and concerns that are important to young people. Rather, as noted by Anderson-Nathe (2008) youth workers will often experience, and try to make sense of, 'not knowing' in the context of their engagement and relationships with young people.

Fusco (2012) has spoken of how youth work practice develops from years of 'trying and testing approaches', yet contends that the percentage of youth workers who 'stick-with-it' long enough to 'develop mastery' through a 'deep and layered understanding of practice' that leads to positive outcomes for young people 'is slim' (p. 111). Magnuson

(2009) also identified gaps between ideas about youth work and ground-level practice in conflict societies, and called for more study to better understand the daily realities of youth work practices in these settings.

Lederach (2002, 2003) identified the often undervalued role played by local practitioners on a day-to-day basis in conflict resolution as a way of viewing social conflict. Grassroots youth workers in Northern Ireland were often 'mediators between paramilitary organisations, the wider community authorities and politicians, and between the various communities in conflict' (Grattan & Morgan, 2007, p. 173). Indigenous youth workers practising at a grassroots level perceived their local knowledge as increasing their empathy towards young people's actual lived experiences of conflict (Harland, 2007). For these youth workers their practice interventions were not necessarily the result of a prescribed curriculum. Rather, relationships evolved through a mutual process of conversation, trust and dialogue – something that the youth workers and young person negotiated together. Youth workers believed that it was this approach that helped break the 'norm of silence' that is so often a feature when attempting to address potentially contentious and controversial issues affecting young people living with conflict. While youth work has developed an ever-expanding body of knowledge within different global contexts, less has been written about youth work and conflict within local contexts. In response to this, we specifically identify and discuss some of the opportunities and tensions through which youth work evolved and developed within our own localised context of Northern Ireland.

YOUTH WORK AND CONFLICT: NORTHERN IRELAND

Northern Ireland, variously described as a province of Ireland or a country of the United Kingdom depending on one's political perspective, is a region in the north east of Ireland where the role, purpose and functions of youth work practice have been significantly shaped by the region's ethno-political conflict, known locally as 'the Troubles'. In a relatively small country with a population of 1.8 million, there are relatively few people whose lives have been unaffected by the violence that resulted in over 3,500 deaths and other extreme manifestations of violence from 1969 until the paramilitary ceasefires of 1994. During this period young people grew up experiencing the tension of being perceived as both the 'hope for the future' and also the 'guardians of the sectarian tradition' (McMaster, 1993). Young people were also both victims and perpetrators of the conflict in Northern Ireland (Smyth & Hamilton, 2003). The conflict was primarily inflicted upon working-class communities by working-class men and entailed young men dying at the hands of other young men (Shirlow & Coulter, 2014). Ninety-one per cent of deaths were male, with 32 percent aged 17–24 (Smyth & Hamilton, 2003). Males were also the primary victims of paramilitary style 'punishment' such as shootings in the knees and ankles that served as a brutal form of social justice and so-called 'community policing' (Topping & Byrne, 2012).

For over forty years, youth workers in Northern Ireland have been at the coalface of responding to the complex needs of young people in a deeply divided and contested society. Throughout this period youth work pioneered and delivered a wide and diverse range of local and international initiatives that attempted to creatively engage and support young people in response to the daily rituals of extreme manifestations of violence. While myriads of youth projects were developed during 'the Troubles', much of this work was exploratory in nature – with no blueprint to follow.

As violence escalated in the early 1970s, youth workers were increasingly engaged on a statutory basis to deliver diversionary programmes aimed at keeping young people, particularly young men, off the streets

and away from violence – effectively a 'peace-keeping' role. One key reason for this was the fact that young men were predominantly at the forefront of community violence and being actively recruited by paramilitary organisations (Harland, 2007). The annual youth work budget from the state rose from £125,500 in 1972 to £3.5 million during 1975 and to £8 million in 1980. This funding resulted in 143 purpose-built youth centres, a host of full-time youth work posts and an increase in professional training (DENI, 1986). The Youth Service during this time positioned itself within a reactive needs-response approach, which the UK government appeared to endorse. While this approach undoubtedly created a safer environment for young people (Smyth, 2007), there was recognition that it also created an over-emphasis on the 'assumed' needs of young men (Harland & Morgan, 2003). In essence the 'hidden curriculum' of this time was about diversion – preventing civil unrest and keeping young people 'off the streets'. The early lessons from youth work practices were nevertheless integrated into a central youth work curriculum, which released government funding and significantly influenced youth policy alongside the establishment of inaugural professional training for Community Youth Workers at Ulster University in 1972 (McCready & Loudon, 2015).

Developing Community Relations Practice

A youth service review in 1985 (DENI, 1986) and a 1986 conference entitled, *The Development of a Youth Service Curriculum*, signalled a change in the youth work policy landscape (McCormick, 1998). In September 1987, a policy for the youth service in Northern Ireland (DENI, 1987) was published which included the introduction of a central 'core curriculum' for youth work. The document also identified the need for a more pronounced thrust towards cross-community activity.

The push reflected government priorities at the time and complemented similar policy changes in formal education.

In addition to the curriculum document in 1987, the Department of Education launched the Cross-Community Contact Scheme (DENI, 1987). This was a funding scheme designed to encourage youth groups (and schools) to bring together young people of different community backgrounds with a view to fostering the development of positive, cross-community relations. It was a voluntary scheme with an annual budget of £3.5 million each year. Crucially however, much of this contact work (see for example, Amir, 1969; Pettigrew, 1997; Neins et al., 2003) avoided the more challenging and controversial issues associated with political education and civic responsibility (Smyth, 2007). As the Youth Service in Northern Ireland evolved, cross-community work and building community relations between the two main Catholic and Protestant traditions were given higher priority by policy makers and funders.

As part of the new 1989 order, the Youth Council for Northern Ireland was established and attracted funding for the creation of curriculum guidance for the youth work sector. Its first priority was to produce *Community Relations Guidelines*, which were developed alongside an added £3.5 million in funding from government (YCNI, 1992). The Guidelines outlined several forms of work, firstly single identity work giving Protestant and Catholic young people independent opportunities to reflect on their identity, hopes and fears before engaging in cross-community activities (Hammond, 2008). This work did not always produce cross-community contact, but it did create a dialogue with young people about diversity, difference and their own culture, providing a form of cultural validation (Church & Visser, 2002). The work involved creating environments and programmes where Catholic and Protestant young people could build relationships using recreational activities, residential experiences and non-controversial discussion.

The curriculum guidance (YCNI, 1992) recognised the need for practice that addressed issues related directly to conflict and provided for dialogue around more controversial issues and personal encounter, although practice of this nature was less prevalent at the time. This practice involved facilitated discussion and dialogue around the more difficult issues of culture, religion and politics, exploring issues of culture, identity, symbols, prejudice, stereotypes and discrimination. However, it was still narrowly defined within the polarity of competing national identity centres, that is, Catholic/Nationalist and Protestant/Unionist, and was not what Smyth (2007) termed 'peacemaking', which necessitated a longer developmental, often programmatic approach that involved supporting young people to engage with political processes, training young people to become peer educators around conflict issues, and facilitating young people to engage with other international conflict regions.

Paramilitary ceasefires in 1994 and the Belfast agreement in 1998 paved the way for a return to devolution and the removal of direct rule. A route and branch review of public administration was announced, signalling a shake-up of local government. The 'peace process' brought an influx of European Union Peace funding, which created new opportunities for the development of local community and voluntary groups and wider sector initiatives. However, only a small proportion of this went to youth work projects.

As the peace process led to increased political settlement, the conservative pluralism of youth work in the 1970s and 1980s was transformed into a more radical pluralism buoyed by the positive political developments. Lederach (2008) posits that after violent conflict has receded peace-building creates a platform from which it is possible to respond creatively to evolving situations. One key initiative within youth work during the peace-building phase in Northern Ireland was the EU-funded Joined in Equity, Diversity and Interdependence (JEDI). The twin aims were: to develop a coherent strategy for community relations youth work and education for citizenship in the Northern Ireland youth work sector; and to imbed the interrelated principles of equity, diversity and interdependence into the ethos, policies and programmes of the organisations that make up the youth sector.

The initiative was informed by the 'Future Ways Project' and the belief that a sustainable and prosperous society is underpinned by fairness (Equity), an acknowledgement of differences (Diversity) and a relational understanding of the ways in which we work together (Interdependence) (Eyben et al., 2002). These three principals were presented as the building blocks of a sustainable, inclusive and forward-moving society. The JEDI project emphasised policy change that reflected the Equality Legislation of the Northern Ireland Act 1998 that emanated from the Belfast Agreement. Section 75 of this legislation required public bodies to give due regard to the need to promote equality of opportunity. The JEDI initiative worked under several strands: it reviewed the inter-linked areas of research, training, policy, and practice and produced a series of publications that significantly influenced the local youth work sector. This included a replacement of the 1992 Community Relations Curriculum Guidelines (Smyth, 2007), which presented a much more radical approach to community relations work in Northern Ireland. It offered a vision of a fairer society, at ease with difference and promoting improved relations between all. The values of Equity, Diversity and Interdependence suggested that a more radical engagement with intersectionality was needed in order to emerge from conflict and underpin the transition towards peace (Eyben et al., 2002).

CONSIDERATIONS FOR YOUTH WORKERS NAVIGATING THE TENSIONS IN CONFLICT SOCIETIES

We propose there are a number of key tensions to consider that are relevant to youth work in conflict and post-conflict societies. These tensions operate at a number of levels: firstly the personal, how can a practitioner be more reflexive? Secondly, within the environment of everyday practice, how can a practitioner remain open to the lived experience of those they work with? Thirdly, in a rapidly changing context, how can the practitioner remain focused? And finally, at the level of policy discourse, how can practitioners be critical and ensure that youth work maintains fidelity with values within our rapidly changing organisations?

Personal Reflection and Awareness

Let us first consider the personal. For practitioners in areas of conflict, it can be difficult to locate oneself. Neutrality is fallacious and reflexivity is vital. In the Northern Ireland context, like all conflict contexts, we are in part defined by the conflict and the complexity of our personal experiences. However, we can aspire to greater neutrality. An important part of this process is that practitioners become aware of their own partisanship and the possibility of bias that they bring to their practice. This can be difficult, for as Wilson (2015) reminds us, we cannot claim to be completely free of moments when we have given in to our own narrow 'ethnocentric emotions' or support religious or political impulses associated with exclusion and denial of different others.

A vital element of the practitioner's practice then, is that they engage in critical reflection concerning their mental model of a society in conflict and that they are able to recognise, acknowledge and reject bias and partisanship in themselves. However, it is also vitally important that they are clear about the mental model to which they aspire and how this informs their practice. Wilson (2015) argues that a mental model based on democratic values and understood within a human rights frame of reference is fundamental in societies in, or emerging from, conflict as it helps provide clarity about the work, its aims and what changes it is trying to affect in society.

Community relations work that involves reconciliation means engaging with young people in activity, dialogue and questioning which allows young people to clarify their own thinking. Youth workers are in a unique position to engage relationally and meaningfully with young people in order to create safe practice spaces for conversation, dialogue and the identification of points of connection. By creating secure spaces, young people can share their stories of conflict with other young people and be supported to make sense of their experiences and explore new possibilities. We have an Irish Gaelic saying: *Tarraingíonn sceal sceal eile* – One story leads to another. Our stories cannot be separated from the story of our neighbour, but also our stories have the potential to lead us somewhere new, possibilities that are liberating and hopeful. Youth workers and young people can bring questions as opposed to issues or a prescribed curriculum with predefined outcomes or unrealistic expectations. Young people can re-imagine their communities, ask what it would be like if the peace walls were removed, ask what it would be like if we re-painted the sectarian murals in our communities. This enables a more organic, as opposed to instrumental, approach, where young people can identify their own defining moments, moments of transformation, and hopes for the future.

Experience in Northern Ireland has shown that practitioners must become much more transparent to themselves, within their organisations and crucially to the young people they are working with. Transparency builds trust, sustains practice and provides a basis on which practitioners can challenge partisan attitudes or behaviour in themselves or our organisations.

Open to Diverse Lived Experiences

Our second consideration is: how can practitioners remain open to the diverse lived experiences of those we work with? In the Northern Ireland context, the meta-narrative about conflict is characterised by a 'them' and 'us' mentality in regard to 'Catholic' and 'Protestant', 'Republican' and 'Unionist'. This raises the danger that practitioners make assumptions about identity. We can assume wrongly that all Catholic experience is the same; all Unionist experience is the same. We cannot short-circuit dialogue or assume understanding. These identities are not monoliths. We must recognise that there is nuance in these identities, while they still essentially reflect a narrative of polarity. Wright (1994) conceives of this as 'an ethnic frontier', two sides with divided loyalties and opposing national identities, but with an inability for one group to dominate. In such polarity there is a real danger that this main story nullifies experience, that is, the experiences of others, individuals and groups with different and diverse needs. In polarised societies it can be difficult to create spaces for experience and issues related to gender, race, sexuality, wider religious identity and disabilities to be aired. As Batsleer reminds us when she quotes novelist Arundhati Roy: 'there are only the silenced and the deliberately misheard' (cited in Batsleer, 2008, p. 12). In societies in conflict this effect can be amplified and experience only deemed valid within the binary of the conflict. The challenge is in acknowledging how different experiences intersect within and outside the conflict. It is important for practitioners to be aware of this tension, to actively seek to achieve balance in addressing experiences dominated by conflict, but also to acknowledge and actively recognise the other diverse experiences that are also present within society. It is also important that practitioners do not allow the meta-narrative to become totalising and obliterate alterity.

Our concept of democratic values must be expansive, radically pluralist, extending to include and recognise diversity, moving from seeing diversity as a threat, to something that enriches us – a place where different cultures and experiences are appreciated and nuances of shared commonality identified and valued. A wider shift in Northern Ireland youth work practice occurred in the late 1990s and early 2000s where the 'the focus on the Catholic/Protestant divide broadened to include a more overarching view of relationship between all citizens in all their diversity' (JEDI, 2002, p. 8). Youth work practice in Northern Ireland has more actively taken on the challenges of inequality and exclusion, working to ensure that our everyday practice and organisational services are more inclusive. Youth work organisations now take seriously their responsibility to prevent exclusion and promote inclusion at a structural level and within government itself.

Maintaining Focus in a Volatile and Changing Political Context

We move now to our third consideration: how can practitioners remain focused in a volatile and rapidly changing political context? Further challenges that practitioners face are those presented by location and time. In conflict societies geography becomes associated with 'territory' and as a result is constructed, negotiated and contested – places become 'our side' and 'their side', safe and unsafe (Leonard, 2006). Some communities in Northern Ireland, especially in interface areas (areas where two different cultures butt against one another geographically – often divided by 'peace walls'), experience regular tension and low-level violence in the form of civil unrest and rioting. While this can be short-lived and is sometimes predictable, it can have intense impacts upon young people's lives. In these situations there is an expectation that youth work practitioners are responsive to the needs of young people, once again reverting to a peace-keeping or diversionary role. The positive improvements in young people's attitudes to the 'other side' can fluctuate positively or negatively in response to these violent events or even broader political setbacks (Devine and Schubotz, 2014).

However, there is a challenge here for the practitioner not to get caught in a responsive orientation, but also to be future orientated, to work 'unambiguously to promote a shared society' (Wilson, 2015, p. 4). Many professional youth workers would recognise practice across a wide continuum, from work that is localised and responsive, to work that is more programmatic, creating shared space, building new relationships, facilitating dialogue, through to work that is civic and concerned with sustaining long-term relationships, structures and a wider civil society. All of these forms of work are important, but an explicit orientation to a better future for all citizens of Northern Ireland is crucial.

Maintaining Fidelity of Youth Work Values

This brings us to our final consideration: how can practitioners be critical and ensure that youth work maintains fidelity with its values within our rapidly changing organisations? Northern Ireland has benefited greatly from international support, both political and financial. External political encouragement and pressure from the USA and European Union funding has buttressed the peace process and the determination for political progress (Darby, 2003). The European Union has brought a rich history of work around intercultural learning and a growing interest in democratic competency. The European Union is also a significant funder alongside financial support from the USA, the UK and Republic of Ireland Governments, while significant charitable trusts have been at the forefront of funding peace-building programmes – all of which have in no small part helped to create and sustain the peace and stability that we now experience. They have provided much needed funds for reconciliation work, the transformation of civic society and economic development. This has both provided opportunities and presented challenges. However, these perspectives should not be accepted uncritically; by this we mean, funding and support often carry with them other external interpretations, for example what makes good policy. Ball (2008) describes the 'soft-law' mechanisms of guidelines, indicators, benchmarking and sharing of best practice that can permeate international policy agendas. For example, the European Union funding has also brought with it other policy and administrative procedural practice. The process for receiving grants has been excessively time-consuming and very competitive. Grants for addressing youth work in contested spaces are typically short-term and therefore raise concerns about sustainability. Ironically, youth workers have often had to apply for funding for their own posts, which can deflect them from their work with young people (Harland, 2007).

Northern Ireland youth work's exposure to international funding has been an additional route for the concepts of 'public sector reform', 'new public sector management', 'performativity', 'marketisation' and 'competition' to reach youth work (Ball, 2008, 2013; Morgan, 2009; Ord, 2011). A key experience of practitioners has been the emergence of a performance-related culture where practice has to be justified in management and policy terms and outcomes measured. Harland, Morgan and Muldoon (2005) reported that as a result of substantial funding from the EU, youth workers experienced increasing pressure to evidence specific outcomes for their work. Ball (2008) refers to this overemphasis as an increase in 'transaction costs'; the work of collecting performance data, monitoring and reporting having the effect of reducing the time and energy available for the actual work. In addition, the coherence and understanding of youth work's key concepts and practice, as well as professional judgement and values are challenged, and there is often values drift as work is reoriented to meet managerial demands. Practitioners, but perhaps more importantly organisations, need to be mindful of this and not apply for funding uncritically; this means being cognisant

of the unexpected transference of values and concepts that come with external and international funding.

FUTURE CHALLENGES OF PEACE-SUSTAINING YOUTH WORK

The new political dispensation and devolved political settlement in Northern Ireland has brought with it public sector and youth work sector re-organisation (Knox, 2008) and new youth work priorities (DE, 2013). The 2013 Youth Work Policy in Northern Ireland calls for new policy technologies, outcomes, measurement and management information systems. There is an emphasis on young people's academic attainment (reducing the performance gap), skills development and employability. Crucially, there is a notable side-lining of community relations work and a lack of investment in youth work that addresses conflict and the legacy of conflict. Yet, young people's everyday lives in Northern Ireland continue to be characterised by segregation, symbolic violence and actual violence. Young people still live with the legacy of violence; they live in communities with peace walls (Byrne et al., 2012); they negotiate sectarian interfaces (Leonard, 2006); and the majority live and are educated separately (Nolan, 2014).

In effect, young people inherit political identities. It is our contention that even though we have a broadly accepted political settlement, the work of peace making is still required. Northern Ireland still accounts for a large proportion of terrorist-related incidents within the European Union (Europol, 2015). As politicians focus on economic development and the development of a competent workforce so that Northern Ireland can compete in a global capitalist market, it is clear that youth workers are being co-opted to address other social-economic issues such as educational underachievement and employability as the immediacy of conflict recedes.

This economic political agenda is echoed across the UK, Ireland, much of Europe and also in the United States.

Devine and Schubotz (2014) points to two contradictory perspectives on the future of community relations work: firstly, that a new generation of young people who have not experienced 'the Troubles' will naturally see a society with reduced community divisions develop; and secondly, in contrast, that our partisan identities are so embedded that they will not easily change. Hamber and Kelly (2005) suggest that a more robust approach to reconciliation is needed but acknowledge, 'reconciliation is a difficult and complex process that needs to be championed at the highest level' (p. 18).

In a society emerging from conflict we contend it is important to re-imagine youth work's role in developing political awareness and supporting the development of democratic values and young people's ability to actively participate in that process. Economic, employment and formal education priorities, while important, cannot take precedence over our society's need to address intersectionality – 'the complex interweaving of diverse social inequalities [such as race, class and gender] which shapes individual lives' (Giddens & Sutton, 2013, p. 491) – and the development of a pluralist, sustainable, democratic future in which young people are included as active participants in a vibrant civic society. Ultimately peace making and politics are too important in a society emerging from conflict to be left to politicians. Hamber and Kelly's research (2005) suggests that community relations are not taken seriously by council officials or elected representatives. In this climate it is particularly important that young people in Northern Ireland are not disenfranchised from local politics and political processes – especially as supporting and involving young people's participation in shaping the future of Northern Ireland is so high on the agenda of funders and policy makers. Peace-sustaining work is linked to the wider work on intersectionality, a more radical interpretation of pluralism and concepts of a participative democracy in which young people are included in civic society.

CONCLUSION

Throughout our world, increasing numbers of children and young people grow up in conflict societies and war zones experiencing manifest atrocities and the very real threats of exploitation and radicalisation. While there have been some examples of local discourse describing youth work practices in conflict societies across the globe (see for example, Magnuson & Baizerman, 2007), there remains a paucity of debate concerning the actual role and purpose of youth work practice in conflict societies. In our own local context of Northern Ireland youth work practice has been delivered within the values and underpinning principles of equity, diversity and interdependence. We have discussed how youth work practices can potentially make a significant and meaningful contribution to supporting young people in conflict societies or societies emerging from conflict. We have also discussed how by creating 'safe secure spaces' youth workers can meaningfully engage young people to make sense of their experiences of conflict and explore new possibilities.

We acknowledge that the practice of youth work in conflict societies is undoubtedly a challenging task and assumes that youth workers possess certain skills, knowledge and attitudes. Importantly however, as Baizerman (2007) reminds us, youth work in conflict societies is not solely about young people; it involves 'educating broader society about young people and the rights, opportunities and channels of participation they deserve' (p. 2). This viewpoint affirms the importance of youth work strategies that engage with parents, members of local communities and other organisations working with young people. It requires a much more inclusive and efficacious response to the realities of young people living in conflict societies as opposed to young people who live in non-conflict societies. It necessitates a type of youth work that helps build towards a civic society in which young people are active, as opposed to marginalised observers in the co-creation of their preferred future. This approach requires that youth work practices exert influence and have impact, not only at the grassroots level, but also on multiple levels, including the civic structures of government and meaningful engagement with policy and decision makers.

Ultimately youth work is about relationships and relationships are about conversations and dialogue. In conflict societies youth workers foster dialogue not only with young people, but also between young people and the contested society in which they live in order to help imagine and build an 'unambiguously shared society'. In the words of Northern Ireland's Nobel Laureate Seamus Heaney, 'If you have the words, there's always a chance that you'll find the way'.

REFERENCES

Amir, Y. (1969). Contact hypothesis in ethnic relations. *Psychological Bulletin*, *71*(5), 319–342.

Anderson-Nathe, B. (2008). Investigating not-knowing. *Child and Youth Services*, *30*(1–2), 27–42.

Baizerman, M. (2007). Introduction. In D. Magnuson & M. Baizerman (Eds.), *Work with youth in divided and contested societies* (pp. 1–3). Rotterdam: Sense Publishers.

Ball, S.J. (2008). *The education debate: Policy and politics in the twenty-first century*. Bristol: Policy Press.

Ball, S.J. (2013). *Foucault, power and education*. Abingdon: Routledge.

Batsleer, J. (2008). *Informal learning and youth work*. London: Sage.

Batsleer, J. (2010). Youth work prospects: Back to the future. In J. Batsleer and B. Davies (Eds.), *What is Youth Work?* (pp. 153–165). Exeter: Learning Matters.

Blacker, H. (2010). Relationships, friendship and youth. In T. Jeffs & M.K. Smith (Eds.), *Youth work practice* (pp. 15–30). Basingstoke: Palgrave.

Browne, B. & Dwyer, C. (2014). Navigating risk: Understanding the impact of the conflict on children and young people in Northern Ireland. *Studies in Conflict and Terrorism*, *37*(9), 792–805.

Buzinkic, E., Cullum, B., Horvat, M. & Kovacic, M. (2015). Youth work in Croatia: Collecting pieces for a mosaic. *Child and Youth Services*, *36*(1), 30–55.

Byrne, J., Gormley, H.C. & Robinson, G. (2012). *Attitudes to peace walls. Research Report to Office of First Minister and Deputy First Minister*. University of Ulster.

Church, C. & Visser, A. (2002). *Local and International Learning Project (LILP): Single identity work*. University of Ulster, INCORE. Retrieved from http://www.incore.ulst.ac.uk/publications/occasional/single_i.pdf

Crownover, J. (2009). Youth work in South East Europe: Youth transitions and challenges in a post conflict environment. *Youth & Policy*, *102*, 67–80.

Darby, J. (2003). Northern Ireland: The background to the peace process. Retrieved from http://cain.ulst.ac.uk/events/peace/darby03.htm

Davies, B. (2010). What do we mean by youth work? In J. Batsleer & B. Davies (Eds.), *What is youth work?* (pp. 1–6). Exeter: Learning Matters.

DE (Department of Education) (2013). *Priorities for youth*. Department of Education for Northern Ireland.

DENI (Department of Education Northern Ireland) (1986). *Northern Ireland Youth Service: A review*. Department of Education for Northern Ireland.

DENI (Department of Education Northern Ireland) (1987). *Policy for the Youth Service in Northern Ireland*. Department of Education for Northern Ireland.

Devine, P. and Schubotz, D. (2014). *Not so different Teenage attitudes across a decade of change in Northern Ireland*. Lyme Regis: Russell House Publishing Ltd.

Europol (2015). *The EU terrorism situation and trend report (TE-SAT)*, European Police Office. Retrieved from https://www.europol

.europa.eu/activities-services/main-reports/european-union-terrorism-situation-and-trend-report-2015

Eyben, K., Morrow, D., Wilson, D. & Robinson, B. (2002). *The equity, diversity and interdependence framework: A framework for organisational learning and development.* University of Ulster.

Freire, P. (2006). *Pedagogy of the oppressed.* New York: Continuum.

Fusco, D. (2012). On becoming an academic profession. In D. Fusco (Ed.), *Advancing youth work: Current trends, critical questions* (pp. 111–126). New York: Routledge.

Fusco, D. & Baizerman, M. (2013). Professionalization in youth work? Opening and deepening circles of inquiry. *Child and Youth Services, 34*(2), 89–99.

Giddens, A. & Sutton, P.W. (2013). *Sociology* (7th edn). Cambridge, UK: Polity Press.

Grattan, A. & Morgan, S. (2007). Youthwork in conflict societies: From divergence to convergence. In D. Magnuson & M. Baizerman (Eds.), *Work with youth in divided and contested societies* (pp. 165–177). Rotterdam: Sense Publishers.

Hamber, B. & Kelly, G. (2005). *A place for reconciliation? Conflict and locality in Northern Ireland.* Democratic Dialogue, Belfast.

Hammond, M. (2008). Cross community youth work training in a divided society. *Youth & Policy, 97&98,* 47–56.

Harland, K. (2007). The legacy of conflict in Northern Ireland: Paramilitarism, violence and youth work in contested spaces. In D. Magnuson & M. Baizerman (Eds.), *Work with youth in divided and contested societies* (pp. 177–190). Rotterdam: Sense Publishers.

Harland, K. & McCready, S. (2014). Rough justice: Considerations on the role of violence, masculinity, and the alienation of young men in communities and peacebuilding processes in Northern Ireland. *Youth Justice, 14*(3), 269–283.

Harland, K. & McCready, S. (2015). *Boys, young men and violence: Masculinities, education and practice.* Basingstoke: Palgrave.

Harland, K. & Morgan, S. (2003). Youth work with young men in Northern Ireland: An 'advocacy approach'. *Youth & Policy, 81,* 74–85.

Harland, K. & Morgan, T. (2006). Youth work in Northern Ireland: An exploration of emerging themes and challenges. *Youth Studies Ireland, 1*(1), 4–18.

Harland, K., Morgan, T. & Muldoon, O. (2005). *The nature of youth work in Northern Ireland: Purpose, contribution and challenges.* Belfast: Department of Education.

JEDI (2002). *A framework for reflections on practice: Guidelines for embedding EDI principles in youth work practice.* Joined in Equity Diversity and Interdependence, Youth Council for Northern Ireland.

Knox, C. (2008). Policy Making in Northern Ireland: Ignoring the Evidence. *Policy and Politics, 36*(3), 343–345.

Lederach, J.P. (2002). *Building peaceful societies.* Washington: Institute of Peace Press.

Lederach, J.P. (2003). *Conflict transformation.* Intercourse, PA: Good Books.

Lederach, J.P. (2008). *Building peace: Sustainable reconciliation in divided societies* (8th edn). Washington, DC: US Institute of Peace Press.

Ledwith, M. (2011). *Community development: A critical approach.* Bristol: Policy Press.

Leonard, M. (2006). Teens and territory in contested spaces: Negotiating sectarian interfaces in Northern Ireland. *Children's Geographies, 4*(2), 225–238.

Leonard, M., McKnight, M. & Spyrou, S. (2011). Child soldiers: Our representation challenged by their reality. *International Journal of Sociology and Social Policy, 31*(9/10), 583–593.

Magnuson, D. (2007). The perils, promise and practice of youth work in conflict societies. In D. Magnuson & M. Baizerman (Eds.), *Work with youth in divided and contested societies* (pp. 3–10). Rotterdam: Sense Publishers.

Magnuson, D. (2009). The need for the study of everyday life about youth work practice in divided societies. *Youth & Policy, 102,* 21–34.

Magnuson, D. & Baizerman, M. (Eds.), *Work with youth in divided and contested societies.* Rotterdam: Sense Publishers.

McCormick, J. (1998). An enquiry into the process involved in the formulation of a new youth work curriculum and considerations for its implementation. MSc. thesis, Faculty of Education, University of Ulster.

McCready, S. & Loudon, R. (2015). *Investing in lives: The history of the youth service in*

Northern Ireland 1844–1973. Youth Council for Northern Ireland/ Corporate Document Services Belfast.

McGrellis, S. (2011). *Growing up in Northern Ireland*. London: Joseph Rowntree Foundation.

McMaster, J. (1993). *Young people as the guardians of sectarian tradition*. Youth Link, Belfast.

Morgan, T. (2009). Measuring outcomes in youth work in Northern Ireland. *Youth & Policy*, *103*, 49–64.

Morrow, D., Eyben, K. & Wilson, D. (2003). From the margin to the middle: Taking equity, diversity and interdependence seriously. In O. Hargie & D. Dickson (Eds.), *Researching the troubles: Social science perspectives on the Northern Ireland conflict* (pp. 163–181). Edinburgh, UK: Mainstream Publishing.

Muldoon, O.T. (2004). Children of the troubles: The impact of political violence in Northern Ireland. *Journal of Social Issues*, *60*(3), 453–468.

Muldoon, O.T., Trew, K. & Kilpatrick, R. (2000). The legacy of the troubles on young peoples' psychological and social development and their school life. *Youth & Society*, *32*(1), 6–28.

Neins, U., Cairns, E. & Hewstone, M. (2003). Contact and conflict in Northern Ireland. In O. Hargie & D. Dickson (Eds.), *Researching the troubles: Social science perspectives on the Northern Ireland conflict* (pp. 123–140). Edinburgh, UK: Mainstream Publishing.

Nolan, P. (2014). *Northern Ireland* Peace Monitoring Report (Number Three). Community Relations Council. Retrieved from http://cain.ulst.ac.uk/events/peace/docs/nipmr_2014-03_1-Intro.pdf

Ord, J. (2011). (Ed.), *Critical issues in youth work management*. Abingdon: Routledge.

Pettigrew, T.F. (1997). Generalized intergroup contact effects on prejudice. *Personality and Social Psychology Bulletin*, *23*(2), 173–185.

Sercombe, H. (2004). Youth work: The professionalization dilemma. *Youth Studies Australia*, *23*(4), 20–25.

Shirlow, P. & Coulter, C. (2014). Northern Ireland: 20 years after the ceasefires. *Studies in Conflict and Terrorism*, *37*(9), 713–719.

Smith, M.K. (2002). Social education – the evolution of an idea. The encyclopedia of informal education. Retrieved from http://www.infed.org/biblio/b-soced.htm

Smith, H. (2010). Engaging in conversation. In T. Jeffs & M.K. Smith (Eds.), *Youth work practice* (pp. 31–40). Basingstoke: Palgrave.

Smyth, M. & Hamilton, J. (2003). The human costs of the troubles. In O. Hargie & D. Dickson (Eds.), *Researching the troubles: Social science perspectives on the Northern Ireland conflict* (pp. 15–36). Edinburgh, UK: Mainstream.

Smyth, P. (2001). Working with children and young people in violently divided societies: Papers from South Africa and Northern Ireland. In M. Smyth & K. Thompson (Eds.), *Community conflict impact on children* (pp. 215–230). Belfast: Incore.

Smyth, P. (2007). The stumbling progress of community relations youth work in Northern Ireland: 1968–2005. In D. Magnuson & M. Baizerman (Eds.), *Work with youth in divided and contested societies* (pp. 46–60). Rotterdam: Sense Publishers.

Spence, J., Devanney, C. & Noonan, K. (2006). *Youth work: Voices of practice*. Leicester: The National Youth Agency.

Stein, J. & Baizerman, M. (2007). Being addressed and obsessed by questions: Calls and cries from the meetings of youth work in contested spaces. In D. Magnuson and M. Baizerman (Eds.), *Work with youth in divided and contested societies* (pp. 325–335). Rotterdam: Sense Publishers.

Topping, J. & Byrne, J. (2012). Paramilitary punishments in Belfast: Policing beneath the peace. *Behavioral Sciences of Terrorism and Political Aggression*, *4*(1), 41–59.

VeLure Roholt, R. & Baizerman, M. (2013). *Civic youth work*. New York: Peter Lang Publications.

VeLure Roholt, R. & Culter, J. (2012). Youth work as engagement. In D. Fusco (Ed.), *Advancing youth work: Current trends, critical questions* (pp. 173–180). New York: Routledge.

Walker, J. & Walker, K. (2012). Establishing expertise in an emerging field. In D. Fusco (Ed.). *Advancing youth work: Current trends, critical questions* (pp. 39–51). New York: Routledge.

Wilson, D. (2015). Envisioning our young people as citizens of a shared society: The current and future task of the Youth Service in Northern Ireland. Celebrating 40 Years of Community Youth Work at Ulster. Keynote Address, Ulster University.

Wright, F. (1994). *Two lands on one soil*. Dublin and London: Gill and Macmillan.

YCNI (1992). *Community relations guidelines: Youth work curriculum*. Youth Council for Northern Ireland.

Young, K. (2006). *The art of youth work* (2nd edn). Lyme Regis: Russell House Publications.

37

Popular Education and Youth Work: Learnings from Ghana

Marion Thomson and Kodzo Chapman

INTRODUCTION

Our passion lies in creating critical spaces where youth uncover the hidden injuries of oppression related to class, race, gender and sexual preference, while questioning the cruelty of extreme poverty and wealth. We feel this as a pedagogical solidarity rooted in the foundations of popular education. This chapter highlights the dynamism of popular education as a guiding principle of critical youth work. We draw on our experiences designing and leading a youth and human rights education program with a youth organization in Ghana. Approximately 150 youth received intensive training in popular education and human rights, while many more community members – children, youth and older adults – were impacted by 80 community theater events throughout five regions of Ghana. Later in this chapter we draw on the ideas and reflections of youth members to strengthen and highlight the culmination of critical theory and a popular education

approach. Our chapter begins with an exploration of popular education theory, including the role of the educator/youth worker, the learner's relationship to knowledge and the ethical basis of popular education where knowledge (knowing) connects to ontology (becoming). Following this we investigate the key tenets of popular education that strengthen and push youth work to new boundaries with poor and disenfranchised youth across racial, class and gender boundaries.

POPULAR EDUCATION

What is Popular Education?

Popular education is intentionally political and can never be neutral. At the heart of this educational practice is the creation of learning spaces that aim to foster transformation and fundamental social change by and for the popular class (working class). Apple (2013) believes critical education programs provide avenues for youth to question 'what is' and pry open possibilities which do not accept globalization and neoliberal paradigms as natural facts but see them as human-made systems which impact communities in various detrimental ways. Marginalized youth need these inclusive spaces to dislodge the logic of capital: an education for liberation and not domestication (Friere, 1972). A youth participant from Ghana comments: 'The program provided me an opportunity to be freed from oppression ... it was liberating' (YPEC focus group, March 2016).

Curriculum design uses a variety of participatory methods and cultural forms that provide opportunities to critique social, political, cultural and economic power and the social relations of capitalism, globalization and neoliberalism. Accompanying systemic analysis is used to examine the ways the dominant ideology oppresses the poor in and through their everyday lives – where learners step back and reflect on practice and their own and societies' mechanisms of 'common sense' (Gramsci cited in Hill, 2010).

All people are philosophers in that they hold some conceptions of the world (Allman, 2001). Analyzing class, race and gender provides opportunities for learners to work across boundaries and explore how colonialism has shaped social relations and development to benefit the accumulation of capital and labor relations across the Global South and Global North. By investigating people's history, locally and globally, learners review community resistance and anti-colonial struggles, which made and changed history. They learn that ordinary people, just like them, act on their world to change it – to resist oppression.

Men make their own history, but they do not make it as they please; they do not make it under self-selected circumstances, but under circumstances existing already, given and transmitted from the past. (Marx, 1852, p. 1)

Knowledge and Epistemology

The relationship between power and what constitutes knowledge is a central pedagogical question for popular educators. A crucial concern is creating a democratic space where learners dissect and critique their own history and ideas about social issues. How do they comprehend their present understanding of reality? These opportunities turn learning relationships to knowledge upside down. In learning and organizing spaces where communities 'read their world' (Freire & Macedo, 1987) newly found knowledge and awareness supports the agency of working-class communities. Learners assert their power acting on and through their world while changing ways of being, not only within the learning community but also within life, community and society. Learners begin to see a clearer picture of oppression in everyday life through re-reading current events in local, national and international contexts. Young people develop critical consciousness through a process of conscientization (a term used by Nkrumah (1964) before Freire). An awakening of critical consciousness creates possibilities to never again read the world in the same way. Such an outcome can be unsettling and lead some learners to retrench and resist seeing and acting on the topsy-turvyness of the world (Zinn, 2004). Freire (1972) refers to this resistance as the fear of freedom, while other writers highlight processes of colonization resulting in appropriating the ideas and practices of the oppressor or dominant colonial class (also see Cabral, 1970; Fanon, 1965; Memmi, 1967).

Ontology and Ethics

Popular education acknowledges the holistic view of how consciousness is internalized and related to our own ways of being and acting with one another and with our world. This sets popular education apart from other educational theories. The philosophy or ethical components are crucial to the humanistic effects of the method – as changes in consciousness lead to further change in our own selves and collectively in community with our world. Change is displayed with our actions in and against dehumanizing systems and relations of capitalism. This is referred to as our ontological being. Linked with this idea, Freire's work has a collective foundation in finding freedom with other oppressed people, encapsulated in 'I cannot be unless you are' (Freire, 1972). Freire was concerned about the social conditions that inhibit humanity from becoming more fully human, as not merely being inserted into the world but belonging essentially to it (Freire, 1998). Through a human responsibility to others, we navigate and act in and to our world as a search to fulfill our human-ness as a lifelong vocation. Apple (2013) refers to the act of becoming as a project, for one is never finished but always becoming.

The importance of learning spaces to build community while exploring our experiences of oppression through questioning and trying on different social identities cannot be ignored. The bonds which grow between group members accentuate the depth of feeling and collective being as learners work through their own feelings and desire 'to be' the best human being they can be working through their own unfinished-ness. In essence, learners find glimpses of freedom and create opportunities to experience a deep understanding and social love for one another and the community. Most importantly, in youth work these questions around caring, relationships, belonging, gender and sexual identities are often posited with the question: what is love?

The Role of the Educator/Youth Worker

The role of the popular educator – or in this case, youth worker as popular educator – centers on a critical education and the relationship between ontology and epistemology. Fusco (2016) describes this role as: 'an awakener of critical consciousness, imagination and deep intellectual pursuit' (p. 36), where the youth worker is 'always operating from their own set of beliefs, their own experiences, history, bias and understanding of cultural, social, political awareness, context and skills through a "relational use of self" with youth' (pp. 46–47). An educator's historical memory and ideology also play a key role in interpreting experience, perceptions and the way a radical educator designs, facilitates and engages in relationship with learners (Kane, 2005). The ability of the educator to question and mobilize students in a dynamic dialogue presumes a non-hierarchal relationship between learners and educator. Freire (1972), however, is a proponent of the directive role of the educator, facilitating learners to redeem their own agency and historical subjectivity. Freire suggests courage is required, a courage to generate other acts of freedom. One cannot free another through generosity but through a social love reflected in a commitment to finding freedom and liberation.

POPULAR EDUCATION WITH YOUNG PEOPLE IN GHANA

Our work is premised on the strength and wealth (social capital) that poor communities and youth bring to the table. Popular education nourishes and builds on that social capital as a collective endeavor whilst embedding, integrating and prioritizing youth experience and youth culture as a central tenet of this mix. Daily, poor youth and their families experience a myriad of potential conflicts with state institutions or ideologies which belittle working-class experience and sanction the reproduction of unequal social relations of class, race, gender, sexuality and ability. Such areas of contestation and surveillance include engagement with public/state officials and/or social workers and/or police and/or the justice system and schools. For young people, schools are major sites of alienation and resistance as working-class and racialized, gendered and indigenous realities, knowledge, expertise, bodies and histories are not respected or recognized by, or integrated into, educational resources and practice. Dei (2004) discusses the legacy of colonial schooling in Ghana whereby indigenous knowledge of subordinated groups was delegitimized against inclusion. He proposes an anti-colonial framework to theorize issues:

> It interrogates the configuration of power embedded in ideas, cultures and histories of knowledge production and use (Fanon 1963, Foucault 1980, and Memmi 1967). It also recognizes the importance of locally produced knowledges emanating from cultural history and daily human experiences and social interactions. Certainly the creation of knowledge begins 'where people are at'. (p. 15)

Generally, schools do not relate to or acknowledge the culture, local languages, learning preferences or diversity of the student populations, but instead tend to reflect the dominant relations of the colonizer: white, middle- and upper-class Western heterosexual men. Like all educational orthodoxies, this process of epistemological filtering of what is worth knowing and learning is, as Jane Thompson (1997) remarks, almost invariably a 'highly particular (dead, white, male, middle class and European) selection of knowledge and culture confirmed as truth' (cited in Martin, 1999, p. 6).

With popular education, youth become creators of cultural form, shifting their passive location as consumers of a dominant heteronormative colonized culture to makers of alternative equitable cultural forms. In and through these processes multiple leadership opportunities arise through the engagement of youth as collective investigators, re-creators and re-presenters of alternative more equitable cultural forms. These opportunities are immersed in a democratic culture of learning which models, interrogates

and supports a critical leadership that shares power, as opposed to a dominant way of withholding and dominating leadership as autocratic power. Youth experience and embrace democratic power-sharing within the learning environment that spills over to civic, social and political spheres. Next we discuss why this type of youth work as popular education is critical in Ghana and other colonized locations globally.

A Colonial Legacy

Colonialism in Ghana involved British rule, with earlier shorter periods of Portuguese and German colonial infiltration. Colonial exploitation was founded on the violent trade in black bodies through the transatlantic slave trade. Ghana, then the Gold Coast, had several key coastal ports involved in the transportation of slaves from the surrounding West African region. At the beginning of the 19th century, slavery was abolished in Britain and the Ghanaian economy began to center on the extraction of the rich natural resources of cocoa, gold and timber. Infrastructure developed according to these resource industries and not the needs of Ghanaians. Railway lines, the main ports, and roads all served the needs of the colonial administration acting on behalf of colonial powers and British merchants. Towns and rural areas did not have the ability to expand their own productive capacity or base.

These 'developments' also brought changes in land ownership as the colonial powers created treaties with local chiefs (but not always to Ghanaians' benefit). People's access to and ownership of land influenced a family's ability to provide for their children and livelihood. As rural towns and villages lost able-bodied men, women, elders and children were left to tend small agricultural holdings to meet basic subsistence needs. Colonial activities such as mining, logging and cash-crop farming speeded up the decay of 'traditional' African life.

Land use changed the African tradition of a diversified agriculture system. Monoculture farming was a colonialist invention whereby cash crops were grown instead of a diversity of staple foods. These practices contributed to periods of food scarcity and problems of desertification. Laborers had no choice but to leave the rural areas and find work in the new centers of business. These key towns and cities were based around the production, extraction and transport of three resource industries. Large numbers of Ghanaians experienced unstable lives in unskilled and irregular employment. During the colonial era there was no sustained development agenda.

An important effect of colonialism was that schools promoted capitalist individualism, which champions and protects the rights of the individual property owners against the collective rights of the people, or ethnic group. Thus, the Ghanaian practice of collective labor and egalitarian social distribution of land, property and resources gave way to wage labor and the individual landowner and entrepreneur. Pre-colonial education centered on the needs of the social, economic, cultural and spiritual life of Ghanaian communities. It was also centered on the collective nature of life and the progressive development of the life cycle, considering the physical, emotional and mental development of the Ghanaian child. There was no distinct separation of education and productive activity, or manual and intellectual educational activity. Elders were crucial teachers of indigenous wisdom, passing on traditions, culture and history through oral storytelling practices. These intergenerational exchanges instilled a strong sense of identity and agency among the young.

During colonialism, schooling had attempted to take on this teaching role of the young. Missionaries engaged in schooling as a means to Christianize Ghanaians. This was especially prevalent in the coastal towns. It was not uncommon for the church to act as an agent of colonial repression by preaching what was culturally correct. The school

curriculum was developed in the metropole countries, resulting in Ghanaian children learning about English literature, colonial wars, the royal family and the geography of Britain, subjects alien to a Ghanaian child. The curriculum did not focus on or celebrate the rich history of literature, arts and the sciences within Ghana and Africa. The colonial curriculum was to promote European society as a superior canon of knowledge and culture, whereby Ghanaian elites would align themselves with the colonizer. These were acts of cultural imperialism and racism.

Problems of access to primary schooling throughout Ghana contributed to inequality, particularly in the North. The colonial administration deliberately kept the Northern–Southern divide owing to the need to exploit the laborforce and the ongoing discrimination against the Muslim religion in Northern Ghana. Only in 1957, after independence, did Kwame Nkrumah remedy this situation through the introduction of compulsory and free education in the Northern region.

Ghana Today

Continuous imperial and globalization trade policies continue to foster underdevelopment, neo-colonialism and globalization. There remain scarce employment opportunities for young people and a constant struggle for parents to provide basic needs for their children and families. The lack of public sector investment is a result of the repayment of outstanding government debt owed to the Western, ex-colonial powers. The strict conditions of loan and trade agreements determine what and how much social and public services are to be freed to market forces. The community pays for health, water and education services through private services and user fees. Undue hardship faced by families and communities leads to the economic migration of youth and 70 per cent of workers struggling in the Ghanaian informal economy.

Schooling opportunities have increased but the challenges of paying teachers, managing scarce school resources, foreign donors acting as education experts in Ghana and the continuation of a colonizing curriculum still remain. Access to education amidst a lack of educational and social infrastructure and the lack of good jobs at the end of schooling pose additional problems for youth.

The existence of a white expatriate class of professionals in the Ghanaian mining and construction industries continue an African brain drain amid new forms of colonization. In contrast, we witness the phenomenon of young Africans making dangerous journeys across the Sahara and the Mediterranean Sea to find work and prosperity in Europe.

The Youth and Human Rights Project (YHRP) with Young Peoples Experience for Change (YPEC)

The Youth and Human Rights Project (YHRP) was a popular education space that nourished the formation of YPEC during an intensive human rights education program. In the beginning, youth aged 14–20 were intentionally drawn from five poor, strong and resilient neighborhoods of Accra. We sought youth who demonstrated skills of resilience in their communities but were not involved in youth organizations. Elder community members suggested youth who they thought might benefit from this program – youth displaying lesser or greater challenges to existing power relations in schools or communities. After Year 2, YPEC was formed and Accra youth co-led training with similar youth groups in the Upper West and Volta Regions of Ghana.

The following excerpt describes the founding principles of YPEC:

The goal of YPEC is to create a culture of human rights whereby human rights principles are popularized and embodied in youth culture. Using popular education methods and popular theatre, which focus on the 'lived' experience of the

participants, the objective is to create an enabling environment whereby young people and students:

- Become sensitized on human rights issues based on the Ghanaian Constitution
- Examine and simplify human rights terminology, linking it to their real lived everyday reality
- Explore and analyze their own ideas and behaviors and work towards the ideal of a human rights culture based on principles of respect, tolerance, equity, diversity, gender equality, etc.
- Are exposed to popular education as an effective teaching and learning tool in Ghana
- Reclaim popular theatre as an important aspect of Ghanaian culture, tackling social and human rights issues in an entertaining and educative manner
- Through a focus on the constitution, build civic culture awareness and lay the groundwork for democracy and good governance
- Expand their world view from the local to the national and the global. (YPEC Outreach pamphlet, Accra 2001)

Historical analysis was a key tenet of the Young Peoples Experience for Change (YPEC) project in Ghana. Oral history activities provided opportunities to compare youth experience of the present with elder women's recollections from the past. Young people interviewed women in one of Accra's poorest neighborhoods while seeking additional literary and historical resources to further study the social context and intersectionality of gender, family, work, education, traditional culture and youth experience. They discovered many similarities and differences, from slavery (pre-colonial) to colonial, independence and post-independence eras. Young people realized the 'development agenda' has never been favorable to their communities but reinforces existing inequalities within neoliberal and post-colonial power structures according to class, race and gender. Dei also questions the development agenda in Ghana:

The international financial community's domination of the development discourse ensures that African governments gear their domestic economic and social policies to suit the prescriptions of the West and those of international finance capital. (2004, p. 24)

Opportunities were created for the young people to create a comic book of their findings and represent the data back to community elders. These activities reflected the ability of youth to research social problems, design questions and conduct research through interviews. The power of also sharing data across generations empowered the interviewees (poor racialized women) through validating and documenting their lives, history and experience while building local youth leadership and expertise within the community.

A series of intensive human rights and civic education workshops created educational and performative spaces to study and analyze the 'historic and current damage of colonialism' (Heathfield & Fusco, 2016, p. 298). Youth dissected their everyday realities in contradiction with the values of human rights espoused in the newly formatted Ghanaian Constitution. Through inquiry-based learning opportunities, they began to see the contradictions in Western-based constructions of human rights, which were in direct opposition to the policies and strategies of neoliberalism and globalization. The program's ability to create an environment for youth to openly question, work through and apply a rights and social justice framework to their own embodied realities was very powerful. Program leaders as popular educators did not judge the young peoples' opinions but allowed their independent thoughts to evolve through serious questioning and interrogation, and by soliciting deep thought and discussion. As Darder eloquently describes:

> Literacy education in the interest of freedom can never make marginal what adult learners already understand about their world. On the contrary, this must serve as the site of departure, in this intense critical journey toward not only learning to communicat[e] graphically, but becoming more deeply conscious of life conditions that stifle freedom and the right to be. (2016, p. 2)

Young people found their voice through these opportunities and asserted their power as human rights advocates. YPEC youth commented:

> You are given freedom to say what's on your mind, certain things you have never said before and you could not say in the house. You did not need to worry about disappointing anyone with your ideas/ views. I could talk and talk in the program. The atmosphere was there to talk, to share what I know. I learnt for change. I had to share, to hear what other people have to say. (YPEC evaluation, December 2007)

CREATIVE METHODS OF POPULAR EDUCATION

A critical factor to ensure the sustainability of an indigenous youth leadership in Ghana was to pry open the increasing globalization and colonization of youth culture. As Jane Thompson reminds us, knowledge, art and culture are all social constructs:

> They can be used to free people or constrain them, to empower them or weaken them, to include or exclude them. They can act to reinforce the status quo and conform people to the logic of the present system. Or they can be a powerful tonic for the imagination and a necessary resource for progressive social change. (2002, p. 3)

Through an arts-based popular education approach the YHRP became a powerful vehicle for youth to 'read the word and the world' (Freire & Macedo, 1987). It also cultivated an environment to build community and new social relations against capitalism (Allman, 2001). During the 1980s, the Ghanaian economy became a poster child for neoliberalist and 'structural adjustment' policies – widespread privatization and retrenchment of the public sector and the devaluation of the Ghanaian Cedi currency (Clark, 2012). Young people turned to the informal and illegal economy for a livelihood, especially in urban neighborhoods such as Accra and Kumasi. They also tuned to the lyrics of many hip-life artists who were using their music as social commentary to talk about these problems (Clark, 2012). Hip-life emerged as an indigenous fusing of Ghanaian traditions of spoken word, proverbs and African high-life, which contains African, and global soul rhythms. In comparison, Dei researched schooling and education in Ghana and concluded teachers and students reflected local views of spirituality and spiritual consciousness not necessarily attached to a religious institution but rather to the spirit and sense of community and the values of its people (2004, p. 186). The YHRP built on this spiritual link to community, place, ancestry and cultural work, which opposed the logic of globalization, capital and oppressive relations.

Youth workers provided space for young people to articulate and speak openly about their own needs as a new approach to youth work as few avenues existed for youth, especially poor youth, to co-lead a program with adults. Popular educators sought collaboration with youth to design program material and identify ways to increase access across all areas of program development, leadership and administration.

Cartoon training manuals depicted violations of human rights in young people's lives contrasted with the newly founded human rights provisions of the Ghanaian Constitution. Through a series of intensive workshops young people investigated each manual scenario through arts-based exercises. Such an example would be the right to safe and healthy working conditions for domestic servants (mostly young teenage girls). Young people discussed the inhumane treatment of servants – working excessive hours, receiving inadequate food and possibly experiencing physical, emotional, psychological and sexual abuse. The group also 'played out' domestic servant scenarios from popular Ghanaian films re-framing each scene by inserting the young women's voice. The young woman talks with neighborhood peers devising strategies to leave the household, access education and find better work opportunities advocating for her rights. Using pertinent clauses of the Ghanaian Constitution, NGOs and government agencies brought the abusive adults to justice within the scenario. Further analysis focused on gender discrimination, patriarchy, family relations and the negligence in schooling girl children.

The topic of gender discrimination also led to young people's interest in culture, history and the practice of widowhood rights. Traditional marriage practices can lead to discrimination after a husband's death. The widow can suffer loss of property rights, housing or inheritance. The young people created a powerful performance piece on widowhood rights using traditional Ghanaian songs to emote the pain of inhumane treatment and the discrimination shown to an estranged widow. During community performances the audience and the YPEC actress felt the widow's pain and anguish, weeping tears of sorrow. Meanwhile another YPEC youth was so moved by gender discrimination that he created a poem 'Is it a human being or a girl?' Young people created a series of dramatic poses to accompany a reading of each verse during community events and it became a YPEC favorite.

The group specifically identified the need to create workshops which examined ways in which globalization is undermining indigenous cultures in the south, particularly in terms of youth culture and identity. Western-style music videos and lyrics centered on consumerism, materialism and acquiring 'things' to measure success while young people and their families were finding it harder and harder to support even their basic needs. These cultural forms also promoted highly sexualized, homophobic, racist, misogynist and violent depictions of gender. Young people researched various music videos from Ghanaian hip-life, gospel and reggae artists and Western hip hop and soul artists. They explored the lyrics and also the video images. What gender roles were depicted? What else was being conveyed regarding class, race, Ghana and Africa?

Together, the group 'played out' these identities and collectively discussed relations of power and the saturation of a multinational corporate music, news, media and advertising industry. Another YPEC module explored various news channels, questioning how news is edited and presented and asking 'what stories are we not hearing?' They also looked at print media, comparing coverage of events and types of news stories published. CNN news stories provided interesting opportunities for youth to role play important national and international debates as Western journalists, World Bank officials, Ghanaian government, NGOs, union leaders and community members. This highlighted the many ways news is created, edited, interpreted and packaged from a particular lens and colonized worldview which undermines Africa.

Creators of Culture through Popular Theatre

YPEC drew on the past tradition of social development theater, 'Concert Party'. During the pre-independence to post-independence era of the 1960s this form of popular theatre experienced its highest profile during the presidency of Kwame Nkrumah (Barber, Collins & Ricard, 1997; Cole, 2001). Concert Party was resurrected to a mass audience through the advent of television. Well-known Ghanaian 'players' enacted live televised drama performances from the National Theater in Accra every weekend.

YPEC youth became excited about using the genre, craft and tradition of Ghanaian popular theatre to explore their own experiences of human rights infractions. They tackled difficult conversations as witnesses and victims of family violence, relationship violence, teacher violence and police violence. Drama became a useful medium to examine

how inhumane practices, relations of violence and oppression are woven into the fabric of our bodies. The roots of violence and relations of power in society and interpersonal relationships were connected and interwoven with colonization, religion, gender and class inequality.

Popular educators built on young people's requests to add an advocacy component to the program. This enabled youth human rights leadership to spread awareness in communities and schools across Accra. There emerged two drama streams: within the education program through human rights workshops which examined experiences of oppression and the human rights provisions of the Ghanaian Constitution, and an advocacy component using popular theatre to create human rights awareness in community venues.

Community drama events also provided a platform to solicit information about further abuses from community members. One such instance was in Northern Ghana during a series of YPEC drama events on gender discrimination and domestic violence. Some community members and community organizations attended the event and became engulfed in a deep discussion about domestic violence within several families residing in the village. The next day the village chief organized a community meeting to support women experiencing violence in the local vicinity. The Commission for Human Rights and Administrative Justice also worked with the local assembly, women and the chief to bring the perpetrators to justice. Young people became the documenters of human rights abuses and the catalysts to ignite agency among the community members.

YPEC formed a concert party drama troupe to provoke community discussions on social issues the society wanted to silence. These were difficult and uncomfortable conversations made easier by young people who acted as leaders, enablers and promoters of a human rights culture, which fostered democracy 'by doing it' (Schugurensky, 2002). Real living democratic spaces were sparked through the group's interpretations of how to use the genre of popular theatre, accompanied by their own history of popular and indigenous culture. As this form does not depend on text or a written script, engagement in the design and performance itself was wide open to all members of the group (see Wright, 2004). The accessibility of popular theatre and use of local languages meant the chasm that usually appears between communities and the theatre performers on stage was eliminated. Audience and players interact. The audience does not consume culture but participates in its living creation. George Dei concludes that language carries cultural values and collective identities as well as social and ancestral histories; language is also connected to the natural world spiritually, physically, emotionally and intellectually (2004, p. 205). The YHRP built on these connections through the use of arts, local languages and collective meaning making. After each performance, the YPEC players led small discussion groups on topics raised in the drama scenarios. YPEC youth became the catalysts and filters, further theorizing the social issues and reinventing drama scenarios for future community events (Thomson, 2011). They treated knowledge as an object, subjected to collective critical scrutiny, to be considered, rejected or transformed (Allman, 2001, p. 173).

The latter highlights that popular education and community arts approaches were not transposed from the Global North, but are a dynamic process drawing on and forged in the specific cultural context of Ghanaian indigenous forms (Mayo, 2004; Steele, 1999). YPEC pursued their craft as messengers of cultural production to interrupt common sense as formulated by Gramsci (1971). Youth agency was built throughout the process – trying on different identities:

> The method made us think and analyze what's around us, for example the drama on widowhood rights – by seeing it, you feel it and by being it, acting it, it frees the imagination, you can think of anything. It shows things can be learnt and

unlearnt. It makes you produce action and express your own lives and other community people's lives. You gain a new identity. You are not the same in the community. You are recreating yourself. (YPEC evaluation, January, 2008)

Allman talks about the need to develop transformative education projects that foster modes of democracy and entice a collective will.

> This type of truly felt will or commitment to alternative values can never be built by social engineering, but transformed social relations created within transformative projects at whatever level or of whatever scope can support such change. (1999, p. 133)

Through these group interactions the young people built their analytical and social skills while developing democracy and a collective solidarity. Galloway (1999) describes this process:

> It is also about broader social, educational and cultural relationships with other students in the group. Working with others in dialogue demands these new ways of being and new forms of behaviour. These must be learned. Skills like active listening, paraphrasing, critical thinking and personal expression are essential for building new ways of relating to others. The combination of transparent teaching methodology and dialogical relationship building is the key to democratizing the culture of the classroom and turning it into a setting where real transformations can occur ... where creative responses to the challenges of the world outside may be imagined and tested. (pp. 235–236)

PRAXIS, ONTOLOGY AND ACTION: A LABORATORY OF LEARNING

Through historical analyses, and youth cultural activities like hip-life and popular theatre, the YPEC program placed radical ontology at the center of programming – the very concept of human beings as a collective entity. According to Allman and Wallis (2005):

> A radical ontology is both critical and hopeful because it requires us to analyse being with a criteria derived from a concretely based vision of

becoming. Concretely based visions are not uto-pian. They are derived from evidence of what some people, through struggle, manage to achieve even in oppressive circumstances. (p. 20)

The program's network of peer support, youth leadership and confidence found on and through the program were crucial for youth asserting their own agency and con-tinuing with educational pursuits. As Dei reminds us, only a quarter of school-age children have access to basic education and few graduates enter employment after they leave school (2004, p. 6). It is therefore a great testament to the YHRP that many young people graduated from secondary school and pursued post-secondary educa-tion, college diplomas, HNCs, and under-graduate and Masters degrees. As community leaders throughout Accra and Ghana, YPEC lead programs in youth centers and commu-nity organizations in the areas of human rights, popular theatre, youth leadership, gender equality, gender violence, children's rights, HIV/AIDS, social enterprise, gay rights and economic justice. In the workplace YPEC are encouraging democratic and criti-cal modes of leadership and management – as trade union activists asserting the rights of workers and as managers building collabora-tive practice with workers. YPEC particpant analyzes power relations in his present career as a popular educator and youth worker:

Personally, I had challenges with the power rela-tions of the top executive level of organisations that I worked for or partnered. ... I never felt comfortable with their methodology or way of working with young people. You're forced to be a part [of] something that you don't like ... I like to work at a low-key level rather than as a boss. I'm aware of the power relations and how it could impede someone's growth and learned how to equalize it to help young people ... it's about respecting the rights of the people. (YPEC focus group, March 2016)

In their own relationships with spouses, friends, family, workplace colleagues and community members gender equality is pro-moted. A participant from YPEC asserts how

community work has forced her to use a power analysis:

There's a woman in my house who I support to stand up for her rights. I have told her man that it is not right what he does to the woman. I have also told the women in my neighborhood that they should go to the police to report when they are abused by their partners. In my workplace too they say I talk too much ... because I am very vocal and outspoken. I don't allow them to infringe on my rights. (YPEC focus group, March 2016)

YPEC women have asserted their own agency negotiating equal and respectful rela-tionships whilst assisting other young women to walk away from abuse and violence.

The training has really impacted on me. For me it's about finding my voice so now I'm able to speak out for myself especially in my marriage ... we dialogue (my husband and I) and come to a conclusion. My husband knows who I am and so he helps me manage the house ... we share the house chores. The social identity analysis of power relations on the YHRP helped me decide on improving myself through education. This, in order not to look up to my husband but to have my independence. I educated myself to a Masters Degree level in order to maintain my independ-ence. When I made this decision, I was already battling with power relations in my relationship with my husband. (YPEC focus group, March 2016)

This demonstrates the relationship between ontology and epistemology and how YPEC internalized and embodied the methodology of popular education and living human rights – to be the best human being one can be. It also demonstrated a new type of collec-tive and critical youth leadership, forged in solidarity within a context of real democracy through/in the practice ground and contact zones of popular education.

CONCLUSION

Today, there exists an even more pressing need for popular education in Ghana as few organizations use popular education or a critical approach in youth work. The general negation of critical education, youth and community work in Ghana (and globally) is paralyzing the sector owing to new managerial approaches, which infect the NGO and development sector. An obsession with measurement, indicators and outcomes can divert funders from programs that highlight participatory processes, youth-centered approaches, community outreach, leadership development and collective social change.

Yet, we know, as demonstrated throughout this chapter, that popular education is a training ground for democracy. Working-class youth need this most – to shape a better future as responsive civic leaders collaborating with allies across boundaries of race, class, gender, age and place in the precarious world of extreme wealth and extreme poverty exacerbated by systems of neoliberalism and globalization in the Global South and Global North. The methodology is a dynamic tool to bridge a guided exchange of ideas between young people in the Global South and their counterparts in the Global North by opening up safe and democratic spaces for researching existing commonalities and similarities.

We will end with an inspiring quote by Antonia Darder:

Such a liberatory pedagogical process, guides students to work together, in order to recapture the power of epistemological curiosity nurtured by reflection, the social imagination rooted in dialogue, the conviction anchored in their own voices, the social agency to act upon their lives, and the pedagogical solidarity and grace necessary for the transformation of their communities and the world. (2016, p. 4)

ACKNOWLEDGEMENT

The authors would like to acknowledge that the chapter would not be possible without the work of YPEC.

REFERENCES

Allman, P. (1999). *Critical education against capitalism*. Westport, CT: Bergin & Harvey.

Allman, P. (2001). *Revolutionary social transformation: Democratic hopes, political possibilities and critical education*. Westport, CT: Bergin and Harvey.

Allman, P. & Wallis, J. (2005). Challenging the postmodern condition. In M. Mayo & J. Thompson (Eds.), *Adult learning, critical learning and social change* (pp. 18–33). Leicester, England: NIACE.

Apple, M. (2013). *Can education change society?* New York, NY: Routledge.

Barber, S., Collins, J. & Ricard, A. (1997). *West African popular theatre*. Bloomington, IN: Indiana University Press.

Cabral, A. (1970). *National liberation and culture* (M. Webster, Trans). Syracuse, NY: Syracuse University.

Clark, M.K. (2012). Hip hop as social commentary in Accra and Dar es Salaam. *African Studies Quarterly, 13*(3), 23–46.

Cole, C. (2001). *Ghana's concert party theatre*. Bloomington, IN: Arizona University Press.

Darder, A. (2016). Paulo Freire and the politics of literacy: The struggle for a revolutionary praxis of adult education. Abstract for SHREA Conference, University of Maynooth, Ireland. Retrieved from https://www.maynoothuniversity.ie/node/393719

Dei, G.J. Sefa (2004). *Schooling & education in Africa: The case of Ghana*. Trenton, NJ: Africa World Press.

Fanon, F. (1963). *The wretched of the earth*. New York: Grove Weidenfeld.

Fanon, F. (1965). *The wretched of the earth* (C. Farrington, Trans.). London: MacGibbon & Kee.

Foucault, M. (1980). *Power/knowledge: selected interviews and other writings, 1972–1977*. New York: Pantheon Books.

Freire, P. (1972). *Pedagogy of the oppressed*. Harmondsworth, England: Penguin.

Freire, P. (1998). *Pedagogy of freedom, ethics, democracy, and civic courage*. Lanham, MD: Rowman & Littlefield.

Freire, P. & Macedo, D. (1987). *Literacy: Reading the word and the world*. London: Routledge Taylor and Francis Group

Fusco, D. (2016). History of youth work: Transitions, illuminations and refractions. In M. Heathfield & D. Fusco (Eds.), *Youth and inequality in education: Global actions in youth work* (pp. 36–52). New York, NY: Routledge.

Galloway, V. (1999). Building a pedagogy of hope: The experience of the adult learning project. In J. Crowther, I. Martin & M. Shaw (Eds.), *Popular education and social movements in Scotland today* (pp. 226–239). London: NIACE.

Giroux, H.A. (2005). *Border crossings: Cultural workers and the politics of education.* London: Routledge & Kegan Paul.

Giroux, H.A. (2012). *Disposable youth, racialized memories and the culture of cruelty.* New York, NY: Routledge.

Gramsci, A. (1971). (Edited and translated by Q. Hoare and G. Nowell-Smith). *Selections from the prison notebooks.* London: Lawrence & Wishart.

Heathfield, M. (2016). Youth and inequality: Weaving complexities, commonalities and courage. In M. Heathfield & D. Fusco (Eds.), *Youth and inequality in education: Global actions in youth work* (pp. 3–18). New York, NY: Routledge.

Heathfield, M. & Fusco, D. (2016). From hope to wise action: The future of youth work and other global actions in education. In M. Heathfield & D. Fusco (Eds.), *Youth and inequality in education: Global actions in youth work* (pp. 295–308). New York, NY: Routledge.

Hill, D.J. (2010). A brief commentary on the Hegelian-Marxist origins of Gramsci's philosophy of praxis. In P. Mayo (Ed.), *Gramsci and educational thought* (pp. 5–20). Chichester, England: Wiley-Blackwell.

Kane, L. (2005). Ideology matters. In J. Crowther, V. Galloway & I. Martin (Eds.), *Popular education: Engaging the academy: International perspectives* (pp. 32–42). London: NIACE.

Martin, I. (1999). Introductory essay: Popular education and social movements in Scotland today. In J. Crowther, I. Martin & M. Shaw (Eds.), *Popular education and social movements in Scotland today* (pp. 1–28). London: NIACE.

Marx, K. (1852). The Eighteenth Brumaire of Luis Napoleon Bonaparte. Retrieved from https://libcom.org/library/18th-brumaire-louis-napoleon-marx

Mayo, P. (2004). *Liberating praxis: Paulo Freire's legacy for radical education and politics.* West Port, CT: Praeger.

Memmi, A. (1967). *The colonizer and the colonized.* Boston: Beacon Press.

Nkrumah, K. (1964). *Consciencism: Philosophy and ideology for de-colonization and development with particular reference to the African Revolution.* New York: Monthly Review Press.

Schugurensky, D. (2002). Transformative learning and transformative politics: The pedagogical dimension of participatory democracy and social action. In E. O'Sullivan, A. Morrell & M. A. O'Connor (Eds.), *Expanding the boundaries of transformative learning: Essays on theory and praxis* (pp. 59–76). New York: Palgrave.

Steele, T. (1999). With 'real feeling and just sense': Rehistoricising popular education. In J. Crowther, I. Martin & M. Shaw (Eds.), *Popular education and social movements in Scotland today* (pp. 95–105). London: NIACE.

Thompson, J. (1997). *Words in edgeways: Radical learning for social change.* Leicester, England: NIACE.

Thompson, J. (2002). *Bread and roses: Arts, culture and lifelong learning.* Leicester, England: NIACE.

Thomson, M. (2011). Researching class consciousness: The transgression of a radical educator across three continents. Unpublished PhD thesis. OISE, University of Toronto.

Wright, H.K. (2004). *A prescience of African cultural studies: The future of literature in Africa is not what it was.* New York: Peter Lang.

Zinn, H. (2004). *You can't be neutral on a moving train: A personal history of our times.* A film by Deb Ellis and Denis Mueller. Brooklyn, NY: First Run/Icarus Films.

38

Roma Youth and Global Youth Work

Brian Belton

INTRODUCTION

Historically the name attributed to Roma in Romania, 'tsigan' originally meant 'slave'. This understanding (and the 'tsigan' epithet) was, up to the late 19th century, pretty consistent across much of Eastern Europe. Indeed, to this day, Roma groups are often referred to in this way (Belton, 2015a; Nicolae, 2013). As late as the 20th century, and still today in small pockets across Eastern Europe, Roma lived in slave settlements, outside villages, with no access to formal education or social support. Marriage between Roma and non-Roma was in most areas strictly forbidden by law and Roma even had separate graveyards. This was a slave and an apartheid system, wherein to be Roma was to be a 'non-person'. Slavery was not abolished in law in Europe until well into the second part of the 19th century (Dawson, 2001; Hancock, 1987), but persisted as a social practice well after that date. Subsequent to slavery, Roma were turned off the lands

they formally worked and were evicted from their huts and other dwelling places. This meant they were without the means of life and labor, literally bereft. As such, a proportion of Roma were obliged to become itinerant, looking for work and temporary shelter. Many stayed on as a kind of serf labor with their former masters, or simply had no other recourse but to beg for food and shelter, having only their labor to offer in exchange. Thus former slaves remained trapped in a semi-slave state, laboring on the land or gaining positions as the most lowly of household servants. The majority had no access to any type of formal education or alternative means of survival. The social situation and pariah status of Roma (see Hancock, 1987) created fertile ground for the unabashed racism that continued for the best part of the next century, up to today.

The appellation 'Roma' is the political replacement for the generic identity 'Gypsy', which covers a huge number of highly diverse communities with different political needs, aspirations, capabilities and interests, living in a wide variety of economic, political, social and cultural environments. While there are pulls towards a sort of shared political identity (Bunescu, 2014), beyond social generation considerations (Belton, 2005a, 2005b), this fictional community has no shared language. A tiny minority might use one of the numerous Romani dialects, many of which are so unlike any other that they are incomprehensible to speakers of other dialects, often being used as a second or domestic language. There is also a panoply of cultural, religious, historical and ethnic differences between groups who might be called Roma. Many of these groups do not call themselves or others 'Roma' (Bunescu, 2014). The list below is not exhaustive but includes:

- Spanish Calé and Gitanos
- Portuguese Ciganos
- French Manush (a sub-group of Sinti)
- German and Northern Italian Sinti
- Hungarian Lovari (Lovara) and Romungro (Modyar or Modgar)
- Austrian/German/Czech Lalleri
- Serbian Machvaya (Machavaya, Machwaya, or Macwaia)
- Greek/Turkish Xoraxai (Horahane)
- Bashaldé
- Boyash
- Lingurari
- Ludar
- Ludari
- Rudari
- Churari
- Erlides
- Yerlii
- Arli
- Kalderash
- Lăutari
- Luri
- Ungaritza
- Ursari
- Zlătari/Aurari.

The isolation and marginalization of Roma embeds forms of cultural, economic, political and social exclusion. Today, with the rise of political extremism, coupled with economic migration in the wake of austerity conditions, the situation of Roma has become concerning, perhaps more than at any other time since the Second World War (Bíró, Gheorghe, Kovats & Guy, 2013; Pusca 2012a, 2012b). In this chapter I will look at Roma identity and how political responses to this group are so enmeshed in ethnic considerations, which undermine understanding of this group's economic and political position. This constitutes forms of intersectional discrimination and social exclusion, which limit opportunity and create social tension (Filčák, 2012; Grzanka, 2014). I will also argue that young people experience something of the same via an age-related deficit categorization, and suggest that this 'treatment', exacerbated by the intersectional pressures and consequences of a Roma identity, lays the ground for disaffection and extremism. Just as young people are understood to be intrinsically challenging (a group that is seen both as a threat and an object in need of support) young Roma are objectified as inherently problematic (Gatti, Karacsony, Kosuke, Ferré & de Paz Nieves, 2016); they are 'this' because they are 'that' – the young are challenging because they are young/immature/childish/adolescent/not grown up – all these epithets might be regarded as insults if applied to 'non-youth' (adults). This is an inherently deficient perspective that if applied to other groups (say people of color, women, LGBT groups) would quite appropriately meet with mass consternation and in many contexts potential legal consequences. Finally, I will argue that innovative youth work responses provide the means to short-circuit the sometimes resultant cycle of radicalization.

ROMA/YOUTH IDENTITY

In the last part of the 20th century and the first part of the 21st century Roma have migrated to every corner of Europe (and across the world) with the legacy of the above cultural and social history. They arrived as what can be understood to be an outsider/outcast group. However, contemporaneous debates in Europe surrounding immigration, premised on the impact of social policy, austerity economics, the refugee crisis and concomitant concerns related to employment, housing, education and healthcare, have exacerbated fears, anxieties and defensive responses to Roma. The general apprehension has been confirmed, exaggerated, fueled, provoked and encouraged by political and media responses (Belton, 2010b; Majtényi 2016). As such, the position of Roma in Europe today is complex. They are a socially, culturally and ethnically rich/diverse/heterogeneous grouping, often from indistinct but varied origins. This being the case there is no one appropriate, overarching cultural response to Roma. At the same time, the social and economic position of Roma groups varies from state to state, sometimes dependent on the political and/or economic environment, as well as the length of time Roma have resided in a particular locality, region or nation.

Youth are also a diverse group in terms of age; in the UK for example, it can encompass everyone from 13 to 19 years of age; other contexts take this category to be anything from 10 to 40. Of course, youth diversity extends over ethnic, social, religious, sexuality and relative ability considerations having intersectional consequences. Thus, the issues relating to Roma youth identity can be understood to have a broadly dual foundation: one grounded in the political and socioeconomic situation and another grounded in constructs of the youth category.

Given the current situation of Roma in the European context, coupled with a history of oppression, and the understandable attendant cultural defensiveness, which might be expected of any group experiencing continuous and unremitting inequality, these groups place little faith in institutions and organizations they perceive or suspect to be part of the general environment of social subjugation.

This might be dismissed as naiveté or ignorance, stoked by a sort of inverted prejudice, but this would be an incorrect and unsophisticated perspective. Roma have, by necessity, become reliant, first and foremost, on the social nexus of the family. Looking for security beyond the familial framework has proved to be not only unsuccessful and so disenchanting for these groups historically speaking, but also dangerous and thus foolish (Belton, 2015a; Nicolae, 2013).

Likewise, youth can be understood as a group subjected to incessant discrimination and inequality (Belton, 2010a). Variously, they are, among other restrictions, unable in law to independently purchase a huge range of commodities and services, including the buying, selling or renting of property, apply for a passport, vote (so being unrepresented politically), receive benefits in their own right, pay taxes, smoke, drive a car, or gain anything but the most restricted, often illegal and poorly paid work. Youth are legally restricted right across the sexual horizon; even in mid/late teenage they are often regarded as non-sexual beings. They are forbidden from frequenting certain forms or categories of entertainment, buying or consuming alcohol and have rights that are only translatable via adult duties and responsibilities. Added to all this, increasingly across the globe, youth are by law required to attend and be subject to the disciplinary regimes and surveillance of state institutions and their professional gaze for the better part of their teen years. In this controlled environment they are obliged to ingest an educational curriculum they have little or no say in (Clark, 1975). Although 'one way education' is not education at all, it is a form of indoctrination.

In the light of these circumstances it is not surprising that some youth have traditionally rebelled against the values of adult society in terms of cultural and countercultural responses, but also outright (if limited) rebellion, uprising and what is labeled 'mindless violence', when any response other than aggressive insurgence would seem illogically passive. Roma youth justifiably have little or no confidence in social intuitions and like youth generally often look to social networks for security, support and interaction (Bunescu, 2014; McGarry, 2010; Milcher, 2011; Nicolae, 2013; Pusca, 2012b; Raykova, Garcia Lopez, Paddison & Belton, 2016). These resorts are currently under attack from adult society; almost any informal group of young people being quickly labeled 'a gang' and therefore, a threat. At the same time, designated youth facilities are limited or completely eradicated due to economic belt tightening. These are replaced by formalized, not unusually commercialized, local bastions of institutional state control, employability projects, training agencies, targeted youth provision – 'fugitive' youth are literally 'hunted' (see Bright, 2015).

Racism/Ageism and Colonized Psyches

Across Europe, the discourse defining Roma, both historically and presently, which has become central to research connected with Roma, is anti-racism. 'Roma' people and their interests as individuals and as a collective are explained via inequality in terms of culture, race and/or ethnicity (Stewart, 2012). As such, issues related to Roma have become increasingly addressed by relatively low-cost (in comparison to developing social infrastructure, etc.), moralistic (rights-based) 'solutions'. Roma are essentially seen as 'racially challenged' and this is put at the core of their experience of disadvantage. Prejudice and discrimination present authentically serious difficulties for the majority of Roma people, but anti-Roma racism is a multifaceted set of phenomena, altering over time, place and arguably sometimes from person to person. It is also dependent on the position any particular individual or group of Roma find themselves in relative to the wider community or society. The nature of prejudice is manifested in and through a range of social, cultural and economic factors. However, racism has become a functional means to explain disadvantage – unemployment, low life expectancy, slum housing; it has been made a 'route one' rationalization of disadvantage and it is what is targeted to alleviate the same (Gatti et al., 2016). At an institutional and state level, this enables the denial of political responsibility by blaming popular prejudices for failures to act politically and socially.

The circumstances of youth are also polygonal; different contexts, including national, regional, familial, religious and cultural mores prevail over the category. Youth populations are also subject to differing responses according to their intersectional profile; faith, sexuality, gender, ethnicity and so on. However, across these considerations they are defined and confined by 'age enclosure'. The perspective of both Roma and youth essentially reflects the promotion of false consciousness within and towards these groups. The story we are confronted with when thinking of Roma is ethnic discourse, addressable via the promotion of an ethical/moral response ('rights'). Youth too are addressed socially by way of ethical and morality discourse, but this is premised on the duties and responsibilities of adults. Youth have little if any authority or influence over how their position is responded to – it is literally out of their hands (despite Articles 12 and 13 of the UN Convention of the Rights of the Child).

The above undermines and detracts from the possibility of understanding the impacts of capitalist social formation, and conflates and camouflages the social imperative of inequality inherent in state-sponsored capitalism. As such, issues pertaining to, or said to be pertaining to, Roma are made to appear almost purely as an uncomplicated struggle for rights by and for an oppressed ethnic minority, thereby negating a process of reassignment of most Roma to their traditional social position as a reserve of cheap labor, maintained at minimal cost to the state and a continuance of the deficit response to young people and the perpetuation of their inequality and control.

At the same time, while identity as race, ethnicity and culture in terms of Roma are relatively ethereal categorizations (Belton, 2005a, 2005b), their disadvantage (in a direct experiential sense) is mechanistic – it is a consequence of the interplay between their economic and social position (along with many other groups) which is instrumentally related to the nature of the social formation over and above relative identity (Milcher, 2011). While racism and bigotry are present, they are at least as much a product of the Roma disadvantage as they are the cause of it. Added to the social malevolence by-product of capitalism, youth are also a categorical consequence of the social formation; their circumstances are often exacerbated by intersectional considerations; they are 'this' but also 'that'. However, as many Roma often seem to 'ethically disappear' into host communities after achieving a level of social economic parity, one is left to conclude that for Roma, race is at best a secondary causation in terms of their collective experience of disadvantage. Youth too vanish as they reach adulthood; they achieve equivalence with age that allows entry into society. This demonstrates that age as such was never the cause of their relative inequality; it was always access to social and economic resources.

Roma access to resources and a voice are increasingly channeled via this narrative, giving rise to what I have elsewhere called (following on from Hall, 1991) 'weak power' – the means to influence is accessed by defining oneself as the oppressed pariah, which in the process confirms notions of the 'born victim', the necessarily oppressed (Belton, 2005a). At once one adopts the psychological disposition: *The most potent weapon of the oppressor is the mind of the oppressed* (Biko & Stubbs, 1979, p. 69). As soon as one accepts one's oppression one is truly oppressed – which, echoing Fanon (1965, 1967a, 1967b), might be understood as the 'colonial mentality'.

Effectively youth are bound to 'weak power' discourses, subject as they are to adult regimes that are close in psychological character to colonial contexts (see Belton, 2010a). This being the case, we can understand that social and economic mechanisms and circumstances, reinterpreted and understood as almost exclusively arising as cultural, racial or ethnic difference, give rise to both internal and external pressures on Roma individuals and groups. For youth, apart from intersectional considerations, relative age is the camouflage. The consequences are the same for continued discrimination, social exclusion, limited opportunities and social tension. In terms of youth, they remain an essentially colonized group.

THE DISENFRANCHISEMENT OF ROMA/YOUTH

Young people are curtailed politically within the limits of Roma and youth identity. Roma politics is restricted to them identifying themselves as Roma and others as not being Roma. What is produced among Roma youth is a cycle of reaction. The claim that Roma constitute a single and distinct community requiring its own separate representation has been expressed by the International Romani Union's (IRU) Declaration of a Nation. This is antithetical to the objective of equality, and as such it is probably not surprising that in more than thirty years, the IRU has failed to generate grassroots support among Roma. However, the IRU has functioned as the forum for a few dozen international activists (Roma and non-Roma) sustained by the patronage of established political interests. Operationally, it is but a voice for segregation and forms of separate development (apartheid). Youth councils and parliaments are something of an echo of this (Wall, 2012); representing no one, with no actual power.

Kovats (2003) argues that Roma as a category represents the racial myth of the Gypsy.

The application of 'Gypsy' identity has traditionally been used to marginalize the status of these communities. For him Roma, being pushed to the degree of separation as a distinct nation, '... accords with this tradition by legitimating the ideology of segregation and suppressing democratic political development in order to sustain the marginalisation and isolation of "Roma" people ...'. This situation, which promotes the understanding of Roma as a discrete racial, ethnic or cultural group, at the micro level of local community, fosters personal and group alienation. Discarded at the margins of society, society acts like and so becomes the enemy or probably more realistically the constant threat. At the same time society understands Roma as a sort of human peril.

The continued allegiance with racial identification poses a huge danger. The ethnic categorization of Roma not only asserts the legitimacy of polity premised on ethnicity, it also provides the basis for the ideological, political and institutional dislocation of 'Roma' minorities from the 'majority', thus freeing governments from their social and moral responsibility for a whole swath of their citizenry. Thus, Roma ethnic categorization can be understood as a reactionary phenomenon, resonant of a far-right political order in which people are increasingly divided by ethnic boundaries, rather than united by their common social interests.

As things stand, Europe-wide, Roma and youth are grossly over represented among the long-term unemployed (Cairns, de Almeida Alves & Alexandre, 2016; Coppola & O'Higgins, 2015; Hammer, 2003; Milcher, 2011). Roma experience massive inequality in regard to housing and healthcare. Like youth, they have few recourses or alternatives. Their consequent dependency on shrinking welfare resources and declining public services are an obvious manifestation of growing social inequality. The 'prohibitive' costs of improving Roma living conditions and of returning their labor to 'profitability' provides a strong incentive for the state to define Roma as a distinct racial community, thereby allowing policy to focus on the far cheaper and simplistic promotion of ethnic difference. Once the majority identifies a minority group as incorrigibly distinctive it is a small step to depicting them as irredeemably defective. The latter is the experience of youth – youth are by their categorization, under-developed. Is it any wonder that some are drawn towards so-called extremist positions and situations wherein they might find the promise of social solidarity and regard as a valued, fully armed resource?

Tyyskä (2014) argues that social institutions neglect, exploit and penalize young people. This demonstrates that the disadvantaged position of youth is by and large explained by their designation. They are the social construct and their issues, condition and circumstances are unproblematically understood to be a result of the same. What they are said (variously) to need is discipline, support, understanding, education, love, training, information, advice, conscription and so on. Their general lack of knowing what they want is articulated in all sorts of ways, codifications and languages, from the banal to the professional ('help them make informed choices', for example).

POTENTIAL FOR COHESION AND HUMAN SOLIDARITY

The meaning of 'Roma' isn't 'slave'; it is 'man', not in the masculine sense but as a referral to being human; you and me, we are Roma! Being part of cross-national and international collaboration, focused on work with and amongst Roma, but as part of an understanding of these groups having commonalities and overlaps with other marginalized groups and communities, is also progressive, both politically and socially. This nexus of approach can help build contemporary models of good and better political, professional and social practices. But such work needs to include members of such groups who should be involved in research as well as the leadership and delivery of practice. In the light of growing political extremism across Europe, such cooperation, via the promotion of understanding and cultural/ethnic interaction and co-working, has the potential to alleviate and counter exclusion, prejudice, exploitation and oppression.

Working with Roma, I have seen and am seeing possibilities for social cohesion between Roma and the host communities (Raykova et al., 2016). This is promoted via community and cultural action/solidarity as first and foremost human beings (as opposed to types of human beings). Such processes can be developmental of new interpretations of social relations and promote cultural cross-fertilization, and so growth, understanding, harmony and community integrity, dignity and civility. But what of youth?

Throughout the world, there has been huge concern about young people finding themselves increasingly unable to identify with and/or engage in the life of their communities, nation or society. This has caused many to make alliances with alternative, often immoderate, anti-social or even negatively activist groups. The Commonwealth Commission on Respect and Understanding (2008) has it that terrorism, extremism, conflict and violence are '… in ascendancy in the contemporary world and afflict Commonwealth countries as well as the rest of the world' (p. 10). It goes on to argue that:

> While the cultural influences are among the forces that can contribute to disrespect, misunderstanding and violence, they are not the only causal factors, nor are they immutable or irresistible. Indeed, much can be done to prevent the violence that may be thrust on us by promoters of belligerent agendas. For this we need a departure from old ways of thinking about the centrality and the alleged inviolability of cultural confrontations. (ibid.)

Part of the problem of grasping the root and nature of considerations such as terrorism, extremism and organized violence is that we often analyze them as if they come into the world as fully formed responses, with no root cause. This is seeking to address the symptom of negative social situations rather than the source. Violence and aggressive agitation do indeed appear to be endemic in the world, but, to take this as a sort of lightning strike that incarnates itself 'out of the blue' would be incorrect, analogous to the pre-Darwinian idea of an instant generation.

There are any number of policy and academic definitions of disaffection and extremism. However, to experienced youth workers the apparent positions are multiple points on the same continuum. Straightforwardly, to be disaffected is a result of dissatisfaction, but simple feelings of dissatisfaction do not automatically give rise to behavior associated with disaffection, which is seen to be anything from problematic to anti-social. If a young person is continually dissatisfied, finding no way to achieve or even express personal aspiration, it is not surprising if she might become hostile and rebellious towards those forces or authorities she understands to be preventing her from voicing and achieving those ambitions and desires. If this young person is unable to find the means to communicate her hopes or grievances, it is likely she will experience frustration. This frustration would logically be made worse when no one responds to that frustration when it is actually expressed. At this point, when the mutinous, disruptive, non-conformist or delinquent behavior associated with disaffection proves to be insufficient to address apparent injustice, or simply to draw attention to the plight or the troubles of young people and/or their communities, regions or nations, etc., all that is left for the aggrieved person is to become more extreme. Then 'they' (those in authority) will be obliged to hear; then 'they' (those seen as relatively powerful) must respond.

For generations, youth workers have adopted a value base that includes listening and responding to the views, perspectives, wants and needs of young people, but in truth, this has had limited impact. This is because the extent to which any one youth worker (or group of youth workers) can respond is restricted by the limitations of their authority. Youth workers are subject to organizational, regional, national and international policy and legislation. At the same time, no matter how attentive or active a listener one might be, the simple act of giving an ear, while helpful to a point in terms of disaffection, will be insufficient with regard to addressing the anguish and frustration that might lead to extremism.

Positively speaking, extremism might be understood as an effort to change the world (something disaffection cannot achieve) and it would be untrue to say it does not have a track record of doing this; many anti-colonial movements for instance were interpreted in their historical contexts as extremist. However, meeting extremist regimes with extremism has been a terribly wasteful habit of humanity, firstly in the terms of direct human suffering, but also with regard to general social resources. If you shout at someone you are inviting that someone to shout at you; this is fairly predictable all things being equal, but this does not translate into shouting being the best way to proceed in a debate or argument. Likewise, because counter-extremism has undermined extremist regimes, it doesn't mean extremism is a 'good thing' generally. In fact the cost of such extremist dynamics shows them to be utterly counterproductive. The initial extremism will always result in (at least) equal and opposite extremism – one is the logical progeny of the other – extremism has proved not to be the midwife of peace.

This is discernible at the micro level of youth work; for example, the bully is punished for their bullying by the youth worker. The bully, who has already shown themselves to define the world in terms of 'might is right' experiences the condemnation of the youth worker as bullying (the youth worker has the 'might' to enforce the 'right'). The bully and the bullied have learned (effectively) that bullying 'works'.

Short-circuiting the Cycle of Radicalization

Given this, how do youth workers engage young people in the contexts of disaffection and extremism without becoming one of the sources of disaffection? We can see that disaffection might be a stepping stone to extremism; that is, it is hard to see how one might jump from being satisfied to an extremist point of view. Thus, extremism can be understood as the wayward child of disaffection, and it is at this source where youth workers can be most effectively deployed with regard to short-circuiting extremism.

But how is this to be done? The cycle begins with dissatisfaction (see Figure 38.1). If this remains unexpressed or unexamined it invites people (not just young people) to look for convenient or quickly identified causes (blame). We know that there are groups with an interest in directing dissatisfaction towards those they see as their rivals or those that detract from their interests. Often young people with unspoken or unexamined discontents are easy prey for such factions.

Youth workers can address this cycle at its very source by working with young people to examine and voice their thoughts and feelings; explore how they might address any issues, looking to themselves, their peers and society as a resource (rather than a source of

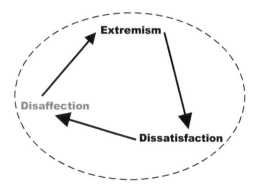

Figure 38.1   The cycle of extremism (adapted from Belton, 2015b)

blame); and consider what interests particular groups have when looking to place responsibility for personal or social problems on rivals, while directing others to take action against these people. The same process might be initiated at any of the three points in the cycle. However, it is likely that young people who have become disaffected or who have taken on extreme views will demand more intensive and longer-term interaction. Currently there are youth work responses in highly disaffected, or post-extreme situations (those who survive the cycle of dissatisfaction, disaffection and extremism might be the most likely to repeat this cycle). These responses go beyond merely listening; they involve energetically supported dialogue, a resulting dialectic and action capable of instigating perceivable social change and concomitant personal and social development. The proposal is that the antidote to disaffection is the generation of the means to address dissatisfaction, thus circumventing extremism.

Deconstructing 'Empowerment'

Standing back, the bigger picture reveals the paucity of understanding and appreciation of the growing disconnection between young people and adult society. The social response to youth has been premised on 'doing stuff to/for them' rather than 'them doing stuff' (Belton, 2010a, 2012). Perhaps too often the youth work response is to call for 'empowerment' of youth. Empowerment, if it is actually to be what the word implies, needs to be founded on organizations working with but also for youth, more as service providers than philanthropic enterprises, generating the means, skills and attitudes to take and ultimately exert power.

All too often this expression suggests (and in practice plays out) a 'passing on' of power from those taken to be relatively powerful to those deemed by this process to be relatively powerless. This is essentially a deficit model, built on subtle but prejudicial assumptions.

Power, by its nature, cannot be given. Any power given is, by definition, an act of patronization; the powerful bestow the power, while the recipient of this power is totally reliant on the powerful for their supply of power. But how often in practice do the powerful literally 'give up' power and become relatively less powerful? Power, if it is power, if it is transferable at all, is taken rather than given; the taking of power is a powerful act (see Belton, 2010a).

This said, 'power' is probably the wrong word to use in relation to state, government and institutional entities. In democratic and developing democratic contexts authority structures are usually administrative in their functioning and are premised on the use and application of relative authority. As such, what youth working with local agencies are involved with when it comes to gaining resources and raising consciousness is access to and gaining influence in relation to authority; one gains authority in these contexts by way of learning to use one's influence. At a foundational level this is what agencies working with youth, by deploying policies of inclusion and participation, can realistically, and most usefully, work towards.

Action as an Avenue of Influence

The most useful emphasis of effective youth work, given the contemporary position of youth, might be understood as that placed on young people taking action; that is, using influence, which is the means to realizing personal and collective authority. However, action cannot be the starting point of youth work. The practice of youth work and the dialogue and dialectic it promotes between young people, and between adults and young people, is the logical means to plan, contextualize, frame, promote and undertake action.

It is noticeable that as welfare economies develop, a gap appears between young people in need of social work intervention and those not in need (see Belton, 2014). At the same time, the world of the child is more than home and school; the 'life territory' of youth includes the boondocks of experience that often remain invisible to adult eyes. It is these apparent voids that youth work has traditionally broached and inhabited. This area has been acknowledged and/or referred to in a number of ways. The organization Pravah in India describes it as the Fifth Space: 'We believe that as a society we have "legitimized" four spaces for young people – that of family, friends, career/career-related education and leisure or recreation. There is on the margins – a Fifth Space – a space where young people discover themselves' (Pravah, 2009, p. 3). From this perspective this space provides the opportunity for young people to build 'on the aspects of understanding the self, developing meaningful relationships and impacting society … While impacting society, young people impact themselves …' (ibid).

The youth work approach here is 'facilitative'. Ultimately the youth worker role is set on 'confirming' young people in a position of responsibility for self, other and the whole. Overall this demonstrates a commitment to 'expediate' (from the Latin – to 'set loose' or 'free the feet') rather than 'welfaring' or an entirely educative model of service delivery. This can be understood as a de-colonizing approach, in that it is based on an asset model that sees young people as vibrant wells of potential rather than inherently powerless, which is what the ambition to empower logically assumes. There is an expectation that youth can and will act out of their own intrinsic spirit and (albeit) latent power, so developing access to their own influence and thus wider authority mechanisms. The latter is not given, it is realized via action that exerts influence and so achieves authority.

The following example is a situation that simply illustrates this type of approach.

> Youth workers in a big city had been involved with a large group of young people who were obliged to sleep on the street. Such were the numbers of these young people that they were causing concern and consternation to the point where the police were instructed to move them along en masse. On picking up on this policy the youth workers intervened, approaching the police to negotiate a more humane and perhaps gradual response. Ultimately a solution was brokered and the youth workers approached the young people's representatives, put forward by the young people themselves. The response was unexpected. It amounted to: 'Who are you to represent and commit to action on our behalf – who gave you this authority?' The workers took this as a valuable lesson. They had in fact been confronted with the consequence of their own practice principles. They went back to the police and informed them that they (the police) would need to negotiate with the representatives of the young people and explain how they, the youth workers, did not represent the young people, but were straightforwardly messengers.

Of course the story could have ended badly, with the police hammering home their legitimate power. However, the results of this, in the full view of the 'messengers', was seen to be undesirable, so negotiations between the police and the young people went forward and a compromise was reached. This was power realized via the use of influence and authority taken. A recognition of young people's political potential might have diverted the potential for disaffection and perhaps more extreme reaction into a means for constructive progressive action.

Thomas (2009) argues that young people are often understood to be apolitical. In terms of social inclusion this puts them in much the same position as Roma. While there has been a global emphasis on developing strategies that ostensibly look to heighten the participation of young people in society, these are by-and-large conceived and led by adults, as such opportunities for young people to take autonomous action is limited. Thomas however believes young people, often those on the margins or who are part of 'communities of revolt', can be understood as 'political actors' via what he calls the 'micro-politics' of their interaction with adults and each other. This political animation is, according to Thomas, a means by which young people take charge of their lives by way of action as varied as organizing clubs and generating websites.

As adults understand these phenomena, they can more effectively associate with young people, engaging with them as autonomous political agents. Often the micro-political statement made by a young person is taken as merely a complaint or just personal avowal, relating to an almost entirely emotional reaction to the world; 'it isn't fair' or 'you are always picking on me' for example. But if such statements can be heard differently, not necessarily but potentially as observations about the impact of circumstance or structural inequality, they can be understood as political observations and declarations.

A Foucauldian understanding of micro-politics includes discourse politics, which is used by marginal groups to contest the hegemonic discourses that position individuals within the confines of accepted identities. Discourse is power because the rubrics shaping discourse enforce norms of what is seen as true, rational, sensible or sane. To make declarations outside the parameters of these rules runs the risk of exclusion and/or marginalization. Every discourse is the product of power, but is not necessarily completely compliant with it; discourses can be deployed as 'a point of resistance and a starting point for an opposing strategy' (Foucault, 1978, p. 101). Counter-discourses afford a means of political resistance by relating personal experience of oppression and struggle to the wider context, so making them means of expressing more general needs and demands.

It is at this level that activists and practitioners might work with Roma/youth to undermine the potential for disaffection. The open and generous exploration of statements of seemingly simple dissatisfaction and frustration, in sympathy with the 'Fifth Space' notion, can lead to a mutual understanding between adults and youth, Roma and non-Roma that can foster novel and collective forms of engagement and re-engagement with society, and the consciousness of the potential and wholeness of humanity that is not partitioned by age or other limiting categorizations.

CONCLUSION

The point of comparative analysis is to reveal something about the character of what is being compared, in this case Roma and youth. However, perhaps more importantly such exercises can also expose the nature of the context we live and work in. As a youth worker and trainer/educator of youth workers, I am consistently reminded of our propensity to work with circumstances as presented to us: we are drawn to a tight focus on the immediate situation – the individual and/or the group. While this is understandable and often necessary, without developing our consciousness of the extended social and political environment that in effect forms ethnic, age and other categorical corrals, our work is almost entirely devoted to alleviating symptoms (discrimination, inequality, disaffection, etc.).

A social worker I put this too responded by saying; 'Well, keep that old deprivation coming!' He was making the point that it is this system of categorization that keeps him in employment. Perhaps he had a point, but a grasp on the wider social prospect can open new vistas on the nature of things that can potentially enable the development of a broader plan for practice. Such a strategy might help us begin to address the root and cause of social maladies; what are often portrayed or perceived as issues specific to one group are not unusually more broadly applicable. While I'm not quite saying 'a problem shared is a problem halved', I am making a case to short-circuit a type of what Illich (1976, p. 294) called 'iatrogenesis'; we can find ourselves emphasizing difference rather commonality and the recognition of a general oppression of people. This risks propagating what we seek to assuage. We find ourselves acting in isolation (with 'our' chosen group) when we could gear our responses to a more oceanic condition and in the process find allies and collaborators within and across social and professional boundaries.

REFERENCES

Belton, B. (2005a). *Gypsy and traveller ethnicity*. London: Routledge.

Belton, B. (2005b). *Questioning gypsy identity*. Walnut Creek, CA: AltaMira Press.

Belton, B. (2010a). *Radical youth work*. Lyme Regis, Dorset: Russell House.

Belton, B. (2010b). Knowing gypsies. In T. Acton & D. De Bas (Eds.), *All change! Romani studies through Romani eyes* (pp. 39–48). Hatfield: University of Hertfordshire Press.

Belton, B. (2012). *Professional youth work*. London: Commonwealth Secretariat.

Belton, B. (2014). *Cadjan – Kiduhu: Global perspectives on youth work*. Rotterdam: Sense Publishers.

Belton, B. (2015a). *Li Sobindoy – Roma in action*. Nottingham: JMD Media.

Belton, B. (2015b). *Youth workers creating paths to peace*. London: Commonwealth Secretariat.

Biko, S., & Stubbs, A. (1979). *I write what I like*. New York: Harper & Row.

Bíró, A., Gheorghe, N., Kovats, M., & Guy, W. (2013). *From victimhood to citizenship*. Budapest: Central European University Press.

Bright, G. (Ed.) (2015). *Youth work: Histories, policy and contexts*. London: Palgrave.

Bunescu, I. (2014). *Roma in Europe: The politics of collective identity formation*. Farnham, Surrey: Ashgate Publishing Group.

Cairns, D., de Almeida Alves, N., & Alexandre, A. (2016). *Youth unemployment and job precariousness*. London: Palgrave Macmillan.

Clark, T. (1975). *The oppression of youth*. New York: Harper Colophon.

Commonwealth Commission on Respect and Understanding (2008). *Civil paths to peace*. London, UK: Commonwealth Secretariat.

Coppola, G., & O'Higgins, N. (Eds.) (2015). *Youth and the crisis: Unemployment, education and health in Europe*. Abingdon: Routledge.

Dawson, R. (2001). *British gypsy slavery*. Alfredon: Dawson.

Fanon, F. (1965). *The wretched of the earth*. New York: Grove Press.

Fanon, F. (1967a). *A dying colonialism*. New York: Grove Press.

Fanon, F. (1967b). *Black skin, white masks*. New York: Grove Press.

Filčák, R. (2012). *Living beyond the pale*. Budapest: Central European University Press.

Foucault, M. (1978). *The history of sexuality*. New York: Pantheon Books.

Gatti, R., Karacsony, S., Kosuke, A., Ferré, C., & de Paz Nieves, C. (2016). *Being fair, faring better*. Washington DC: World Bank Publications.

Grzanka, P.R. (2014). *Intersectionality*. Boulder, CO: Westview Press.

Hall, S. (1991). The local and the global. In A.D. King (Ed.), *Culture, globalization and the world system* (pp. 32–40). London: Macmillan.

Hammer, T. (2003). *Youth unemployment and social exclusion in Europe*. Bristol: Policy Press.

Hancock, I. (1987). *The pariah syndrome*. Ann Arbor, MI: Karoma Publishers.

Illich, I. (1976). *Medical nemesis*. New York: Pantheon.

Kovats, M. (2003). The politics of Roma identity: Between nationalism and destitution. Open Democracy [online]. Retrieved from https://www.opendemocracy.net/people-migrationeurope/article_1399.jsp

Majtényi, B. (2016). *A contemporary history of exclusion*. Budapest: Central European University Press.

Mattson, K. (2001). *Engaging youth*. New York: Century Foundation.

McGarry, A. (2010). *Who speaks for Roma?* New York: Continuum.

Milcher, S. (2011). *On vulnerability and labour market discrimination of Roma*. Saarbrücken: Südwestdeutscher Verlag für Hochschulschriften.

Nicolae, V. (2013). *We are the Roma!* London: Seagull Books.

Parkin, F. (1979). *Marxism and class theory*. New York: Columbia University Press.

Pravah (2009). *Annual report*. Retrieved from http://www.pravah.org/content/files/Pravah%20Annual%20Report%20final%20for%20web3.pdf

Pusca, A. (Ed.) (2012a). *Eastern European Roma in the EU*. New York: International Debate Education Association.

Pusca, A. (2012b). *Roma in Europe*. New York: International Debate Education Association.

Raykova, A., Garcia Lopez, M.A., Paddison, N., & Belton, B. (2016). *Roma youth participation in action*. Strasbourg: Council of Europe.

Stewart, M. (Ed.) (2012). *The gypsy 'menace'*. New York: Columbia University Press.

Thomas, N. (2009). *Children, politics and communication*. Bristol: Policy Press.

Tyyskä, V. (2014). *Youth and society: The long and winding road*. Toronto: Canadian Scholars' Press Inc.

Wall, J. (2012). Can democracy represent children? Toward a politics of difference. *Childhood, 19*(1), 86–100.

39

Community Development with Young People – Exploring a New Model

Helen Bartlett and Adam Muirhead

INTRODUCTION

Youth work within the UK is currently in something of a state of crisis. The slashing of local government budgets in a time of austerity politics has led to the closing and loss of youth clubs and projects across the country. UNISON research (2014) across 168 local authorities showed that nationally 350 youth centres had closed and over 2,000 jobs had been lost in just two years between 2011/12 and 2013/14. Between 2011/12 and 2016/17 the average cut to youth service spending across London Boroughs was 34 percent. 457 (Full Time Equivalency) youth work posts lost and 36 youth centres closed of the 157 that had been open in 2011/12 (Berry, 2017). Meanwhile, money is being poured into the government's National Citizen Service scheme, which aims to reach 300,000 young people per year by 2020, at a cost of £1.1 billion (Ainsworth, 2015). The National Citizen Service is a three-week program of team-building and social action, intended to

act as a 'rite of passage' for 15–17-year-olds. Many of the activities employed in the scheme – group-building days, residential visits, community projects – are familiar to a youth work perspective. However, the scheme marks a complete shift of focus from the longer-term relationships and developmental processes embedded within the notion of youth work to a short-term, time-specific methodology, replicable within and across groups. This shift is epitomized in the fact that as of May 2016, it was announced that the National Citizen Service was to achieve statutory footing, something that youth work has consistently tried to achieve, but been unsuccessful.

These changes of emphasis – in terms of a government perspective on work with young people – are not shifts that have just happened in recent years, but are a continuation of a process that can be traced back to before the current austerity politics (and indeed the current government) as part of the wider expansion of the neoliberal project. Over this time, youth work's original focus on informal education through leisure time activities, and the value of voluntary and collective association and its embeddedness within the notion of community have also shifted. The New Labour years began the exponential rise of 'evidence-based practice' (Alcock, 2008; Farthing, 2012; IDYW, 2009) where increasing processes of managerialism placed priority on targets and short-term interventions (Bright, 2015a; Davies, 2013; IDYW 2014), and a framework of individualized outcomes often based on specific agendas around employment, educational attainment, or offending, became the yardstick by which 'good' youth work was measured. Yet if you ask young people (who after all, should be the subject as well as the object of youth work) about what they value most, they continue to reflect many of youth work's earlier aims: 'to see their friends'; 'to take part in our programmes'; 'a safe space to go' (UK Youth, 2016). Our experience of asking the same question to young people in our settings sees responses reference the relationship with youth workers: having someone to talk to who will listen, support, and not judge.

Although at times it seems as though the neoliberal tide under which youth work (like many sectors) is struggling is inescapable, there is of course active resistance. It is a time of questioning, as academics and practitioners debate the current situation and future direction of youth work. Histories and traditions are being engaged to better understand the present and attempt to determine the future (Bright, 2015b). De St Croix's (2013) grassroots research is a timely reminder of the care and passion felt by youth workers for their work and their affection for young people, set against a field increasingly driven by market principles. Notions of community alongside youth work offer us a way forward as well.

The Milson-Fairbairn Report of 1969 set youth work within the context of community development and by the early 1970s 'youth work' had become 'youth and community

work' (Thomas, 1983). Education courses were aligned to this focus and, as of 2016, 76 percent of all validated youth work courses in the UK were entitled 'Youth and Community' or some variation, as opposed to straight-up 'Youth Work' or 'Youth Ministry'. Considering this, and that the two professions share a union, one might expect that there was a large crossover in the theory and practice of both community development and youth work. In fact, despite the alignment of many of the core values and contexts of each, they remain separate in terms of heritage, literature and practice.

We write this chapter as youth workers and as practitioners of community development with young people, located in specific geographically based, materially poor communities in Brighton & Hove in the UK. Our aim is to contribute to these debates with a proposal for youth work provision grounded in community development processes that challenges the contemporary youth work discourse and the focus on individual outcomes. In this chapter we discuss a model of community development that can be used with young people and illustrate the process with examples from our own practices.

COMMUNITY AND YOUNG PEOPLE

Community is a concept that holds diverse and often conflicting meanings; it both has and continues to be utilized by the range and gamut of different political positions and agendas (Anthias & Yuval-Davis, 1992; Baumann, 1996; Cavalcanti, Goldsmith, Lea, Measor, Squires & Wolff, 2011; Hill Collins, 2010; Rose, 1999). Rose (1999) highlights the ambivalent position that community occupies within social and political discourse, noting how it features as 'both the object and target for the exercise of political power, whilst remaining, somehow, external to politics and a counterweight to it' (p. 168). In everyday, common usage 'community' carries with it a strong sense of something that is good, something that we want: 'It feels good: whatever the word "community" may mean, it is good to "have a community"; to be in a community' (Bauman, 2001, p. 1). And yet as it is manifested within social policy, not everyone is seen to need community in the same way – it is ascribed to specific groups: racial, ethnic and sexual minorities, the poor, and women, for example. When talking about community, as it is most commonly used, and as we are referring to it here, refers to materially poor neighborhoods. In this sense, community is an ascription, holding within it narratives around class and poverty, the causes of it, and potential solutions. Through this construction, community becomes a tool of policy organization, implementation, and management. At the same time, it is an idea around which marginalized and less powerful groups have mobilized (Meekosha, 2011): used as a means to challenge the very systems of social inequality that from a different perspective, it reinforces (Hill Collins, 2010). It can provide a catalyst for political activity; as Hill Collins (2010) comments, the notion provokes strong feelings of identification, affiliation, and care that motivate people to action.

If community is a problematic concept, the relation of young people to community is even more so. Measor and Squires (2000) describe youth as community's Achilles' heel. Despite substantial bodies of work within both 'community' and 'youth' fields, there is little to be found in the literature about the connections and areas of disconnection between the two. Cavalcanti, Goldsmith, Lea, Measor, Squires and Wolff (2011) attribute this disconnect to the development of sub-cultural studies and deviancy studies, focusing on young people's attempt to escape from societal norms, represented in the confining repository of community. Much of what has been written focuses on young people as a community 'problem' to be solved, reinforcing the notion of young people as 'deficit' (Jeffs & Smith, 1999). While the tendency to demonize young

people has been around for centuries (Plato is attributed as having bemoaned the disrespect and disobedience of the young in 4th century BC), and young people have been the topic of media panics throughout the ages, it was during the New Labour period of government in the UK that constructions of young people really became consolidated in social policy. This was epitomized in the 1998 Crime and Disorder Act and accompanying Respect Agenda, with the development of interventions such as Anti-Social Behaviour Orders (ASBOs) and Acceptable Behaviour Contracts (ABCs) and corresponding institutions, such as Youth Offending Teams, to manage these. Although these interventions were not intended to solely target youth, statistics from the period show that young people became the primary focus of the use of ASBOs as 'teenagers hanging around' became seen as a form of anti-social behavior, alongside vandalism, drug-dealing, and fly-tipping (Jacobs, 2010). The discourse that developed at this time meant that anti-social behavior became synonymous with youth, and that this not only became naturalized, but was seen as a form of individual responsibility or failing (Squires, 2008).

This discourse manifests itself in community settings. In one of our organizations, the development of work with young people happened later than that of work with adults, and was a direct response by a local Community Action Forum to the adult-perceived issue of teenagers 'causing trouble' around the neighborhood. Within this context, youth work becomes a community development intervention designed to solve the 'problem' of young people in community. Of course, in messy real-life contexts, the picture is much more complicated than this. Ongoing work with both adults and young people within communities highlights that when asked what they would most like to change in their area: 'things to do for children and young people' frequently tops the list. And certainly in materially poor communities, where transport links are often infrequent and/or unaffordable, where young people are not afforded the same opportunities as their wealthier peers, and where public spaces have become contested sites, this is a valid aim. Young people themselves highlight the links between lack of things to do and 'negative' behaviors. A Youth Manifesto website developed by young people to outline local youth priorities specifically stated: '54.6% of young people asked said that the main problem was not enough to do locally. This has caused boredom and antisocial behaviour throughout the area' (HKYM, 2013).

Young people, like everyone, are involved in internalizing and replicating discourses. Of importance here is the way that 'young people' become discursively constructed as separate from 'community' and how responses are shaped around this principle. There are, of course, concurrent appeals to and with community in relation to young people. It is particularly useful here to consider how these have come into focus and been manifested within New Labour policies concerning participation and subsequent Conservative government commitments to social action. These are key in demonstrating how young people become situated in relationship to 'community', and how this relationship is always shifting and contingent.

Deconstructing New Labour Policies and Conservative Commitments to Social Action

The New Labour period of government was marked by fears of a 'crisis in citizenship increasingly directed towards youth' (Hart, 2009, p. 641). This fear reverberated through the discourses around anti-social behavior, around the introduction during this period of citizenship education into schools, and in the response to a series of disturbances that took place in the North of England in 2001, which called for a common citizenship based around notions of shared identity and values. The policies that were formulated in and

around these occurrences can be seen as an attempt to either educate or control behaviors of young people in order that they become more appropriate citizens. Communities, primarily local communities and within this, primarily local *poor* communities (amply evidenced by Tony Blair's Respect agenda), became the focal point of such policies (Hart, 2009; Jacobs, 2010). Young people were in need of 'learning about and becoming helpfully involved in the lives and concerns of their communities' (CAG, 1998, p. 12).

The given importance of young people's involvement in and relation to their communities is directly relational to the construction of youth as problems within said communities (see also DCLG, 2013). The focus of the proposed involvement was in the form of volunteering and service: it was definitively individual attitudes and values that needed changing, rather than any form of structural or institutional explanation (de St Croix, 2012). Meanwhile, the other method through which New Labour sought to extend their youth participation agenda – through the promotion of Youth Councils and Youth Parliaments as a means to bring young people into the political process (Jeffs, 2005) – has (reflecting representative democracy as a whole) failed to be inclusive of marginalized young people (Turkie, 2010).

The language of 'social action' has come into predominance with the current Conservative government, although it is influenced by many similar ideological underpinnings. The literature around social action in general divides it into two defining approaches: transformational and ameliorative (Morsillo & Prilleltensky, 2007). Social action, defined in the contemporary context as being 'practical action in the service of others' (Cabinet Office, 2013) falls definitively into the latter category: exemplified by such acts as volunteering, giving to charity and 'everyday neighbourly acts' and linked closely to the government focus on the development of specific, traditionalist moral character virtues – curiosity, honesty, perseverance, and service – believed to be key to success in life (PM Office, 2016). Within the context of the wider social action agenda, as epitomized by the National Citizen Service scheme, 'communities' become a tool to act upon or do things unto; the means through which young people enact actions to gain individual outcomes, with the ultimate goal of increased employability and life prospects formulated as intrinsically linked to this (Shukra, Ball & Brown, 2012). There is no evaluation or attention paid to the impact – positive or negative – on the communities in question. Additionally, this form of social action does not seek to encourage any wider questioning of social inequality or the possibility of dissent regarding inherent power structures; there is no recognition that community involvement might provoke a greater awareness of such inequalities or structures (de St Croix, 2011).

COMMUNITY DEVELOPMENT: PRINCIPLES AND PRACTICES

Community development, as a practice and a process, is underpinned by an enduring set of principles (CLG, 2006). Within the UK, community development is most commonly situated within materially poor neighborhoods, in the sense of spatial or geographical communities but also communities of interest or identity. As community is a term that is ascribed to specific groups, community development therefore is always located in communities that have been marginalized in some way. Community development aims to:

> release the potential in communities [by, firstly] bringing people together to address issues of common concern and to develop the skills, confidence and resources to address those problems ... [Secondly,] it works ... to change the relationship between people in communities and the institutions that shape their lives. It enables people acting together to be partners in development rather than objects of decision and policies made by others. (Taylor, Barr & West, 2000, p. 3)

Based around a core set of principles highlighted in the National Occupational Standards: equality, anti-discrimination, social justice, collective action, community empowerment, working and learning together (FCDL, 2015), community development takes as its starting point the everyday realities of people's lives and concerns, but aims to link these into wider structures and contexts. Much like youth work, the history of community development is embedded with tensions; from a colonial history that carries echoes around how and why specific communities are in need of 'development', to its relationship to the state. Arguments have been made that a focus on community detracts from a wider critique of social and economic structures and draws boundaries around groups and neighborhoods who would be better served working together (CDP, 1976; Craig, 2011). In addition, critics have highlighted the potential of such an approach to be ameliorative rather than transformational, focusing on making existing structures work more smoothly and aiming to create a level playing field, rather than fundamentally changing power (Gilchrist & Taylor, 2011). Perhaps most pertinently in the current contexts of austerity and the dismantling of the welfare state, there are concerns that it pushes the responsibility for welfare into the hands of those who can least afford it (one need only refer to the Big Society rhetoric to evidence this) (Miller & Ahmad, 2011; Taylor, 2011).

Despite all of these areas of problem and contradiction, community development retains something of its radical appeal (Mayo, 2016). For us, this appeal is linked to the way in which it enables people who may not traditionally have had a voice to take collective action around the issues that they choose. In so doing it aims to give greater political power to communities (Craig, 2011) and the people that live within them. This needs to be situated in a context in which many traditional spaces for and forms of working-class organization have disappeared

(Gilchrist & Taylor, 2011). In a time and landscape where inequality is increasing and political decisions are hitting the poorest communities hardest, it is more vital than ever that there are spaces and avenues through which these marginalized voices can be heard. In this, the collective element is critical.

The literature around community development however has tended to fail to make the case for how and where young people have been and can be included. In cases where young people are specifically mentioned, it is generally – as described above – in the form of a community intervention. This exclusion, we would argue, is not always intentional. Community development, when seen as a process or approach, can be argued to be overarching: applicable to any particular group within a defined community. However, as demonstrated, young people are not situated within a community; they are constructed as different, as separate, and as problematic. The means of participation and decision-making that develop within communities or neighborhoods do so around existing constructions and power structures, and therefore come to represent prevailing patterns of exclusion. These exclusions are supplemented by practical barriers.

Community development still draws much from the original texts and ways of working outlined in its earlier history. For example, Goetschius (1969) details the development of a group, from conception to established association, and the role of the community development worker at each stage, with the aim of ultimate withdrawal by the worker, and sustainability and independence on the part of the group. Although writers (Gilchrist & Taylor, 2011; Ledwith, 2011) emphasize that organizational development is not necessarily an essential part of the community development process, it remains a key constituent of many of the texts and models, tied up as it is with notions of sustainability and independence. This becomes an issue when working with under-18-year-olds, who are not legally entitled to financially manage and run their own groups/organizations. Similarly, the way and form in which meetings are run can also be a barrier to involving young people. First, and perhaps most obviously, is the timing, given that young people are legally obliged to be in school, college or training until the age of 18 in the UK, while for meetings where the presence of decision-makers and service providers is wanted, more standard timings are during the working day. Furthermore, the often formal, round-table style of meeting – run through the meeting chair, with agendas and minutes – while arguably a useful experience, can be intimidating and exclusive. These of course are not barriers that are solely applicable to young people – adults can also find meeting styles intimidating and daytime hours are not necessarily helpful to those who work. Rather this highlights the ways in which young people, already constructed as separate or distinct, are further excluded by day-to-day practices.

If community development is to adhere to its principles and actively work towards social justice and transformational aims, it needs to consider how it involves young people, as well as other marginalized groups. Meekosha (2011) usefully describes how essentialist notions of community have assumed and embedded white privilege. Without questioning how community is being constructed in any given situation, who is included and excluded from this construction, and continually challenging itself, community development fails in these aims. This is of course also true if we consider the inclusion of young people. Young people's links to community – in our case of neighborhood and of place – are affected by complex constellations of intersecting factors such as class, race, ethnicity, age, gender, sexuality, and disability, both in terms of the individual and of the community in question. If young people become included, but those young people are majority white and non-disabled, how does this affect young people of color, young disabled people or those whose identities and experiences intersect the two? How does the construction of community around these factors affect the ways in which people identify or indeed distance themselves from that community? How do we discuss or consider such questions without essentializing these groups or identities?

This chapter does not provide the space to explore these questions in detail. Our aim is to reinforce the notion that 'community' in itself is never fixed or coherent, as well as to highlight how such processes of questioning need to be integral to any consideration of community development as a political project. Although we are arguing that community development needs to include young people, this is not the extent of our position. Our argument instead situates youth work practice – as a specific way of working with and for young people – within the broader processes of community development. In so doing, young people's own priorities are placed at the heart of the approach, while linking into wider structures and processes and emphasizing social and collective as well as individual outcomes; something that youth work has been forced away from in recent times.

Applying Community Development Processes to Youth Work Practice

> Youth and community work is about dialogue, about conversation. What do youth and community workers do? Listen and talk. Make relationships. Enable young people to come to voice. (Batsleer, 2008, p. 5)

This statement grounds the focus of our practice in the essential interlinking of youth and community, as well as highlighting the aspects of dialogue and of relationship that we consider essential to youth work and that we carry with us into our practice of community development with young people. It is these aspects that our young people consistently reference when they talk about what

youth work means to them. From our perspective of working within community organizations, it is also often the means through which young people are supported to enter into forms of community and collective action. Our experience is contrary to much popular and media-perpetuated, 'vox-pop' opinion which sees young people as disconnected from community, unconcerned about what is happening around them or their potential role in impacting this. Rather we see that the multiple and complex ways in which young people engage and interact with the community around them, and how links to place, neighborhood and networks – especially for young people from materially-poor communities – are often vital (Cavalcanti et al., 2011). Within these engagements, young people need to be recognized (and celebrated!) in terms of their social location as young people, but, at the same time, the means through which they are constructed and excluded as such has to be acknowledged. As Finn and Checkoway (1998) observe: 'when young people are viewed as victims or problems, they see their social role as marginal and question their relationships to wider contexts'; they ask: 'what would happen if, instead of problems, society viewed young people as competent community builders?' (p. 336). It is this question that we aim to support and explore through our practice.

A community development approach necessitates the viewing of young people as resources. Delgado (2015) describes how involving youth in community practices sees the transformation of deficit into asset. This is critical at a time when the deficit model has become all-pervasive, cascading down from policy to everyday practice. Any youth worker today involved in monitoring, evaluation, or fundraising will know the prevailing pressures of describing just how 'in need' or 'at risk' young people are. There are frequently targets to meet surrounding this and it has often become the grounds on which a defense of our work is located. Without care, it is easy to become both implicated and implicit in such discourses. These discourses dehumanize and pathologize young people, as well as placing the emphasis firmly on the individual without providing structural explanations for young people's needs and situations. Working within a model that is solely premised around youth as resources or as assets by necessity challenges this discourse. The model relies wholly on the understanding and premise that young people want to and have the capacity to engage with, be involved in, and affect processes of deliberative democracy and community and social change. This involvement is also critical because as a process it traditionally works with young people who are excluded from many of the other structures that impact their lives. Whether viewed in a positive or negative light, community is the site in which, to a great extent, young people live their citizenship (Hart, 2009). It is therefore key that this becomes the site through which to engage young people, and to bring them into wider contexts: 'community narratives offer dynamic personal and political vocabularies for consciousness and experience, allowing individuals and groups to articulate a sense of self, voice their mistrust and mobilise resistance' (Cavalcanti et al., 2011, p. 7).

Furthermore, a model of community development with young people needs to focus on the impact (both potential and actual) that takes place at community and wider structural, as well as individual, levels – again consistently refocusing our attention on wider contexts. Within 'an increasingly marketised youth sector' (de St Croix, 2013) we are asked to lead young people towards predetermined outcomes, whether to do with employment, health (as for example through teenage pregnancy agendas), or simply attendance. Our aim, in proposing this approach is not to throw away the concept of outcomes in its entirety but rather to question the hegemony with which every interaction with young people becomes prescribed, legitimized, and time-bound within a solely individualized

neoliberal ideology (Taylor, 2013). Here we have drawn and learned from examples from the United States, where more literature has been produced in terms of envisaging how youth development and community development both can and need to be combined. For example, Christens and Dolan (2011) propose an interwoven model, where community-level outcomes might focus around policy change, program implementation and institution building, while also looking at individual outcomes related to psychological empowerment, leadership development and sociopolitical development. Our aims in working with young people who have been excluded and marginalized are often based around the development of the self-esteem, agency, and sense of belonging required to access and get involved in community practices – echoing Batsleer: 'to enable young people to come to voice'. Ironically, this approach might in turn result in the sort of outcome that policy interventions stipulate (employment, improved sexual health, reduced substance misuse, etc.); however, it is not the basis on which we build our practice.

A community development approach also challenges the prevalent notion of the short-term intervention. Rather, the focus is on long-term involvement, built up and over time, and allowing developing skills and capacities to be fed back into the organization and the community. Qualitative methods of monitoring are much more supportive of quality, longer-term youth work, but are found to be less in favor in a market economy where tick-box pro forma charts offer quick, comparable, but hugely oversimplified accounts of the work's progress and results. This is argued through the 'storytelling in youth work' movement developed by In Defence of Youth Work, which advocates for interrogation and analysis of youth work stories submitted as robust evidence, much like cross-examined legal testimony submitted to courts.

It is important to consider what it means to apply community development processes to youth work practice, what this might look like and how it might differ from other forms of youth work. This also serves to challenge some of the assumptions by which young people have typically been left out of community development histories.

Community development begins through getting to know the community in question: the different projects, groups, bodies, people, organizations, and institutions impacting on a specific community, as well as how processes of decision-making and structures of power operate in and between these. Young people and other community members should be involved in these processes, drawing out how people see and experience the community around them: who it consists of; what the boundaries are; the conflicts, the strengths, the needs, the emotions it evokes. Within a neighborhood-based community, this aspect aims to develop a lived understanding of the area, the spaces that are available both in terms of buildings but also of day-to-day practices, people and places: streets, parks, community centers, bus stops, churches, mosques, cafés, pubs. As youth workers, it is about finding out where young people are at, where they hang out, as well as how they relate to and are situated within the wider community. Our own practice of community development with young people is intrinsically tied up with the practice of detached youth work. This in itself can be both challenging and challenged. There is a long-running tension between youth work as a force for social change and as a means of social control, and this is particularly evident within detached youth work, which often contains problematic relationships and crossovers with forms of surveillance (de St Croix, 2016; Jeffs & Smith, 1999). In Brighton & Hove for example, the Local Authority detached team is sent to specific 'hot spots', where young people are alleged to be causing anti-social behavior. Likewise in our own community settings and meetings, as youth workers we are often expected to manage the behavior of young people in specific locations. These tensions

need constant negotiation. However, this also provides a space through which to negotiate and discuss the areas of tension with young people (de St Croix, 2016). In our work, such conversations led to a media project in which younger and older generations were brought together to discuss how the public space available to young people had changed over time. The resulting film highlighted the ways in which youth occupation of public spaces, such as parks, and the actions permissible within these spaces, had become increasingly prohibited. This in turn had an effect on the community discourse that was used to describe the ways in which young people occupied public spaces, as well as impacting on local police practices around moving groups of young people on.

As youth work's impact paradigm became one of individualized outcomes, much youth work provision seemed to become more insular. Anecdotally, many modern center-based youth workers never came into contact with the local Councilors, shopkeepers or pub landlords – or even knew where the local park was. Relationships with both young people and other members of the community are essential when adopting a community development with young people approach. Where intentional linkages can be made between uniformed youth groups, faith organizations, local businesses, community groups, sports clubs, etc., the new opportunities and benefits are greater than the sum of one's input. We have certainly found this to be the case in terms of shared training, new avenues of fundraising and resource pooling. Likewise, these linkages have proved to be avenues of critical support while defending youth work that is under threat.

Gilchrist and Taylor's (2011) three aspects to community development – informal education, collective action and organizational development – provide a useful framework within which we can situate a young people approach. Within this framework, informal education takes place through involvement in community activities; through groups of people coming together to work and learn from each other, recognizing and acknowledging different people's capacities and contributions. Collective action is then the means through which people organize to identify and achieve the meeting of shared needs and interests. Collective action may fall into a range of categories depending on what young people have identified: from politically based activities – campaigning/ lobbying/protesting – to developing a new group in the area, a community event, an intergenerational meeting, social action or practical community change. Actions young people identify with may well be similar to the projects typified within the government construction of social action. Where a community development approach differs is in the ways in which young people have come together to talk about the issues in their community, and have had the opportunity to research, discuss, and contextualize these problems, and follow through with social action (Christens & Dolan, 2011). For example, through highlighting the need for additional youth space (as well as housing options for young people), we supported a partnership that drew a group of young people together with local housing and co-operative movements to protest against a specific private housing development in the local neighborhood. Likewise, bullying in schools was raised as an ongoing problem by young people within the community. The resulting project moved beyond supporting young people to deal with the effects of bullying, but engaged with teachers and schools in order to impact policies: thereby shifting the focus from the individual to the structural.

As highlighted, it is the aspect of community development that involves organizational development that we consider to have been most problematic in terms of the involvement of young people. Through organizational development, groups of people formalize their relation and structure in order to administrate finances, be accountable, be legally compliant, and take actions independently.

This ties in with the generally intrinsic aim of community development to withdraw worker support once the group is sufficiently 'developed' and can act on its own. This aspect is more problematic when it comes to young people, both because of the legal and financial implications and also because the long-term commitments tied up with this might not be in line with young people's own agendas and life transitions. This is not to say that young people cannot be involved in the long term; we worked with a group of young people who met every week for three years to redevelop a sports court in their local neighborhood. We have equally supported young people's groups to achieve organizational independence; in one organization, older young people set up a local youth bank to enable groups of younger people to plan, fundraise for and deliver their own community-based projects. In another, a summer activities group, again supported by older members, set up a formally constituted organization and an award-winning social enterprise. Great individual and social benefits have been derived from these youth projects and they aptly demonstrate why young people should not automatically be excluded from longer or more structured community development activities simply because they are young. However, it is equally important not to focus too heavily on this aspect when working with young people. Even working with adults, groups often may not reach the stage of formal independence and total sustainability. For us, the approach is more about keeping in mind the ways in which a process can be supported and handed over, to the greatest possible extent, in any given circumstance.

CONCLUSION

We argue that community development with young people is a possible way forward for situating youth work in current challenging contexts. This approach draws on the strengths and principles of community development, particularly as a means of giving priority to marginalized voices and as a potential impetus for social change. Intrinsically, notions of community and practices of community development need to include young people, and we have focused on what the model might look like in practice, in addition to discussing some of the barriers. We also argue that resituating youth work in this way benefits youth work itself, providing a potential way to challenge current neoliberal hegemonies.

For our practice, operating within a community development model has allowed us to defend some of the youth work spaces that have come under threat. Placing young people's needs and priorities at the heart of the approach means that we are obliged to listen when they outline 'safe spaces to go' and places to 'see their friends' as of utmost importance. Such spaces and places serve as the grounds through which further engagement happens. Also, enabling these spaces to continue is the way in which we have been able to include young people themselves in the preservation of specific projects, for example through fundraising or through increased volunteer involvement. We say this with caution. We are in no way advocating (as for example David Cameron's Big Society rhetoric did) that all responsibility for groups and projects should be transferred directly into the hands of already targeted communities without support and resources for this to take place. However, the model has also proved a means of survival in times when this is a priority. As workers, and generally as advocates of youth work, we both need to be able to focus on day-to-day survival as well as constantly engaging in conversations about, critiques of, and considerations about youth work as a whole.

In order for community development to work towards transformational or social change aims, it is critical that it does not just focus on change within the boundaries of the community, but that it seeks to link into and ally and connect with other groups, communities, and movements. Without this wider linking, efforts for change become imbued with processes of isolation and self-interest. Our aim is for this chapter to serve as part of a wider conversation, including around the need for bringing together and developing alliances between different youth and community organizations, operating not just with young people but with adults and other groups within communities. Just as we need to continue to argue for the value of collective and associational practices within our work, we also, in these times, need to engage in such practices as organizations and with each other.

REFERENCES

Ainsworth, D. (2015). Charity finance news – national citizen service to serve 300,000 a year and cost £1.1bn by 2020. Retrieved from https://www.civilsociety.co.uk/news/national-citizen-service-to-serve-300000-a-year-and-cost-1bn-by-2020-.html

Alcock, P. (2008). *Social policy in Britain*. Basingstoke: Palgrave Macmillan.

Anthias, F. & Yuval-Davis, N. (in association with Harriet Cain) (1992). *Racialized boundaries: Race, nation, gender, colour and class and the anti-racist struggle*. London: Routledge.

Batstleer, J. (2008). *Informal learning in youth work*. London: Sage.

Bauman, Z. (2001). *Community: Seeking safety in an insecure world*. Cambridge: Polity Press.

Baumann, G. (1996). *Contesting culture: Discourses of identity in multi-ethnic London*. Cambridge: Cambridge University Press.

Berry, S. (2017). *Youth Service Cuts in London – What Next?* London Assembly: Retrieved from https://www.london.gov.uk/sites/default/files/final_sian_berry_youth_services_update_mar2017.pdf

Bright, G. (2015a). In search of soul. In G. Bright (Ed.), *Youth work: Histories, policy and contexts* (pp. 236–248). Basingstoke: Palgrave Macmillan.

Bright, G. (2015b). The early history of youth work practice. In Bright, G. (Ed.), *Youth work: Histories, policy and contexts* (pp. 1–21). Basingstoke: Palgrave Macmillan.

Cabinet Office. (2013). In the service of others: A vision for youth social action by 2020. Retrieved from https://www.gov.uk/government/uploads/system/uploads/attachment_data/file/211937/In_the_Service_of_Others_-_A_vision_for_youth_social_action_by_2020.pdf

CAG (Citizenship Advisory Group). (1998). *Education for citizenship and the teaching of democracy in schools*. London: Qualifications and Curriculum Authority. Retrieved from http://dera.ioe.ac.uk/4385/1/crickreport1998.pdf

Cavalcanti, R., Goldsmith, C., Lea, J., Measor, L., Squires, P., & Wolff, D. (2011). *Youth and community: connections and disconnections*. Arts & Humanities Research Council (Connected Communities Programme), Brighton.

CDP. (1976). *Gilding the ghetto*. Community Development Project, London.

Christens, B. & Dolan, T. (2011). Interweaving youth development, community development and social change through youth organising. *Youth & Society*, *43*(2), 528–548.

CLG (Communities and Local Government). (2006). The community development challenge. Retrieved from https://www.bl.uk/collection-items/community-development-challenge

Craig, G. (2011). Community capacity building. In G. Craig, M. Mayo, K. Popple, M. Shaw, & M. Taylor (Eds.), *The community development reader* (pp. 273–282). Bristol: The Policy Press.

Davies, B. (2013). Youth work in a changing policy landscape: The view from England. *Youth & Policy*, *110*, 6–32.

DCLG (Department of Community and Local Government). (2013). *Government response to the riots, communities and victims. Panel's final report*. Retrieved from https://www.gov.uk/government/uploads/system/uploads/attachment_data/file/211617/Govt_Response_to_the_Riots_-_Final_Report.pdf

Delgado, M. (2015). *Community practice and urban youth: Social justice service learning and civic engagement*. New York: Routledge.

de St Croix, T. (2011). Struggles and silences: Policy, youth work and the national citizen service. *Youth & Policy*, *106*, 48–59.

de St Croix, T. (2012). If someone is not a success in life it's their own fault: What coalition youth policy says about young people and youth workers. In Defence of Youth Work. Retrieved from http://www.indefenceofyouthwork.org.uk/wordpress/?p=2561

de St Croix, T. (2013). 'I just love youth work!' Emotional labour, passion and resilience. *Youth & Policy*, *110*, 33–51.

de St Croix, T. (2016). *Grassroots youth work: Policy, passion and resistance in practice*. Bristol: The Policy Press.

Farthing, R. (2012). Why youth participation? Some justifications and critiques of youth participation using New Labour's youth policies as a case study. *Youth & Policy*, *109*, 71–97.

FCDL (Federation for Community Development Learning). (2015). Community Development National Occupational Standards. Retrieved from https://www.lemosandcrane.co.uk/dev/resources/cdw_nos.pdf

Finn, J. & Checkoway, B. (1998). Young people as competent community builders: A challenge to social work. *Social Work*, *43*(4), 335–345.

Gilchrist, A. & Taylor, M. (2011). *The short guide to community development*. Bristol: The Policy Press.

Goetschius, G. (1969). *Working with community groups: Using community development as a method of social work*. London: Routledge.

Hart, S. (2009). The 'problem' with youth: Young people, citizenship and the community. *Citizenship Studies*, *13*(6), 641–657.

Hill Collins, P. (2010). The new politics of community. *American Sociological Review*, *75*(1), 7–30.

HKYM. (2013). Hangleton and Knoll Youth Manifesto. Retrieved from http://www.hkym.co.uk/

IDYW (In Defence of Youth Work). (2009). The open letter. Retrieved from https://indefenceofyouthwork.com/the-in-defence-of-youth-work-letter-2/

IDYW (In Defence of Youth Work). (2014). IDYW Statement 2014. Retrieved from https://indefenceofyouthwork.com/idyw-statement-2014/

Jacobs, J. (2010). Spaces of New Labour youth policy. PhD thesis, University of Birmingham. Retrieved from http://etheses.bham.ac.uk/1490/1/Jacobs_11_PhD.pdf

Jeffs, T. (2005). Citizenship, youth work and democratic renewal. *The encyclopedia of informal education*. Retrieved from http://infed.org/mobi/citizenship-youth-work-and-democratic-renewal/

Jeffs, T. & Smith, M. (1999). The problem of 'youth' for youth work. *Youth & Policy, 62*, 45–66.

Ledwith, M. (2011). *Community development: A critical approach*. Bristol: The Policy Press.

Mayo, M. (2016). CDJ 50 year anniversary conference presentation: Looking backwards, looking forwards – from the present. *Community Development Journal, 51*(1), 8–22.

Measor, L. & Squires, P. (2000). *Young people and community safety: Inclusion, risk, tolerance and disorder*. Aldershot: Ashgate.

Meekosha, H. (2011). Equality and difference – what's in a concept? In G. Craig, M. Mayo, K. Popple, M. Shaw, & M. Taylor (Eds.), *The community development reader* (pp. 171–183). Bristol: The Policy Press.

Miller, C. & Ahmad, Y. (2011). Community development at the crossroads: A way forward. In G. Craig, M. Mayo, K. Popple, M. Shaw, & M. Taylor (Eds.), *The community development reader* (pp. 223–234). Bristol: The Policy Press.

Morsillo, J. & Prilleltensky, I. (2007). Social action with youth: Interventions, evaluation, and psychopolitical validity. *Journal of Community Psychology, 35*(6), 725–740.

NYA (National Youth Agency). (2015). Cuts watch. Retrieved from http://www.nya.org.uk/2015/01/cuts-watch-update/

PM Office. (2016). Prime Minister's speech on life chances. Retrieved from https://www.gov.uk/government/speeches/prime-ministers-speech-on-life-chances

Rose, N. (1999). *Powers of freedom: Reframing political thought*. Cambridge: Cambridge University Press.

Shukra, K., Ball, M., & Brown, K. (2012). Participation and activism: Young people shaping their worlds. *Youth & Policy, 108*, 36–54.

Squires, P. (2008). The politics of anti-social behaviour. *British Politics, 3*(3), 300–332.

Taylor, M. (2011). Community participation in the real world. In G. Craig, M. Mayo, K. Popple, M. Shaw, & M. Taylor (Eds.), *The community development reader* (pp. 291–300). Bristol: The Policy Press.

Taylor, M., Barr, A., & West, A. (2000). *Signposts to community development*. London: Community Development Foundation.

Taylor, T. (2013). Threatening youth work: The illusion of outcomes. Retrieved from https://indefenceofyouthwork.files.wordpress.com/2009/05/threatening-yw-and-illusion-final.pdf

Thomas, D.N. (1983). *The making of community work*. London: George Allen and Unwin.

Turkie, A. (2010). More than crumbs from the table. In B. Percy-Smith & N. Thomas (Eds.), *A handbook of children's and young people's participation: Perspectives from theory and practice* (pp. 260–269). Abingdon: Routledge.

UK Youth. (2016). *Local youth groups today: The value, the challenge, the opportunity*. Retrieved from http://www.ukyouth.org/uploaded/Local_Youth_Groups_Today_Final_14.03.16.pdf

UNISON. (2014). *The damage: The UK's youth services – how cuts are removing opportunities for young people and damaging their lives*. Retrieved from https://www.unison.org.uk/content/uploads/2014/07/On-line-Catalogue225322.pdf

40

Returning to Responsive Youth Work in New York City

Susan Matloff-Nieves, Tanya Wiggins,
Jennifer Fuqua, Marisa Ragonese,
Steve Pullano and Gregory Brender

INTRODUCTION

Youth work as a responsive practice, one that keeps participants at the center, has become tangled up in bureaucracy and top-down requirements. The imperative of centralized management to ensure standardization of measurable 'quality' conflicts with the essential premise that young people are at the center of the work as active agents, and that the best youth work responds to their aspirations, interests and issues and enables their voices to be heard through effective advocacy. We claim that attempts to reconcile these conflicting demands by incorporating 'leadership' skills development and project-based work into program models fall short in developing youth voice. The ultimate goal of youth work is to foster the resilience of young people and enable them to develop the skills that they will need to navigate the adult world. That world is filled with unpredictability and often shaped by toxic social conditions. Within programs, the essential work often

takes place 'outside the lines' as staff counsel young people through life challenges, provide space for them to discuss their differences with each other and stop scheduled activities to process disturbing community and national events. These necessary activities take place in conflict with the pressure to standardize programmatic structures in order to monitor and measure programs within large-scale systems.

New York City (NYC) now boasts the largest municipally funded youth development system in the United States (NYC DYCD, 2016). As a consequence of local growth as well as the national trends of managerialism and increased requirements for easily measurable outcomes, youth programs and practitioners are pressured to respond to emerging and complex needs with limited and pre-determined 'tools'. These include: requirements to report on short-term outcomes; emphasis on following the curriculum on a schedule that limits the time staff have to respond to issues that arise from young people's daily lives; and contracting requirements to establish activities months before youth are engaged. Funding streams for youth programs tend to follow trends that are shaped by public discussion of what is perceived as lacking in the educational system to the exclusion of holistic youth development. For some years, the primary measurable outcome for youth programs was the improvement of reading and writing skills; then, as gym time was reduced in schools and obesity became a concern, fitness was added as a required activity; now the focus is on promoting STEM (Science, Technology, Engineering and Mathematics) and, in particular, computer coding. These requirements impede staff from designing holistic programs that address the interests of youth. The young people who are most disenfranchised (often young people of color and/or those living in poverty) are also those most reliant on publicly funded programs and therefore disproportionately affected by the pendulum swings of public policies. NYC trends are a microcosm of the national and even international development towards bureaucratization, conformity and increased regulation in youth work.

The complexity and responsiveness that characterize the best youth work is stifled and limited by what has been dubbed elsewhere as, *the Accordion Effect* (Fusco, Lawrence, Matloff-Nieves, & Ramos, 2013). As the authors state:

> Top down pressures and growing expectations to do more with less at a time of decreased resources and swelling bottom-up demands are putting the squeeze on organizations like never before witnessed (in our lifetimes). Youth work practitioners are in the middle caught in stressful attempts to keep up and keep on. They are despairingly and tirelessly working to push up, push back and hold on. (Fusco et al., 2013)

The pressure to document short-term outcomes is at odds with fostering the long-term development of young people. People of all ages make mistakes, some serious, and they need to find their paths back. An ideal outcome of youth development is not a young person who has not made mistakes (ranging from minor to serious) but one who knows how to overcome barriers and obstacles, including those that are generated by their own behavior. Programs designed to help young people face challenges and deal with consequences rather than managing their behavior during program hours, contribute in a deeper way to the long-term development of participants but may make it more difficult to meet short-term contractual goals. Giving participants the space to make independent decisions and allowing for unintended consequences opens up risks that are then addressed through education and reflection. Organizations must be able to provide time for continuous patient and persistent fieldwork, self-examination and reflection by workers. Programs must be able to keep activities fine-tuned to the interests of young people, continuously looking for new, different and fun ways to engage in a genuine fashion with youth on their terms in their world. If staff cannot gain entry to the hardest to reach youth, they cannot have an impact. The 'Accordion Effect' has pressed youth workers and programs to view curricula and activities as the agent of change in a young person's life and overlooks the importance of maintaining the complexity of approach and the centrality of relationships in transformative experiences. This leads to creaming: programs that work for the most easily engaged youth and fail to engage those who may most need them. In order to meet the complex needs of all youth, in particular those challenged by poverty, racism, misogyny, homophobia and negative experiences with adult institutions, we must create and maintain programs capable of engaging and supporting them. The long-term outcome of an adult who is resilient and able to take risks may be at variance with the pressure on programs to produce short-term outcomes and youth who avoid all risks.

The future of quality youth work that is meaningful to young people depends on our ability to reclaim practices that have been lost or buried: strategies for establishing, developing and maintaining positive youth relationships; co-creating programs with young people; and facilitating the development of participants' skills to lead programs and to take action on neighborhood issues and broader policies that affect their lives. These strategies and approaches put youth at the center and empower them with voice, thereby maintaining the engagement and participation of those most difficult to engage. Youth workers are pressing back against increased pressures by engaging in advocacy in partnership with youth and informed by young people's experiences. In this chapter, current and former youth workers from different organizations, all in New York City, explored these trends through their lived experiences of youth work and discuss here how these strands weave together to create or impede a future in which all youth are healthy and thriving. We present what we have collectively found to be the tenets of a responsive practice and discuss both how such a practice is threatened and how it can be protected.

TRENDS IN THE ORGANIZATION OF YOUTH WORK IN NEW YORK CITY

Post-World-War-II publicly coordinated and funded youth services were established in New York, with a focus on prevention of delinquency and intervention with youth gangs (NYC DYCD, 2013). In the 1960s, federal War on Poverty initiatives and education reform provided multiple venues and the accompanying resources to fulfill the goals of youth services programming (Fernandes-Alcantara, 2012). New York-based United Way chapters, born out of 'community chest' cooperative fundraising efforts, began to contribute to the strengthening of human service providers, and research and private foundation communities in New York began to focus on youth development

(Peterson & McClure, 2003). This resulted in an increasingly formalized network of local youth-serving nonprofits throughout New York City.

Since 2000, NYC has shifted away from local control of both the public school system and the system of allocating neighborhood youth funding. The NYC Board of Education has been brought under mayoral control. Local school boards, who for decades determined budgets and priorities, have been disbanded. At the same time, Community Planning Boards, which used to have the authority to determine neighborhood youth needs and allocate Youth Development and Delinquency Prevention funds, were stripped of this authority. The funds are now commingled with other youth funds and distributed through a citywide competitive procurement process.

Guidelines for procurement have a great impact on what types of organizations can apply. Smaller community-based organizations, parent groups and organizations serving special populations have been shut out of most competitions for government dollars. In many cases, these are the groups that are best positioned to operate youth-responsive programming because of their closeness to the community and the fact that their governing boards are more likely to be comprised of community leaders. It is difficult for any organization that is not already highly resourced to secure government funds. One reason for this has been the cost per unit, as well as allowing for administrative costs. While the demand for quality programs and highly qualified youth workers has grown, compensation and benefits have not increased based on city contracts. The effect is essentially a cost of living freeze on an already underpaid nonprofit workforce. The procurement process also presents barriers and hardship for organizations that are required to implement timely programs, with delayed contract registration and payments as organizations wait for months to be reimbursed for program costs. The structure of government contracts limits the resources for agency infrastructure costs such as professional development, technology, facilities, senior supervision and fiscal administration; caps on these costs range from zero to 10 percent (actual costs for quality programs tend to be over 20 percent). This has put a particular stress on youth-serving organizations, which generally have a high turnover necessitating ongoing training for new workers, requirements to enter extensive data into online systems and on-going facility improvements to comply with licensing requirements.

Governance structures of organizations and the pressure for sustainability bring another set of tensions for youth-serving organizations. As public dollars shrink in actual value, agencies are pressed to raise private funds from individual donors, philanthropic foundations and corporations. Local community-led boards of directors are sensitive to neighborhood issues but often lack access to wealthy donors. Organizations that were previously led by neighborhood residents are changing the representation on their boards to include members with the ability to raise funds, and may in the process lose the inclusion of community voices in their governing bodies.

The effects of these changes reverberate throughout the city. Neighborhood-based programs are at subsistence level of funding that precludes their ability to respond to local needs creatively or set the organizational direction as all resources are directed towards meeting contractual requirements. Larger organizations are starved for resources to support the necessary infrastructure. For some organizations, their very survival is at risk, and many have not survived. The fragility of the nonprofit human services sector was brought to public attention in March 2015 when one of the largest organizations in New York City, the Federation Employment and Guidance Services (FEGS) imploded. FEGS operated from 1934 and served 120,000 youth and adults annually with a budget of $250 million and 1,900 staff (Human Services Council,

2016). This closure took place in a context of smaller youth-serving agencies merging and closing (Sesso & Wylde, 2016). A subsequent report commissioned by the Human Services Council noted that in a sector largely funded by government contracts, 60 percent of agencies are considered financially distressed, with less than three months of cash reserves, due to underfunded contracts, low salaries, poor facilities and late payments on cost reimbursement (Human Services Council, 2016; Kaplan, 2016; Sesso & Wylde, 2016). With the organizations that work with youth themselves at risk, there is urgency to ensuring that youth work has a future.

TENETS OF RESPONSIVE PRACTICE

Importance of Youth Voice

Experiences of staff from different organizations illuminate the impact of what organizations can accomplish through the tenets of responsive practice. Key was that participating youth were given voice, which the organizations used to improve programming and ensure relevance. The inclusion of youth voice has been associated with positive outcomes for youth such as intrinsic motivation, persistence, sense of belonging and sense of agency (Akiva, 2005; Akiva, Phillips, & McGovern, 2011; McLaughlin, 2000). Limiting youth voice to accommodate top-down requirements impacts the effectiveness, integrity and credibility of the organization's ability to work with young people. When youth voice is authentically acknowledged and considered, young people feel like influential contributors to the context (Evans, 2007). When the voices of young people are ignored, however, an organization may make incorrect assumptions about what is needed or desired by youth (McLaughlin, 2000).

Most NYC contracts require that activities are set months prior to implementation, which limits the input of participants. Excluded from the process of program development, young people may disengage and not attend. The beliefs and attitudes about youth held by adults (executive leadership, board members, funders and youth workers) drive decision-making in organizations. These decisions have implications for which young people are served, as well as how (Baldridge, 2014). While it is more challenging to maintain a practice that is responsive to young people, engaging them in shaping programs ensures that youth workers can sustain a continuous presence to support them.

Creating a youth-driven space requires a high degree of skill and balance on the part of the staff. If boundaries and activities are set by the worker and not promulgated as part of an equitable developmental process, staff members will fail to gain the trust of the youth. Young people must be allowed to test those limits, explore independently and experience the consequences. The youth workers' role is to help them learn, evaluate and think about alternatives and consequences, even if they believe the young person may not be acting in their own best interests. The safe space created by respecting the young person's equality facilitates a deeper level of reflection and the eventual development of decision-making skills. Youth leadership and decision-making skills are developed over time with practice and guidance. Beginning with taking responsibility for concrete activities such as helping to set up a room, taking attendance in activities and inviting friends to events, young people gradually move on to more challenging roles such as facilitating meetings, formulating advocacy agendas and speaking in public meetings.

Youth–Adult Relationships

Youth voice is promulgated through strong youth–adult relationships. These relationships support positive social and emotional development, promote long-term participation by

virtue of the trust and acceptance fostered with youth, and provide youth with sustained access to social capital held by staff (McLaughlin, 2000; Miller, 2003). While a stable and effective staff suggests long-term positive outcomes for youth participants, it takes time to develop reflective and competent youth workers. Budding youth workers need time and support to reflect on their purpose, goals and skills. They must be able to identify their own prejudices, biases and 'hot button' issues. Developing self-awareness requires time and skilled supervisors and is a prerequisite for relationships that are founded on mutual respect and trust. These processes develop over time, during which the youth workers will be tested over and over again by young people wanting to discover that the staff's actions match their words.

To develop trusting, enduring relationships youth workers have to be embedded in the lives of the young people. Youth workers cannot reach every young person within the same time frame or in the same manner. Continuous patient and persistent fieldwork is necessary to be able to develop trust. Unless program designs account for engagement as a separate process, programs will be limited in their ability to reach participants.

Within the context of long-term, trusting relationships with consistent, responsible adult mentors, young people make transformational changes in their lives through their decisions and actions. This requires a stable workforce that can work with youth throughout an extended period and program models that permit multiple years of engagement with young people throughout key transitions such as graduation from middle to high school.

Engagement in the Context of Society and Community

Contrary to the neoliberal narrative that claims individuals alone determine their future, young people are heavily influenced by the social conditions of their lives. Racism, sexism and economic disparities affect access to opportunities and the risks of violence and exploitation. Under-resourced schools, over-policing, sexual abuse, neighborhood conditions, such as lack of safe places for outdoor play, and street violence have negative impacts. The presence of strong community institutions such as youth centers, organizations that work for community improvement, neighborhood institutions such as houses of worship and the presence of adults who are connected in positive ways to each other, strengthen the conditions for youth to develop.

Responsive youth work engages young people with each other and is organized around the importance of peer relationships. It engages adults outside of the program as resources. Engaging young people as change agents in their neighborhoods through opportunities for community leadership and social change projects simultaneously transforms young people and the conditions in which they live. Program models that address these conditions build credibility with youth participants and equip them for life with the tools and strategies for continuing to address the manifestations of injustice that limit their pathways to professional and personal success and satisfaction.

Developing and Keeping the Right Staff

The first step to building a positive youth program is to identify and hire talented workers. This can be a challenge when contract levels are 'frozen' and low salaries do not increase annually. In addition, youth workers are regularly exposed to financial hardships because of uncertain funding streams. They perceive this as an invalidation of their work as well as the field itself. Even as accredited youth development programs in higher education become more and more recognized, the lack of career paths casts a shadow on the entire field. Without job security and career paths, youth workers cannot make a long-term commitment to the field.

The trust and acceptance used to build strong relationships between staff and youth is damaged when staff members leave (Laroche & Klein, 2008). In addition to the loss of trust, youth lose social capital with the departure of staff members and their professional networks. There are particular times of risk for organizations, such as leadership transitions and program budget cuts. Lack of cost of living adjustments, promotional opportunities and clear career ladders also influence staff decisions to remain at or leave an organization, or to leave the youth field altogether. Sometimes the workplace has to support non-traditional environments to encourage staff retention, such as flextime schedules for working parents. Creation of a strong sense of community among staff and between agencies fosters retention and protects against burn out.

Ongoing professional development that incorporates formal training sessions but also mentoring and coaching by more seasoned staff is necessary. Organizations must ensure that supervisory staff understand the methodology and practices of responsive youth work and that they have the time and resources to train and develop newer staff. Journals, relationships with mentors, and genuine curiosity about young people and their concerns and interests, foster enduring self-reflection while continuously building one's knowledge base. The quest for new and fun ways to engage young people is essential to avoid stagnation and to stay fine-tuned in developing trusting positive relationships. Creating an organizational culture that promotes learning fosters staff engagement and nurtures their enthusiasm.

In order to effectively facilitate this complex development of young people, we have a pressing need to retain and sustain seasoned supervisors. Experienced directors guide and train youth workers and create safety for self-development and honest reflection by staff.

It takes time to develop strong youth workers: turnover in the field is mitigated by career development, career ladders, adequate wages and respect. Seasoned staff must be validated with sufficient trust and autonomy to create responsive programming. Higher education options for youth workers that are relevant to the field, such as youth studies majors and minors, enable staff to develop youth-focused professional expertise. Financial aid and scholarships as well as loan forgiveness programs alleviate the financial and debt burden that youth workers face when they pursue the education that makes them more effective. The affordability of higher education is a challenge both for young people and for the staff who work with them. It is a social justice issue that has consequences for individual youth and for program quality.

All of these strategies for staff development and retention are costly and will require advocacy in order to make the case for investment in youth work and the long-term benefits of doing so.

Executive Leaders Who Understand and Foster Impact

Executive leadership plays a major role in an organization's ability to provide effective programming for young people. The leader of the organization is responsible for promoting the cause of the organization, securing funding and working with funders and board members to understand both the constituency and the rationale for service methodology. The executive leader communicates the mission and vision of the organization to staff members, who implement services according to the mission and vision. In an ideal scenario, funders and board members believe in the vision and perspective the executive director presents, and the organization carries out its mission successfully. Balancing the expectations of these stakeholders with those of youth and staff can be a delicate act for a leader.

The ability to listen to youth is one of the key factors of successful youth program leadership (McLaughlin, Irby & Langman, 1994). An assets-focused approach is an organizational practice for engaging youth. Leadership transitions can diminish this practice if the perceptions and voices of funders and board members appear to increase in volume, muting those of youth participants. Youth may be moved down the 'ladder of participation' and included in the most minimal of ways; chosen for token roles to support causes chosen by the adults (Akiva, Phillips, & McGovern, 2011). At risk is that the organization's leadership de-emphasizes youth development in favor of academic activities. Families may be asked to submit personal data not previously required for participation in an effort to document need. Administrative work related to new policies and reporting increases the burden on staff, decreasing the amount of time available to build relationships. Changes in how youth are perceived can be an overarching threat to sustainability that triggers others.

The most successful leaders see youth as key stakeholders whose voices are given as much importance if not more than governance and funding stakeholders. The ability to stay connected to youth and to include their viewpoint is a key factor in the effectiveness of directors of youth programs and agencies. It takes courage to balance community needs and internal integrity with responsiveness to external stakeholders, on whom we depend for sustainability. McLaughlin, Irby and Langman (1994) term these program leaders 'wizards': program leaders who put youth at the center of their work and therefore create the organizational conditions for youth to overcome the challenges of their social conditions. Wizards maintain direct connections with young people, view social conditions as the root cause of young people's challenges, maintain a consistently optimistic attitude towards young people and their abilities, work over an extended period of time, and devote time and energy to advocacy as integral to their role. The ability to create a complex response to complex problems is more conducive to effective practice than the ability to articulate and evaluate single item outcomes (Schorr, 1996). An ability to hold on to the perspective of youth, to conceptualize and then talk about vision and program, enables executives to balance the competing external and internal push and pull of multiple and sometimes contradictory agendas.

Systems that Support Rather than Impede Good Youth Work

Government and philanthropic systems can play a significant role in ensuring a positive role for youth. A system of public funding can ensure the sustainability of excellent technical assistance providers, as well as ensuring that children and youth in low-resourced communities have an equal chance of finding a quality program as those in wealthier neighborhoods. But, such systems are not always flexible. Foundations can pick up the slack and also play a role in supporting innovative youth work and system support such as peer learning circles, practitioner research and roundtable discussions. Funders can play a positive role in creating learning communities, fostering transfer of information and networking between grantees, making research findings accessible and hiring staff with expertise who can offer a critical perspective to help programs develop. Private philanthropic organizations may provide general operating funds to support agency stability and financial support for responsive programs.

Flexible funding that provides for adequate infrastructure including human resources management, information technology systems, evaluation, training and strong supervision best supports program quality. The erosion of infrastructure places a burden on front-line staff and results in overextended supervisors who are limited in their ability to develop staff and ensure program quality.

The seasoned professional able to operate with discretion becomes a worn down administrator absorbing managerial tasks and stretched among too many programs and supervisees. Recently, the federal government mandated that states and cities permit that at least 10 percent of funding in contracts be allocated for indirect costs (infrastructure), a ruling that NYC and New York State (NYS) are interpreting as a non-binding 'guideline'. For most organizations, the 10 percent is woefully inadequate and puts agencies at risk of failure, as witnessed in the 2015 implosion of FEGS already discussed. Foundations that provide general operating support to their grantees enable them to direct these funds as needed most. In the long run, ensuring the continuity and stability of these sustaining institutions has value in the impact that they have on vulnerable young people.

Bureaucratic rules and regulations serve an important protective function, from malfeasance and scandal and to protect participants from poor quality programming and unsafe conditions. Limits on expectations of youth workers can protect them from unreasonably ambitious goals that are beyond their ability to solve. Most importantly, rules protect vulnerable members of society from abuse. The art is to distinguish which rules impede good youth work and which support it. It is also important to recognize that rules such as quality standards without the adequate resources to address them are useless (Schorr, 1996). Further, it is important to note that these systems are subject to public pressure through advocacy and community organizing.

Advocacy and Community Organizing for Justice

Given the direction that our youth-serving systems are headed, preservation and growth of responsive youth work will depend on advocacy. Over time, advocacy transformed relationships within the NYC system to create partnerships between advocates and public agencies. The advocacy network crosses boundaries between practitioners, foundations, technical assistance providers, and citywide policy advocates. In NYC, successful advocacy campaigns have been responsible for maintaining and increasing significant portions of public agency budgets.

Campaigns that engage youth and adults in partnership to change toxic societal conditions and to push back against the 'Accordion Effect' have a double positive impact. The experience of changing governmental policy strengthens the confidence and competence of young people who are engaged in it. Effective organizing with youth includes education about how political systems work, including an understanding of state and local politics and political dynamics and the development of skills such as speaking in front of large groups and to policy-makers. Learning is scaffolded and includes practice sessions that foster successful interactions and engage a wide range of young people in trying new skills. Legislators and other policy-makers are educated on the issues and also experience young people as experts and positive community leaders, which can be transformative for both the young people and the adults who engage in these interactions.

Campaigns that address local decision-making permit young people direct access to policy-makers and are relatively cost effective due to their geographic proximity. In New York City and State, the Campaign for Summer Jobs has been crucial to the survival and growth of New York's program in this area, which served 60,000 young people in 2016. Hundreds of young people annually visit the State Capitol to rally and meet with elected officials. Key to successful advocacy is training youth in advance. Good training includes: an explanation of how government works with a description of some of the more important players in state politics and their political dynamics; an explanation of the 'ask'; and opportunities to role-play a mock meeting with an elected official to practice advocacy. Initial training is best offered locally, at sites that are accessible and familiar to the young people. The training not only teaches specific information but basic skills for presenting oneself appropriately in meetings and making an effective argument.

One challenge to engaging youth in advocacy is the variation in skills levels among participating youth. This can reinforce a lack of self-confidence for youth who have not developed the skills to effectively present themselves in formal, adult situations. Second, youth may be in the position of being seen but not heard by image-conscious government officials who understand the value of being photographed with young people but also believe that young people will not continue to exert pressure after the meeting is over. Lastly, it is important to continue to look for ways to bring the voices and opinions of young people into the formation of an agenda. By embedding advocacy into the ongoing work of youth programs, it is possible to address these challenges beyond single-issue campaigns.

Advocacy can also move beyond budget and program preservation to social injustice. One example is work by LGBTQ youth to change conditions in the educational system. This work amplified youth voice in a broader societal domain. Within schools, children and adolescents are socialized into unequal gendered power relations (Payne & Smith, 2012; Ringrose & Renold, 2010), and often educated away from the critical thinking skills necessary to challenge the pervasive ideologies undergirding them (Allen, Rasmussen & Quinlivan, 2013). Although the digital revolution has created for young people unprecedented access and opportunities to produce media that challenges sexual double standards, traditional gender roles and the sexualization of girls (Brown, El-Toukhy & Ortiz, 2014), youth culture and the wider social landscape in the US is replete with media and real-life situations in which girls and women are continually sexualized and subjugated to boys and men. Meanwhile, popular neoliberal discourses shaping cultural zeitgeist tout the liberation of girls, including their desires and abilities to choose to be sexualized, and the equality of men and women. However, girls are still punished by peers for being sexual while boys are rewarded (Bay-Cheng, 2015; Tolman, 2012), and students in school who challenge the hierarchies between and among boys and girls experience virulent harassment. In this cultural context, young people are inundated with contradictory information about sex, sexuality and power, and forced to navigate this difficult cultural landscape without the tools to do so.

Youth work, free of the structures of federal educational mandates, and often set up to empower youth to contest and ameliorate racism, sexism and classism, is an ideal medium for youth and adults to learn together about complex social systems and structures that undergird manifestations of social power disparities. Youth examine their own experiences of power and oppression, and learn to think critically about these experiences, while adults and older peers work to close the educational gaps between poor and working-class youth and their more privileged cohorts by equipping young people with the skills to conduct formal and informal peer education that can help interrupt the reproduction of inequality. For instance, despite recent public attention on and public concern about homophobic bullying, local and state policy approaches and the most widely adopted school-based interventions (i.e., Olweus, 1993) take gender-neutral approaches to a problem that is gender-laden; although researchers have long documented the centrality of misogyny to homophobic and other popular forms of bullying and sexual harassment (e.g., Connell, 2005, 2014; Kimmel, 1995; Kimmel & Mahler, 2003; Messner, 1989, 1990; Pleck, 1981), teachers are not trained to handle, address or marshal student conversations about gender and power.

Conversely within youth programs, program staff facilitate intergenerational, social justice work, speaking frankly with young members about the often unspoken power relations among young people, and then working alongside young people to develop ways for young people to reduce homophobic bullying and the harassment facing LGBT students. The result is youth-generated tactics and information to be disseminated, including techniques for teaching young people to examine and challenge the tacit power relations between and among boys and girls that hold homophobia in place in their schools. Both youth participants and staff then bring this knowledge and these techniques to their communities informally through daily interpersonal interactions.

Organizations that engage youth and adult stakeholders in advocacy provide a potent tool for changing conditions and developing individual youth. The critical thinking required for social analysis and the ability to work with others in teams are key factors in young people's success. Developing an analysis of the ways that social inequities affect them inoculates young people from internalizing the toxic effects of injustice. The skills required for advocating and organizing for social justice are transferable to the worlds of higher education and employment and enable young people to successfully navigate these adult domains. Creating opportunities for young people to be heard by policy-makers, to create public agendas that reflect their issues and analyses and to bring their issues forward are powerful and effective strategies for creating a future in which all young people can thrive.

CONCLUDING THOUGHTS: PRESERVING THE FUTURE OF YOUTH WORK

Responsive youth work is important for all young people but especially for those who are disenfranchised and voiceless, those to whom we should be most committed. These are also the young people most likely to be depending on programs funded by government and private philanthropy, those most impacted by the Accordion Effect. The pressures placed on youth programs by bureaucratization, rigidly imposed models and insufficient resources parallel the societal pressures on youth who are poor, who are people of color, who are gender nonconforming, and others outside the mainstream. Young people in poor communities are criminalized for behaviors that their wealthier peers are not, overly policed through stop and frisk and violence, and subjected to high-stakes educational testing. The resource starvation of youth programs is paralleled by the increase in youth unemployment and skyrocketing costs of higher education and levels of student debt. These cause increased stress, the diminishing of opportunities and the school-to-prison pipeline. All of these conditions bring increased expenses and the loss of potential tax revenues through underemployment. The greater cost is the damage done to our social fabric when young people's dreams and opportunities are denied and they are left with no way forward to a productive and satisfying life.

No program on its own can address the larger societal forces that pressure organizations and young people. Developing a sense of unity among organizations in spite of the procurement processes that put organizations in competition with each other is a key first step. The benefits of collaborating to protect and preserve responsive youth work are exponential. Face-to-face meetings among line workers create a sense of belonging to a community that fosters retention in the field. Opportunities to exchange ideas and resources are facilitated by contact and communication. Program leaders with the courage to engage in honest dialogue with the leaders of systems – city, state and county officials and philanthropic leaders – can influence the impact of policies and practices on programs. By acting in concert, programs cannot be singled out for repercussions for taking a stand and the collective voice is more likely to be heard. Some agencies have even taken

the step of refusing to accept contracts that do not provide an adequate funding level for the required level of service. Unified action can also create the necessary conditions for programs that are able to engage the most disenfranchised youth, through collective action and the sharing of effective practices.

Injustice damages the healthy development of young people. The conditions of inequity also impair the healthy functioning of our organizations. Youth work as a responsive practice offers part of a solution, yet neither young people nor the organizations that serve them have the support that they need: the young people to thrive or the organizations to support their development. Often at a personal cost, some organizational leaders manage to make it work, taking on the challenges of transforming the social conditions that are the root causes of these impediments. Engaging young people directly in social justice work is achievable in any setting, by fostering critical examination of the broader societal forces that impinge on their lives. The effects of this work for youth participants are powerful and give it inherent value. Social justice work with youth promotes their long-term development by developing their intellectual and analytic gifts, inoculating them against internalizing oppressive experiences and facilitating their mastery of skills that enable them to take action, understand and navigate institutions (Matloff-Nieves, Fusco, Connolly & Maulik, 2016). The value of empowering young people with the skills to challenge social injustice is exponential: they learn lifelong lessons about navigating systems effectively while challenging the toxic conditions that limit their optimal development.

In order to bring back responsive youth work, there must be dialogue at all levels among practitioners and with young people and their families. Frontline workers can be responsive, listen, build their skills to handle difficult conversations, surface youth concerns with program leaders, and develop comfort with advocacy. Program supervisors can build the skills of staff, raise issues to program leaders, and build their own skills in supervision and advocacy. Program leaders can fearlessly balance the demands of stakeholders, prioritize and privilege youth voice, create mechanisms for youth voice to be heard and support dissent within and outside the organization.

Funding stakeholders and government officials can create spaces for discussion and listen. They can create evaluation and accountability systems that allow space for programs to work with young people in all of their complexity. Voice matters: youth can only be heard if their voices are amplified and validated at all levels.

The need for system-wide accountability should not be in conflict with effective program design that is responsive to neighborhood issues and successful in terms of long-term impact. Emphasis on short-term individual outcomes detracts efforts from what really helps young people to thrive. The process of building trust with youth described in the earlier sections requires time. Flexibility is necessary to create youth programs that can be responsive and engaging. The youth most in need are those who are not easily connected with and who, with good reason, distrust adult institutions. Building into contracts and program models resources and time for outreach and point of entry activities is essential. Most programs go right into intervention and many take time to fully enroll because of the time required to meet young people where they are at. Similarly, accountability measures need to take into account young people's engagement patterns.

Accountability should be to communities and youth themselves as well as to government and foundations. This can be done by including young people on boards of directors where possible and by including young people in decision-making structures within programs and within communities. Examples include lowering the age limit on community boards that make decisions on neighborhood land usage and zoning, creating processes

for meaningful input into programs through the creation of youth councils, and instilling democratic decision-making practices that include youth in organizational decision-making. This has a dual goal of fostering youth voice within programs and communities and developing young people who are able to navigate and lead organizations (Heathfield & Fusco, 2016; Wu et al., 2016).

The future of youth work demands the ability of youth workers to simultaneously work in partnership with young people to challenge injustice in their lives while working against the injustice that impedes the implementation of effective programs. As proclaimed by Nelson Mandela: 'Like slavery and apartheid, poverty is not natural. It is man-made and it can be overcome and eradicated by the actions of human beings' (https://www.theguardian.com/world/2005/feb/03/hearafrica05.development). The parallel suppression of young people's opportunities and the compression of the organizations that expand these are social constructs. The future of youth work depends on using the tools the field has at hand to open up space for opportunity and hope. Unless we do so, we fail the young people who most need our support. If we can reshape systems to be responsive, we create programs that address holistic human development; we enlarge the opportunities open for youth who are most in need and hardest to reach; and we develop a generation with the skills to shape a more just world.

REFERENCES

Akiva, T. (2005). Turning training into results: The new youth program quality assessment. *High/Scope ReSource*, Winter, 21–24. Retrieved from https://www.academia.edu/1319423/Turning_training_into_results_The_new_youth_program_quality_assessment?auto=download

Akiva, T., Phillips, S., & McGovern, G. (2011). Youth voice. Ann Arbor, WI: David P. Weikart Center for Youth Program Quality.

Allen, L., Rasmussen, M., & Quinlivan, K. (Eds.) (2013). *The politics of pleasure in sexuality education*. New York, NY: Routledge.

Baldridge, B. J. (2014). Relocating the deficit: Reimagining black youth in neoliberal times. *American Educational Research Journal*, *51*(3), 1–33.

Bay-Cheng, L. Y. (2015). The agency line: A neoliberal metric for appraising young women's sexuality. *Sex Roles*, *73*(7–8), 279–291.

Brown, J. D., El-Toukhy, S., & Ortiz. R. (2014). Growing up sexually in a digital world: The risks and benefits of youths' sexual media use. In A.B. Jordan & D. Romer (Eds.), *Media and the well-being of children and adolescents* (pp. 90–108). New York: Oxford University Press.

Connell, R. W. (2005). *Masculinities*. Berkeley: University of California Press.

Connell, R. W. (2014). *Gender and power: Society, the person and sexual politics*. New York: John Wiley & Sons.

Evans, S. (2007). Youth sense of community: Voice and power in community contexts. *Journal of Community Psychology*, *35*(6), 693–709.

Fernandes-Alcantara, A. L. (2012). *Vulnerable youth: Background and policies*. Washington, DC: Congressional Research Service.

Fusco, D., Lawrence, A., Matloff-Nieves, S., & Ramos, E. (2013). The Accordion Effect: Is quality in afterschool getting the squeeze? *Journal of Youth Development*, *8*. (online). Retrieved from https://www.academia.edu/1319423/Turning_training_into_results_The_new_youth_program_quality_assessment?auto=download

Gorski, P. (2010). Unlearning deficit ideology and the scornful gaze: Thoughts on authenticating the class discourse in education. *EdChange*. Retrieved from http://www.edchange.org/publications/deficit-ideology-scornful-gaze.pdf

Halpern, R. (2002). A different kind of child development institution: The history of afterschool programs for low-income children. *Teachers College Record*, *104*(2), 178–211.

Heathfield, M. & Fusco, D. (2016). From hope to wise action: The future of youth work and other global actions in education. In M. Heathfield & D. Fusco (Eds), *Youth and inequality in education: Global actions in youth work* (pp. 295–307). New York: Routledge.

Human Services Council (2016). New York nonprofits in the aftermath of FEGS: A call to action. Retrieved from https://www.google.com/search?q=human+services+council+fegs+report&oq=human+services+council+report&aqs=chrome.1.69i57j0.12360j0j8&sourceid=chrome&ie=UTF-8

Kaplan, L. (2016). NYC service providers getting squeezed by problematic government contracts. Retrieved from http://nonprofit-quarterly.org/2016/04/11/nyc-service-providers-getting-squeezed-by-problematic-government-contracts/

Kimmel, M. (1995). *Manhood in America*. New York: Free Press.

Kimmel, M. S., & Mahler, M. (2003). Adolescent masculinity, homophobia, and violence: Random school shootings, 1982–2001. *American Behavioral Scientist*, *46*(10), 1439–1458.

Laroche, H., & Klein, J. (2008). Lessons from the front lines: Factors that contribute to turnover among youth development workers. *Journal of Youth Development*, *2* (online).

Matloff-Nieves, S., Fusco, D., Connolly, J., & Maulik, M. (2016). Democratizing urban spaces: A social justice approach to youth work. In M. Heathfield & D. Fusco (Eds.), *Youth and inequality in education: Global actions in youth work* (pp. 175–195). New York: Routledge.

McLaughlin, M. (2000). *Community counts*. Washington, DC: Public Education Network.

McLaughlin, M., Irby, M.A., & Langman, J. (1994). *Urban sanctuaries: Neighborhood organizations in the lives and futures of inner-city youth*. San Francisco, CA: Jossey-Bass; Wiley.

Messner, M. (1989). Masculinities and athletic careers. *Gender & Society*, *3*(1), 71–88.

Messner, M. (1990). Boyhood, organized sports, and the construction of masculinities. *Journal of Contemporary Ethnography*, *18*(4), 416–444.

Miller, B. (2003). *Critical hours: Afterschool programs and educational success*. Quincy, MA: Nellie Mae Education Foundation.

NYC DYCD (New York City Department of Youth and Community Development) (2013). *2002–2013: A DYCD retrospective on quality, equity and accountability*. New York, NY: Department of Youth and Community Development.

NYC DYCD (New York City Department of Youth and Community Development) (2016). History. Retrieved from https://www1.nyc.gov/site/dycd/about/about-dycd/history.page

Olweus, D. (1993). Bullies on the playground: The role of victimization. In C. Hart (Ed.), *Children on playgrounds: Research perspectives and applications* (pp. 85–128). Albany, NY: State University of New York Press.

Payne, E., & Smith, M. (2012). Rethinking safe schools approaches for LGBTQ students: Changing the questions we ask. *Multicultural Perspectives*, *14*(4), 187–193.

Petersen, A. C., & McClure, G. D. (2003). Private foundation support of youth development. In D. Wertlieb, F. Jacobs, & R. M. Lerner (Eds.), *Handbook of applied developmental science* (pp. 403–423). London: Sage.

Pleck, J. H. (1981). *The myth of masculinity*. Cambridge, MA: MIT Press.

Ringrose, J., & Renold, E. (2010). Normative cruelties and gender deviants: The performative effects of bully discourses for girls and boys in school. *British Educational Research Journal*, *36*(4), 573–596.

Schorr, L. (1996). *Common purpose: Strengthening families and neighborhoods to rebuild. America*. New York: Anchor Books.

Sesso, A., & Wylde, K. (2016). Rush to the rescue of NYC's nonprofits: It's a crisis moment. Retrieved from http://nydailynews.com/opinion/sesso-wylde-rush-rescue-nyc-nonprofits-article-1.2549531

Tolman, D. L. (2012). Female adolescents, sexual empowerment and desire: A missing discourse of gender inequity. *Sex Roles*, *66*(11–12), 746–757.

Wu, H., Kornbluh, M, Weiss, J., & Roddy, L. (2016). Measuring and understanding authentic youth engagement: The youth-adult partnership rubric. *After School Matters*, *23*(Spring), 8–17.

41

Uncomfortable Knowledge and the Ethics of Good Practice in Australia's Offshore Refugee Detention Centers

Judith Bessant and Rob Watts

INTRODUCTION

There is a widely shared view that youth work is essentially a 'practical' job. From this perspective wanting to help young people is the basis of good youth work, requiring only the addition of some basic technical or vocational training. According to proponents of this view, university-based education of practitioners promotes an imbalance between theory and practice such that the excessively theoretical character of youth work education leads graduates and employers alike to complain that they do not have the relevant 'practical' skills (Brooker, 2014). This becomes part of a case for removing youth work education from universities.

We are not so sure about this. The question of what youth workers need to know if they are to engage in good practice is a challenge. Good practice involves the idea that we do the right thing for the right reasons. Yet like most simple things it is difficult to achieve.

While it is one of a number of considerations, the emergent field of 'ignorance studies' suggests that professional knowledge is always shadowed by various forms of ignorance, which can frustrate or prevent good practice. This is the case if we opt for 'preferred ignorance', which occurs when we choose not to know things which are difficult or painful, or 'presumed knowledge', which relies on unwarranted confidence in what we think we know (Gross & McGoey, 2015). We argue that good practice involves the capacity of professionals to untangle the relationship between different kinds of knowledge and different forms of ignorance, something university education ought to enable graduates to do.

The need to do this arises especially when professionals encounter 'uncomfortable knowledge' (Flyvbjerg, 2013). Uncomfortable knowledge involves for example, the discovery by youth workers that young people are being treated poorly or that other professionals are engaging in bad practice like bullying, corruption, harassment, and other harmful actions. We argue that recognizing and responding to uncomfortable knowledge is critical for securing the well-being of young people and constitutes good practice, as implied in the fiduciary responsibility all youth work practitioners have for the young people they work with (Flyvbjerg, 2001).

Engaging with good practice necessarily raises difficult questions about what we know and how we are to provide good answers to practical, i.e., ethical questions. The need to address these issues is highlighted by what happened when Save the Children Australia, a major non-government organization took on a tender to work in Australia's asylum-seeker detention camps on Nauru in 2013 and 2014. In a classic example of preferred ignorance, managers in the organization entered into a contract with a major private security company to supply child protection and youth work services to 'help' the children and young people detained on Nauru. They did this knowing the camps breached international legal and human rights conventions. Its youth work employees were forced to face the horrors of the camp and opted to act as 'whistleblowers' which led them to being forcibly removed from Nauru, some of them facing criminal prosecution. Faced with 'uncomfortable knowledge' of an extreme set of circumstances these youth workers opted for good practice. We begin by outlining the case study before considering some of the implications of this for a curriculum that might help prepare youth workers to think about difficult practice issues as they arise in the field.

AUSTRALIAN ASYLUM-SEEKER POLICY: 1989–2016

Since the late 1980s every Australian government has regarded all asylum-seekers arriving on Australian shores without appropriate documentation as illegal entrants. Even though they have a right to seek asylum under international law and should not be penalized for their mode of entry, those asylum-seekers arriving in Australia by boat are treated as 'unlawful non-citizens' (Phillips, 2015, p. 1) and are detained in high security institutions. The policy of mandatory detention involves the incarceration of men, women and children in high-security camps originally in locations around the Australian mainland for the period that their application for refugee status was being processed. It has become one of the most contentious issues in Australia's political history.

Between 2001 and 2008 and again since 2012, Australia moved to redefine its migration zone, and signed memorandums of understanding with Nauru and Papua-New Guinea to establish offshore detention camps. In August 2012, the Gillard Labor government re-opened three camps in Nauru. As has become common in the era of neo-liberal governance, the operation of these detention camps was outsourced to a private asset-management business. The policy of outsourcing the detention and processing of asylum-seekers to a third country has had the effect of thwarting detailed judicial or public scrutiny of the camps (Dastyari, 2015).

As many commentators observe, the establishment of these camps and the arbitrary detention of asylum-seekers without trial or due legal process constitutes a serious contravention of international human rights law, especially of the United Nations Convention on the Rights of the Child. As the Australian Human Rights Commission noted, 'no other country mandates the closed and indefinite detention of children when they arrive on our shores' (AHRC, 2014, p. 11). Australia's asylum-seeker policy operates against a backdrop of a long history of states engaging in illegal detention of selected populations in camps deemed 'sites of legal exception' (Agamben, 1998). The UN Committee on the Rights of the Child (2012) has expressed its deep concern about the mandatory detention policy, while both the UN Committee against Torture and the UN Human Rights Committee have recommended that Australia abolish mandatory detention (United Nations Committee against Torture, 2008; United Nations Human Rights Committee, 2009). The Australian Human Rights Commission (2006, 2014) laid out the grounds for its concern. While Section 4AA of the Commonwealth Migration Act states that 'a minor shall only be detained as a measure of last resort', in practice the detention of young asylum-seekers had become a defining feature of Australian Government policy. By requiring the mandatory detention of all 'non-citizen children' in Australia without a valid visa, Australia's asylum-seeker policy did the opposite of what was required. While successive governments promised repeatedly that children and young people would be removed from the camps, this had not happened: in March 2016 over a hundred people under 18 were still detained in Nauru alone. Australia's asylum-seeker policies reveal the truth of Schattschneider's point that 'the definition of the alternatives is the supreme instrument of power' (1975, p. 66).

Save the Children Australia

What is happening in these sites is an important issue in a book devoted to youth work. This is because, in October 2012, Save the Children Australia (SCA) tendered successfully to Transfield Services, a publicly listed company that specializes in the provision of industrial infrastructure services and that successfully tendered to provide services for Australia's offshore immigration centers. In 2012, Transfield subcontracted SCA to deliver child protection and youth work services on Manus Island.

While SCA had strongly and publicly objected to the policy of mandatory detention, especially of children in offshore immigration detention camps, in 2012 it tendered

to provide education, recreation and child-protection services to unaccompanied children, children in families, childless couples and single mothers in the camps. The decision to tender for a contract to provide these services was justified on grounds frequently adduced by those working in the human services, namely that the children and young people in offshore centers 'need our help'. It also justified its action by claiming it would take every step to ensure that the environment was 'fit for a child' (SCA, 2016b). It claimed the beneficent mantle of professional altruists when it said that its child protection staff and youth workers were all 'well-qualified workers' possessing degrees in social work, human services or psychology, or else had TAFE Certificate IVs in Child Services or Youth Work. While it had agreed to sign off on government-imposed confidentiality clauses and other forms of intellectual property, SCA claimed it would still be able to advocate on behalf of children.

This convergence of philanthropic altruism on the part of an NGO and Hobbesian misanthropy on the part of the state began to unravel in 2014 when a number of the nine or so child protection workers employed by SCA in Nauru became whistleblowers. Through 2014 the Australian Human Rights Commission (AHRC) had been running an inquiry into the approximately 800 children and young people held in mandatory detention. The youth workers on Nauru made an anonymous submission to that inquiry outlining their serious concerns about what was taking place in the camps. The AHRC report subsequently identified 'Submission No. 183' as a submission made by employees of SCA.

Once it became clear who the whistleblowers were, the Australian (Abbott) government, relying on a security report provided by Wilsons Security (sub-contracted by Transfield to provide security in detention centers on Manus and Nauru), claimed that not only had the workers engaged in whistleblowing, they had also actively fomented strife among the detainees by encouraging them to self-harm. The Abbott government ordered the forced removal of those workers from Nauru. Soon after, the government's Department of Immigration and Border Protection referred the matter to the federal police for investigation of possible breaches of Section 70 of the Crimes Act. A subsequent review found the claims that the child protection workers had encouraged detainees on Nauru to self-harm as part of a political campaign to embarrass the government to be groundless (Doogan, 2015). The contract with SCA was not renewed.

GOOD PRACTICE

Good practice involves the idea that when we relate to other people in our capacity as teachers, doctors, parents or strangers we do the right thing for the right reasons. In short, good practice involves three dimensions. Firstly, it requires knowing the truth of what is happening, which entails thinking and knowing. Secondly, good judgments are required about what is the good thing to do. Finally, will and courage are needed to act in ways that are in accord with that judgment. Good practice is different from today's verbiage of 'best practice', derived from the rational-technical model of practice. The origins of 'best practice' are found in business environments and management textbooks and rely heavily on compliance with rules and criteria used as part of accredited management standards.

Human service professions like youth work, social work, psychology, teaching and counseling have long assumed that professional practice can and should emulate the relationship between theory and practice found in professions like medicine and engineering (Schön, 1983). It is a relationship which can be described as a binary in which scientific theory is constructed by academic researchers and models of practice by professional educators (Ord, 2007). According to this account,

practice emerges from and is dependent on theory (Buchroth & Parkin, 2010). In this way there is a tendency to see practice as technical-rational action which involves following rules and protocols.

This account of theory and practice has been durable in spite of warnings from writers like Schön (1983) about the fragile assumptions it relies on. Others like Bourdieu (1977) likewise reject the model of objective and technical practice informed by a scientific body of theory because its advocates fail to acknowledge the power of the state or the way fields of practice are implicated in reproducing fundamental asymmetries of social and economic power. Salkever (1991) and Flyvbjerg (2001) argued against the application of scientific method as used in the physical sciences to social relations and practices. We agree with them that Aristotle's account of three kinds of knowledge helps clarify the kinds of knowledge that human service professionals require, including, above all else, the practical wisdom (*phronesis*) that underpins good (but not necessarily 'best') practice (Flyvbjerg, 2001).

In Aristotle's account, practical wisdom is different from the other two kinds of knowledge, namely *episteme* (theoretical science) and *techne* (technical know-how). *Episteme* refers to abstracted generalized knowledge consisting of timeless scientific and mathematical truths or theories about the natural world and the cosmos. These are often expressed as mathematical equations like Pythagoras's theorem, or as laws about the physical world like Newton's law of gravity. The second kind of knowledge is *poeisis*, which relies on *techne* (skills) used to make 'useful' or 'beautiful' things like clothing, houses, furniture, poetry or medicine. Each of these kinds of knowing and doing are important and valuable. Yet the best use of them depends on understanding their end purpose. If we want to establish how to best live with and engage with other people then it is important to cultivate a capacity for *phronesis* or practical wisdom (Aristotle, 2002).

As Schwartz and Sharpe (2011) argue, practical wisdom is a way of thinking and knowing that does not rely on rules or generalized abstract laws. Unlike *episteme*, practical wisdom does not seek timeless or eternal truth, nor does it pursue technical knowledge: it is context-sensitive and for this reason enquires into the problem of good practice on a case-by-case basis. This requires thinking about each situation and establishing what is actually happening and then working out the best thing to do. It relies on an ethnographic sensibility that involves straddling the local and the global. It relies on having clarity of purpose (*telos*) about our practice framed by an interest in promoting the relevant human goods without which our lives become less valuable. It entails asking questions like: What are our choices? What are the costs? Are they desirable? Who wins? Who loses? In short, practical wisdom is central to good practice. And, as we now argue, it requires an ability to recognize the complex relation between knowledge and various kinds of ignorance generated in the face of uncomfortable knowledge. This is a capability that needs to be embedded in the youth work curriculum.

Knowing and Ignorance

In her discussion of the banality of evil, Arendt (1963) drew our attention to the disposition of 'ordinary people' to do bad things to other people. Midgley (2001) likewise accepts the ubiquity of ordinary 'wickedness'. Observing that ordinary 'people often do treat each other abominably' Midgley asks why this happens (p. 2). She says there are no simple answers, but that it has something to do with whether we know what is happening or what the consequences of our choices might be. This insight raises the question of what we think we know.

Some continue to bear witness to the Enlightenment idea that 'knowledge when systematically produced through adherence to reliable methods of data collection or extraction will inevitably trump superstition' (Gross & McGoey, 2015, p. 8). As recent developments in the field of ignorance studies suggests, there are good reasons to reconsider this. As Gross and McGoey (2015) observe, 'what is not known is often a challenging and unpopular field of research and teaching' (p. 7). Yet this is precisely what Haas and Vogt (2015) suggest when they point to the many kinds of ignorance, each involving the absence of knowledge. While lies and deception matter, we are more interested in two other kinds of ignorance because they both obstruct good practice. The first is preferred ignorance, which is based on a choice or preference not to know, such as when people do bad things because they have not thought about the principles at stake or the consequences of what they are doing. In effect they chose or expressed a preference for ignorance over knowing (Midgley, 2001). The other kind of ignorance is presumed knowledge (Haas & Vogt, 2015). This is a widespread form of ignorance masked by a certainty that we know. It may be based on processes that have us think that the wrong we are doing is a good deed. This is the ignorance of presumed knowledge.

SCA and Ignorance

We argue that SCA began delivering child protection and other welfare services on Nauru in a state of preferred ignorance (the choice to not know). The main justification offered by the organization for the decision to work in the camps on Nauru was that they would provide services to children in offshore camps because 'they need our help'. Moreover, they would take every step to ensure 'the environment was fit for a child'. We ask: what kind of ignorance informed such a statement?

We know that months before SCA arrived in Nauru in 2013, an Amnesty International team visited the camps in Nauru and reported how 'conditions were far worse than anything we'd seen in our tour of Australia's detention centers this year' (Amnesty, 2012). They also pointed to: '… a toxic mix of uncertainty, unlawful detention and inhumane conditions that are creating an increasingly volatile situation, with the Australian Government failing spectacularly in its duty of care to asylum seekers' (Amnesty, 2012). They reported how human rights were 'completely sidelined' and provided a graphic account of the living conditions:

> Asylum seekers are staying in army tents. The standard of life under rough tents (leaky and hot) is even not suitable for cattle. These tents offer absolutely no privacy, and barely have any room between the stretcher beds. In the camp [the] temperature reaches over 40 degrees in the compound and 80 percent humidity. The heat means people can't stay in their tents during the day. Most find it hard to sleep in the tents – either because of the extreme heat, the dampness, or because of men crying during the night. This all exacerbates the deterioration of their mental health. (ibid)

What kind of ignorance might allow people in an organization to ignore what placing a child or a young person into a high security camp would do to those young people? More worrying, 'as the medical evidence … mounted over the last eight months of the Inquiry' (AHRC, 2014), was the inability of the Human Rights Commission to understand the policy of either the Labor or Coalition Governments: both the Hon Chris Bowen MP, as a former Minister for Immigration, and the Hon Scott Morrison MP, the current Minister for Immigration, agreed on oath before the Inquiry that holding children in detention does not deter either asylum-seekers or people smugglers. No satisfactory rationale for the prolonged detention of children seeking asylum in Australia has been offered (AHRC, 2014). The Australian Human Rights Commission had also made it clear that mandatory immigration detention has always contravened Australia's international legal obligations.

The AHRC and respective Presidents and Commissioners over the last 25 years have been unanimous in reporting that such detention, especially of children, breaches the right of people not to be detained arbitrarily (AHRC, 2014).

While raising these questions it is not currently possible to say how or why those responsible for tendering for the Transfield contract came to their decision to work in Nauru. What is clear is that decision subverted everything SCA says it stands for: 'our policies, procedures and guidelines ensure we uphold the integrity of our work and that we are always working in the best interests of children' (SCA, 2016a). Elaborating on that position, SCA says it is a rights-based organization. Those who work for SCA endorse the concept of human rights in general and particularly children's rights. It also argues that its work is 'underpinned by the UN Convention on the Rights of the Child which states that children and young people should be protected from all forms of physical and mental violence, injury, abuse, neglect, maltreatment and exploitation, including sexual abuse' (SCA, 2016a). They declare a commitment to child protection based on the following principles: promoting and protecting the best interests of children at all times; zero tolerance of child abuse; and that child protection is a shared responsibility between the organization, all personnel and associates, its partners and the communities in which it works (SCA, 2016a).

It remains unclear why or how an organization that says it is committed to these principles can knowingly enter a space of 'legal exception' with well-known conditions (like extreme climate and a high-security regime), and run by a government that ignores human rights obligations as part of a commitment to 'deterring' asylum-seekers by making clear to all would-be asylum-seekers the harshness of the regime they would encounter. We accept up to a point that the management of SCA may have sincerely believed they could 'make a difference', just as we might accept that many youth workers go into homes where they know children are being abused by their parents and choose to remove them and put them into poorly funded and managed child-welfare facilities where they are further neglected or abused. However, this decision by SCA is difficult to understand given their acknowledgement that its own 'experience shows that sending people to offshore detention centers threatens their physical, mental and emotional wellbeing' (SCA, 2016b).

Child Protection Workers and Uncomfortable Knowledge

The case of the practitioners employed on Nauru raises the problem of 'uncomfortable knowledge'. Uncomfortable knowledge refers to knowledge of bad things going on that requires some remedial action (Rayner, 2012). For Flyvbjerg (2013) uncomfortable knowledge includes knowledge of corruption, lying, socially harmful practices, poor management and malfeasance. It may include corrupt or illegal conduct including bribery, fraud, sexual assault, manslaughter or culpable negligence leading to death or injury committed by organizations and the state.

Flyvbjerg (2013) argues that when people in organizations come to know certain things like this they typically pursue four options: denial, dismissal, diversion or displacement. These can be treated as modalities of 'preferred ignorance'. The standard approaches to 'uncomfortable knowledge' according to Cohen (2001) include either outright denial that there is a problem or else dismissing or rejecting evidence that there is something wrong. All this diverts attention from the 'uncomfortable knowledge' to some other factor. There are also strategies like diversion, that is, paying attention to some other issue or some kind of displacement by claiming the problem is really something else, which is then addressed (Cohen, 2001). In the case presented here we see two kinds of

responses: in the camps the youth workers paid attention to what they thought they could do by contacting their managers to express their concerns (diversion); those managers in turn responded by dismissing their concerns, telling their workers not to bother as any 'advocacy will not make a difference and will be a waste of time' (dismissal) (Submission No. 183, 2015, p. 18).

What did the workers employed by SCA on Nauru experience? We know something about this because they summarized their experience and the evidence they had of many basic breaches of the UNCRC as well as Australian child protection protocols in their Submission 183 to the Australian Human Rights Commission. The submission provides evidence of their distress in almost every aspect of their workplace. It began with the government-imposed ignorance that is produced when states require by law secrecy about their activities: 'Unfortunately, due to confidentiality clauses that have been imposed by the Department of Immigration and Border Protection, we are unable to provide our full names and previous/current titles with this submission and will remain anonymous' (Submission No. 183, 2015, p. 1).

That did not prevent the practitioners from making a comprehensive submission detailing the conditions operating on Nauru, including the extreme heat, substandard housing, the lack of resources and details about the way the detention camp was operated. Their submission was that the 'children on Nauru had been subjected to multiple violations of their human rights and wrong doing from multiple parties' (Submission No. 183, 2015, p. 1). As Paul Ronalds, CEO of SCA, acknowledged after the event: 'we know from two years on Nauru about the shocking impact that prolonged incarceration has on people seeking asylum. It is unquestioningly harmful to their mental and physical wellbeing' (SCA, 2016a, p. 1). Employees of *Save the Children Australia* forced by confidentiality clauses imposed on them by the Australian government to give anonymous evidence to the Human Rights Commission, emphasised how the general environment of the Nauru camp served as a constant source of emotional and physical stress:

High noise levels, the presence of uniformed security and security in riot gear, frequent episodes of emergencies (self-harming, violence, urgent medical issues) serve as triggers for previous trauma that children have experienced as well as exacerbate distress and mental health issues, delay recovery, and create additional mental health concerns. (National Inquiry into Children in Immigration Detention 2015 Submission No 183: 5)

The indefinite length of detention caused despair, a sense of hopelessness and depression, effecting school attendance and leading in some cases to self-harm. As the workers pointed out, families who had been in the camp since September 2013 had not seen one application for asylum processed by May 2014. These included young people who had fled Syria already traumatized by war, torture killings, and unjust treatment at the hands of security forces and others. Seeing the deterioration of their parents' physical and mental health also harmed already traumatized young people. Each day they remain in detention 'exposes them to witnessing additional traumatic situations ... which serves as triggers to past traumatic events and delays their ability to recover from previous trauma' (ibid, p. 9).

The workers were concerned about the dehumanization of the children and inadequacy of educational services. They reported the practice of referring to young people and children by their 'numbers' instead of their name and noted how even the young people came to 'identify themselves as a number more than by their name' (ibid, p. 53). There were inadequate supplies of books, paper, pens and pencils; there was no specialist curriculum to assist English Language learning or special needs, and there was inadequate access to recreation, education and social engagement. The children and

young people experienced high levels of stress fatigue and found concentrating hard, which in turn effected their capacity to study and impacted on their mental health. They described the cramped living conditions, with 12 to 15 families living in one-room tents with no air-conditioning. This led to a lack of privacy to discuss issues of safety, abuse and health concerns, which made people reluctant to raise issues because they were embarrassed or afraid of retribution, retaliation or stigmatization.

They described the lack of appropriate clothing and footwear, where inadequate underclothes placed them at 'risk of sexual exploitation, shame and social isolation' (ibid, p. 19). One boy 'had his private parts showing in public because the only clothes he was given were two pair of shorts, one of which was badly torn ... he was not provided with any underwear ...' (ibid, pp. 46–47). In the case of a 13-year-old male who bed wets, despite several requests 'from the torture and trauma team regarding the need for extra linen and cleaning detergent, the things requested were not forthcoming' (ibid, p. 46). Another 13-year-old female had only two pairs of underwear and only one she could use while she had her period.

Workers also became aware of criminal and sexual assaults and multiple violations of the human rights of children and young people. They supplied evidence concerning 12 cases of sexual and physical assault affecting children and young people. One young female was 'put at risk of serious sexual assault after one of her relatives made complaints about bullying. Several adult males in the camp were overheard making plans to assault this teenage female. Some of her relatives also received death threats' (ibid, p. 13). The absence of child protection laws in Nauru means it is very difficult to prosecute crimes against children and young people. Many of those victimized in the camp do not report abuse because they know 'nothing will be done' (ibid, p. 10). Workers were equally concerned about their inability to remove children from situations of abuse within the camp or worse, from within their own families. In this respect the framework of government policy and the operating procedures adopted by Transfield and Wilson Security meant that SCA were not able to implement anything like 'normal' child protection practices.

Nauru and Prospects for Good Practice

We know that SCA workers on Nauru raised their concerns with Transfield and Wilson Security, the people responsible for running the camps. We can infer from their submission to the AHRC that they repeatedly attempted to bring their concerns to the attention of company officials. We assume they did so in the light of a clear frame of ethical practice developed by SCA Australia.

SCA Australia has constructed its organizational identity on the basis of its declared commitment to ensuring that all its activities are conducted legally, ethically and in accordance with high standards of integrity. Board members, employees and volunteers are required to signify acceptance of, and compliance with, the organization's Child Protection Policy and Code of Conduct. All employees are also required to sign a statement that includes the following affirmation: 'I understand that it is my responsibility, as a person employed/engaged by SCA Australia, to use common sense and avoid actions that are abusive or exploitative of children and young people, or could be construed as such' (STC, 2010: 9).

In addition, its own code of conduct outlines a clear process for reporting suspected cases of child abuse. It makes it mandatory that in the reporting of alleged or suspected cases of child abuse – 'all personnel, associates and representatives of SCA must report any concerns they have for the safety or wellbeing of a child. Reports will be handled professionally, confidentially and as quickly as possible and will meet country, state or territory specific legislative requirements' (ibid, p. 6). SCA further stipulates that such allegations are to be made to their own Child Protection Technical Unit (CPTU). In addition: SCA must immediately notify the Department of Foreign Affairs and Trade (DFAT), Child Protection Compliance Section, if any DFAT-Australian Aid funded personnel, or DFAT-Australian Aid partner personnel, are accused of, charged with, arrested for, or convicted of criminal offences relating to child exploitation and abuse. Yet, the organization's claim to uphold child protection principles was shown in a new light as workers reported they were 'actively discouraged from advocating for the removal of children by SCA management' (Submission No. 183, 2015, p. 18). They were also frustrated by the absence of mechanisms like the use of police checks on people working with children in Nauru and weak or non-existent Nauruan child protection legislation.

We do not know all the details of how or when workers decided to make the disclosures once it became evident that the two corporations, Transfield and Wilson Security, were not going to address their concerns. What was at stake in this Nauru case is reflected in the following two pieces of research, which ought to have a role in the youth work curriculum.

Obedience and Conscience

Firstly, there is a body of social science research indicating what many of us will do when confronted by uncomfortable knowledge. Milgram's (1974) research designed to test people's ethical values in a social setting obliging them to obey authority still makes for uncomfortable reading. There is no evidence suggesting that human service professionals do any better than other 'ordinary people'.

In the late 1960s Milgram ran experiments at Yale University's Interaction Laboratories to establish the extent to which people would obey a legitimate authority figure requiring them to inflict pain, even lethal force on an innocent person. Those who volunteered to be research subjects were briefed on the experiment before entering the laboratory, where they met a 'scientific figure in a white coat' and the 'experimental subject'. The 'experimental subject' was wired to an instrument panel and the volunteer was asked to sit behind it. Under instruction from the 'scientist' the volunteer was required to administer a series of electric punishments said to assist the subject's memory. The findings of the research were that volunteers complied with the instructions even though they believed they were inflicting pain. Unbeknown to the volunteer at the time, the equipment, the 'experimental subject', the scientist and the electric shocks were all fake (Milgram, 1974).

In many repeated versions of this experiment, 65–75 percent of volunteers went through to the end (Blass, 1991). They did so even when they could see their action was causing the 'experiment subject' pain and even when the subject pleaded for the experiment to stop (Blass, 1991). Milgram found that the 'basic structure of the authority situation' constructed in the scientific laboratory meant that actors could decide not to see themselves as personally responsible for the consequences of their actions. This was because they saw themselves as having no choice with regard to their actions: they were doing as instructed and did not feel personally responsible.

Secondly, on the other hand, Linn's (1996) research reveals how a smaller number of people obey their conscience when told to do something quite bad. Linn's focus was on Israeli troops who refused orders to shoot at young Palestinian protestors in the late 1980s and early 1990s. It is research that contrasts with research like Milgram's (1974) and highlights a disposition toward binding authority and the silencing of conscience. The usual approach to conscience sees it as a highly individual and rational process. The practice of conscience takes on a different

appearance in Linn's study. Linn's research into the work of listening to and obeying the 'voice of conscience' suggests that we need to approach our ethical practices as emotional practices that reflect and draw on the resources of identity and character. She argues there is a complex play of moral emotions operating on the part of those who reject the call to obey authority. Linn's account of conscientious objection revealed how small numbers of soldiers acted against the dominant moral consensus that existed in their national community and rejected the requirements of obedience to orders.

Linn (1996) did not accept the common-sense Durkheimian account of 'the social' as a moral order in which only two options are possible; namely, conformity or deviance. Linn's idea of the social is different in the ways particular organizations like the army or the police force have their own morally coercive qualities and sanctions. Within that specific social-military context, the capacity for moral action she studied was particularly courageous. Linn offers an understanding of social process in which certain dialogical qualities of ethical practices and self-formation are evident in ways suggested by Charles Taylor when he writes how both 'communities' and 'the self' are dialogically constituted: 'We become full human agents capable of understanding ourselves, and hence of defining our identity, through our acquisition of rich human languages of expression ... we learn these modes of expression through exchanges with others' (1992, p. 32).

As Linn argues, the dialogical qualities of self and community require the questioning of the conventional understanding of our conscience as an individual rational process. This requires that we bypass the Kantian idea of conscience as the voice of a completely rational and autonomous individual. According to Habermas (1990), the conscientious objector exercises their own practical judgment by focusing on their moral principles and disconnecting themselves from their social setting. Habermas considers whether social actors have the cognitive ability to be 'rational' and 'distance themselves from the controversy' (p. 162).

Linn agrees that the Israeli soldiers she interviewed distanced themselves from their immediate social and institutional context where military officers required obedience to orders which they found objectionable. Yet for Linn these narratives of moral separateness are actually examples of 'moral connectedness'. The resistor is better understood as tied to the world not only by principles but also by powerful moral emotions – which are social and which constitute and are foundational to their sense of self. As Michael Walzer observed, the conscientious objector is not only committed to moral principles, but also to other people '... from whom or with whom the principles have been learned and by whom they are enforced' (1970, p. 5). The resistor's moral commitment emerges from the conviction and understanding that if injustice is done in the resistor's name '... or it is done to my people, I must speak out against it' (Walzer, 1988, p. 23).

For Linn, conscience was central to the soldiers' resistance because it provided both the incentive to act as well as the rationale for that action. Her account of how this conscience manifested itself illuminates how this process worked emotionally. She explains that there was no lengthy process of deliberation or analysis, but rather a sudden feeling about what the 'right thing to do' was. In the authoritarian settings in which the soldiers lived, the moral resistor did not ask themself what moral principles were violated. As one soldier explained: 'There was no specific reason for my refusal, I just felt I should not be able to do it [reserve service in the occupied territories] to disperse demonstrations of kids and women [where] an old person has been killed ...' (Linn, 1996, p. 102). Another told her: 'In the case of refusal you first feel that you have no option but to act in a certain way. It is a very strong feeling and you cannot stay calm unless you do it. Only then does one's moral thought become clear' (ibid, p. 103).

We expect this may be close to what some workers on Nauru also experienced.

CONCLUSION

The youth workers on Nauru confronted a particularly difficult version of a widespread problem confronting youth workers and other human service professionals in sites of practice now shaped by neoliberalism. Brown (2015) argues that neoliberalism is a specific governing rationality in which everything is 'economized'. This extends even to border protection and the decision to award Transfield, a private company, a billion-dollar contract to run Australia's offshore detention centers. On this account, protecting Australians from asylum-seekers was not merely outsourced but thoroughly recast as a private good for individual investment or consumption. At the same time this encourages the idea that companies and governments alike should focus on 'best practice' (Bardach, 2011; Bogan & English, 1994). At the least this produces serious incongruity.

In Nauru we saw practitioners working within an incongruent policy frame. The Australian government argued that mandatory detention of young asylum-seekers did not hurt them, even as it hastened to transfer responsibility for high-security detention centers to a multi-billion-dollar corporation. Yet it was a transfer that did nothing to protect the government from breaching its own laws. While Section 4AA of the Commonwealth Migration Act states that a minor shall only be detained as a measure of last resort, in practice the detention of children is the first action taken by the Australian Government. A range of respected international agencies, including the United Nations Refugee Agency (UNHCR, 2013) and Amnesty International (Amnesty International, 2014), concur that Australia's arbitrary and indefinite detention of asylum-seekers, including young people and children, in appalling conditions, amounts to grievous harm.

From the welfare sector came claims by a professional child protection and youth work service (SCA) that it could not only help the young victims of an inhumane and unlawful regime, but also convert a mandatory detention center into 'a fit place' in which those young people might thrive. Some of the professionals who worked at Nauru struggled when faced with 'uncomfortable knowledge' like the discovery that the outsourcing of asylum-seeker detention centers involved underfunding and mandatory detention that seriously harmed children and young people to the point of exposing them to serious physical abuse, sexual violence and psychological harm (Submission No. 183, 2015).

Some practitioners on Nauru exhibited a rare capacity for good practice. They worked out what was actually happening. They listened to and followed their conscience. The only kind of good practice available to those workers in Nauru was to speak out. Exhibiting uncommon courage they did so. The only option for good practice available to them was to express their concern, firstly to their own managers in SCA. When that failed, they made disclosures about the harms caused to young people in Nauru detention center, including disclosures to an official enquiry by Australia's Human Rights Commission.

We expect that many other youth workers, social workers, psychologists and managers will see parallels with this case study and their own experiences as they also struggle to work out what is happening and how to respond to particular local versions of 'uncomfortable knowledge'.

There are two questions that need asking: What does good practice look like? How can youth work educators enable their students to do it?

After the introduction of Australia's Border Force Act 2015, Brian Owler, president of the Australian Medical Association, denounced Australia's treatment of asylum-seekers, describing it as 'state-sanctioned child abuse'. Berger and Maas (2016) contended that an appropriate medical response includes public protest, civil disobedience and a boycott on working in those camps. Australian healthcare professionals have subsequently risked imprisonment to speak out about conditions in Nauru and Manus Island that have been likened to concentration camps. Berger and Maas (2016) argued that a code of medical ethics helps guide medical practitioners in their responses, which includes boycotting employment contracts to deliver medical services in the camps. In terms of ethical practice, the Australian Medical Association's code of ethics requires: 'Refrain[ing] from entering into any contract … which may conflict with professional integrity, clinical independence or your primary obligation to the patient' (AMA, 2006). Given recent efforts invested in developing ethical codes of practice and professional associations for youth workers, it seems appropriate and timely for youth work associations to provide statements that declare their ethical position and that provide guidance and protection for practitioners.

Yet teaching about codes of ethics goes only so far. As we saw, the elaborate code of ethics developed by Save the Children did not prevent that organization from getting itself, and its workers into a compromising position, nor did its senior managers actually draw on that framework when responding to anguished pleas from their employees to intervene. With that in mind, we argue that what is needed is a youth work curriculum that embeds the intellectual framework provided by the sociology of ignorance (e.g., Gross and McGoey, 2015) *and* the ethical tradition of virtue ethics and its preoccupation with 'practical wisdom' (Schwartz and Sharpe, 2011). Such a framework can and should be developed in stand-alone youth work subjects as well as informing the design and development of field-based education. While knowing what is actually going on and forming a reasoned ethical response are eminently theoretical tasks, actually doing what you know you should be doing is the pre-eminently practical task.

REFERENCES

Agamben, G. (1998). *Homo sacer: Sovereign power and bare life*. London: Verso.

Al-Kateb v Godwin (2004). High Court of Australia 37. Retrieved from http://www.austlii.edu.au/au/cases/cth/HCA/2004/37.html

AMA (2006). *Code of ethics*, revised 2006. Retrieved from https://ama.com.au/position-statement/ama-code-ethics-2004-editorially-revised-2006

Amar, P. (2013). *The security archipelago: Human-security states, sexuality politics, and the end of neoliberalism*. Duke: Duke University Press.

Amnesty International (2014). This is breaking people. Human rights violations at Australia's asylum seeker processing centre on Manus Island, Papua New Guinea. Retrieved from https://www.amnesty.org.au/wp-content/uploads/2016/09/Amnesty_International_Manus_Island_report-1.pdf

Arendt, H. (1963/1994). *Eichmann in Jerusalem: A report on the banality of evil* (Rev Edn). Harmondsworth: Penguin.

Aristotle (2002). *Aristotle's Nicomachean Ethics: Translation, glossary and introductory essay*. (Ed. and Trans. J. Sachs). Newburyport: Focus Publishing.

Australian Human Rights Commission (AHRC) (2006). Submission of the Human Rights and Equal Opportunity Commission to the Senate Legal and Constitutional Legislation Committee on the Migration Amendment (Designated Unauthorised Arrivals) Bill. Retrieved from http://humanrights.gov.au/submission-migration-amendment-designated-unauthorised-arrivals-bill-2006

Australian Human Rights Commission (AHRC) (2014). *The forgotten children: National inquiry into children held in immigration detention*. Sydney: Australian Human Rights Commission.

Bardach, E. (2011). *A practical guide for policy analysis: The eightfold path to more effective problem solving*. Thousand Oaks: Sage.

Berger, S., & Maas, F. (2016). Should doctors boycott working in Australia's immigration detention centres? *British Medical Journal*, 352 (online).

Blass, T. (1991). Understanding behaviour in the Milgram obedience experiment: The role of personality, situations, and their interactions. *Journal of Personality and Social Psychology*, 60(3), 398–413.

Bogan, C., & English, M. (1994). *Benchmarking for best practices: Winning through innovative adaptation*. New York: McGraw-Hill.

Bourdieu, P. (1977). *Outline of a theory of practice* (Trans. R. Nice). Cambridge: Cambridge University Press.

Brooker, J. (2014). Current issues in youth work training in major English-speaking countries. In B. Belton (Ed.), *Cadjun and Kiduhu: Global perspectives on youth work* (pp. 132–145). Rotterdam: Sense Publishers.

Buchroth, I., & Parkin, C. (Eds) (2010). *Using theory in youth and community development*. Exeter: Learning Matters.

Brown, W. (2015). *Undoing the demos: Neoliberalism's stealth revolution*. Cambridge: Zone Books.

Cohen, S. (2001). *States of denial: Knowing about atrocities and suffering*. Cambridge: Polity Press.

Dastyari, A. (2015). Detention of Australia's asylum seekers in Nauru: Is detention by any other name just as unlawful? *University of New South Wales Law Journal*, 38(2), 669–693.

Doogan, C. (2015). Review of recommendations from the Moss Review. Retrieved from https://www.border.gov.au/ReportsandPublications/Documents/reviews-and-inquiries/doogan-report.pdf

Finnis, J. (1980). *Natural law and natural rights*. Oxford: Oxford University Press.

Flyvbjerg, B. (2001). *Making social science matter*. Cambridge: Cambridge University Press.

Flyvbjerg, B. (2012). *Real social science: Applied phronesis*. Cambridge: Cambridge University Press.

Flyvbjerg, B. (2013). How planners deal with uncomfortable knowledge: The dubious ethics of the American Planning Association. *Cities*, 32, 157–162.

Flyvbjerg, B. (2015). Aristotle, Foucault, and progressive phronesis: Outline of an applied ethics for sustainable development. In A. Madanipour (Ed.), *Planning theory* (pp. 340–354). London: Routledge.

Gross, M., & McGoey, L. (Eds) (2015). *The Routledge international handbook of ignorance studies*. Abingdon: Routledge.

Haas, J., & Vogt, K. (2015). Ignorance and investigation. In M. Gross & L. McGoey (Eds),

The Routledge international handbook of ignorance studies (pp. 17–28). Abingdon: Routledge.

Habermas, J. (1990). *Moral consciousness and communicative action*. Cambridge: MIT Press.

Linn, R. (1996). *Conscience at war: The Israeli soldier as a moral critic*. Albany: State University of New York Press.

Midgley, M. (2001). *Wickedness: A philosophical essay* (2nd edn). London: Routledge.

Milgram, S. (1974). *Obedience to authority*. London: Tavistock.

National Inquiry into Children in Immigration Detention, (2015) Submission No. 183: Names withheld, employees of Save the Children Australia in Nauru, Submission to the National Inquiry into Children in Immigration Detention, http://www.humanrights.gov.au/our-work/asylum-seekers-and-refugees/national-inquiry-children-immigration-detention-2014-0

Ord, J. (2007). *Youth work process, product and practice: Creating an authentic curriculum in work with young people*. London: Russell House Publishing.

Phillips, J. (2015). *Asylum seekers and refugees: What are the facts?* Canberra: Australian Parliamentary Library.

Rayner, S. (2012). Uncomfortable knowledge: The social construction of ignorance in science and environmental policy discourses. *Economy and Society*, 41(1), 107–125.

Salkever, S. (1991). *Finding the mean: Theory and practice in Aristotelian political philosophy*. Princeton: Princeton University Press.

Sawer, M., Abjorensen, N., & Larkin, P. (2009). *Australia: The state of democracy?* Sydney: Federation Press.

Save the Children Australia (2010). Child Protection Policy and Code of Conduct, SCA, Melbourne, https://www.savethechildren.org.au/__data/assets/pdf_file/0019/229114/SCA-Child-Protection-Policy-and-Code-of-Conduct.pdf

SCA (2016a). Doogan review finds removal of SCA staff from Nauru was 'not justified', Media release, 19/01/2016. Retrieved from https://www.savethechildren.org.au/about-us/media-and-publications/media-releases/media-release-archive/years/2016/doogan-review-finds-removal-of-save-the-children-staff-from-nauru-was-not-justisfied (accessed 15 February 2016).

SCA (STC) (2016b). Protecting children on Nauru. Retrieved from http://scasites.org.au/noborders/providing-support-to-vulnerable-children-on-nauru/

Schattschneider, E. (1975). *The Semi-sovereign People: A realist's view of democracy in America*. London: Dryden Press.

Schön, D. (1983). *The reflective practitioner: How professionals think in action*. London: Temple Smith.

Schwartz, B., & Sharpe, K. (2011). *Practical wisdom: The right way to do the right thing*. New York: Riverview Press.

Taylor, C. (1992). *Multiculturalism and the politics of recognition*. Princeton: Princeton University Press, Princeton.

UNHCR (2013). Report of the UNHCR monitoring visit to the Republic of Nauru 7–9 October. Retrieved from http://www.refworld.org/docid/5294a6534.html

United Nations Committee against Torture (2008). Concluding observations on the third periodic report of Australia under the Convention against Torture and Other Cruel, Inhuman or Degrading Treatment or Punishment.

United Nations Committee on the Rights of the Child (2012). Concluding observations on the fourth periodic report of Australia under the Convention on the Rights of the Child, UN Doc CRC/C/AUS/CO/4.

United Nations Human Rights Committee (2009). Concluding observations on the fifth periodic report of Australia under the International Covenant on Civil and Political Rights, UN Doc CCPR/C/AUS/CO/5.

Walzer, M. (1970). *Obligations: Essays on disobedience, war and citizenship*. Cambridge: Harvard University Press.

Walzer, M. (1988). *The company of critics: Social criticism and political commitment in the twentieth century*. New York: Basic Books.

42

The Evolution of Youth Empowerment: From Programming to Partnering

Heather L. Ramey and Heather L. Lawford

I'd rather be the program, than the reason for the program.

INTRODUCTION

This quote, from a participant in a participatory action research project by and for street-involved youth, has been adopted by The Students Commission of Canada as an informal mission statement for their work. The Students Commission is a nonprofit organization that helps young people 'put their ideas for improving themselves, their communities and their world into action' (Students Commission, 2016). It does so by coordinating and supporting projects, training, conferences, and other activities at local, provincial, and national levels. This young person's statement is a call to youth workers and other youth-serving agencies to engage in a process of authentic and meaningful partnering with young people. In

this chapter, we explore the process by which youth are being reconceptualized from program recipients to partners. We argue that youth work offers a way forward to realizing this mission.

For the past several decades, youth services have been criticized as sites of disempowerment for youth (LISTEN, Inc., 2000). This criticism has revolved around the conceptualization of youth as problems to be solved and passive recipients of service, rather than as 'customers of public goods and services' (LISTEN, Inc., 2000, p. 4) and active participants of society. Critique has also included the lack of attention to the sociopolitical conditions of youth's existence, including broader political systems and structures. Partly in response to these criticisms, alternate models of engaging youth have emerged. These approaches fall under a variety of names, including youth development, youth engagement, youth leadership, youth organizing, and youth participation (LISTEN, Inc., 2000). These alternate models were intended to enable youth participation, as per the UN Convention on the Rights of the Child, to optimize youth potential rather than simply minimize problems (Pittman, 1991), and to foster citizenship prior to adulthood (Wong, Zimmerman, & Parker, 2010; Zeldin, Christens, & Powers, 2013). Some models also emerged out of a legacy of other community organizing and progressive change movements. Despite the critical contributions of youth participation efforts, limitations of these models remain. The continuation of youth–adult binaries, the emphasis solely on youth benefits, and lack of attention to youth culture and political systems and structures have created new forms of programming in which youth are still program recipients, rather than equitable partners.

Whether the emphasis is on youth problems or even youth strengths and resiliencies as program recipients, and where youth development is the intended outcome, youth remain disempowered. Their participation necessarily remains limited, as their current contributions are seen as indicators of or means to future, adult participation. This view also reflects our (de)valuing of youth as members of society. Further, research suggests that youth participate in positive development and other programs out of a desire to contribute and as an expression of humanitarian values, and that these are stronger motivators than anticipated social or career-related benefits (McLellan & Youniss, 2003; Ramey, Lawford, & Rose-Krasnor, 2016; Ramey & Rose-Krasnor, 2015; Zeldin, 2004). We propose that the evolution of youth empowerment must include a shift from programming to partnering. This shift would allow young people's contributions to be considered for their own sake, and not as a means to adult development. Furthermore, we suggest that youth work is best suited to lead the field in this shift, and conversely that this shift is an important next step in advancing the discipline of youth work.

In the current chapter, we discuss the programmatization of youth empowerment

and suggest a way forward for youth work practice. We begin with discussion of youth empowerment programs in North America, with a particular view on the context in Ontario and Quebec, Canada. We describe current pressures to retain a programmatic approach to youth participation, before describing some characteristics of more authentic youth empowerment practice. We then move on to articulate an argument for why youth work practice and youth workers in particular are ideally situated to partner with youth at the forefront of change, before suggesting potential next steps in youth work practice.

THE PROGRAMMATIZATION OF YOUTH EMPOWERMENT

The programmatization of youth development and youth empowerment is readily apparent in the United States. Created in response to a tradition of pathologizing and treatment, youth development and youth empowerment programs focused on building youth's strengths rather than engaging them as problems (e.g., Pittman, 1991). Youth empowerment programs (which include leadership initiatives and civic engagement) further involved youth in leadership roles in organizations and communities. In the US, these approaches have developed into a field of practice (LISTEN, Inc., 2000).

Despite their useful contributions, youth development and empowerment approaches have been criticized as paternalistic, focused on individual youth growth, and excluding social justice and community work, thereby failing to address wider social issues (Matloff-Nieves, Fusco, Conolly, & Maulik, 2016; Pope, 2016). Further, despite some attention to youth's culture and context, youth empowerment approaches still function within adult-determined structures (LISTEN, Inc., 2000). In their meta-analysis of youth empowerment programs, Morton and Montgomery (2013) defined youth empowerment programs as intervention programs, which use participatory, youth-driven processes to improve youth functioning. Although participatory and youth driven, the definition of empowerment approaches provided here retains their structure as 'intervention programs' (p. 23), intended to 'improve functioning' (p. 22).

In Ontario and Quebec, Canada, where our own research has centered, youth empowerment approaches have differed from those of the United States and each other in a number of ways. The American history of positive youth development and leadership programs is not readily apparent in Canada. Service delivery to youth has generally been fully funded by provinces, and larger social policy initiatives are usually funded through fundraising or federal grants. Therefore, despite the powerful influence of the United States across domains of life, there is no parallel in Canada to the youth development, asset building, and civic engagement movements (Stuart, 2014). Youth engagement initiatives in Canada appear both broader and more diverse, but also fragmented and isolated (Ho, Clarke, & Dougherty, 2015).

In Ontario and throughout most of Canada, youth engagement has tended to be not only fragmented, but also field-specific. In children's mental health and child welfare, participation has often focused on improving programs and participation in personal care plans. For example, provincial and federal child welfare organizations have consumer-focused programs, to provide a 'unifying voice for youth in care' (e.g., Ontario YouthCAN; www.ontarioyouthcan.org). In the field of public health, government agencies have also made significant efforts to incorporate youth engagement into their policies and practices. Coupling engagement with an asset-based approach, youth participation has been intended as a health promotion strategy (Sahay, Rempel, & Lodge, 2014). Despite examples of innovative practices in which youth are engaged as partners (Halsall, Garinger, & Forneris, 2014), youth

workers and youth services organizations often have difficulty conceptualizing youth outside of the role of client, even as they are engaged in a process of partnering with youth (e.g., Ramey & Rose-Krasnor, 2015). In public health, for example, evaluation research has noted a lack of individual motivation for youth engagement among staff, and a 'lack of true understanding' of youth engagement (Sahay et al., 2014, p. 33).

In the province of Quebec, located beside Ontario, the context for youth democracy and empowerment is quite different from that of the rest of Canada. Quebec is recognized as a distinct society within Canada, including distinctive language and more social programs. Youth in Quebec have a broad history of advocacy, activism, and political work (Gauthier, 2003). For example, in 2012, Quebec experienced North America's largest youth-led movement since the 1960s, in response to the government's plan to increase university tuition fees (Blanchet-Cohen, Warner, Di Mambro, & Bedeaux, 2013). Nonetheless, attempts to engage youth have suffered from the same limitations as other areas in North America. For example, research on engaging youth in municipalities has concluded that youth councils have tended to attract youth who are considered 'high-functioning', and likely to follow city procedures (Blanchet-Cohen, 2006). In language familiar to the field of youth work, municipalities experience difficulties in working *with youth* and not only *for youth* (Blanchet-Cohen & Torres, 2015; Garfat & Fulcher, 2012; Gharabaghi, Skott-Myhre, & Krueger, 2014). Further, in Quebec and Ontario, adults and administration in youth-serving and government youth empowerment initiatives have difficulty perceiving youth outside of the role of service recipient (Blanchet-Cohen & Bedeaux, 2014; Ramey & Rose-Krasnor, 2015).

In sum, despite a steadily growing focus on youth participation and empowerment, spanning different fields of youth work, there remains a continuation of youth–adult binaries, an emphasis on youth benefits, and a lack of attention to youth culture and political systems and structures. Thus, even as youth are contributing to the community, through advocacy efforts, political work, or co-facilitating programs, their contributions are considered a form of treatment.

Current Pressures

A number of pressures and perspectives continue to shape youth work practice in empowerment settings, reinforcing a programmatic approach to youth participation. Perhaps primary among these is the currency that treatment has in professional practice and broader society (Gharabaghi, 2014), which is greater than any currency provided by youth empowerment, collaboration, and democratization. Along these lines, Gharabaghi has described 'the valorization of treatment as the guiding concept of what youth work is all about' (2014, p. 16).

Related to the issue of treatment is the further pressure from the general public and funders regarding what makes youth work, and youth, successful (Gharabaghi, 2014). At a societal level, broader expectations are that successful work with youth creates a young person who is less aggressive, more compliant, and represents the characteristics of positive citizenship. Whether the best way to make a successful young person is treatment or empowerment programs makes little difference. Gharabaghi notes that all of these movements have the intention of 'imposing change on young people' (p. 17), which goes hand-in-hand with the societal conception of youth as problems. Therefore, the movement away from treatment and participation-as-treatment cannot be done without addressing the pressure of societal views of youth as problems.

The field of developmental psychology both informs and holds more power than youth work, and demonstrates little inclination to view youth as partners. Youth care practice is necessarily developmental (Gharabaghi, Skott-Myhre, & Krueger, 2014). Although the role of developmental theory might be shifting toward a platform for youth workers to understand youth's perspective and needs, rather than a means for assessing normality, it continues to be an important basis for youth work practice (Phelan, 2014). An example of the lack of movement in developmental psychology can be found in the study of youth contributions. Youth contributions are studied in psychology literature as part of positive youth development. They have been described as involving 'ideologies and behaviors related to making positive contributions to self, others, and community' (Hershberg, DeSouza, Warren, Lerner, & Lerner, 2014, p. 951). As one of the six Cs of positive youth development, youth contributions to others are primarily considered a developmental outcome *for youth* (Lerner, Lerner, Almerigi, Theokas, Phelps, Gestsdottir et al., 2005). Although attention to reciprocal influences between youth and context have become fundamental to theory in developmental psychology, actual study of youth–context relations in developmental psychology literature appears to focus solely on the influence of context on youth (e.g., Lerner, Lerner, Bowers, & Geldhof, 2015). That youth contribution might, in fact, create good in the world for others, does not appear to have been directly considered by developmental psychology. Indeed, even youth's own perceptions of their contributions to others have not been treated as a topic of interest (Hershberg et al., 2014). Thus, in addition to the positive contributions of developmental psychology, it also furthers an agenda of youth as recipients and creates barriers to a youth-as-partner framework.

For youth work, the desire for professionalization might provide further pressure to retain a focus on treatment. In a field already challenged in trying to establish credibility as a profession, this pressure is especially threatening. Without the legitimacy afforded by the umbrella of treatment, youth workers might further risk the view from those in other professions that youth work is just 'hanging out' (Garfat & Fulcher, 2012, pp. 14–15; Salhani & Charles, 2007). Already poorly understood in comparison to other disciplines, greater shifts away from interventions might mean further marginalization of the field (see Anderson-Nathe, 2014).

Despite pressures to retain a treatment approach to youth work, there is clearly also pressure for youth empowerment. Funders and accreditation bodies are incorporating and requiring program and evaluation components focused on youth engagement (e.g., Blanchet-Cohen, Manolson, & Shaw, 2014). One difficulty related to this pressure for youth empowerment, however, is reflected in the language of youth empowerment itself. Often used interchangeably with the terms youth engagement and youth participation, such language is unidirectional, implying that adults evoke youth's engagement, participation, and empowerment. Moreover, such language fails to articulate in what processes, exactly, youth are to be engaged. As noted by Fusco and Heathfield (2015): 'participation in what? for what purpose?' Although they further suggest that the answer is to engage youth in broad streams of 'public, social and democratic life (of citizen power)' (p. 16), this purpose is not reflected in current models of youth empowerment. As long as the purpose focuses on outcomes for youth (e.g., health promotion, successful development), then participation will be participation-as-treatment.

The Practice of Youth Empowerment

A move forward in youth empowerment requires a shift in current youth work practices. This includes greater attention to social issues, political structures, and commitment to anti-oppressive frameworks, as well as the need to blur youth–adult roles. Empowerment is based on a theoretical framework and a belief in anti-oppressive life contexts and

critical youth work, which underpins all work across an organization. Garfat and Fulcher (2012) have said that each encounter with young people requires a cultural lens; further than this, each encounter requires a sociocultural lens, with attention to the power in the relationship, and the contextual and historical power that exists.

Partnering requires a shift toward radical youth work, and a need to re-think the institutional parameters of the programs and institutions in which we are organized to encounter young people, to share and organize space differently (Skott-Myhre, 2014b). The best way of helping people is to work with them to 'find different ways of being and living in the world' (Garfat & Fulcher, 2012, p. 13). These ways involve changing the structures of the current system toward ways that engage youth and adults' full participation, meaningful voice, and resistance against oppression. This requires re-conceptualizing 'youth' in youth work and in broader society.

Related to this re-conceptualization of youth, partnering, rather than programming, blurs the lines of the youth–adult binary. This is a critical advancement as a continued youth–adult binary reinforces youth as 'the fundamental other' (Anderson-Nathe, 2014, p. 161). Child and youth care literature has pointed to the importance of 'doing with', developing co-created space and facilitating the active participation of both parties (Garfat & Fulcher, 2012; Phelan, 2009). Partnering furthers the concept of 'doing with' by shifting roles from adult/youth binary to a more blurred and less differentiated distinction where people who identify as youth and adults, or some combinations of these, may serve in a number of roles.

As noted by Moss and Petri (2002), different ways of thinking about youth produce different life experiences for youth, different public provisions for youth, and different ways of working with youth.

Taking into consideration wider social issues and societal conceptualizations of youth, and shifting youth–adult binaries, has both risky and positive implications for our position as a profession. Applying concepts such as treatment and clinical work might add validity to youth work as a profession. However, as a practice that centers on being with youth, increasing the divide between youth and practitioners by reinforcing the role of youth as client might simply reinforce our own marginalized position. As noted by Skott-Myhre (2014b), youth workers have struggled to belong to a system that 'dominates, exploits and controls us' (p. 69). Fusco and Heathfield (2015) have argued that institutions of power and policy need to move closer to communities and cultures, as distance between professionals and youth enables youth's disenfranchising and objectification. We would additionally suggest that by moving closer to youth, we can shift not only youth's position of disenfranchisement, but our own.

Youth Work as a Context for Youth–Adult Partnerships

Youth empowerment work is currently being done by people from varied professions. However, youth workers are ideally situated to partner with youth at the forefront of change for a number of reasons. These include our skill set, positionality, and engagement with the political settings of our work and lives. Part of youth workers' skillset involves strength in developing unique forms of relationship, with an intrinsic focus on care and the dynamic nature of daily encounters (Skott-Myhre, 2014a). Relationship building emphasizes the 'interpersonal in-between' (Garfat, 2008), which is not inviting youth to behave as an adult in adult space, as is the intention of many youth engagement programs (e.g., Blanchet-Cohen & Torres, 2015), nor does it create a place of role modelling, as is the intention of many youth development programs, but rather it is a joining of people's worldviews (Phelan, 2014).

Becoming a partner, however, conceptualizes 'being with' differently (Garfat & Fulcher, 2012). As part of relational youth work, it is not adults doing 'for' or 'to' youth; it requires a mutuality that goes beyond the 'with' of walking alongside a youth through their own growth process. Youth–adult partnerships are collaborative, equitable, democratic, sustained, and have a meaningful effect beyond the youth themselves (Checkoway, 2011; Zeldin et al., 2013). Within this partnership, all participants are equally able to make decisions, use skills, learn, and contribute.

Within a framework of partnership, it is possible for youth workers to be open and even welcoming to conflict, resistance, and rebellion; the relaxing of some boundaries and blurring of roles that are avoided in other disciplines are more possible in youth work (Skott-Myhre, 2014a, 2014b). Skott-Myhre's description of a potential social change, in which we move away from the defined structures and regulations of our current work, suggests something akin to chaos. In place of control, such chaos is a healthy indicator of the need for change, and part of the struggle we have in common with youth in our partnerships. Youth workers' nuanced attention to relational work makes them ideally positioned for re-conceptualizing youth in this role, beyond the role of client. This is a potential strength of youth work in comparison with professionals who are not engaged with youth on a more consistent basis, and do not have care as their primary goal (cf. Sahay et al., 2014; Ramey, Rose-Krasnor, & Lawford, 2016).

As is necessary in partnerships, youth workers are responsive to the needs of young people in the here and now (Fusco & Heathfield, 2015). Youth workers privilege process, without eliminating consideration of outcomes (Batsleer & Davies, 2010). The models under which youth workers too often operate, including youth development and youth empowerment models, privilege outcomes over process work (Heathfield & Fusco, 2016).

Youth workers' positionality enables us to manage being in partnership with youth. Youth workers are curious and willing to enter new spaces (Fusco & Heathfield, 2015; Phelan, 2014). Phelan (2014) has discussed a key ingredient of youth work: humility. He has described this as the ability not only to enter the relationship curious and open, but to remain curious and unthreatened when confronted with beliefs and attitudes different from our own. We choose respect and humility rather than power and control. Admittedly, choosing humility, rather than control, is an ongoing goal in our work (Gharabaghi & Phelan, 2012) but one that is valued in our field, making youth workers uniquely prepared for partnership.

Finally, youth work is already inherently political, as can be seen in the debate over professionalization and youth workers' role in society, as well as in arguments regarding our role in reproducing existing institutional systems in youth work (Skott-Myhre, 2014a; Stuart, 2014). In Canada, at least, it is a field that does not shy away from criticism and controversy, or criticism of existing political and systemic structures (e.g., Vachon, 2013).

THE WAY FORWARD: MOVING FROM PROGRAMMING TO PARTNERSHIPS

A number of concrete steps can be taken to evolve our thinking from youth as recipients of programming to partners. Youth workers need, first, to let go of the belief that we need to align ourselves with arguably more powerful professions. Gharabaghi (2014) has discussed the need to stop valorizing treatment, however positively worded, and de-couple from higher professions focused on clinical work. Stuart (2014) has further stated that there is no need to establish ourselves as a legitimate profession in Canada and beyond because 'we already are one' (p. 65). Rather than accommodating the power and regulated decision-making of other professions,

Stuart has further argued for the need to create a new model of professionalism that is more focused on resisting the oppression of the current structures. Stuart has discussed the need to revolutionize the professional structures available to us to fit a child and youth care practitioner view of professionalism. It is possible to be accountable in our work without the power structures of professions such as nursing, social work, and education, while embracing professionalism based on advocacy. Professional youth work models are evolving, and Stuart (2014) argues that a new model should engage in advocacy, and make radical youth work part of our mainstream professionalism.

Partnership, then, is not a domain of youth work separate from traditional or other domains of youth work. For example, civic youth work, in which youth are supported to be active citizens, has been described as a type of youth work, and an emergent field of practice (Velure Roholt, Baizerman, & Hildreth, 2013). Some youth work might fit into this definition. However, rather than considering partnership as only an additional option for youth workers, there is a need to re-situate youth's position as partners in *all* forms of youth work, and in all youth work settings (Batsleer & Davies, 2010; Skott-Myhre, 2014b).

Youth empowerment and youth–adult partnership is a practice, not a program (Pereira, 2007). Although different aspects of an organization or other setting might rightly involve different forms of youth participation, organizations should not be seeking to fulfill funding requirements or even engage young people's voice in a way that segments it into a specific youth role or area of the organization. In contrast to the segmenting of partnerships into programs, youth infusion engages youth participation at all levels of organizations. Infusion thus meets youth's varied abilities and interests, and involves youth in partnerships at all levels of decision-making, including boards of directors (Camino & Zeldin, 2002). When partnership is a practice, it is embedded in all organizational activities.

Meaningful participation requires recognizing youth contributions, and recognizing that they benefit society, rather than only youth's own personal development. This shift again requires the integration of some of the features of civic youth work into more traditional youth work (Velure Roholt & Cutler, 2012). In civic youth work, youth are described as able to 'get something done'. In Canada, youth, aged 15 to 19, have a higher rate of volunteering than any other age group (Turcotte, 2015). Furthermore, in recent studies, youth have identified the desire to mentor, volunteer, and create opportunities for others (Provincial Advocate for Children & Youth, 2013; Ramey & Rose-Krasnor, 2015). Seeing youth contributions conceptualizes youth differently both in youth work and in broader society. In discussing youth participation, Checkoway (2011) has stated that the quality of participation is contingent on young people having an actual effect. Indeed, it is difficult to know how youth might feel valued and ineffectual at the same time.

A means of integrating these different functions is to ensure partnerships have co-created spaces that allow for shared goals and purpose, which engage both youth and adults in multiple ways. At least in Canada, programs and mandates are often set prior to the establishment of youth–adult partnerships and, as programs rarely have a primary mandate of youth empowerment, partnering with youth is, at best, an add-on to the primary mandate. Currently, the same organization might be simultaneously engaging youth in meaningful participation and tokenism because service and leadership are seen as different functions (Fusco & Heathfield, 2015). Co-created purposes would require that service and engagement are integrative functions. They also require that we see youth contributions as an end in themselves, and not a means for greater youth development. This might dictate the need to stop defining ourselves as a 'helping profession', as this definition inherently considers youth in the role of helped, and the focus of youth work to be youth outcomes. In practice, it appears that youth organizations engage youth using multiple approaches simultaneously (Matloff-Nieves et al., 2016).

Youth–adult partnership requires that empowerment and partnering is embedded in teaching from the outset of youth worker's experiences and education. It should be among the first lessons for new youth workers, embedded in all our teaching, and not just in advocacy or in separate courses or modules on youth engagement. Speaking from our own efforts in teaching and training youth workers about youth engagement, it is clear that many people enter the field with the intention of helping children and youth who have experienced abuse, mistreatment, and marginalization. They have been influenced by the valorization of treatment discussed by Gharabaghi (2014), and the desire to contribute, themselves. Although child and youth empowerment is embedded in student teaching and professional competencies (e.g., Child and Youth Care Certification Board, 2016), this form of empowerment tends to be done in a context of designing interventions. Perceptions of youth as partners do not appear to be part of typical youth work competencies.

The Students Commission as a Case Study

The Students Commission was highlighted at the beginning of this chapter as a case study of youth partnering. Founded in 1991, in 2000 The Students Commission became the lead of the Centre of Excellence for Youth Engagement, which networks academics, youth organizations, and young people together to provide research and training to improve youth programs and youth engagement in Canada. They offer support and consultation, and work directly with youth and those who influence youth on various projects.

Some of their recent activities include the development of an ongoing platform for program evaluation, currently used by 270 programs across Canada; involvement in participatory action research on the healthy behaviors of school-aged children; and a national project engaging young men and boys to take action against gender-based violence.

The Students Commission reflects a number of the shifts we have described as needed in youth work in the movement toward partnering. For example, there is no clear marker of division between youth and adults. Frequently, as we are participating in planning meetings, conferences, and other projects at The Students Commission, we are in a group of people, many of whom we are meeting for the first time. Although introductions are made, at no point are people introduced as 'youth' or 'adults'. Indeed, in one activity used by The Students Commission, participants are asked to go into separate parts of a room based on whether they are youth or adults. Although some people quickly choose one role or another, many participants become confused, or protest that the division depends on the circumstance. The activity is designed to surface some of these complexities and to enable people to work together to address power imbalances.

The Students Commission continues to do work that would be conducted within programs in more traditional youth work. The organization cannot be considered a youth advocacy or civic youth work organization. It has received funding for many programs generally provided by more treatment-focused organizations, including gun violence and gangs, substance use prevention, and mental health. Some of this work has been specifically targeted toward positive development and youth empowerment. As reflected by the quote at the beginning of this article, however, it cannot be said that adults deliver programs to youth, either as part of treatment or positive development approaches. Rather, The Students Commission is based on a youth–adult partnership model grounded in

four pillars: respect, listen, understand, and communicate. These four pillars are both the values and process of the organization, beginning from a deep belief that all young people have something valuable to contribute.

Agendas are mutually created, and bidirectional. At conferences, for example, young people take the lead in identifying the issues to explore. All participants are informed at the outset that agendas are fluid, constantly shifting, and co-created. This includes all participants, and it is not unusual to be invited to facilitate an activity or share in the moment, as the need is identified and regardless of expected roles. Formal and informal training is regularly provided, and all participants are expected to make contributions. Young people have the opportunity to explore issues by examining their own experiences and learning about others, to consult different sources of information to inform their ideas, and to make decisions about what actions they want to take and/or recommendations they want to make. The Students Commission acts as a bridge to support young people to put their ideas into action and bring their recommendations to the relevant decision-makers.

There are, at times, tensions between partnering and traditions of programming. For example, although evaluation requirements would be best served by obtaining data from partners and participants upon their early contacts with The Students Commission, this process was perceived to be alienating and unwelcoming. The choice has been made, at least for the time being, to modify evaluation to be more welcoming to participants of all ages and in all roles, although this makes it difficult to assess changes over the course of people's participation. There are also some limits to youth infusion. Although the organization strives to have half of their staff made up of young people, adults hold the executive director and other management roles, though many organizational activities and decisions are, on balance, more youth-led. For example, at the recent national Young Decision Makers conference, young people from every province developed a series of recommendations and wrote a report to share with relevant decision-makers. The process was cyclical and layered, with young people working closely with young adults and adult allies to develop, refine, and prioritize their recommendations. As one way to address power inequities in decision-making, young people are given the opportunity to vote on priorities, while those who have access to other decision-making structures are asked to abstain. The intergenerational space is designed to make roles and opportunities available to anyone interested in taking them on, with support from those who are more experienced in those roles: for example, young adults are paired with younger youth to facilitate groups. The focus on process, a strength of youth work, is apparent in the work of The Students Commission, and all decisions appear to be subject to an ongoing process of re-evaluation.

In summary, as reflected by the work of The Students Commission, we propose that the evolution of youth empowerment should encompass partnering, which includes attention to social issues, commitment to anti-oppressive frameworks, the blurring of youth–adult roles, and co-created purposes. We note that our case study, like most of the literature on which we have drawn, has been from a Canadian context. Youth work in Canada is relatively well situated in the world, in having, for example, legitimate academic training (Velure Roholt et al., 2013). From this Canadian position, as perhaps more privileged than youth work in some other nations, there are some signs that innovations in youth work practice are welcome (Gharabaghi, 2013).

CONCLUSION

Adapting existing models of youth work, regardless of the inclusion of a strengths-based approach, will not work to create equitable youth–adult partnerships. At the same time, the decades-long urge by youth work for legitimacy under these same models has been broadly ineffective. A new model, based on critical youth work and partnering, is needed. Youth's everyday contributions in communities, as well as their leadership in world-altering movements (e.g., Idle No More, Arab Spring, Black Lives Matter), both in Canada and internationally, indicate youth's capacity for making contributions. Youth work also has demonstrated a capacity to engage youth and the broader systems of youth's lives. Herein, we have proposed a rejection of past models of youth work, and replacement with a process intended, ultimately, to strengthen the work within a new system. Thus, we share The Students Commission's vision, in which youth are no longer considered reasons for 'the program', but program partners.

ACKNOWLEDGEMENTS

We would like to acknowledge the support and input of the Students Commission/Centre of Excellence for Youth Engagement, and especially Nishad Khanna, who provided the case study, as well as insightful comments and review.

REFERENCES

Anderson-Nathe, B. (2014). Insider/outsider. In K. Gharabaghi, H. A. Skott-Myhre, & M. Krueger (Eds.), *With children and youth: Emerging theories and practices in child and youth care work* (pp. 149–167). Waterloo, ON: Wilfrid Laurier University Press.

Batsleer, J., & Davies, B. (2010). *What is youth work?* Exeter, UK: Learning Matters Ltd.

Blanchet-Cohen, N. (2006). Young people's participation in Canadian municipalities: Claiming meaningful space. *Canadian Review of Social Policy, 56,* 71–84.

Blanchet-Cohen, N., & Bedeaux, C. (2014). Towards a right-based approach to youth programs: Duty-bearers perspectives in Montreal. *Children and Youth Services Review, 38*, 75–81.

Blanchet-Cohen, N., Manolson, S., & Shaw, K. (2014). Youth-led decision making in community development grants. *Youth & Society, 46*(6), 819–834.

Blanchet-Cohen, N., & Torres, J. (2015). Enhancing citizen engagement at the municipal level: Youth's perspectives. In J. Wyn & H. Cahill (Eds.), *Handbook of Children and Youth Studies* (pp. 319–404). New York: Springer.

Blanchet-Cohen, N., Warner, A., Di Mambro, G., & Bedeaux, C. (2013). 'Du carré rouge aux casseroles': A context for youth–adult partnership in the Québec student movement. *International Journal of Child, Youth and Family Studies, 3*(1), 444–463.

Camino, L., & Zeldin, S. (2002). From periphery to center: Pathways for youth civic engagement in the day-to-day life of communities. *Applied Developmental Science, 6*(4), 213–220.

Checkoway, B. N. (2011). What is youth participation? *Children and Youth Services Review, 33*(2), 340–345.

Child and Youth Care Certification Board (2016). *Competencies.* College Station, TX: Association for Child and Youth Care Practice. Retrieved from https://cyccb.org

Fusco, D., & Heathfield, M. (2015). Modeling democracy: Is youth 'participation' enough? *Italian Journal of Sociology of Education, 7*(1), 12–31.

Garfat, T. (2008). The inter-personal in-between: An exploration of Relational Child and Youth Care practice. In G. Bellefeuille & F. Ricks (Eds.), *Standing on the precipice: Inquiry into the creative potential of Child and Youth Care Practice* (pp. 7–34). Edmonton, AB: MacEwan.

Garfat, T., & Fulcher, L. (2012). Characteristics of a relational child and youth care approach. In T. Garfat & L. C. Fulcher (Eds.), *Child & Youth Care in Practice* (pp. 5–24). Cape Town: Pretext.

Gauthier, M. (2003). The inadequacy of concepts: The rise of youth interest in civic participation in Québec. *Journal of Youth Studies, 6*(3), 265–276.

Gharabaghi, K. (2013). Social innovation and entrepreneurship: Implications for the field of child and youth care practice. *Relational Child and Youth Care Practice, 26*(3), 42–51.

Gharabaghi, K. (2014). The purpose of youth work. In K. Gharabaghi, H. A. Skott-Myhre, & M. Krueger (Eds.), *With children and youth: Emerging theories and practices in child and youth care work* (pp. 3–24). Waterloo, ON: Wilfrid Laurier University Press.

Gharabaghi, K., & Phelan, J. (2012). Beyond control: Staff perceptions of accountability for children and youth in residential group care. *Residential Treatment for Children & Youth, 28*(1), 75–90.

Gharabaghi, K., Skott-Myhre, H. A., & Krueger, M. (Eds.) (2014). *With children and youth: Emerging theories and practices in child and youth care work.* Waterloo, ON: Wilfrid Laurier University Press.

Halsall, T., Garinger, C., & Forneris, T. (2014). mindyourmind: An overview and evaluation of a web-facilitated mental health program that applies empowerment strategies for youth. *Journal of Consumer Health on the Internet, 18*(4), 337–356.

Heathfield, M., & Fusco, D. (2016). From hope to wise action: The future of youth work and other global actions in education. In M. Heathfield & D. Fusco (Eds.), *Youth and inequality in education: Global actions in youth work* (pp. 295–307). New York, NY: Routledge.

Hershberg, R. M., DeSouza, L. M., Warren, A. E. A., Lerner, J. V., & Lerner, R. M. (2014). Illuminating trajectories of adolescent thriving and contribution through the words of youth: Qualitative findings from the 4-H study of positive youth development. *Journal of Youth Adolescence, 43*(6), 950–970.

Ho, E., Clarke, A., & Dougherty, I. (2015). Youth-led social change: Topics, engagement types, organizational types, strategies, and impacts. *Futures, 67*, 52–62.

Lerner, R. M., Lerner, J. V., Almerigi, J., Theokas, C., Phelps, E., Gestsdottir, S., et al. (2005). Positive youth development, participation in community youth development programs, and community contributions of fifth grade adolescents: Findings from the first wave of the 4-H Study of Positive Youth Development. *Journal of Early Adolescence, 25*(1), 17–71.

Lerner, R. M., Lerner, J. V., Bowers, E. P., & Geldhof, G. J. (2015). Positive youth development: A relational developmental systems model. In W. F. Overton & P. C. Molenaar (Eds.) and R. M. Lerner (Editor-in-Chief), *Theory and method. Vol. 1: The handbook of child psychology and developmental science* (7th edn, pp. 607–651). Hoboken, NJ: Wiley.

LISTEN, Inc. (2000). *An emerging model for working with youth. Occasional paper series on youth organizing*, No. 1. Washington, DC: Funders Collaborative on Youth Organizing.

Matloff-Nieves, S., Fusco, D., Conolly, J., & Maulik, M. (2016). Democratizing urban spaces: A social justice approach to youth work. In M. Heathfield & D. Fusco (Eds.), *Youth and inequality in education: Global actions in youth work* (pp. 175–196). New York, NY: Routledge.

McLellan, J. A., & Youniss, J. (2003). Two systems of youth service: Determinants of voluntary and required youth community service. *Journal of Youth and Adolescence*, *32*(1), 47–58.

Morton, M. H., & Montgomery, P. (2013). Youth empowerment programs for improving adolescents' self-efficacy and self-esteem: A systematic review. *Research on Social Work Practice*, *23*(1), 22–33.

Moss, P., & Petrie, P. (2002). *From children's services to children's spaces: Public policy, children and childhood*. New York, NY: Routledge Falmer.

Pereira, N. (2007). *Ready... set... engage! Building effective youth/adult partnerships for a stronger child and youth mental health system*. Toronto, ON: Children's Mental Health Ontario & Ottawa: The Provincial Centre of Excellence for Child and Youth Mental Health at CHEO.

Phelan, J. (2009). The wounded healer as helper and helped: A CYC model. *CYC-OnLine*. (March). Retrieved from http://www.cyc-net.org/cyc-online/cyconline-mar2009-phelan.html

Phelan, J. (2014). Thinking through a relational and development lens. In K. Gharabaghi, H. A. Skott-Myhre, & M. Krueger (Eds.), *With children and youth: Emerging theories and practices in child and youth care work* (pp. 81–99). Waterloo, ON: Wilfrid Laurier University Press.

Pittman, K. (1991). *Promoting youth development: Strengthening the role of youth-serving and community organizations*. Washington, DC: U.S. Department of Agriculture Extension Services.

Pope, M. (2016). Paternalism in educating and developing our youth: The perpetuation of inequality. In M. Heathfield & D. Fusco (Eds.), *Youth and inequality in education: Global actions in youth work* (pp. 275–292). New York, NY: Routledge.

Provincial Advocate for Children & Youth. (2013). *Putting youth in the picture: A mental health community snapshot*. Toronto, ON: Provincial Advocate for Children & Youth.

Ramey, H. L., Lawford, H. L., & Rose-Krasnor, L. (2016). Motivations for activity participation as predictors of emerging adults' psychological engagement in leisure activities. *Leisure Sciences*, *38*(4): 338–356.

Ramey, H. L., & Rose-Krasnor, L. (2015). The New Mentality: Youth–adult partnerships in a community mental health promotion program. *Children and Youth Services Review*, *50*: 28–37.

Ramey, H. L., Rose-Krasnor, L., & Lawford, H. L. (2016). Youth–adult partnerships and youth identity style. *Journal of Youth and Adolescence (online)*. doi:10.1007/s10964-016-0474-6

Sahay, T. B., Rempel, B., & Lodge, J. (2014). Equipping public health professionals for youth engagement: Lessons learned from a 2-year pilot study. *Health Promotion Practice*, *15*(1), 28–34.

Salhani, D., & Charles, G. (2007). The dynamics of an inter-professional team: The interplay of child and youth care with other professions within a residential treatment milieu. *Relational Child and Youth Care Practice*, *20*(4), 12–20.

Skott-Myhre, H. (2014a). Becoming the common. In K. Gharabaghi, H. A., Skott-Myhre, & M. Krueger (Eds.), *With children and youth: Emerging theories and practices in child and youth care work* (pp. 25–42). Waterloo, ON: Wilfrid Laurier University Press.

Skott-Myhre, H. (2014b). Building a new common: Youth work and the question of transitional institutions of care. In B. Belton (Ed.), *'Cadjan – Kiduhu' Global perspectives on youth work* (pp. 61–75). Boston, MA: Sense Publishers.

Stuart, C. (2014). Developing the profession from adolescence into adulthood: Generativity versus stagnation. In K. Gharabaghi, H. A. Skott-Myhre, & M. Krueger (Eds.), *With children and youth: Emerging theories and practices in child and youth care work* (pp. 57–78). Waterloo, ON: Wilfrid Laurier University Press.

Students Commission (2016). About us. Toronto, ON: The Students Commission. Retrieved from http://www.studentscommission.ca/aorg/aboutusref_e.php

Turcotte, M. (2015). *Spotlight on Canadians: Results from the General Social Survey. Volunteering and charitable giving in Canada*. Ottawa, ON: Statistics Canada, Ministry of Industry. Retrieved from http://www.statcan.gc.ca/pub/89-652-x/89-652-x2015001-eng.pdf.

Vachon, W. (2013). Do not enter: What are the risks of gatekeeping child and youth care? *Child & Youth Services*, 34(2), 156–171.

Velure Roholt, R. V., Baizerman, M., & Hildreth, R. W. (2013). *Civic youth work*. Chicago, IL: Lyceum Books.

Velure Roholt, R. V., & Cutler, J. (2012). Youth work as engagement. In D. Fusco (Ed.), *Advancing youth work: Current trends, critical questions* (pp. 173–189). New York, NY: Routledge.

Wong, N. T., Zimmerman, M. A., & Parker, E. A. (2010). A typology of youth participation and empowerment for child and adolescent health promotion. *American Journal of Community Psychology*, 46(1–2), 100–114.

Zeldin, S. (2004). Youth as agents of adult and community development: Mapping the processes and outcomes of youth engaged in organizational governance. *Applied Developmental Science*, 8(2), 75–90. doi:10.1207/s1532480xads0802_2.

Zeldin, Z., Christens, B., & Powers, C. (2013). The psychology and practice of Youth-Adult Partnership: Bridging generations for youth development and community change. *American Journal of Community Psychology*, 51(3–4), 385–397.

43

Towards a Shared Vision of Youth Work: Developing a Worker-Based Youth Work Curriculum

Tomi Kiilakoski, Viljami Kinnunen
and Ronnie Djupsund

INTRODUCTION

One of the most persistent problems of youth work is the difficulty of explicating what youth work is about. This professional dilemma was manifested in many levels during a practice-based research project aimed at constructing a curriculum for youth work performed on a local level in Finland. In the research interviews conducted for the project, youth workers reflected both their professional history and the status of their local work community. An experienced youth worker talked about his past career and stated: 'It has always been difficult for me to justify youth work to the politicians and others'. Another youth worker described the same thing by saying, 'When somebody says, "Oh, you are a youth worker, what exactly do you do?" I have never been able to answer'. This problem obviously affects youth workers as individuals, but also youth work as a profession.

The two above statements can be taken to indicate that the role of tacit knowledge in the professional culture of youth work is significant. According to Michael Polanyi, a classic theorist of this type of knowledge, 'we can know more than we can tell' (Polanyi, 2009, p. 4). He was first to formulate this concept, pointing out that there is a form of knowledge tied to professional traditions, human relations, sociocultural norms and practices, and even bodily behavior, that is difficult to name. There are at least two reasons for knowledge in any profession remaining tacit. The first relates to the fact that some forms of knowing are impossible to articulate (a classic example being describing how one rides a bicycle). In youth work, these may be connected to understanding a mood and situation intuitively, or 'by merely looking at the position of her shoes' (youth worker interview cited in Kiilakoski, 2011). The second reason for tacit knowledge is that for some reason youth workers are not willing to or even capable of explicating it, possibly because they simply lack the time to reflect on the matter.

Some may say that given the mutable nature of youth work (Kivijärvi & Heino, 2013), the problem of explicating youth work is a perennial one. At least, it has been a problem for youth work for quite some time. A scholar of youth work and youth policy, Howard Williamson states, 'the challenge has always been persuading others that youth work is anything more than "ping pong and pool"' (Williamson, 2012, p. 41–42). Be that as it may, the dominance of tacit knowledge in the youth work field has become increasingly problematic in a current political climate that emphasizes the three E's of New Public Management: economy, effectiveness and efficiency (Otrusinova & Pastuszkova, 2012). The research has indicated that the role of tacit knowledge in the practice of youth work is rather significant. The challenge in a political climate that emphasizes transparency and measurability is explicating the goals, methods and ways of evaluating youth work (Honkasalo, 2011; Kiilakoski, 2011; Kivijärvi, 2015). This means that youth workers should be able to offer clear and articulated descriptions of their distinctive contribution to the network of services (Davies, 2015). If the ontological question regarding the nature and essence of youth work remains vague or unanswered, it will be difficult to explain how youth work should be publicly financed and valued as a profession. Also, if youth workers are unable to articulate their ethos and goals, their ability to work in multi-professional settings is likely to be limited.

A WORKER-BASED YOUTH WORK CURRICULUM IN FINLAND

The social and professional problem described above was taken as the starting point for a practice-based study in the town of Kokkola, Finland. The aim was to articulate what youth work is about by creating a worker-based youth work curriculum that explicated how youth workers themselves view their work. To achieve this, a five-year study was initiated, during which a youth researcher and youth work community in Kokkola worked to create a process-based curriculum.

The youth work curriculum project in the town of Kokkola is a unique effort in Europe, firstly because of the participatory and worker-based methods of developing the curriculum as a form of self-expression. Usually, the youth work curriculum is designed using a top-down approach. Secondly, the project has created a theory of youth work as relational pedagogy that has been used as a basis for describing the essence of youth work. This theory is a result of the dialogues between research and practice in which those involved agreed to the principles that no one knows the truth and everyone has a right to be understood (Doll, 1993). This formal theory challenges the ideals of knowing as decontextualized practice detached from the praxis the theory is supposed to describe. Thirdly, the project is a long lasting (from 2010 to 2016) joint project between all the local youth workers in the town of Kokkola and a youth researcher. The long timespan of the process makes it possible to analyze the organizational learning changes in the work culture during the process.

We believe that the curriculum as both a product and the process of making it are of interest to youth work. The methods of using practice-based research as 'a practice-changing practice' (Kemmis, 2010, p. 464) aimed at transforming and improving current practices include both the research and the praxis of youth work as equal participants in constructing knowledge. Attention is paid both to the process of developing youth work using practice-based research and to the final product, which offers a vision for and a theory of youth work.

The chapter offers an interpretation of how youth workers can explicate the tacit knowledge of the profession and create a community of practice (Wenger, 2008). It also offers a perspective on the nature of youth work as a pedagogical process that supports the individual and social identities of the young. We will begin by contextualizing youth work on the national level in Finland and on the local level in the town of Kokkola. In the second section, we present the idea of curriculum and the methods used and describe the changes in the process. In the third section, we will introduce the conceptual tools used in describing youth work. As a practical example, we analyze how the curriculum changed the management of youth work.

THE LOCAL AND NATIONAL CONTEXTS OF YOUTH WORK

Finland is a relatively small northern European country with 5.4 million inhabitants. Finland is a paradigmatic example of a Nordic welfare state, with a relatively high level of welfare spending, a high degree of equality, and a large public sector (Nygård, 2006, p. 357). Youth work, as a public service, is financed both by the state and local governments, in addition to being a form of voluntary work organized by civil society. Municipalities are important providers of youth work (currently, 3,400 people are employed as professional youth workers). Parishes and NGOs also organize youth work services (Kivijärvi & Heino, 2013). Youth work is seen as part of the network of welfare services, but the related political guidance, or quality assurance and evaluation, is quite thin. This means that many decisions regarding scope, target group and methods are made on the local level (Forkby & Kiilakoski, 2014).

Youth work in Finland has clear professional structures. There has been national legislation governing youth work since 1972, when the first act on youth affairs was passed. At the time our practice-based research,

Youth Act (passed in 2006, a new act was passed in December 2016) defined youth work as the 'promotion of active citizenship in young people's leisure time, their empowerment, support to young people's growth and independence, and interaction between generations' (Youth Act 72/2006, §2). This definition emphasizes the pedagogical and democratic nature of youth work. There is tertiary education in youth work inside universities and applied universities. In addition, there is a growing body of scientific literature on youth work, mostly written in Finnish and accessible to youth workers.

Historically, youth work in Finland has been defined in many ways. Using historical analysis, it can be claimed that, 'there is no unambiguous or generally accepted concept of youth work in Finland' (Nieminen, 2012, p. 72). There are some general guidelines, such as voluntarism, an emphasis on the young as a resource instead of a problem, and the importance of group activities. In accordance with the general idea of a welfare state, youth work is seen as a universal service.

There are 47,031 people living in Kokkola, which makes it the 23rd largest town in the country. This bilingual town, speaking Swedish and Finnish, currently has around 30 youth workers employed by the local government. The youth services belong to the Department of Educational and Cultural Services – a fact that itself emphasizes the long-lasting tradition of seeing youth work as a pedagogical activity. Like most professions in the Nordic welfare states, youth work is expected to autonomously decide on the activities provided and to develop and evaluate them.

Recently, the fields of youth research and youth work have been converging (Kiilakoski, 2011; Kiilakoski, Kinnunen & Djupsund, 2015). Kokkola, along with 17 other municipalities, was part of a research and development study on youth clubs, which have traditionally been one of the centerpieces of municipal youth work in Finland. According to the results of the study, the traditional format of organizing non-formal services for a group of active users in a youth club was transforming into regional and communal youth work with a growing interest in multi-professional co-operation, an increased number of learning environments, and expanding co-operation with formal education in schools (Forkby & Kiilakoski, 2014; Kiilakoski, 2011). This indicates that youth workers should explicate the manner of their work, engage in reconceptualizing the praxis of youth work, and attempt to integrate their educational aims with the aspirations of other professionals (Kiilakoski, 2011). These interpretations and results were negotiated with the town of Kokkola. The discussions led to a proposal to construct a local youth work curriculum, an idea that was strongly influenced by British experiences (Ord, 2007). The project was to be a dialogical enterprise between research and practice and have a bottom-up participatory approach, instead of being led by the administration.

In accordance with the tradition of youth work as a profession in Nordic welfare services, the community took matters into its own hands and decided to provide a description of the youth work themselves – in a dialogical relationship with the research. This could be seen as a manifestation of the zeitgeist regarding current youth work. There have been various ways of explicating youth work in Finland, such as financing practice-oriented research on youth work, developing indicators, quality assurance and evaluation, productization, and the description of the basic tasks and missions of the youth work organization. The starting point of the curriculum was describing the nature of youth work as a pedagogical activity.

Engaging in Practice-changing Practice

Motivation to change

Practice-based research is about changes in practice; the willingness to improve and change is a key factor in engaging in a dialogue between research and practice

(Kemmis, 2010). The main motivations for constructing a curriculum were two-fold. There was an intrinsic need to help the youth work community learn to better negotiate and evaluate the services for young people. In addition to this, there was an extrinsic need to explicate the contributions of youth work to multi-professional co-operation and to prioritize what youth workers do as part of these networks.

During the early 2000s the implementation of youth work in Kokkola was strongly guided by youth workers' personal and varied understandings of the views, goals and values of youth work. There was even a competition between different youth clubs, a dominant method of youth work in Kokkola at the time. Youth clubs worked independently and implemented youth work as they saw fit. One indication of the change in the social climate of youth work was that people seriously debated whether they should lend sport equipment of a certain youth club to another club. Five years later, the same clubs were discussing the shared goals of youth work (Kiilakoski, Kinnunen & Djupsund, 2015).

In 2010, the local youth work community felt the need to change things. Curriculum development required the shared motivation to devote time and resources to the project and also gaining support from the management of the organization. The workers decided that the process should seek to answer the following three questions: What is youth work in Kokkola? What are the desired outcomes of youth work? Which methods are used to achieve these outcomes? Following an intense debate about the curriculum, a number of general expectations for the pros and cons of the process were analyzed (see Table 43.1).

With the advantages outweighing the potential disadvantages, the youth work community decided to move forward. The fear of formalizing youth work was overcome by the promise of simultaneously explicating youth work to different partners and helping the community to deepen a shared understanding

Table 43.1 Initial expectations for the project

Pros of creating a curriculum	Cons
Clarifies the nature of youth work	May end up being just another paper on the shelf
Defines goals	May hinder creative ways of carrying out youth work
Helps recognizability of youth	May be too rigid
Provides a better understanding of successes and failures	Everyone will be forced to work the same way
Helps in understanding and recognizing different methods and ways of working	
Unites the work community	
Generates a common language	
Helps find and recognize common major goals	
Increases the effectiveness of youth work	
Clarifies job descriptions	

about the nature of youth work. It was time to critically examine what youth work actually does, what it claims to do, and how these two questions are interconnected. By doing this, we responded to the overall challenge in youth work: strengthening its professional identity by aiming 'to determine what we are and what we are not'. This 'requires articulating our philosophy and principles for work with young people as well as naming the proven research-based methods and techniques that make sense in light of our goals' (Walker, 2016, p. 14). The goal was to explicate the Selbst-Verständnis [self-understanding] of youth work as a profession, which also meant, at that time, the process had more to do with working *on* young people, instead of working *with* the young people (Belton & Frost, 2010), a point to which we return.

The method

A founder of action research, social psychologist Kurt Levin has famously said that 'If you want to truly understand something, try to change it' (quoted in Snyder, 2009, p. 226). The method of practice-based research is based on the belief that there is a form of knowing that is different from the logico-paradigmatic knowledge of science. Stephen Kemmis talks about the difference between *knowledge about practice* and *knowledge in practice*. The first is a form of knowledge

commonly seen as a product of scientific methodologies. However, the latter is knowledge that is context-dependent and exists in the community of practice, uniting practitioners as members of a work community (Kemmis, 2010). This is not to claim that the knowledge of the community is most valuable or not subject to criticism. Practice-based research is committed to transformation, which means that it is inherently empathetic and critical in its stance towards practice.

> It is not that practitioners have privileged knowledge that is somehow superior to the knowledge or theories others may have about their praxis; rather, it is that they are the only ones who have in their collective care the individual and social project of education (and, in the European sense, of pedagogy). (Kemmis 2010, pp. 20–21)

We are committed to the assumption that both for practice and for research, this means that we should engage in a dialogue – debating, critically questioning, reformulating, and learning from one another's perspectives. For that reason, this article is written jointly by representatives of youth research, of youth work management, and of the practice of youth work. This is a call for 'dirtying hands' and engaging with practice: '[I]t is not by looking at things, but by dwelling within them, that we understand their joint meaning' (Polanyi, 1966/2009, p. 18).

In concrete terms, our project can be described as consisting of three cycles. The first two cycles were local and focused on youth work in one town, Kokkola (2010–2014). The third cycle, which is ongoing at the time of writing (2014–2016), is a co-operative project between five towns that aims to upgrade the curriculum from the local to the national level. The aim of the first two cycles was to collect information from the youth workers and construct conceptual tools with which to talk about youth work. The most important tools were a theory of youth work as relational pedagogy and the concept of a form of work. Using these tools, the youth work curriculum was created. The starting point of the work was to focus on the pedagogical processes taking place in youth work. The third cycle expanded the process used in Kokkola to other towns. The participating towns of Tornio, Oulu, Hämeenlinna and Kouvola are located in various parts of Finland. They differ in size and number of inhabitants. They also have different histories regarding youth work and, to some extent, different methods and arenas of youth work.

The study combines various methodologies. The empirical data of the study consist of 26 diaries of the youth workers, 26 individual research interviews, participatory observations and field notes from these, two quantitative surveys of the young people in the town of Kokkola (N = 1,105 in 2012; N = 1,208 in 2015), and the material produced by the workers. This vast data corpus is typical of practice-based research in that the research data does not necessarily have to be a well-organized and easily codable entity. The most important issue is understanding and transforming practices. During this work, the roles of the researcher and the youth workers were negotiated, reconstructed and, to some extent, even converged, resulting in the final national publication in Finnish, which was written jointly with the authors of this article (Kiilakoski, Kinnunen & Djupsund, 2015).

Curriculum

Curriculum is one of the most contested, debated and deconstructed concepts of the educational sciences. The traditional view of curriculum, as an example of means-end rationality (Weber, 1976), has been called into question in numerous studies. There is an entire paradigm that attempts to conceptualize curriculum and see it as, for example, an autobiographical or hermeneutic text (Pinar, 2011, 2012). According to Pinar, curriculum is about 'complicated conversation encouraging educational experience' (2012, p. 2).

For youth work, the most promising perspective on curriculum emphasizes the centrality of the process instead of preset goals or outcomes (Ord, 2007). A process-oriented curriculum claims that the outcomes regarding preset goals are subservient to the process, or that the process itself is the key (Kelly, 1999). For youth work, this means that engaging in doing something meaningful with the young will likely produce desirable outcomes – paradoxically, this will occur simply because the process was never about producing those outcomes. The curriculum can then be described as an emergent curriculum. This type of curriculum abandons the means-end rationality and the idea that a curriculum is successful if and only if vaguely defined educational goals are met. To replace this, an ideal of open-endedness is offered. 'One does not know, cannot know, what will happen, only that something will happen' (Osberg & Biesta, 2008, p. 325).

An emergent youth work curriculum does not offer the controlled, measurable and predictable results required by McDonaldized societies (Ritzer, 1993). Instead, it places trust in the belief that the process of youth work will be useful to the young. By emphasizing process, the youth work curriculum can serve as a counter-narrative to the neo-liberal tendencies of those mesmerized by the requirements of calculative rationality. The standpoint of the reconceptualizing paradigm of curriculum studies supports the ideals of our project. According to Beyer and Apple (1998), what unites the long line of curriculum theorists is the fact that they

> [a]ll recognize the inherent complexity of education and reject the comforting illusion that we can ever find the one right set of techniques that will guarantee security of outcome. Finally, all of them take education seriously, as worthy of our best thoughts. Education is a process that must embody the finest elements of what makes us human, that frees us in the process of teaching us what is of value. (Beyer & Apple, 1998, p. 6)

YOUTH WORK AS A RELATIONAL PEDAGOGY AND PROCESS

William F. Pinar says curriculum is about 'the everyday experience of the individual and his or her capacity to learn from that experience' (Pinar, 2012, p. 2). It seemed obvious that youth work was not about producing preset outcomes. However, the problem was how to describe the broad aims of youth work. To achieve this, a perspective on the daily interactions and educational intentions of youth workers was needed to create an authentic youth work curriculum (Ord, 2007). A quote from a youth worker's diary describes a situation in which a new group of young people was attending a local youth club, but the workers were too busy to pay attention to their peer dynamics:

> A group of seemingly uncertain girls has come to the youth club. They are trying to play some sort of power game on the boys. In addition, a group of boys who are shy and socially excluded at school have begun attending the club. At the youth club, they are strongly seeking the company of male youth workers. It bugs me that the group dynamics of school affects the youth club as well. These kids have 'a label' that seems to define their social position in the youth clubs as well. I think that we could arrange group activities for them that would help them redefine their positions, but I do not have the time. Hopefully, others will catch onto this. I feel irritated not having done something about this. I hope we can create an open atmosphere so that everyone will find space in a group. (A worker's diary)

This excerpt shows that a youth worker is paying a great deal of attention to the group dynamics and reflecting on the nature of the youth club as a learning environment that will be supportive of the young and redefine their social roles. It also points out that youth work is not only about individual young people, but also about relationships.

To describe what youth work is about, we needed to come up with a theory that would describe what youth work brings to the lives of the young. When youth work is successful, it creates processes that help young people develop as individuals and also supports their social relations. This means that growth, in youth work, is not only seen as an inner process, but also a social process that requires paying attention to the various life worlds and situations in which a young person engages. To capture the individual and social dimensions of youth work, we came up with the idea of youth work as supporting relations. Later, we found that these ideas share similarities to theories of relational pedagogy, which are based on the assumption that we do not have relationships, but rather relations have us (Bingham & Sidorkin, 2004).

A theory of youth as relational pedagogy describes the features of the young with regard to: peers; adults, such as parents, teachers, etc. (inter-generational relations); social structures, such as schooling and welfare systems (relations to other youth services); the local area and communal networks; society (active citizenship, participation in political life); and the world and the eco-system. By using this theory, it was possible to describe youth work as a pedagogical process that creates emergent outcomes (i.e., personal growth and support of relations), which avoids the pitfalls of individualized atomism in describing youth work and also utilizes the processual view of youth work.

Forms of Work

The central assumption was that youth work is a pedagogical process that creates possibilities for achieving educational outcomes despite the fact that it is not oriented toward producing those outcomes. After having formed a theory of youth work as a relational pedagogy, further theoretical elements were required. We wished to differentiate the broad process from mere methods. We defined the concept of *a form of work* to answer the question '*What does youth work do?*' After a heated debate over grouping and regrouping the broad processes of youth work over a time period of one year, we identified five forms of work: communal, societal, participation activities, cultural and focused. Work methods, in turn, were used to answer the question '*How does youth work do what it does?*'

The structure of the youth work curriculum consists of these five forms of work, which reflect the processes of youth work. The overall model is described in Table 43.2. Each form of work has unique methods, distinct aims and a time frame for working with the young. The central relations supported by each form of work also differ.

The curriculum of youth work in Kokkola describes five processes by using the concept of the form of work. Forms of youth work are linked to the broad goals of youth work and cannot easily be measured, as they are multilayered and inter-linked. They have long-term goals and require town-wide analysis of the condition of young people's lives to begin to appreciate the benefits (Kiilakoski, Kinnunen & Djupsund, 2015). Each form of work supports different relations and has a unique length.

This categorization of different processes has several benefits, as described by the workers. First, it enables workers to discuss the broad aims and goals instead of being stuck with mere methods of youth work. This brings unity to the work community because people start to see bridges between different methods. Secondly, it helps in prioritizing the use of time in youth work. When the work community has defined clear and explicit goals, the individual workers are better able

to choose what they will venture to do in multi-professional networks. Instead of having to make individual decisions, they can talk about shared identities. Third, by discussing and debating together, one gets a perspective on the different and shared ways of thinking in the community – as well as different contributions by each worker. The former condition in which '*amazingly little was known what each does in the youth-work community*' (research interview) and the dominance of tacit knowledge are changing into the perspective of the sustained pursuit of a shared pedagogical enterprise (cf. Wenger, 2008).

COMMUNITY AND MANAGEMENT PERSPECTIVES

The process of creating an authentic youth work curriculum (Ord, 2007) is a time-consuming affair that requires support and resources from management. In this section, the benefits of the process are analyzed by looking at the increased ability of youth work to communicate its distinctive practice and the greater coherence of the teams of youth work.

Constructing a curriculum and debating about words are also a quest to understand the nature of the youth work community. Creating a common understanding requires coming to grips with the essence of youth work and theorizing based on the practical wisdom of youth workers. As Stanley Cavell (1999) says:

> The philosophical appeal to what we say, and the search for our criteria on the basis of which we say what we say, are claims to community. And the claim to community is always a search for the basis upon which it can be or has been established. (p. 20)

The above quote implies that even theoretical talk about words will touch on the solid ground of youth work practices because our intuitions and articulated expressions about the nature of the words are also constitutive

Table 43.2 Youth work curriculum

Form of Youth Work	Methods Used	Aims	Time Scale and Target Group	Supports Relations of the Young to
Communal Youth Work	Youth clubs Cooperation with School Local cooperation that enables long-term support for young people	Offers guidance and support for young people Works locally to improve the quality of life and the status of young people	Key age range is 9–17. The duration of the relationship with the young varies from months up to four years	Other young people Adults Local area and communal networks
Societal Youth Work	Operates at the macro level Assisting Youth organizations Collecting data about the living conditions and situations of the young Evaluation of the Youth work and guiding resources	Improves the living conditions of young people in cooperation with young people, networks, and decision-makers. Promotes youth affairs in municipal decision-making as well as in regional cooperation	Indirectly targeting all young people of Kokkola, the main target group being 12–18 year old Implementation requires long-term multi-disciplinary co-operation with other sectors and decision-maker partners.	Society Local area and communal networks
Participation Activities	Activity groups Youth Council	Promotes youth activity in democratic decision, making Develops inclusive practices in co-operation with partners	13–29-year-old interested in influencing the living conditions of young people. From a couple of weeks to 3 years, depending on the activity or group.	Society Other young people
Cultural Youth Work	Rock school Hobby groups Organizing events	Amplifies the voice of youth on local using art-based and cultural methods Supports the personal growth of young people through cultural events and performances Supports youth cultures Promotes cultural diversity	The age of young people usually between 10 and 20. Duration of contact varies strongly. A young person can participate in an event or participate in organized recreational activities for up to several years	Personal development (tolerance, self-expression, creativity, and social skills) Local area and communal networks Other young people Society
Focused Youth Work	Small group activities Outreach youth work Substance-abuse prevention Multi-professional collaboration with social services and the police	Supports the individual development and transitions of the young Builds the capacity to cope with difficulties related to life management, growth, or social relations Supports inclusion into society	Key age group 10-25 years The contact varies between a couple of weeks to several years	Personal growth Social structures Local area and communal network

of our ideas about the nature of the profession. Curriculum is about constructing a text that reflects the context of youth work. The curriculum design is a search for words that would reflect the realities and potential realities of youth work (Seal, 2014, p. 21). Youth work as a pedagogical practice involves doing something 'in a historical and social context that gives structure and meaning to what we do' (Wenger, 2008, p. 47). Understanding and communicating this context of youth work probably requires becoming more reflective on the nature of this practice. By engaging in the dialogue, criticizing and being criticized, categorizing, sharing ideas and interpretations and even enthusiasm, the identity of the youth work community became stronger.

> Our team spirit has changed tremendously. One cannot even [imagine the nature of change], coming to think of it. We used to have common meetings quite seldom. We just went through things and it did not involve any group activities. This [the curriculum] has really tied us together. (Research interview)

The working culture of the work community contributes to being able to describe the realities of youth work. On the other hand, creating authentic descriptions contributes to the working culture. 'The more we talk and discuss about things' (research interview) the stronger the community gets (Kiilakoski, Kinnunen & Djupsund, 2015). According to theory-of-practice architectures, this is because sayings, doings and relatings – the basic elements of social practices – are interlinked, in a constant ballet with each other (Kemmis, 2010). It is no wonder, then, that the curriculum has had a profound effect on the management as well.

During the curriculum project, the organization of youth work in Kokkola was divided into three sub-areas (living conditions of the young, social empowerment and active citizenship) in accordance with the Youth Act of Finland. This division of the organization began to seem artificial when, in the second cycle of the curriculum process, consensus was achieved regarding the forms of working in youth work. Because the forms of work were conceptualized by the entire work community on the basis of practical activities, the relevant teams in question seemed the most natural and appropriate for the tasks. During the spring of 2015, the new team structure, in line with forms of work, became an established element of Kokkola's youth services (Figure 43.1).

The new team divisions were executed in accordance with the forms of work defined in the curriculum. Each sub-area will be implemented by a team, which the organization will endeavor to prevent from becoming hierarchical. Each worker is part of the communal youth work and part of another team that is selected on the basis of a competency assessment and discussions held with the worker in question. Each team consists of employees who will be allocated a specific number of working hours to achieve the team's goals. In the present situation, in which the personnel for the teams have been selected and the number of working hours has been separately specified, the curriculum accurately describes how much time has been invested in each form of youth work.

Through the curricular division of youth work into various forms of work, it is possible to estimate the amount of municipal taxes used in these various forms of youth work. It is thus possible to estimate the performance achieved in a specific form of work, such as the number of young people reached or which youth relationships have been supported. Work-form-specific assessment throughout the curriculum can only be utilized locally, however. This is because work-form-specific assessment requires in-depth situational knowledge and an understanding of the multi-dimensional goal setting of youth work. The implementation of work-form-specific assessments in relation to resources used requires that local youth policy and the living conditions of local young people are assessed as well. This assessment should take into account that the forms of work described by

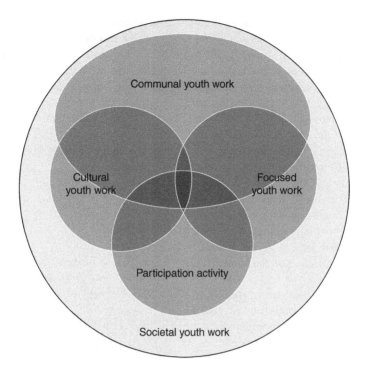

Figure 43.1 New organizational chart based on curriculum

the curriculum cannot be undertaken without including partially overlapping functions that have similar goals.

It should be taken into account that the main aim of the curriculum has never been to determine resourcing for youth work. The utilization of curriculum in the local management and evaluation of youth work is more of a by-product that emerges from the verbalization of youth work, as the transparency of the forms of work is increased and the goal setting is clarified. This, too, can be taken as an example of the importance of emergent learning outcomes.

CONCLUSION

The purpose of using practice-based research in constructing a curriculum was to verbalize tacit knowledge and describe to the general

public, the professional network and the profession itself what youth work, as a non-formal part of educational services, is about. The results show that in addition to individual support, youth work is interested in promoting the relationships of the young with others, with civil society, and with society at large. This has served to explain what youth work is about. Local youth work has become more transparent. This research also has been used in the management of local youth work.

By examining the process and the relationships supported, the curriculum process has verbalized the nature of youth work. Practice-based research does not share traditional ideals of reliability and validity (Heikkinen et al., 2016). The applicability of this type of research can be seen by examining the pragmatic consequences. The project has had an impact in the town of Kokkola on the level of individual worker identity and also on the level of the management of youth work. In addition to this, four more towns have participated, and there is growing interest in the process in various parts of Finland. Therefore, it is safe to assume that the validity of the approach is high because the profession itself has accepted it, and the process has generated further action. After the acceptance of the Curriculum document as a tool describing and guiding the youth work in Kokkola, there has been an intention to increase youth participation in the management of youth work, in evaluation and in allocation of resources, but the process is still ongoing: the participation activity team is developing a tool for evaluating the level of participation in different methods of youth work.

We feel that the in-depth process of explaining the methods and aims of youth work by using top-down approaches is a lasting solution to the requirements of transparency, measurability and effectivity. But, the authenticity of the curriculum is created by the bottom-up, participatory manner of the curriculum design. Also, the interest and approval of other towns in Finland validates the results. By the same token, we do not wish our project to be copied lightly. The most important parts of the project are the reflections on the part of the practitioners themselves. These require time, perhaps more than expected. The potential pitfalls of the process are that youth work, as a creative process, may be over-shadowed by a curriculum, thereby formalizing youth work instead of supporting and empowering the praxis of youth work. To avoid this, one has to emphasize that the authentic discussions on curriculum require a lot of effort and cannot be easily replicated by merely copying the ideas and concepts.

The necessary conditions for development have spanned a long time, enabling different voices to emerge and interact with each other. The discussions have had a clear and explicitly shared goal. There is continuous support and allocation of resources by the management, and there is a connection between

discussions and practice, between theory and the daily realities of youth work (Kivijärvi, 2012; Kiilakoski, Kinnunen & Djupsund, 2015). This way, the whole community has had a chance to contribute to the process. Also, the involvement of the research perspective has meant that youth workers have been able to compare the work done locally with the image of youth work as described by the research.

REFERENCES

Belton, B. & Frost, S. (2010). *Differentiated teaching and learning in youth work training*. Rotterdam: Sense.

Beyer, L.E. & Apple, M. (1998). Values and politics in the curriculum. In L.E. Beyer & M. Apple (Eds.), *The curriculum: Problems, politics and possibilities* (pp. 3–7). Albany, NY: State University of New York Press.

Bingham, C. & Sidorkin, A. (Eds.) (2004). *No education without relation*. New York: Peter Lang.

Cavell, S. (1999). *The claim of reason*. Oxford: Oxford University Press.

Davies, B. (2015). Youth work: A manifesto for our times – revisited. *Youth & Policy, 114*, 96–117.

Doll, W.E. (1993). *Post-modern perspective on curriculum*. New York: Teachers College Press.

Forkby, T. & Kiilakoski, T. (2014). Building capacity in youth work: Perspective and practice in youth clubs in Finland and Sweden. *Youth & Policy, 112*, 1–17.

Heikkinen, H., de Jong, F. & Vanderlinde, R. (2016). What is (good) practitioner research? Reflections in the special issue: Improving professional practice and competencies within practice-based research. *Vocation and Learning, 9*, 1–19.

Honkasalo, V. (2011). Tyttöjen kesken. Monikulttuurisuus ja sukupuolten tasa-arvo nuorisotyössä. Helsinki: Finnish Youth Research Society.

Kelly, A.V. (1999). *The curriculum: Theory and practice*. 4th edition. London: Paul Chapman.

Kemmis, S. (2009). Action research as a practice-based practice. *Educational Action Research*, *17*(3), 463–474.

Kemmis, S. (2010). Knowing doing. *Pedagogy, Culture & Society*, *18*(1), 9–27.

Kiilakoski, T. (2011). Talotyön ja alueellisen nuorisotyön kehittäminen. In Veronika Honkasalo, Tomi Kiilakoski & Antti Kivijärvi *Tutkijat ja nuorisotyö liikkeellä*, Helsinki: Finnish Youth Research Society, pp. 153–252.

Kiilakoski, T. (2015). Youth work and non-formal learning in Europe's education landscape and the call for a shift in education. In *Youth work and non-formal learning in Europe's education landscape*. European Commission, 26–38.

Kiilakoski, T., Kinnunen, V. & Djupsund, R. (2015). *Miksi nuorisotyötä tehdään? Tietokirja nuorisotyön opetussuunnitelmasta*. Helsinki: Humak University of Applied Sciences & Finnish Youth Research Society.

Kivijärvi, A. (2012). Nuorisotointen kehittämistyö monikulttuurisessa yhteiskunnassa. In Katja Komonen, Leena Suurpää & Markus Söderlund (Eds.), *Kehittyvä nuorisotyö*. Helsinki: Finnish Youth Research Society, 299–314.

Kivijärvi, A. (2015). *Etnisyyden merkityksiä nuorten vertaissuhteissa*. Helsinki: Finnish Youth Research Society.

Kivijärvi, A. & Heino, E. (2013). Ethnic minority youth and youth work in Finland: Everyday anti-racism engendering empowering conditions. In M. Törrönen, O. Borodkina, V. Samoylova & E. Heino (Eds.), *Empowering social work: Research & practice* (pp. 222–242). Kotka: Palmenia Centre for Continuing Education, University of Helsinki.

Nieminen, J. (2012). A Finnish perspective: Features of the history of modern youth work and youth organisations. In F. Coussée, H. Williamson & G. Verschelden (Eds.), *The history of youth work in Europe: Relevance for today's youth policy* (pp. 65–74). Strasbourg: Council of Europe Publishing.

Nygård, M. (2006). Welfare-ideological change in Scandinavia: A comparative analysis of partisan welfare state positions in four Nordic countries, 1970–2003. *Scandinavian Political Studies*, *29*(4), 356–385.

Ord, J. (2007). *Youth work process, product and practice: Creating an authentic curriculum in work with young people*. Dorset: Russell House.

Osberg, D. & Biesta, G. (2008). The emergent curriculum: Navigating a complex course between unguided learning and planned enculturation. *Journal of Curriculum Studies*, *40*(3), 313–328.

Otrusinova, M. & Pastuszkova, E. (2012). Concept of 3 E's and public administration performance. *International Journal of System Applications, Engineering & Development*, *6*(2), 171–178.

Pinar, W.F. (2011). *The character of curriculum studies*. New York: Palgrave Macmillan.

Pinar, W.F. (2012). *What is curriculum theory?* New York: Routledge.

Polanyi, M. (2009). *The tacit dimension*. Chicago: University of Chicago Press.

Ritzer, G. (1993). *The McDonaldization of society*. Thousand Oaks, CA: Pine Forge Press.

Seal, M. (2014). Youth work is just common sense … The relevance of philosophy to everyday youth and community work. In M. Seal & S. Frost (Eds.), *Philosophy in youth and community work* (pp. 8–22). Dorset: Russell House.

Snyder, M. (2009). In the footsteps of Kurt Lewin: Practical theorizing, action research, and the psychology of social action. *Journal of Social Issues*, *65*(1), 225–245.

Walker, J. (2016). Crafting the space between either and or: Attending to the role of words, young people and public will. In L. Siurala, F. Coussée, L. Suurpää & H. Williamson (Eds.), *Autonomy through dependency – Histories of co-operation, conflict and innovation in youth work* (pp. 11–23). Strasbourg: Council of Europe Publishing.

Weber, M. (1976). *Witschaft und Gesellschaft*. Tübingen: J.C.B. Mohr.

Wenger, E. (2008). *Communities of practice, learning, meaning and identity*. Cambridge: Cambridge University Press.

Williamson, H. (2012). The wonderful world of youth work. Youth Department, the City of Helsinki.

Youth Act (2006). Youth Act (unofficial translation). Ministry of Education and Culture, Finland. Retrieved from http://www.ilo.org/dyn/natlex/docs/ELECTRONIC/73188/97071/F30481611/FIN73188%20English.pdf

44

Evaluating Youth Work in its Contexts

Susan Cooper and Anu Gretschel

INTRODUCTION

One of the biggest challenges facing youth work today is the need to articulate its intrinsic and extrinsic value, its worth to young people and communities, and its worth to society. Perhaps now, more than ever, it is vital that we demonstrate this worth to policy makers and funders. The way in which this challenge has been taken on is however problematic. The need to be accountable has been interpreted very narrowly and this has led to the dominance of an experimental evaluation paradigm. Quasi-scientific methods, such as random-controlled trials and control groups are seen as the gold standard in producing evidence of effectiveness and worth. We argue that accountability is important but that a range of methods are required if we are to adequately account for the impact and effectiveness of youth work. In this chapter we draw on our research from two participatory evaluation examples: Transformative Evaluation from England and the Deliberative Discussion Day

from Finland. Here, we describe the processes and the kinds of evidence these examples provide about the importance of youth work. In both examples there is a foundational aim to inform youth work practice during the process of evaluation, to evidence existing successful forms of practice, to identify where practice can be improved, and to respond to the demands of funders and stakeholders (see Chelimsky, 1997). Both examples have been developed for evaluating youth work within its contexts, and both seek to develop coherence between youth work, an educational activity based on dialogical relationships, and the processes we use to evaluate it in order that these processes do not change the very nature of the practice being evaluated.

TWO COUNTRIES, TWO PARTICIPATORY EVALUATION EXAMPLES

Transformative Evaluation (TE) was developed in 2011, at a time when the youth work sector in England was experiencing signifi-cant reduction in funding (Davies, 2013). Economic constraints imposed by austerity measures paved the way for a 'payment-by-results' culture that emphasized pre-determined outcomes that were measurable as the basis for evaluation. According to the National Youth Agency, there is no longer a common form of youth service across England. The youth work 'offer' has dimin-ished and in some areas councils no longer publish a youth offer (NYA, 2014). The impe-tus for the development of TE was a need to create an evaluation methodology that enabled youth workers to take a more active role in demonstrating effectiveness and impact. Rather than using pre-determined indicators, the Transformative Evaluation process begins with young people's accounts of impact, about how their involvement has supported them to address the issues in their everyday lives (Cooper, 2012). It is an adapted form of the 'Most Significant Change' (MSC) technique (Davies, 1998). Essentially the MSC technique involves the generation of a number of participants' significant change stories during a given time period and the systematic collective analysis of the stories (see Davies & Dart, 2005 for detailed infor-mation about the MSC technique).

Transformative Evaluation is informed by appreciative inquiry, a strength-based approach that works from the premise that if we ask questions about problems we create a reality of problems; if we ask questions about 'what works' we create a reality of potential (Reed, 2007). All involved, young people, youth workers and stakeholders, engage in appreciative reflection, which according to Marchi (2011) involves the development of action and learning processes based on valuing and building upon what works, what makes us feel good, what we perceive as positive, and what gives us a sense of strength and well-being in the work we do.

The origins of the Deliberative Discussion Day in Finland are quite different. Here youth work is still defined as one the basic services

provided by the state. The Youth Act (72/2006) states youth work is the responsibility of local authorities, even when it is organized by other actors like NGOs and parishes. However, as elsewhere, youth work is coming under assault in Finland. For example, the ways in which youth work is offered are no longer explicitly defined in the new Youth Act draft produced in 2015. Up to this point, the outcomes of youth work had been mainly measured by the number of young people participating and the availability of statutory services in each municipality. The 'payment-by-results' culture is also now seen to be emerging in Finland. In line with its commitment to open-ness, the Ministry of Education and Culture financed a network-based research project to prepare its principles and indicators for youth work. Over 600 young people, youth work-ers, administrators and decision makers from local, regional and national levels participated (Gretschel, Junttila-Vitikka & Puuronen, 2016). The Deliberative Discussion Day was used in the research project as one of the methods for bringing together the different stakeholders' opinions.

Broadly, both methods offer insights as to how youth work organizations can improve their need-responsiveness; in other words how they might re-shape or improve practices to meet the needs of young people and com-munities. Transformative Evaluation authen-ticates why it is important to have youth work in society: it evidences what kind of local-level needs can be met by youth work and how practice can be developed to address those needs even more effectively. The Deliberative Discussion Day works more on a structural level: it provides information about how and where youth work service offerings are organized, what kind of provision there is, and information about quality, sufficiency and availability for those who need it most.

In short, evaluation does not benignly enable judgment; it influences our view of the purpose of youth work and raises fundamen-tal questions about power, about whose needs are prioritized, and whose voices are heard.

Participatory approaches offer a way forward in addressing these questions. The commitment to local control and capacity building enables young people, practitioners and decision makers to generate their own learning, and through this develop their agency as they learn more about themselves and the context and situation in which they find themselves (Forss, Rebien & Carlsson, 2002). The participatory and collective nature of enquiry creates better, more in-depth and more accurate knowledge of the performance and impacts of a practice intervention (Jackson & Kassam, 1998).

Participatory evaluation is a 'doing-with' rather than a 'doing-to' practice, and as such supports a more democratic and political approach to evaluation (Estrella, 2000; Ledwith & Springett, 2010). It raises important questions about who defines and measures change and for whose benefit this is done. The very fact that it is participatory implies democracy in that it provides a vehicle for people to have a voice in the decisions that affect their lives and act collectively for the common good (Freire, 2005; Torres & Reyes, 2011). The examples from practice used in this chapter have a commitment to participation, and thus aim to significantly contribute to empowerment through centralizing the voice of all involved. However, it cannot be assumed that just because something is called 'participatory', it is empowering. Critical attention to the ways in which the *meaningful participation* (Geissel, 2013) of a range of stakeholders can be achieved is a vital aspect of both methods. In the following we seek to use the practice examples to illuminate the benefits of adopting participatory approaches to evaluation in youth work.

USING TRANSFORMATIVE EVALUATION TO MEASURE YOUTH OUTCOMES

In England, considerable attention has been paid to developing evaluation frameworks and tools to aid practitioners in meeting the challenge of evidencing the impact of their work. Our argument is that while these advances are welcome, they have been of a technical nature and aimed at a surface level. If the goal is to develop understanding of 'what works and how' so that we are better able to articulate the value of youth work, then we need more than an enhanced toolkit; we need to critically consider the evaluative practices themselves, to question whether these practices enable or disenable youth workers to articulate the value of youth work. The dominant discourse of evaluation is problematic for youth and community workers on two counts. Firstly, the experimental paradigm can be seen as incongruent with the ethos of youth work in that it is underpinned by the notion that a problem is identified (the 'ill'), action is taken ('the medication'), and a desired outcome is achieved (the 'cure'). This can result in a 'problematizing' agenda. Youth work is a relational practice that centralizes the issues that young people bring from their everyday lives (Batsleer, 2008). The commitment to working in partnership with young people on issues that they identify as important is central to youth work. Young people in this context are viewed as active agents in the process of change, but this way of working is at odds with the notion of pre-determined outcomes. Further, it has been argued that the experimental paradigm is inadequate for capturing the complexity and demonstrating the value of this work to policy makers and funders. Complementary evaluation processes such as Transformative Evaluation can generate evidence of impact and effectiveness that tells a more nuanced story.

Secondly, the experimental paradigm is generally informed by a technocratic conception of accountability that is based on control and regulation, and in this context evaluation can be reduced to upward compliance (Ellis, 2008). This affects the way in which youth workers perceive and experience evaluation, often resulting in fear and suspicion (Derrick-Mills, 2011). Either way, the knowledge and understanding of youth workers' daily practice is lost, reducing the potential to articulate and promote the value of youth work. Workers are 'caught between a rock and a hard place'. On the one hand, they are criticized for not adequately demonstrating the impact of their work and, on the other, they feel a loss of control over the direction of their work as day-to-day practice changes because of imposed evaluation mechanisms that rely solely on quantification (Cooper, 2011). Our argument is that if youth work is to be enabled to account for itself then a range of approaches is required. Participatory approaches to evaluation that are more akin to youth work practice and potentially more able to capture the richness of the impact of youth work's relational practice need to be part of the mix (Cooper, 2012; Patton, 2008; Powers & Tiffany, 2006).

PRACTICE Context: The TRANSFORM Project

The first of our two practice examples draws on an evaluation project implemented in Footsteps (pseudonym), a small voluntary-sector, community-based youth organization in England. Footsteps' aim is to work with disadvantaged young people who do not receive the support and opportunities they need. They take a collaborative approach, working closely with communities and partners to meet local needs. In 2014 Footsteps made a successful grant application to the Big Lottery 'Reaching Communities' fund to run a three-year youth project. In order to do this it was necessary for them to agree to achieve the following predefined outcomes:

Outcome 1: Young people involved in the project will show an increase in community participation and there will be less anti-social behaviour in the area.

Outcome 2: Young people involved in the project will increase their confidence and self-esteem.
Outcome 3: Young people will have increased awareness and be supported to make safer and healthier life-style choices, reducing self-harming behaviour.

Each outcome was assigned quantitative targets across the three years of the project. The funding enabled Footsteps to run two generic and three specialized youth work sessions a week and a program of weekend excursions, and residential and weekly expert-led activities to engage young people in the 11–19 age-group. These sessions aimed to attract young people off the streets into positive activities and relationships, allowing professional workers to engage them in taking responsibility for decision making in the day-to-day running and future developments of the project. Footsteps had in place a system for gathering numeric data to account for their work but they also wanted to use a complementary evaluative process that went beyond the numbers, a process that could provide them with qualitative evidence to demonstrate how their interventions impacted the young people who used their services and on the wider community. To this end they adopted Transformative Evaluation.

Transformative Evaluation addresses the three purposes of evaluation: accountability, project development and practice knowledge development (Chelimsky, 1997). In doing this, it seeks to address youth workers' sense of exclusion from the evaluation process (Ellis, 2008) and support their re-engagement as researchers of their own practice as opposed to acting as mere 'data collectors' (Cooper, 2014; Kajamaa, 2011). TE has been shown to generate evidence of impact and, at the same time, positively impact youth work practice (Cooper, 2013). Its participatory and dialogical nature enables practitioners to be active agents in the evaluation process and is congruent with youth work values. Establishing dialogue between the evaluators (in this case, the youth workers), young people, and other community members is a critical element of a transformative paradigm (Whitmore et al., 2006).

As seen in Figure 44.1, TE follows a four-stage process that is repeated every three to four months: (1) story generation; (2) analysis and selection; (3) final selection and feedback; and (4) meta-evaluation. The process begins with youth workers generating significant change stories with young people that emerge from the open question: 'Looking back, what do you think has been the most significant change that occurred for you as a result of coming here?' The youth workers engaged young people in conversation and recorded the responses. The young people were encouraged to explain how the intervention had enabled the change and why the change was significant to them, promoting reflective dialogue between the young person and the youth worker. The young person's words form the first part of the story as shown in the example of Lara's story below:

> We're always asking each other 'when's the youthy on this week?' and 'when's youthy open?' We don't have much else to do other than coming here. This place keeps us out of trouble and we're not intimidating people here like we are at the shops. Coming here has helped me grow up more and act more mature too.

Generating the stories involved facilitating young people to reflect on the outcome of their engagement, illuminating their learning journeys. The process also supported the youth worker's learning in that the conversations often revealed a different picture, as shown by this worker's comment:

> Just reminiscing [with the young person] about that experience, for both of us was really interesting, and her perspective of that experience was different to what mine was, a different view of the outcome, a different view than I expected of what she got out of it.

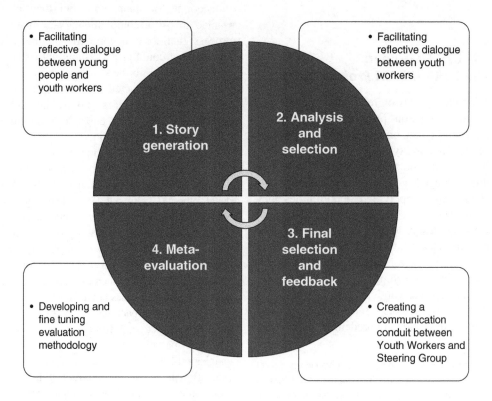

Figure 44.1   The Transformative Evaluation model (Cooper, 2014)

Importantly, learning is extended or solidified as a result of that illumination. One worker articulated this well when she said *'the process of generating the story is a journey in itself'*. Story generation validates the activity of 'sitting down and talking' with young people and promotes a shift from everyday surface conversation to deeper and more meaningful educative conversations that constitute skilful youth work. The story generation stage enhanced existing relationships between the youth workers and the young people and thus improved practice 'in the moment', as demonstrated by the following comments from youth workers:

… because you're asking them questions which are kind of difficult rather than just offhand comments about things, you create a bit more of a relationship, you develop a relationship with people a bit more.

… the stories they told were meaningful to both of us, from the experiences that had gone on in the Centre so, there was a bit of bonding there whilst we discussed the stories.

The evaluation process enabled workers to develop deeper relationships with young people, and this is significant in regards to changing the connection many practitioners have with evaluation. It becomes meaningful and valuable to them; it becomes congruent with their youth work practice and is seen as embedded within that practice.

Stage 2 involved the analysis and selection of the generated change stories. The youth workers met to discuss and analyse the 12 stories they had generated during the three-month period. This analysis process began with the sorting of stories into domains and assigning domain names based on the content of the stories and the workers' interpretation of this content in relation to the purpose of youth work. This led to in-depth discussion and reflection. Following this, the originating youth worker added context and professional commentary to the young person's story – the 'back story'. Engagement in reflective dialogue with peers

about their understanding of the young person's story and their intervention supported the youth worker in the co-construction of the story. Returning to Lara's story, the youth worker added the following commentary:

Lara is a regular member of the youth group. She often gets frustrated by the treatment her group of friends receive from local residents and business owners in the area, and feels 'hard done by' as she believes she has done nothing wrong. Recently though, Lara has attended some community events such as a coffee morning held at the youth centre and is beginning to see the perspectives of other people in the area, and how their group could be intimidating to some even if nobody is actually doing anything 'wrong'.

The final act of this stage was for the youth workers to reach consensus on the most significant change story for each domain, and their reason for selection, which was then added to the story. The analysis and selection stages provide a space for in-depth discussion and reflection. The collective reflective dialogue that is central to the methodology involves an examination of the articulated values of the youth workers. One worker explained the process as follows:

Discussing why a story should go through and why it shouldn't and finding out what everyone thought, either individually or as a group as to what is distance travelled and what is an achievement for a young person and working out who has come the furthest and who has achieved the most.

You can see from this quotation that the process prompted some fundamental questioning, for example the meaning of 'distance travelled', 'achievement' and judgment-making in regards to these often taken-for-granted terms. The process requires practitioners to move from micro-level analysis towards mezzo-level analysis through active collective reflection on the educational goals and values of youth work (Ng & Tan, 2009). Returning to Lara's story, the youth worker added the group's reason for selecting her story as the most significant change story:

> The Youth Workers Group selected this story because it highlights the important advocacy role of youth workers, as they act as a bridge to build relationships between young people and their community. This bridge building requires both support and challenge on both sides and careful, thoughtful facilitation. It is at the core of sustainable development.

At this point, the selected contextualized stories were sent to the steering group for stage 3 of the process. Membership of the steering group includes people who have a stake in the project but are not practitioners, for example it could include managers, leaders of partnership organizations, and community representatives. Members are selected on the basis that they have an interest in the outcomes of the project. In this case, the membership consisted of the organization's manager and three partner representatives. The steering group discussed the selected contextualized stories and selected the MSC story for the whole cycle. Having made their selection they added their reason for selection and then returned this MSC story to the youth workers' group. Transformative Evaluation creates a knowledge conduit as the bottom-up approach recognizes that those engaged in the delivery of services often know more about the activities than their managers and leaders. Importantly, it provides a process to move knowledge from one part of the organization to another, up, down and across (Cooper, 2013). We return to Lara's story to see the reason given by the steering group for their selection:

> The Steering Group selected this story as it demonstrates the impact of youth work on the wider community. It shows how the 'Youthy' has become central in young people's lives but also highlights the link between what happens in the club and what happens beyond the club – in the community. The youth workers have been able to build a safe environment in which young people have felt able and enabled to firstly develop effective relationships with each other and with the youth

workers. This has developed their confidence, self-awareness and broadened their understanding of their community, and these combined have led to an emerging empathy.

Stage 4, the concluding stage, involved a process of meta-evaluation. At the end of each cycle both groups reviewed their experience of using the methodology with the purpose of developing skills and understanding to inform the next cycle.

Benefits of Transformative Evaluation

The benefits of using Transformative Evaluation can be seen at multiple levels (see Table 44.1). The impact of TE can be seen at the macro level in that it produces a collection of Significant Change stories, which, using the words of the young people, youth workers and stakeholders, provide 'rich' descriptions of the impact of interventions on the lives of young people which can then be used to demonstrate the value of youth work at a societal level. Potentially, it can change the knowledge base and thus affect policy making. We assert that Transformative Evaluation also improves practice, it has 'process use' (Patton, 2008); this can be seen at the micro level where it enhances practice 'in the moment', and supports practitioners to become critically reflective. At the mezzo level, Transformative Evaluation provides a conduit for 'bottom-up' learning in organizations (Cooper, 2013).

It is important to acknowledge that TE is not a 'silver bullet' and has its limitations. For some, the process of generating stories may raise concerns about validity in regards to sampling; for others the concern might be that youth workers may lead or manipulate young people's voices. The notion of 'generating' rather than 'collecting' stories is used to make the 'evaluator involvement' in the process transparent. The use of purposive sampling can be seen as a weakness

Table 44.1 The benefits of using Transformative Evaluation

Data from Transformative Evaluation	Data from existing evaluation	Benefits of Transformative Evaluation		
		Micro level	Mezzo level	Macro level
Stories of changes in young people's attitudes and behaviours that originated from their perspectives. Importantly, this data provided examples of both anticipated and unanticipated outcomes.	Number of young people participating in community events. Number of young people attending the youth project. Number of young people participating in health-related focused activities.	Young people able to articulate their learning; learning enhanced by process. Enhanced relationships between young people and youth workers.	Youth workers engaged in critical reflection (double loop learning). Communication conduit opened between young people, workers and organization leaders. Organizational learning.	Production of a new source of knowledge to inform decision making for funders and policy makers. Value of youth work to society is expressed.

in the experimental paradigm; however, in Transformative Evaluation it is seen as strength. It is entirely appropriate to select 'excellent informants' (Spradley, 1979) on the basis that they are able to tell us the most about the questions we ask. Selecting young people based on prior knowledge that they have experienced a change as a result of being involved with the organization is purposefully 'biased', not to make the organization look good but in order to learn from those cases of good practice (Patton, 2002). Some may question whether young people are willing to share the negative when youth workers serve as the evaluator, but this is to misunderstand the purpose. Transformative Evaluation is underpinned by appreciative enquiry; it does not seek to identify what is not working, but what is, in order that we develop understanding about why it is working. The 'appreciative gaze' (Ghaye et al., 2008) of this form of evaluation counters the effects of performativity and the deficit-based discourse associated with accountability and managerialism. Lastly, critics of participatory evaluation often raise questions about validity, reliability and generalizability, yet these concerns are clearly located in positivist-inspired aspirations. Participatory evaluation is informed by the interpretive paradigm and does not draw on these positivist criteria,

rather it uses terms such as credibility, transferability, dependability and confirmability (Guba & Lincoln, 2005). To those aligned with the experimental paradigm and published standards of evidence who may question whether or not these stories count as 'evidence', our response is clear: certainly, the stories do not demonstrate causality using a control group; this is not their intention. However, arguably, the stories do provide a reasonable and credible expression of the contribution that the project interventions made in changing lives. The participatory nature of co-constructing stories, together with the contribution analysis that takes place at stage 2, is fundamental in producing trustworthy and authentic primary data.

DELIBERATIVE DISCUSSION DAY

The first example demonstrates how participatory evaluation can create knowledge about the impact of youth work for young people, groups, the community and society. It demonstrates the potential of participatory approaches to develop the effectiveness of the work by enabling a more nuanced understanding of the youth work process. In this second example of participatory evaluation the approach is quite different. Here, the participants of the evaluation highlighted the equality and ease of access to service provision as important factors when considering the quality, impact and effectiveness of youth work.

The second practice example of participatory evaluation followed the Deliberative Discussion Day procedure (from now on referred to as DDD) and was organized in Lahti, a city of about 100,000 inhabitants in southern Finland in spring 2014 (Gretschel, 2016). The method follows some general criteria of deliberative methods. These criteria have been interpreted as inclusiveness, quality discussions and the connection to decision making (see for example, Carson & Hartz-Karp, 2005). In the case presented here, the process started with young people evaluating youth services in their area. A range of young people were asked to work as evaluators, this included those known to be active from youth or pupil council work, and, importantly, other young people, for example, those that lived in a particular neighbourhood, those that used the youth centre and those that spent their spare time in the local park. Altogether 50 13–19-year-olds participated in the process. Following the young peoples' evaluation, the youth workers and decision makers were invited to evaluate the same services, but from perspectives prioritized by the young people involved. The process ended with consensus negotiations in which the stakeholders discussed how the services could be best developed. As a result, everyone learnt something and the services were developed to be more needs-responsive.

According to the young people, there was nothing to do after the age of 13 in their neighbourhood called Renkomäki, in the most southern part of Lahti city. Activities and in and outdoor places of assembly were needed. True, admitted the youth workers and decision makers. City youth services, a school for classes 7–9 located further away mainly used by the youth of the area and the parish promised to start some activities immediately. This area was not unknown to these actors; there already had been a long tradition of organizing popular offerings for 12-year-olds and younger children and unsuccessful attempts for older children. (This description was written by researcher AG, who was also facilitating the discussion.)

The evaluation was situated in Lahti because of the city youth service's willingness to cooperate with research and to hear what the young people had to say. In this specific DDD example, the data produced were analysed for two purposes. Firstly, to discover the directions youth work should take and, secondly, to shed new light on how and with which criteria the quality and accessibility of youth work provision should be reported on at local and national levels. The evaluation process was part of a larger study financed by the Ministry of Education and Culture (Gretschel et al., 2016).

Uncovering Contradictions in Service Production

In Lahti, the strategic planning of youth work is done by the Development Program for Youth Services (Lahti city, 2012a). The Youth Act states that a network responsible for the coordination of public services for young people should be named. The main aim of this network is to help young people find services most suitable to their needs. In Lahti, the Group for the Welfare of Children and Young People (from now on referred to as the Welfare Group) is responsible for multi-sector cooperation in the town and the four districts. The law also requires an action plan for how leisure activities provided for young people by the municipality are organized to promote the well-being of children, as described in the Child Welfare Act (417/2007). In Lahti, this was called The Welfare Plan of Children and Young People (Lahti city, 2012b). This plan also includes instructions on how Welfare Groups from different areas of the city should work.

The Youth Act states that offering leisure activities to young people is the responsibility of the municipalities. Lahti's local Welfare Plan aims to offer each young person the opportunity to have a leisure pursuit. It was thought that this could be reached by offering low-threshold, leisure-pursuit groups. The city youth service aimed to develop cooperation with youth work organizations and this was written into the Development Program for Youth Services (Lahti city, 2012a). Staff representatives also played an active role in the Welfare Groups, for example, in the southern area, a youth worker held the role of group secretary.

Following a discussion between the young people of Renkomäki and decision makers, it seemed the area would gain some activities for young people up to the age of 13 as resources were available from the city, a school and the parish. The first problem was that there were no free premises for youth work in the area; the only suitable public building in the area was a primary school, and this was being used to capacity. A longer-term strategy was required to emphasize the need to share by those organizing activities for young people living in each area. The Deliberative Day Discussion also highlighted that the composition of Welfare Groups, as planned by the local authority, did not provide sufficient support for youth work issues. The group members were mainly from the fields of schools, health and education. To address this, another network was created, Bodies Organizing Youth Work, to develop cooperation between youth work bodies in the area.

The Welfare Group later discussed the absence of services for young people in Renkomäki, and decided it should or could conduct a systematic analysis to discover which neighbourhoods failed to respond to the need to provide leisure activities for young people of different ages. However, there were a number of problems, for example a lack of time and resources, no named responsibilities within Welfare Group and no channels for sharing the outcomes of the analysis with decision makers for the purposes of allocating resources. To ensure sustainable youth work provision in Renkomäki, other structural changes were needed. The earlier council decision to have only one centre in each youth work area resulted in an increase in the distances young people had to travel to reach it. Additionally, the centre was already full and did not have the capacity to accommodate young people from Renkomäki. The effect of centralization procedures increased drastically with the Youth Services Development Program, which invested all open youth work staff resources in the above sparsely located facilities. It is not possible to turn back the clock; however in the future at least, youth work could focus more on coordinating the cooperation of the various youth work actors in neighbourhoods to support the more equal distribution of services.

About the Practical and Theoretical Background of Deliberative Discussion Day Procedure

In Finland it has been easy to gather youth workers, administrators and decision makers, including those from the highest level of local authorities, to engage in discussion with young people. Such discussions have occurred in more than seventy municipalities in Finland since 2008. The origins of developing the DDD procedure are rooted in the Youth Act (72/2006) that states: 'Young people must be given opportunities to take part in the handling of matters concerning local and regional youth work and youth policy. Further, young people shall be heard in matters concerning them' (Gretschel & Kauniskangas, 2012). The procedure was developed to help local actors involve young people in the evaluation of youth work in order to identify if services needed fine tuning or even reorientation from the perspectives of young people.

The process is led by facilitators who introduce the young people to the idea of using speech circles, which allows each opinion to be considered as it arises. At this stage, young people are divided into smaller groups to discuss the quality of youth work provision based on their own experiences of using the service under review. Moreover, the DDD process aims not only to ask if services are produced properly but also to allow young people to question whether they are the right services in the first place. For this, an open-ended question layout is used such as, 'Are we satisfied with youth work services, and if not, what should happen?' In this practice example, some groups were based on location, with young people from the same area reflecting on their needs. In others, young people reflected on specific existing services or facilities. This led to theme groups being created according to arising needs, such as a park for young people.

Following the group work, the young people met youth workers and decision makers face-to-face and were able to raise their development proposals with them directly. Altogether, 27 representatives of the bodies producing and allocating resources participated in the process, including representatives from the city's youth services (youth workers, administrators and the Education Committee handling youth work), NGOs and parishes, and other services also used by young people, such as the library.

The facilitators had a vital role to play in enabling a symmetrical relationship between the young people and the adults. It was important to ensure, at the invitation stage, that there were more young people than adults present and that the discussions began with the hearing of a statement, question or proposal prepared by the young people in advance. The young people were also given more weight in terms of speech turns.

One important component of DDD is the aim to offer young people a channel for citizens' participation. In DDD the results of the evaluation are always documented, reported and published. A roadmap instrument was used to transform talk into action. The idea is also to encourage young people to take part in realizing the actions, for example by offering them adult support to do so. As stated earlier, Lahti was prepared to organize some activities for the Renkomäki area. Beyond that, as our example showed, some strategic changes were also needed, and some results will be seen over a longer period. Organizing the evaluation as a regularly repeated process secures follow-up for the issues raised by young people. Arguably, regular interaction between young people and decision-making bodies not only produces more enlightened citizens (Geissel, 2013), but also more enlightened decision makers, and that looks ahead to more sustainable service production in the future.

Added Value of DDD in Youth Work Evaluation

There are several types of indicators already in use for securing the quality of youth work at a city and national level (see Table 44.2); for example the number of participants in the low-threshold, leisure-pursuit groups, user satisfaction and the degree of use of the youth centre premises. These were shown to be at a good level (Lahti city, 2012a, 2012b). On a national level good numbers were reported in relation to the amount of youth centres and state-funded leisure pursuits being offered (Ministry of Finance, 2014). DDD provided a different kind of information, for example knowledge of which principles (like equal access) could be highlighted when selecting evaluation criteria in the future.

An output of the DDD in 2014 was an indication that the accessibility of youth work service provision could be developed. It generated knowledge of how young people use the services, for example the young people in this case were not prepared to visit youth centres in different neighbourhoods. The method also allowed reoriented visions of better service production to enter the discussion.

Table 44.2   Indicators and benefits before and after deliberative discussion day

Data from Deliberative Discussion Day/Lahti 2014	*Former volume-focused indicators of youth work offerings*	*Benefits from DDD (Lahti 2014)*	
		Including elements of equality into the indicators	*Participatory method in ensuring sustainability in decision making*
The lack of youth work offerings in some neighbourhoods and for some age groups, even when needed.	Amount of youth centres and low-threshold leisure-pursuit groups. Amount of participants. Satisfaction of the participants. Utilization degree of the youth house premises. Amount of young people living near youth centres.	Analysing the equality and accessibility of service offerings per each service, neighbourhood and age group.	Evaluating with young people and also with those who are not using the services. Offering a possibility for reciprocal learning between young people, youth workers and decision makers. Using evaluation procedures that support service development, even re-orientation.

Face-to-face dialogues with young people are not the only way for securing quality in youth work services. It would also be undemocratic to rely solely on young people to maintain the quality of youth provision. This means some structural quality assurance methods are also needed. In this case, this could mean regular equality and unrestricted accessibility mapping of each service, based on youth-driven knowledge of typical physical, social and economic barriers. Mapping could also include information about possible improvements and how improved participation is to be supported in the future.

Organizing structural dialogues between decision makers and young people could clip the wings of ever deepening austerity-talk. Young people are clear in their descriptions of which and where youth work services are needed. DDD is a participative evaluation method in which a dialogical arena is created for young people to meet decision makers face-to-face. This provides both the space and the possibility to jointly create the knowledge base used for planning and decision making by the local authorities. The creation of 'dialogical moments' between young people and decision makers serve to safeguard the quality of the services. As

well as providing evaluation results that tell about the level of need-responsiveness of the services provided, DDD also highlights differences between the opinions of young people and decision makers, and the level of awareness of the decision makers about the needs of young people.

CONCLUSION

The two examples used in this chapter present very different evaluation processes. While they are both participatory in nature, they have different purposes and involve different types of participants. Transformative Evaluation is an ongoing process, whereas the Deliberative Discussion Day is an annual or bi-annual event. There are however three important similarities between these processes which are worthy of further examination. Firstly, both processes draw on different types of knowledge (young people's knowledge, youth workers' knowledge and decision makers' knowledge) and value this knowledge for its contribution towards generating a more nuanced understanding of youth work and its ability to improve the lives of young people and communities. As stated at the beginning of this chapter, young people's meaningful participation (Geissel, 2013) is a crucial aspect of participatory evaluation. Both TE and DDD processes begin with young people; it is their participation and the outcomes of that participation that shape the evaluation outcomes. In Transformative Evaluation young people's participation enables an articulation of youth work impact, and in DDD it enables a critical review of strategic decision making.

Secondly, both evaluation methodologies demonstrate the value of the 'process use' of evaluation, which Patton (2008) describes as the learning that is gained from engaging in evaluation itself and which is distinct from learning that arises from findings presented in evaluation reports. Through engaging those who are usually excluded from the evaluation process (young people and youth workers), they develop evaluative skills and thinking that supports a deeper involvement in the evaluation of services promoting a more sustainable future.

Lastly, both Transformative Evaluation and the Deliberative Discussion Day examples provide evidence to support the importance of taking context into account. Young people and the communities in which they live are essentially unique; policy makers and funders are often distant from these. Whilst, in general, it is conceivable that many of the challenges young people face in their everyday lives are shared, context does make a difference to the ways in which individuals and groups access and use services. If evaluation is to inform future services then it needs to take account of context.

In this climate of decreasing resources it can appear that a greater level of scrutiny of how resources are used is sensible and practical. Clearly, measuring the impact of the youth work process whilst demonstrating its effectiveness and how it is delivered are important and valuable, but equally, it is necessary to recognize that these are not neutral concepts. Evaluation is a political activity; it is socially constructed, and, importantly, it is not only informed by, but also contributes to policy discourses of youth work on a range of levels (see for example Taylor and Balloch, 2005). The idea of accountability should be re-conceptualized to also include the quality of the decision-making processes to ensure these are informed by multiple sources of knowledge, particularly when deciding where and to whom youth work is made available or not. Judgments of qualities must include considerations of aspects of equality and access to service provision.

In this chapter we have argued that an over-emphasis on a narrowly formed conception of accountability as the key function of evaluation is risky on a number of levels. There is a risk that the evaluation process itself distorts the fundamental purpose of youth work as practices change to enable organizations to meet its requirements (e.g., allocating time to the creation of checklists and charts). Further, these forms of evaluation often exclude the voices of people who are directly affected – the young people themselves and the workers who engage with them. Participatory evaluation reframes stakeholders as 'experts' and values their contribution to the creation of knowledge. When macro- and mezzo-level decision making is based purely on knowledge created by externally driven evaluation processes, there is a real risk that youth work becomes normative rather than transformative. Both examples in this chapter, Transformative Evaluation and the Deliberative Day Discussion have transformative qualities, albeit at different degrees and levels. They each place central importance on the lives and experience of a broad range of people who are generally excluded from decision-making processes (Mertens, 2009), questioning asymmetric power relations.

Our contention is that it is vital to embrace a pluralistic approach to evaluating the impact of youth work and its value to society. In the short term it will be necessary to address the tensions that clearly exist between the different evaluation paradigms.

Trust is a central feature here – are policy makers and funders ready to trust young people themselves to identify what it is they need or to judge the shape and extent of their own learning? Equally, are they ready to trust that youth workers and young people can generate honest and meaningful interpretations of youth work? Are they ready to listen to what they have to say in relation to the youth work services available? We believe that youth workers, youth work organizations and the academy can work collectively to address these tensions by using a diversity of approaches to generate different types of evidence that together produce the 'best' available accounts of the difference youth and community work makes to the lives of young people, communities and society. In the long term this will enable us to more clearly articulate the purpose and value of youth work and make best use of the resources available.

REFERENCES

Batsleer, J. (2008). *Informal learning in youth work*. London: Sage.

Carson, L. & Hartz-Karp, J. (2005). Adapting and combining deliberative designs: Juries, polls and forums. In J. Gastil & P. Levine (Eds.), *The deliberative democracy handbook: Strategies for effective civic engagement in the twenty-first century* (pp. 120–138). San Francisco, CA: Jossey-Bass.

Chelimsky, E. (1997). Thoughts for a new evaluation society. *Evaluation, 3*(1), 97–118.

Cooper, S. (2011). Reconnecting with evaluation: The benefits of using a participatory approach to assess impact. *Youth & Policy, 107*, 55–70.

Cooper, S. (2012). Evaluation: Ensuring accountability or improving practice? In J. Ord (Ed.), *Critical issues in youth work management* (pp. 82–95). London: Routledge.

Cooper, S. (2013). Transformative evaluation: Organisational learning through participative practice. *The Learning Organization, 21*(2), 146–157.

Cooper, S. (2014). Putting collective reflective dialogue at the heart of the evaluation process. *Reflective Practice, 15*(5), 563–578.

Davies, B. (2013). Youth work in a changing policy landscape: The view from England. *Youth & Policy, 110*, 6–32.

Davies, R. (1998). An evolutionary approach to facilitating organisational learning: An experiment by the Christian Commission for Development. In D. Mosse, J. Farrington, & A. Rew (Eds.), *Development as process: Concepts and methods for working with complexity* (pp. 68–83). London: Routledge.

Davies, R. & Dart, J. (2005). *The 'most significant change' (MSC) technique: A guide to its use*. Melbourne, Australia: MandE.

Derrick-Mills, T. (2011). Building the value of evaluation: Engaging with reflective practitioners. *New Directions for Evaluation, 131*(Autumn), 83–90.

Ellis, J. (2008). *Accountability and learning: Developing monitoring and evaluation in the third sector*. London: Charities Evaluation Services.

Estrella, M. (2000). Learning from change. In M. Estrella (Ed.), *Learning from change: Issues and experiences in participatory monitoring and evaluation* (pp. 1–14). London: Intermediate Technology Publications Ltd.

Forss, K., Rebien, C. & Carlsson, J. (2002). Process use of evaluations: Types of use that precede lessons learned and feedback. *Evaluation, 8*(1), 29–45.

Freire, P. (2005). *Pedagogy of indignation*. Boulder, CO: Paradigm Publishers.

Geissel, B. (2013). Introduction: On the evaluation of participatory innovations. In B. Geissel & M. Joas (Eds.), *Participatory democratic innovations in Europe: Improving the quality of democracy?* (pp. 8–31). Opladen: Barbara Budrich Publishers.

Ghaye, T., Melander-Wikman, A., Kisare, M., Chambers, P., Bergmark, U., Kostenius, C., & Lillyman, S. (2008). Participatory and appreciative action and reflection (PAAR) – democratizing reflective practices. *Reflective Practice, 9*(4), 361–397.

Gretschel, A. (2016). Developing the evaluation of web based and near services of youth work. In A. Gretschel, P. Junttila-Vitikka & A. Puuronen, *Guidelines for defining and evaluating the youth affairs sector* (pp. 63–113).

Helsinki: Finnish Youth Research Society. Retrieved from http://www.nuorisotutkimus-seura.fi/images/julkaisuja/suuntaviivoja_nuorisotoimialan_maarittelyyn_ja_arviointiin.pdf (see pages 247–248 for abstract in English).

Gretschel, A., Junttila-Vitikka, P., & Puuronen, A. (2016). *Guidelines for defining and evaluating the youth affairs sector*. Helsinki: Finnish Youth Research Society. Retrieved from http://www.nuorisotutkimusseura.fi/images/julkaisuja/suuntaviivoja_nuorisotoimialan_maarittelyyn_ja_arviointiin.pdf (see pages 247–248 for abstract in English).

Gretschel, A. & Kauniskangas, E. (2012). *Young people evaluating the services of the municipalities – the report of the project: Developing evaluation of basic services 2009–2011*. Helsinki: Finnish Youth Cooperation – Allianssi & Finnish Youth Research Society. Available only in Finnish http://www.alli.fi/binary/file/-/id/665/fid/1683

Guba, E. & Lincoln, Y. (2005). Paradigmatic controversies, contradictions and emerging confluences. In N. Denzin and Y. Lincoln (Eds.), *The Sage handbook of qualitative research* (3rd edn) (pp. 191–215). London: Sage.

Jackson, E. & Kassam, Y. (Eds.) (1998). *Knowledge shared: Participatory evaluation in development cooperation*. Connecticut: IDRC/Kumarian Press.

Kajamaa, A. (2011). Boundary breaking in a hospital: Expansive learning between the worlds of evaluation and frontline work. *The Learning Organization*, *18*(5), 375–391.

Lahti city (2012a). Development program for youth work services, 2013–2016. Unpublished. (available only in Finnish.)

Lahti city (2012b). *The welfare plan of children and young people, 2013–2016*. Retrieved from: https://www.lahti.fi/PalvelutSite/Peru-sopetusSite/Documents/Lasten%20ja%20nuorten%20hyvinvointisuunnitelma%202013-2016.pdf (available only in Finnish.)

Ledwith, M. & Springett, J. (2010). *Participatory practice: Community-based action for transformative change*. Bristol: The Policy Press.

Marchi, S. (2011). Co-constructing an appreciative and collective eye: Appreciative reflection in action in lifelong career guidance. *Reflective Practice*, *12*(2), 179–194.

Mertens, D. (2009). *Transformative research and evaluation*. London: The Guilford Press.

Ministry of Finance (2014). Report on basic public services. Unpublished report. Helsinki: Ministry of Finance.

Ng, P.T. & Tan, C. (2009). Communities of practice for teachers: Sensemaking or critical reflective learning? *Reflective Practice*, *10*(1), 37–44.

NYA (2014). *Youth services in England: Changes and trends in the provision of services*. Accessed at http://www.nya.org.uk/wp-content/uploads/2015/01/Youth-services-in-England-changes-and-trends.pdf

Patton, M. (2002). *Qualitative research and evaluation methods* (3rd edn). London: Sage.

Patton, M. (2008). *Utilization-focused evaluation* (4th edn). London: Sage.

Powers, J. & Tiffany, J. (2006). Engaging youth in participatory research and evaluation. *Public Health Management Practice*, November (Suppl), S79–S87.

Reed, J. (2007). *Appreciative inquiry: Research for change*. London: Sage.

Spradley, J. (1979). *The ethnographic interview*. New York: Holt, Rinehart and Winston.

Taylor, D. & Balloch, S. (Eds.) (2005). *The politics of evaluation*. Bristol: The Policy Press.

The Child Welfare Act (417/2007). Accessed at http://www.finlex.fi/fi/laki/kaannokset/2007/en20070417.pdf

The Local Government Act (410/2015). Accessed at https://www.finlex.fi/en/laki/kaannokset/2015/en20150410?search%5Btype%5D=pika&search%5Bpika%5D=local%20government%20act

The Youth Act (72/2006). Accessed at http://www.youthpolicy.org/national/Finland_2006_Youth_Act.pdf

Torres, M. & Reyes, L. (2011). Announcing possibilities with research as praxis: A counter-hegemonic research paradigm. In M. Torres & L. Reyes (Eds.), *Research as praxis. Democratizing education epistemologies* (pp. 53–103). New York: Peter Lang.

Whitmore, E., Guijt, I., Mertens, D., Imms, P., Chinman, M. & Wandersman, A. (2006). Embedding improvements, lived experience, and social justice in evaluative practice. In I. Shaw, J. Greene & M. Mark (Eds.), *The Sage Handbook of Evaluation* (pp. 340–359). London: Sage.

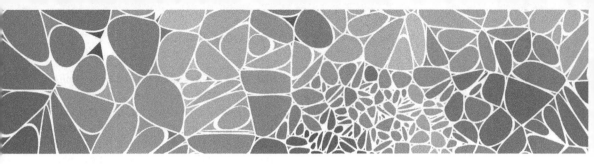

Conclusion

Dana Fusco, Pam Alldred,
Kathy Edwards and Fin Cullen[1]

Forty plus chapters, written separately from different locations and perspectives, offer a wide range of themes. Across the broad and diverse scope of the book, there are four themes that stand out as prominent, offering some common ground for youthwork while not disguising international differences in practice or purpose. They are:

1 **Levels of context:** there are always multiple levels of context at work: a distinct economic and political macro-context for youthwork that shapes, tugs, pulls and only sometimes supports young people and youthwork; on-the-ground micro-contexts for practice that might include sexist, racist, imperialist norms or ideals; and an organizational/professional (or mezzo) context that defines the work.
2 **Lamenting on loss:** in places where youthwork is established, there is a current lamenting of what that context has translated into in terms of loss: loss of a practice tradition, loss of impact in the lives of young people, loss of impact in terms of community outcomes, and loss of opportunity for democracy; yet, also clear is the tenacity of

youthworkers who continue to hold their footing amidst tenuous and sometimes, hostile work environments.
3 **Youthwork values:** throughout the book, and perhaps in response to unwanted changes and macro-influences, there is the repeated naming of youthwork practices that begin with an intentional focus on young people's lives and which, variously, also include, dialogue and inquiry (often yielding social action); the valuing of relationships, democracy, inclusiveness, social justice, rights and ethics.
4 **Hopes and inspiration for the future:** expressed throughout are the hopes and inspiration to create a future that generates fairer, more just and democratic systems of youthwork funding, training and education, research, and evaluation, or which create new youthwork practices that can challenge inequalities and/or be authentically responsive to local places, spaces, peoples and cultures.

Below we attempt to briefly elaborate on these four themes, while recognizing that in so doing we will not capture the nuance of

59 THE SAGE HANDBOOK OF YOUTH WORK PRACTICE

each chapter and context. We hope rather to simply name some themes that struck us (the editors), knowing that readers will find their own and that our conclusion is merely one reading of the book.

LEVELS OF CONTEXT

Too often and in too many parts of the world today, youthworkers are struggling to create or maintain an authentic and dynamic practice with young people shaped by young people's lived experiences. There are many factors that have given rise to this struggle: increased requirements to respond to funding trends that may or may not be applicable to local youth groups; decreased availability of funds for running more responsive youth programs; the need for scientific evidence of program effectiveness that often negates holistic and longitudinal growth and requires measures of accountability that are beyond what most programs are staffed to accomplish; political pressures that lead to directed or token practices or gestures of support; societal/governmental priorities that are not consistent with the priorities of young people and/or even when they are, may not result in the right kinds of change mechanisms; lack of money for adequate staff training and ongoing professional development; not to mention the various pulls and tugs within youthwork itself which lay claim(s) to youthwork being about one thing and not another. There are many complex and often intertwined causal factors here. At a macro level, those that are mentioned most frequently include neoliberalism, globalization and global capitalism. Sometimes it is noted that these overlay older mechanisms of colonialism.

Taking an ecological perspective in which young people as individuals and 'youth' as social constructions or understandings are situated within layers of influences, including those provided by youthwork, we can see

that some influences lie in the *near periphery* of practice and have a direct impact on the work that youthwork practitioners engage in. Youthwork, more often than not, is funded to address societal concerns, and usually those identified and defined by policymakers, government agencies and political officials. Although youthworkers have often fought to challenge and resist, the practice often arises from both real and perceived youth behaviors that are seen as problematic to maintaining social order on both local and grander scales. Lying in the *far periphery* of youthwork practice is the social, political and economic context, which trickles down through policy, legislation, funding streams and regulations, and reaches alas youthwork and youth. As suggested by multiple chapters, this ecological perspective must now include a layer that accounts for global influences and the reach of the interests of global capital that can render invisible or moot the needs and desires of local communities.

Youthwork has not always aimed to illuminate oppression explicitly; sometimes these contexts in our far periphery are notable and easy to 'read'; sometimes they go unnoticed and need a particular type of illumination (Fusco, 2016). Read through this ecological lens, such illumination might help examine contextuality, particularly as it pertains to shaping the conditions of and decisions that impact on the lives of young people. What are the broader global/economic/social/cultural/political/historical context(s) within which young people and youthwork reside? How does that context shape and even limit organizational responses and practices with young people in positive or negative directions? And, how does all of that shape the lives of young people (for better or worse)? Societal conflict and post-conflict (e.g., in Northern Ireland), colonialism, post-colonialism and globalization (e.g., as in 'Roma' or indigenous communities in Ghana, India, Australia, the Maldives and Aotearoa), and most notably, neoliberal economic policies (e.g., in most of Europe, Australia and the

United States) have had enormous impacts on young people, communities, and youthwork – and disproportionately, on indigenous youth and young people in communities of color. Here, it is crucial to mention that core to most understandings and practices of youthwork is that the young people at the center of youthwork and of the aforementioned ecology are vastly different and live lives that are shaped by their sex, gender, race, ethnicity, global location in the metropole and a range of other factors stemming from and reproducing a range of inequalities.

Yet, it is all too typical that decisions about practice, policy, research and funding are made in isolation from these realities. We believe that decisions which affect young people should take into account the nuanced and grounded intersect between the micro context (the situation, area and context for a particular group of youth and the practice of youthwork that responds to these realities), the mezzo context (the nature of organisations in their context, the articulated values and ethics within the profession, the conditions of the sector including social/economic capital, professional education and status – and each of these is set up to support or possibly impede young people's social progress), and the macro context (the larger global, political, cultural, economic, social factors that cast a shadow on how we see/shape/respond to youth and youthwork). By addressing all three aspects, we envision future decision-making about youthwork that has the capacity to be responsive to the actual conditions of young people's lives, the organizational challenges faced by those doing the work, and the larger social forces that support or impede the ability of all young people to thrive. As Brian Belton reflects:

> I am consistently reminded of our propensity to work with circumstances as presented to us: we are drawn to a tight focus on the immediate situation – the individual and/or the group. While this is understandable and often necessary, without developing our consciousness of the extended

social and political environment that in effect forms ethnic, age and other categorical corrals, our work is almost entirely devoted to alleviating symptoms (discrimination, inequality, disaffection, etc.). (Belton, this volume)

That 'extended social and political environment' has created a competitive environment where youthwork is based on predetermined priorities, policies, programs, and outcomes that often are, at best, abstracted from the realities of young people and their communities. For instance, in much of the North and the West today, the focus is on young people gaining skills (academic, vocational and socio-emotional) for tertiary study and careers, and demonstrating results or gains in commoditized educational terms. While there is no intent to critique such a focus per se (after all, it would be difficult to argue that the attainment of such skills could end badly for young people), it is often overlooked that the very act of determining needs and outcomes, and, in the case of locales where youthwork is a form of informal education, curriculum, a prior to engaging young people, removes their agency, rendering youth voice muted and expected outcomes mutated. The stakes are higher than many recognize in terms of multiple layers of loss: to youth, to communities, to society, to our global village and to democracy.

LAMENTING ON LOSS

Although there is a history of tension and opposition in practices, youthwork is usually funded to address societal concerns as defined by policymakers, government agencies and political officials. In its state-funded versions it arises from both real and perceived youth behaviors that are seen as problematic to maintaining social order on local or grander scales. Stated another way, under the guise of youth programs or funding for youth services, it is easy to 'serve' youth, to offer up the latest menu of engaging activities, support or interventions while leaving unexamined structural causes of inequality, poverty, violence and suffering. But at what cost?

We would argue that the current pressure in many geographical regions and nations for youthwork to respond to the above economically and politically constrained and largely adult-directed desires, rather than to the actual wants and needs of young people in the 'here and now' might be effective for creating a society that positions youth as 'on their way' towards meaningful adult roles (if that; we are not so sure), but does little to alter the playing field for youth who can benefit most from the advantages that youth programs and youthwork dialogic relationships or services can offer (see Heathfield and Fusco (2016) for an extensive examination of how youthwork is responding to inequitable conditions around the globe).

The current macro context has not only withered away enormous funding for youth services, it has also put in place systems that work against democratic practices with young people. The losses over the past twenty or so years to young people, to communities and to our field are itself enough to lament over; but the loss to our potential representative democracies is staggering. Participation in pre-packaged programs or otherwise in government-directed youthwork practices with young people does not reflect the practices and principles that most in this *Handbook* hold up as who we are (complicated though that 'we' may be, as shown by many but explicitly by Trudi Cooper in this volume).

RECLAIMING YOUTHWORK VALUES

Youthworkers have learned that the route to success is through focusing on young people, their lives and concerns, and building relationships with young people that are transparent and organic (see the chapters by Andersson, Couch, McNamara, Matloff-Nieves, Jupp-Kina, Spier and Giles, Foley et al., Patel and Trelfa, in this volume). Outside agendas are secondary to the fundamentals of relationships that take center stage; thus, youthworkers are also the frontline receivers of the joys, pains, sufferings, excitements, frustrations, trials, tribulations and trends of young people. It was through real connections with youth that youthwork, not as a field or a profession but as a practice, can be said to have emerged. It was in the relational space that the ethos of youthwork was discovered and refined. The concern raised repeatedly through these pages is that of a loss of a practice tradition that has resulted from what is often termed 'neoliberalism' or the bureaucratization of a practice (see Cullen and Bradford, as well as Thomas, in this volume).

The simple naming of 'new' types of youthwork that boldly and loudly reclaim such values is itself an interesting manifestation of the times. Youthwork it seems, is in search of an emphasis that helps it stand out from the co-opted version of youthwork that is today's institutionalized, bureaucratized version of a practice tradition. The response has been the call for global youthwork (Sallah, 2014), radical youthwork (Belton, 2009), grassroots youthwork (de St Croix, 2013), critical youthwork (Lavie-Ajayi & Krumer-Nevo, 2012), emancipatory youthwork (Ngai, 2006) and civic youthwork (Roholt, Baizerman & Hildreth, 2013).

These narratives specify the need for youthwork to articulate itself in more humanistic and reflexive terms: terms that represent a practice that is participatory and democratic, positioning young people's voice at the center of praxis and youthwork praxis at the center of community. Often these narratives also call for the recognition of gross inequalities in terms of race, sex, ethnicity or global location as a citizen of the global North or South. On these terms, we are called to (re)consider youthwork practices: our aims, principles, values, methods. Collectively, we have seen that youthwork practices have been critically altered by social and political conditions near and far and bear witness to the call to return to something that is 'grassroots' and 'critical'.

In each youthwork context, the relationships between youthworker(s) and youth as a group, and between the young people is a central starting point. Relationships are the vehicle for expressions of care and concern, the basis for trust, the foundation for dialogue, and the tool for communication and learning. Sometimes the relation(s) between and among youthworker(s), young person(s), and the community (whether a geographical or interest-based community) has an immediate role in defining the purpose of youthwork as practices that are closer to traditional social work than educational iterations. Sometimes community development, and sometimes, radical social work informs the relations. Each of these types of social relations requires 'partnering' (see Ramey and Lawford in this volume) and participation (see Cooper and Gretschel in this volume), and challenges the notion of empowerment (see also Belton in this volume), which is embedded in individualistic notions of growth and advancement, and a liberal model of power and justice. Youthworkers in this arrangement are called upon to be responsive to young people (see Matloff-Nieves et al. in this volume), facilitative (see Belton in this volume), and ethical (see Bessant and Watts in this volume) in their actions.

Sometimes understood as informal education, youthwork has no subscription to a particular content: it can reside in everything from basketball, hip hop, ping pong/table tennis, theatre and film, literacy, or community service learning projects such as cleaning a local park. In its myriad of other guises as about youth or community development or radical advocacy, youth participation centrally focuses on young people and their concerns, as well as their social contexts. Intrinsic here is a specific need and a call to engage youth in political

and historical analysis because without so doing, there is no way to heal, restore and challenge inequality and oppression. Of course, analysis without action may not yield the sorts of youth and community actions that many would aim for and certainly runs short of democracy and peace building. As Thomson and Chapman (in this volume) illustrate, there is no such thing as 'common sense' for our sense is always limited to our experiences, which themselves can be contradictory and complex. It is essential for self-growth, as well as the growth of communities to engage in critical analysis and reflection in order to challenge the epistemological frameworks upon which prior learning has been built. The questioning of 'why' and 'what if' are the training ground for democracy.

HOPES AND INSPIRATION

Whereas many chapters in this volume speak of loss, they also chorus the need for hope and inspiration towards new youthwork futures. The IDYW Collective calls for international partnerships to provide challenge, while, in this volume, Sercombe calls for international perspectives to promote reflexivity. Also in this volume, Skott-Myrhe and Skott-Myrhe call for DIY youthwork and Vachon and McConnell for activist alliances across generational and other differences. Beals et al., Edwards and Shaafee, and Nuggehalli each envision postcolonial and decolonized futures that acknowledge the reality of the global, but which are responsive to the local. Sallah et al. argue that youthwork needs to grow and shift focus to challenge growing global inequalities. Howard, Brocken and Sim see new pedagogic possibilities and co-learning between arts education and youthwork, and Heslop, Restler and Luttrell, Wood, and D'Arcy, Thomas and Wallace all illustrate the way that local and particular concerns can be springboards for young people to connect with broader struggles.

The call for youthwork to interrogate concepts of power, inclusion and participation run throughout many of these chapters, especially those by Collin, Lala and Fieldgrass, and by Whelan and Steinkellner. Among the approaches offered to help challenge social inequalities and to promote greater levels of inclusivity are faith-based provision (see the chapter by Bright, Thompson, Hart and Hayden) and the 'alchemy' of feminist traditions of work to promote empowerment and collective action (see Morgan and McArdle's chapter).

Youthwork education is, unsurprisingly, as diverse as youthwork practice. There are a many great models of youthwork education, but they have also suffered massive cutbacks, with many courses closing altogether. Education, research and evaluation might consider modeling the very tenets of practice that they seek to train, understand and evaluate: namely, they should be participatory and democratic. The chapters here point to the use of such models in the design of curriculum (e.g. see the chapter by Kiilakoski, Kinnunen, and Djupsund) and evaluation (e.g. the chapter by Cooper and Gretschel).

For us, we hope that within the mix is the understanding that there is a youthwork practice tradition that aims towards partnering with young people in order to engage intergenerationally in dialogue, examination and inquiry of lived experiences as embedded in structural conditions that also need illumination in the context of youth development. In so doing, young people's own priorities are placed at the heart of the approach, while linking into wider structures and processes and emphasizing social and collective as well as individual outcomes (see the chapters by Bartlett and Muirhead, and Case and Morris).

To finish, we return to the point made in the Introduction about the aim of this *Handbook*.

We see this collection of chapters as a form of conversation started (or sustained) between people in different places, and we hope that it will inspire and sustain their practice with young people towards a more just world.

Note

1 We have retained the authors' own terminology for their practice in each chapter, and similarly here, where Dana Fusco is first author, the Conclusion refers to 'youthwork' and uses US spelling.

REFERENCES

Belton, B. (2009). *Radical youth work: Developing critical perspectives and professional judgment*. Dorset: Russell House Publishing.

de St Croix, T. (2013). 'I just love youth work!' Emotional labour, passion and resistance. *Youth & Policy*, 110, 33–51.

Fusco, D. (2016). History of youth work: Transitions, illuminations, and refractions (pp. 36–52). In M. Heathfield & D. Fusco (Eds.), *Youth and inequality in education: Global actions in youth work*. New York: Routledge.

Heathfield, M. & Fusco, D. (2016). *Youth and inequality in education: Global actions in youth work*. New York: Routledge.

Lavie-Ajayi, M. & Krumer-Nevo, M. (2012). In a different mindset: Critical youth work with marginalized youth. *Children and Youth Services Review*, 35(10), 1698–1704.

Ngai, S. Sek-Yum (2006). Exploring emancipatory youth work: The case of Hong Kong outreach workers. *International Social Work*, 49(4), 471–481.

Roholt, R.V., Baizerman, M., & Hildreth, R.W. (2013). *Civic Youth work: Cocreating democratic youth spaces*. Chicago, IL: Lyceum Books, Inc.

Sallah, M. (2014). *Global youth work: Provoking consciousness and taking action*. Dorset: Russell House Publishing.

Index